Sources of Information in the Social Sciences

Sources of Information in the Social Sciences

A Guide to the Literature

THIRD EDITION

WILLIAM H. WEBB
AND ASSOCIATES

ALAN R. BEALS
WILLIAM W. BRICKMAN
STANLEY CHODOROW
CHAUNCY D. HARRIS
BERT F. HOSELITZ
HOWARD JONES
ROGER T. KAUFMAN
ANN K. PASANELLA
STEVEN SEITZ
TED P. SHELDON
PHILIP SMITH
STEPHEN K. STOAN
CAMILLE WANAT
ROBERT I. WATSON
MARILYN L. WERTHEIMER
MICHAEL WERTHEIMER
ROBERT WESTERMAN
WILEY J. WILLIAMS
ANDREW S. ZIMBALIST

AMERICAN LIBRARY ASSOCIATION
Chicago and London 1986

Designed by Vladimir Reichl

Text composed by Modern Typographers of Florida, Inc.
in Linotron 202 Times Roman.
Index composed by Black Dot, Inc.

Printed on 50-pound Glatfelter,
a pH-neutral stock, and
bound in B-grade Joanna
Arrestox cloth by
Edwards Brothers, Inc.

Library of Congress Cataloging in Publication Data
Main entry under title:
Sources of information in the social sciences.
Rev. ed. of: Sources of information in the
social sciences / Carl M. White and associates.
2nd ed. 1973.
Includes index.
1. Social sciences—Bibliography. I. Webb,
William H., 1935–   . II. Beals, Alan R.
III. White, Carl Milton, 1903–   . Sources of
information in the social sciences.
Z7161.S666 1985   [H61]   016.3   84-20494
ISBN 0-8389-0405-X

Contents

From the Preface
to the Second Edition

The purpose of this book is simple: to make it easier to get at knowledge and information of importance to us all (and becoming more so), to throw light on the workings of the social science information system, and to support subject bibliography as a branch of study.

The book grew out of work in the 1950s with graduate and postgraduate students at Columbia University who had been admitted to the study of library science. Reports on the first edition indicate that a book that meets the needs at their level has additional uses. It serves to remind the searcher who is already at home in one of these subjects of books that he is familiar with and knows to be useful, and serves also to make his literature searches more productive when he turns to adjoining fields where he feels less at home. Awareness of these kindred interests has influenced the revision now in hand. . . .

A book owes its life to the climate of interest and need that sustains it. Librarians, documentalists, and social scientists* on more than one continent have lent their encouragement, counsel, and cooperation. It is impossible to name them all, but I wish heartily to thank them all.

Finally, my colleagues and I are sensible of our indebtedness to a large supporting cast of librarians and bibliographers—some now on campus and others before them—who built the collec-

tions and created the bibliographical tools that have served us so well.

Each contributor worked with a set of editorial guidelines that allowed them to organize the treatment as the internal organization of the literature of the discipline requires. Subject by subject, however, the treatment falls into two parts. First, a subject specialist, chosen for his grasp of the literature, selects, organizes, and reviews monographic works that, if they do not form the core, are at least representative of the core of the substantive literature of that field. This review is followed in each case by a list of reference works to round out the picture. In the first edition, reference works were for the most part annotated individually, and this remains the rule. Faced this time, however, with more titles, contributors were encouraged to make greater use of group annotations when connected discussion would compress essential information or more clearly bring out the interrelationships of works that form a cluster or constellation. Relationships of titles to one another are further brought out, this time, by subject and form indexing.

Certain fields are included that do not fall wholly within the social sciences, but it is simpler to include than to cull them. This tendency toward inclusiveness has another aspect. Sociology includes reference works on demography, social service, minorities, race relations, communication, public opinon, gerontology; works on anthropology, ethnology, ethnography, folklore, linguistics, prehistory, and nonclassical archaeology, and it also bears the brunt of re-

*If for brevity this book hereafter uses but a single inclusive term like "subject bibliographer" or "librarian," the contributions of documentalists and subject specialists who are interested in the organization and communication of information are thereby intended to be in no way minimized.

sponsibility for area studies. Political science includes works on public administration and international relations, as well as selected works in law and government publications.

Research is creating an increasingly luxuriant crop of publications that spill across the lines commonly used to departmentalize academic activity for administrative purposes. The resultant crisscrossing explains two features of this book. First, books that are inseparably related to, and supplement, those described in one chapter are sometimes to be found in other chapters. Consult these other chapters or the index to find these books. Bear in mind, particularly, that the first, general chapter supplements all the others.

Second, the interlocking interests of the social sciences may make an interdisciplinary guide such as this desirable and necessary, but these interests—very unobligingly—get in the way of hulling out some topics so as to eliminate plural reference to those titles that are of interest to more than one discipline. Cross-references have been relied on as far as possible, but now and then a rounded picture of information sources requires more than one entry for a book.

Normally, a chapter treats in one place all sources that furnish a distinctive *type* of information, but the listing is influenced by *where* the sources will be the most useful, as in listing appropriate bibliographies with atlases under the heading "Maps and atlases: bibliographical sources" in the chapter on geography. Basic works are coded to facilitate indexing and cross-reference unless the purpose of the citation is to document or amplify the text.† Space is saved by the heavy use of abbreviations.

CARL M. WHITE

†The opportunity given authors to add and delete titles in the proof stage has resulted, in some instances, in gaps in the numbering of entries. The reader should be assured that when the numbers are not consecutive, they are accurately used in cross-references and the index.—Ed.

Abbreviations

Each chapter contains, usually, under the heading "Sources of scholarly contributions: journals," a representative list of journals that are devoted to the interests of scholarship in the field, with the title, date of origin, place of publication, publisher, frequency, and information as to where its contents are indexed or abstracted. Care has been taken to gather the latter information in one place since it is not widely available elsewhere.

AA	*African abstracts*
ABC	*ABC political science*
AbstAnthro	*Abstracts in anthropology*
AbstFolk	*Abstracts of folklore studies*
AmH&L	*America: history and life*
AustPAIS	*Australian public affairs information service*
BGI	*Bibliographie geographie internationale*
BiolAbst	*Biological abstracts*
BPIA	*Business publications index and abstracts*
BrEdInd	*British education index*
BrHumInd	*British humanities index*
BullAnal	*Bulletin analytique de documentation politique, économique et sociale contemporaine*
BullSig	*Bulletin signalétique*
BusPerInd	*Business periodicals index*
CanEdInd	*Canadian Education Index*
CanInd	*Canadian index to periodicals and documentary films; an author and subject index*
Cc	*Current contents*
ChDevAbst	*Child development abstracts and bibliography*
ChemAbst	*Chemical abstracts*
CIJE	*Current index to journals in education*
CJPI	*Criminal justice periodical index*
CollStudPers-Abst	*College student personnel abstracts*
CommunAbst	*Communication abstracts*
CompRev	*Computing reviews*
CrimPenAbst	*Criminology and penology abstracts*
DataProcDig	*Data processing digest*
EdAdmAbst	*Educational administration abstracts*
EdInd	*Education index*
EM	*Excerpta medica*
EngrInd	*Engineering index*
GeoAbst	*Geo abstracts (formerly Geographical abstracts)*
HistAbst	*Historical abstracts*
HumInd	*Humanities index*
HumResAbst	*Human resources abstracts*
IndLegPer	*Index to legal periodicals*
IndPerArt	*Index to periodical articles by and about blacks*
IntBibPolSci	*International bibliography of political science*
IntBibSocSci	*International bibliography of social sciences*
IntBibZeit	*Internationale bibliographie der zeitschriftenliteratur aus allen gebieten des wissens*
IntPolSciAbst	*International political science abstracts*
JEconLit	*Journal of economic literature*

Abbreviations

LangTeach	*Language teaching and linguistics abstracts*
LLBA	*LLBA: language and language behavior abstracts*
MgtInd	*Management index*
MLA	*MLA international bibliography*
MusicInd	*Music index*
NutrAbst	*Nutrition abstracts and reviews*
PAIS	*Public affairs information service*
PersMgtAbst	*Personnel management abstracts*
PopInd	*Population index*
PsychAbst	*Psychological abstracts*
ResHighEd	*Research into higher education*
RG	*Readers' guide*
RIE	*Research in education*
SagePubAd-minAbst	*Sage public administration abstracts*
SageUrbStud-Abst	*Sage urban studies abstracts*
SciAbst	*Science abstracts*
SSCI	*Social science citation index*
SSI	*Social sciences index*
SocAbst	*Sociological abstracts*
SocEdAbst	*Sociological education abstracts*
SocWkRes&-Abst	*Social work research and abstracts*
UNESCO	*United Nations Educational, Scientific and Cultural Organization*
UNLib	*United Nations Library, Geneva. Monthly list of selected articles.*
UrbAffAbst	*Urban affairs abstracts*
USPSD	*United States political science documents*

WkRelAbst	*Work related abstracts*
WomStudAbst	*Women studies abstracts*
assn.	association
Aufl.	Auflage
augm.	augmented
Ausg.	Ausgabe
bear.	bearbeitet
ca.	circa
comp.	compiled, compiler
corr.	corrected
dept.	department
ed.	editor, edited, edition, édition, edicion, edicão, edizióne, editóre
eds.	editors
enl.	enlarged
gänz	gänzlich
Hrsg.	Herausgeben
in prep.	in preparation
introd.	introduction
Jahrg.	Jahrgang
Lfg.	Lieferung
n.F.	neue Folge
nouv.	nouvelle
n.s.	new series
pa.	paperback
pr.	press
pref.	preface
prelim.	preliminary
pt.	part, parts
ptg.	printing
publ.	published
pubns.	publications
rev.	revised
ser.	series
SIC	Standard industrial classification
supt.	superintendent
tr.	translated, translator
UDC	Universal decimal classification
umgearb.	umgearbeitet
univ.	university
verb.	verbessert
verm.	vermehrt

1 Social Science Literature

Evolution of the social sciences. Developments through the nineteenth century. From World War through World War. 1945 to the present A1–9. *Evolution of the literature of the social sciences*. Developments through the nineteenth century. From World War through World War. 1945 to the present A10–11. *Social science literature and its uses today*. Patterns of use A12–15. Characteristics of the literature A16–21. *Structure of the information system*. A conceptualization of the literature of the social sciences. Scholarly literature. Primary data in published form. Incidental professional and scholarly information. Monographs. Guides to the literature. Reviews. Abstracts, summaries, précis, and digests. Bibliographies and indexes. Directories. Biographical tools. Dictionaries. Encyclopedias and encyclopedic sets. Handbooks, manuals, almanacs, and compendia. Yearbooks. Original sources. Statistical sources. Atlases, pictorial works, and kindred graphic sources. Sources of scholarly contributions. Sources of current information. *Monographs*. Introductions and systematic works A21A–30. Histories A31–41. The scientific method A42–50. Philosophy of the social sciences. The positivistic tradition A51–56. Symbolic interactionism A57–61. Exchange theory A62–66. Middle range theory A67. Anti-positivistic approaches A68–72. Functionalism A73–76. Conflict theory A77–89. General systems theory A90–92. Recent research trends. Futures research A93–98. Policy sciences A99–103. Evaluation research A104–7. Sociobiology A108–11. Structuralism A112–13. Research methods in the social sciences A114–15.

Guides to the literature. General A116–23. Specialized A124–29. *Reviews*. Reviews of the literature and research A130–38. Reviews of bibliographic control A139–48. *Abstracts and digests*. A149–66. Current digests A167–71.

Bibliographies of bibliographies A172–91. *Current bibliographies and indexes.* Aids essential to all disciplines A192–213. Aids with social science emphasis A214–39. Aids with regional emphasis A240–48. Current bibliographies of published proceedings A249–52. Current newspaper indexes A253–55. *Retrospective bibliographies.* General records of accumulated learning A256–57. National library and national union catalogs A258–63. Other library catalogs A264–82. Interdisciplinary bibliographies and indexes A283–96. Bibliographies of directories A297–302. Bibliographies of newspapers A303–13. Bibliographies of periodicals A314–21. Bibliographies of statistical sources A322–38. *Directories and biographical information.* Biographical information for social scientists A339–46. Research organizations, learned societies, and associations A347–59. Calendars of congresses and other meetings A360–63. Information centers. A364–72. Directories of databases A373–80. Directories for social science periodicals A381–88. Grants and awards A389–401. *Dictionaries* A402–12. *Encyclopedias and encyclopedic sets* A413–16. *Handbooks* A417–31. *Yearbooks.* General and global yearbooks A432–39. Regional and national yearbooks A440–58. *Statistical sources.* National statistical sources A459–75. Historical statistical sources A476–82. Regional and international statistical sources A483–500. *Sources of scholarly contributions.* Journals A501. Monograph series A502–3. Organizations A504. *Sources of current information.* Journals A505–20. Selected daily newspapers A521.

Scope and Purpose

The purpose of this book is to provide a systematic guide to the literature of eight fields commonly classified among the social sciences: history, geography, economics and business administration, sociology, anthropology, psychology, education, and political science. This selection of disciplines is somewhat arbitrary, since linguistics, statistics, and demography are often considered social sciences where history is frequently thought of as one of the humanities. Moreover, education and business, like public administration, social work, criminology, and law, are generally thought of as applied rather than theoretical fields. It should also be noted that a number of the disciplines under study here are more commonly referred to by scholars as behavioral sciences, since their research methods frequently involve direct observations of human behavior. Such a definition would exclude history, economics, and geography. The eight fields selected, however, have in common a concern for the behavior of man in relation to his fellow men and to the environment they share. In this sense, we can distinguish them from the sciences, which deal with the physical world, and from the humanities, which concentrate on the unique and essentially timeless works of human artistic creativity and speculation. So the term social sciences can be considered appropriate for the disciplines we are covering.

Survey of the Field

EVOLUTION OF THE SOCIAL SCIENCES

Though our task is essentially bibliographic, it would be useful to present a brief survey of the evolution and growing complexity of the social sciences up to the present, for the bibliographic apparatus has developed partially as a response to the internal dynamic of social scientific research. As we shall see, however, that bibliographic apparatus has not proven to be fully adequate for social scientists. This is so for two reasons. First, the nature of the social sciences, with their imprecise terminology, overlapping disciplinary boundaries, ideological partiality, and relative lack of cumulativeness, makes it difficult to define the literature needs of each discipline. Second, the tendency of bibliographers to use the literature of the sciences as a model in designing bibliographic tools for the social sciences has narrowed the focus largely to literature in the journals when monographs are at least as important for social scientists. But these topics will be developed more fully later.

Developments through the Nineteenth Century

Until the nineteenth century the study of man and society was largely deductive in approach and given to system-building. These systems were modeled on ideas derived from theology or from the emerging physical sciences and generally had a powerful normative and prescriptive content. The few individuals involved in these speculative enterprises had no clear-cut professional identity.

As the nineteenth century progressed, emphasis switched to the empirical and supposedly impartial gathering of facts which would, when properly classified, provide obvious and incontrovertible truths. Thus was born the positivistic approach to the social sciences which with modifications has held a powerful sway up to the present, particularly in the Anglo-American world. The numbers of people involved in the active study of society grew considerably and disciplinary lines emerged. German universities,

from which American universities borrowed heavily, had a strong impact on these developments. Departments specializing in history, anthropology, economics, and so on, emerged in the latter years of the nineteenth century.

A measure of the increasing specialization in the social sciences was the appearance of professional organizations: the American Historical Association, 1884; the American Economics Association, 1885; the American Psychological Association, 1892; the American Sociological Association, 1895; the American Anthropological Association, 1902; and the American Political Science Association, 1903. These bodies all created journals designed to disseminate professional news and provide their members with a forum for the exchange of ideas, both in the form of correspondence and of articles reporting the results of research.

From World War through World War

The period around the time of the First World War formed an important transition in the development of the social sciences. Wartime activities gave a new prestige both to psychologists, who developed testing instruments used in evaluating the abilities of recruits, and to economists, who became involved in the regulation and planning that accompanied the substantial reorientation of economic resources. The emergence of Soviet Russia, with its claim to speak for an alternative socioeconomic and political system opposed to imperialism and racism, further shook a Western society whose complacent faith in the inherent goodness of its system had already been jolted by the bloodletting of the war years.

Even as society was developing new concerns about socioeconomic, political, and international problems, the Einsteinian revolution in the sciences began to make itself felt among social scientists. The concepts of relativity and statistical probability came to be interpreted as obviating the need to establish true predictability in behavioral research. Social scientists also borrowed a new understanding of the research process from the sciences, in which theory-construction, hypothesizing, research design, gathering and analyzing empirical data, and positing tentative conclusions became key elements. This hypothetico-deductive model, incorporating both inductive and deductive reasoning, recognized the indispensable role of the human mind in creating the links between fact and theory, and further encouraged the belief that human behavior could be studied using a scientific mode of enquiry. Increasing sophistication in statistical methodology became an important tool of the more "behaviorally" oriented social scientists.

Two significant developments of the postwar years that helped cement the growing influence of the social sciences were the creation in 1920 of the National Bureau of Economic Research and in 1923 of the Social Science Research Council (SSRC). The former gave considerable impetus to the collection of economic data for purposes of analyzing the functioning of the economy. The latter played an important role in fostering the development of new methodologies and empirical research in the social sciences by awarding grants and fellowships and sponsoring a number of research projects itself. The guidelines laid down by the SSRC in giving out monies had a strong influence on the methodological orientation of researchers who desired financial assistance. One enduring legacy of the work of the SSRC in the interwar years was sponsorship of the 15-volume *Encyclopedia of the social sciences*, published between 1928 and 1933 in an effort to encourage a "scientific" approach to society on all disciplinary fronts.

The Great Depression and the Second World War heightened interest in the potential use of the ever more scientific social sciences to generate knowledge that might ultimately have direct application in social melioration. The socioeconomic, political, international, military, and racial problems afflicting Western society became more obvious as economic stagnation, massive unemployment, imperialist ideologies, international war, and genocide occupied world attention. The aftermath of the war brought decolonization, the emergence of a Third World, stirrings of racial unrest at home, the expansion of Marxist ideology, and the rise of hitherto undreamed of destructive power. It appeared that the evolution of man's scientific and technological knowledge had outpaced his ability to organize and manage his social affairs. If solutions were to be found to human problems, they were to be found in the social realm, not the purely technological.

1945 to the Present

In this postwar atmosphere, the social sciences came to enjoy an enhanced prestige. Social scientists had contributed in significant ways to the war effort, especially in the areas of morale and propaganda. Their statistical and analytical techniques had become impressive. Inasmuch as the war had demonstrated the advantages of organized effort in the sciences, some now argued that similar mobilization of social science expertise might produce striking results. The cold war demanded that we demonstrate to the world the superiority of our system in generating the good life at home and in the Third World, where social scientists had identified a "revolution of rising expectations." Domestic social problems, particularly the racial one that heated up after 1954, demanded some attempts at solution. Poverty discrimination, criminality, poor housing, broken homes, inadequate medical care, and domestic violence were seen as problems in need of redress.

These trends seemed to peak and converge in the early 1960s as the Kennedy-Johnson administrations courted the social sciences openly. Already, in 1960, the government had created a Division of Social Science in the National Science Foundation, as if to symbolize that the social sciences had achieved complete respectability as sciences. Kennedy's Science Advisory Committee produced a report in 1962 entitled *Strengthening the behavioral sciences* (Washington, D.C.: 1962 [19p.]) (**A1**). The National Science Foundation generated three reports in the late sixties entitled *The behavioral sciences and the federal government* (Washington, D.C.: National Academy of Sciences, 1968 [107p.]) (**A2**); *The behavioral and social sciences: outlook and needs* (Washington, D.C.: National Academy of Sciences, 1969 [320p.]) (**A3**); and *Knowledge into action: improving the nation's use of the social sciences* (Washington, D.C.: Govt. Print. Off., 1969 [95p.]) (**A4**). The main thrust of all these reports was that federal support for applied research in the social sciences could produce beneficial social results.

Though many in the government were suspicious of the ideological bent of the social scientists who proposed solutions to social problems, and many in the academy were fearful of losing their scholarly detachment to the ideological demands of the government, the social sciences seemed to have matured as legitimate sciences capable of generating knowledge applicable to the solution of social problems. Overall, a sense

4

of optimism prevailed in the aura of the Great Society of the sixties. HEW created a panel in 1966 out of which emerged the concept of "social indicators," sets of statistics designed to parallel the economic indicators already in use. Social forecasting and futurism became respectable intellectual activities. Evaluation research emerged as a field of endeavor whose purpose was to study the impact of social programs to determine their effectiveness. Policy studies developed as a branch of the social sciences concerned specifically with the formulation and implementation of successful governmental policies. The increasing sophistication and use of the elaboration model of multivariate analysis seemed to offer a powerful statistical tool for social research.

The 1970s, however, brought retreat and disillusionment. The economy failed to respond to Keynesianism and welfare economics. Social problems, made more visible by the anti-Vietnam War forces, proved to be more intractable than hypothesized. A report sponsored by the National Science Foundation in 1976, *Social and behavioral science programs in the National Science Foundation* (Washington, D.C.: National Academy of Sciences, 1976 [103p.]) (**A5**), offered the sobering assessment that most federally sponsored social research was undistinguished and held out little promise for useful application. A National Research Council study, the Study Project on Social Research and Development (four out of six projected volumes appeared in 1978–79), resulted in divided counsel on the value of government-sponsored research and development programs in the social sciences.

A6   The federal investment in knowledge of social problems. Washington, D.C.: National Academy of Sciences, 1978. 114p.

A7   The funding of social knowledge production and applications: a survey of federal agencies. Washington, D.C.: National Academy of Sciences, 1978. 478p.

A8   Studies in the management of social r & d: selected policy areas. Washington, D.C.: National Academy of Sciences, 1979. 218p.

A9   Lynn, Laurence. Knowledge and policy: the uncertain connection. Washington, D.C.: National Academy of Sciences, 1978. 183p.

In government and in academic ranks, the retreat was general. Some academicians in the social sciences pulled in their horns, as it were, and tended to revert to smaller, more empirical studies of limited scope that avoided systems approaches like Keynesianism or Parsonianism. Sociobiology arose to challenge the hitherto regnant belief in the dominance of environmental factors in shaping human conduct. Neo-Marxian ideas challenged the social science establishment. Structuralism began to permeate many areas of the social sciences. General systems theory received more attention. Last but not least, the humanist elements that have always been present in social science ranks took advantage of the disarray to condemn the "scientism" of the behaviorists. Everywhere, fragmentation seemed to characterize the social science endeavor of the mid-eighties.

The present mood in the social sciences, therefore, has been one of introspection and tentativeness. At the same time, Reaganism has moved the government toward a non-interventionist stance with regard to social problems. These trends, however, are giving the social sciences an opportunity to undertake necessary reappraisals that should result in a new understanding of their strengths, weaknesses, and potentials. Already there is emerging a more sophisticated perception of the nature of the scientific endeavor, as social scientists have acquired greater awareness of the influence of politics, prejudice, ideology, and conflicting paradigms in shaping research approaches in many areas of the physical sciences, which are still often looked to as models. At the same time, social scientists continue to grapple with a variety of long-standing issues: cumulativeness in the social sciences, normative vs. empirical approaches, heredity vs. environment, subjectivity vs. objectivity, conflict vs. equilibrium, theoretical vs. applied social research, free will vs. determinism, the individual vs. the collectivity, and a number of other issues that fall under the rubric "philosophy of the social sciences." What will emerge as the dominant trends of the next generation, however, is guesswork in this period of fluidity and transition.

EVOLUTION OF THE LITERATURE OF THE SOCIAL SCIENCES

The research literature of the social sciences and the secondary tools for controlling it have grown in a pattern that, as might be expected, closely parallels the development of the disciplines themselves. In the same way that social scientists looked toward the sciences for their models, bibliographers of the social sciences looked toward the secondary literature of the sciences for their models, with results that have not, as we shall see, always been felicitous.

Developments through the Nineteenth Century

Throughout the early modern era, from the sixteenth into the nineteenth centuries, savants had made sporadic and unconnected efforts to create bibliographies of the slowly emerging literature generated by scholars. Not until the late nineteenth century, as disciplines developed with more or less defined areas of intellectual endeavor and identifiable bodies of research literature produced by trained professionals, did there appear a somewhat sustained interest in bibliographic control. This interest appeared on two fronts. First, the scholars themselves, usually working through their newly formed professional organizations, sometimes encouraged the development of indexing systems designed to give access to the research literature. Second, and equally important, librarians, who were beginning to define their own professional role with its heavy emphasis on bibliographic expertise, became concerned about access problems, particularly to the journal literature.

History, the oldest, best defined, and largest of the social science disciplines, was an early leader in attempts at bibliographic control. Beginning in 1880 and continuing until the war terminated it permanently in 1913, the *Jahresberichte der Geschichtswissenschaft* appeared annually in Berlin under the sponsorship of the Historical Society. Similar annual bibliographies covering the field of history appeared in a number of other European countries. In the United States, the American Historical Association undertook in 1902 to produce *Writings on American history*, an annual inventory of literature published in the field of American history. It is still being published. The field of psychology began efforts at systematic bibliographic control in 1890 with the annual publication of *Psychological bulletin*, sponsored by the journal *Psychological review*. The *Bulletin* continued until 1935. Geography followed in 1891 with the *Bibliographie géographique internationale*, an annual produced by the Association de Géographes Français. It continues to the present day under different sponsorship. Other areas of the social sciences, with fewer scholars, smaller bodies of literature, and less clearly defined boundaries, were more poorly served. The *Bibliographie der Sozialwissenschaften*, still in existence, originated in Berlin in 1905 as an inventory of mainly economic and political literature.

The preceding titles were all sponsored by scholars themselves. In the United States, the major burden of attempting to index scholarly literature in the social sciences other than history and psychology fell to library-sponsored publications. The Wilson Company initiated the *International index* in 1907. It included the social sciences and humanities generally. The *Public Affairs Information Service bulletin*, generally called *PAIS*, which was also originated by librarians, was equally important as a bibliographic source for the social sciences after its creation in 1915. It included selected books and government publications as well as journal literature. In Britain, the *Subject index to periodicals*, later renamed the *British humanities index*, began in 1915, fulfilling the same role as the *International index* and *PAIS*. It too was a librarian-sponsored publication.

By the advent of World War I, therefore, there had been efforts by both scholars and librarians to create bibliographic control of the literature of the social sciences. In assessing the adequacy of these efforts, it must be kept in mind that as of 1910, there were only about 3,200 social scientists in the United States, more than 2,000 of whom were historians, and only about forty major scholarly journals. It was possible for scholars to keep current using informal techniques.

From World War through World War

Some limited progress in bibliographic control was made in the interwar years, with advances continuing to come on both the library and academic fronts. Business literature was included in the *Industrial arts index* created by the Wilson Company in 1926. Three years later, Wilson began publishing the *Education index*. Two other secondary services for the field of education appeared at about the same time. The Society for Research in Child Development began *Child development abstracts* in 1927; and the American Educational Research Association created the *Review of educational research* in 1931. Other professional efforts included the highly selective but still useful *International bibliography of historical sciences*, begun by the International Committee of Historical Sciences in 1926; *Psychological abstracts*, started by the American Psychological Association in 1927; and the *Population index*, sponsored by the Population Association of America beginning in 1935.

One other tool that deserves some mention at this point is *Social science abstracts*, created by the Social Science Research Council in 1928 to abstract the journal literature of economics, sociology, anthropology, geography, political science, and history. The publication was discontinued in 1932 when its costs became incommensurate with its use. The venture is instructive for what it tells us of the still modest dimensions of research activity in many of the social sciences and the tendency of researchers to continue to rely on more informal techniques of keeping abreast of a growing but still small literature.

1945 to the Present

As might be surmised from our earlier survey of the evolution of the social sciences, rapid expansion of the access literature occurred only after World War II. Two landmark studies contributed to new developments. One was carried out by the Graduate Library School and the Division of the Social Sciences at the University of Chicago in 1948 under the sponsorship of the Carnegie Foundation.

A10 "Bibliographic services in the social sciences." *Library quarterly* 20: 79–100 (1950).

The study concluded that, although the number of social scientists in the United States was now about 12,000 and the number of scholarly journals around 500, only the fields of psychology, demography, and education were reasonably well served bibliographically. It recommended abstracting services for other social science disciplines. The second study was sponsored jointly by the United Nations Educational, Social, and Cultural Organization and the Library of Congress.

A11 UNESCO/Library of Congress Bibliographical Survey. Bibliographical services, their present state and possibilities of improvement. Washington, D.C., 1950. 2v.

It too discovered grave lacunae in coverage of all types of literature, especially social science. As a result, UNESCO undertook remedial measures of its own.

UNESCO sponsored the *International bibliography of the social sciences*, which appears in four series: *International bibliography of sociology* (1951), *International bibliography of political science* (1952), *International bibliography of economics* (1952), and *International bibliography of social and cultural anthropology* (1955). At the same time, the International Committee for Social Sciences Documentation initiated *International political science abstracts* (1951).

Thereafter, numerous new indexing and abstracting services were added, being sponsored now not only by scholars and the Wilson Company, but also by commercial sources and governmental bodies. The list could become boring if made too comprehensive. In 1953, the American Sociological Association started *Sociological abstracts*. *Historical abstracts* appeared in 1955 from a commercial source, ABC-Clio. The *American behavioral scientist*, a journal, began publishing the *ABS guide to recent publications in the social and behavioral sciences* in 1957. In 1958, *Business periodicals index* emerged from the *Industrial arts index*.

Expansion in the 1960s and after was equally rapid. In 1961, the Centre Nationale de la Recherche Scientifique in France began the *Bulletin signalétique*, with sections on ethnology, sociology, education, and psychology. The American Economics Association started the *Index of economic journals* (now called *Index of economic articles*) in 1961 and followed up with the *Journal of economic literature* in 1969. The *Funk & Scott index of corporations and industries*, a commercial tool for business research, was begun in 1962. The Royal Anthropological Institute began *Anthropological index* in 1963, ABC-Clio added *America: history and life* in 1964, and the federal government initiated the ERIC system for unpublished educational research, *Resources in education*, in 1966, and for journal literature, *Current index to journals in education*, in 1969. *Geographical abstracts* came out of England in 1966, *ABC-pol sci* appeared in 1969, *Abstracts in anthropology* was started independently by American anthropologists in 1970, and the Wilson Company converted the *International index* to the *Social sciences and humanities index* in 1966. Eight years later, in 1974, this tool was divided into two more specialized indexes: the *Humanities index* and the *Social sciences index*. With the creation of *United States political science documents* (USPSD) in 1976, the American Political Science Association became involved in bibliographic activity.

Two particularly significant bibliographic developments of the late sixties and the seventies related to emerging computer technology. In the first place, efforts were made to utilize computers for the generation of print indexes by selecting key words from titles. The most sophisticated and useful tool to develop from this technology was the *Social sciences citation index*, begun by the Institute for Scientific Information in Philadelphia in 1969. It indexes hundreds of journals from all areas of the social sciences, deciding which are worth inclusion on the basis of citation analysis. Another set of tools generated by computer is the *Combined retrospective index series* (CRIS), published in 1974. It includes a *Combined retrospective index to journals in sociology*, *Journals in history*, and *Journals in political science*, as well as to *Book reviews in scholarly journals*. Though subject indexing is poor because of the approach used, the series has the merit of indexing journal articles and book reviews going back to the nineteenth century.

A second area in which the utilization of computer technology is having a significant impact is the development of machine-readable indexing/abstracting systems. The electronic format offers possibilities for quicker retrieval using a wider range of search keys than the traditional author and subject indexes available in print format. Retrieval by title words, abstract words, journal name, publication date, language, and other criteria, combined with the ability to apply Boolean logic in combining concepts, offers an enhanced ability to locate useful and recent leads in the literature. The principal drawbacks of the computerized bibliographic systems are that their chronological coverage is often more limited than that of the corresponding print indexes and that they eliminate patron browsing of the index.

The ever-expanding number of bibliographic databases available includes most of the more important print indexes and abstracts, among them *Sociological abstracts*, *Psychological abstracts*, ERIC, USPSD, PAIS, *America: history and life*, *Historical abstracts*, *Social sciences citation index*, *Language and language behavior abstracts* (LLBA), *F & S index*, and *Wilsonline* (the Wilson indexes). Online files also include indexes developed specifically for the computer, such as *Agricola*; indexes to government publications, including the *Monthly catalog*, the *Publication reference file*, and the *CIS index*; indexes to sources of statistics, such as the *American statistics index* (ASI); and indexes to newspaper and magazine literature, including the *National newspaper index* and the *Magazine index*.

Besides these bibliographic files, there is also a growing number of factual databases from which raw data may be extracted. Among these are the Predicast databases of business and economic statistics; files containing census data; and growing numbers of databases of traditional reference tools, such as *Foundation grants directory* or *American men and women of science*, becoming available online.

Several hundred files available for online searching can be accessed through three major vendors: Dialog Information Services, Bibliographic Retrieval Services (BRS), and System Development Corporation (SDC). Most academic libraries, large or medium-sized public libraries, and many special libraries now subscribe to one or more of these systems. In addition, there is a plethora of databases of a specialized nature available elsewhere.

SOCIAL SCIENCE LITERATURE AND ITS USES TODAY

The rapid expansion of the social sciences after World War II, as seen, occasioned a corresponding growth in the research literature generated. In response, the access literature underwent an era of unparalleled expansion as librarians, scholars, commercial sources, and the government made efforts to establish effective bibliographic control, first with new print tools, later with computerized sources that sometimes duplicated, sometimes supplemented, the hard copy. Yet, there was a feeling among librarians and information specialists who worked with the secondary literature that its use by social scientists was limited and sporadic. This impressionistic evidence stimulated some efforts to collect empirical data that might (1) determine how social scientists really work in satisfying their information needs, and (2) suggest ways of improving information systems and services in the social sciences.

Patterns of Use

Among the more significant studies designed to analyze use of social science materials are one conducted by the American Psychological Association in 1969, *Reports on the projects on scientific information exchange in psychology*, v. 3 (**A12**); the project published by D.F. Swift and V. Winn, "The 'Sociology of education abstracts' research report," *Education libraries bulletin* 38: 12–19 (1970) (**A13**); and the two sizable investigations carried out at the Bath University of Technology in England. The first of these, published in five parts in 1971, was called INFROSS, or *Investigation into information requirements of the social sciences* (**A14**); the second, published in parts in 1973–76, with a final report in 1980, was called DISISS, or *Design of information systems in the social sciences* (**A15**). These studies and several lesser ones of similar import constitute for the library world part of its own much needed labor of introspection and reassessment with regard to the social sciences—a labor that is still in progress.

The picture that emerges from these studies of how social scientists work can be summarized as follows.

—In tracking down bibliography, social scientists rely heavily on citations found in books and journal articles and on a variety of informal means, including personal recommendations and serendipitous discovery. Their use of formal bibliographic tools is sporadic and limited.

—Social science researchers rely equally heavily on book and journal literature, suggesting that bibliographic systems modeled on the literature of the physical sciences, where periodical literature predominates, are of limited utility to social researchers. Moreover, citations to book and journal literature together constitute only a third of the citations in the typical social science research project. The remaining two-thirds of the citations refer to either published or unpublished primary data.

—The wide variety of sources of primary data cited by social scientists, including such things as correspondence, government publications, printed document collections, memoirs and diaries, statistics, newspaper articles, magazine literature, published testing instruments, speeches, and a variety of others, may or may not have been produced by social scientists, and may have been produced for purposes other than social scientific research. Thus, they often cannot be indexed or cataloged as social science material per se.

—With the exception of psychologists and economists, who tend to cite their own literatures rather heavily, social researchers draw from a broad spectrum of social science disciplines. This is especially true of sociologists, political scientists, geographers, historians, and education specialists. This fact suggests that "discipline-centered" indexing systems are of limited value to social scientists, who must work extensively across disciplinary lines. Efforts to remedy this situation by trying to familiarize researchers with the dozens of indexing systems that might be of value to them have met with little success. Physical scientists, on the other hand, are generally well served with only a few comprehensive services.

—The "research process" of each social scientist is so highly individualized with regard to the conceptual and chronological relationship of such factors as idea generation, background reading and discussion, literature searching, data collection, research design, data analysis, hypothesis formulation, writing, and theorizing that it is impossible to come up with a generalization that approximates a complex reality. Consulting the literature is so often interrelated, in an inseparable intellectual process, with other aspects of the research project as it germinates, evolves, matures, and bears fruit in the mind of the researcher that the comprehensive, one-time literature search generally associated with the physical sciences may be an entirely inappropriate model for the social sciences generally.

—The demand for social science literature is not limited to academic researchers and specialists, as tends to be the case with scientific and much humanistic literature. Both practitioners—social workers, teachers, counselors, criminologists, etc.—and policymakers—politicians, administrators, planners, businessmen, etc.—are also users of social science literature. In each case, there are special nuances in their understanding of and approach to the literature. Practitioners have some theoretical grounding in the social sciences. However, because they are mainly occupied in working with clients, they use bibliographic tools very seldom, do not generally make efforts to keep current with the literature or the latest theoretical work, prefer informal channels of communication, and often need highly specific information for immediate application to a current problem. Policymakers generally have little or no theoretical grounding in the social sciences and tend to require specialized services in which information is distilled and packaged for them to serve as a guide in choosing from among several options.

Characteristics of the Literature

Besides these generalizations about the way social scientists and other users of social science information work, several studies, including the ones conducted at Bath University (A14, A15), have also identified some special characteristics of the literature of the social sciences.

9

A16   Hogeweg-DeHaart, H.P. "Social science and the characteristics of social science information and its users." *International forum on information and documentation* 8: 11–15 (1983).

A17   Brittain, J.M. "Information services and the structure of knowledge in the social sciences." *International social science journal* 31: 711–28 (1979).

A18   Line, Maurice B. "The information uses and needs of social scientists: an overview of INFROSS." *Aslib proceedings* 23: 412–34 (1971).

A19   ———. "Secondary services in the social sciences: the need for improvement and the role of librarians." *Behavioral & social science librarian* 1: 263–73 (1980).

A20   ———. "The structure of social science literature as shown by large scale citation analysis." *Social science information studies* 2: 67–87 (1981).

A21   ———, and Stephen Roberts. "The size, growth and composition of social science literature." *International social science journal* 28: 122–59 (1976).

The principal findings of these studies can be summarized as follows.

—Since World War II, the literature of the social sciences has grown more rapidly than either science or humanities literature. Perhaps 20 percent of current scholarly serials and an even higher percentage of scholarly books may be social science publications.

—Line and Roberts (A21) calculated from DISISS and other data that the total number of journal articles published in academic social science journals in 1970 came to about 140,000 (3,900 journals multiplied by 36 articles/title/year), compared to 130,000 social science monographs published in the same year. These figures would yield a ratio of journal articles to books of about 1.1:1, a marked contrast from the situation in the sciences, where the ratio is about 8:1. The social science figure dovetails with the results of a DISISS citation analysis revealing a ratio of 1.3:1 in citing the two forms of literature. Line cautioned that the figures for books include a great many popular or semipopular titles used by social scientists, whereas the figures for journals are limited to scholarly publications.

—The ratio of secondary services to journals in the social sciences increased from about 1:42 in 1920 to about 1:15 in 1970. According to Line, who did a detailed analysis of this situation in DISISS (A19), this statistic indicates an abundance of small, overlapping bibliographic services within each discipline that still fail to cover the literature adequately even when used in conjunction with other works. In other words, social researchers may have to consult a large number of secondary services in their own and related disciplines without identifying a significant percentage of potentially useful materials. This unfavorable reward-cost ratio discourages regular use of tools that seem to turn up few new leads at the expense of considerable personal effort. The INFROSS study indicated that at best social scientists use an average of 1.7 secondary services.

—The best coverage of the literature by secondary services occurs in psychology and economics. These are disciplines that are heavily self-citing, rely strongly on journal literature, and evince a high concentration of use in a relatively small number of journals. At the other extreme, geography, sociology, education, and political science make relatively few references to their own literatures, cite monographs heavily, and demonstrate a broad scatter of journal literature cited, both within themselves and from other disciplines. Line postulated that one possible reason for the smaller, more inexpensive secondary services in the social sciences is the lack of a wealthy market such as that for scientific and technological literature, demanded as it is by business, industry, and government. Another factor is the difficulty in defining just what constitutes the literature of most of the social sciences.

—Terminological problems abound in the social sciences, both within and between disciplines. Social science terms are often natural language terms with popular connotations and susceptible to numerous definitions; may be used in different ways in different disciplines; may have varied ideological connotations; and often overlap in confusing ways with similar or related terms. Such everyday words as imperialism, colonialism, exploitation, militarism, expansionism, racism, Marxism, and democracy, for example, may be interpreted and defined in many different ways. A coined expression like "groupthink" does not show up as a descriptor or subject heading. This terminological "softness" makes for greater difficulty in effective indexing and subsequent retrieval.

—Since most social science research projects are unique, with little replication carried out or even able to be carried out, the penalties for failing to identify potentially useful prior research are relatively mild. This characteristic of the literature relates to the lack of cumulativeness observed in much social scientific research.

—The social sciences seem to be lacking in reviews of research, a fact that may also be related to the lack of cumulativeness. A survey by Maurice Line and Stephen Roberts (A21) in the mid-1970s indicated a ratio of reviews to primary articles of 1:133, compared with a ratio of 1:45 in the sciences.

These findings indicate a complex of interrelated factors in the dialogue between social science researchers and the literature that have far-reaching and sometimes disturbing implications for librarians and information specialists. Those who create secondary services, too frequently influenced by models derived from the physical sciences, have created access tools that are often only marginally useful to social science researchers. Above all, the secondary tools generally fail to cover book literature, fail to take into account the cross-disciplinary nature of social science research, and frequently fail to cover even disciplinary journal literature very comprehensively. Moreover, access to the numerous printed sources of primary data that are also used extensively by social scientists is even less systematic. At the same time, the cognitive approaches utilized by social researchers because of the nature of their disciplines seem to make systematic exploitation of secondary services difficult. The result is a tendency on the part of researchers to avoid a bibliographic apparatus that is difficult to utilize because of its size and complexity, is poorly adapted to the peculiarities of their research and their disciplines, and yields only modest returns at the expense of considerable effort. This situation contrasts markedly with that of physical scientists, who may need to master only a few comprehensive bibliographic services for literature searching and who do not, as we shall see, use the library at all for primary data.

The INFROSS study, directed by Maurice Line, did reveal that most social scientists would be amenable to some or even considerable delegation of literature searching and other types of retrieval to an "information officer." Because of this, Line postulated that rather than continuing uninstitutionalized and sporadic attempts to "educate" social scientists to the tools, whose numbers and structure they find bewildering and frustrating, academic librarians should consider setting themselves up as intermediaries between social researchers and the bibliographic apparatus in imitation of special librarians. A trial run of just such an arrangement lasting for three years proved to be quite successful at Bath University, with the bibliographic tools receiving heavier use (by the information officers, of course) than they ever had before.

Line further noted that bibliographic tools could be developed to greater levels of complexity if it were understood that information specialists rather than patrons would be the principal users. As a matter of fact, the rise of online retrieval in the last ten years has to some extent created just such a situation, in which the search analyst serves as intermediary between the end user and the bibliographic tool. However, the question of the role of the academic librarian—intermediary or teacher—is one that must yet be resolved, for it is fraught with philosophical implications concerning the professional identity of librarians within the academy.

One last corollary to be derived from our present understanding of the weaknesses of the secondary literature in the social sciences is this. Since librarians, not end users, are the sole purchasers of these bibliographic tools, and since social scientists generally manage without being conversant with the tools, any impetus toward improvement in the quality and comprehensiveness of the access literature must come from the library world. The alternatives may be either to use librarians as intermediaries to tap the literature for the researchers, or to continue expending sizable amounts of money on seldom used materials.

STRUCTURE OF THE INFORMATION SYSTEM

An introduction to the variety of sources available to social scientists for research purposes must make one critical clarification at the outset. We must understand the distinction between primary data, on the one hand, and the written record, on the other. The hard core of a social science research project, like that of a physical science research project, consists of essentially uninterpreted data. In the sciences, such data nearly always come from outside the library—from laboratories, geological field trips, observation of marine life, astronomical observations, and what have you. In the social sciences, however, though primary data may come from outside the library, a great deal of it may also be in published form. Thus, historians may use memoirs, autobiographies, archival materials, government publications, printed document collections, newspapers, magazines, statistics, and so on. Psychologists may use data generated from laboratory experiments with animals, case studies of human beings, psychological tests, or a variety of types of behavioral observations. Sociologists may use data gathered from questionnaires, interviews, field research, content analysis, published statistics, or behavioral observation. Anthropologists may analyze artifacts, bones, and linguistics structure, or engage in field work. Economists rely heavily on statistics gathered and published by official sources, which they manipulate and subject to complex mathematical analysis. Political scientists may use many of the techniques of historians and sociologists in gathering and analyzing primary data. A moment's reflection on the types of data mentioned in the preceding sentences will make it obvious that some of it is generated outside the library, while much of it is to be found within the library.

The books and journal articles written by scholars to communicate to other researchers what they believe they have learned become part of the written record of published research. It is this literature, called "primary" by many information specialists, that bibliographers are attempting to control and make accessible. The bibliographic sources thus become "secondary" literature. Researchers, therefore, are involved not only in gathering and analyzing primary data, which make their research projects distinctive, but also in "consulting the record" to determine what research may already have been done by others in this same area.

The preceding discussion should make it obvious that in the physical sciences the distinction between the literature search, conducted in the library, and research, almost always conducted elsewhere, is fairly clear-cut. In the social sciences, however, the literature search and research may seem intertwined, for a great deal of primary data for many social scientists, as seen, can also be found in the library. In tracking down these primary data in published form, the social researcher will be using bibliographic techniques similar to those utilized in literature searching. Thus, the political scientist who consults USPSD, PAIS, and the *Social sciences index* in doing a literature search may then consult *American statistics index* (ASI) to track down sources of economic statistics, *America votes* to obtain election statistics, the *Almanac of American politics* to study the biographical background and

voting records of candidates, the *Monthly catalog* and *CIS index* to seek out hearings on electoral reform, and the card catalog to obtain the published results of Gallup polls. In the latter five cases, the researcher is seeking not research literature but primary data in published form.

To summarize, then, whereas physical scientists use bibliographic tools only to seek literature, social scientists use them to seek both literature and primary data in published form. The result is that scientists can manage well by mastering only a few comprehensive bibliographic tools, whereas social scientists may need to consult staggeringly large numbers of library resources in their quest for both literature and primary data.

A Conceptualization of the Literature of the Social Sciences

An important characteristic of social scientific literature, therefore—one that distinguishes it from scientific literature—is that much of it either contains primary data or is designed to access primary data. For example, the *Digest of educational statistics* contains primary data; ASI accesses those data by guiding the researcher to the *Digest*. If, therefore, we keep in mind that social science literature encompasses both scholarly literature and primary data, as well as access tools to both scholarly literature and primary data, we may be able to construct a somewhat different framework in which to fit the various categories of reference tools, documents, and other library materials used by social researchers. We must always keep in mind, however, that no conceptual framework will be entirely neat. Printed materials can be used for different purposes at different times, and some materials, such as national bibliographies or general guides to the literature, may provide access both to scholarly literature and to primary data sources.

With these reservations in mind, we may conceptualize three major categories of literature which, with their various subdivisions, reflect the functional role of different types of library materials as used by social scientists. We can call them Scholarly Literature, Primary Data in Published Form, and Incidental Professional and Scholarly Information.

Scholarly Literature

In this category are included (1) materials generated by scholars and (2) the access tools designed to locate those materials. This literature falls into four major categories.

1. *Original Research Literature.* This grouping includes books, journal articles, research reports, theses, and dissertations in which scholars report to others the results of specific research projects.
2. *Derivative Research Literature.* This category includes books and journal materials that function as textbooks, introductions, systematic works, histories of disciplines, works on theory, method, and philosophy, treatises on progress and problems of the discipline, book reviews, and reviews of research.
3. *Synthetic Literature.* This category includes encyclopedias, dictionaries, atlases, and many kinds of handbooks and compendia.
4. *Bibliographic Literature.* These are tools designed to provide access to the first three categories of literature. They may be subdivided in a variety of different ways. They include individual bibliographies, indexing systems, abstracting systems, other types of serial bibliographies, bibliographies of bibliographies, book review indexes, library catalogs, national and trade bibliographies, and guides to the literature, both specialized and general. Library catalogs and national and trade bibliographies are not social science tools per se, but in the absence of discipline-centered sources seeking systematic control of the book literature they must be used to perform this function.

Primary Data in Published Form

In this category are included (1) materials providing primary data and (2) the access tools designed to identify them. These materials fall into two logical subdivisions.

1. *Published Primary Data.* This disparate category can include memoirs; diaries; printed correspondence; printed document collections; government publications; collections of laws, treaties, and constitutions; judicial opinions; published results of polls; collections of validated and unvalidated testing instruments; newspapers; magazines; news-

reporting services; yearbooks; almanacs; compendia; biographical tools; certain types of handbooks and manuals; statistical compilations; speeches; looseleaf services; and others. These materials may be found in the general collection, the reference collection, or the documents collection. Many of them cannot be identified as social science materials per se.

2. *Access Tools to Primary Data.* This category includes indexes to statistics, biographical sources, newspapers, and magazines; directories of directories; guides to archival sources; indexes to government publications, including state, federal, and international documents; looseleaf services; library catalogs; national and trade bibliographies; and guides to the literature. An interesting aspect of this category of access tools is that they may index not only published primary data but also primary materials of a non-library nature, e.g., a guide to manuscript materials in the National Archives. Like the published primary data they access, many cannot be identified as social science materials per se.

Incidental Professional and Scholarly Information

Besides the several categories of literature that fall under the previous two classifications, both of which are intimately related to mastery of and research in the discipline, there also exists a category of literature, primarily of a reference nature, that provides incidental information to the scholar. Included are style manuals, guides to nonprint media like filmstrips, motion pictures, audiocassettes, etc., for use in the classroom, and biographical materials. Most important, however, are the great majority of directories providing names, addresses, and phone numbers of such disparate individuals and organizations as research centers, publishers, journal editors, newspapers, Chambers of Commerce, institutions of higher education, social work agencies, juvenile detention centers, prisons, homes for the aged, public school systems, state and local historical societies, federal, state, or local government agencies, international agencies and organizations, politicians, diplomats, professional associations, businesses, and so on.

This tripartite classification does not conform to the schemes generally used by librarians, most of whom think in terms of the general collection, composed of books and journals; the documents collection; and the reference collection, whose materials are subdivided according to format, i.e., bibliographies, biographical tools, directories, indexes, atlases, etc. It would be valuable for those working with social scientists, however, to keep in mind the functional relationship of all types of library materials to the research process, which this scheme attempts to delineate. With this conceptual framework in mind, individual types of sources may be treated in any order. For simplicity's sake, the remainder of this chapter will roughly follow the format used in the second edition of this book, since the subject chapters have also retained such a format. A brief characterization of each subcategory of sources follows.

Monographs

With rare exceptions, the treatment will be limited to the two more learned branches of this large family of sources, that is, to (1) reports, in separate publications or in series, of original research and (2) treatises designed to serve other scholarly purposes besides reporting research. Types of sources in this second branch include general introductions and systematic works, milestones in the development of major branches of learning, histories that trace the development of the discipline and record contributions of those who have done the most to further it, works on theory and method, and treatises on the progress and problems of the profession to which the discipline is entrusted.

Guides to the Literature

Loosely used, this term refers to any work that helps someone use books. It is used here in a narrower sense to refer to the type of source designed to map the way through the literature of a reasonably extensive area, the type which in so doing helps evaluate, organize, and introduce the literature. This distinguishes it from its two cousins: the bibliographical list (whether annotated or unannotated) and the introductory treatise. It is more versatile, more informative than the one, and, unlike the other, it introduces the literature, not the content of the subject.

Reviews

This versatile type of source is being put to increased use as the literature to be scanned proliferates. One use is to review the literature. The oldest channel for the purpose is the book review section of the multipurpose journal. Psychology spearheaded two moves to improve this long-accepted model. One is to abandon the scatter-

ing of book reviews among journals (which normally have to subordinate book reviewing to the publication of original papers) and to centralize current book reviews in one organ. The older method is still widespread, however. The other move is to produce periodic reviews of research based on the relevant literature, and this can be done in several ways. The annual review of research in an area is the most popular.

The third type of review differs from all of these: its emphasis falls on gathering objective data on the overall communication process within a field. It has obvious uses for planning how to organize the process so as to facilitate access to information. We shall, accordingly, include studies of significance for bibliographic policy along with conventional reviews.

Abstracts, Summaries, Précis, and Digests

These sources offer no critical assessments, and do not relate individual works to one another, but stand next to reviews in informative quality. Abstracts that are accurately indicative or fully descriptive of the nature of a contribution are a popular approach to indexing the journal literature, and have proliferated in the last several decades. The sources most in demand are current, but some are retrospective. Like other current bibliographic services, abstracts and related summaries acquire retrospective research uses as the date of publication recedes.

Bibliographies and Indexes

Exhibiting extremes in scope, purpose, and makeup, bibliographies and indexes share responsibility for *listing* books, articles, maps, films, etc., according to some pattern—whether by author, subject, title, form, date of publication, or some other means. The material may be current or retrospective. A valuable subclass is the bibliography of bibliographies. The information a bibliography provides is often limited to selection, organization, and a bare listing of items, but annotations may add expository, critical, or promotional information. Here and there, bibliographies take on the more instructive characteristics associated with one or the other of the three preceding types of sources.

Directories

The minimum object of this heavily used class of tools is to supply accurate identification and addresses of people, organizations, places, periodicals, and other things. It is the principal type of source providing incidental professional information.

Biographical Tools

This diverse class of sources may provide either incidental professional information or primary data for research purposes. The former category would include, for example, membership directories of professional organizations. The latter could include a wide range of biographical dictionaries, encyclopedias, and directories providing information on deceased or living persons.

Dictionaries

A classic example of the synthetic tool, their first object is to define the meaning of words and phrases. They may be general or subject-oriented.

Encyclopedias and Encyclopedic Sets

This type of source represents man's most ambitious efforts to sum up the knowledge he accumulates. It is further distinguished by scholarly treatment that places the subject in historical perspective, identifies those who have furthered its advancement, and introduces the most pertinent literature. The customary style is to break down the treatment into an alphabetical arrangement, but the arrangement may be systematic, as in an encyclopedic set. It is the purpose and scope of the information, not the style of presentation, that determine whether a source is encyclopedic.

Handbooks, Manuals, Almanacs, and Compendia

This type of work is so useful that a person wants to keep it near at hand—the *vade mecum* of a world of information users. These works vary extraordinarily in content, as the insistent, specialized needs that generate them require. They include parliamentary manuals, foreign exchange tables, date chronologies for students of history, and (not least) the learned handbook, pioneered by the German *Handbuch*. The latter is sometimes looked upon as a small encyclopedia with good reason, for it is an authoritative synthesis of the work, and/or productive methods of work, in an established field of scholarship.

Yearbooks

Information on current developments is indispensable in any field, and particularly in one that is of interest to many people. The structure of news reporting is by recency, dailies and annuals being in general more popular than reports at in-between intervals. The annual reporting of yearbooks is prized for the solid perspective such an interval makes possible. Certain yearbooks prove so handy that they are indistinguishable from handbooks as above defined.

Original Sources

Containing primary data for research but too vast to be treated thoroughly, this type and its role in the system will be depicted mainly by published collections of original sources.

Statistical Sources

It will be convenient to treat this special type of original material as a separate class because of (1) the importance of statistical information and (2) the desirability of bringing such sources together in one place. The best examples play roles that are comparable to those of handbooks and yearbooks.

Atlases, Pictorial Works, and Kindred Graphic Sources

These are compilations of information that depend less on the printed word than on some other medium. Social sciences vary in the amount and kind of nonprint sources they use.

Sources of Scholarly Contributions

These are the journals that form the heart of the established system of reporting research, monograph series that help round out the reporting system, and organizations that stimulate research or in other ways significantly influence the development of scholarly literature.

Sources of Current Information

Social scientists rely on a variety of media to keep up with news that bears on their professional activities, and three classes of first importance are (1) separately published news organs, specifically designed for members of the profession, which are increasing in number; (2) ancillary news channels, of which the news sections of multipurpose journals are most typical; and (3) the more important general news media.

MONOGRAPHS

The substantive literature presented here, more limited in quantity that in the subject chapters that are to follow, centers primarily on contributions of an interdisciplinary nature. Because of the centrality of sociological thought to social science thinking in general, many titles will of necessity be derived from that discipline.

Introductions and Systematic Works

Among the most important types of derivative research literature are those works that seek to synthesize the current state of our understanding of a field. To the extent that cumulativeness does exist in the social sciences, it receives expression in attempts to systematize and generalize from the multitude of individual research projects that find their way into print as journal articles or as books. The last attempt at systematization of social science knowledge on a grand scale can be found in the *International encyclopedia of the social sciences* (A415), now a generation out of date. Though still useful, it must nonetheless be supplemented with shorter and more recent summaries. Among the best of these are the following.

A21A Apsler, Alfred. An introduction to social science. 3d ed. New York: Random, 1980. 541p.

A22   Berelson, Bernard, ed. The behavioral sciences today. New York: Basic Books, 1963. 278p.

A23   Bierstedt, Robert. Modern social science. New York: McGraw-Hill, 1964. 725p.

A24   Brown, Gary D. A survey of the social sciences. New York: McGraw-Hill, 1975. 374p.

A25   Homans, George C. The nature of social science. New York: Harcourt, 1967. 109p.

A27   Hunt, Elgin F. Social science: an introduction to the study of society. 5th ed. New York: Macmillan, 1984. 557p.

A28   Kuhn, Alfred. Unified social science: a system-based introduction. Homewood, Ill.: Dorsey, 1975. 540p.

A29   MacRae, Duncan. The social function of social science. New Haven, Conn.: Yale Univ. Pr., 1976. 352p.

A30   McIntosh, Donald. The foundations of human society. Chicago: Univ. of Chicago Pr., 1969. 341p.

Also see Berthold F. Hoselitz, *A reader's guide to the social sciences,* described at A125.

Histories

Though systematic treatments of a field of intellectual endeavor sometimes include a historical component, their major thrust is to summarize our present state of knowledge. To achieve a complete appreciation of where scholarship now stands and how it got there, however, it is essential to plunge into full-fledged historical analysis. Our interpretation of the past is conditioned by our perceptions of present problems; our view of the present is shaped by our understanding of the evolution of ideas and events that brought us to this juncture. Such introspective evaluation is essential to a full and mature appreciation of present problems and future prospects.

Though the best histories are to be found in the component disciplines, there are a number of more general ones that merit consideration. Barnes and Becker still come closest to a satisfactory unified history of the social sciences. A number of the better historical works deal more specifically with sociology, but the catholicity of this discipline causes it to lap over naturally into the literature of other fields, contributing thus to a fuller understanding of all social science endeavor. Two good works that establish a solid historical base for further study are Philip Abrams, *The origins of British sociology, 1834–1914: an essay with selected papers* (Chicago: Univ. of Chicago Pr., 1968 [304p.]) **(A31)** and Albion W. Small, *Origins of sociology* (New York: Russell, 1967, 1924 [359p.]). **(A32)**.

A33   Abel, Theodore. The foundation of sociological theory. New York: Random, 1970. 258p.

A34   Aron, Raymond. Main currents in sociological thought; tr. by Richard Howard and Helen Weaver. Garden City, N.Y.: Anchor, 1968. 2v.

A35   Bell, Daniel. The social sciences since the Second World War. New Brunswick, N.J.: Transaction, 1982. 102p.

A36   Becker, Howard, and H.E. Barnes. Social thought from lore to science. 3d ed., exp. and rev. Gloucester, Mass.: Peter Smith, 1978. 3v.

A37   Bernard, Luther L., and Jessie Bernard. Origins of American sociology: the social science movement in the United States. New York: Russell, 1965, 1943. 866p.

A38   Bogardus, Emory S. The development of social thought. 4th ed. Westport, Conn.: Greenwood, 1979, 1960. 689p.

A39   Bonner, Thomas N. The contemporary world: the social sciences in historical perspective. Englewood Cliffs, N.J.: Prentice-Hall, 1960. 594p.

A40   Johnson, Doyle Paul. Sociological theory: classical founders and contemporary perspectives. New York: Wiley, 1981. 597p.

A41   Nisbet, Robert. The sociological tradition. New York: Basic Books, 1966. 349p.

The Scientific Method

Debates over the scientific method are central to philosophical arguments over the nature of the social sciences, their research methods, and what social scientists can reasonably expect to achieve. Some theorists reject the assumption that the social sciences are even "scientific" or can be modeled on the physical sciences. Most theorists, however, still accept the thesis that social research can be scientific. They debate, rather, the exact definition of "the scientific method," if such a thing even exists, in the physical sciences and the implications thereof for social research. The role of theory, of subjectivity, of commitment, of paradigm, and of methodology in the scientific enterprise are topics of ever current interest. Important books on the scientific method, nearly all of which touch on the social sciences, are these.

A42   Hanson, Norwood Russell. Patterns of discovery: an inquiry into the conceptual foundations of science. Cambridge: Cambridge Univ. Pr., 1958. 240p.

A43   Holton, Gerald. Thematic origins of scientific thought: Kepler to Einstein. Cambridge, Mass. Harvard Univ. Pr., 1973. 495p.

A44   Kaplan, Abraham. The conduct of inquiry. San Francisco: Chandler, 1964. 428p.

A45   Kuhn, Thomas S. The structure of scientific revolutions. 2d ed., enl. Chicago: Univ. of Chicago Pr., 1970. 210p.

A46   Polanyi, Michael. Personal knowledge: toward a post-critical philosophy. Chicago: Univ. of Chicago Pr., 1974, 1962. 428p.

A47   Popper, Karl R. Objective knowledge: an evolutionary approach. Rev. ed. Oxford: Clarendon, 1971. 396p.

A48   Ravetz, Jerome R. Scientific knowledge and its social problems. Oxford: Clarendon, 1971. 449p.

A49   Scheffler, Israel. Science and subjectivity. 2d ed. Indianapolis: Haskett, 1982. 166p.

A50   Toulmin, Stephen. Human understanding. Vol. 1: The collective use and evolution of concepts. Princeton, N.J.: Princeton Univ. Pr., 1972. 520p.

Philosophy of the Social Sciences

Any attempt at examining the philosophy of the social sciences will necessarily be closely linked to the history of these disciplines, since schools of thought can be explained only in terms of their origins, development, and evolution through time. Any attempt to list the major writings that have contributed to the changing philosophies of the social sciences will necessarily be somewhat subjective and often ideologically discriminatory. Nevertheless, the presentation of even a good sample of important titles, however arbitrarily selected, will be enough to get the reader into an intellectual realm in which citation patterns alone will ultimately lead to virtually every other work that might prove to be of value. Nearly every title mentioned in this section is amply laden with bibliographic references to relevant portions of the literature.

One could simply elaborate a long list of writers who have made significant contributions to thought on the epistemological foundations of the social sciences. In conceptual terms, however, it would be more beneficial to consider thinkers in relation to the powerful positivistic tradition, for the history of philosophical conflict within the social sciences can be viewed, somewhat arbitrarily, in terms of (1) debates within the positivistic tradition and (2) attacks upon the positivistic tradition. We will proceed accordingly.

The Positivistic Tradition

What many call the "positivist orthodoxy" emerged gradually out of the thought of Francis Bacon (1561–1626), René Descartes (1596–1650), Auguste Comte (1798–1857), John Stuart Mill (1806–73), and Herbert Spencer (1820–1903). Of the great trio of classical social thinkers of the nineteenth century—Émile Durkheim (1858–1917), Max Weber (1818–83), and Karl Marx (1864–1920)—Durkheim best fits into the early positivistic tradition. The other two, as we shall see, were not positivists. Weber, whose thought grew out of the Continental idealist tradition, influenced the development of Parsonian functionalism, which will be discussed later. Marx had a powerful impact on all forms of conflict theory, which will also be discussed shortly.

In the twentieth century, positivism, in either its original "radical" form or its later "logical empirical" form, became so widespread, especially in the Anglo-American world, that its enemies came to see it as the unarticulated philosophy of the social science establishment. Its basic elements can be presented, somewhat crudely, in the following terms. First, reality consists essentially of what is available to the senses. Second, metaphysical issues have no place in the practice of essentially empirical disciplines. Third, the social sciences share with the sciences a common logic and methodological foundation. And fourth, normative concerns are beyond the scope of social scientific research. This last element results in strong emphasis on the empirically verifiable accompanied by a suspicion of value-laden theorizing, speculation, or interpretation.

It is perhaps a bit bold to list thinkers who fit at

least loosely into the positivistic intellectual stream, for not only do they not form a self-conscious school but they exhibit a wide range of tendencies and emphases with regard to the nuances of their research philosophies. The following list, however, is fairly representative.

A51 Catton, William R., Jr. From animistic to naturalistic sociology. New York: McGraw-Hill, 1966. 364p.

A52 Goode, William J. Explorations in social theory. New York: Oxford Univ. Pr., 1973. 449p.

A53 Nagel, Ernest. The structure of science: problems in the logic of scientific explanation. New York: Harcourt, 1961. 618p.

A54 Stinchcombe, Arthur. Constructing sociological theories. New York: Harcourt, 1968. 303p.

A55 Wallace, Walter L., ed. Sociological theory: an introduction. Chicago: Aldine, 1969. 296p.

A56 Zetterberg, Hans L. On theory and verification in sociology. 3d ed., enl. Totowa, N.J.: Bedminster Pr., 1965. 177p.

In twentieth-century American positivistic thought, several theoretical positions of considerable influence have appeared. They are symbolic interactionism, exchange theory, and middle range theory. Each will be dealt with briefly.

SYMBOLIC INTERACTIONISM

George Herbert Mead must rank as the founding father of this theory of behavior and organization. Drawing on social psychological theories, Mead emphasized the importance of self-consciousness, of being able to analyze and interpret our own behavior from the perspective of others, as giving rise to shared subjective definitions through which human beings negotiate their social relationships. The creation and manipulation of symbols is thus crucial in explaining, not merely describing, human conduct and social organization. Some important writers who fit into the symbolic interactionist tradition are as follows.

A57 Blumer, Herbert. Symbolic interactionism: perspective and method. Englewood Cliffs, N.J.: Prentice-Hall, 1969. 208p.

A58 Cooley, Charles H. Human nature and social order. New Brunswick, N.J.: Transaction, 1983, 1902. 414p.

A59 Goffman, Erving. The presentation of self in everyday life. Woodstock, N.Y.: Overlook Pr., 1973, 1959. 259p.

A60 McCall, George, and J.L. Simmons. Identities and interactions. Rev. ed. New York: Free Pr., 1978. 288p.

A61 Mead, George Herbert. Mind, self, and society; ed. with an introd. by Charles W. Morris. Chicago: Univ. of Chicago Pr., 1974, 1934. 401p.

EXCHANGE THEORY

Like other strains of American positivism, exchange theory emphasizes the typical American emphasis on individualism as a touchstone for understanding social behavior. George C. Homans, powerfully influenced by the ideas of B.F. Skinner, was one of the pioneers in the development of the theory. He emphasized the influence of positive and negative reinforcement in shaping how human beings choose to conduct themselves, for some behaviors offer a more favorable reward-cost ratio. Though Homans emphasized primarily face-to-face encounters, Thibaut and Kelley and Blau made efforts to expand the theory to encompass larger and more complex social processes.

A62 Blau, Peter M. Exchange and power in social life. New York: Wiley, 1964. 352p.

A63 ———. On the nature of organizations. Malabar, Fla.: Krieger, 1983, 1974. 358p.

A64 Homans, George C. The human group. London: Routledge & Paul, 1975, 1950. 484p.

A65 ———. Social behavior: its elementary forms. Rev. ed. New York: Harcourt, 1974. 386p.

A66 Thibaut, John W., and Harold H. Kelley. The social psychology of groups. New York: Wiley, 1959. 313p.

MIDDLE RANGE THEORY

The man strongly identified with middle range theory is Robert K. Merton. Educated in the anti-positivistic functionalist tradition (by Talcott Parsons himself), Merton ultimately shrank from the "grand theory" approach of his mentor to a more empirical posture that emphasized a "middle range" between the abstract systematic theorizing of the Parsonians and the often theory-poor microanalysis of many positivists. His middle range theory was not a comprehensive social theory but a strategy for analyzing and explaining empirical data.

A67 Merton, Robert K. Social theory and social structure. Enl. ed. New York: Free Pr., 1968. 702p.

Anti-Positivistic Approaches

Anti-positivistic social theories are susceptible to various classification schemes. Among the earlier ones in this century was the "human studies" critique that frankly rejected the "objectivism" of the positivist tradition. A thinker strongly identified with this critique, Wilhelm Dilthey, rejected the natural sciences as a model for the social sciences, since the former can only *explain* observed events by relating them to each other in accordance with natural laws. With human behavior, however, it should be possible to *understand* actions in terms of inner feelings, thoughts, and desires. Knowledge of human behavior is not simply external, but is based on insight into psychological motivation.

A68 Dilthey, Wilhelm. Selected writings. New York: Cambridge Univ. Pr., 1976. 268p.

A second early critique of positivism was phenomenology, which traces itself to Edmund Husserl. His powerful critique of the positivistic position, *The crisis of European sciences and transcendental phenomenology; an introduction to phenomenological philosophy*; tr. by David Carr (Evanston, Ill.: Northwestern Univ. Pr., 1970 [405p.]) (A69) appeared originally in 1935 and has influenced thinkers in several of the social sciences. Husserl denied that human beings can know social reality as such through any empirical approach. They see what they have been culturally conditioned to see, and can only study the beliefs people have about reality. Husserl's subjectivist orientation (in contrast to the objectivist orientation of positivism) has appeared in the thought of the following writers.

A70 Berger, Peter L., and Thomas Luckmann. The social construction of reality. New York: Irvington, 1980, 1966. 203p.

A71 Merleau-Ponty, Maurice. Science and nonsense. Evanston, Ill.: Northwestern Univ. Pr., 1964. 193p.

A72 Schutz, Alfred. The phenomenology of the social world. Evanston, Ill.: Northwestern Univ. Pr., 1967. 255p.

Among the antipositivist strains of thought, however, the most powerful have been the functionalism of Talcott Parsons and his followers, various categories of conflict theory, many of them Marxist or influenced to some extent by Marxism, and an increasingly influential "general systems" theory.

FUNCTIONALISM

It is difficult to do justice to the theories of Talcott Parsons, founder of functionalism. He brought back from his education in Germany a powerful attachment to European theoretical social thinking that conflicted sharply with the empirical tradition dominant in the United States. Beginning with his classic *The structure of social action* (New York: McGraw-Hill, 1937 [817p.]) (A73), he succeeded in injecting into American social thinking a powerful dose of the thought of Max Weber. Villified by his enemies as a disguised idealist attempting to parade as scientific, Parsons nonetheless forced nearly every thinker to attempt to come to grips with his grand theory approach, which sought to state general principles of individual and social behavior, applicable to micro- or macro-analysis, that cut across cultural boundaries. Through the 1950s and 1960s, his functionalism was a major force in American social thinking, and a "third generation" Parsonian, Jeffrey Alexander, is presently attempting to perpetuate a now much weakened legacy. Some important Parsonian thinkers are as follows.

A74 Alexander, Jeffrey C. Theoretical logic in sociology. Berkeley: Univ. of California Pr., 1982.

    v. 1. Positivism, presuppositions, and current controversies

    v. 2. The antinomies of classical thought: Marx and Durkheim

    v. 3. The classical attempt at theoretical synthesis: Max Weber

    v. 4. The modern reconstruction of classical thought: Talcott Parsons

A75 Smelser, Neil J. Essays in sociological explanation. Englewood Cliffs, N.J.: Prentice-Hall, 1968. 280p.

A76 ———. Sociology. Englewood Cliffs, N.J.: Prentice-Hall, 1981. 552p.

CONFLICT THEORY

Conflict theorists usually draw at least to some extent on Marxist ideas in emphasizing the role of social conflict in bringing about internal modifications and adaptations in social systems, whether as a way of arriving at a new equilibrium or of bringing about a fundamental restructuring of socioeconomic and political relationships. Like the functionalists, they are given to social theorizing at the grand level, divorced from close attention to empirical corroboration.

The Marxist strain of thought, like thought in other traditions, has been characterized by evolution, fragmentation, conflict, and divergent philosophical nuances and tendencies, both within and without Marxist nations. Our primary concern here is to list some of the more prominent Western Marxists and neo-Marxists of the last generation, for they form a loose ideological family whose fundamental precepts are in conflict with the positivist tradition. A fairly well-defined group of Marxists is the so-called Frankfurt School, which emerged in the 1930s at the Institute for Social Research at the University of Frankfurt. Its earliest devotees were Adorno, Horkheimer, and Marcuse. A younger follower is Habermas.

A77   Adorno, Theodor W. Prisms; tr. by Samuel and Sherry Weber. London: Spearman, 1967. 272p.

A78   Habermas, Jürgen. Knowledge and human interests. Boston: Beacon, 1971. 356p.

A79   ———. Toward a rational society. Boston: Beacon, 1970. 132p.

A80   Horkheimer, Max, and Theodor W. Adorno. Dialectic of enlightenment. New York: Seabury, 1972. 258p.

A81   Marcuse, Herbert. One dimensional man: studies in the ideology of advanced industrial society. Boston: Beacon, 1964. 260p.

Other important Marxist writers have been as follows.

A82   Althusser, Louis. For Marx. London: Allen Lane, 1969. 272p.

A83   Giddens, Anthony. Capitalism and modern social theory. Cambridge, Mass.: Cambridge Univ. Pr., 1971. 261p.

A84   Gouldner, Alvin W. The coming crisis of Western sociology. New York: Basic Books, 1970. 528p.

A85   Lukács, György. History and class consciousness: studies in Marxist dialectics. Cambridge, Mass.: MIT Pr., 1971. 356p.

A86   Sartre, Jean-Paul. Critique of dialectical reason, theory of practical ensembles; tr. by Alan Sheridan-Smith. Atlantic Highlands, N.J.: Humanities, 1976. 835p.

The exact dividing line between Marxists and non-Marxists is often vague, since the latter usually derive ideas from the former. Among other important conflict thinkers are the following:

A87   Collins, Randall. Conflict sociology: toward an explanatory science. New York: Academic, 1975. 548p.

A88   Dahrendorf, Ralf. Class and class conflict in industrial society. Stanford, Calif.: Stanford Univ. Pr., 1959. 336p.

A89   Mills, C. Wright. The sociological imagination. Oxford: Oxford Univ. Pr., 1967, 1959. 234p.

GENERAL SYSTEMS THEORY

General or open systems theory, which traces itself to the biologist Ludwig von Bertalanffy, seeks to analyze social behavior in the broadest possible context, including the biological, the environmental, and the behavioral. It sees a basic unity in the sciences—whether physical, biological, or social—as they seek out patterns of interdependence between interrelated elements. A change in any part of the total organization, however small, sets off a chain of readjustments throughout the entire system as it seeks to maintain or change itself. Thus, general systems theorists incorporate both material and social elements in their models, and claim to be able to make use of symbolic interactionism, exchange theory, functionalism, and conflict theory in a single conceptual framework. They also make some use of sociobiology. Important thinkers in this tradition are as follows.

A90   Allen, T. Harrell. New methods in social science research: policy sciences and futures research. New York: Praeger, 1978. 157p.

A91   Bertalanffy, Ludwig von. General systems theory: foundations, development, applications. Rev. ed. New York: Braziller, 1980, 1968. 295p.

A92   Buckley, Walter. Sociology and modern systems theory. New York: Prentice-Hall, 1967. 227p.

Recent Research Trends

The preceding sections dealt with broader philosophical issues of social science research and its relationship to research in the sciences. In this section, we will deal with more specific areas of recent research interest, though we must offer two cautions at the outset. First, the selections will, as in the preceding sections, be somewhat arbitrary, and titles mentioned earlier will not be repeated routinely even where they could be mentioned again in the narrower context under consideration here. Second, we will make some effort to avoid writings that are too narrow in disciplinary scope, preferring instead to seek out more general works. Two excellent books to start with are those of Daniel Bell (A35) and T. Harrell Allen (A90). In succeeding sections, we will deal in turn with five important areas of investigation in recent years: futures research, policy sciences, evaluation research, sociobiology, and structuralism.

Futures Research

As an area of research interest, futures research began to flourish only in the late sixties. Though some of the more "philosophical" and "intuitive" approaches to the field are suspect in academic social science circles, approaches that use statistics and other empirical techniques in forecasting social change have become rather influential and respectable. Such specific methods as trend extrapolation, scenarios, the Delphi technique, cross-impact analysis, simulation modeling, simulation gaming, decision trees, and technological forecasting are among those used by futures researchers.

A93 Ascher, William. Forecasting: an appraisal for policy-makers and planners. Baltimore: Johns Hopkins Univ. Pr., 1978. 239p.

A94 Cornish, Edward. The study of the future: an introduction to the art and science of understanding and shaping tomorrow's world. Washington, D.C.: World Future Society, 1977. 307p.

A95 Fowles, Jib, ed. Handbook of futures research. Westport, Conn.: Greenwood, 1978. 815p.

A96 Jantsch, Erich. Technological planning and social futures. New York: Wiley, 1972. 256p.

A97 Jouvenel, Bertrand de. The art of conjecture; tr. by Nikita Lary. New York: Basic Books, 1967. 307p.

A98 Schwartz, Brita, and others. Methods in futures studies: problems and applications. Boulder, Colo.: Westview, 1982. 175p.

Policy Sciences

The idea of utilizing research as a way of improving policy-making goes back at least to the classic book *The policy sciences: recent developments in scope and method*, edited by Harold Lasswell and Daniel Lerner (Stanford, Calif.: Stanford Univ. Pr., 1951 [344p.]) **(A99)**. Lasswell eventually came out with a more fully developed work entitled *A pre-view of policy sciences* (New York: Elsevier, 1971 [173p.]) **(A100)**. Some other important writings in this area are these:

A101 Coleman, James S. Policy research in the social sciences. Morristown, N.J.: General Learning Pr., 1972. 23p.

A102 Dror, Yehezkel. Design for policy sciences. New York: Elsevier, 1971. 156p.

A103 Horowitz, Irving Louis, and James Everett Katz. Social science and public policy in the United States. New York: Praeger, 1975. 187p.

Evaluation Research

Closely related to the development of policy sciences has been the area of evaluation research or program evaluation. Its purpose is to assess, in a deliberate and structured way, the impact of a program of social intervention to determine if the consequences do indeed fulfill the expectations of the policymakers. Several excellent books dealing in detail with evaluation research are as follows.

A104 Bennett, Carl A., and Arthur A. Lumsdaine, eds. Evaluation and experiment: some critical issues in assessing social programs. New York: Academic, 1975. 553p.

A105 Finsterbusch, Kurt, and Annabelle Motz. Social research for policy decisions. Belmont, Calif.: Wadsworth, 1980. 199p.

A106 Nachmias, David, ed. The practice of policy evaluation. New York: St. Martin's, 1980. 478p.

A107 Riecken, Henry W., and Robert F. Boruch, eds. Social experimentation: a method of planning and evaluating social intervention. New York: Academic, 1974. 339p.

Sociobiology

This strain of thought owes its recent influence to several thinkers, though Wilson is perhaps the one who attracted the most attention.

A108 Wilson, Edward O. Sociobiology: the new synthesis. Cambridge, Mass.: Belknap, 1975. 697p.

Wilson, in an effort to relate biology and the social sciences in such a way as to explain basic patterns of social behavior in terms of evolutionary biology, created quite a stir because of his strong emphasis on the impact of heredity on human behavior, thus contributing another powerful argument to one side of the never ending nature vs. nurture controversy. Other writers of note are these:

A109 Barash, David P. Sociobiology and behavior. 2d ed. New York: Elsevier, 1982, 1977. 426p.

A110 Berghe, Pierre L. van den. Man in society: a biosocial view. 2d ed. New York: Elsevier, 1978. 349p.

A111 Tiger, Lionel, and Robin Fox. The imperial animal. New York: Holt, 1971. 308p.

Structuralism

Guided by a belief that it is possible to identify in an objective way invariant relationships in the social world using a human mind whose underlying structure is rational, the structural movement has permeated a number of fields, especially psychology, anthropology, educational theory, psychoanalysis, linguistics, and literary criticism. Some strains of Neo-Marxism have been influenced by it. Jean Piaget, Claude Lévi-Strauss, Louis Althusser, Jacques Derrida, Roland Barthes, Jacques Lacan, and Michel Foucault are prominent names identified with the movement in recent times. Two useful books dealing with structuralism are as follows.

A112 Benoist, Jean-Marie. The structural revolution. New York: St. Martin's, 1978. 247p.

A113 Gardner, Howard. The quest for mind: Piaget, Lévi-Strauss, and the structuralist movement. 2d ed. Chicago: Univ. of Chicago Pr., 1981. 303p.

Research Methods in the Social Sciences

There is a plethora of books dealing with research methods in general or with specific areas of methodology. These generally concentrate on the hypothetico-inductive model of current empirical research, describing the relationship of theory, models, and hypotheses to the gathering and analyzing of empirical data drawn from the social world. Consequently, they cover such areas as sampling, questionnaires, interviews, experiments, survey research, field research, unobtrusive investigation, measurement issues, the use of statistical analysis to evaluate data, and, increasingly, the uses of computers in social science research. No good purpose would be served by presenting a long list of such titles, for a good general text will contain a bibliography adequate to direct the investigator toward any aspect of methodology. We will, therefore, mention only two solid introductions.

A114 Babbie, Earl. The practice of social research. 3d ed. Belmont, Calif.: Wadsworth, 1983. 551p.

A115 Nachmias, David, and Chava Nachmias. Research methods in the social sciences. 2d ed. New York: St. Martin's, 1981. 585p.

Survey of the Reference Works

The classes of material to which we now turn contribute differing types of information but, as a group, can be said to play a supporting role in instruction, research, and communication. Reference works are emphasized that supplement more specialized works in the chapters that follow.

GUIDES TO THE LITERATURE

General

A116 Cheney, Frances Neel, and Wiley J. Williams. Fundamental reference sources. 2d ed. Chicago: American Library Assn., 1980. 351p.

A substantial expansion and updating of the 1971 edition, this work remains one of the best introductions to principles and general purpose tools of library research. Addressed primarily to librarians, it bears on the work of all practitioners.

A117 Maichel, Karol. Guide to Russian reference books; ed. by J.S.G. Simmons. Stanford, Calif.: Hoover Institution, 1962– .

Originally projected at 6 volumes, only v.1, 2, and 5 ever appeared. They cover, respectively, general bib-

liographies and reference books; history, auxiliary historical sciences, ethnography, geography; and science, technology and medicine.

A118 Malclès, Louise-Noëlle. Les sources du travail bibliographique. Geneva: Droz; Lille: Girard, 1950–58. 3v. in 4.

The outstanding French guide. Bibliographies, encyclopedias, dictionaries, atlases, texts, important periodicals, collections. A supplement to Sheehy (A121) and Walford (A123) for European and Middle Eastern materials, though it is considerably dated now. The 3 volumes cover (1) bibliographies générales, (2) bibliographies spécialisées (sciences humaines), and (3) bibliographies spécialisées (science exactes et techniques). Author, subject, and title index for each volume. Reprinted by Droz in 1965.

A119 Robinson, Judith S. Subject guide to U.S. government reference sources. Rev. ed. Littleton, Colo.: Libraries Unlimited, 1985. 333p.

Revision of Sally Wynkoop's *Subject guide to government reference books* (1972). An annotated guide that presents more than a thousand reference books selected for their coverage of federal government publications. The social sciences receive heavy emphasis.

A120 Ryder, Dorothy E. Canadian reference sources: a selective guide. 2d ed. Ottawa: Canadian Library Assn., 1981. 311p.

Vastly expanded over the 1973 edition, this work includes over 1,900 titles organized in 5 sections (general reference, history and allied subjects, humanities, science, and social sciences). Extensively indexed by author, title, and subject.

A121 Sheehy, Eugene P. Guide to reference books. 9th ed. Chicago: American Library Assn., 1976. 1,015p.

A venerable standard guide to general works of reference that are fundamental to research in all major fields. Its predecessors were edited by Constance Winchell and Isadore Mudge, respectively. Works having greatest breadth of interest are followed by more specialized works in the social sciences, humanities, and pure and applied sciences. The arrangement is classified, annotations are compact and brief, and the index includes authors, subjects, and most titles. The cutoff date is late 1974, but 2 supplements have appeared, in 1980 and 1982. New edition in progress. In the meantime, Sheehy edits a column of new reference tools in the January and July issues of *College & research libraries*.

A122 Totok, Wilhelm, and others. Handbuch der bibliographischen Nachschlagewerke. 6th enl. ed. Frankfurt-am-Main: Klostermann, 1984– .

A German counterpart of Malclès, Sheehy, and Walford, the *Handbuch* is now appearing in its 6th edition, projected for the first time to occupy 2 volumes. It includes encyclopedias, dictionaries, directories, biographical sources, journals, and treatises, but the emphasis continues to be on bibliographic tools. Brief annotations. Authors and titles are included in the index.

A123 Walford, Albert J. Walford's guide to reference material. 4th ed. London: Library Assn., 1980– . 3v.

Well chosen, extensively annotated list of over 10,000 sources with several thousand additional titles included as subsumed entries. Concentrates on reference material of recent years that can be considered basic for both general and special library work. Though it is international in scope, Walford is especially strong on Anglo-American sources. The 4th edition, of which only v. 1 (science and technology [1980]), and 2 (social and historical sciences, philosophy and religion [1982]) have appeared, is considerably larger than preceding ones. The researcher must still use v. 3 (generalia, language and literature, the arts) from the 3d edition. A classified arrangement that includes a comprehensive author, title, and subject index.

Specialized

A124 Freides, Thelma. Literature and bibliography of the social sciences. Los Angeles: Melville, 1973. 284p.

An excellent introduction to social science literature and its structure. Covers the eight disciplines included in this book with business excluded. Freides also has fine chapters on the characteristics of science and on the social sciences as branches of the scientific enterprise. Especially strong in categorizing social scientific literature in relation to the mechanisms for disseminating scholarly research. Includes name-title and subject indexes.

A125 Hoselitz, Bert F., ed. A reader's guide to the social sciences. Rev. ed. New York: Free Pr., 1970. 425p.

Originated in postwar effort to improve library education by providing more knowledge about contents of books and criteria used in evaluating them. Describes literary output of major disciplines and nature of available tools in the form of books, journals, pamphlets, and reference works that social scientists consult and use in teaching and research. Includes sociology, anthropology, psychology, political science, economics, and geography. Has useful bibliography of titles discussed in the essays.

A126 Li, Tze-chung. Social science reference sources: a practical guide. Westport, Conn.: Greenwood, 1980. 315p.

A substantial recent addition to the literature. It emerged out of Li's library school courses on the literature of the social sciences. It includes general tools and material on statistics, government documents, archival sources, and database services. Deals specifically with cultural anthropology, economics and business, education, history, law, political science, psychology, and sociology. Includes name and title indexes.

A127 Lu, Joseph K. U.S. government publications relating to the social sciences: a selected annotated guide. Beverly Hills, Calif.: Sage, 1975. 260p.

Lu lists reference books, bibliographies, statistical sources, and other publications issued by the U.S. government that would be of interest to social scientists. Each entry in his classified arrangement consists of a complete citation with its Sudocs number. Subjects covered include history, business and economics, communism, Congress, education, foreign affairs, foreign countries, labor, law, the President, and social conditions and services. The book includes personal name and title indexes.

A128 McInnis, Raymond G., and James W. Scott. Social science research handbook. New York: Garland, 1984. 436p.

An invaluable contribution to the literature of the social sciences. McInnis and Scott include anthropology, demography, economics, geography, history, political science, sociology, and a good survey of area studies covering the entire globe. Published in 1975, reprinted in 1984.

A129 Roberts, N., ed. Use of social sciences literature. London: Butterworth, 1977. 326p.

This guide to the literature has a British emphasis. It omits psychology, history, and geography, but includes economics, sociology, political science, social anthropology, management, education, environmental planning, public administration, and criminology. The chapters, each done by a different specialist, generally offer excellent conceptual introductions to the literature of the fields dealt with.

REVIEWS
Reviews of the Literature and Research

A130 American Academy of Political and Social Science. Annals. v. 1–   , 1891– . Beverly Hills, Calif.: Sage. Bimonthly.

Includes extensive "book department" that surveys hundreds of new titles a year. Signed critical reviews classified by broad headings that cover all of the social sciences. Mainly English-language materials. Five-year indexes devote separate section to book reviews.

A131 American reference books annual. 1970– . Littleton, Colo.: Libraries Unlimited. Annual.

A now venerable reviewing service. Seeks to provide thorough, critical reviews of output of reference books (general as well as in special fields) and to disseminate the results in 4 to 5 months following the calendar year covered. Classified arrangement includes all social sciences. Author, title, subject index. More selective reviewing of reference books is done by *College & research libraries* (A121), *Library journal*, *RQ*, and *Booklist*. See also annotations for *Choice* (A133) and *Government reference books* (A134).

A132 Book review digest. v.1– , 1905– . New York: Wilson. Monthly.

Indexes and quotes from selected book reviews in about 85 English-language journals. Some leading social science journals are represented, but in general coverage is spotty. Annual cumulations. Author approach supplemented by title and subject indexes, which cumulate every 5 years.

A133 Choice. v.1– , 1964– . Chicago: American Library Assn. 11/yr.

Outcome of years of effort to produce a channel for reviewing new books in time to be of practical use in developing undergraduate college library collections. Compact reviews, prepared with the aid of some 1,000 specialists, concentrate on assessing the professional merits of books and placing them with reference to the literature of the field. Reference and general works added as special area. Author and title index cumulates annually in February. Editorial columns have many useful bibliographies, comments, and lists designed to further collection development and bibliography.

A134 Government reference books, a biennial guide to U.S. government publications, 1969– . Littleton, Colo.: Libraries Unlimited. Biennial.

A companion to *American reference books annual* (A131), this series represents a commitment to comb through the titles of the world's most prolific publisher to locate and review every 2 years the reference books it publishes. The latest issue includes nearly 1,200 titles, all well annotated individually or in groups. The entries cover a vast range of subjects, a majority of them in the social sciences.

A135 International review of social history. v.1– , 1956– . Assen, Netherlands: Van Woerden. 3/yr.

Issued in 1937–40 and 1950–55 as *Bulletin* of the International Institute of Social History. Features bibliography of around 1,000 books a year, predominantly European. Interdisciplinary in scope. Each title is abstracted or commented on.

A136 Urban affairs annual reviews, 1967– . Beverly Hills, Calif.: Sage. Annual.

Under Philip M. Hauser and L.F. Schnore, eds., *The study of urbanization* (New York: Wiley, 1965 [554p.]) (**A137**), with a superb bibliography, grew out of the Social Science Research Council's recognition of urban problems as a neglected interdisciplinary area. This series, an indirect outcome, is designed for long-term facilitation of more effective handling of problems, policies, and current developments in all areas of concern to urban specialists.

A138 Wissenschaftlicher Literaturanzeiger. v.1– , 1962– . Freiburg, W. Germany: Verlag Rombach. Bimonthly.

This tool reviews German books and books translated into German in all fields of knowledge. Between 1962 and 1964, it was entitled *Neuer Literatur Anzeiger*.

Reviews of Bibliographic Control

The post-World War II years produced a number of efforts to review bibliographic problems with a view to seeking effective solutions. Two of the more influential were the studies sponsored by the Graduate Library School of the University of Chicago (A10) and by UNESCO and the Library of Congress (A11). A valuable preliminary to the latter study had been prepared by Luther H. Evans, *Preliminary outline of a working paper for an international conference on the improvement and coordination of bibliographic services on a world-wide basis*, ed. by Katharine Oliver Murra (Washington, D.C.: Library of Congress, 1949 [57p.]) (**A139**). It laid the basis of the UNESCO Meeting on Improvement of Bibliographic Services held in Paris in 1950. These joint ventures of UNESCO with the Library of Congress seem to have resulted in the coining of the term "bibliographic control" and did much to shape postwar bibliographic strategy.

A140 Boehm, Eric H. Blueprint for bibliography: a system for the social sciences and humanities. Santa Barbara, Calif.: Chico, 1965. 22p.

Boehm's study was carried out for the International Social Science Institute under commission from the Carnegie Endowment for International Peace. Recognizing the still grave problems of bibliographic control and dissemination in the social sciences, Boehm made a series of 6 recommendations for improvement, the most important of which was the creation of a single, comprehensive, integrated bibliographic system for the social sciences and humanities. He also recommended the use of computers, better education in bibliography, and a multilevel bibliographic approach with one level consisting of (1) a basic citation enhanced by subject headings and (2) another offering abstracts of only selected titles.

A141 Collison, Robert L. Bibliographical services throughout the world, 1950–1959. Paris: UNESCO, 1961. 240p.

Culmination of a series of reports inaugurated in 1955. Pt. 1, arranged by country, describes bibliographical achievements in over 100 countries or territories. Indicates the progress in national bibliography, library cooperation, current special and retrospective bibliography. Pt. 2 summarizes bibliographical work of more than 80 international organizations. No index.

Continued by Paul Avicenne, *Bibliographical services throughout the world, 1960–1964* (Paris: UNESCO, 1969 [228p.]) (**A142**), a systematic survey by country of national and union bibliographies, bibliographic cooperation, legal deposits, archives, and related problems of exercising broad, effective bibliographic control. Synoptic table of services in each country in appendix. Avicenne also produced an update for the period 1965–69 in 303p. (1972).

The work of Collison and Avicenne has been continued by Marcelle Beaudiquez, who has edited a 419p. update for the period 1970–74 (1977) and a 462p. update for the period 1975–79 (1984). All titles in this series have been published in Paris by UNESCO. A closely related tool is UNESCO's *Bibliography, documentation, terminology*, v.1– , 1962–   (Paris: UNESCO [bimonthly]) (**A143**).

A144 Downs, Robert B., and F.B. Jenkins, eds. Bibliography: current state and future trends. Urbana: Univ. of Illinois Pr., 1967. 611p.

A good general review of subject. "Designed to review comprehensively the current status and future outlook of bibliography, general and special, at home and abroad, in every major area." All social sciences covered except sociology. Helps sort out and organize the literature, with choice bibliographies following essays. Author, subject, and title index.

A145 Ferguson, Jack. Specialized social science information services in the United States. Springfield, Va.: National Bureau of Standards, 1965. 40p.

Analysis of characteristics of organizations that participate in knowledge-production by making available specialized information (in form of literature or data) of potential use to social scientists. Based on a sample of 650 replies to questionnaires prepared and analyzed by the Bureau of Applied Social Research, Columbia University. Distinguishes 5 types of organizations: libraries and museums (as facilitators rather than initiators of research), research organizations whose input and output include literature and research of both types, statistical organizations whose input and major output are data, and such "service" organizations as the Internal Revenue Service, which provide social science information as a by-product of their primary purpose. Attention centers on the purposes, methods, and operating problems of these services.

A146 Freides, Thelma. "The state of secondary access services: social sciences." *Journal of the American Society for Information Science* 33: 157–61 (1982).

A solid current analysis of the problems encountered in controlling social sciences literature. Freides summarizes many of the findings of the Bath University studies (A14, A15). Some related studies that merit mention in this context are the ones by J.M. Brittain (A17) and Maurice Line (A19).

A147 Hale, Barbara M. The subject bibliography of the social sciences and humanities. Oxford: Pergamon, 1970. 149p.

On the basis of analysis of the development of bibliography and limited empirical findings, Hale raises questions about the meaning and place of subject bibliography in the handling of information. She sees a furtherance of subject bibliography as hinging on knowledge of communication and on clarification of theory. Contains a helpful list of the bibliographic tools cited in the study.

A148 Inter-American review of bibliography. v.1– , 1951– . Washington, D.C.: Organization of American States. Quarterly.

Begun by the Pan American Union, which acted as a bibliographical center for the Organization of American States. Facilitates exchange of thought and information through the review of current books and activities closely related to books. Issues contain articles, many with a bibliographic slant, and news and reviews of books of special interest to scholars and librarians of the Western Hemisphere. News includes new publications of the OAS and its specialized organizations. Accents the social sciences and librarianship.

ABSTRACTS AND DIGESTS

A149 Bulletin signalétique. v.1– , 1940– . Paris: Centre Nationale de la Recherche Scientifique. Frequency varies.

This major abstracting service is difficult to handle because of its publishing history, program, and organization. Envisaged as a continuing record of advances in various branches of science, it provides coverage of world literature of exceptional breadth. Its early handling of social science literature was marked by neglect, an outdated philosophic emphasis, and a changing pattern of organization that impaired continuity, in some cases seriously. Orderly treatment has improved tremendously. The present method is to use short, indicative abstracts to report on the significant professional literature of psychology, education, sociology, ethnology, linguistics, archeology, some aspects of history, and political philosophy. Annual indexes of authors and subjects.

To understand sequence and interrelationship of the subseries it is useful to keep three major changes in mind. One is the maturing of the conception between 1940 and 1956, when the title changed from *Bulletin analytique* to *Bulletin signalétique*. The original was issued in two parts, one dealing generally with the physical sciences, the other with the biological sciences and agriculture. A separate publication, beginning in 1947, was the *Bulletin analytique: philosophie, sciences humaines*, which attempted to roll philosophy, religion, art, psychology, sociology, political philosophy, and history of the sciences into a single package. This companion series became pt. 3 of the newly named *Bulletin signalétique* (1956–60).

From 1961 to 1964, the total program was decentralized into subseries renumbered 1–24. Pt. 3 of the old program was split into 4 sections and the quality of the treatment was improved:

> sec. 19. Sciences humaines, philosophie, v. 1– , 1947– . Quarterly.
>
> sec. 20. Psychologie, pédagogie, v.15– , 1961– . Quarterly.
>
> sec. 21. Sociologie, sciences du langage, v. 15– , 1961– . Quarterly.
>
> sec. 22. Histoire des sciences et des techniques, v. 15– , 1961– . Quarterly.

Further reorganization, mainly in 1969 and after, has introduced fresh subject alignments and new sections and replaced the older numbering system with a more flexible one. V.30, 1970 (i.e., v.24 in terms of pt. 3, which originated in 1947), was issued in 36 sections with numbers ranging from 101 to 970. Social science literature is presently treated in the following manner.

> part 390. Psychologie, psychopathologie, psychiatrie, 1961– . Monthly.
>
> part 520. Sciences de l'éducation, 1947– . Quarterly.
>
> part 521. Sociologie-ethnologie, 1947– . Quarterly.
>
> part 522. Histoire des sciences et des techniques, 1947– . Quarterly.
>
> part 523. Histoire et sciences de la littérature, 1947– . Quarterly.
>
> part 524. Sciences du langage, 1947– . Quarterly.
>
> part 525. Préhistoire et protohistoire, 1947– . Quarterly.
>
> part 526. Art et archéologie; Proche-Orient, Asie, Amérique, 1947– . Quarterly.
>
> part 528. Bibliographie internationale de science administrative, 1971– . Quarterly.

Other sections include material of social science interest, such as 519, "Philosophie," and 527, "Histoire et sciences des religions."

A150 Dissertation abstracts international. v.1– , 1938– . Ann Arbor, Mich.: University Microfilms. Monthly.

Contains abstracts of doctoral dissertations submitted to University Microfilms by more than 450 cooperating institutions. Since July 1965, a current list of participating institutions with their entry date has been included. Originally a single list, DAI was divided into 2 sections in 1966: A. Humanities and social sciences; and B. Sciences and engineering. Abstracts are listed alphabetically by author under subjects, as outlined in the table of contents.

To supplement DAI, one can consult a number of listings, without abstracts, that go back into the 19th century. Eleven research centers published their own lists before 1912: University of California, 1885–1931; Catholic University, 1897–1928; Chicago (education only), 1893–1931; Clark, 1889–1920; Columbia, 1872–1910; Harvard, 1873–1926; Johns Hopkins, 1876–1926; Michigan, n.d.; Minnesota, 1888–1932; Pennsylvania, 1889–1912; and Yale, 1861–1912.

Next in point of time was the *List of American doctoral dissertations printed in 1912–1938*, drawn up by the Library of Congress (Washington, D.C.: Govt. Print. Off., 1913–40 [2v.]) **(A151)**. The next aid to appear was *Doctoral dissertations accepted by American universities, 1933/34–1954/55* (New York: Wilson, 1934–55 [22v.]) **(A152)**. This annual is a more complete listing than DAI, though it does not, as mentioned, contain abstracts. It is currently being compiled as an independent series for the Association of Research Libraries and published by University Microfilms.

The most complete subject and author index to doctoral dissertations written in the United States is now provided by *Comprehensive dissertation index: 1861–1972* (Ann Arbor, Mich.: Xerox University Microfilm, 1973 [37v.]) **(A153)**, supplemented with a 38-volume cumulation for 1973–82 and annual supplements. CDI indexes not only the dissertations contained in DAI, but also every dissertation it could identify produced anywhere in the country since 1861. The volumes are organized by subject area, then by title keyword retrieved by computer. There are separate author volumes.

Retrospective lists of dissertations are common among nations active in research, but current national lists are less common. The United Kingdom has no listing before *Index to theses accepted for higher degrees in the universities of Great Britain and Ireland and the Council for National Academic Awards* (v.1– , 1950/51– ; London: Aslib, 1954– [annual]) **(A154)**. This thorough and classified list includes author and subject indexes.

The official French list is France, Ministère de l'Éducation Nationale, Direction des Bibliothèques, des musées et de l'information scientifique et technique, *Catalogue des thèses de doctorat soutenues devant les universités françaises* (1959– ; Paris, 1960– [annual]) **(A155)**. The title of the old series (1884–1958) was *Catalogue des thèses et écrits académiques*.

. . . Since 1914, the theses have been listed by "faculties." Author and subject indexes were not issued from 1929 to 1958.

Other current national lists include National Library of Canada, *Canadian theses. Thèses canadiennes* (1960/61– ; Ottawa [annual]) (**A156**), and *Jahresverzeichnis der deutschen Hochschulschriften* (1884/85– ; Liepzig: VEB Verlag für Buch- und Bibliothekswesen [annual]) (**A157**). Publishers, titles, and arrangement vary. The official German listing includes all universities since 1885, all Technische Hochschulen since 1913, and Hochschulen der Länder since 1924.

A158 UNESCO. Thèses de sciences sociales; catalogue analytique internationale des thèses inédites de doctorat, 1940–1950. Paris: 1952. 236p.

A retrospective list for a decade of war and educational reconstruction. It publishes information supplied by 22 member countries and Germany on doctoral dissertations completed and accepted by universities but unpublished during this period. 3,215 entries by subject. For more specialized dissertation lists, consult the index.

A159 Excerpta medica, 1947– . Amsterdam: Excerpta Medica. Frequency varies depending on the section.

This comprehensive service has given increasing attention to world literature on social aspects of health and medicine. Of the 51 sections, the following are of interest to social scientists: 17: Public health, social medicine and hygiene (1955– [20/yr.]); 19: Rehabilitation and physical medicine (1958– [10/yr.]); 20: Gerontology and geriatrics (1958– [10/yr.]); 32: Psychiatry (1948– [20/yr.]); 35: Occupational health and industrial medicine (1971– [10/yr.]); 36: Health economics and hospital management (1971– [10/yr.]); 37: Drug literature index (1969– [24/yr.]); 40: Drug dependence (1973– [10/yr.]); 46: Environmental health and pollution control (1971– [10/yr.]); 49: Forensic science (1975– [10/yr.]).

A160 Government reports announcements & index. v.1– , 1946– . Springfield, Va.: National Technical Information Service. Semimonthly.

Cites and abstracts the reports released to the public through NTIS by U.S. government agencies. Includes some government translations and some reports in foreign languages. Arranged in 22 subject fields (field 5 is "Behavioral and social science"). Citations bearing on human behavior appear in other fields. Title has varied: *Bibliography of scientific and industrial reports* (1946–49); *Bibliography of technical reports* (1949–54); *U.S. government research reports* (1954–64); *U.S. government research and development reports* (1965–71); and *Government reports announcements* (1971–75). Indexing has also varied. Until 1965, the indexing was included with the reports. From 1965 to 1975, an index was published separately under three different names: *Government-wide index to federal research and development reports* (1965–67); *U.S. government research and development reports index* (1968–70); and *Government reports index* (1971–75). In 1975, *Government reports announcements* and *Government reports index* were merged to form the present *Government reports announcements & index*. Indexing is by personal and corporate author, subject, contract number, and accession/report number.

A161 Human resources abstracts; an international information service. v.1– , 1966– . Beverly Hills, Calif.: Sage. Quarterly.

Formerly called *Poverty and human resources*. Each issue has a rounded program of (1) abstracts of several hundred articles, books, parts of books, government reports, and some unpublished material selected as most significant for poverty, manpower, and human resources; (2) feature articles; and (3) special analyses of current problems. Oriented to research and action mainly in the U.S. Author and subject index cumulates annually.

A162 Hydro-abstracts, 1968– . Minneapolis: Environmental Hydrology. Monthly.

Hydata, a monthly awareness journal published by the American Water Resources Assn. between 1965 and 1978, sought to index the world's literature on water resources planning, research, management, development, sciences, and education. *Hydro-abstracts*, originally called *Water resources abstracts*, was begun by the same association to make abstracts of that literature available in looseleaf. It is now also available in microfiche. Not all sections are of direct interest to social scientists.

A163 LLBA: language and language behavior abstracts. v.1– , 1967– . San Diego: Sociological Abstracts. Quarterly.

This abstracting service seeks to meet the needs of all researchers and practitioners in the various disciplines concerned with the nature and use of language. It screens around 1,000 publications, including periodicals, progress and technical reports, occasional papers, monographs, and conference proceedings. LLBA covers exhaustively articles that report language-related research in 25 disciplines. Subject and author indexes are included. Now searchable online.

A164 Selected Rand abstracts; to provide a timely and comprehensive index-guide to the Rand Corporation unclassified publications. v.1– , 1963– . Santa Monica, Calif.: Rand. Quarterly.

A high proportion of these studies, while not limited by subject, have social science interest because of Rand's emphasis on research having application to problems of policy and planning in domestic and foreign affairs. Supersedes its *Index of selected publications, 1946–1962*. Abstracts all unclassified books and reports currently published by the corporation. Quarterly issues progressively cumulate into an annual volume.

A165 Statistical theory and method abstracts. v.1– , 1959– . Voorburg, Netherlands: International Statistical Inst. Quarterly.

Formerly *International journal of abstracts*. Articles on statistical theory and method appear at a rate of well over 1,000 a year. Scattered sources, some relatively inaccessible, threatened to get out of hand by the 1950s. Coordinated planning resulted in preparation of *Bibliography of statistical literature* (A333) for retrospective coverage and the launching of this abstracting journal to provide "complete coverage" of significant new contributions. Language of original papers is indicated, but all abstracts are in English. Classified arrangement, with annual author index and index to book reviews in major journals.

A166 World agricultural economics and rural sociology abstracts; abstracts of world literature. v.1– , 1959– . Slough, Eng.: Commonwealth Agricultural Bureau. Monthly.

This comprehensive service, with abstracts in English, construes agricultural economics and rural sociology broadly to include agricultural policy, legislation, agrarian reform, international trade, geography, history, and agricultural education. Well classified, with cumulative author, subject, and geographic index.

Current Digests

A167 Asian recorder: weekly record of Asian events with index. 1955– . New Delhi: M.S.R. Khemchand. Weekly.

A looseleaf service in the style of *Keesing's contemporary archives* (A171). The news items are summarized from Asian and other newspapers, periodicals, official publications, and reports. Sources are identified and references to previous articles are given. Geographical coverage includes all of Asia and the Middle East, as well as some African areas, with emphasis on India. Quarterly index with annual cumulation.

A168 Current digest of the Soviet press. v.1– , 1949– . Columbus, Ohio: American Assn. for the Advancement of Slavic Studies. Weekly.

Originated to meet the need for documents, statistics, and reliable indication of official attitudes and policies of the USSR, this useful source translates and presents in full the important items from the two newspapers of highest authority, *Pravda* and *Izvestiia*. Other items are condensed or mentioned by title in its "Weekly index to *Pravda* and *Izvestiia*." Additional material of permanent reference value from around a hundred other Soviet newspapers and magazines. Quarterly index.

A169 Editorial research reports. 1923– . Washington, D.C.: Congressional Quarterly. 4/mo. (collected in semiannual bound volumes)

Made up of two services. (1) *Situation reports* of around 6,000 words on major issues at the focus of public attention are prepared at about the rate of one a week. Prefaced by an outline of the text, the typical report starts with a summary of current developments, followed by analysis of the main elements of controversy, the arguments on both sides, and the major influences at work. *Report* then digs further into background and concludes with outlook, including proposals and anticipated action. (2) *Daily reminders* consists of chronologically arranged background briefs prepared at a rate of nine or ten a week. Each dated brief

is a succinct background story of 200–500 words on a single spot-news development, which often updates a *Report*. Marginal cross-references to earlier coverage. Each semiannual volume contains a 15-year subject-title index to *Reports*, 5-year combined index to *Reports* and *Daily reminders*, and index to *Daily reminders* for the preceding 6 months.

A170 Facts on file: weekly world news digest with index. v.1– , 1940– . New York: Facts On File. Weekly.

A looseleaf service that in brief form presents the most newsworthy developments week by week the world over. Does not miss the spectacular news, from sports to disasters, but balances the record with obituaries, book news, and significant developments in science and the arts. The news section is continuously paged; stories cite location of related articles for background. Stairstep cumulation of bi-weekly index, yielding 3-month, 6-month, 9-month, annual, and (beginning with 1946–50) 5-year indexes.

A171 Keesing's contemporary archives. v.1– , 1931– . Essex, Eng.: Keesing. Monthly.

Looseleaf "reports, statistics and data selected, condensed, translated, summarized and indexed from newspapers, periodicals and official publications of the United Kingdom, the Commonwealth and foreign countries, as well as from information supplied by the recognized international news agencies." Items tend to be political and economic in nature, and are more fully reported than in the comparable *Facts on file*. Each of these tools reflects news interests of the country of origin. *Keesing's* reproduces speeches and text of documents (often in full), as well as statistical tables and maps. Sources of each report are briefly identified.

BIBLIOGRAPHIES OF BIBLIOGRAPHIES

A172 Besterman, Theodore. A world bibliography of bibliographies and bibliographical catalogues, calendars, abstracts, digests, indexes and the like. 4th rev. and greatly enl. ed. Lausanne: Societas Bibliographica, 1965–66. 5v.

A formidable accomplishment. An alphabetical subject arrangement of 117,187 bibliographies with cross-references. Annotations are sparse and lean. An estimate of the number of items in each work is given, as is relevant information about publication history, including supplements. V. 5 is a 1,742-column alphabetical index, mainly of authors, editors, translators, etc., titles of serials and anonymous works, and libraries and archives. Little left out except anonymous bibliographies. Besterman included bibliographies in more than 50 languages.

An effort to "update" Besterman was made by Alice F. Toomey, *A world bibliography of bibliographies, 1964–1974: a list of works represented by Library of Congress printed catalog cards, a decennial supplement to Theodore Besterman, A world bibliography of bibliographies* (Totowa, N.J.: Rowman & Littlefield, 1977 [2v.]) **(A173)**. Nothing at all like the original, Toomey's work is really a photographic reproduction of some 18,000 Library of Congress cards with subject headings. It has no index.

A174 Bibliografia sovetskoi bibliografii. 1939– . Moscow. Annual.

This annual publication, which was suspended only during the war years of 1940–45, is a classified index to bibliographies published separately or as parts of books or articles in the Soviet Union. It comprises a segment of the *Soviet national bibliography*.

A175 Bibliographic index; a cumulative bibliography of bibliographies. v.1– , 1938– . New York: Wilson. Publ. in April, August, and (with a bound cumulation) December.

Extensive international coverage, concentrating primarily on the Germanic and Romance languages, of bibliographies of at least 50 citations published separately, as parts of books or as articles. Drawn from around 2,600 publications scanned each year. Selective notice of supplements and new editions. Subject headings make it possible to pinpoint specific interests down to elusive minor subjects.

A176 Bibliographie der deutschen Bibliographien. 1954– . Leipzig: Verlag für Buch– und Bibliothekswesen. Annual.

An annual listing of bibliographies published in Germany. It includes both separately published bibliographies as well as those contained in books and periodicals. Covers all subject areas. Much of the coverage is of social science materials.

A177 Garling, Anthea. Bibliography of African bibliographies. Cambridge: African Studies Centre, 1968. 138p.

This slender volume represents a first attempt to systematize and make available bibliographies dealing with Africa. The entries, arranged by region, then by country, cover all major subject areas.

A178 Gray, Richard A. A guide to book review citations; a bibliography of sources. Columbus: Ohio State Univ. Pr., 1969. 221p.

A small volume that fills a large gap. For various subject fields, identifies and describes 512 sources of book reviews, roughly half in the social sciences. To be included, a source "must cite reviews from more than one journal or periodical, and . . . must cite book reviews in contradistinction to critical studies." To supplement the classified arrangement, there are 5 indexes: subject, personal name, title, chronology (to facilitate locating reviews before the 20th century), and a country-of-origin index for identifying sources that (1) list books published in only one country or (2) cite reviews in journals of only one country.

A179 ———, and Dorothy Villmow. Serial bibliographies in the humanities and social sciences. Ann Arbor, Mich.: Pierian, 1969. 345p.

This list passes over works that everyone knows about and concentrates on bringing to light valuable, continuing bibliographies that tend to be hidden and unknown. Tireless effort turned up 1,409 such titles.

They are described, arranged by the Dewey system, and numbered consecutively. For each title, coded information brings out such basic features as scope, frequency, country of origin, language of publications covered, and organization and type of annotation (if any). A title index identifies (1) separately published bibliographies, (2) periodicals that contain bibliography sections, and (3) concealed bibliography sections. There are 3 other indexes for (4) author, sponsor, and publisher, (5) subject and keyword approaches, and (6) characteristics of the material, that is, whether it is an article, book, dissertation, review, and so on.

A180 Gropp, Arthur E. A bibliography of Latin American bibliographies. Metuchen, N.J.: Scarecrow, 1968. 515p.

The unsuperseded pioneer work in this field is Cecil Knight Jones's *A bibliography of Latin American bibliographies*, 2d ed., rev. and enl. (Washington, D.C.: Govt. Print. Off., 1942 [311p.]) **(A181)**, which includes—besides separates—numerous bibliographies in journals and as parts of books. The Gropp bibliography is a worthy successor that, obliged to limit treatment to bibliographies of a monographic nature, nevertheless cites a bulky 7,000 titles, including selected titles in the Jones list. Numerous bibliographical notes, some of which refer to additional titles. Subject arrangement (subdivided geographically, with A–Z entries thereunder) locates copies. Detailed index of persons, corporate bodies, government offices, titles of series and subjects. Brought up to date by "Bibliographies" in *Handbook of Latin American studies* (A245), and by the following series of supplements to the Jones and Gropp works.

A182 ———.———Supplement. Metuchen, N.J.: Scarecrow, 1971. 277p.

Conforms to the format of the main volume. Adds to the above total more than 1,400 bibliographies in monograph form. The majority of these were published between 1965 and 1969, but some titles were not discovered in time to include in the 1968 edition. New citations include 64 bibliographic journals.

A183 Cordeiro, Daniel Reposo. A bibliography of Latin American bibliographies: social sciences and humanities. Metuchen, N.J.: Scarecrow, 1977. 272p.

Designated as supplement 2 to Gropp's work of 1968, Cordeiro's bibliography continues with the same format as previous editions. Includes the period 1969–1974 for monographs and 1966–1974 for journal articles. It adds some 1,750 bibliographies, though Cordeiro's work, unlike Gropp's, centers exclusively on the social sciences and humanities.

A184 Piedracueva, Haydée. A bibliography of Latin American bibliographies, 1975–1979: social sciences and humanities. Metuchen, N.J.: Scarecrow, 1982. 313p.

Piedracueva's supplement 3 to Gropp's original work, a worthy continuation of the endeavors of Jones, Gropp, and Cordeiro, carries the chronological listing up to 1979. It retains the format of earlier editions and includes an additional 2,122 bibliographies relating to Latin America. Like Cordeiro, Piedracueva includes only the social sciences and humanities.

A185 Gropp, Arthur E. A bibliography of Latin American bibliographies published in periodicals. Metuchen, N.J.: Scarecrow, 1976. 2v.

Gropp has supplemented his splendid bibliographic endeavors in updating Jones by publishing this companion set concentrating on bibliographies published in periodicals during the years 1929–65. He includes not only bibliographic articles but topical articles that include good bibliographies. In total, Gropp lists 9,715 citations covering all disciplines drawn from 1,044 periodicals. Most social science materials are included in v. 2. A lengthy author-subject index rounds out the work.

A186 Lancaster, Henry O. Bibliography of statistical bibliographies. Edinburgh: Oliver & Boyd for the International Statistical Inst., 1968. 103p.

Selected bibliographies on statistics as a discipline. Sec. 1, "Personal bibliographies," is directed to the life and works of important contributors to statistical theory and method. Sec. 2, "Subject bibliographies," covers methodology and applications and is arranged alphabetically by bibliographer and indexed by subject and national origin. Author index has entries for all persons in the bibliography, including editors and joint compilers.

A187 Lochhead, Douglas. Bibliography of Canadian bibliographies. 2d ed., rev. and enl. Toronto: publ. in association with the Bibliographical Society of Canada by the Univ. of Toronto Pr., 1972. 312p.

Lochhead's revision of Raymond Tanghe's original work of 1960 is a thorough updating and expansion. It includes more than 2,300 bibliographies bearing on all aspects of Canada. Arrangement is alphabetical by author with a subject and compiler index.

A188 Scull, Roberta A. A bibliography of United States government bibliographies, 1968–1973: Ann Arbor, Mich.: Pierian, 1974.

A work that fills a need in attempting some control over the difficult-to-locate publications of the U.S. government. Scull lists bibliographies in all disciplines. The bibliographies included cover not only government but non-government publications as well. Scull updated this tool in 1979 with *A bibliography of United States government bibliographies, 1974–1976*, also published by Pierian (**A189**). Scull's efforts have been splendidly supplemented by Edna A. Kanely with her 7-volume *Cumulative subject guide to U.S. government bibliographies, 1924–1973* (Arlington, Va.: Carrollton, 1976) (**A190**).

A191 Tsien, Tsuen-Hsuin. China: an annotated bibliography of bibliographies. Comp. in collaboration with James K. M. Cheng. Boston: Hall, 1978. 604p.

An excellent selected listing of some 2,500 bibliographies on one of the world's most important nations. The entries, covering all fields of study, are mainly in English, Chinese, and Japanese. There are good author, title, and subject indexes included.

CURRENT BIBLIOGRAPHIES AND INDEXES

Aids Essential to All Disciplines

Because book literature is so critical to social scientists, research aids that permit any type of subject access to such publications deserve considerable attention. The best guides to general reference books describe scores of under-used national and book-trade bibliographies that are essential to sophisticated work in subject bibliography. Prominent "musts" among these book-finding tools for American books are:

A192 Books in print: an author-title-series index to the Publishers trade list annual. 1948– . New York: Bowker. Annual.

A multivolume set, *Publishers trade list annual*, 1873– (New York: Bowker [annual]) (**A193**), combines the most recent catalogs of all publishers and is an authoritative record of their current stock. BIP ferrets out the most-in-demand information (author, title, publisher, price, etc.) about all these books and presents it in an easily accessible format. *Subject guide to books in print; an index to the Publishers trade list annual*, 1957– (New York: Bowker [annual]) (**A194**) provides another approach to the same publications, making it possible to locate a book when one is not sure of the author or title. Above all, it offers *subject* access to currently available book literature. *Paperbound books in print*, 1955– (New York: Bowker [monthly]) (**A195**) cumulates 3 times a year and provides an approach by author, title, and subject for paperbacks.

A196 Cumulative book index. 1898– . New York: Wilson. Monthly

CBI, a world list of books in English but strongest for the United States and Canada, features an author-title-subject approach and cumulates quarterly. Back volumes, the result of further cumulations, are invaluable for retrospective searching.

A197 Publishers weekly, the book industry journal. 1872– . New York: Bowker. Weekly.

Provides, through weekly lists of new books, later information on the industry's output than the above-mentioned tools. These weekly lists cumulate in the companion *American book publishing record*, 1960– (New York: Bowker [monthly]) (**A198**), in which all these new publications are classified and indexed by author and title. The monthlies cumulate into an annual record, which in turn cumulates into the 5-year *American book publishing record: BPR cumulative*, beginning with the 4-volume set for 1960–64, published 1968– (New York: Bowker) (**A199**).

A200 Forthcoming books, now including new books in print; a forecast of books to come. v.1– , 1966– . New York: Bowker. Bimonthly.

Limited at the outset to books to be published within the next 5 months, this list now goes a step further and supplements *Books in print* by listing (cumulatively) all books published since the latest annual BIP. This chain of book-finding tools covering the recent output of the American book trade is completed by *Subject guide to forthcoming books, a bimonthly subject forecast of books to come*, v.1– , 1967– (New York: Bowker [bimonthly]) (**A201**). It provides a dictionary arrangement by subject of all titles except fiction listed in A200.

A202 Union list of serials in libraries of the United States and Canada. 3d ed. New York: Wilson, 1965. 5v.

This work on serial publications is a cornerstone of subject bibliography and an indispensable aid to scholarship. It briefly describes and gives library locations for more than 150,000 serials, providing all important information on name changes, cessations, and dates of publication. A supplement entitled *New serial titles, 1950–1970: a union list of serials commencing publication after December 31, 1949* (New York: Bowker; Washington, D.C.: Library of Congress, 1973 [4v.]) (**A203**) continues the work of the earlier publication. A series of later NSTs have appeared, published by the Library of Congress, covering the years 1971–75, 1976–80, 1981–84, and later.

The structure of national and trade bibliography varies from country to country, but one of the marks of a nation's bibliographical maturity is the availability of tools that provide book-finding apparatus comparable to the foregoing. No nation has produced a current record of national output more versatile than the weekly *British national bibliography*, 1950– (London: Council of the British National Bibliography, British Museum) (**A204**), with its 4 cumulations a year. It promptly lists, classifies, and indexes all new works published in Great Britain.

BNB is flanked by the Whitaker program, which announces forthcoming books in *Whitaker's books of the month and books to come*, 1970– (London: Whitaker [monthly]) (**A205**), and lists new books each week in *The bookseller; the organ of the booktrade* (1858–) (**A206**). These weekly lists build into the quarterly, annual, and 5-year cumulations of *Whitaker's cumulative book list* (1924–) (**A207**). The Whitaker system goes farther and tells what titles are still in print in the annual *British books in print, the reference catalog of current literature* (1874–) (**A208**) and its companion *Paperbacks in print* (1960–) (**A209**).

The English catalogue of books, 1801–1966 (London: Low, 1864–1901; Publishers' Circular, 1906–1966) (**A210**), while less satisfactory as a searching aid, recorded books published for a century and more before the time of the BNB and the Whitaker cumulations. It even included selected American and continental books for some years in the late 19th century.

Central in a cluster of aids to searches involv-

ing serial publications is the *British union-catalogue of periodicals; a record of the periodicals of the world, from the seventeenth century to the present day, in British libraries* (London: Butterworth, 1955–58 [4v.]) (**A211**). It lists more than 140,000 titles. A *Supplement to 1960* for the British union-catalogue of periodicals was prepared by James D. Stewart and others in 1962 (London: Butterworth, 1962) (**A212**). Butterworths continued its fine work of bibliographic control of serial publications with the following self-explanatory publication.

A213 British union-catalogue of periodicals, incorporating World list of scientific periodicals. New periodical titles. v.1– , 1964– . London: Butterworth. Quarterly, with annual cumulations.

Though we have dealt here only with the national and trade bibliographies of the United States and Great Britain, comparable tools are available for many other countries in the world. The researcher should consult the appropriate sections of Sheehy and its supplements (A121) and Walford (A123).

Aids with Social Science Emphasis

A214 Bibliographie der Wirtschaftswissenschaften. v.1– , 1968– . Göttingen: Vandenhoeck & Ruprecht. Annual.

Successor to the venerable *Bibliographie der Sozialwissenschaften*, published annually with several name changes and changing subject content from 1905 to 1967. An extensive, classified bibliography of German and foreign-language books, parts of books, and journal articles dealing with all aspects of the social sciences. Always had author and subject index. Currently has title index as well.

A215 Book review index. v.1– , 1965– . Detroit: Gale. Bimonthly.

Cites reviews, by author, in some 455 North American and British journals, magazines, and newspapers. Strong in the social sciences. Publication was suspended in 1969–71, but was resumed in 1972 with the gap being closed retrospectively. The 1984 cumulation included 128,000 reviews of 68,000 individual books. Quarterly cumulations build into annual volumes.

A216 Book review index to social science periodicals. Ed. by Arnold M. Rzepecki. Ann Arbor, Mich.: Pierian, 1978. 4v.

Designed to provide indexing to book reviews in the social sciences from 1964 until the advent of the *Social science index* in 1974, thus complementing the coverage in *Index to book reviews in the humanities*. V. 1 covers the years 1964–70; v. 2 through 4 cover the years 1971–73. Since 1974, the best coverage of book reviews in the social sciences is provided by the *Social sciences index* (A234) and the *Humanities index* (A235). The *Social sciences citation index*, operative since 1969, also includes book reviews in the *Citation index* (A231). Another book reviewing tool that might be mentioned in this context is the *Combined retrospective index to book reviews in scholarly journals, 1886–1974* (Woodbridge, Conn.: Research Pubns., 1979–82 [15v.]) (**A217**). This computer-generated listing of reviews of books in all disciplines, is organized by author. The last 3 volumes contain a title listing that refers the searcher to the appropriate author in the first 12 volumes. The citations to book reviewing sources, though abbreviated, are adequate for identifying the source, year, volume number, and page.

A218 British humanities index. 1962– . London: Library Assn. Quarterly.

Subject guide to periodicals (1915–61) expanded into the *British technology index* and the *BHI*. The latter indexes some 400 widely read British periodicals—general, humanities, and social sciences (exclusive of education). Arrangement is by author and subject in separate alphabets. Cumulates annually.

A219 Current contents. 1961– . Philadelphia: Inst. for Scientific Information. Weekly.

This series has appeared with various subject coverages since its inception. Presently, it consists of 6 series, which may be purchased separately: Physical and chemical sciences; Engineering technology and applied sciences; Social and behavioral sciences; Life sciences: agriculture, biology, and environmental sciences; and Clinical practice. Each number reproduces the tables of content of the most recent issues of leading journals in the respective subject fields. This is one of the more valuable current awareness tools presently available to researchers in keeping up with the journal literature.

A220 Fondation Nationale des Sciences Politiques. Bulletin analytique de documentation politique, économique et social contemporaine. v.1– , 1946– . Paris: Presses Universitaires de France. Monthly.

Informative thumbnail annotations or contents notes for articles in French and other European-language periodicals. Some publications of governments and international organizations are also included. Title accurately describes contents. Classified arrangement with annual subject index. Replaces *Bulletin bibliographique de documentation internationale contemporaine* (1926–40).

A221 ———. Bibliographie courante d'articles de périodiques postérieurs à 1944 sur les problèmes politiques, économiques et sociaux. Boston: Hall, 1968. 17v.

A cumulative postwar index based on a file of 300,000 cards, classified by country or region and then by subject. Entry usually accompanied by a note or précis of contents. Twenty volumes of supplements have been published between 1969 and 1979.

A222 International bibliography of the social sciences. 1955– . London: Tavistock; Chicago: Aldine. Annual.

The International Committee for Social Science Documentation, having originated with the aid of UNESCO in 1950, followed up studies showing urgent need for action at the international level to strengthen current bibliography, especially in anthropology (F468), economics (D567), political science (I735), and sociology (E236). These four services, treated independently at the outset, currently draw from the same global list of several thousand journals. They are in effect part of a single, comprehensive selecting and indexing program. Title pages began to show the general series title for material in 1955. Further information for each bibliography and its subject at numbers cited above.

A223 Internationale Bibliographie der Zeitschriftenliteratur; aus allen Gebieten des Wissens. v.1– , 1963/64– . Osnabruck, W. Germany: Dietrich, 1965– . Semiannual.

A current index of unsurpassed breadth. Prepared to simplify use by English-language searchers. Produced by combining its 2 historic components: *Bibliographie der deutschen Zeitschriftenliteratur* (1897–1964) and *Bibliographie der Fremdsprachigen Zeitschriftenliteratur* (1911–64). The first covered periodical literature in German; the second covered periodical literature in foreign languages. Presently offers a subject approach to the contents of thousands of periodicals, yearbooks, composite works, society proceedings, transactions, and symposia. Journals of scholarship in the social sciences are strongly represented.

A224 MLA international bibliography of books and articles of the modern languages and literatures. 1921– . New York: Modern Language Assn. Annual.

This tool, which has undergone considerable evolution since its creation, is presently an international classified listing of books and articles dealing with modern languages, literature, folklore, and linguistics. Until 1955, it limited itself to materials written by American scholars. From 1956 to 1969 it evolved gradually to encompass ever more literature produced around the world. From 1969 to 1980, it came to be divided into 3 volumes which were gathered annually into a single-volume library edition. The first two covered literature arranged by country; the third volume dealt with linguistics. Beginning in 1981, MLA is published in 5 volumes which appear as a single-volume library edition. V.1 and 2 deal exclusively with literature arranged by country. V.3 deals with linguistics, v.4 with general literature and related topics, and v.5 with folklore. Also, a subject index began to appear with the revision of 1981. Of greatest interest to social scientists are the sections on folklore, linguistics, and language teaching. MLA is searchable online.

A225 Public Affairs Information Service bulletin. v.1– , 1915– . New York: PAIS. Semimonthly, with 3 quarterly and one annual cumulations.

One of the mainstays in social science information, PAIS is a comprehensive subject index to "the latest books, pamphlets, government publications, reports of public and private agencies and periodical articles relating to economic and social conditions, public administration and international relations published throughout the world." A first-rate source for authoritative material, including statistics, originating outside as well as inside the book trade. Starting in 1972, *PAIS* began publishing a separate *Foreign language index* (**A226**), with material primarily in French, Italian, German, Spanish, and Portuguese. The indexing here is by subject, but within subject categories the listing is by author rather than by title, as in the original *PAIS*. Both *PAIS* and the *Foreign language index* are searchable online, the former from 1976, the latter from 1972. An additional enhancement to PAIS is the *Cumulative subject index to the P.A.I.S. annual bulletin, 1915–1974* (Arlington, Va.: Carrollton, 1977–78 [15v.]) (**A227**). It refers the searcher to the year, pages, and column of the *Bulletin* where the complete entry can be found. One last enhancement is the *Cumulative author index, 1965–69* to the *PAIS*, edited by C. Edward Wall (Ann Arbor, Mich.: Pierian, 1973) (**A228**), with the promise of similar indexes for earlier years.

A229 Recent publications in the social and behavioral sciences: the ABS guide supplement. 1966–75. Beverly Hills, Calif.: Sage. Annual.

The *American behavioral scientist*, a journal that began in 1957, included in its monthly issues a section called "New studies" in which it listed between 20 and 80 recent books, articles, government publications, or research reports that it considered to be particularly solid examples of good behaviorally oriented research. In 1965, the journal decided to publish the complete list of these highly selective publications in cumulative form and continue thereafter with an annual cumulation. The initial cumulation was the *ABS guide to recent publications in the social and behavioral sciences* (New York: ABS, 1965 [781p.]) (**A230**), which brought together in a single author list the 6,664 items previously listed in the monthly *New studies* along with title, proper name, and subject indexes. The annual supplements being mentioned here only lasted until 1975. Their value was always limited by the considerable selectiveness of the list and its extensive duplication of other bibliographical sources.

A231 Social sciences citation index. v.1– , 1969– . Philadelphia: Inst. for Scientific Information. 3/yr. with annual cumulation.

The citation indexes published by ISI should be considered together, for they are organized on similar principles and overlap where the social sciences are concerned. The original *Science citation index* (**A232**), begun in 1961 and now issued bimonthly, includes psychology journals and some multidisciplinary journals of interest to social scientists. The *Arts & humanities citation index* (**A233**), initiated in 1976 and published 3 times a year, also contains materials in the areas of linguistics, folklore, philosophy, etc., of possible use to social scientists. The *SSCI* itself indexes about 4,500 social science journals in all disciplines and major languages. It covers 1,400 of these journals fully. The citation indexes, all computer-generated and searchable online, were devised under the rationale that authors who cite a particular work are likely to be doing research similar to that reported in the cited work. Thus, it would be useful to researchers to be able to identify later articles that have cited an earlier article determined to be useful. The citation indexes, therefore, consist of three separate indexes. The *Source index* lists in alphabetical order by author all articles indexed during the year from the journals scanned, giving a complete bibliographic citation, the number of references contained in each article, and, in the case of *SSCI* and *A&HCI*, a listing with truncated citation of those references. The *Citation index* lists in alphabetical order by author all works cited during the year in any of the articles listed in the *Source index*. Thus, the *Citation index* may list books or articles 30 or 40 years old provided they were cited during the current year. Lastly, the *Permuterm subject index* provides subject access to the items listed in the *Source index* by linking keywords that appear together in titles. One of the advantages of the citation indexes is that the subject searching ignores disciplinary boundaries. One of the disadvantages, especially in *SSCI* and *A&HCI*, is the lack of controlled vocabulary access. The citation indexes are an excellent source of book reviews, which are listed in the *Citation index* under the name of the author. ISI decides which journals to index on the basis of citation counts.

A234 Social sciences index. v.1– , 1974– . New York: Wilson. Quarterly.

The *Social sciences index* should be considered in conjunction with the *Humanities index* (**A235**), since they appeared in 1974 by breaking up the *Social sciences and humanities index* (1965–74) (**A236**). The latter title, in turn, emerged out of the older *International index* (1907–65) (**A237**). Like other Wilson indexes, these are organized around the familiar author and subject indexing integrated into a single alphabetical sequence. Whereas the *Social sciences index* covers most of the social sciences per se, the *Humanities index* includes history, archeology, linguistics, philosophy, religion, and classical studies that are of value to many social scientists. The journals indexed vary through the years. A particularly useful feature of both indexes since 1974 is the extensive listing of book reviews at the end of each year's cumulative volume. These indexes are now searchable online.

A238 United Nations. Library. Monthly list of selected articles. Liste mensuelle d'articles selectionnés. v.1– , 1929– . New York: United Nations. Monthly.

Begun by the League of Nations and continued by the UN, this current bibliography (in English and French) provides survey of articles selected from several thousand periodicals on political, legal, economic, financial, and social problems. The entries are classified broadly by subject, with subdivisions. No annotations, cumulations, or annual indexes. Wide international coverage.

A239 United Nations. Library. Monthly list of books catalogued in the library of the United Nations. Liste mensuelle d'ouvrages catalogués à la bibliothèques des Nations Unis. v.1– , 1928– . Geneva: League of Nations, 1928–45; New York: United Nations, 1946– . Monthly.

"A selected list of works relating to questions of every kind studied by the organs of the United Nations." Several thousands of items listed annually in a systematic arrangement in 7 groups, including sections devoted to reference tools and library science. Full bibliographic details but no annotations. UN publications are specifically excluded. In 1978, the 2 previous titles were merged into a single *Monthly bibliography* divided into 2 parts. The first is entitled *Books, official documents, serials*; the second is entitled *Selected articles.*

Aids with Regional Emphasis

A240 American bibliography of Slavic and East European studies. 1967– . Columbus: Ohio State Univ. Pr. Annual.

Supersedes the *American bibliography of Russian and East European studies* (1965–66) published by Indiana University. Lists books and journal articles, mainly by American authors, covering all subject fields related to Russia and Eastern Europe. Includes book reviews as well. The entries are not annotated. For the period 1945–57, see Robert F. Byrnes' *Bibliography of American publications on East Central Europe, 1945–1957* (Bloomington: Indiana Univ. Pr., 1958 [213p.]), a classified listing of 2,810 items. It excludes the U.S.S.R., East Germany, and Greece.

A241 Arctic Institute of North America. Arctic bibliography; prepared for and in cooperation with the Department of Defense. v.1– , 1953– . Washington, D.C.: Govt. Print. Off.

Comprehensive annotated bibliography in all languages of publications relating to the Arctic and sub-Arctic. Transliteration or translation of Cyrillic titles. Includes material on administration and government, Eskimos, archaeology, economic and social conditions, expeditions, mapping, population, communication, psychology, education, colonization, transportation, and ethnography. Especially valuable for Russian and Scandinavian sources.

A242 Australian Public Affairs Information Service; a subject index to current literature. 1945– . Canberra: Commonwealth Natl. Library. Monthly.

Part of a program of National Library of Australia that includes *Australian national bibliography* and more specialized current lists. *APAIS* indexes material on Australian political, economic, and social and cultural affairs, consisting of some official publications and books but mainly of articles selected from over a thousand periodicals published in Australia or overseas during the current or 2 preceding years. All articles are indexed in certain Australian periodicals that are chosen for their importance in the social sciences and humanities. Author index with annual cumulations since 1955.

A243 "Bibliography of Asian studies." *Journal of Asian studies.* v.1– , 1941– . Coral Gables, Fla.: Assn. for Asian Studies. Annual.

Title and scope of this excellent source vary. "At present the *Bibliography of Asian studies* aims at making available as complete a listing as possible of significant books and articles in European languages concerning countries of the Far East, Southeast Asia, and South Asia in the general fields of philosophy, religion, history, economics, social science, education, language and literature, and political science." The list dates from the American Council of Learned Societies' lists of periodical articles on Chinese subjects, which originated in 1934. Expanded mimeographed lists appeared from 1936 through 1940. Stable publication dates from 1941, when *Far Eastern quarterly* began publishing the list in each issue. It became an annual in v.9 (1949–50). The present title dates from 1956, when the *Quarterly* became the *Journal of Asian studies*. Lists more than 20,000 books, articles, and government reports a year. The range and growing significance of the service led to publication by AAS of the *Cumulative bibliography of Asian studies, 1941–1965* (Boston: Hall, 1969–70 [8v.]) (**A244**), and a later 6-volume set covering the years 1966–70, published in 1972–73.

A245 Handbook of Latin American studies. v.1– , 1935– . Cambridge, Mass.: Harvard Univ. Pr., 1935–47; Gainesville, Fla.: Univ. of Florida Pr. 1948– . Annual.

A notable annotated bibliography of books, articles, pamphlets, maps, and documents relating to Latin America. Originally a listing of publications of the preceding year, each volume since 1957 has included important older publications coming to the attention of the editors for the first time. Entries are classified according to discipline. Annotations, mostly in English, are critical as well as descriptive. Beginning in 1964, the handbook has been divided into 2 parts, even years being devoted to the humanities, odd years to the social sciences. Two other sources of current bibliographic information dealing with Latin America are *Current Caribbean bibliography* (v.1– , 1951– ; San Juan, P.R.: Caribbean Commission [annual]) (**A246**), and *Hispanic American periodical index* (v.1– , 1975– ; Los Angeles, Calif.: UCLA Latin American Center [annual]) (**A247**). The latter tool indexes some 200 journals published in Latin America, the U.S., and Europe, confining itself to social science and humanities materials. The indexing is by subject and author.

A248 Kyoto Imperial University. Research Institute for Humanistic Science. Annual bibliography of Oriental studies. v.1– , 1934– . Kyoto. Annual.

A companion to the "Bibliography of Asian studies" (A243), it has a more selective list of books and articles, in Western and Oriental languages, pertaining to all countries of the Orient except Japan. Classified with author index.

Current Bibliographies of Published Proceedings

A249 Directory of published proceedings, series SSH—social sciences/humanities. v.1– , 1968– . Harrison, N.Y.: Interdok. Quarterly.

Primarily a bibliography of preprints and published proceedings. Originally published in combination with the science series in 1965. In a list arranged chronologically by date of conference combines (1) a directory of places of meetings, conference names, and sponsors, and (2) bibliographical and other information needed to order the published reports. Subject/ sponsor, editor, and location indexes cumulate annually. Materials are mainly worldwide in scope and not exclusively in English.

A250 Index to social sciences and humanities proceedings. v.1– , 1979– . Philadelphia: Inst. for Scientific Information. Quarterly.

Another valuable contribution by ISI. Indexes in great detail published proceedings that appear as books, journal literature, reports, or preprint sets. The 7 parts include: (1) bibliographic information; (2) category (broad subject) index; (3) title keyword index to papers as well as conferences themselves; (4) sponsor index; (5) author/editor index; (6) meeting location index; and (7) corporate index, arranged by geographic location and by organization.

A251 Proceedings in print. 1964– . Arlington, Mass.: Proceedings in Print. Bimonthly.

This service, which offers access to conference proceedings in all areas and languages, is arranged by unique titles of conferences that are broadly interpreted to include lecture series, courses, and hearings. The entries are arranged alphabetically. The index is a single alphabet, combining corporate authors, sponsoring agencies, editors, and keywords.

A252 Yearbook of international congress proceedings; bibliography of reports arising out of meetings held by international organizations. 1969– . Brussels: Union of International Assns. Annual.

Companion to *Yearbook of international organizations* (A438). Lists reports of proceedings (minutes, summaries, working papers, etc., of over 10 pages) arising out of international meetings and indicates how to obtain them. Entries give year and date of meetings, place, subject matter, all titles of the publication, addresses of sponsoring organizations, and commercial publisher (if any). Concentrates on substantive results of meetings, and therefore excludes reports for internal administration of associations, as well as reports from the UN and its specialized agencies, although bibliographic access is described in an appendix. Basic listing of reports is chronological, supplemented by 3 indexes: by organization, author/editor, and subject/keyword. Since reports arise at varying times from the date of the meetings, the *Year-*

book includes reports arising during the preceding 8 years.

Current Newspaper Indexes

A253 New York times index v.1– , 1913– . New York: New York Times. Semimonthly, with annual cumulation.

Detailed subject index to a newspaper intent from its inception on serving as a reliable contemporary record. Notably successful in opening up the contents of this record, with exact citation of page and column. Ample cross-references. Bowker has produced an index to the *New York times* for the years 1851–1912. The newspaper is now accessible online, through a database made available directly by the *New York times*, and through the mediation of vendors.

A254 Times (London). Official index. 1906– . London: The Times. Bimonthly, with semiannual cumulations.

Detailed alphabetical index referring to date, page, and column. Complemented by *Palmer's index to the Times newspaper, 1790–1941* (London: Palmer, 1868–1943) (**A254A**); reprinted by Kraus (1966).

A255 Wall Street journal index. v.1– , 1958– . New York: Dow Jones. Monthly, with annual cumulation.

A detailed index in 2 parts, general and company, to one of the influential newspapers in the United States. The "company" section is designed to give access to articles dealing with specific business firms. The *Wall Street journal* can also be searched online, through vendor-supplied files.

The Micro Photo Division of Bell & Howell in Wooster, Ohio, has published indexes to a number of leading papers in the United States. These include: *Chicago sun-times* (1979–); *Chicago tribune* (1972–); *Christian Science monitor* (1960–); *Denver post* (1979–); *Detroit news* (1976–); *Los Angeles times* (1972–); *Saint Louis post-dispatch* (1980–); *San Francisco chronicle* (1976–); and the *Washington post* (1971–). The *Post*, one of the more important newspapers in the nation, has, since 1979, been indexed as well by Research Publications of Woodbridge, Conn.

Besides print indexes, there is a rapidly growing trend toward computerized indexing of newspapers. The *New York times*, as mentioned earlier, has developed its own online system that can be subscribed to. In addition, the *National newspaper index*, a database available through several vendors, indexes the *New York times*, the *Wall Street journal*, the *Washington post*, the *Christian Science monitor*, and the *Los Angeles times*.

An even more recent development is the advent of full-text searching by computer. A new database called *VuText*, developed by the *Phil-*

adelphia enquirer and available since 1984, stores the complete text of newspaper articles for online retrieval. *VuText* already indexes a number of Knight-Ridder newspapers and is rapidly expanding its coverage. Currently indexed are such newspapers as the *Akron beacon-journal*, the *Sacramento bee*, and the *Wichita eagle-beacon*.

RETROSPECTIVE BIBLIOGRAPHIES

General Records of Accumulated Learning

A256 Books for college libraries; a core collection of 40,000 titles. 2d ed. Chicago: American Library Assn., 1975. 6v.

This extensively revised edition of an earlier work with the same title (1967) seeks to select a core of 40,000 titles covering all subject fields that would constitute "the bare minimum of titles needed to support an average college instructional program of good quality." Selections were made by teaching scholars, specialist librarians, and staff members of a number of professional associations. The titles selected are arranged by LC classification in the 5 bibliographic volumes, with v. 3 and 4, covering history and the social sciences, respectively, including a total of 15,801 of the 38,651 items included. Psychology, included in another volume, would add several hundred more titles. V. 6 is devoted exclusively to author and title indexes. New edition in progress.

A257 Harvard University. Library. Widener Library shelflist. no. 1– , 1965– . Cambridge, Mass.: Harvard Univ. Pr.

Based on one of the ranking accumulations of learning, this monumental set presents a far more detailed record of learning than the preceding select list. Easy to use, this shelflist provides for each subject dealt with (1) a classified catalog (printout of the books in shelflist sequence, with outline of the classification scheme adjoining the list); (2) a listing of the same books in alphabetical sequence; and (3) a listing by date of publication. These subject bibliographies of book literature are so important that they deserve to be listed.

1. Crusades. 1965. 82p. 1,202 titles. Superseded by no. 32.
2. Africa. 1965. 790p. 13,335 titles. Superseded by no. 34.
3. Twentieth-century Russian literature. 1965. 428p. 9,430 titles.
4. Russian history since 1917. 1966. 698p. 13,722 titles.
5–6. Latin America and Latin American periodicals. 1966. 2v. 27,292 titles.
7. Bibliography and bibliography periodicals. 1966. 1,066p. 19,643 titles.
8. Reference collections. 1966. 187p. 4,300 titles. Superseded by no. 33.
9–13. American history. 1967. 5v. 83,867 titles.
14. China, Japan and Korea. 1968. 494p. 11,388 titles.
15. Periodical classes. 1968. 758p. 25,685 titles.
16–17. Education and education periodicals. 1968. 2v. 32,722 titles.
18. Literature: general and comparative. 1968. 189p. 5,065 titles.
19. Southern Asia: Afghanistan, Bhutan, Burma, Cambodia, Ceylon, India, Laos, Malaya, Nepal, Pakistan, Sikkim, Singapore, Thailand, and Vietnam. 1968. 543p. 10,292 titles.
20. Canadian history and literature. 1968. 411p. 10,212 titles.
21. Latin American literature. 1969. 498p. 16,900 titles.
22. Government. 1969. 263p. 7,190 titles.
23–24. Economics. 1970. 2v. 65,000 titles.
25. Celtic literatures. 1970. 192p. 7,500 titles.
26–27. American literature. 1970. 2v. 50,000 titles.
28–31. Slavic history and literatures. 1970. 4v. 93,000 titles.
32. General European and world history. 1970. 959p. 35,000 titles.
33. Reference collections. 1970. 160p. 5,000 titles. Supersedes no. 8.
34. African history and literatures. 1970. 500p. 20,000 titles. Supersedes no. 2.
35–38. English literature. 1971. 4v. 112,000 titles.
39. Judaica. 1971. 302p. 9,000 titles.
40. Finnish and Baltic history and literatures. 1972. 250p. 8,600 titles.
41. Spanish history and literature. 1972. 771p. 30,000 titles.
42–43. Philosophy and psychology. 1973. 2v. 59,000 titles.
44. Hungarian history and literature. 1974. 186p. 6,550 titles.
45–46. Sociology. 1973. 2v. 49,000 titles.
47–48. French literature. 1973. 2v. 52,000 titles.
49–50. German literature. 1974. 2v. 46,000 titles.
51–52. Italian history and literature. 1974. 2v. 72,000 titles.
53–54. British history. 1975. 2v. 45,000 titles.
55. Ancient history. 1975. 363p. 11,000 titles.
56. Archaeology. 1979. 442p. 14,300 titles.
57. Classical studies. 1979. 215p. 6,700 titles.
58. Ancient Greek literature. 1979. 638p. 19,800 titles.
59. Latin literature. 1979. 610p. 18,600 titles.
60. Geography and anthropology. 1979. 270p. 9,000 titles.

National Library and National Union Catalogs

The bibliographies whose range of subjects and publications overshadows all others have been built around the holdings of the two ranking national libraries of the English-speaking world. The British Museum's (Department of Printed Books) *General catalogue of printed books* (London: Trustees of the British Museum, 1960–66 [263v.]) **(A258)** contains more than four million entries. The following 3 supplements complete the printed version of the *General catalogue*, for records after 1975 are available only in microform.

> 10-year supp., 1956–65. 1968. 50v.
> 5-year supp., 1966–70. 1971–72. 26v.
> 5-year supp., 1971–75. 1978. 13v.

The first microfiche supplement, now available, covers the years 1976–82.

The K.G. Saur Company is producing a comprehensive 360-volume set of the *General catalogue* up to 1975 in a single dictionary sequence that will considerably simplify searching. Saur has also already published a print counterpart to the British Museum's microfiche supplement for the years 1976–82. It is in 50 volumes.

Subject access to the monumental book collections of the British Museum is provided by:

A259   British Museum. Department of Printed Books. Subject index of the modern works added to the library, 1881–1900. London: British Museum, 1902–3. 3v.

This original source has now been supplemented numerous times, bringing the coverage up to the year 1970. The supplements are currently titled *Subject index of modern books acquired* **(A260)**.

For the United States, a similar effort at massive bibliographic control of literature is represented by the *National union catalog, pre-1956 imprints; a cumulative author list representing Library of Congress cards and titles reported by other American libraries* (London: Mansell, 1968–84 [754v.]) **(A261)**. The NUC has been supplemented for the years 1956–67, 1968–72, 1973–77, and annually from 1978 through 1982, after which the publication is available only on microfiche. Subject access to American holdings was not originally as far-reaching as for British holdings, since efforts only covered literature printed in 1945 or later, and was limited to the holdings of the Library of Congress itself: United States. Library of Congress. *Library of Congress catalog. Books: subjects, 1950–1954* (Ann Arbor, Mich.: Edwards, 1955 [20v.]) **(A262)**. Supplements carried the indexing up through 1974. This publication is currently being made available only on microfiche.

The K.G. Saur Company is now doing a monumental bibliographic service for the world of scholarship by making available on microfiche the entire Library of Congress catalog for the years 1898–1980: *Main catalog of the Library of Congress* (New York: Saur, 1984–   [10,000 fiches]) **(A263)**. The collection includes author, title, subject, series, etc., cards in a single dictionary sequence.

Other Library Catalogs

An increasingly popular method of making book literature available to the scholarly world is the photographic reproduction of the card catalog for a subject collection of a major research library. Though this approach inevitably entails some duplication of other bibliographic sources, it is nonetheless of great value to researchers. Some catalogs that cut across the interests of more than one social science are listed here, particularly those that lend themselves to area studies. Others are listed with the special subjects to which they limit themselves.

A264   University of London. School of Oriental and African Studies. Library. Library catalogue. Boston: Hall, 1963. 28v.

Based on a collection of over a quarter million volumes dealing with the whole of Asia, Africa, and Oceania, this catalog excludes only science, medicine, and technology. It is especially strong in history, anthropology, and law. It includes author, title, and subject access, along with a catalog of manuscripts and microfilms, a Chinese catalog, and a Japanese catalog. Three supplements of 16, 16, and 19 volumes, respectively, published by Hall between 1968 and 1979, bring coverage up to 1978 and include maps, recorded disks, and tapes.

A number of other library catalogs of notable collections on Asia or parts of Asia could also be mentioned here. The University of California, East Asiatic Library, *Author-title catalog; subject catalog* (Boston: Hall, 1968 [19v]) **(A265)**, and a supplement of 4 volumes published by Hall in 1973, are especially strong on China, Japan, and Korea. The University of Chicago Oriental Institute Library, *Catalog* (Boston: Hall, 1971 [16v.]) **(A266)** emphasizes the Near East. Also published by the University of Chicago, Far Eastern Library is the *Catalogs of the Far Eastern Library* (Boston: Hall, 1973 [18v.]) **(A267)**, which is especially strong on Japan and China. Both involve author, title, and subject access. Cornell University, Libraries, *Southeast Asia catalog* (Boston: Hall, 1976 [3v.] **(A268)**, with a 3-volume supplement published by Hall in 1983, covers Burma, Cambodia, Indonesia, Laos, Malaysia, Singapore, Brunei, the Philippines, Portuguese Timor, Thailand, and Vietnam.

Several other excellent library catalogs round out this presentation on Asia. The University of Michigan, Asia Library, has produced the *Catalogs of the Asia Library* (Boston: Hall, 1978 [25v.]) **(A269)**, which strongly emphasizes China, Japan, and Korea. The University of Minnesota, Ames Library of South Asia, *Catalog* (Boston: Hall, 1980 [16v.]) **(A270)** is a fine source of material on India, Pakistan, Nepal, Bhutan, Sikkim, Sri Lanka, Bangladesh, Afghanistan, and Burma. The New York Public Library, Reference Department, *Dictionary catalog of the Oriental collection* (Boston: Hall, 1960 [16v.]) **(A271)**, supplemented with 8 additional volumes published by Hall in 1976, is especially strong on the Arabic, Indic, and Ancient Near East. It now covers publications up to 1971.

A272 A London bibliography of the social sciences. . . . Comp. under the direction of B. M. Headicar and C. Fuller, with an introd. by Sidney Webb (Lord Passfield). London: London School of Economics, 1931–32. 4v.

Nineteen supplements now carry this classic work up through v.42 (1984). Beginning with the sixth supplement (additions to the library 1962–68), this major bibliography is reproduced from cards that form the subject catalog of its sponsor, the British Library of Political and Economic Science, London School of Economics. This growing library collects extensively in social sciences other than economics, political science, and law, the areas of its greatest strength. It is strong in legislative and administrative reports and official publications. The original 4 volumes included complementary holdings of 8 additional London social sciences libraries, a cooperative feature that has continued. Each supplement forms an independent alphabet, and headings conform closely to the LC subject heading list. Form subdivisions help locate bibliographies and government publications.

A273 Royal Commonwealth Society. Library. Subject catalogue of the Library of the Royal Empire Society; with new introduction by Donald H. Simpson. London: The Society, 1930–37. Reprint, London: Dawsons for the Royal Commonwealth Society, 1967. 4v.

A library of distinction that deals with interdisciplinary aspects of the areas encompassed by the collection. Contents: v.1, British Empire and Africa; v.2, Commonwealth of Australia, Dominion of New Zealand, South Pacific, general voyages and travels, Arctic and Antarctic regions; v.3, Dominion of Canada and its provinces, Dominion of Newfoundland, West Indies, colonial America; v.4, Mediterranean col-

onies, Middle East, Indian empire, Burma, Ceylon, British Malaya, East Indian islands, Far East. The main set, going only into the 1930s, was supplemented by Donald H. Simpson, *Biography catalogue* (London: Royal Commonwealth Society, 1961 [511p.]) **(A274)**. Hall published an updated version of the *Subject catalogue* in 7 volumes in 1971, and followed up with a 2-volume supplement in 1977, thus bringing the original and Simpson's *Biography catalogue* up through the mid-seventies.

A275 Texas. University (Austin). Library. Catalog of the Latin American collection. Boston: Hall, 1969. 31v.

A dictionary catalog of one of the premier Latin American collections in the world, the original included about 175,000 printed books, pamphlets, periodicals, microfilms, and newspapers, particularly those published before 1890. Supplements of 5 volumes (1971), 3 volumes (1973), and 8 volumes (1975) have brought the bibliography up into the 1970s.

Several other catalogs of Latin American material are also extremely valuable. The University of Florida Libraries produced a *Catalog of the Latin American collection* (Boston: Hall, 1973 [13v.]) **(A276)**, with a 7-volume supplement in 1979. Another major collection is: Tulane University of Louisiana, Latin American Library, *Catalog of the Latin American Library of the Tulane University Library, New Orleans* (Boston: Hall, 1970 [9v.]) **(A277)**. It has now been supplemented with 3 additions totaling 5 volumes published in 1973, 1975, and 1978.

These holdings are complemented by the Canning House collections, which comprise the largest publicly available British library on the cultures of Spain, Portugal, and Latin America. Canning House is headquarters of two councils that have joined in making catalogs of these collections available: Hispanic Council, *Canning House Library* (Boston: Hall, 1967 [4v.]) **(A278)** and Luso-Brazilian Council, *Canning House Library* (Boston: Hall, 1967 [286p.]) **(A279)**. The Luso-Brazilian holdings concentrate on Portugal and Brazil. These original catalogs have now been supplemented with a single-volume addition published by Hall in 1973. One other library catalog that deserves mention in dealing with Latin America is the Hispanic Society of America, *Library catalogue* (Boston: Hall, 1962 [10v.]) **(A280)**. It is especially strong in the humanities and history, concentrating primarily on Spain, Portugal, and colonial Hispanic America.

A281 U.S. Department of Health, Education, and Welfare. Author-title catalog of the department library. Boston: Hall, 1965. 29v.

850,000 entries for a half-million volume collection representing various social sciences but especially strong in education and related subjects, including law. An asset in working with U.S. government publications because of the completeness of the set for departments and operating agencies.

A282 ———. Subject catalog of the department library. Boston: Hall, 1965. 20v.

Contains some 350,000 subject entries. Merging of predecessor collections meant combining catalogs that had not followed the same subject heading practices. Numerous cross-references help the searcher cope with this difficult problem. Hall has subsequently published a 7-volume supplement to the former title and a 4-volume supplement to the latter, both in 1973.

Interdisciplinary Bibliographies and Indexes

A283 Air pollution and the social sciences: formulating and implementing control programs. Ed. by Paul B. Downing. New York: Praeger, 1971. 270p.

Reviews the literature in sociology, psychology, political science, law, and economics dealing with the air quality issue. With less emphasis on the economic aspects of the problem, Nedjelko D. Suljak, *Public policymaking and environmental quality: an annotated interdisciplinary bibliography* (Davis, Calif.: Univ. of California Inst. of Governmental Affairs, 1971 [176p.]) (**A284**), helps round out coverage of the literature. Both bibliographies are dated but still standard.

A285 Grandin. A. Bibliographie générale des sciences juridiques, politiques, économiques et sociales de 1800 à 1925. Paris: Recueil Sirey, 1926. 3v.

Nineteen supplements published between 1928 and 1951 carried the coverage of this classic retrospective bibliography up to 1950. Extensive coverage of monographic works, mainly in law, politics, economics, and sociology. Legal literature constitutes at least half of the average volume. Very strong on France, Switzerland, and Belgium; less so for other countries. Full bibliographical details but no annotations. Subject and author indexes.

A286 Groennings, Sven. Scandinavia in social science literature, an English language bibliography. Bloomington: Indiana Univ. Pr. for the International Affairs Center, 1970. 284p.

Comprehensive classified listing of 20th-century books, dissertations, and articles relevant to comparative social science research on Denmark, Finland, Iceland, Norway, and Sweden. Introductory essays for the broad categories of economics, education, geography, history, international relations, law, political science, and sociology, emphasizing trends in research, highlighting most important contributions, and pointing to gaps and deficiencies in research efforts.

A287 Index translationum. Répertoire internationale des traductions. Nos. 1–31, 1932–40. Paris: International Inst. of Intellectual Cooperation. n.s., v.1– , 1948– . Paris: UNESCO, 1949– .

The original series (1932–40) appeared quarterly; the new series (1948–) is an annual. This tool is extremely valuable but does not fit well under the categories used in this chapter. It amounts to a bibliography of translations covering all subject areas. The translations are arranged first by the country in which they were published and then by subject, under the 10 general Dewey headings. Complete bibliographical information is given, including the original language, title, publisher, and date when available. Both series include indexes of authors, publishers, and translators. Social science and social problems are prominent.

A288 Ouvrages cyrilliques concernant les sciences sociales; liste des réproductions disponibles. Paris: Mouton, 1964–65. 2v.

Compilation from then current sources of reproductions (by reprint or microcopy) of books and periodicals primarily in Russian. The scope of the reproductions is really broader than the social sciences. For more updated material on the Soviet Union, one can consult William S. Heiliger, *Bibliography of the Soviet social sciences, 1965–1975* (Troy, N.Y.: Whitston, 1978 [2v.]) (**A289**). It is a fairly comprehensive list of books, journal articles, dissertations, and a few pamphlets—some 9,318 entries in all—published by 15 Soviet agencies. All entries are translated into English, and there are author and subject indexes besides the detailed table of contents.

A290 Pan American Union. Columbus Memorial Library. Index to Latin American periodical literature, 1929–1960. Boston: Hall, 1962. 8v.

This valuable access tool to journal literature dealing with Latin America and mostly of Latin American origin, covers some 3,000 journals, reproducing the entries photographically from imbricated library cards. Preference given to economic, political, social, and cultural material. Dictionary arrangement by author and subject, with cross-references. Two supplements have appeared, in 1968 and 1980, covering the periods 1961–65 and 1966–70.

Sturgis E. Leavitt and others, *Revistas hispanoamericanas: índice bibliográfico, 1843–1935* (Santiago, Chile: Fondo Histórico y Bibliográfico José Toribio Medina, 1960 [589p.]) (**A291**), provides a much needed access to much 19th-century periodical literature from Latin America with more than 30,000 entries from 56 leading Spanish-language journals. The cutoff date of 1935 corresponds to the initiation of the *Handbook of Latin American studies* (A245).

A292 Pearson, James D. Index Islamicus, 1906–1955; a catalogue of articles on Islamic subjects in periodicals and other collective publications. London: Mansell, 1972. 897p.

Supplements in 1962, 1967, 1972, 1977, and 1982 bring coverage up to the year 1980. One of the single most important sources of periodical literature on the Muslim world of North Africa, Middle East, and East and Central Asia, this tool includes law, geography, history, anthropology, demography, folklore, and education. It dovetails neatly with the published catalog of the library of the London University School of Oriental and African Studies (A264) and is further supplemented by the annual "Abstracta islamica," which itself appears as a supplement to the *Revue des études islamiques*, v.1– , 1927– (Paris: Librairie orientaliste Paul Geuthner [3/yr.]) (**A293**).

A294 UNESCO. List of UNESCO documents and publications. Paris: UNESCO, 1973. 13v.

A295 UNESCO list of documents and publications. 1972– . Paris: Computerized Documentation Service. Annual.

The first title mentioned is a cumulative subject listing of UNESCO publications from the years 1951–73. The second title is intended to be an annual that continues providing subject access to this body's publication. An earlier publication that sought to provide access to UNESCO publications was UNESCO, *General catalogue of UNESCO publications and UNESCO sponsored publications, 1946–1959* (Paris: UNESCO, 1962 [217p.]) (**A296**). With supplements published in 1964 and 1969, it listed several thousand items with full bibliographical detail with indexes by author, title, and series. The arrangement itself was classified.

Thus far, we have been listing bibliographies of interdisciplinary social science interest according to subject content. We will now list bibliographies of material according to form: directories, newspapers, periodicals, and statistical sources.

Bibliographies of Directories

A297 Current African directories, incorporating African companies—a guide to sources of information: a guide to directories published in or relating to Africa, and to sources of information on business enterprises in Africa. Ed. by I. G. Anderson. Beckenham, Eng.: CBD Research, 1972. 187p.

Now somewhat dated, but in the absence of a successor the best guide available. The first part lists African directories alphabetically with descriptive information; the second part lists African companies on a country-by-country basis. A subject index is included.

A298 Current Asian & Australasian directories: a guide to directories published in or relating to all countries in Asia, Australasia & Oceania. Ed. by I. G. Anderson. Beckenham, Eng.: CBD Research, 1978. 264p.

The title adequately describes this alphabetical listing of directories with descriptive information for each. A subject index is included.

A299 Current British directories: a guide to the directories published in Great Britain, Ireland, the Commonwealth, Pakistan, and South Africa. Ed. by I. G. Anderson. 9th ed. Beckenham, Eng.: CBD Research, 1979. 370p.

A comprehensive list for the countries included in the title. Each entry includes title, publisher, date of first edition, and description of contents. A topical index assists in use.

A300 Directory of directories: an annotated guide to business and industrial directories, professional and scientific rosters, directory databases, and other lists and guides of all kinds. Ed. by James M. Ethridge. 3d ed. Detroit: Gale, 1984. 1,322p.

The single best place to begin in seeking a directory. Classified listing of 7,280 directories, with address and phone number of publisher, summary of contents, description of arrangement, pagination, frequency, name of editor, circulation, price, and whether it accepts advertising. Includes both title and subject index.

A301 Guide to American directories; a guide to the major business directories of the United States; covering all trade, professional, and industrial categories. Ed. by Bernard Klein. 11th ed. Coral Springs, Fla.: Klein, 1982. 572p.

A classic tool dealing essentially with business directories in the United States. It also includes numerous directories prepared by and for other professions.

A302 Larson, Donna Rae. Guide to U.S. government directories. v.1: 1970–1980; v.2: 1980–1984. Phoenix, Ariz.: Oryx, 1981, 1985. 2v.

A successor to an earlier work by Sally Wynkoop (1969), this tool lists 1,631 directories published by the federal government arranged by Sudocs classification number. There is comprehensive bibliographic information on each entry, including depository item availability, GPO stock number, and descriptive material about the format of the directory. Included is a detailed subject index.

Bibliographies of Newspapers

A303 American newspapers, 1821–1936; a union list of files available in the United States and Canada. Ed. by Winifred Gregory. New York: Wilson, 1937. 791p.

Invaluable for full utilization of newspapers in research. Companion to *Union list of serials* (A202), it records newspaper files of some 5,700 libraries, newspaper offices, and other owners, public and private.

Similar information for the period before 1821 is provided by Clarence S. Brigham, *History and bibliography of American newspapers, 1690–1820* (Worcester, Mass.: American Antiquarian Soc., 1947 [2v.]) **(A304)**.

These sources must be supplemented with two excellent publications of the Library of Congress.

A305 Newspapers in microform: United States, 1948–1983. Comp. and ed. by the Catalog Management and Publication Division, Library of Congress. Washington, D.C.: Library of Congress, 1984. 2v.

A306 Newspapers in microform: foreign countries, 1948–1983. Comp. and ed. by the Catalog Management and Publication Division, Library of Congress. Washington, D.C.: Library of Congress, 1984. 504 p.

Each tool provides an extensive list of retrospective and current newspapers, published in the U.S. and in other countries, respectively, that are available on microfilm. The entries, arranged geographically, contain information on title changes, mergers, supersedes, and cessations, along with holdings locations for use in interlibrary loan. Another tool of use in interlibrary loan is: Chicago, Center for Research Libraries, *The Center for Research Libraries catalogue, newspapers*, 2d ed. (Chicago: The Center, 1978 [233p.]) **(A307)**. It lists the extensive holdings of the Center in alphabetical order.

More specialized sources for specific regions or countries of the world can be identified through Sheehy (A121) and Walford (A123). Several major bibliographic tools, however, could be included here because of their importance. For the Soviet Union, one should consult *Soviet and Russian newspapers at the Hoover Institution*, comp. by Karol Maichel (Stanford, Calif.: The Institution, 1966 [235p.]) **(A308)**, which contains 1,108 entries in alphabetical order. The Library of Congress has published 2 companion works of great historical value: *Russian, Ukrainian, and Belorussian newspapers, 1917–1953: a union list*, comp. by Paul L. Horecky (Washington, D.C.: Library of Congress, 1953 [218p.]) **(A309)**; and *Newspapers of the Soviet Union in the Library of Congress (Slavic, 1954–1960; non-Slavic, 1917–1960)*, comp. by Paul L. Horecky (Washington, D.C.: Library of Congress, 1962 [73p.]) **(A310)**. Together, they cover Soviet newspapers from 1917 up to 1960. For the rest of Eastern Europe, the Library of Congress has published: *Newspapers of east central and southeastern Europe in the Library of Congress*, ed. by Robert G. Carlton (Washington, D.C.: Govt. Print. Off. 1965 [204p.]) **(A311)**. It includes newspapers published in Albania, Bulgaria, Czechoslovakia, Hungary, Poland, Rumania, and Yugoslavia since World War I and in Estonia, Latvia, and Lithuania between 1917 and 1940.

Major bibliographies of newspapers for 2 other regions of the world can also be mentioned. For Latin America, one should consult: Library of Congress Serial Division, *Latin American newspapers in United States libraries; a union list*, comp. by Steven M. Charno (Austin: Univ. of Texas, 1968 [619p.]) **(A312)**. And for Africa, there is *African newspapers in selected American libraries, a union list*, comp. by Rozanne M. Barry, 3d ed. (Washington, D.C.: Govt. Print. Off. 1965 [135p.]) **(A313)**.

Bibliographies of Periodicals

A314 Andriot, John L. Guide to U.S. government publications. McLean, Va.: Documents Index, 1984. 2v.

A comprehensive listing of journals and other serial publications of the federal government. The first volume includes current agencies; the second includes non-current agencies. The latter volume covers agencies existing up to 1980 and will only be published every 5 years. The entries are arranged by agency and Sudocs number and include item numbers and depository designation. Indexes by agency and by title round out this indispensable tool.

A315 Katz, William A., and Linda Sternberg. Magazines for libraries: for the general reader and school, junior college, college, university, and public libraries. 4th ed. New York: Bowker, 1982. 958p.

A selective, classified, annotated list of periodicals in major and a few minor subjects, compiled for all types of readers and libraries. "It represents the views and experiences of the compiler, his science editor, librarians, teachers, subject specialists, students and informed magazine readers." Social science journals receive considerable emphasis. The annotations are supplemented by coded information on the audience the title can be expected to reach, its permanent reference value, and its standing in its field.

A316 Liste mondiale des périodiques spécialisés dans les sciences sociales. 6th ed., rev. Paris: UNESCO, 1983. 446p.

For scholars, this UNESCO publication is a valuable contribution, listing periodicals that specialize in (1) the social sciences as a whole or one discipline (e.g., sociology) and (2) studies along scientific lines. General arrangement is alphabetical by country, with indexes by title, institutional sponsor, and subject. Periodicals sponsored by international organizations are also included. The entries include editorial information; data on frequency, publisher, tables, indexes, date of first issue; and a description of the average issue (pages, number and length of articles, subjects covered, etc.). Titles are listed in French and English, but the text is in French.

Another tool that lists serials from around the world, though without a social science emphasis, is: Chicago, Center for Research Libraries, *The Center for Research Libraries catalogue: serials* (Chicago: The Center, 1972 [2v.]) (**A317**). With its 1-volume supplement published in 1978, this tools lists all of the journal and newspaper holdings of the Center in alphabetical order. It is valuable as an interlibrary loan tool.

A319 Bureau of the Census. Bibliography of social science periodicals and monograph series. Washington, D.C.: Govt. Print. Off., 1961–65. [Foreign social science bibliographies series P92, no. 1–22]

A valuable tool that concentrates essentially on non-journal continuations. It includes about 2,000 selected English-language titles, arranged by discipline. A few irregular serials are included. The bibliographic information provided for each entry is extensive, and descriptive annotations are added. The work is rounded out with author-title and subject indexes.

A319 U.S. Department of Commerce. Bureau of the Census. Bibliography of social science periodicals and monograph series. Washington, D.C.: Govt. Print. Off., 1961–65. [Foreign social science bibliographies series P92, no. 1–22]

Originated to bring information published in the more "difficult" languages under better control, this project concentrates on series for the period between 1945 and the early sixties. It is restricted to the holdings of the Library of Congress. Each bibliography includes titles under 15 subject headings, with uniform information for each type of material. For periodicals: issuing agency (transliterated and translated); title (in original language, transliterated and translated); publication information; indication of book reviews; news notes; summaries; brief statement of coverage; 5 representative recent articles; and Library of Congress holdings. For monographic series: issuing agency; series title; details of each title in series. Indexes of subjects, titles, authors, and issuing agencies are included in each bibliography.

The resultant publications, with years covered, date of publication, and number within the series, are as follows: Albania, 1944–61 (1962), 12p. [no.6]; Bulgaria, 1944–60 (1961), 36p. [no. 2]; Czechoslovakia, 1948–63 (1965), 129p. [no. 19]; Denmark, 1945–61 (1963), 111p. [no. 11]; Finland, 1950–62 (1963), 85p. [no. 12]; Greece, 1950–61 (1962), 19p. [no. 5]; Hong Kong, 1950–61 (1962), 13p. [no. 7]; Hungary, 1947–62 (1964), 137p. [no. 13]; Iceland, 1950–62 (1962), 10p. [no. 10]; Japan, 1950–63 (1965), 346p. [no. 20]; Mainland China, 1949–60 (1961), 32p. [no. 3]; North Korea, 1945–61 (1962), 12p. [no. 8]; Norway, 1945–62 (1964), 59p. [no. 15]; Poland, 1945–62 (1964), 312p. [no. 16];

Republic of China, 1949–61 (1962), 24p. [no. 4]; Republic of Korea, 1945–61 (1962), 48p. [no. 9]; Rumania, 1947–60 (1961), 27p. [no. 1]; Soviet zone of Germany, 1948–63 (1965), 190p. [no. 21]; Sweden, 1950–63 (1965), 83p. [no. 22]; Turkey, 1950–62 (1964), 88p. [no. 14]; USSR, 1950–63 (1965), 443p. [no. 17]; Yugoslavia, 1945–63 (1965), 152p. [no. 18].

A320 Vesenyi, Paul E. European periodical literature in the social sciences and the humanities. Metuchen, N.J.: Scarecrow, 1969, 226p.

Inventory with brief descriptive information of aids for the subject bibliographer in handling information in European periodicals: abstracting services, bibliographies, union lists, directories. Social sciences emphasized are sociology, economics, political science, public administration, international relations, law, history, geography, and statistics. Book bibliographies are omitted unless a significant portion of the entries is from periodicals. Arrangement of publications is by country of origin.

A321 Woodsworth, David. Guide to current British journals. 2d ed. London: Library Assn., 1973. 2v.

A classified arrangement by UDC of over 4,700 current British periodicals. It includes more than just social sciences serials. Appendixes include journals that carry abstracts, discontinued journals, and societies and their publications. All of volume 2 constitutes a "Directory of publishers of British journals," and may be purchased separately.

The single most comprehensive subject bibliography of *currently published* periodicals from around the world is *Ulrich's international periodicals directory* (A381).

Bibliographies of Statistical Sources

A322 American statistics index (ASI) 1974– . Washington, D.C.: Congressional Information Service. Annual, with monthly supplements.

Control of published statistics took a giant step forward with the initiation of this publication. *ASI* indexes as many statistics as can be found that are published by any agency of the United States government. Organization of the entries, which give extensive bibliographic information, a Sudocs number, and a lengthy abstract, is by government department, agency, and subagency. A separate volume provides indexing by subject headings, by titles, by agency report numbers, and by a variety of economic, geographic, and demographic categories. Extensive *see* and *see also* references further enhance the value of this indispensable tool. In 1984, it indexed 6,500 titles, including over 700 periodicals. The publication seeks to be "a master guide and index to all the statistical publications of the U.S. government." The base volume, published in 1974, covered the years 1960–73. Succeeding annuals bring the series up to date. ASI has an accompanying microfiche set containing texts of all documents indexed. It is now also searchable online.

In broadening its coverage of statistical sources, Congressional Information Service also initiated *Statistical reference index* (SRI) **(A323)** in 1980 to include statistics published by thousands of private organizations and state government agencies in the United States. It also initiated *Index to international statistics* (IIS) **(A324)** in 1983 to cover sources of international statistics, including the UN, OECD, EC, Organization of American States, and some 30 other intergovernmental bodies of significance. Organization of these sources is similar to that of the original *ASI*. Microfiche sets of the source documents are also available on subscription for *SRI* and *IIS*.

A325 Ball, Joyce, ed. Foreign statistical documents: a bibliography of general, international trade, and agriculture statistics. Stanford, Calif.: Hoover Institution, 1967. 173p.

This source systematically records, alphabetically by country, statistical documents of all nations produced in or translated into Western European languages. Based largely on the excellent collections of Stanford University libraries, with some additions. Retrospective and current acquisitions are described. Entries are identified by author or issuing agencies, title, and publication date, with helpful notes on cessations and continuations for serials.

A326 Harvey, Joan M. Sources of statistics. 2d ed., rev. and enl. Hamden, Conn.: Linnet, 1971. 126p.

A British bibliography that describes the main sources of governmental statistical information in the United Kingdom. Includes important U.S. and international sources. Arranged as a running commentary, the book is divided into broad subject areas (population, social problems, education, labor, production, etc.) with abbreviated citations for each title discussed. Subject and title index.

Harvey has also published an invaluable set of guides to statistics on all major areas of the world. They are as follows.

A327 ———. Statistics Africa: sources for social, economic, and market research. 2d ed., rev. and enl. Beckenham, Eng.: CBD Research, 1978. 374p.

A328 ———. Statistics America: sources for social, economic, and market research (North, Central, and South America). 2d ed., rev. and enl. Beckenham, Eng.: CBD Research, 1978. 385p.

A329 ———. Statistics Asia and Australasia: sources for social, economic, and market research. 2d ed., rev. and enl. Beckenham, Eng.: CBD Research, 1983. 440p.

A330 ———. Statistics Europe: sources for social, economic, and market research. 4th ed., rev.

and enl. Beckenham, Eng.: CBD Research, 1981. 508p.

The U.S.S.R. is included in the volume on Europe. The bibliographic entries are arranged first by country, then by category, e.g., public finance, production, health and welfare, etc. Each entry contains a complete bibliographic citation, the time period covered, the address of the issuing organization, cross-references where necessary, and brief description of contents. Each volume is rounded out with indexes of titles and of subjects.

A331 Inter-American Statistical Institute. Bibliography of selected statistical sources of the American nations. Washington, D.C.: The Institute, 1947. Reprint, Detroit: Blaine-Ethridge, 1974. 689p.

Comprehensive bibliographical guide to principal statistical materials of 22 American nations, including data, analyses, methodology, laws, and organization of statistical agencies. 2,500 titles classified first by country and then by subject, with detailed alphabetical and classified indexes. Annotations are factual in content and are given in 2 languages (English being one). Gives detailed information on statistical publications of each country and has section on general statistical works. Kept up to date by the quarterly bibliography in *Estadística: journal of the Inter-American Statistical Institute*, v.1– , 1948– (Washington, D.C.) **(A332)**.

A333 Kendall, Maurice G., and Alison G. Doig. Bibliography of statistical literature. Edinburgh: Oliver & Boyd, 1962–68. Reprint, New York: Arno, 1981. 3v.

Another example of the use of conventional bibliography to stem loss of control over expanding information. The compilers undertook to ferret out, list, and organize significant literature from the 16th century to the end of 1958. The object was sound retrospective coverage that could be kept current by the quarterly *Statistical theory and method abstracts* (A165).

A333 Manheim, Jarol B., and Allison Ondrasik.
A DataMap: index of published tables of statistical data. New York: Longman, 1984. 1,069p.

An invaluable index of considerable originality in conception, *DataMap* indexes the tables contained in 29 leading statistical sources of national and international scope. The emphasis is heavily on data of use to social researchers.

A334 Pieper, F. C. Subject index to sources of comparative international statistics. Beckenham, Eng.: CBD Research, 1978. 745p.

Another of the splendid new indexes to statistics to have appeared in the last twelve years. Detailed subject indexing of over 53,000 separate entries to statistics gathered from 358 publications. Covers the entire world. Complete list of publications indexed appears in the back. Along with *ASI, SRI, IIS*, and the series of tools by Harvey, the Pieper work represents a significant contribution to the effort to provide adequate access to sources of current statistics.

A335 U.S. Bureau of the Budget. Office of Statistical Standards. Statistical services of the United States government. Rev. ed. Washington, D.C.: Govt. Print. Off., 1976. 234p.

A periodically published tool appearing previously in 1968, this source introduces the statistical system of the federal government and briefly describes the principal statistical series within the system. Under each of about 50 subject headings, it is possible to determine what agencies are responsible for various categories of data. A last part provides an annotated bibliography of principal periodical statistical publications, arranged by agency.

A336 U.S. Library of Congress. Census Library Project. General censuses and vital statistics in the Americas: an annotated bibliography of the historical censuses and current vital statistics of the 21 American republics. Washington, D.C.: Govt. Print. Off., 1943. Reprint, Detroit: Blaine-Ethridge, 1974. 151p.

A classic work of value especially for identification of retrospective statistics for the Latin American nations. It is arranged by country, with all entries annotated. Used in conjunction with A331 and A332, it gives the searcher a good introduction to the major statistical series of the Latin American nations.

A337 ———. ———. Statistical yearbooks; an annotated bibliography of the general statistical yearbooks of major political subdivisions of the world; prep. by Phyllis G. Carter. Washington, D.C.: Govt. Print. Off., 1953. 123p.

Comprehensive survey of statistical annuals published by governments of around 200 countries or areas. Arrangement is by continent, subdivided by country. Each entry is annotated. Information on historical background, data covered, and contents of most recent issue. Included (in absence of a regular statistical yearbook) is any reasonable equivalent that may serve the same purpose. Of value primarily for historical statistical work.

A338 Wasserman, Paul. Statistics sources: a subject guide to data on industrial, business, social, educational, financial and other topics for the United States and internationally. 9th ed. Detroit: Gale, 1984. 2v.

A venerable and still useful guide to locating statistics, both domestic and international, on a wide range of topics. Organized by subject.

DIRECTORIES AND BIOGRAPHICAL INFORMATION

Biographical Information for Social Scientists

A339 American men and women of science: social and behavioral sciences. 13th ed. New York: Bowker, 1978.

Prepared with the aid of an advisory committee representing key professional associations, this directory adheres to high standards both as to selection of subjects and quality of information. It is, in addition, the most comprehensive directory in the field, providing data on Americans and Canadians in administration and management, area studies, business, communications and information sciences, community and urban studies, political science, psychology, and sociology. Professional information includes field of specialization, education, positions held, memberships, major publications, honors and distinguished services. Included are a discipline index, listing individuals under their fields of endeavor, and a geographic index, listing individuals by city under the appropriate state or province (for Canada). This addition to *American men and women of science* was made beginning with the 9th ed. (1956) with around 18,000 names and continued to the 13th, with some 24,000 names. The 14th and 15th eds. did not include a social and behavioral sciences section. Its future is undecided.

Most of the biographical directories of social scientists are to be found within individual subject disciplines. There are a few interdisciplinary directories that should be mentioned, though some of them are now so old that their value is now semi-historical. UNESCO, *Social scientists specializing in African studies* (Paris: Mouton, 1963 [375p.]) (A340), contains sketches for 2,072 scholars from various countries in economics, anthropology, linguistics, archaeology, history, political science, and law.

U.S. Library of Congress, Hispanic Division, *National directory of Latin Americanists: biographies of 2,695 specialists in the social sciences and humanities*, 2d ed. (Washington, D.C.: Library of Congress, 1971 [684p.]) (A341), is a response to inquiries for current information on persons with specialized knowledge about Latin America. It highlights performance record and language skills. Sophie Bassili Rentz has produced *A directory of social scientists in the Middle East* (Cairo: Organization for the Promotion of Social Sciences in the Middle East, 1977 [249p.]) (A342). It provides background on more than 200 social scientists, listed by country, then by area of subject specialization. Emphasizes behavioral scientists.

Who's who in Soviet social sciences, humanities, art and government, comp. by Ina Telberg (New York: Telberg, 1961 [147p.]) (**A343**), contains sketches in English of 700 persons, with party officials, political scientists, and economists prominent in the meager list of social scientists. It is based on the third edition of *Malaia sovetskaia entsiklopediia*.

Social Science Research Council, *Fellows of the Social Science Research Council, 1925–1951* (New York: The Council, 1951 [473p.]) (**A344**), contains information, including work done under the fellowship program from the council's earliest days, on 1,028 scholars. It documents, as it were, the evolution of the philosophy of the SSRC from its inception until after World War II, providing a look at the changing patterns of research that the Council emphasized. One can also find biographical information on social scientists in the *Encyclopedia of the social sciences* (A414), the *International encyclopedia of the social sciences* (A415), and the *Handwörterbuch der Sozialwissenschaften* (A416).

The preceding section has dealt with sources that may lead social scientists to biographical information on other social scientists, past or present, who have contributed to the development of knowledge in the field. Social researchers, however, may also need biographical data on the lives and careers of non-social scientists, which can serve as primary data for their research. Though it would be tedious and unnecessary to list even a sample of the hundreds of bibliographic sources, including dozens of national who's whos, retrospective dictionaries of national biography, and specialized directories, that could be useful, it will suffice to name two *indexes* to sources of biographical information.

A345 Biography and genealogy master index: a consolidated index to more than 3,200,000 biographical sketches in over 350 current and retrospective biographical ·dictionaries. 2d ed. Detroit: Gale, 1980. 8v. Supps. through 1984 have been published.

An extraordinarily useful tool that uses a computer-generated indexing system to identify biographical information in a large number of sources, from the *Dictionary of American biography* to *Foremost women in communication* to *Who's who in the socialist countries*. It obviates the need to consult numerous sources by indexing every major biographical tool and many relatively obscure ones. It is the single best place to start in seeking biographical information on anyone, living or dead.

A346 Biography index, 1946–   . New York: Wilson. Quarterly, with annual cumulations.

Organized in the fashion of all the Wilson indexes, this serial indexes biographical material appearing in several hundred magazines and books each year. Each entry identifies the dates and the profession of the individual, then lists citations, including obituaries, where biographical material can be found.

Research Organizations, Learned Societies, and Associations

A347 Conference of Social Science Councils and Analogous Bodies. International directory of social science research councils and analogous bodies. 1978–   New York: Saur. Annual.

This useful source contains entries for several regional and many national organizations, including detailed information on their history, structure, funding, grants, publications, and international cooperative programs.

A348 Encyclopedia of associations. 19th ed. Detroit: Gale, 1984. 5v.

A classified directory of over 18,000 organized groups of people who have voluntarily associated themselves for stated purposes. V.1, in 2 parts, lists over 10,000 national organizations of the U.S.; v.2 contains geographic and executive indexes; v.3 is a supplement, listing new associations and projects; v.4 includes around 8,000 international organizations; and v.5 lists "research programs and activities carried on by non-profit organizations and foundations." The entries are by principal interest of the associated group (agriculture, business, etc.) and are indexed by name, keyword, and subject. Details for each association include name, address, acronym, chief officer, membership, purpose and activities, staff size, special committees, publications, and meetings. Also has lists of inactive and defunct organizations and former names.

The British counterpart, the *Directory of British associations and associations in Ireland*, 7th ed. (Beckenham, Eng.: CBD Research, 1982 [473p.]) (**A349**), provides similar information on over 9,000 associations, societies, institutes, chambers of commerce, trade unions, and other organizations in Great Britain and the Irish Republic. Entries are arranged in one alphabet and indexed by abbreviations, publications, and subject of activities and groups served. A complementary publication for Britain is *Councils, committees, and boards: a handbook of advisory, consultative, executive and similar bodies in British public life*, 6th ed. (Beckenham, Eng.: CBD Research, 1984 [430p.]) (**A349A**), which lists more or less official bodies specifically excluded from the former.

There are comparable tools for continental Europe: *Directory of European associations*, 3d ed. (Beckenham, Eng.: CBD Research; Detroit: Gale, 1981–84 [2v.]) **(A350)**; and for Canada: *Directory of associations in Canada*, 5th ed. (Toronto: Micromedia, 1984 [346p.]) **(A351)**.

A352 Government research centers directory. 2d ed. Detroit: Gale, 1982. 434p.

A listing of over 1,600 research centers of the federal government. Included are those owned by the government, those contracting with the government, and university and independent laboratories receiving federal support. Entries include name, address, phone number, date established, director, size of staff, and activity. Name/keyword index, agency index, and geographic index are included.

A353 Research centers directory. 9th ed. Detroit: Gale, 1984. 1,308p.

Originally published in 1960 as *Directory of university research bureaus and institutes*. It presently lists more than 6,300 nonprofit, permanent research units sponsored by universities or operating independently. Supporting service units, such as computation centers, are included; primarily instructional laboratories are excluded. All major research fields, including the social sciences, are represented. Classified arrangement by field is supplemented by institutional research unit, personal name, and subject indexes, and each center is listed by subject as its range of activities requires.

A354 Scientific, technical, and related societies of the United States. 9th ed. Washington, D.C.: National Academy of Sciences, 1971. 213p.

A directory of professional and selected amateur societies of science and technology, including anthropology, archaeology, geography, and psychology. Both national and local membership societies are included in the alphabetical listing, which gives addresses, officers, history, purpose, membership, library, research funds, publications and activities, and keyword and geographical indexes. Has more detailed descriptions than the *Encyclopedia of associations* (A348). Canadian societies, formerly included, are now compiled in a separate directory, *Scientific and technical societies of Canada* (Ottawa: National Research Council of Canada, 1982 [150p.]) **(A355)**.

A similar British directory, *Scientific and learned societies of Great Britain; a handbook compiled from official sources*, 61st ed. (London: Allen & Unwin, 1964 [222p.]) **(A356)**, has a section on government and public research bodies, a classified arrangement that includes social science associations and provides directory information similar to the American version and an alphabetic organization index. Since it has not been updated in a long time, it is somewhat dated.

A357 World directory of social science institutions; research, advanced training, documentation, professional bodies. 3d rev. ed. Paris: UNESCO, 1982. 535p.

Compact, easy-to-use directory of organizations registered in UNESCO Social Science Documentation Centre Files, with updating service provided by the *International social science journal*. Entries include address, presiding officer, founding date, and publications, with coded information on research activities and facilities. Following the international section, organizations are alphabetically filed by country. Supersedes various earlier lists.

A358 World guide to scientific and learned societies. 4th ed. Munich: Saur, 1984. 947p.

A directory of more than 11,000 national and international societies and organizations in the sciences, technology, social sciences, and humanities. Brief information on each entry includes name, address, director, founding date, and membership. Arrangement is by continent, then by country. Subject index is included.

A359 World of learning. 1947– . London: Europa. Annual.

This magnificent annual must be included here because, in addition to universities from around the world, it also includes learned societies, research institutions, libraries, museums, and other institutions of higher education. Arranged by country, with a separate index of institutions. Completeness of information on bodies included varies considerably, but name, address, staff, and publications are fairly uniform.

Calendars of Congresses and Other Meetings

A360 "Annual international congress calendar," *Transnational Associations*, v.1– , 1949– . Brussels: Union of International Assns. Monthly.

This journal was formerly called *International associations*. The December issue features an annual calendar of future meetings, with location, organization, and keyword indexes. This information is supplemented monthly with additions to keep the calendar current.

A361 Union of International Associations. Les congrès internationaux de 1681 à 1899, liste complète. Brussels: The Union, 1960. 76p.

A chronological listing of 1,414 international congresses that gives the name of each meeting, the city where held, and the inclusive dates. Preface and analytical index are in French and English. A supplement that includes 2,528 congresses held between 1900 and 1919, along with a cumulative subject index to both volumes, was published in 1964 as *Les congrès internationaux de 1900 à 1919, liste complète* (Brussels: The Union, 1964 [143p.]) **(A362)**.

A363 World meetings: social and behavioral sciences, human services and management. v.1– , 1971– . New York: Macmillan. Quarterly.

Formerly called *World meetings: social and behavioral sciences, education and management*. A 2-year registry of future meetings. Entries include sponsor, source to use for inquiries, summary of content, language(s) used, expected attendance, report deadline, projected publications, and exhibits. They are arranged at random in serial-number sequence. Access through introductory computer printout indexes by meeting dates, keywords, locations, deadlines for reports, and sponsor directory index.

Information Centers

A364 Ash, Lee, comp. Subject collections: a guide to special collections and subject emphases as reported by university, college, public, and special libraries and museums in the United States and Canada. 5th ed., rev. and enl. New York: Bowker, 1978. 1,184p.

A standard source listing well over 70,000 references arranged by subject headings, then alphabetically by state, city, and library. It includes notes on collection peculiarities, size, and availability through loan or photocopy. Good cross-references.

Another approach to special collections is Robert Bingham Downs' *American library resources; a bibliographical guide* (Chicago: American Library Assn., 1951 [428p.]) **(A365)** and its supplements for the years 1950–61, 1961–70, and 1971–80, all published by the ALA in the years 1962, 1972, and 1981, respectively. Downs includes classified and annotated lists of library catalogs, union lists, and reports of holdings indexed by institution, subject, and editor.

For resources in European libraries, the pioneer has been Richard C. Lewanski, *Subject collections in European libraries*, 2d ed. (New York: Bowker, 1978 [495p.]) **(A366)**. Lewanski lists collections by Dewey classification along with an analytical subject index.

A367 Aslib directory of information sources in the United Kingdom. 5th ed. London: Aslib, 1982–84. 2v.

A directory of British libraries, information services, and organizations with specialized sources of information. Arrangement is alphabetical with good subject indexing but difficult geographical indexing. Pertinent data, including name, address, phone number, contact person, subject coverage, and so on, are included with each entry.

A369 Directory of special libraries and information centers: a guide to special libraries, research libraries, information centers, archives, and data centers maintained by government agencies. Ed. by Brigitte T. Darnay. 8th ed. Detroit: Gale, 1983. 1v. in 2.

A listing of around 16,000 special libraries and information centers. Included are subject divisions and departmental or professional libraries on university campuses, branches and divisions of large public libraries, company libraries, governmental libraries, and libraries of nonprofit organizations (learned societies, bar associations, museums, hospitals, civic, social, and religious organizations, etc.). Each entry includes name, address, phone number, contact person, staffing, year of founding, and a description of holdings and publications. Subject, geographic, and personnel indexes are included.

To facilitate more specialized subject access to this valuable directory, Gale publishes a separate *Subject directory of special libraries and information centers*, ed. by Brigitte T. Darnay (Detroit: Gale, 1983 [5v.]) **(A370)**. The 5 volumes cover: business and law libraries; education and information science libraries; health science libraries; social sciences and humanities libraries; and science and technology libraries.

A371 UNESCO. Guide to national bibliographical information centres. 3d ed., rev. Paris: UNESCO: 1970. 195p.

Lists major bibliographical centers for most of the countries of the world. Provides full name and address, phone number, founding date, purpose, specialization, statement of resources, availability, and reproduction services.

A372 U.S. Library of Congress. National Referral Center. A directory of information resources in the United States: social sciences. Rev. ed. Washington, D.C.: Govt. Print. Off., 1973. 700p.

A listing of organizations in social science information activities, with descriptions of their resources and services arranged alphabetically by main institutions. Small research units may be found through organization and subject indexes. Complete addresses and phone numbers provided for all organizations.

Directories of Databases

The rapid spread of databases, both bibliographic and factual, in the last decade has necessitated efforts to provide access to them. An entirely new class of reference tool has consequently sprung up. The following list of sources, many now appearing in updated editions every few years or even as regularly updated subscriptions, will give the researcher excellent guidance in identifying potentially useful databases for research purposes.

A373 Computer-readable databases: a directory and data sourcebook; ed. by Martha E. Williams. Chicago: American Library Assn., 1979. 2v.

This edition succeeds and updates an earlier effort by Williams in 1976, which limited itself to bibliographic files and was itself a successor to an earlier tool first published in 1973. The original publication covered only 81 databases, the 1976 volume included about 300, and the 1979 edition expanded to 528. Each entry includes name, address, chronological coverage, frequency of update, subject matter and scope of data, indexable fields, user aids, costs of subscribing, languages, countries providing source materials included, and other useful information. There are indexes by name, subject, producer, and processor (vendor). *Computer-readable databases* is itself searchable online.

A374 Data base directory. 1984–   . White Plains, N.Y.: Knowledge Industries. Expected to appear 2/yr.

Includes about 2,100 bibliographic and factual databases, especially those available in the U.S. and Canada. Alphabetical listing of entries, which include name, subject headings assigned by the producer, summary of scope and content, corresponding print sources, name of producer, information on the file itself, vendor, price, and other data. Vendor, producer, and subject indexes round out this excellent tool. It is itself available online.

A375 Datapro directory of on-line services. 1982–   . Delran, N.J.: Datapro. 2v.

This new source includes a monthly update service. It describes more than 1,400 publicly available databases, arranged alphabetically with detailed information on each file. A subject index helps in the identification of appropriate databases.

A376 Directory of online databases. v.1–   , 1979–   . Santa Monica, Calif.: Cuadra. Quarterly.

Now including around 2,760 databases available through vendors, this source cumulates into annual directories. Entries include name, type, subject, producer, vendor, content, coverage, and updating. There are 5 indexes: subject; producer, listing all databases created by each producer; online service, listing databases available through specific vendors; telecommunications, listing networks that can be used to access each file; and a master index of databases, producers, and vendors. This tool is also searchable online.

A377 Directory of online information resources. 1978–   . Kensington, Md.: CSG Pr. 2/yr.

This tool aims to cover both bibliographic and non-bibliographic databases that meet the needs of American and Canadian scholars. It is therefore selective rather than comprehensive, choosing those files it deems most popular. The databases are listed alphabetically, with general description of subject content, coverage, size of file, unit record (citation, abstract, etc.), vendor, and cost. There are subject and vendor indexes and a list of producers and vendors with name, address, and databases produced.

A378 Encyclopedia of information systems and services. Ed. by John Schmittroth, Jr. 5th ed. Detroit: Gale, 1983. 1,242p.

This work includes among its more than 2,000 entries publishers, professional associations, libraries, commercial firms, networks, governmental agencies, consultants, online services, time-sharing companies, telecommunications networks, fee-based information services, associations that promote the interests of the information community, and research projects and reference services that study and supply information in the field of information. Nearly everyone dealing with computer-processed information is included. The entries, arranged alphabetically, include name, address, phone number, chief administrator, description of system or service, scope of subject matter, input sources, computer-based products and services, publications, clientele, and other materials in whatever combination is appropriate for the organization or database mentioned. A long list of indexes is appended, including lists of databases, software products, abstracting and indexing services, database producers and publishers, geographic index, subject index, and many others.

A379 EUSIDIC: database guide. Medford, N.J.: Learned Information, 1983. 324p.

Includes 982 entries for organizations located in Europe, the U.S., Africa, and Asia that serve as producers, networks, vendors, or other agencies associated with bibliographic and non-bibliographic databases available in Europe. Each entry includes name, address, telephone number, databases produced, marketed, or operated, subject content of databases, and other details. Five indexes are by organization, subject, network, geographical locale, and database.

A380 Hall, James L., and Marjorie J. Brown. Online bibliographic databases. 3d ed. London: Aslib, 1983. 383p.

Covers 179 databases of interest in Britain, and consequently concentrates on English-language databases. Gives extensive information on each database as well as a sample printout. Other valuable features are addresses of online service suppliers, a selected bibliography of 215 items on online searching, a broad subject arrangement of databases, a listing of most important word in title or implicit in title, and a good general index. Specifically excludes non-bibliographic databases.

Directories for Social Science Periodicals

A381 Ulrich's international periodicals directory: a classified guide to current periodicals, foreign and domestic, 1984. 23d ed. New York: Bowker, 1984. 2v. Biennial.

Crammed with much-used information on some 66,000 current periodicals, with strong representation of social sciences and contiguous areas. Easy to use classified arrangement, with an "Index to publications of international organizations" and an alphabetical title index. Now also includes a valuable subject listing of abstracting and indexing services as well as an alphabetical index to these services. Information about titles includes: name of publication, translated title, subtitle, title change, sponsor, languages used in text, year first published, frequency, price, editor, address, noteworthy features (inclusion of book or film reviews, abstracts, bibliography section, statistics, cumulative indexes, etc.), and where the contents are indexed (although this is not done thoroughly). It also lists publications that have ceased since the last edition. Limited to publications issued more frequently than once a year.

For yearbooks, proceedings, and other serials published annually, less often, or irregularly, see *Irregular serials and annuals; an international directory*, 1967– (New York: Bowker [biennial]) (**A382**). The latest edition supplies information for over 30,000 such publications, arranged by subject area. Both *Ulrich's international periodicals directory* and *Irregular serials and annuals* are now updated between their biennial appearances by *Ulrich's quarterly*, 1977– (New York: Bowker) (**A383**), which follows the format of the parent publications. Yet another invaluable tool now being made available by Bowker is *Sources of serials: an international publisher and corporate author directory*, 2d ed. (New York: Bowker, 1981 [1,824p.]) (**A384**). This directory "provides comprehensive and authoritative author/publisher access to the world's periodicals." It includes 65,000 publishers and corporate authors of the 96,600 titles listed in the 3 previous publications.

IMS/Ayer directory of publications, 1869– (Fort Washington, Pa.: IMS) (**A385**) provides annual access not only to journals and magazines, but also newspapers and newsletters. It includes titles not found in *Ulrich's* that are published in the United States, Canada, Puerto Rico, the Virgin Islands, Bermuda, and the Philippines. The arrangement is geographical, by state, then by city. The latest edition lists 22,238 publications. The *IMS/Ayer directory* was formerly called the *Ayer directory of publications* and, even earlier, the *N.W. Ayer & Son's directory of newspapers and periodicals. Standard periodical directory*, 1964/65– (New York: Oxbridge [bienniel]) (**A386**), also limited to the United States and Canada, duplicates some of the information in *Ulrich's* and *IMS/Ayer's*, but is very strong on such elusive titles as house organs, yearbooks, government publications, newsletters, directories, transactions and proceedings of scientific societies, and publications of religious, ethnic, literary, and social groups. The latest edition makes available the names of some 65,000 periodicals (defined as any publication that appears at least once every 2 years) organized under 246 subject categories. For the U.S. and Canada, it is the single most comprehensive source, and it provides excellent data on each title.

Better coverage of non-U.S. newspapers and periodicals, though with only brief information about each title, is supplied by *Willing's press guide*, 1874– (London: Willing [annual]) (**A387**), now subtitled *A guide to the press of the United Kingdom and to the principal publications*

of Europe, the Americas, Australasia, the Far East and the Middle East. The 111th ed. lists 20,290 newspapers, periodicals, and annuals. The Union of International Associations, *Directory of periodicals published by international organizations*, 3d ed. (Brussels: The Union, 1969 [240p.]) (**A388**), gives directory information and descriptive comments for around 1,500 titles arranged by subject under 2 broad subdivisions: (1) supranational and intergovernmental organizations, and (2) international nongovernmental organizations. It is now somewhat dated.

Grants and Awards

A389 Annual register of grant support. 1967– . Chicago: Marquis Academic Media. Annual.

A major guide, originally published as a serial called *Grant data quarterly*. Comprehensive classified directory of current sources of financial aid for general categories, arts and humanities, social sciences, and sciences from federal agencies, foundations, and business and professional organizations, all but a few in the U.S. Each entry describes type of stipend, purpose, eligibility, financial data, application information, deadline, and address. Subject, organizational, and geographic indexes.

A390 Catalog of federal domestic assistance. 1965– . Washington, D.C.: Govt. Print. Off. Annual.

Published by the Office of Management and Budget, the *Catalog* provides data on all federal assistance programs, including scholarships, loan guarantees, grants, exchange programs, technical assistance and others. The 1984 *Catalog* contains 989 programs administered by 51 federal agencies. Includes indexes by agency, applicant eligibility, function, deadline, and subject. Each entry gives extensive information about the program in question.

A391 Directory of grant-making trusts. 6th comp. Tonbridge, Eng.: Charities Aid Foundation, 1978. 973p.

A guide to major British foundations organized to give support to other organizations for social welfare and community betterment. There are classified and alphabetical listings of the trusts. Each is identified by name, address, correspondent, trustees, purpose, and scope.

A392 Directory of research grants. 1975– . Phoenix: Oryx. Annual.

Beginning as a slender volume in 1975, this tool has been greatly expanded. It seeks to provide "information about grant, contract and fellowship support programs available for federal and state governments, private foundations, associations, and corporations for research, training, and innovative efforts."

The Foundation Center of New York makes available a group of publications essential for identifying information on grants made available by non-governmental, nonprofit organizations. The basic publication is the *Foundation directory*, 9th ed. (New York: Foundation Center, 1983 [762p.]) (**A393**) and its supplement (1984 [428p.]). It lists 4,063 nonprofit, private organizations with assets of at least one million dollars and annual contributions of $100,000 or more. The *Foundation grants index*, 1970/71– (New York: Foundation Center [annual]) (**A394**), is an annual adjunct to the preceding tool, listing the recipients of grants of at least $10,000 or more. Individuals who are recipients are not included. Both the *Foundation directory* and *Foundation grants index* are available online.

Yet another tool now available through the Foundation Center is *Foundation Center national data book*, 1975– (New York: Foundation Center [annual]) (**A395**), which lists more than 22,000 smaller foundations that give grants to nonprofit organizations. It also is available online. To round out its offerings, the Center also publishes *Foundation grants to individuals*, ed. by Claude Barilleaux, 4th ed. (New York: Foundation Center, 1984 [243p.]) (**A396**). It provides data as indicated in its name.

A397 The grants register. 1969/70– . Chicago & London: St. James. Biennial.

Subtitle: *Postgraduate awards in the English-speaking world*. A major guide to scholarships and fellowships at all levels of graduate study from regional, national, and international sources tenable in the home country and abroad, plus funds for advanced professional and vocational training, exchange opportunities, travel, special courses, conferences, equipment, and publications. Excludes awards sponsored solely by universities. Emphasis on Great Britain, the U.S., and developing nations. Good bibliography of other grant guides in separate section.

A398 Guide to European foundations. 3d ed. Turin: Fondazione Giovanni Agnelli, 1978. 467p.

Successor to the *Directory of European foundations*. Provides information on several hundred foundations, arranged by country, that support activities in the sciences, arts, and education.

A399 International foundation directory. Ed. by H.V. Hodson. 3d ed., rev. and enl. Detroit: Gale, 1983. 401p.

Describes more than 700 philanthropic foundations, arranged under 46 countries, that provide research and other types of grants. Each entry describes activities, publications, finances, trustees, officers, and address. Included are an index of foundations and an index of main activities.

A400 Millard, Patricia. Awards and prizes. Havant, Eng.: Kenneth Mason, 1970. 249p.

Directory of British awards given on regular basis for outstanding achievement, excluding competitive sports and advertising campaigns. Concise statements of awards are listed under 700 administering agencies, arranged alphabetically and giving address and phone number. Explanations are simple, not detailed. Indexed by subject, type of award (e.g., medal, certificate, grant, etc.) and names of awards.

A401 Wasserman, Paul. Awards, honors, and prizes: an international directory of awards and their donors. 5th ed. Detroit: Gale, 1982. 2v.

The first volume includes the United States and Canada; the second the rest of the world. The current edition lists more than 11,000 entries in alphabetical order by name of awarding agency. A subject index of awards and an alphabetical index of awards facilitate use. The entries list all awards given by each organization listed along with a description of the award and the year of its inception.

DICTIONARIES

A402 Acronyms, initialisms & abbreviations dictionary. Ed. by Ellen T. Crowley and Helen E. Sheppard. 9th ed. Detroit: Gale, 1984. 2v.

Subtitled "A guide to over 300,000 acronyms, initialism, abbreviations, contractions, alphabetical symbols, and similar condensed appellations." V.1 is in 2 bound parts; v.2 is a paperback supplement entitled *New acronyms, initialisms & abbreviations*. It is regularly updated until a new edition of the publication appears. A separate publication by Gale entitled *Reverse acronyms, initialisms, & abbreviations dictionary*, 8th ed. (Detroit: Gale, 1982 [2v.]) (**A403**), produces an alphabetical list by meaning of acronyms, initialisms, and abbreviations.

A404 Gould, Julius, and William L. Kolb, eds. A dictionary of the social sciences. New York: Free Pr. 1964. 761p.

In 1952 UNESCO began to encourage preparation of dictionaries in the principal languages for purposes of refining social terminology and facilitating international acquaintance with technical concepts. This work, produced by 270 scholars in the U. S. and Great Britain, is one outcome. Using A to D sections beneath a term, the editors first define its meanings (A), then supply background for divergencies of usage (B–D). Noticeable freedom is exercised in applying this formula. In general, the 1,000 terms represent (1) key concepts in political science and sociology (which are best represented), economics, social anthropology, and psychology, (2) meanings too technical to be found in an unabridged dictionary, and (3) meanings that need clarification. All definition articles are signed. Numerous citations document the text. There are also numerous cross-references.

A405 Kendall, Maurice G., and William R. Buckland. A dictionary of statistical terms. 4th ed., rev. and enl. London & New York: Longman for International Statistical Inst., 1982. 213p.

Authoritative compilation of generally accepted definitions for nearly 3,000 statistical terms with evaluations of controversial usage. For German, French, Italian, and Spanish equivalents, it is still necessary to consult the supplementary glossaries of the 2d ed. of Kendall and Buckland's *Dictionary of statistical terms*. Samuel Kotz's *Russian-English/English-Russian glossary of statistical terms* (London: Oliver & Boyd for International Statistical Inst., 1971 [87p.]) (**A406**) is based on the earlier publication.

Another glossary, designed to promote uniform inter-American usage of terminology, is the Inter-American Statistical Institute's *Statistical vocabulary*, 2d ed. (Washington, D.C.: Pan American Union, 1960 [83p.]) (**A407**). It consists of a basic list of 1,300 English terms with Spanish, Portuguese, and French equivalents and separate Spanish, Portuguese, and French indexes.

A408 Mitchell, Geoffrey Duncan. A new dictionary of the social sciences. Hawthorne, N.Y.: Aldine, 1979. 244p.

Aimed primarily at students and concentrating on sociology, this work includes about 350 articles, many signed. Many of the entries are biographical sketches; a few contain bibliographic references. Of use primarily to beginners.

A409 Nixon, James W. Glossary of terms in official statistics: English-French, French-English. London: Oliver & Boyd for International Statistical Inst., 1964. 106p.

List of more 1,500 main terms and approximately 3,000 subsidiary variations used in official statistics. Excludes words already explained in technological and methodological statistical dictionaries and in classifications of economic or other activities (i.e., industries, occupations, diseases).

A410 Reading, Hugo F. A dictionary of the social sciences. London: Sociologia Pubns., 1976. 231p.

Reading offers brief definitions of over 7,500 terms drawn from all of the social sciences except economics and linguistics. The tool is useful primarily for beginners.

A411 Smith, Robert E.F. A Russian-English dictionary of social science terms. London: Butterworth, 1962. 495p.

An aid to translating Russian words apt to occur in social science work, and a guide to words used in technical or special senses in sociology, political science, economics, accounting, public administration, welfare, and education, plus selected abbreviations.

A412 Zadrozny, John T. Dictionary of social science. Washington, D.C.: Public Affairs Pr., 1959. 367p.

Introduction by William F. Ogburn and author's preface develop the thesis that differentiation of language nowadays results more from occupational differences than from geography, and they present a strong case for the technical dictionary. This dictionary is intended to help broaden understanding of social science by broadening comprehension of its vocabulary. Defines about 4,500 terms from sociology, political science, economics, and—to a lesser extent—from population, psychology, physical anthropology, prehistory, jurisprudence, and statistics. Concise definitions reflect usage, including divergent usage. Some overlapping with unabridged dictionaries.

ENCYCLOPEDIAS AND ENCYCLOPEDIC SETS

A413 Encyclopedia of statistical sciences. Ed. by Samuel Kotz and Normal L. Johnson. New York: Wiley, 1982– . Projected at 8v.

Thus far, the first 5 volumes of this fine encyclopedia have appeared, carrying it into the *M*s. The articles, all signed and generally including bibliographies for further consultation, include not only statistical terms but also prominent persons identified with the field of statistics, important organizations, leading journals, and other materials of interest to statisticians in whatever subject field. A good system of cross-references furthers its value.

A414 Encyclopedia of the social sciences. New York: Macmillan, 1930–35. 15v.

Excellent survey of the social sciences as of the 1930s, prepared under the auspices of 10 learned societies with assistance from scholars from many nations. The Social Science Research Council was the motivating spirit in publishing this now classic work. The first part of its 349-page introduction has a notable discussion of the nature and scope of the social sciences, a history of their development, and a country-by-country survey of their position. The main portion of the work covers important concepts and advances in political science, economics, law, anthropology, sociology, penology, and social work, and in addition the social aspects of cognate subjects. Brief biographical articles make up 20 percent of the contents—a timeless contribution. The articles are accompanied by judiciously selected bibliographies. There are ample cross-references and a subject index.

A415 International encyclopedia of the social sciences. Ed. by David L. Sills. New York: Macmillan & Free Pr., 1968. 17v.

The product of well-coordinated efforts by 1,500 scholars from 30 countries, this tool synthesizes the concepts, theories, methods, and empirical regularities of 10 disciplines—anthropology, economics, geography, history, law, political science, psychiatry, psychology, sociology, and statistics. Interdisciplinary and cognate subject are included: area studies, behavioral sciences, and major societies of the world, as well as modern social thought about the arts, principal religions, and selected professions. The work treats broad subjects, often groups related topics within the alphabetical sequence, and seeks coherence by making use of interdisciplinary collaboration. The general level of authoritativeness of the encyclopedia is high. It is stronger in the then-current state of the art than in the historical approach, and thus replaces its predecessor (A414) only in part. The earlier also was much stronger in biography, though the later edition has partially compensated by publishing a separate *Biographical supplement* in 1979. The bibliographies include not only works cited but also additional works to help round out study of the subject. The index volume contains a detailed subject index, together with alphabetical and classified lists of articles.

A416 Handwörterbuch der Sozialwissenschaften. Stuttgart: G. Fischer, 1956–68. 12v. plus index.

This comprehensive encyclopedia is the successor to *Handwörterbuch der Staatswissenschaften* and covers all branches of social science, whereas its predecessor was primarily concerned with political science. Articles are long, signed, and have excellent bibliographies. International in scope, with articles on countries, geographical areas, international organizations, noteworthy contributions and concepts in anthropology, economics, education, political science, psychology, and sociology. Twenty percent of the articles are biographical, with citations to works by and about the persons. Index volume is in 3 parts: contributors, personal names, and subjects.

HANDBOOKS

A417 Blake, Judith, and J.J. Donovan. Western European censuses, 1960: an English language guide. Berkeley: Univ. of California Pr., 1971. Reprint, Westport, Conn.: Greenwood, 1976. 421p.

A handy aid to research. Undertakes to answer the following questions about 22 Western European censuses for 1960: whether comparative analysis of a particular topic is possible; which specific tables, if any, in the 22 censuses bear on the topic; where and how to get photocopies if the data are not available locally.

A418 The environmental law handbook. 7th ed. Washington, D.C.: Government Institutes, 1983. 507p.

Specialists summarize laws and regulations on pollution, review pertinent cases, and discuss methods of investigation and how to prepare for court action. Includes a glossary and further readings.

A419 Great Britain. Central Office of Information. Britain: an official handbook. v.1– , 1948/49– . London: HMSO. Annual.

A current compendium of factual information on the state of the nation and its administration, covering the economy, industry, labor, social welfare, education, the churches, etc. Neither a directory nor a prime source of statistical data, the handbook provides a broad current survey of the country and its institutions, with some attention given to historical developments.

A420 Kurian, George Thomas. Encyclopedia of the Third World. Rev. ed. New York: Facts On File, 1982. 3v.

An excellent source of quick information on the 122 nations of the Third World, arranged alphabetically through the 3 volumes. Provides political, economic, and social data. Among the topics covered for each country are weather, population, ethnic groups, languages, religion, constitution and government, local government, foreign policy, political parties, various subsectors of the economy, education, and so on. Many current statistics. Ten appendixes of statistical data, a selected bibliography of the Third World since 1970, and a general index enhance the value of the set.

A421 Lincoln library of social studies. 8th ed. Columbus, Ohio: Frontier, 1978. 3v.

An elementary, easy-to-use series of A–Z summaries, divided into subject sections that capsulize and tabulate information on people, events, and subjects. V.1 deals with history, government, politics; v.2 covers geography, economics, sociology; and v.3 deals with biography, space exploration, miscellany. Bibliographies and a master index are included.

A422 Miller, Delbert C. Handbook of research design and social measurement. 4th ed. New York: Longman, 1983. 678p.

The title is slightly misleading. The tool is intended to help researchers find practical information on research design, the most common methods of social science research, and methods of data collection. It has instructions for questionnaire construction, statistical analysis, selection of sociometric scales or indexes, research costing and reporting. Short bibliographies are included as further aids.

A423 Robert, Henry M. Robert's rules of order newly revised; comp. by Sarah Corbin Robert and others. New and enl. ed. Glenview, Ill.: Scott, Foresman, 1984. 594p.

The standard manual of parliamentary procedure. New edition greatly improved in organization while retaining essential continuity of content with earlier versions. Sets basic procedures for deliberative assemblies. Gives attention to bylaws, voting, and problems of conducting various types of organized meetings. Excellent subject index.

A424 Ronart, Stephan, and Nandy Ronart. Concise encyclopaedia of Arabic civilization. New York: Praeger, 1960–66. 2v.

Deals with the cultural, social, economic, and political aspects of the Arab world identified through historical and current issues, ideas, places, events, political parties, sects, and organizations, together with treatment of people of its past and their achievements. Arranged as a dictionary with cross-references and maps. V.1 covers the Arab east and v.2 the Arab west. There is a selected bibliography but no index.

A425 Tendances principales de la recherche dans les sciences sociales et humaines. Paris: UNESCO; The Hague: Mouton, 1970–78. 2v.

The product of many years of international effort, this report skips over familiar ground covered by standard textbooks and over areas where only limited progress has been made of late. It seeks, rather, to discern, summarize, and focus attention on recent developments of major importance, and is a first-rate interdisciplinary assessment of the state of the art. V.1 treats sociology, political science, psychology, economics, demography, linguistics, major interdisciplinary aspects of research, and the vital issue of science policy and social science research. V.2 covers jurisprudence, history, archaeology, art, literature and philosophy. Good bibliographies and a subject index.

A426 World almanac and book of facts. 1868– . New York: Newspaper Enterprise Assn. Annual.

This tool has unsurpassed score for packing heavy-demand, quick reference information between a pair of covers. Year after year the content has had no unifying theme except handiness, facilitated by around 30,000 index entries, but it is strongly weighted with social science data. A British counterpart, *Whitaker's almanack*, 1869– (London: Whitaker [annual]) **(A427)**, devotes more attention to statistics, especially for the Commonwealth and foreign countries. It also concentrates on material of interest to the British.

The success of these annually revised handbooks, designed to meet quick reference needs, has produced additional sources of high quality. Of front rank are the *Information please almanac*, 1947– (Boston: Houghton [annual]) **(A428)**; and the *Official Associated Press almanac*, 1970– (Maplewood, N.J.: Hammond [annual]) **(A429)**, formerly titled *New York Times encyclopedic almanac*.

A430 Worldmark encyclopedia of the nations. 6th ed. New York: Worldmark, 1984. 5v.

V.1 is a compendium of information on the UN and 17 related international agencies and on 172 nations arranged by continent: v.2, Africa; v.3, Americas; v.4, Asia & Oceania; and v.5, Europe. There is a systematic survey of each country under about 50 headings (e.g., population, ethnic groups, religion, history, government, international cooperation, economic policy, etc.), plus identifying symbols, small maps, and short bibliographies. It is a very handy set, though much material is duplicated elsewhere.

A431 Worldmark encyclopedia of the states. New York: Worldmark, 1981. 690p.

A companion publication to the preceding item, this tool presents handy data on all 50 states, the District of Columbia, Puerto Rico, and the U.S. dependencies in the Caribbean and the Pacific. A final section presents data on the United States as a whole. For each entry, material is presented under 50 subject headings, with a bibliography being the final heading.

YEARBOOKS
General and Global Yearbooks

A432 Annual register of world events; a review of the year . . . . v.1– , 1758– . London: Longman. Annual.

A durable symbol of the tradition of taking annual stock of man's affairs in an effort to gain perspective on present trends and possible future developments. First edited by Edmund Burke, who saw in the tool an aid to statecraft, the *Annual register* consists of essays on suitable topics prepared by specialists who seek out the major developments of the preceding year. Although the yearbook is global in scope, British affairs receive the fullest treatment. Organization of contents has varied, but in general the following topics are covered: history of the United Kingdom, Commonwealth, international organizations, and foreign countries (by country or regional group); religion; science; law; arts and literature; economics; texts of important documents; maps; obituaries; and a chronicle of world events. Includes an index of names and subjects.

Among other yearbooks of encyclopedic range, two in particular stand out. One is the *Americana annual*, 1923– (New York: Grolier) **(A433)**, which presents under broad subject headings arranged alphabetically interpretive articles on events of the preceding year. The other is *Britannica book of the year*, 1938– (Chicago: Encyclopaedia Britannica [annual]) **(A434)**, whose format has been similar. It presents the major events of the preceding year in the form of broad interpretive articles.

A435 The Europa yearbook: a world survey. 1959– . London: Europa. 2v./yr.

This title supersedes *Europa: the encyclopaedia of Europe* (1926–58) and *Orbis: the encyclopaedia of extra-European countries* (1938–58), which were published in looseleaf format. It is a reliable, much used source for current facts and figures of global scope. It contains much more directory information than the *Statesman's yearbook* (A437). V.1 contains international statistical comparisons, data on international organizations, and data on the countries of Europe. V.2 presents data on the remaining nations of the world. The format for each country includes a general survey and economic/demographic survey, and material on politics, government, religion, the press, publishers, radio and television, finance, trade, industry, transportation and tourism, atomic energy, and universities. Narrative, statistical tables, and directory information are provided for each section where appropriate. It is the most comprehensive of the Europa publications, which include the *World of learning* (A359), *Africa south of the Sahara* (A442), *Far East and Australasia* (A446), and *Middle East and North Africa* (A452).

A436 International yearbook and statesmen's who's who. v.1– , 1953– . West Sussex, Eng.: Thomas Skinner. Annual.

In addition to biographical information for statesmen as well as other international leaders, this book provides extensive political and economic data of global scope. The information on various countries, arranged alphabetically, is much the same as in *Statesman's yearbook*, but with more detailed statistical information.

A437 Statesman's yearbook; statistical and historical annual for the states of the world for the year . . . . v.1– , 1964– . New York: St. Martin's. Annual.

A comprehensive, up-to-date, and reliable compendium of information on all countries of the world. Pt.1 covers international organizations; pt.2 deals with the countries of the world alphabetically. The section on the United States includes a state-by-state breakdown besides the national data. The book presents for each nation material on area and population, constitution and government, defense, international relations, economy, energy and natural resources, industry and trade, communications, justice, religion, education, and welfare. Diplomatic representatives to and from Great Britain are also listed. Included with each national description is a bibliography of further works to consult. The statistics presented are not as extensive as in the *International yearbook* (A436).

A438 Yearbook of international organizations. v.1– , 1948– . Brussels: Union of International Assns. Biennial.

This useful source brings together in the main alphabetical section extensive information about individual governmental and nongovernmental international organizations. It includes data on origins, structure, purpose, basis of financing, activities, and membership, besides the usual directory information of address. Gives truly comprehensive data on the UN family of organizations. Future meetings of organizations and publications resulting therefrom are left respectively to the Union's *Annual international congress calendar* (A360) and the *Yearbook of international congress proceedings* (A252). News of current activities of international organizations is reported in the Union's monthly *International transactions* (**A439**), formerly titled *International associations*.

Regional and National Yearbooks

A440 Africa annual: the "New Africa" reference book. v.1– , 1958– . London: Foreign Correspondents.

For the most part duplicates standard directory and handbook information to be found elsewhere, but contains some information not readily identified in other sources, such as full lists of diplomatic missions at home and abroad. The initial section contains a good summary of foreign economic assistance to African states.

A441 Africa contemporary record, annual survey and documents. v.1– , 1969– . New York: Holmes & Meier.

A splendid country-by-country narrative of major developments in each of the nations of Africa during the year. Deals with political changes, foreign affairs, economic developments, social affairs, foreign investment, and other categories. Includes statistical tables. Also included are general articles dealing with special issues or continental affairs, and the text of important documents. Subject and name indexes add to the usefulness of the tool. Companion publications, similarly organized, are the *Middle East contemporary survey* (A453) and *Latin America and Caribbean contemporary record* (A451).

A442 Africa south of the Sahara. v.1– , 1971– . London: Europa. Annual.

A typical Europa regional yearbook that describes the physical, political, and economic features of the countries. General introductory articles place the countries covered within the framework of Africa as a whole. Descriptions of regional organizations precede those of the countries, with entries systematically treating geography, 20th-century history, economy, statistics, directory information, and bibliography. Includes a lengthy who's who for the area covered. Related Europa publications are *Europa yearbook* (A435), *Far East and Australasia* (A446), and *Middle East and North Africa* (A452).

A443 Canadian almanac and directory. v.1– , 1848– . Toronto: Richard de Boo. Annual.

A handbook of facts, general and Canadian, plus a collection of detailed social, economic, and political directories, such as banks, stock exchanges, governmental agencies, educational and learned institutions, postal guide, etc. Also a legal directory and digest of laws. Alphabetical table of contents and detailed index.

A444 Canadian annual review of politics and public affairs. v.1– , 1960– . Toronto: Univ. of Toronto Pr.

A far-ranging narrative overview of Canadian society and culture for the report year. Divided into the following basic sections: parliament and politics; external affairs and defense; national economy; life and leisure. Relatively few notes and bibliographic citations. Contains an index and list of contributors.

A445 Caribbean year book. v.1– , 1927– . Toronto: Caribook. Annual.

Formerly called *West Indies and Caribbean year book* (1927–77). Substantial, well constructed country-by-country annual guide with capsule information on social and economic conditions. Good general coverage, but a strong commercial orientation is displayed in export-import and tourist information, business and trade directories, and tables of trade statistics for each nation.

A446 The Far East and Australasia. v.1– , 1969– . London: Europa. Annual.

This Europa publication encompasses South Asia, Southeast Asia, East Asia, Australia, and the

Pacific islands. It provides the same type of narrative and statistical information on these nations as do the other Europa publications: *Europa yearbook* (A435), *Africa south of the Sahara* (A442), and *Middle East and North Africa* (A452).

A447 India: a reference annual. v.1– , 1953– . New Delhi: Ministry of Information and Broadcasting.

A rich source of statistical data. Official sources are used to compile summary statements on the current state of education, finance, scientific research, government, etc. Contains bibliographies.

A448 Iran almanac and book of facts. v.1– , 1961– . Teheran: Echo of Iran. Annual.

This tool provides standard, almanac-type information. The emphasis is on economics. It contains good directory information, statistical summaries, and an index.

A449 Japan statistical yearbook. v.1– , 1949– . Tokyo: Bureau of Statistics. Annual.

The text of this source is in Japanese and English. It is an official publication compiling current social and economic statistics for Japan.

A450 Korea annual. v.1– , 1964– . Seoul: Hapdong News Agency.

The standard national yearbook on Korean government, politics, economy, and foreign relations. It contains current statistical summaries and chronologies. Indexed.

A451 Latin America and Caribbean contemporary record. v.1– , 1982– . New York: Holmes & Meier. Annual.

Like its counterparts, the *Africa contemporary record* (A441) and *Middle East contemporary survey* (A453), this annual provides excellent current information in narrative form, supplemented by statistical tables, of recent developments in Latin America. Besides the country-by-country chapters, each written by a known expert in the field, there are chapters on general topics as well as texts of important documents. A bibliography with abstracts of recent book publications is another enhancement. Subject and name indexes.

A452 The Middle East and North Africa. v.1– , 1948– . London: Europa. Annual.

A political, economic, and social survey, similar in format to the other Europa publications: *Europa yearbook* (A435), *Africa south of the Sahara* (A442), and *Far East and Australasia* (A446). Excellent sections on religious diversity, calendars, holy places, regional cooperation, oil, the Suez Canal, and other problems unique to the area. These essays and the convenience of having statistics and directories of scholarly institutions of the countries of this region in one volume are its assets.

A453 Middle East contemporary survey. v.1– , 1976/77– . New York: Holmes & Meier. Annual.

Provides scholarly evaluation of recent developments in the Middle East on a country-by-country basis as well as articles of a more general nature. Statistical tables included with the narrative. Also included are subject and name indexes. With its companions, *Africa contemporary record* (A441) and *Latin America and Caribbean contemporary record* (A451), this annual is a very valuable source of current scholarly assessment of developments in an important region of the world.

A454 The New Zealand official year book. v.1– , 1893– . Wellington: Dept. of Statistics. Annual.

An accurate yearly record in text and statistical summaries of governmental, social, and economic developments. This standard source book is rich in detail and wide in scope. It includes historical chronologies, bibliographies, and index.

A455 South American handbook. v.1– , 1924– . Bath, Eng.: Trade & Travel Pubns. Annual.

A reliable, standard travel guide to 33 nations south of the United States, with up-to-date descriptive and statistical summaries. Detailed place-name index useful for location and identification of cultural features of cities is an addition.

A457 The Times of India directory and yearbook including who's who. v.1– , 1927– . New Delhi: Bennet, Coleman. Annual.

The best and most complete single-volume compilation of statistical and factual data on the economy, government, politics, commerce, banking, currency, etc., of India. Also a brief biographical dictionary of major figures. It is indexed. The government of India also publishes an annual volume, *India: a reference annual* (A447), described briefly earlier. The *Times of India directory* is more satisfactory because of the excellent directory information it contains on the trade and professional associations of India and the biographical section.

A458 A year book of the Commonwealth. v.1– , 1969– . London: HMSO. Annual.

Currently issued by the British Foreign and Commonwealth Office. It supersedes the *Colonial office list*, 1862–1966 (London: HMSO [annual]) and the *Commonwealth office year book*, 1967–68 (London: HMSO [annual]). It also incorporates the *Commonwealth relations office list*, 1951–65 (London: HMSO [annual]). Heavily weighted with handbook and directory governmental information. Main contributions: current and historical diplomatic lists; constitutional developments of the Commonwealth; digests of constitutions; lists of regional organizations and cooperative activities of member nations. The historical, social, and political digests for each year are somewhat repetitive from year to year and extensively overlap such sources as *Europa yearbook* (A435) and the *Statesman's yearbook* (A437). General name and subject index.

STATISTICAL SOURCES

Statistics are critical to the work of many social scientists, including economists, geographers, sociologists, political scientists, and historians. We have already dealt with statistics in this chapter from another angle. We have discussed bibliographies of statistical sources, i.e., guides to statistical compilations (A322–38). In this section, we will mention a number of the more important statistical compilations themselves.

National governments have become master compilers of statistical data. Various countries now have centralized statistical services and regularly publish a general statistical abstract or digest of basic national data. The *Statistical abstract of the United States* is a good example. National governments, in turn, report data to international organizations, which makes comparisons and summaries of international scope possible. Agencies like the International Statistical Association and organizations associated with the United Nations have encouraged national governments to cooperate in standardizing reporting to ensure accuracy and comparability of data. Where necessary, documents issued by these agencies use explanatory notes to describe their scope and any limitations of reliability.

The following statistical compilations are arranged under 3 broad categories: national, historical, and regional and international statistical sources.

National Statistical Sources

A459 U.S. Bureau of the Census. Statistical abstract of the United States. v.1– , 1878– . Washington, D.C.: Govt. Print. Off. Annual.

An indispensable summary of social, political, and economic statistics of the United States. Also a guide to further data from over 100 federal agencies and an equal number of private organizations through the introductory text to each section, the source notes for each table, and the "Guide to sources of statistics," a subject index to important sources of statistical information for the United States. To satisfy the need for more detailed information on specific areas, supplements, based on the most recent census material, have been issued. Among the oldest is the *County and city data book* (**A460**), which appeared in 1949, 1952, 1956, 1962, 1967, 1979, and 1983. The *State and metropolitan area data book* (**A461**), published in 1979 and 1982, presents statistics on states and SMSAs under 2,008 categories. And in line with trends emerging in the 1960s, the Bureau of the Census is also now publishing *Social indicators: selected data on social conditions and trends in the United States* (**A462**). These compendia have appeared in 1973, 1976, and 1979.

Though they are not technically compilations of statistics but guides to statistics, the following publications of the Bureau of the Census can best be mentioned at this point, for they form an integral part of the complex of Census Bureau materials.

A463 ———. Directory of federal statistics for local areas: a guide to sources, 1976. Washington, D.C.: Govt. Print. Off., 1978. 359p.

A464 ———. Directory of federal statistics for local areas: a guide to sources, urban update, 1977–78. Washington, D.C.: Govt. Print. Off., 1980. 490p.

A465 ———. Directory of federal statistics for states. Washington, D.C.: Govt. Print. Off., 1967. 380p.

A466 ———. Directory of non-federal statistics for states and local areas. Washington, D.C.: Govt. Print. Off., 1970. 678p.

A selection of other useful statistical digests follows. Many nations also publish monthly reports, all of which have a similar format and strong emphasis on demographic and economic factors. The most complete available lists of official statistical publications of nations around the world can be found in Pieper (A334) and in the series compiled by Harvey (A326–30). Ball, though a bit dated, is still useful (A325).

A467 Canada. Bureau of Statistics. Canada yearbook; official annual. 1905– . Ottawa: Statistics Canada.

A468 France. Institut National de la Statistique et des Études Économiques. Annuaire statistique de la France. 1878– . Paris: Imprimerie Nationale.

A469 Germany (Democratic Republic, 1949–). Staatliche Zentralverwaltung für Statistik. Statistiches Jahrbuch der deutschen Demokratischen Republik. 1955– . Berlin: Deutscher Zentralverlag. Annual.

A470 Germany (Federal Republic, 1949–). Statistiches Bundesamt Wiesbaden. Statistiches Jahrbuch für die Bundesrepublik Deutschland. 1952– . Stuttgart-Mainz: Kohlhammer. Annual.

A471 Great Britain. Central Statistical Office. Annual abstract of statistics. 1840/53– . London: HMSO.

A472 Italy. Istituto Centrale di Statistica. Annuario statistico italiano. 1878– . Rome: Istituto Poligrafico dello Stato.

A474 Narodnoe khoziaistvo SSSR. Statisticheskii ezhegodnik. 1955– . Moscow: Gos. Statisticheskoe Izd-vo. Annual.

See also the official publication of the Japanese Bureau of Statistics, *Japan statistical yearbook* at A449. Another serial publication presenting statistics on the Soviet Union is *USSR facts and figures,* 1977–   (Gulf Breeze, Fla.: Academic International [annual]) **(A475)**. This is probably the most carefully prepared and well-documented source of statistics on the Soviet Union today, especially in view of the problems inherent in attempting to interpret the official statistics listed above.

Historical Statistical Sources

In a special research project, the U.S. Bureau of the Census, in cooperation with the Social Science Research Council, reconstituted the data history of the nation in *Historical statistics of the United States, colonial times to 1970* (Washington, D.C.: Govt. Print. Off., 1975 [2v.]) **(A476)**. This edition supersedes the original published in 1960. It includes more than 12,500 time series, mostly on an annual basis, for the period 1610–1970. Included are data on every major aspect of the nation's social and economic development. Text notes specify the sources of the data, provide references to other sources, discuss the historical development of data, and evaluate their reliability. Also included are a chapter on colonial statistics and a subject index. Similar compilations for other countries include F. H. Leahy, *Historical statistics of Canada,* 2d ed. (Ottawa: Statistics Canada, 1983 [900p.]) **(A477)**; B. R. Mitchell and P. Deane, *Abstract of British historical statistics* (Cambridge: Cambridge Univ. Pr., 1962; reprinted 1976 [513p.]) **(A478)**; B. R. Mitchell and H. G. Jones, *Second abstract of British historical statistics* (Cambridge: Cambridge Univ. Pr., 1971 [227p.]) **(A479)**; and Italy, Istituto Centrale di Statistica, *Sommario di statistiche storiche dell' Italia, 1861–1975* (Rome: The Institute, 1976 [187p.]) **(A480)**. A very useful general compilation of historical statistics for all of Europe is Brian R. Mitchell, *European historical statistics, 1750–1975,* 2d ed. (New York: Facts On File, 1980 [868p.]) **(A481)**. Another helpful tool of a historical nature is Paul S. Shoup, *The East European and Soviet data handbook: political, social, and developmental indicators, 1945–1975* (New York: Columbia Univ. Pr., 1981 [482p.]) **(A482)**. It includes statistics on Albania, Bulgaria, Czechoslovakia, German Democratic Republic, Hungary, Poland, Rumania, the USSR, and Yugoslavia.

Regional and International Statistical Sources

A483 *América en cifras.* 1960–   . Washington, D.C.: Organization of American States. Irregular.

A comprehensive statistical source on all the American nations, with a master design to incorporate tables on demographic, economic, social, political, and cultural features. Each issue includes analytical indexes and a bibliography of sources. Because each edition appears as a lengthy series of reports, the OAS began publishing, in 1969, a handy summary entitled *Statistical compendium of the Americas* (Washington, D.C.: OAS [irregular]) **(A484)**. It is based on the fuller statistics contained in *América en cifras.* Statistical control became even tighter and more frequent with the creation by the OAS of *Statistical bulletin of the OAS,* 1979–   (Washington, D.C.: OAS [monthly]) **(A485)**. It includes analytical articles, regional statistical tables, and tables of economic indicators by country.

A486 Annuaire de statistique internationale des grandes villes. v.1–   , 1961–   . The Hague: International Statistical Inst. Biennial.

Comparative data on European cities of 100,000 or more population and cities outside Europe with over 750,000 population, including urban agglomerations similar to U.S. standard metropolitan statistical areas. Tables on population, vital statistics, housing and construction, public utilities, motor vehicles and urban transport, communications, water supply, cultural institutions, and sports. Expanded tabulations on special topics are sometimes issued as supplements.

A487 California. University (Los Angeles). Latin American Center. Statistical abstract of Latin America. 1955–   . Los Angeles: UCLA. Annual (irregular).

Presents current and comparative statistical data on the American nations south of the United States. Has excluded the non-Latin areas since 1976. Information on population; social, economic, financial and trade categories; coverage of religion, elections, and political developments. Beginning in 1970, the Center has also published a separate series of supplements dealing with special topics.

A488 European Communities. Statistical Office. Basic statistics of the Community. 1961–   . Luxembourg. Annual.

Compilation of statistics from the European Community, together with comparisons with some European countries, Canada, the U.S., Japan, and the USSR. Another publication, *ACP: statistical yearbook, 1972–78* (Luxembourg, 1980 [603p.]) **(A489)**, now presents statistics from 59 of the 61 signatories of the Lomé Convention of 1975, which created special trading relationships between the European Community and its former "Overseas Associates," now called the ACP (African, Caribbean, and Pacific) countries. This latter publication supersedes the *Associés d'outre-mer: annuaire de statistiques générales* (Luxembourg, 1966–67 [2v.]) **(A490)**.

A491 United Nations. Economic Commission for Asia and the Pacific. Statistical yearbook for Asia and the Pacific. 1970– . Bangkok. Annual.

This publication contains data for 34 nations, including Australia, New Zealand, and Japan but excluding China, North Korea, Vietnam, and countries of Western Asia. It is updated with the *Quarterly bulletin of statistics for Asia and the Pacific*, 1971– (Bangkok) **(A492)**.

A493 United Nations. Economic Commission for Latin America. Statistical yearbook for Latin America. 1973– . Santiago de Chile. Annual.

Contains statistical series for countries and for regional associations, such as the Latin American Free Trade Association, the Andean Group, the Central American Common Market, and the Caribbean Free Trade Association. The statistics are heavily economic.

A494 United Nations. Educational, Scientific and Cultural Organization. Statistical yearbook. 1964– . Paris: United Nations. Annual.

A successor to UNESCO's *Basic facts and figures*, the *Statistical yearbook* contains a wide variety of data on education, radio and television, publications, libraries, museums, population, and other measures of cultural and intellectual life in countries around the world.

A495 United Nations. Statistical Office. Compendium of social statistics, 1977. 3d ed. New York: United Nations, 1980. 1,325p.

The compendium appears irregularly (earlier editions were in 1963 and 1967) with the goal of providing essentially social statistics on demography, health, nutrition, housing, education, working conditions, and employment for nations around the world. It emerged through the efforts of the Inter-Agency Working Party on Statistics for Social Programmes.

A496 ———. Demographic yearbook. 1948– . New York: United Nations. Annual.

A valuable UN publication that compiles statistics on demography, mortality, natality, marriage, and divorce from all countries in the world. It includes a subject index.

A497 ———. Statistical yearbook. 1948– . New York: United Nations. Annual.

A master digest of statistics for over 200 countries, continuing the *Statistical yearbook of the League of Nations* (1926–1942/44; Geneva). The tables cover 10- to 20-year spans for agriculture, manufacturing and extractive industries, trade and transport, finance and national accounts, construction, housing, education, and mass communications. World summary tables emphasize population and economic growth trends. The text is in English and in French. The *Statistical yearbook* is supplemented with the *Monthly bulletin of statistics*, 1947– (New York: United Nations) **(A498)**, which provides updates and special expansions. Two special supplements have thus far appeared, in 1967 and 1974, with the purpose of describing the methodology and definitions in a fuller

way than can be accomplished in the explanatory notes of the previous two publications. These supplements have also contained a bibliography of the statistical yearbooks and bulletins from countries around the world. The latest supplement is: *Supplement to the Statistical yearbook and the Monthly bulletin of statistics; methodology and definitions*, 2d ed. (New York: United Nations, 1974 [424p.]) **(A499)**. An additional tool published by the United Nations, though not a statistical compilation, should be mentioned here. It is the *Directory of international statistics* (New York: United Nations, 1982 [274p.]) **(A500)**, first published in 1975. It describes the statistical publications of the UN, presents a classified list of its statistical series, describes methodological concepts, standards, etc., and inventories databases used in the system.

SOURCES OF SCHOLARLY CONTRIBUTIONS

Journals

A501

African affairs. v.1– , 1901– . Oxford: Oxford Univ. Pr. for the Royal African Society. Quarterly.
AbstAnthro; BrHumInd; Cc; HistAbst; HumInd; IntBibSocSci; IntBibZeit; IntPolSciAbst; PAIS; SocAbst.

American behavioral scientist. v.1– , 1957– . Beverly Hills, Calif.: Sage. Bimonthly
BullSig; Cc; ChDevAbst; IntBibSocSci; LLBA; PAIS; PsychAbst; SocAbst; SSCI; SSI; UrbAffAbst.

American journal of economics and sociology. v.1– , 1941– . New York. Quarterly.
AmH&L; AustPAIS; BullSig; CIJE; Cc; HistAbst; IntBibSocSci; IntBibZeit; IntPolSciAbst; JEconLit; PAIS; PopInd; PsychAbst; SocAbst; SSCI; SSI.

American Philosophical Society. Proceedings. v.1– , 1838– . Philadelphia. Quarterly.
AbstFolk; BiolAbst; BullSig; ChemAbst; Cc; HistAbst; IntBibZeit; LLBA; PAIS; SSCI.

Annales—Économies, Sociétés, Civilisations. v.1– , 1929– . Paris: Colin. Bimonthly.
AbstAnthro; BullSig; Cc; HistAbst; IntBibSocSci; SSCI.

Behavior science research; HRAF journal of worldwide comparative studies. v.1– , 1966– . New York: Human Sci. Pr. Quarterly.
AbstAnthro; PsychAbst; SSCI.

Behavioral science. v.1– , 1956– . Santa Barbara, Calif.: Inst. of Management Sciences, Univ. of California. Quarterly.
BiolAbst; Cc; EM; IntBibSocSci; IntBibZeit; IntPolSciAbst; LLBA; PsychAbst; SciAbst; SocAbst; SSCI; SSI.

Comparative studies in society and history; an international quarterly. v.1– , 1958– . Cambridge: Cambridge Univ. Pr. Quarterly.
AbstAnthro; AustPAIS; BullSig; Cc; HistAbst; HumInd; IntBibSocSci; IntBibZeit; IntPolSciAbst; LLBA; SocAbst; SSCI.

Daedalus. v.1– , 1958– . Cambridge, Mass.: American Academy of Arts and Sciences. Quarterly.
BiolAbst; BullSig; ChemAbst; Cc; HumInd; IntBibSocSci; IntBibZeit; IntPolSciAbst; PAIS; PsychAbst; SciAbst.

Diogenes; an international review of philosophy and human studies. v.1– , 1953– . Paris: International Council for Philosophy and Humanistic Studies. Quarterly.
AbstAnthro; AbstFolk; AmH&L; BullSig; Cc; HistAbst; HumInd; IntBibSocSci; IntBibZeit; IntPolSciAbst; LLBA; MLA; PAIS; SocAbst.

Ethnohistory; devoted to original research in the documentary history of the culture and movements of primitive peoples and related problems of broader scope. v.1– , 1954– . Tucson: Univ. of Arizona, Arizona State Museum. Quarterly.
AbstAnthro; AbstFolk; HistAbst; SSI.

Evaluation review; a journal of applied social research. v.1– , 1977– . Beverly Hills, Calif.: Sage. Bimonthly.
Cc; PAIS; PsychAbst; SocAbst; SSCI; SSI.

Health and society. v.1– , 1923– . Cambridge, Mass.: MIT Pr. Quarterly. (Formerly: Milbank Memorial Fund quarterly)
BiolAbst; ChemAbst; Cc; IntBibSocSci; IntBibZeit; NutrAbst; PAIS; SocAbst; SSCI.

Human relations; a journal of studies toward the integration of the social sciences. v.1– , 1947– . New York: Plenum. Monthly.
BrHumInd; BullSig; ChDevAbst; Cc; IntBibSocSci; IntBibZeit; PAIS; PsychAbst; SocAbst; SSI.

Impact of science on society. v.1– , 1950– . Paris: UNESCO. Quarterly.
BiolAbst; BullSig; ChemAbst; Cc; PAIS; SocAbst; SSI.

International social science journal. v.1– , 1949– . Paris: UNESCO. Quarterly.
Cc; EM; PAIS; PsychAbst; SSCI; SSI.

International social science review. v.1– , 1925– . Toledo, Ohio: Toledo Univ. Quarterly.
Cc; HistAbst; IntBibSocSci; IntBibZeit; IntPolSciAbst; PAIS; SocAbst; SSCI.

Jahrbuch für Sozialwissenschaften. v.1– , 1950– . Göttingen: Vendenhöck und Ruprecht. 3/yr.
BullSig; Cc; IntBibSocSci; SSCI.

Journal of applied behavioral research. v.1– , 1965– . Greenwich, Conn.: JAI Pr. Quarterly.
Cc; EdInd; PsychAbst; SSCI; SSI.

Journal of Asian and African studies. v.1– , 1966– . Leiden, Netherlands: Brill. Quarterly.
BullSig; Cc; IntBibSocSci; IntPolSciAbst.

Journal of conflict resolution; research on war and peace between and within nations. v.1– , 1957– . Beverly Hills, Calif.: Sage. Quarterly.
ABC; Cc; HistAbst; IntBibSocSci; IntPolSciAbst; PAIS; PsychAbst; SocWkRes&Abst; SSCI; SSI.

Journal of interamerican studies and world affairs. v.1– , 1959– . Beverly Hills, Calif.: Sage. Quarterly.
Cc; HistAbst; IntBibSocSci; IntPolSciAbst; PAIS; SSCI; SSI.

Kyklos; internationale Zeitschrift für Sozialwissenschaften. v.1– , 1948– . Basel, Switzerland: Kyklos. Quarterly.
Cc; EM; IntBibSocSci; IntBibZeit; JEconLit; PAIS; SSCI; SSI.

Philosophy of the social sciences. v.1– , 1971– . Waterloo, Ont.: Wilfred Laurier Univ. Quarterly.
Cc; SSCI.

Policy sciences; an international journal devoted to the improvement of policy making. v.1– , 1970– . Amsterdam: Elsevier. Quarterly.
ABC; Cc; IntPolSciAbst; SocAbst; SSCI.

Policy studies journal. v.1– , 1972– . Urbana: Univ. of Illinois, Policy Studies Organization. Quarterly.
ABC; AmH&L; Cc; HistAbst; IntPolSciAbst; PAIS; SocAbst; SSCI.

Royal Statistical Society. Journal. v.1– , 1838– . London: The Society. ser. A: General, 4pts./yr.; ser. B: Methodological, 3pts./yr.; ser. C: Applied statistics, 3pts./yr.
BullSig; Cc; IntBibSocSci; IntBibZeit; SSCI.

Science and society. v.1– , 1936– . New York: Science & Society. Quarterly.
ABC; AmH&L; BullSig; Cc; HistAbst; IntBibSocSci; IntPolSciAbst; PAIS; SocAbst; SSCI.

Slavic review; American quarterly of Soviet and East European studies. v.1– , 1941– . Stanford, Calif.: American Assn. for the Advancement of Slavic Studies. Quarterly.
HistAbst; HumInd; IntBibSocSci; IntBibZeit; PAIS; SocAbst.

Social forces. v.1– , 1922– . Chapel Hill: Univ. of North Carolina. Quarterly.
BullSig; Cc; EM; IntBibSocSci; IntBibZeit; IntPolSciAbst; LLBA; PAIS; PsychAbst; SocAbst; SocWkRes&Abst; SSCI; SSI.

Social problems. v.1– , 1953– . Buffalo: Society for the Study of Social Problems. 5/yr.
AbstSocWork; BullSig; Cc; EM; IntBibSocSci; IntBibZeit; IntPolSciAbst; LLBA; PAIS; PsychAbst; SocAbst; SSCI; SSI.

Social research; an international journal of political and social science. v.1– , 1934– . New York: New School for Social Research. Quarterly.
BullSig; Cc; IntBibSocSci; IntBibZeit; IntPolSciAbst; PAIS; SocAbst; SSCI; SSI.

Social science journal. v.1– , 1963– . Fort Collins, Colo.: Western Social Science Assn. Quarterly.
AmH&L; Cc; HistAbst; IntPolSciAbst; PAIS; SocAbst; SocWkRes&Abst; SSCI.

Social science quarterly. v.1– , 1920– . Austin: Southwestern Social Science Assn. Quarterly.
ABCPolSci; AmH&L; CIJE; Cc; HistAbst; IntBibSocSci; IntBibZeit; IntPolSciAbst; PAIS; SocAbst; SSCI; SSI.

Social science research; a quarterly journal of social science methodology and quantitative research. v.1– , 1972– . New York: Academic Pr. Quarterly.
Cc; PsychAbst; SocAbst; SSCI; SSI.

Society; social science and modern society. v.1– , 1962– . New Brunswick, N.J.: Rutgers Univ. Bimonthly.
Cc; RG; SocAbst; SSCI.

Technology and culture. v.1– , 1960– . Chicago: Society for the History of Technology. Quarterly.
AbstFolk; AmH&L; Cc; EM; HistAbst; IntBibZeit; SocAbst; SSCI; SSI.

Monograph Series

Major monographic series of a general social science nature can be identified in several sources. Perhaps the best is *Books in series in the United States: original, reprinted, in-print, and out-of-print books published or distributed in the U.S. in popular, scholarly and professional series*, 2d ed. (New York: Bowker, 1979 [3,273p.]) (**A502**). It includes a subject index to book series. Another source of information that includes a subject index to monographic series is the *Publishers' trade list annual* (A193), already mentioned in another context. Unlike the Bowker tool mentioned previously, it includes only current series. Some important monographic series of a general social science nature are:

A503

American Academy of Political and Social Science. Monographs. ser. 1, 1933–39; ser. 2, 1962– . Philadelphia.

American Philosophical Society. Memoirs. 1935– . Philadelphia.

Columbia University. Columbia studies in the social sciences. 1891– . New York.

Human Relations Area Files. Survey of world cultures. 1958– . New Haven, Conn.

Indiana University. Social science series. 1939– . Bloomington.

Johns Hopkins University. Studies in historical and political science. 1883– . Baltimore.

Jossey-Bass social and behavioral science series. 1967– . San Francisco.

National Institute of Economic and Social Research. Economic and social studies. 1942– . London.

Sage library of social research. 1973– . Rye, N.Y.

Sage research papers in the social sciences. 1973– . Rye, N.Y.

Social Science Research Council. Bulletin. 1930– . New York.

———. Monographs. 1948– . New York.

Stanford University. Stanford studies in history, economics, and political science. 1922– . Stanford, Calif.

University of California. Ibero-Americana. 1932– . Berkeley.

University of Chicago. Studies in social science. 1924– . Chicago.

University of Florida. Social science monographs. 1959– . Gainesville.

University of Illinois. Illinois studies in the social sciences. 1912– . Champaign-Urbana.

University of Michigan. Publications in history and political science. 1911– . Ann Arbor.

Organizations

A504

American Academy of Political and Social Science. Philadelphia. Founded 1889.

American Assn. for the Advancement of Science. Washington, D.C. Founded 1848.

American Institute for Research in the Behavioral Sciences. Washington, D.C. Founded 1946.

American Philosophical Society. Philadelphia. Founded 1743.

Brookings Institution. Washington, D.C. Founded 1927.

Bureau of Social Science Research. Washington, D.C. Founded 1950.

Center for Advanced Study in Behavioral Sciences. Stanford, Calif. Founded 1954.

Centro Latinoamericano de Investigaciones en Ciencias Sociales. Rio de Janeiro. Founded 1957.

Columbia Univ. Center for the Social Sciences. New York. Founded 1976.

Consortium of Social Science Assns. Washington, D.C. Founded 1981.

George Washington Univ. Human Resources Research Office. Alexandria, Va. Founded 1951.

Hoover Institution on War, Revolution, and Peace. Stanford, Calif. Founded 1919.

Institute for Social Science Research. Washington, D.C. Founded 1956.

Institute of Social Studies. The Hague. Founded 1956.

Inter-American Economic and Social Council. Washington, D.C. Founded 1945.

Intl. Committee for Social Science Information and Documentation. Paris. Founded 1950.

Intl. Federation of Social Science Organizations. Copenhagen. Founded 1979.

Intl. Institute of Differing Civilizations. Brussels. Founded 1894.

Intl. Social Science Council. Paris. Founded 1952.

Intl. Statistical Institute. Voorburg, Netherlands. Founded 1885.

Latin American Social Sciences Council. Buenos Aires. Founded 1967.

Milbank Memorial Fund. New York. Founded 1905.

National Institute of Economic and Social Research. London. Founded 1938.

National Institute of Social Sciences. New York. Founded 1912.

National Research Council. Washington, D.C. Founded 1916.

PEP (Political and Economic Planning) Trust. London. Founded 1931.

Resources for the Future, Inc. Washington, D.C. Founded 1952.

Social Science Research Council. New York. Founded 1923.

Social Science Research Council of Canada. Ottawa. Founded 1952.

Society for the Study of Social Problems. Buffalo, N.Y. Founded 1951.

Union of Intl. Assns. Brussels. Founded 1907.

Univ. of Colorado. Institute of Behavioral Science. Boulder. Founded 1957.

Univ. of Hawaii. Social Science Research Institute. Honolulu. Founded 1962.

Univ. of Michigan. Center for Human Growth and Development. Ann Arbor. Founded 1964.

————. Institute for Social Research. Ann Arbor. Founded 1946.

Univ. of North Carolina. Institute for Research in Social Science. Chapel Hill. Founded 1924.

Univ. of Wisconsin. Social Systems Research Institute. Madison. Founded 1924.

Urban Institute. Washington, D.C. Founded 1968.

Wright State Univ. Intl. Society for the Comparative Study of Civilizations. Dayton, Ohio. Founded 1961.

SOURCES OF CURRENT INFORMATION

Journals

Many of the general purpose journals listed earlier include not only researched articles and book reviews but also current information of value to social scientists in pursuing their professional activities. Excellent examples are the *International social science journal*, published by UNESCO, and *Society: social science and modern society* (A501). In addition, there are other publications of a newsletter or magazine nature that are more specifically directed at providing current information rather than scholarly articles. Two good sources that can assist researchers in identifying such publications by subject area are these.

A505 National directory of newsletters and reporting services: a reference guide to national and international information services, financial services, association bulletins, and training and educational services. 2d ed. Detroit: Gale, 1981. 8v.

A506 Oxbridge directory of newsletters, 1983–84: the most comprehensive guide to U.S. and Canadian newsletters available. New York: Oxbridge Communications, 1983. 508p.

Though most newsletters are discipline-centered, there are a number of a broad social science tools that deserve to be mentioned.

A507 BSSR newsletter. 1950– . Washington, D.C.: Bureau of Social Science Research. Quarterly.
Aimed primarily at describing the current research of the Bureau and the activities of its staff. Of use not only to academicians, but also to policymakers, practitioners in the social sciences, and the media.

A508 COSSA Washington update. 1982– . Washington, D.C.: Consortium of Social Science Assns. Biweekly.
Seeks "to inform and educate members of Congress, congressional staff, and officials in the administration and in federal agencies about recent research in the social and behavioral sciences, its importance, and the need to maintain adequate financial support for research." Interested in all aspects of federal activity that affect or can be affected by the social sciences.

A509 Center for the social sciences—newsletter. 1979– . New York: Columbia Univ. 2–3/yr.

Presents information on research conducted at the Center itself and throughout the university, including coming events, new grants, and the activities of researchers.

A510 Foundation news; the magazine of philanthropy. 1960– . Washington, D.C.: Council on Foundations. Bimonthly.

Devoted to news of activities of foundations in the United States.

A511 HRAF newsletter. 1976– . Amherst, N.Y.: Human Relations Area Files. Quarterly.

Though the main emphasis is on anthropology, this newsletter includes news of research in related fields and of an interdisciplinary nature.

A512 ISR newsletter. 1968– . Ann Arbor: Inst. for Social Research. Quarterly.

A high circulation newsletter describing the ongoing research and the research findings of the staff of the institute. It includes book reviews.

A513 New society. 1962– . London: IPC Magazines. Weekly.

Sees present-day society as requiring closer links between scholarship and public affairs and between intelligence and human behavior, and undertakes to serve as a broker of information and promoter of rational ties. A similar American journal in its inception is *Society; social science & modern society* (A501), formerly called *Trans-action*.

A514 Social action & the law. 1973– . Brooklyn: Center for Responsive Psychology. Bimonthly.

Seeks to keep legal practitioners informed of relevant social science research findings. Includes book reviews, statistics, a section on research progress, summaries of important court cases being argued, and an editorial.

A515 Social science information. 1962– . London: Sage. Quarterly.

Produced by the International Social Science Research Council with the aid of UNESCO and L'École Pratique des Hautes Études. The focus of the news reports and articles is on global progress in teaching and scholarship in the social sciences. News reports feature professional activities at the international level and newsworthy research and training programs. The text and title are in English and French.

A516 Social science news letter. 1914– . Chapel Hill, N.C.: Inst. for Research in Social Science. Quarterly.

"Disseminates current research findings and developments in social science theory and method to a state, regional, and national audience of social scientists and government officials." Includes current information on the Institute and its activities as well as articles of a scholarly nature.

A517 Social Science Research Council. Items. 1947– . New York. Quarterly.

News and information medium for the Council. Includes articles on current developments, committee reports, personal news, publications, grants, etc. A newsletter that is not as directly related to the social sciences but touches on many of them is *ACLS newsletter*, 1949– (New York; American Council of Learned Societies [2/yr.]) (**A518**). It includes information on the activities of ACLS and its 43 constituent societies. A report on the annual meeting of ACLS and lists of recipients of fellowships and grants-in-aid are standard features, along with announcements from the member organizations, many of which are social science bodies.

A519 Social Science Research Council. Newsletter. 1967– . London. 3/yr.

Its purpose is "to make available information on the undertakings and achievements of the Council."

A520 UN chronicle. 1954– . New York: United Nations. 11/yr.

Earlier titles were: *United Nations review* (1954–64) and *UN monthly chronicle* (1964–75). It contains information on the activities of the UN and its principal organs. Includes data on important resolutions and UN documents.

Selected Daily Newspapers

A521

Il corriere della sera, Milan, 1876– ; Daily telegraph, London, 1855– ; Excelsior, Mexico City, 1917– ; Le figaro, Paris, 1854– ; Frankfurter Allgemeine Zeitung, Frankfurt, 1949– ; Globe and mail, Toronto, 1844– ; La prensa, Buenos Aires, 1869– ; The guardian, London and Manchester, 1821– ; Le monde, Paris, 1861– ; Neue Zürcher Zeitung, Zurich, 1779– ; Pravda, Moscow, 1912– ; The times, London, 1785– .

Atlanta constitution, Atlanta, Ga., 1868– ; Chicago tribune, Chicago, 1847– ; Christian Science monitor, Boston, 1908– ; Los Angeles times, Los Angeles, 1881– ; New York times, New York, 1851– ; St. Louis post-dispatch, St. Louis, 1878– ; Wall Street journal, New York, 1889– ; Washington post, Washington, D.C., 1877– .

Stephen K. Stoan

2 History

Survey of the Field

Survey of the Reference Works

B1671–78. *Dictionaries, handbooks, manuals, and compendia* B1679–1721. *Original sources* B1722–29. *Atlases, maps, and pictorial works* B1730–54. *Sources of scholarly contributions.* Journals B1755. Monograph series B1756. Organizations B1757. *Sources of current information* B1758–63.

Survey of the Field

BASIC WORKS ON THE DISCIPLINE

Historical writing, in the context of Western culture, stems from both its Hebrew and Greek antecedents. Before the rise of the Hebrews and Greeks, little historical consciousness is known to have existed among the peoples of the world. What we have of a historical nature from the Egyptians and Mesopotamians, and their successors, provides little more than fragmentary lists of kings to posterity. The first history of the Egyptians that we know about was written in Greek, the result of Greek influence in Egypt.

Among the Hebrews, history became an important religious and intellectual undertaking. The writers of the Old Testament, adopting much of the cosmology of their Near Eastern neighbors, sought to justify their religious practices and their self-image as the chosen people. They did so by recounting their history. Thus was history made a basic element of Hebrew religion, and culture as a whole.

The Greek historical tradition, like the Hebrew, sought to prove the importance of Greek civilization. The Greeks had been a migrant people who conquered the earlier inhabitants of their land area, then developed their own culture. Like the Bible, Greek historical writing explained and justified these developments through explanations of social origins. And among both peoples, great events stimulated new historical writings. The writing of the Old Testament continued until about 168 B.C. The Homeric epics recorded the Trojan War, and the meaningful events of the fifth century B.C. led other writers to produce prominent historical works. The Persian Wars found their historian in Herodotus, whose work went far beyond the wars themselves, and who may be seen as the first self-conscious historian, aware of the need to criticize sources and verify his story. As a result, he is generally considered the "father" of history.

The Peloponnesian War inspired another Greek historian, Thucydides, a younger contemporary of Herodotus. He achieved a new consciousness of purpose and a new level of criticism in his work; he also introduced a new element to the historian's task. For the Hebrew writers, as for Herodotus, the purpose of history had been the glorification of the nation. Thucydides conceived of history as an educational tool, a teacher of men. This expanded attitude toward historical knowledge demanded both a stronger effort to analyze events and their causes and a more critical approach to the sources.

In its origins, then, historical writing had two main purposes. It glorified and explained the identity of the people who produced it, and it had educational value. These purposes retained their importance for the Romans, who developed a rich and important historiographical tradition. In fact Roman historical writing, like other aspects of Roman cultural and intellectual life, borrowed heavily from the Greeks. One of the earliest and best histories of Rome was written in Greek by Polybius. Among prominent Roman historians writing in Latin, Sallust and Cicero told the story of the troubled last years of the Republic. After the establishment of the Principate by Augustus (30 B.C.–A.D. 14), Roman historians sought to survey the whole history of the Republic, now become Empire. The sense of Rome's having achieved its final goal in the time of Augustus infused the writing of Titus Livy, who extolled the glory of Rome.

Later some Romans recognized that Imperial Rome in its golden age had significant problems, and this recognition is reflected in the brilliantly written *Histories* and *Annals* of Tacitus. Writing in the second century after Christ, Tacitus saw beneath the surface to the realities of power, and in terse and subtle Latin expressed anger and disgust at what he saw. His work was an exposé of imperial government written for the senatorial class. In his hands, history became an objective evaluation of positive and negative characteristics.

The historiographical traditions of the Hebrews and of Greco-Roman civilization served as the foundation for the historical writing of the Christian Middle Ages. Christian writers saw religious significance in history just as biblical writers had, while also feeling the strong influence of the Greco-Roman intellectual tradition. They tried to bring these two approaches together, looking upon both Old Testament and Greco-Roman history as their own history. Medieval writers reflected the view of history which held mankind to be forever evil, and awaiting the end of history in the second coming of Christ.

Medieval historical writing, notwithstanding its clearly indicated and determinedly held religious point of view, achieved excellence. The work of the Venerable Bede shows that excellence depends more on the critical acumen and skill of the author than on his underlying assumptions. In such comparisons a fundamental truth emerges. All historians make assumptions, based on the culture and society they live in, and none escapes those assumptions. Thus the value of historical work lies in its ability to reflect the historian's particular set of biases, as well as in his critical abilities and his power of reasoning and interpretation. On these criteria, Bede stands very high among historical writers of any age.

The chief difference between medieval historical writers and the humanist-historians of the Renaissance period—the late fifteenth and sixteenth century—appears in the new historical viewpoint that characterizes the work of the latter. The humanists were conscious of a separation between themselves and their subjects that medieval writers did not appreciate. By separating the past from the present, the humanists looked at earlier periods with greater detachment than their predecessors, and this detachment led to an increasingly critical attitude toward their sources. The ancient age received praise because of its concern for this world, while the Middle Ages were pictured as a time of stagnation because of the emphasis on other worldly rewards.

But many similarities exist between Renaissance and medieval historians. Like their medieval predecessors, the humanist-historians looked upon the history of man as a story of progress, but that progress now aimed at more perfect human values, toward civilization in the Greco-Roman sense, and not toward spiritual salvation. Attention focused on the character of human society, government and the improvement of life in this world. This extremely important change in emphasis and point of view brought with it the new critical attitude toward historical sources and legends. But it is important to note that this critical attitude was exercised selectively—that it destroyed the veracity of only some of the long-honored sources and authorities. When it came to the sources relative to ancient civilization and history, the humanists proved no better than their predecessors. The humanist point of view precluded complete objectivity and the honest employment of critical skills just as the Christian point of view had obscured the vision of medieval historians.

One of the results of the humanist reaction to medieval intellectual tendencies and to medieval historiography was the production of civic histories. The civic histories, like Machiavelli's history of Florence, emphasized civic pride that had been identified as one of the touchstones of ancient civilization. Universal history, like the medieval world chronicles that began with the Creation and ended in the time of the writing, fell into disfavor among the humanists and their successors. Yet resistance to the humanist approach continued among some Catholics, the most important of whom was Bossuet (1627–1704). For him, only universal history had validity because only in that kind of history could God's hand be seen working in the whole of history.

This attitude became the target for the new generation of historians associated with the Enlightenment of the eighteenth century. In many ways the Enlightenment historians—Hume, Voltaire, Montesquieu, among others—continued the tradition of the humanists. They emphasized human values and were sensitive to differences between national groups. Geography, climate, and religious mores served to explain historical patterns and developments. These factors were, for them, the natural laws of human life, analogous to the principles of natural law being discovered at that time by Newton and others. Enlightenment historians avowed their faith in the power of human reason to grasp the laws of nature and human behavior, and they dispensed with Providence in historical as well as physical explanations. For Voltaire, Bossuet's history was nonsense. It was neither truly universal nor valid as an interpretation of the nature of man or of man's history.

Much of the historical writing of the Age of Reason exhibited high literary quality, and the intellectual and factual content of works often suffered in the drive for literary excellence. Yet much of great importance was introduced to the historical discipline in this period. Historical writers became interested in social and economic history, and the Germans heightened attention paid to the history of art and literature. But Enlightenment history preserved some of the more questionable characteristics of earlier historical writing. It was based on the assumption that the use of reason would result in perfect understanding of man and his world. Now that man understood his potential, he would consummate his development as a rational being.

The attitude of Enlightenment writers toward history and historical scholarship was in fact antihistorical. Since they thought that man had progressed toward perfection, the only goal for historical scholarship lay in providing evidence for the argument that man was in the process of achieving perfection. By studying history, the Enlightenment authors—most of whom were primarily philosophers—sought to demonstrate that man was now "better" than in earlier times. History served as an adjunct to philosophy.

The intellectual movement called Romanticism provided a reaction to this view. The Romanticists—Herder, Goethe, Hegel, and others—argued that man was a product of his history. In historical scholarship they sought a way to understand humanity and, in particular, human nature, for human nature was viewed as a product of history in the same sense that a mature individual was the product of his childhood and adolescence. Begun in the 1770s and 1780s, the Romantic reaction reached its apex in the first half of the nineteenth century. The French revolution had promised the rationalization of politics and society that the Enlightenment *philosophes* had been calling for. But as this dream turned to ashes in the revolutionary violence and terror, the intellectual reaction to the ideas supposedly embodied in the conflict became a major factor in European intellectual life. This reaction centered in Germany and England.

The Romantic historians wanted to find the foundations of the present; thus they went in search of the past. Their writings show a strong interest in the ancient mythology and folklore of the peoples of Europe. Interest in the cultural development of Europe led to an interest in languages, oral tradition, and religion, as well as economic and social history. The Middle Ages, so long consigned to the shadows by the attitudes passed on by the Renaissance humanists, again became a period of vital interest to historians.

The Romantics' emphasis on the past had a profound effect on historical writing. Since history was the basis of, and in fact part of, the present, it had to be studied in all its aspects. Historians sought ways of increasing their knowledge by developing new ways to analyze and interpret the sources. Libraries were searched for historical sources and new disciplines, like comparative philology and paleography, came into existence. The *Monumenta Germaniae Historica*, the Rolls series in England, and similar large-scale projects designed to make the sources of European history readily available published the records, chronicles, accounts, journals and other historical sources from earlier periods. At the same time, editions of historically important texts were printed in large collections, such as the famous *Patrologiae* of J. P. Migne.

Accompanying the broadening and deepening of historical research, the reaction against Enlightenment ideas brought about a critical evaluation of the eighteenth-century philosophies of history. The most important figure in this reevaluation, Hegel, rejected the idea of historical progress toward the realization of perfect reason but did not reject the notion that history had meaning. He saw in history a dialectic between the status quo and elements representing revolutionary new forms of organization and culture. He called the prevailing mores and systems the *thesis* and the challenge to it the *antithesis*, and he argued that every thesis, every historical status quo, contains in itself its antithesis, the radically different form of life destined to destroy it. The struggle between the two produce a synthesis, which became the new thesis. The whole process represented the continuing realization of God in the world, and like all progressions, this process had an end-point. Hegel identified the nation-state as the thesis, as the social and cultural entity destined to prevail with finality. Only the nation-state did not contain the seeds of its own destruction, for in its perfect development it is identical to that divine order toward which all history is directed. Thus Hegel glorified the nation-state and raised *raison d'etat* and nationalism to the status of divine obligations.

This philosophy of history was profoundly influential in the early decades of the nineteenth century, and in Karl Marx it found its most famous and important adherent. Marx seized upon the dialectic of thesis and antithesis while transforming its content. He saw the economic system, not the social and political system, as the determining factor in the progress of history from one age to another. Simply stated, Marx argued that the progress of history is determined not by the locus of political and cultural power but by the locus of the means of production. Marx's ideas, with the Hegelian dialectic at its core, became an important factor in historical thought. Its influence remained strong until the mid-twentieth century.

Modern historical writing stems from the early nineteenth century. Particularly in Germany, but also elsewhere in Europe, schools of professional historians emerged. These schools differed from one another according to their interests and methods of obtaining historical information. Improvements in method brought increases in self-confidence, and the conviction that the historical treatises based on the new methods were objectively true. One of the greatest nineteenth-century historians, Leopold von Ranke, said he depicted historical events as they actually happened. The great French historian, Fustel de Coulanges, said that it was not he, the historian, who spoke in his work but history itself. The decisive advances in the establishment of historical facts created an opinion among historians that the facts were objective and that their histories stated absolute truth.

Twentieth-century historians have reacted sharply to this idea. As Carl Becker said in an article reprinted in Robin Winks' collection cited below, historical facts are not like so many bricks dumped out of a barrow and left to speak their eloquent message. The literary and intellectual medium in which the facts are presented shape and color them. History did not speak through Fustel de Coulanges' work; rather Fustel de Coulanges spoke through history. Historical writing is the product of a mind, and it expresses the needs, both intellectual and emotional, of that mind. The finished product results from the process of research and the focus of the intellect.

Students of history quickly learn that the discipline is divided into many fields and subfields, which makes it possible for the historian to contribute to knowledge of the past by focusing his attention and by choosing a manageable subject. There are two principles according to which the division into fields has been made: (1) the type of questions asked by historians and (2) the relevant time period.

All historical research begins with the posing of questions. As in all disciplines, knowledge of the past is increased by answering the questions raised by earlier contributions or by developing new perspectives; but the questions the historian poses direct his or her reading of the sources and more sharply focus the historian's attention. Furthermore, the questions can be grouped into political, economic, intellectual, social and other categories.

But in order to work in any one of these fields it is necessary that the historian have considerable knowledge of the others. Thus we come to the second division in historical writing, periodization. By breaking man's history into periods, historians have enabled themselves to obtain general knowledge about a period that is the foundation for original research. While this division according to periods can be defended, it is recognized by the great majority of historians to be a matter of convenience that—like the division according to questions posed—can be taken too far.

History is a field that demands extraordinarily large library resources, for the basic source material for the historian's work is the written record of the past. But the use of this material demands skills not normally considered part of the historian's intellectual arsenal. For example, paleography is essential for the historian who uses materials that must be dated and placed without the aid of the original author, or materials in which establishing the true text is difficult because of the script, copyists' errors, abbreviations, and the like. Special skills also are necessary when the historian must distinguish between authentic and forged documents.

Likewise, work in other disciplines aids historical writing. The geography of an area is often a factor of extreme importance in historical events, and the historian must know the geography of his subject, including the geographical changes that have taken place.

But the specifically historical sciences, like paleography and historical geography, do not circumscribe the interests and skills of historians; they borrow methods and insights from the social sciences and humanities in a process of interdisciplinary exchange that is advantageous to all. For when the historian uses the methodology and insight of the social sciences, he or she "returns the favor" by providing colleagues in those fields with significant test cases for their theories and ideas. Humanities such as literary criticism help assure the accuracy of meaning in historical records, and historical research provides the context for understanding literary sources. History is interdisciplinary; a comprehensive field of knowledge, it is concerned with all aspects of human past experience.

For the evolution of historical writing and the methods and epistemology of the discipline, see the following books.

B1   Barker, John. The superhistorians. New York: Scribner, 1982. 365p.

B2   Barraclough, Geoffrey. History in a changing world. Oxford: Basil Blackwell, 1955. 246p.

B3   Berlin, Isaiah. Historical inevitability. London: Oxford Univ. Pr., 1954. 78p.

B4   Bloch, Marc. The historian's craft. New York: Knopf, 1953. 197p.

B5   Bury, John B. The ancient Greek historians. New York: Macmillan, 1909. 281p.

B6   Butterfield, Herbert. Man on his past; the study of the history of historical scholarship. Cambridge: Cambridge Univ. Pr., 1955. 237p.

B7   Carr, Edward H. What is history? New York: St. Martin's, 1961. 154p.

B8   Collingwood, Robin G. The idea of history. New York: Oxford Univ. Pr., 1946. 339p.

B9   Fischer, David H. Historians' fallacies; toward a logic of historical thought. New York: Harper, 1970. 338p.

B10   Gooch, George P. History and historians in the nineteenth century. Boston: Beacon, 1959. 547p.

B11   Hegel, Georg W. The philosophy of history. New York: Dover, 1956. 457p.

B12   Hexter, Jack H. The history primer. New York: Basic Books, 1971. 297p.

B13   Higham, John, et al. History. Englewood Cliffs, N.J.: Prentice-Hall, 1965. 402p.

B14   Hofstadter, Richard. The progressive historians. New York: Knopf, 1970. 498p.

B15   Hughes, H. Stuart. History as art and science; twin vistas on the past. New York: Harper, 1964. 107p.

B16   Huizinga, Johan. Men and ideas: history, the Middle Ages, the Renaissance; essays. New York: Meridian, 1959. 378p.

B17   Kammen, Michael, ed. The past before us; contemporary historical writing in the United States. Ithaca, N.Y.: Cornell Univ. Pr., 1980. 524p.

B18   Kelley, Donald R. Foundations of modern historical scholarship: language, law, and history in the French Renaissance. New York: Columbia Univ. Pr., 1970. 321p.

B19   Krieger, Leonard. Ranke: the meaning of history. Chicago: Univ. of Chicago Pr., 1977. 402p.

B20   Laistner, Max L. W. The greater Roman historians. Berkeley: Univ. of California Pr., 1947. 196p.

B21   Marx, Karl. Capital: a critique of political economy. New York: Modern Library, 1936. 869p.

B22   Namier, Lewis B. Avenues of history. New York: Macmillan, 1952. 202p.

B23   Plumb, J. H. The death of the past. London: Macmillan, 1969. 153p.

B24   Popper, Karl. The poverty of historicism. Boston: Beacon, 1957. 166p.

B25   Stern, Fritz. The varieties of history, from Voltaire to the present. New York: Meridian, 1956. 427p.

B26   White, Hayden V. Metahistory: the historical imagination in nineteenth-century Europe. Baltimore: Johns Hopkins Univ. Pr., 1973. 448p.

B27   Wilcox, Donald J. The development of Florentine humanistic historiography in the fifteenth century. Cambridge, Mass.: Harvard Univ. Pr., 1969. 223p.

B28   Winks, Robin, ed. The historian as detective; essays on evidence. New York: Harper, 1969. 543p.

Stanley Chodorow
revised by Ted P. Sheldon

BASIC WORKS IN HISTORY

Because its subject encompasses the totality of humanity's past, the discipline of history is unique. All other fields of knowledge are subsumed within it, and all of its parts are necessarily interrelated. The structure of knowledge within the field, emphasizing the importance of both old and new scholarship, old and new methods, old and new interpretations, accommodates cross-fertilization between subfields and finds meaning for the multiplicity of human existence. The repository of historical knowledge lies in part in its accumulated monographic literature. The annotated bibliography which follows divides historical literature into traditional periods and areas, and presents the major interpretations representing various schools of thought.

Prehistory and the Ancient Near East

The work of anthropologists and archeologists sheds light on mankind before the invention of writing. The insights of anthropologists are presented in Marvin Harris, *The rise of anthropological theory: a history of theories of culture* (New York: Crowell, 1968) (**B29**), and William W. Howells, *Mankind in the making: the story of human evolution*, rev. ed. (Garden City, N.Y.: Doubleday, 1967) (**B30**). Insightful surveys of prehistory include J. Grahame Clark, *World prehistory: a new outline*, 2d ed. (London: Cambridge Univ. Pr., 1969) (**B31**), and Glyn Daniel, *The idea of pre-history* (New York: Penguin, 1971) (**B32**). Recent discoveries in East Africa are discussed in Richard E. Leakey and Roger Lewin, *Origins: what new discoveries reveal about the emergence of our species and its possible future* (New York: Dutton, 1977) (**B33**), while Grahame Clark's *Stone Age hunters* (New York: McGraw-Hill, 1967) (**B34**) discusses the Paleolithic Age and V. Gordon Childe's *What happened in history?*, rev. ed. (New York: Penguin, 1954) (**B35**) describes the Neolithic Age, including the concept of "urban revolution" in fourth-century Mesopotamia.

For an introduction to the civilizations of the ancient Near East, consult Henri Frankfort, *The birth of civilization in the Near East* (Bloomington: Indiana Univ. Pr., 1951) (**B36**). An exciting personal description of Sumerian excavation is provided in Sir Leonard Woolley, *Ur of the Chaldees: a record of seven years of excavation* (New York: Scribner, 1930) (**B37**), while H. W. F. Saggs, *The greatness that was Babylon* (New York: Praeger, 1969) (**B38**) presents a history of Babylon especially rich for social and economic life. Assyrian society and culture is an important part of A. Leo Oppenheim, *Ancient Mesopotamia: portrait of a dead civilization*, rev. ed. (Chicago: Univ. of Chicago Pr., 1977) (**B39**). Mason Hammond, *The city in the ancient world* (Cambridge, Mass.: Harvard Univ. Pr., 1972) (**B40**) provides an economic and social analysis of the role of early cities. Important books on the various ancient peoples include Sabatino Moscati's *The face of the ancient Orient* (Chicago: Quadrangle, 1960) (**B41**) introducing the peoples of Syria and Palestine, Donald B. Harden's *The Phoenicians* (New York: Penguin, 1980) (**B42**) treating their life, history and art, Giuseppe Riccioti's *The history of Israel*, 2v. (Milwaukee: Bruce, 1955) (**B43**) and Harry M. Orlinsky, *Ancient Israel* (Ithaca, N.Y.: Cornell Univ. Pr., 1954) (**B44**) treating the Israelites. James G. MacQueen, *The Hittites and their contemporaries in Asia Minor* (Boulder, Colo.: Westview, 1975) (**B45**) argues that economic need caused the movement of that people.

Good introductions to the history of ancient Egypt appear in Cyril Aldred, *The Egyptians* (New York: Praeger, 1961) (**B46**) and Alan Gardiner, *Egypt of the pharaohs* (Oxford: Clarendon, 1961) (**B47**). Mesopotamian and Egyptian scientific developments are evaluated in Otto Neugebauer, *The exact sciences in antiquity*, 2d ed. (New York: Dover, 1969) (**B48**).

Ancient Greece and Rome

Few textbooks deal adequately with both Greek and Roman history in the ancient period,

among the best being Chester G. Starr, *A history of the ancient world*, 3d ed. (New York: Oxford Univ. Pr., 1983) (**B49**). Among the better general histories of Greece is Humphrey D. F. Kitto, *The Greeks* (Baltimore: Penguin, 1951) (**B50**) which is delightfully informative, and Anthony Andrewes, *The Greeks* (New York: Knopf, 1967) (**B51**) which has a political focus. Victor Ehrenberg covers much of Greek history in *From Solon to Socrates*, 2d ed. (London: Methuen, 1973) (**B52**) and *The Greek state*, 2d ed. (London: Methuen, 1974) (**B53**). John M. Cook skillfully summarizes developments in *The Persian Empire* (New York: Schocken, 1983) (**B54**). Early Greece receives admirable treatment in Chester G. Starr, *The origins of Greek civilization, 1100–650 B.C.* (New York: Knopf, 1961) (**B55**), and in *The economic and social growth of early Greece, 800–500 B.C.* (New York: Oxford Univ. Pr., 1977) (**B56**) which seeks causes for economic development in the eastern Mediterranean. On the Golden Age of fifth century B.C. Athens, consult Andrew R. Burn, *Pericles and Athens* (London: English Univ. Pr., 1956) (**B57**) and Robert Flacelière, *Daily life in the Athens of Pericles* (New York: Macmillan, 1964) (**B58**). Russell Meiggs provides the best treatment available in *The Athenian Empire* (Oxford: Clarendon, 1972) (**B59**). The end of Athenian supremacy is ably described in Donald Kagan, *The Archidamian war* (Ithaca, N.Y.: Cornell Univ. Pr., 1974) (**B60**).

The two centuries following the defeat of Athens in 404 B.C. saw the rise of Hellenistic culture, ably described in William W. Tarn and G. T. Griffith, *Hellenistic civilization*, 3d ed. (London: Methuen, 1966) (**B61**), and in Michael Grant, *From Alexander to Cleopatra* (New York: Scribner, 1982) (**B62**). The foundation laid by Mikhail Rostovtseff, *The social and economic history of the hellenistic world* (Oxford: Clarendon, 1941) (**B63**) has been modified by many studies, among them Charles Bradford Welles, *Alexander and the hellenistic world* (Toronto: Hakkert, 1970) (**B64**), and Claude Mossé, *Athens in decline, 404–86 B.C.* (Boston: Routledge & Paul, 1973) (**B65**). Among biographies of Alexander the Great are Robin L. Fox's very readable *Alexander the Great* (London: Lane, 1973) (**B66**) and Joel R. Hamilton's *Alexander the Great* (Pittsburgh: Univ. of Pittsburgh Pr., 1973) (**B67**), the latter seeing Alexander as a ruthless, power-hungry despot.

Rome developed under the influence of the Etruscans to the north and the Greek colonies to the south. For a balanced introduction to Etruscan culture, see Massimo Pallottino, *The Etrus-*

cans, rev. ed. (Bloomington: Indiana Univ. Pr., 1975) **(B68)**. Raymond Bloch, *The origins of Rome*, rev. ed. (London: Thames & Hudson, 1960) **(B69)** discusses Greek influence as an element in the history of Rome to the founding of the Republic. Livy provided Romans with the story of their origins in *The early history of Rome* (Harmondsworth, Eng.: Penguin, 1973) **(B70)**. Ronald Syme's classic *Roman revolution* (Oxford: Oxford Univ. Pr., 1939) **(B71)** describes the politics of Republican Rome. The rise of the Roman Empire is discussed in Robert M. Errington, *The dawn of empire: Rome's rise to world power* (London: H. Hamilton, 1971) **(B72)**.

Life in imperial Rome is vividly portrayed in Thomas W. Africa, *Rome of the caesars* (New York: Wiley, 1965) **(B73)**. John P. V. D. Balsdon, *Rome: the story of an empire* (London: Weidenfield & Nicolson, 1970) **(B74)** discusses the achievements of the Roman Empire in an analysis of individual provinces.

Changes manifest in the later Roman Empire, as it melted into the Middle Ages in the West and the Byzantine Empire in the East, are interpreted in Peter Brown's *The world of late antiquity, A.D. 150–750* (New York: HBJ, 1971) **(B75)** and his *The making of late antiquity* (Cambridge, Mass.: Harvard Univ. Pr., 1978) **(B76)**. Arnold H. M. Jones presents the degenerative forces acting within the empire in *The decline of the ancient world* (New York: Holt, 1966) **(B77)**. Solomon Katz, *The decline of Rome and the rise of medieval Europe* (Ithaca, N.Y.: Cornell Univ. Pr., 1955) **(B78)** discusses the transition to the medieval period while avoiding the cataclysmic views of Edward Gibbon in *The decline and fall of the Roman Empire*, edited by Dero A. Saunders (New York: Viking, 1952) **(B79)**.

On Christianity in the late ancient period, Robert A. Markus, *Christianity in the Roman world* (New York: Scribner, 1974) **(B80)** discusses the rise of Christianity. Arnold H. M. Jones's *Constantine and the conversion of Europe* (London: English Univ. Pr., 1961) **(B81)** describes the conversion of the emperor and its implications. The pivotal role of St. Augustine emerges in Peter Brown, *Augustine of Hippo: a biography* (Berkeley: Univ. of California Pr., 1967) **(B82)**, and the leaders of the early Christian church gain stature in Edward K. Rand, *Founders of the Middle Ages* (Cambridge, Mass.: Harvard Univ. Pr., 1957) **(B83)**.

The Byzantine Empire

An altered empire lived on in the eastern Mediterranean after the Roman Empire dis-

appeared in the West, and continued to 1453. The politics and culture of this Byzantine Empire have held a special fascination for historians. Among valuable surveys are Steven Runciman, *Byzantine civilization* (New York: Longmans, Green, 1933) **(B84)** and Georgije Ostrogorsky, *History of the Byzantine state*, rev. ed. (New Brunswick, N.J.: Rutgers Univ. Pr., 1969) **(B85)** on politics, and Peter Arnott, *The Byzantines and their world* (New York: St. Martin's, 1973) **(B86)**. Glanville Downey, *Constantinople in the age of Justinian* (Norman: Univ. of Oklahoma Pr., 1960) **(B87)** focuses on the capital city of the Byzantine Empire, while John W. Barker, *Justinian and the later Roman Empire* (Madison: Univ. of Wisconsin Pr., 1966) **(B88)** discusses the contributions of its most well-known emperor, and Robert Browning, *Justinian and Theodora* (New York: Praeger, 1971) **(B89)** describes the sixth century in terms of its two most important figures. The end of the Byzantine Empire at the hands of the Turkish Ottoman emperors is described vividly in Steven Runciman, *The fall of Constantinople* (Cambridge: Cambridge Univ. Pr., 1965) **(B90)**. For a history of the Ottoman Empire by a distinguished Turkish historian, see Halil Inaluik, *The Ottoman Empire: the classical age, 1300–1600* (New York: Praeger, 1973) **(B91)**.

Medieval Europe

The Germanic successor kingdoms, culminating in the Carolingian Empire, and the Christian church dominated the early Middle Ages. Among many excellent introductions are John M. Wallace-Hadrill, *The barbarian west, 400–1000* (London: Hutchinson, 1952) **(B92)** on political evolution, Robert S. Lopez, *The birth of Europe* (New York: Evans, 1967) **(B93)** which presents clear and insightful discussions of feudalism and manorialism, and George Duby, *The early growth of the European economy* (Ithaca, N.Y.: Cornell Univ. Pr., 1974) **(B94)**.

The economic history of the medieval period has received much attention recently. Especially valuable are Norman J. G. Pounds, *An economic history of medieval Europe* (New York: Longman, 1974) **(B95)** which also discusses societal relationships, Michael M. Postan, *The Cambridge economic history of Europe*, v.1, *The agrarian life of the Middle Ages* (Cambridge: Cambridge Univ. Pr., 1966) **(B96)**, Postan's *Medieval trade and finance* (Cambridge: Cambridge Univ. Pr., 1973) **(B97)** and Robert H. Bautier, *The economic development of medieval*

Europe (New York: HBJ, 1971) **(B98)** which emphasizes developments in France.

Politics in early medieval Europe focused first on the Carolingian Empire and the dominant figure of Charlemagne who styled himself the reviver of Roman unity. Arthur J. Grant, *Early lives of Charlemagne* (New York: Cooper Square, 1966) **(B99)** includes Einhard's *Life of Charlemagne*. Heinrich Fichtenau, *The Carolingian Empire* (Oxford: Basil Blackwell, 1957) **(B100)** introduces the period. Friederich Heer's well-illustrated *Charlemagne and his world* (New York: Macmillan, 1975) **(B101)** discusses society and culture in the ninth century and Charlemagne's achievements.

The rapid expansion of Arab power and culture in the seventh century and its subsequent influence played a formative role in Western Europe. Henri Pirenne discusses that role in *Mohammed and Charlemagne* (New York: Barnes & Noble, 1957) **(B102)**. Among the results was the rise of feudalism. Marc Bloch's *Feudal society* (Chicago: Univ. of Chicago Pr., 1961) **(B103)** and Carl Stephenson, *Feudalism* (Ithaca, N.Y.: Cornell Univ. Pr., 1942) **(B104)**, present the traditional understandings. For recent interpretations, consult David Herlihy, ed., *The history of feudalism* (New York: Harper, 1970) **(B105)**.

The three centuries from 1000 to 1300 witnessed an economic revival which served as the context for the rule of the feudal monarchies and the papacy, as well as the maturing of medieval culture.

Among older works dealing with the economic revival are two works of Henri Pirenne, *Medieval cities: their origins and the revival of trade* (Princeton, N.J.: Princeton Univ. Pr., 1925) **(B106)**, and *Belgian democracy* (Manchester, Eng.: Manchester Univ. Pr., 1915) **(B107)**, both of which deal with the growth of Flemish towns. Among more recent works are the authoritative Michael M. Postan, *The medieval economy and society: an economic history of Britain, 1100–1500* (Berkeley: Univ. of California Pr., 1972) **(B108)**, Fritz Rörig, *The medieval town* (Berkeley: Univ. of California Pr., 1967) **(B109)** which focuses on Germany, Robert S. Lopez, *The commercial revolution of the Middle Ages, 950–1350*, (Englewood Cliffs, N.J.: Prentice-Hall, 1971) **(B110)**, and Robert S. Lopez and Irving W. Raymond, *Medieval trade in the Mediterranean world* (New York: Columbia Univ. Pr., 1955) **(B111)**.

Studies of the feudal monarchies are many. Among general surveys is Sidney Painter's, *The rise of the feudal monarchies* (Ithaca, N.Y.: Cornell Univ. Pr., 1951) **(B112)**. Geoffrey Barraclough, *Medieval Germany, 911–1250*, 2v. (New York: Barnes & Noble, 1938) **(B113)** surveys the Holy Roman Empire, while Charles H. Haskins' masterful *The Normans in European history* (Boston: Houghton, 1915) **(B114)** lays the groundwork for understanding the feudal monarchies in England and Sicily. David C. Douglas, *The Norman achievement, 1050–1100* (Berkeley: Univ. of California Pr., 1969) **(B115)** discusses the establishment of Norman rule in England by William the Conqueror. See also his *The Norman fate* (Berkeley: Univ. of California Pr., 1976) **(B116)**. Carrying on the story are Charles Petit Dutaillis, *The feudal monarchy in France and England: from the tenth century to the thirteenth century* (London: K. Paul, Trensh & Trubner, 1936) **(B117)**, Wilfred L. Warren, *Henry II* (Berkeley: Univ. of California Pr., 1973) **(B118)**, and Sidney Painter, *The reign of King John* (Baltimore: Johns Hopkins Univ. Pr., 1949) **(B119)**. On France, consult Robert Fawtier, *The Capetian kings of France* (New York: St. Martin's, 1960) **(B120)**. The power of the papacy is analyzed in Walter Ullmann, *Growth of papal government in the Middle Ages*, 2d ed. (London: Methuen, 1962) **(B121)** and Geoffrey Barraclough's *The medieval papacy* (New York: HBJ, 1968) **(B122)**. The opposition to papal power within the Church is discussed in Brian Tierney, *The foundations of the conciliar theory* (Cambridge: Cambridge Univ. Pr., 1955) **(B123)**. On monasticism, Christopher N. Brooke, *The monastic world* (New York: Random, 1974) **(B124)** presents a recent synthesis with illustrations. The most reliable summary of the place of the Christian church in the Middle Ages appears in R. W. Southern, *Western society and the church in the Middle Ages* (Harmondsworth, Eng.: Penguin, 1970) **(B125)**.

The Crusades, which focused on the capture of Jerusalem from the "infidels," are treated in Steven Runciman's classic three-volume *A history of the Crusades* (Cambridge: Cambridge Univ. Pr., 1951–54) **(B126)**, which makes delightful reading. See also Joshua Prawer's short but well-illustrated *The world of the Crusaders* (New York: Quadrangle, 1972) **(B127)**.

The cultural flowering of the High Middle Ages is treated well in Charles H. Haskins, *The Renaissance of the twelfth century* (Cambridge, Mass.: Harvard Univ. Pr., 1927) **(B128)**, which redirected historians' views, and Christopher Brooke, *The twelfth century Renaissance* (Cambridge, Mass.: Harvard Univ. Pr., 1969) **(B129)** which synthesizes recent scholarship. On universities, Haskins' *The rise of the universities* (New

York: Holt, 1923) **(B130)** provides a short introduction which may be supplemented by Gordon Leff, *Paris and Oxford universities in the thirteenth and fourteenth centuries: an institutional and intellectual history* (New York: Wiley, 1968) **(B131)**. Medieval philosophy is well summarized in David Knowles, *The evolution of medieval thought* (New York: Vintage, 1962) **(B132)**. For discussions of technology in the Middle Ages, see the watershed study of Lynn White, *Medieval technology and social change* (Oxford: Clarendon, 1962) **(B133)**, Edward Grant, *Physical science in the Middle Ages* (New York: Wiley, 1971) **(B134)**, and Jean Gimpel, *The medieval machine: the industrial revolution of the Middle Ages* (New York: Holt, 1976) **(B135)**.

The Fourteenth and Fifteenth Centuries

The fourteenth and fifteenth centuries often receive attention as the period when the "modern era" began. Such a view matches that of the period's intellectual elite, the humanists. Certainly it was a time of numerous cross-currents; economic decline accompanied the evolution of the national monarchies save in Germany and Italy, while humanist writers, artists and thinkers explored new ground, and the decadence of the papacy set the stage for the reform movements of the next century.

Among valuable general surveys of the fourteenth and fifteenth centuries are Denys Hay, *Europe in the fourteenth and fifteenth centuries* (New York: Holt, 1966) **(B136)**, John R. Hale, *Renaissance Europe, 1480–1520* (New York: Random, 1971) **(B137)**, and Wallace K. Ferguson, *Europe in transition, 1300–1520* (Boston: Houghton, 1962) **(B138)**. Among surveys of economic developments, B. H. Slicher van Bath, *The agrarian history of Western Europe, A.D. 500–1850* (London: Edward Arnold, 1963) **(B139)** synthesizes European scholarship documenting the agrarian crisis of the late Middle Ages, while Harry A. Miskimin, *The economy of the early Renaissance, 1300–1460* (Cambridge: Cambridge Univ. Pr., 1975) **(B140)** concentrates on urban economic change. Raymond de Roover, *The rise and decline of the Medici bank* (Cambridge, Mass.: Harvard Univ. Pr., 1963) **(B141)** discusses the great Florentine banking house in the context of economic trade and civil politics. The Black Death exerted a pivotal influence on all aspects of European life from its outbreak in 1347. A fine survey of its impact is

Philip Zeigler, *The Black Death* (New York: Day, 1969) **(B142)**.

The rise of the "new" monarchies occurred in the context of the Hundred Years' War which is well surveyed by Edouard Perroy in *The Hundred Years War* (New York: Oxford Univ. Pr., 1951) **(B143)**. Changes in the French and English monarchies are summarized by Joseph R. Strayer in *On the medieval origins of the modern state* (Princeton, N.J.: Princeton Univ. Pr., 1970) **(B144)**. For treatments of individual countries, consult Peter S. Lewis, ed., *The recovery of France in the fifteenth century* (New York: Harper, 1972) **(B145)**, Richard Vaughan, *Valois Burgundy* (Hamden, Conn.: Archon, 1975) **(B146)**, John H. Elliott, *Imperial Spain, 1469–1716* (Harmondsworth, Eng.: Penguin, 1963) **(B147)**, and on England, May McKisack, *The fourteenth century* (Oxford: Clarendon, 1959) **(B148)** and Ernest F. Jacobs, *The fifteenth century* (Oxford: Clarendon, 1961) **(B149)**, volumes 6 and 7 respectively of the *Oxford history of England*. For other areas, Philippe Dollinger, *The German Hansa* (Stanford, Calif.: Stanford Univ. Pr., 1970) **(B150)** discusses the German trading towns, while David Herlihy, *Medieval and Renaissance Pistoia: the social history of an Italian town* (New Haven, Conn.: Yale Univ. Pr., 1967) **(B151)**, John K. Hyde, *Padua in the age of Dante* (New York: Barnes & Noble, 1966) **(B152)** and Gene Brucker, *Renaissance Florence* (New York: Wiley, 1969) **(B153)** study Italian towns. Excellent summaries of the growth of Italian towns is provided by Daniel Waley, *The Italian city-republic* (New York: McGraw-Hill, 1969) **(B154)** and Lauro Martines, *Power and imagination: city-states in Renaissance Italy* (New York: Knopf, 1979) **(B155)**.

Renaissance humanism as a concept in historical thought is surveyed in Wallace K. Ferguson, *The Renaissance in historical thought* (Boston: Houghton, 1948) **(B156)**. The use of the works of classical authors by humanists receives attention in Paul Oskar Kristeller, *The classics and Renaissance thought* (Cambridge, Mass.: Harvard Univ. Pr., 1955) **(B157)**, and R. R. Bolgar, *The classical heritage and its beneficiaries* (Cambridge: Cambridge Univ. Pr., 1954) **(B158)**, while Eugenio Garin, *Italian humanism: philosophy and civic life in the Renaissance* (New York: Harper, 1965) **(B159)** and Denys Hay, *The Italian Renaissance in its historical background* (Cambridge: Cambridge Univ. Pr., 1961) **(B160)** provide excellent overviews. For an insightful biography of the most well-known humanist, consult Johan Huizinga, *Erasmus of Rotterdam* (London: Phaidon, 1952) **(B161)**.

The history of the church in the later Middle Ages and early Renaissance period involved the competing claims of popes and church councils. Ludwig von Pastor, *History of the popes*, 2d ed. (St. Louis: Herder, 1902) **(B162)** is still a valuable survey in spite of the author's viewpoint. Guillaume Mollat, *The popes of Avignon, 1305–1378* (New York: Nelson, 1963) **(B163)** concentrates on the papacy away from Rome as does Walter Ullmann, *The origins of the great schism* (London: Burns, Oates & Washbourne, 1948) **(B164)**.

The Reformation Century

The Reformation movement shattered the political and social, as well as religious life of Europeans. Among general works are Lewis Spitz, *The Reformation movement* (Chicago: Rand McNally, 1971) **(B165)**, and Arthur G. Dickens, *Reformation and society in sixteenth century Europe* (New York: Harcourt, Brace & World, 1966) **(B166)** which is well illustrated. Hans Hillerbrand offers a finely crafted selection of source readings summarizing Reformation ideas in *The Reformation in its own words* (New York: Harper, 1964) **(B167)**.

Books on Martin Luther abound, and among the better analyses of his life and contributions are the classic by Roland H. Bainton, *Here I stand: a life of Martin Luther* (New York: Abingdon-Cokesbury, 1950) **(B168)**, Gordon Rupp, *Luther's progress to the Diet of Worms* (New York: Harper, 1964) **(B169)**, and Harry G. Haile, *Luther: an experiment in biography* (Garden City, N.Y.: Doubleday, 1980) **(B170)**.

Following Luther's lead others proclaimed independence from the Roman church, among the most prominent John Calvin and Ulrich Zwingli. François Wendel, *Calvin: the origins and development of his religious thought* (New York: Harper, 1963) **(B171)**, discusses the man, while Calvinism as a movement received systematic treatment in John T. McNeil, *The history and character of Calvinism* (New York: Oxford Univ. Pr., 1954) **(B172)**. Two classics evaluate the relationship between religion and capitalism—Max Weber, *The Protestant ethic and the spirit of capitalism*, 2d ed. (London: Allen & Unwin, 1976) **(B173)** and Richard H. Tawney, *Religion and the rise of capitalism* (New York: Harcourt, Brace, 1926) **(B174)**. Zwingli's views and contribution receive attention in George R. Potter, *Zwingli* (New York: Cambridge Univ. Pr., 1976) **(B175)**. Claus-Peter Clasen, *Anabaptism: a social history, 1525–1618* (Ithaca, N.Y.: Cornell Univ. Pr., 1972) **(B176)** presents one of the most prominent "radical reform" movements.

The struggle for religious control in England dominated the sixteenth century. Arthur G. Dickens, *The English Reformation* (New York: Schocken, 1964) **(B177)**, discusses religious forces and issues while J. J. Scarisbrick, *Henry VIII* (Berkeley: Univ. of California Pr., 1968) **(B178)**, Garrett Mattingly, *Catherine of Aragon* (Boston: Little, 1941) **(B179)**, and Geoffrey R. Elton, *Reform and Reformation, 1509–1558* (Cambridge, Mass.: Harvard Univ. Pr., 1977) **(B180)** discuss political developments.

The reaction to Protestant criticism known as the Catholic Reformation is surveyed by Marvin R. O'Connell, *The counter Reformation, 1560–1610* (New York: Harper, 1974) **(B181)**. For a biography of the founder of the Jesuit order which played such a prominent role in the resurgence of Catholicism, see Paul Dudon, *St. Ignatius of Loyola* (Milwaukee: Bruce, 1949) **(B182)**. On the Council of Trent, where reform efforts focused, consult Hubert Jedin, *A history of the Council of Trent*, 2v. (St. Louis: Herder, 1957–61) **(B183)**.

The fracturing of the Roman church occurred as Europeans discovered overseas land, and struggled with internal political change within countries and for hegemony among countries. On overseas exploration and expansion, John H. Parry, *The age of reconnaissance* (Cleveland: World, 1963) **(B184)** examines the causes and consequences of the voyages of discovery. Carlo M. Cipolla, *Guns, sails and empires: technological innovation and the early phases of European expansion, 1400–1700* (New York: Pantheon, 1966) **(B185)** adds another perspective. Charles R. Boxer, *The Portuguese seaborne empire, 1415–1825* (New York: Knopf, 1969) **(B186)** discusses Portuguese society as well as the explorations of Portuguese sailors. Spanish overseas exploration and colonization are treated in John H. Parry, *The Spanish seaborne empire* (New York: Knopf, 1966) **(B187)** which provides a valuable discussion of Spanish trade with the Americas. Spanish politics, society and culture are related to overseas expansion in John H. Elliott, *Imperial Spain, 1496–1716* (described at B147). The effects of overseas discovery on Europeans are ably evaluated in Fredi Chiappelli, *First images of America: the impact of the New World on the old* (Berkeley: Univ. of California Pr., 1976) **(B189),** and in Earl Hamilton, *American treasure and the price revolution in Spain, 1501–1650* (Cambridge, Mass.: Harvard Univ. Pr., 1934) **(B190)**. For an innovative and influential study of Mediterranean life in the sixteenth century, sample Fernand Braudel, *The Mediterranean and the Mediterranean world in the age of Philip II*, 2v.

(New York: Harper, 1972–73) (**B191**). A superb example of excellence in historical research as well as writing is found in Garrett Mattingly, *The Armada* (Boston: Houghton, 1959) (**B192**).

Discussion of the religious wars in France in the sixteenth century appears in John H. M. Salmon, *Society in crisis: France in the sixteenth century* (New York: St. Martin's, 1975) (**B193**). Nancy Roelker's, *Queen of Navarre, Jeanne d'Albret* (Cambridge, Mass.: Harvard Univ. Pr., 1968) (**B194**) is a superb biography dealing with sectarian conflict. The standard work on the Netherlands remains Pieter Geyl, *The revolt of the Netherlands, 1555–1609* (New York: Barnes & Noble, 1958) (**B195**).

The England of the late sixteenth century changed drastically under Elizabeth I, and John E. Neale has chronicled and analyzed those changes in Queen Elizabeth (New York: Harcourt, 1934) (**B196**) and *Elizabeth I and her parliaments, 1559–1581* (London: Cape, 1953) (**B197**), Alfred L. Rowse's trilogy, *The England of Elizabeth* (New York: Macmillan, 1950) (**B198**), *The expansion of Elizabethan England* (New York: St. Martin's, 1955) (**B199**) and *The Elizabethan Renaissance: the life of the society*, 2v. (New York: Scribner, 1971–72) (**B200**) describes the structure of English society and government, overseas expansion and artistic and intellectual achievements.

Severely divided, particularistic Germany is well surveyed by Hajo Holborn, *A history of modern Germany: the Reformation* (New York: Knopf, 1967) (**B201**). Karl Brandi, *The Emperor Charles V* (London: Cape, 1939) (**B202**) discusses the man who became King of Spain and Holy Roman Emperor simultaneously.

Several surveys of the sixteenth century digest the wealth of material dealing with the century's diversity and conflict. They are Helmut G. Koenigsberger and George L. Mosse, *Europe in the sixteenth century* (New York: Holt, 1968) (**B203**), Geoffrey R. Elton, *Reformation Europe, 1517–1559* (New York: Harper, 1963) (**B204**), and John H. Elliott, *Europe divided, 1559–1598* (New York: Harper, 1968) (**B205**).

The Seventeenth Century

The seventeenth century witnessed continuing religious wars, the emergence of France as a dominant power, and the institution of the modern state, as absolute monarchy in France and constitutional monarchy in England. Spain declined, Central Europe experienced the Thirty Years War, Sweden and Holland enjoyed short

ascendancies and Russia began to emerge from Muscovy.

Among general surveys of the seventeenth century, Carl J. Friedrich, *The age of the baroque, 1610–1660* (New York: Harper, 1958) (**B206**) and Frederick L. Nussbaum, *The triumph of science and reason, 1660–1685* (New York: Harper, 1953) (**B207**) have not been entirely superseded by the more recent Donald H. Pennington, *Seventeenth century Europe* (New York: Holt, 1970) (**B208**), or Henry A. Kamen, *The iron century: social change in Europe, 1550–1660* (New York: Praeger, 1971) (**B209**). Theodore K. Rabb, *The struggle for political stability in early modern Europe* (New York: Oxford Univ. Pr., 1975) (**B210**) surveys political stresses.

The emergence of absolute monarchy in France is treated by Victor L. Tapié, *France in the age of Louis XIII and Richelieu* (New York: Macmillan, 1974) (**B211**), A. D. Liublinskaia, *French absolutism: The crucial phases, 1620–1629* (London: Cambridge Univ. Pr., 1968) (**B212**), and Aldous Huxley, *Grey eminence* (New York: Harper, 1941) (**B213**). The perfection of absolute monarchy came with Louis XIV. John B. Wolf, *Louis XIV* (New York: Norton, 1968) (**B214**) provides the best biography. Pierre Goubert, *Louis XIV and twenty million Frenchmen* (New York: Pantheon, 1970) (**B215**) discusses the king's policies in an economic and social context. The social life of seventeenth-century France is portrayed in a lively manner in Warren H. Lewis, *The splendid century* (London: Eyre & Spottiswoode, 1953) (**B216**), and peasant life is brilliantly analyzed in Emmanuel La Roi Ladurie, *The peasants of Languedoc* (Urbana: Univ. of Illinois Pr., 1974) (**B217**).

England in the time of the Stuarts and the "glorious revolution" is surveyed in J. E. Christopher Hill, *The century of revolution, 1603–1714*, new ed. (London: Sphere, 1974) (**B218**), Perez Zagorin, *The court and the country* (New York: Atheneum, 1970) (**B219**), and Ivan A. Roots, *The great rebellion, 1642–1660* (London: Batsford, 1966) (**B220**). On the revolution consult Lawrence Stone, *The causes of the English revolution, 1529–1642* (New York: Harper, 1972) (**B221**) and Cicely V. Wedgwood, *Oliver Cromwell*, rev. ed. (London: Duckworth, 1973) (**B222**), an excellent biography.

The best short discussions of the Netherlands are found in Charles Wilson, *The Dutch republic and the civilization of the seventeenth century* (New York: McGraw-Hill, 1968) (**B223**) and Charles R. Boxer, *The Dutch seaborne empire, 1600–1800* (London: Hutchinson, 1965) (**B224**) which also deals with homeland conditions.

Cicely V. Wedgewood's *The Thirty Years War* (London: Cape, 1939) (**B225**) discusses the series of wars which ravaged central Europe, while Michael Roberts, *Gustavus Adolphus and the rise of Sweden* (London: English Univ. Pr., 1973) (**B226**) discusses the Swedish role in the wars.

The emergence of Russia as a unified, independent political force is summarized admirably in Nicholas V. Riasanovsky, *A history of Russia*, 4th ed. (New York: Oxford Univ. Pr., 1984) (**B227**). The repulsing of the Tartars is described in John L. Fennell, *The emergence of Moscow, 1304–1359* (Berkeley: Univ. of California Pr., 1968) (**B228**) and in his *Ivan the Great of Moscow* (New York: St. Martin's, 1962) (**B229**). The role of Peter the Great is depicted in Benedict H. Sumner, *Peter the Great and the emergence of Russia* (New York: Macmillan, 1951) (**B230**) and more recently in Alex de Jonge, *Fire and water: a life of Peter the Great* (New York: Coward, 1980) (**B231**).

The Eighteenth Century

The primary characteristic of the eighteenth century proved to be French dominance in political influence and cultural authority. Though the Revolution of 1789 shattered that ascendancy, it furnishes the key to understanding eighteenth-century life. France occupied the central position in war and diplomacy, both within Europe and overseas, and in the culture of the Enlightenment. Elsewhere, the rise of Brandenburg-Russia and the continued growth of Russia foretold the shape of the nineteenth century.

Insightful general surveys of the eighteenth century include Matthew S. Anderson, *Europe in the eighteenth century, 1713–1783*, 2d ed. (New York: Longman, 1976) (**B232**), and the four relevant volumes in the *Rise of modern Europe* series: John B. Wolf, *The emergence of the great powers, 1685–1715* (New York: Harper, 1951) (**B233**), Penfield Roberts, *The quest for security, 1715–1740* (New York: Harper, 1947) (**B234**), Walter L. Dorn, *Competition for empire, 1740–1763* (New York: Harper, 1940) (**B235**), and Leo Gershoy, *From despotism to revolution, 1763–1789* (New York: Harper, 1944) (**B236**). The nature of society is examined in Robert Forster and Elborg Forster, *European society in the eighteenth century* (New York: Walker, 1969) (**B237**), while Albert Goodwin, ed., *The European nobility in the eighteenth century*, 2d ed. (London: Black, 1967) (**B238**) focuses on one social group, albeit a stratified one. E. Neville Williams, *The ancien régime in Europe: government and society in the major states, 1648–1789* (New York: Harper, 1970) (**B239**) discusses methods of political control, including those of the "enlightened despots." On individual rulers see George P. Gooch, *Frederick the Great: the ruler, the writer, the man* (New York: Longman, Green, 1947) (**B240**), Gladys S. Thomson, *Catherine the Great and the expansion of Russia* (London: Hodder & Stoughton, 1947) (**B241**) and Saul K. Padover, *The revolutionary emperor, Joseph II of Austria*, rev. ed. (Hamden, Conn.: Archon, 1967) (**B242**), all older works which retain their importance.

The thinkers of the Enlightenment, many of them French, including Voltaire, Diderot, Rousseau and Montesquieu, affirmed the ability of mankind to apply reason to understand the world, the universe and man's role. Those who stress reason often are not as reasonable as they think themselves to be. This theme is discussed in Carl L. Becker, *The heavenly city of the eighteenth century philosophers* (New Haven, Conn.: Yale Univ. Pr., 1932) (**B243**). Kingsley Martin, *French liberal thought in the eighteenth century*, 3d ed. (New York: Harper, 1963) (**B244**) provides a survey of Enlightenment thought which treats the *philosophes* in a generally favorable light. Peter Gay has provided two recent works analyzing the thought of Enlightenment figures. His *Party of humanity: essays in the French enlightenment* (New York: Knopf, 1964) (**B245**) and *The enlightenment: an interpretation*, 2v. (New York: Knopf, 1966–69) (**B246**) serve as reinterpretations of the Enlightenment and its major participants.

Studies of individual *philosophes* are numerous. On Quesnay and the physiocrats consult Elizabeth Fox-Genovese, *The origins of physiocracy: economic revolution and social order in eighteenth century France* (Ithaca, N.Y.: Cornell Univ. Pr., 1976) (**B247**). Peter Gay, *Voltaire's politics: the poet as realist* (Princeton, N.J.: Princeton Univ. Pr., 1959) (**B248**) provides an interesting, insightful and sympathetic biography of the leading thinker of the Enlightenment. A detailed biography of Diderot appears in Arthur M. Wilson, *Diderot* (New York: Oxford Univ. Pr., 1972) (**B249**), while Robert Shackleton, *Montesquieu: a critical biography* (London: Oxford Univ. Pr., 1961) (**B250**) presents the life and thought of the author of *The spirit of the laws*.

The Industrial Revolution

As important as any political or social force active in eighteenth-century Europe, the Industrial Revolution, now often referred to as the "first" such revolution, worked to transform every aspect of life. From its origins in England, the industrialization of society spread to the United States and continental Europe.

Among the better surveys of early industrial development in Great Britain are Phyllis Deane, *The first Industrial Revolution* (Cambridge: Cambridge Univ. Pr., 1965) **(B251)**, Paul Mantoux, *The Industrial Revolution in the eighteenth century*, new and rev. ed. (New York: Macmillan, 1961) **(B252)** and the shorter Thomas S. Ashton, *The Industrial Revolution, 1760–1830* (New York: Oxford Univ. Pr., 1968) **(B253)**. These works may be complemented by the leftist approach of Eric J. Hobsbawm in *Industry and empire: an economic history of Britain since 1750* (New York: Pantheon, 1968) **(B254)**. Phyllis Deane and William A. Cole, *British economic growth, 1688–1959: trends and structures*, 2d ed. (London: Cambridge Univ. Pr., 1967) **(B255)** utilizes the analytical techniques of research in economics to depict trends and developments. A provocative interpretation of the conditions present in the early stages of economic growth appears in Walt W. Rostow, *The stages of economic growth: a non-Communist manifesto* (Cambridge: Cambridge Univ. Pr., 1960) **(B256)**.

Perhaps the major recent interpretation of industrial growth in a Western European context is David S. Landes, *The unbound Prometheus: technological change and industrial development in western Europe from 1750 to the present* (London: Cambridge Univ. Pr., 1969) **(B257)**. The spread of industrial techniques and methods on the continent, particularly the influence of British capital and inventions, is well covered in William O. Henderson, *Britain and industrial Europe, 1750–1870*, 3d ed. (Leicester, Eng.: Leicester Univ. Pr., 1972) **(B258)**. Henderson focuses more specifically on Germany, France and Russia in *The Industrial Revolution on the Continent: Germany, France, Russia, 1800–1914*, 2d ed. (London: Cass, 1967) **(B259)**. John H. Clapham, *The economic development of France and Germany, 1815–1914*, 4th ed. (Cambridge: Cambridge Univ. Pr., 1936) **(B260)** is witty, sophisticated and readable. On Germany, William O. Henderson discusses the role of the well-known German customs union in *The Zollverein*, 2d ed. (London: Cass, 1968) **(B261)**, and Theodore S. Hamerow, *Restoration, revolution, reaction: economics and politics in Germany, 1815–1871* (Princeton, N.J.: Princeton Univ. Pr., 1958) **(B262)** evaluates economic growth in terms of politics.

The social and political implications of early industrialization have been studied from several directions. Jürgen Kuczynski, *The rise of the working class* (New York: McGraw-Hill, 1967) **(B263)** is a leftist analysis of the nature of the working class in different countries. For an analysis of the structure and makeup of the laboring class in England, see Edward P. Thompson, *The making of the English working class* (New York: Pantheon, 1963) **(B264)**. Also, Asa Briggs, *Victorian cities*, new ed. (Harmondsworth, Eng: Penguin, 1968) **(B265)** studies the industrial centers of Britain and their impact on English life. For France, see Louis Chevalier, *Laboring classes and dangerous classes in Paris during the first half of the nineteenth century* (New York: Fertig, 1973) **(B266)**.

By-products of the Industrial Revolution included both liberal and socialist thought. The major liberal thinkers are introduced by Robert L. Heilbroner, *The worldly philosopher*, 5th ed. (New York: Simon & Schuster, 1980) **(B267)**, a popular work, and in the classic study by Guido de Ruggiero, *The history of European liberalism* (New York: Oxford Univ. Pr., 1927) **(B268)**. A fine recent and controversial analysis of John Stuart Mill is found in Gertrude Himmelfarb, *On liberty and liberalism: the case of John Stuart Mill* (New York: Knopf, 1974) **(B269)**.

Among many discussions of socialism, George Lichtheim, *A short history of socialism* (New York: Praeger, 1970) **(B270)** presents the evolution of socialist thought in its historical context. George D. H. Cole analyzes the various socialist movements and schools of thought in *A history of socialist thought*, 5v. (New York: St. Martin's, 1953–60) **(B271)**. Edmund Wilson, *To the Finland Station: a study in the writing and acting of history* (New York: Harcourt, 1940) **(B272)** presents a history of socialism drawing on personal experience and concentrating on Karl Marx and Friedrich Engels. Franz Mehring, *Karl Marx: the story of his life* (Ann Arbor: Univ. of Michigan Pr., 1962) **(B273)** provides an insightful biography of this pivotal figure, while Steven Marcus, *Engels, Manchester and the working class* (New York: Random, 1974) **(B274)** provides valuable insight into Engels' ideas. For a discussion of French utopian thinkers and movements, consult Frank E. Manuel, *The prophets of Paris* (Cambridge, Mass.: Harvard Univ. Pr., 1962) **(B275)**. The role of women in early industrial society has received attention in Theresa M. McBride, *The domestic revolution: the modernization of household service in England and France, 1820–1920* (New York: Holmes & Meier, 1976) **(B276)**, and in Louise A. Tilly and Joan W. Scott, *Women, work, and family* (New York: Holt, 1978) **(B277)**.

where the change to a "family wage economy" is presented.

The Revolutionary Era and Napoleon

The problems of the later eighteenth century, especially in France, formed the foundation for revolution. Georges Lefebvre, *The coming of the French Revolution* (Princeton, N.J.: Princeton Univ. Pr., 1947) (**B278**) has become a classic synthesis, though it now requires some modification. Lefebvre's view that the French Revolution reflected stress in the major classes of French society is rejected in Alfred Cobban's concise survey, *The history of modern France, vol. 1: 1715–1799* (Harmondsworth, Eng.: Penguin, 1957) (**B279**).

Specialized studies have focused on particular aspects of eighteenth-century society to explain the outbreak of the revolution. On economic conditions, consult Tom Kemp, *Economic forces in French history, 1760–1914* (London: Dobson, 1971) (**B280**) which reports on the recent research in economic history. The condition of the poor is presented in Olwen Hufton's important *The poor in eighteenth century France* (Oxford: Clarendon, 1974) (**B281**).

Franklin L. Ford, *The robe and the sword: the regrouping of the French aristocracy after Louis XIV* (Cambridge, Mass.: Harvard Univ. Pr., 1953) (**B282**) examines the revival of the French aristocracy, while Elinor Barber, *The bourgeoisie in eighteenth-century France* (Princeton, N.J.: Princeton Univ. Pr., 1955) (**B283**) reveals the importance of social nobility as a cause of social stress. See also George Rudé's, *Paris and London in the eighteenth century: studies in popular protest* (London: Collins, 1970) (**B284**).

Several studies of the French Revolution hold center stage for their insightful analysis of its many complex cross-currents. Georges Lefebvre's *The French Revolution*, 2v. (New York: Columbia Univ. Pr., 1962–64) (**B285**) should be complemented with Albert Soboul, *The French Revolution, 1787–1799* (New York: Random, 1975) (**B286**) which presents the views of a noted Marxist historian. An interesting antidote is Alfred Cobban, *The social interpretation of the French Revolution* (Cambridge: Cambridge Univ. Pr., 1964) (**B287**). The roles of crowds and crowd psychology are examined in George Rudé, *The crowd in the French Revolution* (Oxford: Clarendon, 1959) (**B288**) while Soboul examines the aspirations and motivations of those composing "crowds" in *The Parisian sans-*

culottes and the French Revolution, 1793-94 (Oxford: Clarendon, 1972) (**B289**). Robert R. Palmer's *Twelve who ruled: the year of terror in the French Revolution* (Princeton, N.J.: Princeton Univ. Pr., 1970) (**B290**) analyzes the Jacobin leaders of the Reign of Terror. The Directory ruled France following the Reign of Terror until Napoleon seized the government. Lefebvre's *The Directory* (London: Routledge & Paul, 1965) (**B291**) should be supplemented by Martyn Lyons, *France under the Directory* (New York: Cambridge Univ. Pr., 1975) (**B292**).

Napoleon Bonaparte subverted the Directory, then sought to reestablish the Roman Empire through military conquest. Conflicting opinions have always surrounded him. For a quick survey of those opinions, see Pieter Geyl, *Napoleon: for and against* (New Haven, Conn.: Yale Univ. Pr., 1949) (**B293**). Among insightful biographies of Napoleon are James M. Thompson, *Napoleon Bonaparte: his rise and fall* (New York: Oxford Univ. Pr., 1952) (**B294**) and Felix Markham, *Napoleon and the awakening of Europe* (London: English Univ. Pr., 1954) (**B295**). Among works which view Napoleon as a key figure on a wider stage are Geoffrey Bruun, *Europe and the French imperium, 1799–1814* (New York: Harper, 1938) (**B296**), J. Christopher Herold's *Age of Napoleon* (New York: American Heritage, 1963) (**B297**), a fine example of popular history, and Jacques Godechot, *The Napoleonic era in Europe* (New York: Holt, 1971) (**B298**).

The reactions to Napoleon in Germany focused within the "Prussian reform" movement. Hans Rosenberg, *Bureaucracy, aristocracy and autocracy: the Prussian experience, 1660–1815* (Cambridge, Mass.: Harvard Univ. Pr., 1958) (**B299**) examines changes in a deep historical context, while George P. Gooch, *Germany and the French Revolution* (New York: Longman, Green, 1920) (**B300**) presents an older but still relevant view. The effect of Bonaparte on nascent Italian nationalism is studied in Emiliana P. Noether, *Seeds of Italian nationalism, 1789–1815* (New York: Columbia Univ. Pr., 1951) (**B301**). See also two works by Owen Connally, *Napoleon's satellite kingdom* (New York: Free Pr., 1966) (**B302**) and his *The gentle Bonaparte: a biography of Joseph, Napoleon's elder brother* (New York: Macmillan, 1968) (**B303**).

The Nineteenth Century

The removal of Napoleon from the European scene and the meeting of the Congress of Vienna set the stage for a century of change and of struggle between "reform and reaction." France, the birthplace of the "revolution of 1789" and Napoleon saw the conflict of old and new erupt into violence and strife in 1830, 1848 and 1871. In England, Gladstone, Disraeli, the Chartists and Victoria represent forces of change and continuity. Germany struggled with disunity, then under Bismarck achieved unification, as did Italy through the actions of Cavour, Garibaldi and Mazzini. The Hapsburg Empire, focused on Vienna, became gradually more anachronistic. Poland tried to exist between Germany and Russia, and failed, while Russia itself freed its serfs and fought change, setting the stage for the demise of the Romanovs and autocratic monarchy in the heat of World War I and revolution. Nationalism and industrialization proved vital forces in a century which by 1900 sought security, tranquility and an end to revolution and war. By the early twentieth century, that hope seemed assured.

The Congress of Vienna, which sought to reconstruct Europe after the "interlude" of Napoleon, is admirably studied by Harold Nicolson in *The Congress of Vienna, a study in allied unity, 1812–1822* (New York: Harcourt, Brace, 1946) (**B304**). Among the valuable biographies of Clemens von Metternich is Guillaume de Bertier de Sauvigny's *Metternich and the times* (London: Darton, Longman & Todd, 1962) (**B305**) which relies extensively on Metternich's own *Memoirs*. Henry A. Kissinger, *A world restored* (Boston: Houghton, 1957) (**B306**) provides a fast-paced look at the diplomacy of the Congress through 1829.

General works on nineteenth-century Europe have generally proved of limited value. Those offering well-reasoned approaches include Frederick B. Artz, *Reaction and revolution, 1815–1832* (New York: Harper, 1934) (**B307**), Robert C. Binkley, *Realism and nationalism, 1852–1871* (New York: Harper, 1935) (**B308**) and Carleton J. H. Hayes, *A generation of materialism, 1871–1900* (New York: Harper, 1941) (**B309**), all of which remain important despite their age. See also William L. Langer, *Political and social upheaval, 1832–1852* (New York: Harper, 1969) (**B310**) and Oron J. Hale, *The great illusion, 1900–1914* (New York: Harper, 1971) (**B311**). Works encompassing many decades which offer insights into the tenor of the century include the following. Eugene N. Anderson and Pauline R. Anderson, *Political institutions and social change in the nineteenth century* (Berkeley: Univ. of California Pr., 1967) (**B312**) present a comprehensive view of constitutional and legal change, while Raymond Grew, ed., *The crisis of political development in Europe and the United States* (Princeton, N.J.: Princeton Univ. Pr., 1978) (**B313**) evaluates political modernization. An interesting Marxist assessment appears in Eric J. Hobsbawm, *The age of revolution, 1789–1848* (Cleveland: World, 1962) (**B314**). Alan J. P. Taylor, *The struggle for mastery in Europe, 1848–1918* (Oxford: Clarendon, 1954) (**B315**) treats international relations in a highly controversial way, and David K. Fieldhouse, *Economics and empire, 1830–1914* (Ithaca, N.Y.: Cornell Univ. Pr., 1973) (**B316**) demonstrates that economic conditions may have been less influential than many believe.

The pivotal revolutions of 1848 are skillfully analyzed in Priscilla Robertson, *The revolutions of 1848* (Princeton, N.J.: Princeton Univ. Pr., 1952) (**B317**), and more recently in great detail by Jean Sigmann, *1848: The romantic and democratic revolutions in Europe* (New York: Harper, 1973) (**B318**). Peter N. Stearns, *The revolutions of 1848* (London: Weidenfield & Nicolson, 1974) (**B319**) is more readable as well as historically interesting. The Balkans took center stage in the events leading up to World War I. The historical context for those events, as well as other nineteenth-century themes, is recreated in L. S. Stavrianos, *The Balkans, 1815–1914* (New York: Holt, 1963) (**B320**) and by Carlile A. Macartney, *The Hapsburg Empire, 1790–1918* (New York: Macmillan, 1969) (**B321**). Karl Löwith, *From Hegel to Nietzsche: the revolution in nineteenth century thought* (New York: Holt, 1964) (**B322**) surveys the evolution in modern thought, and W. Warren Wagar, *Good tidings: the belief in progress from Darwin to Marcuse* (Bloomington: Indiana Univ. Pr., 1972) (**B323**) surveys the theme that dominated the end of the century. Also focusing on the end of the century is Edward R. Tannenbaum, *1900: the generation before the Great War* (Garden City, N.Y.: Anchor, 1976) (**B324**).

France

Several valuable general histories of France in the nineteenth century are available. Alfred Cobban's *A history of modern France, vol. 2, 1799–1871*, new ed., rev. and enl. (London: Cape, 1963) (**B325**) and *vol. 3, 1871–1961* (London: Cape, 1965) (**B326**) provide interesting interpretations in the context of readable narrative. John P. Plamenatz, *The revolutionary movement in France, 1815–1871* (New York: Longman, Green, 1952) (**B327**) concentrates on the republican and anti-monarchical trends and movements. On the French Second Republic, consult Roger Price, *The French Second Republic: a social history* (Ithaca, N.Y.: Cornell Univ.

Pr., 1972) **(B328)**. The work of Frederick A. Simpson remains the definitive detailed treatment of Napoleon III; consult his *The rise of Louis Napoleon*, 3d ed. (New York: Longman, Green, 1950) **(B329)**, and his *Louis Napoleon and the recovery of France, 1848–1856*, 3d rev. ed. (London: Longman, 1965) **(B330)**. George P. Gooch, *The second empire* (London: Longman, 1960) **(B331)** is quite readable. The revolution of 1871 and the creation of the French Third Republic are ably examined in Denis W. Brogan, *The development of modern France, 1870–1939*, new ed. (New York: Harper, 1966) **(B332)**, while Stewart Edwards, *The Paris commune, 1871* (London: Eyre & Spottiswoode, 1971) **(B333)** and John P. T. Bury, *Gambetta and the making of the Third Republic* (London: Longman, 1973) **(B334)** analyze the birth of the new republic. An important overview is provided by Theodore Zeldin, *France, 1848–1945*, 2v. (Oxford: Clarendon, 1973–77) **(B335)**, wherein a suggestive synthesis is presented. Guy Chapman, *The Third Republic of France; the first phase, 1871–1894* (New York: St. Martin's, 1963) **(B336)** is one of the better surveys in English.

Great Britain

The many facets of the Victorian age come together in good surveys by David Thomson, *England in the nineteenth century, 1815–1914* (Baltimore: Penguin, 1950) **(B337)**, and more recently Asa Briggs, *The making of modern England, 1783–1867: the age of improvement* (New York: Harper, 1965) **(B338)**, and Robert K. Webb, *Modern England: from the eighteenth century to the present*, 2d ed. (New York: Harper, 1980) **(B339)**. George Kitson Clark, *The making of Victorian England* (New York: Atheneum, 1966) **(B340)** weighs the various forces at work, especially religion. Asa Briggs' *Victorian people*, rev. ed. (Chicago: Univ. of Chicago Pr., 1970) **(B341)** describes prominent Victorians including Benjamin Disraeli, but Robert Blake, *Disraeli* (New York: St. Martin's, 1967) **(B342)** remains prominent among recent full-length biographies of this central figure. For a biography of Queen Victoria, consult Elizabeth Longford, *Queen Victoria: born to succeed* (New York: Harper, 1965) **(B343)**.

The social history of Victorian England has received much attention. Among the better analyses of urban life are Aldon D. Bell, *London in the age of Dickens* (Norman: Univ. of Oklahoma Pr., 1967) **(B344)**, Asa Briggs, *Victorian cities* (see description at B265), which concentrates on Manchester, and Francis M. L. Thompson, *Hampstead: building a borough,*

1650–1964 (Boston: Routledge & Paul, 1974) **(B346)**. Of particular interest are the works of Charles Dickens, which may be supplemented by the amply illustrated work of Angus Wilson, *The world of Charles Dickens* (New York: Viking, 1970) **(B347)**.

The classic study of working women in nineteenth-century England is Ivy Pinchbeck, *Women workers and the Industrial Revolution, 1750–1850* (London: Routledge, 1930) **(B348)**. Middle class women's roles emerge in studies by Lee Holcombe, *Victorian ladies at work: middle class working women in England and Wales, 1850–1914* (Hamden, Conn.: Archon Books, 1973) **(B349)**, and in Patricia Branca's essay in Mary S. Hartman and Lois Banner, eds., *Clio's consciousness raised: new perspectives on the history of women* (New York: Harper, 1974) **(B350)**.

George Dangerfield, *The strange death of liberal England* (New York: Smith & Haas, 1935) **(B351)** describes the crisis in nineteenth-century English society.

Germany

The growing strength of Prussia, which led the movement culminating in 1871 in unification, is surveyed creditably in Hajo Holborn, *A history of modern Germany, vol. 3, 1840–1945* (New York: Knopf, 1969) **(B352)**, Golo Mann, *The history of Germany since 1789* (New York: Praeger, 1968) **(B353)**, and Koppel S. Pinson, *Modern Germany*, 2d ed. (New York: Macmillan, 1966) **(B354)**. The importance of the Prussian army is established in Gordon A. Craig, *The politics of the Prussian army, 1640–1945* (New York: Oxford Univ. Pr., 1955) **(B355)**. German nationalism is analyzed in Hans Kohn, *The mind of Germany: the education of a nation* (New York: Scribner, 1960) **(B356)**, and Fritz Stern, *The politics of cultural despair: a study in the rise of the Germanic ideology* (Berkeley: Univ. of California Pr., 1961) **(B357)**. Broader in scope is George L. Mosse, *The nationalization of the masses: political symbolism and mass movements in Germany from the Napoleonic Wars through the Third Reich* (New York: Fertig, 1975) **(B358)**, which seeks the roots of Nazism in nineteenth- and early twentieth-century Germany. Theodore S. Hamerow, *The social foundations of German unification, 1858–1871*, 2v. (Princeton, N.J.: Princeton Univ. Pr., 1969–72) **(B359)** deals with social and economic change, while Otto Pflanze, *Bismarck and the development of Germany* (Princeton, N.J.: Princeton Univ. Pr., 1963) **(B360)** provides a widely accepted recent reinterpretation. Louis L. Snyder, *The blood* *and iron chancellor: a documentary-biography of Otto von Bismarck* (Princeton, N.J.: Van Nostrand, 1967) **(B361)**, the readable Werner Richter, *Bismarck* (New York: Putnam, 1965) **(B362)** and Erich Eyck, *Bismarck and the German nation* (London: Allen & Unwin, 1950) **(B363)** are among the better works on Bismarck.

Italy

As important for twentieth-century developments as German unity was Italian unification and national feeling. A somewhat skeptical but insightful survey of the unification process appears in Derek Beales, *The risorgimento and the unification of Italy* (New York: Barnes & Noble, 1971) **(B364)**. Jasper Ridley's *Garibaldi* (London: Constable, 1974) **(B365)**, in addition to filling the need for a strong biography, throws much light on the progress of unification. For the contribution of another major figure, consult Arthur J. Whyte, *The early life and letters of Cavour, 1810–1848* (London: Oxford Univ. Pr., 1925) **(B366)** and *The political life and letters of Cavour, 1848–1861* (London: Oxford Univ. Pr., 1930) **(B367)**, which remain the best English works though now somewhat dated.

Austria, the Balkans, Iberia, and Poland

The Hapsburg Empire, with its capital in Vienna, plodded through the nineteenth century toward its dissolution in World War I. Reuben J. Rath, *The Viennese revolution of 1848* (Austin: Univ. of Texas Pr., 1957) **(B368)** focuses on the events which broke down Metternich's policies. Arthur J. May, *The Hapsburg monarchy, 1867–1914* (Cambridge, Mass.: Harvard Univ. Pr., 1951) **(B369)** shows the influence of the classic work of Oszkár Jászi, *The dissolution of the Hapsburg Empire* (Chicago: Univ. of Chicago Pr., 1929) **(B370)**. The welter of divergent national feelings within the Hapsburg Empire provides the focus for Robert A. Kann, *The multinational empire: nationalism and national reform in the Hapsburg monarchy, 1848–1918*, 2v. (New York: Octagon, 1950) **(B371)**.

The Iberian peninsula has been less well studied in English, but several valuable works survey the two countries. For Spain, consult Raymond Carr, *Spain, 1808–1975*, 2d ed. (Oxford: Clarendon, 1982) **(B372)**, and Gerald Brenan, *The Spanish labyrinth: an account of the social and political background of the civil war* (Cambridge: Cambridge Univ. Pr., 1950) **(B373)**. Harold V. Livermore, *A new history of Portugal*, 2d ed. (Cambridge: Cambridge Univ. Pr., 1976) **(B374)** surveys that country's development.

For Poland, Oskar Halecki, *A history of Poland*, 9th ed. (New York: McKay, 1976) **(B375)** presents the several partitions of Poland during the nineteenth century as a part of Polish historical development. Robert H. Lord, *The second partition of Poland* (Cambridge, Mass.: Harvard Univ. Pr., 1915) **(B376)** emphasizes the factors threatening the Polish national state, both internal and external.

Russia

Several general surveys of wide repute provide an understanding of Russian development in the nineteenth century. James Billington, *The icon and the ax: an interpretive history of Russian culture* (New York: Knopf, 1966) **(B377)** discusses church and state in Russian culture while the relations of landlords, peasants and serfs are examined in Jerome Blum, *Lord and peasant in Russia from the ninth century to the nineteenth century* (Princeton, N.J.: Princeton Univ. Pr., 1961) **(B378)**.

The course of events and movements during the century hold particular interest as the antecedents of the 1917 revolution. Among older works Michael Karpovich, *Imperial Russia, 1801–1917* (New York: Holt, 1932) **(B379)** remains prominent, but should be followed by more recent interpretations, such as Hugh Seton-Watson, *The Russian Empire, 1801–1917* (Oxford: Clarendon, 1967) **(B380)** and Bernard Pares, *Russia: between reform and revolution* (New York: Schocken, 1962) **(B381)**. Barbara Jelavich, *A century of Russian foreign policy, 1814–1914* (Philadelphia: Lippincott, 1964) **(B382)** surveys foreign relationships. F. Venturi, *The roots of revolution: a history of the populist and socialist movements in nineteenth century Russia* (New York: Knopf, 1960) **(B383)** surveys anti-imperial movements with skill and insight.

As the century unfolded, reform failed repeatedly, and revolution became more possible. Special studies covering specific periods, events and people are many, among them several on individual rulers. On Alexander I consult Georges M. Paléologue, *The enigmatic tsar: the life of Alexander I of Russia* (New York: Harper, 1938) **(B384)**. Nicholas V. Riasanovsky, *Nicholas I and official nationality in Russia, 1825–1855* (Berkeley: Univ. of California Pr., 1959) **(B385)** discusses that ruler's repressive actions. The freeing of the serfs and Alexander II's other reforms receive attention in Werner Mosse, *Alexander II and the modernization of Russia* (New York: Macmillan, 1958) **(B386)**. Nicholas II's reign is vividly portrayed in Robert K. Massie, *Nicholas* *and Alexandra* (New York: Atheneum, 1967) (**B387**).

The road to 1917 begins with Antole Mazour, *The first Russian revolution, 1825: the Decembrist movement* (Berkeley: Univ. of California Pr., 1937) (**B388**). Subsequent events and personages are surveyed in Avrahm Yarmolinsky, *Road to revolution: a century of Russian radicalism* (London: Cassell, 1957) (**B389**). Adam B. Ulam, *The Bolsheviks* (New York: Macmillan, 1965) (**B390**) traces the history of the party of Lenin and Trotsky, while the anarchists are treated in Paul Avrich, *The Russian anarchists* (Princeton, N.J.: Princeton Univ. Pr., 1967) (**B391**).

World War I and Revolution in Russia

World War I shattered the illusion of security in early twentieth-century Europe. The classic explanation of World War I origins written between the two world wars is Sidney B. Fay, *The origins of the World War*, 2v. (New York: Macmillan, 1928) (**B392**). Another view is apparent in Laurence Lafore, *The long fuse: an interpretation of the origins of World War I* (Philadelphia: Lippincott, 1965) (**B393**), while Barbara Tuchman, *The guns of August* (New York: Macmillan, 1962) (**B394**) describes the outbreak of war with graphic realism. The goals of German expansionists are discussed in Fritz Fischer, *Germany's war aims in the First World War* (New York: Norton, 1967) (**B395**). A short history of the war concentrating on the incompetence of military leaders is Alan J. P. Taylor, *The First World War* (London: H. Hamilton, 1963) (**B396**). Erich Maria Remarque's moving novel, *All quiet on the western front* (Boston: Little, 1929) (**B397**) presents the author's own feelings while fighting in World War I. The domestic impact of the war is assessed in John Williams, *The home fronts: Britain, France, and Germany, 1914–1918* (London: Constable, 1972) (**B398**). The best discussion of the process which ended the war and created the Treaty of Versailles appears in Harold Nicolson, *Peacemaking, 1919* (Boston: Houghton, 1933) (**B399**). The problems with the treaty were immediately spelled out in John Maynard Keynes, *The economic consequences of the peace* (New York: Harcourt, Brace & Howe, 1920) (**B400**). For a recent Marxist interpretation consult Arno J. Mayer, *Politics and diplomacy of peacemaking* (New York: Knopf, 1967) (**B401**).

Strained by the demands of the World War, Russia fell into revolution in 1917 and emerged as the Union of Soviet Socialist Republics. An informative survey of the century is Donald W. Treadgold, *Twentieth century Russia*, 5th ed. (Boston: Houghton, 1981) (**B402**). The events of 1917 are interpreted in Robert V. Daniels, *Red October: the Bolshevik revolution of 1917* (New York: Scribner, 1967) (**B403**), and in Robert Conquest, *V. I. Lenin* (New York: Viking, 1972) (**B404**) where the failures of Bolshevik leaders are emphasized. Among the best accounts of the "October Days" is John Reed, *Ten days that shook the world* (New York: International Pub., 1919) (**B405**) written with intense conviction by an eyewitness. Several biographies help capture the events of the revolution and their meaning. Bertram E. Wolfe, *Three who made a revolution: a biographical history* (New York: Dial, 1948) (**B406**) covers the efforts of Lenin, Trotsky and Stalin. Isaac Deutscher has contributed a landmark three-volume biography of Leon Trotsky, *The prophet armed: Trotsky, 1879–1921* (New York: Oxford Univ. Pr., 1954) (**B407**), *The prophet unarmed: Trotsky, 1921–1929* (New York: Oxford Univ. Pr., 1959) (**B408**), and *The prophet outcast, Trotsky, 1929–1940* (New York: Oxford Univ. Pr., 1963) (**B409**), as well as *Stalin: a political biography*, rev. ed. (Harmondsworth, Eng.: Penguin, 1966) (**B410**). For another view of Stalin consult Adam B. Ulam, *Stalin: the man and his era* (New York: Viking, 1973) (**B411**). Among the several biographers of Lenin, David Shub, *Lenin: a biography*, rev. ed. (Harmondsworth, Eng.: Penguin, 1966) (**B412**) contains primary materials, and Michael C. Morgan, *Lenin* (New York: Free Pr., 1973) (**B413**) treats the subject favorably in contrast to Ulam's interpretations.

Between World Wars, 1919–1939

The interwar period saw the western democracies mired in cultural malaise accompanied by economic uncertainty and depression. These circumstances provided fertile soil for fascist totalitarian rulers to seize control of governments in Germany, Italy and Spain. While the East European republics struggled to survive, the Soviet state fell under the ruthless dictatorship of Stalin.

Perhaps the most complete survey of the period is Raymond J. Sontag, *A broken world, 1919–1939* (New York: Harper, 1971) (**B414**). Edward H. Carr, *The twenty years' crisis, 1919–1939* (London: Macmillan, 1940) (**B415**) captures the sense of failure which gradually pervaded supporters of democracy. The role of the middle classes is studied in Charles S. Maier, *Recasting bourgeois Europe: stabilization in France, Germany and Italy in the decade after World War I* (Princeton, N.J.: Princeton Univ. Pr., 1975) (**B416**). The diplomacy of the 1920s is briefly surveyed in Sally Marks, *The illusion of peace: international relations in Europe, 1918–1933* (New York: St. Martin's, 1976) (**B417**), and Charles P. Kindleberger, *The world in depression, 1929–1939* (Berkeley: Univ. of California Pr., 1973) (**B418**) interprets and surveys economic development. Attention focuses on the relations between France and Great Britain and the crumbling of the Versailles system in Arnold Wolfers, *Britain and France between the two wars* (New York: Harcourt, Brace, 1940) (**B419**).

Depression, social unrest and economic exhaustion are depicted in Alan J. P. Taylor's controversial *English history, 1914–1945* (New York: Oxford Univ. Pr., 1965) (**B420**). The role of the Labour Party is sympathetically portrayed in George D. H. Cole, *A history of the Labour Party from 1914* (London: Routledge & Paul, 1948) (**B421**), while Trevor Wilson, *The downfall of the Liberal Party, 1914–1935* (Ithaca, N.Y.: Cornell Univ. Pr., 1966) (**B422**) examines political realignments. Sean Glynn and John Oxborrow, *Interwar Britain: a social and economic history* (New York: Barnes & Noble, 1976) (**B423**) discusses economic growth and commerce, while Robert Graves and Alan Hodge, *The long weekend: a social history of Great Britain, 1918–1939* (New York: Macmillan, 1941) (**B424**) captures the ethics of middle class life.

The history of the French Third Republic is effectively surveyed in Nathanael Greene, *From Versailles to Vichy: the Third Republic, 1919–1940* (New York: Crowell, 1970) (**B425**). Joel Colton, *Leon Blum: humanist in politics* (New York: Knopf, 1966) (**B426**) places this exceptional French politician in the context of his country and his times, while Val R. Lorwin, *The French labor movement* (Cambridge, Mass.: Harvard Univ. Pr., 1954) (**B427**) discusses a major factor in French politics of the 1920s and 1930s. The East European democracies during two decades of independence are surveyed with insight and understanding by John Rothschild, *East central Europe between the two world wars* (Seattle: Univ. of Washington Pr., 1974) (**B428**). Another excellent survey is Carlile A. Macartney and A. W. Palmer, *Independent Eastern Europe: a history* (New York: St. Martin's, 1962) (**B429**).

Germany, Italy and Spain saw the rise of fascist dictatorships between the wars. Ernst Nolte,

Three faces of fascism (New York: Holt, 1966) (**B430**) presents a complex sociological and philosophical comparison which is difficult but very important. On Germany, the political history of the enfeebled Weimar Republic receives the attention of Erich Eyck in *A history of the Weimar Republic*, 2v. (Cambridge, Mass.: Harvard Univ. Pr., 1962) (**B431**). For German culture in the 1920s consult Peter Gay, *Weimar culture: the outsider as insider* (New York: Harper, 1968) (**B432**). The rise of Hitler and the Nazi party have received much attention. Alan Bullock, *Hitler: a study in tyranny*, rev. ed. (New York: Harper, 1964) (**B433**) best captures the life and motivation of its subject. K. D. Bracher, *The German dictatorship* (New York: Praeger, 1970) (**B434**) comprehensively treats the origins and functioning of the Nazi movement and government. William S. Allen, *The Nazi seizure of power*, rev. ed. (New York: Watts, 1984) (**B435**) relates the experience in one town. Jill Stephenson, *Women in Nazi society* (New York: Barnes & Noble, 1975) (**B436**) demonstrates that Hitler intended no change in the traditional role of women. Valuable works on other aspects of Germany in the 1930s include John W. Wheeler-Bennett, *The nemesis of power: the German army in politics, 1918–1945*, 2d ed. (New York: St. Martin's, 1964) (**B437**), John S. Conway, *The Nazi persecution of the churches, 1933–1945* (New York: Basic Books, 1968) (**B438**), and David Schoenbaum, *Hitler's social revolution* (Garden City, N.Y.: Doubleday, 1967) (**B439**).

Italian fascism is comprehensively treated in Elizabeth Wiskemann, *Fascism in Italy: its development and influence* (New York: St. Martin's, 1969) (**B440**). An important survey which is especially good on Mussolini and Italian fascism is Denis Mack Smith, *Italy: a modern history*, new ed. (Ann Arbor: Univ. of Michigan Pr., 1969) (**B441**). Adrian Lyttleton, *The seizure of power: Fascism in Italy, 1919–1929* (New York: Scribner, 1973) (**B442**) describes the complicated process which led to Mussolini's ascendancy. Important works on Spain include Hugh Thomas, *The Spanish civil war*, rev. and enl. ed. (New York: Harper, 1977) (**B443**), which presents the war in narrative form, and Stanley G. Payne's two works, *The Spanish revolution* (New York: Norton, 1970) (**B444**) and *Politics and the military in modern Spain* (Stanford, Calif.: Stanford Univ. Pr., 1967) (**B445**), which discuss the causes for the fall of the Spanish republic and the rise of Franco. Several works detail the "appeasement" of Hitler. Among the best are Alfred L. Rowse, *Appeasement: a study in political decline, 1933–1939* (New York: Norton, 1961) (**B446**) and

Lewis Namier, *Diplomatic prelude, 1938–1939* (London: Macmillan, 1948) (**B447**).

The Soviet Union in the decades after the Bolshevik revolution is surveyed in Edward H. Carr, *A history of Soviet Russia* (London: Macmillan, 1950–) (**B448**). The Communist takeover in one city is analyzed in Merle Fainsod, *Smolensk under Soviet rule* (New York: Vintage, 1958) (**B449**) which utilizes documents captured in World War II. Soviet internal policy, especially relating to minorities, receives careful explanation in Richard Pipe's *The formation of the Soviet Union*, rev. ed. (Cambridge, Mass.: Harvard Univ. Pr., 1964) (**B450**). Robert Conquest, *The great terror: Stalin's purge of the thirties* (New York: Macmillan, 1968) (**B451**) objectively evaluates the paranoid author of the five-year plans, the "purges," and Soviet strategy in World War II. Naum Jasny, *Soviet industrialization, 1928–1952* (Chicago: Univ. of Chicago Pr., 1961) (**B452**) discusses economic development under Stalin. On Soviet foreign relations, contrast the classic work of George F. Kennan, *Russia and the West under Lenin and Stalin* (Boston: Little, 1961) (**B453**) with the more recent analysis of Adam B. Ulam, *Expansion and coexistence: a history of Soviet foreign policy, 1917–1973*, 2d ed. (New York: Praeger, 1974) (**B454**).

World War II and Post-War Europe

The best survey of the Second World War is Gordon Wright, *The ordeal of total war, 1939–1945* (New York: Harper, 1968) (**B455**). See also Cyril Falls, *The Second World War: a short history*, 3d ed. (London: Methuen, 1950) (**B456**) and Basil Liddell Hart, *History of the Second World War* (London: Cassell, 1970) (**B457**). On the concentration camps see the powerful work of Eugen Kogon, *The theory and practice of hell* (New York: Farrar, 1950) (**B458**) and Raoul Hilberg, *The destruction of the European Jews*, rev. ed. (New York: Holmes & Meier, 1984) (**B459**). F. W. Deakin, *The brutal friendship: Mussolini, Hitler and the fall of Italian fascism*, rev. ed. (Harmondsworth, Eng.: Penguin, 1966) (**B460**), Robert Aron, *The Vichy regime, 1940–44* (New York: Macmillan, 1958) (**B461**), and Alexander Dallin, *German rule in Russia, 1941–1945* (New York: St. Martin's, 1957) (**B462**) all discuss aspects of World War II. Nigel Hamilton, *Master of the battlefield, Monty's war years, 1942–44* (New York: McGraw-Hill, 1983) (**B463**) follows one of Great Britain's foremost generals while Iris Origo, *War in Val d'Orcia, 1943–1944: a diary* (London: Cape, 1947) (**B464**) relates how a small Italian community survived the ravages of civil war and foreign invasion. Among popular accounts William L. Shirer, *The rise and fall of the Third Reich* (New York: Simon & Schuster, 1960) (**B465**) is a long but readable journalistic account of Germany under Hitler. For an excellent study of Mussolini's aggressive aims, consult the well-researched work of Denis Mack Smith, *Mussolini's Roman Empire* (New York: Viking, 1976) (**B466**). The most readable account of Allied diplomacy during the war is John Snell, *Illusion and necessity: the diplomacy of global war, 1939–1945* (Boston: Houghton, 1963) (**B467**).

Europe Eclipsed

World War II marks the end of European dominance in the world. During ensuing decades the cold war and the end of colonization moved the focus of world affairs away from Europe with deceptive gradualism. At the same time, Western Europe seemed to move haltingly toward integration and unity. A strong basis for understanding postwar Europe appears in Michael M. Postan, *An economic history of Western Europe, 1945–1964* (London: Methuen, 1967) (**B468**). Surveys of political developments include Jacques Freymond, *Western Europe since the war* (New York: Praeger, 1964) (**B469**), Walter Laqueur, *Europe since Hitler*, rev. ed. (New York: Penguin, 1982) (**B470**), Frank Roy Willis, *European integration* (New York: New Viewpoints, 1975) (**B471**), and Richard J. Mayne, *The recovery of Europe, 1945–1973* (New York: Harper, 1970) (**B472**).

On specific countries, writings display the contradictory currents blowing across the continent. The British ruling elite is castigated in Anthony Sampson, *The new anatomy of Britain* (New York: Stein & Day, 1972) (**B473**), with a more objective survey presented by Francis Boyd, *British politics in transition, 1945–1963* (New York: Praeger, 1964) (**B474**). For France, John Ardagh, *The new France: a society in transition, 1945–1977*, 3d ed. (Harmondsworth, Eng.: Penguin, 1977) (**B475**) offers interesting new interpretations, while Henry W. Ehrmann, *Politics in France*, 4th ed. (Boston: Little, 1983) (**B476**) emphasizes social and institutional change. The turmoil of the French Fourth Republic is analyzed in Duncan MacRae, *Parliament, parties and society in France, 1946–1958* (New York: St. Martin's, 1967) (**B477**). The regime of Francisco Franco is studied in Brian Crozier, *Franco* (Boston: Little, 1967) (**B478**), while his country is the subject of works by Stanley G. Payne, *Franco's Spain* (New York: Crowell, 1967) **(B479)** and George Hills, *Spain* (New York: Praeger, 1970) **(B480)**.

On Eastern Europe under Soviet domination, see Hugh Seton-Watson, *The Eastern European revolution*, 2d ed. (London: Methuen, 1952) **(B481)** which describes the communization of the area, and Zbigniew K. Brzezinski, *The Soviet bloc: unity and conflict*, rev. ed. (Cambridge, Mass.: Harvard Univ. Pr., 1967) **(B482)**.

Germany's postwar development led by Konrad Adenauer is the subject of Richard Hiscocks, *The Adenauer era* (Philadelphia: Lippincott, 1966) **(B483)**. Alfred Grosser, *Germany in our time* (New York: Praeger, 1971) **(B484)** provides a discussion of Germany's place in modern Europe. On Italy, political developments are surveyed in Norman Kogan, *A political history of postwar Italy: from the old to the new center left* (New York: Praeger, 1981) **(B485)**.

Among the mass of generally unimaginative and shallow works on the cold war, several stand out. Andre Fontaine, *A history of the cold war*, 2v. (New York: Pantheon, 1968–69) **(B486)** presents a balanced European point of view, while Louis J. Halle, *The cold war as history* (New York: Harper, 1967) **(B487)** and the pro-United States work of John Lukacs, *A new history of the cold war*, 3d ed. (Garden City, N.Y.: Anchor, 1966) **(B488)** render contrasting portrayals. For works on the United States, see below. On the Soviet Union, consult Merle Fainsod, *How Russia is ruled*, rev. ed. (Cambridge, Mass.: Harvard Univ. Pr., 1963) **(B489)** and W. Leonhard, *The Kremlin since Stalin* (New York: Praeger, 1962) **(B490)**.

Ted P. Sheldon

UNITED STATES HISTORY

Historians of the United States are particularly fortunate because of their government's generosity in allowing the use of its documents relating to both domestic and foreign policy. Whereas other countries have placed stringent restrictions on their primary materials which range from outright refusal to an inordinately lengthy period of time, the United States has a twenty-year waiting period, which researchers can often circumvent by appealing for the release of documents through the Freedom-of-Information Act. The result is that numerous first-rate works have appeared on nearly all phases of America's history. The following bibliographical essay contains many of the most important works related to the United States, some of which are monographs on specialized subjects, whereas the others are textbook surveys, syntheses of monographs, personal accounts, or memoirs. Combined, they constitute a rich history of America's past.

General Works

There are numerous surveys of America's history, but among the best are: Samuel Eliot Morison, Henry Steele Commager, and William E. Leuchtenburg, *The growth of the American Republic*, 2v., 6th ed. (New York: Oxford Univ. Pr., 1969) **(B491)**; Richard N. Current, et al., *American history: a survey*, 2v., 6th ed. (New York: Knopf, 1983) **(B492)**, an excellent, well-written coverage, containing maps, pictures, and illustrations, as well as sections on historians' interpretations of controversial issues; Thomas A. Bailey and David M. Kennedy, *The American pageant: a history of the Republic*, 2v., 7th ed. (Lexington, Mass.: Heath, 1983) **(B493)**, sprightly and colorfully written, amply illustrated with maps, cartoons, and other attractions for students; John A. Garraty, *The American nation*, 2v., 5th ed. (New York: Harper, 1982) **(B494)**, clearly written and interpretive, and beautifully illustrated with pictures from *American heritage*; and John Morton Blum, et al., *The national experience: a history of the United States*, 2v., 5th ed. (New York: HBJ, 1981) **(B495)**, also highly readable.

On the nation's foreign policy, the following surveys are useful: Thomas A. Bailey, *A diplomatic history of the American people*, 10th ed. (Englewood Cliffs, N. J.: Prentice-Hall, 1980) **(B496)**, an anecdotal and scholarly account of America's foreign policy that is filled with maps, cartoons, and illustrations; Howard Jones, *The course of American diplomacy: from the Revolution to the present* (New York: Watts, 1984) **(B497)**, a balanced survey containing maps and illustrations that help to highlight the "makers" of American foreign policy along with the major events; Thomas G. Paterson, J. Garry Clifford, and Kenneth J. Hagan, *American foreign policy: a history*, 2v., 2d ed. (Lexington, Mass.: Heath, 1983) **(B498)**, often critical of the nation's diplomacy. Still helpful, although in need of updating, are: Julius W. Pratt, Vincent P. De Santis, and Joseph M. Siracusa, *A history of United States foreign policy*, 4th ed. (Englewood Cliffs, N.J.: Prentice-Hall, 1980) **(B499)**, a longtime standard survey; Alexander DeConde, *A history of American foreign policy*, 3d ed. (New York: Scribner, 1978) **(B500)**, heavily detailed; and Robert H. Ferrell, *American diplomacy: a history*, 3d ed. (New York: Norton, 1975) **(B501)**, elegantly written and highly interpretive.

There are useful histories of the American West. They include: Ray A. Billington, *Westward expansion: a history of the American frontier*, 4th ed. (New York: Macmillan, 1974) **(B502)**, the standard coverage of the subject; Thomas D. Clark, *Frontier America: The story of the westward movement*, 2d ed. (New York: Scribner, 1969) **(B503)**, a sound study and nicely written; Frederick Merk, *History of the westward movement* (New York: Knopf, 1978) **(B504)**; and LeRoy R. Hafen and Carl C. Rister, *Western America*, 3d ed. (Englewood Cliffs, N. J.: Prentice-Hall, 1970) **(B505)**.

The intellectual history of the United States is the subject of many fine studies. Some of the most ambitious are: Vernon L. Parrington, *Main currents in American thought*, 3v. (New York: Harcourt, Brace, 1927–30) **(B506)**; Henry S. Commager, *The American mind: an interpretation of American thought and character since the 1880's* (New Haven, Conn.: Yale Univ. Pr., 1950) **(B507)**; Harvey Wish, *Society and thought in America*, 2v. (New York: McKay, 1950–62) **(B508)**; Ralph H. Gabriel, *The course of American democratic thought*, rev. ed. (New York: Wiley, 1956) **(B509)**; and Merle Curti, *The growth of American thought*, 3d ed. (New York: Harper, 1964) **(B510)**.

Other aspects of America's history have appeared in full-scale scholarly works. On black history, see John Hope Franklin, *From slavery to freedom: a history of Negro Americans*, 5th ed. (New York: Knopf, 1980) **(B511)**, the basic survey of the subject. But also see August Meier and Elliott M. Rudwick, *From plantation to ghetto: an interpretive history of American Negroes* (New York: Hill & Wang, 1966) **(B512)**. Urban America has attracted the interest of many historians. The best works include: two volumes by Blake McKelvey, *The urbanization of America, 1860–*

1915 (New Brunswick, N. J.: Rutgers Univ. Pr., 1963) **(B513)**, and *The emergence of metropolitan America, 1915–1966* (New Brunswick, N. J.: Rutgers Univ. Pr., 1968) **(B514)**; and Charles N. Glaab and A. Theodore Brown, *A history of urban America* (New York: Macmillan, 1967) **(B515)**. For the nation's constitutional history, see the longtime basic study, Alfred H. Kelly and Winfred A. Harbison, *The American Constitution: its origins and development*, 5th ed. (New York: Norton, 1979) **(B516)**. A solid history of immigration is that by Maldwyn A. Jones, *American immigration* (Chicago: Univ. of Chicago Pr., 1960) **(B517)**, while of several sound works on economic history, see Harold U. Faulkner, *American economic history*, 8th ed. (New York: Harper, 1960) **(B518)**. On American labor, there are: Joseph G. Rayback, *A history of American labor* (New York: Free Pr., 1966) **(B519)**; Foster R. Dulles, *Labor in America: a history*, 3d ed. (New York: Crowell, 1966) **(B520)**; and Henry Pelling, *American labor* (Chicago: Univ. of Chicago Pr., 1960) **(B521)**, a brief survey.

Colonial Beginnings to 1763

There are several important surveys of America's colonial history. Perhaps the most readable and interpretive is David Hawke, *The colonial experience* (Indianapolis: Bobbs-Merrill, 1966) **(B522)**. Another first-rate study is Max Savelle and Darold D. Wax, *A history of colonial America*, 3d ed. (Hinsdale, Ill.: Dryden, 1973) **(B523)**, while still valuable are Curtis P. Nettels, *The roots of American civilization: a history of American colonial life*, 2d ed. (New York: Appleton, 1963) **(B524)**, and Oscar T. Barck, Jr., and Hugh T. Lefler, *Colonial America*, 2d ed. (New York: Macmillan, 1969) **(B525)**. Another survey, recently published, is Paul R. Lucas, *American odyssey, 1607–1789* (Englewood Cliffs, N. J.: Prentice-Hall, 1983) **(B526)**. For the cultural life of the colonies, consult Daniel J. Boorstin, *The Americans: the colonial experience* (New York: Random, 1958) **(B527)**.

On the European background of American colonization, see two works by Edward P. Cheyney: *The dawn of a new era, 1250–1453* (New York: Harper, 1936) **(B528)**, and *European background of American history, 1300–1600* (New York: Collier, 1904) **(B529)**, and one by John H. Parry, *The age of reconnaissance* (B184). Samuel Eliot Morison has contributed three major studies on the European exploration of the New World: *Admiral of the ocean sea: a life* *of Christopher Columbus*, 2v. (Boston: Little, 1942) **(B531)**, the classic biography of the man, which also appears in a one-volume abridgment entitled *Christopher Columbus, mariner* (New York: Mentor, 1942) **(B532)**; *The European discovery of America: the northern voyages, A.D. 500–1600* (New York: Oxford Univ. Pr., 1971) **(B533)**; and *The European discovery of America: the southern voyages* (New York: Oxford Univ. Pr., 1974) **(B534)**. The discovery and settlement of America is the subject of many studies. See two works by David B. Quinn: *England and the discovery of America, 1481–1620* (New York: Knopf, 1974) **(B535)**, which covers England's early relations with America; and *North America from earliest discovery to first settlements: the Norse voyages to 1612* (New York: Harper, 1977) **(B536)**. The best coverage of the Spanish experience in America is Charles Gibson, *Spain in America* (New York: Harper, 1966) **(B537)**. But also helpful are Edward G. Bourne, *Spain in America, 1450–1580* (New York: Barnes & Noble, 1904) **(B538)**, and Clarence H. Haring, *The Spanish Empire in America* (New York: Harcourt, 1947) **(B539)**. A general study is John B. Brebner, *The explorers of North America, 1492–1806* (New York: Meridian, 1933) **(B540)**, whereas the role of France in the New World is the subject of William J. Eccles, *France in America* (New York: Harper, 1972) **(B541)**.

There are numerous works on the English background of colonization. A sound introduction to the subject is Wallace Notestein, *The English people on the eve of colonization, 1603–1630* (New York: Harper, 1954) **(B542)**. See also Peter Laslett, *The world we have lost: England before the industrial age* (New York: Scribner, 1965) **(B543)**, for a pathbreaking and colorful study of the social and demographic factors preceding England's entrance into the modern industrial age. Carl Bridenbaugh, *Vexed and troubled Englishmen, 1590–1642* (New York: Oxford Univ. Pr., 1968) **(B544)**, also deals with social and demographic factors in premodern England. Religious concerns dominated Elizabethan society in England and thus deeply affected colonization in the New World. For a sound survey, see Alfred L. Rowse, *The Elizabethans and America* (New York: Harper, 1959) **(B545)**. On the religious background of English colonization, Charles H. George and Katherine George have studied *The Protestant mind of the English Reformation, 1570–1640* (Princeton, N. J.: Princeton Univ. Pr., 1961) **(B546)**, and Patrick Collinson has a superb account of the Puritans in England in *The Elizabethan Puritan movement* (Berkeley: Univ. of

California Pr., 1967) **(B547)**. For a provocative treatment of the subject, see Michael Walzer, *The revolution of the saints: a study in the origins of radical politics* (Cambridge, Mass.: Harvard Univ. Pr., 1965) **(B548)**. And for an examination of the English civil war and its ramifications for America, see Lawrence Stone, *The crisis of the aristocracy, 1558–1641* (New York: Oxford Univ. Pr., 1965) **(B549)**.

The early years of the American colonies have stimulated great interest among historians. A sound survey is Clarence L. Ver Steeg's *The formative years, 1607–1763* (New York: Hill & Wang, 1964) **(B550)**. Detailed coverages of the early English colonies in North America are in the following monumental studies: Herbert L. Osgood, *American colonies in the seventeenth century*, 3v. (New York: Macmillan, 1904–7) **(B551)**, and his *The American colonies in the eighteenth century*, 4v. (New York: Columbia Univ. Pr., 1924–25) **(B552)**; and Charles M. Andrews, *The colonial period of American history*, 4v. (New Haven, Conn.: Yale Univ. Pr., 1934–38) **(B553)**. For a good survey of the Chesapeake colonies, see Wesley Frank Craven, *The southern colonies in the seventeenth century, 1607–1689* (Baton Rouge: Louisiana State Univ. Pr., 1949) **(B554)**. See the same author's *The colonies in transition, 1660–1713* (New York: Harper, 1968) **(B555)**. Alden T. Vaughan discusses the first English success in colonization in *American genesis: Captain John Smith and the founding of Virginia* (Boston: Little, 1975) **(B556)**. Carl Bridenbaugh offers a social history of the Southern plantation economy in *Myths and realities: societies of the colonial South* (Baton Rouge: Louisiana State Univ. Pr., 1952) **(B557)**.

Religion permeated all of the American colonies. For a general survey, see Sydney E. Ahlstrom, *A religious history of the American people* (New Haven, Conn.: Yale Univ. Pr., 1972) **(B558)**. William W. Sweet's *Religion in colonial America* (New York: Scribner, 1942) **(B559)** is an institutional approach to church groups, whereas Edwin S. Gaustad covers *The Great Awakening in New England* (New York: Harper, 1957) **(B560)**. Alan E. Heimert, *Religion and the American mind, from the Great Awakening to the Revolution* (Cambridge, Mass.: Harvard Univ. Pr., 1966) **(B561)**, tries to show the connection between the religious unrest of the early 1700s and the political upheaval of 1776 by following the development of religious divisions during the Great Awakening and into the revolutionary period and afterward. For the relationship between religious and political life, consult Carl

Bridenbaugh, *Mitre and sceptre: transatlantic faiths, ideas, personalities, and politics, 1689–1775* (New York: Oxford Univ. Pr., 1962) **(B562)**, which shows the colonists' fear that Britain might force them to accept Anglicanism.

Northern settlements—especially in Massachusetts Bay—are the focus of numerous studies. On Plymouth Plantation, see the valuable contemporary account by William Bradford, *Of Plymouth Plantation: the Pilgrims in America*, edited by Harvey Wish (New York: Capricorn, 1962) **(B563)**. Also helpful is John Demos, *A little commonwealth: family life in Plymouth colony* (New York: Oxford Univ. Pr., 1970) **(B564)**, a social history of the Pilgrims of Plymouth. The establishment of Boston and Massachusetts Bay Colony is the subject of Samuel Eliot Morison, *Builders of the Bay colony* (Boston: Houghton, 1958) **(B565)**, whereas Darrett B. Rutman, in *Winthrop's Boston: a portrait of a Puritan town, 1630–1649* (Chapel Hill: Univ. of North Carolina Pr., 1965) **(B566)**, shows that within a decade of Boston's establishment, economic interests had become more important than religion in determining many citizens' lives. For colonial commerce, see Bernard Bailyn, *The New England merchants in the seventeenth century* (Cambridge, Mass.: Harvard Univ. Pr., 1955) **(B567)**; and Frederick B. Tolles, *Meeting house and counting house: the Quaker merchants of colonial Philadelphia, 1682–1763* (Chapel Hill: Univ. of North Carolina Pr., 1948) **(B568)**. Jackson Turner Main, *The social structure of revolutionary America* (Princeton, N. J.: Princeton Univ. Pr., 1965) **(B569)** shows how the lack of economic equality had an impact on America before the Revolution.

There are many admirable studies of Puritanism in Massachusetts Bay. A highly readable account is Edmund S. Morgan, *The Puritan dilemma: the story of John Winthrop* (Boston: Little, 1958) **(B570)**, which shows the interrelationship of political and religious issues in Massachusetts Bay and notes how Winthrop dealt with the Puritans' dilemma of attempting to live *in* the world without becoming part *of* it. See also Darrett B. Rutman, *American Puritanism: faith and practice* (New York: Lippincott, 1970) **(B571)**. Perry Miller has written a series of complex studies of Puritan theology, which nevertheless are the beginning point for any serious study of the subject. See *Orthodoxy in Massachusetts, 1630–1650* (New York: Harper, 1933) **(B572)**; *The New England mind: the seventeenth century* (New York: Macmillan, 1939) **(B573)**; *The New England mind: from colony to province* (Cambridge, Mass.: Harvard Univ. Pr., 1953) **(B574)**;

Errand into the wilderness (Cambridge, Mass.: Belknap, 1956) **(B575)**; and *Jonathan Edwards* (New York: Sloane, 1949) **(B576)**, the last an intellectual study of the foremost American religious leader of the Great Awakening. Edmund S. Morgan, in *The Puritan family: religion and domestic relations in seventeenth-century New England* (New York: Harper, 1966) **(B577)**, covers local life and social history in Massachusetts Bay, whereas his *Visible saints: the history of a Puritan idea* (New York: New York Univ. Pr., 1963) **(B578)**, discusses the Puritans' use of the "half-way covenant" in trying to combat their children's declining religious zeal. Sacvan Bercovitch, in *The Puritan origins of the American self* (New Haven, Conn.: Yale Univ. Pr., 1975) **(B579)**, focuses on the impact of the New England way of life on the American individual. For a leading Puritan family, see Robert Middlekauff, *The Mathers: three generations of Puritan intellectuals, 1596–1728* (New York: Oxford Univ. Pr., 1971) **(B580)**.

Despite the emphasis on Puritan orthodoxy, not all was harmonious in the Bay colony. One of the most dangerous dissenters in Massachusetts is the subject of Perry Miller, *Roger Williams: his contribution to the American tradition* (Indianapolis: Bobbs-Merrill, 1953) **(B581)**, and Edmund S. Morgan, *Roger Williams: the church and the state* (New York: Harcourt, 1967) **(B582)**. Williams, among other contentions, argued for the separation of church and state. Another dissenter was Anne Hutchinson, whose ideas on the "inner light" are the subject of Kai T. Erikson, *Wayward Puritans: a study in the sociology of deviance* (New York: Wiley, 1966) **(B583)**. One should read the following two studies in conjunction with Erikson's work: Emery Battis, *Saints and sectaries* (Chapel Hill: Univ. of North Carolina Pr., 1962) **(B584)**, and William K. B. Stoever, *A faire and easie way to heaven: Covenant theology and antinominianism in early Massachusetts* (Middletown, Conn.: Wesleyan Univ. Pr., 1978) **(B585)**. Paul R. Lucas, *Valley of discord: church and society along the Connecticut River, 1636–1725* (Hanover, N. H.: Univ. Pr. of New England, 1976) **(B586)**, examines Rhode Island and Connecticut, both founded as a result of the dissension in Massachusetts Bay. On the witchcraft phenomena, see Chadwick Hansen, *Witchcraft at Salem* (New York: Braziller, 1969) **(B587)**; Paul Boyer and Stephen Nissenbaum, *Salem possessed: the social origins of witchcraft* (Cambridge, Mass.: Harvard Univ. Pr., 1974) **(B588)**; Marian L. Starkey, *The devil in Massachusetts: a modern enquiry into the Salem witch trials* (New York: Knopf, 1949) **(B589)**; and a recent study by John Demos, *Entertaining Satan: witchcraft and the culture of early New England* (New York: Oxford Univ. Pr., 1982) (**B590**).

For an introduction to the subject of Indians, both in the period before and after the entrance of the Europeans, see Wilcomb E. Washburn, *The Indian in America* (New York: Harper, 1975) (**B591**). On the northern colonists' relations with the Indians, see Alden T. Vaughan, *New England frontier: Puritans and Indians, 1620–1675* (Boston: Little, 1965) (**B592**). See also Douglas E. Leach, *Flintlock and tomahawk: New England in King Philip's War* (New York: Norton, 1958) (**B593**).

For early colonial politics, see Bernard Bailyn, *The origins of American politics* (New York: Knopf, 1968) (**B594**). Charles S. Sydnor notes the importance of "deference" in *Gentlemen freeholders: political practices in Washington's Virginia* (Chapel Hill: Univ. of North Carolina Pr., 1952) (**B595**). On the intellectual background of colonial politics, see Caroline Robbins, *The eighteenth-century commonwealthman: studies in the transmission, development and circumstance of English liberal thought from the restoration of Charles II until the war with the thirteen colonies* (Cambridge, Mass.: Harvard Univ. Pr., 1959) (**B596**), who emphasizes the colonists' aim of an integrated society. A first-rate analysis of colonial assemblies is Jack P. Greene's *The quest for power: the lower houses of assembly in the southern royal colonies, 1689–1776* (Chapel Hill: Univ. of North Carolina Pr., 1963) (**B597**).

The New England town has been the subject of many demographic studies. An early model for other historians is Sumner Chilton Powell's *Puritan village: the formation of a New England town* (Middletown, Conn.: Wesleyan Univ. Pr., 1963) (**B598**), a social history of the town of Sudsbury, Massachusetts. In a previously mentioned work, Darrett B. Rutman, in *Winthrop's Boston* (B566), focuses on changes in early seventeenth-century Boston that increasingly shifted the locus of authority from the Puritans' religious leaders. Other demographic works include: Kenneth A. Lockridge, *A New England town: the first hundred years* (New York: Norton, 1970) (**B599**), which deals with Dedham, Massachusetts; Philip J. Greven, Jr., *Four generations: population, land, and family in colonial Andover, Massachusetts* (Ithaca, N. Y.: Cornell Univ. Pr., 1970) (**B600**); and Michael Zuckerman, *Peaceable kingdoms: New England towns in the eighteenth century* (New York: Knopf, 1970) (**B601**), which disputes the traditional interpretation that tensions permeated Puritan communities. Urban colonial America is the subject of two works by Carl Bridenbaugh: *Cities in the wilderness: urban life in America, 1625–1742* (New York: Capricorn, 1938) (**B602**), and *Cities in revolt: urban life in America, 1743–1776* (New York: Capricorn, 1955) (**B603**).

American colonial society was in a constant state of social, political, and economic change. For the shaping of America's national character, see Michael Kammen, *People of paradox: an inquiry concerning the origins of American civilization* (New York: Knopf, 1972) (**B604**). For colonial culture and the effect of the Enlightenment, see Louis B. Wright, *The cultural life of the American colonies, 1607–1763* (New York: Harper, 1957) (**B605**), and Howard M. Jones, *O strange new world: American culture: the formative years* (New York: Viking, 1964) (**B606**). A more specific study is Henry F. May, *The enlightenment in America* (New York: Oxford, 1976) (**B607**). On education, see Lawrence A. Cremin, *American education: the colonial experience, 1607–1783* (New York: Harper, 1970) (**B608**), volume 1 of a projected full-scale study of the subject of education in America. Samuel Eliot Morison, *The founding of Harvard College* (Cambridge, Mass.: Harvard Univ. Pr., 1935) (**B609**), deals with the establishment of the first college in America. See also his *The intellectual life of colonial New England* (New York: New York Univ. Pr., 1936) (**B610**). Bernard Bailyn shows the effects of *Education in the forming of American society* (New York: Random, 1960) (**B611**), and Brooke Hindle focuses on *The pursuit of science in revolutionary America, 1735–1789* (Chapel Hill: Univ. of North Carolina Pr., 1956) (**B612**). Perhaps the embodiment of the Enlightenment in America was Benjamin Franklin, who has been the subject of numerous biographies. See Carl C. Van Doren, *Benjamin Franklin* (New York: Viking, 1938) (**B613**); Verner W. Crane, *Benjamin Franklin and a rising people* (Boston: Little, 1954) (**B614**); and Ronald W. Clark, *Benjamin Franklin: a biography* (New York: Random, 1983) (**B615**). See also Franklin's *Autobiography*, which has appeared in many editions.

Despite the attempt by many colonists to escape Old World problems, they found it impossible to do so. Howard H. Peckham, *The colonial wars, 1689–1762* (Chicago: Univ. of Chicago Pr., 1964) (**B616**), examines how Anglo-French rivalry and wars in Europe stirred conflict in the New World as well. A valuable study is Max Savelle's *The origins of American diplomacy: the international history of Angloamerica, 1492–1763* (New York: Macmillan, 1967) (**B617**), which contains a discussion of the Anglo-French struggle for North America. For a literary masterpiece, see Francis Parkman's *France and England in North America*, 2v. (New York: Literary Classics, dist. by Viking, 1983) (**B618**), which is available in several editions.

The American Revolution, 1763–1789

The American revolutionary era extends from the first events pointing toward upheaval to the culmination with the ratification of the Constitution and the inauguration of George Washington as president in 1789. Useful surveys include: Robert Middlekauff, *The glorious cause: the American Revolution, 1763–1789* (New York: Oxford Univ. Pr., 1982) (**B619**), a superb blend of the military events with the overall revolutionary struggle; Edmund S. Morgan, *The birth of the Republic, 1763–1789* (Chicago: Univ. of Chicago Pr., 1956) (**B620**), a clearly written study extolling the Americans' drive for liberty against oppression; two works by John C. Miller: *Origins of the American Revolution* (Boston: Little, 1943) (**B621**), and *Triumph of freedom: 1775–1783* (Boston: Little, 1948) (**B622**), both highly readable; Merrill Jensen, *The founding of a nation: a history of the American Revolution, 1763–1776* (New York: Oxford Univ. Pr., 1968) (**B623**); John R. Alden, *The American Revolution, 1775–1783* (New York: Harper, 1954) (**B624**); Ian R. Christie and Benjamin W. Labaree, *Empire or independence, 1760–1776* (New York: Norton, 1977) (**B625**), which tries to mesh American and British perspectives on events; and Esmond Wright, *Fabric of freedom, 1763–1800* (New York: Hill & Wang, 1961) (**B626**). The most comprehensive and detailed study is a multivolume work by Lawrence Henry Gipson, who in *The British empire before the American Revolution*, 15v. (New York: Knopf, 1936–70) (**B627**) shows the changes in the imperial system of the 1760s that encouraged revolutionary sentiment in America. In his shorter work, *The coming of the Revolution, 1763–1775* (New York: Harper, 1954) (**B628**), Gipson stresses the importance of the outcome of the French and Indian War, as he more aptly called "The Great War for the Empire," in the approaching American Revolution. According to Gipson, the outcome of the Anglo-French struggle was monumental: it changed England's mood from "salutary neglect" to enforcement of

imperial decrees, which in turn altered America's desire for autonomy within the empire in 1763 to a demand for independence by the middle of the following decade. Also helpful is Charles M. Andrews, *The colonial background of the American Revolution*, rev. ed. (New Haven, Conn.: Yale Univ. Pr., 1931) (**B629**), and Howard H. Peckham, *The colonial wars, 1689–1762* (described at B616), which contains an examination of the French and Indian War.

The causes and meaning of the American Revolution have been the focal points of historians' concern about the period. For a valuable bibliographical source, see Jack P. Greene, ed., *The reinterpretation of the American Revolution, 1763–1789* (New York: Harper, 1968) (**B631**). Though in need of updating, Greene has masterfully capsulized the central ideas of the leading books and articles on the subject. Historians for many years assumed that British mercantile policies were vital to the coming of the Revolution, but Oliver M. Dickerson, in *The Navigation Acts and the American Revolution* (Philadelphia: Univ. of Pennsylvania Pr., 1951) (**B632**), shows that the acts were the "cement" of empire and that the causes of the insurrection had to lie elsewhere. Bernhard Knollenberg, *Origin of the American Revolution, 1759–1766* (New York: Free Pr., 1961) (**B633**), analyzes the impact of Britain's decision to enforce imperial regulations in America during the 1760s. British historian Lewis B. Namier, in two works, shows the effect on the American colonies of King George III's ascension to the throne: *England in the age of the American Revolution*, rev. ed. (New York: St. Martin's, 1961) (**B634**), and *The structure of politics at the accession of George III*, rev. ed. (New York: St. Martin's, 1961) (**B635**). Arthur M. Schlesinger, *The colonial merchants and the American Revolution, 1763–1776* (New York: Columbia Univ. Pr., 1918) (**B636**), argues that out of economic interests, colonial merchants led the resistance against the British. Once the Revolution was underway, however, it escaped merchant control and became a widely based social upheaval. Carl L. Becker, *The history of political parties in the province of New York, 1760–1776* (Madison: Univ. of Wisconsin Pr., 1909) (**B637**), shows how the Revolution had two sides: the question of "home rule"—the problems between the mother country and colonies—and "who should rule at home"—those among the colonies themselves over who would govern once they had achieved independence. In another study by Becker, *The heavenly city of the eighteenth-century philosophers* (B243), he explores the intellectual context of the American revolutionary era. J. Franklin Jameson, *The American Revolution considered as a social movement* (Princeton, N. J.: Princeton Univ. Pr., 1926) **(B639)**, discerns a power struggle between "radical" and "conservative" elements in America that culminated in the "democratization of American politics and society." In a similar manner, Robert E. Brown argues in *Middle-class democracy and the revolution in Massachusetts, 1691–1780* (Ithaca, N. Y.: Cornell Univ. Pr., 1955) **(B640)**, that well before 1776, Massachusetts had approached the status of a "complete democracy" and that the social tensions often attributed to the revolutionary period were a myth. In a work mentioned already, Edmund S. Morgan, *Birth of the Republic* (B620), argues that the American revolutionists' cry for political liberties was the central reason for the unrest, but that interests and principles ultimately came together during the period. Robert R. Palmer, *The age of the democratic revolution: a political history of Europe and America, 1760–1800*, 2v. (Princeton, N. J.: Princeton Univ. Pr., 1959) **(B641)**, places America's revolutionary changes within the perspective of the West's history.

Several historians have emphasized the constitutional bases of the Revolution. For the most important analysis, see Bernard Bailyn, *The ideological origins of the American Revolution* (Cambridge, Mass.: Harvard Univ. Pr., 1967) **(B642)**, who uses hundreds of pamphlets of the revolutionary era to show that the upheaval was primarily "an ideological, constitutional, political struggle." The American colonists, he insists, became convinced that a conspiracy against liberty had developed among the king's advisers in England. See also Bailyn, ed., *Pamphlets of the American Revolution, 1750–1776* (Cambridge, Mass.: Harvard Univ. Pr., 1965–) **(B643)**, for not only a first-hand examination of American revolutionary thought, but also for Bailyn's lengthy introductory essay. Along these same lines, see Caroline Robbins, *The eighteenth-century commonwealthman* (B596), and H. Trevor Colbourn, *The lamp of experience: Whig history and the intellectual origins of the American Revolution* (Chapel Hill: Univ. of North Carolina Pr., 1965) **(B644)**, the latter of which rests on the "marginalia" among numerous other pieces of evidence to show that America's Founding Fathers were well-read in intellectual history and that they based their ideas of liberty on the early English Whigs. Clinton L. Rossiter, *Seedtime of the Republic: the origin of the American tradition of political liberty* (New York: Harcourt, Brace, 1953) **(B645)**, emphasizes the conservatism of the Revolution in showing how Americans tried to restore liberties that they believed once existed. In a more broadly based study, Gary B. Nash, *The urban crucible: social change, political consciousness, and the origins of the American Revolution* (Cambridge, Mass.: Harvard Univ. Pr., 1979) **(B646)**, asserts that economic interests combined with ideological concerns to shape an atmosphere conducive to revolution.

Most of the events in the decade preceding the outbreak of the American Revolution have received careful historical attention. Edmund S. and Helen M. Morgan, in *The Stamp Act crisis: prologue to revolution* (Chapel Hill: Univ. of North Carolina Pr., 1953) **(B647)**, find the first feelings of "Americanism" in the greatest political crisis of the 1760s, whereas Pauline Meier, in *From resistance to revolution: colonial radicals and the development of American opposition to Britain, 1765–1776* (New York: Knopf, 1972) **(B648)**, links political ideas to the beginnings of "mob" resistance, showing how colonial leaders won a popular following. Hiller B. Zobel, *The Boston massacre* (New York: Norton, 1970) **(B649)**, is particularly strong on the legal aspects of the episode. Benjamin W. Labaree, *The Boston Tea Party* (New York: Oxford Univ. Pr., 1964) **(B650)**, offers an excellent account of the relationship of that event to the Americans' call for individual liberty, whereas one of the perpetrators of the "party" is the subject of *Sam Adams: pioneer in propaganda* (Boston: Little, 1936) **(B651)**, by John C. Miller. See also Pauline Meier, *The old revolutionaries: political lives in the age of Samuel Adams* (New York: Knopf, 1980) **(B652)**. Carl L. Becker's *The Declaration of Independence: a study in the history of political ideas* (New York: Knopf, 1922) **(B653)** is a classic study that highlights the effect of John Locke's ideas on the intellectual leaders of the Revolution, but one should also consult Morton G. White, *The philosophy of the American Revolution* (New York: Oxford, 1978) **(B654)**, and Garry Wills, *Inventing America: Jefferson's Declaration of Independence* (Garden City, N. Y.: Doubleday, 1978) **(B655)**, the latter of whom argues that Scottish radical thinkers affected Jefferson's philosophy. On Tom Paine, see: Eric Foner, *Tom Paine and revolutionary America* (New York: Oxford Univ. Pr., 1976) **(B656)**, a highly interpretive study, and David Hawke, *Paine* (New York: Harper, 1974) **(B657)**, a biography.

The war itself has been the subject of several studies. Among the best are: Christopher Ward, *The war of the Revolution*, 2v. (New York: Macmillan, 1952) **(B658)**; Howard H. Peckham, *The* *war for independence: a military history* (Chicago: Univ. of Chicago Pr., 1958) **(B659)**; John R. Alden, *A history of the American Revolution* (New York: Knopf, 1969) **(B660)**; Don Higginbotham, *The war of American independence: military attitudes, policies, and practice, 1763–1789* (New York: Macmillan, 1971) **(B661)**; Marshall Smelser, *The winning of independence* (Chicago: Quadrangle, 1972) **(B662)**; and James K. Martin and Mark E. Lender, *A respectable army: the military origins of the Republic, 1763–1789* (Arlington Heights, Ill.: Harlan Davidson, 1982) **(B663)**. Piers Mackesy, *The war for America, 1775–1783* (Cambridge, Mass.: Harvard Univ. Pr., 1964) **(B664)**, places the American War within the European context. Two recent studies by John S. Pancake emphasize particular aspects of the war: *1777: The year of the hangman* (University: Univ. of Alabama Pr., 1977) **(B665)**, and *This destructive war: the British campaign in the Carolinas, 1780–1782* (University: Univ. of Alabama Pr., 1984) **(B666)**. For the impact of social factors on the American military in the war, see John Shy, *A people numerous and armed: reflections on the military struggle for American independence* (New York: Oxford Univ. Pr., 1976) **(B667)**. Charles Royster, *A revolutionary people at war: the Continental army and American character, 1775–1783* (Chapel Hill: Univ. of North Carolina Pr., 1979) **(B668)**, explains the relationship of political thought to the military aspects of the war. On the Loyalists, see: William H. Nelson, *The American Tory* (New York: Oxford Univ. Pr., 1961) **(B669)**; Wallace Brown, *The good Americans: the Loyalists in the American Revolution* (New York: Morrow, 1969) **(B670)**; Robert M. Calhoon, *The Loyalists in revolutionary America, 1760–1781* (New York: HBJ, 1973) **(B671)**; and Bernard Bailyn's biography of the governor of colonial Massachusetts, *The ordeal of Thomas Hutchinson* (Cambridge, Mass.: Harvard Univ. Pr., 1974) **(B672)**.

There have been several works on the foreign policy of the period. For emphasis on ideological factors, see Paul A. Varg, *Foreign policies of the Founding Fathers* (East Lansing: Michigan State Univ. Pr., 1963) **(B673)**. The standard work on the wartime era remains Samuel F. Bemis, *The diplomacy of the American Revolution* (New York: Appleton-Century, 1935) **(B674)**, but also see: Richard W. Van Alstyne, *Empire and independence: the international history of the American Revolution* (New York: Wiley, 1965) **(B675)**; Richard B. Morris' study of the Paris peace talks, *The peacemakers: the great powers and American independence* (New York: Har-

per, 1965) **(B676)**, and Gerald Stourzh's examination of *Benjamin Franklin and American foreign policy* (Chicago: Univ. of Chicago Pr., 1954) **(B677)**. For the making of the Franco-American Treaty of 1778, see William C. Stinchcombe, *The American Revolution and the French alliance* (Syracuse, N. Y.: Syracuse Univ. Pr., 1969) **(B678)**.

The culmination of the revolutionary era, the making of the United States Constitution, has drawn considerable attention and has caused great controversy among historians. Gordon S. Wood, *The creation of the American Republic, 1776–1787* (Chapel Hill: Univ. of North Carolina Pr., 1969) **(B679)**, examines the establishment of state governments, and shows how Americans formed a "mixed government" that achieved a balance among the three branches of government to control man's worst passions. John Fiske, *The critical period of American history, 1783–1789* (Boston: Houghton, 1888) **(B680)**, examines the era under the Articles of Confederation and calls attention to the weaknesses of the national government in dealing with the economic depression at home and the external threats from Britain and Spain. Merrill Jensen has offered important correctives to Fiske's dire assessment of the period. In *The new nation: a history of the United States during the Confederation, 1781–1789* (New York: Knopf, 1950) **(B681)**, Jensen argues that the Confederation period was a time of postwar adjustment, and in his other study of the period, *The Articles of Confederation* (Madison: Univ. of Wisconsin Pr., 1940; new preface, 1959) **(B682)**, he cites accomplishments such as the Northwest Ordinances of 1785 and 1787. On the drafting of the Constitution, one of the most solid accounts of the Philadelphia proceedings still is Max Farrand's *The framing of the Constitution of the United States* (New Haven, Conn.: Yale Univ. Pr., 1913) **(B683)**, although one should also consult colorful accounts by Catherine D. Bowen, *Miracle at Philadelphia: the story of the Constitutional Convention, May to September, 1787* (Boston: Little, 1966) **(B684)**, and Clinton L. Rossiter, *1787: The grand convention* (New York: Macmillan, 1966) **(B685)**.

Controversy began over the Constitution itself with the publication of Charles A. Beard's *An economic interpretation of the Constitution of the United States* (New York: Macmillan, 1913) **(B686)**. Writing in the Progressive reform era in America, Beard argues that the Constitution was "an economic document drawn with superb skill by men whose property interests were immediately at stake." Conservative economic interests, he continued, sought to discard the decentralized form of government under the Articles of Confederation because it endangered their properties. Robert E. Brown, in *Charles Beard and the Constitution: a critical analysis of "An Economic Interpretation of the Constitution"* (Princeton, N. J.: Princeton Univ. Pr., 1956) **(B687)**, is sharply critical of Beard's thesis. Brown finds "absolutely no correlation" between the Philadelphia delegates with economic interests at stake and their stand on the Constitution. Forrest McDonald also has published a rebuttal of Beard. In *We the people: the economic origins of the Constitution* (Chicago: Univ. of Chicago Pr., 1958) **(B688)**, McDonald examines the debate between the Federalists and anti-Federalists and, like Brown, discovers no clear relation between private property interests and public positions on the Constitution. He does argue, however, that groups satisfied with their plight in life often opposed the Constitution, while those dissatisfied supported it. Beard has had supporters. Jackson Turner Main, *The antifederalists: critics of the Constitution, 1781–1788* (Chapel Hill: Univ. of North Carolina Pr., 1961) **(B689)**, focuses on the economic and social reasons for favoring the new system of government under the Constitution, and asserts that in general terms the proponents of the Constitution were from well-to-do classes who favored the social and economic status quo. But, Main insists, the lines of distinction were nowhere as rigid as Beard seemed to argue. In a work already cited, *The creation of the American Republic* (B679), Gordon S. Wood also downplays the economic factors while arguing that distinct social differences became preponderant in the debate over the state constitutions advocated in the 1770s and 1780s and then manifested themselves again during the debates over the Constitution itself. Thus, according to Wood, the major determinant in the Constitutional struggle was domestic stability and order, not economic interests or ideals.

The Early Republic, 1789–1825

The Federalist period in American history, which encompasses the presidencies of George Washington and John Adams from 1789 to 1801, has drawn much attention among historians. Good surveys include: Marcus Cunliffe, *The nation takes shape: 1789–1837* (Chicago: Univ. of Chicago Pr., 1959) **(B690)**, written from a British historian's perspective; John C. Miller, *The Federalist era, 1789–1801* (New York: Harper, 1960) **(B691)**, a solid work; Charles M. Wiltse, *The new nation, 1800–1845* (New York: Hill & Wang, 1961; recently revised by John Mayfield) **(B692)**, also useful; and an administrative history of the new government by Leonard D. White, *The Federalists: a study in administrative history, 1789–1801* (New York: Macmillan, 1948) **(B693)**. Cunliffe also has examined the myths around Washington. In *George Washington: man and monument* (Boston: Little, 1958) **(B694)**, he concludes that it is futile to try to separate the "man" from the "monument." Forrest McDonald has written a book on *The presidency of George Washington* (Lawrence: Univ. Pr. of Kansas, 1974) **(B695)**. Among the numerous biographical accounts of the first president, the most solid works include: Douglas S. Freeman, *George Washington: a biography*, 7v. (New York: Scribner, 1948–57) **(B696)**, and James T. Flexner, *George Washington: a biography*, 4v. (Boston: Little, 1965–72) **(B697)**. Also helpful is Flexner's one-volume abridgment of his longer study, *Washington: the indispensable man* (Boston: Little, 1969) **(B698)**.

For other aspects of the early republic, see Russel B. Nye, *The cultural life of the new nation, 1776–1830* (New York: Harper, 1960) **(B699)**, and Lawrence A. Cremin, *American education: the national experience, 1783–1876* (New York: Harper, 1981) **(B700)**. Economic studies include: Thomas C. Cochran and William Miller, *The age of enterprise: a social history of industrial America*, rev. ed. (New York: Harper, 1961) **(B701)**, a longtime standard; George R. Taylor, *The transportation revolution, 1815–1860* (New York: Holt, 1951) **(B702)**, which shows the economic impact of America's revolution in transportation; two important studies by Douglass C. North, *The economic growth of the United States, 1790–1860* (Englewood Cliffs, N. J.: Prentice-Hall, 1961) **(B703)**, and *Growth and welfare in the American past: a new economic history*, rev. ed. (Englewood Cliffs, N. J.: Prentice-Hall, 1974) **(B704)**; and Stuart Bruchey, *The roots of American economic growth, 1607–1861: an essay in social causation* (New York: Harper, 1965) **(B705)**, provide sound introductions to the beginnings of industrialization in America.

The origins of political parties in the United States was one of many important developments of the Federalist era. For this subject, see: Joseph M. Charles, *The origins of the American party system* (Williamsburg, Va.: The Institute of Early American History and Culture, 1956) **(B706)**; Noble E. Cunningham, Jr., *The Jeffersonian Republicans: the formation of party organization, 1789–1801* (Chapel Hill: Univ. of North Carolina Pr., 1957) **(B707)**; William N. Chambers, *Political parties in a new nation: the American experience, 1776–1809* (New York: Oxford Univ. Pr., 1963) **(B708)**; Morton Borden, *Parties and politics in the early Republic, 1789–1815* (New York: Crowell, 1967) **(B709)**; and Richard Hofstadter, *The idea of a party system: the rise of legitimate opposition in the United States, 1780–1840* (Berkeley: Univ. of California Pr., 1969) **(B710)**. In a controversial study by Charles A. Beard, *Economic origins of Jeffersonian democracy* (New York: Macmillan, 1915) **(B711)**, he argues that Jeffersonians in the Federalist era were extensions of the anti-Federalists, or the agricultural spokesmen of the 1780s.

The two major protagonists of the period were Alexander Hamilton and Thomas Jefferson. On Hamilton and Federalist thought, see John C. Miller, *Alexander Hamilton and the growth of the new nation* (New York: Harper, 1964) **(B712)**; Forrest McDonald, *Alexander Hamilton: a biography* (New York: Norton, 1979) **(B713)**; and Jacob E. Cooke, *Alexander Hamilton* (New York: Scribner, 1982) **(B714)**. On Jefferson and Republican thought, see the monumental study by Dumas Malone, *Jefferson and his time*, 6v. (Boston: Little, 1948–81) **(B715)**, which is, as near as seems possible, the definitive study of the subject. But also see: Adrienne Koch, *The philosophy of Thomas Jefferson* (New York: Columbia Univ. Pr., 1943) **(B716)**, which is particularly useful on the Kentucky and Virginia resolutions; Daniel J. Boorstin, *The lost world of Thomas Jefferson* (New York: Holt, 1948) **(B717)**, which is a sound description of the intellectual atmosphere of the period; Merrill D. Peterson's two works: *The Jeffersonian image in the American mind* (New York: Oxford Univ. Pr., 1960) **(B718)**, and *Thomas Jefferson and the new nation: a biography* (New York: Oxford Univ. Pr., 1970) **(B719)**. In *The beginnings of American foreign policy: to the Farewell Address* (New York: Harper, 1965) **(B720)**, Felix Gilbert highlights the role of Hamilton in formulating Washington's Farewell Address of 1796, which warned against the formation of political parties and the establishment of permanent entangling alliances.

Washington's successor receives attention in Stephen G. Kurtz, *The presidency of John Adams: the collapse of Federalism, 1795–1800* (Philadelphia: Univ. of Pennsylvania Pr., 1957) **(B721)**; Gilbert Chinard, *Honest John Adams* (Boston: Little, 1933) **(B722)**; and Page Smith, *John Adams*, 2v. (Garden City, N.Y.: Doubleday, 1962) **(B723)**. For the alien and sedition law controversy, see John C. Miller, *Crisis in freedom: The Alien and Sedition Acts* (Boston: Lit-

tle, 1951) **(B724)**, and James M. Smith, *Freedom's fetters: the alien and sedition laws and American civil liberties* (Ithaca, N.Y.: Cornell Univ. Pr., 1956) **(B725)**.

The Republican presidencies of Thomas Jefferson, James Madison, and James Monroe, from 1801 to 1825, also were characterized by deep party division inside the United States. For the classic account of the political aspects of the period, see Henry Adams, *History of the United States of America during the administrations of Thomas Jefferson and of James Madison*, 9v. (New York: Scribner, 1889–91) **(B726)**. Marshall Smelser's *The Democratic Republic, 1801–1815* (New York: Harper, 1968) **(B727)** is a sprightly survey. For Jefferson's struggle with the slavery question, see John C. Miller, *The wolf by the ears: Thomas Jefferson and slavery* (New York: Macmillan, 1977) **(B728)**. Bernard W. Sheehan explores the Jeffersonians' attitudes and policies toward the Indians in *Seeds of extinction: Jeffersonian philanthropy and the American Indian* (Chapel Hill: Univ. of North Carolina Pr., 1973) **(B729)**. For Jefferson's two terms as president, see Noble E. Cunningham, Jr., *The Jeffersonian Republicans in power: party operations, 1801–1809* (Chapel Hill: Univ. of North Carolina Pr., 1963) **(B730)**. The standard biography of Madison is Irving Brant, *James Madison*, 6v. (Indianapolis: Bobbs-Merrill, 1941–61) **(B731)**. On Monroe, see Harry Ammon, *James Monroe and the quest for national identity* (New York: McGraw-Hill, 1971) **(B732)**. For other domestic aspects of the period, see George Dangerfield's two masterfully written studies: *The era of good feelings* (New York: Harcourt, Brace, 1952) **(B733)**, an account of the Monroe presidency and the growth of nationalism inside the United States, and *The awakening of American nationalism, 1815–1828* (New York: Harper, 1965) **(B734)**, a valuable survey of the period following the War of 1812 and continuing through the presidency of John Quincy Adams.

Other subjects have drawn attention. Frederick Jackson Turner highlights the *Rise of the new West, 1819–1829* (New York: Harper, 1906) **(B735)** in the early nineteenth century, and in *The frontier in American history* (New York: Holt, 1920) **(B736)** argues that the Western frontier was a major impetus to democracy and nationalism in the United States. For disagreement with Turner's thesis, see Francis S. Philbrick, *The rise of the West, 1754–1830* (New York: Harper, 1965) **(B737)**. The starting point for examining the Missouri crisis of 1820 is still Glover Moore, *The Missouri controversy, 1819–1821* (Lexington: Univ. of Kentucky Pr., 1953)

(**B738**), who considers the episode a "rehearsal" for the American Civil War of four decades afterward. For the Supreme Court, see Albert J. Beveridge, *The life of John Marshall*, 4v. (Boston: Houghton, 1916–19) (**B739**), a monumental study of the chief justice's part in the important court decisions of the early nineteenth century; Maurice G. Baxter, *Daniel Webster and the Supreme Court* (Amherst: Univ. of Massachusetts Pr., 1966) (**B740**), a superb study of the famous Massachusetts lawyer's arguments before the court; and R. Kent Newmyer's useful and bibliographically oriented short account, *The Supreme Court under Marshall and Taney* (New York: Crowell, 1968) (**B741**). A solid scholarly treatment of the Marshall Court is found in Charles G. Haines, *The role of the Supreme Court in American government and politics, 1789–1835* (Berkeley: Univ. of California Pr., 1944) (**B742**).

Foreign affairs in the early Republic were inseparable from domestic matters. For a useful overview of the period before the War of 1812, see Lawrence S. Kaplan, *Colonies into nation: American diplomacy, 1763–1801* (New York: Macmillan, 1972) (**B743**). See also Paul A. Varg, *Foreign policies of the Founding Fathers* (B673). For specialized topics, see: Samuel F. Bemis' two major works, *Jay's treaty: a study in commerce and diplomacy*, rev. ed. (New Haven, Conn.: Yale Univ. Pr., 1962) (**B745**), and *Pinckney's treaty: America's advantage from Europe's distress, 1783–1800*, rev. ed. (New Haven, Conn.: Yale Univ. Pr., 1960) (**B746**), both demonstrating how America's diplomats exploited Europe's problems to achieve American objectives. Jerald A. Combs relates domestic politics to *The Jay treaty: political battleground of the Founding Fathers* (Berkeley: Univ. of California Pr., 1970) (**B747**). Bradford Perkins, *The first rapprochement: England and the United States, 1795–1805* (Philadelphia: Univ. of Pennsylvania Pr., 1955) (**B748**), focuses on the factors involved in the establishment of the first Anglo-American rapprochement in the decade following Jay's treaty. Harry Ammon analyzes the importance of *The Genet mission* (New York: Norton, 1973) (**B749**) in solidifying political party division during the Washington presidency. Alexander DeConde considers the impact of foreign entanglements on domestic affairs in *Entangling alliance: politics and diplomacy under George Washington* (Durham, N.C.: Duke Univ. Pr., 1958) (**B750**). DeConde then emphasizes America's problems with France during the Federalist presidency of John Adams in *The quasi-war: the politics and diplomacy of the undeclared war with France,*

1797–1801 (New York: Scribner, 1966) (**B751**). See also William C. Stinchcombe, *The XYZ affair* (Westport, Conn.: Greenwood, 1981) (**B752**). Brant's biography of Madison (B731) recounts Republican foreign policy, whereas DeConde focuses on the "imperialist thrust" as the basis of the Louisiana Purchase of 1803 and America's expansion west in *This affair of Louisiana* (Baton Rouge: Louisiana State Univ. Pr., 1976) (**B753**). Another useful study is Arthur P. Whitaker's *The Mississippi question, 1795–1803: a study in trade, politics, and diplomacy* (New York: Appleton-Century, 1934) (**B754**). For a colorful account of the Lewis and Clark expedition, see Bernard DeVoto, *The course of empire* (Boston: Houghton, 1952) (**B755**).

The War of 1812 has been the subject of numerous studies. For its causes, see: Julius W. Pratt, who argues that the *Expansionists of 1812* (New York: Macmillan, 1925) (**B756**) were interested in the Floridas and Canada; Reginald Horsman, *The causes of the War of 1812* (Philadelphia: Univ. of Pennsylvania Pr., 1962) (**B757**), who emphasizes maritime difficulties; Bradford Perkins, *Prologue to war: England and the United States, 1805–1812* (Berkeley: Univ. of California Pr., 1961) (**B758**), who also highlights maritime issues and relates them to America's drive for international respect; Alfred L. Burt, *The United States, Great Britain and British North America: from the Revolution to the establishment of peace after the war of 1812* (New Haven, Conn.: Yale Univ. Pr., 1940) (**B759**), a Canadian historian who shows how impressment insulted American sovereignty and was a central cause of the War of 1812; Roger H. Brown, *The Republic in peril: 1812* (New York: Columbia Univ. Pr., 1964) (**B760**), who notes that from the Republican party's point of view, the American republic was in danger both from England on the outside and from the monarchical-minded Federalists inside the United States. Failure to fight England, according to Brown, would have meant submission by the Republican party to domestic and foreign enemies and the collapse of the great republican experiment. Useful military accounts include: Harry L. Coles, *The War of 1812* (Chicago: Univ. of Chicago Pr., 1965) (**B761**), and Patrick C. T. White, *A nation on trial: America and the War of 1812* (New York: Wiley, 1965) (**B762**), who also covers the diplomatic aspects of the period.

The aftermath of the War of 1812 also has been the focus of many historians' work. For an overview, see Kenneth Bourne, *Britain and the balance of power in North America, 1815–1908* (Berkeley: Univ. of California Pr., 1967) (**B763**).

On the Monroe presidency, see Dangerfield's studies mentioned earlier in this section (B733, 734); also see Harry Ammon's biography of Monroe, cited earlier (B732). Samuel F. Bemis' *John Quincy Adams and the foundations of American foreign policy* (New York: Knopf, 1949) **(B764)** is the first volume of a major biography of the secretary of state whom the author calls the leading "continentalist" of the period. Bradford Perkins, *Castlereagh and Adams: England and the United States, 1812–1823* (Berkeley: Univ. of California Pr., 1964) **(B765)**, examines the war, the Ghent peace talks, and Anglo-American relations throughout the period, including the Monroe Doctrine, in his admirable study of the relationship between Adams and Britain's Lord Castlereagh. For the Monroe Doctrine, which is the subject of countless studies, see: Dexter Perkins, *A history of the Monroe Doctrine*, rev. ed. (Boston: Little, 1941) **(B766)**, still the standard work; Arthur P. Whitaker, *The United States and the independence of Latin America, 1800–1830* (Baltimore: Johns Hopkins Univ. Pr., 1941) **(B767)**, solid on the background of the Monroe Doctrine; and Ernest R. May, *The making of the Monroe Doctrine* (Cambridge, Mass.: Harvard Univ. Pr., 1975) **(B768)**, who attempts to relate the Monroe Doctrine to domestic political issues and the presidential election of 1824. For the broad picture, see Samuel F. Bemis, *The Latin American policy of the United States: an historical interpretation* (New York: Harcourt, Brace, 1943) **(B769)**.

The Age of Jackson, Slavery, and Reform, 1825–1840s

There are many useful surveys of this period so heavily marked by Andrew Jackson. George Dangerfield, *The awakening of American nationalism, 1815–1828* (B734), explains the nationalistic context for the rise of the folk hero. Glyndon G. Van Deusen, *The Jacksonian era, 1828–1848* (New York: Harper, 1959) **(B771)**, emphasizes, among other things, the ideological and social factors determining party allegiances. See also James C. Curtis, *Andrew Jackson and the search for vindication* (Boston: Little, 1976) **(B772)**. For a solid account of President John Quincy Adams' fight with the Jacksonians in Congress after his victory in the bitter presidential election of 1824, see Samuel F. Bemis, *John Quincy Adams and the union* (New York: Knopf, 1956) **(B773)**. Charles M. Wiltse, *The new nation, 1800–1845* (B692), recently revised

by John Mayfield, is still helpful, as is Leonard D. White, *The Jacksonians: a study in administrative history, 1829–1861* (New York: Macmillan, 1954) **(B775)**. On Jackson, see: Robert V. Remini's three-volume biography, *Andrew Jackson and the course of American empire: 1767–1821* (New York: Harper, 1977) **(B776)**, *Andrew Jackson and the course of American freedom: 1822–1832* (New York: Harper, 1981) **(B777)**, and *Andrew Jackson and the course of American democracy: 1833–1845* (New York: Harper, 1984) **(B778)**; and Marquis James' old but still useful, entertaining, and beautifully written two-volume biography, *Andrew Jackson: the border captain* (New York: Literary Guild, 1933) **(B779)**, and *Andrew Jackson: portrait of a president* (Indianapolis: Bobbs-Merrill, 1937) **(B780)**. On social, political, and cultural life of Jacksonian America, see: Alexis de Tocqueville, *Democracy in America*, 2v. (1835) **(B781)**, which appears in numerous editions and is the classic examination based on first-hand observations; and two detailed studies by Russel B. Nye—*The cultural life of the new nation, 1776–1830* (described at B699), and *Society and culture in America, 1830–1860* (New York, Harper, 1974) **(B783)**.

The economic growth of the period is the subject of several works. Among these, see: Stuart Bruchey, *The roots of American economic growth, 1607–1861: an essay in social causation* (B705); two studies by Douglass C. North—*The economic growth of the United States, 1790–1860* (B703), and *Growth and welfare in the American past: a new economic history*, rev. ed. (B704); Thomas C. Cochran and William Miller, *The age of enterprise: a social history of industrial America*, rev. ed. (B701); Paul W. Gates, *The farmer's age: agriculture, 1815–1860* (New York: Holt, 1960) **(B788)**; George R. Taylor, *The transportation revolution, 1815–1860* (B702); and Norman Ware, *The industrial worker, 1840–1860: the reaction of American industrial society to the advance of the Industrial Revolution* (Boston: Houghton, 1924) **(B790)**.

Historians still disagree over the myth and the reality of Jacksonian democracy. Two studies by Frederick Jackson Turner emphasize the role of the West in promoting democracy. In *Rise of the new West, 1819–1829* (B735) and *The frontier in American history* (B736), Turner argues that Jackson spoke for frontiersmen who advocated freedom of opportunity and fought entrenched conservative interests from the East. Arthur M. Schlesinger, Jr., *The age of Jackson* (Boston: Little, 1945) **(B791)**, agrees with Turner in praising Jackson as the source of a political democracy that emphasized equal opportunity. But instead of finding the origins of Jacksonian Democracy in the West, Schlesinger argues that it emanated from a class conflict whereby the Jacksonians drew Eastern labor support and tried to place restrictions on wealthy Eastern capitalists for the good of the "common man" throughout the nation. Lee Benson, *The concept of Jacksonian democracy: New York as a test case* (Princeton, N.J.: Princeton Univ. Pr., 1961) **(B792)**, offers a quantitative study of political parties in New York, in which he disagrees with Schlesinger by discerning no substantial differences between the Jacksonians and others. According to Benson, all parties favored increasing equality of opportunity and participatory democracy. Only local and cultural concerns distinguished one party from another; thus the period was not the Age of Jackson, but the Age of Egalitarianism. Marvin Meyers, *The Jacksonian persuasion: politics and belief* (Stanford, Calif.: Stanford Univ. Pr., 1957) **(B793)**, emphasizes the ideological basis of Jacksonian democracy. The Jacksonians, he claims, regarded the new industrial America with suspicion and sought a return to the agrarian republicanism of the Jeffersonian period. The "image" of Jackson is also important in John W. Ward, *Andrew Jackson—symbol for an age* (New York: Oxford Univ. Pr., 1953) **(B794)**.

Not all historians emphasize ideological factors. Richard Hofstadter disagrees with those who highlighted democracy in the period. In *The American political tradition and the men who made it* (New York: Knopf, 1948) **(B795)**, he regards Jackson as the leader of a new and rising business class that sought to break the Eastern aristocracy's monopolistic control of the economy. Bray Hammond, *Banks and politics in America from the Revolution to the Civil War* (Princeton, N.J.: Princeton Univ. Pr., 1957) **(B796)**, agrees with Hofstadter and uses the struggle over the Second Bank of the United States as evidence of a rising capitalist group trying to break the hold of others. According to Robert V. Remini, *Andrew Jackson and the bank war* (New York: Norton, 1967) **(B797)**, the battle over the bank was political and personal in nature, as Jackson took on opponents he believed used the bank's funds to try to defeat his bid for the presidency. Edward M. Pessen, *Jacksonian America: society, personality, and politics*, rev. ed. (Homewood, Ill.: Dorsey Pr., 1978) **(B798)**, argues that social and economic considerations were more important than political party denominations in understanding the period. The mid-nineteenth century, Pessen insists, was a period of *inequality*. Richard P. McCormick, *The second American party system: party formation in the Jacksonian era* (Chapel Hill: Univ. of North Carolina Pr., 1966) **(B799)**, analyzes party politics and agrees with Glyndon G. Van Deusen, *The Jacksonian era, 1828–1848* (B771), that local and personal considerations were more important than social and ideological factors in determining loyalties.

Many emotional issues arose during the Jackson presidency. For the controversy over states' rights in South Carolina, see William W. Freehling, *Prelude to civil war: the nullification controversy in South Carolina, 1816–1836* (New York: Harper, 1965) **(B800)**, an admirable study that argues that South Carolinians feared the tariff of 1828 as a precedent for federal intervention into the realm of states' rights that would eventually lead to antislavery legislation. Jackson's Indian policy has not drawn a favorable press. See: Arthur H. DeRosier, Jr., *The removal of the Choctaw Indians* (Knoxville: Univ. of Tennessee Pr., 1970) **(B801)**; Ronald N. Satz, *American Indian policy in the Jacksonian era* (Lincoln: Univ. of Nebraska Pr., 1975) **(B802)**; and Michael P. Rogin, *Fathers and children: Andrew Jackson and the subjugation of the American Indian* (New York: Knopf, 1975) **(B803)**, the last of which is a psychohistorical study of Jackson.

Perhaps the most profound development of the Jacksonian era was the rapid growth of slavery in the South. Winthrop D. Jordan, *White over black: American attitudes toward the Negro, 1550–1812* (Chapel Hill: Univ. of North Carolina Pr., 1968) **(B804)**, argues that American slavery had its origins in the Western tradition—that Europe had long regarded black Africans as inferior to whites. Thus American slavery derived from white racism. David B. Davis, *The problem of slavery in Western culture* (Ithaca, N.Y.: Cornell Univ. Pr., 1966) **(B805)**, also asserts that American slavery developed as part of Western culture and was therefore not much different from the institutions found in other societies. Edmund S. Morgan, *American slavery, American freedom: the ordeal of colonial Virginia* (New York: Norton, 1975) **(B806)**, focuses on colonial Virginia in showing that Americans did not purposely establish slavery; instead, he argues, the thriving tobacco industry created a demand for cheap labor that for ideological and economic reasons was suited better for blacks than whites. Although the African slave trade had been abolished by both the United States and England in 1807, it managed to survive throughout the period and afterward. On this subject, see: W.E.B. DuBois, *The suppression of the African slave-trade to the United States of America, 1638–1870* (New York: Longman, Green, 1896) (**B807**); Daniel P. Mannix and Malcolm Cowley, *Black cargoes: a history of the Atlantic slave trade, 1518–1865* (New York: Viking, 1962) (**B808**); Peter Duignan and Clarence Clendenen, *The United States and the African slave trade, 1619–1862* (Stanford, Calif.: Stanford Univ. Pr., 1962) (**B809**); and Warren S. Howard, *American slavers and the Federal law, 1837–1862* (Berkeley: Univ. of California Pr., 1963) (**B810**). For a statistical study, see Philip D. Curtin, *The Atlantic slave trade: a census* (Madison: Univ. of Wisconsin Pr., 1969) (**B811**).

Arguments still continue over many aspects of the institution of slavery in the antebellum South. Ulrich B. Phillips, *American Negro slavery* (New York: Appleton, 1918) (**B812**), presents an apologetic survey of American slavery in which he argues that blacks were happy with the institution, and that whites, having established a system of labor and social control, had time for other pursuits in life. Slavery, Phillips insisted, was economically unprofitable but socially beneficial as a means of race control. Herbert Aptheker, *Negro slave revolts in the United States, 1526–1860* (New York: International Pub., 1939) (**B813**), disagrees with Phillips' view by arguing that blacks retained their African heritage, that they were not contented with the institution of slavery, and that an almost continuous strain of rebelliousness characterized the system. On the most famous slave revolt of the antebellum South, see Stephen B. Oates, *The fires of jubilee: Nat Turner's fierce rebellion* (New York: Harper, 1975) (**B814**). Another staunch opponent of the Phillips interpretation is Kenneth M. Stampp, who in *The peculiar institution: slavery in the ante-bellum South* (New York: Knopf, 1956) (**B815**), regards slavery as economically profitable and highly cruel—both physically and psychologically. Slaves, he insists, were generally rebellious; if not often rising in revolt, they at least tried to obstruct work on the plantation. Stanley M. Elkins, *Slavery: a problem in American institutional and intellectual life* (Chicago: Univ. of Chicago Pr., 1959) (**B816**), caused widespread indignation among blacks during the 1960s when he argued that slavery created a "Sambo-like" being—childlike and submissive and having lost all African identity. According to Elkins, this situation resulted from an institution that was similar to the Nazis' concentration camps during World War II in which the psychological impact was to blur all sense of identity among captive Jews. John W. Blassingame, *The slave community: plantation life in the antebellum South*, rev. ed. (New York: Oxford Univ. Pr., 1979) (**B817**), argues that America's slaves retained their African past and made notable social and cultural achievements. Though Blassingame admits that it is difficult to generalize about the slaves' character, he believes that most male slaves hated bondage and would attempt to escape when the opportunity arose. Another book that aroused great controversy was that by Robert W. Fogel and Stanley L. Engerman, *Time on the cross: the economics of American Negro slavery* (Boston: Little, 1974) (**B818**). According to this quantitative study, slaves were good workers, the black family remained intact, and slavery itself was beneficial for both blacks and whites. Treatment of slaves was fair and the overall conditions of the institution were better than those of industrial laborers in the North.

The institution of slavery has caused other controversies as well. A slant different from Fogel's and Engerman's appears in the works of Eugene D. Genovese. In *Roll, Jordan, roll: the world the slaves made* (New York: Random, 1972) (**B819**), he notes the paternal nature of slavery in showing how whites maintained rigid control over blacks. But instead of whites being the system's sole benefactor, Genovese declares, blacks maintained a type of life that enabled them to retain their traditions and cultural life. In a real sense, he asserts, the slaves had come to consider themselves as a distinct "nation" by the middle of the nineteenth century. In two of his other works, *The political economy of slavery: studies in the economy and society of the slave South* (New York: Random, 1965) (**B820**), and *The world the slaveholders made: two essays in interpretation* (New York: Random, 1969) (**B821**), Genovese argues that slavery retarded the industrial development of the South by helping to prevent the establishment of a substantial middle class. Herbert G. Gutman, *The black family in slavery and freedom, 1750–1925* (New York: Random, 1976) (**B822**), argues that the black family held together extremely well under slavery. For blacks in the North, see Leon F. Litwack, *North of slavery: the negro in the free states, 1790–1860* (Chicago: Univ. of Chicago Pr., 1961) (**B823**).

The Jacksonian period was an age of reform. For the standard survey of this reform spirit, see Alice Felt Tyler, *Freedom's ferment: phases of American social history from the colonial period to the outbreak of the Civil War* (Minneapolis: Univ. of Minnesota Pr., 1944) (**B824**). See also: Whitney R. Cross, *The burned-over district: the social and intellectual history of enthusiastic reli-*

gion in western New York, 1800–1850 (Ithaca, N.Y.: Cornell Univ. Pr., 1950) (**B825**); C.S. Griffin, *The ferment of reform, 1830–1860* (New York: Crowell, 1967) (**B826**); and Daniel J. Boorstin, *The Americans: the national experience* (New York: Random, 1965) (**B827**). There are many fine studies of antislavery sentiment during this period. Gilbert H. Barnes, *The antislavery impulse, 1830–1844* (New York: Appleton-Century, 1933) (**B828**), emphasizes the leadership of Theodore Dwight Weld in a work favorable to the abolitionists, those who wanted immediate emancipation of the slaves without compensation to their owners. See also: Louis Filler, *The crusade against slavery, 1830–1860* (New York: Harper, 1960) (**B829**), a survey of the antislavery and abolitionist movements; and Aileen S. Kraditor, *Means and ends in American abolitionism: Garrison and his critics on strategy and tactics, 1834–1850* (New York: Random, 1967) (**B830**), an important and favorable examination of William Lloyd Garrison, founder of the Boston *Liberator* and the first major abolitionist in the United States. In this connection, see Russel B. Nye, *William Lloyd Garrison and the humanitarian reformers* (Boston: Little, 1955) (**B831**).

Manifest Destiny and the Disruption of the Union, 1840s–1861

Among the best surveys of the period are: James G. Randall and David H. Donald, *The Civil War and Reconstruction*, rev. ed. (Lexington, Mass.: Heath, 1969) (**B832**); James M. McPherson, *Ordeal by fire: the Civil War and Reconstruction* (New York: Knopf, 1982) (**B833**); Allan Nevins, *Ordeal of the Union*, 8v. (New York: Scribner, 1947–71) (**B834**); Roy F. Nichols, *The disruption of American democracy* (New York: Macmillan, 1948) (**B835**); Avery Craven, *The coming of the Civil War*, rev. ed. (Chicago: Univ. of Chicago Pr., 1957) (**B836**); David M. Potter, *The impending crisis, 1848–1861* (New York: Harper, 1976) (**B837**); and Ray A. Billington, *The Far Western frontier, 1830–1860* (New York: Harper, 1956) (**B838**).

The antebellum South has drawn considerable interest. Wilbur J. Cash, *The mind of the South* (New York: Knopf, 1941) (**B839**), attempts to explain why the South was different from the rest of the nation, whereas Charles S. Sydnor explores *The development of Southern sectionalism, 1819–1848* (Baton Rouge: Louisiana State Univ. Pr., 1948) (**B840**). Avery Craven comes from a different direction by highlighting the

political, social, and cultural ingredients involved in *The growth of Southern nationalism, 1848–1861* (Baton Rouge: Louisiana State Univ. Pr., 1953) (**B841**). David M. Potter, *The South and the sectional conflict* (Baton Rouge: Louisiana State Univ. Pr., 1968) (**B842**), is also first-rate. Clement Eaton has contributed three valuable studies of the period: *The freedom-of-thought struggle in the Old South* (New York: Harper, 1964) (**B843**); *The growth of Southern civilization, 1790–1860* (New York: Harper, 1961) (**B844**), which focuses on the intellectual history of the region; and *The mind of the Old South*, rev. ed. (Baton Rouge: Louisiana State Univ. Pr., 1967) (**B845**). John Hope Franklin, *The militant South, 1800–1861* (Cambridge, Mass.: Harvard Univ. Pr., 1956) (**B846**), emphasizes the tradition of violence in the South, whereas John McCardell, *The idea of a Southern nation: Southern nationalists and Southern nationalism, 1830–1860* (New York: Norton, 1979) (**B847**), examines the social and intellectual bases of Southern nationalism. See also Bertram Wyatt-Brown, *Southern honor* (New York: Oxford Univ. Pr., 1982) (**B848**).

The diplomacy of the 1840s also has attracted much interest among historians. Albert B. Corey, *The crisis of 1830–1842 in Canadian-American relations* (New Haven, Conn.: Carnegie Endowment for International Peace, 1941) (**B849**), is strong on the border troubles that preceded the signing of the Webster-Ashburton Treaty in 1842. Howard Jones, *To the Webster-Ashburton Treaty: a study in Anglo-American relations, 1783–1843* (Chapel Hill: Univ. of North Carolina Pr., 1977) (**B850**), emphasizes Webster's successful compromises of the Maine boundary and other disputes that led to a mid-nineteenth-century rapprochement between England and the United States, which in turn permitted Americans to turn their goals westward. On manifest destiny, the starting point for its intellectual base remains Albert K. Weinberg, *Manifest destiny: a study of nationalist expansionism in American history* (Baltimore: Johns Hopkins Univ. Pr., 1935) (**B851**), but Frederick Merk has written several important studies touching upon the subject: *Manifest destiny and mission in American history: a reinterpretation* (New York: Random, 1963) (**B852**) examines the expansionist drive; *The Monroe Doctrine and American expansionism, 1843–1849* (New York: Random, 1966) (**B853**) relates the Monroe Doctrine to the expansionist impulse; and *Slavery and the annexation of Texas* (New York: Knopf, 1972) (**B854**) examines the intricate relationship between two of the biggest issues of the period. William H. Goetzmann, *Exploration and* empire: the explorer and the scientist in the winning of the American West (New York: Random, 1966) **(B855)**, shows the impact of explorers and scientists in America's expansionism, whereas Norman A. Graebner, *Empire on the Pacific: a study in American continental expansion* (New York: Ronald, 1955) **(B856)**, examines the commercial motives behind America's Western interests.

Other useful studies on the American West include: Walter P. Webb, *The Great Plains* (New York: Ginn, 1931) **(B857)**, a standard work; R. Carlyle Buley, *The old Northwest: pioneer period, 1815–1840*, 2v. (Bloomington: Indiana Univ. Pr., 1950) **(B858)**; Oscar O. Winther, *The great Northwest: a history*, rev. ed. (New York: Knopf, 1960) **(B859)**; and three studies by Bernard DeVoto—*Year of decision, 1846* (Boston: Little, 1943) **(B860)**, *Across the wide Missouri* (Boston: Houghton, 1947) **(B861)**, and *The course of empire* (B755). Also insightful is the classic account of America's migration to the Pacific—Francis Parkman, *Oregon Trail* (1849) **(B863)**, which is available in many editions. On the Mormons, see: Nels Anderson, *Desert saints: the Mormon frontier in Utah* (Chicago: Univ. of Chicago Pr., 1942) **(B864)**; Thomas F. O'Dea, *The Mormons* (Chicago: Univ. of Chicago Pr., 1957) **(B865)**; Norman F. Furniss, *The Mormon conflict, 1850–1859* (New Haven, Conn.: Yale Univ. Pr., 1960) **(B866)**; Robert Mullen, *The Latter-Day Saints: the Mormons yesterday and today* (Garden City, N.Y.: Doubleday, 1966) **(B867)**; and Leonard J. Arrington and Davis Bitton, *The Mormon experience: a history of the Latter-Day Saints* (New York: Random, 1979) **(B868)**. Richard C. Wade discusses the growth of frontier cities in *The urban frontier: the rise of Western cities, 1790–1830* (Cambridge, Mass.: Harvard Univ. Pr., 1959) **(B869)**.

President James K. Polk and the Mexican War have been the focus of several studies. For Polk, see Charles G. Sellers, *James K. Polk: continentalist, 1843–1846* (Princeton, N.J.: Princeton Univ. Pr., 1966) **(B870)**, who examines the president's role in the expansionist 1840s. David M. Pletcher, *The diplomacy of annexation: Texas, Oregon, and the Mexican War* (Columbia: Univ. of Missouri Pr., 1973) **(B871)**, is a masterful demonstration of how President Polk, who did not want a war with either Britain or Mexico, followed a series of provocative policies that escalated the United States into a near war with England over Oregon and into war with Mexico over Texas and California. John H. Schroeder is heavily critical of the president in *Mr. Polk's war: American opposition and dissent, 1846–1848* (Madison: Univ. of Wisconsin Pr., 1973)

(B872). For the Mexican side of the dispute, see Gene M. Brack, *Mexico views manifest destiny, 1821–1846: an essay on the origins of the Mexican War* (Albuquerque: Univ. of New Mexico Pr., 1975) **(B873)**. On the war itself, see: Justin H. Smith's old but still important work, *War with Mexico*, 2v. (New York: Macmillan, 1919) **(B874)**; Otis A. Singletary's brief but useful study, *The Mexican War* (Chicago: Univ. of Chicago Pr., 1960) **(B875)**; Seymour V. Connor and Odie B. Faulk, *North America divided: the Mexican War, 1846–1848* (New York: Oxford Univ. Pr., 1971) **(B876)**; and K. Jack Bauer, *The Mexican-American War, 1846–1848* (New York: Macmillan, 1974) **(B877)**.

The turbulent decade of the 1850s in the United States has stimulated many fine works. Holman Hamilton, *Prologue to conflict: the crisis and Compromise of 1850* (Lexington: Univ. of Kentucky Pr., 1964) **(B878)**, emphasizes the role of Stephen A. Douglas in pushing the Compromise through the Senate. For specific subjects during the decade, see: Stanley W. Campbell, *The slave catchers: enforcement of the Fugitive Slave Law, 1850–1860* (Chapel Hill: Univ. of North Carolina Pr., 1968) **(B879)**; James A. Rawley, *Race and politics: "Bleeding Kansas" and the coming of the Civil War* (New York: Lippincott, 1969) **(B880)**, who emphasizes "race" over slavery as the essential ingredient in the Kansas crisis; Stephen B. Oates, *To purge this land with blood: a biography of John Brown* (New York: Harper, 1970) **(B881)**, a first-rate biography; Don E. Fehrenbacher, *The Dred Scott case: its significance in American law and politics* (New York: Oxford Univ. Pr., 1978) **(B882)**, a model work on the monumental Supreme Court decision of 1857; Robert E. May, *The Southern dream of a Caribbean empire, 1854–1861* (Baton Rouge: Louisiana State Univ. Pr., 1973) **(B883)**, a solid analysis of the Cuban question and others that shows the impact of slavery in obstructing America's expansion south; Stephen A. Channing, *Crisis of fear: secession in South Carolina* (New York: Norton, 1970) **(B884)**, a sound study; David M. Potter, *Lincoln and his party in the secession crisis* (New Haven, Conn.: Yale Univ. Pr., 1942) **(B885)**, which focuses on the last days before the war broke out; and Kenneth M. Stampp, *And the war came: the North and the secession crisis, 1860–61* (Baton Rouge: Louisiana State Univ. Pr., 1950) **(B886)**, which raises the question of what might have happened had the North not resisted secession.

The leading personalities of the period have been the subjects of numerous studies. For Clay, see Glyndon G. Van Deusen, *The life of Henry*

Clay (Boston: Little, 1937) (**B887**), which is a biography of the Kentucky statesman instrumental in several political compromises during the early and mid-nineteenth century, including the Missouri Compromise, Compromise of 1833, and Compromise of 1850. See also Clement Eaton, *Henry Clay and the art of American politics* (Boston: Little, 1957) (**B888**). Charles M. Wiltse, *John C. Calhoun*, 3v. (Indianapolis: Bobbs-Merrill, 1944–51) (**B889**), traces the South Carolinian from his early years as a nationalist to his change into a sectionalist. Also on Calhoun, see: Margaret L. Coit, *John C. Calhoun: American portrait* (Boston: Houghton, 1950) (**B890**), and Gerald M. Capers, *John C. Calhoun—opportunist: a reappraisal* (Gainesville: Univ. of Florida Pr., 1960) (**B891**). Other leading works include: Richard N. Current, *Daniel Webster and the rise of national conservatism* (Boston: Little, 1955) (**B892**); Robert F. Dalzell, Jr., *Daniel Webster and the trial of American nationalism, 1843–1852* (Boston: Houghton, 1973) (**B893**); Robert W. Johannsen, *Stephen A. Douglas* (New York: Knopf, 1973) (**B894**); Gerald M. Capers, *Stephen A. Douglas: defender of the Union* (Boston: Little, 1959) (**B895**); and David H. Donald, *Charles Sumner and the coming of the Civil War* (New York: Knopf, 1960) (**B896**), which is particularly strong on the "Sumner-Brooks affair" of 1856.

Civil War and Reconstruction, 1861–1877

There are several fine surveys of this tumultuous period. Allan Nevins, *The ordeal of the Union* (B834) is a monumental work that, among other attributes, traces the emergence of Lincoln to national prominence. James G. Randall and David H. Donald, *The Civil War and Reconstruction* (B832), and James M. McPherson, *Ordeal by fire: the Civil War and Reconstruction* (B833), are superb analyses of the breakup of the Union and the period after the war.

For the war's causes, see Thomas J. Pressly, *Americans interpret their Civil War* (Princeton, N.J.: Princeton Univ. Pr., 1954) (**B897**), which describes the "confusion of voices" in trying to understand the causes of the Civil War. James Ford Rhodes' *History of the United States from the Compromise of 1850*, 9v. (New York: Macmillan, 1892–1928) (**B898**), is the first scholarly study of the war. Rhodes argues that the moral issue of slavery was the central cause of the war; no compromise was possible, making the war "inevitable." Charles A. and Mary Beard, *The rise of American civilization*, 2v. (New York: Macmillan, 1927) (**B899**), assert that economic differences between North and South caused "inherent antagonisms" over slavery, states' rights, and other matters to make the war one over the protection of self-interest. Avery Craven, *The coming of the Civil War*, rev. ed. (B836), presents a "revisionist" view in declaring that the war could have been averted by compromise. Slavery, he insists, would have collapsed on its own had it not become part of the political arena. But conflict developed over the Southern argument for "rights" assured by the Constitution, and the Northern appeal to what it deemed "right" in moral terms. Nevins, in *Ordeal of the Union* (B834), maintains that the North and South had become "separate peoples" primarily over the problem of slavery and the issue of "race adjustment" that would result should the war destroy the institution of slavery.

On disloyalty in the North during the war, see two studies: Wood Gray, *The hidden Civil War: the story of the copperheads* (New York: Macmillan, 1942) (**B901**), and Frank L. Klement, *The copperheads in the Middle West* (Chicago: Univ. of Chicago Pr., 1960) (**B902**).

As with the 1850s, leaders in America in the following decade, both North and South, have drawn special attention by historians. On Lincoln, the best one-volume biography remains Benjamin P. Thomas, *Abraham Lincoln: a biography* (New York: Knopf, 1952) (**B903**). But another excellent biography is Stephen B. Oates, *With malice toward none: the life of Abraham Lincoln* (New York: Harper, 1977) (**B904**). A richly detailed study is James G. Randall, *Lincoln the president*, 4v. (New York: Dodd, 1945–55) (**B905**). The famous poet, Carl Sandburg, has contributed *Abraham Lincoln*, 6v. (New York: Harcourt, Brace, 1929–39) (**B906**), an anecdotal but literary masterpiece that is heavily pro-Lincoln. See also Oscar and Lilian Handlin, *Abraham Lincoln and the Union* (Boston: Little, 1980) (**B907**). A superb biography of the leading "radical" of the Republican party is David H. Donald's *Charles Sumner and the rights of man* (New York: Knopf, 1970) (**B908**). For members of Lincoln's cabinet, see the following biographies: Benjamin P. Thomas and Harold M. Hyman, *Stanton: the life and times of Lincoln's secretary of war* (New York: Knopf, 1962) (**B909**); Glyndon G. Van Deusen, *William Henry Seward* (New York: Oxford Univ. Pr., 1967) (**B910**), the secretary of state; and John Niven, *Gideon Welles, Lincoln's secretary of the navy* (New York: Oxford Univ. Pr., 1973) (**B911**). The best study of the Union's most successful military commander is William S. McFeely, *Grant: a biography* (New York: Norton, 1981) **(B912)**. For the Confederate States of America, see: E. Merton Coulter, *The Confederate States of America, 1861–1865* (Baton Rouge: Louisiana State Univ. Pr., 1950) **(B913)**; Clement Eaton, *A history of the Southern Confederacy* (New York: Macmillan, 1954) **(B914)**, a solid account; Charles P. Roland, *The Confederacy* (Chicago: Univ. of Chicago Pr., 1960) **(B915)**, a short survey; and Emory M. Thomas, *The Confederate nation: 1861–1865* (New York: Harper, 1979) **(B916)**, now the best study of the South during the war. For Southern leaders, see: Clement Eaton, *Jefferson Davis* (New York: Macmillan, 1977) **(B917)**, an adequate biography; and two magisterial works by Douglas S. Freeman: *Robert E. Lee*, 4v. (New York: Scribner, 1934–35) **(B918)**, the classic biography of the South's foremost leader; and *Lee's lieutenants*, 3v. (New York: Scribner, 1942–44) **(B919)**, detailed but highly readable.

There is almost no limit to the number of books on the war itself. Nevins' eight-volume work, *Ordeal of the Union* (B834), contains four volumes on *The war for the Union*. Bruce Catton has written numerous books on the war. Among these, see his trilogy on *The army of the Potomac: Mr. Lincoln's army* (Garden City, N.Y.: Doubleday, 1951) **(B920)**, *Glory road* (Garden City, N.Y.: Doubleday, 1952) **(B921)**, and *A Stillness at Appomattox* (Garden City, N.Y.: Doubleday, 1953) **(B922)**. Another of his studies, *This hallowed ground: the story of the Union side of the Civil War* (Garden City, N.Y.: Doubleday, 1956) **(B923)**, is a solid and beautifully written one-volume survey of the war from the Northern viewpoint. Shelby Foote's *The Civil War: a narrative*, 3v. (New York: Random, 1958–74) **(B924)**, is an elegant account. For the soldier's life, see two short works by Bell I. Wiley: *The life of Johnny Reb, the common soldier of the Confederacy* (Indianapolis: Bobbs-Merrill, 1943) **(B925)**, for the Southerner; and *The life of Billy Yank, the common soldier of the Union* (Indianapolis: Bobbs-Merrill, 1952) **(B926)**, for the Northerner. Useful works on the diplomacy of the war include: David P. Crook, *The North, the South, and the powers, 1861–1865* (New York: Wiley, 1974) **(B927)**, and his shortened version of the same book—*Diplomacy during the Civil War* (New York: Wiley, 1975) **(B928)**. For Southern diplomacy, see Frank L. Owsley, *King cotton diplomacy: foreign relations of the Confederate States of America*, 2d ed. (Chicago: Univ. of Chicago Pr., 1959) **(B929)**, a superb study of why the South failed in its efforts to use cotton as diplomatic leverage in Europe. David H. Donald, ed., *Why the North won the Civil War* (Baton Rouge: Louisiana State Univ. Pr., 1960) **(B930)**, is a useful collection of essays by various historians having differing views on the subject.

There are several useful studies on the Reconstruction period after the war. William A. Dunning's *Reconstruction: political and economic, 1865–1877* (New York: Harper, 1907) **(B931)**, is a pro-Southern account that heavily criticizes Northern vindictiveness in establishing "bayonet rule" in the South, following exploitative policies, and causing widespread corruption and misery. Howard K. Beale's *The critical year: a study of Andrew Johnson and Reconstruction* (New York: Harcourt, Brace, 1930) **(B932)**, is also a traditional pro-Southern work that is sympathetic with Johnson and emphasizes the role of Northern business groups in exploiting the prostrate postwar region. Another strongly pro-Southern study is E. Merton Coulter, *The South during Reconstruction, 1865–1877* (Baton Rouge: Louisiana State Univ. Pr., 1947) **(B933)**, who calls the Reconstruction period in the South the "Blackout of Honest Government" and criticizes the blacks, carpetbaggers, and scalawags for the region's problems. Kenneth M. Stampp's *The era of Reconstruction, 1865–1877* (New York: Knopf, 1965) **(B934)**, is part of the "revisionist" works that began to appear in the early 1960s. He argues that the tragedy of Reconstruction was the *nation's* failure to ensure racial equality for blacks—that the racism usually attributable to the South was part of a nationwide racist view that had impact on other minorities as well as the blacks. Along this line, John Hope Franklin, *Reconstruction after the Civil War* (Chicago: Univ. of Chicago Pr., 1961) **(B935)**, shows that the Republican party had tried to solve racial problems in the South by helping freedmen, but the issue got enmeshed in postwar corruption that was bisectional, bipartisan, and biracial. According to Franklin, racial relations in this period in Southern history fell under the category of "Reconstruction, Confederate style." W.E.B. DuBois, *Black Reconstruction in America, 1860–1880* (New York: Harcourt, Brace, 1935) **(B936)**, claims that blacks and whites in North and South sincerely tried to establish a democratic society and that the Reconstruction government established in the South had accomplished more than could have been expected given the bitter atmosphere. Herman Belz, *A new birth of freedom: the Republican party and freedmen's rights, 1861–1866* (Westport, Conn.: Greenwood, 1976) **(B937)**, focuses on the accomplishments of the Reconstruction period, most particularly the Fourteenth and Fifteenth amendments, which helped make the federal government, rather than the states, the guarantor of civil rights.

Other aspects of the period have drawn attention. Studies sympathetic to President Johnson include: Eric L. McKitrick, *Andrew Johnson and Reconstruction* (Chicago: Univ. of Chicago Pr., 1960) (**B938**), who also argues that Southerners failed to fulfill the "symbolic requirements" of a vanquished people after the war, thereby deepening the Northerners' hostility toward the postwar South; Michael Les Benedict's two works: *A compromise of principle: congressional Republicans and Reconstruction, 1863–1869* (New York: Norton, 1975) (**B939**), and *The impeachment and trial of Andrew Johnson* (New York: Norton, 1973) (**B940**), both of which favor the Radicals and argue that Johnson's impeachment was justified. Two other works critical of Johnson are W. R. Brock, *An American crisis: Congress and Reconstruction, 1865–1867* (New York: St. Martin's, 1963) (**B941**), and LaWanda Cox and John H. Cox, *Politics, principle, and prejudice, 1865–1866* (New York: Macmillan, 1963) (**B942**). The Radicals draw favor in James M. McPherson, *The struggle for equality: abolitionists and the Negro in the Civil War and Reconstruction* (Princeton, N.J.: Princeton Univ. Pr., 1964) (**B943**). Other important studies include: C. Vann Woodward, *Reunion and reaction: the Compromise of 1877 and the end of Reconstruction* (Boston: Little, 1951) (**B944**), who analyzes the political deals that comprised the Compromise of 1877; William S. McFeely, *Yankee stepfather: General O. O. Howard and the freedmen* (New Haven, Conn.: Yale Univ. Pr., 1968) (**B945**), who examines the head of the Freedmen's Bureau; and Leon F. Litwack, *Been in the storm so long: the aftermath of slavery* (New York: Knopf, 1979) (**B946**), who studies the impact of Reconstruction on black Americans. Paul H. Buck, *The road to reunion, 1865–1900* (Boston: Little, 1937) (**B947**), focuses on the reconciliation of North and South in the Reconstruction era and afterward, and Rayford W. Logan, *The Negro in American life and thought: the nadir, 1877–1901* (New York: Macmillan, 1954) (**B948**), discusses the "betrayal of the Negro" caused by the provision of the Compromise of 1877 which permitted federal non-enforcement of the Fifteenth Amendment in the South. His book later appeared in an enlarged edition under the title *The betrayal of the Negro: from Rutherford B. Hayes to Woodrow Wilson* (New York: Macmillan, 1965) (**B949**).

The Late Nineteenth Century, 1877–1900

The post-Reconstruction period in American history is a confusing, chaotic time that is understandable only within the context of attempts by Americans to reestablish social, political, and economic order after the cataclysmic events of civil war. For a highly critical examination of the period that soon became known by the title of their best-selling novel, see Mark Twain and Charles Dudley Warner, *The Gilded Age: a tale of to-day* (Indianapolis: Bobbs-Merrill, 1972, orig. pub. 1873) (**B950**). Though the two writers concentrate on the Grant presidency, their use of the term *Gilded Age*, with its condemnation of materialism, has become a somewhat unfair label for the last quarter of the nineteenth century. Another unfavorable analysis of the period is Ray Ginger's *Age of excess: the United States from 1877 to 1914* (New York: Macmillan, 1965) (**B951**). John A. Garraty, *The new commonwealth, 1877–1890* (New York: Harper, 1968) (**B952**), presents a balanced survey of the political and industrial changes of the period and their ramifications for the country. Robert H. Wiebe, *The search for order, 1877–1920* (New York: Hill & Wang, 1967) (**B953**), has written a seminal work that examines the rise of bureaucracy in America as leaders tried to establish a new system of order in the United States after the Civil War and Reconstruction. H. Wayne Morgan's *From Hayes to McKinley: national party politics, 1877–1896* (Syracuse, N.Y.: Syracuse Univ. Pr., 1969) (**B954**), is a sound political overview of the period. For the Republican party, see Robert D. Marcus, *Grand Old Party: political structure in the Gilded Age, 1880–1896* (New York: Oxford Univ. Pr., 1971) (**B955**). Other political studies include: Matthew Josephson, *The politicos, 1865–1896* (New York: Harcourt, Brace, 1938) (**B956**), a highly critical view of American politicians of the late nineteenth century; David J. Rothman, *Politics and power: the United States Senate, 1869–1901* (Cambridge, Mass.: Harvard Univ. Pr., 1966) (**B957**), an important analysis of the rise of the Senate to political power; and Leonard D. White, *The Republican era: a study in administrative history, 1869–1901* (New York: Macmillan, 1958) (**B958**).

The postwar South continued to draw nationwide attention. See: Paul H. Buck, *The road to reunion, 1865–1900* (B947), who emphasizes the conciliatory aftermath of Reconstruction in the region; C. Vann Woodward, *Origins of the New South, 1877–1913* (Baton Rouge: Louisiana

State Univ. Pr., 1951) **(B959)**, the beginning point for any study of the subject; and Wilbur J. Cash, *The mind of the South* (B839), a controversial interpretation. Two valuable studies recount the Republican party's futile efforts to build a political following in the New South: Vincent P. De Santis, *Republicans face the Southern question: the new departure years, 1877–1897* (Baltimore: Johns Hopkins Univ. Pr., 1959) **(B961)**, and Stanley P. Hirshson, *Farewell to the bloody shirt: Northern Republicans and the Southern Negro, 1877–1893* (Bloomington: Indiana Univ. Pr., 1962) **(B962)**. On Southern politics, the classic work is V. O. Key, Jr., *Southern politics in state and nation* (New York: Random, 1949) **(B963)**. Southern spokesmen have been the subject of numerous works. Among them, see: C. Vann Woodward, *Tom Watson: agrarian rebel* (New York: Macmillan, 1938) **(B964)**, a model biography of the famous Georgia Populist; and Francis B. Simkins, *Pitchfork Ben Tillman: South Carolinian* (Baton Rouge: Louisiana State Univ. Pr., 1944) **(B965)**, a study of the fiery Democrat.

Race relations permeated nearly every important topic during the period. A sound survey is August Meier, *Negro thought in America, 1880–1915: racial ideologies in the age of Booker T. Washington* (Ann Arbor: Univ. of Michigan Pr., 1963) **(B966)**. Perhaps the most thought-provoking study is C. Vann Woodward's *The strange career of Jim Crow*, rev. ed. (New York: Oxford Univ. Pr., 1974) **(B967)**, which finds the origins of segregation in the *post*-Reconstruction era South and then highlights the "Second Reconstruction Era" of the 1960s. Joel Williamson's *After slavery: the Negro in South Carolina during Reconstruction, 1861–1877* (Chapel Hill: Univ. of North Carolina Pr., 1965) **(B968)**, is a good balance to Woodward's interpretation. The two leading black spokesmen of the time were Booker T. Washington and W.E.B. DuBois. Louis R. Harlan, *Booker T. Washington*, 2v. (New York: Oxford Univ. Pr., 1972–83) **(B969)**, has a superb account of the premier black leader of the New South who called for accommodation with the whites until the blacks could improve their lot in life. See Washington's own *Up from slavery: an autobiography* (Garden City, N.Y.: Doubleday, 1900) **(B970)**. For DuBois, who founded the NAACP and called for confrontation in attacking America's racial policies, see: Elliott M. Rudwick, *W.E.B. DuBois, propagandist of the Negro protest*, rev. ed. (Philadelphia: Univ. of Pennsylvania Pr., 1968) **(B971)**, and Francis L. Broderick, *W.E.B. DuBois: Negro*

leader in a time of crisis (Stanford, Calif.: Stanford Univ. Pr., 1959) **(B972)**.

Many of the most revolutionary changes of the period centered on industrialization, immigration, and urbanization. For the importance of industrial development, see Edward C. Kirkland, *Industry comes of age: business, labor, and public policy, 1860–1897* (New York: Holt, 1961) **(B973)**. Thomas C. Cochran and William Miller, *The age of enterprise: a social history of industrial America*, rev. ed. (B701), highlight the economic aspects of the industrial changes. A pathbreaking study is Samuel P. Hays' *The response to industrialism: 1885–1914* (Chicago: Univ. of Chicago Pr., 1957) **(B975)**, which sees the drive for "efficiency" as the central ingredient in America's industrial revolution. George R. Taylor and Irene D. Neu, *The American railroad network, 1861–1890* (Cambridge, Mass.: Harvard Univ. Pr., 1956) **(B976)**, show how railroad development was the major impetus to America's industrial expansion. Alfred D. Chandler, Jr., *The visible hand: the managerial revolution in American business* (Cambridge, Mass.: Harvard Univ. Pr., 1977) **(B977)**, traces the rise of the modern corporation in this period. Melvyn Dubofsky's *Industrialism and the American worker, 1865–1920* (Arlington Heights, Ill.: Harlan Davidson, 1975) **(B978)**, is a superb account. A highly critical examination of America's industrial leaders is Matthew Josephson, *The robber barons: the great American capitalists, 1861–1901* (New York: Harcourt, Brace, 1934) **(B979)**, who wrote during the early years of the Great Depression after becoming disenchanted with capitalism.

On industrialism's ideological base, see: Edward C. Kirkland, *Dream and thought in the business community, 1860–1900* (Ithaca, N.Y.: Cornell Univ. Pr., 1956) **(B980)**, who examines the ideology of capitalism; Richard Hofstadter, *Social Darwinism in American thought*, rev. ed. (Boston: Beacon, 1955) **(B981)**, the basic work on the subject; Sidney Fine, *Laissez faire and the general-welfare state: a study of conflict in American thought, 1865–1901* (Ann Arbor: Univ. of Michigan Pr., 1956) **(B982)**, who analyzes opposing attitudes on one of the most important subjects of the period. See also Morton G. White, *Social thought in America: the revolt against formalism* (New York: Viking, 1949) **(B983)**, a good intellectual study, and Robert G. McCloskey, *American conservatism in the age of enterprise, 1865–1910* (Cambridge, Mass.: Harvard Univ. Pr., 1951) **(B984)**, a solid explanation of conservative thought. See also Harold U. Faulkner, *The decline of laissez faire, 1897–1917* (New

York: Holt, 1951) (**B985**). Daniel J. Boorstin's *The Americans: the democratic experience* (New York: Random, 1973) (**B986**), is a social and cultural examination of the time.

On immigration, see: Oscar Handlin, *The uprooted: the epic story of the great migrations that made the American people*, rev. ed. (Boston: Little, 1973) (**B987**), for a moving account of the personal impact of immigration on the people uprooted from Europe; Marcus L. Hansen, *The immigrant in American history* (Cambridge, Mass.: Harvard Univ. Pr., 1940) (**B988**); Nathan Glazer and Daniel P. Moynihan, *Beyond the melting pot: the Negroes, Puerto Ricans, Jews, Italians, and Irish of New York City* (Cambridge, Mass.: MIT Pr., 1963) (**B989**), for a highly controversial examination of assimilation in America; Moses Rischin, *The promised city: New York's Jews, 1870–1914* (Cambridge, Mass.: Harvard Univ. Pr., 1962) (**B990**); and John Higham, *Strangers in the land: patterns of American nativism, 1860–1925* (New Brunswick, N.J.: Rutgers Univ. Pr., 1955 (**B991**), for a classic account of nativism in America. See also Alan M. Kraut, *The huddled masses: the immigrant in American society, 1880–1921* (Arlington Heights, Ill.: Harlan Davidson, 1982) (**B992**).

On urbanization, see Arthur M. Schlesinger, *The rise of the city, 1878–1898* (New York: Macmillan, 1933) (**B993**), for the basic study. Other important works include: two general examinations by Lewis Mumford—*The culture of cities* (New York: Harcourt, Brace, 1938) (**B994**), and *The city in history: its origins, its transformations, and its prospects* (New York: Harcourt, Brace, 1961) (**B995**); and three specialized studies by Sam Bass Warner, Jr.—*Streetcar suburbs: The process of growth in Boston, 1870–1900* (Cambridge, Mass.: Harvard Univ. Pr., 1962) (**B996**), which examines the impact of improved transportation on developing Boston's suburbs; *The private city: Philadelphia in three periods of its growth* (Philadelphia: Univ. of Pennsylvania Pr., 1968) (**B997**); and *The urban wilderness: a history of the American city* (New York: Harper, 1972) (**B998**), a discussion of the physical characteristics of the city. On poverty in the cities, see: Robert H. Bremner, *From the depths: the discovery of poverty in the United States* (New York: New York Univ. Pr., 1956) (**B999**), a sound examination of the subject; and Stephan Thernstrom, *Poverty and progress: social mobility in a nineteenth century city* (Cambridge, Mass.: Harvard Univ. Pr., 1964) (**B1000**), which deals with social mobility in the cities.

The development of the American West in this period has also received serious attention. For the "frontier thesis," see Frederick Jackson Turner, *The frontier in American history* (B736). See also his seminal essay, "The Significance of the Frontier in American History," read at the Chicago World's Fair of 1893 and reprinted in numerous collections. Henry Nash Smith, *Virgin land: the American West as symbol and myth* (Cambridge, Mass.: Harvard Univ. Pr., 1950) (**B1001**), focuses on the image of the West found in American literature. Walter P. Webb, *The Great Plains* (B857), is a classic account of the end of America's last agricultural frontier. See also Ernest S. Osgood, *The day of the cattleman* (Minneapolis: Univ. of Minn. Pr., 1929) (**B1003**). On the Indians, see: Wilcomb E. Washburn, *The Indian in America* (New York: Harper, 1975) (**B1004**), for a useful survey of the subject; Ralph K. Andrist, *The long death: the last days of the plains Indian* (New York: Macmillan, 1964) (**B1005**); and Francis Paul Prucha, *American Indian policy in crisis: Christian reformers and the Indian, 1865–1900* (Norman: Univ. of Oklahoma Pr., 1975) (**B1006**).

The plight of the farmers and their protests that grew into political movements and the Populist party have attracted considerable interest among historians. Two sound works are Fred A. Shannon, *The farmer's last frontier: agriculture, 1860–1897* (New York: Holt, 1945) (**B1007**), and Gilbert C. Fite, *The farmers' frontier, 1865–1900* (New York: Holt, 1966) (**B1008**). John D. Hicks, *The Populist revolt: a history of the Farmers' alliance and the People's Party* (Minneapolis: Univ. of Minnesota Pr., 1931) (**B1009**), remains the starting point on the subject. Hicks argues that the farmers' revolt emanated from genuine economic problems—both of a natural origin and those caused by industrialized America. Lawrence Goodwyn's *Democratic promise: the Populist moment in America* (New York: Oxford Univ. Pr., 1976) (**B1010**), is a first-rate study of the Populists that also has appeared in an abridged paperback under the title of *The Populist moment: a short history of the agrarian revolt in America* (New York: Oxford Univ. Pr., 1978) (**B1011**). He argues that the Populists were engaged in a crusade against the "emerging corporate state" and that they aimed to establish a democratic society. Richard Hofstadter, *The age of reform: from Bryan to F.D.R.* (New York: Knopf, 1955) (**B1012**), considers the Populists to have been nostalgic conservatives who strived to restore what he called the "agrarian myth" of a Jeffersonian, idyllic America; rather than being democrats, Hofstadter insists, the Populists were guilty of bigotry and ignorance. Norman Pollack, *The Populist response to industrial America:*

midwestern *Populist thought* (Cambridge, Mass.: Harvard Univ. Pr., 1962) **(B1013)**, disagrees with Hofstadter and argues that the Populists were radicals trying to deal with the problems of an industrialized America, not by destroying the country but by making it more democratic. Walter T. K. Nugent's *The tolerant Populists: Kansas Populism and nativism* (Chicago: Univ. of Chicago Pr., 1963) **(B1014)**, is an important study of Kansas Populism which challenges Hofstadter's claim that the Populists were backward and racist.

Other important studies include: C. Vann Woodward, *Origins of the New South, 1877–1913* (B959), which contains a superb section on Populism in the New South; Robert C. McMath, Jr., *Populist vanguard: a history of the Southern Farmers' alliance* (Chapel Hill: Univ. of North Carolina Pr., 1975) **(B1016)**, which examines the Farmers' alliances that became a foundation of the Populist party; and Theodore Saloutos, *Farmer movements in the South, 1865–1933* (Berkeley: Univ. of California Pr., 1960) **(B1017)**, which shows how the Populist movement fitted with other developments in America at the time. On William Jennings Bryan and the presidential election of 1896, see two studies by Paul W. Glad—*The trumpet soundeth: William Jennings Bryan and his democracy, 1896–1912* (Lincoln: Univ. of Nebraska Pr., 1960) **(B1018)**, and *McKinley, Bryan, and the people* (New York: Lippincott, 1964) **(B1019)**; Robert F. Durden, *The climax of Populism: the election of 1896* (Lexington: Univ. of Kentucky Pr., 1965) **(B1020)**; and Paolo E. Coletta, *William Jennings Bryan*, 3v. (Lincoln: Univ. of Nebraska Pr., 1964–69) **(B1021)**, the standard biography.

Foreign affairs by the 1890s had captured the attention of Americans for the first important time since before the Civil War era. For useful surveys, see: Milton Plesur, *America's outward thrust: approaches to foreign affairs, 1865–1890* (DeKalb: Northern Illinois Univ. Pr., 1971) **(B1022)**; Robert L. Beisner, *From the old diplomacy to the new, 1865–1900* (New York: Crowell, 1975) **(B1023)**; and Charles S. Campbell, *The transformation of American foreign relations, 1865–1900* (New York: Harper, 1976) **(B1024)**. Interpretive studies include: Albert K. Weinberg, *Manifest destiny: a study of nationalist expansionism in American history* (B851), an ideological work; Frederick Merk, *Manifest destiny and mission in American history: a reinterpretation* (B852), an examination of the ideas underlying manifest destiny and mission that stirred the expansionism of the 1890s; Walter LaFeber, *The new empire: an interpretation of*

American expansion, 1860–1898 (Ithaca, N.Y.: Cornell Univ. Pr., 1963) **(B1027)**, an economic interpretation of the period stressing America's search for markets and raw materials as the basic impetus to expansion; William A. Williams, *The tragedy of American diplomacy*, rev. ed. (New York: Dell, 1962) **(B1028)**, who emphasizes the "open door" as the fundamental economic motive behind expansion; and two works by Ernest R. May—*Imperial democracy: the emergence of America as a great power* (New York: HBJ, 1961) **(B1029)**, and *American imperialism: a speculative essay* (New York: Atheneum, 1968) **(B1030)**. On the 1890s and the "new" manifest destiny, see David F. Healy, *U.S. expansionism: the imperialist urge in the 1890s* (Madison: Univ. of Wisconsin Pr., 1970) **(B1031)**; Harold U. Faulkner, *Politics, reform and expansion: 1890–1900* (New York: Harper, 1959) **(B1032)**; H. Wayne Morgan, *William McKinley and his America* (Syracuse, N.Y.: Syracuse Univ. Pr., 1963) **(B1033)**.

The Spanish-American War and other foreign events of the late 1890s have been the subject of numerous historical works. See: Julius W. Pratt, *Expansionists of 1898: the acquisition of Hawaii and the Spanish Islands* (Baltimore: Johns Hopkins Univ. Pr., 1936) **(B1034)**, an important study of the expansionist interests of the United States that led to war with Spain in 1898; Margaret Leech, *In the days of McKinley* (New York: Harper, 1959) **(B1035)**; H. Wayne Morgan, *America's road to empire: the war with Spain and overseas expansion* (New York: Wiley, 1965) **(B1036)**, a good account of the background, highlights, and results of the Spanish-American War; Walter Millis, *The martial spirit* (Cambridge, Mass.: Riverside, 1931) **(B1037)**, an examination of the mood of the country during its first outward thrust of the 1890s; David F. Trask, *The war with Spain in 1898* (New York: Macmillan, 1981) **(B1038)**, a solid account; Frank Freidel, *The splendid little war* (New York: Dell, 1958) **(B1039)**, an absorbing account of the war with Spain; Foster R. Dulles, *America's rise to world power, 1898–1954* (New York: Harper, 1954) **(B1040)**, helpful on the events of the late 1890s; and Bradford Perkins, *The great rapprochement: England and the United States, 1895–1914* (New York: Atheneum, 1968) **(B1041)**, which traces the history of perhaps the most important development in foreign affairs during the period from the Venezuelan crisis through the outbreak of World War I. For the rise of the leading national personality of the time, see Edmund Morris, *The rise of Theodore Roosevelt* (New York: Coward, 1979) **(B1042)**, who has a sprightly account of Roosevelt's role in the war with Spain.

Progressivism and World War I, 1900–1920

The onset of the twentieth century was characterized by a reform spirit that became a central part of America's decision to enter the First World War. There are several important surveys of the ideological bases of reform. Robert H. Wiebe, *The search for order, 1877–1920* (B953), argues that "Progressivism" was the wide-ranging result of the attempts by a new middle class to safeguard its place in society by bringing social and political order to the chaos stemming from the rapid industrial changes of the period. The goal, Wiebe declares, was the establishment of national institutions to replace those of a local nature. See also his *Businessmen and reform: a study of the Progressive movement* (Cambridge, Mass.: Harvard Univ. Pr., 1962) **(B1044)**. Gabriel Kolko, *The triumph of conservatism: a reinterpretation of American history, 1900–1916* (New York: Macmillan, 1963) **(B1045)**, asserts that Progressivism was democratic in rhetoric only—that big business interests quietly supported regulatory controls by Congress in an effort to avert more rigid restraints by state legislatures that would stimulate damaging competition. Samuel P. Hays, *The response to industrialism: 1885–1914* (B975), agrees with Kolko that businessmen and Progressives were oftentimes one and the same, but insists that their common aim was to establish efficiency in American political and economic life and thus protect their own positions in society. For the same theme tied to the subject of conservation of natural resources, see Hays' *Conservation and the gospel of efficiency: the Progressive conservation movement, 1890–1920* (Cambridge, Mass.: Harvard Univ. Pr., 1959) **(B1047)**. See also Samuel Haber, *Efficiency and uplift: scientific management in the Progressive era, 1890–1920* (Chicago: Univ. of Chicago Pr., 1964) **(B1048)**. Richard Hofstadter, *The age of reform: from Bryan to F.D.R.* (B1012), argues for the "status thesis" in explaining the Progressive upheaval—that former holders of social, political, and economic power had tried to regain their positions by using reforms to control the new corporations and other enterprises. See also John Chamberlain, *Farewell to reform: the rise, life and decay of the Progressive mind in America* (New York: Day, 1932) **(B1049)**.

For the ideological bases of Progressivism, see: Morton G. White, *Social thought in America: the revolt against formalism* (B983); Eric F. Goldman, *Rendezvous with destiny: a history of modern American reform*, rev. ed. (New York: Knopf, 1956) **(B1051)**, a liberal interpretation of reformism; Daniel Aaron, *Men of good hope: a story of American Progressives* (New York: Oxford Univ. Pr., 1951) **(B1052)**; Arthur Mann, *Yankee reformers in the urban age: social reform in Boston, 1880–1900* (Cambridge, Mass.: Harvard Univ. Pr., 1954) **(B1053)**; Sidney Fine, *Laissez faire and the general-welfare state: a study of conflict in American thought, 1865–1901* (B982); Harold U. Faulkner, *The decline of laissez faire, 1897–1917* (B985); Henry F. May, *The end of American innocence: a study of the first years of our own time, 1912–1917* (New York: Knopf, 1959) **(B1054)**, who examines intellectual and social developments; and Aileen S. Kraditor, *The ideas of the woman suffrage movement, 1890–1920* (New York: Columbia Univ. Pr., 1965) **(B1055)**.

There have been several studies of the state and regional aspects of Progressivism. See: George E. Mowry, *The California Progressives* (Berkeley: Univ. of California Pr., 1951) **(B1056)**, who like Hofstadter uses the "status thesis" in explaining Progressivism in California. According to Mowry, a small but privileged class of businessmen and professionals sought to regain social and economic position by restraining the growth of new corporations. David P. Thelen, *The new citizenship: origins of Progressivism in Wisconsin, 1885–1900* (Columbia: Univ. of Missouri Pr., 1972) **(B1057)**, discerns a major conflict between the "public interest" and "corporate privileges" in Wisconsin. The depression of the 1890s had brought together a disparate group of Americans who wanted to tie government and corporate interests to what the people wanted. According to Thelen, rhetoric matched reality in Wisconsin. On Progressivism in the Midwest, see Russel B. Nye, *Midwestern Progressive politics: a historical study of its origins and development, 1870–1958* (East Lansing: Michigan State Univ. Pr., 1959) **(B1058)**. For the South, see: C. Vann Woodward, *Origins of the New South, 1877–1913* (B959), and George B. Tindall, *The emergence of the New South, 1913–1945* (Baton Rouge: Louisiana State Univ. Pr., 1967) **(B1059)**. Of the many specialized studies of the era, see James H. Jones, *Bad blood: the Tuskegee syphilis experiment* (New York: Macmillan, 1981) **(B1060)**, a masterful study; David P. Thelen, *Robert M. LaFollette and the insurgent spirit* (Boston: Little, 1976) **(B1061)**, an analysis of the leading Wisconsin Progressive;

Louis Filler, *Crusaders for American liberalism* (New York: Harcourt, Brace, 1939) **(B1062)**, an examination of "muckraking" writers and other publicists who exposed the injustices in the United States during the period; and James T. Patterson, *America's struggle against poverty, 1900–1980* (Cambridge, Mass.: Harvard Univ. Pr., 1981) **(B1063)**, a study of rural and urban poverty in the twentieth century.

On the national level, the two most famous spokesmen of Progressive reform were Presidents Theodore Roosevelt and Woodrow Wilson. On Roosevelt, see: Henry F. Pringle, *Theodore Roosevelt: a biography* (New York: Harcourt, Brace, 1931) **(B1064)**, an anecdotal and critical biography; John Morton Blum, *The Republican Roosevelt* (Cambridge, Mass.: Harvard Univ. Pr., 1954) **(B1065)**, an interpretive account of Roosevelt's use of power in public life; two studies by George E. Mowry—*The era of Theodore Roosevelt and the birth of modern America, 1900–1912* (New York: Harper, 1958) **(B1066)**, a solid survey of Roosevelt's presidential years and the country's politics; and *Theodore Roosevelt and the Progressive movement* (Madison: Univ. of Wisconsin Pr., 1946) **(B1067)**; William H. Harbaugh, *The life and times of Theodore Roosevelt*, rev. ed. (New York: Collier, 1963) **(B1068)**, a valuable interpretive account of how Roosevelt meshed power and responsibility; G. Wallace Chessman, *Theodore Roosevelt and the politics of power* (Boston: Little, 1969) **(B1069)**, a useful coverage. For Wilson, consult: Arthur S. Link, *Woodrow Wilson*, 5v. to date (Princeton, N.J.: Princeton Univ. Pr., 1947–65) **(B1070)**, who will have, when completed, the definitive biography of Wilson. Link's work presently carries the story to America's entry into World War I. Link has written two other studies of Wilson: *Woodrow Wilson and the Progressive era, 1910–1917* (New York: Harper, 1954) **(B1071)**, an excellent political survey of the period, and *Wilson the diplomatist: a look at his major foreign policies* (Baltimore: Johns Hopkins Univ. Pr., 1957) **(B1072)**, which has appeared as an extensive revision under the title of *Woodrow Wilson: revolution, war, and peace* (Arlington Heights, Ill.: AHM, 1979) **(B1073)**. Among several other important studies of Wilson, see: John Morton Blum, *Woodrow Wilson and the politics of morality* (Boston: Little, 1956) **(B1074)**, and Alexander George and Juliette George, *Woodrow Wilson and Colonel House: a personality study* (New York: Day, 1956) **(B1075)**, a psychoanalytic examination of the two men who at one time were the closest of friends. For a comparative biography, see John Milton Cooper, Jr., *The warrior and the priest: Woodrow Wilson and Theodore Roosevelt* (Cambridge, Mass.: Harvard Univ. Pr., 1983) **(B1076)**.

Foreign policy during the early years of the twentieth century was a dominant force in the country's history. For a broad survey, see Julius W. Pratt, *Challenge and rejection: The United States and world leadership, 1900–1921* (New York: Macmillan, 1967) **(B1077)**. Numerous works highlight Roosevelt's profound impact on the nation's growing role in foreign affairs: Foster R. Dulles, *America's rise to world power, 1898–1954* (B1040), which covers broad themes; Howard K. Beale, *Theodore Roosevelt and the rise of America to world power* (Baltimore: Johns Hopkins Univ. Pr., 1956) **(B1079)**, which remains the standard account of Roosevelt's foreign policy, except for its sparse coverage of Latin American affairs; and Frederick W. Marks, *Velvet on iron: the diplomacy of Theodore Roosevelt* (Lincoln: Univ. of Nebraska Pr., 1979) **(B1080)**, a useful account. On the Roosevelt administration's relations with the Far East, see: Thomas A. Bailey, *Theodore Roosevelt and Japanese-American crises* (Stanford, Calif.: Stanford Univ. Pr., 1934) **(B1081)**; Roger Daniels, *The politics of prejudice: the anti-Japanese movement in California and the struggle for Japanese exclusion* (Berkeley: Univ. of California Pr., 1962) **(B1082)**, which shows how America's treatment of the Japanese in the United States indirectly affected the nation's foreign policy; Raymond A. Esthus, *Theodore Roosevelt and Japan* (Seattle: Univ. of Washington Pr., 1966) **(B1083)**; two studies by Charles E. Neu—*An uncertain friendship: Theodore Roosevelt and Japan, 1906–1909* (Cambridge, Mass.: Harvard Univ. Pr., 1967) **(B1084)**, and *The troubled encounter: the United States and Japan* (New York: Wiley, 1975) **(B1085)**, both excellent accounts of Roosevelt's efforts to defuse problems with Japan, which he regarded as America's greatest potential rival in the Pacific; and two works by Akira Iriye—*Across the Pacific: an inner history of American-East Asian relations* (New York: Harcourt, Brace, 1967) **(B1086)**, and *Pacific estrangement: Japanese and American expansion, 1897–1911* (Cambridge, Mass.: Harvard Univ. Pr., 1972) **(B1087)**. On the administration's problems with Europe, see Raymond A. Esthus, *Theodore Roosevelt and the international rivalries* (Waltham, Mass.: Ginn-Blaisdell, 1970) **(B1088)**. Roosevelt's role in the Panama Canal controversy becomes clear in Walter LaFeber, *The Panama Canal: the crisis in historical perspective*, expanded ed. (New York: Oxford Univ. Pr., 1979) **(B1089)**. See also

David McCullough's colorful account, *The path between the seas: the creation of the Panama Canal, 1870–1914* (New York: Simon & Schuster, 1977) **(B1090)**.

Whereas Roosevelt's brand of diplomacy revolved around "realism" in foreign affairs, that of Wilson's focused on "morality." For Wilsonian diplomacy in Mexico, see: Kenneth J. Grieb, *The United States and Huerta* (Lincoln: Univ. of Nebraska Pr., 1969) **(B1091)**, and two excellent studies by Robert E. Quirk—*The Mexican Revolution, 1914–1915* (Bloomington: Indiana Univ. Pr., 1960) **(B1092)**, which explores the context of American involvement, and *An affair of honor: Woodrow Wilson and the occupation of Veracruz* (Lexington: Univ. of Kentucky Pr., 1962) **(B1093)**, an absorbing account of how "honor" almost caused war between the nations in 1914. On Wilsonian diplomacy in Europe, see: William E. Leuchtenburg, *The perils of prosperity, 1914–32* (Chicago: Univ. of Chicago Pr., 1958) **(B1094)**; Ernest R. May, *The World War and American isolation, 1914–1917* (Cambridge, Mass.: Harvard Univ. Pr., 1959) **(B1095)**, who examines America's domestic attitudes toward events in Europe, and argues that poor diplomacy by the Wilson administration—especially during the *Sussex* crisis—was a major reason for the United States' entry into the Great War; Daniel M. Smith, *The great departure: the United States and World War I, 1914–1920* (New York: Wiley, 1965) **(B1096)**, who offers a comprehensive account dealing with America's neutrality, its entrance into the war, and the controversy over the League of Nations. Like Link's works on Wilson, Smith argues that Wilson took the nation into the war to win a spot at the negotiating table and thus to guarantee permanent peace. Also strong on the neutrality period are: John Milton Cooper, Jr., *The vanity of power: American isolationism and the First World War, 1914–1917* (Westport, Conn.: Greenwood, 1969) **(B1097)**, and Patrick Devlin, *Too proud to fight: Woodrow Wilson's neutrality* (New York: Oxford Univ. Pr., 1974) **(B1098)**. On the *Lusitania* controversy, Thomas A. Bailey and Paul B. Ryan, *The Lusitania disaster: an episode in modern warfare and diplomacy* (New York: Macmillan, 1975) **(B1099)**, show that there was no Anglo-American collusion designed to force the United States into the war. On one of the most explosive issues encouraging America's entry into the war, see Barbara W. Tuchman's colorful *The Zimmermann telegram* (New York: Macmillan, 1958) **(B1100)**. A useful and brief interpretive work is Ross Gregory's *The origins of American intervention in the First World War* (New York: Norton, 1971) **(B1101)**.

There have been numerous studies on both the war and the League of Nations controversy afterward. On the war, see: H. C. Peterson and Gilbert C. Fite, *Opponents of war, 1917–1918* (Madison: Univ. of Wisconsin Pr., 1957) **(B1102)**, a description of the wartime restrictions on civil liberties in the United States; and Paul L. Murphy, *World War I and the origin of civil liberties in the United States* (New York: Norton, 1979) **(B1103)**, who argues that the movement for civil liberties began during the war. For a valuable military history, see Edward M. Coffman, *The war to end all wars: the American military experience in World War I* (New York: Oxford Univ. Pr., 1968) **(B1104)**. America's Siberian venture has been the subject of numerous accounts. See: George F. Kennan, *Soviet-American relations, 1917–1920*, 2v. (Princeton, N.J.: Princeton Univ. Pr., 1956–58) **(B1105)**, who argues that the Wilson administration sent troops into Russia to save Czech soldiers marooned after the Bolsheviks withdrew from the war by the Treaty of Brest-Litovsk; Betty M. Unterberger, *America's Siberian expedition, 1918–1920: a study of national policy* (Durham, N.C.: Duke Univ. Pr., 1956) **(B1106)**, who also discerns no ulterior political motives in the episode; and Richard Goldhurst, *The midnight war: the American intervention in Russia, 1918–1920* (New York: McGraw-Hill, 1978) **(B1107)**, who asserts that the United States initially entered Russia as part of an international expedition designed to guarantee that German soldiers would not confiscate Western weapons in Russia after its withdrawal from the war. But as events progressed, Goldhurst continues, the American soldiers found themselves engaged in the Russian civil war and thus vulnerable to charges of seeking to determine its outcome. A highly critical account of Wilsonian interventionism is N. Gordon Levin, Jr., *Woodrow Wilson and world politics: America's response to war and revolution* (New York: Oxford Univ. Pr., 1968) **(B1108)**.

The postwar period in America was a time of disillusionment. The most colorfully written accounts of the League of Nations issue remain the two volumes by Thomas A. Bailey—*Woodrow Wilson and the lost peace* (New York: Macmillan, 1944) **(B1109)**, which focuses on the Versailles proceedings, and *Woodrow Wilson and the great betrayal* (New York: Macmillan, 1945) **(B1110)**, which concentrates on events inside the United States and contains Bailey's argument that Wilson's refusal to compromise with the

Senate on the league and treaty constituted his "supreme infanticide." On Senate opposition to the league, see Ralph Stone, *The irreconcilables: the fight against the League of Nations* (Lexington: Univ. of Kentucky Pr., 1970) (**B1111**). For the Bolshevik scare in the United States, see Robert K. Murray's engrossing work, *Red scare: a study of national hysteria, 1919–1920* (Minneapolis: Univ. of Minnesota Pr., 1955) (**B1112**).

The Twenties and Depression–New Deal, 1920–1937

There are several useful surveys of the period. See: Arthur M. Schlesinger, Jr., *The age of Roosevelt*, 3v. (Boston: Houghton, 1957–60) (**B1113**) for a highly favorable view of the Roosevelt era; William E. Leuchtenburg, *The perils of prosperity, 1914–32* (B1094), a sprightly account of the social and political life of the 1920s; John D. Hicks, *Republican ascendancy, 1921–1933* (New York: Harper, 1965) (**B1115**); David A. Shannon, *Between the wars: America, 1919–1941* (Boston: Houghton, 1965) (**B1116**); George B. Tindall, *The emergence of the New South, 1913–1945* (B1059), for a study of Southern politics; Daniel J. Boorstin, *The Americans: the democratic experience* (B986), which includes a survey of American culture during the twenties. On that decade, the classic popular survey, written by a contemporary, is Frederick Lewis Allen, *Only yesterday: an informal history of the 1920's* (New York: Harper, 1957, orig. pub. 1931) (**B1118**). But also see: Paul A. Carter, *The twenties in America* (New York: Crowell, 1968) (**B1119**), and Robert K. Murray, *The politics of normalcy: governmental theory and practice in the Harding-Coolidge Era* (New York: Norton, 1973) (**B1120**).

Specific topics have drawn considerable interest among historians. On blacks, see: Gilbert Osofsky, *Harlem: The making of a ghetto: Negro New York, 1890–1930*, 2d ed. (New York: Harper, 1971) (**B1121**), who discusses the background of the "Harlem Renaissance"; and Nathan I. Huggins, *Harlem renaissance* (New York: Oxford Univ. Pr., 1971) (**B1122**), who analyzes black culture during the decade. Nativism was one of the dominant themes of the post-World War I era. See: John Higham, *Strangers in the land: patterns of American nativism, 1860–1925* (B991), for the standard work on the subject; David M. Chalmers, *Hooded Americanism: the history of the Ku Klux Klan* (New York:

Watts, 1981) (**B1124**), for a detailed account of the rise of the KKK during the 1920s; Charles C. Alexander, *The Ku Klux Klan in the Southwest* (Lexington: Univ. of Kentucky Pr., 1965) (**B1125**); and Kenneth T. Jackson, *The Ku Klux Klan in the city, 1915–1930* (New York: Oxford Univ. Pr., 1967) (**B1126**), for evidence that the Klan's popularity was not confined to rural, fundamentalist areas in America. On prohibition, see: Andrew Sinclair, *Era of excess: a social history of the Prohibition movement* (Boston: Little, 1962) (**B1127**), a lively account of the era of Prohibition; and Norman H. Clark, *Deliver us from evil: an interpretation of American Prohibition* (New York: Norton, 1976) (**B1128**), a history of prohibition from its origins in the Progressive period. Burl Noggle, *Teapot Dome: oil and politics in the 1920's* (Baton Rouge: Louisiana State Univ. Pr., 1962) (**B1129**), analyzes the biggest scandal of the Harding years. Fundamentalism was also a major theme of the decade. See: Ray Ginger, *Six days or forever? Tennessee v. John Thomas Scopes* (Boston: Beacon, 1958) (**B1130**), for an entertaining account of the Scopes trial over the evolution controversy. Two general accounts of fundamentalism are: Norman F. Furniss, *The fundamentalist controversy, 1918–1931* (New Haven, Conn.: Yale Univ. Pr., 1954) (**B1131**), and George M. Marsden, *Fundamentalism and American culture: the shaping of twentieth century evangelicalism, 1870–1925* (New York: Oxford Univ. Pr., 1980) (**B1132**). On the economy of the twenties, see: George Soule, *Prosperity decade: from war to depression, 1917–1929* (New York: Holt, 1947) (**B1133**); and Robert Sobel, *The great bull market: Wall Street in the 1920s* (New York: Norton, 1968) (**B1134**). See also: Irving Bernstein, *The lean years: a history of the American worker, 1920–1933* (Boston: Houghton, 1960) (**B1135**), for an examination of the labor movement; and Alfred D. Chandler, Jr., *Strategy and structure: chapters in the history of the industrial enterprise* (Cambridge, Mass.: MIT Pr., 1962) (**B1136**), an analysis of American corporate development.

The presidents during the "Golden Twenties" have received ample attention. For Warren G. Harding, see: Andrew Sinclair, *The available man: the life behind the masks of Warren Gamaliel Harding* (New York: Macmillan, 1965) (**B1137**), a favorable account; Francis Russell, *The shadow of Blooming Grove: Warren G. Harding in his times* (New York: McGraw-Hill, 1968) (**B1138**), a critical work; and Robert K. Murray, *The Harding era: Warren G. Harding and his administration* (Minneapolis: Univ. of

Minnesota Pr., 1969) (**B1139**), a balanced view. On Calvin Coolidge, see William Allen White, *A Puritan in Babylon: the story of Calvin Coolidge* (New York: Macmillan, 1938) (**B1140**), a journalist's biography of the president; and Donald R. McCoy, *Calvin Coolidge: the quiet president* (New York: Macmillan, 1967) (**B1141**), a scholarly account of the presidency.

The Great Depression era has been the subject of many works. For the Stock Market Crash of 1929, see John Kenneth Galbraith, *The Great Crash, 1929* (Boston: Houghton, 1954) (**B1142**), who attributes the collapse to a combination of faulty government policies along with a weak economy. A thorough account of the monetary problems of the 1930s appears in the study by Milton Friedman and Anna J. Schwartz, *Monetary history of the United States, 1867–1960* (Princeton, N.J.: Princeton Univ. Pr., 1963) (**B1143**). For useful surveys of the 1930s, see: Broadus Mitchell, *Depression decade: from new era through New Deal, 1929–1941* (New York: Holt, 1947) (**B1144**), which contains a discussion of the economy during the Great Depression; Dixon Wecter, *Age of the Great Depression* (New York: Macmillan, 1948) (**B1145**), a social history; Dexter Perkins, *The new age of Franklin Roosevelt, 1932–45* (Chicago: Univ. of Chicago Pr., 1957) (**B1146**); Studs Terkel, *Hard times: an oral history of the Great Depression* (New York: Random, 1970) (**B1147**), which shows the social impact of the depression. For Herbert Hoover, see: Harris G. Warren, *Herbert Hoover and the Great Depression* (New York: Oxford Univ. Pr., 1959) (**B1148**), a sympathetic account; Joan Hoff Wilson, *Herbert Hoover: forgotten Progressive* (Boston: Little, 1975) (**B1149**), a brief though sound biography; and David Burner, *Herbert Hoover: the public life* (New York: Knopf, 1978) (**B1150**). Roger Daniels, *The Bonus March: an episode of the Great Depression* (Westport, Conn.: Greenwood, 1971) (**B1151**), focuses on the march on Washington during the summer of 1932 that ended in violence and even stronger criticism of the Hoover presidency.

Franklin D. Roosevelt and the New Deal have received great attention among historians. A recent work is Nathan Miller, *FDR: an intimate history* (Garden City, N.Y.: Doubleday, 1983) (**B1152**). For the rise of Roosevelt and his reform program, see Frank Freidel, *Franklin D. Roosevelt*, 4v. completed to date (Boston: Little, 1952–73) (**B1153**), which ends after Roosevelt's first hundred days in office. Considerable controversy still surrounds the meaning and impact of the New Deal. William E. Leuchtenburg, *Franklin D. Roosevelt and the New Deal, 1932–*

1940 (New York: Harper, 1963) (**B1154**), is the most solid one-volume account. The New Deal, he argues, was not a full-fledged revolution because of restrictions imposed by political, economic, and ideological realities. Held back by these restraints, the program was able to help only some unfortunate groups (labor and agriculture in particular), while failing to do much if anything for others (blacks, sharecroppers, and poverty-stricken people in the cities). Arthur M. Schlesinger, Jr., in volume 2 of his study of Roosevelt, *The coming of the New Deal* (Boston: Houghton, 1959) (**B1155**), considers the New Deal an extension of the long conflict between public and private interests. According to Schlesinger, the government finally placed effective restraints on big business, thus reforming the capitalist system to enable more Americans to share in its benefits. Eric F. Goldman, *Rendezvous with destiny: a history of modern American reform*, rev. ed. (B1051), claims that the New Deal went farther than merely establishing what earlier reformers had advocated—social security for example, was a notable step in a new direction. Richard Hofstadter, *The age of reform: from Bryan to F.D.R.* (B1012) criticizes the New Deal on several counts, but agrees with other writers that the program was a "drastic new departure" from anything ever staged before in the United States. The basic change, he declares, was that the government assumed the responsibilities of striking out at special privileges and caring for the general welfare of Americans.

Other aspects of the period have received extensive attention. James M. Burns' *Roosevelt: the lion and the fox* (New York: Harcourt, Brace, 1956) (**B1157**), is a major study of Roosevelt's early years that criticizes the man for sometimes allowing his political maneuverings to get in the way of needed reforms. Ellis W. Hawley's *The New Deal and the problem of monopoly* (Princeton, N.J.: Princeton Univ. Pr., 1966) (**B1158**), is an excellent study of economic policy under the New Deal. He argues that the program helped private business groups, even if it sometimes entailed foregoing some of the liberal measures called for by the administration. Otis L. Graham, Jr.'s *An encore for reform: the old Progressives and the New Deal* (New York: Oxford Univ. Pr., 1967) (**B1159**), highlights the impact that the "Old Progressives" had on the New Deal. Bernard Bellush, *The failure of the NRA* (New York: Norton, 1975) (**B1160**), closely studies the failure of the New Deal's most ambitious reform bill. Paul K. Conkin, *The New Deal* (New York: Crowell, 1967) (**B1161**), argues that the reform program failed to help many farmers, did not establish real tax reforms or treat all business concerns equally, and did not properly fund the Social Security Act.

There are several sound studies of the opposition to the New Deal. See: Arthur M. Schlesinger, Jr., *The politics of upheaval*, volume 3 of his trilogy on Roosevelt (Boston: Houghton, 1960) **(B1162)**; T. Harry Williams, *Huey Long* (New York: Knopf, 1969) **(B1163)**, the leading biography of the Louisiana proponent of the Every Man a King program; and Alan Brinkley, *Voices of protest: Huey Long, Father Coughlin, and the Great Depression* (New York: Knopf, 1982) **(B1164)**, a superb study. For the Pulitzer Prize winning novel based on Huey Long, see Robert Penn Warren, *All the king's men* (New York: HBJ, 1946) **(B1165)**.

For other aspects of the reform era, see: Frank Freidel, *F.D.R. and the South* (Baton Rouge: Louisiana State Univ. Pr., 1965) **(B1166)**, which discusses the conservative opposition to the New Deal; and two studies by James T. Patterson— *Congressional Conservatism and the New Deal: the growth of the conservative coalition in Congress, 1933–1939* (Lexington: Univ. of Kentucky Pr., 1967) **(B1167)**, which examines the rise of the conservative opposition in Congress; and *The New Deal and the states: federalism in transition* (Princeton, N.J.: Princeton Univ. Pr., 1969) **(B1168)**, which focuses on the relationship between the federal and state governments. Frederick Lewis Allen's *Since yesterday: the nineteen-thirties in America* (New York: Harper, 1939) **(B1169)**, is a social history of the decade. On blacks, see Dan T. Carter, *Scottsboro: a tragedy of the American South* (Baton Rouge: Louisiana State Univ. Pr., 1979) **(B1170)**, a superb account of perhaps the most famous racial event of the 1930s. See also Harvard Sitkoff, *A New Deal for blacks: the emergence of civil rights as a national issue* (New York: Oxford Univ. Pr., 1978) **(B1171)**, a study of the impact of the depression and New Deal on black Americans. Donald L. Parman, *The Navajos and the New Deal* (New Haven, Conn.: Yale Univ. Pr., 1976) **(B1172)**, focuses on the Navajos' reaction to the New Deal's Indian policy. Irving Bernstein's *Turbulent years: a history of the American worker, 1933–1941* (Boston: Houghton, 1969) **(B1173)**, is a comprehensive study of the subject.

Though emphasis in the period was on domestic troubles, foreign affairs became a growing concern of the Roosevelt administration by the mid-1930s. For a survey of America's foreign policy in these years, see Selig Adler, *The uncertain giant, 1921–1941: American foreign policy between the wars* (New York: Macmillan, 1965) **(B1174)**. See also L. Ethan Ellis, *Republican foreign policy, 1921–1933* (New Brunswick, N.J.: Rutgers Univ. Pr., 1968) **(B1175)**, and Joan Hoff Wilson, *American business and foreign policy, 1920–1933* (Lexington: Univ. of Kentucky Pr., 1971) **(B1176)**, the latter showing the influence of big business on foreign policy and America's relations with the Soviet Union. For a biography of Harding's secretary of state, see Merlo J. Pusey, *Charles Evans Hughes*, 2v. (New York: Columbia Univ. Pr., 1963) **(B1177)**. A. Whitney Griswold's *The Far Eastern policy of the United States* (New York: Harcourt, Brace, 1938) **(B1178)**, is an excellent examination of America's Asian policy. Thomas H. Buckley, *The United States and the Washington Conference, 1921–1922* (Knoxville: Univ. of Tennessee Pr., 1970) **(B1179)**, focuses on the naval disarmament conference called by the Harding administration. For a careful analysis of the pact of 1928 "outlawing" war, see Robert H. Ferrell, *Peace in their time: the origins of the Kellogg-Briand Pact* (New Haven, Conn.: Yale Univ. Pr., 1952) **(B1180)**. See also Ferrell's *American diplomacy in the Great Depression: Hoover-Stimson foreign policy, 1929–1933* (New Haven, Conn.: Yale Univ. Pr., 1957) **(B1181)**, which deals with the growing crisis in the Far East during the Hoover administration. Elting E. Morison's *Turmoil and tradition: a study of the life and times of Henry L. Stimson* (Boston: Houghton, 1960) **(B1182)**, is a biography of Hoover's secretary of state and later Roosevelt's secretary of war, who was largely responsible for America's nonrecognition policy of 1932 toward Japan's expansionist activities in Manchuria.

Several world issues drew America's attention during the 1930s. For an admirable study of Roosevelt's foreign policy, see Robert Dallek, *Franklin D. Roosevelt and American foreign policy, 1932–1945* (New York: Oxford Univ. Pr., 1979) **(B1183)**. United States recognition of Russia in 1933 was a major decision by the administration. See Robert P. Browder, *The origins of Soviet-American diplomacy* (Princeton, N.J.: Princeton Univ. Pr., 1953) **(B1184)**, and Edward M. Bennett, *Recognition of Russia: an American foreign policy dilemma* (Waltham, Mass.: Ginn-Blaisdell, 1970) **(B1185)**. Bryce Wood's *The making of the good neighbor policy* (New York: Columbia Univ. Pr., 1961) **(B1186)**, is a sound examination of America's new policy toward Latin America. John E. Wiltz, *In search of peace: the Senate munitions inquiry, 1934–36* (Baton Rouge: Louisiana State Univ. Pr., 1963) **(B1187)**, and Wayne S. Cole, *Senator Gerald P. Nye and American foreign relations* (Minneapolis: Univ. of Minnesota Pr., 1962) **(B1188)**, emphasize the Senate's investigation into the charges that American munitions industries profited from World War I. Manfred Jonas' *Isolationism in America, 1935–1941* (Ithaca, N.Y.: Cornell Univ. Pr., 1966) **(B1189)**, is a sound survey of a major theme during the period. Dorothy Borg's *The United States and the Far Eastern crisis of 1933–1938* (Cambridge, Mass.: Harvard Univ. Pr., 1964) **(B1190)**, is a solid study of the problems in China during the late 1930s that helped lead to World War II.

The Era of World War II, 1937–1945

There are many sound studies of the United States' role in World War II. For the diplomatic aspects of the period following 1938, see Stephen E. Ambrose, *Rise to globalism: American foreign policy since 1938*, 3d ed. (New York: Penguin, 1983) **(B1191)**. Two works by Selig Adler are useful: *The isolationist impulse: its twentieth century reaction* (New York: Abelard-Schuman, 1957) **(B1192)**, and *The uncertain giant, 1921–1941: American foreign policy between the wars* (B1174). Several historians focus on the impact of isolationism on America's foreign outlook during the 1930s and early 1940s. Among them, see: Manfred Jonas, *Isolationism in America, 1935–1941* (B1189); two works by Wayne S. Cole that emphasize the central organization and its major spokesman for isolationism—*America first: the battle against intervention, 1940–1941* (Madison: Univ. of Wisconsin Pr., 1953) **(B1194)**, and *Charles A. Lindbergh and the battle against American intervention in World War II* (New York: HBJ, 1974) **(B1195)**. For an interpretive study that questions the impact of isolationism in pre-World War II America, see Robert A. Divine, *The reluctant belligerent: American entry into World War II* (New York: Wiley, 1979) **(B1196)**.

Other important works on America before Pearl Harbor include: James R. Leutze, *Bargaining for supremacy: Anglo-American naval collaboration, 1937–1941* (Chapel Hill: Univ. of North Carolina Pr., 1977) **(B1197)**, which focuses on tightening Anglo-American relations during the period; Warren F. Kimball, *The most unsordid act: Lend-Lease, 1939–1941* (Baltimore: Johns Hopkins Univ. Pr., 1969) **(B1198)**, a study of the Lend-Lease controversy; George C. Herring, Jr., *Aid to Russia, 1941–1946: strategy, diplomacy, the origins of the cold war* (New York: Columbia Univ. Pr., 1973) **(B1199)**, which in-

cludes an analysis of the most controversial aspect of the Lend-Lease Act; John L. Snell, *Illusion and necessity: the diplomacy of global war, 1939–1945* (Boston: Houghton, 1963) **(B1200)**; Robert A. Divine, *The illusion of neutrality* (Chicago: Univ. of Chicago Pr., 1962) **(B1201)**; and William L. Langer and S. Everett Gleason, *The challenge to isolation, 1937–1940* (New York: Harper, 1952) **(B1202)**, a standard history of the period before United States entry into the war. An admirable examination of the president's foreign policy is Robert Dallek's *Franklin D. Roosevelt and American foreign policy, 1932–1945* (B1183). On the Far East, see: A. Whitney Griswold, *The Far Eastern policy of the United States* (B1178), and Dorothy Borg, *The United States and the Far Eastern crisis of 1933–1938* (B1190).

The controversy over Pearl Harbor has attracted enormous interest among historians. Within ten years of the event, Charles A. Beard, *President Roosevelt and the coming of the war, 1941: a study in appearances and realities* (New Haven, Conn.: Yale Univ. Pr., 1948) **(B1205)**, accused the Roosevelt administration of maneuvering the Japanese into attacking Pearl Harbor. Charles C. Tansill, among others, argues in *Back door to war: the Roosevelt foreign policy, 1933–1941* (Chicago: Regnery, 1952) **(B1206)**, that Roosevelt failed to convince Americans that Hitler was a threat and managed to get the United States into the war through the "back door" by luring the Japanese into the attack. Richard N. Current, *Secretary Stimson: a study in statecraft* (New Brunswick, N.J.: Rutgers Univ. Pr., 1954) **(B1207)**, refutes the Beard-Tansill argument by asserting that even though Stimson expected a Japanese attack, he thought it would be on either British or Dutch holdings in the Pacific. Thus the White House's problem was how to convince Americans and Congress that such an assault constituted a threat to United States security as well. A sound defense of the Roosevelt administration, based on State Department materials, is Herbert Feis' *The road to Pearl Harbor: the coming of the war between the United States and Japan* (Princeton, N.J.: Princeton Univ. Pr., 1950) **(B1208)**. One of the most convincing arguments against the accusations is Roberta Wohlstetter's study, *Pearl Harbor: warning and decision* (Stanford, Calif.: Stanford Univ. Pr., 1962) **(B1209)**, which attributes the disaster to "noise" in the American intelligence network that confused the warning signals and permitted the Japanese to launch the surprise attack. Another important defense of the administration is the long work by Gordon W. Prange,

At dawn we slept: the untold story of Pearl Harbor (New York: McGraw-Hill, 1981) **(B1210)**, who made extensive use of Japanese and American sources in showing that the attack on Pearl Harbor was the result of mistakes and not a calculated effort to draw the United States into the war. For an intriguing study, see Ladislas Farago, *The broken seal: the story of "Operation Magic" and the Pearl Harbor disaster* (New York: Random, 1967) **(B1211)**. The most recent attack on the Roosevelt administration's alleged culpabilities is John Toland's *Infamy: Pearl Harbor and its aftermath* (Garden City, N.Y.: Doubleday, 1982) **(B1212)**, who claims to have interviewed someone (left unnamed) with proof of the president's role. For a dramatic account of the Japanese attack on Pearl Harbor, see Walter Lord, *Day of infamy* (New York: Holt, 1957) **(B1213)**. See also Walter Millis, *This is Pearl: the United States and Japan, 1941* (New York: Morrow, 1947) **(B1214)**.

Numerous works encompass the war years. For a comprehensive survey of the domestic and foreign aspects of America's involvement, see A. Russell Buchanan, *The United States and World War II*, 2v. (New York: Harper, 1964) **(B1215)**. James M. Burns' *Roosevelt: the soldier of freedom* (New York: HBJ, 1970) **(B1216)**, is a beautifully written, interpretive survey of the domestic, foreign, and military affairs of the war years. See Robert A. Divine, *Roosevelt and World War II* (Baltimore: Johns Hopkins Univ. Pr., 1969) **(B1217)**, for a series of interpretive essays on Roosevelt and foreign affairs. The most useful survey of wartime diplomacy is Gaddis Smith's *American diplomacy during the Second World War, 1941–1945* (New York: Wiley, 1965) **(B1218)**. Wartime strategy is the subject of two works: Samuel Eliot Morison, *Strategy and compromise* (Boston: Little, 1958) **(B1219)**, and Kent R. Greenfield, *American strategy in World War II: a reconsideration* (Baltimore: Johns Hopkins Univ. Pr., 1963) **(B1220)**. On the war itself, see two studies by Hanson W. Baldwin—*Great mistakes of the war* (New York: Harper, 1950) **(B1221)**, and *Battles lost and won: great campaigns of World War II* (New York: Harper, 1966) **(B1222)**. For the naval aspects, see Samuel Eliot Morison, *History of United States naval operations in World War II*, 15v. (Boston: Little, 1947–62) **(B1223)**. A useful broad study of the war is B. H. Liddell Hart's *History of the Second World War* (see description at B457). Dwight D. Eisenhower's *Crusade in Europe* (Garden City, N.Y.: Doubleday, 1948) **(B1225)** is a wartime account by America's chief military commander in Europe. On another American military leader, see Forrest C. Pogue, *George C. Marshall*, 3v. (New York: Viking, 1963–73) **(B1226)**, the first part of a biography of a major wartime strategist. See also Chester Wilmot, *The struggle for Europe* (New York: Harper, 1952) **(B1227)**, and Gordon Wright, *The ordeal of total war, 1939–1945* (see the description at B455). Also useful are: Robert A. Divine, *Second chance: the triumph of internationalism in America during World War II* (New York: Atheneum, 1967) **(B1229)**, and Randall B. Woods, *The Roosevelt foreign-policy establishment and the "Good Neighbor": the United States and Argentina, 1941–1945* (Lawrence: Univ. of Kansas Pr., 1979) **(B1230)**, a solid study of an important subject.

There are several useful works on wartime conferences and the last days of the war. On Roosevelt's decision at Casablanca in 1943 to push for unconditional surrender of Germany, Italy, and Japan, see Raymond G. O'Connor, *Diplomacy for victory: FDR and unconditional surrender* (New York: Norton, 1971) **(B1231)**. Diane S. Clemens, *Yalta* (New York: Oxford Univ. Pr., 1970) **(B1232)**, is highly critical of the president's performance at Yalta in 1945. For a defense of the Yalta decisions, see John L. Snell, ed., *The meaning of Yalta: Big Three diplomacy and the new balance of power* (Baton Rouge: Louisiana State Univ. Pr., 1956) **(B1233)**, a collection of essays by historians on the questions that came before the conference. Athan G. Theoharis, *The Yalta myths: an issue in U.S. politics, 1945–1955* (Columbia: Univ. of Missouri Pr., 1970) **(B1234)**, deals with the controversy over Yalta in the decade following the conference. On the Potsdam conference, see Herbert Feis, *Between war and peace: the Potsdam Conference* (Princeton, N.J.: Princeton Univ. Pr., 1960) **(B1235)**, and Charles L. Mee, Jr., *Meeting at Potsdam* (New York: M. Evans, 1975) **(B1236)**. On the final days of the war in Europe, see two works by Cornelius Ryan—*The longest day: June 6, 1944* (New York: Simon & Schuster, 1959) **(B1237)**, an account of the Allied landing at Normandy Beach; and *The last battle* (New York: Simon & Schuster, 1966) **(B1238)**; John Toland, *The last 100 days* (New York: Random, 1965) **(B1239)**; and Stephen E. Ambrose, *Eisenhower and Berlin, 1945: the decision to halt at the Elbe* (New York: Norton, 1967) **(B1240)**, which absolves Roosevelt of responsibility for ordering American troops to halt their drive toward Berlin, and places it on General Eisenhower, who for sound logistical and military reasons made the decision to stop at the Elbe River.

Some historians believe the cold war had its origins in World War II. A highly important study that ties in the events of the war with the origins of the cold war afterward is John L. Gaddis, *The United States and the origins of the cold war, 1941–1947* (New York: Columbia Univ. Pr., 1972) (**B1241**). For "revisionist" studies criticizing America's wartime policy as contributory to the aftermath of cold war, see Gabriel Kolko, *The policies of war: the world and United States foreign policy, 1943–1945* (New York: Random, 1968) (**B1242**); and Lloyd C. Gardner, *Architects of illusion: men and ideas in American foreign policy, 1941–1949* (Chicago: Quadrangle, 1970) (**B1243**). William H. McNeill, *America, Britain, and Russia: their co-operation and conflict, 1941–1946* (New York: Oxford Univ. Pr., 1953) (**B1244**), covers wartime diplomacy and presents strong analyses of the problems in Soviet-American relations. For the diplomacy of the "strange alliance," see Herbert Feis, *Churchill-Roosevelt-Stalin: the war they waged and the peace they sought* (Princeton, N.J.: Princeton Univ. Pr., 1957) (**B1245**). An indispensable British view of the conflict is Winston S. Churchill's classic study, *The Second World War*, 6v. (Boston: Houghton, 1948–53) (**B1246**).

The domestic aspects of the war were important. See: Richard Polenberg, *War and society: the United States, 1941–1945* (New York: Lippincott, 1972) (**B1247**), and John Morton Blum, *V was for victory: politics and American culture during World War II* (New York: HBJ, 1976) (**B1248**). After Pearl Harbor, Americans feared that Japanese-Americans might attempt to sabotage the war effort against Japan, and favored a federal program calling for their relocation in centralized camps for surveillance reasons until the war was over. Roger Daniels argues that America's racial prejudice against the Japanese was vital to the establishment of these wartime relocation centers. See his *Concentration camps USA: Japanese Americans and World War II* (New York: Holt, 1972) (**B1249**).

The Asian side of the war has drawn considerable attention among historians. On China, see: John K. Fairbank, *The United States and China*, 4th ed. (Cambridge, Mass.: Harvard Univ. Pr., 1982) (**B1250**); Tang Tsou, *America's failure in China, 1941–1950*, 2v. (Chicago: Univ. of Chicago Pr., 1963) (**B1251**), who blames the United States for the fall of China to communism in 1949; Barbara W. Tuchman, *Stilwell and the American experience in China, 1911–1945* (New York: Macmillan, 1970) (**B1252**), who shows the complexity of the China situation and asserts that the United States could not have halted the

events leading to the communist takeover; and Herbert Feis, *The China tangle: the American effort in China from Pearl Harbor to the Marshall mission* (Princeton, N.J.: Princeton Univ. Pr., 1953) (**B1253**), also a defense of the administration's policies in China. On Japan, see: Christopher Thorne's splendid *Allies of a kind: The United States, Britain, and the war against Japan, 1941–1945* (New York: Oxford Univ. Pr., 1978) (**B1254**).

There are several works on the atomic bomb and the collapse of Japan. See: John Toland's *The rising sun: The decline and fall of the Japanese empire, 1936–1945* (New York: Random, 1970) (**B1255**); Martin J. Sherwin's *A world destroyed: the atomic bomb and the Grand Alliance* (New York: Knopf, 1975) (**B1256**), which examines the decision-making process that led to the use of the bomb; Gar Alperovitz's *Atomic diplomacy: Hiroshima and Potsdam—the use of the Atomic Bomb and the American confrontation with Soviet power* (New York: Knopf, 1965) (**B1257**), which argues that the use of the bomb was militarily unnecessary but that the United States used it as "atomic diplomacy" to place pressure on the Soviet Union in the postwar period; and Robert J. Donovan's *Conflict and crisis: the presidency of Harry S Truman, 1945–1948* (New York: Norton, 1977) (**B1258**), which contains a discussion of the president's decision to use the bomb. John Hersey's *Hiroshima* (New York: Knopf, 1946) (**B1259**) is a dramatic and graphic account of the impact of the bomb on Hiroshima. For the period afterward, see Gregg Herken, *The winning weapon: the atomic bomb in the cold war, 1945–1950* (New York: Knopf, 1980) (**B1260**). For the final collapse of Japan, see: Robert J.C. Butow, *Japan's decision to surrender* (Stanford, Calif.: Stanford Univ. Pr., 1954) (**B1261**); William Craig, *The fall of Japan* (New York: Dial, 1967) (**B1262**); and Lester Brooks, *Behind Japan's surrender: the secret struggle that ended an empire* (New York: McGraw-Hill, 1968) (**B1263**).

The United States since 1945

There are several helpful surveys of the period, but unfortunately most of them are already outdated. Among the best, see: Eric F. Goldman, *The crucial decade—and after: America, 1945–1960* (New York: Random, 1960) (**B1264**), a spirited and lighthearted account of postwar America that focuses on both the domestic and foreign aspects of what Goldman calls the "half-century of revolution" beginning with the New Deal; William E. Leuchtenburg, *A* *troubled feast: American society since 1945* (Boston: Little, 1979) **(B1265)**, a lively and anecdotal survey; Dewey W. Grantham, *The United States since 1945: the ordeal of power* (New York: McGraw-Hill, 1976) **(B1266)**; Carl N. Degler, *Affluence and anxiety: America since 1945* (Glenview, Ill.: Scott, Foresman, 1975) **(B1267)**, a sound overview; John Brooks, *The great leap: the past twenty-five years in America* (New York: Harper, 1966) **(B1268)**, which focuses on the rapid changes in American society after World War II; Godfrey Hodgson, *America in our time* (New York: Random, 1976) **(B1269)**; James Gilbert, *Another chance: postwar America, 1945–1968* (New York: Knopf, 1981) **(B1270)**; and Herbert Agar, *The price of power: America since 1945* (Chicago: Univ. of Chicago Pr., 1957) **(B1271)**, a useful introduction to the argument that with power comes responsibility.

Domestic Affairs

The revolution in civil rights in America received a tremendous boost with World War II and exploded in violence by the decade of the 1960s. On the Truman period, see: William C. Berman, *Politics of civil rights in the Truman administration* (Columbus: Ohio State Univ. Pr., 1970) **(B1272)**; and Richard M. Dalfiume, *Desegregation of the United States armed forces: fighting on two fronts, 1939–1953* (Columbia: Univ. of Missouri Pr., 1969) **(B1273)**, which shows how one of the most controversial moves of the period culminated in Truman's decision to complete the process begun during the war. For a first-rate study of the Earl Warren Supreme Court, see Paul L. Murphy, *The Constitution in crisis times, 1918–1969* (New York: Harper, 1972) **(B1274)**, and the more recent work by Bernard Schwartz, *Super chief: Earl Warren and his Supreme Court—a judicial biography* (New York: New York Univ. Pr., 1983) **(B1275)**. On the *Brown* decision of 1954, see Richard Kluger, *Simple justice: the history of Brown v. Board of Education and black America's struggle for equality* (New York: Random, 1975) **(B1276)**. Anthony Lewis, *Portrait of a decade: the second American revolution* (New York: Random, 1964) **(B1277)**, is solid on the rise of the civil rights movement. A superb examination of the sit-ins and the civil rights revolution in Greensboro, North Carolina, is William H. Chafe's study, *Civilities and civil rights: Greensboro, North Carolina, and the black struggle for freedom* (New York: Oxford Univ. Pr., 1980) **(B1278)**.

On the turbulent sixties, see: James Baldwin, *The fire next time* (New York: Dell, 1962) **(B1279)**, who warned that failure to grant needed reforms to blacks would lead to violence in the streets; Louis E. Lomax, *The Negro revolt* (New York: Harper, 1962) **(B1280)**, for a sound overview; Robert Conot, *Rivers of blood, years of darkness* (New York: Bantam, 1967) **(B1281)**, for a gripping account of the riot in Watts that helped launch four summers of violence in the nation's cities; and Numan V. Bartley, *The rise of massive resistance: race-politics in the South during the 1950s* (Baton Rouge: Louisiana State Univ. Pr., 1969) **(B1282)**. On Martin Luther King, Jr., the foremost spokesman of the black movement, see: Stephen B. Oates, *Let the trumpet sound: the life of Martin Luther King, Jr.* (New York: Harper, 1982) **(B1283)**, an excellent biography; David J. Garrow, *Protest at Selma: Martin Luther King, Jr., and the Voting Rights Act of 1965* (New Haven, Conn.: Yale Univ. Pr., 1978) **(B1284)**, a superb account of the march on that Alabama city; and Martin Luther King, Jr., *Why we can't wait* (New York: Harper, 1963) **(B1285)**, for the reasons behind black pressure for change. For black leaders who did not fall into the category of moderates like King, see Stokely S. Carmichael and Charles V. Hamilton, *Black power: the politics of liberation in America* (New York: Random, 1967) **(B1286)**, who show how the term *black power* became affixed to the movement; and Malcolm X (ghostwritten by Alex Haley), *The autobiography of Malcolm X* (New York: Random, 1964) **(B1287)** for a superb odyssey of one of the black leaders of the 1960s who was gunned down by other blacks.

There are numerous useful studies of the Truman period. The most recent and now the best account is a two-volume work by Robert J. Donovan, *Conflict and crisis: the presidency of Harry S Truman, 1945–1948* (B1258), and *Tumultuous years: the presidency of Harry S Truman, 1949–1953* (New York: Norton, 1982) **(B1289)**. See also Robert H. Ferrell, *Harry S. Truman and the modern American presidency* (Boston: Little, 1983) **(B1290)**. Dated but still useful is Cabell Phillips' *The Truman presidency: the history of a triumphant succession* (New York: Macmillan, 1966) **(B1291)**. For intellectual strains during the period, see Alonzo L. Hamby, *Beyond the New Deal: Harry S. Truman and American liberalism* (New York: Columbia Univ. Pr., 1973) **(B1292)**. On politics, see Samuel Lubell, *The future of American politics*, rev. ed. (Garden City, N.Y.: Doubleday, 1955) **(B1293)**, which examines the impact of the presidential election of 1948. A colorful account of Truman's upset victory in that year is Irwin Ross' *The loneliest campaign: the Truman victory of 1948* (New

York: New American Library, 1968) (**B1294**). For the president's view of these and many other events, see Harry S. Truman, *Memoirs*, 2v. (Garden City, N.Y.: Doubleday, 1955–56) (**B1295**). James T. Patterson's *Mr. Republican: a biography of Robert A. Taft* (Boston: Houghton, 1972) (**B1296**), is a first-rate biography of perhaps the leading conservative of the era.

Fear of communism in the United States was a major theme of the postwar period. Earl Latham, *The communist controversy in Washington: from the New Deal to McCarthy* (Cambridge, Mass.: Harvard Univ. Pr., 1966) (**B1297**), discusses the background of "McCarthyism" from the 1930s through the rise of Senator Joe McCarthy himself. Latham emphasizes the impact of the Republicans' loss in the presidential election of 1948 upon the decision of many to support McCarthy's attacks upon the Truman administration. Allen Weinstein, *Perjury: the Hiss-Chambers case* (New York: Knopf, 1978) (**B1298**), argues on admittedly limited documentary evidence that Alger Hiss was guilty of the charges made by Whittaker Chambers. Three works examine the effect of the Truman administration's policies in stirring the anticommunist fear: Alan Harper, *The politics of loyalty* (Westport, Conn.: Greenwood, 1969) (**B1299**); Athan G. Theoharis, *Seeds of repression: Harry S. Truman and the origins of McCarthyism* (New York: Times Books, 1971) (**B1300**); and Richard M. Freeland, *The Truman doctrine and the origins of McCarthyism: foreign policy, domestic politics, and international security, 1946–1948* (New York: Knopf, 1970) (**B1301**). On McCarthy, see Richard H. Rovere, *Senator Joe McCarthy* (New York: Harcourt, Brace, 1959) (**B1302**), a highly critical account by a journalist who traveled with the senator; and Thomas C. Reeves, *The life and times of Joe McCarthy* (New York: Stein & Day, 1981) (**B1303**), now the most important biography of the man. Robert W. Griffith's *The politics of fear: Joseph R. McCarthy and the Senate* (Lexington: Univ. of Kentucky Pr., 1970) (**B1304**), is an important analysis of why American senators and other public figures were afraid to criticize McCarthy's tactics. For McCarthy's opponents, see Richard M. Fried, *Men against McCarthy* (New York: Columbia Univ. Pr., 1976) (**B1305**). Edwin R. Bayley explores the relationship between *Joe McCarthy and the press* (Madison: Univ. of Wisconsin Pr., 1981) (**B1306**). And see David Caute, *The great fear: the anti-communist purge under Truman and Eisenhower* (New York: Simon & Schuster, 1978) (**B1307**).

On the espionage charges involving Julius and Ethel Rosenberg, see Walter and Miriam Schneir, *Invitation to an inquest*, rev. ed. (New York: Random, 1983) (**B1308**); Ronald Radosh and Joyce Milton, *The Rosenberg file: a search for the truth* (New York: Holt, 1983) (**B1309**); and Robert and Michael Meeropol, *We are your sons: The legacy of Ethel and Julius Rosenberg* (Boston: Houghton, 1975) (**B1310**), an account by the Rosenbergs' children who are trying to prove their parents' innocence.

The Eisenhower presidency was also a time of great unrest, despite the distorted arguments that the 1950s were a period of placidity at home and abroad. The best overview of both domestic and foreign affairs is Charles C. Alexander's *Holding the line: the Eisenhower era, 1952–1961* (Bloomington: Indiana Univ. Pr., 1975) (**B1311**), but also see Herbert S. Parmet, *Eisenhower and the American crusades* (New York: Macmillan, 1972) (**B1312**). For personal accounts by the president and administration members, see Dwight D. Eisenhower, *The White House years*, 2v. (Garden City, N.Y.: Doubleday, 1963–65) (**B1313**); Sherman Adams, *Firsthand report: the story of the Eisenhower administration* (New York: Harper, 1961) (**B1314**); and Emmet John Hughes, *The ordeal of power: a political memoir of the Eisenhower years* (New York: Atheneum, 1963) (**B1315**). For the intellectual and political context of the decade, see: Richard Hofstadter, *The age of reform: from Bryan to F.D.R.* (B1012), and Daniel Bell, *The end of ideology: on the exhaustion of political ideas in the fifties*, rev. ed. (New York: Macmillan, 1961) (**B1316**).

Influential works written during the period include John Kenneth Galbraith's *The affluent society* (Boston: Houghton, 1958) (**B1317**), which focuses on the theme of affluence in postwar America; David Riesman's *The lonely crowd: a study of the changing American character* (New Haven, Conn.: Yale Univ. Pr., 1950 (**B1318**), which shows how modern society helped to make the individual become "otherdirected" toward conformity rather than "innerdirected" toward individualism; and William H. Whyte, Jr.'s *The organization man* (New York: Simon & Schuster, 1956) (**B1319**), which describes the impact of the corporation on molding American lives and aspirations.

The abbreviated John F. Kennedy administration also has stimulated numerous studies. Theodore H. White's *The making of the president, 1960* (New York: Atheneum, 1961) (**B1320**), is the classic account of Kennedy's election to the White House. For a solid overview of the Kennedy (and Johnson) years, see Jim F. Heath, *Decade of disillusionment: the Kennedy-Johnson years* (Bloomington: Indiana Univ. Pr., 1975) **(B1321)**. See also Tom Wicker, *JFK and LBJ: the influence of personality upon politics* (New York: Morrow, 1968) **(B1322)**, for a useful study of the political relations between Congress and the presidency over the passage of domestic legislation. Arthur M. Schlesinger, Jr.'s *A thousand days: John F. Kennedy in the White House* (Boston: Houghton, 1965) **(B1323)**, is a highly useful though pro-Kennedy examination of the administration by the "historian-in-residence" in the White House. Another pro-Kennedy account is Theodore C. Sorensen, *Kennedy* (New York: Harper, 1965) **(B1324)**, a memoir by one of the president's chief speechwriters. See Michael Harrington, *The other America: poverty in the United States* (New York: Macmillan, 1962) **(B1325)**, for the book read by Kennedy that sparked the later war on poverty. Henry Fairlie's *The Kennedy promise: the politics of expectation* (Garden City, N.Y.: Doubleday, 1973) **(B1326)**, is a critical assessment of the Kennedy promise and the Kennedy reality. For the commission investigating the assassination of President Kennedy, see *Report of the Warren Commission on the assassination of President Kennedy* (New York: McGraw-Hill, 1964) **(B1327)**.

On the Johnson presidency, see the studies by Heath and Wicker mentioned above. The most comprehensive work is Vaughn D. Bornet, *The presidency of Lyndon B. Johnson* (Lawrence: Univ. of Kansas Pr., 1983) **(B1328)**. Also useful are: Theodore H. White, *The making of the president, 1964* (New York: Atheneum, 1965) **(B1329)**; Doris Kearns, *Lyndon Johnson and the American dream* (New York: Harper, 1976) **(B1330)**, a psychoanalytic study of the president; Eric F. Goldman, *The tragedy of Lyndon Johnson* (New York: Knopf, 1968) **(B1331)**, a critical account of the Johnson presidency by the "historian-in-residence" in the White House for part of the period; and Lyndon B. Johnson, *The vantage point: perspectives of the president, 1963–1969* (New York: Holt, 1971) **(B1332)**, for his memoirs. See also Robert A. Caro, *The years of Lyndon Johnson: the path to power* (New York: Knopf, 1982) **(B1333)**, volume 1 of a projected trilogy that will constitute a monumental political biography of the man.

Domestic unrest during the sixties became so serious that many Americans, as in the period one hundred years earlier, feared for the safety of the Union. The starting point now is Allen J. Matusow's *The unraveling of America: a history of liberalism in the 1960s* (New York: Harper, 1984) **(B1334)**, which highlights the reasons for the revival of conservatism in the 1970s and afterward. John P. Diggins, *The American left in the twentieth century* (New York: HBJ, 1973) **(B1335)**, examines the social and political underpinnings of the movement. Irwin Unger, *The movement: a history of the American New Left, 1959–1972* (New York: Dodd, 1974) **(B1336)**, highlights the domestic protests against the Vietnam War. Theodore Roszak's *The making of a counter culture: reflections on the technocratic society and its youthful opposition* (Garden City, N.Y.: Doubleday, 1969) **(B1337)**, is a strongly sympathetic account of the turmoil of the decade, and Charles A. Reich's *The greening of America* (New York: Random, 1970) **(B1338)**, had a major impact on the participants in the demonstrations. Also helpful are William L. O'Neill, *Coming apart: an informal history of America in the 1960s* (New York: Times Books, 1971) **(B1339)**; Ronald Berman, *America in the sixties: an intellectual history* (New York: Free Pr., 1968) **(B1340)**, an unfavorable view of the decade; and Milton Viorst, *Fire in the streets: America in the 1960s* (New York: Simon & Schuster, 1979) **(B1341)**, a discussion of the social and cultural features of the decade. For the rise of the feminist movement, see Betty Friedan, *The feminine mystique* (New York: Norton, 1963) **(B1342)**, which was an influential work of the period; and William H. Chafe's *The American woman: her changing social, economic and political roles, 1920–1970* (New York: Oxford Univ. Pr., 1972) **(B1343)**, which focuses on the rise of feminism since the 1920s. Alexander Kendrick, *The wound within: America in the Vietnam years, 1945–1974* (Boston: Little, 1974) **(B1344)**, relates the Vietnam War to internal unrest in the United States. Theodore H. White's *The making of the president, 1968* (New York: Atheneum, 1969) **(B1345)**, is another excellent study of a presidential election, this one putting Richard M. Nixon into the Executive Office.

The Nixon administration was marked by a drive for law and order at home in the midst of continued problems caused by the war in Vietnam and by what many perceived to be presidential callousness toward domestic injustices. For the first part of the period, see Rowland Evans, Jr., and Robert D. Novak, *Nixon in the White House: the frustration of power* (New York: Random, 1971) **(B1346)**. Jonathan Schell, *The time of illusion* (New York: Knopf, 1975) **(B1347)**, examines the impact of the Watergate crisis on

America's spirit and institutions. Garry Wills, *Nixon Agonistes: the crisis of the self-made man* (Boston: Houghton, 1969) **(B1348)**, analyzes Nixon's personality in the early period of his presidency. For a valuable account of Nixon's reelection, see Theodore H. White, *The making of the president, 1972* (New York: Atheneum, 1973) **(B1349)**. Also useful on the Nixon years is the president's own account: *RN: the memoirs of Richard Nixon* (New York: Warner, 1978) **(B1350)**.

On the president's fall from power, see: Carl Bernstein and Bob Woodward, *All the president's men* (New York: Simon & Schuster, 1974) **(B1351)**, a personal account by the two *Washington Post* reporters who helped to tie the Watergate scandal to the White House itself. The same two reporters have also detailed Nixon's last days in office in *The final days* (New York: Simon & Schuster, 1976) **(B1352)**. For a balanced account of Nixon's alleged violation of Americans' faith in the office of the presidency, see Theodore H. White, *Breach of faith: the fall of Richard Nixon* (New York: Atheneum, 1975) **(B1353)**. Two of many accounts by administration members involved in the Watergate scandal are: *Blind ambition: the White House years* (New York: Simon & Schuster, 1976) **(B1354)**, by John W. Dean III, counsel for the Nixon administration who gave the congressional investigating committee the most damaging testimony against the White House role in Watergate; and *Witness to power: the Nixon years* (New York: Simon & Schuster, 1982) **(B1355)**, by John Ehrlichman, who defends the Nixon presidency against Dean's charges. Arthur M. Schlesinger, Jr., *The imperial presidency* (Boston: Houghton, 1973) **(B1356)**, fits Watergate within the long-range development of the increasing powers of the Executive Office.

There are understandably few important works on the period after the Nixon years. On the brief Ford presidency, see Gerald R. Ford's *A time to heal: the autobiography of Gerald R. Ford* (New York: Harper, 1979) **(B1357)**. On Jimmy Carter, see two accounts of the presidential campaign of 1976: Jules Witcover, *Marathon: the pursuit of the presidency, 1972–1976* (New York: Viking, 1977) **(B1358)** and James Wooten, *Dasher: the roots and the rising of Jimmy Carter* (New York: Summit, 1978) **(B1359)**. Clark R. Mollenhoff, *The president who failed: Carter out of control* (New York: Macmillan, 1980) **(B1360)**, critically examines the Carter presidency. See also Carter's own work, *Why not the best?* (Nashville: Broadman, 1975) **(B1361)**. On the Ronald Reagan years, Theodore H.

White, in *America in search of itself: the making of the president, 1956–1980* (New York: Harper, 1982) **(B1362)**, relates the presidential election of 1980 to America's social and political problems of the times. Rowland Evans, Jr., and Robert D. Novak, in *The Reagan revolution: a blueprint for the next four years* (New York: Dutton, 1981) **(B1363)**, offers a sympathetic account of the early part of the presidency.

Foreign Affairs

For useful surveys of postwar foreign policy and the origins of the cold war, see: Stephen E. Ambrose, *Rise to globalism: American foreign policy since 1938*, 3d ed. (B1191); Walter LaFeber, *America, Russia, and the cold war, 1945–1980*, 4th ed. (New York: Wiley, 1980) **(B1365)**; and John Spanier, *American foreign policy since World War II*, 9th ed. (New York: Holt, 1983) **(B1366)**.

Controversy has raged for a long time over the origins of the cold war between the United States and the Soviet Union. Though the intensity of the argument has dissipated, disagreements have ranged from one extreme—the orthodox or traditional view of blaming the Soviet Union—to the other—the revisionist or New Left view of blaming the United States itself. Recently a consensus has begun to develop which has adapted some of the arguments of both schools in an effort to reach a balanced interpretation. A leading orthodox account is an article by Arthur M. Schlesinger, Jr., "Origins of the cold war," in *Foreign affairs* (October 1967), pp. 22–52 **(B1367)**. He admits that the Soviet Union may not have been set on world control, but asserts that Premier Joseph Stalin and others were paranoid about the West and capitalism and demanded hegemony over Eastern Europe, thus making the cold war virtually inescapable. Another defense of the United States is Herbert Feis' *From trust to terror: the onset of the cold war, 1945–1950* (New York: Norton, 1970) **(B1368)**. Revisionists often follow the critical line set by William A. Williams, who in *The tragedy of American diplomacy*, rev. ed. (B1028), argues that America's foreign policy was committed to the "open door" in expanding the nation's foreign trade. Thus, to Williams, capitalist expansion was more important than Russian aggression in bringing on the cold war. Joyce and Gabriel Kolko's study, *The limits of power: the world and United States foreign policy, 1945–1954* (New York: Harper, 1972) **(B1370)**, also criticizes American foreign policy for being, among other things, self-righteous in tone. Another revisionist work is Lloyd C. Gardner's

Architects of illusion: men and ideas in American foreign policy, 1941–1949 (B1243), which examines several personalities instrumental in molding the policy of the period. Thomas G. Paterson, *Soviet-American confrontation: postwar reconstruction and the origins of the cold war* (Baltimore: Johns Hopkins Univ. Pr., 1973) **(B1372)**, distributes the blame for the cold war between the United States and the Soviet Union, the former in wanting to dominate the postwar era, the latter for its basic hostility toward the West. See also Daniel Yergin, *Shattered peace: the origins of the cold war and the national security state* (Boston: Houghton, 1977) **(B1373)**. Perhaps the most solid and balanced view is the model study by John L. Gaddis, *The United States and the origins of the cold war, 1941–1947* (B1241), who spreads the causes between the two superpowers, the United States because its policymakers were subject to domestic political pressures, the Soviets because Stalin was determined to keep his own power and to guarantee security along his nation's borders. Of the two, however, Gaddis holds the Soviets more responsible because Stalin was freer to compromise than was Truman. For a work that is highly critical of the revisionists' historical methodology as well as their ideas, see Robert J. Maddox, *The New Left and the origins of the cold war* (Princeton, N.J.: Princeton Univ. Pr., 1973) **(B1374)**.

The American decision to use the atomic bomb in the war has caused much disagreement among historians. Gar Alperovitz, *Atomic diplomacy: Hiroshima and Potsdam* (B1257), insists that the United States did not believe the bomb to be militarily necessary, but used it as "atomic diplomacy" to scare the Russians into submission during the postwar period. The result was cold war. Herbert Feis, *The atomic bomb and the end of World War II*, rev. ed. (Princeton, N.J.: Princeton Univ. Pr., 1966) **(B1375)**, sharply disagrees with Alperovitz. According to Feis, even though the bomb may have been unnecessary to win the war, the president's best military advice in 1945 was that its use would end the war quicker, thus saving perhaps a half million American lives. Martin J. Sherwin, *A world destroyed: the atomic bomb and the Grand Alliance* (B1256), shows how the decision to use the bomb was inseparable from scientific developments and congressional politics. See also Gregg Herken, *The winning weapon: the atomic bomb in the cold war, 1945–1950* (B1260).

Containment of Soviet communism became the central theme of the Truman period. Several accounts by participants in the administration are important. On containment theory, see two items by George F. Kennan, often called the architect of the policy: *American diplomacy: 1900–1950* (Chicago: Univ. of Chicago Pr., 1951) **(B1377)**, a collection of essays that includes his highly influential article from *Foreign affairs* magazine in July 1947: "The sources of Soviet conduct," pp. 566–82 **(B1378)**; and his *Memoirs, 1925–1950* (Boston: Little, 1967) **(B1379)**, in which he argues that he had not intended for containment policy to become military oriented. See also John L. Gaddis' superb analysis, *Strategies of containment: a critical appraisal of postwar American national security policy* (New York: Oxford Univ. Pr., 1982) **(B1380)**. For an administration member's account of the making of the Truman doctrine and Marshall Plan, see Joseph M. Jones, *The fifteen weeks (February 21–June 5, 1947)* (New York: Viking, 1955) **(B1381)**. Dean Acheson's *Present at the creation: my years in the State Department* (New York: Norton, 1969) **(B1382)**, is valuable on nearly all aspects of the Truman administration's foreign policy. Charles E. Bohlen's *Witness to history, 1929–1969* (New York: Norton, 1973) **(B1383)**, is an insightful memoir by another leading member of the administration. Two works by historian John Gimbel are important: *The American occupation of Germany: politics and the military, 1945–1949* (Stanford, Calif.: Stanford Univ. Pr., 1968) **(B1384)**, and *The origins of the Marshall Plan* (Stanford, Calif.: Stanford Univ. Pr., 1976) **(B1385)**. On the establishment of the Central Intelligence Agency, see Bradley F. Smith, *The shadow warriors: O.S.S. and the origins of the C.I.A.* (New York: Basic Books, 1983) **(B1386)**. See also previously mentioned works on the domestic aspects of the Truman period that contain material on foreign affairs as well.

There are several studies of the crises in the Far East during the Truman presidency. For two standard accounts of their subjects, see John K. Fairbank, *The United States and China*, 4th ed. (B1250), and Edwin O. Reischauer, *The United States and Japan*, 3rd ed. (Cambridge, Mass.: Harvard Univ. Pr., 1965) **(B1388)**. On the struggle between the United States and the Soviet Union over the occupation of Japan, see Herbert Feis, *Contest over Japan* (New York: Norton, 1967) **(B1389)**. For the China issue, see: Tang Tsou, *America's failure in China, 1941–1950* (B1251), who blames the United States for the fall of China to communism in 1949; Herbert Feis, *The China tangle: the American effort in China from Pearl Harbor to the Marshall mission* (B1253), who defends the administration against the charge; Barbara W. Tuchman, *Stilwell and* *the American experience in China, 1911–1945* (B1252), who shows that the Americans repeatedly failed to find someone other than Chiang Kai-shek to support in China; and Akira Iriye, *The cold war in Asia* (Englewood Cliffs, N.J.: Prentice-Hall, 1974) **(B1390)**, for a balanced analysis.

On the Korean War, see: David Rees, *Korea: the limited war* (New York: St. Martin's, 1964) **(B1391)**, for a discussion of the place of limited warfare in postwar America; Robert Leckie, *Conflict: the history of the Korean War, 1950–1953* (New York: Putnam, 1962) **(B1392)**, for a military history; Allen S. Whiting, *China crosses the Yalu: the decision to enter the Korean War* (New York: Macmillan, 1960) **(B1393)**, for one of the most decisive moments in the war—China's decision to intervene; Glenn D. Paige, *The Korean decision [June 24–30, 1950]* (New York: Macmillan, 1968) **(B1394)**; and Joseph C. Goulden, *Korea: the untold story of the war* (New York: McGraw-Hill, 1982) **(B1395)**. John W. Spanier's *The Truman–MacArthur controversy and the Korean War* (Cambridge, Mass.: Harvard Univ. Pr., 1959) **(B1396)**, is indispensable to understanding the controversy between the president and the general that brought together all issues of such a limited war, including the constitutional question of who was to make policy—the civilian or the military. See also Douglas MacArthur, *Reminiscences* (New York: McGraw-Hill, 1964) **(B1397)**, for a defense of his strategy for winning the Korean War.

The foreign policy of the Eisenhower administration is undergoing an important revision by historians. Whereas earlier writers stressed the do-nothing policy of the president, recent scholars are finding that even though President Eisenhower was not publicly forceful and dynamic, he maintained firm control over events, preferring to make decisions in a quiet and undramatic fashion. For an important work propounding that view, see Robert A. Divine, *Eisenhower and the cold war* (New York: Oxford Univ. Pr., 1981) **(B1398)**. On the Suez crisis of the 1950s, see: Herman Finer, *Dulles over Suez: the theory and practice of his diplomacy* (London: Heinemann, 1964) **(B1399)**, a sharply critical view of Secretary of State John Foster Dulles; Hugh Thomas, *Suez* (New York: Harper, 1967) **(B1400)**; and Donald Neff, *Warriors at Suez: Eisenhower takes America into the Middle East* (New York: Simon & Schuster, 1981) **(B1401)**. See other works on the Eisenhower presidency mentioned earlier in this section.

The foreign policy of the Kennedy-Johnson years was also marked by tumult and conflict.

For Kennedy's problems in Cuba and the disaster at the Bay of Pigs in April 1961, see Tad Szulc and Karl E. Meyer, *The Cuban invasion: the chronicle of a disaster* (New York: Ballantine, 1962) **(B1402)**, an account written by two reporters who, independently of each other, uncovered the makings of the fiasco. Two other works showing America's involvement in the attempt to overthrow Fidel Castro are: Haynes Johnson, *The Bay of Pigs: The leaders' story of Brigade 2506* (New York: Norton, 1964) **(B1403)**, and Peter Wyden, *Bay of Pigs: the untold story* (New York: Simon & Schuster, 1979) **(B1404)**. On the Cuban missile crisis, see: Elie Abel, *The missile crisis* (New York: Lippincott, 1966) **(B1405)**, for a compelling account by a journalist; Graham T. Allison, *Essence of decision: explaining the Cuban missile crisis* (Boston: Little, 1971) **(B1406)**, a study of the decision-making process behind America's handling of the crisis; Herbert S. Dinerstein, *The making of a missile crisis, October 1962* (Baltimore: Johns Hopkins Univ. Pr., 1976) **(B1407)**, an examination of the Soviet stance in the controversy; and Robert F. Kennedy, *Thirteen days: a memoir of the Cuban missile crisis* (New York: Norton, 1969) **(B1408)**, a dramatic account of the crisis by the president's brother and attorney general, who played a central role in resolving the matter peaceably. For a critical work referring to President Kennedy as the "Cold Warrior," see Robert J. Walton, *Cold war and counterrevolution: the foreign policy of John F. Kennedy* (New York: Viking, 1972) **(B1409)**. Richard J. Barnet, *Intervention and revolution: the United States in the Third World* (New York: New American Library, 1968) **(B1410)**, criticizes the administration's policies toward the Third World. Roger Hilsman's *To move a nation: the politics of foreign policy in the administration of John F. Kennedy* (New York: Dell, 1964) **(B1411)**, is a valuable account of the Kennedy foreign policy by a member of the administration. See also the relevant chapters in works cited earlier in the section on domestic affairs.

The Vietnam War is rapidly becoming one of the most written about topics in American foreign policy. Many previously cited works on post-World War II foreign policy touch upon various aspects of the Vietnam experience. For the best overview, see George C. Herring, Jr., *America's longest war: the United States and Vietnam, 1950–1975* (New York: Wiley, 1979) **(B1412)**, for a strong criticism of America's policy of containment in Southeast Asia. See also George M. Kahin and John W. Lewis, *The United States in Vietnam* (New York: Dial, 1969)

(B1413), and Stanley Karnow's new work, *Vietnam: a history* (New York: Viking-Penguin, 1983) (B1414). For a sharp criticism of America's involvement in Vietnam, see *The best and the brightest* (New York: Random, 1969) (B1415), by David Halberstam, a journalist who criticizes the decision-makers in Washington. For a defense of the White House based on Defense Department documents, see Guenter Lewy, *America in Vietnam* (New York: Oxford Univ. Pr., 1978) (B1416). On the background and context of America's involvement in Vietnam, see: Joseph Buttinger, *Vietnam: a dragon embattled*, 2v. (New York: Praeger, 1967) (B1417), and Frances FitzGerald, *Fire in the lake: the Vietnamese and the Americans in Vietnam* (New York: Random, 1972) (B1418), the latter a study which critics complained tended to romanticize the Vietcong, making the American position even more difficult to defend. Melvin Gurtov's *The first Vietnam crisis: Chinese communist strategy and United States involvement, 1953–1954* (New York: Columbia Univ. Pr., 1967) (B1419), is a useful coverage of America's decision against intervening to save the French at Dienbienphu in 1954. The journalist Bernard B. Fall contributed three first-rate accounts before his death in 1967: *The two Viet-Nams: a political and military analysis*, rev. ed. (New York: Praeger, 1967) (B1420); *Last reflections on a war* (Garden City, N.Y.: Doubleday, 1967) (B1421); and *Viet-Nam witness, 1953–66* (New York: Praeger, 1966) (B1422). Three other important journalistic works are Robert Shaplen's *The lost revolution: the United States in Vietnam, 1946–1966*, rev. ed. (New York: Harper, 1966) (B1423); *Time out of hand: revolution and reaction in Southeast Asia* (New York: Harper, 1969) (B1424); and *The road from war: Vietnam 1965–1970* (New York: Harper, 1970) (B1425). For a

critical analysis of the Diem regime and the American military escalation of the mid-1960s, see Jean Lacouture, *Vietnam: between two truces* (New York: Random, 1966) (B1426).

On the beginnings of what would be called "Vietnamization," see Townsend Hoopes, *The limits of intervention: the inside account of how the Johnson policy of escalation in Vietnam was reversed* (New York: McKay, 1969) (B1427). On the Gulf of Tonkin controversy, see Joseph C. Goulden, *Truth is the first casualty: the Gulf of Tonkin affair—illusion and reality* (Chicago: Rand McNally, 1969) (B1428). The publication in 1971 of *The Pentagon papers* by the *New York Times* revealed through classified Defense Department documents that the White House had been less than truthful in its explanations of the Vietnam involvement to the American public almost from the first year of its intervention. Leslie H. Gelb and Richard K. Betts, *The irony of Vietnam: the system worked* (Washington, D.C.: Brookings, 1979) (B1429), offer a controversial examination of America's experience in Vietnam. For an important study criticizing America's military strategy in the war, see Harry G. Summers, Jr., *On strategy: a critical analysis of the Vietnam War* (Novato, Calif.: Presidio, 1982) (B1430). See also Warren I. Cohen, *Dean Rusk* (Totowa, N.J.: Cooper Square, 1980) (B1431), a volume in the American Secretaries of State series; and Henry A. Kissinger's two volumes of memoirs—*White House years* (Boston: Little, 1979) (B1432), which covers the Nixon-Kissinger foreign policy and is especially strong on Southeast Asia; and *Years of upheaval* (Boston: Little, 1982) (B1433), which deals with the period from 1973 to 1975. See also Seymour M. Hersh's controversial study, *The price of power: Kissinger in the Nixon White House* (New York: Simon & Schuster, 1983) (B1434).

Howard Jones

Survey of the Reference Works

GUIDES TO THE LITERATURE
Basic and General Guides

B1435 American Historical Association. Guide to historical literature. New York: Macmillan, 1961. 962p.

Though more than 20 years old, and despite the fact that recent historical research has restructured the study of history in many areas, the *Guide* continues to provide information necessary for historical research. The value of the *Guide* lies in its presentation of seminal works in all subfields. Its 20,000 items are grouped into 35 major sections, some arranged by general topic (history of religions) and others by geographical area. Most entries are briefly annotated. When used in conjunction with the 1931 *Guide*, which includes older works not cited in this edition, and with sources reflecting scholarship of recent decades, the *Guide* helps provide a rounded approach to historical research.

B1436 Freidel, Frank, ed. Harvard guide to American history. Rev. ed. 2v. Cambridge, Mass.: Harvard Univ. Pr., 1974. 1,290p.

This edition of the standard guide to study and research in United States history represents a departure from the 1954 edition. Though still selective, opening chapters are now devoted to finding aids while the syllabi introducing bibliographic chapters are absent. One-third of the citations is to books and articles not listed in the 1954 *Guide*; publications appearing after June 30, 1970 are not included. In v.1, citations are arranged by general topic; those in v.2 by chronological period. Though citations are not annotated, the reputation of the *Guide* for the high quality of selections is deserved. Consult book reviews in the *Journal of American history* (B1486) for relevant recent articles and book reviews published after mid-1970. Expanded coverage of social and economic history is evident. See the 1954 edition of the *Harvard guide* for extensive sections on historical sources.

B1437 Griffin, Charles C., ed. Latin America: a guide to the historical literature. Austin: Univ. of Texas Pr., 1971. 700p.

This attempt to provide a basic research tool introducing the most important sources and histories covering the whole of Latin American history succeeds admirably. Introductory chapters on bibliography and broad subjects (e.g., art, economy, politics) are followed by others arranged chronologically and geographically. A critical paragraph accompanies each citation. The annual *Handbook of Latin American studies* (B1600) serves as an update by providing citations to current historical publications.

B1438 Henry Adams History Club, Harvard University. A select bibliography of history. 4th ed. Cambridge, Mass.: The Club, Dept. of History, Harvard Univ., 1970. 428p.

Aimed as it is at "young scholars, graduate students and the intelligent general reader," the work seeks to provide a bibliographic orientation to those "beginning a study of the field in question." Historical scholarship is divided into 42 fields, with each section including appropriate bibliographic and reference sources, periodicals, and general works, with a subject breakdown governed by the field of study itself. The limited purpose of the volume is fulfilled through discriminating selection of materials.

B1439 Paetow, Louis J. A guide to the study of medieval history. Rev. and corr. ed. Prepared under the auspices of the Medieval Academy of America. Millwood, N. Y.: Kraus, 1980. 643p.

B1440 Boyce, Gray Cowan. The literature of medieval history, 1930–1975; a supplement to Louis John Paetow's A guide to the study of medieval history. 5v. Millwood, N. Y.: Kraus, 1981. 2,630p.

The 1980 edition of Paetow is a reprint of the 1931 edition which includes materials published through 1928, along with an *Errata* compiled by Gray Boyce and a significant *Addendum* by Lynn Thorndike. Boyce's *Literature* serves as an update to Paetow and includes works published up to 1975. Organized on the same principles, these two works complement each other as exemplary scholarly guides. They are divided into three main parts: major general works (bibliographic works, reference sources, auxiliaries to the study of medieval history and original sources); general history of the Middle Ages (500–1500), and medieval culture. Extensive coverage of works in English, German and French, and more selective coverage of Spanish and Italian is evident. English history is not treated fully, the reader being referred to Charles Gross' *Sources and literature of English history . . . to about 1485* (2v., 1974) (B1589). Both Paetow and Boyce are extensively indexed.

B1441 Sauvaget, Jean. Introduction to the history of the Muslim East; a bibliographical guide. Based on the 2d ed. as recast by Claude Cohen. Berkeley: Univ. of California Pr., 1965. 252p.

This English translation of the standard guide to Islamic history in the Middle East contains revisions and corrections by the Near Eastern Center staff at UCLA. Prose-style bibliographic essays covering all aspects of cultural, religious, political, economic and social history are divided into three sections: sources of Muslim history, tools of research and general works, and historical bibliography. The last section provides valuable critical notes. Errors found in previous French editions have been corrected. For more recent literature, consult Albert Houvanis' "History," in Leonard Binder, *The study of the Middle East* (New York: Wiley, 1976), pp. 92–135 (**B1442**).

B1443 United States. Library of Congress. General Reference and Bibliography Division. A guide to the study of the United States of America: representative books reflecting the development of American life and thought. Washington, D.C.: Govt. Print. Off., 1960. 1,193p. Supplement, 1956–1965. Washington, D.C.: Govt. Print. Off., 1975. 526p.

Selective listing of approximately 10,000 titles organized in 32 chapters dealing with such broad topics as literature; geography; diplomatic, military, intellectual and local history; economic life; politics; science and technology. Annotations judge the contributions of works and cite related titles. Covers works published through 1965. Index of authors, subjects and titles. Especially useful to the general reader.

Specialized Guides

B1444 Beers, Henry P. The French and British in the old Northwest, a bibliographic guide to archives and manuscript sources. Detroit: Wayne State Univ. Pr., 1964. 297p.

Provides an historical account of the acquisition, preservation and publication of original records created by French and British officials in the old Northwest. A concluding chapter presents a bibliography of manuscripts, printed books and articles. An excellent source of information for researchers. For related material, see the author's *The French in North America: a bibliographical guide to French archives, reproductions, and research missions* (Baton Rouge: Louisiana State Univ. Pr., 1957) (**B1445**); for a discussion of manuscripts and records of Spanish and Mexican origin relating to the southwestern United States, see Beers' *Spanish and Mexican records of the American Southwest: a bibliographical guide to archives and manuscript sources* (Tucson: Univ. of Arizona Pr., 1979) (**B1446**).

B1447 Carnegie Institution, Washington, D.C. Guides to manuscript materials for the history of the United States. Washington, D.C.: 1906–43. Reprint, New York: Kraus, 1965. 23v.

Individual monographs provide guides, inventories, calendars, lists of archives, manuscripts and other unpublished material in American and European repositories. Valuable tools for research are discussed, especially those on British, British-American, European, Spanish and Spanish-American archives. Some have been superseded. Among recent revisions are B. R. Crick and Miriam Alman. *A guide to manuscripts relating to America in Great Britain and Ireland* (London: Oxford Univ. Pr., 1961 [667p.]) (**B1448**), and John W. Raimo's revision of Crick and Alman (Westport, Conn.: Meckler, 1979) (**B1449**).

B1450 Foster, Janet and Julia Sheppard. British archives: a guide to archive resources in the United Kingdom. London: Macmillan, 1982. 533p.

Covers all types of repositories, aiming to provide "a starting point for first time users of [British] archives." Listings for 708 repositories appear describing collections held, guides and publications available to assist researchers, and address information. A key subject word index and a general index to collections increase the usefulness of the volume, while a selected bibliography leads to more detailed guides, among them M. D. Wainwright, *A guide to western manuscripts and documents in the British Isles relating to South and Southeast Asia* (New York: Oxford Univ. Pr., 1965) (**B1451**); P. Walne, *A guide to manuscript sources for the history of Latin America and the Caribbean in the British Isles* (London: Oxford Univ. Pr. for the Institute of Latin American Studies, Univ. of London, 1973) (**B1452**); Noel Matthews, *A guide to manuscripts and documents relating to the Far East* (Oxford: Oxford Univ. Pr., 1977) (**B1453**); Noel Matthews and M. D. Wainwright, *A guide to manuscripts and documents in the British Isles relating to the Middle East and North Africa* (New York: Oxford Univ. Pr., 1980) (**B1454**).

B1455 Gipson, Lawrence H. A bibliographical guide to the history of the British Empire, 1748–1776. v.14 of The British Empire before the American Revolution. New York: Knopf, 1969. 478p.

B1456 ———. A guide to the manuscripts relating to the history of the British Empire, 1745–1776. v.15 of The British Empire before the American Revolution. New York: Knopf, 1970. 490p.

The 2 concluding volumes of Gipson's respected multivolume work serve as a guide to the vast majority of printed and manuscript materials in major repositories in Great Britain, France, Spain, Canada, the West Indies and the United States. Some entries, arranged basically by geographical area, are annotated. Indexes are quite helpful. Provides information of great value for a much longer time period than indicated by the title. These volumes serve to complement relevant volumes in the Carnegie guide series.

B1457 Great Britain. Public Record Office. Guide to the contents of the Public Record Office. 3v. London: HMSO, 1963–68. 850p.

A revision of M. S. Giuseppi's *Guide to the manuscripts preserved in the Public Record Office*, 2v. (London: HMSO, 1923–24) (**B1458**), updated to include holdings accessioned through December, 1966. Provides information essential to the effective use of documents found in the Public Record Office by presenting a brief introduction to the source of records, dates and organization of records, and notation of specific printed guides to special parts of collections. Indexes of persons, places and subjects assist readers. Students and scholars new to the use of the Public Record Office will still profit from V. H. Galbraith, *An introduction to the use of the public records* (Oxford: Clarendon, 1934 [112p.]; reprint, London: Oxford Univ. Pr., 1971) (**B1459**).

B1460 Higham, Robin, ed. A guide to the sources of United States military history. Hamden, Conn.: Archon Books, 1975. Supplement I, 1981. 859p.

Bibliographical essays deal with broad topics arranged chronologically (e.g., "Colonial forces, 1607–1776"; "Sciences and technology in the nineteenth century"; "The army, 1945–1973"), with a concluding chapter on museums. The authors, all well-known scholars, present essays discussing titles which are keyed to a bibliography which follows. All types of historical sources are covered and critical comments help evaluate sources.

B1461 Meckler, Alan M. and Ruth McMullin. Oral history collections. New York: Bowker, 1975. 344p.

Provides a "comprehensive" annotated listing of oral history collections located in libraries, oral history centers and archives. A name/subject index leads to descriptions of holdings by institution. Institutional listings discuss the contents of collections and provide location information, while name entries include an indication of profession, years of the subject's life, subject of holdings, number of pages and location. Organized generally following the pattern used by Elizabeth B. Mason and Louis M. Starr in *The oral history collection of Columbia University* (New York: Oral History Research Office, Columbia Univ., 1979 [306p.]) **(B1462)**.

B1463 Newberry Library Center for the History of the American Indian. Bibliographical series. Bloomington: Indiana Univ. Pr., various dates.

A continuing series of volumes designed to help advanced scholars as well as new students cope with the uneven quality of literature on the history and culture of American Indians. Intended as guides to reliable sources and studies, some titles are devoted to culture areas, others to individual tribes and still others to contemporary and historical issues. Bibliographical essays critically evaluate works which are listed alphabetically by author following the essay. Among individual titles are Francis Paul Prucha, *United States Indian policy* (1977) **(B1464)**; Robert J. Surtees, *Canadian Indian policy* (1982) **(B1465)**; Henry F. Dobyns and Robert C. Euter, *Indians of the Southwest* (1980) **(B1466)** and C. A. Weslager, *The Delawares* (1978) **(B1467)**.

B1468 Nunn, G. Raymond. Asia; reference works, a select annotated guide. London: Mansell, 1980. 365p.

A guide to reference works on Asian studies, including India, Pakistan, Kampuchea, Indonesia, China, Japan, Korea and Mongolia. Nunn provides annotated citations which inform readers of the content and merits of various sources of information. A large percentage of cited titles is of interest for historical research. Entries are arranged by country, then by type of work. An author-title index assists readers.

B1469 Poulton, Helen J. The historian's handbook: a descriptive guide to reference works. Norman: Univ. of Oklahoma Pr., 1972. 304p.

Discusses the merits of over 700 sources of information for the historian, including national and trade bibliographies; guides; encyclopedias; serial and newspaper guides; geographical, biographical and legal sources; dissertations; and government publications. An easily used guide to a wide range of reference sources which supplements material contained in this chapter. Index of titles, general index and detailed table of contents make it a fine reference work.

B1470 Rubicam, Milton, ed. Genealogical research: methods and research, v. 1. Rev. ed. Washington, D.C.: American Society of Genealogists, 1980. 579p.

Following an introductory section on general methods of genealogical research, discussions of genealogical sources are organized into sections on original sources, public records, secondary materials, regional sources (arranged by state or province) and pre-American ancestry. A concluding section deals with heraldry, genealogy and the law, and surnames. Essays describe and evaluate the contents of relevant documents in a clear, concise manner which is useful for historical as well as genealogical research.

B1471 United States. Library of Congress. Manuscript sources in the Library of Congress for research on the American Revolution. Washington, D.C.: Library of Congress, 1975. 372p.

Presents descriptions of manuscripts relevant to the study of the American Revolution which are held by the Library of Congress. Divided into "Domestic collections" and "Foreign reproductions," entries describe the contents of record groups along with biographical information and guides which are available. Indexed by subject.

B1472 United States. National Archives and Records Service. Guide to the National Archives of the United States. Washington, D.C.: Supt. of Doc., 1974. 884p.

Superseding the 1948 *Guide*, coverage includes all official records of the U.S. government accessioned before June 30, 1970. Papers and manuscripts held by presidential libraries are not included. Entries cover more than 1 million cubic feet of records, as well as maps, microfilm, motion pictures, photographs and sound recordings, and are arranged by record group and introduced by a short administrative history of each agency. Descriptions of contents also appear. Ease of use is assured through indexes by record group and administrative units, and by broad subjects. Updates to the *Guide* are found principally in *Prologue* **(B1473)**, the periodical publication of the National Archives and Records Service.

Supplementing this general volume, from time to time the National Archives and Records Service has published subject guides to federal records aimed at a broad spectrum of scholars. Among recent volumes are the *Guide to federal records relating to the Civil War* (1962) **(B1474)**; *Guide to the archives of the government of the Confederate States of America* (1968) **(B1475)**; and *Guide to materials on Latin America in the National Archives of the United States* (1974) **(B1476)**.

B1477 United States. National Historical Publications and Records Commission. Directory of archives and manuscripts repositories in the United States. Washington, D.C.: The Commission, 1978. 905p.

Presents full entries for 2,675 archives and repositories, with abbreviated entries for others. Describes holdings of photographs, machine-readable data records, sound recordings and other types of historical documents as well as manuscripts and correspondence. Entries are arranged by state with subject/corporate body index and a directory of repositories by type (e.g., medical, local, historical). Complements the well-respected work by Philip M. Hamer, *A guide to archives and manuscripts in the United States* (New Haven, Conn.: Yale Univ. Pr., 1961 [775p.]) **(B1478)**.

REVIEWS OF THE LITERATURE

B1479 The American historical review. v.1– , Oct., 1895– . Washington, D.C. 5/yr.

More than half of this premier journal is devoted to book reviews of historical literature covering all periods and all areas. Editorial policy regarding materials chosen for review and reviewers is conservative. Major festschriften and collections are analyzed, and a listing of documents and bibliographies, international in scope, appears in each issue. The annual index includes book reviews. Articles published here carry footnotes which indicate other writings to be consulted. The American Historical Association also publishes *AHA perspectives* (B1758) which serves as its newsletter, carrying historiographical and bibliographical comments and controversy as well as notes on research and publications in progress.

B1480 Economic history review. First ser., v.1–18, 1927–48; second ser., v.1– , 1948– . Cambridge. Quarterly.

An important source for scholarly reviews of both current monographic and periodical literature, approximately 35 monographs are reviewed in each issue, mainly by well-known British scholars. Reviews concentrate on the economic history of the British Isles and Europe, but also deal with other areas. Articles generally avoid theoretical discussions in economic modeling. An annual review of periodical literature is published, as are bibliographic essays reviewing the literature on selected topics in economic history (e.g., "The population history of England, 1541–1871"), and annual lists of publications on the economic and social history of Great Britain and Ireland.

B1481 English historical review. v.1– , 1886– . London. Quarterly.

A major British historical journal which provides 60–80 reviews and an average of 300 "short notices" annually. All periods of history and all geographical areas are covered, with emphasis on Great Britain and Europe. The July number contains "Notices of periodical and occasional publications" for the preceding calendar year, where coverage is international in scope, and entries are organized by country or continent with emphasis on Europe. The annual index provides a listing of reviews and short notices.

B1482 Hispanic American historical review. v.1– , 1918– . Durham, N.C. Quarterly.

In this English-language source for reviews of books dealing with Latin American history, reviews are divided into three broad chronological periods along with general works and related topics. English and foreign language monographs, festschriften and reference works are reviewed by respected scholars in the field. Book reviews are followed by a limited number of abstracts of books not chosen for review, and a list of other books received. Reviews follow between 1 and 2 years after publication.

B1483 Historical Association, London. Annual bulletin of historical literature. v.1– , 1911– .

Emphasizing European history, especially Great Britain, each issue presents selective bibliographies of publications devoted almost exclusively to the year in question. Arrangement is by period for Europe and geographically for other parts of the world. Both monographic and periodical literature are covered with brief citations. The subject of history is broadly construed when scholar-contributors choose works for inclusion. A name index concludes each volume.

B1484 The historical journal. v.1– , 1958– . London. Quarterly.

Reviews appear in three settings. A limited number of individual monographs are reviewed in each issue 1 to 2 years following publication in the "Other reviews" section. In the "Review articles" section, between 3 and 10 monographs are discussed on their merits and in relation to one another. Twice each year, historiographical reviews cover recent studies on more general topics (e.g., the English Reformation, Scottish independence). Editorial policy is conservative and emphasis strongly favors British history. The annual index includes separate sections on "Books reviewed" and "Review articles and historiographical reviews."

B1485 Historische Zeitschrift. v.1– , 1859– . Munich. Bimonthly.

History is defined very broadly here, and coverage is international in this respected European historical journal. Roughly 50 percent of each issue is devoted to book reviews, and concludes with a review of recent periodical contents. Both sections are organized by historical period. Reviews written generally by German scholars serve to effectively survey German language historical scholarship. Because of its excellence, *Historische zeitschrift* is perhaps the most important single source of international scope for reviews of the literature. The *Sonderheften* (v.1– , 1962–) offer specialized bibliographic studies of recent literature on such topics as France in the Middle Ages (1982). Authors are recognized scholars and fine indexing makes each volume very usable.

B1486 Journal of American history. v.1– , 1914– .
    Bloomington, Ind. Quarterly.
    The 400 book reviews published annually deal with all aspects of American history, including Canada and the diplomatic history of the United States and Canada. Coverage concentrates on monographs published in North America, but occasionally includes works on North American history published in Europe. This most respected of journals devoted to American history appeared as the *Mississippi Valley Historical Review* until 1964 when its publisher, the Organization of American Historians, renamed it. Scholarly articles are well-documented and serve as bibliographic sources for specific topics. A list of recently published articles also appears in each issue, as does a list of books received but not reviewed entitled "Book notes" which includes most textbooks, collections, anthologies and reference works.

B1487 Journal of modern history. v.1– , 1929– .
    Chicago. Quarterly.
    Reviews cover the diplomatic, political, social, cultural, philosophical, intellectual, economic and technological history of Europe (including Russia) since the Renaissance. Prominent American and British scholars are called upon as reviewers, also contributing review articles evaluating work on specific topics (e.g., "History of European Jewry"). An annual index assists the reader seeking reviews of the literature.

B1488 Reviews in American history. v.1– , 1973– .
    Baltimore. Quarterly.
    Each issue reviews approximately 25 monographs. Reviews by published American scholars take the form of essays, some with footnotes, which evaluate works in their scholarly context. When appropriate, reviewers treat several related publications. Unique because of the extended depth of the reviews, the lag time between publication and the appearance of the review remains typical for the field at between 1 and 2 years. The quality of the reviews, limited almost exclusively to United States history, has improved since the appearance of v.1.

B1489 Revue historique. v.1– , 1876– . Paris.
    Quarterly.
    Including historical studies and those in related fields, this prominent French historical journal presents upwards of 100 reviews in each issue concentrating on the history of France. Reviewers are French scholars, and emphasis is more heavily on subjects in social and economic history, reflecting the influence of social historians such as Lefebvre, Marc Bloch and Braudel. Twice each year, essays summarizing recent scholarship on a particular topic are published, and each issue contains a section devoted to short reviews ("Notes bibliographique"), another to dissertations in progress and dissertation defenses, and a third to recent periodical literature. A list of books received concludes each issue. An annual index is provided.

B1490 Speculum; a journal of medieval studies. v.1– , 1926– . Cambridge, Mass. Quarterly.
    Devoted to all aspects of medieval studies, *Speculum* publishes more than 200 full length reviews annually as well as numerous shorter notices and lists of books received. Coverage is limited to the Middle Ages in European history, and works on the arts, literature and religious studies mix with more narrowly defined historical studies. While English language scholarly works receive greater attention, studies in West European languages also are reviewed along with published documents and writings of the medieval period. Consult the annual "Contents" for a list of the year's major reviews.

ONLINE DATABASES FOR HISTORICAL RESEARCH

Many online databases contain some information relevant to historical research. As time passes and the depth of available databases grows, their usefulness to historians will increase. Two online databases, using similar indexing systems, survey the periodical literature of history.

B1491 America: history and life, 1964– . (DIALOG: File 38) Published by ABC-Clio, Inc.
    Online coverage of U.S. and Canadian history and culture in all periods and fields begins with 1964. Journal articles and essays in collections are included; in 1974 some books and dissertations were added. Among the roughly 2,000 journals surveyed are those of national, regional, state and local historical associations and societies, along with journals in related fields. Over 1,000 foreign periodicals also receive treatment. Indexing has been somewhat erratic. The SPIndex system is used allowing free text searching with general and specific terms as well as chronological periods in both titles and abstracts. Coverage of 1954–74 is incomplete in online mode. Available printed with 5-year cumulations, as well as online.

B1492 Historical abstracts, 1973– . (DIALOG: File 39) Published by ABC-Clio, Inc.
    Unlike the paper edition, *Historical abstracts* online begins coverage with 1973 and includes articles and essays in collections dealing with world history since 1450 excluding North America. Surveys the same list of periodicals as its brother, *America: history and life*, with a necessarily higher incidence of foreign language citations. English translations of titles and annotations in English provide assistance. The inconsistent nature of the database is apparent when searching chronologically, and employing search terms with variant definitions and usages. Coverage varies in printed volumes covering 1955 to present.
    Many other online databases offer assistance for historical research. Among them are *Comprehensive dissertation index*, 1973– (**B1493**), *ERIC*, 1966– (**B1494**), *Social scisearch*, 1972– (**B1495**), *PAIS international*, 1972– (**B1496**), and *United States political science documents*, 1975– (**B1497**).

BIBLIOGRAPHIES OF BIBLIOGRAPHIES

B1498 Beers, Henry Putney. Bibliographies in American history, 1942–78. 2v. Woodbridge, Conn.: Research Pubns., 1982. 946p.

Organized on the same subject pattern as the author's *Bibliographies in American history* (New York: Wilson, 1942; reprinted 1959 and 1963) **(B1499)**, resources for the study of American history which appeared between 1942 and 1978 are cited. Used together, the 1942 edition and this volume provide valuable bibliographic listings, including articles, manuscript bibliographies and compilations. Coverage is limited to the United States, though actual sources and other materials from Canada, France, Great Britain, South and Central America have been included when they relate to United States history. Political, social, military, religious, economic and cultural history receive treatment, along with regional, state and, to a limited extent, local history. V.2 provides a state-by-state listing of bibliographic sources relating to each state. Government documents are covered, and an index of personal names, subjects and place names is helpful.

B1500 Coulter, Edith M. and Melanie Gerstenfeld. Historical bibliographies; a systematic and annotated guide. Berkeley: Univ. of California Pr., 1935. 206p.

Covering bibliographies published before 1935, this well-annotated list dealing only with printed materials provides readers with information on important early bibliographies. Entries indicate where reviews of cited works are found. International in scope, the work concludes with a name/subject index.

B1501 Rouse, Richard H. Serial bibliographies for medieval studies. Berkeley: Univ. of California Pr., 1969. 170p.

Provides an introduction to 294 serial bibliographies which pertain wholly or in part to medieval studies. Entries list the title, publisher, place of publication, date of first publications and a descriptive annotation outlining its coverages, organization and features. Arranged by broad subjects with cross-references to similar titles listed elsewhere. Successfully presents this difficult-to-assemble-and-use body of literature.

For a more general source covering many fields related to history, see Richard A. Gray and Dorothy Villmow, *Serial bibliographies in the humanities and social sciences* (Ann Arbor, Mich.: Pierian, 1969) **(B1502)** which provides (now somewhat dated) selective coverage.

The *Bibliographic index* (A175) is useful for updating works such as Gray and Villmore, and for discovering more current bibliographies.

CURRENT BIBLIOGRAPHIES

B1503 L'Année philologique; bibliographie critique et analytique de l'antiquité greco-latine 1924/26– . Paris: Société d'Edition "Les Belles Lettres," 1928– . Annual.

Annual volumes present publications for the year in 2 parts. Pt. 1, "Auteurs et textes," is arranged by classical authors and lists texts and studies relating to that author. Pt. 2 classifies entries by subject, listing works on the history and culture of the classical world (e.g., literary history, paleography, archeology, history). Publications relating to Greece and Rome from prehistoric times to approximately 800 A.D. are included. Coverage includes books with their reviews, and periodical articles often with annotation. Festschriften are listed separately. Volumes conclude with an index of classical names, a geographical name index, an index of humanists who utilized classical authors, and an index of authors. For coverage of earlier periods, consult S. Lambino's *Bibliographie classique des années 1896 à 1914* (Paris: 1951) **(B1504)**, of which only v.1 has been published, and Jules Marouzeau, *Dix années de bibliographie classique . . . 1914–1924* (Paris: 1927–28) **(B1505)**.

B1506 Bibliografia storica nazionale. v.1– , 1939– . Rome: Scalia Editore, 1939–41; Rome: Laterza, 1942– .

Annual volumes list books, articles and sources on Italian history published during the year in question, beginning with 1939. The whole of Italian history is covered, from prehistory to 1978. Local, regional and national history receives attention, with foreign publications included very rarely, but many translations of foreign works into Italian appear in their Italian editions. A name index concludes each volume.

B1507 Bibliografía histórica mexicana, v.1– , 1967–. Guanajuato: El Colegio de Mexico, 1967–. Annual.

Including books, articles and dissertations relating the history of Mexico for all periods, the *Bibliografía* is international in scope and cites works principally in Spanish, English and French. Coverage is not comprehensive, but does provide information on works published in the Western Hemisphere. Citations in each volume lead to publications of the last 2 years with a few exceptions. Entries are arranged by subjects, among them general histories of Mexico, ethnic history, prehistory, colonial history, the Mexican Revolution, regional histories by region, as well as diplomatic, agrarian, social, religious and similar subjects. Of importance is the section on bibliographic studies, and that on documents and archives. Citations are in the language of publication, and an author index contributes to ease of use.

B1508 Bibliographie annuelle de l'histoire de France du cinquième siècle à 1939. 1953– . Paris: CNRS, 1956– .

Indexes numerous French and foreign periodicals, papers presented at congresses and the contents of "melanges," both French and foreign, citing works on French history from the 5th century A.D. The terminal date has advanced to 1958. Citations are arranged by subject classifications, with no annotations provided. In addition to the current annual volumes, volumes covering earlier years are in preparation. The goal is to fill the gap between the *Bibliographie annuelle* and its predecessor, the *Répertoire bibliographique de l'histoire de France* (Paris: Picard, 1923–38; reprint, Aalen: Scientia, 1972 [6v.]) **(B1509)**. This biennial classified bibliography of books and articles on the history of France from earliest times to 1914 was snuffed out by World War II. It cites books reviews, gives explanatory notes and is a valuable source for the years it covers, 1920–31. The classified arrangement of the *Répertoire* has been adopted by the *Bibliographie*.

B1510 Bibliographie internationale de l'humanisme et de la Renaissance. v.1– , 1965– . Geneva: Droz, 1966– .

With the cooperation of scholarly societies in Europe and the United States, all aspects of human activity in the 15th and 16th centuries in Europe and related areas which appear in monographs, periodicals and series have been included. Chronological limits are loosely adhered to. The first part of the bibliography lists works by and about individuals by personal name, while the second part is arranged by subject. Works in all European languages appear, with a name and subject index concluding this valuable source. The volume for 1977 appeared in 1982.

B1511 Indice historico español. v.1– , 1953– . Barcelona: Ed. Teide, 1953– .

A quarterly review providing extensive lists of books and articles on the history of Spain and Spanish America in all languages and published in all countries. Citations include signed critical annotations. Author and subject indexes are provided.

B1512 International bibliography of historical sciences. v.1– , 1926– . Paris: Colin, 1930– .

Each volume for given years presents selective lists of major published historical works, both monographs and periodical articles, dealing with all geographical areas and all periods. No evaluation or annotation is provided. The subject of history is divided into broad areas focusing on European history by period with separate lists for Africa, Asia and America. The value of selections varies from volume to volume, and within volumes. Recently, coverage of the Western Hemisphere has been of little value. The volume for 1978–79 appeared in 1982.

B1513 International medieval bibliography. 1967– . Dept. of History, Univ. of Minnesota and Univ. of Leeds (Eng.): 1968– .

Semiannual volumes list articles, notes and review articles, but not book reviews, on all aspects of medieval studies, arranged by subject (e.g., demography, literature-verse, sources). The 1981 volumes examined nearly 1,000 journals, festschriften, colloquium papers and collections. Coverage is limited to Europe, including Russia, North Africa and the Byzantine Empire between the years 500–1500 A.D.

The *IMB* is supplemented by the now defunct *International guide to medieval studies; a quarterly index to periodical literature* (v. 1–12, 1961–73) **(B1514)** for the period before 1967.

B1515 Jahresberichte der Geschichtswissenschaft; im Auftrage der Historischen Gesellschaft zu Berlin. v.1–36, 1878–1913. Berlin: Mittler, 1880–1916.

This annual compilation, international in scope, presents comprehensive and accurate classified listings of historical studies published each year (in narrative form). Review articles written by acknowledged authorities cover books and periodical articles in the major European languages.

Limited to Germany, coverage continued in the *Jahresberichte der deutschen Geschichte* (v. 1–7; 1918–24; Breslau: Priebalschs, 1920–26) **(B1516)**. It was superseded in turn by the *Jahresberichte für deutsche Geschichte* (B1517).

B1517 Jahresberichte für deutsche Geschichte. v. 1–15/16, 1925–39/40. Leipzig: Koeler, 1927–42. new ser., v. 1– , 1941– . Berlin: Academie-Verlag, 1952– .

Continues the *Jahresberichte der deutschen Geschichte* (B1516). In volumes for 1925–39/40, the first part lists citations by period up to 1919. The second part provides evaluations of material presented in pt. 1. Volumes in the new series contain only the bibliography, which lists writings in European languages on German history through 1945. Books, articles and collections are covered, though works of local interest are omitted. Helpful author and subject indexes. Volumes are published approximately 2 years after the year(s) in question.

B1518 Recently published articles. 1976– . Washington, D.C.: American Historical Assn., 1976– . 3/yr.

Previously published as a part of the *American historical review*, this publication provides current listings of articles of interest to historians appearing in some 4,000 journals from around the world. Journals of related disciplines which publish articles important for historical study also receive treatment. All periods of history and all areas of the world fall under scrutiny. Arrangement is geographical and chronological, with citations including no annotations. The thrice yearly issues are not cumulated and no indexes are provided, forcing readers to rely on the broad subject categories. While currency is its strong point, individual issues are intended for browsing rather than sophisticated subject searching.

B1519 Writings on American history. 1902– . Various publishers.

Publishers of this valuable bibliography of works relating to American history have changed. Current periodical literature is covered on a worldwide basis in recent volumes, though coverage varies somewhat during the history of the series. Many volumes contain annotations, with citations to critical reviews found in pre-World War II volumes.

Writings began in 1902 as a continuation of *The*

literature of American history (Chicago: American Library Assn., 1902) **(B1520)** which covered works published in 1899–1901. Volumes for 1902–60 were issued as supplementary volumes to the *Annual reports* of the American Historical Association. No volumes have been published for 1904, 1905 and 1941–47, but recent volumes appear on a timely basis.

Annual volumes have individual indexes. The need for a cumulative index was met in part by the *Index to the "Writings on American history,"* 1902–40 (Washington, D.C.: American Historical Assn., 1956) **(B1521)**.

RETROSPECTIVE BIBLIOGRAPHIES
General and by Period

B1522 Chevalier, Cyr Ulysse J. Répertoire des sources historiques du Moyen Age. Nouv. éd., refondue, corr. et augm. Paris: Picard, 1894–1907. Reprint, New York: Kraus, 1959–60.

Divided into 2 parts: The topo-bibliographie, providing bibliographic citations to books, periodicals, society publications, and other printed sources, arranged alphabetically under the French form of names, along with very brief explanatory notes; the biobibliographie provides similar citations for people following very brief biographical notes. Publications listed are not evaluated, and coverage of the literature is selective, emphasizing 19th-century publications.

B1523 Combined retrospective index set to journals in history, 1838–1974. Washington, D.C.: Carrollton Pr., 1977–   . 11v.

Drawing together into a single publication subject access to 243 English-language history periodicals from their beginning—as early as 1838—through 1974, *CRIS* lists articles under key word and assigned subject words with each article identified by an assigned number. Journal codes are identified in the front end papers of each volume. The vast majority of journals covered were published in the United States, and all were active as of 1974. Despite limited coverage, failure to list superseded journal titles, and indexing inconsistencies, *CRIS-history* proves helpful in developing bibliographies on specific topics.

B1524 Czarra, Fred. A guide to historical reading: non-fiction; for the use of schools, libraries and the general reader. 11th rev. ed. Washington, D.C.: Heldref, 1983. 312p.

This well-known work aims at providing public and school librarians and teachers, as well as those interested in the past, with books on historical subjects that are easy to read and worthwhile. The nonscholarly audience will find books on the United States and Europe, but little on other areas. Annotations are informative and the selective character of the volume suggests that only books of merit are included.

This edition is based on the earlier editions which Hannah Logasa compiled. See her *Historical fiction: guide for junior and senior high schools and colleges, also for the general reader*, 9th rev. and enl. ed. (Brooklawn, N.J.: McKinley, 1968 [383p.]) **(B1525)** for complementing fictional listings.

B1526 Frewer, Louis B. Bibliography of historical writings published in Great Britain and the Empire, 1940–1945. Oxford, Eng.: Basil Blackwell, 1947. Reprint, Westport, Conn.: Greenwood, 1974. 346p.

Intended to fill the gap in the *International bibliography of historical sciences* (B1512) created by World War II, this work is edited on the same principles and uses the same subject headings. Only the British books, articles and reviews intended for the *IBHS* are cited. Continued by Joan C. Lancaster, *Bibliography of historical works issued in the United Kingdom, 1946–1956* (London: 1957 [388p.]) **(B1527)**, and William Kellaway, *Bibliography of historical works issued . . . 1957–1960* (London: 1962 [236p.]) **(B1528)**; *1961–1965* (London: 1967 [298p.]) **(B1529)**; *1966–1970* (London: 1972 [322p.]) **(B1530)**. The latter 4 volumes exclude articles and reviews.

B1531 International Committee of Historical Sciences. Bibliographie internationale des travaux historiques publiés dans les volumes de "Mélanges," 1880–1939; 1940–1950. Paris: Colin, 1955–65. 443p.

Presenting an international bibliography of articles and miscellanies, pt. 1 contains a list of volumes which are indexed, and arranged by country. Pt. 2 arranges citations for indexed articles by subject classification. An index of subjects treated in enumerated volumes along with an index of personal names, historical events, institutes and societies, and an author index make the work easier to use. Coverage is limited to works published in Europe. V.2 covering festschriften published between 1940 and 1950 was published in 1965.

More recent, but arranged somewhat differently, are three titles which inform readers about festschriften. The New York Public Library, Research Libraries, *Guide to festschriften; the retrospective festschriften collection of the New York Public Library: materials cataloged through 1971*, 2v. (Boston: Hall, 1977) **(B1532)** presents the rich holdings of the library. Otto Leistner, *International bibliography of festschriften* (Osnabruck, 1976 [893p.]) **(B1533)** covers 1850–1974, and may in part be updated by the *Internationale Jahresbibliographie der Festschriften*, v. 1– , 1980–   (1982–   ) **(B1534)**.

B1535 Mayer, Hans Eberhard. Bibliographie zur Geschichte der Kreuzzuge. Hanover: Hahnsche, 1960. 270p.

A valuable detailed bibliography for the Crusades. The 5,300 citations to books and periodical articles in all relevant languages are arranged by type of material and by subject. Particularly valuable is the section on primary sources. Related subjects such as geography are covered. No annotations are provided, but an index of authors, editors and translators proves helpful.

For a more current bibliography consult Gray

C. Boyce, *The literature of medieval history, 1930–1975* . . . (B1440), and the bibliographic notes in Kenneth M. Setton, *History of the crusades*, 2d ed.(Madison: Univ. of Wisconsin Pr., 1969–)(**B1536**).

An earlier English language introduction to Crusade literature is found in Aziz S. Atiya, *The crusade; historiography and bibliography* (Bloomington: Indiana Univ. Pr., 1962 [170p.])(**B1537**) which outlines the monumental works and covers primary and secondary sources.

B1538 New York Public Library. Dictionary catalog of the Research Libraries of the New York Public Library, 1911–1971. New York: The Library, 1979. 800v.

This monumental bibliographic compilation provides probably the single most useful bibliography for the study of historical subjects produced in the United States. The card catalog of the Research Libraries is reproduced, cards having been analyzed for accuracy before inclusion. Represents collections in the Astor, Tilden and Lenox libraries before 1895. The catalog is continued by the *Dictionary catalog of the Research Libraries, 1972–* (**B1539**).

B1540 Repertorium fontium historiae medii aevi; primum ab Augusto Potthast digestum, nunc cura collegii historicorum e pluribus nationibus emendalum et auctum. Rome: Instituto storico italiano per il medio evo, 1962– .

Known as the "new Potthast," it supersedes the classic *Bibliotheca historica Medii Aevi: Wegweiser durch die Geschichtswerke des europäischen Mittelalters bis 1500. 2. Verm. und verb. Aufl.* (Berlin: Weber, 1896 [2 v.]; reprint, Graz: Akademische Druck-u. Verlagsanstalt, 1957) (**B1541**). V.1 (1962, 819p.) lists all major collections of sources relating to the European Middle Ages and analyzes individual volumes by title and date. An Additamenta (1973)(**B1542**) updates these lists with collections published between 1962 and 1973, and concludes with a list of corrections for the 1962 volume.

The central bibliography of the "new Potthast" will encompass many volumes, the fourth of which appeared in 1976. Entries are arranged alphabetically by original name or title. After a brief geographical note, the location of the manuscript is given, and editions and variants noted along with commentaries, translations and special studies. As of 1983, volumes for A–Gez were available.

B1543 Roach, John. A bibliography of modern history. Cambridge: Cambridge Univ. Pr., 1968. 388p.

This companion bibliographic volume to the *New Cambridge modern history* (B1677) is intended to provide "useful introductions to new subjects" for serious students of history. Emphasis lies on monographs with articles cited sparingly and manuscript sources excluded. Coverage includes European Russia and the overseas expansion of European power and influence. Among the 6,000 cited works, few were published after 1960. Many citations carry short annotations.

B1544 Rounds, Dorothy. Articles on antiquity in festschriften. The ancient Near East, the Old Testament, Greece, Rome, Roman law, Byzantium. An index. Cambridge, Mass.: Harvard Univ. Pr., 1962. 560p.

Analyzing festschriften published between 1863 and 1954, work dealing with the period from the end of the Neolithic period in Egypt, Mesopotamia, Syria, Asia Minor, the Aegean area, Crete, Greek lands and Italy (from the early Bronze Age, and including the whole of the Roman Empire) is included. Terminal dates vary: Byzantium—1453 A.D., Rome about 400 A.D. Indexes all authors, titles of articles and the person or institution honored.

For updated listings see the *American historical review* (B1479) and other journals listed above under "Reviews of the literature."

Asia and Australia

Much of the bibliography of Asian history is found in Asian studies sources evaluated elsewhere in this volume (see chap. 6). In particular see the *Bibliography of Asian studies*, 1956– (Ann Arbor: Assoc. for Asian Studies, 1957– [Annual])(**B1545**), which succeeds the *Far Eastern bibliography*, 1941–55 (**B1546**) and the *Bulletin of Far Eastern bibliography*, 1936–1940 (**B1547**).

B1548 Ferguson, John A. Bibliography of Australia. Sydney: Angus & Robertson, 1941–69. 7v.

This major work identifies, describes and locates virtually every important book, pamphlet, broadside, newspaper, magazine and government document relating to Australia which was printed between 1784 and 1900. Entries are arranged chronologically by date of publication. V.4 (1955) contains an addenda to the first 3 volumes. An additional volume, containing addenda along with indexes, is not yet completed.

B1549 Kerner, Robert J. Northeastern Asia: a selected bibliography. . . . Berkeley: Univ. of California Pr., 1939. 2v.

Nearly 14,000 citations for printed works, most in Oriental or Russian languages, are contained in these volumes, with coverage extending to China, the Soviet Union, Japan and Mongolia. Titles have been transliterated and translated. Treatment is uneven and no author index is provided. The usefulness of this work continues despite limitations.

B1550 London University. School of Oriental and African Studies. Historical writings on the peoples of Asia. London: Oxford Univ. Pr., 1961–62. 4v.

Essays presented here were prepared for conferences held at London University between 1956 and 1958. Each volume provides an historiographic and bibliographic survey of work published through the mid-1950s. Historians of India, Pakistan and Ceylon are treated in v.1, those of Southeast Asia in v.2, China and Japan in v.3 and the Middle East in v.4.

B1551 Patterson, Maureen L. P. and Ronald B. Inden. South Asia: an introductory bibliography. Chicago: Univ. of Chicago Pr., 1962. 412p.

Limited to English language works, unannotated citations are arranged by subject and period within country and grouped in six major sections (general, history, social structure and organization, political and economic structure, religion and philosophy, and literature, science and the arts). An author-title index is provided to the more than 4,000 entries.

For a selected bibliography of some 2,000 works with short descriptive annotations, see J. Michael Mohar, *India: a critical bibliography* (Tucson: Univ. of Arizona Pr., 1964 [119p.]) (**B1552**). Entries for books, government documents and a few articles are arranged by subject.

Margaret H. Case has provided valuable help for readers with her *South Asian history, 1750–1950: a guide to periodicals, dissertations and newspapers* (Princeton, N.J.: Princeton Univ. Pr., 1968 [561p.]) (**B1553**). 351 periodicals have been indexed here, along with 650 dissertations. Listings for 600 newspapers include holdings for major American research libraries.

B1554 Pearson, J. D. South Asian bibliography, a handbook and guide. Atlantic Highlands, N.J.: Humanities Pr., 1979. 381p.

Covering the Indian subcontinent and the neighboring regions of Sri Lanka, Burma, Afghanistan, Tibet, the Himalayas and the Maldive Islands, essays by English scholars discuss published works, including government documents, and archival sources for the study of South Asia. Commentaries contained in essays evaluate the content of sources, relate them to each other, and weave together the fabric of information. Essays take different forms, a few being little more than lists of books. But that on historical writings contributed by Kenneth Ballhatchet (pp. 202–11) and those on archives and religions are particularly useful. The index is marginally helpful.

B1555 Tregonning, Kennedy G. Southeast Asia: a critical bibliography. Tucson: Univ. of Arizona Pr., 1969. 103p.

This selected bibliography of works on Southeast Asia presents citations to books, parts of books, articles and government documents written in English. Southeast Asia is defined to include Burma, Thailand, Cambodia (Kampuchea), Laos, Vietnam, Malaysia, Indonesia and the Philippines. Entries are arranged by subject within country. The reputation of this work is well established.

In the same series are Charles O. Hucker, *China: a critical bibliography* (Tucson: Univ. of Arizona Pr., 1962 [125p.])(**B1556**) and Bernard S. Silberman's *Japan and Korea: a critical bibliography* (Tucson: Univ. of Arizona Pr., 1962 [120p.]) (**B1557**).

For an important bibliography of earlier works see John F. Embree and Lillian O. Dotson, *Bibliography of the peoples and cultures of mainland Southeast Asia* (New Haven: Yale Univ. Pr., 1950 [821p.])

(**B1558**). Coverage ends with 1949. A more selective list is provided by Stephen N. Hay and Margaret H. Case, *Southeast Asian history: a bibliographic guide* (New York: Praeger, 1962 [138p.])(**B1559**). Hay may be supplemented with Gayle Morrison, *A guide to books on Southeast Asian history (1961–1966)* (Santa Barbara, Calif.: ABC-Clio Pr., 1969 [105p.])(**B1560**).

Europe

B1561 Caron, Pierre. Bibliographie des travaux publiés des 1866 à 1897 sur l'histoire de la France depuis 1789. Paris: Cornély, 1912. 831p.

Continues the coverage of Saulnier and Martin (B1573), presenting a bibliography of books, periodical articles, documents, pamphlets and society publications published during 1866–97. For bibliographies of material on the history of France published after 1897, see the *Répertoire méthodique de l'histoire moderne et contemporaine de la France* (B1572) and the *Bibliographie annuelle de l'histoire de France du cinquieme siècle à 1939* (B1508).

B1562 European bibliography of Soviet, East European and Slavonic studies. v. 1– , 1975– . Paris: Editions de l'école des hautes études en sciences sociales, Institut d'Etudes Slaves, 1978– .

Citations contained here are to books, articles from periodicals and symposia and scholarly reviews dealing with the Soviet Union and the 8 communist countries of Eastern Europe, and published in Great Britain, West Germany and France, as well as Austria, Belgium and French-speaking Switzerland which are treated on a less systematic basis. Entries are not annotated. The volume of 1978 publications appeared in late 1983.

For works on East European history up to 1945, published between 1939 and 1964 in West European languages, see Klaus Meyer, *Bibliographie zur osteuropäischen Geschichte* (Wiesbaden, W. Germany: Harrassowitz, 1972 [649p.]) (**B1563**).

For manuscripts and archival materials on Russia and the Soviet Union, see Steven A. Grant and John H. Brown, *The Russian Empire and the Soviet Empire: a guide to manuscripts and archival materials in the United States* (Boston: Hall, 1981 [632p.]) (**B1564**).

B1565 Heimpel, Hermann and Herbert Geuss, eds. Dahlmann-Waitz. Quellenkunde der deutschen Geschichte; Bibliographie der Quellen und der Literatur zur deutschen Geschichte. Stuttgart: Hiersemann, 1969– .

This new edition greatly expands the 2-volume 9th edition of the Dahlmann-Waitz of 1931–32, and will serve as the most complete bibliography of German-language works on German history to 1945 when completed. A detailed subject arrangement governs the placement of citations. Only German-language works are included. Consult the earlier 1931–32 edition for sections of this "new Dahlmann-Waitz" which have not yet appeared.

B1566 Holtzmann, Walther and Gerhard Ritter. Die deutsche Geschichtswissenschaft im zweiten Weltkrieg. Marburg/Lahn: Simons, 1951. 2v.

Includes citations to German historical works published between 1939 and 1945 on all areas of historical inquiry. Entries are arranged by subject, with political history divided into broad periods. Its coverage supplements the *Jahresberichte für deutsche Geschichte* (B1517) and the *International bibliography of historical sciences* (B1512), both of which were not published during World War II.

B1567 Horecky, Paul L. Russia and the Soviet Union: a bibliographic guide to Western-language publications. Chicago: Univ. of Chicago Pr., 1965. 473p.

B1568 ———. East central Europe: a guide to basic publications. Chicago: Univ. of Chicago Pr., 1969. 956p.

B1569 ———. Southeastern Europe: a guide to basic publications. Chicago: Univ. of Chicago Pr., 1969. 755p.

Each volume is intended to provide "highly selective and judiciously evaluated inventories of the most important publications" relating to the areas in question. The emphasis in each is on the "area studies" approach, but separate chapters on the history of countries and regions, and the retrospective character of other sections make these volumes very valuable to historians and interested readers. Books, articles, government documents and other sources of information are arranged by broad subject within country and further divided in accord with accepted scholarly practice. Citations carry critical annotations, and extensive author-title-subject indexes help make these volumes important for researchers.

Updating Horecky's works to some extent is Stephan M. Horak, *Russia, the USSR, and Eastern Europe; a bibliographic guide to English language publications, 1964–1974; and 1975–1980* Littleton, Colo.: Libraries Unlimited, 1978, 1982) (**B1570**). Horak arranges citations in a manner similar to Horecky, with annotations drawn from scholarly reviews which are cited.

B1571 Institut für Zeitgeschichte. Bibliothek. Alphabetischer Katalog, 5v. and supp.; Sachkatalog [Subjects], 6v. and supp.; Landerkatalog [Countries, regions, geographic units], 2v.; Biographischer Katalog, 1v. Boston: Hall, 1967–73.

Reproduces the card catalogs of the Institute for Contemporary History in Munich, whose holdings amounted to some 61,000 volumes as of 1973. Contemporary history is defined for collecting purposes as "the history of the most recent past insofar as it directly influences the history of those now living." In practical terms, recent German history since 1918 is the focus of the collection. The alphabetical catalog includes all titles of books, serials, volumes in series and selected journal articles.

B1572 Répertoire méthodique de l'histoire moderne et contemporaine de la France, pour les années 1898–1913. Paris: Rieder, 1899–1932. Reprint, Nendeln, Liechtenstein: Kraus, 1977. 11v.

Continues Pierre Caron's work covering the period 1866–97, *Bibliographie des travaux publiés de 1866 à 1897 sur l'histoire de la France depuis 1789* (B1561). Classified by broad subjects and by historical period, entries cover books and articles published in French on the history of France since 1500. Occasional cross-references, annotations and references to book reviews appear. Publication of v.8 (for 1907–9) in 1965 closed a long standing gap, but the projected v.12 for 1914–19 is still awaited. Continued by P. Caron and H. Stein's *Répertoire bibliographique de l'histoire de France* (B1509), which begins with 1920.

B1573 Sauluier, Eugene and A. Martin. Bibliographie des travaux publiés de 1866 à 1897 sur l'histoire de la France de 1500 à 1789. Paris: Presses Universitaire de France, 1932–38. 2v.

A listing of books and periodical articles on the early modern period in France published predominantly in Western Europe, continued by P. Caron, *Bibliographie des travaux publiés de 1866 à 1897 sur l'histoire de la France depuis 1789* (B1561)

Great Britain

B1574 Altschul, Michael. Anglo-Norman England, 1066–1154. Cambridge: Cambridge Univ. Pr., 1969. 83p.

This lead volume in the Conference on British Studies, Bibliographical Handbook series, lists 1,800 titles of books and articles under 14 headings established for the series, among them general surveys, foreign relations, social history, science and technology. Short annotations accompany some entries. Intended as very selective bibliographies, each volume in the series is limited to no more than 2,500 entries. An author, editor, translator index concludes each volume. Other volumes in the series include Delloyd J. Guth, *Late medieval England, 1377–1485* (Cambridge: Cambridge Univ. Pr., 1976 [143p.]) (**B1575**); Mortimer Levine, *Tudor England, 1485–1603* (Cambridge: Cambridge Univ. Pr., 1968 [115p.]) (**B1576**); William L. Sachse, *Restoration England, 1660–1689* (Cambridge: Cambridge Univ. Pr., 1971 [115p.]) (**B1577**); and Josef L. Altholz, *Victorian England, 1837–1901* (Cambridge: Cambridge Univ. Pr., 1970 [100p.]) (**B1578**). Other volumes are planned.

B1579 Bibliography of British history to 1485. Ed. by Edgar B. Graves. Oxford: Clarendon, 1975. 1,103p.

B1580 Bibliography of British history, Tudor period, 1485–1603. Ed. by Conyers Read. 2d ed. Oxford: Clarendon, 1959. 624p.

B1581 Bibliography of British history; Stuart period, 1603–1714. Ed. by Godfrey Davies. 2d rev. ed. by Mary F. Keeler. Oxford: Clarendon, 1970. 734p.

B1582 Bibliography of British history, the eighteenth century, 1714–1789. Ed. by Stanley Pargellis and D. J. Medley. Oxford: Clarendon, 1951. 642p.

B1583 Bibliography of British history, 1789–1851. Ed. by Lucy M. Brown and Ian R. Christie. Oxford: Clarendon, 1977. 759p.

B1584 Bibliography of British history, 1851–1914. Comp. and ed. by H. J. Hanham. Oxford: Clarendon, 1976. 1,606p.

Following the tradition established by Gross (B1589), these 6 volumes provide selective, annotated, critical bibliographies made up of citations to primary and secondary sources, pamphlets and articles in periodicals, collections and society publications. British history is defined broadly here. The goal has been "to list the major works which a student is likely to wish to consult, a selection of other works which makes clear the scope of contemporary printed materials, and a selection of biographies and autobiographies." These are extensive bibliographies which may be updated by consulting *Writings on British history* (B1593–1594).

B1585 Bonser, Wilfrid. An Anglo-Saxon and Celtic bibliography (450–1087). Oxford, Eng.: Basil Blackwell, 1957. 2v.

V.1 contains over 12,000 entries drawn from nearly 400 British and foreign periodicals and collected works published before 1954. Coverage encompasses "all aspects of the period, as pertaining to the whole of the British Isles," with the exception of purely literary and linguistic materials and the source material which can be found in Gross (B1589). Citations are arranged by a subject classification. V.2 provides very helpful author and subject-topographical indexes which lead directly to the citation. Helpful for identifying articles. Equally valuable is Bonser's *A Romano-British bibliography (55 B.C.–A.D. 449)* (Oxford, Eng.: Basil Blackwell, 1964 [2v.]) (**B1586**), which follows the same principles and covers articles published in some 250 periodicals and collected works before 1960.

B1587 Elton, G. R. Modern historians on British history, 1485–1945; a critical bibliography. London: Methuen, 1970. 239p.

Including material published from 1945 through 1969, Elton discusses changes in historical methods and knowledge and provides citations to important works which altered the view expressed by earlier historians. The whole range of historical literature has been examined by Elton, who first composed a shorter edition for *Historische Zeitschrift* (B1485). An author-editor and a subject index make the volume more usable.

B1588 Great Britain. Colonial Office. Library. Catalogue. Boston: Hall, 1964. 15v. Supplement, 1963–67. Boston: Hall, 1967.

A reproduction of the Colonial Office Library card catalog. The Library seeks to acquire, as extensively as possible, publications on dependent territories and Commonwealth countries. Citations for books, pamphlets, reports, documents, periodicals and articles contained in serial publications are included, some from as far back as the 17th century.

B1589 Gross, Charles. The sources and literature of English history from the earliest times to about 1485. 2d ed. London: Longmans, Green, 1915. 820p.

The classic critical bibliography of British history, it has become a standard by which later bibliographic work is judged. Covering books, pamphlets, articles in journals and collections, as well as the transactions of societies, Gross provides a "systematic survey of the printed materials relating to the political, constitutional, legal, social and economic history of England, Wales and Ireland." Continental publications of value to students of English history are included, but manuscripts are omitted. Short critical annotations for many cited works, as well as introductory paragraphs, serve to guide readers to related sources. Edgar B. Graves has revised and updated the work of Gross in his *Bibliography of British history to 1485* (B1579).

B1590 Mullins, E. L. C. A guide to the historical and archeological publications of societies in England and Wales, 1901–1933. London: Univ. of London, Athlone Pr., 1968. 850p.

As a complement to *Writings on British history, 1901–1933* (B1593), this volume lists and indexes the titles and authors of books and articles bearing upon the history and archeology of England and Wales, the Isle of Man and the Channel Islands. Continued by *Writings on British history, 1934–* (B1594).

For Scotland, see Charles S. Terry, *A catalogue of the publications of Scottish historical and kindred clubs and societies . . . , 1780–1908* (Glasgow: Maclehose, 1909 [253p.]) (**B1591**), and Cyril Matheson, *A catalogue of the publications of Scottish historical and kindred clubs and societies . . . , 1908–1927* (Aberdeen: Milne & Hutchison, 1928 [232p.]) (**B1592**).

B1593 Writings on British history, 1901–1933. A bibliography of books and articles on the history of Great Britain from about 400 A.D. to 1914. Ed. by H. Hale Bellot. London: Cape, 1968–70. 5v. in 7.

B1594 Writings on British history, 1934– . A. T. Milne, ed. London: Cape, 1937– .

Lists the majority of books and articles published in the years covered, as well as citations to major reviews of books. Most items cited are in English, though some foreign language works appear. Coverage includes writings on French territories in the Middle Ages and 20th-century Commonwealth countries when they directly concern England and Britain respectively. Entries are arranged by historical period and subject. Name indexes lead to specific items.

The original series of 7 volumes continues in volumes covering 1934–45 under the general editorship of A. T. Milne, and from 1946 in volumes listing publications of 2 or 3 years. The most recent volume, that for 1967–68 edited by Heather J. Creaton, appeared in 1982. Recent volumes have followed the scope, arrangement and method of compilation of earlier ones, and seek to provide a "full list of books and articles on British history."

The Royal Historical Society, which sponsors *Writings on British history*, is attempting to deal with long lag time by publishing the new *Annual bibliography of British and Irish history* (London: Harvester Pr., 1982–) **(B1595)**. While somewhat less inclusive than *Writings*, it is much more timely.

Latin America

B1596 Gonzalez, Luis. Fuentes de la historia contemporanea de Mexico. Mexico City: El Colegio de Mexico, 1961–67. 5v.

Coverage of books, shorter published works, articles and reviews are divided into 2 parts, the first for "libros y folletos" and the second for "periodicos y revistas." Publications by or about Mexicans or Mexico published between 1910 and 1940, and works published since 1940 dealing with the period 1910–40 are included. Citations are arranged by broad subject and contain short descriptive annotations. Appropriate indexes assist readers.

B1597 Sable, Martin H., ed. A guide to Latin American studies. Los Angeles: Univ. of California, Latin American Center, 1967. 2v. 783p.

A critical and descriptive guide arranged by subject, then geographically within subject, the *Guide* is designed as a successor to *Latin America in periodical literature* (Los Angeles: Univ. of California Center of Latin American Studies, 1962–63) **(B1598)**. The focus is on bibliography. The historical section is arranged by periods, with extensive indexes to subjects and authors leading to annotated entries. Emphasis lies on publication from 1955 to 1966.

B1599 Sanchez Alonso, Benito. Fuentes de la historia española e hispanoamericana: ensayo de bibliografía sistemática de impresos y manuscritos que ilustran la historia política de España y sus antiguas provincias de ultramar. 3d ed. Madrid: Consejo Superior de Investigaciones Cientificas, 1952. 3v.

The most comprehensive modern guide to the printed sources and scholarly studies dealing with Spanish and Spanish-American history. Arranged chronologically, the focus is on political history from early times to 1950. Books and articles are cited. An author index is supplemented by a biographical index, a geographical index and a miscellaneous index to manuscript sources, abbreviations, anonymous works and such.

For updates consult the annual volumes of the *Handbook of Latin American studies* (Gainesville: Univ. of Florida Pr., 1936–) **(B1600)** which is the single most important bibliographic source on Latin American studies. See also the *Hispanic American historical review* (1918–) (B1755).

For British manuscript sources see Peter Walne, *A guide to manuscript sources for the history of Latin America and the Caribbean in the British Isles* (B1452).

North America

B1602 Burr, Nelson R. A critical bibliography of religion in America. Princeton, N.J.: Princeton Univ. Pr., 1961. 2v.

Still the most complete bibliography on religion in American life, the bibliography grew out of a desire to provide "a general review of the history of religion in the United States, and to apply references to illustrate the manifold influences of religion in American life and thought." A vigorous though selective work, it includes monographs, articles, essays and theses deemed to be essential and illustrative of movements and influences. Works are cited and evaluated in essays which successfully interrelate sources of information. An author index concludes the second volume. The bibliography is v.4 of James Ward Smith and A. Leland Jamison, *Religion in American life* (Princeton, N.J.: Princeton Univ. Pr., 1961–) **(B1603)**. Nelson R. Burr, *Religion in American life* (New York: Appleton, 1971 [171p.]) **(B1604)** provides an update.

B1605 Clark, Thomas D. ed. Travels in the Old South; a bibliography. Norman: Univ. of Oklahoma Pr., 1956–59. 3v.

B1606 ———. Travels in the New South; a bibliography. Norman: Univ. of Oklahoma Pr., 1962. 2v.

The most complete compilations of travel narratives relating to the South, the "Old" South encompasses 1527–1860, the "New" South 1865–1955. The 2,500 entries are arranged in broad chronological periods, with annotations extensive and critical in content. See also E. Merton Coulter's *Travels in the Confederate states; a bibliography* (Norman: Univ. of Oklahoma Pr., 1948 [289p.]) **(B1607)** for similar treatment of 492 narratives from the Civil War period (1861–65). Each of the 6 volumes has its own index.

For a bibliography of travel narratives on the Trans-Mississippi West, see Henry R. Wagner, *The plains and the Rockies; a bibliography of original narratives of travel and adventure, 1800–1865* (Columbus, Ohio: Long's, 1953 [601p.]) **(B1608)**.

B1609 Crandall, Marjorie Lyle. Confederate imprints; a check list based principally on the collection of the Boston Athenaeum. Boston: Athenaeum, 1955. 2v.

V.1 deals with 2,400 official and v.2 with 2,700 unofficial publications. Included are citations to printed materials owned by the Boston Athenaeum, listed in the Library of Congress catalog, reported to the Boston Athenaeum by their owners, or listed in selected modern bibliographies. The result is a valuable listing of Confederate printed matter. Richard B. Harwell, *More Confederate imprints* (Richmond: Virginia State Library, 1957 [345p.]) **(B1610)** provides citations to nearly 1,800 additional items.

B1611 Cripe, Helen and Diane Campbell. American manuscripts, 1763–1815: an index to documents described in auction records and dealer's catalogues. Wilmington, Del.: Scholarly Resources, 1977. 704p.

Included are citations to all letters and manuscripts which are identifiable, have some meaningful context, were written between 1763 and 1815, and appeared in auction records and dealer catalogs. Only American dealers' records are analyzed, with auction catalogs indexed through 1895 and dealer's catalogs through 1970.

Entries are arranged in a chronological index according to the date written, alphabetically in a name index, and in the Dealer's Catalogue Index by dealer name. The volume will prove very helpful in tracing the location of items.

B1612 Goldentree bibliographies in American history. Arthur S. Link, ed. Various places and publishers.

Intended as a series of volumes dealing with the major periods of United States history, recent new titles have been issued irregularly. Each bibliography includes selected books, articles and dissertations arranged by easily understood subdivisions. No annotations are found, but an author index is provided. Recent volumes include Robert H. Bremner, *American social history since 1860* (New York: Appleton, 1971) (**B1613**); E. David Cronon, *The Second World War and the atomic age, 1940–1973* (Northbrook, Ill.: AHM, 1975) (**B1614**); William M. Leary and Arthur S. Link, *The Progressive Era and the Great War, 1896–1920* (Arlington Heights, Ill.: AHM, 1978) (**B1615**); Norman A. Graebner, *American diplomatic history before 1900* (Arlington Heights, Ill.: AHM, 1978) (**B1616**); and Vincent P. De Santis, *The Gilded Age, 1877–1896* (Northbrook, Ill.: AHM, 1973) (**B1617**).

B1618 Griffin, Appleton P.C. Bibliography of American historical societies. 2d ed., rev. and enl. Washington, D.C.: Govt. Print. Off., 1907. 1,374p. In American Historical Assn., *Annual report, 1905*, v.2. Reprint, Detroit: Gale, 1966.

An index to reports, proceedings, transactions, historical records and studies, historical collections, diaries and other publications of some 500 United States and Canadian historical societies from their commencement to 1905. United States national societies are listed first, followed by state and local societies arranged by state, followed by the Canadian section. Subject, author, biography and society indexes are provided. Griffin's work is continued by the *Annual magazine subject index, 1907–1949* (Boston: Faxon, 1908–52 [43v.]) (**B1619**), which lists society publications it covers in the front of each volume. Searching is made easier by the 2-volume photo reprint of the entries in *Cumulated magazine subject index, 1907–1949* (Boston: Hall, 1964) (**B1620**). For the period after 1949, consult *Writings on American history* (B1519).

B1621 Miller, Elizabeth W. and Mary L. Fisher. The Negro in America: a bibliography. 2d ed., rev. and enl. Cambridge, Mass.: Harvard Univ. Pr., 1970. 351p.

An important bibliography for the study of blacks in America, historical studies occupy a significant place. Concentrating on English language monographs and periodical articles, entries represent "clinical, empirical, prescriptive and polemical material" which "identify the problems and mark the urgency of their solution." The "guide to further research" which concludes the volume is of value though some titles are no longer published.

For an older, well respected bibliography which is itself an historical document, see Monroe N. Work, *A bibliography of the Negro in Africa and America* (New York: Wilson, 1928 [698p.]) (**B1622**). For an introductory bibliography of monographs, articles, and in some cases pamphlets, see Wayne C. Miller, *A comprehensive bibliography for the study of American minorities*, 2v. (New York: New York Univ. Pr., 1976) (**B1623**).

B1624 Nevins, Allan and others. Civil War books; a critical bibliography. Baton Rouge: Louisiana State Univ. Pr., 1967–69. 2v.

Aimed at both scholars and general readers, only books and pamphlets are included. The 5,700 citations are arranged by subject under 15 general headings. Short critical annotations mention strong and weak characteristics of works. Indexed.

B1625 Trask, David F., and others. A bibliography of United States-Latin American relations since 1810; a selected list. . . . Lincoln: Univ. of Nebraska Pr., 1968. 441p. Supplement, 1979. 193p.

Seeking to "collate and expand the corpus of previous general lists of references for the history of United States-Latin American relations," entries are organized into two sections. The first presents a chronological survey of relations from 1810 to 1976, the second a country-by-country survey. A wide variety of materials appear, with language no obstacle to inclusion. Cross-references link related sections together. Chapter 1 provides a list of guides and bibliographies. An author index concludes the volume. The original volume carries coverage to about 1963, the supplement through 1976.

B1626 United States. Library of Congress. National union catalog of manuscript collections. Washington, D.C.: Library of Congress, 1962– .

An index of manuscript collections which describes collections located in public or quasi-public repositories. With the 1981 volume, 48,600 collections in 1,132 repositories had been indexed using over 500,000 references to topical subjects, and personal, family, corporate and geographical names. Recently, entries have been published in annual volumes with indexes cumulated in 5-year periods. For purposes of inclusion, a collection is defined as "a group of manuscripts consisting of letters, memoranda, accounts and the like, either in original handwritten or typewritten form or in the form of photocopies, typescripts or facsimiles of originals." Transcripts of oral recordings and single items of "great historical importance" also appear. Entries are arranged by accession number and include a physical description, indication of scope and content, and location. The indexes provide access to entries, and include names of persons, families and corporate entities, places and subject/topical terms. The catalog relies on solicited information and therefore is not a complete index to all manuscript collections. Nonetheless, it is the most complete listing available.

B1627 United States local histories in the Library of Congress; a bibliography. Baltimore: Magna Carta, 1975. 4v. and supp.

The most complete bibliography of local history dealing with the United States, inclusion is determined by Library of Congress classification. Entries are arranged by region and state in accord with the classification scheme. Occasionally, notes are included with citations to assist with identification of items. The original 4 volumes contain entries for works cataloged at the Library of Congress before mid-1972. Following citations for each region and state is a supplementary index of places. V.5 contains entries cataloged between mid-1972 and January, 1976. Also found there are corrections to the first 4 volumes, as well as a supplementary index of places for v.5, and a general index to all 5 volumes.

B1628 Wiltz, John E. and Nancy C. Cridland. Books in American history. 2d ed. Bloomington: Indiana Univ. Pr., 1981. 113p.

As in the first edition which it does not entirely replace, this edition lists very selectively those books which form the core of a high school library history collection. Among criteria for inclusion are easy availability, low cost and readability. Coverage has been expanded through 1974, with sections on historical fiction and nonprint materials added. Entries include an informative annotation discussing the viewpoints and merits of books. After a series of chronological chapters, a list of 100 selected titles and an index appear.

B1629 Winther, Oscar O. A classified bibliography of the periodical literature of the trans-Mississippi West, 1811–1957. Bloomington: Indiana Univ. Pr., 1961. 626p. Supp., 1957–67. 1970. 340p.

An updating of the 1942 edition titled *The trans-Mississippi West: a guide to its periodical literature, 1811–1938* (Bloomington: Indiana Univ. Pr., 1942 [278p.]) (**B1630**). Lists nearly 14,000 articles in some 80 state, regional and national historical journals. Entries are arranged by subject, with cross-references to related topics noted in the table of contents. A name index also facilitates use. An excellent source for scholars and general readers alike.

Biography and Genealogy

B1631 Filby, P. William. American and British genealogy and heraldry: a selected list of books. 2d ed. Chicago: American Library Assn., 1975. 467p.

Intended for the beginning researcher, this edition cites 5,000 titles of books basic to the study of genealogy and heraldry. The major emphasis rests on the United States. The opening section covers bibliographies, guides, indexes and series useful as reference sources. Organization is by country, then generally by type of materials, except for the United States, which is arranged by state, and Latin America and the British dominions, which are organized by country. The combined author, serial title, and subject index proves helpful.

B1632 Jarboe, Betty M. Obituaries: a guide to sources. Boston: Hall, 1982. 370p.

An index to sources of biographical information found in obituaries. After a short section on international sources, the majority of citations are to United States sources. Included are books and articles referring to obituary information in newspapers and periodicals. Organized by state, or country, with a subject and an author index.

B1633 Kaplan, Louis. A bibliography of American autobiographies. Madison: Univ. of Wisconsin Pr., 1961. 372p.

B1633 Briscoe, Mary Louise. American autobiogra-
A phy, 1945–1980; a bibliography. Madison: Univ. of Wisconsin Pr., 1982. 365p.

Kaplan provides a comprehensive compilation of 6,377 autobiographies published from the colonial period to 1945. Citations for each autobiography include the author's occupation, dates, the state in which he/she lived, and the library location(s) of copies of the autobiography. Episodic accounts, travel narratives, journals, diaries, collections of letters, autobiographies, serially published works, manuscript autobiographies, and fictional and spurious works are excluded. Many rare items are listed. A subject index reveals the occupations of the autobiographers, where they lived and the important events in which they played a part. Briscoe's work, intended as a companion to update Kaplan, covers autobiographies published by private and commercial presses between 1945 and 1980, as well as pre-1945 works not included by Kaplan. Entries include short annotations.

B1634 Matthews, William. American diaries; an annotated bibliography of American diaries written prior to 1861. Berkeley: Univ. of California Pr., 1945. 383p.

Includes diaries written in or translated into English by Americans or foreign visitors between 1629 and 1861, as well as separately published works containing diaries. Brief geographical notes provide information on each diarist, accompanied by descriptive notes and occasionally an evaluative comment. Arrangement of entries is chronological by date of first entry in the diary. For unpublished diaries see William Matthews, *American diaries in manuscript, 1580–1954;*

a descriptive bibliography (Athens: Univ. of Georgia Pr., 1974 [176p.]) **(B1635)**, which is intended as a companion volume and organized on principles similar to those used in the 1945 volume.

B1636 ———. British autobiographies; an annotated bibliography of British autobiographies published or written before 1951. Berkeley: Univ. of California Pr., 1955. 376p.

Contains autobiographies written by persons born in the British Isles and naturalized British subjects. Autobiographies relating wholly to life in Canada, South Africa, New Zealand, Australia or the United States have been eliminated. Citations are arranged alphabetically by author, and brief annotations indicate the focus of the subject's life. A subject index is provided.

B1637 ———. British diaries; an annotated bibliography of British diaries written between 1442 and 1942. Berkeley: Univ. of California Pr., 1950. 339p.

A listing of some 2,000 diaries, both published and in manuscript form, written in the course of 500 years by English, Scotch, Welsh and Irish writers. Diaries of foreign travelers in England which were published in England appear. Many cited diaries form a part of biographies, histories or other works. Entries appear chronologically by date of first entry, and include a brief statement identifying each diarist followed by a concise description of the diary's contents. Diaries covering more than 10 years are listed chronologically in a separate index. The location of manuscript material is indicated, and an index of diarists provided.

B1638 ———. Canadian diaries and autobiographies. Berkeley: Univ. of California Pr., 1950. 136p.

Intended as a companion to other bibliographies of diaries and autobiographies compiled by Matthews (see above), 1,300 published and unpublished "personal records relating to Canadian life" are cited with locations provided for manuscripts. The arrangement is alphabetical by author with subject index to the main concerns of the diaries.

B1639 O'Neill, Edward H. Biography by Americans, 1658–1936; a subject bibliography. Philadelphia: Univ. of Pennsylvania Pr., 1939. 465p.

Listing biographical material written by Americans, O'Neill includes some 7,000 separately published items. Autobiographies, diaries and journals are excluded, and in the case of famous persons listings are selective. Entries are arranged alphabetically by the name of the subject. A rather unhelpful listing of collective biographies arranged by author concludes the volume. No index.

B1640 Riches, Phyllis M. An analytical bibliography of universal collected biography, comprising books published in the English tongue in Great Britain and Ireland, America and the British dominions. London: Library Assn., 1934. 709p.

An attempt to index every volume of traceable collected biography published through 1933. Citations to some 56,000 biographies are arranged alphabetically by names of persons and indicating where biographical material may be found. An alphabetical list of indexed books follows, providing fuller citations to sources. Three indexes are provided: a chronological list of persons arranged by century, a list arranged by occupation, and an author and subject bibliography of biographical dictionaries. Valuable for obscure biography.

B1641 Slocum, Robert B. Biographical dictionaries and related works. Detroit: Gale, 1967. 1,056p. 1st supp. Detroit: Gale, 1972. 852p. 2d supp. Detroit: Gale, 1978. 922p.

Coverage of this wide-ranging work focuses on biographical dictionaries, but also includes bio-bibliographies, collections of epitaphs, genealogical works having biographical value, dictionaries, anonyms and pseudonyms, portrait dictionaries, government and legislative manuals, bibliographies of individual and collective biography, biographical indexes and selected portrait catalogs. Entries are divided into 3 parts; universal biography, national or area biography arranged by country, and biography by location. Two supplements have thus far updated the original volume. Separate author, title and subject indexes appear in each volume.

Dissertations

B1642 Jacobs, P. M. History theses, 1901–70; historical research for higher degrees in the universities of the United Kingdom. London: Institute of Historical Research, 1976. 456p.

Provides a listing of all theses presumed to have been completed, many of which may not be readily available. Entries are arranged within a traditional subject breakdown of historical fields. Author and subject indexes complete the volume.

B1643 Kuehl, Warren F. Dissertations in history; an index to dissertations completed in history departments of United States and Canadian universities, 1873–June, 1970. Lexington: Univ. of Kentucky Pr., 1965, 1972. 2v.

An alphabetically arranged listing by author, v.1 covers 1873–1960; v.2 includes dissertations completed between 1961 and June, 1970. A subject index with cross-references assists readers. All historical subjects are included. Listings should be supplemented by the American Historical Association's *List of doctoral dissertations in history in progress in the United States* (Washington, D.C., 1947–73) **(B1644)** and its *Doctoral dissertations in history* (Washington, D.C., 1973–   ) **(B1645)**, both of which list research in progress. Not all dissertations appear in these sources.

For abstracts of completed dissertations, and for dissertations done in other academic departments which are important for historical research, see *Dissertation abstracts international* (A150).

DIRECTORIES AND BIOGRAPHICAL INFORMATION

B1646 Biography and genealogy master index; a consolidated index . . . . 2d ed. plus supps. Detroit: Gale, 1980– .

Presented here in a single publication are brief citations to biographical information published in some 350 current and retrospective biographical dictionaries, subject encyclopedias, volumes of literary criticism and biographical indexes. Emphasis rests on the United States with very limited coverage of other countries. Indexed sources provide "who's who" type information as a rule. Entries, arranged alphabetically by the author's name, indicate the dates of life, and provide a coded reference to the biographical sketch. This 2d edition will be supplemented by annual or biennial sets running to several volumes, two of which appeared by late 1983. End papers list titles indexed and a "bibliographic key" tells which edition is indexed in the pertinent edition or supplement. Important and valuable.

B1647 Boorman, Howard L. Biographical dictionary of republican China. New York: Columbia Univ. Pr., 1967–79. 5v.

Accurate and objective presentation of information on persons who played a role in China during the Republican period, including non-Chinese. V.4 is in part devoted to a bibliography listing the writings of persons included, and sources used in preparing entries. V.5 provides a personal name index. For an earlier period, consult Arthur W. Hummel, *Eminent Chinese of the Ching period*, 2v. (Washington, D.C.: Govt. Print. Off., 1943–44) (**B1648**), which identifies 800 prominent Chinese from 1644–1912. For the Communist movement, see *Biographic dictionary of Chinese communism, 1921–1965*, ed. by Donald W. Klein and Anne B. Clark, 2v. (Cambridge, Mass.: Harvard Univ. Pr., 1971) (**B1649**), which emphasizes political and military figures.

B1650 Burke's genealogical and heraldic history of the peerage, baronetage and knightage. London: Burke, 1826– .

The standard source for information on the family history and lineage of the British nobility, published irregularly (105th ed., 1970). Full family histories are provided for every peer and baronet, arranged alphabetically by title. Also provided are the royal lineage and a general index.

Supplementing *Burke's peerage* is *Burke's genealogical and heraldic history of the landed gentry*, 18th ed. (London: Burke, 1965–72 [3v.]) (**B1651**), and *Burke's dormant and extinct peerages* (1883; reprint, London: Burke, 1969) (**B1652**).

B1653 Centre National de la Recherche Scientifique. Institut de Recherche et d'Histoire des Textes. Répertoire international des medievistes. 2v. Paris: Saur, 1979. 811p.

This most recent edition presents names, titles, academic affiliations, addresses, special fields of study, and selected publications for some 6,000 medievalists from nearly 40 countries. Unlike earlier editions, persons are listed in a single alphabet with no indexes provided. Previous editions were published in 1953, 1960 and 1965, the earliest two being limited to European medievalists and entitled *Répertoire des medïevistes d'Europe* and *Répertoire des medievistes Européens* respectively. The 1965 edition follows the plan of this latest edition and carries the same title.

B1654 Concise dictionary of American biography. 3d ed. New York: Scribner, 1980. 1,333p.

A 1-volume summary of each of the more than 17,000 entries in the authoritative *Dictionary of American biography*, 20v. and supp. (New York: Scribner, 1928–) (**B1655**). While the *Concise dictionary* covers deceased Americans as of 1960, the *DAB* is regularly extended with supplements. Rayford W. Logan and Michael R. Winston, *Dictionary of American Negro biography* (New York: Norton, 1982 [680p.]) (**B1656**) provides well-researched and scholarly biographical sketches with annotated lists of additional readings.

Serving a similar purpose for Canada is the *Dictionary of Canadian biography* (Toronto: Univ. of Toronto Pr., 1966–) (**B1657**). Volumes are devoted to specific time periods, with appropriate indexes. Entries conclude with relevant bibliographic information. A French edition titled the *Dictionnaire biographique du Canada* (Québec: Presses de l'Université Laval, 1965–) (**B1658**), is being published simultaneously. Matt S. Meier and Feliciano Rivera, *Dictionary of Mexican American history* (B1704), is less scholarly but one of the best efforts to date.

For Great Britain, the standard source is the *Dictionary of national biography, from the earliest times to 1900* (London: various eds., supps. and reprints) (**B1660**). Eight supplements now extend coverage to persons who died before January 1, 1971. All supplement volumes are indexed in the 8th supplement (1981). *The concise dictionary of national biography* (Oxford: Oxford Univ. Pr., 1953, 1982) (**B1661**) presents capsulized sketches drawn from the larger work.

Organized in 3 historical periods (1788–1850, 1851–1890, 1891–1938) is the *Australian dictionary of biography* (Melbourne: Melbourne Univ. Pr., 1966–) (**B1662**), which is expected to run to 12 volumes when complete, and provides trustworthy information about prominent Australians.

B1663 Craig, Tracey L. Directory of historical societies and agencies in the United States and Canada. 12th ed. Nashville, Tenn.: American Assn. for State and Local History, 1982. 416p.

Lists some 5,800 societies and agencies arranged by state or province, then by city or town. Entries tell name, address, date founded, chief officer, number of members, staff size, publications, major programs and periods of collections. Does not generally cover library and museum holdings.

B1664 de Boer, S. P., E. J. Driessen, and H. L. Verhaar. Biographical dictionary of dissidents in the Soviet Union, 1956–1975. The Hague: Nijhoff, 1982. 679p.

Provides information on some 10,000 dissidents in the Soviet Union, including unverified facts which are identified by a question mark. Names for the most part appear in Russian. The texts of major criminal code articles concerning political offenses, and a glossary of terms are found at the end of the volume with a selected bibliography.

B1665 Iwao, Seiichi. Biographical dictionary of Japanese history. New York: Kodansha, 1978. 655p.

Divides Japanese history into four periods, presenting important people alphabetically within those periods. Sketches are in English and present the contributions of prominent Japanese who with few exceptions were deceased as of 1978. Information is well researched and aimed at non-Japanese audiences. Charts of family lineages, a list of major military events, charts of army and navy cliques, a bibliography and a personal name index conclude the volume.

B1666 James, Edward T. and others, eds. Notable American women, 1607–1950; a biographical dictionary. Cambridge, Mass.: Harvard Univ. Pr., 1971. 3v.

An unusually fine, short introduction on the role of women in American history, culture and society precedes 3 volumes of extended biographical essays on American women who died before 1951. Essays are well researched by scholars and concentrate on events in the lives of subjects and contributions made by them. A discussion of sources concludes each essay. A "classified list of selected biographies" groups prominent women by occupation. *Notable American women, the modern period; a biographical dictionary* (Cambridge, Mass.: Harvard Univ. Pr., 1980) **(B1667)** provides biographical essays on women who died between 1951 and 1975.

B1668 Rössler, Hellmuth and Gunther Franz. Biographisches Wörterbuch zur deutschen Geschichte. Munich: Francke, 1973–75. 3v.

Biographical sketches and essays are provided for historical figures who were prominent in German history through the early 1970s. Well-researched entries include lists of the subjects' works and further reading. V.3 concludes with a name index.

B1669 Who was who in America. Chicago: Marquis, 1963–

Self-described as "a compilation of sketches of individuals, both of the United States of America and other countries, who have made a contribution to, or whose activity was in some manner related to the history of the United States, from the founding of Jamestown Colony . . . ," volumes include persons now dead who were listed in *Who's who in America*. Following the *Historical volume* which covers the period through 1896, subsequent volumes bring coverage forward, v.7 dealing with the period 1977–81.

For an index to historical figures, see *Notable names in American history, a tabulated register: 3d ed. of White's conspectus of American biography* (Clifton, N.J.: White, 1973) **(B1670)**.

ENCYCLOPEDIAS AND ENCYCLOPEDIC SETS

B1671 Cambridge ancient history. Cambridge: Cambridge Univ. Pr., 1923–39. 12v. of text, 5v. of plates.

A scholarly, comprehensive history of the ancient Mediterranean world covering Egyptian and Babylonian times through the early 4th century A.D. Emphasis rests on political history, with each volume composed of independent chapters. Maps and line drawings accompany the text, and extensive bibliographies are provided. Five volumes of plates are integrated into the texts by way of a reference connecting particular plates with pages in the text. Each volume concludes with a separate index. V.3–11 were reissued with corrections in 1951–54.

A 3d edition (Cambridge: Cambridge Univ. Pr., 1970–) is in progress. Modeled on the 1st edition, the text has doubled in length and now includes a chapter on geological ages while footnotes in code form accompany the text. The revision of v.3 (1982) was called the 2d edition, adding some confusion. Volumes published after 1970 reflect the consensus and interests of historians since World War II, and expand upon but do not replace earlier volumes and versions. The first in a series of volumes devoted to plates for the 3d edition appeared in 1977.

B1672 Cambridge medieval history. Cambridge: Cambridge Univ. Pr., 1911–36. 8v.

A reference work for the history of the European Middle Ages following a plan similar to that for the *Cambridge modern history* (B1678). Emphasis rests on political and administrative history, with each chapter an independent entity written by a renowned English scholar. A bibliography and an extensive index end each volume. Maps and illustrations are found in a separate portfolio for each volume. A 2d edition of v.4 on the Byzantine Empire was published in 1966–67.

For a shorter version see C. W. Previté-Orton, *The shorter Cambridge medieval history* (Cambridge: Cambridge Univ. Pr., 1952 [2v.]) **(B1673)** which is a separately written work accompanied by maps, illustrations, and genealogical tables and aimed at the general reader.

For discussions and bibliographies of the economic and social history of the medieval period, see the *Cambridge economic history of Europe from the decline of the Roman Empire*, v.1–3 (Cambridge: Cambridge Univ. Pr., 1941–) **(B1674)**.

B1675 Gebhardt, Bruno. Handbuch der deutschen Geschichte. 9 Aufl. Hrsg. von Herbert Grundman. Stuttgart: Union, 1970–76. 5v.

Originally published in 1891–92, this edition is arranged chronologically by subject, with articles written by well-known German scholars. Short articles present events in German history followed by extensive bibliographies of monographs and articles. Covers German history from earliest times to 1950.

B1676 Handbuch der Altertumswissenschaft; begrundet von I. V. Miller, erweitert von W. Otto, forgeführt von H. Bengtson. Munich: Beck, 1897– .

A massive cooperative work made up of a series of scholarly treatises covering the whole field of classical antiquity. Many of the volumes in the 12 sections have appeared in several editions and many others have new editions in preparation. Some of the treatises are the most comprehensive in their field, others comparatively brief. Early volumes previously published as the *Handbuch der klassischen Altertumswissenschaft.*

B1677 The new Cambridge modern history. Cambridge: Cambridge Univ. Pr., 1957–79. 12v.

Based on the earlier *Cambridge modern history* (Cambridge: Cambridge Univ. Pr., 1902–12) (**B1678**), this completely revised work covers the history of Europe from the Renaissance to 1945. Following the directions taken by historical scholarship since 1945, this "new" edition devotes more space to economic, social and cultural history, though political history still predominates. A revised edition of v.12 was published in 1968. Bibliographies do not appear in each volume; rather, they are collected in a separate book, John Roach, *A bibliography of modern history* (B1543). An atlas accompanies the set as v.14 (B1736). A companion volume, v.13, examines long-term continuity and change in modern European history.

For the economic and, to a lesser extent, social history of early modern and modern Europe, see the *Cambridge economic history of Europe from the decline of the Roman Empire*, v.4–7 (B1674).

DICTIONARIES, HANDBOOKS, MANUALS, AND COMPENDIA

B1679 Almanach de Gotha; annuaire genealogique, diplomatique et statistique. Gotha, E. Germany: Perthes, 1763–1944. Annual.

This standard source on the nobility in European and non-European countries is divided into 2 parts. Pt. 1, The "Annuaire genealogique," presents the genealogies of royal and princely houses, including those dispossessed. Pt. 2, the "Annuaire diplomatique et statistique," provides descriptions of various countries which list principal government officials including the foreign diplomatic corps.

The "Annuaire genealogique" is continued by *Genealogisches Handbuch des Adels* (Limburg a.d. Lahn: Starke, 1951–) (**B1680**), which supplies the same information as its predecessor, with concentration on the German nobility.

B1681 Avery, Catherine B. The new century classical handbook. New York: Appleton, 1962. 1,162p.

Information about classical myths, legends, gods and heroes, persons and places, presented in dictionary format. Entries give pronunciation, and sketches emphasize "stories the ancients told each other, and believed." Plot summaries are provided for important literary works.

B1682 Boatner, Mark M. Encyclopedia of the American Revolution. Bicentennial ed. New York: McKay, 1974. 1,290p.

A somewhat idiosyncratic work in dictionary form which provides information on people, places, events, and emphasizes biographical data and military affairs, especially battles. Coverage is limited to 1763–83. A bibliography of titles cited in the articles concludes the volume.

For information on the Civil War, see Boatner's *Civil War dictionary* (New York: McKay, 1959 [974p.]) (**B1683**) which follows a similar plan.

B1684 Boehm, Eric H. and others, eds. Historical periodicals directory. Santa Barbara, Calif.: ABC-Clio Pr., 1981– .

In the three volumes published, history is defined in the broadest sense encompassing all periods, countries and fields as well as auxiliary historical disciplines in establishing the parameters for inclusion. Only periodicals published more than twice each year and containing "articles" are found. Within these definitions the goal is a comprehensive listing of current publications, including interdisciplinary journals, and local and regional historical journals. Entries are listed alphabetically by title within country of publication. Superseded titles are cross-referenced to the newer title, and publications of societies and other corporate bodies may appear under the corporate heading. Entries list the publisher, subjects covered, languages used, indexes listing the periodical and earlier titles. A title index concludes each volume. Updates and expands *Historical periodicals: an annotated world list of historical and related serial publications*, Eric H. Boehm, ed. (Santa Barbara, Calif.: 1961) (**B1685**), and P. Caron and M. Jaryc, *World list of historical periodicals and bibliographies* (New York: Wilson, 1939) (**B1686**) which lists the 3,100 titles surveyed for the *International bibliography of historical sciences* (B1512).

B1687 Carruth, Gorton, and others. The encyclopedia of American facts and dates. 7th ed. New York: Crowell, 1979. 1,015p.

Chronologically arranged coverage for the period 986–1978, information is presented in 4 categories: (1) politics and government, war, disasters, vital statistics; (2) books, painting, dance, architecture, sculpture; (3) science, industry, economics, education, religion, philosophy; (4) sports, fashion, popular entertainmant, folklore, society. Extensive index covers all entries and refers to the appropriate year and column.

B1688 Diccionário de história de España. Madrid: Allanza, 1979. 3v.

Entries present the historical significance of places, events, persons and examine terminology relevant to the history of Spain and the Spanish empire.

B1689 Dicionário de história de Portugal. Porto: Iniciatinas Editoriais, 1979. 6v.

Provides information on Portugese history, culture and society as well as prominent personages.

B1690 Dictionary of American history. Rev. ed. New York: Scribner, 1976. 8v.

Its 7,200 articles provide concise information on American history defined very broadly to include political, economic, social, cultural, and industrial aspects. Signed articles provide basic information and bibliographic citations to further reading. A few longer articles cover broad topics (e.g., agriculture), and biographical articles are omitted (see the *Dictionary of American biography*, [B1655]). Many catch words and popular names of laws are described. V.8 contains an index which draws together references to subjects from throughout the 7 volumes of articles. More than 500 new articles and substantial revision make this an effective updating of earlier editions.

B1691 Dictionary of the Middle Ages. Joseph R. Strayer, ed. New York: Scribner, 1982– .

Defining the Middle Ages as encompassing 500 A.D. to 1500 and covering the Latin West, the Slavic world, Asia Minor, the lands of the caliphate in the East, and the Muslim-Christian areas of North Africa, the projected 12 volumes of the dictionary hope to define and explain ideas, movements, individuals, institutions and places associated with the Middle Ages. Entries vary from short sketches to 10,000 word essays with bibliographies of further reading emphasizing English works. Cross-references link related entries and assist readers in finding needed information. More detailed and scholarly is the *Lexicon des Mittelalters* (Munich: Artemis, 1977–   ) **(B1692)**, which treats the period 300 A.D. to the early 16th century in European history, including the Byzantine Empire, and provides bibliographic citations for sources mainly in European languages.

B1693 Dupuy, R. Ernest and Trevor N. Dupuy. The encyclopedia of military history from 3500 B.C. to the present. Rev. ed. New York: Harper, 1977. 1,464p.

Chapters on chronological periods cover military trends, then provide short definitions of military events arranged by geographical area. A general index and indexes of wars, battles and sieges, along with maps, help explain events.

B1694 Freeman-Grenville, G. S. P. Chronology of world history; a calendar of principal events from 3000 B.C. to A.D. 1976. 2d ed. London: Collings, 1978. 746p.

A number of "chronologies" trace the development of mankind in chart form, creating lists of events thousands of years long. Freeman-Grenville's work divides into 6 columns, all geographical save the last on religion and culture. Using a similar format, Bernard Grun, *The timetables of history*, new, updated ed. (New York: Simon & Schuster, 1979 [676p.]) **(B1695)** deals more heavily with cultural events, science and technology.

For an emphasis on European history, especially Britain, try S. H. Steinberg, *Historical tables*, 9th ed. (London: Macmillan, 1973 [269p.]) **(B1696)**. James Trager, *The people's chronology; a year by year record of human events from prehistory to the present* (New York: Holt, 1979 [1,206p.]) **(B1697)** provides an anecdotal survey of man's history in the vein of "popular culture." Not scholarly. For coverage of American history, see Laurence Urdang, *The timetables of American history* (New York: Simon & Schuster, 1981 [470p.]) **(B1698)**. E. J. Bickerman, *Chronology of the Ancient World*, 2d ed. (Ithaca, N.Y.: Cornell Univ. Pr., 1980 [223p.]) **(B1699)** supplies a chronological listing of events in Greek and Roman history from 776 B.C. to A.D. 476, along with tables and discussions on calendars and time measurement in the ancient period.

B1700 Howat, G.M.D. Dictionary of world history. London: Nelson, 1973. 1,720p.

Covering prehistory through 1970, short articles state the historical importance of some 8,000 persons, while another 7,000 describe institutions, cultural movements, trading interests and "some of the great 'isms' of history." 5,000 entries discuss prominent events, such as treaties, battles and conferences. Emphasis lies on the 20th century. No bibliographies.

B1701 Johnson, Thomas H. The Oxford companion to American history. New York: Oxford Univ. Pr., 1966. 906p.

Short entries provide a reliable source for factual information, with a minimum of interpretation, on the "lives, events and places significant in the founding and growth of the nation." No bibliographies for further reading.

B1702 Langer, William L. An encyclopedia of world history; ancient, medieval and modern, chronologically arranged. 5th ed. Boston: Houghton, 1972. 1,569p.

A valuable handbook of historical facts arranged chronologically and presented in highly condensed prose which allows quick access to essential information on individuals, events or topics. Emphasis is placed on Western civilization and on the period since 1500. Lists of kings and rulers, genealogical tables and a few maps, along with an index of people, places and events and other tables provide for easy use.

B1703 Martin, Michael R. and Gabriel H. Lovett. Encyclopedia of Latin-American history. Indianapolis: Bobbs-Merrill, 1968. 348p.

A concise compendium of basic information on Latin-American history, society and culture, from pre–Columbian times to the 1960s. Material is arranged alphabetically, with some cross-references. Special articles appear for major pre–Columbian civilizations and for individual countries, and complement biographical information on major and minor persons, as well as definitions of Spanish and Portuguese terms having historical significance. No index or bibliographic citations.

B1704 Meier, Matt S. and Feliciano Rivera. Dictionary of Mexican American history. Westport, Conn.: Greenwood, 1981. 498p.

Defining history broadly, and covering 1519 to 1980, entries for persons, places, events, documents and institutions are presented alphabetically with cross-references. Short articles focus on Mexican-American developments and concerns. Appendixes include a chronology, a glossary of frequently used Chicano terms, an annotated list of Chicano journals and general historical works, as well as maps and statistical tables. Some entries list titles for futher reading.

B1705 Morris, Richard B. Encyclopedia of American history. 6th ed. New York: Harper, 1982. 1,285p.

A reliable chronological manual rather than encyclopedia which presents the essential facts of American history through 1981. Information is divided into three parts: (1) basic chronology, wherein comments on specific events are woven together to read as a narrative; (2) topical chronology, presenting such aspects of American life as population, economic development, science and technology, thought and culture and Supreme Court decisions; (3) biographical sketches of 500 notable Americans. More than 40 maps and charts help present developments. Subject and name index.

For a similar approach to the modern world, see Richard B. Morris and Graham W. Irwin, *Harper encyclopedia of the modern world; a concise reference history from 1760 to the present* (New York: Harper, 1970 [1,271p.]) (**B1706**) which covers economic development, technology, scientific discovery and culture as well as presenting a basic overview of political developments throughout the world.

B1707 The Oxford classical dictionary. Ed. by N. G. L. Hammond and H. H. Scullard. 2d ed. Oxford: Clarendon, 1970.

A valuable scholarly English language dictionary of classical subjects through the later Roman empire. Articles are often by recognized scholars and include bibliographic notes. For major classical authors, notes refer to texts, commentaries, translations and major scholarly interpretations. A general bibliography and an index of names which are not titles of entries end the dictionary.

For information of an archeological nature on classical sites, see Richard Stillwell, *The Princeton encyclopedia of classical sites.* (Princeton, N.J.: Princeton Univ. Pr., 1976 [1,019p.]) (**B1708**), which contains helpful site maps.

B1709 Paulys Realencyclopaedie der classischen Altertumswissenschaft. Neue Bearbeitung begonnen von George Wissowa, et al. Stuttgart: Metzler, 1894– .

A standard encyclopedia for classical studies in general. Scholarly articles include valuable bibliographies. Volumes published in two concurrent series that cover the letters A–P and R–Z. Supplementary volumes serve to update information.

Der kleine Pauly. Lexicon der Antike . . . , bear. und Hrsg. von Konrat Ziegler und Walther Southeimer (Stuttgart: Druckenmuller, 1964–75 [5v.]) (**B1710**) is a condensation of the above work.

B1711 Ploski, Harry A. and Roscoe C. Brown, Jr. The Negro almanac. 4th ed. New York: Bellweather, 1983. 1,550p.

One of the more reliable of several handbooks on the history and culture of the Negro, principally in the United States. Includes considerable biographical and statistical information. The appendix lists and gives page locations of tables, illustrations and charts. Heavily historical in content.

For an attempt to provide an encyclopedic history of Afro-Americans, see W. Augustus Low and Virgil A. Clift, *Encyclopedia of black America* (New York: McGraw-Hill, 1981 [921p.]) (**B1712**) which concludes some general articles with short bibliographies.

B1713 Powicke, Frederick M. and E. B. Fryde. Handbook of British chronology. 2d ed. London: Royal Historical Society, 1961. 565p.

A valuable work listing rulers of England, Ireland and Scotland; English and Scottish officers of state; bishops of England, Scotland and Wales; dukes, marquesses and earls; tables of parliaments and councils. Sources are cited in many cases, and a bibliographical guide to the lists of English office-holders to about 1800 provides additional sources.

B1714 Roller, David C. and Robert W. Twyman. The encyclopedia of Southern history. Baton Rouge: Louisiana State Univ. Pr., 1979. 1,421p.

Defining the South as that area which practiced slavery in 1860, short articles appearing in dictionary form discuss persons, places, events, institutions and terms prominent in the history of the South. Longer articles present condensed histories of the states. Articles are signed and have bibliographies pointing readers to additional information sources. Appropriate maps and charts prove helpful. Subject-name index.

B1715 Schlesinger, Arthur M., Jr. The almanac of American history. New York: Putnam, 1983. 623p.

Each of 5 chronologically defined sections begins with a short introductory essay by a noted historian which describes the major themes of the period. There follow listings of events, which focus on national politics and international relations, but also deal extensively with science, the arts, and social history. Some events are explained in greater detail relating their significance. Capsule biographies of prominent figures and brief discussions of major themes are interspersed throughout. The index helps locate subjects. Issues of interpretation and controversy receive attention. Succinctly covers American historical development through the early 1980s with appropriate maps and interesting illustrations.

B1716 Story, Norah. The Oxford companion to Canadian history and literature. Toronto: Oxford Univ. Pr., 1967. 935p. William Toye, ed. Supplement. Toronto: Oxford Univ. Pr., 1973. 318p.

Modeled on other "Oxford companions," Story presents in dictionary form articles on political and constitutional issues, forts, important places and special topics such as Indian groups, the fur trade, arctic exploration, the territories and provinces, and political parties. Bibliographies provide for further reading. William Toye, editor of the *Supplement*, renders 2 interesting essays, "History studies in English," and "History studies in French," which survey historical publication in Canada between 1967 and 1972.

B1717 Taddey, Gerhard. Lexicon der deutschen Geschichte; Personen, Ereignisse, Institutionen von der Zeitwende bis zum Ausgang des 2. Weltkrieges. Stuttgart: Alfred Krömer, 1977. 1,352p.

Provides short articles on prominent people, places and institutions in German history from early times to the close of World War I. References to further reading conclude many entries.

B1718 Williams, Neville. Chronology of the modern world, 1763 to the present time. Rev. American ed. New York: McKay, 1968. 923p.

Entries are arranged chronologically by year and month. Left-hand pages relate political events, while right-hand pages mention prominent published works and important events in science and technology, philosophy, religion, fine arts, literature and other aspects, as well as births of important figures and statistics. An index of persons, places, subjects and titles of books is provided.

For other periods, consult Neville Williams, *Chronology of the expanding world, 1492 to 1762* (New York: McKay, 1969 [700p.]) (**B1719**). R. L. Storey, *Chronology of the medieval world, 800–1491* (London: Barrie & Jenkins, 1973 [705p.]) (**B1720**); and H. E. L. Mellersh, *Chronology of the ancient world, 10,000 B.C. to A.D. 799* (London: Barrie & Jenkins, 1976 [500p.]) (**B1721**) which are organized on the same pattern.

ORIGINAL SOURCES

B1722 Aptheker, Herbert. A documentary history of the Negro people in the United States. New York: Citadel, 1951–73. 3v.

A collection of original sources relating to the Negro experience in the United States, chronologically arranged, with a brief introduction to each group of documents. Covers developments up to 1945.

B1723 Commager, Henry S. Documents in American history. 9th ed. Englewood Cliffs, N.J.: Prentice-Hall, 1973. 815p.

A judicious selection of basic source documents from the age of discovery to 1973. The 695 "documents" are limited to official or quasi-official items. Many are complete, others edited to present important segments. A paragraph giving title, date, reference to source used, a note on its historical significance and brief references to related works prefaces each document. Chronologically arranged with index.

B1724 Donald, David, ed. A documentary history of American life. New York: McGraw-Hill, 1966. 8v.

Each volume of this well-edited series contains 40–50 groups of documents. The volume editors briefly introduce each group of texts. Most documents deal with political history, but a refreshing mixture of social, religious and cultural materials, plus cartoons presents a broad picture of American life. Individual volumes have different titles and cover different periods (e.g., v.1: *Settlements to society, 1584–1763*; v.8: *Anxiety and affluence, 1945–1965*).

B1725 English historical documents. Ed. by David C. Douglas. London: Eyre & Spottiswoode, 1953– .

A comprehensive selection of fundamental source documents covering ca. 500–1914 in 14 volumes, 11 of which had been published by late 1983, as well as 2d editions of v.1 and 2. Each volume contains an introductory survey of the period and a general selected bibliography. Documents are arranged by topic (e.g., parliament, economic structure, education), with each group of documents accompanied by a topical introduction and a selected bibliography. All documents appear in modern English. A well-respected compilation.

B1726 Israel, Fred L. Major peace treaties of modern history: 1648–1967. New York: Chelsea House and McGraw-Hill, 1967. 4v.

One hundred treaties, dating from the Peace of Westphalia to the Tashkent Declaration (1966), are printed here in English, each with a commentary. Substantive elements in the treaties are indexed, and 28 maps reprinted from Shepherd's *Historical atlas* (B1750) illustrate major treaty boundaries.

For 203 treaties in U.S. history, see Francis G. Davenport, ed., *European treaties bearing on the history of the United States and its dependencies* (Washington, D.C.: Carnegie, 1917–37 [4v.]; reprint, Gloucester, Mass.: Peter Smith, 1967) (**B1727**). The text and English translation of each treaty between 1455 and

1815 are preceded by a summary of the history associated with the treaty, location of the original text, important printed editions and bibliographical references.

B1728 Monumenta Germaniae Historica. Georg H. Pertz et al., eds. Hanover and Berlin: 1826– .

The most famous collection of medieval historical sources, it consists of many of the principal documents for the study of medieval Germany. Many of the volumes have been reedited or reprinted, and work continues on new volumes. For a listing of volumes in the series, see Repertorium fontium historiae medii aevi, v.1 (B1540).

B1729 Royal Historical Society, London. Camden series. 1838– .

Ser.1 (105v.) and most of ser.2 (62v.) were published by the Camden Society. The Royal Historical Society has published the series ever since (3d ser., 94v. [1900–63]; 4th ser., v.1– [1964–]). The series includes chronicles, letters, memoirs and documents significant in English history. Each volume is edited by a respected scholar, and often includes a full introduction to the text and an index.

ATLASES, MAPS, AND PICTORIAL WORKS

B1730 Adams, James T. and others, eds. Album of American history. New York: Scribner, 1944–61. 5v.

Illustrations of many types are used to depict the historical development of the United States from colonial times to the early 1950s. The last volume is a name-subject index.

The *Album* is a part of Adams' survey of the United States which also includes the *Atlas of American history* (B1740), the *Dictionary of American history* (B1690) and the *Dictionary of American biography* (B1655).

B1731 Barraclough, Geoffrey, ed. The Times concise atlas of world history. London: Times Books, 1982; Maplewood, N.J.: Hammond, 1982. 184p.

Like its larger predecessor, the *Times atlas of world history* (London: Times Books, 1978 [360p.]) **(B1732)**, the "concise" edition is truly universal in scope, depicting historical developments on all continents and such areas as Micronesia. Using modern graphic and cartographic techniques, economic, social, demographic and cultural, as well as political and military developments are pictured. Clarity and accuracy characterize maps. Graphs are employed often to show the significance of events. Of the 320 maps presented, 32 did not appear in the larger 1978 edition, and others have been redesigned. The whole period of mankind's existence on earth is covered. A very helpful index is arranged by geographic name. Consult also R. R. Palmer's *Atlas of world history*, rev. ed. (New York: Rand McNally, 1965) **(B1733)**, a highly respected atlas which covers the entire world.

B1734 Brice, William C. An historical atlas of Islam. Leiden, Netherlands: Brill, 1981. 71p.

Multicolor maps which combine political and topographic features explain the spatial distribution of Islam from 632 A.D. to 1900. All geographic areas with concentration of Muslim populations are represented. A place-name index, astronomical index and economic index assist readers. The best available atlas, though imprecise information is at times a problem.

B1735 Cambridge modern history atlas. 2d ed. Cambridge: Cambridge Univ. Pr., 1924. 229p.

B1736 New Cambridge modern history atlas. H. C. Darby and Harold Fullard, eds. Cambridge: Cambridge Univ. Pr., 1970. 319p.

Because both volumes are intended as companions to their respective narrative series (B1678, B1677), they reflect the emphases of those series. The 1924 edition concentrates heavily on Europe, particularly the British Isles. The 1970 edition places more emphasis on non-European areas (about 50 percent). In addition, the 1970 volume allots more space to social and economic subjects, though political and military affairs still predominate. Both volumes present skillfully drawn color maps which clearly depict events and spatial distributions. The 1970 volume does not supersede the 1924 edition, both being useful to readers.

B1737 Cirker, Hayward and others. Dictionary of American portraits. New York: Dover, 1967. 756p.

Presents over 4,000 portraits of distinguished Americans, all of uniform size. In the absence of photographs, line drawings are provided. Limited to prominent figures before 1900, but also U.S. presidents and their wives through 1967. A bibliography of published sources of portraits, a name index arranged by occupation or activity and a variant name index conclude the volume.

B1738 Gabriel, Ralph H., ed. Pageant of America; a pictorial history. New Haven: Yale Univ. Pr., 1925–29. 15v.

Each of the 15 volumes traces, through numerous photographs, line drawings, maps, portraits and charts, the history of an aspect of American life. Examples include the "Epic of industry," "March of commerce," and "Love of the frontier." Among the more than 10,000 illustrations are many which remain rare and unreproduced. Each volume is indexed and interpretation is aided by "Notes on the pictures" found in each volume. Coverage necessarily ends with the early 20th century.

B1739 Gaustad, Edwin Scott. Historical atlas of religion in America. Rev. ed. New York: Harper, 1976. 189p.

Presents charts, graphs and maps which show the demographic and geographic distribution of religious groups in the United States from 1650 to 1970. County level populations by religious group for 1850 are based on the 7th Decennial Census (1850) and can be compared with 1950 maps based on denominational sources. Many charts and maps provide information for the 1950s and 1960s as well. Explanatory text accompanying maps aids greatly in the interpretation of data, and contains citations, now somewhat dated, to related studies and sources for those wishing to read further on the history of religions in the United States.

B1740 Jackson, Kenneth T. Atlas of American history. Rev. ed. New York: Scribner, 1978. 294p.

This new edition supersedes James Truslow Adams, *Atlas of American history* (New York: Scribner, 1943) **(B1741)**, retaining all of the 147 maps contained in the earlier ed., and supplemented by 51 new maps. Coverage now extends from the origins of the United States to the mid-1970s. The black-and-white line drawing maps are arranged in chronological fashion, showing the settlement of the United States, military history, and social and economic development. The use of most commonly used place names as well as the clarity with which maps present information and the accuracy of information make this a most important source.

B1742 Kouwenhoven, John A. Columbia historical portrait of New York; an essay in graphic history. . . . New York: Doubleday, 1953. 550p.

Among the best early attempts at "graphic history" which became the model for many later volumes. Photographs, drawings, paintings and other graphic forms are used to tell the story of New York City's development and life in the city. Text explains the context and importance of illustrations.

Works which tell the history of events, social and economic change, and cultural development are numerous. Examples include Langston Hughes and Milton Meltzer, *A pictorial history of the Negro in America*, 3d ed. (New York: Crown, 1968 [380p.]) **(B1743)**; Stefan Lorant, *Sieg heil! an illustrated history of Germany from Bismarck to Hitler* (New York: Norton, 1974 [452p.]) **(B1744)**; Rupert Furneaux, *Pictorial history of the American Revolution as told by eyewitnesses and participants* (Chicago: Ferguson, 1973 [400p.]) **(B1745)**. For an early example of this genre see Henry W. Elson, *The Civil War through the camera* (New York: McKinley, Stone & MacKenzie, 1912) **(B1746)** which is now succeeded by William C. Davis, ed., *The image of war, 1861–1865* (New York: Doubleday, 1981–83 [5v.]) **(B1747)**.

B1748 Paullin, Charles O. Atlas of the historical geography of the United States. Washington, D.C.: Carnegie Institution, 1932. 162p.

Following an extended introduction, old and rare maps and cartographic representations (e.g., the Mercator map of 1569) are reproduced showing early views of North America. Now classic maps showing voting patterns and votes on various political issues accompany others depicting political, cultural and social developments. The introduction explains the documentation upon which maps are based and an index of names and subjects complements the highly informative table of contents.

B1749 Schwartzberg, Joseph E. A historical atlas of South Asia. Chicago: Univ. of Chicago Pr., 1978. 352p.

Provides a cartographic record of the history of South Asia from the Old Stone Age. Political, social, cultural, demographic and economic developments are treated. Maps are supplemented with textual explanations, an extensive bibliography, index, and 3 chronological charts. The most valuable atlas for South Asia.

B1750 Shepherd, William R. Shepherd's historical atlas. 9th ed., rev. and updated. New York: Barnes & Noble, 1973. 226, 115p.

The 9th edition, reprinted with revisions (1973), follows the pattern developed by Shepherd in the 1920s and uses maps which he drew that have become classics. Coverage is limited to Europe and follows the traditional chronological approach to European historical development. Focus rests on political change. Multicolor maps have a well-deserved reputation for clarity and accuracy. A full index of place names, including classical and medieval Latin names cross-referenced to the modern forms used, provides assistance. Shepherd's maps are supplemented by others covering 1930 through 1973 (plates 218–26).

B1751 Treharne, R. F. and Harold Fullard, eds. Muir's historical atlas; ancient, medieval and modern. New York: Barnes & Noble, 1956, 1962. No pagination.

Maps are divided into 2 sections, the first covering ancient and classical times, and the second medieval and modern periods through 1962. Multicolor maps depict political divisions and migration routes, as well as the expansion of important world powers. Heavily emphasizes European historical development, with other areas depicted when they become important in European history. Two separate indexes indicate the location of place-names in maps by map number and reference coordinates. Maps for the ancient period use Latin and Greek place names except when commonly used English names are employed. Maps for the medieval and modern periods utilize common spellings used in English-speaking countries.

B1752 United States Military Academy (West Point). The West Point atlas of American wars. New York: Praeger, 1959. 2v.

Clear, detailed maps tell of battles and campaigns from the Colonial period through the Korean War. Military units and directions of battle are indicated, and accompanying brief commentary explains map information. V.1 covers wars fought before 1900 and emphasizes the Civil War. V.2 emphasizes the World Wars. For more detailed coverage of the Civil War, consult the *West Point atlas of the Civil War* (New York: Praeger, 1962) **(B1753)**.

B1754 Westermann, Georg. Atlas zur Weltgeschichte: Vorzeit-Altertum, Mittelalter, Neuzeit. Hrsg. von Hans-Erich Slier, et al. Braunschweig: Westermann, 1956. 160p.

Among the best historical atlases, Westermann's is divided into 3 parts, Vorzeit und Altertum, Mittelalter and Neuzeit. Coverage is limited to the development of European civilization from its origins in the Middle East and North Africa. Multicolor maps depicting political divisions are accompanied by many maps not found in other atlases. Among them, town maps, river basin maps and maps depicting cultural dispersion are among the most valuable. All maps are clearly drawn and printed, with place names and legends in German. The scholarly reputation of Westermann is well established.

SOURCES OF SCHOLARLY CONTRIBUTIONS

Journals

B1755

The American historical review. v.1– , Oct. 1895– . Washington, D.C.: American Historical Assn. 5/yr.
Cc; HumInd; RG; SSCI.

The Canadian historical review. v.1– , 1920– . Toronto: Canadian Historical Assn., Univ. of Toronto Pr. Quarterly.
Cc; HistAbst, HumInd; SSCI.

Current history: a world affairs monthly. v.1– , 1914– . Philadelphia. Monthly.
Cc; PAIS; RG; SSCI.

Diplomatic history. v.1– , 1977– . Wilmington, Del.: Scholarly Resources (for the Society for Historians of American Foreign Relations). Quarterly.
AmH&L; HistAbst.

The English historical review. v.1– , 1886– . London: Longman. Quarterly.
Cc; HumInd.

The Hispanic American historical review. v.1– , 1918– . Durham, N.C.: Duke Univ. Pr. Quarterly.
Cc; HumInd.

Historical methods. v.1– , 1967– . Chicago: Univ. of Illinois at Chicago. Quarterly.
AmH&L; Cc; HistAbst; SSCI.

Historische Zeitschrift. v.1– , 1859– . Munich: Oldenbourg. Bimonthly.
Cc; SSCI.

Isis: international review devoted to the history of science and its cultural influences. v.1– , 1912– . Philadelphia: History of Science Society. 5/yr.
HistAbst; HumInd; SSCI.

The journal of African history. v.1– , 1960– . Cambridge: Cambridge Univ. Pr. Quarterly.
BrHumInd; Cc; HistAbst; HumInd; SSCI.

The journal of American history. v.1– , 1914– . Bloomington, Ind.: Organization of American Historians. Quarterly.
Cc; HumInd; SSCI.

The journal of Asian studies. v.1– , 1941– . Ann Arbor, Mich.: Assn. for Asian Studies. Quarterly.
HistAbst; HumInd; SSCI.

The journal of modern history. v.1– , 1929– . Chicago: Univ. of Chicago Pr. Quarterly.
AmH&L; Cc; HumInd; SSCI.

Journal of Negro history. v.1– , 1916– . Washington, D.C.: Assn. for the Study of Negro Life and History. Quarterly.
Cc; HumInd; SSCI.

The Journal of Southern history. v.1– , 1935– . Houston: Southern Historical Assn. Quarterly.
AmH&L; Cc; HistAbst; HumInd; SSCI.

Pacific historical review. v.1– , 1932– . Berkeley: Univ. of California Pr. (for American Historical Assn., Pacific Coast Branch). Quarterly.
Cc; HistAbst; HumInd; SSCI.

Revista de historia de America. v.1– , 1938– . Mexico City: Instituto Panamericano de Geografia e Historia. Semiannual.
Cc; HistAbst.

Rivista storica Italiana. v.1– , 1884– . Naples: Edizioni Scientifiche Italiane. Quarterly.
Cc.

Revue d'histoire moderne et contemporaine. v.1– , 1954– . Paris: Colin (for the Société d'Histoire Moderne et Contemporaine). Quarterly.
Cc.

Revue historique. v.1– , Jan.–June, 1876– . Paris: Presses Universitaires de France. Quarterly.
Cc.

The Slavic review; American quarterly of Soviet and East European studies. v.1– , 1941– . Stanford, Calif.: American Assn. for the Advancement of Slavic Studies. Quarterly.
HumInd; PAIS.

Speculum; a journal of medieval studies. v.1– , 1926– . Cambridge, Mass.: Medieval Academy of America. Quarterly.
Cc; HumInd.

Vierteljahrshefte für Zeitgeschichte. v.1– , 1953– . Stuttgart: Deutsche Verlags-Anstalt. Quarterly.
Cc.

Western historical quarterly. v.1– , 1970– . Logan, Utah: Western History Assn. Quarterly.
AmH&L; Cc; HumInd.

William and Mary quarterly. v.1– , 1892– . Williamsburg, Va.: Inst. for Early American History and Culture.
Cc; HistAbst; HumInd.

Monograph Series

B1756

Harvard historical monographs. v.1– , 1932– . Cambridge, Mass.

Harvard historical studies. v.1– , 1896– . Cambridge, Mass.

Historical problems: studies and documents. v.1– , 1968– . New York.

Historical studies (London University). v.1– , 1954– . London.

Historische Studien. v.1– , 1896– . Husum, W. Germany.

History of Europe series. v.1– , 1966– .

Johns Hopkins University studies in historical and political science. v.1– , 1882– .

Louvain. Université Catholique. Recueil de travaux d'histoire et de philologie.

    ser.1. v.1–50, 1890–1923.

    ser.2. v.1–50, 1923–39.

    ser.3. v.1–50, 1940–52.

    ser.4. v.1– , 1953– .

    ser.5. v.1– , 1967– .

    ser.6. v.1– , 1972– .

New American nation series. v.1– , 1954– . New York.

Oxford historical monographs. v.1– , 1968– . Oxford.

Records of civilization: sources and studies. v.1– , 1915– . New York.

Smith College studies in history. v.1– , 1915– . Northampton, Mass.

Southern historical publications. v.1– , 1964– . Tuscaloosa, Ala.

University of California publications in history. v.1– , 1911– . Berkeley, Calif.

Organizations

B1757

American Historical Assn. Washington, D.C. Founded 1884.

Economic History Society. Cambridge. Founded 1926.

Historical Assn. London. Founded 1869.

Medieval Academy of America. Cambridge, Mass. Founded 1925.

Organization of American Historians. Bloomington, Ind. Founded 1970.

Société de l'Histoire de France. Paris. Founded 1833.

Society of American Archivists. Chicago. Founded 1936.

Southern Historical Assn. Athens, Ga. Founded 1933.

Western History Assn. Reno, Nev. Founded 1960.

SOURCES OF CURRENT INFORMATION

Most historical societies and associations publish news about society business, activities of members, conferences, symposia and scholarly controversy. Consult the journals listed above which are published by associations, as in the case of the *Journal of American history* (B1486), and *Journal of Southern history* (B1755).
Also see the following titles.

B1758 AHA perspectives. American Historical Assn. Washington, D.C. v.1– , 1962– . Monthly.
Formerly titled the *AHA newsletter*, it now appears monthly; a membership directory is published periodically. *Perspectives* reports minutes of the AHA Council; association items and special reports; comments and controversy in the form of letters; awards and fellowships; research and publications; notices of meetings; promotions, appointments and retirements; and news of visiting foreign scholars and international conferences.

B1759 French historical studies. Society for French Historical Studies. Columbus, Ohio. v.1– , 1958– . Semiannually.
In addition to current bibliographies and articles, news of the association, its members, awards and seminars appears.

B1760 Latin American research review. Latin American Studies Assn. Austin, Tex. v.1– , 1965– . 3/yr.
Intended to "achieve greater and more systematic communication among individuals and institutions concerned with scholarly studies of Latin America," its news section contains institutional news, a calendar of meetings, library information and publication data. A regular feature, "Current research inventory," attempts to systematically list postdoctoral research related to Latin America.

B1761 Renaissance quarterly. Renaissance Society of America. New York. v.1– , 1948– .
Formerly titled *Renaissance news*, and now incorporating *Studies in the Renaissance*, this journal serves the advancement of learning in Renaissance studies, and especially the promotion of interchange among the various fields of specialization through the publishing of articles, book reviews, news of publica-

tions, projects, conferences and a membership directory.

B1762 Royal Historical Society. Transactions. ser. 1, v.1–10, 1869/71–82; new ser., v.1–20, 1883–1906; ser. 3, v.1–11, 1907–17; ser. 4, v.1–32, 1918–50; ser. 5, v.1– , 1951– . London: The Society. Annual.

In addition to papers read before the society, volumes contain presidential addresses, reports of the council, awards, officers and committees of the society, lists of associates and fellows, and essential information about the society's publishing activities. For a detailed retrospective index to society publications, consult Alexander A. Milne, *A centenary guide to the publications of the Royal Historical Society, 1868–1968, and the former Camden Society, 1838–1897* (London: The Society, University College, 1968 [249p.]) **(B1763)**.

Ted P. Sheldon

3   Geography

Survey of the Field

Introduction C1. *General reports* C2–13. *Methodology*. Field methods C14–17. Remote sensing C18–26A. Cartography C27–33. Quantitative methods C34–46. General methodology C47–52. *History of geography* C53–69A. *Historical geography* C70–101. *Human geography* C102–4. Spatial systems C105–13. Diffusion C114–18A. Behavioral geography C119–33A. *Social geography* C134–57. *Cultural geography* C158–72C. *Political geography* C173–91. *Economic geography*. General treatises C192–202. Agricultural geography C203–15A. Manufacturing geography C216–30. Marketing geography C231–34. International trade C235–36. Transportation geography C237–44A. Energy C245–47. Recreation and tourism C248–51A. *Urban geography*. Systematic urban geography C252–92. Regional urban geography C293–327. *Rural geography* C328–29. *Population geography* C330–60. *Medical geography* C361–75D. *People and environment* C376–94. *Applied geography* C395. *Regional geography* C396–454.

Survey of the Reference Works

Guides to the literature. Basic guides C455–69. *Review of the literature:* Progress in geography *and* Progress in human geography C471–72. (General, p.180; Methodology, philosophy, and history of geography, p.180; Cartography, p.180; Quantitative methods, p.181; Historical geography, p.181; Human geography, p.181; Perceptual geography, p.182; Space and time, p.182; Diffusion research, p.182; Social geography, p.182; Cultural geography, p.182; Political geography, p.183; Economic geography, p.183; Agricultural geography, p.183; Manufacturing geography, p.183; Trade, p.183; Energy, p.183; Transportation geography, p.183; Location theory, p.184; Recreation, p.184; Regional development, p.184; Economic regionalization, p.184; Urban geography, p.184; Rural settlements, p.185; Population geography and migration, p.185; Medical geography, p.185; Environment and resources, p.185; Regional geography, p.186; Geography in education, p.186.) *Other reviews of the literature* C473–78. *Current bibliographies and abstracts.* Current bibliographies C479–80. Current abstracts C481–82. *Retrospective bibliographies.*

Comprehensive C483–86. General C487–91. Cartography C492–98. Quantitative methods C499–503. Historical geography C504–8. Social geography C509–15. Perceptual geography C516–17. Cultural geography C518. Political geography C519–20. Economic geography C521–28. Transportation geography C529–32. Regional development C533. Economic regions C534–35. Recreational geography and tourism C536–39. Urban geography C540–53. Population geography C554–57. Medical geography C557A. Resource use and management C558–59. Teaching of geography C560–64. *Regional geographical bibliographies* C565–610. *Biographical directories* C611–16. *Dictionaries* C617–21. *Gazetteers* C622–27. *Geographical encyclopedias* C628–29. *Theses and dissertations* C630–33A. *Maps and atlases*. Bibliographical sources C634–51. Lists of maps and atlases C652–53. Directories of map collections C654–55. *Atlases*. General-reference large world atlases C656–65. Smaller atlases C666–70. Thematic atlases C671–80. National and regional atlases C681–92. *Geographical serials*. Inventories C693–96. Periodicals in geography C697. Interdisciplinary serials C698. Monograph series in geography C699. *Organizations* C700–704. *Sources of current information* C705–7.

Survey of the Field

INTRODUCTION

Geography is a complex subject with features of both the social and the natural sciences. Recent American trends have emphasized its social science orientation. Geography deals fundamentally with human societies in their spatial and ecological setting. It views humans, their culture, and their activities as areally distributed or interconnected over the face of the globe. The patterns may be the worldwide distribution of population, cities, languages, religions, political states, agricultural systems, industries, types of transportation, climates, or land forms, or they may be the intricate patterns of land use, poverty, crime, health, retail trade, or air pollution in a single city. Or the object of study may be flows or interconnections among areas, as of air-passenger traffic, ocean shipping, or international trade.

Three characteristics tend to distinguish geography from the other social sciences: its concerns for spatial patterns, for regional complexes, and for human-nature relationships.

Geography attempts to extract from the enormously diverse data of the biological, physical, and social worlds those elements that display significant variations in space and that have meaningful interrelationships with other phenomena. Thus rainfall is geographically significant in that it exhibits sharp areal differences over the face of the globe, and these contrasts are interrelated in important ways with the distribution of vegetation, agricultural production, population density, and types of societies.

Geography also has a long regional tradition in the analysis of the areal association and functional interrelationships among social, cultural, economic, and physical phenomena in specific regions, as in the rice-culture areas of monsoon Asia or the coal-mining and industrial district of the Ruhr in Germany, to cite two regions of high-density population—one rural and the other urban, but both revealing the most intimate interplay of physical resources, human culture and technology, historical evolution, and location.

Interest in human/land relationships has recently been revived with the heightened public concern for ecology and environment. In their anxiety to avoid the simplistic generalizations of environmental determinism, geographers for a time neglected the ecological approach and tended to speak of associations in contrast to functional interrelationships. Culture, including technology, obviously establishes the way humans perceive and utilize their terrestrial home. With evolving technology, available resources increase, but these resources of spaceship earth are physically finite. Humankind's relationship with environmental elements is complex, interconnected, and reciprocal. In geography, as in

150

anthropology, there recently has been an increased, but more sophisticated, appreciation of the importance of resources and environmental elements.

The field of geography includes the systematic study of cultural, economic, or physical phenomena, not only in areal, regional, or ecological aspects but also—though less distinctively—in genetic, generic, or theoretical terms.

In a very broad sense, human geography can be considered to include social, cultural, political, economic, urban, and population geography.

The systematic fields of geography have close connections with the other social sciences. Cultural geography and anthropology have a common interest in the ecological setting of rural cultures and societies. Social geography and urban geography share with sociology the study of communities within a city, in which the key elements of the environment are almost entirely social. Economic geography, political geography, and historical geography touch the neighboring disciplines of economics, political science, and history, and utilize common data while also viewing these data as ordered in space, region, or environmental setting (both physical and human). Emerging fields of behavioral geography and perceptual geography have both interests and methods in common with psychology and the behavioral sciences. The teaching of geography obviously has close ties with the field of education. Recently there have been calls for a more humanistic geography and attention to human values. Landscape appreciation lies close to aesthetics and art.

Regional geography and area studies share interest in the "areal character of the earth in which man lives—the form, the content, and the function of each areal part, region, or place and the pattern of and interconnections between the area parts," to quote Richard Hartshorne in *International encyclopedia of the social sciences* (6:115). Although regional geography has often been regarded as the culmination of geography, the most vigorous thrusts in current research come mainly from the systematic branches of the discipline.

The following survey of the monographic literature in geography does not cover equally all segments of the total corpus of scholarly materials in the field. First of all, emphasis is placed on works in human geography in contrast to physical geography. In the United States, possibly three-fourths of geographical publications fall into this sector, but in the Soviet Union the proportions are reversed, with about three-fourths

of published work being in physical geography. Second, the stress is on works in English, particularly the "A-B-C" literature: American, British, and Canadian. Approximately 35 percent of the current scholarly geographical publications of the world are in English. About 35 percent are in three other major languages of science—French, German, and Russian—in roughly equal proportions. Another 30 percent is in one or another of 50 other languages, among which Spanish, Italian, Portuguese, Polish, and Japanese figure prominently. The reference section of this chapter lists the more important bibliographical guides for the geographical literature in these other languages. Third, the monographic section cites works mainly from the 1970s and early 1980s and is highly selective in inclusion of works from earlier periods. For fuller coverage of the 1960s and earlier periods, the reader may consult chapter 3, "Geography," in the second edition of *Sources of information in the social sciences: a guide to the literature*, edited by Carl M. White (Chicago: American Library Assn., 1973, p.139–80) **(C1)**. Finally the works listed are mainly monographs published by regular presses. The reference section of this chapter treats those bibliographies that provide access to articles in periodicals and serials and to government documents, dissertations, discussion papers, reports, fugitive materials, and maps.

GENERAL REPORTS

The world as viewed by geographers can be seen in any of a number of recent textbooks with modern viewpoints, such as the ones by Haggett (C2), Kolars and Nystuen (C3), Broek and Webb (C4), or by Murphey (C5), the first two using spatial structure as a frame of reference, the third cultures, and the fourth regions.

For current trends in human geography as a field of learning, one can turn to a recent special issue of the *American behavioral scientist*, edited by Zelinsky (C6), which provides critical reviews by leading scholars of developments over the past quarter-century in the most active segments: cultural, social, perceptual, ecological, historical, urban, and economic geography. These reveal shifting centers of interest, increased attention to a behavioral approach, and growing concern with environmental problems (such as pollution) or with limited and limiting resources, such as energy. Mikesell has written a brief review (C7) of the relationship of geography to the other social sciences: anthropology, sociology, political science, economics, demography, psychology, history, and area studies.

Authoritative summaries of the major systematic social science subdivisions of geography are provided in articles in the *International encyclopedia of the social sciences* (C8)—the field of geography by Richard Hartshorne, political geography by Harold H. Sprout, economic geography by Richard S. Thoman, cultural geography by Edward T. Price, social geography by Anne Buttimer, and statistical geography by Brian J. L. Berry. Older, still-valuable summaries of the development and status of the fields of geography were published in the *Encyclopedia of the social sciences* (C9)—cultural geography by Carl Sauer, human geography by Camille Vallaux, and economic geography by Karl Sapper. A recent nontechnical report by Taaffe and others (C10) in the volume on geography in the "Behavioral and Social Sciences Survey" presents some of the major growing aspects of the field, conceived as "spatial organization expressed as patterns and processes." Also valuable is the report *The science of geography* (C11), which views geography's overriding problem as "a full understanding of the vast system on the earth's surface comprising man and the natural environment." Major reviews of American contributions to the various subfields in the first half of the century, with extensive bibliographies, are given in James and Jones (C12) and in Taylor (C13).

C2   Haggett, Peter. Geography: a modern synthesis. 3d rev. ed. New York: Harper, 1983. 644p. (1st ed. 1972. 483p.)

C3   Kolars, John F., and John D. Nystuen. Geography: the study of location, culture, and environment. New York: McGraw-Hill, 1974. 448p.

C4   Broek, Jan O. M., and John W. Webb. A geography of mankind. 3d ed. New York: McGraw-Hill, 1978. 494p. (1st ed. 1968. 527p.)

C5   Murphey, Rhoads. Patterns on the earth: an introduction to geography. 4th ed. Chicago: Rand McNally, 1978. 544p. (1st ed. 1961. 699p.)

C6   Zelinsky, Wilbur, ed. "Human geography: coming of age," *American behavioral scientist* 22, no.1 (Sept.–Oct. 1978). 167p. Reprint, Beverly Hills, Calif.: Sage, 1978.

C7   Mikesell, Marvin W. "The borderlands of geography as a social science." *In* Interdisciplinary relationships in the social sciences, ed. by Muzafer Sherif and Carolyn W. Sherif, p.227–48. Chicago: Aldine, 1969.

C8   "Geography." *In* International encyclopedia of the social sciences, ed. by David L. Sills, 6:114–51. New York: Macmillan and Free Pr., 1968.

C9   "Geography." *In* Encyclopaedia of the social sciences, ed. by Edwin R. A. Seligman and Alvin Johnson, 6:621–29. New York: Macmillan, 1931.

C10   Taaffe, Edward J., ed. Geography. Englewood Cliffs, N.J.: Prentice-Hall, 1970. 143p. [The behavioral and social sciences survey]

C11   The science of geography: report of the ad hoc Committee on Geography, Earth Sciences Division, National Academy of Sciences—National Research Council. Washington, D.C.: National Academy of Sciences—National Research Council, 1965. 80p. (The Ackerman committee) [Publication 1277]

C12   James, Preston E., and Clarence F. Jones, eds. American geography: inventory and prospect. Syracuse: publ. by Syracuse Univ. Pr. for the Assn. of American Geographers, 1954. 590p.

C13   Taylor, T. Griffith, ed. Geography in the twentieth century: a study of growth, fields, techniques, aims and trends. 3d ed. enl. New York: Philosophical Library, 1957. 674p. (1st ed. 1951. 630p.)

METHODOLOGY

The ultimate source of geographical data is direct field observation, but most scholarly treatises depend on observation by someone other than the writers for much of their information. Therefore the reliability, quality, relevance, and adequacy of data must always be examined. In the use of written material, however, the problems of geography do not differ markedly from those of the other social sciences. Geography is also similar to the other social sciences in its use of numerical data by quantitative or statistical methods, except for the special problem of the importance of place-specific and sometimes time-specific figures and their generalization into areal patterns or flows.

The geographer, of course, makes extensive use of special sources: maps, photographs, and remote-sensing data. The map is the geographer's computer data bank, enabling him or her to store thousands—or millions—of pieces of information that are always available for quick inspection, extended study, or exact measurement. Maps are also a device for generalization and pattern recognition. Who doesn't recognize the shape of Africa, even though because of cloud cover no one has ever seen the entire land mass at one time? The map is also an instrument for studying such relationships as the limits of the Corn Belt in association with mean July temperatures, annual precipitation, glacial deposits, soils, roughness of terrain, or proximity to urban markets for products of competing systems of agriculture (such as dairying). Thus the geographer has special concern for the field of cartography in the production and utilization of maps, together with historical cartography, atlases, and map collections.

The use of photographs recently has been expanded to the whole field of remote sensing. Ground and aerial photographs record the landscape as it exists at a particular place and time. Aerial photographs have been used for the construction of maps, for plotting the land use, and for detailed investigation of the geography of cities. With the development of artificial earth satellites, the use of many sensors, either visual (as in ordinary photographs) or nonvisual (as in infrared sensors), has opened new possibilities for the exact recording of a vast range of physical and human data, from the state of vegetation in Africa to the traffic patterns of the metropolitan areas of the United States. One of the problems for the geographer is to recognize patterns not immediately apparent from direct observation of a mass of data, just as an ant crawling over a halftone photograph would see only dots, not a portrait. Now weather satellites with the perspective of greater distance reveal great nebula-like swirling patterns of clouds not previously clear from study of detailed ground data. Like maps, photographs are bulky to store and awkward to use, and pose special problems of preservation and retrieval.

A general introduction to field methods is offered by Lounsbury and Aldrich (C14). The Association of American Geographers has produced two guides—one for college instructors (C15), the other for high school teachers (C16). Platt examines diverse points of view and approaches to field observations and reports (C17).

The most exciting development of the 1970s was the rapid development of remote sensing techniques and applications. Many treatises have been published. Particularly useful are Richason (C18), Sabins (C19), Barrett and Curtis (C20), Lintz and Simonett (C21), Estes and Senger (C22), Rudd (C23), and Holz (C24). Lo treats the use of air photographs in geography (C25). Campbell examines the use of aerial imagery for land use information (C26). An authoritative and comprehensive manual of remote sensing has been provided by the American Society of Photogrammetry (C26A).

The best general introduction to cartography is by Robinson, Sale, and Morrison (C27). Monkhouse and Wilkinson emphasize diagrams

and graphic materials (C28). Muehrcke (C29) and Robinson (C30) treat thematic maps. The reading and meaning of maps are discussed by Monmonier (C31) and by Muehrcke (C32). Robinson and Petchenik (C33) explore maps as a means of communication. The emerging field of perceptual geography has begun to examine mental maps and cognitive mapping.

Application of quantitative methods to geographical problems developed rapidly in both the 1960s and 1970s. The literature is now very large. Perhaps the best introductions are by Taylor (C34) and by Hammond and McCullagh (C35). Other surveys of the field are by Gregory (C36), Yeates (C37), Berry and Marble (C38), King (C39), and Cole and King (C40). Recent British work is summarized in Wrigley and Bennett (C41) and European work in Bennett (C42). Models are treated by Chorley and Haggett (C43) and networks by Haggett and Chorley (C44). Useful texts have recently appeared by Wilson and Kirkby (C45) treating the mathematical background of quantitative methods and another by Dawson and Unwin (C46) on computer programs.

Basic questions concerning general methodology, scientific reasoning, explanations, and ideology have been explored by a number of recent writers. Sack examines conceptions of space (C47), a basic phenomenon studied by geography. General scientific methodology is treated by Amedeo and Golledge (C48) and by Harvey (C49). Chapman attempts to apply general systems analysis (C50). Gregory examines ideology (C51). Chorley looks at new directions (C52). These works, which vary greatly in orientation, present stimulating challenges to established methods and viewpoints.

Field Methods

C14   Lounsbury, John F., and Frank T. Aldrich. Introduction to geographic field methods and techniques. Columbus, Ohio: Merrill, 1979. 181p.

C15   Association of American Geographers. Field training in geography. Washington, D.C.: Assn. of American Geographers, 1968. 69p. [Commission on College Geography, Technical paper no.1]

C16   Association of American Geographers. High School Geography Project. Committee on Local Geography. The local community: a handbook for teachers. New York: Macmillan, 1971. 255p.

C17   Platt, Robert S. Field study in American geography: the development of theory and method exemplified by selections. Chicago: Univ. of Chicago Dept. of Geography, 1959. 405p. [Research paper 61]

Remote Sensing

C18   Richason, Benjamin F., Jr., ed. Introduction to remote sensing of the environment. 2d ed. Dubuque, Iowa: Kendall Hunt, 1983. 582p. (1st ed. 1978. 496p.)

C19   Sabins, Floyd F., Jr. Remote sensing: principles and interpretations. San Francisco: Freeman, 1978. 426p.

C20   Barrett, Eric C., and Leonard F. Curtis. Introduction to environmental remote sensing. 2d ed. New York: Chapman & Hall, 1982. 352p. (1st ed. 1976. 336p.)

C21   Lintz, Joseph, Jr., and David S. Simonett, eds. Remote sensing of environment. Reading, Mass.: Addison-Wesley, 1976. 694p.

C22   Estes, John E., and Leslie W. Senger, eds. Remote sensing: techniques for environmental analysis. Santa Barbara, Calif.: Hamilton (a division of Wiley), 1974. 340p.

C23   Rudd, Robert D. Remote sensing: a better view. North Scituate, Mass.: Duxbury, 1974. 135p.

C24   Holz, Robert K., ed. The surveillant science: remote sensing of the environment. Boston: Houghton, 1973. 390p.

C25   Lo, C. P. Geographic applications of aerial photography. New York: Crane, Russak, 1976. 336p. [420 references]

C26   Campbell, James B. Mapping the land: aerial imagery for land use information. Washington, D.C.: Assn. of American Geographers, 1983. 96p. [Resource publications in geography]

C26A Colwell, Robert N., ed. Manual of remote sensing. 2d ed. Falls Church, Va.: American Society of Photogrammetry, 1983. 2v. 2,440p. (1st ed. 1975. 2v.)

Cartography

C27   Robinson, Arthur H., and others. Elements of cartography. 5th ed. New York: Wiley, 1984. 544p. (1st ed. 1953. 254p.)

C28   Monkhouse, Francis J., and Henry R. Wilkinson. Maps and diagrams: their compilation and construction. 3d ed., rev. London: Methuen, 1978. 527p. (1st ed. 1952. 330p.)

C29   Muehrcke, Phillip. Thematic cartography. Washington, D.C.: Assn. of American Geographers, 1972. 66p. [Commission on College Geography, Resource paper no.19]

C30   Robinson, Arthur H. Early thematic mapping in the history of cartography. Chicago: Univ. of Chicago Pr., 1982. 266p.

C31   Monmonier, Mark S. Maps, distortion, and meaning. Washington, D.C.: Assn. of American Geographers, 1977. 51p. [Resource papers for college geography, no.75-4]

C32   Muehrcke, Phillip C. Map use: reading, analysis and interpretation. Rev. ed. Madison, Wis.: JP Pubns., 1980. 469p. (1st ed. 1978. 469p.)

C33   Robinson, Arthur H., and Barbara Bartz Petchenik. The nature of maps: essays toward understanding maps and mapping. Chicago: Univ. of Chicago Pr., 1976. 138p.

Quantitative Methods

C34   Taylor, Peter J. Quantitative methods in geography: an introduction to spatial analysis. Boston and London: Houghton, 1977. 386p.

C35   Hammond, Robert, and Patrick McCullagh. Quantitative techniques in geography: an introduction. 2d ed. London: Oxford Univ. Pr., 1978. 364p. (1st ed. 1974. 318p.)

C36   Gregory, Stanley. Statistical methods and the geographer. 4th ed. London: Longman, 1978. 240p. (1st ed. 1963. 240p.)

C37   Yeates, Maurice H. Introduction to quantitative analysis in human geography. New York: McGraw-Hill, 1974. 300p. First published as An introduction to quantitative analysis in economic geography (1968), 182p.

C38   Berry, Brian J. L., and Duane F. Marble, eds. Spatial analysis: a reader in statistical geography. Englewood Cliffs, N.J.: Prentice-Hall, 1968. 512p.

C39   King, Leslie J. Statistical analysis in geography. Englewood Cliffs, N.J.: Prentice-Hall, 1969. 288p.

C40   Cole, John P., and Cuchlaine A. M. King. Quantitative geography: techniques and theories in geography. New York and London: Wiley, 1968. 692p.

C41   Wrigley, Neil, and Robert J. Bennett, eds. Quantitative geography: a British view. London: Routledge & Paul, 1981. 419p.

C42   Bennett, Robert J., ed. European progress in spatial analysis. 2d European colloquium on quantitative and theoretical geography, 11–14 September 1980, Cambridge. London: Pion, 1981. 305p.

C43   Chorley, Richard J., and Peter Haggett, eds. Models in geography. London: Methuen; New York: Barnes & Noble, 1967. 816p.

C44   Haggett, Peter, and Richard J. Chorley. Network analysis in geography. London: Edward Arnold, 1969; New York: St. Martin's, 1970. 348p.

C45   Wilson, Alan G., and Michael J. Kirkby. Mathematics for geographers and planners. 2d ed.

Oxford: Clarendon, 1980. 408p. (1st ed. 1975. 325p.)

C46   Dawson, John A., and David J. Unwin. Computing for geographers. Newton Abbot, Eng.: David & Charles; New York: Crane, Russak, 1976. 362p.

General Methodology

C47   Sack, Robert D. Conceptions of space in social thought: a geographic perspective. Minneapolis: Univ. of Minnesota Pr., 1981. 231p.

C48   Amedeo, Douglas, and Reginald G. Golledge. An introduction to scientific reasoning in geography. New York: Wiley, 1975. 431p.

C49   Harvey, David. Explanation in geography. London: Edward Arnold, 1969; New York: St. Martin's, 1970. 521p.

C50   Chapman, Geoffrey P. Human and environmental systems: a geographer's appraisal. London and New York: Academic, 1977. 421p.

C51   Gregory, Derek. Ideology, science, and human geography. London: Hutchinson, 1978; New York: St. Martin's, 1979. 198p.

C52   Chorley, Richard J., ed. Directions in geography. London: Methuen; New York: Barnes & Noble, 1973. 331p.

HISTORY OF GEOGRAPHY

Geography as an intellectual discipline dates from the Greeks. Two major strands in modern geography developed early: regional geography, in descriptions by Herodotus and Strabo of specific peoples and places, and systematic geography, in the attempts by Eratosthenes and Ptolemy to give mathematical precision to the shape and size of the earth, its distances, and the distribution of its principal features. Modern geography found its earliest strong expression in Germany in the nineteenth century under the leadership of Alexander von Humboldt and Carl Ritter, the former most interested in systematic physical geography and the latter in regional and human geography. By tradition and practice, geography has always included both human and inanimate objects and both regional and systematic fields, although the relative emphasis has varied over time, among various national traditions, and even between centers of learning.

Kish has recently published, with introductory comments, 123 original texts (C53) that provide vistas of geographical thought from the earliest times through Alexander von Humboldt and Carl Ritter, both of whom died in 1859. James and Martin present panoramas of geographical concepts through the ages (C54). The most exhaustive investigation of the nature and philosophy of geography as a modern discipline is provided in two volumes by Hartshorne (C55, C56). A briefer account with emphasis on more recent developments is by Holt-Jensen (C57). The contributions of leading Anglo-American geographers to the development of the field are discussed by Dickinson (C58) and by Johnston (C59). Dickinson also has a similar work on German and French geographers (C60). Gilbert (C61), Freeman (C62), and Brown (C63) treat British geographers and geography, and Buttimore (C64), the French school. In a new publication, *Geographers: biobibliographical studies* (C65), biographical sketches on geographers from all parts of the world are written by authors from many countries; it is sponsored by the International Geographical Union. Histories of organizations of geographers are provided by James and Martin for the Association of American Geographers, 1904–79 (C66), and for the International Geographical Union and International Geographical Congresses, 1871–1972, by *La géographie à travers un siècle de congrès internationaux* (C67). A volume edited by Blouet examines the origins of academic geography in the United States (C68). The best history of cartography is the volume by Bagrow as revised by Skelton (C69). A recent collection edited by Johnston and Claval interprets the main trends in geography since World War II in 11 countries (C69A).

C53   Kish, George, ed. A source book in geography. Cambridge, Mass.: Harvard Univ. Pr., 1978. 453p.

C54   James, Preston E., and Geoffrey J. Martin. All possible worlds: a history of geographical ideas. 2d ed. New York: Wiley, 1981. 508p. (1st ed. 1972. 622p.)

C55   Hartshorne, Richard. The nature of geography: a critical survey of current thought in the light of the past. Washington, D.C.: Assn. of American Geographers, 1939. 482p. Reprinted from *Annals of the Association of American Geographers* 29:171–658 (1939), with addition of "Abstract" and "Corrections and supplementary notes." Reprint, Westport, Conn.: Greenwood, 1977.

C56   ———. Perspective on the nature of geography. Washington, D.C.: Assn. of American Geographers, 1959. 201p. [Monograph no. 1]

C57   Holt-Jensen, Arild. Geography: its history and concepts: a student's guide. Totowa, N.J.: Barnes & Noble, 1982. 171p.

C58   Dickinson, Robert E., comp. Regional concept: the Anglo-American leaders. London and Boston: Routledge & Paul, 1976. 408p.

C59   Johnston, Ronald J. Geography and geographers: Anglo-American human geography since 1945. 2d ed. London and Baltimore: Edward Arnold. 1983. 264p. (1st ed. 1980. 232p.)

C60   Dickinson, Robert E. The makers of modern geography. London: Routledge & Paul; New York: Praeger, 1969. 305p.

C61   Gilbert, Edmund W. British pioneers in geography. Newton Abbot, England: David & Charles; New York: Barnes & Noble, 1972. 271p.

C62   Freeman, T. Walter. A history of modern British geography. London and New York: Longman, 1980. 258p.

C63   Brown, Eric H., ed. Geography: yesterday and tomorrow. Oxford: Oxford Univ. Pr., 1980. 302p.

C64   Buttimer, Anne. Society and milieu in the French geographic tradition. Washington, D.C.: Assn. of American geographers, 1971. 226p. [Monograph no.6]

C65   Geographers: biobibliographical studies. Ed. by Thomas Walter Freeman and others on behalf of the Commission on the History of Geographical Thought of the International Geographical Union. London: Mansell, 1– (1977–) annual.

C66   James, Preston E., and Geoffrey J. Martin. The Association of American Geographers: the first seventy-five years 1904–1979. Washington, D.C.: Assn. of American Geographers, 1979. 279p.

C67   La géographie à travers un siècle de congrès internationaux. Geography through a century of international congresses. Chicago: International Geographical Union. Commission on History of Geographical Thought. 1972. 252p. [Union géographique internationale. Commission histoire de la pensée géographique].

C68   Blouet, Brian W., and Teresa L. Stitcher, eds. The origins of academic geography in the United States. Hamden, Conn.: Archon Books, 1981. 342p.

C69   Bagrow, Leo. History of cartography. Rev. and enl. by R. A. Skelton. Tr. by D. L. Paisey. Cambridge, Mass.: Harvard Univ. Pr., 1964. 312p. (1st ed. Die Geschichte der Kartographie. Berlin: Safari, 1951. 383p.)

C69A   Johnston, Ronald J., and Paul Claval, eds. Geography since the Second World War: an international survey. London: Croom Helm; Totowa, N. J.: Barnes & Noble, 1984. 290p.

HISTORICAL GEOGRAPHY

Historical geography, the reconstruction of the geography of the past, should be differentiated from the geographical background of historical events. The former is a subdivision of geography, the latter of history, though both utilize the methods and viewpoints of both geography and history.

Judged by the last decade, the future of the past appears assured. Historical geography has "exploded," with a new periodical, *Journal of Historical Geography*, and with an outpouring of monographs.

Baker edited a valuable and informative survey of the development and status of historical geography in Britain, France, Germany, Austria and Switzerland, Scandinavia, the Soviet Union, North America, Australia and New Zealand, and Latin America (C70). Baker and others also assembled a volume of readings (C71) and collections of articles on research methods and interpretations in historical geography (C71A and C71B).

For North America, Meinig presents a prospectus of work (C72). A collected volume, *European settlement and development in North America: essays on geographical change in honour and memory of Andrew Hill Clark*, edited by Gibson, suitably recalls the contributions of a leading scholar and teacher through essays by the next generation of active young practitioners (C73).

Brown's *Historical geography of the United States*, written more than 35 years ago, remains the best overall synthesis (C74). Ward has assembled a book of readings of later articles (C75). Ehrenberg's volume treats archival and other sources, and research based on them (C76). Cities and immigrants have been studied by Ward (C77), and urban growth by Pred (C78). Many valuable studies devoted to a particular region or even locality have appeared. Particularly noteworthy are McManis on colonial New England (C79), Lemon on southeastern Pennsylvania (C80), Earle on a tidewater parish in Maryland (C81), Mitchell on the Shenandoah Valley (C82), Johnson on the land survey of the upper Mississippi country (C83), Blouet and Lawson on images of the Plains (C84), and Meinig on Imperial Texas (C85) and on the Great Columbia Plain (C86).

Similar studies have appeared on Canada: Harris and Warkentin on Canada before Confederation (C87), Harris on the seigneurial system (C88), Clark on Nova Scotia (C89), Knight on the capital for Canada (C90), and Goheen on Victorian Toronto (C91).

The British Isles offer unusually rich materials for historical geography, a field that has long flourished in Britain. The towering figure in the field, Darby, has edited a new volume on England (C92), which stands in interesting contrast to the older series of studies published some 45 years ago (C93). The seven volumes on the Domesday geography of England stand as a monumental scholarly achievement (C94). Dodgshon and Butlin provide a shorter and more recent set of papers on England and Wales (C95).

Clifford Smith (C96) provides a good survey of Western Europe up to 1800, Catherine Smith of the Western Mediterranean Europe (C97), and Mead of Scandinavia (C97A). Butzer has an extensive synthesis of the ecological setting for prehistory (C98, C99).

Then there is the study of the landscape, product of past human efforts and of current social values. Newcomb has examined the preservation of historical landscapes (C100) and Meinig has edited a series of essays on observation and interpretation of the landscape (C101).

C70 Baker, Alan R. H., ed. Progress in historical geography. Newton Abbot, Eng.: David & Charles; New York: Wiley, 1972. 311p.

C71 ———, and others. Geographical interpretations of historical sources: readings in historical geography. Newton Abbot, Eng.: David & Charles; New York: Barnes & Noble, 1970. 452p.

C71A Baker, Alan R. H., and Mark Billinge, eds. Period and place: research methods in historical geography. Cambridge and New York: Cambridge Univ. Pr., 1982. 377p.

C71B Baker, Alan R. H., and Derek Gregory, eds. Explorations in historical geography: interpretative essays. Cambridge and New York: Cambridge Univ. Pr., 1984. 252p.

C72 Meinig, Donald W. "The continuous shaping of America: a prospectus for geographers and historians," *American historical review* 83, no.5:1186–1217 (Dec. 1978). Reprint, Washington, D.C.: American Historical Assn., 1978.

C73 Gibson, James R., ed. European settlement and development in North America: essays on geographical change in honour and memory of Andrew Hill Clark. Toronto and Buffalo: Univ. of Toronto Pr., 1978. 230p.

C74 Brown, Ralph H.; under the editorship of J. Russell Whitaker. Historical geography of the United States. New York: Harcourt, 1948. 596p.

C75 Ward, David, ed. Geographic perspectives on America's past: readings on the historical geography of the United States. New York: Oxford Univ. Pr., 1979. 364p.

C76 Ehrenberg, Ralph E., ed. Pattern and process: research in historical geography. Washington, D.C.: Howard Univ. Pr., 1975. 360p.

C77 Ward, David. Cities and immigrants: a geography of change in nineteenth century America. New York: Oxford Univ. Pr., 1971. 164p.

C78 Pred, Allan R. Urban growth and the circulation of information: the United States system of cities, 1790–1840. Cambridge, Mass.: Harvard Univ. Pr., 1973. 348p.

C79 McManis, Douglas R. Colonial New England: a historical geography. New York: Oxford Univ. Pr., 1975. 159p.

C80 Lemon, James T. The best poor man's country: a geographical study of early southeastern Pennsylvania. New York: Norton, 1972. 295p.

C81 Earle, Carville V. The evolution of a tidewater settlement system: All Hallow's Parish, Maryland, 1650–1783. Chicago: Univ. of Chicago Dept. of Geography, 1975. 239p. [Research paper no. 170]

C82 Mitchell, Robert D. Commercialism and frontier: perspectives on the early Shenandoah Valley. Charlottesville: Univ. Pr. of Virginia, 1977. 251p.

C83 Johnson, Hildegard Binder. Order upon the land: the U.S. rectangular land survey and the upper Mississippi country. New York: Oxford Univ. Pr., 1976. 268p.

C84 Blouet, Brian W., and Merlin P. Lawson, eds. Images of the plains: the role of human nature in settlement. Lincoln: Univ. of Nebraska Pr., 1975. 214p.

C85 Meinig, Donald W. Imperial Texas: an interpretive essay in cultural geography. Austin: Univ. of Texas Pr., 1969. 145p.

C86 ———. The Great Columbia Plain: a historical geography, 1805–1910. Seattle: Univ. of Washington Pr., 1968. 576p.

C87 Harris, R[ichard] Cole[brook] and John Warkentin. Canada before Confederation: a study in historical geography. New York and London: Oxford Univ. Pr., 1974. 338p.

C88 Harris, R[ichard] Cole[brook]. The seigneurial system in early Canada: a geographical study. Madison: Univ. of Wisconsin Pr., 1966. 247p.

C89 Clark, Andrew H. Acadia: the geography of early Nova Scotia to 1760. Madison: Univ. of Wisconsin Pr., 1968. 450p.

C90 Knight, David B. A capital for Canada: conflict and compromise in the 19th century. Chicago:

Univ. of Chicago Dept. of Geography, 1977. 341p. [Research paper no.182]

C91   Goheen, Peter G. Victorian Toronto, 1850 to 1900; pattern and process of growth. Chicago: Univ. of Chicago Dept. of Geography, 1970. 278p. [Research paper no.127]

C92   Darby, H[enry] Clifford, ed. A new historical geography of England. Cambridge: Cambridge Univ. Pr., 1973. 767p.

C93   ———. An historical geography of England before A.D. 1800; fourteen studies. Cambridge: Cambridge Univ. Pr., 1936. 566p.

C94   ———. The Domesday geography of England. Cambridge and New York: Cambridge Univ. Pr., 1952–1977. 7v.

   v.1.   The Domesday geography of Eastern England. 3d ed. 1971. 400p. (1st ed. 1952. 400p.)

   v.2.   . . . of Midland England. 2d rev. ed. 1971. 490p. (1st ed. 1954. 482p.)

   v.3.   . . . of South-East England. 1962. 658p.

   v.4.   . . . of Northern England. 1962, 1977. 540p.

   v.5.   . . . of South-West England. 1967. 469p.

   Domesday Gazetteer. 1975. [544, 65p.]

   Domesday, England. 1977. 416p.

C95   Dodgshon, Robert A., and Robin A. Butlin, eds. An historical geography of England and Wales. London and New York: Academic, 1978. 257p.

C96   Smith, Clifford T. An historical geography of Western Europe before 1800. Rev. ed. London and New York: Longman, 1978. 622p. (1st ed. 1967. 604p.)

C97   Smith, Catherine Delano. Western Mediterranean Europe: a historical geography of Italy, Spain, and Southern France since the Neolithic. London and New York: Academic, 1979. 453p.

C97A   Mead, William Richard. An historical geography of Scandinavia. London and New York: Academic, 1981. 313p.

C98   Butzer, Karl W. Archaeology as human ecology: methods and theory for a contextual approach. Cambridge and New York: Cambridge Univ. Pr., 1982. 364p.

C99   ———. Environment and archeology: an ecological approach to prehistory. 2d ed. Chicago: Aldine-Atherton, 1971. 703p. (1st ed. 1964. 524p.)

C100   Newcomb, Robert M. Planning the past: historical landscape resources and recreation. Folkestone, Eng.: William Dawson; Hamden, Conn.: Archon Books, 1979. 255p. [Studies in historical geography]

C101   Meinig, Donald W., ed. The interpretation of ordinary landscapes: geographical essays. New York: Oxford Univ. Pr., 1979. 255p.

HUMAN GEOGRAPHY

The term *human geography* is used to distinguish all phases of geography other than physical geography or to emphasize the human aspects of geography. It is not really a unified field, although the term is used in a number of useful textbooks and in titles of conferences on trends in geography.

Good general treatises are by Chisholm (C102) and by de Blij (C103). Buttimer has called for more attention to value systems in human geography (C104).

C102   Chisholm, Michael. Human geography: evolution or revolution? Harmondsworth, Eng., and Baltimore: Penguin, 1975. 207p.

C103   de Blij, Harm J. Human geography: culture, society, and space. 2d ed. New York: Wiley, 1982. 656p. (1st ed. 1977. 444p.)

C104   Buttimer, Anne. Values in geography. Washington, D.C.: Assn. of American Geographers, 1974. 58p. [Commission on College Geography. Resource paper no.24]

Among developments of the last two decades have been the elaboration of theories of spatial systems, studies of diffusion processes, and the rise of behavioral geography.

Spatial Systems

Haggett has been a leader in the view of geography as a spatial system with attention to location theories (C105). He has recently reviewed the field and with coauthors has revised his very influential book, *Locational analysis in human geography* (C106). Morrill and Dormitzer (C107), Cliff and others (C108), Cox (C109), and Abler and others (C110) also have general presentations of the spatial order. Massam has applied location theory to the placement of public facilities in relation to service areas (C111–12). Comparisons of the qualities of space and time have been made by Carlstein and others (C113).

C105   Haggett, Peter. "The spatial economy," *American behavioral scientist* 22, no.1:151–67 (Sept.–Oct. 1978).

C106 ———, and others. Locational analysis in human geography. 2d ed. London: Edward Arnold; New York: Wiley, 1977. 605p. (1st ed. 1965. 339p.)

C107 Morrill, Richard L., and Jacqueline M. Dormitzer. The spatial order: an introduction to modern geography. North Scituate, Mass.: Duxbury, 1979. 483p.

C108 Cliff, Andrew D., and others. Elements of spatial structure: a quantitative approach. Cambridge and New York: Cambridge Univ. Pr., 1975. 258p.

C109 Cox, Kevin R. Man, location, and behavior: an introduction to human geography. New York and London: Wiley, 1972. 399p.

C110 Abler, Ronald, and others. Spatial organization: the geographer's view of the world. Englewood Cliffs, N.J.: Prentice-Hall, 1971. 587p.

C111 Massam, Bryan H. Location and space in social administration. London: Edward Arnold; New York: Wiley, 1975. 192p.

C112 ———. Spatial search: application to planning problems in the public sector. Oxford and New York: Pergamon, 1980. 294p.

C113 Carlstein, Tommy, and others, eds. Timing space and spacing time. London: Edward Arnold; New York: Wiley. 1978. 3v.

v.1.   Making sense of time.

v.2.   Human activity and time geography.

v.3.   Time and regional dynamics.

Diffusion

The pioneer in sophisticated diffusion studies is Hägerstrand. His seminal study of the diffusion of innovations in Sweden is now available in English (C114). Pred, Brown, and Hudson have also made important contributions (C115–18). Windhorst provides a bibliography with about 750 references (C118A).

C114 Hägerstrand, Torsten. Innovation diffusion as a spatial process. Tr. by Allan Pred and Greta Haag. Chicago: Univ. of Chicago Pr., 1967. 334p. (Innovationsförloppet ur Korologisk synpunkt. Lund: Gleerup, 1953. 304p.)

C115 Pred, Allan R. Behavior and location: foundations for a geographic and dynamic location theory. Lund, Sweden: Gleerup, 1967–69. 2v. 128p., 152p. [Lund studies in geography, ser. B. Human geography, no.27–28.]

C116 Brown, Lawrence A., ed. "Studies in spatial diffusion processes. I. Empirical. II. Conceptual." *Economic geography* 50, no.4:285–374 (1974); 51, no.3:185–304 (1975). Special issues.

C117 ———. Innovation diffusion: a new perspective. London and New York: Methuen, 1981. 345p.

C118 Hudson, John C. Geographical diffusion theory. Evanston, Ill.: Northwestern Univ. Dept. of Geography, 1972. 179p. [Studies in geography, no.19]

C118 Windhorst, Hans W. Geographische Innova-
A   tions- und Diffusionsforschung. Darmstadt, W. Germany: Wissenschaftliche Buchgesellschaft, 1984. 209p. [Erträge der Forschung, Band 189]

Behavioral Geography

A striking development in geography in the 1970s was the application of behavioral approaches to studies of urban and environmental problems. Gold (C119), Porteous (C120), Jakle and others (C121), Relph (C122), and Webber (C123) have useful treatments of various aspects of this new field. Collected works have been edited by Ley and Samuels (C124) and by Cox and Golledge (C125–26).

Closely related is perceptual geography, an analysis of how individuals perceive specific aspects of their social or physical environment, problems, or possible solutions. Downs and Meyer review this somewhat ill-defined field (C127). General surveys of the state of the art are provided by Saarinen (C128) and Tuan (C129). Pocock and Hudson present a British viewpoint (C130). Collected works have been edited by Moore and Golledge (C131), by Golledge and Rushton (C132), and by Downs and Stea (C133). The most recent work by Saarinen and others provides a wide-ranging overview of the dynamism and diversity of the field (C133A).

C119 Gold, John R. An introduction to behavioural geography. Oxford and New York: Oxford Univ. Pr., 1980. 290p.

C120 Porteous, J. Douglas. Environment and behavior: planning and everyday urban life. Reading, Mass.: Addison-Wesley, 1977. 446p.

C121 Jakle, John A., and others. Human spatial behavior. North Scituate, Mass.: Duxbury, 1976. 315p.

C122 Relph, Edward C. Place and placelessness. London: Pion, 1976. 156p.

C123 Webber, Michael J. Impact of uncertainty on location. Cambridge, Mass.: MIT Pr., 1972. 310p.

C124 Ley, David, and Marwyn Samuels, eds. Humanistic geography: prospects and problems. Chicago: Maaroufa, 1978. 337p.

C125 Cox, Kevin R., and Reginald G. Golledge, eds. Behavioral problems in geography; a symposium. Evanston, Ill.: Northwestern Univ. Dept. of Geography, 1969. 276p. [Studies in geography, no.17]

C126 ———. Behavioral problems in geography revisited. New York and London: Methuen, 1981. 290p.

C127 Downs, Roger M., and James T. Meyer. "Geography of the mind: an exploration of perceptual geography," *American behavioral scientist* 22, no.1:59–77 (Sept.–Oct. 1978).

C128 Saarinen, Thomas F. Environmental planning: perception and behavior. Prospect Heights, Ill: Waveland, 1984. 262p. Reissue of Boston: Houghton, 1976.

C129 Tuan, Yi-Fu. Topophilia: a study of environmental perception, attitudes, and values. Englewood Cliffs, N.J.: Prentice-Hall, 1974. 260p.

C130 Pocock, Douglas C. D., and Ray Hudson. Images of the urban environment. New York: Columbia Univ. Pr., 1978. 181p.

C131 Moore, Gary T., and Reginald G. Golledge, eds. Environmental knowing: theories, research, and methods. Stroudsburg, Pa.: Dowden, Hutchinson & Ross, 1976. 441p.

C132 Golledge, Reginald G., and Gerard Rushton, eds. Spatial choice and spatial behavior: geographical essays on the analysis of preference and perception. Columbus: Ohio State Univ. Pr., 1976. 321p.

C133 Downs, Roger M., and David Stea. Maps in minds: reflections on cognitive mapping. New York: Harper, 1977. 284p.

C133 A Saarinen, Thomas F., and others, eds. Environmental perception and behavior: an inventory and prospect. Chicago: Univ. of Chicago Dept. of Geography, 1984. 362p. [Research paper 209]

SOCIAL GEOGRAPHY

The term *social geography* was little used in the United States until very recently, and in Britian was earlier employed merely as loosely synonymous with the whole of human geography. But during the 1970s, intense concern with social problems led to investigation of their geographic aspects in a rapidly growing literature. The rise and characteristics of this field have been discussed by Eyles and Smith (C134). Smith has taken a welfare approach to geography (C135). Fielding treats social geography in the context of related fields in geography and in the other social sciences (C136). Jones and Eyles provide a general introduction to the field (C137). Jones has edited a coordinated set of readings (C138). Herbert and Johnston have edited two volumes on social areas in cities (C139). The social geography of the United States has been treated by Watson (C140) and by Smith (C141). In the United States, problems faced by the black minority have been extensively described in works by Rose (C142) and by Ley (C143). Morrill and Wohlenberg opened vistas on poverty (C144). Spatial aspects of crime have been treated by Georges-Abeyie and Harries (C145), by Herbert (C146), and by Harries and Brunn (C147). Symanski has studied prostitution (C148). Smith and Hanham summarize the problem of alcohol abuse (C149). Golant has investigated the problems of the elderly coping with urban transport and other problems (C150, C151). Warnes presents a variety of studies on the elderly (C152). Albaum and Davies have addressed a wide range of contemporary issues (C153). In three very recent books Jackson and Smith provide a broad introduction to social geography (C153A), Clarke and Ley include case studies of ethnic pluralism from many parts of the world (C153B), and White examines the social geography of West European cities (C153C).

Concerned with social problems in Western and Third World societies, a group of geographers has emphasized inequality and conflict. The problem of inequality has been discussed by Smith (C154) and by Coates and others (C155). Harvey has examined social justice (C156). Peet has edited papers of highly variable quality into a volume on radical geography (C157).

C134 Eyles, John C., and David M. Smith. "Social geography," *American behavioral scientist* 22, no.1:41–58 (Sept.–Oct. 1978).

C135 Smith, David M. Human geography: a welfare approach. London: Edward Arnold; New York: St. Martin's, 1977. 402p.

C136 Fielding, Gordon J. Geography as social science. New York: Harper, 1974. 336p.

C137 Jones, Emrys, and John Eyles. An introduction to social geography. New York: Oxford Univ. Pr., 1977. 273p.

C138 Jones, Emrys, ed. Readings in social geography. London: Oxford Univ. Pr., 1975. 328p.

C139 Herbert, David T., and Ronald J. Johnston, eds. Social areas in cities. London and New York: Wiley, 1976. 2v.

v.1. Spatial processes and form.

v.2. Spatial perspectives on problems and policies.

C140 Watson, J. Wreford. Social geography of the United States. London and New York: Longman, 1979. 290p.

C141 Smith, David M. The geography of social well-being in the United States: an introduction to territorial social indicators. New York: McGraw-Hill, 1973. 144p.

C142 Rose, Harold M. The black ghetto: a spatial behavioral perspective. New York: McGraw-Hill, 1971. 147p.

C143 Ley, David. The black inner city as frontier outpost: images and behavior of a Philadelphia neighborhood. Washington, D.C.: Assn. of American Geographers, 1974. 282p. [Monograph series no.7]

C144 Morrill, Richard L., and Ernest H. Wohlenberg. The geography of poverty in the United States. New York: McGraw-Hill, 1971. 148p.

C145 Georges-Abeyie, Daniel E., and Keith D. Harries, eds. Crime: a spatial perspective. New York: Columbia Univ. Pr., 1980. 301p.

C146 Herbert, David T. The geography of urban crime. London and New York: Longman, 1982. 120p.

C147 Harries, Keith D., and Stanley D. Brunn. The geography of laws and justice: spatial perspectives on the criminal justice system. New York: Praeger, 1978. 175p.

C148 Symanski, Richard. The immoral landscape: female prostitution in Western societies. Toronto: Butterworths, 1981. 349p.

C149 Smith, Christopher J., and Robert Q. Hanham. Alcohol abuse: geographical perspectives. Washington, D.C.: Assn. of American Geographers, 1982. 84p. [Resource publications in geography]

C150 Golant, Stephen M., ed. Location and environment of elderly population. New York: Wiley, 1979. 214p.

C151 ———. The residential location and spatial behavior of the elderly: a Canadian example. Chicago: Univ. of Chicago Dept. of Geography, 1972. 226p. [Research paper no.143]

C152 Warnes, Anthony M., ed. Geographical perspectives on the elderly. New York: Wiley, 1982. 478p.

C153 Albaum, Melvin, and Shane Davies, comps. Geography and contemporary issues: studies in relevant problems. New York: Wiley, 1973. 590p.

C153 A Jackson, Peter, and Susan J. Smith. Exploring social geography. Boston: Allen & Unwin, 1984. 239p.

C153 B Clarke, Colin, and David Ley, eds. Geography and ethnic pluralism. Boston: Allen & Unwin, 1984. 294p.

C153 C White, Paul. The West European city: a social geography. London and New York: Longman, 1984. 269p.

C154 Smith, David M. Geographical perspectives on inequality. Harmondsworth, Eng.: Penguin, 1977; New York: Harper, 1979. 386p.

C155 Coates, Bryan E., and others. Geography and inequality. Oxford and New York: Oxford Univ. Pr., 1977. 292p.

C156 Harvey, David. Social justice and the city. London: Edward Arnold; Baltimore: Johns Hopkins Univ. Pr., 1973. 336p.

C157 Peet, Richard, ed. Radical geography: alternative viewpoints on contemporary social issues. Chicago: Maaroufa, 1977; London: Methuen, 1978. 387p.

CULTURAL GEOGRAPHY

Cultural geography, as defined by Wagner and Mikesell (C158), deals with five principal themes: culture, culture area, cultural landscape, cultural history, and cultural ecology. Thus the cultural geographer studies the distribution in time and space of cultures and the elements of culture (such as artifacts and tools, techniques, attitudes, customs, languages, and religious belief); cultural complexes in space; the cultural landscape or the association of human and physical features on the surface of the earth; the succession of cultures and the history of cultural origins and dispersals; and the intimate and interrelated association of culture and nature, as in the study of the agricultural practice of shifting cultivation in association with rapid depletion of soil fertility in low-latitude areas.

Two thoughtful essays on recent trends in cultural geography are by Mikesell as his presidential address to the Association of American Geographers (C159) and by Spencer in the *American behavioral scientist* (C160). A recent, highly recommended introduction to the field by Jordan and Rowntree treats culture region, culture diffusion, cultural ecology, cultural integration, and cultural landscape (C161). Spencer and Thomas also provide a good synthesis of the field (C162). *Man's role in changing the face of the earth*, edited by Thomas and others, touches on numerous aspects of man's impact on the surface of the globe (C163). Evolving concepts of nature and culture, basic themes in cultural geography, have been traced by Glacken (C164). Zelinsky has a short cultural geography of the United States (C165). Isaac has studied domestication (C166). The cultural landscape has been the object of attention by Hart (C167) and Donald

Meinig, in *The interpretation of ordinary land-scapes,* already described at C101. Overall treatments of the geography of religion are presented by Sopher (C169) and Schwind (C170). De Planhol has investigated geographic aspects of the history of Islam (C171). Sopher and Agnew have studied varied aspects of the cultural geography of India (C172) and cities (C172A). The textbook of Jan Broek and John W. Webb, *A geography of mankind,* in a revised edition (see description at C4), retains its continuing value, while Jackson (C172C) interprets the American landscape.

C158   Wagner, Philip L., and Marvin W. Mikesell, eds. Readings in cultural geography. Chicago: Univ. of Chicago Pr., 1962. 589p.

C159   Mikesell, Marvin W. "Tradition and innovation in cultural geography," *Annals of the Association of American Geographers* 68:1–16 (1978).

C160   Spencer, Joseph E. "The growth of cultural geography," *American behavioral scientist* 22, no.1:79–92 (Sept.–Oct. 1978).

C161   Jordan, Terry G., and Lester Rowntree. The human mosaic: a thematic introduction to cultural geography. 3d ed. New York: Harper, 1982. 444p. (1st ed. 1976. 430p.)

C162   Spencer, Joseph E., and William L. Thomas. Introducing cultural geography. 2d ed. New York: Wiley, 1978. 428p. (1st ed. 1973. 409p.)

C163   Thomas, William L., Jr., and others, eds. Man's role in changing the face of the earth. Chicago: publ. by Univ. of Chicago Pr. for Wenner-Gren Foundation for Anthropological Research and National Science Foundation, 1956. 1,193p.

C164   Glacken, Clarence J. Traces on the Rhodian shore: nature and culture in Western thought from ancient times to the end of the eighteenth century. Berkeley: Univ. of California Pr., 1967. 763p.

C165   Zelinsky, Wilbur. The cultural geography of the United States. Englewood Cliffs, N.J.: Prentice-Hall, 1973. 176p.

C166   Isaac, Erich. Geography of domestication. Englewood Cliffs, N.J.: Prentice-Hall, 1970. 132p.

C167   Hart, John F. The look of the land. Englewood Cliffs, N.J.: Prentice-Hall, 1975. 210p.

C169   Sopher, David E. Geography of religions. Englewood Cliffs, N.J.: Prentice-Hall, 1967. 118p.

C170   Schwind, Martin, ed. Religionsgeographie. Darmstadt, W. Germany: Wissenschaftliche Buchgesellschaft, 1975. 404p.

C171   Planhol, Xavier de. Les fondements géographiques de l'histoire de l'Islam. Paris: Flammarion, 1968. 443p.

C172   Sopher, David E., ed. An exploration of India: geographical perspectives on society and culture. Ithaca, N.Y.: Cornell Univ. Pr., 1980. 334p.

C172 A   Agnew, John, and others, eds. The city in cultural context. Boston: Allen & Unwin, 1984. 299p.

C172 C   Jackson, John B. Discovering the vernacular landscape. New Haven, Conn.: Yale Univ. Pr., 1984. 165p.

POLITICAL GEOGRAPHY

Political geography examines the areal organization of the world into states; their larger political groupings on one hand and their subordinate administrative units on the other; frontiers and boundaries; capitals, core areas, peripheral areas, and colonies or dependent units; the basis of political power in terms of population and resources; the relations among states, including international trade or aid; international organizations; and the territorial sea and maritime boundaries.

During the 1970s there has been particular concern with what components in a society have political power and with conflicts, patterns of voting behavior, and public policy.

A straightforward, balanced introduction to political geography is Bergman (C173). Other good general treatments are by Cohen (C174), Glassner and de Blij (C175), and Pounds (C176). Books of readings have been assembled by Jackson and Samuels (C177), and by Kasperson and Minghi (C178). Morrill has addressed the problem of political redistricting in the United States (C179). Prescott in short monographs has examined boundaries and oceans (C180–81). Cox and others have been particularly concerned with power and conflicts (C182–83). The geography of politics is treated by Brunn (C184). Taylor and Johnston have studied voting behavior (C185–86). Soja has examined the administrative organization of space (C187). Gottmann emphasizes the significance of territory (C188). Bennett has pioneered in the analysis of spatial aspects of public finance (C189). Boateng treats the political geography of Africa (C190). Whitney has constructed a systematic approach to political geography through a case study of China (C191).

C173 Bergman, Edward F. Modern political geography. Dubuque, Iowa: W. C. Brown, 1975. 408p.

C174 Cohen, Saul B. Geography and politics in a world divided. 2d ed. New York: Oxford Univ. Pr., 1973. 334p. (1st ed. 1963. 347p.)

C175 Glassner, Martin I., and Harm J. de Blij. Systematic political geography. 3d ed. New York: Wiley, 1980. 537p. (1st ed. 1967. 618p.)

C176 Pounds, Norman J. G. Political geography. 2d ed. New York: McGraw-Hill, 1972. 453p. (1st ed. 1963. 422p.)

C177 Jackson, W[illiam] A. Douglas, and Marwyn S. Samuels, eds. Politics and geographic relationships: towards a new focus. 2d ed. Englewood Cliffs, N.J.: Prentice-Hall, 1971. 528p. (1st ed. 1964. 411p.)

C178 Kasperson, Roger E., and Julian V. Minghi, eds. The structure of political geography. Chicago: Aldine, 1969. 528p.

C179 Morrill, Richard L. Political redistricting and geographic theory. Washington, D.C.: Assn. of American Geographers, 1981. 76p. [Resource publications in geography]

C180 Prescott, John R. V. Boundaries and frontiers. London: Croom Helm; Totowa, N.J.: Rowman & Littlefield, 1978. 210p.

C181 ———. The political geography of the oceans. Newton Abbot, England: David & Charles; New York: Wiley, 1975. 247p.

C182 Cox, Kevin R., and others, eds. Locational approaches to power and conflict. New York: Wiley, 1974. 345p.

C183 Cox, Kevin R. Location and public problems: a political geography of the contemporary world. Chicago: Maaroufa, 1979. 352p.

C184 Brunn, Stanley D. Geography and politics in America. New York: Harper, 1974. 443p.

C185 Taylor, Peter J., and Ronald J. Johnston. Geography of elections. Harmondsworth, Eng.: Penguin, 1978; New York: Holmes & Meier, 1979. 528p.

C186 Johnston, Ronald J. Political, electoral and spatial systems. Oxford: Clarendon Pr.; New York: Oxford Univ. Pr., 1979. 221p.

C187 Soja, Edward W. The political organization of space. Washington, D.C.: Assn. of American Geographers, 1971. 54p. [Commission on College Geography. Resource paper no.8.]

C188 Gottmann, Jean. The significance of territory. Charlottesville: Univ. Pr. of Virginia, 1973. 169p.

C189 Bennett, Robert. Geography of public finance: welfare under fiscal federalism and local government finance. London and New York: Methuen, 1980. 498p.

C190 Boateng, E. A. A political geography of Africa. Cambridge and New York: Cambridge Univ. Pr., 1978. 292p.

C191 Whitney, Joseph B. R. China: area, administration, and nation building. Chicago: Univ. of Chicago Dept. of Geography, 1970. 198p. [Research paper no.123]

ECONOMIC GEOGRAPHY

Economic geography is the study of the characteristics of, differences among, and movements between areas in the production, exchange, transfer, and consumption of goods and services. Of special interest are the location of economic activity as historically evolved and currently developed, and the principles of location theory. Geographers have been particularly interested in and strongly influenced by studies in industrial location by economists Walter Isard, August Lösch, and Edgar M. Hoover (see the section "Time and space in economic theory" in chapter 4, "Economics" (D167–85)). The economic geography of a particular area typically includes consideration of the interrelationships within the area itself of production with both economic and noneconomic factors, both cultural and physical. Linkages with other areas through trade or competition are also of concern. Thus in an analysis of an industrial district specializing in iron and steel, account is taken of the availability of raw materials such as iron ore, scrap, limestone, coking coal and other fuel, and labor; of the effects of inertia in the form of past capital investments in plant and social overhead; of markets; of changes in past location with changing resource bases or technology; of linkages with other areas for raw materials or markets; and of the competitive position with respect to other centers of production.

General Treatises

General treatises on economic geography may be organized by activities (systems of livelihood), by commodities, by regions, or by principles—or by some combination of them. Among the numerous introductory textbooks, Thoman and Corbin (C192), Wheeler and Muller (C193), and Alexander and Gibson (C194) may be especially recommended for their coverage of the field as a whole. Somewhat more theoretical from the viewpoint of the space economy are Berry and Conkling (C195), Boyce (C196), and Lloyd and Dicken (C197). De Souza and Foust attempt to encompass alternative and controversial conservative, liberal, and radical approaches to understanding the world's space economy (C198).

Of particular interest is the study of the geography of economic development. Here the reader needs to be particularly careful to note the particular approach or bias of the writer. Much of the writing has assumed that economic development is primarily a worldwide diffusion from Western Europe and Anglo-America of economic modernization; yet others take a Marxian stand that development has been part of a process of exploitation by the developed world of the developing world, and still others take a more ecological approach, with emphasis on local environmental systems and on diverse cultures involved. A good summary of different approaches is in Brookfield (C199), of regional factors in Cole (C200) and of resource factors in Chisholm (C201).

Multinational corporations are playing an increasing role in the world economy. Taylor and Thrift have edited a collection of studies on various geographic aspects of this development (C202).

C192 Thoman, Richard S., and Peter Corbin. The geography of economic activity. 3d ed. New York: McGraw-Hill, 1974. 420p. (1st ed. 1962. 602p.)

C193 Wheeler, James O., and Peter O. Muller. Economic geography. New York: Wiley, 1981. 395p.

C194 Alexander, John W., and Lay J. Gibson. Economic geography. 2d ed. Englewood Cliffs, N.J.: Prentice-Hall, 1979. 480p. (1st ed. 1963. 661p.)

C195 Berry, Brian J. L., and others. The geography of economic systems. Englewood Cliffs, N.J.: Prentice-Hall, 1976. 529p.

C196 Boyce, Ronald Reed. The bases of economic geography. 2d ed. New York: Holt, 1978. 433p. (1st ed. 1974. 358p.)

C197 Lloyd, Peter E., and Peter Dicken. Location in space: a theoretical approach to economic geography. 2d ed. London and New York: Harper, 1977. 474p. (1st ed. 1972. 292p.)

C198 de Souza, Anthony R., and J. Brady Foust. World space-economy. Columbus, Ohio: Merrill, 1979. 615p.

C199 Brookfield, Harold C. Interdependent development. London: Methuen; Pittsburgh: Univ. of Pittsburgh Pr., 1975. 234p.

C200 Cole, John P. The development gap. Chichester and New York: Wiley, 1981. 454p.

C201 Chisholm, Michael. Modern world development: a geographic perspective. Totowa, N.J.: Barnes & Noble, 1982. 216p.

C202 Taylor, Michael J., and Nigel Thrift, eds. The geography of multinationals: studies in the spatial development and economic consequences of multinational corporations. New York: St. Martin's, 1982. 338p.

The principal subfields of economic geography are agricultural, manufacturing, marketing, and transportation geography. In addition, special attention has been paid recently to the geography of energy, to recreation and tourism, and to economic development.

Agricultural Geography

Good introductions to agricultural geography are provided by Symons, Andreae, Grigg, Tarrant, Morgan and Munton, and Gregor (C203–8). The series *Geography of world agriculture*, published in English in Hungary, contain regional studies of agriculture, including monographs on the Southeastern United States and California (C209). Monographs of special interest are Chisholm on rural settlement and land use (C210), Coppock on Great Britain (C211), Grigg on harsh lands (C212), Knight and Wilcox on world food problems (C213), Dando on famines (C214) and Furuseth and Pierce on agricultural land (C215). Grigg provides a systematic historical geography of agriculture with emphasis on the role of technology and economic trends (C215A).

C203 Symons, Leslie. Agricultural geography. Rev. ed. London: G. Bell; Boulder, Colo.: Westview, 1979. 285p. (1st ed. 1967. 272p.)

C204 Andreae, Bernd. Farming development and space: a world agricultural geography. Tr. by Howard F. Gregor. Berlin and New York: de Gruyter, 1981. 345p.

C205 Grigg, David B. The agricultural systems of the world: an evolutionary approach. London and New York: Cambridge Univ. Pr., 1974. 358p.

C206 Tarrant, John R. Agricultural geography: problems in modern geography. North Pomfret, Vt.: David & Charles, 1980. (1st ed. New York: Wiley, 1974. 279p.)

C207 Morgan, William B., and Richard J. C. Munton. Agricultural geography. London: Methuen; New York: St. Martin's, 1971. 175p.

C208 Gregor, Howard F. Geography of agriculture: themes in research. Englewood Cliffs, N.J.: Prentice-Hall, 1970. 181p.

C209 Geography of world agriculture. György Enyedi, ed. in chief. Budapest: Akademiai Kiadó, 1972– .

v.1. Poland, by Jerzy Kostrowicki, 1972.

v.2. Southeast of the United States, by James R. Anderson, 1973.

v.3. Land supply and specialization, by Norbert Csáki, 1974.

v.4. California, by Howard F. Gregor, 1974.

v.5. Denmark, by Aage H. Kampp, 1975.

v.6. Finland, by Uuno Varjo, 1977.

v.7. Ireland, by Desmond A. Gillmor, 1977.

v.8. Eastern Siberia, by Vladimir P. Shotskii, 1979.

v.9. Australia, by Peter Scott, 1981.

v.10. Canada, by Michael J. Troughton, 1982.

v.11. Malaysian region, by R. D. Hill, 1982.

C210 Chisholm, Michael D. I. Rural settlement and land use: an essay in location. 3d ed. London: Hutchinson, 1979. 189p. (1st ed. 1962. 207p.)

C211 Coppock, John Terence. An agricultural geography of Great Britain. London: Bell, 1971. 345p.

C212 Grigg, David. The harsh lands: a study in agricultural development. London: Macmillan; New York: St. Martin's, 1970. 321p.

C213 Knight, C. Gregory, and R. Paul Wilcox. Triumph or triage? The world food problem in geographical perspective. Washington, D.C.: Assn. of American Geographers, 1977. 63p. [Commission on College Geography. Resource paper no.75–3.]

C214 Dando, William A. The geography of famine. New York: Wiley, 1980. 209p.

C215 Furuseth, Owen J., and John T. Pierce. Agricultural land in an urban society. Washington, D.C.: Assn. of American Geographers, 1982. 89p. [Resource publications in geography]

C215 Grigg, David B. The dynamics of agricultural
A   change: the historical experience. London: Hutchinson Educational, 1982. New York: St. Martin's, 1983. 260p.

Manufacturing Geography

Industrial development has been studied in several books written or edited by Hamilton (C216–19) and a symposium edited by Rees and others (C220). A particular favorite of geographers has been the study of industrial location patterns and factors, as by Miller, Keeble, Bale, Collins and Walker, Estall and Buchanan, Smith, and Karaska and Bramhall (C221–27).

Nonmetropolitan industrialization has been examined by Lonsdale and Seyler (C228), the automobile industry by Bloomfield (C229), and the iron and steel industry by Warren (C230).

C216 Hamilton, F. E. Ian, ed. Spatial perspectives on industrial organization and decision-making. London and New York: Wiley, 1974. 533p.

C217 ———. Industrial change: international experience and public policy. London and New York: Longman, 1978. 183p.

C218 ———, ed. Contemporary industrialization: spatial analysis and regional development. London and New York: Longman, 1978. 203p.

C219 Hamilton, F. E. Ian, and G. J. R. Linge, eds. Spatial analysis, industry and the environment. Chichester and New York: Wiley.

v.1. Industrial systems. 1979. 289p.

v.2. International industrial systems. 1981. 652p.

v.3. Regional economics and industrial systems. 1984. 680p.

C220 Rees, John, and others, eds. Industrial location and regional systems: spatial organization in the economic sector. Brooklyn: J. F. Bergen, 1981. 260p.

C221 Miller, E[ugene] Willard. Manufacturing: a study of industrial location. University Park: Pennsylvania State Univ. Pr., 1977. 286p.

C222 Keeble, David E. Industrial location and planning in the United Kingdom. London and New York: Methuen, 1976. 317p.

C223 Bale, John. The location of manufacturing industry; an introductory approach. 2d ed. Edinburgh: Oliver & Boyd, 1981. 224p. (1st ed. 1976. 223p.)

C224 Collins, Lyndhurst, and David F. Walker, eds. Locational dynamics of manufacturing activity. London and New York: Wiley, 1975. 402p.

C225 Estall, Robert C., and R. Ogilvie Buchanan. Industrial activity and economic geography: a study of the forces behind the geographical location of productive activity in the manufacturing industry. 3d rev. ed. London: Hutchinson, 1973. 252p. (1st ed. 1961. 232p.)

C226 Smith, David M. Industrial location: an economic geographical analysis. 2d ed. New York: Wiley, 1981. 492p. (1st ed. 1971. 553p.)

C227 Karaska, Gerald J., and David F. Bramhall, eds. Locational analysis for manufacturing: a selection of readings. Cambridge, Mass.: MIT Pr., 1969. 515p.

C228 Lonsdale, Richard E., and H. L. Seyler, eds. Nonmetropolitan industrialization. Washington, D.C.: V. H. Winston, 1979. 196p.

C229   Bloomfield, Gerald. The world automotive industry. Newton Abbot, Eng. and North Pomfret, Vt.: David & Charles, 1978. 368p.

C230   Warren, Kenneth. World steel: an economic geography. Newton Abbot, Eng.: David & Charles; New York: Crane, Russak, 1975. 335p.

Marketing Geography

The three principal studies of retail marketing are by Davies, Scott, and Berry (C231–33). Vance has turned attention to wholesaling (C234).

C231   Davies, Ross L. Marketing geography with special reference to retailing. London: Methuen, 1977. 300p.

C232   Scott, Peter. Geography and retailing. London: Hutchinson; Chicago: Aldine, 1970. 192p.

C233   Berry, Brian J. L. Geography of market centers and retail distribution. Englewood Cliffs, N.J.: Prentice-Hall, 1967. 146p.

C234   Vance, James E., Jr. The merchant's world: a geography of wholesaling. Englewood Cliffs, N.J.: Prentice-Hall, 1970. 167p.

International Trade

Brief introductions to international trade are presented by Thoman and Conkling, and by Johnston (C235–36).

C235   Thoman, Richard S., and Edgar C. Conkling. Geography of international trade. Englewood Cliffs, N.J.: Prentice-Hall, 1967. 186p.

C236   Johnston, Ronald J. The world trade system: some enquiries into its spatial structure. London: Bell; New York: St. Martin's, 1976. 208p.

Transportation Geography

Four general treatises of transportation geography are provided by Taaffe and Gauthier, Lowe and Moryadas, Eliot Hurst, and Hay (C237–40). Good studies by Alexandersson and Norström are available on ocean shipping (C241), by O'Dell and Richards on railroads (C242), and by Ducharry (C243), and by Sealy (C244) on air transport. The most recent general study is by White and Senior (244A).

C237   Taaffe, Edward J., and Howard L. Gauthier, Jr. Geography of transportation. Englewood Cliffs, N.J.: Prentice-Hall, 1973. 224p.

C238   Lowe, John C., and S. Moryadas. The geography of movement. Boston: Houghton, 1975. 333p.

C239   Eliot Hurst, Michael E., ed. Transportation geography: comments and readings. New York: McGraw-Hill, 1974. 528p.

C240   Hay, Alan M. Transport for the space economy: a geographical study. London: Macmillan; Seattle: Univ. of Washington Pr., 1973. 192p.

C241   Alexandersson, Gunnar, and Göran Norström. World shipping: an economic geography of ports and seaborne trade. Stockholm: Almquist & Wiksell; New York: Wiley, 1963. 507p.

C242   O'Dell, Andrew C., and Peter S. Richards. Railways and geography. 2d rev. ed. London: Hutchinson, 1971. 248p. (1st ed. 1957. 200p.)

C243   Ducharry, Monique. Géographie du transport aérien. Paris: Librairies Techniques (LITEC), 1981. 370p.

C244   Sealy, Kenneth R. The geography of air transport. Rev. ed. London: Hutchinson, 1966; Chicago: Aldine, 1968. 198p. (1st ed. 1957. 207p.)

C244   White, Henry P., and M. L. Senior. Transport
A   geography. London and New York: Longman, 1983. 224p.

Energy

General background studies on energy as a whole are contained in Wagstaff (C245) and Manners (C246). Odell has turned attention to the role of petroleum in world power (C247).

C245   Wagstaff, H. Reid. A geography of energy. Dubuque, Iowa: W. C. Brown, 1974. 122p.

C246   Manners, Gerald. The geography of energy. London: Hutchinson; Chicago: Aldine, 1967. 205p.

C247   Odell, Peter R. Oil and world power: background to the oil crisis. 5th ed. Harmondsworth, Eng., and New York: Penguin, 1979. 272p. (1st ed. 1970. 188p.)

Recreation and Tourism

Increasing attention has been given to recreational geography in recent years. Matley has a short review of the field (C248). More detailed studies are by Robinson on tourism (C249) and by the Chubbs, by Coppock and Duffield and by Smith on recreation (C250–51A).

C248   Matley, Ian M. The geography of international tourism. Washington, D.C.: Assn. of American Geographers, 1976. 40p. [Resource papers for college geography no.76-1]

C249   Robinson, Harry. A geography of tourism. London: Macdonald & Evans, 1976. 476p.

C250   Chubb, Michael, and Holly R. Chubb. One third of our time? An introduction to recreation behavior and resources. New York and Chichester: Wiley, 1981. 742p.

C251 Coppock, John Terence and B. S. Duffield. Recreation in the countryside: a spatial analysis. London: Macmillan; New York: St. Martin's, 1975. 262p.

C251 Smith, Stephen L. J. Recreation geography.
A   London and New York: Longman, 1983. 220p.

URBAN GEOGRAPHY

Urban geography is one of the best-developed branches of geography in the United States. Geographers have been particularly active in investigating the following aspects of cities: factors in their location; the urban system as a network of settlement points; urbanization as a characteristic of population distribution and growth; cities in relation to tributary areas or spheres of influence; the hierarchy of central places; characteristics of city-size regularities, such as rank-size rule; functional types of cities (economic classification); the expansion of the built-up city or metropolitan area in relation to political segmentation of central city, suburbs, and urban sprawl; internal structure of cities, especially in terms of areal differentiation of land use and localization of industry, residences, and business; community or neighborhood characteristics; urban transportation, including the journey to work and origin and destination studies; social areas within cities; spatial aspects of urban problems such as poverty and crime; minorities; housing; and cities as growth points in the economy. In addition, other branches of geography often deal particularly with the urban scene—social geography, for example.

Systematic Urban Geography

Pacione edits 10 British surveys of the present status and recent trends in the major subfields of urban geography as of 1983 (C252). Vance, Herbert and Johnston, Berry and Horton, and Berry have also surveyed recent trends and the present status of the field of urban geography. Vance concentrates on developments during the past 25 years in the United States (C253). Herbert and Johnston's books contain extensive bibliographies (C254). Berry and Horton provide an integrated set of readings (C255). The volume edited by Berry consists of 13 papers on urbanization and counterurbanization in major regions of the world (C256). Berry and Kasarda emphasize the ecology of the city (C257). *Geographical*

perspectives and urban problems treats some of the frontiers and current research needs (C258).

King and Golledge (C259), Carter (C260), Herbert and Thomas (C261), Beaujeu-Garnier (C262), Rugg (C263), and Hartshorn (C264) present introductions to urban geography. Vance (C265) and Berry (C266) provide historical and comparative depth. Ley and Knox examine the social geography of the city (C267–68). Four small volumes published by the Association of American Geographers treat employment (Pred, C269), social aspects (Harvey, C270), transportation (Stutz, C271), and spatial growth (Mayer, C272). Central-place theory has been reinterpreted by Beavon (C272) and further examined by Alao and others (C274). Systems of cities have been fruitfully studied by Bourne and Simmons (C275), Morrill (C276), Pred and Törnqvist (C277–78), and Wilson (C279). Residential mobility has been investigated by Clark (C280) and Moore (C281–82), and housing by Bourne (C283). Murphy has summarized his studies of the central business district (C284). Johnson looks at suburbanization (C285). Detwyler and Marcus treat the physical geography of the city (C286). In recent years concern has grown about the impact of the city on the environment, especially in generating pollution, as described by Lakshmanan and Chatterjee (C287), Berry and others (C288), Berry and Horton (C289), Detwyler (C290), and many others. A book edited by Dear and Scott provides a broad range of analyses of urbanization in Western societies from a leftist perspective (C291), and Harvey attempts a theoretical Marxian approach to the functioning of capital (C292).

C252 Pacione, Michael, ed. Progress in urban geography. London: Croom Helm; Totowa, N.J.: Barnes & Noble, 1983. 281p.

C253 Vance, James E., Jr. "Geography and the study of cities." *American behavioral scientist* 22, no.1: 131–49 (Sept.–Oct. 1978).

C254 Herbert, D. T., and R. J. Johnston, eds. Geography and the urban environment: progress in research and applications. Chichester and New York: Wiley.

V.1, 1978. 363p. V.2, 1979. 308p. V.3, 1980. 428p. V.4, 1982. 354p. V.5, 1983. 419p. V.6, 1984. 406p.

C255 Berry, Brian J. L., and Frank E. Horton. Geographic perspectives on urban systems with integrated readings. Englewood Cliffs, N.J.: Prentice-Hall, 1970. 564p.

C256 Berry, Brian J. L., ed. Urbanization and counterurbanization. Beverly Hills, Calif.: Sage

Publications, 1976. 334p. [Urban affairs annual reviews, v.11]

C257 ——, and John D. Kasarda. Contemporary urban ecology. New York: Macmillan, 1977. 497p.

C258 Geographical perspectives and urban problems. Washington, D.C.: National Academy of Sciences, 1973. 107p. [National Research Council. Committee on Geography.]

C259 King, Leslie J., and Reginald G. Golledge. Cities, space, and behavior: the elements of urban geography. Englewood Cliffs, N.J.: Prentice-Hall, 1978. 393p.

C260 Carter, Harold. The study of urban geography. 3d ed. London: Edward Arnold; Philadelphia: International Ideas, 1981. 434p. (1st ed. 1972. 346p.)

C261 Herbert, David T., and Colin J. Thomas. Urban geography: a first approach. Chichester and New York: Wiley, 1982. 508p.

C262 Beaujeu-Garnier, Jacqueline. Géographie urbaine. Paris: Armand Colin, 1980. 360p.

C263 Rugg, Dean S. Spatial foundations of urbanism. 2d ed. Dubuque, Iowa: W. C. Brown, 1979. 375p. (1st ed. 1972. 313p.)

C264 Hartshorn, Truman A. Interpreting the city: an urban geography. New York: Wiley, 1980. 498p.

C265 Vance, James E., Jr. This scene of man: the role and structure of the city in the geography of Western civilization. New York: Harper, 1977. 437p.

C266 Berry, Brian J. L. Comparative urbanization: divergent paths in the twentieth century. 2d ed. New York: St. Martin's, 1982. 235p. (1st ed. as The human consequences of urbanization: divergent paths in the urban experience of the twentieth century, 1973. 205p.)

C267 Ley, David. A social geography of the city. New York: Harper, 1983. 449p.

C268 Knox, Paul. Urban social geography: an introduction. London and New York: Longman, 1982. 243p.

C269 Pred, Allan R. Major job-providing organizations and systems of cities. Washington, D.C.: Assn. of American Geographers, 1974. 69p. [Commission on College Geography. Resource paper no.27]

C270 Harvey, David. Society, the city, and the space-economy of urbanism. Washington, D.C.: Assn. of American Geographers, 1972. 56p. [Commission on College Geography. Resource paper no.18.]

C271 Stutz, Frederick P. Social aspects of interaction and transportation. Washington, D.C.: Assn. of American Geographers, 1976. 74p. [Resource papers for college geography, no.76-2]

C272 Mayer, Harold M. The spatial expression of urban growth. Washington, D.C.: Assn. of American Geographers, 1969. 57p. [Commission on college geography. Resource paper no.7.]

C273 Beavon, Keith S. O. Central place theory: a reinterpretation. London and New York: Longman, 1977. 157p.

C274 Alao, Nurudeen, and others. Christaller central place structures: an introductory statement. Evanston, Ill.: Northwestern Univ. Dept. of Geography, 1977. 314p. [Studies in geography, no.22]

C275 Bourne, Larry S., and James W. Simmons, eds. Systems of cities: readings on structure, growth, and policy. New York: Oxford Univ. Pr., 1978. 565p.

C276 Morrill, Richard L. Migration and the spread and growth of urban settlement. Lund studies in geography, series B, Human geography, no.26, 1965. 208p.

C277 Pred, Allan R. City systems in advanced economies: past growth, present processes, and future development options. New York: Wiley; London: Longman, 1977. 256p.

C278 ——, and Gunnar E. Törnqvist. Systems of cities and information flows. Lund studies in geography, series B, Human geography, no.38, 1973. 121p.

C279 Wilson, Alan G. Urban and regional models in geography and planning. London and New York: Wiley, 1974. 418p.

C280 Clark, William A. V., and Eric G. Moore, eds. Population mobility and residential change. Evanston, Ill.: Northwestern Univ. Dept. of Geography, 1978. 288p. [Studies in geography, no.25]

C281 Moore, Eric G., ed. Models of residential location and relocation in the city. Evanston, Ill.: Northwestern Univ. Dept. of Geography, 1973. 199p. [Studies in geography, no.20]

C282 Moore, Eric G. Residential mobility in the city. Washington, D.C.: Assn. of American Geographers, 1972. 50p. [Commission on College Geography. Resource paper no.13.]

C283 Bourne, Larry S. The geography of housing. New York: Wiley, 1981. 288p.

C284 Murphy, Raymond E. The central business district. Chicago: Aldine-Atherton, 1972. 193p.

C285 Johnson, James H., ed. Suburban growth: geographical processes at the edge of the Western city. London and New York: Wiley, 1974. 257p.

C286 Detwyler, Thomas R., and others. Urbanization and environment: the physical geography of the city. Belmont, Calif.: Duxbury, 1972. 287p.

C287 Lakshmanan, T. R., and Lata R. Chatterjee. Urbanization and environmental quality. Washington, D.C.: Assn. of American Geographers, 1977. 35p. [Resource papers for college geography, no.77-1]

C288 Berry, Brian J. L., and others. The social burdens of environmental pollution: a comparative metropolitan data source. Cambridge, Mass.: Ballinger, 1977. 613p.

C289 Berry, Brian J. L., and Frank E. Horton, comps. Urban environmental management: planning for pollution control: an original text with integrated readings. Englewood Cliffs, N.J.: Prentice-Hall, 1974. 425p.

C290 Detwyler, Thomas R., comp. Man's impact on the environment. New York: McGraw-Hill, 1971. 731p.

C291 Dear, Michael, and Allen J. Scott, eds. Urbanization and urban planning in capitalist society. London and New York: Methuen, 1981. 619p.

C292 Harvey, David. The limits to capital. Oxford: Blackwell; Chicago: Univ. of Chicago Pr., 1982. 478p.

Regional Urban Geography

The best worldwide surveys of urban geography as a field of study and research are edited by Jones, with articles on 28 countries by specialists on each (C293), and by Schöller, with articles on trends by major language areas, particularly valuable for coverage of work in German, Portuguese, Dutch, Polish, and Japanese (C294). Both of these surveys contain extensive bibliographies. They were sponsored by the Commission on Processes and Patterns of Urbanization of the International Geographical Union. Brunn and Williams provide a world regional survey of urbanization (C295), and Hall describes the larger world cities individually (C296). North American cities are treated by Christian and Harper, Murphy, Yeates and Garner, Brunn and Wheeler, Palm, Johnston, and Yeates (C297–303), and the suburban trend by Muller (C304) and Lake (C305). The Comparative Metropolitan Analysis Project of the Association of American Geographers, edited by Adams and Abler, includes volumes of comparative analysis (C306), descriptions of 20 individual metropolitan areas (C307), and an atlas based mostly on 1970 census material (C308). Gottmann describes the largest metropolitan agglomeration of the United States (C309), and Yeates discusses the main urban corridor of Canada (C310). At the other end of the scale, Jakle evokes images of the small town (C311). Holcomb and Beauregard provide a critical view of programs of redeveloping cities (C312). Among the numerous monographs on individual American cities, Chicago by Cutler (C313) and Los Angeles by Nelson (C314) are worthy of special mention. A worldwide overview of urbanization and settlement systems has resulted from the work of the Commission on National Settlement Systems of the International Geographical Union (C294A).

Cities in other areas of the world also have been the object of recent studies: cities in the socialist realm by French and Hamilton (C315); Czechoslovakia by Kansky (C316); the Soviet Union by Harris (C317); the Third World by McGee (C318), Dwyer (emphasis on squatter settlements) (C319), and Alam and Pokshishevsky (based on Soviet-Indian collaboration) (C320); and Mabogunje on Nigeria (C321), and Western on the social geography of apartheid in Cape Town (C322). *Japanese cities*, published by the Association of Japanese Geographers, discusses Japanese research in the exploding cities of Japan (C323). Urban origins in China have been investigated by Wheatley (C324), in Japan by Wheatley and See (C325), and in Southeast Asia by Wheatley (C325A). The cities of Australia are treated by Burnley (C326), and those of New Zealand by Johnston (C327).

C293 Jones, Ronald, ed. Essays on world urbanization. London: Phillip, 1975. 402p.

C294 Schöller, Peter, ed. Trends in urban geography: reports on research in major language areas. Paderborn, W. Germany: Ferdinand Schöningh, 1973. 72p. [Bochumer geographische Arbeiten, Heft 13]

C294 A Bourne, Larry S., and others, eds. Urbanization and settlement systems; international perspectives. Oxford: Oxford Univ. Pr., 1984. 475p.

C295 Brunn, Stanley D., and others. Cities of the world: world regional urban development. New York: Harper, 1983. 506p.

C296 Hall, Peter G. The world cities. 2d ed. New York: McGraw-Hill, 1977; London: Weidenfeld & Nicolson, 1978. 271p. (1st ed. 1966. 256p.)

C297 Christian, Charles M., and Robert A. Harper, eds. Modern metropolitan systems. Columbus, Ohio: Merrill, 1982. 495p.

C298 Murphy, Raymond E. The American city: an urban geography. 2d ed. New York: McGraw-Hill, 1974. 556p. (1st ed. 1966. 464p.)

C299 Yeates, Maurice H., and Barry J. Garner. The North American city. 3d ed. New York: Harper, 1980. 557p. (1st ed. 1971. 536p.)

C300 Brunn, Stanley D., and James O. Wheeler, eds.

The American metropolitan system: present and future. New York: Wiley, 1980. 216p.

C301 Palm, Risa. The geography of American cities. New York and Oxford: Oxford Univ. Pr., 1981. 365p.

C302 Johnston, Ronald J. The American urban system: a geographical perspective. New York: St. Martin's, 1982. 348p.

C303 Yeates, Maurice H. North American urban patterns. New York: Wiley; London: Edward Arnold, 1980. 168p.

C304 Muller, Peter O. Contemporary suburban American. Englewood Cliffs, N.J.: Prentice-Hall, 1981. 218p.

C305 Lake, Robert W. The new suburbanites: race and housing in the suburbs. New Brunswick, N.J.: Rutgers Univ. Center for Urban Policy Research, 1981. 303p.

C306 Adams, John S., ed. Urban policymaking and metropolitan dynamics: a comparative geographical analysis. Cambridge, Mass.: Ballinger, 1976. 576p. [Assn. of American Geographers, Comparative Metropolitan Analysis Project]

C307 ———. Contemporary metropolitan America: twenty geographical vignettes. Cambridge, Mass.: Ballinger, 1976. 4v. 354, 314, 507, and 350p. [Assn. of American Geographers, Comparative Metropolitan Analysis Project]

C308 Abler, Ronald, and John S. Adams, eds. A comparative atlas of America's great cities; twenty metropolitan regions. Minneapolis: Univ. of Minnesota Pr., 1976. 503p. [Assn. of American Geographers, Comparative Metropolitan Analysis Project]

C309 Gottmann, Jean. Megalopolis: the urbanized northeastern seaboard of the United States. New York: Twentieth Century Fund, 1961. 810p.

C310 Yeates, Maurice. Main Street: Windsor to Quebec city. Toronto: Macmillan of Canada, in association with the Ministry of State for Urban Affairs and Information Canada, 1975. 431p.

C311 Jakle, John A. The American small town: twentieth-century place images. Hamden, Conn.: Archon Books, 1982. 195p.

C312 Holcomb, H. Briavel, and Robert A. Beauregard. Revitalizing cities. Washington, D.C.: Assn. of American Geographers, 1981. 84p. [Resource publications in geography]

C313 Cutler, Irving. Chicago: metropolis of the Mid-Continent. 3d ed. Dubuque, Iowa: Kendall Hunt, 1982. 319p. (1st ed. 1973. 128p.)

C314 Nelson, Howard J. The Los Angeles metropolis. Dubuque, Iowa: Kendall Hunt, 1983. 344p.

C315 French, R. A., and F. E. Ian Hamilton, eds. The socialist city: spatial structure and urban policy. Chichester and New York: Wiley, 1979. 541p.

C316 Kansky, Karel Joseph. Urbanization under socialism: the case of Czechoslovakia. New York: Praeger, 1976. 313p.

C317 Harris, Chauncy D. Cities of the Soviet Union: studies in their functions, size, density, and growth. Washington, D.C.: Assn. of American Geographers, 1970. 484p. [Monograph series, no.5]

C318 McGee, Terence G. The urbanization process in the Third World: explorations in search of a theory. London: Bell, 1971. 179p.

C319 Dwyer, Donald J. People and housing in Third World cities: perspectives on the problem of spontaneous settlements. London and New York: Longman, 1975. 286p.

C320 Alam, S. Manzoor, and Vadim Pokshishevsky, eds. Urbanization in developing countries. Hyderabad, India: Osmania Univ., 1976. 583p. [Indo-Soviet collaborative volume]

C321 Mabogunje, Akin L. Urbanization in Nigeria. London: Univ. of London Pr. [Holmes & Meier], 1968. 353p.

C322 Western, John C. Outcast Cape Town. Minneapolis: Univ. of Minnesota Pr., 1981. 373p.

C323 Japanese cities: a geographical approach. Tokyo: Assn. of Japanese Geographers, 1970. 264p. [Special publication no.2]

C324 Wheatley, Paul. The pivot of the four quarters: a preliminary enquiry into the origins and character of the ancient Chinese city. Chicago: Aldine; Edinburgh: Edinburgh Univ. Pr., 1971. 602p.

C325 ———, and Thomas See. From court to capital: a tentative interpretation of the origins of the Japanese urban tradition. Chicago: Univ. of Chicago Pr., 1978. 242p.

C325 A Wheatley, Paul. Nagara and commandery: origins of the Southeast Asian urban tradition. Chicago: Univ. of Chicago Dept. of Geography, 1983. 472p. [Research papers nos. 207–208]

C326 Burnley, I. H., ed. Urbanization in Australia: the post-war experience. Cambridge and New York: Cambridge Univ. Pr., 1974. 248p.

C327 Johnston, Ronald J. Urbanisation in New Zealand: geographical essays. Wellington and London: Reed Education, 1973. 328p.

RURAL GEOGRAPHY

In contrast to numerous studies of urban areas, there are few recent studies of rural areas. However, Platt and Macinko provide a recent survey of many aspects of rural land use in the United States (C328), and Lewis of rural communities (C329).

C328 Platt, Rutherford H., and George Macinko, eds. Beyond the urban fringe: land use issues of nonmetropolitan America. Minneapolis: Univ. of Minnesota Pr., 1983. 416p.

C329 Lewis, G. J. Rural communities. Newton Abbot, Eng., and North Pomfret, Vt.: David & Charles, 1979. 255p.

POPULATION GEOGRAPHY

Although geography has always been concerned with the distribution of people, population geography as a separate field is a recent development. It examines such questions as the growth and areal distribution of population and its major characteristics—number, density, age, sex, occupations, division into rural and urban, fertility, mortality and natural increase, migrations, and ethnic, linguistic, or religious groupings. Also, these traits are usually studied in relation to resources and to other economic and cultural factors, and often in terms of regional groupings.

Effective introductions to the field are offered by Jones, Noin, Woods, Schnell and Monmonier, Beaujeu-Garnier, and Clarke (C330–35A). Other good treatments of the entire field are two volumes by George (especially good in its treatment of economic and urban factors) (C336–37), Zelinsky (good treatment of cultural factors) (C338), and three volumes by Trewartha (C339–41). The collected volumes edited by Demko and others (C342) and Griffin (C343) open vistas into the range and diversity of research. Rees and Wilson provide models for spatial analysis of population (C344).

The Commission on Population Geography of the International Geographical Union in a series of international seminars has produced three important volumes which have examined in turn three important objects of population geography: *Geography and a crowding world*, edited by Zelinsky and others, examines population pressures upon resources (C345); *Population at microscale*, edited by Kosiński and Webb, pioneered in study of small areal units (C346); and *People on the move*, edited by Kosiński and Prothero, brought together many studies on migration (C347). Migration turns out to be a topic of lively investigation, with an overview by Lewis (C348) and with studies on the United States by Roseman and Clark (C349–50), on

Europe by Salt and Clout (C351), on Britain by Sant (C352), on Eastern Europe by Kostanick (C353), and on West Africa by Mabogunje (C354). General studies of population geography are also available for Europe by Kosiński (C355); for Eastern Europe, also by Kosiński (C356); for the Soviet Union by Lewis and others (C357–57A); and for developing countries by Clarke (C358). Denevan has edited a study of the native population of the Americas in 1492 at the time of the arrival of Columbus (C359). Grigg has examined the relationship of population growth to agrarian change in Western and Northern Europe over the last several centuries (C360).

C330 Jones, Huw R. A population geography. London and New York: Harper, 1981. 330p.

C331 Noin, Daniel. Géographie de la population. Paris and New York: Masson, 1979. 320p.

C332 Woods, Robert. Theoretical population geography. London and New York: Longman, 1982. 220p.

C333 Schnell, George A., and Mark Stephen Monmonier. The study of population: elements, patterns, processes. Columbus, Ohio: Merrill, 1983. 371p.

C334 Beaujeu-Garnier, Jacqueline. Geography of population. 2d ed. Tr. by Stanley H. Beaver. London and New York: Longman, 1978. 400p. (1st ed. 1966. 386p.)

C335 Clarke, John I. Population geography. 2d ed. Oxford and New York: Pergamon, 1972. 176p. (1st ed. 1965. 164p.)

C335 ———, ed. Geography and population: apA proaches and applications. Oxford and New York: Pergamon, 1984. 245p.

C336 George, Pierre. Populations actives: introduction à une géographie du travail. Paris: Presses Universitaires de France, 1978. 237p.

C337 ———. Population et peuplement. Paris: Presses Universitaires de France, 1969. 212p.

C338 Zelinsky, Wilbur. A prologue to population geography. Englewood Cliffs, N.J.: Prentice-Hall, 1966. 150p.

C339 Trewartha, Glenn T., A geography of population: world patterns. New York: Wiley, 1969. 186p.

C340 ———, ed. The more developed realm: a geography of its population. Oxford and New York: Pergamon, 1978. 275p.

C341 ———. Less developed realm: a geography of its population. New York and London: Wiley, 1972. 449p.

C342 Demko, George J., and others, eds. Population geography; a reader. New York: McGraw-Hill, 1970. 526p.

C343 Griffin, Paul F., ed. Geography of population: a teacher's guide. Palo Alto, Calif.: Fearon, 1969. 370p. [National Council for Geographic Education Yearbook, 1970]

C344 Rees, Philip H., and Alan G. Wilson. Spatial population analysis. London: Edward Arnold; New York: Academic, 1977. 356p.

C345 Zelinsky, Wilbur, and others, eds. Geography and a crowding world. Symposium on Population Pressures upon Physical and Social Resources in the Developing Lands. Pennsylvania State Univ., 1967. New York: Oxford Univ. Pr., 1970. 601p.

C346 Kosiński, Leszek A., and John W. Webb, eds. Population at microscale. Edmonton, Canada: IGU Commission on Population Geography. Dept. of Geography. Univ. of Alberta, 1976. 193p. [New Zealand Geographical Society. Special publication no.8.]

C347 Kosiński, Leszek A., and R. Mansell Prothero, eds. People on the move: studies on internal migration. London and New York: Methuen, 1975. 393p.

C348 Lewis, G. J. Human migration: a geographical perspective. New York: St. Martin's, 1982. 220p.

C349 Roseman, Curtis C. Changing migration patterns within the United States. Washington, D.C.: Assn. of American Geographers, 1977. 34p. [Resource papers for college geography, no.77-2]

C350 Clark, Gordon L. Interregional migration, national policy, and social justice. Totowa, N.J.: Rowman & Allanheld, 1983. 191p.

C351 Salt, John, and Hugh D. Clout, eds. Migration in post-war Europe: geographical essays. London and New York: Oxford Univ. Pr., 1976. 228p.

C352 Sant, Morgan E. C. Industrial movement and regional development: the British case. Oxford: Pergamon, 1975. 253p.

C353 Kostanick, Huey Louis, ed. Population and migration trends in Eastern Europe. Boulder, Colo.: Westview, 1977. 247p.

C354 Mabogunje, Akin L. Regional mobility and resource development in West Africa. Montreal: McGill-Queens Univ. Pr., 1972. 154p.

C355 Kosiński, Leszek A. The population of Europe: a geographical perspective. London: Longman, 1970. 161p.

C356 ———. Demographic developments in Eastern Europe. New York: Praeger, 1977. 343p. [International Slavic Conference, 1st, Banff, Alta., 1974. v.8]

C357 Lewis, Robert A., and others. Nationality and population change in Russia and the USSR; an evaluation of census data, 1897–1970. New York: Praeger, 1976. 456p.

C357 Lewis, Robert A., and Richard H. Rowland.
A Population redistribution in the USSR: its impact on society, 1897–1977. New York: Praeger, 1979. 485p.

C358 Clarke, John I. Population geography and developing countries. New York: Pergamon, 1971. 282p.

C359 Denevan, William M., ed. The native population of the Americas in 1492. Madison: Univ. of Wisconsin Pr., 1976. 353p.

C360 Grigg, David B. Population growth and agrarian change: an historical perspective. Cambridge and New York: Cambridge Univ. Pr., 1980. 340p.

MEDICAL GEOGRAPHY

Learmonth provides a good introduction to the field (C361). Medical geography includes three quite different types of studies. First are studies of diseases, particularly infectious ones, as in epidemiology. A series of monographs by Howe represents this line of investigation (C362–65). The work by Cliff and others provides excellent examples of research (C366). Second are studies of the ecology of malnutrition in relation to medical problems. The series of studies by May (C367) and the Geomedical monograph series (C368) illustrate this approach. Third, research on the best distribution of health care facilities has been carried out by Pyle, de Vise, and Shannon and Dever (C369–73). Smith has examined the geography of mental health (C374). A good symposium of medical geography was edited by Hunter (C375). Four recent publications by Learmonth, Gesler, McGlashan and Blunden, and Eyles and Woods (C375A–D) examine the geography of health care with papers and examples from many parts of the world.

C361 Learmonth, Andrew T. A. Patterns of disease and hunger: a study in medical geography. Newton Abbot, Eng. and North Pomfret, Vt.: David & Charles, 1978. 256p.

C362 Howe, George Melvyn, ed. A world geography of human diseases. London and New York: Academic, 1977. 621p.

C363 ———. Man, environment and disease in Britain: a medical geography of Britain through the ages. Newton Abbot, Eng.: David & Charles; New York: Barnes & Noble, 1972. 285p.

C364 ——, and John A. Loraine, eds. Environmental medicine. 2d ed. London: Heinemann, 1981. 375p. (1st ed. 1973. 271p.)

C365 ——. National atlas of disease mortality in the United Kingdom. Rev. and enl. ed. London: Nelson, 1970. 197p. (1st ed. 1963. 111p.)

C366 Cliff, Andrew D., and others. Spatial diffusion: an historical geography of epidemics in an island community. Cambridge: Cambridge Univ. Pr., 1981. 283p.

C367 May, Jacques M. [and Donna L. McLellan], eds. Studies in medical geography. v.1, New York: MD Publications, 1959. v.2–14, New York: Hafner, 1961–74.

v.1.   Ecology of human disease. 1959. 327p.

v.2.   Studies in disease ecology. 1961. 613p.

The ecology of malnutrition in:

v.3.   . . . The Far and Near East: food resources, habits and deficiencies. 1961. 688p.

v.4.   . . . Five countries of Eastern and Central Europe. 1963. 292p.

v.5.   . . . Middle Africa. 1965. 255p.

v.6.   . . . Central and Southeastern Europe. 1966. 290p.

v.7.   . . . Northern Africa. 1967. 275p.

v.8.   . . . French speaking countries of West Africa and Madagascar. 1968. 433p.

v.9.   . . . Eastern Africa and four countries of Western Africa. 1970. 675p.

v.10.   . . . Seven countries of Southern Africa and in Portuguese Guinea. 1971. 432p.

v.11.   . . . Mexico and Central America. 1972. 395p.

v.12.   . . . The Caribbean. 1973. 490p.

v.13.   . . . Eastern South America. 1974. 558p.

v.14.   . . . Western South America. 1974. 365p.

C368 Geomedical monograph series: regional studies in geographical medicine. Medizinische Länderkunde: Beiträge zur geographischen Medizin. (Heidelberger Akademie der Wissenschaften. Mathematischnaturwissenschaftliche Klasse). Heidelberg, Berlin, and New York: Springer Verlag, 1967– . Irregular. Monographs have been published on Libya, Afghanistan, Kuwait, Ethiopia, Kenya, and Korea.

C369 Pyle, Gerald F. Applied medical geography. New York: Wiley, 1979. 282p.

C370 ——. "Human health problems: spatial perspectives," *Economic geography* 52, no.2:95–191 (1976). Special issue.

C371 ——. Heart disease, cancer and stroke in Chicago: a geographical analysis with facilities plans for 1980. Chicago: Univ. of Chicago Dept. of Geography, 1971. 292p. [Research paper no.134]

C372 de Vise, Pierre. Misused and misplaced hospitals and doctors: a locational analysis of the urban health care crisis. Washington, D.C.: Assn. of American Geographers, 1973. 96p. [Commission on college geography. Resource paper no.22.]

C373 Shannon, Gary William, and G. E. Alan Dever. Health care delivery: spatial perspectives. New York: McGraw-Hill, 1974. 141p.

C374 Smith, Christopher J. Geography and mental health. Washington, D.C.: Assn. of American Geographers, 1976. 51p. [Resource papers for college geography, no.76-4]

C375 Hunter, John Melton, ed. The geography of health and disease. Chapel Hill: Univ. of North Carolina Dept. of Geography, 1974. 193p. [Papers of the First Carolina Geographical Symposium. Studies in geography, no.6.]

C375 Learmonth, Andrew T. A., ed. The geography
A   of health. Oxford: Pergamon, 1981. 262p.

C375 Gesler, Wilbert M. Health care in developing
B   countries. Washington, D.C.: Assn. of American Geographers, 1984. 88p. [Resource publications in geography]

C375 McGlashan, Neil D., and John R. Blunden,
C   eds. Geographical aspects of health. London: Academic, 1983. 392p.

C375 Eyles, John, and Kevin J. Woods. The social
D   geography of medicine and health. London: Croom Helm; New York: St. Martin's, 1983. 272p.

PEOPLE AND ENVIRONMENT

The best guide to the vast literature of environmental studies in geography is *Sourcebook on the environment,* by 26 specialists edited by Hammond and others, with extensive bibliographies (C376). It covers a wide range of topics from conceptual frameworks for the study of humankind and its environment, to environment and quality of life, resource scarcity, urban settlements and land use, the limits-to-growth controversy, and the impact of human activities on the environment. Another particularly valuable volume is *Perspectives on environment,* edited by Manners and Mikesell (C377). It reviews the status of knowledge on environmental problems and interaction of humans with the environment, also with extensive bibliographies. Another review, much briefer, by Porter, is of geography as human ecology (C378). Other studies of natural resources and of the human environment are by Simmons and by Dawson and Doornkamp (C379–80). Borgstrom has examined the biological limitations of the earth (C381). White has been an outstanding leader in the analysis of water problems. Three of his volumes reveal a very wide range of scale and of approaches; one examines the environmental effects of development of large river basins (C382), another looks at management of water in the United States (C383), and a third studies domestic water use in East Africa (C384). Desertification, the absence of water, was the subject of a special issue of *Economic geography*, edited by Johnson (C385). Natural hazards affecting humankind have been the object of analysis by Burton and others, and by White (C386–87). Five resource papers issued by the Association of American Geographers illustrate the range of topics of concern: a general conceptual framework for study of humankind and environment by Hewitt and Hare (C388), water resources for cities by Baumann and Dworkin (C390), land-use controls by Platt (C391), and environmental impact statements by Greenberg and others (C392). Environmental impact statements in Britain are disucssed by O'Riordan and Hey (C393). Finally, at the opposite end of resource management or development is the concept of wilderness preservation, examined by Graber (C394). In addition, see a work on the world food problem described earlier, C. Gregory Knight and R. Paul Wilcox, *Triumph or triage? The world food problem in geographical perspective,* at C213.

C376 Hammond, Kenneth A., and others. Sourcebook on the environment: a guide to the literature. Chicago: Univ. of Chicago Pr., 1978. 613p.

C377 Manners, Ian A., and Marvin W. Mikesell, eds. Perspectives on environment: essays requested by the Panel on Environmental Education, Commission on College Geography. Washington, D.C.: Assn. of American Geographers, 1974. 395p. [Publication no.13]

C378 Porter, Philip W. "Geography as human ecology: a decade of progress in a quarter century." *American behavioral scientist* 22, no.1:15–39 (Sept.–Oct. 1978).

C379 Simmons, Ian Gordon. The ecology of natural resources. 2d ed. New York: Wiley, 1981. 438p. (1st ed. 1974. 424p.)

C380 Dawson, John A., and John C. Doornkamp, eds. Evaluating the human environment: essays in applied geography. London: Edward Arnold, 1973. 288p.

C381 Borgstrom, Georg. Too many: a study of earth's biological limitations. London: Collier-Macmillan; New York: Macmillan, 1969. 368p.

C382 White, Gilbert F., ed. Environmental effects of complex river development. Boulder, Colo.: Westview, 1977. 172p.

C383 ———. Strategies of American water management. Ann Arbor: Univ. of Michigan Pr., 1969. 155p.

C384 White, Gilbert F., and others. Drawers of water: domestic water use in East Africa. Chicago and London: Univ. of Chicago Pr., 1972. 306p.

C385 Johnson, Douglas L., ed. "The human face of desertification." *Economic geography* 53, no.4: 317–432 (1977). Special issue.

C386 Burton, Ian, and others. The environment as hazard. New York: Oxford Univ. Pr., 1978. 240p.

C387 White, Gilbert F., ed. Natural hazards: local, national, global. New York: Oxford Univ. Pr., 1974. 288p.

C388 Hewitt, Kenneth, and F. Kenneth Hare. Man and environment: conceptual frameworks. Washington, D.C.: Assn. of American Geographers, 1973. 39p. [Commission on College Geography. Resource paper no.20.]

C390 Baumann, Duane D., and Daniel Dworkin. Water resources for our cities. Washington, D.C.: Assn. of American Geographers, 1978. 35p. [Resource papers for college geography, no.78-2]

C391 Platt, Rutherford H. Land use control: interface of law and geography. Washington, D.C.: Assn. of American Geographers, 1975. 39p. [Resource papers for college geography, no.75-1]

C392 Greenberg, Michael, and others. Environmental impact statements. Washington, D.C.: Assn. of American Geographers, 1978. 35p. [Resource papers for college geography, no.78-3]

C393 O'Riordan, Timothy, and R. Hey, eds. Environmental impact assessment. Farnborough, Eng.: Saxon House, 1976; Lexington, Mass.: Lexington Books, 1977. 232p.

C394 Graber, Linda H. Wilderness as sacred space. Washington, D.C.: Assn. of American Geographers, 1976. 124p. [Monograph series, no.8]

APPLIED GEOGRAPHY

Geography can be applied to many practical problems of society, and there is an active interest in applied geography; however, the field is ill-defined and highly diverse. Frazier provides a useful perspective (C395).

C395 Frazier, John W., ed. Applied geography: selected perspectives. Englewood Cliffs, N.J.: Prentice-Hall, 1982. 333p.

REGIONAL GEOGRAPHY

Problems and possibilities of field work around the world by scholars from outside the areas involved are discussed by a group of specialists on the world's major cultural regions in the volume *Geographers abroad*, edited by Mikesell (C396). McGee has also examined the interactions of Western and Third World geographers in studies of the Third World (C397).

Geographic literature is enormously rich in detailed regional studies of continents, major cultural areas, countries, subregions within countries, and even individual cities. Within the scope of this chapter, it is possible to mention only the outstanding works on the larger regions. For North America, or more properly Anglo-America, the leading general syntheses are by White and coauthors, Starkey and coauthors, and Paterson (C398–400). *Studies in Canadian geography* is the best regional treatment of Canada (C401). For Latin America, James' text remains the best overall coverage, with somewhat fuller attention to Brazil (C402). Middle America is excellently treated by West and Augelli (C403). For the West Indies, Blume and Lowenthal provide contrasting emphases (C404–5).

Europe is the best-investigated continent, with a wealth of monographs on all regions at many scales from diverse viewpoints. Hoffman and coauthors provide a good overall view (C406). Nystrom and Hoffman (C407) and Parker (C408) focus on the Common Market. For the British Isles, Stamp and Beaver remain valuable (C409), though Watson and Sissons now provide the best systematic geography (C410) and Johnston and Doornkamp, the best review of recent changes (C410A). For France, one can turn to House (C411), for Germany to Mellor and Elkins (C412–13), for Northern Europe to Sømme (C414), for Southern Europe to the Beckinsales (C415), for Italy to a collected volume, *Italy: a geographical survey* (C416), and for Eastern Europe to Turnock (C417) or Pounds (C418).

For the Soviet Union, Lydolph provides either a systematic or a regional treatment (C419–20). Dienes and Shabad effectively treat energy (C421), and Symons, agriculture (C422). Demko and Fuchs provide a large volume of readings, translations from Russian studies by Soviet geographers (C423), while Jensen and others have examined in great detail the natural resources of Siberia (C424).

Hodder discusses economic development (C425), and De Souza and Porter modernization of the Third World (C426). Recent active interest in Africa is reflected in the availability of a large number of works, among which Hance, Harrison Church and others, Grove, Best and de Blij (C427–30), Boateng (C190), and O'Connor (C432) provide particularly good introductions. More specialized treatments are by Udo for West Africa (C433) and by Morgan for East Africa (C434). For the Middle East, Fisher's volume remains a durable, widely used introduction (C435). Beaumont and coauthors offer a new approach (C436).

Asia is the largest and most populous continent. Ginsburg and coauthors provide a treatment of the entire continent (C437). Spencer concentrates on the southern and eastern countries of large population and monsoon climate (C438). Spate and Learmonth provide the best overall monograph on India and Southern Asia (C439), and Fryer of Southeast Asia (C440). The classic study by Gourou on the Far East (C441) and the more recent monograph by Kolb (C442) have both been recently translated into English. For Japan, the most authoritative works are *Geography of Japan* by a group of Japanese geographers (C443) and Trewartha (C444). For recent spectacular developments, one turns to Kornhauser (C445), to Nō and Gordon (C446), to Hall (C447), or to the monograph in German by Boesch (C448). Work by Japanese geographers on Japan is effectively summarized in the volume *Geography in Japan*, edited by Kiuchi, including surveys of 30 fields by 42 authors (see C478). For China, Cressey remains the best treatment, although it is somewhat dated (C450).

For the Pacific, Brookfield is useful (C451); for the Southwest Pacific, Cumberland (C452); and for Australia, Jeans (C453).

Finally, Arctic regions are effectively treated by Armstrong and coauthors (C454).

C396 Mikesell, Marvin W., ed. Geographers abroad: essays on the problems and prospects of research in foreign areas. Chicago: Univ. of Chicago Dept. of Geography, 1973. 296p. [Research paper no.152]

C397 McGee, Terence G. "Western geography and the Third World," *American behavioral scientist* 22, no.1:93–114 (Sept.–Oct. 1978).

C398 White, C[harles] Langdon, and others. Regional geography of Anglo-America. 5th ed. Englewood Cliffs, N.J.: Prentice-Hall, 1979. 585p. (1st ed. 1943. 898p.)

C399 Starkey, Otis P., and others. The Anglo-American realm. 2d ed. New York: McGraw-Hill, 1975. 369p. (1st ed. 1969. 533p.)

C400 · Paterson, John H. North America. 6th ed. London and New York: Oxford Univ. Pr., 1979. 463p. (1st ed. 1960. 454p.)

C401 Studies in Canadian geography, ed. by Louis Trotier. Toronto: Univ. of Toronto Pr., 1972. 6 v. (22nd International Geographical Congress).

The Atlantic provinces, ed. by Alan G. Macpherson, 182p.

Québec, ed. by Fernand Grenier, 110p.

Ontario, ed. by Louis Gentilcore, 126p.

The Prairie provinces, ed. by P. J. Smith, 141p.

British Columbia, ed. by J. Lewis Robinson, 139p.

The North, ed. by William C. Wonders, 151p.

C402 James, Preston E. Latin America. 4th ed. New York: Odyssey, 1969. 949p. (1st ed. 1942. 908p.)

C403 West, Robert C., and John P. Augelli. Middle America: its lands and peoples. 2d ed. Englewood Cliffs, N.J.: Prentice-Hall, 1976. 494p. (1st ed. 1966. 482p.)

C404 Blume, Helmut. The Caribbean islands. Tr. by Johannes Maczewski and Ann Norton. London and New York: Longman, 1974. 464p. (Die Westindischen Inseln. Braunschweig: Westermann, 1968. 352p.)

C405 Lowenthal, David. West Indian societies. London and New York: Oxford Univ. Pr., 1972. 385p.

C406 Hoffman, George W., and others. Geography of Europe: problems and prospects. 5th ed. New York: Wiley, 1983. 647p. (1st ed. 1953. 775p.)

C407 Nystrom, J[ohn] Warren, and George W. Hoffman. The Common Market. 2d ed. New York: Van Nostrand, 1976. 147p. (1st ed. 1962. 134p.)

C408 Parker, Geoffrey. The logic of unity: a geography of the European Economic Community. 3d ed. London and New York: Longman, 1981. 208p. (1st ed. 1969. 178p.)

C409 Stamp, L. Dudley, and Stanley H. Beaver. The British Isles: a geographic and economic survey. 6th ed. London: Longman; New York: St. Martin's, 1971. 881p. (1st ed. 1933. 719p.)

C410 Watson, J. Wreford, and J. B. Sissons, eds. The British Isles: a systematic geography. Edinburgh: Nelson, 1964. 452p.

C410 A Johnston, Ronald J., and John C. Doornkamp, eds. The changing geography of the United Kingdom. London and New York: Methuen for the Institute of British Geographers, 1982. 430p.

C411 House, John W. France: an applied geography. London and New York: Methuen, 1979. 478p.

C412 Mellor, Roy E. H. The two Germanies: a modern geography. London and New York: Harper, 1978. 461p.

C413 Elkins, Thomas H. Germany. 2d ed. London: Chatto & Windus, 1968. 334p. (1st ed. 1960. 272p.)

C414 Sømme, Axel, ed. A geography of Norden: Denmark, Finland, Iceland, Norway, Sweden. Oslo: J. W. Cappelens; London: Heinemann; New York: International Pubns. Serv. 1968. 343p. (1st ed. 1962. 363p.)

C415 Beckinsale, Monica, and Robert P. Beckinsale. Southern Europe: the Mediterranean and Alpine lands. London: Univ. of London Pr.; New York: Holmes & Meier, 1975. 334p.

C416 Italy: a geographical survey. Ed. by Mario Pinna and Domenico Ruocco. Published for the 24th International Geographical Congress, Tokyo, 1980. Pisa: Pacini, 1980. 567p. [Associazione dei Geografi Italiani]

C417 Turnock, David. Eastern Europe. Folkestone, Eng.: Dawson; Boulder, Colo.: Westview, 1978. 273p.

C418 Pounds, Norman J. G. Eastern Europe. London: Longman; Chicago: Aldine, 1969. 912p.

C419 Lydolph, Paul E. Geography of the U.S.S.R.: topical analysis. Elkhart Lake, Wis.: Misty Valley, 1979. 522p. 1984 supplement, 37p.

C420 ———. Geography of the U.S.S.R. 3d ed. New York: Wiley, 1977. 495p. (1st ed. 1964. 451p.)

C421 Dienes, Leslie, and Theodore Shabad. The Soviet energy system: resource use and policies. New York: Wiley, 1979. 298p. [Scripta series in geography]

C422 Symons, Leslie. Russian agriculture: a geographic survey. London: Bell; Boulder, Colo.: Westview, 1972. 348p.

C423 Demko, George J., and Roland J. Fuchs, eds. Geographical perspectives in the Soviet Union: a selection of readings. Columbus: Ohio State Univ. Pr., 1974. 742p.

C424 Jensen, Robert G., and others, eds. Soviet natural resources in the world economy. Chicago and London: Univ. of Chicago Pr., 1983. 700p.

C425 Hodder, Branwell W. Economic development in the Tropics. 3d ed. London; New York: Methuen, 1980. 255p. (1st ed. 1968. 258p.)

C426 De Souza, Anthony R., and Philip W. Porter. The underdevelopment and modernization of the Third World. Washington, D.C.: Assn. of American Geographers, 1974. 94p. [Commission on College Geography. Resource paper no.28.]

C427 Hance, William A. The geography of modern Africa. 2d ed. New York: Columbia Univ. Pr., 1975. 657p. (1st ed. 1964. 653p.)

C428 Harrison Church, Ronald J., and others. Africa and the islands. 4th ed. London: Longman; New York: Wiley, 1977. 542p. (1st ed. 1964. 494p.)

C429 Grove, Alfred T. Africa. 3d ed. London and New York: Oxford Univ. Pr., 1978. 337p. (1st ed. 1967. 275p.)

C430 Best, Alan C. G., and Harm J. de Blij. African survey. New York: Wiley, 1977. 626p.

C432 O'Connor, Anthony M. The geography of Tropical African development: a study of spatial patterns of economic change since independence. 2d ed. Oxford and New York: Pergamon, 1978. 255p. (1st ed., 1971. 207p.)

C433 Udo, Reuben K. A comprehensive geography of West Africa. London: Heinemann; New York: Holmes & Meier, 1978. 304p.

C434 Morgan, W[illiam] T. W. East Africa. London and New York: Longman, 1973. 410p.

C435 Fisher, William B. The Middle East: a physical, social, and regional geography. 7th ed. London and New York: Methuen, 1978. 615p. (1st ed. 1950. 514p.)

C436 Beaumont, Peter, and others. The Middle East: a geographical study. Chichester and New York: Wiley, 1976. 572p.

C437 Ginsburg, Norton S., and others. The pattern of Asia. Englewood Cliffs, N.J.: Prentice-Hall, 1958. 929p.

C438 Spencer, Joseph E. Asia, east by south: a cultural geography. 2d ed. New York: Wiley, 1971. 669p. (1st ed. 1954. 453p.)

C439 Spate, Oskar H. K., and A. T. A. Learmonth. India and Pakistan: a general and regional geography. 3d ed. rev. London: Methuen; New York: Barnes & Noble, 1967. 877p. (1st ed. 1954. 827p.)

C440 Fryer, Donald W. Emerging Southeast Asia: a study in growth and stagnation. 2d ed. New York: Wiley, 1979. 540p. (1st ed. 1970. 486p.)

C441 Gourou, Pierre. Man and land in the Far East. Tr. by Stanley H. Beaver. London and New York: Longman, 1975. 239p. (La terre et l'homme en Extrême-Orient. Paris: A. Colin, 1940)

C442 Kolb, Albert. East Asia: China, Japan, Korea, Vietnam; the geography of a cultural region. Tr. by C. A. M. Sym. London: Methuen; New York: Barnes & Noble, 1971. 591p. (Ostasien. Heidelberg: Quelle & Meyer, 1963. 608p.)

C443 Geography of Japan. Ed. by the Assn. of Japanese Geographers. Tokyo: Teikoku-Shoin, 1980. 440p. [Association of Japanese Geographers. Special publication no.4.]

C444 Trewartha, Glenn T. Japan: a geography. Madison: Univ. of Wisconsin Pr., 1965. 652p. (1st ed. 1945. 607p.)

C445 Kornhauser, David. Japan: geographical background to urban-industrial development. 2d ed. London and New York: Longman, 1982. 189p. First published as Urban Japan; its foundations and growth (1976). 180p.

C446 Nō, Toshio, and Douglas H. Gordon, eds. Modern Japan: land and man. 2d ed. Tokyo: Teikoku-Shoin, 1978. 146p. (1st ed. 1974. 146p.)

C447 Hall, Robert B., Jr. Japan: industrial power of Asia. 2d ed. New York: Van Nostrand Reinhold, 1976. 150p. (1st ed. 1963. 127p.)

C448 Boesch, Hans. Japan. Bern: Kümmerly & Frey, 1978. 257p.

C450 Cressey, George B. Land of the 500 million: a geography of China. New York: McGraw-Hill, 1955. 387p.

C451 Brookfield, Harold C., ed. The Pacific in transition: geographical perspectives on adaptation and change. London: Edward Arnold; New York: St. Martin's, 1973. 332p.

C452 Cumberland, Kenneth B. Southwest Pacific; a geography of Australia, New Zealand, and their Pacific island neighbors. Rev. ed. New York: Praeger, 1968. 423p. (1st ed. Christchurch, N.Z.: Whitcombe & Tombs, 1954. 365p.)

C453 Jeans, Dennis N., ed. Australia: a geography. London: Kegan Paul; New York: St. Martin's, 1978. 571p.

C454 Armstrong, Terence E., and others. The circumpolar north: a political and economic geography of the Arctic and Sub-Arctic. London: Methuen, 1978; New York: Wiley, 1979. 303p.

Survey of the Reference Works

GUIDES TO THE LITERATURE

The best guides to the literature of geography are Harris, Brewer, and *A geographical bibliography for American college libraries*. Harris (C455) is the most specialized, being limited to bibliographies proper and to reference aids for geography as a whole, but it treats these in great depth both historically and on an international scale with coverage of the most important works in English, French, German, and Russian. Brewer (C456) is the most extensive, treating some 2,400 works in the running text, including substantive monographs, bibliographies, and reference books for the systematic and regional field of geography. *A geographical bibliography for American college libraries*, published by the Association of American Geographers (C457), is a collaborative volume involving specialists in many fields. It provides an excellent selection of the best books and serials as of 1970 but is already somewhat dated, particularly for segments of the field that are evolving rapidly. Goddard includes a very good chapter by Jesse H. Wheeler on the United States (C458). Martinson

is designed particularly as an introduction for students (C459). Durrenberger is useful for its listing materials in related fields (C460). Ginsburg discusses the fields of geography (C461). Wright and Platt, although unequaled in the high quality of its annotations and critical comments, is now largely of historical interest (C462).

The other guides here cited are particularly useful in coverage of other languages. Dion is especially good for French and Canadian materials (C463). Josuweit is international in coverage of bibliographies and reference works but, of course, is of particular value in its fuller treatment of German publications (C464). Nolzen discusses substantive works in German (C465). Blotevogel and Heineberg provide a detailed, four-volume annotated bibliography of publications in German and English, and less fully in other languages (C466–69). Harris has an extensive annotated listing of bibliographies and reference works in Russian; for full description of *Guide to geographical bibliographies and reference works in Russian or on the Soviet Union*, see C585.

BASIC GUIDES

C455 Harris, Chauncy D. Bibliography of geography. Part I. Introduction to general aids. Chicago: Univ. of Chicago Dept. of Geography, 1976. 276p. [Research paper no.179]

Covers bibliographies of bibliographies, current and retrospective bibliographies of geography, books, serials, government documents, dissertations, photographs, maps and atlases, gazetteers, dictionaries, encyclopedias, statistics, and methodology. Includes 585 main entries. Current and retrospective comprehensive bibliographies of geography analyzed in detail. Author and title index.

C456 Brewer, J. Gordon. The literature of geography; a guide to its organisation and use. 2d ed. London: Clive Bingley; Hamden, Conn.: Linnet, 1978. 264p. (1st ed. 1973. 208p.)

Extensive discussion of principal guides and bibliographies, and the major substantive works in geography. Emphasis on recently published English-language material. Especially full coverage of works published in Britain but international in scope. Author and title index.

C457 A geographical bibliography for American college libraries. Ed. by Gordon R. Lewthwaite and others. Washington, D.C.: Assn. of American Geographers, 1970. 214p. [Commission on College Geography publication no.9] Revision of A basic geographical library; a selected and annotated book list for American colleges, ed. by Martha Church and others. Washington, D.C.: The Assn., 1966.

Substantive books in all fields of geography considered appropriate as a core for the geographic collection of an American college library. Critical evaluations and notes by specialists in each field. Books in English have been favored, mainly for the period 1945–69. Four main sections: (1) general aids and sources; (2) history, philosophy, and methods; (3) works grouped by topic; (4) works grouped by regions, each subdivided and carefully articulated. 1,760 entries. Items recommended for junior college libraries are noted. Author index.

A successor to this volume to be entitled *A geographical bibliography for American libraries*, edited by Chauncy D. Harris and others, is planned for publication by the Association of American Geographers in 1985. More than 70 geographers and librarians contributed. Emphasis is on publications of 1970–84. For 1945–69 see C457 and for the period before 1945, C462.

C458 Goddard, Stephen, ed. Guide to information sources in the geographical sciences. London: Croom Helm; Totowa, N. J.: Barnes & Noble, 1983. 273p.

Chapters devoted to the systematic approach (geomorphology, historical geography, agricultural geography, and industrial geography), sources of regional information (Africa, South Asia, U. S. A., and the U. S. S. R.), and tools for the geographer (maps, atlases and gazetteers, and list of current cartographic serials, aerial photographs and satellite information, statistical materials and the computer, and archival materials—governmental and otherwise) by 12 specialists.

C459 Martinson, Tom L. Introduction to library research in geography: an instruction manual and short bibliography. Metuchen, N.J.: Scarecrow, 1972. 168p.

938 main entries. Emphasis on works in the United States. Brief introductions to the utilization of each main type of material of geographic value.

C460 Durrenberger, Robert W. Geographical research and writing. New York: Crowell, 1971. 246p.

Simple listing without annotations or textual comments.

C461 Ginsburg, Norton S. "Geography [bibliography]." *In* A reader's guide to the social sciences. Rev. ed. Ed. by Bert F. Hoselitz, 293–318 and 420–25. New York: Free Pr., 1970. (1st ed. 1959, p. 70–88)

Discussion of the nature and fields of geography, with introduction to reference materials.

C462 Wright, John K., and Elizabeth T. Platt. Aids to geographical research; bibliographies, periodicals, atlases, gazetteers and other reference books. 2d ed. New York: pub. by Columbia Univ. Pr. for the American Geographical Society, 1947. 331p. Reprint, Westport, Conn.: Greenwood, 1971. [American Geographical Society. Research series no.22.] (1st ed. 1923. 243p.)

Best bibliography for the period before 1945.

C463 Dion, Louise. Introduction aux ouvrages de référence en géographie. Choix d'ouvrages de la collection de la Bibliothèque de l'Université Laval. Quebec: Université Laval, 1970. 107p. [Publications de la Bibliothèque] 268 entries.

C464 Josuweit, Werner. Studienbibliographie Geographie: Bibliographien und Nachschlagewerke. Wiesbaden, W. Germany: Steiner, 1973. 122p. [Wissenschaftliche Paperbacks. Studienbibliographien.]

365 numbered entries for bibliographies and reference works in classed arrangement. Good coverage of sources in German, English, French, and Russian.

C465 Nolzen, Heinz. Bibliographie allgemeine Geographie; Grundlagenliteratur der Geographie als Wissenschaft. Paderborn, W. Germany: Schöningh. 1976. 185p.

Listing of more-important substantive works, especially in German, for all systematic fields of geography.

C466 Blotevogel, Hans H., and Heinz Heineberg. Bibliographie zum Geographiestudium. Teil 1. Fachtheorie. Didaktik der Geographie. Arbeitsmethoden. Physische Geographie. Geoökologie. Paderborn, W. Germany: Schöningh, 1976. 236p.

Annotated bibliography of major works on theory, teaching, and methods in geography. Covers systematic fields of physical geography. Thorough coverage of German literature. Good selection of works in English.

C467 ———. ———. Teil 2. Kulturgeographie. Sozialgeographie. Raumplanung. Entwicklungsländerforschung. Statistische Quellen. Paderborn, W. Germany: Schöningh, 1976. 346p.

Annotated bibliography of substantive works in social science fields in geography, cultural geography, social geography, and studies of developing regions. Statistical sources. Thorough coverage of German literature. Selective coverage of works in English.

C468 ———. ———. Teil 3. Regionale Geographie: Deutschland, Europa, Sowjetunion. Paderborn, W. Germany: Schöningh, 1980. 304p.

C469 ———. ———. Teil 4. Regionale Geographie: Asien, Afrika, Nordamerika, Lateinamerika, Australien, Ozeanien, Ozeane, Polargebiete. Paderborn, W. Germany: Schöningh, 1981. 372p.

Annotated bibliography of substantive works in regional geography on all parts of the world, arranged by regions and countries. The most extensive annotated bibliography of regional geography. Especially full for works in German but also includes a good selection of works in English. Less-complete coverage of works in other languages.

REVIEW OF THE LITERATURE: *PROGRESS IN GEOGRAPHY* AND *PROGRESS IN HUMAN GEOGRAPHY*

The best series of reviews of the literature of geography are contained in *Progress in geography* and in its successors *Progress in human geography* and *Progress in physical geography*. These reviews are distinguished by thoughtful essays on the development and state of various subfields of human geography and of special areas of active current research, accompanied by extensive bibliographies. They sensitively reflect the dynamic research frontiers of geography and thus stand in contrast to the organization of the field as formalized in library classification systems, which, once established, must endure changing clusters of research activities, permeable boundaries of fields, restructuring of fields and subfields, and even the rise of new technologies (such as remote sensing from artificial earth satellites) or the rise of new subfields, such as perceptual geography, which did not exist a few years ago.

Review and note sections of the key international geographical periodicals also provide a continuing overview of the new literature. See the section "Periodicals," especially the *Annals of the Association of American Geographers, Geographical review, Professional geographer, Geographical journal, Geography, Canadian geographer, Annales de géographie, Cahiers d'Outre-mer, Erde, Erdkunde, Geographische Zeitschrift,* and *Petermanns geographische Mitteilungen.*

The principal reviews of the field in *Progress in geography* (PG) (C471) and *Progress in human geography* (PHG) (C472) are listed below grouped by subfields. These reviews generally provide the most up-to-date, comprehensive, and critical reviews of recent publications, trends, and progress in geographical work in the social sciences and humanities. They are written by leading scholars in each field and represent evaluative essays—sometimes controversial but generally well balanced—of current research activity. Extensive bibliographies are appended to each review.

C471 Progress in geography: international reviews of current research. General editors: Christopher Board and others. London: Edward Arnold, v. 1–9 (1969–1976). Annual. Abbreviated as PG.

C472 Progress in human geography. Managing editor: Christopher Board. Review editor: Ron Johnston. London: Edward Arnold, 1– (1977–). Four nos. a year. v. 1–2 (1977–78) had 3 nos. Distributed in the United States and Canada by Cambridge Univ. Pr., New York. Abbreviated as PHG.

General

Wise, Michael J. "On progress and geography," PHG 1, no.1:1–11 (1977). 28 references.

Walford, Rex. "Geographical education in Britain," PHG 1, no.3:503–509 (1977). 14 references.

Methodology, Philosophy, and History of Geography

Claval, Paul. "Epistemology and the history of geographical thought," PHG 4, no.3:371–84 (1980). 28 references.

———. "Methodology and geography," PHG 5, no.1:97–103 (1981). 31 references. "Methodology and philosophy," PHG 6, no.3:449–54 (1982). 33 references.

Agnew, John A., and James S. Duncan. "The transfer of ideas into Anglo-American human geography," PHG 5, no. 1:42–57 (1981). 70 references. Discussion by Michael Curry, 6, no.4:593–603 (1982). 24 references.

Bird, James. "Methodology and philosophy," PHG 1, no.1:104–110 (1977); 2, no.1:133–40 (1978); 3, no.1:117–25 (1979). 90 references.

Smith, Neil. "Geography, science and post-positivist modes of explanation." PHG 3, no.3:356–83 (1979). 120 references. [Marxism as science in geography]

Peet, Richard. "The development of radical geography in the United States," PHG 1, no.2:240–63 (1977). 75 references.

Doughty, Robin W. "Environmental theology: trends and prospects in Christian thought," PHG 5, no.2:234–48 (1981). 90 references. Discussion by David N. Livingstone, and rejoinder, 7, no.1:133–41 (1983). 45 references.

Gould, Peter C. "Methodological developments since the fifties," PG 1:1–49 (1969). 438 references.

Glick, Thomas F. "History and philosophy of geography," PHG 8, no.2:275–83 (1984). 21 references.

Griffith, Daniel A. "Reexamining the question 'are locations unique?'," PHG 8, no.1:82–94 (1984). 35 references.

Cartography

Board, Christopher. "Maps and mapping," PHG 1, no.2:288–95 (1977): 6, no.1:106–113 (1982). 72 references.

———. "Maps in the mind's eye: maps on paper and maps in the mind," PHG 3, no.3:434–41 (1979). 43 references.

———. "Map design and evaluations: lessons for geographers," PHG 4, no.3:433–37 (1980). 10 references.

Monmonier, Mark Stephen. "Cartography and mapping," PHG 6, no.3:441–48 (1982). 43 references.

———. "Cartography, mapping and geographic information," PHG 7, no.3:420–28. (1983). 42 references.

———. "Geographic information and cartography," PHG 8, no.3:381–91 (1984). 49 references.

Blakemore, Michael. "From way-finding to map-making: the spatial information fields of aboriginal peoples," PHG 5, no.1:1–24 (1981). 85 references.

Haining, R. P. "Analysing univariate maps," PHG 5, no.1:58–78 (1981). 51 references.

Chen, Cheng-siang. "The historical development of cartography in China," PHG 2, no.1:101–120 (1978). 26 references.

Quantitative Methods

Cliff, Andrew D. "Quantitative methods," PHG 1, no.3:492–502 (1977); 3, no.1:143–52 (1979); 4, no.4:568–76 (1980). 75 references.

Wrigley, Neil. "Quantitative methods . . . ," PHG 5, no.4:548–61 (1981); 6, no.4:547–62 (1982); 7, no.4:567–77 (1983); 8, no.4 525-35 (1984). 251 references.

———. "Developments in the statistical analysis of categorical data," PHG 3, no.3:315–55 (1979). 112 references.

Baxter, Mike. "Estimation and inference in spatial interaction models," PHG 7, no.1:40–59 (1983). 78 references.

Senior, Martyn L. "From gravity modelling to entropy maximizing: a pedagogic guide," PHG 3, no.2:175–210 (1979). 41 references.

Tinkler, Keith J. "Graph theory," PHG 3, no.1: 85–116 (1979). 249 references.

Holmes, John H. "Dyadic interaction matrices; a review of transformation purposes and procedures," PHG 2, no.3:467–93 (1978). 46 references.

Boots, Barry N., and Arthur Getis. "Probability model approach to map pattern analysis," PHG 1, no.2:264–86 (1977). 112 references.

Hepple, Leslie W. "The impact of stochastic process theory upon spatial analysis in human geography," PG 6:89–142 (1974). 254 references.

Bassett, Keith. "Numerical methods for map analysis," PG 4:217–54 (1972). 76 references.

Bosque-Sendra, J., and others. "Quantitative geography in Spain," PHG 7, no.3:370–85 (1983). 111 references.

Timmermans, Harry J. P. "Decompositional multiattribute preference models in spatial choice analysis: a review of some recent developments," PHG 8, no.2:189–221 (1984). 97 references.

Historical Geography

Baker, Alan R. H. "Historical geography," PHG 1, no.3:465–74 (1977); 2, no.3:495–504 (1978); 3, no.4:560–70 (1979). 209 references.

Conzen, Michael P. "Historical geography: North American progress during the 1970s," PHG 4, no.4:549–59 (1980). 86 references.

———. "Historical geography: changing spatial structure and social patterns," PHG 7, no.1:88–107 (1983). 98 references.

Dennis, Richard. "Rethinking historical geography," PHG 7, no.4:587–94 (1983). 48 references.

———. "Historical geography: theory and progress," PHG 8, no.4:536–43 (1984). 47 references.

Crush, Jonathan, and Christian Rogerson. "New wave African historiography and African historical geography," PHG 7, no.2:203–231 (1983). 253 references.

Perry, P. J. "Beyond Domesday," PHG 3, no.3: 407–16 (1979). 30 references.

Hodder, Ian. "Spatial studies in archaeology," PHG 1, no.1:33–64 (1977). 81 references.

Dilke, O. A. W., and Margaret S. Dilke, "Perception of the Roman world," PG 9:39–72 (1976). 118 references.

Taylor, James A. "Chronometers and chronicles: a study of palaeo-environments in west central Wales," PG 5:247–334 (1973). 231 references.

Prince, Hugh. "Real, imagined and abstract worlds of the past," PG 3: 1–86 (1971). 548 references.

Human Geography

Johnson, Hildegard Binder, and Gerald R. Pitzl. "Viewing and perceiving the rural scene: visualization in human geography," PHG 5, no.2:211–33 (1981). 98 references.

Pacione, Michael. "The use of objective and subjective measures of life quality in human geography," PHG 6, no.4:495–514 (1982). 111 references.

Johnston, Ronald J. "Paradigms and revolutions or evolutions: observations on human geography since the Second World War," PHG 2, no.2:189–206 (1978). 53 references.

Guelke, Leonard. "The role of laws in human geography," PHG 1, no.3:376–86 (1977). 15 references.

Mead, William R. "Recent developments in human geography in Finland," PHG 1, no.3:361–75 (1977). 104 references.

Claval, Paul. "Contemporary human geography in France," PG 7:253–92 (1975). 168 references.

Reboratti, Carlos E. "Human geography in Latin America," PHG 6, no. 3:397–407 (1982). 33 references.

Jeans, D. N. "Experiments of fruit and experiments of light: human geography in Australia and New Zealand," PHG 7, no.3:313–43 (1983). 299 references.

Bailly, Antoine S., and Bryn Greer-Wootten, "Behavioural geography in Francophone countries," PHG 7, no.3:344–56 (1983). 71 references.

Tuan, Yi-Fu. "Space and place: humanistic perspective," PG 6:211–52 (1974). 114 references.

Langton, John. "Potentialities and problems of adopting a systems approach to the study of change in human geography," PG 4:125–79 (1972). 146 references.

Chouinard, Vera, and others. "Empirical research in scientific human geography," PHG 8, no.3:347–80 (1984). 93 references.

Perceptual Geography

Saarinen, Thomas F., and James L. Sell. "Environmental perception," PHG 4, no.4:525–48 (1980); 5, no.4:525–47 (1981); 6, no.4:515–47 (1982) (with Eliza Husband). 1,020 references.

Gold, John R., and Brian Goodey. "Behavioural and perceptual geography . . . ," PHG 7, no.4:578–86 (1983); 8, no.4:544–50 (1984). 104 references.

Lowenthal, David. "Environmental perception: preserving the past," PHG 3, no.4:549–59 (1979). 82 references.

Hudson, Ray. "Personal construct theory, the repertory grid method and human geography," PHG 4, no.3:346–59 (1980). 61 references.

Penning-Rowsell, Edmund C. "Fluctuating fortunes in gauging landscape value," PHG 5, no.1:25–41 (1981). 84 references.

Sack, Robert. "Conceptions of geographic space," PHG 4, no.3:313–45 (1980). 96 references.

Downs, Roger M. "Geographic space perception: past approaches and future prospects," PG 2:65–108 (1970). 89 references.

Brookfield, Harold C. "On the environment as perceived," PG 1:51–80 (1969). 51 references.

Space and Time

Gold, John R. "Territoriality and human spatial behaviour," PHG 6, no.1:44–67 (1982). 197 references.

Thrift, Nigel. "Time and theory in human geography," PHG 1, no.1:65–101 (1977), and 1, no.3:413–57 (1977). 358 references.

Forer, Pip. "A place for plastic space?" PHG 2, no.2:230–67 (1978). 155 references.

Diffusion Research

Blaikie, Piers. "The theory of the spatial diffusion of innovations: a spacious cul-de-sac," PHG 2, no.2:268–95 (1978). 11 references.

Brown, Lawrence A., and Eric G. Moore. "Diffusion research in geography: a perspective," PG 1:119–57 (1969). 106 references.

Browett, John. "Development: the diffusionist paradigm and geography," PHG 4, no.1:57–79 (1980). 221 references.

Social Geography

Robson, Brian T. "Social geography," PHG 1, no.3:481–86 (1977); 2, no.3:512–17 (1978); 3, no.4:571–75 (1979); 6, no. 1:96–101 (1982). 94 references.

Jackson, Peter. "Social Geography . . . ," PHG 7, no.1:116–21 (1983); 8, no.1:105–12 (1984). 77 references.

Williams, Colin, and Anthony D. Smith, "The national construction of social space," PHG 7, no.4:502–18 (1983). 53 references.

Herbert, David. "Crime, delinquency and the urban environment," PHG 1, no.2:208–239 (1977). 136 references.

Eyles, John C. "Social theory and social geography," PG 6:27–87 (1974). 458 references.

Smith, Christopher J. "Social networks as metaphors, models and methods," PHG 4, no.4:500–524 (1980). 81 references.

Zelinsky, Wilbur, and others. "Women and geography: a review and prospectus," PHG 6, no.4:317–67 (1982). 251 references.

Warnes, A. M. "Towards a geographical contribution to gerontology," PHG 5, no.3:317–41 (1981). 259 references.

Cultural Geography

Mikesell, Marvin W. "Cultural geography," PHG 1, no.3:460–64 (1977). 30 references.

Ley, David. "Cultural/humanistic geography," PHG 5, no.2:249–57 (1981); 7, no.2:267–75 (1983). 131 references.

Sopher, David E. "Geography and religion," PHG 5, no.4:510–24 (1981). 121 references.

Trudgill, Peter. "Linguistic geography and geographical linguistics," PG 7:227–52 (1975). 139 references.

Political Geography

Taylor, Peter J. "Political geography," PHG 1, no.1:130–35 (1977); 2, no. 1:153–62 (1978); 3, no. 1:139–42 (1979). 160 references.

Archer, J. Clark. "Political geography," PHG 4, no.2:255–64 (1980); 6, no.2:231–41 (1982). 145 references.

Short, J. R. "Political geography," PHG 7, no.1: 122–25 (1983); 8, no.1:127–30 (1984). 49 references.

Johnston, Ronald J. "Marxist political economy, the state and political geography," PHG 8, no.4:473–92 (1984). 44 references.

Knox, Paul. "Planning and applied geography," PHG 8, no.4:515–24 (1984). 99 references.

Massam, Bryan. "Political geography and the provision of public services," PG 6:179–210 (1974). 117 references.

Cox, Kevin R. "The voting decision in a spatial context," PG 1:81–117 (1969). 75 references.

Economic Geography

Sayer, Andrew. "Explanation in economic geography," PHG 6, no.1:68–88 (1982). 37 references.

Hayter, Roger, and H. D. Watts. "The geography of enterprise: a reappraisal," PHG 7, no.2:157–81 (1983). 125 references.

Clark, Gordon L. "Critical problems of geographical unemployment models," PHG 4, no.2:157–80 (1980). 79 references.

Walker, Richard, and Michael Storper. "Capital and industrial location," PHG 5, no.4:473–509 (1981). 159 references.

Jones, Donald W. "A geography of money," PHG 5, no.3:342–69 (1981). 50 references.

Scott, Allen J. "Land and land rent: an interpretative review of the French literature," PG 9:101–145 (1976). 110 references.

Cooke, Philip. "Labour market discontinuity and spatial development," PHG 7, no.4:543–65 (1983). 77 references.

Gettler, Meric S. "Regional capital theory," PHG 8, no.1:50–81 (1984). 146 references.

Agricultural Geography

Grigg, David. "Agricultural geography," PHG 5, no.2:268–76 (1981); 6, no.2:242–46 (1982); 7, no.2: 255–60 (1983). 215 references.

———. "Ester Boserup's theory of agrarian change: a critical review," PHG 3, no.1:64–84 (1979). 107 references.

———. "Population pressure and agricultural change," PG 8:133–76 (1976). 266 references.

Bowler, I. B. "Agricultural geography," PHG 8, no.2:255–62 (1984). 70 references.

King, Russell, and Steve Burton, "Structural change in agriculture: the geography of land consolidation," PHG 7, no.4:471–501 (1983). 93 references.

Dickenson, J. P., and J. Salt. "In vino veritas: an introduction to the geography of wine," PHG 6, no.2:159–89 (1982). 155 references.

Ilbery, Brian W. "Agricultural decision-making: a behavioral perspective," PHG 2, no.3:448–66 (1978). 86 references.

Manufacturing Geography

Keeble, David. "Industrial geography," PHG 1, no.2:304–312 (1977); 2, no.2:318–23 (1978); 3, no.3:425–33 (1979). 167 references.

Wood, Peter A. "Industrial geography," PHG 4, no.3:406–416 (1980); 5, no.3:414–19 (1981); 6, no.4:576–83 (1982). 85 references.

Taylor, Michael. "Industrial geography," PHG 8, no.2:263–74 (1984). 60 references.

Warren, Kenneth. "The study of the economic geography of steel," PHG 3, no.4:538–47 (1979). 61 references.

Collins, Lyndhurst. "Industrial size distributions and stochastic processes," PG 5:119–65 (1973). 56 references.

Stafford, Howard A. "The geography of manufacturers," PG 4:181–215 (1972). 36 references.

Trade

Smith, Robert H. T. "Periodic market-places and periodic marketing: review and prospect," I, PHG 3, no.4:471–505 (1979); II, 4, no.1:1–31 (1980). 268 references.

Energy

Hoare, Anthony. "Alternative energies: alternative geographies?" PHG 3, no.4:506–537 (1979). 153 references.

Spencer, D. J., and Frank J. Calzonetti. "Geography and coal revisited: Anglo-American perspectives," PHG 8, no.1:1–25 (1984). 99 references.

Transportation Geography

Hay, Alan M. "Transport geography," PHG 1, no.2:313–18 (1977); 2, no.2:324–29 (1978); 3, no.2:267–72 (1979); 4, no.2:271–75 (1980); 5, no.2:263–67 (1981). 171 references.

———. "The geographical explanation of commodity flow," PHG 3, no.1:1–12 (1979). 21 references.

Rimmer, Peter J. "Redirections in transport geography," PHG 2, no.1:76–100 (1978). 92 references.

McKinnon, Ross D., and Gerald M. Barber. "Optimization models of transportation network improvement," PHG 1, no.3:387–412 (1977). 132 references.

Leinbach, Thomas R. "Transportation geography I: networks and flows," PG 8:177–207 (1976). 115 references.

Muller, Peter O. "Transportation geography II: social transportation," PG 8:208–231 (1976). 54 references.

O'Connor, Kevin. "The analysis of journey to work patterns in human geography," PHG 4, no.4:475–99 (1980). 153 references.

Location Theory

Wood, Peter A. "Location theory and spatial analysis," PHG 1, no.3:487–91 (1977); 2, no.3:518–25 (1978); 3, no.4:585–89 (1979). 42 references.

Martin, J. E. "Location theory and spatial analysis," PHG 4, no.2:265–70 (1980); 5, no.2:258–62 (1981); 6, no.2:260–64 (1982). 65 references.

Carr, Martyn. "A contribution to the review and critique of behavioural industrial location theory," PHG 7, no.3:386–401 (1983). 51 references.

Hodgart, R. L. "Optimizing access to public services: a review of problems, models and methods of locating central facilities," PHG 2, no.1:17–48 (1978). 95 references.

Chisholm, Michael. "In search of a basis for location theory: micro-economics or welfare economics?" PG 3:111–33 (1971). 37 references.

Nishioka, Hisao. "Location theory in Japan," PG 7:133–99 (1975). 413 references.

Recreation

Patmore, J. Allan, and Michael F. Collins (in various combinations). "Recreation and leisure," PHG 1, no.1:111–17 (1977); 2, no.1:141–47 (1978); 3, no.1:126–32 (1979); 4, no.1:91–97 (1980); 5, no.1:87–92 (1981); 6, no.2:254–59 (1982). 190 references.

Lowenthal, David. "Finding valued landscapes," PHG 2, no.3:373–418 (1978). 159 references.

Owens, Peter L. "Rural leisure and recreation research: a retrospective evaluation," PHG 8, no.2:157–88 (1984). 244 references.

Regional Development

Harriss, John, and Barbara Harriss (in alternating order). "Development studies," PHG 3, no.4:576–84 (1979); 4, no.4:577–88 (1980); 5, no.4:572–81 (1981); 6, no.4:584–92 (1982). 252 references.

King, Leslie J., and Gordon L. Clark. "Government policy and regional development," PHG 2, no.1:1–16 (1978). 75 references.

Funnell, D. C. "Development studies," PHG 8, no.1:113–19 (1984). 42 references.

Economic Regionalization

Pokshishevsky, Vadim Viacheslavovich. "On the Soviet concept of economic regionalization: a review of geographical research in the USSR on the problems of economic regionalisation," PG 7:1–52 (1975). 179 references.

Urban Geography

Johnston, Ronald J. "Urban geography: city structures," PHG 1, no.1:118–29 (1977); 2, no.1:148–52 (1978); 3, no.1:133–38 (1979); 4, no.1:81–85 (1980). 221 references.

Palm, Risa. "Urban geography: city structures," PHG 5, no.1:79–86 (1981); 6, no.1:89–95 (1982); 7, no.1:109–115 (1983). 126 references.

Whitehand, J. W. R. "Urban geography: the internal structure of cities," PHG 8, no.1:95–104 (1984). 77 references.

Bourne, L. S. "Urban and regional systems," PHG 4, no.3:399–405 (1980). 49 references.

Simmons, James W., and Larry S. Bourne. "Urban and regional systems . . . ," PHG 5, no.3:420–31 (1981); 6, no.3:431–40 (1982). 100 references.

Whitelaw, Jim. "Urban and regional systems," PHG 7, no.3:414–19 (1983); 8, no.3:406–12 (1984). 66 references.

Goddard, J. B. "Urban geography: city and regional systems," PHG 1, no.2:296–303 (1977); 2, no.2:309–317 (1978). 52 references.

Warnes, A. M., and P. W. Daniels. "Spatial aspects of an intrametropolitan central place hierarchy," PHG 3, no.3:384–406 (1979). 71 references.

Ford, Larry R. "Urban preservation and the geography of the city in the USA," PHG 3, no. 2:211–38 (1979). 67 references.

Short, John R. "Residential mobility," PHG 2, no.3:419–47 (1978). 109 references.

Bracken, Ian. "Simulation: methodology for urban study," PHG 2, no.1:49–75 (1978). 114 references.

Carter, Harold. "Urban origins: a review," PHG 1, no.1:12–33 (1977). 41 references.

Bater, James H. "Soviet town planning: theory and practice in the 1970s," PHG 1, no.2:177–207 (1977). 80 references.

McGee, Terence G. "The persistence of the proto-proletariat: occupational structures and planning of the future of Third World cities," PG 9:1–38 (1976). 101 references.

Friedmann, John, and Robert Wulff. "The urban transition: comparative studies of newly industrializing societies," PG 8:1–93 (1976). 482 references.

Pred, Allan R. "Urbanisation, domestic planning problems and Swedish geographical research," PG 5:1–76 (1973). 262 references.

Corna Pellegrini, Giacomo, and Maria Chiara Zerbi. "Urban geography and urban problems in Italy, 1945–81," PHG 7, no.3:357–69 (1983). 87 references.

Greer-Wootten, Bryn. "Metropolitan regional analysis," PG 4:255–99 (1972). 157 references.

Johnston, Ronald J. "Towards a general model of intra-urban residential patterns: some cross-cultural observations," PG 4:83–124 (1972). 163 references.

Taylor, John L. "Urban gaming simulation systems," PG 3:135–71 (1971). 93 references.

Colenutt, Robert J. "Building models of urban growth and spatial structure," PG 2:109–152 (1970). 130 references.

Leonard, Simon. "Urban managerialism: a period of transition?" PHG 6, no.2:190–215 (1982). 130 references.

Carroll, Glenn R. "National city-size distributions: what do we know after 67 years of research?" PHG 6, no.1:1–43 (1982). 120 references.

Bird, James. "Seaports as a subset of gateways for regions: a research survey," PHG 4, no.3:360–70 (1980). 57 references.

Kellerman, Aharon. "Telecommunications and the geography of metropolitan areas," PHG 8, no.2:222–46 (1984). 86 references.

Harris, Richard. "Residential segregation and class formation in the capitalist city: a review and direction for research," PHG 8, no.1:26–49 (1984). 133 references.

Simon, David. "Third world colonial cities in context: conceptual and theoretical approaches with particular reference to Africa," PHG 8, no.4:493–514 (1984). 109 references.

Rural Settlements

Clout, Hugh. "Rural settlements," PHG 1, no.3:475–80 (1977); 2, no.3:505–511 (1978); 3, no.3:417–24 (1979); 4, no.3:392–98 (1980); 5, no.3:408–413 (1981); 6, no.3:425–30 (1982). 241 references.

Cloke, Paul J. "New emphases for applied rural geography," PHG 4, no.2:181–217 (1980). 241 references.

King, Russell, and Steve Burton. "Land fragmentation: notes on a fundamental rural spatial problem," PHG 6, no.4:475–94 (1982). 105 references.

Population Geography and Migration

Clarke, John I. "Population geography," PHG 1, no.1:136–41 (1977); 2, no.1:163–69 (1978); 3, no.2:261–66 (1979); 4, no.3:385–91 (1980). 109 references.

Woods, Robert, "Population studies," PHG 6, no.2:247–53 (1982); 7, no.2:261–66 (1983); 8, no.2:247–54 (1984). 173 references.

Boots, Barry N. "Population density, crowding and human behaviour," PHG 3, no.1:13–63 (1979). 179 references.

Swindell, Kenneth. "Labour migration in under-developed countries; the case of subSaharan Africa," PHG 3, no.2:239–59 (1979). 67 references.

Riddell, J. Barry. "Beyond the description of spatial pattern: the process of proletarianization as a factor in population migration in West Africa," PHG 5, no.3:370–92 (1981). 84 references.

Gober-Meyers, Patricia. "Employment-motivated migration and economic growth in post-industrial market economies," PHG 2, no.2:207–29 (1978). 72 references.

Medical Geography

Learmonth, Andrew T. A. "Ecological medical geography," PG 7:201–226 (1976). 61 references.

Mayer, Jonathan D. "Relations between two traditions of medical geography: health systems planning and geographical epidemiology," PHG 6, no.2:216–30 (1982). 64 references.

Drury, Peter. "Some spatial aspects of health service developments: the British experience," PHG 7, no.1:60–77 (1983). 85 references.

Rosenberg, Mark W. "Accessibility to health care: a North American perspective," PHG 7, no.1:78–87 (1983). 38 references.

Environment and Resources

Simmons, Ian Gordon. "Natural resources and their management," PHG 1, no.2:319–26 (1977); 2, no.2:330–35 (1978); 3, no.2:273–77 (1979). 89 references.

———. "Resource management and conservation," PHG 4, no.1:86–90 (1980); 5, no.1:93–96 (1981); 6, no.1:102–105 (1982). 28 references.

Munton, Richard. "Resource management and conservation," PHG 7, no.1:126–32 (1983). 53 references.

Mitchell, Bruce. "Models of resource management," PHG 4, no.1:32–56 (1980). 125 references.

O'Riordan, Timothy. "Environmental issues," PHG 4, no.3:417–32 (1980); 5, no.3:393–407 (1981); 6, no.3:409–424 (1982); 7, no.3:403–413 (1983); 8, no.3:392–405 (1984). 241 references.

Chapman, Keith. "Issues in environmental impact assessment," PHG 5, no.2:190–210 (1981). 85 references.

Matley, Ian M. "Nature and society: the continuing Soviet debate," PHG 6, no.3:367–96 (1982). 77 references.

Parker, Dennis J., and Edmund C. Penning-Rowsell, "Flood hazard research in Britain," PHG 7, no.2:182–202 (1983). 158 references.

Couper, Alastair D. "Marine resources and environment," PHG 2, no.2:296–308 (1978). 15 references.

Gerasimov, Innokenti Petrovich. "Problems of natural environment transformation in Soviet constructive geography," PG 9:73–99 (1976). 36 references.

Wall, Geoffrey, "Some contemporary problems in research on 'air pollution,'" PG 8:95–131 (1976). 205 references.

O'Riordan, Timothy. "Environmental management," PG 3:173–231 (1971). 287 references.

Munton, Richard. "Resource management and conservation: the UK response to the World Conservation Strategy," PHG 8, no. 1:120–26 (1984). 34 references.

Regional Geography

Spence, Nigel A., and Peter J. Taylor. "Quantitative methods in regional taxonomy," PG 2:1–64 (1970). 258 references.

Paterson, John H. "Writing regional geography and progress in the Anglo-American realm," PG 6:1–26 (1974). 48 references.

Preston, David A. "Geographers among the peasants: research on rural societies in Latin America," PG 6:143–78 (1974). 209 references.

Gilbert, Alan G. "Latin American studies . . . ," PHG 5, no. 4:582–92 (1981); 7, no. 4:595–601 (1983). 69 references.

Preston, David A. ". . . Rural Latin America," PHG 4, no.4:601–10 (1980); 7, no.2:276–82 (1983). 127 references.

Turnock, David. "Postwar studies on the human geography of Eastern Europe," PHG 8, no. 3:315–46 (1984). 370 references.

Pallet, Judith. "Recent approaches in the geography of the Soviet Union," PHG 7, no.4:519–42 (1983). 283 references.

Richards, Paul. "The environmental factor in African studies," PHG 4, no.4:589–600 (1980). 116 references.

———. "Farming systems and agrarian change in West Africa," PHG 7, no.1:1–39 (1983). 235 references.

———. "Spatial organization as a theme in African studies," PHG 8, no.4:551–61 (1984). 56 references.

Beavon, K. S. O., and C. M. Rogerson. "Trekking on; recent trends in the human geography of southern Africa," PHG 5, no.2:159–89 (1981). 288 references.

Fisher, W. B. "Middle East," PHG 5, no.3:432–38 (1981); 7, no.3:429–35 (1983). 96 references.

Schwartzberg, Joseph E. "The state of south Asian geography," PHG 7, no.2:232–53 (1983). 82 references.

Spencer, J. E. "Southeast Asia," PHG 4, no.2:249–54 (1980); 6, no.2:265–69 (1982); 8, no.2:284–88 (1984). 39 references.

Takeuchi, Keiichi. "Some remarks on the history of regional description and the tradition of regionalism in modern Japan," PHG 4, no.2:238–48 (1980). 16 references.

Leeming, Frank. "On Chinese geography," PHG 4, no.2:218–37 (1980). 26 references.

Brookfield, Harold. "Third World development," PHG 2, no.1:121–32 (1978). 40 references.

Geography in Education

Graves, Norman J. "Geographical education," PHG 4, no.4:560–67 (1980); 5, no.4:562–71 (1981); 6, no.4:563–75 (1982). 150 references.

OTHER REVIEWS OF THE LITERATURE ON TRENDS IN GEOGRAPHY

Five other volumes that reviewed the status and literature of geography are of particular value. One deals with systematic fields, and the other four with geography within major countries. Chisholm and Rodgers discuss the fields of human geography, particularly in Britain, as of 1973 (C473). Summaries of geographical research in France (C474, C474A) were prepared for International Geographical Congresses in 1972 and 1984. Similar appraisals of work in the United Kingdom have appeared at 4-year intervals (C475, C476, C476A). Work in the Soviet Union (C477) for the 23rd International Geographical Congress was reviewed in 1976. Appraisals of scholarly effort in geography in Italy over the past twenty years have been published in both Italian and English (C477A, C477B). Especially useful is a volume by the Association of Japanese Geographers which presents in English a panorama of developments in major fields of geography in Japan, with rich citations of the literature in Japanese and in English (C478).

C473 Chisholm, Michael, and Brian Rodgers, eds. Studies in human geography. London: publ. by Heinemann for the Social Science Research Council, 1973. 305p.
Specialists review the states of various fields of human geography: David Grigg, agriculture and economic development; John Clarke, population migration; Ross Davies, service activities; Harold Carter and Brian Robson, urban geography; Gerald Manners, regional development; and John House, public policy.

C474 Comité National Français de Géographie. Recherches géographiques en France. Paris: Comité National Français de Géographie, 1972. 238p. [Ouvrage offert en hommage aux membres du 22d Congrès International de Géographie, Montréal, Août 1972]
28 chapters by specialists on current geographical research in France. In French, with brief abstracts in English.

C474 ———. La recherche géographique française
A (structures, thèmes et perspectives). Paris-Alpes, Août 1984. French geographical research (structures, topics and perspectives). Paris: Président du Comité National Français de Géographie, 1984. 261p.
15 major chapters on recent developments in French geography: schools of thought, natural environment, nature and society, space and society, and development and regional and economic planning. Each chapter includes a substantial bibliography.

C475 Cooke, R. U., and B. T. Robson, "Geography in the United Kingdom 1972–76. Report to the 23rd International Geographical Congress in Moscow, USSR, in July 1976," *Geographical journal* 142, pt. 1:81–100 (March 1976). Also separately issued.

C476 Doornkamp, J. C., and K. Warren. "Geography in the United Kingdom, 1976–80. Report to the 24th International Geographical Congress in Tokyo, Japan, in August 1980," *Geographical journal* 146, pt. 1:94–110 (March 1980).

C476 Munton, R. J. C., and A. S. Goudie. "Geogra-
A phy in the United Kingdom 1980–84. Submitted

to the XXV International Geographical Congress, Paris, August 1984," *Geographical journal* 150, part 1:27–47 (March 1984). Also separately issued.
Appraisals of developments in geography in the United Kingdom, with extensive bibliography.

C477 USSR Academy of Sciences. National Committee of Soviet Geographers. Soviet geographical studies. Moscow: Social Sciences Today, 1976. 287p. [Problems of the contemporary world, no.39]
Articles by leading Soviet geographers on current developments in geography, prepared for the 23d International Geographical Congress, 1976, in Moscow.

C477 Corna Pellegrini, Giacomo, and Carlo Brusa,
A eds. La ricerca geografica in Italia 1960–1980. Varese: Ask Edizioni, 1981. 1,007p. [Associazione dei Geografi Italiani]
Thorough review of all aspects of modern geography as practiced in Italy.

C477 ———. Italian geography 1960–80: general and
B physical geography. Varese: Ask Edizioni, 1982 (i.e., 1984). 312p.
Abridged and selective English translation of part of the above work.

C478 Geography in Japan. Ed. by Shinzo Kiuchi. Tokyo: Univ. of Tokyo Pr., 1976. 294p. [Assn. of Japanese Geographers. Special publ. no.3.]
Reviews of the development of each field in geography in Japan by specialists. Extensive bibliographies.

CURRENT BIBLIOGRAPHIES AND ABSTRACTS

Current Bibliographies

The quarterly *Bibliographie géographique internationale* (C479) provides the most convenient, best balanced, and fullest current international coverage of the geographical literature of the world. An international group of collaborators insures treatment of all regions of the earth. Specialists in the systematic subfields of geography, mostly from France, uphold a high scholarly level. Bibliographic personnel from the Laboratoire d'Information et de Documentation en Géographie maintain the regular flow of information. Computer storage of entries makes possible rapid indexing of each issue and of annual supplements. A supplementary table of contents in English facilitates the international utilization of this bibliography.

Current geographical publications (C480), now published by the American Geographical Society Collection of the University of Wisconsin–Milwaukee Library, is particularly useful in its coverage of publications from the United States and other English-speaking countries. It provides a detailed listing of individual monographs, articles, and documents in topical and regional sections. Smaller sections list selected maps and selected books and monographs. These sections are useful as a convenient checklist of items for consideration for acquisition by libraries, even though the entries are not annotated.

For a comparative analysis of current comprehensive geographical bibliographies, see Harris, *Bibliography of geography* (C455), p.25–56.

C479 Bibliographie géographique internationale. v.1– , 1891– . Paris: Centre National de la Recherche Scientifique. Laboratoire d'Information et de Documentation en Géographie. Annual. 1891–1975/76. Quarterly 1977– . v.1–23/24 (1891–1914) are issues or supplements to *Annales de géographie*, successively entitled *Bibliographie de l'année, Bibliographie annuelle*, and *Bibliographie géographique annuelle*; v.25–41 (1915–31) are entitled *Bibliographie géographique*. v.1–60 (1891–1953) were published by Armand Colin; v.61– (1954–) by Centre National de la Recherche Scientifique.
Geographic bibliography of international value, wide coverage, and long duration. No other work so fully records the corpus of geographic literature over the last 95 years. Critical or analytical notes. Organized systematically and regionally. Includes books and periodical articles. Indexes for authors, subjects, places, and serials.

C480 Current geographical publications: additions to research catalogue of the American Geographical Society Collection of the University of Wisconsin–Milwaukee Library. v.1– , 1938– . Monthly except July and Aug. v.1–41, no.2 (Jan. 1938–Feb. 1978), published by the American Geographical Society in New York.
A classified index covering books (with analytical entries for chapters or sections of multiauthor collections), periodical articles, and maps received at the library. Arranged first by general subject and then by region and country. Annual index. Section 3, maps, from Nov. 1964. No annotations. For 1938–76, the society's *Research catalogue* (C483–85) provides a cumulation, but for 1977 and later the monthly issues and annual indexes need to be consulted.

Current Abstracts

The most comprehensive and useful abstracts in English of the geographical literature of the world are in the seven series of *Geo abstracts* (C481), each published six times a year. It is particularly superior in coverage of the system-

atic fields of geography. Of especial value in the human side of geography are series C, Economic geography; D, Social and historical geography; F, Regional and community planning; and G, Remote sensing, photogrammetry, and cartography. Annual and quinquennial cumulative indexes increase the efficiency of searching.

Referativnyi zhurnal: geografiia (C482) provides massive coverage, especially of physical geography, but also on regional economic geography. It is entirely in Russian.

C481 Geo abstracts. 1966– . Norwich, Eng.: Geo Abstracts, Ltd. 7 ser., each with 6 nos. a year. (1966–71: Geographical abstracts).

   A. Landforms and the Quaternary (preceded by Geomorphological abstracts [no.1–27, 1960–65]. Cumulative subject and author index, 1960–65). (1966–71 as A. Geomorphology)

   B. Climatology and hydrology.

   C. Economic geography.

   D. Social and historical geography.

   E. Sedimentology. 1972– .

   F. Regional and community planning. 1972– .

   G. Remote sensing, photogrammetry, and cartography. 1974– .

Abstracts in English of the geographical literature of the world in many languages. Series C, D, and F are of particular interest to social scientists.

In series C, Economic geography, abstracts are under the following headings: economic geography (methodology, philosophy, and education); location theory and spatial analysis; urban and household studies; general and regional economic development; environmental economics; labor, capital, and income; international trade and economic association; manufacturing and industry; general resources and technology; fuel and energy (general, hydrocarbons, other sources); minerals; water; forestry; fisheries; agriculture (general, policy, arable, livestock); tertiary; tourism and recreation; transport and communications; and regional studies. About 2,800 abstracts a year.

In series D, Social and historical geography, abstracts are under the following headings: social; population distribution; population change; population migration; population fertility; man and environment; natural hazards; perception; medical; regional; cultural; historical—field evidence; historical—documentary evidence; regional historical; political; urban; rural; methodology; biography; and education. About 3,700 abstracts a year.

In series F, Regional and community planning, abstracts are under the following headings: planning theory and research; statistical techniques and data; national planning; regional and economic planning; sub-regional and structure planning; urban planning (processes and techniques; projects and policies; renewal, rehabilitation, and conservation; retail planning); rural planning; transportation planning; social planning; housing; environmental planning: (1) general, (2) recreation, (3) coastal conservation and development, (4) pollution and waste disposal, (5) air, (6) water, (7) minerals, and (8) planning law and administration; and participation and decision making. About 4,200 abstracts a year.

A series of indexes facilitate access. An annual author index for each series is included in issue no.6. Comprehensive annual indexes for authors, titles, key words, subjects (average of seven entries for each abstract) covered all four series, A–D, 1966–71. From 1972, two annual indexes were published, one covering series A, B, E, and (from 1974) G; the other covering series C, D, and F (human geography). Cumulative indexes for five years, 1966–70 and 1970–75, were published separately for each of the four series, A–D, 1972–76 for series E and F, and 1974–78 for series G.

C482 Referativnyi zhurnal: geografiia. Vsesoiuznyi Institut Nauchnoi i Tekhnicheskoi Informatsii. 1954– . Moscow. 12/yr.

The most massive publication of geographic abstracts in any language. Abstracts are signed, and quite full, but are informative rather than critical. Includes books, articles, maps, and reviews. Abstracts on physical geography organized topically; those on economic geography arranged regionally. Some sections have author index in each no. Sections available separately.

RETROSPECTIVE BIBLIOGRAPHIES

Comprehensive

The most comprehensive and useful retrospective bibliography covering the entire field of geography is the *Research catalogue* of the

American Geographical Society (C483). With two supplements (C484–85), it consists of 21 large volumes covering the years 1923–76. All the major systematic and regional fields of geography are covered. Books, periodical articles, government documents, pamphlets, sections in books, and fugitive materials are included. The basic publication is a little difficult to use, but the two supplements show enormous improvement in legibility, in articulated tables of contents, and in listing of entries by both systematic field and by locality.

Two other general comprehensive bibliographies should also be mentioned. *Geographisches Jahrbuch* (C486) provided excellent coverage of many fields of geography from 1866 to the mid-1930s, the exact dates varying by fields. *Bibliographie géographique internationale* (C479) has been published since 1891 and although not cumulated can be utilized over about 95 years, through annual volumes and, since 1977, in quarterly issues (with annual indexes).

Of the three, the *Research catalogue* is the largest with about 350,000 entries (1923–76) compared with about 300,000 for *Bibliographie géographique internationale* (1891–1984) and about 250,000 for *Geographisches Jahrbuch* (1866–ca. 1943). *Geo abstracts* (C481), also not cumulated but with cumulated indexes, published about 290,000 abstracts in the period 1966–84. In the length of time covered, *Bibliographie géographique internationale* is longest with about 95 years, compared with about 70 years for *Geographisches Jahrbuch* and 54 years of full coverage for the *Research catalogue*. Since the *Geographisches Jahrbuch* was regularly published only up to the 1930s, it is now badly outdated. The other three are being continued.

For a comparative analysis of comprehensive retrospective bibliographies of geography see Harris, *Bibliography of geography* (C455), p. 57–86.

C483 American Geographical Society Library. Research catalogue. Boston: Hall, 1962. 15v.

Covers mainly 1923–61. About 220,000 entries. Emphasis on regional geography, with 13 of the 15v. devoted to listings by region or subregion and breakdown by systematic topics within regions, with latest works listed first.

Additions to *Research catalogue* are published in *Current geographical publications* (C480).

C484 ——. ——. First supp. [1962–71]. Boston: Hall, 1972–74. 4v. Pt. 1. Regional. 2v. 1972. Pt. 2. Topical. 2v. 1974.

Extends the Research catalogue for the ten years 1962–71, with improvements that make it much easier to use. Greater emphasis on systematic fields of geography. About 90,000 entries.

C485 ——. ——. Second supp. [1972–76]. Boston: Hall, 1978. 2v.
About 40,000 entries.

C486 Geographisches Jahrbuch. 1866– . Gotha, E. Germany: Perthes (later, VEB Hermann Haack). 1 or 2v. yearly from 1866 to 1943. Occasionally from 1947 to 1956. Very infrequent since 1956.
For many years, the most valuable bibliographic source for an overview of the literature of the topical and regional fields of geography. The various fields were covered in a series of cycles: each year a half-dozen fields were covered, and any given field was summarized about once a decade. Surveys were made by experts. Critical evaluations excellent. Author index in each volume. A key bibliographical resource for the period 1866 to the 1930s. About 250,000 entries. Harris, *Bibliography of geography* (C455), p.83–86, provides a list of fields covered.

General

Five other general retrospective bibliographies are of particular value. Wheeler provides a selected set of references on the philosophy and methodology of geography (C487). Van Balen lists all books in geography reviewed in the principal geographical periodicals and thus indicates sources of critical evaluations of books published 1968–75 (C488). Kish has indexed some 7,000 papers presented at International Geographical Congresses (C489). Vinge selects United States government documents of potential geographic value (C490). Arnim inventories the rich monographic literature in German (C491).

C487 Wheeler, James O. Bibliography on geographic thought, 1950–1982. Athens: Univ. of Georgia Dept. of Geography, 1983. 98p. [Aids to geographic research series, no.5] (Previous editions, 1975, 1978)
226 books and 1,326 articles. Articles classified into biographical; geography in relation to other disciplines; geography in various countries; methodology; philosophy; training; quantitative geography; subdisciplines; and theoretical approaches.

C488 Van Balen, John, comp. Geography and earth sciences publications: an author, title and subject guide to books reviewed, and an index to the reviews. Ann Arbor, Mich.: Pierian Pr., 1978. v.1, 1968–72, 313p.; v.2, 1973–75, 232p.
Bibliographic listing of books in geography and related earth sciences reviewed in geographical periodicals and a record of the reviews published in 21 periodicals in the first volume and 38 in the second. Works listed alphabetically by author. Subject, regional, and title indexes.

C489 Kish, George. Bibliography of international geographic congresses, 1871–1976. Boston: Hall, 1979. 540p.
Lists about 7,000 papers presented at the first 23 international geographical congresses by congress and section, with indexes of subject groups and of author.

C490 Vinge, Clarence L., and Ada G. Vinge. U.S. government publications for research and teaching in geography and related social and natural sciences. Totowa, N.J.: Littlefield, 1967. 360p.
From more than 500,000 documents issued by the federal government between 1945 and 1966, this work lists 3,500 of direct or tangential value to geographers. Arranged by departments and bureaus.

C491 Arnim, Helmuth. Bibliographie der geographischen Literatur in deutscher Sprache. Baden-Baden: Heitz, 1970. 177p. Reprint, Baden-Baden: Valentin Koerner, 1980. 177p.
A bibliography of monographs in German on all fields of geography. 1,545 entries. Especially good for bibliographies of geography, with 291 items. Covers both systematic and regional geography, as well as cartography, up to 1970.

Cartography

C492 U.S. Library of Congress. Geography and Map Division. The bibliography of cartography. Boston: Hall, 1973. 5v.

C493 ——. ——. First supplement. Boston: Hall, 1980. 2v.
About 110,000 entries. The most comprehensive bibliography of cartography. The supplement includes a list of serials analyzed.

C494 Ristow, Walter W. Guide to the history of cartography: an annotated list of references on the history of maps and mapmaking. Washington, D.C.: Govt. Print. Off., 1973. 96p. [Library of Congress. Geography and Map Division.]
398 numbered entries in alphabetical order on history and evolution of maps and mapmaking.

C495 Kosack, Hans-Peter, and Karl Heinz Meine. Die Kartographie 1943–1954: eine bibliographische Übersicht. Lahr/Schwarzwald: Astra Verlag, 1955. 216p. [Kartographische Schriftenreihe, Band 4]

C496 Bibliotheca cartographica. Bibliographie des kartographischen Schrifttums; bibliography of cartographic literature. 1/2–29/30, 1957–72. Bonn-Bad Godesberg, W. Germany: Institut für Landeskunde und Deutsche Gesellschaft für Kartographie.

C497 Bibliographia cartographica: Internationale Dokumentation des kartographischen Schrifttums. International documentation of cartographical literature. 1– , 1974– . Annual. Berlin: Staatsbibliothek Preussischer Kulturbesitz with Deutsche Gesellschaft für Kartog-

raphie. Dist. by München: Verlag Dokumentation Saur; New York: K. G. Saur.
Trilingual in German, English, and French. Continuation of *Bibliotheca cartographica*.

C498 International Cartographic Association. Commission V. Communication in Cartography. Bibliography of works on cartographic communication. Ed. by Christopher Board. Provisional ed. London: [Intl. Cartographic Assn. Com. 5]. 1976. 147p.
870 references arranged by author with key words. Subject index.

Quantitative Methods

C499 Greer-Wootten, Bryn. A bibliography of statistical applications in geography. Washington, D.C.: Assn. of American Geographers, 1972. 91p. [Commission on College Geography. Technical paper no.9.]
Comprehensive treatment of 34 types of statistical applications in geography, with introductory explanation and bibliography of relevant papers.

C500 Lea, Anthony C. Location-allocation systems: an annotated bibliography. Toronto: Univ. of Toronto Dept. of Geography, 1973. 273p. [Discussion paper no.13]

C501 Anderson, Marc. A working bibliography of mathematical geography. Ann Arbor: Univ. of Michigan Dept. of Geography, 1963. 52p. [Michigan Inter-University Community of Mathematical Geographers. Discussion paper no.2.]
Application of mathematical techniques to geographical problems. Covers substantive and methodological publications and is arranged alphabetically by author.

C502 Porter, Philip W. A bibliography of statistical cartography. Minneapolis: Univ. of Minnesota Bookstore, 1964. 66p.
982 entries, arranged alphabetically by author, with marginal key to topics covered: bibliography, history, or serials; automation and computers; central-place theory; graphs and diagrams; general methods and textbooks; interaction, migration, diffusion, and social physics; population mapping; quantitative methods of spatial description and regionalization; and symbols.

C503 Lichtenberger, Elisabeth. "Die 'Quantitative Geographie' im deutschen Sprachraum: eine Bibliographie," *Mitteilungen der Österreichischen geographischen Gesellschaft* 119, no.1: 114–29 (1977).
Bibliography with 440 references on quantitative geography in the German literature.

Historical Geography

C504 Grim, Ronald E. Historical geography of the United States: a guide to information sources. Detroit: Gale, 1982. 291p. [Geography and travel information guide series, v.5]
686 annotated entries arranged by three major parts: cartographic sources; archival and other historical sources; and selected literature in historical geography. These are further divided into 20 chapters. A basic source.

C505 McManis, Douglas R. Historical geography of the United States: a bibliography excluding Alaska and Hawaii. Ypsilanti: Eastern Michigan Univ. Div. of Field Services, 1965. 249p.
3,500 books, monographs, and periodical articles listed by region and state, with topical breakdown in each region or state.

C506 Jakle, John A. Past landscapes: a bibliography for historic preservationists selected from the literature of historical geography. Monticello, Ill.: Council of Planning Librarians, 1974. 56p. [Exchange bibliog. 651]
About 650 entries.

C507 Denevan, William M. A bibliography of Latin American historical geography. Washington, D.C.: Pan American Institute of Geography and History. United States National Section. Special publication no.6, 1971. 32p. Regional and country index.
560 entries.

C508 Narweleit, Gerhard, and others. Historische Geographie der Deutschen Demokratischen Republik. 1945–1968. Gotha-Leipzig: Hermann Haack. 1976–79. Teil 1, 1976, 359p.; Teil 2, 1977, 379p.; Teil 3, 1979, 571p. [Geographisches Jahrbuch, 63–65]
15,178 entries arranged first by regions then by 17 subjects.

Social Geography

C509 Jakle, John A. The spatial dimensions of social organization: a selected bibliography for urban social geography. Monticello, Ill.: Council of Planning Librarians, 1970. 50p. [Exchange bibliog. 118]
About 750 entries.

C510 Thomale, Eckhard. Sozialgeographie: eine disziplingeschichtliche Untersuchung zur Entwicklung der Anthropogeographie. Mit einer Bibliographie. Marburg: Geographisches Institut der Universität, Marburg, 1972. 264p. Separately paged bibliography. 85p. [Marburger geographische Schriften, 53]
950 entries in bibliography arranged alphabetically by authors with subject index. Entries mainly from Germany, Austria, the Netherlands, France, and Sweden.

C511 Reynaud, A. La géographie, science sociale. Travaux de l'Institut de géographie de Reims. 49–50, special. 1982. 164p.
645 references, mostly but not exclusively in French, on all branches of geography in relation to the social sciences.

C512 Hafner, James A. Perspectives on poverty: a reference bibliography. Monticello, Ill.: Council of Planning Librarians, 1974. 39p. [Exchange bibliog. 693]
About 600 references.

C513 Ernst, Robert T. The geographical literature of black America, 1949–1972: a selected bibliography of journal articles, serial publications, theses, and dissertations. Monticello, Ill.: Council of Planning Librarians, 1973. 29p. [Exchange bibliog. 492]
About 300 entries.

C514 Jakle, John A., and Cynthia A. Jakle. Ethnic and racial minorities in North America: a selected bibliography. Monticello, Ill.: Council of Planning Librarians, 1973. 71p. [Exchange bibliog. 459–60]
About 900 entries.

C515 Hanson, Perry O. III, and Barbara Boehnke. The spatial analysis of crime: a bibliography. Monticello, Ill.: Council of Planning Librarians, 1976. 25p. [Exchange bibliog. 1166]
About 325 references in classed arrangement.

Perceptual Geography

C516 Harrison, James D. The perception and cognition of environment (annotated). Monticello, Ill.: Council of Planning Librarians, 1974. 79p. [Exchange bibliog. 516]
158 annotated entries plus about 550 other references.

C517 Lieber, Stanley R. A working bibliography on geographic and psychological perception and related subjects. Monticello, Ill.: Council of Planning Librarians, 1972. 25p. [Exchange bibliog. 299]
About 300 entries.

Cultural Geography

C518 Ravenau, J., and others. "Ouvrages récents (1973–1977) pertinents à la géographie culturelle," *Cahiers de géographie du Québec* 21, no.53/54:309–18 (1977).

Political Geography

C519 Sanguin, André-Louis. Géographie politique: bibliographie internationale. Montréal: Presses de l'Université du Québec, 1976. 232p.
3,138 entries in classed arrangement. Index of authors.

C520 Hoggart, Keith. Geography and local administration: a bibliography. Monticello, Ill.: Vance Bibliographies, 1980. 84p. [Public administration series, bibliography no.P-530]
1,005 references by subjects such as political geography, territorial needs, and spatial structure of local government, particularly in the United Kingdom and the United States.

Economic Geography

C521 Muller, Peter O. Locational analysis and economic geography: a comprehensive bibliography of recent literature on theory, techniques, and the spatial organization of agriculture, manufacturing, and transportation. Philadelphia: Temple Univ. The Samuel Paley Library, 1972. 94p.
Nearly 2,000 entries, more than half for the period 1968–71. Pt. 1 covers the scope, theory, and methods of economic geography; pt. 2 covers location and other theory in agriculture, manufacturing, and transportation of geography.

C522 ———. ———. Supp. 1971–77. 1977. 57p.
About 900 entries. Accurate and useful listing of books and serial articles in English.

C523 Wheeler, James O. Industrial location: a bibliography, 1966–1972. Monticello, Ill.: Council of Planning Librarians, 1973. 68p. [Exchange bibliog. 436]
About 750 entries.

C524 Fisher, James S., and others. Industrial location analysis: a bibliography, 1966–1979. Athens: Univ. of Georgia Dept. of Geography, 1979. 76p. [Aids to geographic research, bibliography no.1]

C525 Rowe, James E. Industrial plant location. Monticello, Ill.: Vance Bibliographies, 1980. 52p. [Public administration series, bibliography no.P-575]
About 750 references to empirical studies.

C526 ———. The theory of industrial location. Monticello, Ill.: Vance Bibliographies, 1980. 32p. [Public administration series, bibliography no.P-576]
About 450 references to theoretical studies, mainly in geography, economics, and sociology.

C527 Miller, E. Willard, and Ruby M. Miller. Economic, political and regional aspects of the world's energy problems. Monticello, Ill.: Vance Bibliographies, 1979. 99p. [Public administration series, bibliography no.P-360]
About 1,400 references arranged in two parts: topical and regional.

C528 Bromley, R. J. Periodic markets, daily markets and fairs: a bibliography. Melbourne, Australia: Monash Univ. Dept. of Geography, 1974. 116p.
[Monash publ. in geography, no.10]

Transportation Geography

C529 Wheeler, James O. Spatial studies in transportation: introduction and annotated bibliography. Monticello, Ill.: Council of Planning Librarians, 1972. 161p. [Exchange bibliog. 324–25]

About 1,000 annotated entries arranged alphabetically by author. Subject index.

C530 Adams, Russell B., and Mark C. Geyer. Transportation: a geographical bibliography. Minneapolis: Univ. of Minnesota Dept. of Geography, 1970. 154p.

Almost 2,000 references, including books, journals, and articles, with emphasis on urban transportation and theoretical and quantitative studies but with wide coverage of historical, economic, and regional studies on one hand and the principal modes on the other. Author index.

C531 Siddall, William R. Transportation geography: a bibliography. 3d ed. Manhattan: Kansas State Univ. Library, 1969. 94p. [Bibliography series no.1] (1st ed. 1964. 46p.)

About 1,700 articles or books in English, primarily from the period 1950–69, mainly organized according to type of transportation: ocean shipping, seaports, inland waterways, railroads, highways, pipelines, and air transportation but including general and regional studies in transportation geography.

C532 Hsu, Ann Yi-rong, and James O. Wheeler. A bibliography of highway impact studies, 1966–1976. Monticello, Ill.: Council of Planning Librarians, 1977. 29p. [Exchange bibliog. 1401] About 400 references.

Regional Development

C533 Thoman, Richard S. Selected bibliography on regional development in Canada and the United States with special reference to 1965–1971. Kingston, Ont.: Richard S. Thoman, Prof. of Geography, Queen's Univ., 1971. 93p. Mimeo.

About 1,100 entries arranged alphabetically by author under three headings: general method and policy, application to Canada, and application to the U.S.

Economic Regions

C534 Berry, Brian J. L., and Thomas D. Hankins. A bibliographic guide to the economic regions of the United States. Chicago: Univ. of Chicago Dept. of Geography, 1963. 101p. [Research paper no.87] Reprint, Westport, Conn.: Greenwood, 1975.

378 entries arranged by concept or type of regions: regions in geography and other social sciences, economic regions, regions of uniformity, organizational regions, regional science, regional planning, and textbooks on North American regions. Introductory text and supplementary list of articles by journal.

C535 Hamilton, F. E. Ian. Regional economic analysis in Britain and the Commonwealth: a bibliographic guide. London: Schocken, 1970. 410p.

5,117 entries organized regionally by continent and country. The major entries for the British Isles have extensive annotations. Introductory text on concepts and types of regions, and introductions to chapters on specific regions.

Recreational Geography and Tourism

C536 Lancaster, Joel R., and Leland I. Nichols. A selected bibliography of geographical references and related research in outdoor recreation and tourism: 1930–1971. Monticello, Ill.: Council of Planning Librarians, 1971. 41p. [Exchange bibliog. 190]

Books, articles in geographical journals or by geographers, geographical theses and dissertations, government publications, study of tourism in related fields, and bibliographies. About 600 entries.

C537 Mings, Robert C. The tourist industry in Latin America: a bibliography for planning and research. Monticello, Ill.: Council of Planning Librarians, 1974. 62p. [Exchange bibliog. 614] About 750 entries.

C538 ———, and Steve Quello. The tourist industry in Latin America, 1974–1979: a bibliography for planning and research. Monticello, Ill.: Vance Bibliographies, 1979. 32p. [Public administration series, bibliography no.P-333] About 400 entries.

C538 Carlson, Alvar W. "A bibliography of geoA graphical research on tourism," *Journal of cultural geography* 1, no.1:161–84 (1980).

Comprehensive bibliography of geographical publications on tourism published in English up to 1980. 369 references including 31 bibliographies.

C538 Steinecke, Albrecht, ed. Interdisziplinäre BibB liographie zur Fremdenverkehrs- und Naherholungsforschung, Beiträge zur allgemeinen Fremdenverkehrs- und Naherholungsforschung. Berlin: Institut für Geographie der Technischen Universität Berlin, 1981. 583, 305p. [Berliner geographische Studien, 8 and 9] About 6,500 entries on tourism and recreation.

C539 Kemper, Franz-Josef. Probleme der Geographie der Freizeit: ein Literaturbericht über raumorientierte Arbeiten aus den Bereichen Freizeit, Erholung und Fremdenverkehr. Bonn: Dümmler, 1978. 149p. [Bonner geographische Abhandlungen, Heft 59] Bibliography: p. 85–149.

Review of the studies of leisure, recreation, and tourism with a bibliography of about 1,600 references, primarily in German, English, and French.

Urban Geography

C540 Green, Jerry E., and Mark Middagh. Human settlement in the perspective of geography. Monticello, Ill.: Council of Planning Librarians, 1976. 34p. [Exchange bibliog. 1161]
About 475 references in regional arrangement.

C541 Strand, Sverre. Urban geography 1950–70: a comprehensive bibliography of urbanism as reflected in the articles and book reviews of 72 American, Canadian, British, Dutch, and Scandinavian geographical periodicals. Monticello, Ill.: Council of Planning Librarians, 1973. 272p. [Exchange bibliog. 358–60]
2,949 entries in classed arrangement. 2 regional indexes. Author index.

C542 Sommer, John W. Bibliography of urban geography, 1940–1964. Hanover, N.H.: Dartmouth College Dept. of Geography, 1966. 94p. [Geography publications no.5]
Listing of 1,310 articles on urban geography published over 25 years in 71 geographical periodicals. Articles arranged by region, but author index and topical index provide alternate routes of access.

C543 Salinari, Marina E. Bibliografia degli scritti di geografia urbana, 1901–1954. Rome: Consiglio Nazionale delle Ricerche, 1948–56. 2 no. [Consiglio Nazionale delle Ricerche. Centro di Studi per la Geografia antropica. Memorie di geografia antropica, v.2 and 11.]
A bibliography of writings on urban geography published in all countries between 1901 and 1954. No.1 (1948) covers the years 1901–1944 in 1,955 entries. No.2 (1956) covers the years 1944–54 in 1,995 entries. Following a section on general works, the entries are arranged by geographical area. Index of authors in no.2. Includes books and articles. Some brief annotations.

C544 Ray, William W. Urban studies in geography: a bibliography of dissertations and theses in geography, 1960–1970. Monticello, Ill.: Council of Planning Librarians, 1971. 60p. [Exchange bibliog. 189]
Simple listing, alphabetically by author, of more than 200 doctoral dissertations and nearly 700 master's theses in urban geography presented at universities in the U.S. and Canada in 11-year period.

C545 Brunn, Stanley D. Urbanization in developing countries: an international bibliography. East Lansing: Michigan State Univ. Latin American Studies Center and Center for Urban Affairs, 1971. 693p. [Latin American Studies Center research report no.8]
7,138 entries, arranged regionally, with a subject index by 17 systematic categories; 2,599 entries on Latin America, 1,624 on Africa, and 2,431 on Asia. Emphasis on economic, population, housing, and social and cultural aspects of cities.

C546 Sable, Martin H. Latin American urbanization: a guide to the literature, organizations, and personnel. Metuchen, N.J.: Scarecrow, 1971. 1,077p.
Bibliography of 6,903 items arranged topically within the major categories of aesthetics and humanities; economics, industry, and commerce; government and law; sociology and urbanization as a phenomenon. Directory of 1,978 research centers, institutes, and organizations; working organizations; and specialists. Author and subject indexes to the bibliography section. Index of fields of activity of organizations and individuals in the directory section.

C547 Rubio, Angel. Bibliografía de geografía urbana de América. Rio de Janeiro: Instituto Pan Americano de Geografía e Historia. Comissão de Geografia, 1961. 229p. [Publicación no.220]
2,112 comprehensive entries arranged chronologically by country, and alphabetically by cities within each country. Includes books, monographs, articles, reports, theses, and surveys. Covers all the Americas, including North America in general (18 entries), Canada (316 entries), the United States (803 entries), and Latin America (975 entries). List of sources. Chronological index, index of cities, and index of authors and institutions.

C548 O'Connor, Anthony M. Urbanization in tropical Africa: an annotated bibliography. Boston: Hall, 1981. 381p.
Includes books, periodical articles, atlases, and dissertations, 1960–79, arranged by region and then by country.

C549 La recherche urbaine en France, 1978: Fiches analytiques. Urban research in France, 1978: analytical cards. La investigación urbana en Francia. 1979. Paris: Ministère de l'Environnement et du Cadre de vie, centre de documentation sur l'urbanisme, 1979. 314p.
193 research contracts with summaries of research and findings in French, English, and Spanish. List of organizations and authors. Subject index.

C550 Schöller, Peter, and others. Bibliographie zur Stadtgeographie. Deutschsprachige Literatur 1952–1970. Paderborn, W. Germany: Schöningh Verlag, 1973. 139p. [Bochumer geographische Arbeiten, 14]
1,455 entries in classed arrangement.

C551 Harris, Chauncy D., and Richard Louis Edmonds. "Urban geography in Japan: a survey of recent literature," *Urban geography* 3, no.1:1–21 (1982).
86 references.

C552 Berry, Brian J. L., and Allan R. Pred. Central place studies: a bibliography of theory and applications, including supplement through 1964 by H. G. Barnum and others. Philadelphia: Regional Science Research Institute, 1965. 203p. [Bibliography series no.1 with supplement] (1st ed. 1961. 153p.)
Annotated bibliography of more than 1,000 items on various aspects of central-place theory or

related concepts, organized topically, with author index and list of journals in which articles appear. Includes a useful textual review of the field and a brief summary of Christaller's theory and findings.

C553 Andrews, Howard F. Working notes and bibliography of central place studies, 1965–1969. Monticello, Ill.: Council of Planning Librarians, 1971. 41p. [Exchange bibliog. 209]
About 350 entries, partly annotated.

Population Geography

C554 Zelinsky, Wilbur. A bibliographic guide to population geography. Chicago: Univ. of Chicago Dept. of Geography, 1962. 257p. [Research paper no.80] Reprint, Westport, Conn.: Greenwood Press, 1976.
A list of 2,588 writings on some phase of population geography from the late nineteenth century to mid-1961. Studies arranged by region unless of a general character. A valuable finding list but without critical annotations. Author index.

C555 Thomas, Robert N. "Population bibliography of Latin America." *In* Population dynamics of Latin America: proceedings of the 2nd Conference of Latin Americanist Geographers 1971, ed. by R. N. Thomas, p.121–200. East Lansing, Mich.: CLAG Pubns., 1973.
About 1,000 entries in classed arrangement.

C556 Weber, Peter. Geographische Mobilitätsforschung. Darmstadt, W. Germany: Wissenschaftliche Buchgesellschaft, 1982. 190p. [Erträge der Forschung, Band 179]
532 references on research on geographical mobility in all its forms of migration, emigration, and immigration and their geographic conditions and impacts.

C557 Hermanns, Hartmut, and others. Arbeiterwanderungen zwischen Mittelmeerländern und den mittel-und westeuropäischen Industrieländern: eine annotierte Auswahl-Bibliographie unter geographischem Aspekt. München and New York: Saur, 1979. 245p.
Annotated bibliography of geography of worker migration from the Mediterranean to industrial areas in Central and Western Europe.

Medical Geography

C557 Akhtar, Rais. The geography of health: an
A essay and bibliography. New Delhi, India: Marwah Publications, 1982. 194p.
About 1,800 references arranged by sections.

Resource Use and Management

C558 Brunn, Stanley D. Key word identifiers of theses and dissertations from departments of geography in Canada and the United States on land use, water use, resource conflict, resource policy, and facility location. Monticello, Ill.: Council of Planning Librarians, 1978. 71p. [Exchange bibliog. 1512]
Lists 236 doctoral dissertations and 546 master's theses in departments of geography of universities in the United States and Canada, 1926–76. Topical index. Regional index.

C559 Mitchell, Bruce, and Joan Mitchell. Law of the sea and international fisheries management. Monticello, Ill.: Council of Planning Librarians, 1976. 48p. [Exchange bibliog. 1162]
About 650 references in classed arrangement.

Teaching of Geography

C560 Ball, John M. A bibliography for geographic education. Athens: University of Georgia, 1976. 113p. [Geography curriculum project, no.21] (previous ed. 1969. 91p.)
Covers particularly curriculum and teaching methods in the United States.

C561 Lukehurst, Clare T., and Norman J. Graves, eds. Geography in education: a bibliography of British sources, 1870–1970. Sheffield: Geographical Assn., 1972. 86p.
1,400 entries.

C562 Handbook for geography teachers. Ed. M. Long. 6th ed. London: Methuen Educational, 1974. 724p. (1st ed. 1932)
General reference book for teachers of geography in the United Kingdom. Includes sections on teaching of geography; outdoor geography; indoor geography; atlases, globes and maps; visual aids; geographical societies; books for primary stage; books for secondary stage; books for teachers.

C563 Sperling, Walter. Geographiedidaktische Quellenkunde: internationale Basisbibliographie und Einführung in die wissenschaftlichen Hilfsmittel (Ende 17. Jh. bis 1978). Duisburg: Verlag für Pädagogische Dokumentation, 1978. 897p. [Beiheft zum BIB report, 4]
The most comprehensive bibliography of the teaching of geography. Detailed information on many general bibliographic aids in geography. Facsimile reproduction of sample sheets from about 100 bibliographic sources. About 2,700 annotated entries in classed arrangement (93 categories). Author and subject indexes.

C564 Birkenhauer, Josef. Bibliographie Didaktik der Geographie. Paderborn, W. Germany: Schöningh, 1976. 194p. [Uni-Taschenbücher 554]
Bibliography on teaching of geography. Includes articles, sections in books or collected works, and pamphlets as well as books and monographs.

REGIONAL GEOGRAPHICAL BIBLIOGRAPHIES

In the broad spectrum of numerous regional bibliographies we here report only a rather narrow band. On the one hand are the general bibliographies of regions or countries, which include works from a wide range of fields; these are too broad for inclusion in this chapter, although many of them have a significant geographic content. One should consult also other sections of this book: "Aids with regional emphasis" in chapter 1, Social Science Literature; "Retrospective bibliographies" in chapter 2, History; and "Retrospective bibliographies: geographical bibliographies" and "Handbooks, manuals, and scholarly compendiums: geographical areas" in chapter 6, Anthropology. On the other hand, there are many regional bibliographies too specialized for inclusion in a general work of this scope either because the area is too small or because the bibliography treats only one topic in a region.

Many current bibliographies are published in regional geographical periodicals, often annually. These provide excellent coverage of many regions of the world. The following are particularly well covered: Chile in *Informaciones geográficas*, Brazil in *Boletim geográfico*, Scotland in the *Scottish geographical magazine*, Ireland in *Irish geography*, Normandy and West Central France in *Norois*, the French South in *Bulletin de la Société Languedocienne de géographie*, the Pyrenees in *Revue géographique des Pyrénées et du Sud-Ouest*, the Rhône basin in *Revue de géographie de Lyon*, the Alps in *Revue de géographie alpine*, Franche-Comté in *Cahiers de géographie de Besançon*, the French North in *Hommes et terres du Nord*, all of France in *Bibliographie géographique internationale*, the Federal Republic of Germany in *Neues Schrifttum zur deutschen Landeskunde*, Norway in *Norsk geografisk tidsskrift*, Sweden in *Svensk geografisk årsbok*, Finland in *Terra*, Czechoslovakia in *Československa geograficka společnost, Sborník*, Austria in *Mitteilungen der Österreichischen geographischen Gesellschaft*, northern Switzerland in *Regio Basiliensis*, Portugal in *Finisterra*, Zaïre in *Bulletin de la Société belge d'études géographiques*, and Madagascar in *Madagascar, Revue de géographie*.

C565 Walford, Albert John, ed. "Area studies." *In* Walford's guide to reference materials. 4th ed. v.2, section 908, p.365–433. London: Library Assn., 1982.
Of great value for regional bibliography and regional geography.

C566 Miller, E. Willard, and Ruby M. Miller. A bibliography on the Third World. Monticello, Ill.: Vance Bibliographies. [Public administration series]

Latin America, P-1062, 1982. 33p. 407 entries.

Middle America and the Caribbean, P-1063, 1982. 98p. 1,141 entries.

South America, P-1064, 1982. 81p. 993 entries.

Africa, P-817, 1981. 32p. 370 entries.

Northern and Western Africa, P-818, 1981. 96p. 1,189 entries.

Tropical, Eastern, and Southern Africa, P-819, 1981. 82p. 1,008 entries.

Asia, P-919, 1982. 45p. 525 entries.

References on political, economic, and social aspects; natural resources; and general—arranged first by field (within each volume) and then by region and country.

C567 Nō, Toshio. Bibliography of regional geography in western languages and regional bibliographies with emphasis on geography. Sendai, Japan: 1969. 58p. [Science reports of Tohoku Univ. 7th ser. Geography. 19, no.1.]
About 725 substantive monographs and 67 bibliographies listed by continent and region. Author index.

C568 Paylore, Patricia. Desertification: a world bibliography. Comp. for the 23d International Geographical Congress, Moscow, 1976. Pre-conference meeting of the IGU working group on desertification, Desert Research Institute, Ashkhabad, Turkmen SSR, July 20–26, 1976. Tucson: Univ. of Arizona Office of Arid Lands Studies, 1976. 664p.
1,645 entries with substantial abstracts compiled by 15 regional collaborators. Organized regionally. Each region has separate author index and keyword index.

C568 ——, and J. A. Mabbutt, eds. Desertification
A world bibliography update, 1976–1980. Tucson: Univ. of Arizona Office of Arid Lands Studies, 1980. 196p.
402 annotated references including material of the 1977 United Nations Conference on Desertification.

C568 Spooner, Brian, and H. S. Mann, eds. Deser-
B tification and development: dryland ecology in social perspective. London and Orlando, Fla.: Academic, 1982, 1983. 407p.
About 500 references.

C568 Hopkins, Stephen T., and Douglas E. Jones,
C with the technical assistance of John A. Rogers. Research guide to the arid lands of the world. Phoenix: Oryx Pr., 1983. 391p.
3,199 entries in two parts. Pt. 1 arranged by major regions, continents, and 120 countries. Pt. 2 arranged by fields, such as earth sciences and human geography.

C569 Hills, Theo L. A select annotated bibliography of the humid tropics. Montreal: McGill Univ. Geography Dept., 1960. 238p.
About 2,500 items arranged by continent, country, and smaller areas. Some annotations.

C570 Hodson, Dean R. A bibliography of dissertations in geography on Anglo-America, 1960–1972. Monticello, Ill.: Council of Planning Librarians, 1974. 202p. [Exchange bibliog. 583–84]
About 2,900 entries arranged by regions.

C570 Harris, Chauncy D. United States of America,
A   Bibliography of geography, part II, volume 1. Chicago: Univ. of Chicago Dept. of Geography, 1984. 178p. [Research paper no.206]
1,257 entries, mostly annotated, arranged by general aids; physical and related earth sciences, the environment, and resources; human geography and related social sciences; and regions of the United States, each with subdivisions. Part III, Human geography, includes sections on urban, economic, social, cultural, population, medical, political, and historical geography of the United States. Some entries cover many references, as, for example, the one for the National Technical Information Service, which lists 262 bibliographies and other reports for 17 major subject categories, or the one for the research catalog of the American Geographical Society, which analyzes references on the United States by 69 topical and regional subdivisions.

C571 Canada. Department of Mines and Technical Surveys. Geographical Branch. Bibliographical series. Ottawa. v.1–34, 1950–67. (No.34 [1967] by Dept. of Energy, Mines and Resources)
Bibliographies of Canadian geography, with annual general listings and retrospective summaries for special topics or regions.

C572 Handbook of Latin American studies. v.1– , 1936– . Austin: Univ. of Texas Pr. Annual.
The section on geography provides the best review of scholarly publications in geography and therefore typically the most convenient and useful foundation for following the literature in geography on Latin America. The reviews were annual before 1964 but thereafter biennial as volumes on the social sciences and humanities appear in alternate years. Geography appears in the social science volume.

C573 Hoy, Don R., and Tim Wall. Agricultural and livestock activities in Latin America: a partial bibliography. Athens: University of Georgia Dept. of Geography, 1980. 171p. [Aids to geographic research series, bibliography no.2]
2,616 entries arranged by topic and crop. Lists of entry numbers relevant to each region and country.

C574 Hoy, Don R., and Samuel Macfie. Manufacturing and mining activities in Latin America: a partial bibliography. Athens: Univ. of Georgia Dept. of Geography, 1981. 131p. [Aids to geographic research series, bibliography no.3]
1,744 entries arranged by topic, with lists of entry numbers relevant to each region and country.

C575 Mexico. Dirección de Geografía y Meteorología. Bibliografía de México. Ed. by Angel Bassols Batalla. Mexico City: 1955. 652p.
Comprehensive bibliography of the geography of Mexico. 4,600 entries by systematic and regional breakdown. Author and place indexes.

C576 Hoy, Don R., and Samuel Macfie.Central America: a bibliography of economic, political, and cultural conditions. Athens: Univ. of Georgia Dept. of Geography, 1982. 134p. [Aids to geographic research series, bibliography no. 4]
1,727 entries arranged by topic, with lists of entries relevant to each region and country.

C577 Norton, Ann V., comp. A bibliography of the Caribbean area for geographers. Mona, Kingston, Jamaica: Univ. of the West Indies Geography Dept., 1971. 3v. 418p. Mimeo. Bibliographies, p.407–16. [Occasional publ. 7]
About 5,000 entries organized topically and within topics by regions.

C578 Dolphin, Philippa, and others. The London region: an annotated geographical bibliography. London: Mansell, 1981. 379p.

C579 "France." *In* Bibliographie géographique internationale, v.1– , 1891– . (C479).
Comprehensive coverage of publications on the geography of France, annually 1891–1976 and quarterly 1977– .

C580 Dumont, Maurice E., and Lucien de Smet. Aardrijkskundige bibliographie van België. Bibliographie géographique de la Belgique. Gent: Seminarie voor Menselijke Aardrijkskunde der Rijksuniversiteit, 1954–56. 4v. 450p. [Bibliographia belgica, 14–17]

1st supp. 1954–58 (1960). 210p. [Bibliographia belgica, 48]

2d supp. 1959–63 (1965). 280p. [Bibliographia belgica, 82]

3d supp. 1964–68 (1970). 247p. [Bibliographia belgica, 113]

4th supp. 1969–73 (1978). 243p. [Publicatie no. 14]

5th supp. 1974–78 (1980). 197p. [Publicatie no.15]

Comprehensive bibliography of all aspects of the physical and human geography of Belgium. Arranged by systematic subdivisions. Within each category, entries in reverse chronological order. Index of authors, places, and subjects (in Dutch and French).

C580 Denis, Jacques, and others, eds. Geography in
A   Belgium. Namur: Comité National de Géographie, 1984. 167p. [Reprinted from Bulletin de la Société Belge d'Études Géographiques 53, no.2:1–167 (1984)]
Extensive bibliography.

C581 Berichte zur deutschen Landeskunde. v.1– , 1941– . Trier, W. Germany: Selbstverlag des

Zentralausschuss für deutsche Landeskunde. Semiannual.

Detailed and comprehensive bibliography of geography and related fields for Germany, Austria, and Switzerland through 1971. Thereafter includes only short articles and extensive reviews. Bibliography continued, after a break, in *Neues Schrifttum zur deutschen Landeskunde* (C581A).

C581 Neues Schrifttum zur deutschen Landeskunde.
A 1– , 1979– . 2 nos. a year. Trier, W. Germany: Selbstverlag des Zentralausschuss für deutsche Landeskunde, 1981– .
Detailed bibliography on German geography from 1979.

C582 Sperling, Walter. Landeskunde DDR; eine annotierte Auswahlbibliographie. München, New York: Verlag Dokumentation Saur, 1978. 456p. [Bibliographien zur regionalen Geographie und Landeskunde, Band 1]
More than 2,000 entries, 1945–77, in classed arrangement (38 categories) with short annotations; 240 bibliographical entries; 130 periodicals; 124 references on maps and atlases. Indexes of authors and places.

C582 ———. Ergänzungsband 1978–1983. München:
A K. G. Saur, 1984. [Bibliographie zur regionalen Geographie und Landeskunde, Band 5]

C583 Rostankowski, Peter, and others. Aktuelle Bibliographie Deutsch-, Englisch- und Französischsprachiger Arbeiten zur Geographie Osteuropas. Wiesbaden, W. Germany: Harrassowitz, 1978. 205p. [Berlin. Freie Universität. Osteuropa Institut. Bibliographische Mitteilungen, Heft 17.]
More than 2,000 references on the geography of Eastern Europe.

C583 ———. Teil II, 1982. 216p. [. . . Heft 23]
A
2,218 additional references, particularly for the later years 1978–80 but including also additional entries for an earlier period 1960–66.

C584 Bibliografia geografii polskiej. Bibliography of Polish geography. (Polska Akademia Nauk. Instytut Geografii i Przestrzennego Zagospodarowania). Warszawa. 1956– . Irregular.
Annual bibliography of geography in Poland. Retrospective volumes cover earlier years, 1918–27; 1936–44; 1945–51. Current years have covered 1952–77, usually in annual volume but occasionally in volume covering two years. Bibliography for 1977, published in 1982 (413p.) has 3,056 entries in classed and regional arrangement, with author index. Principal compiler: Halina Tuszyńska-Rękawek.

C585 Harris, Chauncy D. Guide to geographical bibliographies and reference works in Russian or on the Soviet Union. Chicago: Univ. of Chicago Dept. of Geography, 1975. 475p. [Research paper no.164]
The sections on bibliographies of regional geography of the Soviet Union contain 351 entries in Russian and other languages of the Soviet Union

(p.281–333) and 220 entries in Western languages, mainly English, French, and German (p.353–88).

C586 Maichel, Karol. History, auxiliary historical sciences, ethnography, and geography. v.2 of Guide to Russian reference books. Stanford: Hoover Institution, 1964. 297p. [Hoover Institution Bibliographical series 18]
Section F (Geography, p.189–227, entries F1–F300) provides a comprehensive retrospective bibliography of bibliographies on the geography of Russia and the Soviet Union. Extensive annotations include English translation of titles and full information on the scope, contents, and value of each bibliography. Includes general and selective bibliographies, dissertations, institutions, periodicals, abstracts and indexes, regional physical geographies, special-subject bibliographies, cartography, maps and atlases, administrative regions, encyclopedias, dictionaries and gazetteers, biography, and handbooks.

C587 Geografska bibliografija slovenije. Geographic bibliography of Slovenia. (Ljubljana. Univerza. Inštitut za Geografijo). 1960– . Annual. 1960–65 as Slovenska geografska bibliografija. Slovene geographic bibliography.
Bibliography of Slovenia in Yugoslavia in classed arrangement.

C588 Collana di bibliografie geografiche delle regioni italiane. v.1– , 1959– . Rome. Irregularly. [Italy. Consiglio Nazionale delle Ricerche. Comitato per le Scienze Storiche, Filologiche e Filosofiche.]
Comprehensive and retrospective bibliographies of Italy, region by region.

C589 Società Geografica Italiana. Bibliografia geografica delle regione Italiana. v.1– , 1925– . Rome. Annual. Indexes v.1–10 (1925–34), v.11–19/20 (1935–43/44), v.21–30 (1945–54), v.31–40 (1955–64).
Comprehensive annual bibliography on geography of Italy, organized systematically. Author index. Long delay in publication.

C590 Bibliografia geografica de Portugal, v.2. Lisboa: Centro de Estudos geográficos, 1982. 432p.
Covers the years 1947–74. V.1, published in 1948, was reprinted in 1973.

C591 Bederman, Sanford H. Africa: a bibliography of geography and related disciplines: a selected listing of recent literature published in the English language. 3d ed. Atlanta: Georgia State Univ. Bureau of Business and Economic Research, 1974. 334p. (1st ed. 1970. 212p.).
3,629 entries arranged alphabetically by author within regions and countries. Subject indexes for each region and country. Author index.

C592 Sommer, John W. Bibliography of African geography, 1940–1964. Hanover, N.H.: Dartmouth College Dept. of Geography, 1965. 139p. [Geography publications no.3]
1,724 articles from 58 geographical periodicals are arranged topically by subfields of human geogra-

phy, economic geography, and physical geography. Author index.

C593 Leng, G. Desertification: a bibliography with regional emphasis on Africa. Bremen: Universität Bremen, 1982. 177p. Bremer Beiträge zur Geographie und Raumplanung, v.4.
Covers all parts of Africa, with some emphasis on the Sahel.

C594 Barth, Hans Karl, ed. Egypt: geographical bibliography. Bremen: Universität Bremen, 1981. 197p.
Entries mainly in English, German, and French.

C595 Aiyepeku, Wilson O. Geographical literature on Nigeria, 1901–1970: an annotated bibliography. Boston: Hall, 1974. 214p.
1,441 annotated entries, in classed arrangement (38 divisions) of books and periodical articles in English. Author, place, and subject indexes.

C595 Williams, Geoffrey J. A bibliography of geo-
A graphical writing on Zambia 1900–1979. Lusaka: Zambia Geographical Association, 1982. 33p. [Z.G.A. Bibliographies no. 4]
525 references.

C596 Logan, Richard F. Bibliography of South West Africa: geography and related fields. Windhoek: Committee of the S.W.A. Scientific Society, 1969. 152p. [Scientific research in South West Africa, 8th ser.]
About 2,000 entries up to 1966, by author, with indexing and coding by 89 subjects and 20 regions.

C597 Sukhwal, Bheru Lal. South Asia: a systematic geographic bibliography. Metuchen, N.J.: Scarecrow Pr., 1974. 827p. Author index.
10,346 entries, arranged in nine sections, the first devoted to South Asia generally, the other eight to individual regions: India, Pakistan, Bangladesh, Sri Lanka, Tibet, Nepal, Bhutan and Sikkim, and the Indian Ocean and islands. Within each section, organization is systematic, with books, articles, and dissertations listed separately. Most entries are in English, but works in other languages are also included.

C598 Rahman, Mushtaqur. Bibliography of Pakistan geography, 1947–1973. Monticello, Ill.: Council of Planning Librarians, 1974. 117p. [Exchange bibliog. 656]
1,452 entries. Author index.

C599 Carlson, Alvar W. A bibliography of the geographical literature on Southeast Asia, 1920–1972. Monticello, Ill.: Council of Planning Librarians, 1974. 127p. [Exchange bibliog. 598–600]
1,312 entries arranged by regions subdivided by fields. Author index.

C600 Pelzer, Karl J. Selected bibliography on the geography of Southeast Asia. New Haven, Conn.: Yale Univ. Southeast Asia Studies, 1949–56. 3v.
A selective guide to the physical, cultural, eco-nomic, and political geography of Southeast Asia. V.1 deals with Southeast Asia in general, v.2 with the Philippines, v.3 with Malaya. Entries are arranged under broad subject heading with subdivisions. Includes books and articles.

C601 ———. West Malaysia and Singapore: a selected bibliography. New Haven, Conn.: Human Relations Area Files Pr., 1971. 394p. [Behavior science bibliographies]
A revision, expansion, and updating of previous entry, v.3, *Malaya*.

C602 Huke, Robert E. Bibliography of Philippine geography, 1940–1963: a select list. Hanover, N.H.: Dartmouth College Dept. of Geography, 1964. 84p. [Geography publications no.1]
Reprint, New York: Kraus Reprint, 1976.
A detailed bibliography of the topical fields of geography in the Philippines. Particularly strong on economic and human geography. More than 1,000 entries. Author index.

C603 Kornhauser, David H. Studies of Japan in Western languages of special interest to geographers. Tokyo: Kokon-Shoin, 1984. 99p. (Revision of A selected list of writings on Japan pertinent to geography in Western languages, with emphasis on the work of Japan specialists. Hiroshima: Univ. of Hiroshima Research and Sources Unit for Regional Geography, 1979. 71p.)
About 1,200 entries on the physical, human, and regional geography of Japan.

C604 Hall, Robert B., and Toshio Noh. Japanese geography: a guide to Japanese reference and research materials. Rev. ed. Ann Arbor: Univ. of Michigan Pr., 1970. 233p. [Univ. of Michigan Center for Japanese Studies. Bibliographical series no.6.] (1st ed. 1956. 128p.)
Excellent annotated bibliography of Japanese-language materials on geography of Japan. 1,486 entries with titles and authors in romanized form, in the original Japanese, and in English translation. Provides a discriminating introduction to the vast Japanese literature. Covers bibliographies, encyclopedias, dictionaries, gazetteers, travel guides, yearbooks and statistical sources, sets and collections, periodicals, atlases, maps, cartography, air-photo coverage, and the major fields of geography grouped under history of Japanese geography, physical geography, historical and cultural geography, economic geography, and regional descriptive geography.

C605 K.B.S. bibliography of standard reference books for Japanese studies with descriptive notes: geography. Rev. ed. Tokyo: The Japan Foundation (Kokusai Koryu Kikin), 1973. 224p. (1st ed. 1962)
Titles given in Romanized form, in Japanese writing, and in translation.

C606 Herman, Theodore, ed. The geography of China: a selected and annotated bibliography. New York: Univ. of the State of New York

Foreign Area Materials Center, 1967. 44p. [Occasional publication 7]

Introduction to English-language materials on the geography of China. Annotations are informative and evaluative. Covers reference materials, human geography, and physical geography. Author index.

C607 Reiner, Ernst. Literaturbericht über Australien und Neuseeland, 1938–1963. Gotha/Leipzig: Hermann Haack, 1967. 294p. [Geographisches Jahrbuch, Band 62]

2,677 entries for Australia and 943 for New Zealand.

C608 ———. Geographischer Literaturbericht Neuseeland, 1962–1972. Niedergelpe, W. Germany: Author, Gelpestr. 46, D-5251 Post Kalkkuhl, 1974. 38p.

223 entries in classed arrangement.

C609 ———. Geographischer Literaturbericht Australien, 1962–1972. 1975. 302p. Niedergelpe, W. Germany: Author, 1974. 300p.

2,078 entries in classed arrangement.

C609 Jeans, D. N., and J. L. Davies. "Australian
A   geography 1972–1982," *Australian geographical studies* 22, no. 1:3–35 (1984).

C610 Lea, David A.M., and others. "Geographers in Papua, New Guinea: a preliminary bibliography," *Australian geographer* 13, no.2:104–145 (1975).

Lists about 650 publications by geographers.

BIOGRAPHICAL DIRECTORIES

C611 Orbis geographicus 1980/84: world directory of geography. Ed. by Emil Meynen. Wiesbaden, W. Germany: Steiner, 1982. 962p.

The standard international source of biographical information on geographers. Name, date of birth, degrees, positions, editorial activities, and residence and office address of about 7,000 geographers, arranged by country. Alphabetical index. Previous editions in 1960, 1967, and 1974. Supersedes *World directory of geographers* (1952).

C612 Association of American Geographers. Directory, 1982. Washington, D.C.: The Association, 1982. 186p.

Name, mailing address, birth date, birth place, education, employment, speciality, and geographic area of interest. 5,402 members. Earlier editions 1949, 1952, 1956, 1961, 1967, 1970, 1974, and 1978.

C613 Canadian Association of Geographers. Directory. Ed. by Brenton M. Barr. Montreal: Association of Canadian Geographers, 1978– . Annual.

The 1983 directory listed 1,259 names and addresses of members as of September 30, 1983, and faculty, research, and publications of 65 departments of geography in Canada.

C614 Répertoire des géographes français 1984. 2d ed. Paris: Centre National de la Recherche Scientifique. Laboratoire Intergéo, 1984. 313p.

Name, addresses, and specializations of 1,070 French geographers. Indexes of organizations, research themes, and countries studied.

C615 "Anschriften von Personen," *Geographisches Taschenbuch und Jahrweiser für Landeskunde,* hrsg. E. Ehlers and E. Meynen. 1949– . Wiesbaden, W. Germany: Franz Steiner. About every 2 years.

The 1983/1984 issue provides the names, birth dates, degrees, positions, addresses, and specializations of nearly 2,000 geographers in the Federal Republic of Germany, Austria, and Switzerland.

C616 Directory of Soviet geographers, comp. by Theodore Shabad. *Soviet geography: review and translation* 28, no.7:433–538 (Sept. 1977). Special issue, also separately paged, 102p.

Names, degrees, present positions, and fields of interest of about 3,000 Soviet geographers.

DICTIONARIES

C617 International Geographical Union. Commission on international geographical terminology. Bibliography of mono- and multilingual dictionaries and glossaries of technical terms used in geography as well as in related natural and social sciences. Comp. by Emil Meynen. Wiesbaden, W. Germany: Steiner, 1974. 246p.

3,211 entries in classed arrangement by fields of geography and related disciplines. Most entries are for related fields. 49 monolingual dictionaries of terms in geography as a whole in 10 languages. 38 bilingual or multilingual dictionaries of terms in geography as a whole.

C618 Johnston, Ronald J., and others. The dictionary of human geography. Oxford: Basil Blackwell; New York: Free Pr., 1981. 411p.

The best reference work on English terms in human geography.

C619 Stamp, L. Dudley, and Audrey N. Clark, eds. A glossary of geographical terms based on a list prepared by a committee of the British Assn. for the Advancement of Science. 3d ed. London: Longman, 1979. 571p. (1st ed. 1961. 539p.)

The most comprehensive and ambitious attempt to define terms in modern geography and to show their origin. Includes definitions from other dictionaries. Cites original usage and development of variations. Appendixes include Greek and Latin roots commonly used in the construction of terms and lists of words in foreign languages that have been absorbed into English (grouped by language).

C620 Quencez, G. Vocabularium geographicum. Brussels: Presses Académiques Européennes, 1968. 298p.

Vocabularies in parallel column—in French, German, Italian, Dutch, English, and Spanish—of 3,100 basic terms arranged in 617 closely related concepts and grouped in 42 fields, with alphabetical index for each language of all terms. Compiled with cooperation of many international specialists to facilitate and give effect to the work of the Council of Europe's Council for Cultural Co-Operation.

C621   George, Pierre. Dictionnaire de la géographie. 2d ed. Paris: Presses universitaires de France, 1974. 451p. (1st ed. 1970. 448p.)

Comprehensive coverage of geographical terms and concepts in French by 20 specialists, ranging from physical to human geography. Modern, clear, and accurate.

GAZETTEERS

C622   Sheehy, Eugene P., and others, comps. "Gazetteers." *In* Guide to reference books, p.576–82. 9th ed. Chicago: American Library Assn., 1976. Entries CL55–112. Supp., 1980, p.175. Entries CL29–37. Second supp., 1982, p.147. Entries 2CL18–22.

Annotated list of major gazetteers of the principal countries of the world.

C622   Meynen, Emil. Gazetteers and glossaries of
A   geographical names of the member countries of the United Nations and the agencies in relationship with the United Nations: bibliography 1946–1976. Wiesbaden, W. Germany: Steiner, 1984. 518p.

Detailed bibliography.

C623   Webster's new geographical dictionary. Springfield, Mass.: Merriam, 1984. 1,376p. 218 maps. (revised from 1972 ed.; 1st ed. 1949. 1,293p.)

Frequently reprinted.

Up-to-date, handy-sized gazetteer, adequate for most immediate-reference uses, particularly in the United States or Canada. Includes in one alphabet more than 47,000 geographical names and 15,000 cross-references for equivalent and alternative spellings. Gives spelling, pronunciation, location, size, population (as of approximately 1980), and description. For the largest cities, important countries, and each state in the United States, fuller descriptive and historical information is given. Includes all incorporated places with a population of 2,500 or more in the United States and Canada, of more than 8,000 in Australia and New Zealand, of more than 10,000 in the United Kingdom, of more than 20,000 in most countries of Latin America or Europe, and of generally higher figures in other areas (for example, 40,000 in the USSR, 50,000 in India and Japan, and 100,000 in China). "Geographical terms," p.xvii–xxiv, provides a selection of geographical terms in various languages and their equivalents in English and a list of terms in English with foreign-language equivalents.

C624   Columbia Lippincott gazetteer of the world. Ed. by Leon Seltzer. New York: Columbia Univ. Pr., 1952. 2,148p.

The best and most complete English-language world gazetteer. It lists (in one alphabet) the political subdivisions and geographic features of the world, giving variant spellings and pronunciation, population (with date), altitude, historical, economic, social, and cultural information and other pertinent facts. Places are generally located by straight-line distances (in miles) from larger features. Lists some 130,000 names and has 30,000 cross-references. Updated by a 36-page 1961 supplement.

C625   The Times index-gazetteer of the world. London: The Times, 1965. 956p.

Names, latitude and longitude, and map location of 345,000 towns, villages, rivers, mountains, and other geographical features, about 198,000 of which are on plates of the *Times atlas of the world*. The most comprehensive one volume worldwide location index of places. Not a descriptive gazetteer.

C626   U.S. Board on Geographic Names. Gazetteers; official standard names. Washington, D.C.: no.1–116, 1955–70. No.1–68 (1955–62) issued by Superintendent of Documents, Govt. Print. Off.; no.69–104 (1962–67) issued by the Office of Geography, U.S. Department of Interior; no.105–16 (1968–70) and later unnumbered gazetteers issued by U.S. Army Topographic Command or the Defense Mapping Agency.

This world series of gazetteers of official standard names includes more than 3,500,000 places and geographic features. Each volume devoted to a country or area. Entries give geographic coordinates, identification (e.g., island, mountain, region), and map source from which the name was taken. Each volume contains a list of generic geographical terms. Cross-references from variant spelling. Individual gazetteers are listed both by number and by country in Harris *Bibliography of geography* (C455), Appendix 1, p.237–42.

C627   The National Gazetteer of the United States, Geological Survey Professional Paper 1200. Washington, D.C.: Govt. Print. Off., 1982– . In process.

The New Jersey volume (1982, 220p.) contained about 10,000 names. The National Geographic Names Data Base of the U.S. Geological Survey contains information on about 2 million names used throughout the United States and its territories. Various listings are available in the form of computer printouts, magnetic tapes, and microfiche. Lists of names by states are available on microfiche from the National Cartographic Information Center, 507 National Center, Reston, VA 22092.

GEOGRAPHICAL ENCYCLOPEDIAS

Two modern comprehensive geographical encyclopedias cover the regions and places of the world (much like a regional geography and a gazetteer) and the fields and topics of geography, and each is the work of many scholars. *Westermann Lexikon der Geographie* (C628) is more recent and generally more useful to the Western scholar, but *Kratkaia geograficheskaia entsiklopediia* (C629) is also modern and is particularly useful for its coverage of the Soviet Union and the other socialist countries. There are no comparable works in English or French.

C628 Westermann Lexikon der Geographie. Ed. by Wolf Tietze. Brunswick, W. Germany: Westermann, 1968–72. 5v.

Excellent geographic encyclopedia with articles by more than 125 leading German specialists on geography and its related disciplines, topics, regions, cities, geographic features, and technical terms, with references. High-quality scholarship. V. 1–4, text; v.5, index.

C629 Kratkaia geograficheskaia entsiklopediia. Moscow: Sovetskaia Entsiklopediia, 1960–66. 5v.

A major geographical reference work with articles on places, fields of geography, regions, and topics. V.5 contains many geographical tables and general articles, articles on peoples of the world, and a biographical index of all geographers cited in the bibliographies.

THESES AND DISSERTATIONS

C630 Browning, Clyde E. A bibliography of dissertations in geography; 1901 to 1969: American and Canadian universities. Chapel Hill: Univ. of North Carolina Dept. of Geography, 1970. 96p. [Studies in geography no.1]

1,582 doctoral dissertations in geography arranged by 23 subject categories. A regional classification records the entry numbers by large regions.

C630 ———. ———. 1969 to 1982. Chapel Hill:
A Univ. of North Carolina Dept. of Geography, 1983. 145p. [Studies in geography no.18]

2,270 additional doctoral dissertations in geography arranged by 30 subject categories.

C631 Stuart, Merrill M. A bibliography of master's theses in geography: American and Canadian universities. Tualatin, Ore.: Geographic and Area Study Publications, 1973. 274p.

5,054 master's theses arranged by 27 fields alphabetically by author in each field. Regional classification index.

C632 Recent geography theses completed and in preparation. *In* Professional geographer. Washington, D.C.: Assn. of American Geographers, 1950–79.

Titles of geography theses completed in the United States and Canada were published in the March and November issues, 1950–60; in the November issue, 1961–70; and in the February issues, 1972–79. Lists by author, Ph.D. dissertations completed and in progress, and master's theses completed. Each entry gives title, university, indication of the publication (including microfilming), and availability through interlibrary loan. 1950–72 by Leslie Hewes; 1973–79 by Robert H. Stoddard. The lists in 1950 and 1951 are retrospective to 1946. Continues two works: (1) Derwent Whittlesey, "Dissertations in geography accepted in the United States for the degree of Ph.D. as of May, 1935," *Annals of the Association of American Geographers* 25:211–37 (Dec. 1935), and (2) Leslie Hewes, "Dissertations in geography accepted by universities in the United States and Canada for the degree of Ph.D., June 1935–June 1945, and those currently in progress," *Annals of the Association of American Geographers* 36:215–54 (Dec. 1946).

From 1978/79 completed theses and dissertations are listed under each department in *Guide to graduate departments of geography in the United States and Canada* 1979/80–1983/84 and *Guide to departments of geography in the United States and Canada* 1984/85– (C701).

C633 Fraser, J. Keith, and Mary C. Hynes, comps. List of theses and dissertations on Canadian geography. Rev. ed. Ottawa: Dept. of the Environment, Lands Directorate, 1972. 114p. [Geographical paper, no.51]

2,418 entries for theses produced in geography departments of universities in Canada (1) on the geography of Canada, (2) on foreign areas, (3) on methodological topics. List includes baccalaureate, master's, or doctoral theses or dissertations. Arrangement is regional. Author and subject indexes.

———. ———. 1972 supplement. Ottawa: Canadian Committee on Geography, Environment Canada, 1973. 40p.

473 entries.

———. ———. Supplement 1972–1975. Ottawa: Canadian Committee for Geography.

C633 Marsden, B. S., and E. E. Tugby. Bibliography
A of Australian geography theses. Preliminary edition: 1933–1971. Brisbane, Australia: Univ. of Queensland Dept. of Geography, 1981. 2d ed. 77p.

1,468 theses, mainly on Australia, New Zealand, and Papua-New Guinea. Index by 31 subjects. A supplement for 1972–80 has been prepared by D. Wadley and E. Tugby.

MAPS AND ATLASES
Bibliographical Sources

C634 British Museum. Catalogue of printed maps, charts, and plans. Photolithographic edition to 1964. London: British Museum, 1967. 15v. (Corrections and additions, 1968. 55p.)

A complete inventory of the great collection of printed maps, atlases, globes, and other cartographic material in the Map Room and other parts of the British Museum at the end of 1964. About 225,000 entries. Alphabetical arrangement.

C635 British Museum. Catalogue of printed maps, charts, and plans. Ten-year supplement 1965–1974. London: publ. by British Museum Publications for the British Library, 1978. 1,380 cols.

About 14,000 entries.

C636 New York Public Library. Map Division. Dictionary catalog. Boston: Hall, 1971. 10v.

186,748 cards representing some 280,000 sheet maps, 6,000 atlases, other cartographic publications, and 11,000 volumes other than atlases on the history of mapmaking, bibliographies, and related topics—all in a single alphabetical order.

C637 Canada. Public Archives. Catalogue of the national map collection, Ottawa. Boston: Hall, 1976. 16v. 12,011p.

About 96,000 cards arranged by an area classification. Area, author, and subject cross-references. Most comprehensive record of Canadian maps.

C638 American Geographical Society. Map Department. Index to maps in books and periodicals. Boston: Hall, 1968. 10v.

A comprehensive and unique bibliography of 164,338 cards of maps that appear in books or articles, not as separate publications. Alphabetical arrangement by subject, place, and author.

C639 ———. ———. First supp. Boston: Hall, 1971. 603p. 12,654 cards for the period 1968–71.

C639 A ———. ———. Second supp. Boston: Hall, 1976. 568p. 11,924 cards for the period 1972–75.

Later additions are entered into a card file at the American Geographical Society Collection at the University of Wisconsin-Milwaukee Library.

C640 Bibliographie cartographique internationale. 1936–75. Paris: Colin, 1938–70; Librairie de la Faculté de Sciences, and Nendeln, Liechtenstein: Kraus-Thomson, 1972–79. Annual. Closed 1979.

Issued in 1936 as *Bibliographie cartographique de la France;* in 1937–45 as *Bibliographie cartographique française.* An international bibliography of maps, charts, and atlases arranged by continent and country. Indexes of authors, publishers, and subjects. About 3,000 items a year.

C641 U.S. Library of Congress. Map Division. A list of geographical atlases in the Library of Congress, with bibliographical notes. v.1–4 by Philip Lee Phillips; v.5–8 by Clara Egli LeGear. Washington, D.C.: Govt. Print. Off., 1909–74. 8v.

v. 1–4 cover 5,324 atlases in the Library of Congress in 1920; v.5, 2,326 world atlases acquired 1920–55; v.6, 2,647 atlases acquired 1920–60 for Europe, Asia, Africa, Oceania, and polar regions; v.7 Western Hemisphere 1920–69; v.8 index to v.7.

A key major inventory of 18,478 atlases, the most extensive of its kind, with full bibliographical information and analytical notes on contents. Author and place indexes.

C642 Alexander, Gerard L. Guide to atlases: world, regional, national, thematic: an international listing of atlases published since 1950. Metuchen, N.J.: Scarecrow, 1971. 671p.

5,556 entries. 1,786 world atlases arranged chronologically by date and, within each year, alphabetically by publisher; 393 regional atlases, covering whole continents or major regions; 1,809 national atlases; and 1,568 thematic atlases. List of publishers by continent and country. Alphabetical publishers index to entries. Language index. Index of authors, cartographers, and editors. In part, updates C641.

C643 ———. ———. Supplement: an international listing of atlases published 1971 through 1975 with comprehensive indexes. Metuchen, N.J.: Scarecrow, 1977. 362p.

2,993 entries (no.5557–8549).

C644 Bibliographic guide to maps and atlases. 1979– . Boston: Hall, 1980– . Annual.

Lists materials cataloged during each year by the Map Division of the New York Public Library and the Geography and Map Division of the Library of Congress in one alphabetical listing.

C645 U.S. Library of Congress. Map Division. United States atlases: a catalog of national, state, county, city, and regional atlases in the Library of Congress and cooperating libraries. Comp. by Clara Egli LeGear. Washington, D.C.: Govt. Print. Off., 1950–53. 2v.

Title of v.1 varies slightly. The most comprehensive list of atlases of the United States and its states, counties, cities, and regions. Lists 7,064 atlases, of which 2,173 are not in the Library of Congress but in the collections of 132 cooperating libraries.

C646 McGaugh, Maurice E. Geographies, atlases, and special references on the states and provinces of Anglo-America. Special Libraries Association, Geography and Map Division. Bulletin. 83: 40–47, 84: 31–39, 85: 13–18 (1971). Also Mt. Pleasant: Central Michigan Univ. Dept. of Geography, 1970. 36p.

About 450 entries arranged by state and province.

C647 Walford, Albert John, ed. "Atlases and maps."
In Walford's guide to reference materials. 4th
ed. v.2, section 912, p.448–69. London: Library
Assn., 1982.
Good selection of major atlases.

C648 Sheehy, Eugene P., and others. "Atlases." *In*
Guide to reference books. 9th ed. Chicago:
American Library Assn., 1976. Entries CL165–
263. Supp., 1980. p.176–77. Entries CL45–67.
Second supp., 1982. p.148–50. [Entries 2CL32–
44.]
Good selection of guides to bibliographies,
general atlases, and national and regional atlases.

C649 Yonge, Ena L. "National atlases: a summary,"
Geographical review 47:570–78 (1957); "Regional atlases: a summary survey," ibid.,
52:407–32 (1962); and "World and thematic
atlases: a summary survey," ibid., 52:583–96
(1962).
A review and evaluation of 28 major national,
about 100 regional, 33 world, and 31 thematic atlases.

C650 Stephenson, Richard W. "Atlases of the Western Hemisphere: a summary survey," *Geographical review* 62:92–119 (1972).
Review of 147 atlases of the Western Hemisphere published in the period 1962–71.

C651 Murphy, Mary. "Atlases of the Eastern Hemisphere: a summary survey," *Geographical review* 64:111–39 (1974).
Review of 156 atlases of the Eastern Hemisphere published 1962–1973 with bibliographical
notes.

Lists of Maps and Atlases
Currently Available

C652 Winch, Kenneth L., ed. International maps and
atlases in print. 2d ed. London and New York:
Bowker, 1976. 866p. (1st ed. 1974. 864p.).
List of more than 15,000 maps and atlases currently available from about a thousand official and
commercial publishers. Almost 400 index maps record
coverage of multisheet series. Extensive map indexes.

C653 Geo-katalog. In two parts. Band 1. Touristische
Veröffentlichungen. Landkarten, Reiseführer,
Pläne, Atlanten, Globen aus aller Welt. Maps
plans, guides, atlases, globes. München:
GeoCenter Verlagsbetrieb, 1972– . Annual
[1983. 612p. plus Blattschnitt-Teil]. Band 2.
International. Amtliche geographisch-the-
matische Karten und Atlanten. Schnittüber-
sichten von Kartenwerken. Official geogra-
phic-thematic maps and atlases. Indexes of map
series. [Geowissenschaften. Liefbare Karten,
Atlanten und ausgewählte Handbücher aus
allen Themenbereichen der regionalen Geographie. Blattschnitte für alle Kartenwerke.
Available maps, atlases and selected books
comprising topics in the field of regional geography. Indexes for all map series.] Stuttgart:

GeoCenter Internationales Landkartenhaus,
1976– .
In two looseleaf volumes, with distribution
several times each year of groups of sheets to replace
provisional or earlier indexes.

Directories of Map Collections

C654 World directory of map collections. Comp. by
the Geography and Map Libraries Sub-Section.
Ed. by Walter W. Ristow. München: Verlag
Dokumentation; distr. New York: Unipub,
1976. 326p. [International Federation of Library Associations publications 8]
Information on 285 map collections in 45
countries.

C655 Map collections in the United States and Canada; a directory. Comp. by David K. Carrington
and Richard W. Stephenson. 3d ed. New York:
Special Libraries Assn., 1978. 230p. [A project
of the Geography and Map Div., Special Libraries Assn.] (1st ed. 1954).
Information on 743 map collections.

ATLASES
General-Reference Large
World Atlases

C656 The Times atlas of the world, comprehensive
edition. 6th ed. London: Times Books, 1980.
123 plates; 227p. (first pub. 1955–59, in 5v.; 1v.
ed. first pub. 1967)
The outstanding general-reference large-format
world atlas. Excellent cartography. Physical-political
maps show locations and relief. Thematic maps.
Gazetteer (see C625) has more than 200,000 place
names, with map location and latitude and longitude.

C657 Rand McNally and Co. The new international
atlas. Chicago: Rand McNally, 1984. 320p. of
maps and text; 231p. index and tables. (updated
reprinting of 1980 ed.; 1st ed. 1969.)
A major, high-quality general-reference world
atlas based on international collaboration in editing
and production, with text in English, German, Spanish, and French. To facilitate comparison among
areas, only four scales are used on regional
maps: 1:12,000,000, 1:6,000,000, 1:3,000,000, and
1:1,000,000. Special maps of the world's major urban
areas are scaled at 1:300,000. Primarily physical-
political maps, with relief shown by shading. Index has
about 160,000 names and indicates map location and
latitude and longitude. Includes glossary of geographical terms, world information table, and population of cities and town.

C658 Britannica atlas. Chicago: Encyclopaedia Britannica, 1979. 312p.; 222p. index. (Present ed.
basically from 1969)
Basic maps the same as in Rand McNally *Inter-*

national atlas. Feature of special interest is the "World scene" (p.283–320), with thematic maps of political, cultural, economic, and physical phenomena.

C659 Hammond, Inc. Hammond medallion world atlas. New census ed. Maplewood, N.J.: Hammond, 1982. Various paging. [672p.]

World and regional maps. Special features: (1) combines maps, index, and statistical data on each double-page layout; (2) political subdivisions of each country are shown. A complex assemblage of basic political maps supplemented by many smaller maps of physical features, economic characteristics, and special maps. Master index of more than 100,000 names. Includes separately paged sections: atlas of Bible lands (32p.), historical atlas (48p.), and U.S. history atlas (64p.). Very legible.

C660 Cosmopolitan world atlas. Census ed. Chicago: Rand McNally, 1981. Various paging.

About 300 maps, primarily political, with emphasis on the United States and Canada (separate map of each state and province). Index with 82,000 entries.

C661 The great geographical atlas. Chicago: Rand McNally in association with Istituto Geografico de Agostini, Novara, Italy, and Mitchell Beazley Publishers, London, 1982. 304p. Index.

Maps are by the Istituto Geografico de Agostini, supplemented by Rand McNally maps for North America. A 112-page encyclopedia section, prepared by Mitchell Beazley, discusses and illustrates astronomy, earth science, life sciences, environmental science, and cartography. The international map index contains more than 75,000 names; a separate index for Canada and the United States contains 24,000 names.

C662 Kartographisches Institut. Bertelsmann Atlas international. Ed. by W. Bormann. Text in English, French, and German. Gütersloh, W. Germany: C. Bertelsmann, 1975. Various pagings. (1st ed. 1963) (Amer. ed. McGraw-Hill international atlas. New York: McGraw-Hill, 1964. 544p.)

Regional physical maps. Special detailed section for Central Europe. Map scales comparable in various sections. Two separate indexes: world series of plates and Central European section. Total of about 175,000 names.

C663 Pergamon world atlas. Oxford and New York: Pergamon, 1968. 525p. Prepared and printed by the Polish Army Topographical Service (Wojsko Polskie, Służba Topograficzna).

Distinguished by large map-surface area, made possible by foldouts. Physical, thematic, and regional maps. Index of 150,000 names.

C664 Atlante internazionale del Touring Club Italiano. 8th ed. Milan: Consociazione Turistica Italiana, 1968. 2v. Maps and index. Updated reprinting 1977.

Detailed reference atlas with large number of place names. Well-designed and well-produced location maps. 93 maps on 173 plates. Relief by hachuring and shading. Index of about 250,000 names.

C665 Russia (1923– USSR). Glavnoe Upravlenie Geodezii i Kartografii (Chief Administration of Geodesy and Cartography). The world atlas. 2d ed. Moscow: 1967. 250 plates. (1st ed. 1954. 283 plates in Russian only)

English-language version of the revised 2d ed. of *Atlas Mira,* with all names in Latin letters and text in English. One of the really fine world atlases. The *Index-gazetteer* (Moscow: 1968, 1,010p.) includes all proper names found on the maps of the atlas, and indicates map location. About 200,000 names. Glossary of geographical terms and key to transliteration system.

Smaller Atlases

C666 Goode's world atlas. 16th ed. Ed. by Edward B. Espenshade, Jr., and Joel L. Morrison. Chicago: Rand McNally, 1982. 368p. (first pub. as Goode's school atlas, 1923. 96, 41p.)

The most widely used, and generally the best, American world atlas for school, home, or office. Convenient and up-to-date small atlas with thematic world maps of physical, cultural, and economic features and regional physical-political maps. Maps of major cities and environs with separate index. Table of world comparisons and data on principal countries and regions of the world. Pronouncing index of 32,000 geographical names, with map locations and latitude and longitude. Recommended for even the smallest library and as a convenient shelf-size atlas to be kept handy for frequent consultation, a source of first resort.

C667 The New York Times atlas of the world: in collaboration with the Times of London. Rev. ed. New York: Times Books, 1981. Various pagings. (1st ed. 1972; rev. ed. 1975, as The Times concise atlas of the world)

Excellent medium-size atlas. Introduction with thematic maps. General reference regional maps. Special maps of metropolitan areas. Index with 90,000 entries.

C668 The new Oxford atlas. Rev. ed. Prepared by the Cartographic Dept. of the Oxford Univ. Pr. London and New York: Oxford Univ. Pr., 1978. 202p. (Oxford atlas, first pub. 1951; New Oxford atlas, 1975)

Regional reference physical-political maps. Maps of oceans, physical environment of the continents. Thematic maps of the world and of the United Kingdom. Gazetteer with about 55,000 entries.

C669 National Geographic Society. Cartographic Div. National Geographic atlas of the world. Rev. 5th ed. Washington, D.C.: The Society, 1981. 383p. (1st ed. 1963. 300p.)

Primarily a location atlas with a large number of place names but also clear depiction of railroads, roads, and various cultural features and physical forms. Index records map location of about 150,000 place-names.

C670 Philip (George) and Son. The university atlas. 17th ed. Ed. by Harold Fullard and H.C.

Darby. London: Philip, 1975. 111p. (1st ed. 1937. 96p.)

High-quality small atlas with thematic world maps and regional physical-political maps. Tables of statistical information. Index of 46,000 names indicates map location and latitude and longitude.

Thematic Atlases

C671 Atlas international Larousse, politique et économique (Larousse international atlas, political and economic). Ed. by Ivan du Jonchay and Sandor Radó. Rev. ed. Paris: Larousse, 1965. 73 plates (some folded); 55p. index; 45p. statistical tables. (1st ed. 1950. 172p.)

Maps of physical, political, economic, and historical features. 300 statistical tables. Index-gazetteer with 30,000 entries. Text and annotations in English, French, and Spanish.

C672 Russia (1923–   , USSR). Glavnoe Upravlenie Geodezii i Kartografii: Institut Etnografii im. N.N. Miklukho-Maklaia Akademii Nauk SSR. Atlas narodov mira. Moscow: 1964. 184p.

Finest atlas of the world distribution of ethnic groups. Regional maps cover all parts of the world and give detailed distribution of each group. Excellent detail on minorities in traditional and rural societies, but less successful for Western and urban societies (which are more difficult to depict cartographically). Tables of numbers in each ethnic group in 1961 (based primarily on language), by group and by region. In Russian. Alphabetical index of names of groups with equivalents in Latin letters.

C673 Al-Faruqi, Isma'il R., and David E. Sopher. Historical atlas of the religions of the world. New York: Macmillan, 1974. 346p.

Discusses religions of the past, ethnic religions of the present, and universalistic religions of the present. 65 maps. Chronologies. Illustrations. Bibliographies.

C674 Oxford economic atlas of the world. 4th ed. Prepared by the Cartographic Dept. of Clarendon Pr. London: Oxford Univ. Pr., 1972. 248p. (1st ed. 1955. 113, 152p.)

World dot maps of production areas of major commodities, especially agricultural and mineral. Regional reference maps. Extensive statistical tables of yields, production, and trade by country. Subject index to the maps and country index to the tables. Accompanying text. Also available as *The shorter Oxford economic atlas of the world*, without country statistical tables (128p.).

C675 Humlum, Johannes, and H. Sylvain Thomson. Kulturgeografisk atlas. Atlas of economic geography. 7th ed. Copenhagen: Gyldendal, 1975. 142p. (1st ed. 1944. 88p.)

Production and trade in agricultural, mineral, and industrial products, water-power, and traffic by various means of transportation. World maps of production and trade by country, with insets of major

areas of production. Subject and place index. Captions and text in Danish and English.

C676 Ginsburg, Norton S. Atlas of economic development. Chicago: Univ. of Chicago Pr., 1961. 119p.

World maps with text and tables of factors in economic development. Ranking of countries on diverse characteristics of the population, resource endowment, accessibility, technology and industrialization, and external relations.

C677 World atlas of agriculture: under the aegis of the International Association of Agricultural Economists. Land utilization maps and relief maps prepared by the Committee for the World atlas of agriculture. Novara, Italy: Istituto Geografico de Agostini; New York: Unipub, 1969–76. 62 plates.

Land utilization maps by major world regions. Sources indicated for each map. Accompanied by monographs on major world regions, edited by the Committee for the *World atlas of agriculture:*

v.1. Europe, U.S.S.R., Asia Minor. 1972.

v.2. South and East Asia, Oceania. 1973. 671p.

v.3. The Americas. 1970. 497p.

v.4. Africa. 1976. 760p.

C678 Van Royen, William. The agricultural resources of the world. v.1 of Atlas of the world's resources. New York: Prentice-Hall, 1954. 258p.

Prepared in cooperation with the U.S. Bureau of Agricultural Economics. Worldwide survey by crops and types of livestock. Maps, tables, and text. References. Basic data on areal distribution of production and factors in that distribution.

C679 ——, and Oliver Bowles. The mineral resources of the world. v.2 of Atlas of the world's resources. New York: Prentice-Hall, 1952. 181p.

Survey of the world's mineral resources, including major resources, such as coal, petroleum, waterpower, and iron ore, and minor minerals. Maps, tables, and text by specialists for each mineral. Authoritative, informative, and useful.

C680 Russia (1923–   , USSR). Akademiia Nauk SSSR: Glavnoe Upravlenie Geodezii i Kartografii GGK SSSR. Fizikogeograficheskii atlas mira. Moscow: 1964. 289p.

Superb atlas of distribution of principal physical features of the earth. World thematic maps and a series of continental maps, including many maps of the USSR. Includes relief, tectonics, geology, minerals, earthquakes and volcanoes, quaternary deposits, sediments of the oceans, geomorphology, climatic zones and regions, annual march of climatic elements, radiation, evaporation, radiation balance, heat loss and exchange, air temperature, frost-free periods, circulation of the atmosphere, air pressure and winds, precipitation, characteristics of ocean waters, lakes, runoff, soils, vegetation, zoogeography, and natural landscapes. Prepared in Russian by scientists of the Academy of Sciences of the USSR. An English translation of all legends and text is available as "Physical-geographic atlas of the world, Moscow, 1964," a special issue of *Soviet geography: review and translation* (May–June 1965, 403p.).

National and Regional Atlases

C681   The national atlas of the United States of America. Washington, D.C.: U.S. Geological Survey, 1970. 417p.

Beautiful atlas of the United States, its regions, and major characteristics depicted on special-subject maps of land forms, geophysical forces, geology, marine features, soil, climate, water, history, fishing and forestry, agriculture, mineral and energy resources, manufacturing, business, transportation, socio-cultural characteristics, administrative structure, and mapping and charting. Produced in cooperation with many governmental agencies and non-governmental institutions. Index of 41,000 names showing map location, population, and latitude and longitude.

C682   Rand McNally and Co. Commercial atlas and marketing guide. 1984. 115th ed. Chicago: Rand McNally, 1984. 562p. (first pub. as Rand McNally & Co.'s Business atlas . . . , 1876–1877. 112p.)

The most detailed listing and mapping of cities and towns of the United States with over 128,000 places described in the index, with data on U.S. transportation and communication systems, economics, and population figures from the 1980 census. Also sections of data for Canada and the rest of the world. Maps of each state emphasize railroads.

C683   Oxford University Press. The United States and Canada. 2d ed. Prepared by the Cartographic Dept. of the Oxford Univ. Pr., John D. Chapman and John C. Sherman, advisory eds. Prepared with the assistance of Quentin H. Stanford. London and New York: Oxford Univ. Pr. 1975. 128p. Unpaged index. (1st ed. 1967. 128p.) [Oxford regional economic atlas]

Well-done atlas of Anglo-America; particularly useful in treating the United States and Canada together. Urban plans (of larger cities), regional relief maps, and many aspects of physical geography, demography, agriculture, forestry, fishing, fuels and energy, mining and industry, and transport. Gazetteer index gives map location and latitude and longitude of about 10,000 places.

C684   Rooney, John F., Jr., and others, eds. This remarkable continent: an atlas of United States and Canadian society and culture. College Station: Texas A & M Univ. Pr. for the Soc. for the North American Cultural Survey, 1982. 316p.

Wide-ranging coverage of cultural and popular regions, settlement, division of the land, structures, social organization and behavior, language and place names, ethnicity, religion, politics, foodways, music and dance, sports and games, and place perception.

C685   The national atlas of Canada. 4th ed. Toronto: Macmillan of Canada, in association with the Department of Energy, Mines and Resources, and Information Canada, Ottawa; New York: Books Canada, 1974. 254p., plus sources, 12p. (1st ed. 1906; 3d ed. 1957)

All major aspects of the physical and economic geography and demography of Canada.

C686   Canada gazetteer atlas. Toronto: Macmillan of Canada in cooperation with Energy, Mines and Resources Canada, and the Canadian Government Publishing Centre. Supply and Services Canada; Chicago: Univ. of Chicago Pr., 1980. 164p.

Consists of 48 regional maps and a detailed index, with population data collected for the 1976 Census on Canada.

C687   Kerr, Donald G.G. An historical atlas of Canada. 3d ed. Toronto: Nelson, 1975. 100p. (1st ed. 1960. 120p.; 2d ed. 1966. 120p.)

Canadian exploration, settlement, socioeconomic development, and international relations are depicted in new maps, contemporary drawings, and text.

C688   Atlas of Britain and North Ireland. Executed by the Cartographic Dept. of the Clarendon Pr. Oxford: Clarendon, 1963. 200p. 24p. gazetteer.

Excellent maps of the United Kingdom as a whole, covering a wide range of physical, economic, and demographic features. Regional maps for physical features, population, and general reference.

C689   Russia (1923– , USSR). Glavnoe Upravlenie Geodezii i Kartografii (Chief Administration of Geodesy and Cartography). Atlas SSSR. 3d ed. Moscow: 1983. 259p. (1st ed. 1962. 185p.; 2d ed. 1969. 199p.)

Best available current atlas of the vast territory of the Soviet Union. Regional physical-administrative maps. Thematic maps of the Soviet Union as a whole, both physical and economic. Maps of economic regions record types of agriculture, mining, and manufacturing. Index of about 25,000 names.

C690   Atlas of Africa. Prepared by Jeune Afrique under direction of Regine van Chi-Bonnardel. New York: Free Pr., 1973. 335p. (French ed. Paris: Editions Jeune Afrique).

Includes both general thematic maps for Africa as a whole and individual maps for each country. Maps and text valuable for reference and study.

C691   Schwartzberg, Joseph E., ed. A historical atlas of South Asia. Chicago: Univ. of Chicago Pr., 1978. 352p.

Superb record of the development of culture in South Asia, with text, illustrations, and maps by leading specialists. Extensive bibliography.

C692 The Times atlas of China. P. J.M. Geelan and D.C. Twitchett, eds. New York: Quadrangle/ New York Times, 1974. 144, 27p.

125 colored maps or map insets. Index with 20,000 entries.

GEOGRAPHICAL SERIALS
Inventories

C693 Harris, Chauncy D., and Jerome D. Fellmann. International list of geographical serials. 3d ed. Chicago: Univ. of Chicago Dept. of Geography, 1980. 457p. [Research paper no. 193]

A comprehensive inventory of geographical serials both current and closed. Lists 3,445 serials from 107 countries in 55 languages. Arranged by country. Entries include reference to the title location in *Union list of serials, New serial titles,* or *British union catalogue of periodicals* where library holdings are recorded for the United States, Canada, and the United Kingdom. Entries in non-Latin alphabets and other writing systems are given both in transliterated form and in the original (such as Chinese and Japanese characters and the Cyrillic alphabet). Addresses of publishers given for current serials. Indexes noted. Alphabetical index includes former and variant names.

C694 Harris, Chauncy D. Annotated world list of selected current geographical serials. 4th ed. Chicago: Univ. of Chicago Dept. of Geography, 1980. 165p. [Research paper 194]

443 current geographical serials from 72 countries selected on the basis of quality of geographic material; frequency, regularity and longevity of publication; number of citations in international bibliographies; and availability in major libraries. Information provided on title, issuing agency, place of publication, date of first issue, frequency of publication, name and address of editor, name and address of publisher, abstracts, basic and supplementary languages. Annotations note nature of contents and coverage. (Includes study of serials most cited in geographical bibliographies.)

C695 Bibliography and review of geography department discussion papers, occasional papers, and monographs, comp. by Bruce Young. v.4. Waterloo, Ontario: Wilfrid Laurier Univ. Dept. of Geography, June 1980. 167p. (v.1, 1974; v.2, 1976, v.3, 1978).

Geographical series in English from 109 universities: Australia and New Zealand (10), United Kingdom (24), Canada (27), United States (42), and other countries (6). List of papers in each series but often without the number, date, or other bibliographical data. Each volume includes all entries from previous volumes, so only the latest is needed. Particularly valuable in tracing fugitive materials in semipublished discussion papers.

C696 Schmidt, Rolf D., and Charlotte Streumann. Verzeichnis der geographischen Zeitschriften, periodischen Veröffentlichungen und Schriftenreihen Deutschlands und der in den letzeren erschienenen Arbeiten. Bad Godesberg, W. Germany: Bundesanstalt für Landeskunde und Raumforschung, 1964. 303p. [Berichte zur deutschen Landeskunde. Sonderheft 7.]

Lists 393 German geographical serials with full bibliographical details, including name changes, issuing agencies, names of editors. Indexes for names of authors and editors, titles, sponsoring institutions and places, and places treated in the listed monographs. Covers directories, bibliographies, periodicals, and nonperiodical series. Particularly useful in listing individual titles in the many German monographic series.

Periodicals in Geography

C697 Forty-seven geographical periodicals in Western languages of the widest international scholarly and bibliographical interest are listed below in alphabetical order. These are published in 18 countries in 6 languages: 28 are in English, 8 in French, 6 in German, 2 each in Spanish and Italian, and 1 in Portuguese.

American cartographer. v.1– , 1974– . Falls Church, Va.: American Congress on Surveying and Mapping. Semiannual.

Articles on all aspects of cartography. Reviews. Recent literature.

BGI; Cc; GeoAbst.

Annales de géographie: bulletin de la Société de Géographie. v.1– , 1891– . Paris: Colin. Bimonthly. Indexes: 1891–1901, 1902–11, 1912–21, 1922–31, 1932–51, 1952–61, 1962–71, 1972–81.

A key international journal with broad coverage of the field and the literature. In French. Abstracts in English.

BGI; GeoAbst; SSCI.

Association de géographes français. Bulletin. v.1– , 1924– . Paris. Bimonthly. Indexes: 1924–34, 1955–75.

A leading scholarly French geographical periodical with articles often in the forefront of geographic thought. In French. Abstracts in English.

BGI; GeoAbst.

Assn. of American Geographers. Annals. v.1– , 1911– . Washington, D.C. Quarterly. Indexes: v.1–25 (1910–35), v.26–55 (1936–65), v.56–65 (1966–75).

The leading scholarly geographical periodical of the U.S.

BGI; BiolAbst; GeoAbst; SSCI; SSI.

Australian geographer. (Geographical Society of New South Wales) v.1– , 1928– . North Ryde, New South Wales. Semiannual. Index every 3 years.

Specializes in Australia.

AustPAIS; BGI; GeoAbst.

Australian geographical studies. 1963– . Canberra: Australian National Univ. Institute of Australian Geographers. Semiannual.
Scholarly journal of academic geographers of Australia.
AustPAIS; BGI; Cc; GeoAbst; SSCI.

Cahiers de géographie du Québec. v.1– , 1956– . Québec: Les Presses de l'Université Laval. 3 per annum. Indexes: 1956–73, 1974–81.
Devoted to French Canada and to general problems of cultural, economic, and regional geography. In French or occasionally English.
Abstracts in French and English.
BGI; GeoAbst.

Cahiers d'Outre-Mer: revue de géographie. v.1– , 1948– . Bordeaux. Quarterly. Indexes: 1948–57, 1958–67, 1968–77.
Geographical articles of wide interest on all parts of the Third World in Latin America, Africa, and Asia. In French. Abstracts in English.
BGI; GeoAbst.

Canadian geographer. (Canadian Assn. of Geographers) v.1– , 1951– . Montreal: McGill Univ. Quarterly. Index: 1951–67.
The principal scholarly and professional geographical periodical of Canada.
BGI; BullSig; Cc; Chem Abst; GeoAbst; SSCI; SSI.

Cartographica. v.1– , 1964– . Toronto: Univ. of Toronto Pr. Quarterly. Index: 1964–73.
(Formerly: the Canadian cartographer and Cartographica monographs)
Contributions to geographical cartography. Book reviews. Recent cartographic literature. Cartographic monographs.
BGI; Cc; GeoAbst.

Economic geography. v.1– , 1925– . Worcester, Mass.: Clark Univ. Quarterly. Indexes: v.1–25 (1925–49), v.26–41 (1950–65).
International journal devoted entirely to economic geography.
BGI; BiolAbst; Cc; GeoAbst; PAIS; SSCI; SSI.

Erde: Zeitschrift der Gesellschaft für Erdkunde zu Berlin. v.1– , 1853– . Berlin. Quarterly. Indexes: 1853–63, 1863–1901.
Major international scholarly journal of long standing and high current value. In German. English titles in table of contents and English abstracts.
BGI; BiolAbst; GeoAbst.

Erdkunde: Archiv für wissenschaftliche Geographie. v.1– , 1947– . Bonn: Ferd. Dümmler. Quarterly. Index: v.1–17 (1947–63).
A key international scientific periodical with wide range of coverage. In German. English titles in table of contents, long English abstracts, and some articles in English. Reviews.
BGI; GeoAbst.

Estudios geográficos. v.1– , 1940– . Madrid: Consejo Superior de Investigaciones Científicas.

Quarterly. Indexes: v.1–37 (1940–49), v.38–77 (1950–59), v.78–117 (1960–69), v.118–57 (1970–79).
Leading geographical periodical of Spain. In Spanish. Abstracts in English.
BGI; GeoAbst.

Geoforum: the international multi-disciplinary journal for the rapid publication of research results and critical review articles in the physical, human, and regional geosciences. v.1– , 1970– . Oxford: Pergamon. Quarterly.
Part of each issue is usually devoted to a particular aspect of human-land relationships.
BGI; GeoAbst.

Geografiska annaler. Ser. B. Human geography. v.47B– , 1965– . v.1– , 1919– . Stockholm: Almqvist and Wiksell. Semiannual.
An outstanding international scientific periodical, largely in English.
BGI; GeoAbst.

Geographica Helvetica. v.1– , 1946– . Egg/ZH, Switzerland: Fotorotor AG. Quarterly.
Some specialization on Switzerland but articles on other parts of the world and systematic topics. In German.
BiolAbst; BGI; GeoAbst.

Geographical analysis; an international journal of theoretical geography. v.1– , 1969– . Columbus: Ohio State Univ. Pr. Quarterly. Index for v.1–10 (1969–78) in v.10.
Theoretical, systematic, and quantitative studies in geography.
BGI; Cc; GeoAbst; SSCI.

Geographical journal. v.1– , 1893– . London: Royal Geographical Society. Quarterly. Indexes: v.1–20 (1893-1902), v.21–40 (1903–12), v.41–60 (1913–22), v.61–80 (1923–32), v.81–100 (1933–42), v.101–20 (1943–54), v.121–30 (1955–64), 131–40 (1965–74).
International journal of long standing. Strong on geographic exploration and physical geography of deserts, glaciers, and mountains. Extensive review section.
BGI; BrHumInd; Cc; GeoAbst; PAIS; SSCI; SSI.

Geographical magazine. v.1– , 1935– . London: Magnum Distribution. Monthly. Index: v.23–45 (1950–72).
Combines sound scholarship with nontechnical, popular, interesting, and well-illustrated presentation. Informative professional news and notes, particularly on British geography and geographers.
BGI; BrHumInd; GeoAbst; PAIS; SSI.

Geographical review. v.1– , 1916– . New York: American Geographical Society. Quarterly. Indexes: v.1–15 (1916–25), v.16–25 (1926–35), v.26–35 (1936–45), v.36–45 (1946–55), v.46–55 (1956–65).
Key international journal with well-edited, authoritative articles on wide range of topics and exten-

sive and comprehensive signed notes and critical reviews.

> AbstAnthro; BGI; BiolAbst; Cc; ChemAbst; GeoAbst; HistAbst; PAIS; SSCI; SSI.

Geographische Zeitschrift. v.1–50, 1895–1944; v.51– , 1963– . Wiesbaden, W. Germany: Steiner. Quarterly. Index: v.1–50 (1895–1944).

> Scholarly articles. In German. English titles in table of contents and English abstracts.
> BGI; GeoAbst; SSCI.

Geography. (Geographical Association) v.1– , 1901– . London: George Philip and Son. Quarterly. Index: v.1–54 (1901–69).

> Substantive articles and articles on geography in education.
> BGI; BrEdInd; Cc; GeoAbst; SSI.

GeoJournal: international journal for physical, biological and human geosciences and their application in environmental planning and ecology. v.1– , 1977– . Wiesbaden, W. Germany: Akademische Verlagsgesellschaft. Bimonthly.

> International authorship. Each issue devoted in part to papers on a related theme. In English.
> BGI; GeoAbst.

Institute of British Geographers. Transactions. v.1–66, 1935–75; n.s. v.1– , 1976. London Quarterly. Index for v.1–42 (1935–67) in v.42.

> The leading British scholarly periodical in geography.
> BGI; GeoAbst; SSCI.

Journal of historical geography. v.1– , 1975– . London: Academic Pr. Quarterly.

> Scholarly articles on historical geography, with a wide range of areas and periods covered. Extensive reviews.
> BGI; Cc; GeoAbst; SSI.

Méditerranée: revue géographique des pays Méditerranéens. v.1– , 1960– . Aix-en-Provence: Université d'Aix Marseille II. Quarterly. Indexes: v.1–10 (1960–69).

> Devoted to all aspects of the geography of the Mediterranean region. In French. Abstracts in English.
> BGI; GeoAbst.

New Zealand geographer. (New Zealand Geographical Society) v.1– , 1945– . Christchurch, New Zealand: Univ. of Canterbury. Semiannual. Index: v.1–25 (1945–69).

> Specializes in New Zealand but has broad interest.
> BGI; BiolAbst; GeoAbst.

Norois: revue géographique de l'Ouest et des pays de l'Atlantique Nord. v.1– , 1954– . Poitiers. Quarterly. Indexes: 1954–63, 1964–73.

> Of international interest for articles on West of France, the Low Countries, Britain, the North Atlantic, and North America. Table of contents in English and in French. English abstracts.
> BGI; GeoAbst.

Österreichische Geographische Gesellschaft. Mitteilungen. v.1– , 1857– . Vienna. Semiannual. Indexes: 1857–1907, 1908–59, 1960–80.

> Long-established major scholarly geographical periodical. Bibliography of Austrian geography. In German. English abstracts.
> BGI; GeoAbst; SSCI.

Pacific viewpoint. v.1– , 1960– . Wellington, New Zealand: Victoria Univ. of Wellington Dept. of Geography. Semiannual. Index: 1960–64.

> Articles on Asian and Pacific areas and on economic growth and social change.
> BGI; GeoAbst.

Petermanns geographische Mitteilungen (Geographische Gesellschaft der DDR). v.1– , 1855– . Gotha, E. Germany: Hermann Haack. Quarterly. Indexes: 1855–64, 1865–74, 1875–84, 1885–94, 1895–1904, 1905–34.

> International scholarly geographical periodical of long standing. Some specialization on Central and Eastern Europe. Reviews. In German. English titles in table of contents and English abstracts.
> BGI; Cc; GeoAbst; SSCI.

Polar geography and geology. v.1– , 1977– . Silver Spring, Md.: V.H. Winston. Quarterly.

> English translations of current Soviet, Japanese, and West European research on the Arctic and Antarctic.
> BGI; GeoAbst.

Political geography quarterly. v.1– , 1982– . Guildford, Eng.: Butterworth Scientific. Journals Div. Quarterly.

> New journal devoted to the field of political geography.
> BGI; GeoAbst.

Professional geographer. n.s. v.1– , 1949– . Washington, D.C.: Assn. of American Geographers. Quarterly. Index for 1946–66 in v.19, no.2 (1967).

> Short articles, professional notes, official notices and reports of the association, news of members and centers of geographic work, short book reviews, discussions, and contents of foreign journals.
> BGI; Cc; GeoAbst; SSI.

Progress in human geography: an international review of geographical work in the social sciences and humanities. v.1– , 1977– . London: Edward Arnold; New York: Cambridge Univ. Pr. Quarterly.

> Surveys of the state of the art in the fields of human geography. Progress reports. Book review essays and book reviews. Best journal for following the literature and frontiers in human geography. See C472 for analysis.
> BGI; GeoAbst.

Revista brasileira de geografia. v.1– , 1939– . Rio de Janeiro: Fundação Instituto Brasileiro de Geografia e Estatística. Quarterly. Index: v.1–10 (1939–48).

The most substantial national geographic periodical publication of Latin America. Research articles on all aspects of geography of Brazil. In Portuguese. Abstracts in English.
BGI; BiolAbst; BullSig; GeoAbst.

Revista geográfica. v.1– , 1941– . Mexico: Instituto Panamericano de Geografía e História. Semiannual. Indexes: v.1–63 (1941–65), 64–77 (1966–72), 78–90 (1973–79).
The leading international geographical periodical devoted to the Americas. In Spanish, English, Portuguese, or French, with abstracts in a second language.
BGI; GeoAbst.

Rivista geografica italiana. v.1– , 1893– . Pisa: Pacini Editore. Quarterly. Indexes: v.1–50 (1894–1943), v.51–60 (1944–53).
Scholarly Italian geographical periodical of high quality and international reputation. Bibliographical notes and reviews. In Italian. English titles in annual table of contents and English abstracts.
BGI; GeoAbst.

Revue géographique de l'Est. v.1– , 1961– . Nancy, France: Presses Universitaires de Nancy. Quarterly. Index: v.1–20 (1961–80).
Devoted particularly to the east of France, Central and Eastern Europe, and the Middle East. In French. Abstracts in English.
BGI; GeoAbst.

Società Geografica Italiana. Bollettino. v.1– , 1868– . Rome. Monthly. Numbers often combined. Indexes: 1868–75, 1876–87, 1888–99, 1900–1911, 1912–23, 1924–35.
Major Italian geographical periodical of long standing, with wide range of articles, notes, and reviews. In Italian. English titles in table of contents and English abstracts.
BGI; GeoAbst.

Société Belge d'Études Géographiques. Bulletin. Belgische Vereniging voor Aardrijkskundige Studies. Tijdschrift. v.1– , 1931– . Leuven. Semiannual. In French or Dutch. Abstracts in English in front of each number. Indexes: 1931–40, 1941–50, 1951–60, 1961–70, 1971–80.
Belgian scholarly geographical periodical with reviews and bibliographical notes.
BGI; GeoAbst.

Soviet geography; review and translation. v.1– , 1960– . Silver Spring, Md.: V. H. Winston. Monthly except July and Aug.
Translations into English of major articles from the principal Soviet geographical periodicals. News notes. Tables of contents of latest issues of Soviet geographical journals.
BGI; GeoAbst; SSCI.

Special Libraries Association. Geography and Map Division. Bulletin. v.1– , 1947– . Washington, D.C. Quarterly. Indexes: 1–70 (1947–67), 71–102 (1968–75).

Articles on maps and geography, map and book bibliographies, notes on map libraries. News. Reference aids. New atlases, maps, books, and government publications. Reviews.
GeoAbst.

Tijdschrift voor economische en sociale geografie. Journal of economic and social geography. v.1– , 1910– . Amsterdam: Koninklijk Nederlands Aardrijkskundig Genootschap. Bimonthly. Index: v.1–25 (1910–34), 26–43 (1935–52).
Outstanding international journal of economic and human geography. Worldwide in coverage and authorship. In English. English abstracts.
BGI; Cc; GeoAbst; PAIS; SSCI.

Urban geography. v.1– , 1980– . Silver Spring, Md.: V. H. Winston. Quarterly.
New journal devoted to research articles and book reviews in urban geography.
BGI; GeoAbst.

Interdisciplinary Serials

C698 Four interdisciplinary serials in English include substantial fractions of articles and reviews of geographic work in the study of cities and regions.

Environment and planning A. International journal of urban and regional research. v.1– , 1969– . London: Pion. Monthly.
BGI; Cc; GeoAbst.

Regional Science Association. Papers. v.1– , 1954– . Urbana, Ill.: Regional Science Association. 3v. a year.
BGI; GeoAbst.

Regional studies. Journal of the Regional Studies Association. v.1– . 1967– . Cambridge: Cambridge Univ. Pr. Bimonthly.
BGI; Cc; GeoAbst; SSCI.

Society and space. Environment and planning D. v.1– , 1983– . London: Pion. Quarterly.

Monograph Series in Geography

C699

California Univ. Publications in geography. v.1– , 1915– . Berkeley and Los Angeles. Irregularly.
Original research monographs, especially in cultural, historical, and physical geography.

Univ. of Chicago Dept. of Geography. Research papers. v.1– , 1948– . Chicago. Irregularly.
Original research monographs, collected works, and bibliographies in cultural, economic, urban, historical, regional, and ecological geography.

ORGANIZATIONS

The International Geographical Union has about 90 member countries. The location of the secretariat changes. For the period 1984–88 the Secretary-General is Prof. Leszek A. Kosinski, Dept. of Geography, University of Alberta, Edmonton, Alberta, Canada T6G 2H4.

The principal geographical organization in the United States is the Association of American Geographers, 1710 16th St., N.W., Washington, DC 20009.

The principal geographical organization in Canada is the Canadian Association of Geographers, Burnside Hall, McGill University, 805 Sherbrooke St. West, Montreal, P.Q. H3A 2K6, Canada.

The main association of geographers in Britain is the Institute of British Geographers, 1 Kensington Gore, London, SW7 2AR, England. The Royal Geographical Society, Kensington Gore, London, SW7 2AR, England, is the most important geographical society in the English-speaking world.

C700 Orbis geographicus 1980/1984. World directory of geography. Ed. by E. Meynen. Wiesbaden, W. Germany: Steiner, 1982. Pt. 1, societies, institutes, agencies, p.1–246 (Previous eds. 1960, 1964, 1970).

Best worldwide source of comprehensive information on geographical centers. Names, addresses, and personnel of geographical and cartographical societies, departments of geography in universities, and official governmental agencies for general or regional geography. Also information on polar studies, cartographic and topographic surveys, hydrographic and oceanographic offices, map collections, and geographical names. Includes national committees, commissions, officers, and statutes of the International Geographical Union. Index of persons.

C701 Association of American Geographers. Guide to departments of geography in the United States and Canada. 1968/1969– . Annual. Washington, D.C.: 1968– . (1968/1969–1983/1984 as Guide to graduate departments . . .)

Annual guide to departments of geography in the U.S. and Canada. Information includes addresses and telephone numbers, degrees offered, number of degrees awarded and number of graduate students in residence, programs and research facilities, academic plans and requirements, financial aid, list of staff with degrees and specializations, and titles of dissertations and theses completed in previous years. Handy, authoritative, up to date.

For information on staff, research, and publications of university departments of geography and government departments in Canada, see the annual *Directory* of the Canadian Association of Geographers discussed at C613.

C703 "Anschriften von Behörden, Institutionen und Organisationen," *Geographisches Taschenbuch und Jahrweiser für Landeskunde*, hrsg. E. Ehlers and E. Meynen. 1949– . Wiesbaden, W. Germany: Franz Steiner. About every two years.

The 1983/1984 issue, p.121-293, provides a detailed listing of geographical institutes in universities, geographical societies, cartographic establishments, and government agencies in the Federal Republic of Germany, Austria, and Switzerland, and a briefer list of such centers in the German Democratic Republic.

C704 Fuchs, Roland J., and John M. Street, eds. Geography in Asian universities. Honolulu: Oriental Publishing [1975]. 522p.

Survey of university work in geography, country by country, in Asia.

SOURCES OF CURRENT INFORMATION

C705 The geographical digest. London: Philip, 1963– . Annual.

Concise data on recent changes in the world: political, administrative, names, population, agricultural production, manufacturing and mining, trade, projects, communications, conservation, exploration, and natural catastrophes.

C706 Cartactual: map service bi-monthly. v.1– , 1965– . Budapest. Bimonthly. Index for v.1–16 (1965–68).

Special maps on timely topics, such as new countries and administrative divisions, disputed areas, pipelines, canals, highways, railroads, air routes, ports, city population and boundaries, reservoirs, gas fields, power plants, and place names. In English, French, and German.

C707 U.S. Department of State. Office of the Geographer. International boundary studies. v.1– , 1961– . Irregularly.

Authoritative studies of the official status of international boundaries. Each number is devoted to a single boundary or country. Maps.

Chauncy D. Harris

4 Economics and Business Administration

213

Survey of the Field

Economics is a social science that is concerned with how people, either individually or in groups, attempt to accommodate scarce resources to their wants through the processes of production, substitution, and exchange. In other words, economics may be described as the study of the production, distribution, and consumption of material goods and services that are destined to fulfill the needs of persons and groups in human societies. This definition of economics is both too wide and too narrow, depending upon one's point of view, but it describes rather well the common concern of most persons who regard themselves as economists.

SYSTEMATIC SURVEYS

In the course of its development since the eighteenth century, when the first systematic attempt was made to treat economics in its entirety, students of economics have given major stress to different parts of the discipline at different times. At all times, however, economists have been concerned with four main problems. (1) They have attempted to develop a body of general principles of human behavior in the realms of production, distribution, and consumption of goods and services. This is economic theory. (2) They have attempted to find ways and means of measuring (more or less accurately) the performance of an economic system and the magnitude of certain rates of change that seemed significant. This is economic methodology and measurement. (3) They have attempted to discuss the steps that should be taken by governments or private groups and individuals to bring about certain desired results within the realm of economic activity. This is economic policy. (4) They have tried to explain the state of the economy of their time as a result of developments in the past, with the hope of adding

thereby to their insight into theoretical, methodological, and policy prescriptions. This is economic history. This survey of the literature will take up all these fields in order.

In the course of the development of economics as a discipline, many attempts were made to provide all-embracing systematic surveys of the field. In the following, we list a few of the most successful and representative studies of different periods.

D1   Boulding, Kenneth E. Economics as a science. New York: McGraw-Hill, 1970. 157p.

D2   Lipsey, Richard G., and Peter Steiner. Economics. 7th ed. New York: Harper, 1983. 1,024p.

D3   Marshall, Alfred. Principles of economics. 9th (variorum) ed., with annotations by C. W. Guillebaud. London: Macmillan, 1961. 2v.

D4   Mill, John Stuart. Principles of political economy. New York: Kelley, 1965. 1,013p. (reprint of 1909 ed.)

D5   Samuelson, Paul A., and William Nordhaus. Economics. 12th ed. New York: McGraw-Hill, 1984. 950p.

In addition to the treatises and comprehensive textbooks that purport to deal with economics as a whole, some attempts have been made to enlist the collaboration of several workers for the purpose of producing encyclopedic treatments of economics. There is no genuine encyclopedia of economics, but economics has been made the major center of a quasi-encyclopedic handbook edited by R. H. Inglis Palgrave and reprinted several times, with additions and changes. For a fuller description see the entry at D682. Moreover, several social science encyclopedias have given a prominent place to economics. The two recent encyclopedic productions in the social sciences that devote well over a quarter of their space to economics are listed below, in addition to the work by Palgrave.

D7   Seligman, Edwin R. A., and others. Encyclopaedia of the social sciences. New York: Macmillan, 1930–35. 15v.

D8   Sills, David L., ed. International encyclopedia of the social sciences. New York: Macmillan and Free Pr., 1968. 17v.

HISTORICAL DEVELOPMENT

Although comprehensive treatments of economics do not antedate the late eighteenth century, economic problems had been the subject of literary efforts long before that time. The catalogs of the Kress Collection at Harvard University and the Goldsmith Library of Economic Literature at London University, for example, mention several hundred tracts and pamphlets, as well as books, that appeared long before Adam Smith's *The wealth of nations* (see D35). Some of these publications are extremely interesting, not merely from an antiquarian standpoint but also as contributions to history and the development of theoretical ideas—and in some instances even as guides for policy. They and, of course, the later economic literature have been dealt with descriptively and analytically in a number of ways. First, there is a series of general histories of economic thought, many of which are textbooks that were occasioned by the fact that courses in this field are common in American colleges and universities. But there also are some highly original works in this field, ranging from compilations of titles that are scarcely more than annotated bibliographies to original analyses. Some treat the whole sweep of economic history, from its earliest manifestations in the writings of authors of antiquity to authors of the present century.

D9   Blaug, Mark. Economic theory in retrospect. 3d ed. London: Cambridge Univ. Pr., 1978. 756p.

D10 Roll, Erich. History of economic thought. 4th ed. Homewood, Ill.: Irwin, 1974. 626p.

D11 Schumpeter, Joseph A. History of economic analysis. Ed. by Elizabeth B. Schumpeter. New York: Oxford Univ. Pr., 1954. 1,260p.

D12 Spengler, Joseph J., and William R. Allen, eds. Essays in economic thought: Aristotle to Marshall. Chicago: Rand McNally, 1960. 800p.

D13 Stigler, George J. Essays in the history of economics. Chicago: Univ. of Chicago Pr., 1965. 206p.

Other works deal with special periods or "schools" of economics. The period before the crystallization of economics as a discipline has been very attractive to many students, and proportionally more publications are available on economic thought before the year 1800 than on the period during which economic thought grew to full stature. The best works in this literature cover a broader area than merely technical economics. In tracing the development of economic ideas it is often necessary to include the general political and philosophical thought of a period, and some of these works, though principally in economics, should be considered general intellectual histories of a particular period or movement.

D14 Cannan, Edwin. A history of the theories of production and distribution in English political economy from 1776 to 1848. New York: Kelley, 1967. 336p. (reprint of 1917 ed.)

D15 Gruchy, Allan G. Contemporary economic thought: the American contribution. Clifton, N.J.: Kelley, 1972. 360p.

D16 Halévy, Elie. The growth of philosophic radicalism. 3d ed. London: Faber, 1972. 554p.

D17 Heckscher, Eli F. Mercantilism. 2d ed. New York: Macmillan, 1962. 2v.

D18 Hume, David. Writings on economics. Ed., with introduction by E. Rotwein. Madison: Univ. of Wisconsin Pr., 1955. 224p.

D19 Johnson, Edgar A. J. Predecessors of Adam Smith. New York: Kelley, 1960. 426p. (reprint of 1937 ed.)

D20 Maddison, Angus. Economic growth in the West; comparative experience in Europe and North America. New York: Twentieth Century, 1964. 246p.

D21 Robbins, Lionel. The theory of economic policy in English classical political economy. 2d ed. Philadelphia: Porcupine Pr., 1978. 217p.

D22 Stephen, Leslie. The English utilitarians. New York: Kelley, 1968. 3v. (reprint of 1900 ed.)

D23 Weulersse, Georges. Le mouvement physiocratique en France. New York: Johnson Reprint, 1968. 2v. (reprint of 1910 Paris ed.)

COLLECTED WORKS AND TRACTS

All these works are secondary sources; although they discuss the development of economic ideas and theories, they present only excerpts from the works of the authors of these ideas, and in many cases they discuss, question, alter, and interpret these ideas in ways that would have surprised—and sometimes perhaps even shocked—the original writers. Yet the continuing concern with these works reflects, in large measure, the challenge that these older writers presented and the many instructive lessons that could be learned from them. Hence it is not surprising that, at various times, the collected writings of the great economists were published to provide as full and comprehensive a documentation as possible of their own words and reasoning. For example, at the time of the 1976 celebration of the two hundredth anniversary of the publication of *The wealth of nations* by Adam Smith, a list of his major works and important books by and about him was issued. It is too long to include here, but the chief works are cited. In some instances, nationalistic or other political considerations played a role. For example, the publication of the writings of Friedrich List was motivated, in part, by the urge to present to the German public the challenging ideas of a great German economist. Many of these editions, however, were produced on thoroughly scholarly lines, and several may be regarded as constituting the *editio princeps* of the writings of several great economists.

Listed below is a series of the most interesting sets of these collected works. All of them comprise the writings of great and important economists, and some have brought to light various previously unknown manuscripts, letters, and other ephemera and thereby have greatly enriched our knowledge of the writings of these authors.

D24   Bentham, Jeremy. Economic writings. Ed. by W. Stark. London: Allen & Unwin, 1952–54. 3v.

D25   Edgeworth, Francis Y. Papers relating to political economy. 3v. in 1. New York: Franklin, 1970. (reprint of 1925 ed.)

D26   International Association for Research in Income and Wealth. Income and wealth. Series 1–11. Cambridge: Bowes, 1951–65. Succeeded by Review of income and wealth. v.12– , 1966– . New Haven, Conn.: publ. by Yale Univ. Pr. for the Assn. Quarterly.

D27   Keynes, John Maynard. The collected writings of John Maynard Keynes. Donald Moggridge and Elizabeth Johnson, eds. Cambridge: Cambridge Univ. Pr., 1971. 30v.

D28   Law, John. Oeuvres completes. Ed. by Paul Harsin. Paris: Recueil Sirey, 1934. 3v. in 2. Fairfield, N.J.: Kelley, 1976. (reprint of 1934 ed.)

D29   List, Friedrich. Schriften, Reden, Briefe, hrsg. von Erwin V. Beckerath and others. Berlin: Hobbing, 1932–35. 12v.

D30   Marx, Karl, and Friedrich Engels. Werke. Berlin: Dietz, 1959–70. 40v., 2 Ergänzungsbände, and 2 Verzeichnis.

D31   Menger, Karl. The collected works of Carl Menger. London: London School of Economics and Political Science, 1933–36. 4v.

D32   Petty, William. The economic writings of Sir William Petty. Ed. by Charles H. Hull. 2v. New York: Kelley, 1963. (reprint of 1899 ed.)

D33   Quesnay, François. Oeuvres économiques et philosophiques. Ed. by Auguste Oncken. New York: Franklin, 1970. 814p. (reprint of 1888 ed.)

D34   Ricardo, David. The works and correspondence. Ed. by Piero Sraffa and M. H. Dobb. Cambridge: Cambridge Univ. Pr., 1955–73. 11v.

D35   Smith, Adam. An inquiry into the nature and causes of the wealth of nations. Ed. by Edwin Cannan. New York: Modern Library, 1937. 976p.

D36   ———. The early writings of Adam Smith. Ed. by J. Ralph Lindgren. New York: Kelley, 1967. 254p.

D37   ———. The theory of moral sentiments. Oxford: Clarendon, 1976. 412p.

D38   Turgot, Anne R. J. Oeuvres de Turgot et documents le concernant, avec biographie et notes. Ed. by Gustave Schelle. Paris: F. Alcan, 1913–23. 5v.

In addition to the works of the masters that have been made available to the general student in convenient new editions, some of the scarce older tracts have been collected and reprinted. Here again, antiquarianism, pride in the early achievements of a national culture, a search for intellectual origins, and competition for finding priorities among theories have played a role, but, as in the case of reprints of collected works, the republication of scarce tracts and other books on economics has had the additional advantage of making otherwise rare but interesting works more readily available to the student. It is eloquent testimony to the utility and value of these reprints that several series are again out of print and that several reprints had to be made of some items. Among the more interesting collections and series of this kind are the following.

D39   Scrittori classici italiani di economia politica. Milan: G. G. Destefanis, 1803–16. 50v. (Half-title: Economisti classici italiani)

D40   Dubois, A., ed. Collection des économistes et des réformateurs sociaux de la France. Paris: Paul Geuthner, 1911–13. 12v.

D41   Hollander, Jacob H. Reprints of economic tracts. Baltimore: Johns Hopkins Univ. Pr., 1903– . (Several volumes, many now out of print)

D42   McCulloch, John R., ed. A select collection of scarce and valuable tracts on money. New York: Kelley, 1966. 637p. (first published in 1856)

D43   ———. Early English tracts on commerce. Cambridge: Cambridge Univ. Pr., 1954. 663p. (first published in 1856)

METHOD IN ECONOMICS

The works described thus far may be regarded as providing general surveys of economics and its problems, the history of economic ideas, and the main components of the great corpus of economic writings by the most famous and most widely reputed scholars in the field. These works are the backbone of any collection of books on economics, and it is on the basis of these volumes that more specialized aspects of the literature should be considered.

The first specialized topic to which we turn is the consideration of method in economics. Although today there is a reasonable degree of consensus on the most appropriate method in economics, this has not always been the case. One of the most memorable quarrels in the history of economics has been the so-called *Methodenstreit*, or "battle of methods," between Carl Menger and Gustav Schmoller, which inverted the primacy of generalized theory over particularized empirical support for economic propositions and emphasized the need for economists either to accept current psychological theories or to make their own assumptions about relevant aspects of human behavior. Most of these conflicts have been resolved, although even today there are somewhat different approaches, and the "model builders" do not always see eye to eye with the strict and "simple-minded empiricists." But the conflicts have been greatly mitigated.

In general, economists favor an empirical approach. They collect their own factual data or use those data collected by others (e.g., statistical offices, census bureaus, etc.). They have developed methods for determining factual data from indirect evidence, and have participated in adding to the knowledge and sophistication of the statistical treatment of mass phenomena. On the basis of factual data, various generalizations are attempted and sets of generalizations are built into theories.

Not all the progress, however, has been clarification in language and in the terms used with a specialized meaning in economics. There also has been a clarification of the overall assumptions about human nature and behavior on which economic propositions are built. Whereas the early economists were utilitarians, and later economists assumed an inbred hedonism and rationality, modern economics has dropped these restrictive assumptions about human nature and merely assumes that human beings act reasonably consistently—that is, they continue a particular behavior pattern until they make an explicit change.

The economic method has also progressed in a second field: the integration of historical and contemporary comparative studies. Until very recently, economic history had been regarded by many economists as a separate branch of study, having scarcely any relationship with economics proper. For example, in many British universities economic history is taught in a special academic department, without close contact with economics proper, but this split is disappearing. Economists discover that many facts about the past of some societies are found among other present societies. Certain institutions in historical settings also have analogies or similarities in the present. Thus it has become increasingly common to combine certain historical and comparative studies. At the same time, many of the statistical and mathematical procedures that were developed in economics have been applied to historical problems. In fact, some exercises of this kind have (perhaps somewhat jokingly) been referred to as "Cliometrics."

In brief, the spirit that impinges upon method in economics is strongly influenced by positivism. Economics has ceased to be speculative and based on a priori reasoning—though old habits die slowly, and every now and then a thoroughly speculative book appears. In collecting its data, modern economics applies the various forms of empirical method that are employed in the social sciences generally, and often it processes its data by complex statistical methods.

Economic method has become both narrower and broader in its interrelationship with other social sciences. Economists have become increasingly aware that interrelations with other fields of social research are in many instances indispensable for furthering their knowledge, and hence they look with more sympathy on

217

interdisciplinary treatment of certain problems. The development in the other social sciences of methods similar to those in economics has helped greatly in this process. Although it is premature to expect that this interdependence will lead to a unified social science, a surer command of method in economics and a more modest interpretation of achievements go a long way toward laying the groundwork for the elaboration of more refined methods in economics and the other social sciences.

Much of the literature on method is not contained in special monographs or treatises but is incidental to substantive contributions. However, we list a number of works that concern themselves primarily with method in economics and, on the whole, represent the present state of methodology in the field.

D44 Blaug, Mark. The methodology of economics: or how economists explain. New York and Sidney: Cambridge Univ. Pr., 1980. 296p.

D45 Eucken, Walter. The foundations of economics. Tr. by T.W. Hutchison. Chicago: Univ. of Chicago Pr., 1961. 358p.

D46 Fraser, Lindley M. Economic thought and language: a critique of some fundamental economic concepts. Port Washington, N.Y.: Kennikat, 1971. 411p. (reprint of 1937 ed.)

D47 Hayek, F. A. The counter-revolution of science: studies on the abuse of reason. Glencoe, Ill.: Free Pr., 1952. 255p.

D48 Hutchison, T. W. Knowledge and ignorance in economics. Chicago: Univ. of Chicago Pr., 1977. 186p.

D49 Keynes, John Neville. The scope and method of political economy. 4th ed. New York: Kelley, 1965. 382p. (reprint of 1917 ed.)

D50 Kuhn, Thomas S. The structure of scientific revolutions. 2d ed. Chicago: Univ. of Chicago Pr., 1970. 210p.

D51 Latsis, Spiro, ed. Method and appraisal in economics. Cambridge: Cambridge Univ. Pr., 1980. 230p.

D52 Machlup, Fritz. The methodology of economics and other social sciences. New York: Academic, 1978. 567p.

D53 Robbins, Lionel. An essay on the nature and significance of economic science. 2d ed. New York: St. Martin's, 1969. 160p.

D54 Thurow, Lester. Dangerous currents: the state of economics. New York: Random, 1983. 247p.

ECONOMIC THEORY

As has been pointed out, the "core" of economics is economic theory. Theory formed the basis of Adam Smith's work and has maintained this position in economics writing since that time. The various "schools" of economic thought are distinguished by their variations in theoretical concepts, and the growth of economics as a science is measured by its progress in theory.

The theoretical literature may be classified according to several principles, but the easiest classification is by field of concentration in the academic curriculum. It is around these divisions that certain clusters of literature have grown up, and even the more advanced monographic works may, on the whole, be divided by these criteria.

Theories of Value and Price

Since most of economics deals with the study of quantitative relationships that tend to become established in a market, one of its main theoretical concerns is the analysis of value and price. The problem of value, which at first sight appears a puzzle, is brought into sharp focus when it is observed that some of the most necessary things in life often have little economic value and some of the most "useless" ones have high value. Water and diamonds are two objects whose value is often compared. Since it is so obvious that the more useful of the two has less value than the other, any theories of value that were based on utility were rejected at first. For many decades economists adhered to a labor theory of value almost 200 years old that took various expression but was stated most clearly and unambiguously by David Ricardo and later by Marx.

It was replaced within one generation of its ultimate formulation by a value theory, based on utility, that remained in force for many decades and that still forms the basis of our theorizing on value. Utility was seen not as an indivisible entity but as something that could be split into many small portions. In the example of water and diamonds, it was shown that the choice of a person in assigning a value to each of these objects is not to decide between all the water and all the diamonds, but merely between small quantities of each. If a cup of water is lost, scarcely anything is lost. Hence the decisive unit is this marginal unit—that is, the last cup of water—and therefore the theory came to be called the marginal utility theory of value. Since it was first stated, almost 100 years ago, further developments have taken place, and the emphasis on marginal utility has been replaced by an analysis of situations of preference and indifference, mainly because such situations are closer to measurable and empirically observable relations.

Among the more stimulating works on the theory of value in its various aspects are the following.

D55 Cassel, Gustav. The theory of social economy. Tr. by J. McCabe. New York: Kelley, 1932. 654p.

D56 Debreu, Gerard. Theory of value: an axiomatic analysis of economic equilibrium. New Haven, Conn., and London: Yale Univ. Pr., 1959. 114p.

D57 Dobb, Maurice. Theories of value and distribution since Adam Smith. Cambridge: Cambridge Univ. Pr., 1973. 264p.

D58 Georgescu-Roegen, Nicholas. The entropy law and the economic process. Cambridge, Mass.: Harvard Univ. Pr., 1971. 457p.

D59 Hicks, John R. Value and capital. 2d ed. Oxford: Clarendon, 1946. 340p.

D60 Jevons, William Stanley. The theory of political economy. 5th ed. New York: Kelley, 1965. 343p.

D61 Kaldor, Nicholas. Essays on value and distribution. Glencoe, Ill.: Free Pr., 1960. 238p.

D62 Knight, Frank H. The ethics of competition, and other essays. Chicago: Univ. of Chicago Pr., 363p. (reprint of 1935 ed.)

D63 Lerner, Abba P. Economics of employment. New York: Greenwood, 1978. 397p. (reprint of 1951 ed.)

D64 Meade, James E. Principles of political economy. Chicago: Aldine; Albany: State Univ. of New York Pr., 1965–76. 4v.

D65 Meek, Ronald. Studies in the labor theory of value. London: Lawrence and Wishart, 1973. 332p.

D66 On political economy and econometrics: essays in honour of Oskar Lange. New York: Pergamon, 1965. 661p.

D67 Pigou, Arthur C. Employment and equilibrium: a theoretical discussion. 2d ed. New York: Kelley, 1978. 383p. (reprint of 1949 ed.)

D68 Robinson, Joan. Economic philosophy. London: Aldine, 1964. 150p.

D69 Sraffa, Piero. Production of commodities by means of commodities. Cambridge: Cambridge Univ. Pr., 1960. 98p.

D70 Varian, Hal R. Microeconomic analysis. New York: Norton, 1978. 284p.

D71 Walras, Leon. Elements of pure economics; or, the theory of social wealth. Tr. by William Jaffe.

New York: Kelley, 1969. 620p. (reprint of 1954 ed.)

D72 Wicksell, Knut. Lectures on political economy. Ed. by Lionel Robbins. Tr. by E. Classen. New York: Kelley, 1967. 2v. (reprint of 1934–35 ed.)

Price is closely related to value; in fact, it has been said that price is the monetary expression of value. Some economists have recognized this and have puzzled over the fact that fluctuations in price from hour to hour and day to day are, in many circumstances, more violent than fluctuations in intrinsic value. Surely a chair that is sold for $10 for many weeks and suddenly is put in a clearance sale and offered for $5 has not lost half its value in the few minutes in which the clearance sale is decided upon. It is recognized, therefore, that the external forces of the market influence prices and that conditions of supply and demand, the openness of entry to markets, the smoothness with which markets function, the pattern of governmental regulation of markets, and the presence or absence of monopoly or partial monopoly play a role. Prices may be subject to competition, but it has been found that competition sometimes is caused not by changing prices but by offering more services in connection with a purchase or by a change in quality. In other words, competition can be less than perfect; it can depend upon the relative location of competitors, the influence exerted upon people through advertising, and other factors.

Finally, it has been recognized that the stark dichotomy between the concepts of competition and monopoly (having only one seller or one buyer in a market) was too extreme and that sometimes there is competition among the few. This has led to elaboration of the theory of oligopoly, which is recognized as applicable in many markets in modern free-enterprise economies.

The variety of these patterns of price determination is exhibited in the following books. In addition to purely theoretical contributions, one or two monographs that concentrate on methods of empirical measurement of prices have been listed. Although the latter do not really belong in the field of price theory, they are clearly relevant in this context.

D73 Chamberlin, Edward. The theory of monopolistic competition: a reorientation of the theory of value. 8th ed. Cambridge, Mass.: Harvard Univ. Pr., 1962. 396p.

D74 Friedman, James. Oligopoly theory. Cambridge: Cambridge Univ. Pr., 1983. 240p.

D75   Friedman, Milton. Essays in positive economics. Chicago: Univ. of Chicago Pr., 1953. 328p.

D76   Johnson, Harry G. Money, trade and economic growth; survey lectures in economic theory. Cambridge, Mass.: Harvard Univ. Pr., 1962. 199p.

D77   Robinson, Joan. The economics of imperfect competition. 2d ed. London: Macmillan, 1969. 352p.

D78   Stigler, George J. The theory of price. 3d ed. New York: Macmillan, 1966. 355p.

Theory of Production

As we have seen, the theory of price concentrates on the process of exchange. But economists are also interested in production, and hence have developed extensive theories of production. To some extent these theories are attempts to determine the theoretical relationships between inputs into a production process and outputs from it. They imply certain technologies, but they sometimes consider technology as one of the variables that needs to be analyzed. The research and the development of new technologies, both in the productive and in the organization fields, are now recognized to be costs of production comparable to other costs—raw materials, labor, etc. But the principal inputs in any production process are inputs of labor and capital, and it is in the field of wage theory and capital theory that the most important contributions to the literature of theories of production have been made.

It would lead us too far into technical economics to discuss detailed theories of wages and capital, particularly since each set of theories has its own peculiarities, but it is evident that wage theories tend to be affected by the fact that wages are sticky; that an absolute minimum level of wages is essential for survival, even if the value of labor should be lower than that level; and that, despite great differences in workers' skills, initiative, and intelligence, the power of the labor union of which they are members may affect the wages they receive.

On the side of capital, the problems that have cropped up are ultimately based on the fact that capital assets, though perishable in the long run, have different degrees of durability—that capital, as such, is consumed over a long time in the form of the services it renders. Moreover, the durability of capital goods is affected by the outlays on their maintenance, and, depending on the span of time one has in mind, the distinction between fixed and circulating capital tends to become blurred. All these aspects—as well as the fact that in modern societies capital appears in the form of cash, securities, inventories, machines, and buildings and land, and these objects have different degrees of liquidity—have complicated the theory of capital.

Among the more valuable monographs on the theory of production are the following.

D79   Böhm von Bawerk, Eugen. Capital and interest: a critical history of economic theory. Tr. by George D. Huncke and H. F. Sennholz. South Holland, Ill.: Libertarian Pr., 1959. 3v. in 1.

D80   Clark, John Bates. The distribution of wealth: a theory of wages, interest, and profits. New York: Kelley, 1965. 445p. (reprint of 1899 ed.)

D81   Clark, John M. Studies in the economics of overhead costs. Chicago: Univ. of Chicago Pr., 1923. 502p.

D82   Fisher, Irving. The theory of interest. New York: Macmillan, 1930. 566p.

D83   Harcourt, G. C. Some Cambridge controversies in the theory of capital. Cambridge: Cambridge Univ. Pr., 1973. 272p.

D84   Hayek, F. A. The pure theory of capital. Chicago: Univ. of Chicago Pr., 1975. 454p. [Midway reprint series]

D85   Hicks, John R. Capital and growth. New York: Oxford Univ. Pr., 1965. 339p.

D86   Leontief, Wassily W., ed. Structure, system, and economic policy. Cambridge: Cambridge Univ. Pr., 1977. 223p.

D87   Robinson, Joan. The accumulation of capital. 3d ed. New York: St. Martin's, 1970. 444p.

Theory of Income and Employment

The theories discussed thus far turn on the behavior of individuals or single firms. In other words, the primary question of someone studying the theory of prices is, How will a firm or consumer behave in the market and how, through this behavior, will prices be determined? The study of various forms of competition implies aggregation, but the basic object of study is still the single economic unit rather than the mass of persons or firms in their entirety.

The study of income and the theory of employment, on the other hand, turn on mass behavior; the entities with which these studies deal are the whole society, or a sizable portion of it. Hence, whereas the theory of value, price, and market transactions, including theories of the firm, is usually referred to as microeconomics, the theory of income and employment, as well as the theory of savings and investment (which are sub-topics of the theory of income) are referred to as macroeconomics. Whereas economics began by paying primary attention to macroeconomic problems, it turned in time—under the impact of marginal utility theory—to pay special attention to problems of microeconomics. In the last twenty years, partly under the impact of the Great Depression of the 1930s, it once again focused extensively on macroeconomic problems and paid particular attention to income analysis, the study of investment and savings, the theory of consumption, and, as a consequence, the theory of employment and fluctuations in employment.

D88   Dornbusch, Rudiger, and Stanley Fischer. Macroeconomics. 3d ed. New York: McGraw-Hill, 1984. 723p.

D89   Gordon, Robert J. Macroeconomics. 3d ed. Boston: Little, 1984. 634p.

This change in principal interest was due primarily to the theories of John Maynard Keynes and the subsequent "Keynesian revolution" in economics that was carried on by his students. But Keynes not only stressed the importance of such aggregates as income, investment, and savings; he also related them to new interpretations in the field of monetary theory. Hence, on the macroeconomic level a more intimate relationship was achieved between branches of economics that previously had been treated as rather separate parts. Monetary theory, business cycle theory, and ultimately the theory of secular economic growth were brought within the context of general economic theory, and a more uniform body of economic theory emerged. This, as well as the stress on the aggregate entities, was the chief merit of Keynesianism.

D90   Barro, Robert J., and Hershel I. Grossman. Money, employment, and inflation. Cambridge: Cambridge Univ. Pr., 1976. 304p.

D91   Baumol, William J. Economic dynamics. 3d ed. New York: Macmillan, 1970. 472p.

D92   Denison, Edward F. Why growth rates differ: postwar experience in nine Western countries. Washington, D.C.: Brookings, 1967. 494p.

D93   Hansen, Alvin H. Economic policy and full employment. New York: McGraw-Hill, 1947. 340p.

D94   Keynes, John Maynard. The general theory of employment, interest and money. New York: Harcourt, 1936. 403p. Also included in v.7 of the collected writings of John Maynard Keynes (D27).

D95   Kuznets, Simon. National income and its composition, 1919–1938. New York: National Bureau of Economic Research, 1941. 2v. in 1.

D96   Leijonhufvud, Axel. On Keynesian economics and the economics of Keynes: a study in monetary theory. London and New York: Oxford Univ. Pr., 1968. 431p.

D97   Lerner, Abba P. The economics of control: principles of welfare economics. New York: Kelley, 1970. 428p. (reprint of 1944 ed.)

D98   Okun, Arthur M. Prices and quantities: a macroeconomic analysis. Washington, D.C.: Brookings, 1981. 367p.

D99   Shackle, George L. S. Expectations, investment, and income. 2d ed. Oxford: Clarendon, 1968. 130p.

D100 Tobin, James. Essays in economics, volume 1: macroeconomics. Chicago: Markham, 1971. 526p.

Monetary Theory

As we have seen, recent developments in economics have brought about a closer integration of monetary theory with macroeconomics. But even before this happened, considerations about money were intimately linked to the theory of prices and to market analysis, for the distinction between natural and actual prices—which goes back to the classical economists of the early nineteenth century—was called forth by the fact that under certain circumstances the prices paid for given commodities fluctuated widely and were subject to easily discernible trends. There were periods when all prices rose or declined more or less uniformly, and this phenomenon could be explained only by the general loss or gain in the value of money.

Another difficulty was the explanation required as long as the value of money was tied to some metallic standard, and especially when it was tied to more than one metal, since the price relation between the two metals was also subject to change.

Monetary theory was further complicated when near-moneys were invented and tended to be used widely. Banks could create money, either by printing bank notes or by establishing deposits, and the circulation of means of exchange could vary greatly, depending upon the number of loans banks were willing to make or the rights of overdraft they were willing to authorize. Hence such phenomena as inflation and deflation, the determination of the "adequate and proper" amount of bank credit, the practice of divorcing the circulation of currencies from monetary metals, and sometimes the indiscriminate use of the printing press were developments that brought attention to the conditions regulating the value of money. As the value of money fluctuated, certain persons gained and others lost. Money tended to lose its significance as a store of value if it gradually lost its value through inflationary trends. Men began to speculate in money as they had speculated in other things, and in periods of serious hyperinflation— as in post–World War II Germany—they turned from money to other means of exchange. Foreign currencies, and even such objects as cigarettes, acquired the status of a general means of exchange.

Attention was drawn to such points as the quantity of money in circulation, the velocity of circulation, and the considerations that induced people to hold stocks of money, and reasons for and against their preference for liquidity. Modern monetary theory takes account of all these features, as well as of the impact a generally rising or falling price level has on overall economic prosperity.

The monographs listed below contain extensive discussions of these various aspects of money.

D101 Fisher, Douglas. Monetary theory and the demand for money. New York: Wiley, 1978. 278p.

D102 Fisher, Irving. The purchasing power of money. New York: Kelley, 1963. 515p. (reprint of 1922 ed.)

D103 Friedman, Milton. Price theory. Chicago: Aldine, 1976. 357p.

D104 ———, ed. Studies in the quantity theory of money. Chicago: Univ. of Chicago Pr., 1956. 265p.

D105 Jevons, William S. Money and the mechanism of exchange. London: Routledge & Paul, 1910. 367p.

D106 Johnson, Harry G. Essays in monetary economics. Cambridge, Mass.: Harvard Univ. Pr., 1967. 332p.

D107 Keynes, John Maynard. A treatise on money. New York: AMS Pr., 1976. 2v. (reprint of 1930 ed.) Also included in v.5 and 6 of the collected writings of John Maynard Keynes (D27).

D108 Mundell, Robert. Monetary theory: inflation, interest, and growth in the world economy. Pacific Palisades, Calif.: Goodyear, 1971. 189p.

D109 Patinkin, Don. Money, interest, and prices: an integration of monetary and value theory. 2d ed. New York: Harper, 1965. 708p.

D110 Robertson, Dennis H. Essays in money and interest: selected with a memoir by Sir John Hicks. London: Collins, 1966. 256p.

D111 Wicksell, Knut. Interest and prices. New York: A. M. Kelly, 1962. 239p. (reprint of 1936 ed.)

Theory of Economic Fluctuations

As was noted, one of the peculiarities of economic systems is the fact that they experience periodic fluctuations in the general price level. About 50 years ago it was observed that these fluctuations are associated with fluctuations in output and employment and that they seem to recur with a certain periodicity. Although the peaks and troughs of these fluctuations did not always reach the same height or depth, there were periods during which business activity tended to become increasingly sluggish and others in which it picked up again and became quite buoyant. This led to various attempts at explaining the causes of these fluctuations.

Among the factors that were made responsible for the "business cycles" (as these fluctuations were soon called) were such things as changes in harvests due to a changing reappearance of sunspots, shifts in the attitudes of business leaders between optimism and pessimism, and differences in the growth rate of production and consumption (often referred to as overproduction or underconsumption theories). There are probably few fields in economics that have produced such numerous attempts at theoretical reasoning and such variation in assigning causes for an economic phenomenon as the field of business cycles. In part this is due to the sharpness of some depressions, to the apparent inability to find adequate remedies for the depressed state of business, and to the widespread concern with growing unemployment, falling prices, business failures, and an apparent general loss of vigor in the economy.

In this field, as in others, recent developments have brought some new insights and also raised new questions. Most economists still believe that government's fiscal policies and central banks' monetary policies may be used as instruments in stabilizing the economy and alleviating or avoiding depressions. The distribution of public works over time and space is another instrument, and various relaxations of other regulatory measures (in both domestic and foreign trade) are still others.

D112 Fellner, William. Trends and cycles in economic activity: an introduction to problems of economic growth. New York: Holt, 1956. 411p.

D113 Gordon, Robert A. Economic instability and growth: the American record. New York: Harper, 1974. 216p.

D114 Haberler, Gottfried von. Prosperity and depression: a theoretical analysis of cyclical movements. 4th ed. Cambridge, Mass.: Harvard Univ. Pr., 1960. 520p.

D115 Hansen, Alvin H. Business-cycle theory, its development and present status. Westport, Conn.: Hyperion, 1979. 218p. (reprint of 1927 ed.)

D116 Kalecki, Michael. Essays in the theory of economic fluctuations. New York: Russell & Russell, 1972. 208p. (reprint of 1939 ed.)

D116 Kondratieff, Nikolai. The long wave cycle. Tr.
A   by Guy Daniels. New York: Richard & Snyder, 1984. 128p.

D117 Mitchell, Wesley C. Business cycles: the problem and its setting. New York: National Bureau of Economic Research, 1968. 489p.

D118 Moore, Geoffrey H. Business cycles, inflation, and forecasting. 2d ed. Cambridge, Mass.: Ballinger, 1983. 473p.

D119 Schumpeter, Joseph A. Business cycles: a theoretical, historical and statistical analysis of the capitalist process. Philadelphia: Porcupine Pr., 1982. 2v. (reprint of 1939 ed.)

D120 Tinbergen, Jan. The dynamics of business cycles: a study in economic fluctuations. Tr. and adapted by J. J. Polak. Chicago: Univ. of Chicago Pr., 1950. 366p.

Other economists have recently applied the theory of rational expectations to reach more cautious conclusions about the efficacy of countercyclical monetary and fiscal policies. Rational expectations is a theory that has frequently been used in the finance literature to explain movements in the prices of stocks and bonds. It assumes that people do not make any systematic errors in their predictions of economic variables. When coupled with additional assumptions of perfect competition and continuous market clearing, this theory implies that expected policy changes will have no effect on the level of real output. A brief list of books that explain and pursue this line of thought is given below.

D120 Barro, Robert J. Macroeconomics. New York:
A   Wiley, 1984. 580p.

D121 Begg, David. The rational expectations revolution in macroeconomics. Baltimore: Johns Hopkins Univ. Pr., 1982. 304p.

D122 Lucas, Robert E. Studies in business cycle theory. Cambridge, Mass.: MIT Pr., 1981. 300p.

D123 ———, and Thomas J. Sargent, eds. Rational expectations and econometric practice. Minneapolis: Univ. of Minnesota Pr., 1981. 2v.

D124 Sargent, Thomas J. Macroeconomic theory. New York: Academic, 1979. 404p.

D125 Sheffrin, Steven M. Rational expectations. Cambridge: Cambridge Univ. Pr., 1983. 215p.

Theories of Economic Growth

There is only one stop from theories of economic fluctuations to theories of secular economic growth. Whereas the former are concerned with the determination of the variables responsible for the periodic ups and downs of an economy, the latter try to explain why economies, from a certain point on, tend to progress to higher and higher levels of performance. For even though there are depressions and periods of downturn, the subsequent upturn tends to lead to levels of income and output higher than any peak reached before. In other words, many economies have proved that they experience decided secular growth. These economies may be contrasted with others that have stagnated for a long time, that have apparently been unable to overcome their inherently low productivity, and that do not seem to be able to progress to a point of self-sustained economic growth.

If advancing and stagnating economies are contrasted with one another, the crucial question immediately arises: What factors determine the point of "takeoff"? This is merely another way of asking what factors differentiate advancing from stagnant economies, and is equivalent to pointing to the practical policy problem of what changes must be made in stagnating economies to push them to a level of output where a self-sustained process of growth will begin. The debate on this question is by no means resolved. Some writers assign predominant importance to the supply of capital, others to the skill and education level of the labor force, and still others to noneconomic factors that have their primary basis in the culture, social structure, or political affairs of the societies concerned.

The study of economic growth has also concerned itself with a reexamination of the economic history of the leading countries in the world economy. This has been done in the hope that by examining this history, often from a new point of view, certain strategic factors could be singled out that would point to the most appropriate policies poor and "underdeveloped" countries could embrace in order to enter the stage of economic growth.

In a certain sense, the study of economic growth represents the general state of studies in contemporary economics; it has a theoretical core around which considerations are built that stretch into the applied, the historical, and the noneconomic areas. It is primarily concerned not with static equilibrium, or even a temporary equilibrium in the short run, but rather with a situation into which change is built in a long-run dynamic movement. Finally, it accepts the variability of economic institutions and explicitly recognizes their differentiation in time and space.

D126 Adelman, Irma, and Cynthia T. Morris. Economic growth and social equity in developing countries. Stanford, Calif.: Stanford Univ. Pr., 1973. 257p.

D127 Amin, Samir. Accumulation on a world scale. New York: Monthly Review Pr., 1978. 2v. in 1.

D128 Baran, Paul. Political economy of growth. New York: Monthly Review Pr., 1957. 308p.

D129 Chenery, Hollis, and others. Redistribution with growth: policies to improve income distribution in developing countries in the context of economic growth: a joint study . . . . New York: Oxford Univ. Pr., 1974. 304p.

D130 Clark, Colin. The conditions of economic progress. 3d ed. New York: St. Martin's, 1960. 720p.

D131 Hagen, Everett. On the theory of social change: how economic growth begins. Homewood, Ill.: Dorsey Pr., 1962. 557p.

D132 Harrod, Roy F. Towards a dynamic economics: some recent developments of economic theory and their application to policy. Westport, Conn.: Greenwood, 1980. 168p. (reprint of 1948 ed.)

D133 Higgins, Ben H. Economic development: principles, problems, and policies. Rev. ed. New York: Norton, 1968. 918p.

D134 Hirschman, Albert O. The strategy of economic development. New Haven, Conn.: Yale Univ. Pr., 1966. 217p.

D135 Hoselitz, Bert F. Sociological aspects of economic growth. Glencoe, Ill.: Free Pr., 1960. 250p.

D136 Jameson, Kenneth, and C. Wilber, eds. Directions in economic development. South Bend, Ind.: Univ. of Notre Dame Pr., 1980. 268p.

D137 Kahn, Herman. World economic developments: 1979 and beyond. Boulder, Colo.: Westview, 1979. 519p.

D138 Kuznets, Simon. Modern economic growth: rate, structure, and spread. New Haven, Conn.: Yale Univ. Pr., 1966. 529p.

D139 ———. Economic growth of nations: total output and production structure. Cambridge, Mass.: Harvard Univ. Pr., 1971. 363p.

D140 Leibenstein, Harvey. Economic backwardness and economic growth: studies in the theory of economic development. New York: Wiley, 1957. 295p.

D141 ———. General x-efficiency theory and economic development. New York: Oxford Univ. Pr., 1978. 189p.

D142 Lewis, William Arthur. The theory of economic growth. Homewood, Ill.: Irwin, 1955. 453p.

D143 Meier, Gerald M. Leading issues in economic development. 4th ed. New York: Oxford Univ. Pr., 1984. 862p.

D144 Rostow, Walt W. The stages of economic growth: a non-communist manifesto. 2d ed. Cambridge: Cambridge Univ. Pr., 1971. 253p.

D145 Schumacher, E. F. Small is beautiful: economics as if people mattered. New York: Harper, 1973. 290p.

D146 Todaro, Michael P. Economic development in the Third World. 2d ed. New York: Longman, 1980. 544p.

D147 Wilber, Charles K., ed. The political economy of development and underdevelopment. 3d ed. New York: Random, 1984. 595p.

Mathematical Economics

Until very recently, many relationships among individual magnitudes in all these theories were stated in ordinary language, but now it has become customary to state some of them in mathematical form. Various branches of mathematics have been elaborated by economists because mathematical formulations appear to be of great utility in solving economic problems. In this mathematical approach, two types of problem solving have become apparent. Of the first, dependent to some extent upon nonmathematical thinking, it is difficult to know how much of the solution is due to nonmathematical logical formulation by the solver. The second defines the problem exactly in mathematics; it always recognizes whether it is of great or minute importance, and finds the most elegant mathematical formulation that will solve it.

In the purely theoretical formulation, mathematical economists have given up the less accurate, purely linguistic statements and replaced them with rigorous mathematical ones; but although these statements are in some cases truer than the linguistic ones, the mathematical solution has not yet reached a point where it can supersede the linguistic one. The mathematical statements, in other words, are very frequently accurate, but they are often obliged to make unrealistic assumptions, so that only linguistic economics can give a full accounting of the whole economic system.

The use of many mathematical approaches by economists has resulted in their making a very large number of contributions to mathematical theory. For example, they have made contributions to matrix theory, and linear programming has been developed almost entirely by mathematical economists. Economists also have developed a mathematical theory of games and have made contributions to the mathematical treatment of difference equations and the analysis of time series.

The most important books on mathematical economics are:

D148 Allen, Roy G. D. Mathematical analysis for economists. New York: St. Martin's, 1964. 548p.

D149 Arrow, Kenneth J. Essays in the theory of risk bearing. New York: Elsevier, 1976. 278p.

D150 ———, and Frank H. Hahn. General competitive analysis. San Francisco: Holden-Day, 1971.

D151 ———, and Leonid Hurwicz, eds. Studies in resource allocation processes. Cambridge: Cambridge Univ. Pr., 1977. 482p.

D152 ———, and Michael D. Intriligator. eds. Handbook of mathematical economics. Amsterdam: North-Holland, 1981. 3v.

D153 Box, George E. P., and Gwilym M. Jenkins. Time series analysis, forecasting and control. San Francisco: Holden-Day, 1976. 500p.

D153 Debreu, Gerard. Mathematical economics:
A twenty papers of Gerard Debreu. Cambridge: Cambridge Univ. Pr., 1983. 250p.

D154 Dorfman, Robert P., and others. Linear programming and economic analysis. New York: McGraw-Hill, 1958. 527p.

D155 Fuss, Melvyn, and Daniel McFadden, eds. Production economics: a dual approach to theory and applications. Amsterdam: North-Holland, 1978. 2v.

D155 Griliches, Zvi, and Michael D. Intriligator,
A eds. Handbook of econometrics. Amsterdam: North-Holland, 1983. 3v.

D156 Haavelmo, Trygve. A study in the theory of investment. Chicago: Univ. of Chicago Pr., 1960. 221p.

D157 Intriligator, Michael D. Mathematical optimization and economic theory. Englewood Cliffs, N.J.: Prentice-Hall, 1971. 508p.

D158 Klein, Lawrence R. An introduction to econometrics. New York: Greenwood, 1977. 280p. (reprint of 1962 ed.)

D159 Koopmans, Tjalling C. Three essays on the state of economic science. New York: McGraw-Hill, 1957. 231p.

D160 Nerlove, Marc, and David Grether. Analysis of economic time series: a synthesis. New York: Academic, 1979. 468p.

D161 Samuelson, Paul A. Foundations of economic analysis. Enl. ed. Cambridge, Mass.: Harvard Univ. Pr., 1983. 604p.

D162 Theil, Henri. Introduction to econometrics. Englewood Cliffs, N.J.: Prentice-Hall, 1978. 447p.

D163 Tinbergen, Jan. Economic policy: principles and design. 4th ed. Amsterdam: North-Holland, 1967. 276p.

D164 Von Neumann, John, and Oskar Morgenstern. Theory of games and economic behavior. 3d ed. New York: Wiley, 1964. 641p.

D165 Wold, Herman O., ed. Bibliography on time series and stochastic processes: an international team project. Cambridge, Mass.: MIT Pr., 1965. 516p.

Time and Space in Economic Theory

The consideration of business cycles and secular economic growth has made abundantly clear the need to "date" observations in economics. The earlier economists did not explicitly date their observations, though they assumed, of course, relationships that would undergo change over time. But this practice gradually led to the very central position that the analysis of equilibrium situations achieved in economics. All processes were supposed to be temporary, except certain cases of equilibrium, which could be either stable or unstable. Unstable equilibrium, as its name implies, was not assumed to be permanent, and economists studied the paths that led from one unstable equilibrium position to another until finally a situation of stable equilibrium was reached.

Gradually this conception of the functioning of the economy was replaced by a conception of dynamic equilibrium—that is, equilibrium was not assumed to be a point in time but rather a path through time, and the various economic variables were thought to fluctuate around this path. Problems were posed as to whether certain deviations from the equilibrium path would lead to stable or to "explosive" solutions—that is, whether the variables could be expected to return to some point on the equilibrium path or whether they would move farther and farther from it. In the former case, the model that resulted in tracing the equilibrium path was considered confirmed; in the latter case, it was considered in need of replacement.

Of course there are numerous reasons why certain economic variables may diverge from equilibrium situations. They are subject to various shocks, some of them systematic shocks, but also to many random shocks—shocks that come from outside the economic system. The election of a new president may be such a shock. A war in a foreign country, a natural disaster, etc., may exert shocks on an economic system and prevent the variables from reaching, or even moving closer to, their equilibrium positions. Hence it is important not only to analyze the positions different economic magnitudes (income, prices, etc.) may take over time but also to ascertain what shocks they are subject to and what behavior they exhibit when exposed to certain shocks from outside or inside the economic systems.

The consideration of location of economic activity (i.e., the role of space in economics) has gone through a similar process of clarification. In early writings, space was almost assumed out of existence, except in theories relating to the international division of labor. Gradually, economic considerations of location were introduced explicitly into general theorizing, and at present they have assumed such an important role in the eyes of some students that a separate field of inquiry—regional science—has become crystallized.

Interest in regionalism is not confined to economists but is also found, above all, among geographers and ecologists. However, the economics of transportation—of differential pricing, depending upon the location of the producer and consumer, and the problems arising from the fact that shipments between two points may require different transport facilities and different quantities of transport equipment—has been combined with regional studies and thus provides a more rounded picture of space and location in economic theory.

Some of the outstanding monographs on dynamics, static equilibrium theory, and location theory (including regionalism) are listed below.

D167 Hart, Albert G. Anticipations, uncertainty, and dynamic planning. Chicago: Univ. of Chicago Pr., 1940. 98p.

D168 Heilbrun, James. Urban economics and public policy. 2d ed. New York: St. Martin's, 1981. 556p.

D169 Hoover, Edgar M. An introduction to regional economics. New York: Knopf, 1971. 395p.

D170 Isard, Walter. Methods of regional analysis: an introduction to regional science. Cambridge, Mass.: MIT Pr., 1960. 784p.

D171 Keeler, Theodore, ed. Research in the economics of transportation, v.1. Greenwich, Conn.: JAI Pr., 1983.

D172 Locklin, D. Philip. Economics of transportation. 7th ed. Homewood, Ill.: Irwin, 1972. 882p.

D173 Lösch, August. The economics of location. 2d rev. ed. Tr. by W. H. Woglom and W. F. Stolper. New Haven, Conn.: Yale Univ. Pr., 1954. 520p.

D174 Meyer, J. R., and others. The urban transportation problem. Cambridge, Mass.: Harvard Univ. Pr., 1965. 427p.

D175 ——. The economics of competition in the transportation industries. Cambridge, Mass.: Harvard Univ. Pr., 1959. 359p.

D176 Mieszkowski, Peter, and Mahlon Straszheim. Current issues in urban economics. Baltimore: Johns Hopkins Univ. Pr., 1979. 589p.

D177 Mills, Edwin, and Bruce W. Hamilton. Urban economics. 3d ed. Glenview, Ill.: Scott, Foresman, 1984. 420p.

D178 Mohring, Herbert. Transportation economics. Cambridge: Ballinger, 1976. 174p.

D179 Neenan, William. Urban public economics. Belmont, Calif.: Wadsworth, 1981. 336p.

D180 Nourse, Hugh O. Regional economics: a study in the economic structure, stability and growth of regions. New York: McGraw-Hill, 1968. 247p.

D181 Oates, Wallace E. The political economy of fiscal federalism. Lexington, Mass.: Lexington, 1977. 355p.

D182 Perloff, Harvey S. Regions, resources and economic growth. Baltimore: Johns Hopkins Univ. Pr., 1960. 716p.

D183 Pigou, Arthur C. The economics of stationary states. London: Macmillan, 1935. 326p.

D184 Schumpeter, Joseph A. The theory of economic development: an inquiry into profits, capital, credit, interest, and the business cycle. Tr. by Redvers Opie. London and New York: Oxford Univ. Pr., 1961. 255p.

D185 Shackle, George L. Time in economics. Amsterdam: North-Holland, 1958. 111p.

Theories of Consumption

Thus far we have been concerned primarily with production and distribution and have paid relatively little attention to consumption. To be sure, the subjective value theories, based on considerations of utility, are concerned with the consumer; so are theories of demand, and even theories of business fluctuation. We have seen, for example, that some business cycle theories are based upon assumptions of underconsumption. But, on the whole, consumption and welfare have thus far entered into consideration only accidentally or in a subordinate fashion. Yet it may be argued that all production is ultimately destined for the satisfaction of human needs, through consumption either by individuals or collectivities (e.g., the state). The purchase of armaments and similar objects is also a form of consumption, although these objects are consumed not by private individuals but by a nation—by citizens acting as a collective group.

In the past, not much explicit attention was given to the economics of consumption. Most of the studies that dealt with consumption centered on a specific commodity or group of commodities (e.g., food), and their main purpose was to find the nature of demand for these commodities and their place in the consumer's budget. Yet even at a fairly early stage, a number of rather general propositions were made and common relationships discovered. The best known is perhaps Engel's law, which states that as the income of a household rises the proportion of its expenditure on food declines. Engel, a German statistician, showed that this generalization was widely applicable in the middle of the nineteenth century, and since then it has been confirmed numerous times.

More modern research in the field of consumption has gone beyond the problem of expenditure on food, and students have discovered relationships between a household's income and its expenditures on various perishable, semidurable (clothes, etc.), and durable (furniture and other household equipment) consumer goods. These studies tend to be summarized in works dealing with the function of consumption as a whole, in which various generalizations relating to changes in the level and type of consumption, and changes in income, are discussed.

D188 Duesenberry, James. Income, savings, and the theory of consumer behavior. Cambridge, Mass.: Harvard Univ. Pr., 1952. 128p.

D189 Friedman, Milton. A theory of the consumption function. Princeton, N.J.: Princeton Univ. Pr., 1957. 243p.

D190 Katona, George. The mass consumption society. McGraw-Hill, 1964. 343p.

D191 Katona, George, and Eva Mueller. Consumer response to income increases. Washington, D.C.: Brookings, 1968. 244p.

D192 Kyrk, Hazel. A theory of consumption. New York: Arno, 1976. 298p. (reprint of 1923 ed.)

D193 Modigliani, Franco. The collected papers of Franco Modigliani, v. 2: The life cycle hypothesis of saving. Ed. by Andrew Abel. Cambridge, Mass., and London: MIT Pr., 1980. 527p.

D194 Reid, Margaret G. Consumers and the market. 3d ed. New York: Arno, 1976. 617p. (reprint of 1947 ed.)

Welfare Economics

Considerations of consumption problems lead us straight to the consideration of welfare. The classical economists had their philosophical roots in utilitarianism, and some of them (e.g., John Stuart Mill) explicitly applied utilitarian principles to economics. The question was raised as to how economics could contribute to the utilitarian ideal of attaining the greatest happiness for the greatest number. This background may also be discerned throughout economic reasoning in later periods. For example, F. Y. Edgeworth was very much concerned with this problem in the late nineteenth century.

In the period since the end of the First World War, welfare as an objective of economic activity and economic organization has again become a prominent concern of economists. In this area, as in others, the problem is now posed in a new fashion. Instead of attempting an aggregation of individual satisfaction or "happiness," welfare economics takes into account the fact that every person's welfare depends not only upon the "happiness" that person alone achieves but also on that of his or her family, neighbors, and others in the local community—that is, the concept of a community welfare function must be developed. Here economic reasoning comes close to social philosophy and the problem of societal values, and is clearly influenced by the assumptions made about these values. In the field of welfare economics, we reach, so to speak, the limits of pure economics and come close to politics, philosophy, and the analysis of social psychology.

D195 Arrow, Kenneth J. Social choice and individual values. 2d ed. New York: Wiley, 1963. 124p.

D196 Dobb, Maurice. Welfare economics and the economics of socialism: towards a common-sense critique. London: Cambridge Univ. Pr., 1969. 275p.

D197 Hla Myint, U. Theories of welfare economics. Cambridge, Mass.: Harvard Univ. Pr., 1948. 240p.

D198 Little, Ian M. D. A critique of welfare economics. 2d ed. Oxford: Clarendon, 1957. 302p.

D199 Pigou, Arthur C. The economics of welfare. 4th ed. New York: AMS Pr., 1978. 876p. (reprint of 1932 ed.)

D200 Reder, Melvin W. Studies in the theory of welfare economics. New York: Columbia Univ. Pr., 1947. 208p.

D201 Scitovsky, Tibor. The joyless economy: an inquiry into human satisfaction and consumer dissatisfaction. New York: Oxford Univ. Pr., 1976. 310p.

D202 ———. Welfare and competition. Rev. ed. Homewood, Ill.: Irwin, 1971. 492p.

D203 Tinbergen, Jan, and others. Optimum social welfare and productivity: a comparative view. New York: New York Univ. Pr., 1972. 175p.

ECONOMIC HISTORY

We completed our survey of the major branches of economic theory in the preceding discussion, but we must touch briefly upon one more topic: the study of economic institutions in countries of different cultures. In the customary economics curriculum these problems are usually taught in courses on "comparative economic systems," but this is a restrictive interpretation and it is more suitable to think of differences in economic institutions on a quite general level.

Institutions differ either because they belong to different culturally oriented societies or because they belong to different time periods in the same society. Hence the study of economic history—to the extent it has economic rather than historical or antiquarian objectives—is really a comparison of economic institutions. Some of the most distinguished writings in economic history (which has a vast literature and hence cannot be discussed extensively) are strictly limited in conception and objectives; those works, therefore, are not of interest in the present context. But some monographs on economic history are explicitly devoted to the examination of changing institutions in the field of production, distribution, or exchange, and the relation of these changes to the historical evolution of certain societies. These studies are thus devoted to an examination of comparative economic institutions within the historical context. They may be matched by a series of similar studies that perform the same function of comparison on a cross-cultural basis.

We list here a few of the broadest and most general studies in economic history, some of which are based on viewpoints and methods originally developed by the German historical school in economics.

D204 Braudel, Fernand. Capitalism and material life: 1400–1800. Tr. by Miriam Kochan. New York: Harper, 1973. 478p.

D205 Cipolla, Carlo M., ed. The Fontana economic history of Europe. London: Collins/Fontana, 1972–77. 6v. in 9.

D206 Deane, Phyllis. The first industrial revolution. 2d ed. New York: Cambridge Univ. Pr., 1979. 318p.

D207 Fogel, Robert W., and Stanley L. Engerman. Time on the cross: the economics of American Negro slavery. Boston: Little, 1974. 2v.

D208 Gerschenkron, Alexander. Continuity in history and other essays. Cambridge, Mass.: Harvard Univ. Pr., 1968. 545p.

D208 Habukkah, H. J. American and British technol-
A   ogy in the nineteenth century. Cambridge: Cambridge Univ. Pr., 1962.

D209 Hicks, John. A theory of economic history. Oxford: Oxford Univ. Pr., 1969. 191p.

D210 Landes, David S. The unbound Prometheus: technological change and industrial development in Western Europe from 1750 to the present. London: Cambridge Univ. Pr., 1969. 566p.

D211 North, Douglass C., and Robert Thomas. The rise of the Western world: a new economic history. New York: Cambridge Univ. Pr., 1973. 170p.

D212 Pirenne, Henri. Economic and social history of medieval Europe. Tr. by I. E. Clegg. New York: Harcourt, 1937. 239p.

D213 Postan, Michael M. Essays on medieval agriculture and general problems of the medieval economy. Cambridge: Cambridge Univ. Pr., 1973. 302p.

D214 Sombart, Werner. The quintessence of capitalism: a study of the history and psychology of the modern business man. Tr. by M. Epstein. New York: Fertig, 1967. 400p.

D215 Weber, Max. General economic history. Tr. by H. Knight. New York: Greenberg, 1927. 401p.

INSTITUTIONAL ECONOMICS

One of the consequences of the research of the German historical school in economics was the development of institutional economics, which experienced its main flowering in the United States in the early twentieth century. Its main representatives were Thorstein Veblen and John R. Commons in the United States, and John A. Hobson in Great Britain. The institutionalists had no real quarrel with the prevailing economic theory, though in some of the less friendly reviews of their ideas this opinion is sometimes expressed. They tried to do what some of the more thoughtful members of the German school of historical economics had already attempted; that is, they tried to examine the social role played by economic institutions and the way in which these institutions exerted feedback on the functioning of the economic system itself. They tried to provide answers to questions that general theory had not been able to solve. These answers were not to be found in the economic system as such but in the social relations, in the psychology of the participants in the economic process, and in the distribution of political power throughout a given society.

In its period of flowering (i.e., during the first three decades of this century), institutional economics made a very real contribution. By now many of the suggestions proffered by the institutional economists have been incorporated into the general body of economics. In the postwar period this has been facilitated by the growing interest in the economics of underdeveloped countries and by the fact that their cultural and social conditions, as well as their economic institutions, were patently different from those of Western nations. Hence, contemporary economics, though still predominantly "theoretical and analytical," has become much more "institutional" than the economics of even a generation ago.

D216 Ayres, Clarence E. The theory of economic progress: a study of the fundamentals of economic development and cultural change. 3d ed. Kalamazoo: Western Mich. Univ. Institute of Public Affairs, 1978. 324p.

D217 Commons, John R. Legal foundations of capitalism. Madison: Univ. of Wisconsin Pr., 1957. 394p.

D218 Gordon, Wendell. Institutional economics: the changing system. Austin: Univ. of Texas Pr., 1980. 366p.

D219 Hobson, John A. Work and wealth: a human valuation. New York: Kelley, 1965. 367p. (reprint of 1914 ed.)

D220 Polanyi, Karl. Primitive, archaic, and modern economies: essays of Karl Polanyi. Tr. by George Dalton. Boston: Beacon, 1971. 346p.

D221 Veblen, Thorstein. The theory of business enterprise. New York: Kelley, 1969. 400p. (reprint of 1904 ed.)

D222 ———. The theory of the leisure class: an economic study of institutions. New York: Modern Library, 1934. 404p.

Cross-Cultural Comparison of Economic Institutions

As indicated above, some of the work that has incorporated suggestions originally made by the institutional economists relates to cross-cultural comparisons of economic institutions. The number of studies in this field has been greatly expanded in recent years, and research in this branch of economics has become very popular. A large number of field reports have been made available on the economic institutions of peoples with cultures very different from those of the West, and steps have been taken to develop a field of "economic anthropology." It would be impossible to provide an adequate listing of all the case studies in this field that are now available.

On the basis of these field studies, and through the cooperation of several researchers, some comparative studies have been produced. These tend to incorporate the results of field research from various sources. The economist in search of generalizations is better served by the comparative studies than by the special field studies, since the former already contribute to a certain effort at generalization. Moreover, comparative studies tend to select the major variables from several field studies and to place primary emphasis on them. In an area in which institutional variety is so large, this is an important step forward.

In the following, we present a few studies that may properly be said to fall into the area of the comparative cross-cultural study of economic institutions. Some are case studies, others are more genuine comparative studies. Some deal with relatively simple and primitive societies, others with more advanced societies—notably those in which extensive planning of the socialist variety is practiced. Some are recent attempts to digest and evaluate the field of comparative economic studies. These are merely samples of a rapidly growing literature, which in the not too distant future is likely to supply us with extensive descriptive and analytical accounts of the economic relations in most countries and societies of the world.

D223 Bergson, Abram. The economics of Soviet planning. New Haven, Conn.: Yale Univ. Pr., 1964. 394p.

D224 ———, and H. Levine, eds. The Soviet economy: toward the year 2000. London: Allen & Unwin, 1983. 496p.

D225 Dalton, George, ed. Tribal and peasant economies: readings in economic anthropology. Austin: Univ. of Texas Pr., 1976. 584p.

D226 Eckstein, Alexander. China's economic revolution. New York: Cambridge Univ. Pr., 1977. 340p.

D227 Firth, Raymond W., ed. Themes in economic anthropology. London: Tavistock, 1970. 292p.

D228 Gadgil, Dhananjaya R. Planning and economic policy in India. New York: International Pubns. Serv., 1972. 405p.

D229 Moore, Wilbert E. The impact of industry. Englewood Cliffs, N.J.: Prentice-Hall, 1965. 117p.

D230 Patrick, Hugh, and H. Rosovsky, eds. Asia's new giant: how the Japanese economy works. Washington, D.C.: Brookings, 1976. 943p.

D232 Rosovsky, Henry. Capital formation in Japan, 1868–1949. New York: Free Pr., 1961. 358p.

D233 Schneider, Harold K. Economic man: the anthropology of economics. New York: Free Pr., 1974. 278p.

D234 Schran, Peter. Guerilla economy: the development of the Shensi-Kansu-Ninghsia border region, 1937–1945. Albany: State Univ. of New York Pr., 1976. 323p.

D235 Zimbalist, Andrew, ed. Comparative economic systems: an assessment of knowledge, theory and method. Boston: Kluwer-Nijhoff, 1984. 177p.

D236 ———, and H. Sherman. Comparing economic systems: a political-economic approach. New York: Academic, 1984.

APPLICATION OF ECONOMIC THEORIES

In the preceding discussion, we covered all the fields in which economic theories have been developed, with the exception of theories relating to the international division of labor. These theories have found application in several areas of practical concern, and we shall now turn to a few such applications. We will deal first with agriculture, labor, banking and business man-

agement, industrial organization and regulation, energy and the environment, health, and education, then with applications of economic theory to the activities of governments, and will finally arrive at a general consideration of economic policies and planning.

Agricultural Economics

Agricultural economics is an area in which a literature has developed that in scope and quantity equals, or perhaps even exceeds, that of all other fields combined. Agricultural economists in the United States have their own professional organization, their own journal, and in most universities are organized in their own departments. Hence, there are probably more data available on various aspects of economic matters pertaining to agriculture than on any other field of production. This proliferation of research and publications in agricultural economics has taken place in spite of the fact that an increasingly smaller percentage of the labor force in the United States is employed in agriculture. This has had the effect, however, of bringing to the attention of many agricultural economists the importance of farming in foreign countries, especially the poorer countries of Asia, Africa, and Latin America, where the majority of the labor force is engaged in agriculture and a sizable proportion of their total output is agricultural. Moreover, their techniques of farming are primitive, their organization of agricultural production is backward and clumsy, and their applications of modern methods are lagging behind. There are important needs that call for changes in the structure of landholding, and profound changes also are needed in the patterns of farm management and agricultural marketing. Although the literature does not yet fully represent these concerns, a growing stream of articles and pamphlets is devoted to these problems, and even the official agencies of the U.S. Department of Agriculture are increasingly concerned with the problems of the poorer countries.

It would be impossible within a reasonable space to enter into all the ramifications of empirical, theoretical, and applied studies in the field of agricultural economics. We therefore list only a few of the monographs that seem to be of most general interest and widest applicability. But it should be pointed out that such organizations as the U.S. Bureau of Farm Economics, the Food Research Institute at Stanford University, and many agricultural extension stations and departments of agriculture (especially at the land-grant colleges) supply an abundance of valuable special materials on all aspects of farming, land economics, agricultural marketing, and agricultural management.

D237 de Janvry, Alain. The agrarian question and reformism in Latin America. Baltimore: Johns Hopkins Univ. Pr., 1981. 352p.

D238 Dovring, Folke. Land and labor in Europe in the 20th century: a comparative survey of recent agarian history. 3d rev. ed. The Hague: Nijhoff, 1965. 522p.

D239 Fox, Karl A., and D. Gale Johnson, comps. Readings in the economics of agriculture. Homewood, Ill.: Irwin, 1969. 517p.

D240 Frankel, Francine. India's green revolution: political costs of economic growth. Princeton, N.J.: Princeton Univ. Pr., 1971. 232p.

D241 Hayami, Yujiro, and Vernon W. Ruttan. Agricultural development: an international perspective. Baltimore: Johns Hopkins Univ. Pr., 1971. 367p.

D242 Heady, Earl O. Agricultural policy under economic development. Ames: Iowa State Univ. Pr., 1962. 682p.

D243 Johnson, David Gale. World agriculture in disarray. New York: St. Martin's, 1973. 304p.

D244 Johnston, Bruce F., and Peter Kilby. Agriculture and structural transformation: economic strategies in late-developing countries. New York: Oxford Univ. Pr., 1975. 474p.

D245 Lappé, Frances, and J. Collins. Food first: beyond the myth of scarcity. New York: Ballantine, 1978. 619p.

D246 Mellor, John W. Economics of agricultural development. Ithaca, N.Y.: Cornell Univ. Pr., 1966. 403p.

D247 Schultz, Theodore W. Economic growth and agriculture. New York: McGraw-Hill, 1968. 306p.

D248 ———. Transforming traditional agriculture. New Haven, Conn.: Yale Univ. Pr., 1964. 212p.

D249 Sen, Amartya. Poverty and famines: an essay on entitlement and deprivation. Oxford: Oxford Univ. Pr., 1983. 272p.

D249 A Timmer, C. Peter, and others. Food policy analysis. Baltimore and London: Johns Hopkins Univ. Pr., 1983. 301p.

D250 Wharton, Clifton R., ed. Subsistence agriculture and economic development. Chicago: Aldine, 1969. 481p.

D251 Wortman, Sterling, and Ralph W. Cummings, Jr. To feed this world: the challenge and the strategy. Baltimore and London: Johns Hopkins Univ. Pr., 1978. 440p.

Industrial Labor Force

With agriculture declining in importance in the advanced countries, there has been an increase in the attention given to industrialism and its associated phenomena. At one time principal attention was paid to the standard of living of the laborer, but with the increasing capacity of the more highly developed economies to afford a rising standard of comfort for the average worker, the main attention has turned to other problems, principally the size and composition of the labor force, the impact and strategy of trade unions, the conditions of work on the job, labor-management relations, income distribution, and the specific phenomena of poverty and racial and sexual discrimination.

At first sight the problem of the determination of the labor force appears easiest and most straightforward. Superficially, one would assume that the study of the labor force turns on a primarily statistical problem: counting the number of workers in a series of industries and determining fluctuations and changes in that number over time. But once one penetrates the reasons for these fluctuations, one observes that many difficult and complex social problems are involved.

For example, if we witness a sharp, sudden change in the labor force in a given industry, is this due to technical change, to different social views of the population, to changes in wages or general working conditions, to changes in the requirements of skill in the industry, or to some combination of these forces? What determines the participation of women, especially married women, in the labor force? The income of a household is one factor, its aspirations another; cultural and social attitudes regarding women's work a third; the conditions under which a job may be performed a fourth; hours, wages, and wage differentials a fifth, sixth, and seventh; and so on.

Whether we are interested in the participation of women in industrial and related work, whether we ask what impact the age of leaving school exerts, or whether we study the consequences of automation or the problem of unemployment, we are concerned with some aspect of the analysis of the labor force. Hence studies in the field have appeared in growing numbers and have become oriented toward an increasing variety of questions and problems.

D252 Addison, John T., and W. Stanley Siebert. The market for labor: an analytical treatment. Santa Monica, Calif.: Goodyear, 1979. 500p.

D253 Bakke, Edward W. The unemployed worker: a study of the task of making a living without a job. Hamden, Conn.: Archon, 1969. 465p.

D254 Braverman, Harry. Labor and monopoly capital. New York: Monthly Review, 1974. 465p.

D255 Doeringer, Peter B., and Michael J. Piore. Internal labor markets and manpower analysis. Lexington, Mass.: Heath, 1971. 214p.

D256 Ehrenberg, Ronald G., and Robert S. Smith. Modern labor economics: theory and public policy. Glenview, Ill.: Scott, Foresman, 1982. 514p.

D257 Foner, Philip S. Labor and the American Revolution. Westport, Conn.: Greenwood, 1976. 256p.

D258 Gordon, David, and others. Segmented work, divided workers: the historical transformation of labor in the United States. Cambridge: Cambridge Univ. Pr., 1982. 288p.

D259 Horstein, Zmira, and others, eds. The economics of the labour market. London: Her Majesty's Stationery Office, 1981. 328p.

D260 Kerr, Clark. Labor markets and wage determination: the Balkanization of labor markets and other essays. Berkeley: Univ. of California Pr., 1977. 222p.

D260 Killingsworth, Mark R. Labor supply. Cam-
A   bridge: Cambridge Univ. Pr., 1983. 493p.

D261 Zimbalist, Andrew, ed. Case studies on the labor process. New York: Monthly Review, 1981. 314p.

Wages and Income Distribution

The most important considerations determining the value of the work of a laborer are expressed in the theory of wages. The income of a large segment of the population in the industrial states is determined on the basis of the level of wages. The theory of determination of how high they should be, and whether the wage receivers are exploited, is the subject of one of the longest quarrels among economists. The theory of wages was basic to Karl Marx, and is still basic to John Hicks.

Although wage earnings comprise about two-thirds of national income, differences in earnings from rents, interest payments, and profits also account for the observed pattern of income distribution. Therefore, this has been a related but separate area of research.

D262 Atkinson, A. B. The economics of inequality. 2d ed. New York: Oxford Univ. Pr., 1983. 296p.

D263 ———, ed. Wealth, income, and inequality. 2d ed. Oxford: Oxford Univ. Pr., 1980. 412p.

D264 Dobb, Maurice H. Wages. London: Nisbet, 1956. 201p.

D265 Douglas, Paul H. The theory of wages. New York: Kelley, 1964. 639p. (reprint of 1934 ed.)

D266 Hicks, John R. The theory of wages. 2d ed. New York: St. Martin's, 1963. 388p.

D267 Jencks, Christopher. Who gets ahead? The determinants of economic success in America. New York: Basic Books, 1979. 397p.

D268 Lydall, Harold. A theory of income distribution. New York: Oxford Univ. Pr., 1979. 326p.

D269 McDiarmid, Orville J. Unskilled labor for development: its economic cost. Baltimore: Johns Hopkins Univ. Pr., 1977. 206p.

D270 Rees, Albert, and George P. Schultz. Workers and wages in an urban labor market. Chicago: Univ. of Chicago Pr., 1970. 236p.

Economics of Discrimination

Economists have also analyzed the problems of racial and sexual discrimination, especially within the labor market. Although income differences between blacks and whites have been narrowing slightly, they remain substantial, as do those between men and women. Economic analysis has been used to illustrate the extent of these differences, to indicate which groups within society may actually benefit from such discrimination, and to estimate the impact of government programs developed to eliminate discrimination.

D271 Ashenfelter, Orley, and Albert Rees, eds. Discrimination in labor markets. Princeton, N.J.: Princeton Univ. Pr., 1974. 136p.

D272 Becker, Gary S. The economics of discrimination. 2d ed. Chicago: Univ. of Chicago Pr., 1971. 137p.

D273 Lloyd, Cynthia B., and Beth T. Niemi. The economics of sex differentials. New York: Columbia Univ. Pr., 1979. 355p.

D274 Pascal, A. H., ed. Racial discrimination in economic life. Lexington, Mass.: Heath, 1972, 228p.

D275 Reich, Michael. Racial inequality: a political-economic analysis. Princeton, N.J.: Princeton Univ. Pr., 1981. 345p.

D276 Remick, Helen, ed. Comparable worth and wage discrimination: technical possibilities and political realities. Philadelphia: Temple Univ. Pr., 1984. 320p.

D277 Sowell, Thomas. Race and economics. New York and London: Longman, 1975. 276p.

Economics of Trade Unionism

Of equally great importance as the problems of size, quality, and composition of the labor force is the effect of trade unions. Probably little needs to be said in substantiating the importance of the subject, and so we will merely list a few of the major economic effects associated with the growth and changing structure of labor unionism.

The proper economic purpose of labor organizations is collective bargaining, and it is this aspect of unionism to which economists have paid most attention. To be sure, the internal structure of a union, the degree of free determination of its policies and objectives by the membership, its centralization, and the weight of its financial control play a role, but the major economic problems relate to the methods the union uses in determining wages and associated working conditions. Within this context is a whole set of further considerations, since determination of wages and working conditions by unions has extensive effects upon the economy as a whole. Although unions unquestionably increase the wage rates paid to their working members, recent studies indicate that the net effect of unionization on productivity may also be positive because of the associated "shock effects" upon management. The overall effects on profitability, however, remain negative.

Of equal importance is the problem of negotiations with management. The confrontation of a labor union with the heads of a large enterprise is, economically speaking, an instance of bilateral monopoly. The negotiations under these conditions can best be analyzed by application of the principles of the theory of games. Here again the nonachievement of consensus may lead to strikes or work stoppages that, in the case of some basic industries, may have far-reaching effects upon a country's economy. Hence it is not surprising that most modern nations have passed extensive legislation designed to regulate the organization, internal structure, and activities of labor unions.

D278 Atherton, Wallace. Theory of union bargaining goals. Princeton, N.J.: Princeton Univ. Pr., 1973. 160p.

D279 Bain, George S., and Robert Price. Profiles of union growth: a comparative statistical portrait of eight countries. Oxford: Basil Blackwell, 1981. 304p.

D280 Bok, Derek C., and John T. Dunlop. Labor and the American community. New York: Simon & Schuster, 1970. 542p.

D281 Dunlop, John T. Industrial relations systems. New York: Holt, 1958. 399p.

D282 ———, and Walter Galenson, eds. Labor in the twentieth century. New York: Academic, 1978. 329p.

D283 Freeman, Richard B., and James L. Medoff. What do unions do? New York: Basic Books, 1984. 272p.

D284 Galenson, Walter, ed. Labor in developing economies. Berkeley: Univ. of California Pr., 1962. 299p.

D285 Hoxie, Robert F. Trade unionism in the United States. 2d ed. New York: Russell & Russell, 1966. 468p. (reprint of 1923 ed.)

D286 Perlman, Selig. A theory of the labor movement. New York: Kelley, 1949. 321p. (reprint of 1928 ed.)

D287 Sturmthal, Adolf F. Unity and diversity in European labor: an introduction to contemporary labor movements. Glencoe, Ill.: Free Pr., 1953. 237p.

D288 Webb, Sidney, and Beatrice Webb. Industrial democracy. New York: Kelley, 1965. 929p. (reprint of 1920 ed.)

Labor-Management Relations

Negotiations between management and unions about wages and conditions of work also have an impact upon general labor-management relations. The work situation for an individual is not confined to a day's work in a completely impersonal environment and departure after this work is done, without the factory or the office having any impact whatsoever.

It was discovered early by efficiency experts that the environment in which work is performed has an impact upon productivity. It was discovered later that in many instances workers form informal groups that cooperate and that if these groups are disturbed, productivity declines. In brief, it was shown that the internal organization and layout of the work process, the flow of tasks, and the informal social relations that become established between workers have an effect upon the economic results of an enterprise.

But the relations between management and the workers also play a role. Such problems as grievance procedures, the possibilities of advancement in pay and in rank, and considerations of seniority and rights derived therefrom, and the barriers between the blue- and white-collar portion of the work force are paramount.

Labor-management relations have passed through various phases. They began with emphasis on strong paternalistic features, developed to a situation in which the two parties faced one another as "enemies," and gradually developed into more or less impersonal business relations. It is increasingly recognized that the injection of some added ingredients that will enhance workers' interest in their jobs, their company, and their industry may have beneficial effects upon productivity. A job, as is becoming more and more clearly seen, is not merely a means of earning a living; it is part of an individual's life. In some countries, including the United States, there also has been a renewed interest in worker-owned cooperatives and worker co-determination, whereby workers share in the control and/or ownership of the firm.

D291 Clark, Rodney. The Japanese company. New Haven: Yale Univ. Pr., 1979. 282p.

D292 Clegg, Hugh Armstrong. Trade unionism under collective bargaining: a theory based on comparisons of six countries. Oxford: Basil Blackwell, 1976. 121p.

D293 Espinosa, Juan, and Andrew Zimbalist. Economic democracy: workers' participation in Chilean industry, 1970–1973. New York: Academic, 1978. 211p.

D294 Jones, Derek, and Jan Svejnar, eds. Participatory and self-managed firms: evaluating economic performance. Lexington, Mass.: Lexington Books, 1982. 416p.

D295 Kerr, Clark, and others. Industrialism and industrial man: the problems of labor and management in economic growth. 2d ed. New York: Oxford Univ. Pr., 1964. 263p.

D296 Kochan, Thomas A. Collective bargaining and industrial relations. Homewood, Ill.: Irwin, 1980. 523p.

D298 Mayo, Elton. The human problems of an industrial civilization. New York: Viking, 1960. 187p.

D299 Moore, Wilbert E., and Arnold S. Feldman, eds. Labor commitment and social change in developing areas. New York: Social Science Research Council, 1960. 378p.

D300 Oakeshott, Robert. The case for workers' co-ops. London: Routledge & Paul, 1978. 272p.

D301 Roethlisberger, Fritz J., and William J. Dickson. Management and the worker: an account of a research program conducted by the Western Electric Co., Hawthorne Works, Chicago. Cambridge, Mass.: Harvard Univ. Pr., 1939. 615p.

D302 Slichter, Sumner H., and others. The impact of collective bargaining on management. Washington, D.C.: Brookings, 1960. 982p.

D303 Vanek, Jaroslav. The general theory of labor-managed market economies. Ithaca, N.Y.: Cornell Univ. Pr., 1970. 424p.

D304 Walton, Richard, and Robert McKersie. A behavioral theory of labor negotiations. New York: McGraw-Hill, 1965. 437p.

D305 Whyte, William Foote. Organizational behavior: theory and application. Homewood, Ill.: Irwin, 1969. 807p.

Management

The trends that have been observed in the study and research of labor problems have parallels in the field of management research. On the one hand, there has been a growth of interest in the social position of persons in management jobs, and studies have been extended to cover the psychological pressures and personality characteristics—creativity, achievement orientation, and others—that contribute to the performance of their jobs. On the other hand is the development of "scientific management" and the growing interpretation of business administration as a system of decision-making processes. Decisions of varying importance, under varying constraints, are made on different levels in a management structure, and the organization of decision-making machinery that entails both vertical and horizontal lines of interconnection has become a fascinating field of study.

At the same time, the place and role of business, its structural aspects, and its evolution have become points of interest. Thus the literature may be divided into three parts. The first, which will not be discussed here, is the rather old-fashioned set of studies and texts on technical aspects of business administration, such as accounting practices, advertising, salesmanship, etc. The second part is devoted to management as a set of decisions and considerations underlying this traditional interpretation of management. The third is the interpretation of business leadership as the performance of the entrepreneurial function, its history, and the present challenge to entrepreneurship.

A few of the more important works on management proper are listed below.

D306 Barnard, Chester I. The functions of the executive. Cambridge, Mass.: Harvard Univ. Pr., 1968. 334p.

D307 Chandler, Alfred D. Management strategy and business development. Mystic, Conn.: Verry, 1976. 608p.

D308 Cyert, Richard M., and James G. March. A behavioral theory of the firm. Englewood Cliffs, N.J.: Prentice-Hall, 1963. 332p.

D309 Drucker, Peter F. Technology, management & society: essays. New York: Harper, 1977. 209p.

D310 ———. An introductory view of management. New York: Harper, 1978. 588p. (Based on the author's Management)

D311 Dubin, Robert. Human relations in administration. 4th ed. Englewood Cliffs, N.J.: Prentice-Hall, 1974. 640p.

D312 Koontz, Harold, and others. Management. 7th ed. New York: McGraw-Hill, 1980. 682p.

D313 Lawrence, Paul R., and Jay W. Lorsch. Organization and environment: managing differentiation and integration. Homewood, Ill.: Irwin, 1969. 279p.

D314 Likert, Rensis. The human organization: its management & value. New York: McGraw-Hill, 1967.

D315 March, James G., and Herbert A. Simon. Organizations. New York: Wiley, 1958. 262p.

D316 McGregor, Douglas. The human side of enterprise. New York: McGraw-Hill, 1960. 246p.

D317 Miner, John B. The management process: theory, research and practice. 2d ed. New York: Macmillan, 1978. 559p.

D318 Peters, Thomas J., and Robert H. Waterman, Jr. In search of excellence: lessons from America's best-run companies. New York: Harper, 1982. 360p.

D319 Selznick, Philip. Leadership in administration: a sociological interpretation. Rev. ed. Berkeley: Univ. of California Pr., 1983. 162p.

D320 Simon, Herbert A. Administrative behavior: a study of decision-making processes in administrative organization. 3d ed. New York: Free Pr., 1976. 364p.

D321 Taylor, Frederick Winslow. The principles of scientific management. New York: Harper, 1911. 207p.

D323 Weick, Karl E. The social psychology of organizing. 2d ed. Reading, Mass.: Addison-Wesley, 1979. 294p.

D324 Whyte, William F., and others. Money and motivation: an analysis of incentives in industry. New York: Harper, 1955. 268p.

Entrepreneurship

As we have seen, the various studies of the human element in productive activity—labor, management, salaried officials—have begun to stress the motivational and general psychological background of economic performance in these areas. Of all types of economic activity, entrepreneurship has been studied most intensively, with the personality angle in view, and it was with primary consideration of the performance of entrepreneurship that students wrote monographs that are explicitly devoted to both economics and psychology.

Entrepreneurship has been differently defined; that is, its main characteristics have been given different weights. J.B. Say defined it as the performance of combining productive factors—of drawing labor, capital, and science together for purposes of production. Later writers have stressed the risk element characteristic of entrepreneurs. But Joseph Schumpeter has stressed the innovating activity of enterprisers, and this interpretation has been more or less generally accepted. In a private enterprise economy it is the entrepreneur who performs the crucial function of pushing the system to higher and better standards of performance, who introduces innovations in technology, organization, and marketing activities. But since not every person has the innate or even acquired propensities for entrepreneurship, it is not strange that this question should have been asked: What personality traits are associated with the performance of entrepreneurial functions? The life histories and activities of entrepreneurs have been examined to determine whether any useful generalizations can be derived from this study.

D325 Beard, Miriam. A history of business. Ann Arbor: Univ. of Michigan Pr., 1962–63. 2v.

D326 Casson, Mark. The entrepreneur: an economic theory. Totowa, N.J.: Barnes & Noble, 1982. 418p.

D327 Cochran, Thomas C. Basic history of American business. 2d ed. Princeton, N.J.: Van Nostrand Reinhold, 1968. 191p.

D328 Cole, Arthur H. Business enterprise in its social setting. Cambridge, Mass.: Harvard Univ. Pr., 1959. 286p.

D329 Kilby, Peter. Entrepreneurship and economic development. New York: Free Pr., 1971. 384p.

D330 Lane, Frederic C., and Jelle C. Riemersma, eds. Enterprise and secular change: readings in economic history. Homewood, Ill.: Irwin, 1953. 556p.

D331 McClelland, David C. The achieving society. New York: Irvington, 1976. 512p.

D332 Redlich, Fritz. The molding of American banking: men & ideas. New York: Johnson, 1968. 2v. (reprint of 1951 ed., issued as v.2 of his History of American business leaders: a series of studies)

Invention and Innovation

If entrepreneurship is defined as consisting primarily of the introduction of innovations, the role of invention in economics becomes crucial. Here is a field that is still too little explored for us to have really useful theories. Yet some work has been done both along historical lines and in an analytical direction. Here, as in the general field of business management, the haphazard accidental practices of earlier days are shown to have been replaced by the much more orderly procedures of research and development departments and the planned execution of inventive activity. The economics of the modern research laboratory has not yet been explored as exhaustively as that of the family farm or the industrial plant, but the applicable principles in terms of performance and profitability differ little, if at all, from those applied to other business entities.

D333 Gilfillan, S. C. Sociology of invention. Cambridge, Mass.: MIT Pr., 1970. 185p. (Supplement to Sociology of invention. San Francisco: San Francisco Pr., 1971.)

D334 Gold, Bela, ed. Technological change: economics, management, and environment. New York: Pergamon, 1975. 175p.

D335 Griliches, Zvi, and others, eds. Patents, inventions, and economic change: data and selected essays. Cambridge, Mass.: Harvard Univ. Pr., 1972. 320p.

D335 Griliches, Zvi, ed. R&D, patents, and produc-
A tivity. Chicago and London: Univ. of Chicago Pr., 1984. 512p.

D336 Jewkes, John, and others. The sources of invention. 2d ed. New York: Norton, 1969. 372p.

D337 Kamien, Morton I., and Nancy L. Schwartz. Market structure and innovation. Cambridge: Cambridge Univ. Pr., 1982. 241p.

D338 Mansfield, Edwin. The economics of technological change. New York: Norton, 1968. 257p.

D339 ———, and others. The production and application of new industrial technology. New York: Norton, 1977. 220p.

D340 Meier, Richard L. Science and economic development: new patterns of living. 2d ed. Cambridge, Mass.: MIT Pr., 1966. 273p.

D341 Nelson, Richard R., and others. Technology, economic growth, and public policy. Washington, D.C.: Brookings, 1967. 238p.

D342 Noble, David F. America by design: science, technology, and the rise of corporate capitalism. New York: Knopf, 1977. 384p.

D343 Schmookler, Jacob. Invention and economic growth. Cambridge, Mass.: Harvard Univ. Pr., 1966. 332p.

D344 Stoneman, Paul. The economic analysis of technological change. Oxford: Oxford Univ. Pr., 1983. 256p.

D345 Strassman, W. Paul. Risk and technical innovation: American manufacturing methods during the nineteenth century. Ithaca, N.Y.: Cornell Univ. Pr., 1959. 249p.

Banking and Finance

Although innovation and entrepreneurship are customarily thought of in connection with industry, an important area of entrepreneurial innovation has been the field of finance and banking. The very ordinary commercial bank, with which we are all familiar, is an invention of medieval Europe. In later periods, specialized investment banks were founded, and in the course of the evolution of banking, central banks or central banking systems, such as the Federal Reserve System, have come into prominence. Today the central banks are by far the most important portions of the banking systems of the various countries since they not only perform functions of credit supply but assist the fiscal authorities in the implementation of policies of monetary and price stability.

In the course of time, banks have developed many new techniques and functions, and various banks have specialized in such aspects of business as small loans, mortgage lending, savings deposits, investment trusts, and other financial practices. But the major business of banks has been commercial banking—that is, granting loans to merchants and manufacturers and accepting deposits against which checks can be drawn. Since checks circulate in place of cash and since banks, by granting loans, can influence the number of checks in circulation at any time, they have the power to influence indirectly the quantity of money in circulation and, with this, the level of prices.

Since banks receive interest on loans, their profit motive gives them an incentive to augment the number of loans outstanding as much as possible; but at the same time they must impose self-restraints, since if all outstanding checks were presented at once for payment in cash, the banks could not make these payments. Hence they can expand their loan activities only up to a certain level and must watch that this does not exceed a certain multiple of their cash reserves. This ratio between deposits and cash reserves is the reserve ratio, which is sometimes regulated by government. In some countries a customary limit is self-imposed by the banks.

The central bank may also lend directly to banks at a rate of interest called the rediscount rate. The lower the rediscount rate, the more reserves banks will want to borrow from the central bank, and the easier it will be for banks to make loans themselves.

Rediscounting, reserve requirements, and other measures (e.g., open-market sales and purchases of certain securities) are the main practices employed by central banks to control the expansion and contraction of bank credit and thus to regulate the currency in effective circulation. It is clear that an understanding of banking practices is closely related to the analysis of monetary phenomena and prices.

D346 Bagehot, Walter. Lombard Street: a description of the money market. Westport, Conn.: Hyperion, 1979. 176p. (reprint of 1962 ed.; orig. pub. 1874)

D348 Friedman, Milton. A program for monetary stability. New York: Fordham Univ. Pr., 1959. 110p.

D349 ———, and Anna J. Schwartz. Monetary history of the United States, 1867–1960. Princeton, N.J.: Princeton Univ. Pr., 1963. 860p.

D350 Friedman, Milton. Monetary trends in the United States and the United Kingdom: their relation to income, prices and interest rates, 1867–1975. Chicago: Univ. of Chicago Pr., 1982. 664p.

D351 Gurley, John G., and Edward S. Shaw. Money in a theory of finance. Washington, D.C.: Brookings, 1960. 371p.

D352 Hawtrey, Ralph G. Currency and credit. 4th ed. New York: Arno, 1978. 475p. (reprint of 1919 ed.)

D353 Hester, Donald D., and James L. Pierce. Bank management and portfolio behavior. New Haven, Conn.: Yale Univ. Pr., 1975. 304p.

D354 Hutchinson, Harry D. Money, banking, and the U.S. economy. 5th ed. Englewood Cliffs, N.J.: Prentice-Hall, 1984. 560p.

D355 Johnson, Harry G. Macroeconomics and monetary theory. Chicago: Aldine, 1972. 214p.

D356 Markowitz, Harry. Portfolio selection: efficient diversification of investments. New York: Wiley, 1959. 344p.

D357 Robertson, Dennis H. Essays in monetary theory. London: Staples, 1956. 252p.

D359 Sharpe, William F. Portfolio theory and capital markets. New York: McGraw-Hill, 1970.

D360 Van Horne, James C. Financial management and policy. 6th ed. Englewood Cliffs, N.J.: Prentice-Hall, 1983. 832p.

D361 ———. Financial market rates and flows. 2d ed. Englewood Cliffs, N.J.: Prentice-Hall, 1984. 320p.

Industrial Organization and Regulation

Many theoretical models of the economy treat each firm as if it supplied a tiny portion of the output in its industry and therefore could sell as much as it could produce at the prevailing market price. The classic example is that of the wheat farmer. Economists have also noted that many industries consist of only one firm, several dominant firms, or many smaller firms, each of which produces a slightly different product. These differences in market structures have wide ramifications for industrial behavior and consumer welfare. The study of these structures is called industrial organization.

D362 Adams, Walter, ed. The structure of American industry. 6th ed. New York: Macmillan, 1982. 513p.

D363 Bain, Joe S. Industrial organization. 2d ed. New York: Wiley, 1968. 678p.

D363 A Baumol, William J., and John Panzar. Contestable markets and the theory of industry structure. New York: HBJ, 1982. 510p.

D364 Berle, Adolf, and Gardiner Means. The modern corporation and private property. New York: Macmillan, 1932. 396p.

D366 Phillips, Almarin. Market structure, organization, and performance. Cambridge, Mass.: Harvard Univ. Pr., 1962. 257p.

D367 Posner, Richard A. Antitrust law: an economic perspective. Chicago: Univ. of Chicago Pr., 1976. 262p.

D368 Scherer, F. M. Industrial market structure and economic performance. 2d ed. Boston: Houghton, 1980. 632p.

D368 A Shepherd, William G., and Clair Wilcox. Public policies toward business. 6th ed. Homewood, Ill.: Irwin, 1979. 601p.

D369 Williamson, Oliver E. Markets and hierarchies: analysis and antitrust implications. New York: Free Pr., 1983. 320p.

See also *A behavioral theory of the firm* by Richard Cyert and James G. March, described at D308.

Several industries such as utilities and, until recently, communications and transportation have been heavily regulated by the government. Because of scale economies and other market imperfections, it was felt that these industries would otherwise achieve suboptimal results. Regulators have frequently asked economists their advice on pricing structures, rules of entry, and other regulatory practices. While economists are divided among themselves on the desirability of government regulation in many industries, there is some agreement on which types of regulations are more beneficial (or less harmful) than others.

D370 Bonbright, James C. Principles of public utility rates. New York: Columbia Univ. Pr., 1961. 433p.

D370 Fromm, Gary, ed. Studies in public regulation.
A   Cambridge, Mass.: MIT Pr., 1981. 400p.

D371 Kahn, Alfred E. The economics of regulation. New York: Wiley, 1970. 2v.

D371 Keeler, Theodore E. Railroads, freight, and
A   public policy. Washington, D.C.: Brookings, 1983. 250p.

D372 Kolko, Gabriel. Railroads and regulation, 1877–1916. New York: Norton, 1970.

D373 Lave, Lester B., ed. Quantitative risk assessment in regulation. Washington, D.C.: Brookings, 1982. 264p.

D374 Owen, Bruce, and R. Braeutigan. The regulation game: strategic use of the administrative process. New York: Ballinger, 1978.

D375 Phillips, Almarin, ed. Promoting competition in regulated markets. Washington, D.C.: Brookings, 1975. 397p.

D375 Weiss, Leonard W., and Michael W. Klass, eds.
A   Case studies in regulation: revolution and reform. Boston: Little, 1981. 301p.

ENVIRONMENTAL AND ENERGY ECONOMICS

Two fields of applied microeconomics that have grown rapidly in the last 10 years are environmental and energy economics. The scarcity of energy resources has become increasingly apparent since the initial quadrupling of oil prices engineered by OPEC in late 1973. Similarly, problems of environmental pollution have raised public interest in the issues surrounding the social costs and benefits of preserving a salubrious environment. Work in these areas has produced some theoretical novelties but has mainly focused on the evaluation of policy alternatives.

D376 Adelman, M. A. The world petroleum market. Baltimore: Johns Hopkins Univ. Pr., 1973. 456p.

D377 Baxter, William. People or penguins: the case for optimal pollution. New York: Columbia Univ. Pr., 1974. 110p.

D377 Dasgupta, P. S., and G. M. Heal. Economic
A   theory and exhaustible resources. Cambridge: Cambridge Univ. Pr., 1979.

D378 Dorfman, Nancy, and R. Dorfman, eds. Economics of the environment: selected readings. 2d ed. New York: Norton, 1977. 494p.

D379 Griffin, James, and H. Steele. Energy economics and policy. New York: Academic, 1980. 370p.

D379 Landsberg, Hans, ed. Energy: the next twenty
A   years. Cambridge, Mass.: Ballinger, 1979. 656p.

D380 Lovins, Amory. Soft energy paths. New York: Harper, 1979. 231p.

D381 Mills, Edwin. The economics of environmental quality. New York: Norton, 1978. 304p.

D382 Seneca, Joseph, and M. Taussig. Environmental economics. 3d ed. Englewood Cliffs, N.J.: Prentice-Hall, 1984. 368p.

D383 Smith, V. Kerry, ed. Scarcity and growth reconsidered. Baltimore: Johns Hopkins Univ. Pr., 1979. 298p.

D384 Stobaugh, Robert, and D. Yergin, eds. Energy future. New York: Random, 1982. 368p.

D384 Tietenberg, Tom. Environmental and natural
A   resource economics. Glenview, Ill.; Scott, Foresman, 1984. 482p.

Health Economics

As expenditures on health care have grown rapidly and recently surpassed 10 percent of total national income, economists have applied their tools to this critical area. Although critics have argued that consumers of health care do not treat it like other commodities, economic models have provided many useful insights. Questions that have been addressed include the extent to which health insurance modifies patient behavior; the role of government in financing health care and the proper way to assess these programs; the objectives of physicians, hospitals, and other health care providers; the functioning of the market for pharmaceutical drugs; and the desirability of a national health insurance.

D385 Berki, Sylvester E. Hospital economics. Lexington, Mass.: Lexington Books, 1972. 270p.

D385 Feldstein, Martin. Hospital costs and health in-
A   surance. Cambridge, Mass.: Harvard Univ. Pr., 1981. 327p.

D386 Feldstein, Paul J. Health care economics. 2d ed. New York: Wiley, 1983. 573p.

D387 Fuchs, Victor. Who shall live? Health, economics, and social choice. New York: Basic Books, 1983. 168p.

D388 Greenburg, Warren, ed. Competition in the health care sector: past, present, and future. Germantown, Md.: Aspen Systems Corp., 1979. 420p.

D389 Luke, Roice D., and Jeffrey C. Bauer, ed. Issues in health economics. Rockville, Md.: Aspen Systems Corp., 1982. 624p.

D390 Pauly, Mark V., ed. National health insurance. What now, what later, what never? Washington, D.C.: American Enterprise Institute, 1980. 381p.

D391 Starr, Paul. The social transformation of American medicine. New York: Basic Books, 1982. 514p.

D391 Van der Gaag, Jacques, and Mark Perlman,
A eds. Health, economics, and health economics. Amsterdam: North-Holland, 1981. 400p.

D392 Warner, Kenneth E., and Bryan R. Luce. Cost-benefit and cost-effectiveness analysis in health care. Ann Arbor, Mich.: Health Administration Pr., 1982. 375p.

D393 Yett, D. E., and others. A forecasting and policy simulation model of the health care sector. Lexington, Mass.: Lexington Books, 1979. 204p.

Economics of Education

Economists have long argued that education plays a crucial role in economic development. In the past generation, however, they have examined this relationship more closely to determine the marginal impact of education on income. At the same time, other economists have argued that the educational system of a country preserves the status quo as much as it fosters upward mobility.

D394 Becker, Gary S. Human capital, 2d ed. New York: National Bureau of Economic Research, 1975. 268p.

D395 Bowles, Samuel, and Herbert Gintis. Schooling in capitalist America: educational reform and the contradictions of economic life. New York: Basic Books, 1976. 340p.

D396 Cohn, Elchanan. The economics of education. 2d ed. Cambridge, Mass.: Ballinger, 1978. 480p.

D397 Mincer, Jacob. Schooling, experience, and earnings. New York: National Bureau of Economic Research, 1974. 167p.

D398 Schultz, Theodore. The economic value of education. New York: Columbia Univ. Pr., 1963. 92p.

Public Finance

In a modern nation the policies in the monetary field are closely related to those in the fiscal field. In the present period of the world's development, a large proportion of a nation's income is transferred to government by means of taxes and is spent by the government. Through the budgetary process the government can withdraw or add to the purchasing power of the public, and can affect the level of employment and prosperity in the community. Deficit financing may be a blessing when the economy at large is sluggish, and may be a curse in a situation of full or nearly full employment. Hence the instrumentality of raising revenue and spending it on public works or other projects—together with the monetary policy of the central bank—is an important regulator of general economic activity.

Of all the features of public finance, the problem of taxation is the most controversial. It is not so much the fact of taxation but rather the economic impact of taxes, the kinds of taxes, and the distribution of the burden of taxation that are under discussion. Among the most important and controversial subjects are the question of indirect versus direct taxes, the problem of proportionality versus progressivity of taxation, and the question of the ease of shifting taxes onto the shoulders of someone else (e.g., by price changes or alteration of wage payments). In addition there are problems of the cost of collection, of the possibility of tax evasion and avoidance, and, above all, of the equity and justice of a tax system. It should be remembered that all modern societies have a multiplicity of taxes and that what affects each person is not the impact of a single tax but rather the tax system as a whole. These and many related problems are discussed in the monographs cited below.

D399 Aaron, Henry J. Who pays the property tax? A new view. Washington, D.C.: Brookings, 1975. 110p.

D400 ———, and Michael J. Boskin, eds. The economics of taxation. Washington, D.C.: Brookings, 1980. 418p.

D401 Aaron, Henry J., and Joseph Pechman, eds. How taxes affect economic behavior. Washington, D.C.: Brookings, 1981. 456p.

D402 Atkinson, Anthony B., and Joseph Stiglitz. Lectures on public economics. New York: McGraw-Hill, 1980. 640p.

D403 Blinder, Alan S., and others. The economics of public finance. Washington, D.C.: Brookings, 1974. 435p.

D404 Blum, Walter J., and Harry Kalven, Jr. The uneasy case for progressive taxation. Chicago: Univ. of Chicago Pr., 1953. 108p.

D405 Buchanan, James M. Public finance in democratic process: fiscal institutions and individual choice. Chapel Hill: Univ. of North Carolina Pr., 1967. 307p.

D406 Goode, Richard. The individual income tax. Rev. ed. Washington, D.C.: Brookings, 1976. 746p.

D407 Harberger, Arnold C. Taxation and welfare. Boston: Little, 1974. 304p.

D408 Haveman, Robert H., and Julius Margolis. Public expenditure and policy analysis. 3d ed. Boston: Houghton, 1982. 608p.

D409 King, Mervyn A., and Dan Fullerton, eds. The taxation of income from capital: a comparative study of the U.S., U.K., Sweden, and West Germany. Chicago: Univ. of Chicago Pr., 1984. 352p.

D410 Musgrave, Richard, and Peggy Musgrave. Public finance in theory and practice. 4th ed. New York: McGraw-Hill, 1984. 896p.

D411 Musgrave, Richard, and Alan T. Peacock, eds. Classics in the theory of public finance. New York: Macmillan, 1958. 244p.

D412 Pechman, Joseph A. Federal tax policy. 4th ed. Washington, D.C.: Brookings, 1983. 410p.

D412 ———, and Benjamin A. Okner. Who bears
A   the tax burden? Washington, D.C.: Brookings, 1974. 119p.

D413 Pechman, Joseph A., and P. Michael Timpane, eds. Work incentives and income guarantees: the New Jersey negative income tax experiment. Washington, D.C.: Brookings, 1975. 232p.

D414 Pigou, Arthur C. A study in public finance. 3d ed. New York: Kelley, 1971. 285p. (reprint of 1947 ed.)

D415 Simons, Henry C. Personal income taxation: the definition of income as a problem of fiscal policy. Chicago: Univ. of Chicago Pr., 1938. 238p.

General Role of Government in the Economy

Although the fiscal policies of the government have the most clearly discernible impact on governmental functions in the economy, modern governments enter the economy in many different ways. In the preceding paragraphs we discussed government expenditures as though they were undertaken merely or mainly as a means of economic stabilization, but it will be recalled that at an earlier stage we talked about government consumption. Certain outlays of governments are made precisely for the purchase of goods and services arising from the independent needs of providing the customary government services, rather than from the desire to carry out economic stabilization. In fact, some of the heaviest expenditures undertaken by central and local governments stem from these needs. For example, the expenditures on armaments or education, on dispensing justice, and on general administration

are autonomous expenses; only such expenses as certain relief payments or expenditures on certain public works have primarily a stabilizing function. It is proper, therefore, to study the general level of government activity as it has developed over time and to look into the problems of such governmental activities as the provision of materials and services for defense, education, etc. Recent research has also examined the behavior and objectives of government legislators and bureaucrats, who may not be as altruistic as we often assume.

D416 Baumol, William J. Welfare economics and the theory of the state. 2d ed. Cambridge, Mass.: Harvard Univ. Pr., 1967. 212p.

D417 Buchanan, James M., and Gordon Tullock. The calculus of consent: logical foundations of institutional democracy. Ann Arbor: Univ. of Michigan Pr., 1962. 361p.

D418 Dorfman, Robert, ed. Measuring benefits of government investments. Washington, D.C.: Brookings, 1965. 429p.

D419 Downs, Anthony. An economic theory of democracy. New York: Harper, 1957. 310p.

D420 Fabricant, Solomon. The trend of government activity in the United States since 1900. New York: National Bureau of Economic Research, 1952. 267p.

D421 Friedman, Milton, and Rose Friedman. Free to choose: a personal statement. New York and London: HBJ, 1980. 338p.

D422 Galbraith, John Kenneth. The new industrial state. 3d ed. Boston: Houghton, 1978. 427p.

D423 Gramlich, Edward M. Benefit-cost analysis of government programs. Englewood Cliffs, N.J.: Prentice-Hall, 1981. 304p.

D424 Hitch, Charles J., and Roland N. McKean. The economics of defense in the nuclear age. Cambridge, Mass.: Harvard Univ. Pr., 1960. 422p.

D424 Kuperberg, Mark, and Charles R. Beitz. Law,
A   economics, and philosophy. Totowa, N.J.: Rowman & Allenheld, 1983. 294p.

D425 Mueller, Dennis C. Public choice. New York and London: Cambridge Univ. Pr., 1979. 297p.

D425 Niskanen, William A. Structural reform of the
A   federal budget process. Washington, D.C.: American Enterprise Inst., 1973.

D426 Olson, Mancur. The logic of collective action: public goods and the theory of groups. Rev. ed. Cambridge, Mass.: Harvard Univ. Pr., 1971. 176p.

D427 Posner, Richard A. Economic analysis of law. 2d ed. Boston and Toronto: Little, 1977. 572p.

D429 Stigler, George J. The citizen and the state: essays on regulation. Chciago: Univ. of Chicago Pr., 1977. 209p.

D430 Stokey, Edith, and Richard Zeckhauser. A primer for policy analysis. New York: Norton, 1978. 356p.

Economic Policy and Planning

Fiscal measures, as well as other steps taken by the government, are all part and parcel of the overall economic policy of the government. This policy may have varying objectives; it may be directed primarily toward the welfare of the people, or defense, or maximization of the rate of economic growth. In all instances, there will be efforts to bring some degree of equity to the distribution of goods and services, at least in the modern nations. The steps to these ends may be fiscal or regulatory, but usually they will be combinations of both.

In all instances in which the intervention of government is not inspired by a general production plan, we customarily speak of economic policy or sets of economic policies. Whenever the amount or degree of regulation is ordered according to a systematic, comprehensive schedule, we speak of economic planning. Dahl and Lindblom have shown that the limits between economic policy and economic planning are often blurred and that certain policies shade into planning and certain plans shade into measures of somewhat disjointed policies. In the literature, somewhat sharper distinctions are drawn, and one may make separate lists of studies that are concerned primarily with economic policies, the rationale for certain policies, and the consequences—intended or not—of economic policies. A few of the more challenging books in this vein are listed below.

D431 Clark, John M. Preface to social economics: essays in economic theory and social problems. New York: Kelley, 1967. 435p. (reprint of 1936 ed.)

D432 Dahl, Robert A., and Charles E. Lindblom. Politics, economics, and welfare. New York: Harper, 1953. 556p.

D433 Economic progress, private values, and public policy: essays in honor of William Fellner. Ed. by Bela Belassa and Richard Nelson. New York: Elsevier North-Holland, 1977. 339p.

D434 Galbraith, John Kenneth. The age of uncertainty. Boston: Houghton, 1977. 365p.

D435 Hawtrey, Ralph G. Economic aspects of sovereignty. 2d ed. New York: Longman, 1952. 191p.

D436 Hayek, Friedrich A. Law, legislation and liberty. Chicago: Univ. of Chicago Pr., 1973–79. 3v.

D437 Heller, Walter W. The economy: old myths and new realities. New York: Norton, 1976. 224p.

D438 Hicks, John R. Economic perspectives: further essays on money and growth. Oxford: Clarendon, 1977. 199p.

D439 Holland, Stuart, ed. Beyond capitalist planning. New York: St. Martin's, 1978. 222p.

D440 Johnson, Chalmers. MITI and the Japanese miracle. Stanford, Calif.: Stanford Univ. Pr., 1982. 393p.

D441 Lindblom, Charles. Politics and markets. New York: Basic Books, 1977. 403p.

D441 Magaziner, Ira, and Robert Reich. Minding
A   America's business: the decline and rise of the American economy. New York: HBJ, 1982. 387p.

D442 Shonfield, Andrew. Modern capitalism. London: Oxford Univ. Pr., 1969. 456p.

D443 Tullock, Gordon. Private wants, public means: an economic analysis of the desirable scope of government. New York: Basic Books, 1970. 262p.

Other books concentrate on planning. At some point, the possibility of planning as such is questioned, at another its wisdom, and at some points its efficiency. To all these questions, answers have been given, but the debate continues. However, the proponents of some form of planning are likely to win out. Whether this results from the economic temper of our time or from the greatly improved capacity of planners to draw up realistic plans, or whether it shows an overall trend toward collectivism, is difficult to say. At any rate, the inclination toward planning has become ubiquitous, and anyone advocating it may be following the wave of the future.

D444 Ellman, Michael. Socialist planning. Cambridge: Cambridge Univ. Pr., 1979. 300p.

D445 Hindess, Barry, ed. Sociological theories of the economy. London: Macmillan, 1977. 199p.

D446 Kornai, Janos. Economics of shortage. Amsterdam: North-Holland, 1980.

D447 Lange, Oskar. Essays on economic planning. 2d ed. New York: Asia Publishing House, 1967. 97p.

D448 Lippincott, Benjamin E., ed. On the economic theory of socialism. By Oskar Lange and Fred M. Taylor. New York: Kelley, 1970. 143p. (reprint of 1939 ed.)

D449 Robinson, Joan. Aspects of development and underdevelopment. New York: Cambridge Univ. Pr., 1979. 146p.

D450 Taylor, Lance. Structuralist macroeconomics: applicable models for the Third World. New York: Basic Books, 1983. 234p.

D451 Waterston, Albert. Development planning: lessons of experience. Baltimore: Johns Hopkins Univ. Pr., 1965. 706p.

INTERNATIONAL ECONOMICS

Apart from a few stray comments, our discussion thus far has been concerned with economic relations in general—a situation in which abstractions were made of different nations or in which economic relations were confined to one country. But a large body of economic theory, applied economics, and thinking on economic policy relates explicitly to the problems of international exchanges and international interaction between sovereign nations. We shall briefly take up the various aspects of this part of economics.

The study of international economics may be divided into several branches. First, there is general theory. Then there are problems of international monetary economics (e.g., questions of exchange rates and international debt). Next there are problems of applied economics and economic policy. Finally, there is a literature that is beginning to deal with questions of international economic planning.

One of the main producers of works and sponsors of research in international economics is the United Nations and its specialized agencies. The United Nations itself publishes statistical and general works on international economic relations between all countries. The various regional economic commissions bring out annual reports and occasional studies on the international economic relations pertaining to the regions they serve. The Food and Agriculture Organization publishes works on international aspects of farm production and trade in agricultural commodities, the International Labor Organization on international migration and comparative studies on wages, etc. In addition, other special agencies, such as the Organization of American States, NATO, and the Organization for European Economic Cooperation and Development, sponsor international research and bring out publications in the field of regional or worldwide international economics.

Basic to all this study are works on the general theories of international economics and international trade. The most general works deal with the international, and sometimes the interregional, exchange of goods and services, particularly finished goods. But some studies concentrate on the international movement of productive factors (labor and capital). The basic works in the field are the following.

D452 Bhagwati, Jagdish. Essays in international economic theory. Cambridge, Mass.: MIT Pr., 1983. 2v.

D452 ———, and T. N. Srinivasan. Lectures on interA national trade. Cambridge, Mass.: MIT Pr., 1983. 414p.

D453 Caves, Richard E., and Ronald W. Jones. World trade and payments. 3d ed. Boston: Little, 1981. 548p.

D454 Dixit, A. K., and V. Norman. Theory of international trade. Cambridge: Cambridge Univ. Pr., 1980. 250p.

D455 Ethier, Wilfred. Modern international economics. New York: Norton, 1983. 588p.

D456 Haberler, Gottfried von. The theory of international trade, with its applications to commercial policy. New York: Kelley, 1968. 406p. (reprint of 1936 ed.)

D457 Harrod, Roy. International economics. New York: Cambridge Univ. Pr., 1959. 186p.

D458 Johnson, Harry G. The world economy at the crossroads: a survey of current problems of money, trade, and economic development. Oxford: Clarendon, 1965. 106p.

D458 Jones, Ronald W., and Peter Kenen, eds.
A Handbook of international economics. New York, Amsterdam: North-Holland, 1984. 2v.

D458 Kravis, Irving B., and others. World product
B and income: international comparison of real gross domestic product. Baltimore: Johns Hopkins Univ. Pr., 1982. 400p.

D459 Myrdal, Gunnar. An international economy, problems and prospects. Westport, Conn.: Greenwood, 1978. 381p. (reprint of 1956 ed.)

D460 Ohlin, Bertil. Interregional and international trade. Rev. ed. Cambridge, Mass.: Harvard Univ. Pr., 1967. 324p.

D461 Taussig, Frank W. International trade. Rev. ed. Cambridge, Mass.: Harvard Univ. Pr., 1967. 324p.

D462 Viner, Jacob. Studies in the theory of international trade. New York: Kelley, 650p. (reprint of 1937 ed.)

Balance of Payments and Exchange Rates

The most general treatises in international economics deal primarily with questions of the international exchange of goods and services and the problem of the prices of this exchange. However, as economists before Adam Smith knew, what may matter most for a country is not so much the items that enter into trade, or their prices, but rather the overall impact of international exchange. In other words, does a country come out as a net exporter or a net importer? In the former case it gains currency; in the latter case it loses currency.

The mercantilist writers, to whom the acquisition of gold through international trade was a highly favored objective, all wished a positive balance of payments—that is, a situation in which exports exceeded imports. A government that is welfare-oriented may well take a less extreme view, since an excess of imports over exports may, at certain times, contribute greatly to the country's overall level of welfare. But ultimately the most desirable policy is one of equilibrium in a country's international accounts.

In general, a net inflow of foreign funds, as well as a net outflow of domestic funds abroad, may have inflationary or deflationary results, just as a governmental budgetary deficit or surplus may have these effects. It is not always easy to insulate the domestic economy against the impact of balance-of-payments problems, and so policies designed to bring about equilibrium in the international accounts have certain obvious advantages.

One of the mechanisms by which a country's international indebtedness may be settled is the outflow of currency, especially gold. Another mechanism is the alteration of its rate of exchange—that is, the alteration of the price of foreign currencies in terms of its domestic currency. Depreciation is an alternative to gold outflow. And usually, if a country's balance of payments worsens, both of these adjustments may take place. In contemporary nations a great deal of effort is spent to influence the balance of payments and the exchange rates by various forms of governmental regulation, but before we can consider these we must be clear about the monetary and payment mechanisms involved.

Finally, an important regulatory device may be the international flow of capital, and in fact capital flows have often played a stabilizing role. In the more recent postwar period, the major stabilizing influence has come from foreign aid, although capital flows in certain cases have also been of significance.

D463 Aliber, Robert. The international money game. New York: Basic Books, 1983. 356p.

D464 Argy, Victor. The postwar international monetary crisis. London: Allen & Unwin, 1983. 472p.

D465 Corden, W. M. Inflation, exchange rates, and the world economy: lectures on international monetary economics. Chicago: Univ. of Chicago Pr., 1977. 160p.

D466 Dale, Richard, and R. Mattione. Managing global debt. Washington, D.C.: Brookings, 1983. 50p.

D467 Dornbusch, Rudiger. Open economy macroeconomics. New York: Basic Books, 1980. 293p.

D468 Fair, D. E., and R. Bertrand, eds. International lending in a fragile world economy. The Hague: Martinus Nijhoff, 1983. 421p.

D469 Frenkel, Jacob A., ed. Exchange rates and international macroeconomics. Chicago: Univ. of Chicago Pr., 1984. 400p.

D470 ———, and Harry G. Johnson, eds. The monetary approach to the balance of payments. Toronto: Univ. of Toronto Pr., 1976. 388p.

D471 Iversen, Carl. Aspects of the theory of international capital movements. 2d ed. New York: Kelley, 1967. 536p. (reprint of 1936 ed.)

D472 Kindleberger, Charles P. Europe and the dollar. Cambridge, Mass.: MIT Pr., 1966. 297p.

D473 ———. International money: a collection of essays. London: Allen & Unwin, 1981. 336p.

D474 Machlup, Fritz. International payments, debts and gold: collected essays. 2d ed. New York: New York Univ. Pr., 1976. 514p.

D475 Meier, Gerald M. Problems of a world monetary order. 2d ed. New York and Oxford: Oxford Univ. Pr., 1982. 343p.

D476 Moffit, Michael. The world's money: international banking from Bretton Woods to the brink of insolvency. New York: Simon & Schuster, 1983. 320p.

D477 Snider, Delbert A. International monetary relations. New York: Random, 1966. 141p.

D478 Tinbergen, Jan. Reshaping the international order: a report to the Club of Rome. New York: Dutton, 1976. 325p.

D479 Williams, John B. International trade under flexible exchange rates. Amsterdam: North-Holland, 1954. 332p.

Protectionism

As we have already pointed out, it is rare in our day that the free play of the market is allowed to exert its influence upon international transactions. The regulatory activity may be unilateral or multilateral; that is, it may be imposed by one country without regard to the interests of others or it may be imposed by mutual agreement among the countries concerned.

The first policy is protectionism. It consists of the imposition of tariffs, quotas, exchange controls, and various other measures designed to protect the domestic producers and consumers against foreign competition. Although different protective measures have different degrees of effectiveness, the most appropriate measures vary from country to country and from commodity to commodity. In one country a tariff may be a very effective means of reducing foreign competition, whereas in another country—owing to geographical, or transportation, or institutional factors—the same degree of protection can be achieved only by harsher means (e.g., quotas).

Since protectionism is a form of governmental regulation, most of the considerations apply to it that may be applied to other governmental economic policies. To what extent do considerations of equity, or national power, or economic growth prevail? Depending upon differences in objectives, different forms of the regulation of international economic transactions will be employed.

Finally, it should be remembered that just as economic policies, in general, have become highly refined and specialized, so have measures of international economic policy, and especially protectionist devices. The ingenuity that has gone into the development of new and more highly discriminating measures has been great, and one might well have hoped that it would have been applied to a somewhat worthier cause.

D480 Balassa, Bela. Trade liberalization among industrial countries: objectives and alternatives. New York: McGraw-Hill, 1967. 251p.

D481 Corden, W. M. The theory of protection. Oxford: Clarendon, 1971. 263p.

D482 Griffin, Keith B. International inequality and national poverty. New York: Holmes & Meier, 1978. 191p.

D483 Krauss, Melvyn. The new protectionism: the welfare state and international trade. New York: New York Univ. Pr., 1978. 119p.

D484 Kravis, Irving B. Domestic interests and international obligations: safeguards in international trade organizations. Philadelphia: Univ. of Pennsylvania Pr., 1963. 448p.

D485 Meade, James E. The theory of international economic policy. London: Oxford Univ. Pr., 1951–55. 2v.

D486 Pigou, Arthur C. Protective and preferential import duties. New York: Kelley, 1968. 117p. (reprint of 1906 ed.)

D487 Semmel, Bernard. The rise of free trade imperialism: classical political economy, the empire of free trade and imperialism, 1750–1850. New York: Cambridge Univ. Pr., 1970. 250p.

D488 Taussig, Frank W. Some aspects of the tariff question: an examination of the development of American industries under protection. 3d ed. Westport, Conn.: Greenwood, 1969. 499p. (reprint of 1931 ed.)

International Economic Cooperation

The alternative to regulation of international economic transactions by unilateral action is regulation by bilateral or multilateral action—that is, the arrangement of controls of international exchanges and the international flow of persons, capital, goods, and services by various types of bilateral or multilateral treaties. The place of commercial treaties in the history of international economic relations has often been studied, with special reference to the discrimination these treaties were intended to eradicate. A specially favored topic is the "most favored nation" clause, a provision in commercial treaties designed to ensure to each signatory the same treatment given to any most highly favored third nation. The struggle against discrimination has been long and arduous and has by no means been finally overcome.

Recently, the major effort of finding multilateral patterns for regulating international economic relations has been the formation of customs unions and various other forms of economic union. The European Economic Community (the so-called Common Market) is only the first such device. It is already being imitated in Latin America, and other regional organizations and economic blocs are under discussion or have been formed.

The main problems in the formation of these unions are political; but to the extent that they extend the territory of common trade and related economic actions, they have economic results. It is to these economic results that the more serious literature has been devoted. Most of the popular treatments do not go to the heart of the economic problem but discuss, mainly or exclusively, the political questions involved.

One aspect of the treatment of international diversity of prices has been the formation of multinational corporations engaged in the production of goods, or provision of services such as tourism, technology, health programs, etc. Parent companies are usually based in developed countries, and extensions in underdeveloped countries.

D489 Barnet, Richard J., and Ronald E. Müller. Global reach: the power of the multinational corporations. New York: Simon & Schuster, 1974. 508p.

D490 Bauer, P. T. Equality, the Third World and Economic Delusion. Cambridge, Mass.: Harvard Univ. Pr., 1981. 293p.

D491 Behrman, Jere R. Development, the international economic order, and commodity agreements. Reading, Mass.: Addison-Wesley, 1978. 152p.

D492 The Brandt Commission. Common crisis: north-south cooperation for world recovery. Cambridge, Mass.: MIT Pr., 1983. 184p.

D493 Hirschman, Albert O. Development projects observed. Washington, D.C.: Brookings, 1967. 197p.

D494 Krueger, Anne O. The developmental role of the foreign sector and aid. Cambridge, Mass.: Harvard Univ. Pr., 1979. 256p.

D495 Little, Ian M. D., and J. M. Clifford. International aid: a discussion of the flow of public resources from rich to poor countries. Chicago: Aldine, 1966. 302p.

D496 Meade, James E. The theory of customs unions. Amsterdam: North-Holland, 1955. 121p.

D497 Mikesell, Raymond F. The economics of foreign aid. Chicago: Aldine, 1968. 300p.

D498 Newberry, D., and J. Stiglitz. The theory of commodity price stabilization. Oxford: Oxford Univ. Pr., 1981. 226p.

D499 Payer, Cheryl. The World Bank: a critical analysis. New York: Monthly Review, 1982. 414p.

D500 Pincus, John. Economic aid and international cost sharing. Baltimore: Johns Hopkins Univ. Pr., 1965. 221p.

D501 Ranis, Gustav, ed. The United States and the developing economies. Rev. ed. New York: Norton, 1973. 350p.

D502 Vernon, Raymond. Storm over the multinationals: the real issues. Cambridge, Mass.: Harvard Univ. Pr., 1977. 260p.

D503 Viner, Jacob. The customs union issue. New York: Carnegie Endowment for International Peace, 1950. 221p.

D504 White, John A. The politics of foreign aid. New York: St. Martin's, 1974. 315p.

D505 Wolf, Charles, Jr. Foreign aid: theory and practice in southern Asia. Princeton, N.J.: Princeton Univ. Pr., 1960. 442p.

Bert F. Hoselitz   Roger T. Kaufman   Andrew S. Zimbalist

Survey of the Reference Works

GUIDES TO THE LITERATURE

D506 Brownstone, David M., and Gorton Carruth. Where to find business information: a worldwide guide for everyone who needs the answers to business questions. 2d ed. New York: Wiley, 1982. 632p.

Consists of three sections: (1) Source Finder, an alphabetical arrangement of more than 2,500 subjects, many subdivided geographically (e.g., Advertising lists 38 titles each with an entry no., followed by geographic subheads—Australia, Canada, Delaware, European Economic Community, etc.—in turn followed by such topics as Advertising, Deceptive; Advertising, Direct Mail; Advertising, Television and Radio); (2) Publishers' Index to more than 1,500 publishers; (3) Sources of Business Information, an A–Z list by title of more than 5,100 numbered entries for which publisher, address, phone no., annotation are given. Scope is English-language materials worldwide: directories, journals, looseleaf services, government publications, databases, etc.

D507 Coman, Edwin T., Jr. Sources of business information. Rev. ed. Berkeley: Univ. of California Pr., 1964. 330p.

A very satisfactory retrospective introduction to business information. Suggests basic works, describes simple research methods, and points out the uses of such resources as libraries, trade associations, and chambers of commerce. Each chapter deals with one phase of business (e.g., statistics, finance, accounting, management, basic industries) and has a bibliography and general discussion of sources. Chapter 16 is "A basic bookshelf."

D508 Daniells, Lorna M. Business information sources. Berkeley: Univ. of California Pr., 1976. 439p.

In the tradition of Coman (D507) but neither a revision of nor a replacement for Coman, this work is arranged in two parts. The first eight chapters describe the basic kinds of business reference sources (e.g., bibliographies, indexes and abstracts, statistical and financial sources, directories, databases). Chapters 9–20 describe sources in management or a management function (accounting, marketing, personnel management, etc.). Chapter 21 is "A basic bookshelf." Detailed author, title, subject indexes. Rev. ed. in progress. For comprehensive treatment of Canadian sources (more than 6,500) see: Brown, Barbara, E., ed. *Canadian business and economics: a guide to sources of information* (Ottawa: Canadian Library Assn., 1984; 469p.) **(D508A)**.

D509 Economics information guide series. v.1–16. Detroit: Gale, 1976–80.

Annotated subseries in the Gale Information Guide Library. Examples: v.1, East Asian economies, ed. by Molly K. S. C. Lee; v.2, Economics of minorities, ed. by Kenneth L: Gagala; v.11, Money, banking, and macroeconomics, ed. by James M. Rock; v.12, Soviet-type economic systems, ed. by Z. Edward O'Reilly; v.16, American economic history, ed. by William Kenneth Hutchinson. Other subseries, such as International relations and Man and the environment, may also be useful. See also *Management information guide* (D515).

D510 Encyclopedia of business information sources. Detroit: Gale, 1965– . (5th ed., 1983)

First published in 1965 as *Executive's guide to information sources*. For some 1,300 topics, alphabetically listed, identifies pertinent encyclopedias and dictionaries, handbooks, trade and professional organizations, journals, directories, statistical sources, etc.

D511 Fletcher, John, ed. Information sources in economics. 2d ed. London, Boston: Butterworth, 1984. 339p. [Butterworth guides to information sources]

Twenty-two British librarians and economists provide this superior guide, which "attempts . . . to give economists and would-be economists a guide to three things: (1) what material there is on the various branches of the subject, what is important and valuable, and what level it best serves; (2) what tools are available to assist the researcher to make a more extensive and intensive survey of the literature of his specialized field; (3) where the material can be found." (p.4) Rev. ed. of: *The use of economics literature* (Hamden, Conn.: Archon, 1971).

D512 Harvard Univ. Graduate School of Business Administration. Baker Library. Business reference sources: an annotated guide for Harvard Business School students. Comp. by Lorna M. Daniells. Boston: The Library, 1979. 133p. [Reference list no.30]

Substantially revises a guide originally published in 1963 (Reference list no.21, 46p.) and revised in 1965 (Reference list no.24, 72p.) and in 1971 (Reference list no.27, 108p.). Remarkably clear and precise. 13 sections (e.g., indexes and abstracts, directories, financial sources, basic U.S. statistical sources, statistics for industry analysis, law and government organization) precede an extensive index, primarily to authors and titles.

D513 How to find information about companies. Ed. by Lorna M. Daniells and others. Washington, D.C.: Washington Researchers, 1983. 521p.

This directory draws together a wide variety of public and private information resources: the municipal planning department; state government offices for air pollution, commerce, banking, etc.; federal government offices (e.g., SEC, Internal Revenue Service, Freedom of Information Act offices); court records; trade associations and labor unions, credit reporting and bond rating services, fee-based information services, databases; foreign firms; the public library (with annotations of selected reference titles). Index includes government agencies, private organizations, databases, subjects.

D514 Lovett, Robert W. American economic and business history information sources: an annotated bibliography of recent works pertaining to economic, business, agricultural, and labor history and the history of science and technology for the United States and Canada. Detroit: Gale, 1971. 323p. [Management information guide, 23]

Intended in part as a supplement to Larson's *Guide to business history* (D604), Lovett's guide concentrates on the period 1948–70. One chapter is devoted to each of the five areas of the subtitle; a sixth chapter treats general reference works.

D515 Management information guide. v.1– . Detroit: Gale, 1963– .

"Each volume is edited by one or more individuals known to be expert in the subject matter of the field as well as in the information resources applicable to the problems of that field. . . . Each . . . is designed to direct the user to key sources by arranging, describing, and indexing published sources as well as the programs and services of organizations, agencies and facilities which in combination make up the total information scene of each of the fields covered." (Preface, by Paul Wasserman)

D516 Marketing information: a professional reference guide. Ed. by Jac L. Goldstucker. Atlanta: Georgia State Univ. Business Pub. Div., 1982. 369p.

Includes associations, government agencies, and other organizations active in the field; also includes bibliographies, directories, journals, indexing services, and other media, both print and nonprint and including databases.

D516 Mayros, Van, and D. Michael Werner. Busi-
A   ness information: applications and sources. Radnor, Pa.: Chilton Book, 1983. 490p.

Lists more than 3,800 sources including about 400 databases. Compares favorably with scope and purpose of *Encyclopedia of business information sources* (D510).

D517 Thompson, Marilyn Taylor. Management information: where to find it. Metuchen, N.J.: Scarecrow, 1981. 272p.

In 20 topical chapters (II, Management sources; XIII, Personnel management and industrial relations sources; etc.), annotates more than 1,200 entries— bibliographies, indexes and abstracts, dictionaries, government publications, statistical sources, etc.

REVIEWS OF THE LITERATURE AND RESEARCH

D518 American Economic Assn. The series of republished articles on economics. Philadelphia: Blakiston, 1942–51; Homewood, Ill.: Irwin, 1952– .

Essays with extensive references to economic literature.

D519 Cole, Arthur H. The historical development of economic and business literature. Boston: Harvard Univ. Graduate School of Business Administration. Baker Library, 1957. 56p.

A study in progressive complexity—from scattered pamphlets, sermons, and occasional books of the 16th century to the formidable range and complexity of the literature of the 20th.

D520 Fels, Rendigs, and John J. Siegfried, eds. Recent advances in economics: a book of readings. Homewood, Ill.: publ. by Irwin for the American Economic Assn., 1974. 346p.

Intended "to help economics teachers with teaching loads to keep up with their field [and to be] useful for undergraduate majors in economics . . . and graduate students in the social sciences." (p.v.) Extensive documentation; many charts and tables.

D520 A Readings in the economics of law and regulation. Ed. by A. I. Ogus and C. G. Veljanovski. New York: Oxford Univ. Pr., 1984. 361p.

Readings from both journals and books on such topics as private law (e.g., property, tort, contract), public law (antitrust, theories and techniques of regulation) and legal institutions (law enforcement, procedure).

D521 Research in. . . . Greenwich, Conn.: JAI Pr., 1976– .

Annual compilations of essays—i.e., research papers longer than conventional journal-length articles but shorter than monographs. Examples: *Research in economic history* (1976–), *Research in labor economics* (1977–), *Research in population economics* (1978–), *Research in international business and finance* (1979–). Publisher has some research annuals with titles beginning *Advances in*, e.g., *Advances in the economics of energy and resources* (1979–).

D522 American economic review. v.1– , 1911– . Nashville: American Economic Assn. Quarterly.

Long articles, extensively documented and often graphed.

D523 Economic journal. v.1– , 1891– . Cambridge: Royal Economic Society. Quarterly.

International list of periodical articles (dropped with v.81, 1971) and an annotated list of new books. Several feature articles per issue. Notes on new books.

D524 Journal of accountancy. v.1– , 1905– . New York: American Inst. of Certified Public Accountants. Monthly.

Book reviews and a bibliography of book and periodical literature.

D525 Journal of economic literature. v.1– , 1963– . Nashville: American Economic Assn. Quarterly.

Journal of economic abstracts (v.1–6, 1963–68) was not a literature review source. Beginning with March 1969, the first section of each issue "provides (*a*) comprehensive and balanced review of the recent literature in some sub-field of economics, (*b*) one or more essays giving the reactions of generally recognized leading economists to his (or her) recent professional reading, and (*c*) when appropriate, a review article on some particularly outstanding book. Occasionally . . . an article pertaining to the journals or books generally, or comments on previous contributions, will also appear." (editor's note, 7:iii [1969]) Available for online searching.

D526 Wall Street review of books. v.1– , 1973– . Bedford Hills, N.Y.: Redgrave. Quarterly.

A journal devoted exclusively—like other recently established social science journals—to reviewing books. Although the focus is on books of interest and importance to the securities and financial communities, the scope embraces titles in economics and business viewed in its broad political, social, and historical setting.

ABSTRACTS AND SUMMARIES

D527 Accountants digest. v.1– , 1935– . Boca Raton, Fla.: Florida Atlantic Univ. College of Business and Public Administration. Quarterly.

Abstracts of selected important articles in English-language accounting journals.

D528 Anbar management services. Wembley, England: Anbar Pubns.

Five subseries, each issued 8 times per year: Accounting and Data Processing Abst. (1970–), Marketing and Distribution Abst. (1971–), Personnel and Training Abst. (1971–), Top Management Abst. (1971–), Work Study and O and M Abst. (1973–). *Anbar management services bibliography* (annual) lists books, pamphlets, and films covered by the abstracts in the preceding sections. Worldwide selection of materials, not all in English. Abstracts are in English. The five subseries were preceded by a monthly *Anbar management services abstracts*.

D528 A Business publications index and abstracts, 1983– . Detroit: Gale, 1984– . Annual, with monthly issues and quarterly cumulations.

The *Management contents* database (D874) in hard copy. Separate volumes for index (subject-author citations) and for abstracts. Unlike *Business periodicals index* (D551) covers books and provides author indexes to citations.

D529 Computing reviews. v.1– , 1960– . New York: Assn. for Computing Machinery. Monthly.

D530 Data processing digest. v.1– , 1955– . Los Angeles: Data Processing Digest. Monthly.

D531 Human resources abstracts. v.10– , 1975– . Beverly Hills, Calif.: Sage. Quarterly. (v.1–9: Poverty and human resources abstracts, 1966–74)

D532 International executive. v.1– , 1959– . White River Junction, Vt.: Foundation for the Advancement of International Business Administration. 3/yr.

First half (order varies) includes "Research roundup" (research projects by universities, foundations, etc.), "Books of note," "Articles in brief." Second half ("Reference guide") annotates books, articles, pamphlets.

D534 Key to economic science and managerial sciences. v.25– . Jan. 1, 1978– . The Hague: Library and Documentation Center of the Netherlands Foreign Trade Agency EVD (Ministry of Economic Affairs). Semimonthly.

Abstracts of pamphlets, books, and articles in the original language. Title varies: *Economic abstracts*, v.1–22, June 1, 1953–Dec. 1975; *Key to economic science*, v.23–24, Jan. 1, 1976–1977.

D535 Management review and digest. v.1–10, 1974–83. London: British Inst. of Management. Quarterly.

Incorporates the former *Bulletin*, *Quarterly review*, and *Management abstracts* of the institute. Numbered abstracts and reviews of books and audiovisual items. Continued by: *Management news*, 1983– .

D536 Personnel management abstracts. v.1– , 1955– . Chelsea, Mich.: Personnel Management Abst. Quarterly.

In addition to brief abstracts of important articles and books, each issue has a Periodicals Index, which has 3 sections: authors, subjects, titles.

D537 Work related abstracts. 1973– . Detroit: Information Coordinators. Monthly. Looseleaf. (1951–58, Labor-personnel index; 1959–72, Employment relations abstracts)

Journal of economic literature, another important publication in the field, is published quarterly by the American Economic Assn. The third section of *JEL*, the lineal descendant of *JEA*, has the tables of contents of about 200 current economic journals and a classified listing of all articles in them. Abstracts of some but not all the articles. Title at D568. Available for online searching.

Dissertation Abstracts and Summaries

D538 "Abstracts of doctoral dissertations," *Journal of finance*. v.7–30. 1952–75.
About 10 abstracts (1–2p.) in most issues.

D539 "Dissertation abstracts," *Journal of international business studies*.
A few in each issue.

D540 "Doctoral dissertation abstracts," *Accounting historians journal*.
A few in each issue.

D541 "Summaries of doctoral dissertations," *Journal of economic history*. v.25– , 1965– .

D542 "A summary of doctoral research in retailing," *Journal of retailing*.
In summer (formerly spring) issue. Called "Dissertation reviews" beginning with Spring 1983 issue.

CURRENT BIBLIOGRAPHIES

D543 Accountants' index. New York: American Inst. of Certified Public Accountants, 1921– . Annual (biennial before 1970); quarterly, with annual cumulations, 1973– .

A basic index of English-language literature in periodicals, proceedings, reports, books, and parts of books. Author, subject, and title entries show bibliographic information only. Initial volume (1921) refers to literature in print back to 1912.

D544 Accounting articles. 1965– . Chicago: Commerce Clearing House. Monthly.

Cumulative indexes and abstracts of accounting material not only from journals but also from books and pamphlets. Looseleaf format; organized by large topics. Retrieval enhanced by a small-topical index and author index.

D545 American Economic Assn. Index of economic articles in journals and collective volumes. 1886– . Homewood, Ill.: Irwin, 1961– . Annual.

A classified index of English-language articles from the world's major professional economic journals and collective volumes. Author index. Title for v.1–7: Index of economic journals; for parallel volumes to 6 (1960–63) and 7 (1964–65): *Index of economic articles in collective volumes*.

D546 Assn. for University Business and Economic Research. University research in business and economics. v.1– , 1956– . Title varies. v.1–26: Bibliography of publications of university bureaus of business and economic research; variant title: AUBER bibliography. Morgantown: West Virginia Univ. Bureau of Business Research. Annual.

Divided into 3 principal sections: by subject, institution (association members and those of the American Assembly of Collegiate Schools of Business), and author. Before Oct. 1970 the association's name was Associated University Bureaus of Business and Economic Research. For publications through 1949, consult Fern Wilson's *Index of publications by university bureaus of business research* (Cleveland: Pr. of Western Reserve Univ., 1951).

D547 "Business books [of the year]," *Library journal.* v.75– , 1950– . New York: Bowker. Annual.

Carefully prepared list of the best or most significant business books now appears in Mar. 1 issue. Jesse E. Cross's monthly column on business books began Oct. 1, 1949. His first review of the preceding year's output appeared May 15, 1950 (p.824–31). Title varies. His successors, beginning with Rose Vormelker, have further strengthened the usefulness of the service.

D548 Business and economics books and serials in print. 1981– . New York: Bowker. Annual.

Previous editions called *Business books in print,* (1973, 1974) and *Business books and serials in print* (1977, 1978). Indexes to books by subject, author, title; to serials by subject and title.

D549 Business index. Jan. 1979– . Belmont, Calif.: Information Access Corp., 1980– . Monthly; each issue cumulative to date; computer-output-microfilm.

Covers comprehensively more than 700 business periodicals and the *Wall Street journal* (cover-to-cover); selectively covers the *New York times* and more than 1,000 general and legal periodicals, business books, and reports from the LC MARC database, and government reports from the Supt. of Documents database. Available for online searching.

D550 Business literature. v.1– , Apr. 1928– . Newark: Newark Public Library. Irregularly.

One topic per issue. Accurate bibliographic information and annotations. For information on the work of other libraries in producing timely bibliographies, consult issues of Bulletin, Special Libraries Assn. Business and Finance Division.

D551 Business periodicals index. v.1– , 1958– . New York: Wilson. Monthly with frequent cumulations.

Cumulative subject index to English-language periodicals in accounting, advertising and public relations, automation, banking, communications, economics, finance and investments, general business, insurance, labor, management, marketing, taxation, and specific businesses, industries, and trades. Successor to business portion of *Industrial arts index.* Subject headings constantly revised to assure currency of terminology. Many subheadings and cross-references. Very useful. Available for online searching.

For *Business publications index and abstracts,* see the description at D528A.

D551 Computer contents. v.1– , 1983– . Belmont,
B Calif.: Management Contents. Biweekly.

Contains tables of contents of latest issues of computer, electronic and telecommunications periodicals, other serials, and books.

D552 Consumers index to product evaluations and information sources. 1973– . Ann Arbor: Pierian, 1974– . Quarterly, with annual cumulation.

Aims to provide a current index to consumer information as found in a select list of about 100 sources as diverse as *American home, Backpacker, Changing times, Consumer reports, Stereo review,* and *Yachting.* Classified arrangement consists of 14 sections (Health and Personal Care; Food, Beverages, and Tobacco; Clothing; The Home, etc.) plus a concluding section identifying "books, pamphlets and consumer aids" keyed to the 14 sections. Index to product or consumer aid.

D553 Council of Planning Librarians. CPL bibliography. no.1– , 1979– . Chicago: CPL Bibliographies, 1979– . Irregularly.

The council's *Exchange bibliographies* (1958–78), frequently annotated, treated many business- and economics-related topics. The new series is doing likewise; e.g., no.5, Futures planning in management, and no.18, Government regulations and the cost of housing (both 1979), and no. 99, Valuation and property taxation of nonrenewable resources (1983).

D554 Economic books: current selections. v.1– , March 1974– . Pittsburgh: Univ. of Pittsburgh Pr., 1974– . Quarterly.

A publication of the Univ. of Pittsburgh Dept. of Economics and the University Libraries. Topically annotates English-language books, indicating a code for budget level of library for which each book is recommended. Author index. Continues in part:

D554 Economics and business: an international anno-
A tated bibliography. v. 29– , Dec. 1984– . New York: Gordon & Breach. Quarterly.

Continues *Economics selections: an international annotated bibliography* (D561). Ed. at the Dept. of Economics, Adelphi Univ., Garden City, N.Y.

D555 Economics selections: an international bibliography. 1954–73. Baltimore: Johns Hopkins Univ. Dept. of Political Economy, 1954–62; New York: Gordon & Breach Science Pubs. for the Univ. of Pittsburgh Dept. of Economics, 1963–73.

Entitled *Economics library selections, ser.1: New books in economics,* 1954–65, *International economics selections bibliography, ser.1: New books in economics* in 1966.

D556 ———.

Ser. 2: Basic lists in special fields. An irregular series "designed to assist libraries in building up basic collections of books in the several major fields of economics and in appraising their existing collections." Renders a service of unmatched importance in the areas it covers.

Citation to annotations for the Hopkins period is provided in Univ. of Pittsburgh Dept. of Economics, *Cumulative bibliography of economics books . . . 1954–62* (New York: Gordon & Breach, 1965) **(D557)**. Gordon & Breach has published later cumulations: *Economics selections: an international bibliography, cumulative bibliography,* series 1 and 2, 1963–70 (1975) **(D558)**, *Economics selections: cumulative bibliography,* v.3, 1971–77 (1979) **(D559)**, and *Economics selections: cumulative bibliography,* v.4, 1978–81 (1982) **(D560)**.

D561 Economics selections: an international annotated bibliography. New York: Gordon & Breach, 1980–84. Quarterly.

Issued by the Dept. of Economics and Finance, Baruch College, City Univ. of New York. Annotates new titles (usually in English) in economics, business, and finance. Continues in part the Univ. of Pittsburgh publication of the same title and assumes its numbering (v.21– , Jan. 1976–). Continued by: *Economics and business: an international annotated bibliography.* (D554A).

D562 Economics working papers: a bibliography. Jan./June 1973– . Dobbs Ferry, N.Y.: Trans-Media, 1973– . Semiannual.

Published in association with the University of Warwick. Provides access to working papers—defined as draft papers, not yet in final form for publication—made available for general circulation to interested parties with a view to eliciting comments before being offered for publication.

D563 Harfax directory of industry data sources: the United States of America and Canada. 2d ed. Cambridge, Mass.: Harfax/Ballinger, 1982. 3v.

More than doubles the coverage of the first ed., listing more than 20,000 entries of marketing and financial information, broadly defined, for 65 industries: indexes and abstracts, directories and yearbooks, market research reports, databases, etc. Publisher also has published a similar directory for Western Europe (2v.), *Harfax guide to industry special issues* (1983), and other products. Available for online searching.

D564 Harvard Univ. Graduate School of Business Administration. Baker Library. Core collection: an author and subject guide. 1969/70– . Boston: The Library. Annual.

The core consists of more than 3,000 English-language titles.

D565 ———. ———. Recent additions to Baker Library. v.13– , 1973– . Boston: The Library. Monthly. (Former title: New books in business and economics)

Lists and sometimes describes new books and substantial pamphlets.

D566 ———. ———. Reference list. no.1– , Oct. 1947– . Boston: The Library. Irregularly.

Annotated bibliographies of books, pamphlets, and articles. Recent issues: no.28, *Executive compensation* (1976); no.29, *Business intelligence and strategic planning* (1979); no.30, *Business reference sources* (1979) (D512).

D567 International bibliography of economics. v.1–8, 1952–59. Paris: UNESCO, 1955–61. v.9– , 1960– . London and New York: Tavistock. Annual.

Part of a UNESCO program to supply basic bibliographic tools of international scope for each social science (see A222). Bibliographic information on books, articles, and reports appears under a classified arrangement in both English and French. Separate author and subject indexes. Issued 2 or 3 years after original publication date of material.

The *Journal of economic literature,* in its second section provides a classified, annotated listing of new books in economics, and conventional book reviews of a major portion of new works. Title described at D525.

D569 Management contents. v.1– . 1975– . Belmont, Calif.: Management Contents. Biweekly.

Contains tables of contents of latest issues of business and management periodicals. Available for online searching.

D570 Management review. v.1– . 1914– . New York: American Management Assn. Monthly.

Has digests of current articles and reports, and reviews of new books.

D572 Predicasts F & S index international. 1968– . Cleveland: Predicasts. Monthly, with annual cumulation. (Formerly: F & S Index of Corporations and Industries)

Contains references to articles appearing in foreign and domestic publications. Information is arranged by company, country, and industry. Company listings are alphabetical, and countries alphabetical by region and products are coded by Standard Industrial Classification (SIC). See also *Predicasts F & S index Europe.* 1979– . Monthly, with quarterly and annual cumulations (**D573**). Available for online searching.

D574 Predicasts F & S index United States, 1960– . Cleveland: Predicasts. Weekly, with monthly, quarterly, semiannual, and annual cumulations. (Former titles: F & S Index of Corporations and Industries and Predicasts F & S Index of Corporations and Industries)

Indexes U.S. and Canadian financial, business, and trade journals, and special reports. Available for online searching.

D575 Princeton Univ. Industrial Relations Section. Selected references. no.1– , Jan. 1945– . Princeton, N.J.: The University. 5/yr.

Annotated lists of books, articles, and reports: no. 211, Outstanding books in industrial relations and labor economics, 1981 (1982), is a recent issue in an annual subseries.

For *Public Affairs Information Service bulletin,* see A225.

D576 Technical book review index. Comp. in cooperation with the Science and Technology Dept., Carnegie Library of Pittsburgh, and the Maurice and Laura Falk Library of the Health Professions, Univ. of Pittsburgh. v.1– , 1935– . New York: Special Libraries Assn., 1935–76; Pittsburgh: JAAD Pub. Co., 1977– . Monthly.

Identifies reviews in current scientific, technical, and trade journals, and quotes from these reviews. The original publication covered the years 1917–28 and was published by the Technology Dept. of the Carnegie Library. In 1935, the Special Libraries Assn. revived the project. Cumulative author index in Dec. issue. Although extremely useful in a technical library, this index does not cover all books of interest to business.

D577 U.S. Bureau of the Census. Bureau of the Census catalog. 1946– . Washington, D.C.: Govt. Print. Off. Quarterly and cumulative to annual, with monthly supplements; annual, 1980– .

Divided for the years 1946–80 into 2 sections: (1) publications and (2) data files. Each section is subdivided to reflect bureau's major concerns: agriculture, construction and housing, distribution and services, foreign trade, geography, governments, manufacturing, mineral industries, population, and transportation. A third section lists publications containing information for geographic areas—e.g., state, county, and standard metropolitan areas. More information at D787.

D578 U.S. Dept. of Commerce. Library. Publications catalog. 1979– . Washington, D.C.: Govt. Print. Off. Annual. (Title, 1952–78: United States Department of Commerce publications catalog and index)

Basic volume covers 1790 to 1950 and agency by agency within the department, followed by subject index. Same arrangement for each supplement. Updated by *Business service checklist* (1946–78), *Recent Commerce publications* (Jan. 19–Apr. 27, 1979), *Recent Commerce Department publications* (May 11, 1979–June 6, 1980), and *Commerce publications update* (July 4, 1980–).

D579 U.S. Small Business Administration. Small business bibliography. no.1– . 1954– . Washington, D.C.: Govt. Print. Off. Irregularly.

Selective, classified, annotated bibliographies—e.g., no.13, National directories for use in marketing (rev. 1977); no.18, Basic library reference sources (rev. 1978); no.89, Marketing for small business (rev. 1978); no.90, New product development (1979).

D580 Wall Street Journal index. Dec. 1957– . New York: Dow Jones. Monthly, with annual cumulations. Index to final Eastern ed.

Current Lists of Dissertations and Research

D581 American Bankers Assn. Stonier Graduate School of Banking. Cumulative catalog of theses. Washington, D.C.: The Association.

Brief description of each thesis. Access enhanced by specific subject index. Each new edition supersedes the preceding one. Each is cumulative from 1937.

D582 "Bibliography of recent doctoral dissertations on creativity and problem-solving," *Journal of creative behavior*. v.6– , 1972– . Buffalo: Creative Education Foundation. 1–2 times per year.

D583 "Doctoral dissertations accepted," *Journal of business*. v.29– , 1956– . Chicago: Univ. of Chicago Pr. Annual.

Annual (Jan.) topical list (e.g., accounting, banking and public finance, data processing, insurance, international trade, management organization, theory and practice, personnel and industrial relations, social control, and business law) giving author, institution, and title.

D584 "Doctoral dissertations in insurance and closely related fields, 1940–1962," *Journal of risk and insurance*. v.30– , 1963– . Bloomington, Ill.: American Risk and Insurance Assn. Annual.

Topical arrangement. Supplements appear irregularly.

D585 Doctoral dissertations on transportation. 1961– 1967, and addendum, December 1967–July 1968; a bibliography. Evanston, Ill.: Northwestern Univ. Transportation Center, 1968.

A topical list with supplements issued from time to time.

D586 Industrial relations theses and dissertations. . . . 1949/50. var. places, var. pubs., 1951– .

Frequency and number of institutions reporting vary. Arranged alphabetically by author.

D587 "International register of theses and dissertations," *Omega: international journal of management science*. 1973– . Oxford: Pergamon. Bimonthly.

D588 "List of doctoral dissertations in political economy in American universities and colleges," *American economic review*. v.1– , 1911– . Nashville: American Economic Assn. Annual.

List 1 (1904) sent to membership—not bound in AEA publications; lists 2–4 (1905–7) in third series, v.6, p.737; v.7, no.3, supp., p.43; v.8, no.2, supp., p.42. (Cf. *American economic review* 1:212, Mar. 1911); lists 5–7 (1908–10), in its *Bulletin*. An annual in Dec. (formerly Sept.) issue has classified listing of authors, dissertation titles, and granting institutions. Brief abstracts of some of the titles.

D589 "Ph.D. recipients by subject" and "Ph.D. recipients by institution," *American journal of agricultural economics*. v.34– , 1952– . Lexington: Univ. of Kentucky Dept. of Agricultural Economics. Annual.

Annual list (usually May) of authors, their degrees and granting institutions, and dissertation titles. Title varies. See other issues for additions to the list.

D590 "Research clearinghouse," *Business horizons*. v.5– , 1962– . Bloomington: Indiana Univ. Graduate School of Business. Bimonthly.

Each issue lists current academic and non-academic projects in classified order, with title and purpose of study and researcher's name and address.

D591 "Research in accounting," *Accounting review*. v.12– , 1937– . Sarasota, Fla.: American Accounting Assn.

July 1951 issue (v.26, no.3) contains listing for the period (1941–50/51). Classified annual list (Jan.) identifies doctoral and faculty research, title, institution, and completion date. Jan. 1971 issue has alphabetical list of projects by author or analyst. Another list, "Research projects" (e.g., Apr. 1970, Jan. 1971), often notes ongoing research sponsored by American Accounting Assn.

D592 "Research in progress," *Industrial and labor relations review*. Quarterly.

In every issue. Prior to Oct. 1976, called "Research notes."

D593 "Research studies in business education completed or under way, 1951/52–1968/69," *National business education quarterly*. v.20–38, 1952–70. Washington, D.C.: National Business Education Assn. Annual.

Lists authors, titles, institutions under some 10 topics. For 1970– , this list appears in v.25–34 of *Business education forum*. Lists are in spring (Mar.) issue; lists for 1980– are in *NABTE* (National Assn. for Business Teacher Education) *review*.

D594 U.S. Dept. of Labor. Employment and Training Administration. Research and development projects. 1976– . Washington, D.C.: Govt. Print. Off. Annual.

Projects and basic information and description are classified as active at close of the fiscal year or completed during the fiscal year and by research or evaluation contracts, research grants, dissertation grants, etc. Indexes (e.g., contractor/grantee, individual, contract/grant number, subject) are a necessity. Title varies: *Manpower research projects* (1963–68); *Manpower research and development projects* (1971–75). Former agency name: Manpower Administration.

RETROSPECTIVE BIBLIOGRAPHIES

D595 American economic history before 1860. Ed. by George Rogers Taylor. Northbrook, Ill.: AHM, 1969. 108p.

D596 American economic history since 1860. Comp. by Edward C. Kirkland. Northbrook, Ill.: AHM, 1971. 78p.

Each bibliography is part of the Goldentree Bibliographies in American History series; each is selective, with the sole criterion for inclusion being the significance, not the age, of the particular work. Includes books, periodicals, dissertations. Mostly unannotated.

D597 Batson, Harold E., comp. A select bibliography of modern economic theory, 1870–1929. London: Routledge; New York: Dutton, 1930. 224p. [Studies in economics and political science. Bibliographies no.6.]

Annotated bibliography of books and articles arranged in 2 parts, the first a classified section and the second an author section. Separate parts for English/American, German, and French authors.

D598 British Institute of Management. Basic library of management. London: The Institute, 1964– . Irregularly.

Classifies titles under broad subject headings, with indexes of authors and subjects/titles.

D598 Business & economic books 1876–1983. New
A   York: Bowker, 1983. 4v.

Bibliographic identification of more than 143,000 titles published or distributed in U.S. Indexes to authors and titles.

D599 Cornell Univ. New York State School of Industrial and Labor Relations. Library. Library catalog. Boston: Hall, 1967. 12v. 1st supp.; 1967– .

D600 Harvard Univ. Graduate School of Business Administration. Baker Library. Author-title catalog. Boston: Hall, 1971. 22v. 1st supp.; 1974– .

D601 ———. ———. Subject catalog. Boston: Hall, 1971. 10v. 1st supp.; 1974– .

D602 ———. ———. Kress Library of Business and Economics. Catalogue; with data upon cognate items in other Harvard libraries. Boston: The Library, 1940–67. 5v.

A chronological, unannotated list of economic works, some dating from pre–16th century incunabula. Detailed author and anonymous title index. Outstanding record of early business and economics literature. The original volume (v.1) covers material published through 1776; v.2 is a supplement for the same period. Two other basic volumes cover 1777–1817 (v.3) and 1818–48 (v.4); and there is another supplement for 1473–1848 (v.5).

D603 Institute of Personnel Management. IPM bibliography. London: The Institute, 1973– . (To be in 6 pts.)

Annotated; based on holdings of the Institute's library. Pt.1 (1973): Management—General; Pt.2 (1974): Manpower studies and labour economics; Pt.3 (1975): Education, training and development.

D604 Larson, Henrietta M. Guide to business history: materials for the study of American business history and suggestions for their use. Cambridge, Mass.: Harvard Univ. Pr., 1948. Reprinted, Boston: Canner, 1964; 1,181p. [Harvard studies in business history, v.12]

An outstanding compilation of books and periodical articles. Some 4,900 critically annotated entries are arranged by topic and indexed by author and title. Broad topics include historical background and setting of American business, business history of individual business units. Section on research and reference materials covers business manuscript records, business and technical museums, trade associations, publications, govt. materials, doctoral dissertations, biographical collections, and state and local histories. See also Lovett (D514).

D605 London. University. Goldsmiths' Company's Library of Economic Literature. Catalogue of the Goldsmiths' library of economic literature. Comp. by Margaret Canney and David Knott. London: Athlone, 1970–83. 4v.

Like the Kress Library (D602), this library secured a portion of the collection of the economist H. S. Foxwell. V.1, Printed books to 1800, has more than 18,000 entries; v.2 covers printed books from 1801 to 1850; v.3 includes periodicals and manuscripts; v.4 is an index to the catalog. V.1 and 2 published by Cambridge Univ. Pr.

D606 Goldsmiths'-Kress library of economic literature: a consolidated guide to Segment I of the microfilm collection. Woodbridge, Conn.: Research Pubns., 1976– . (To be in 4v.)

Segment I of the microfilm collection being published by Research Publications is to include about 3,000 titles of pre-1801 holdings of the Goldsmiths' Library of Economic Literature at the Univ. of London and the Kress Library of Business and Economics at the Harvard Univ. Graduate School of Business Administration in Boston. Other segments projected.

D607 McCulloch, John R. The literature of political economy: a classified catalogue of select publications in the different departments of that science, with historical, critical and biographical notices. New York: Kelley, 1964 (1845). 407p. [Reprints of economic classics]

Selective bibliography of 20 chapters on publications of the 17th and 18th centuries and up to ca. 1840. Author and book indexes.

D608 Melnyk, Peter. Economics: bibliographic guide to reference books and information resources. Littleton, Colo.: Libraries Unlimited, 1971. 263p.

1,464 numbered entries are entered in 10 chapters within which listings are alphabetical by type of reference material, starting with guides and current and retrospective bibliographies and followed by dictionaries and encyclopedias, directories, handbooks, etc. Most items are in English, but some are West and East European-language publications. Chapters are on economic theory, economic conditions in various countries, private and public finance, commerce and marketing, international economics, agricultural and land economics, economic geography, industry and transportation, labor economics, population and statistics, periodicals. Extensive index to authors, titles, and some subjects.

Bibliographies of Dissertations and Research

D609 Blum, Albert A. "Report on research in progress in American labor history." *Labor history* 7:78–92 (1966).

Arranged by topics: general history; periods of development; topics in labor history (e.g., American labor and international affairs, Negroes and other minority groups); city, regional, and state labor move-

ments and conditions; individual occupations, trades, industries and unions. Provides author, institution, title of research.

A companion contribution by the same author, and with the same title (ibid., 3:218–25 (1962)), lists research and anticipated dates of publication under issues, people, regions, sources (i.e., source materials and collections for labor history research), and the various unions in labor's past.

The bibliography was resumed in 1975 (covering 1974): Swanson, Dorothy. "Annual bibliography on American labor history: periodicals, dissertations and research in progress," *Labor history* 16:521–40, Fall 1975. **(D610)** See each subsequent fall list.

D611 Marketing doctoral dissertation abstracts, 1974/75. Comp. and ed. by Donald L. Shawver. Chicago: American Marketing Assn., 1977– . (AMA Bibliography series, nos.24, 29, 32, 34, etc.)

See also: *Doctoral dissertations on marketing, sales, and advertising.* Ann Arbor: Univ. Microfilms Intl., 1979. 11p. **(D612)**.

D613 Rosen, Ned, and Ralph E. McCoy. Doctoral dissertations in labor and industrial relations, 1933–1953. Champaign: Univ. of Illinois Institute of Labor and Industrial Relations, 1955. 86p. [The institute's bibliographic contributions, no.5]

Alphabetical author list of 1,031 items, with subject index. See also *Industrial relations theses and dissertations, 1949–1969: a cumulative bibliography,* ed. by John M. Houkes. Ann Arbor, Mich.: Xerox University Microfilms, 1973. 195p. **(D614)**.

D615 Wood, W.D., and others. Canadian graduate theses 1919–1967: an annotated bibliography (covering economics, business and industrial relations). Kingston, Ont.: Queen's Univ. at Kingston Industrial Relations Centre, 1970. 483p. [Bibliography series, no.4]

2,494 items, of which 2,052 were submitted to Canadian universities.

DIRECTORIES AND BIOGRAPHICAL INFORMATION

The following are useful and representative. Many others may be found through *PAIS bulletins* (A225), under "Directories," *Business reference sources* (D512), *Small business bibliography,* (D579), and *Encyclopedia of business information sources* (D510).

Bibliographies of Directories

D616 Guide to American directories. 1st ed.– , 1954– . Coral Springs, Fla.: Klein. (11th ed., 1982)

Lists and describes, by topic, directories from a variety of organizations, governmental and non-governmental. Title index.

D617 Directory of directories. 1st– ed.; 1980– . Detroit: Gale.

The 1st ed. describes and indexes more than 5,000 directories. Detailed subject index; title index. Interedition supplements appear in Gale's *Directory information service,* 1977– . 3/yr. **(D618)**

D619 Trade directories of the world. 1952– . Queens Village, N.Y.: Croner.

Items are arranged geographically by country of publication. Two indexes, geographical and trade or profession, may be used to cross-check each other to locate a specific trade in a specific country. Looseleaf.

Biographical Directories

D620 American Economic Assn. Directory of members, 1938– . Nashville. Irregularly. (Title varies) Issued as a number of American economic review. Formerly: AEA handbook.

Biographical information on members covers range of activities and interests, field of concentration, doctoral dissertation subjects, and publications. See also: *Roster of women economists,* annual (with quarterly supplements) published by the Committee on the Status of Women in the Economics Profession, Tallahassee, Fla. **(D621)**

D622 Directory of directors in the City of New York and Tri-State Area. 1898– . Southport, Conn.: Directory of directors. Annual. (Title varies)

Lists individuals who have one or more directorships in companies located in the New York area. Brief sketches include name, business and home address, and directorships. A second section covers important companies whose boards of directors include a New York area director or maintain principal offices in the New York area, with names and titles of officers and directors and type of business. Such directories, available for many other large cities, supplement the more comprehensive *Who's who* volumes.

D623 Dun & Bradstreet, Inc. Dun & Bradstreet reference book of corporate managements. 1967– . New York. Annual.

Provides brief biographical information about officers of some 2,400 corporations. Arranged by company. Alphabetical index by executive's name.

D624 Fink, Gary M., ed. Biographical dictionary of American labor leaders. Westport, Conn.: Greenwood, 1974. 559p.

Brief sketches of some 500 American labor leaders defined broadly enough to include Walter Reuther, A. Philip Randolph, and Arthur Goldberg.

Most are of the twentieth century, but a few 19th-century figures included. See also: Ingham, John N, *Biographical dictionary of American business leaders* (Westport, Conn.: Greenwood, 1983) 4v. **(D625)** and Fink, Gary M., ed., *Biographical dictionary of American labor* (Westport, Conn.: Greenwood, 1984) **(D625A)**. Rev. ed. of Fink (D624).

D626 Mai, Ludwig H. Men and ideas in economics: a dictionary of world economists past and present. Totowa, N.J.: Littlefield, 1975. 270p.

Includes some 700 persons from ancient times to the present. Appendixes: a list, by country, of current, active economists and their principal works; a brief outline of a history of economic doctrines.

D627 Standard & Poor's register of corporations, directors and executives. New York: Standard & Poor's, 1975– . Annual, with 3 supps. a year.

The main section, arranged alphabetically by corporation/ firm, gives executive rosters and business telephone numbers of 37,000 companies in U.S. and Canada. Section on individuals lists brief biographical information (including business and professional memberships) for about 75,000 directors and executives. Also a most useful source for listing of companies by SIC code. Geographical index. Title, 1928–74: *Poor's register.*

D628 Who's who in consulting. 2d ed. Detroit: Gale, 1973– .

Second ed. includes more than 7,500 entries. Supplements, 1982– .

D629 Who's who in economics: a biographical dictionary of major economists, 1700–1981. Ed. by Mark Blaug and Paul Sturges. Cambridge, Mass.: MIT Pr., 1983. 435p.

Biobibliographical information on 674 living and 397 deceased economists—criteria for inclusion being frequency of citations as determined by *Social sciences citation index.* Entries usually include full name, year and place of birth, title of current and recent previous positions, degrees, professional affiliations, prizes won and honors received, major fields of interest, statement of principal contributions to economics, and chief publications. Indexes: country of residence and country of birth.

D630 Who's who in finance and industry. 1st ed.– , 1936– . Chicago: Marquis.

Title varies. Eds. 1–11: *Who's who in commerce and industry;* eds. 12–15: *World's who's who in commerce and industry;* ed. 16: *World who's who in finance and industry.* A roster, mostly American, of prominent men and women. Useful as specialized biographical tool when user keeps the criteria for inclusion in mind.

D631 Who's who in insurance. 1948– . Englewood, N.J.: Underwriter Printing & Pub. Annual.

Biographical information covers position, address, education, memberships, and professional experience. Before 1948, this information appeared in *Insurance almanac* (D648).

D632 Who's who in labor. New York: Arno, 1976. 807p.

The 3,800 biographees were chosen with the cooperation of AFL-CIO, UMW, UAW, American Arbitration Association, and the Federal Mediation and Conciliation Service. Additional information includes a list of AFL-CIO and other labor federations, glossary, government offices serving labor, bibliography of labor journals. Compare with Fink's *Biographical dictionary of American labor leaders* (D624) and his *Biographical dictionary of American labor* (D625A).

Directories of Associations and Corporations

D633 American exporter register. 1980– . New York: Thomas Intl., 1980– . Annual.

A product index, with text in English, Spanish, and French, to sources of materials, products, and services. Formerly: *American register of exporters and importers,* 1945/46–79.

D634 American Marketing Assn. New York Chapter. International directory of marketing research houses and services. New York, 1962– . Annual.

"The Green Book." Alphabetical, with geographic index. Identifies chief officials and briefly describes each firm's services. Formerly a part of the chapter's *Newsletter.*

D635 Angel, Juvenal L., comp. Directory of American firms operating in foreign countries. 1955/56– . New York: Uniworld Bus. Pubs. Irregularly.

First section is alphabetical arrangement of companies with U.S. addresses, president, and executive in charge of foreign operations. Second section indicates companies by country of operation.

D636 ———. Directory of foreign firms operating in the United States. New York: World Trade, 1971– . [American encyclopedia of international information, v.4]

D637 Arpan, Jeffrey S., and David A. Ricks. Directory of foreign manufacturers in the United States. 2d ed. Atlanta: Georgia State Univ. Business Publishing Division, College of Business Adm., 1979.
Lists 3,400 firms. 3d ed. in progress.

D638 Conference Board. Announcements of mergers and acquisitions. 1964– . New York: Conference Board, 1964– .

Includes announcements of completed mergers and acquisitions, using such sources as *Standard & Poor's corporation news, Moody's manuals, Wall Street journal,* and *the New York times.*

D639 Consultants and consulting organizations directory. 1st ed.– , 1966– . Detroit: Gale. Triennial.
4th ed. (1979) provides information on some

6,000 firms, individuals, organizations: names, addresses, phone numbers, services offered. Approaches: geographic location, subject area, firm name, names of individual consultants. Periodically supplemented by *New consultants,* June 1976– . 1st ed. (1966) published by Cornell Univ. Graduate School of Business and Public Administration **(D640).**

D641 Directory of corporate affiliations ("Who owns whom"). Skokie, Ill.: Natl. Register Pubs., 1967– . Annual, with 5 supplements.

Title varies. Covers over 4,000 companies. Includes index by subsidiary names. Geographical index (a separate publication) lists companies by state and city with name, street address, zip code, and page number of directory listing. Also available are *Who owns whom: North America* (New York: Dun & Bradstreet, 1969–) **(D642)** and companion volumes for Australasia and Far East, Continental Europe, and United Kingdom and Republic of Ireland.

D642 Directory of mail order catalogs. 2d ed. New
A York: Facts On File, 1984. 350p.

Address, telephone number, names of chief officers, and products for more than 5,000 companies.

D643 Dun & Bradstreet, Inc. Middle market directory. 1964– . New York: Dun & Bradstreet. Annual.

D644 ———. Million dollar directory. 1959– . New York: Dun & Bradstreet. Annual.

Companion volumes. The former lists some 31,000 businesses with net worth of $500,000 to $999,999, the latter some 47,000 businesses with net worth of $1 million or more. Each directory gives business name, state of incorporation, address, SIC numbers, annual sales, and number of employees and company officers and directors. Each has 3 parts: alphabetical list by company name, geographical company directory, and classification by SIC number. *Million dollar directory* has a fourth part, an alphabetical list of officers, directors, etc. 1979– . *Middle market directory* issued as v.2 of *Million dollar directory.*

D645 ———. Principal international businesses. New York: Dun & Bradstreet, 1974– . Annual.

More than 50,000 companies in 135 countries. Basic information: chief official, line of business, standard industrial classification (SIC) number, sales, number of employees. Arrangement is alphabetical by country. Indexes by SIC and by company name.

D646 Guide to graduate study in economics and agricultural economics in the United States of America and Canada. 1st ed.– , 1965– . Homewood, Ill.: Irwin. (title and publisher vary)

Prepared under the auspices of the American Economic Assn. and the American Agricultural Economics Assn. by the Economics Institute, Univ. of Colorado, Boulder. 7th ed. (1984) describes more than 300 graduate programs and gives comparative data and information for prospective students.

D647 Industrial research laboratories of the United States. 1st ed.– , 1920–60, 1965– . Washington, D.C.: Natl. Academy of Sciences, 1920–60; New York: Bowker, 1965– . Irregularly.

Supplies information on nongovernmental laboratories. Each entry gives address, names of research staff and administration, and fields of research interest. Subject, personnel, and geographic indexes.

D648 Insurance almanac: who, what, where and when in insurance: an annual of insurance facts. 1912– . Englewood, N.J.: Underwriter Printing & Pub. Annual.

Primarily a directory of companies (arranged by type of insurance written), organizations, state departments of insurance, and agents, brokers, adjusters, the insurance press, etc. Also includes recent laws. Until 1948, when *Who's who in insurance* (D631) began to be published separately, one section was devoted to it. Lists officers and directories of companies and organizations and gives brief history. Index by title of organization.

D649 Kelly's manufacturers and merchants directory. 1880– . West Sussex, Eng.: Kelly's Directories. Annual.

Title varies. International coverage, but comprehensive only for the British Isles. Information fairly limited: name, address, and type of business, product, or service.

D650 Major companies of Europe. 1982– . London: Graham & Trotman, 1982– . (Former titles: 1979/80–81; Principal companies of the European Economic Community; 1970–79: Jane's major companies of Europe; 1965–68: Beerman's financial year book of Europe)

Lists important West European companies in the fields of finance, services, light industries, engineering, building, and metals and natural resources. About 1,000 companies covered in depth; several hundred additional ones in a summary section.

D651 National trade and professional associations of the United States. 1982– . Washington, D.C.: Columbia Bks. (Former title: 1975–81: National trade and professional associations of the United States and Canada and labor unions) Annual.

Title varies. Name, address, chief executive officer, size of staff, membership, year founded, annual budget, and publications of about 300 associations. Keyword and executive indexes. See also *Encyclopedia of associations* (A348). Title, 1966–74: *National trade and professional associations of the United States*.

D652 Norback, Craig T. The international consumer's yellow pages. New York: Facts On File, 1982. 287p.

For both the average consumer and the larger-scale importer. This work is arranged by product categories (antiques, bicycles, fabrics, watches, yarn, etc.). Under that: company information includes name and address, phone and telex numbers, business hours, payment terms, catalog and cost, delivery time. Discusses U.S. customs regulations and consumer complaints; index includes company name and product categories.

D653 Polk's world bank directory. 1895– . Nashville: R.L. Polk. Semiannual, with supplements.

International section issued separately each July, 1970– . North American section, Sept. 1971– , supersedes in part *Polk's world bank directory* and continues its numbering.

D654 Rand McNally international bankers' directory. 1876– . Chicago: Rand McNally. Semiannual, with supplements.

Comparable to *Polk's world bank directory*, this lists banks and branches, their officers and directors, financial statements, etc.

D655 Sheldon's retail. . . . 1884– . New York: Phelon, Sheldon & Marsar. Annual.

Lists department, dry goods, and specialty stores by states and cities. Gives location of buying office in New York and/or other cities and names of resident and department buyers. Primarily U.S. but some Canadian stores.

D656 Standard directory of advertisers. 1964– . Skokie, Ill.: Natl. Register Pubs. Annual, with monthly supplements, weekly news bulletins.

List of national advertisers, arranged by industry, names of officers and executives of the companies, products advertised, agency connections, advertising appropriations, and types of media used. Has "trademark index." Separate geographical index. Supersedes in part the *Standard advertising register* (1915–63) and incorporates *McKittrick directory of advertisers* (1899–1960).

D657 Standard directory of advertising agencies. 1964– . Skokie, Ill.: Natl. Register Pubs. 3/yr.; monthly supplement entitled Agency news.

More than 4,000 U.S. and some foreign agencies, preceded by a geographical index. Supersedes "Agency list" of the *Standard advertising register*.

D658 Thomas register of American manufacturers. New York: Thomas Pub., 1906– . Annual.

This multivolume set includes lists of products and services; alphabetical list of companies, with addresses, branches, subsidiaries, products, approximate capitalization, etc.; index to product classifications, trade names, and commercial organizations; catalogs of companies.

D659 Trade names dictionary. 1st ed.– . Detroit: Gale, 1976– . Triennial.

Currently the most comprehensive list available. Information provided: trade name, product description, company/distributor name, code indicating source of information. Manufacturers' addresses appear in regular alphabetic sequence. Interedition supplements entitled *New trade names. Trade names dictionary: company index* (1979) **(D660)**, a companion to *Trade names dictionary*, alphabetically lists nearly 30,000 companies and thereunder lists the firms' trade names, brief product descriptions, and codes to the list of sources used in compilation. For names and addresses of these companies, see the special section following the main portion.

D661 U.S. Bureau of Labor Statistics. Directory of national unions and employee associations. 1971–79. Washington, D.C.: Govt. Print. Off. [Bulletin series] Continued by: Directory of U.S. labor organizations. 1982/83– . Washington, D.C.: Bureau of National Affairs, 1982– .

Continues *Directory of national and international labor unions in the United States* (1943–70).

D662 Wiesenberger Investment Companies Service. Investment companies. 1941– . Boston: Warren, Gorham & Lamont. Annual.

Published as a source of factual information on investment companies, merits of their management, and status of their securities. Information includes comparison of management results (by changes in net assets and income) and individual firm's background, policy, and results. Supplemented quarterly by *Management results* and monthly by *Current performance and dividend record*.

Other important sources include various regional industrial directories (e.g., *Directory of New England manufacturers*), state manufacturers' directories (see the pamphlet *Sources of state information and state industrial directories*, published irregularly by Chamber of Commerce of the United States), trade directories (e.g., *Lockwood's directory of the paper and allied trades*), telephone and city directories, and directories that appear as special issues of periodicals. For the last-named category, *Guide to special issues and indexes of periodicals* (New York: Special Libs. Assn., 1962, 1975) or *Special issues index* (Westport, Conn.: Greenwood, 1982) are useful.

DICTIONARIES AND ENCYCLOPEDIAS

D663 Ammer, Christine, and Dean S. Ammer. Dictionary of business and economics. Rev. and expanded ed. New York: Free Pr., 1984. 500p.

More than 3,000 entries written for the general reader. Emphasis is in biographies of the most important economists is on their ideas. Charts, graphs, tables.

D664 Arnold, Alvin L., and Jack Kusnet. The Arnold encyclopedia of real estate. Boston: Warren, Gorham & Lamont, 1978. 901p.

Arnold, editor of *Real estate review* and a member of the New York Bar, and attorney Kusnet have compiled "the most comprehensive and useful one-volume real estate encyclopedia currently available. [Their] use of examples and their emphasis on 'the salient features—economic, financial, legal and tax—of the real estate activity to which a term applies' distinguish their work." (*Choice* 16:1283, Dec. 1979)

D665 Auld, Douglas A. L., and others. The American dictionary of economics. New York: Facts on File, 1983. 342p.

Compiled by academics for the general reader and undergraduates. Clear, concise—briefer than *McGraw-Hill dictionary of modern economics* (D679).

A revision of the 1978 ed. of Graham Bannock and others, *Penguin dictionary of economics*.

D666 Davids, Lewis E. Dictionary of banking and finance. Totowa, N.J.: Rowman & Littlefield, 1979. 229p.

A very useful supplement to, but not a substitute for, Munn's *Encyclopedia of banking and finance* (D681). Its more than 5,000 terms and phrases were compiled from more than 100 works carefully identified with definitions. See also *Dictionary of banking and finance,* Jerry M. Rosenberg (New York: Wiley, 1983), 690p. **(D667).**

D668 Dictionary of administration and management. Los Angeles: Systems Research, 1981. 752p.

Includes (1) current terms, concepts, acronyms; (2) descriptions of current professional diagnostic tests and learning instruments for measuring leadership abilities and potential; (3) descriptions of major national and international leadership organizations and educational opportunities they provide; (4) worldwide directory of resources currently in use. Earlier eds. under variant titles.

D669 Encyclopedia of computer science and engineering. 2d ed. Ed. by Anthony Ralston and Edwin D. Reilly, Jr. New York: Van Nostrand Reinhold, 1983. 1,664p.

Comprehensive coverage in 550 articles. Text amplified by numerous charts, graphs, photos, diagrams, cross-references, detailed index, five-language glossary (English, French, German, Spanish, Russian).

D670 Encyclopedia of economics. Ed. by Douglas Greenwald. New York: McGraw-Hill, 1982. 1,070p.

More than 300 signed articles by prominent economists explain the topic and often present opposing viewpoints. Frequent cross-references; chronology of economic events, technological developments, financial changes, and economic thought.

D671 Encyclopedia of investments. Ed. by Marshall E. Blume and Jack P. Friedman. Boston: Warren, Gorham & Lamont, 1982. 1,041p.

Covers both traditional (stocks, bonds, mutual funds) and nontraditional (motion pictures, artworks, period furniture, etc.) investments. For each investment alternative, the following points are included: how to buy and sell the asset, tax implications, a glossary, and suggested readings. Annual supplements projected by publisher.

D672 Graham, Irvin. Encyclopedia of advertising. 2d ed. New York: Fairchild, 1969. 494p.

D673 Gross, Jerome S. Illustrated encyclopedic dictionary of real estate terms. 2d ed. Englewood Cliffs, N.J.: Prentice-Hall, 1978. 418p.

D674 Heyel, Carl, ed. The encyclopedia of management. 3d ed. New York: Van Nostrand Reinhold, 1982. 1,371p.

Superior compendium of more than 300 alphabetically arranged entries, representing the work of more than 200 contributors.

D675 International encyclopedia of statistics. Ed. by William H. Kruskal and Judith M. Tanur. New York: Free Pr., 1978. 2v.

Seventy articles on statistics proper; those reprinted from *International encyclopedia of the social sciences* have been revised, corrected, and updated. Note also: Kendall, M. G., and W. R. Buckland. *A dictionary of statistical terms*, 4th ed. (New York: Longmans, 1982), 213p. **(D676)**.

D677 Johannsen, Hano, and G. Terry Page. International dictionary of business. Englewood Cliffs, N.J.: Prentice-Hall, 1981. 376p. (Previous ed., 1975, and 2d British rev. ed., 1980, published as International dictionary of management)

Defines and explains about 5,000 words, abbreviations, institutions. Numerous cross-references. Appendixes: units of measure, time zones, directory of world stock exchanges.

D677 James, Simon, comp. A dictionary of eco-
A nomics quotations. 2d ed. Totowa, N.J.: Barnes & Noble, 1984. 240p.

More than 2,000 sources.

D678 Kohler, Eric L. Kohler's dictionary for accountants. 6th ed. Englewood Cliffs, N.J.: Prentice-Hall, 1983. 574p.

Authoritative and truly encyclopedic, replete with tables and illustrative material. Many of the terms have been appropriated from other fields, but only their meaning for accounting is given. Excellent.

D679 McGraw-Hill dictionary of modern economics: a handbook of terms and organizations. 3d ed. New York: McGraw-Hill, 1983. 632p.

The first part defines—often in detail and with charts, tables, diagrams— some 1,425 frequently used terms, which may include references to sources of additional information. Pt. 2 describes some 200 private and public organizations.

D680 Moffatt, Donald W. Economics dictionary. 2d ed. New York: Elsevier, 1983. 331p.

Meets the needs of persons without a background in economics to understand expressions found in the popular and trade press and on television. Includes illustrative material: charts, graphs, etc.

D681 Munn, Glenn G. Encyclopedia of banking and finance. 8th ed. Boston: Bankers Publishing Co., 1983. 1,028p.

Encyclopedic information on the American finance field and banking, investment, economic, financial, and related legal terms (some 4,000 in all). Some entries contain bibliographies and explanations with tables and charts. Special features include important acts on banking and finance and a list of New Deal agencies. Definitions are explicit and clear.

D682 Palgrave, Sir Robert H. I. Palgrave's dictionary of political economy. London and New York: Macmillan, 1923–26. 3v.; Reprint, New York: Kelley, 1963; Detroit: Gale, 1976.

First edition appeared in 1894–99 and was reprinted in 1910 with text changes and a supplement of new articles. The 1915–18 reprint contains the same supplement but with cross-references to the supplement from the main sections. This edition is a reprint of the 1915–18 edition, with some changes and an expanded supplement. Original purpose was to provide information to help students understand contemporary economic thought. Articles are complete and authoritative, with bibliographies, and each is signed by a specialist. Oriented toward economic developments in the English-speaking world. Much of the information is out of date, but book is useful for historical and biographical information in economics.

D683 Pearce, David W., ed. The dictionary of modern economics. Rev. ed. Cambridge, Mass.: MIT Pr., 1983. 480p.

More than 2,500 entries, including biographies of celebrated economists.

D684 Shafritz, Jay M. Dictionary of personnel management and labor relations. Oak Park, Ill.: Moore Pub., 1980. 429p.

Brief definitions, ending with references (official documents, articles, books, etc.). Numerous "see" and "see also" references; strong on names of individuals, organizations, journals; charts, graphs.

D685 Sloan, Harold S., and Arnold J. Zurcher. Dictionary of economics. 5th ed. New York: Barnes & Noble, 1971. 520p.

Edited by a professor of economics and a professor of political science, this collection of some 2,500 brief definitions covers a wide range, from economic history to industrial organization. Includes digests and briefs of important American statutes and judicial decisions of American and international agencies. Many cross-references, charts, tables. Appendix classifies terms under 36 topics, such as accounting, economics, financial documents, bills, judicial decisions.

D686 U.S. Dept. of Commerce. Office of the Assistant Secretary for Economic Affairs. Dictionary of economic and statistical terms. Prepared by James M. Howell and others. Washington, D.C.: Govt. Print. Off., 1969. 73p. (2d ed. 1972 [pub. 1973]. 83p.)

Designed as an aid to understanding and using the publications and press releases of the Bureaus of the Census and Economic Analysis in the Dept. of Commerce and for those with a limited background in economic statistics.

D687 Urdang, Laurence. Dictionary of advertising terms. Chicago: Tatham-Laird & Kudner, 1979. 214p.

More than 4,000 entries; some illustrations. "1st published edition": 1977.

D688 Weik, Martin H. Standard dictionary of computers and information processing. Rev. 2d ed. Rochelle Park, N.J.: Hayden, 1977. 390p. (1st ed. 1969)

More than 12,000 terms (in inverted word order), many with examples, illustrations, cross-references. Broad interdisciplinary coverage. Some 80 vocabularies were used as a database and reference source in preparing this dictionary.

To supplement this highly selective list of dictionaries, see Lorna Daniells' *Business information sources* (D508) and the *Encyclopedia of business information sources* (D510).

HANDBOOKS, MANUALS, AND COMPENDIA

Handbooks are good sources of quick, factual information; however, the following list, though representative, is neither comprehensive nor definitive. Additional titles can be found in Daniells' *Business information sources* (D508) and the *Encyclopedia of business information sources* (D510). Cf. James B. Woy, "Basic business handbooks and dictionaries," *RQ* 9:236–38 (Spring 1970) **(D689).**

D690 AMA management handbook. 2d ed. New York: AMACON, 1983. 1,872p.

D691 ASPA [American Society for Personnel Administration] handbook of personnel and industrial relations. Ed. by Dale Yoder and Herbert G. Heneman. Washington, D.C.: Bureau of National Affairs, 1979. 1,697p.

D692 Accountants' handbook. Ed. by Lee J. Seidler and Douglas R. Carmichael. 6th ed. New York: Wiley, 1981. Various pagings.

D693 Advertising age yearbook. 1981– . Chicago: Crain Bks., 1981– .

D694 Advertising manager's handbook. 3d ed. Chicago: Dartnell, 1982.

D695 Almanac of China's economy. 1981– . Comp. by the Economic Research Centre, the State Council of the People's Republic of China, and the State Statistical Bureau. Peking: Modern Cultural Co. (dist. Ballinger), 1982– . (1981 ed.: 1949–80 statistics)

D696 Business systems handbook. [By] John W. Haslett. New York: McGraw-Hill, 1979. 355p.

D697 The complete secretary's handbook. By Lillian Doris and Besse May Miller. 5th ed., rev. by Mary A. DeVries. Englewood Cliffs, N.J.: Prentice-Hall, 1982. 596p.

D698 Dartnell public relations handbook. Chicago: Dartnell, 1979. 1,115p.

D699 Dictionary of occupational titles. 4th ed. U.S. Employment and Training Administration, 1977. Supplement, 1982. 1983.

D699 Direct marketing handbook. Ed. by Edward L.
A   Nash. New York: McGraw-Hill, 1984. 946p.

D700 Dow Jones-Irwin business and investment almanac. 1982– . Homewood, Ill.: Dow Jones-Irwin. Annual. (Title 1977–81: Dow Jones-Irwin business almanac)

D701 Economic handbook of the world. 1981– . New York: McGraw-Hill for the Center for Social Analysis of SUNY—Bingham, 1981– .

D702 Encyclopedia of accounting systems. Rev. and enl. Prentice-Hall editorial staff; Jerome K. Pescow, ed. Englewood Cliffs, N.J.: Prentice-Hall, 1976. 3v.

D703 Encyclopedia of American economic history: studies of the principal movements and ideas. Ed. by Glenn Porter. New York: Scribner, 1980. 3v.

D704 Encyclopedia of information systems and services. Ed. by John Schmittroth. 1st ed.– , 1971– . Detroit: Gale, 1971– .

D705 Everybody's business: an almanac: the irreverent guide to corporate America. Ed. by Milton Moskowitz and others. New York: Harper, 1980. 916p. (Supplements: Everybody's business, 1982 update [San Francisco: Harper, 1981] and Everybody's business scoreboard: corporate America's winners, losers and also-rans [San Francisco: Harper, 1983])

D706 Financial handbook. 5th ed. Ed. by Edward I. Altman. New York: Wiley, 1981. Various pagings.

D707 Foreign commerce handbook. 1st ed.– , 1922– . Washington, D.C.: Chamber of Commerce of the U.S. Irregularly.

D708 Franchise opportunities handbook. 14th ed. Washington, D.C.: U.S. International Trade Administration and U.S. Minority Business Development Agency, 1980– . Annual.

D709 Guidebook to labor relations. 1950, 1960– . Chicago: Commerce Clearing House. Annual.

D709 Handbook of international financial manage-
A   ment. Ed. by Allen Sweeny and Robert Rachlin. New York: McGraw-Hill, 1984. Various pagings.

D710 Handbook of modern accounting. Ed. by Sidney Davidson and Roman L. Weil. 3d ed. New York: McGraw-Hill, 1983. 1,408p.

D711 Handbook of modern marketing. Ed. by Victor P. Buell. New York: McGraw-Hill, 1970. Various pagings.

D712 Handbook of modern personnel administration. Ed. by Joseph J. Famularo. New York: McGraw-Hill, 1972. Various pagings.

D713 Handbook of operations research. New York: Van Nostrand Reinhold, 1978. 2v.

D714 Handbook of public relations. Ed. by Howard Stephenson. 2d ed. New York: McGraw-Hill, 1971. 836p.

D715 Industrial engineering handbook. Ed. by Harold B. Maynard. 1st ed.– , 1956– . New York: McGraw-Hill. Various pagings.

D716 Labor almanac. By Adrian A. Paradis and Grace D. Paradis. Littleton, Colo.: Libraries Unlimited, 1983. 205p.

D717 Labor unions. Ed. by Gary M. Fink. Westport, Conn.: Greenwood, 1977. 520p. [Greenwood encyclopedia of American institutions,1]

D718 Lesly's public relations handbook. 3d. by Philip Lesly. 3d ed. Englewood Cliffs, N.J.: Prentice-Hall, 1983. 718p.

D718 McGraw-Hill real estate handbook. Ed. by
A   Robert Irwin. New York: McGraw-Hill, 1984. Various pagings.

D719 Materials handbook: an encyclopedia for purchasing managers, engineers, executives and foremen. Ed. by George S. Brady. 1st ed.– , 1929– . New York: McGraw-Hill.

D720 The modern accountant's handbook. Ed. by James D. Edwards and Homer A. Black. Homewood, Ill.: Dow Jones-Irwin, 1976. 1,203p.

D720 NTL managers handbook. Arlington, Va.:
A   NTL Institute, 1983. 381p.

D721 Office administration handbook. Ed. by Clark Fetridge and Robert S. Minor. Chicago: Dartnell, 1981. 1,087p.

D722 Personnel administration handbook. 2d ed. Ed. by Wilbert E. Scheer. Chicago: Dartnell, 1979. 1,088p.

D723 Public relations handbook. By Richard W. Darrow and Dan J. Forrestal. 2d ed. Chicago: Dartnell, 1979. 1,115p.

D724 Purchasing handbook. Coordinating ed.: Paul V. Farrell. 4th ed. McGraw-Hill, 1982. Various pagings. (Also called: Aljian's purchasing handbook)

D725 Quality control handbook. Ed. by J. M. Juran and others. Rev. 3d ed. New York: McGraw-Hill, 1974. Various pagings.

D726 Real estate handbook. Ed. by Maury Seldin. Homewood, Ill.: Dow Jones-Irwin, 1980. 1,186p.

D727 Sales manager's handbook. 1st ed.– , 1934– . Chicago: Dartnell.

D728 The small business handbook. Irving Burstiner. Englewood Cliffs, N.J.: Prentice-Hall, 1979. 342p.

D729 Standard industrial classification manual. Washington, D.C.: U.S. Office of Management and Budget, 1972. 649p. (1977 supplement 1980. 15p.)

D730 Stock market handbook. Ed. by Frank G. Zarb and Gabriel T. Kerekes. Homewood, Ill.: Dow Jones-Irwin, 1970. 1,073p.

D731 The successful secretary's handbook. By Esther R. Becker and Evelyn Anders. New York: Harper, 1971. 418p.

D732 Sylvia Porter's your own money book. By Sylvia Porter. New York: Avon, 1983. 768p.

D733 Training and development handbook: a guide to human resource development. 2d ed. New York: McGraw-Hill, 1976. Various pagings.

D734 U.S. Bureau of Labor Statistics. Occupational outlook handbook. 1949– . Washington, D.C.: Govt. Print. Off. Biennial. [Bulletin series]

D735 U.S. Women's Bureau. Handbook on women workers. 1948– . Washington, D.C.: Govt. Print. Off. Biennial. [Bulletin series]

D736 Webster's new world secretarial handbook. New rev. ed. New York: Simon & Schuster, 1981. 530p.

D737 Webster's secretarial handbook. 2d ed. Springfield, Mass.: Merriam, 1983. 550p.

D738 World energy book: an A–Z atlas, and statistical source book. Cambridge, Mass.: MIT Pr., 1979. 259p.

STATISTICAL SOURCES

Data sources such as the *Statistical abstract of the United States* and *County and city data book* (A459, A460), and U.N. *Statistical yearbook* (A497), are of basic importance for this field (as for others). See also "After the Statistical Abstract, what?" by Nathalie D. Frank, *RQ* (14:204–10, [1975]) (**D739**); "International economic statistics: a selected list of documents," by M. Balachandran, *Reference services review* (5:3–57 [1977]) (**D740**); U.S. Domestic and International Business Administration, *A guide to federal data sources on manufacturing* (Washington, D.C.: Govt. Print. Off., 1977; 197p.) (**D741**); U.S. Industry and Trade Administration, *Measuring markets: a guide to the use of federal and state statistical data* (Washington, D.C.: Govt. Print. Off., 1979; 101p.) (**D742**); "Ten basic sources of business and economic statistics," by James B. Woy and others, *RQ* (10:30–32 [1970]) (**D743**); "A student's guide to American federal government statistics," by J. F. Morton, *Journal of economic literature* (10:371–97 [1972]) (**D744**); and "Statistical sources in business and economics," by Lucy Heckman, *Reference services review* (11:72–76 [1983]) (**D745**).

Those who are beginning and those who wish to extend their search will profit by examining— in addition to the statistical sources—aids that are designed to facilitate their use, such as *Busi-*

ness reference sources (D512), which devotes more than a third of its text to a discussion of statistics; *Encyclopedia of business information sources* (D510); and *Bureau of the Census catalog* (D577). *DataMap* (New York: Longmans, 1983– ; annual) **(D746)** indexes all tables— more than 10,000—in 28 published sources of socioeconomic, political statistics in U.S. Government, United Nations, and other sources (e.g., *Statistical abstract of the United States*, *U.N. Statistical yearbook*, the *Information please almanac*, and the *World almanac*).

D747 Balachandran, M. A guide to trade and securities statistics. Ann Arbor: Pierian, 1977. 185p.
A detailed subject analysis of some 30 most-used serials: Standard & Poor's, Moody's, Value Line, *Life insurance fact book*, etc.

D748 Business conditions digest. Jan. 1972– . Washington, D.C.: Bureau of Economic Analysis, U.S. Dept. of Commerce. Monthly.
"Provides a monthly look at many of the economic time series found most useful by business analysts and forecasters" (cover 2). Continues *Business conditions digest* (Nov. 1968–Dec. 1971) and *Business cycle developments* (Oct. 1961–Oct. 1968). *The handbook of cyclical indicators: a supplement to business conditions digest*, 2d ed. (Washington, D.C.: Govt. Print. Off., 1984; 191p.) contains data for all BCD series, 1947–82, assembled in one source.

D749 Carlsen, Robert D., and Donald L. Vest. Encyclopedia of business charts. Englewood Cliffs, N.J.: Prentice-Hall, 1977. 886p.
Examples: costs as a percent of sales; current assets to current liabilities, percent return on gross assets, sales per employee. The encyclopedia is "not limited to a single subject but rather offers a selection of business charts and chart styles." (p.v.)

D750 Commodity year book. v.1– , 1939– . New York: Commodity Research Bureau. Annual.
Statistical information, arranged alphabetically by product, on supply, demand, consumption, prices, and export of raw and semifinished products. Numerous charts illustrate statistics. Update with *Statistical abstract service* **(D751)**, published 3 times a year, and with weekly *Commodity chart service* **(D752)**.

D753 Conference Board. Consumer attitudes and buying plans. New York: Conference Board, 1968– . Monthly.
Commentary, statistics, and charts on consumer expectations for business conditions, employment, and income, and consumer buying plans for autos, homes, major appliances, carpets, and vacations. See also the board's semimonthly *Road maps of industry*, its monthly *Statistical bulletin*, and its bimonthly *International economic scoreboard*.

D754 Current industrial reports. Washington, D.C.: U.S. Bureau of the Census. Monthly, quarterly, and annually.
Formerly *Facts for industry*. Separate reports cover major manufacturing (textile mill products, apparel, pulp and paper, primary metals, machinery, etc.). Statistical data on production, shipments, orders, and inventories.

D755 Dun & Bradstreet. Industry norms and key business ratios: library edition. 1982/83– . New York: Dun & Bradstreet, 1982– . Annual.
An expanded version of the "Key Business Ratios" information in Dun's business month. See also: Robert Morris Associates' *Annual statement studies* and Leo Troy's *Almanac of business and industrial financial ratios* **(D778)**.

D756 Economic indicators. May 1948– . Washington, D.C.: U.S. Council of Economic Advisers. Monthly.
Charts and tables summarize current economic series in such areas as income and spending, employment and wages, production and business activity, prices, credit, and security markets, as well as federal finance. *Historical and descriptive supplement*, revised from time to time, gives data back to 1939 or earlier and explanation of each series, showing relation to other series, limitations, and uses. Concise review of important economic series, current and historical. The council assists in preparation of *Economic report of the President to the Congress* **(D792)**.

D757 The Economist. The world in figures. London: Economist Newspaper Ltd.; New York: Facts On File, etc. Various dates.
Political, economic, and statistical information on more than 200 countries: population, income, standard of living, climate, currency, etc.

D758 Editor & publisher. Market guide. v.1– , 1924– . New York. Annual.
Data on newspaper markets in cities and towns in the U.S. and Canada. Arranged alphabetically by state or province and then alphabetically by town or city. Provides information on transportation facilities, population, housing facilities, savings banks, auto registration, gas meters, telephones, types of industry, colleges and universities, retail outlets, heaviest buying day, chain food stores, newspapers, local contact for advertising, climate, character of water supply. Of use for market research and plant relocation, and useful to individuals who plan to move to a new city.

D759 Federal Reserve bulletin. v.1– , 1915– . Washington, D.C.: U.S. Board of Governors of the Federal Reserve System. Monthly.
Comprehensive presentation of economic and business developments pertaining to banking and finance. Statistics cover information on Federal Reserve banks, department-store trade, consumer credit, production indexes, and international finance. Most statistics based on reports made to the board or from the Treasury Dept. Note: the district Federal Reserve banks publish one or more periodicals pertinent to the economy of their region.

D760 Foreign economic trends and their implications for the United States. Washington, D.C.: U.S.

International Trade Administration, 1969– . Annual or semiannual.

This series analyzes the latest business and economic developments in more than 100 countries, devoting one issue to each country. "Key economic indicators," at the beginning of each report, presents data for the past three years on national income and production, finance, trade balance of payments, and public finance.

D761 Handbook of basic economic statistics. 1947– . Washington, D.C.: Economic Statistics Bureau of Washington, D.C. Annual or quarterly, with monthly supplements; or monthly service.

Current and historical data on industry, commerce, labor, and agriculture.

D762 International financial statistics. 1948– . Washington, D.C.: Intl. Monetary Fund. Monthly.

Statistics for various countries on exchange rates, gold and foreign exchange, balance of payments, government finance, industrial production, etc. Summary tables (by subject) are followed by country section with detailed tables and review of financial situation of the country. All information is from official publications of the respective countries, direct communication, and international agencies. Statistics are both historical and current, permitting a number of comparisons. See also the fund's *International financial statistics yearbook*. 1979– .

D763 International Labour Office. Year-book of labour statistics. 1930– . Geneva: Intl. Labour Office, 1931– . Annual.

Labor statistics for various countries are arranged by subject matter (employment, hours or work, wages, social security, industrial injuries, etc.). Update with Statistical supplement to the monthly *International labour review* (**D764**) through Dec. 1964 and with the office's *Bulletin of labour statistics*, 1965– ; quarterly (**D765**). Both are useful for locating internationally comparable figures.

D766 LNA Multi-Media Reports Service. 1948– . New York: Leading National Advertisers. Quarterly.

In 4 parts: Company/Brand $ (advertising expenditures in 6 media, by company, then by brands); Class/Brand Qtr $ and Class/Brand YTD [year to date] $ (advertising expenditures in 6 media, by industry and product classification); Ad $ Summary (index of brands with year-to-date total advertising dollars ranking of 1,000 top advertisers with expenditures spent in each of 6 media).

D767 Long term economic growth, 1860–1970. Washington, D.C.: U.S. Bureau of Economic Analysis, 1973. 311p.

Brings together some 1,200 annual economic time series.

D768 Monthly labor review. v.1– , 1915– . Washington, D.C.: U.S. Bureau of Labor Statistics. Monthly.

Detailed statistics on employment, work stoppages, payrolls, and other labor topics, as well as statistics on consumer and wholesale prices and building and construction. Features discuss recent events. Book reviews and list of recent publications.

D769 PIB monthly service/Leading national advertisers monthly service: magazine advertising expenditures. 1948– . New York: Publishers' Information Bureau. Looseleaf.

In 7 industry sections: apparel, business-financial, drugs-toiletries, food-beverages, general, home-building, transportation-agriculture.

D770 Pieper, Frank C. SISCIS: subject index to sources of comparative international statistics. Beckenham: CBD Research Ltd. (dist. Detroit: Gale), 1978. 745p.

About 350 recurring statistical publications covered.

D771 Predicasts forecasts. no.1– . Oct. 1960– . Cleveland: Predicasts. Quarterly, with annual cumulation. (Title varies)

Economic and market forecast abstracts arranged by product. Vols. for 1960–66 published by Economic Index & Surveys, Inc. Available for online searching.

D772 Standard Rate and Data Service. Network rates and data. 1951– . Skokie, Ill.: SRDS. Monthly.

Excellent information on rates, audiences, and advertising facilities. Other volumes discuss direct mail lists, business publications, Canadian advertising rates and data, newspapers, spot radio, spot TV, weekly newspapers, consumer magazines, farm publications, etc. Under varying titles and frequencies, the service began publishing in 1919.

D773 "Survey of buying power," *Sales and marketing management*. 1918– . New York: Bill Pubs.

Population, effective buying income, and retail sales: estimates for state, county, and metropolitan areas. Statistics are those of the magazine and are based on government figures and local information. Annually in a July issue, with Pt. 2 in an Oct. issue. "Survey of industrial purchasing power" (title varies) (**D774**) is in an April issue.

D775 Survey of current business. v.1– , Aug. 1921– . Washington, D.C.: U.S. Bureau of Economic Analysis. Monthly.

Analysis of current business trends is followed by statistical series on national income, gross national product, personal and farm income; expenditures for new plant and equipment, retail and wholesale sales, manufacturers' sales, orders, and inventories; estimates of balance of international payments; and production, prices, and shipment for various commodities. Important issues are Feb., which reviews the previous year, and July, on national income. Special supplements are issued from time to time, e.g., *Business statistics*, biennially, in odd-number years (**D776**) and *National income and product accounts of the United States, 1929–1976* (**D777**).

D778 Troy, Leo. Almanac of business and industrial financial ratios. 1971– . Englewood Cliffs, N.J.: Prentice-Hall. Annual.

Ratios and factors for selected industries based on the Internal Revenue Service's analyses of corporate income tax returns.

D779 United Nations. Dept. of Economic and Social Affairs. World economic survey. no.1– , 1945/47– . New York: 1948– . Annual.

Comprehensive review of world economic conditions in text, tables, and charts. The regional UN economic commissions—for Africa, Asia and the Pacific, Europe, Western Asia, and Latin America—also issue economic surveys.

D780 ———. Statistical Off. The growth of world industry. 1967–73. New York. Annual.

Preceded by irregular issues under this title. v.1 contains general industrial statistics for selected countries; v.2 contains information on the production of selected industrial commodities. Title, 1974– : *Yearbook of industrial statistics*.

D781 ———. ———. Yearbook of international trade statistics. 1950– . New York: 1951– . Annual.

Covers 140 or more countries. Continues the League of Nations' *International trade statistics* (issued from 1925 to 1939). Use the office's *Statistical papers: series D: commodity trade statistics* to obtain current statistics.

D782 ———. ———. Yearbook of national accounts statistics. 1957– . New York: 1958– . Annual.

Supersedes UN's *Statistics of national income and expenditures* (no.1–10, 1952–57) (Statistical papers, ser. H), which continued *National income statistics of various countries* (published by the League of Nations from 1938 to 1947).

D783 U.S. Bureau of Labor Statistics. Consumer price index. Jan. 1953– . Washington, D.C. Monthly.

Index numbers measure changes in prices of goods and services purchased by the average consumer. Entitled, Aug. 1974– : *CPI detailed report*.

D784 ———. Employment and earnings. 1954– Washington, D.C.: Govt. Print. Off. Monthly.

Current statistics on hours, trends, turnover rates, earnings, man-hour indexes. Some of the statistics also appear in *Monthly labor review* (D768).

D785 ———. Handbook of labor statistics. 1924/26– . Washington, D.C.: Govt. Print. Off. Irregularly. [Bulletin series]

Makes available in 1 v. the major series produced by the Bureau of Labor Statistics and related series from other governmental agencies and foreign countries. Note: The 1975 Reference edition (Bulletin 1865) provides complete historical data.

D786 ———. Wholesale prices and price indexes. Jan. 1952– . Washington, D.C.: Govt. Print. Off. Monthly.

Index numbers indicating changes in primary market prices of various commodities. Also in *Monthly labor review* (D768). Various title changes. Now called *Producer price indexes*.

D787 U.S. Bureau of the Census. Census of [the year]. 1790– . Washington, D.C.: Govt. Print. Off.

Federal censuses that are useful for business and economic research begin with the decennial *Census of population* (1790–) and the various series of *Current population reports*. Others are Agriculture (1840–), Business (incl. those called Distribution) (1926–), Housing (1940–), Manufactures (1810–), Annual survey of manufactures (1949/50–), Mineral industries (1840–), Transportation (1963–). The Census Bureau now employs the term economic censuses to mean all the above (except population and agriculture) plus the censuses of outlying areas, enterprise statistics, survey of minority-owned business enterprises, and the survey of women-owned businesses.

D788 ———. County business patterns. 1946– . Washington, D.C.: Govt. Print. Off. Annual.

Based upon information obtained directly from employers. Data on number of business establishments, employment, and payroll are shown by state and county as well as by industry and employment-size group. Some SMSA (Standard Metropolitan Statistical Area) statistics are given.

D789 ———. Social indicators III. Washington, D.C.: Govt. Print. Off. 1980. 585p.

Text, charts, statistics on U.S. social conditions and trends: population, housing, family, health and nutrition, education and training, work, etc. 1st ed. (1973) by Statistical Policy Division, U.S. Office of Management and Budget; 2d ed. (1977) by Dept. of Commerce, Office of Federal Statistical Policy and Standards.

D790 U.S. Central Intelligence Agency. Handbook of economic statistics. Washington, D.C.: Govt. Print. Off. Annual.

Provides statistics for selected non-Communist and all Communist countries.

D791 U.S. Dept. of Agriculture. Agricultural statistics. 1936– . Washington, D.C.: Govt. Print. Off. Annual.

Detailed statistics on crops and livestock (acreage, prices, foreign trade, etc.), farm income, and other agricultural economic data.

D792 U.S. President. Economic report of the President to the Congress. 1st ed.– , Jan. 1947– . Washington, D.C.: Govt. Print. Off. Annual.

Review of the national economy with statistical appendixes covering employment, income, and production.

D793 Wasserman, Paul, and Diane Kemmerling. Commodity prices: a source book and index. Detroit: Gale, 1974. 200p.

References to wholesale and retail quotations for more than 5,000 agricultural, commercial, industrial, and consumer products.

ATLASES, MAPS, AND PICTORIAL WORKS

D794 National Planning Assn. Basic maps of the U.S. economy, 1967–1990: population, employment, income. Washington, D.C.: Center for Economic Projections, National Planning Assn. [1979]. 292p.

Pt. 1 is devoted to economic/demographic developments at the state level; Pt. 2 does the same for the economic areas as defined by the U.S. Bureau of Economic Analysis. Maps grouped under four subjects: growth summaries, population characteristics, employment composition, and income by source. Statistical data used to draw each map are presented in tabular form on the facing page. Plastic overlays display boundaries and the numbers for states and economic areas.

D795 Official airline guide. 1943– . Oakbrook, Ill.: Official Airline Guide, etc., 1943– . Monthly.

Guide to airline routes and schedules. North American and worldwide (formerly international) editions.

D796 Oxford economic atlas of the world. Prepared by the Cartographic Dept. of the Clarendon Pr. 4th ed. Oxford and New York: Oxford Univ. Pr. 1972. 248p.

Basic information about the economics of world commodities: maps with information on production and consumption and index by country of statistical information (from official sources) on the importance of various commodities in each country's economy. Series of regional atlases to complement this atlas are available: Africa (1965), Middle East and North Africa (1960), U.S. and Canada (1967, 1975), USSR and Eastern Europe (1956), and Western Europe (1971).

D797 Rand McNally & Co. Rand McNally commercial atlas and marketing guide. 1st ed.– , 1876– . Chicago: Rand McNally. Annual.

Excellent business and marketing statistics for U.S. cities, metropolitan areas, counties, and possessions. Maps are clear and large. Considerably less attention to rest of the world.

D798 U.S. Small Business Administration. Statistics and maps for national market analysis. [Small business bibliography, no.12] 1st ed., June 1959; 7th ed., 1982.

BUSINESS SERVICES

The number of business and economics services, whose raison d'être is the prompt furnishing of usable data, prohibits anything more than a sampling. In addition to those listed below, see the guides to the literature, such as Brownstone and Carruth (D506), Daniells (D508, D512), and Mary McNierney Grant and

Riva Berleant-Schiller, eds., *Directory of business and financial services*, 8th ed. (New York: Special Libraries Assn., 1984) **(D799).** The latter describes more than 1,100 services and is kept up to date by listings in the bulletin of the Business and Finance Division of the Special Libraries Association.

D800 Bureau of National Affairs. Washington, D.C.

Affirmative action compliance manual for federal contractors.

Antitrust and trade regulation report

BNA policy and practice series: for the personnel executive (available in separate parts: Personnel Management, Labor Relations, Wages and Hours, etc.)

Collective bargaining negotiations and contracts

Daily labor report

Daily report for executives

Daily tax report

EEOC compliance manual

Employee relations weekly

Environment reporter

Fair employment practice service

International trade reporter

Labor arbitration reports

Labor relations reference manual

Labor relations reporter

Occupational safety and health reporter

Retail/services labor report

Tax management

Union labor report

United States law week

Wage and hour cases

White collar report

D801 Commerce Clearing House, Chicago

Accounting articles

Common Market reporter

Congressional index

Consumer credit guide

Corporation filled-in tax return forms (also one for individuals' forms)

Corporation law guide

Federal tax course

Government contracts reporter

Guidebook to labor relations

Income tax regulations

Labor law reporter

Standard federal tax reporter

State tax guide; all states

Stock values and dividends for . . . tax purposes

Tax Court memorandum decisions

Tax Court reporter

Trade regulation reporter

Unemployment insurance reporter

U.S. master tax guide

U.S. tax cases

D802 Moody's Investors Service, New York

Bank & finance manual

Bond survey

Dividend record

Fact sheets

Handbook of common stocks

Industrial manual

International manual

Moody's bond record

Municipal & government manual

OTC industrial manual

Public utility manual

Stock survey

Transportation manual

D803 Prentice-Hall, Englewood Cliffs, N.J.

American federal tax reports

Corporation guide

Cumulative changes in Internal Revenue Code and tax regulations

Executive reports

Federal tax handbook

Federal tax service, cumulative

Individual federal income tax specimen returns

Industrial relations guide

Labor relations guide

Personnel communications

Personnel policies and practices

Prentice-Hall federal tax citator

Prentice-Hall federal tax course

Securities regulation guide

State tax guide; all states

Tax Court reported and memorandum decisions

Tax ideas

D804 Standard & Poor's Corp., New York

Bond guide

Dividend record

Industry surveys

Outlook

Over-the-counter and regional exchange stock reports

Security owner's stock guide

Security price index record

Standard ASE stock reports

Standard corporation records

Standard NYSE stock reports

Statistical service

Trade and securities: statistics

D804 Unlisted Market Guide, Glen Head, N.Y.
A   Unlisted market guide

D805 United Business Service Co., Boston

United business & investment report (formerly: United business service)

D806 Arnold Bernhard & Co., New York

Value line investment survey

SOURCES OF SCHOLARLY CONTRIBUTIONS

Journals

D807

Annotations of more than 150 journals (many of which are listed below) may be found in Vasile Tega, *Management and economics journals: a guide to information sources* (Detroit: Gale, 1977 [Management information guide, 33]) (**D808**). Brief notes on some 100 titles are in Agnes O. Hanson, *Executive and management development for business and government: a guide to information sources* (Detroit: Gale, 1976 [Management information guide, 31]), p.255–76 (**D809**).

ACES bulletin v.17– , 1975– . Temple, Ariz.: Dept. of Economics, Arizona State Univ. Quarterly. (Formerly: ASTE bulletin)
JEcon Lit; PAIS.

Academy of Management. Journal. v.1– , 1958– . Mississippi State: Mississippi State Univ. Quarterly.
BusPerInd; Psych Abst; SSCI; WkRelAbst.

Academy of Management review. v.1– , 1976– . Mississippi State: Mississippi State Univ. Quarterly.
BusPerInd; WkRelAbst.

Accounting review. v.1– , 1926– . Sarasota, Fla.: American Accounting Assn. Quarterly.
BullAnal; BusPerInd; IntBibZeit; SSCI.

Across the board. v.13– , 1976– . New York: Conference Board. Monthly.
BusPerInd; PAIS; SSCI; WkRelAbst.

Administrative science quarterly. v.1– , 1956– . Ithaca, N.Y.: Cornell Univ. Graduate School of Business and Public Administration. Quarterly.
BusPerInd; Cc; PAIS; PsychAbst; SocAbst; SSCI.

African economic history. v.1– , 1976– . Madison: Univ. of Wisconsin African Studies Program, Semiannual.
Cc; HistAbst; SSCI.

Agricultural economic research. v.1– , 1949– . Washington, D.C.: U.S. Dept. of Agriculture, Economics Management Staff, Information Div. Quarterly.
BioAbst; Cc; ChemAbst; PAIS.

American economic review. v.1– , 1911– . Nashville: American Economic Assn. Quarterly.
BusPerInd; Cc; PAIS; SSCI; SSI; WkRelAbst.

American economist. v.1– , 1957– . New York: Omicron Delta Epsilon. 2/yr.
SSCI; SSI; WkRelAbst.

American journal of agricultural economics. v.1– , 1919– . Ames: Iowa State Univ., Dept. of Economics for American Agricultural Economics Assn. 5/yr.
Cc; EM; SSCI.

American journal of economics and sociology. v.1– , 1941– . New York: The Journal. Quarterly.
HistAbst; JEconLit; PopInd; PAIS; SocAbst; SSCI; SSI; WkRelAbst.

American Statistical Assn. Journal. v.1– , 1888/89– . Washington, D.C.: American Statistical Assn. Quarterly.
BusPerInd; Cc; PsychAbst; SSCI.

Applied economics. v.1–14, 1969–83. London: Chapman & Hall. Quarterly.
JEconLit; SSCI.

Bell journal of economics. v.1– , 1970– . Hicksville, N.Y.: AT&T. 2/yr. (Now: Rand journal of economics)
Cc; JEconLit; SSCI; SSI; WkRelAbst.

Brookings papers on economic activity. no.1– , 1970– . Washington, D.C.: Brookings. 3/yr.
Cc; PAIS; SSCI; SSI.

Bulletin of economic research. v.1– , 1949– . Oxford: Basil Blackwell. 2/yr. (Formerly: Yorkshire bulletin of economic research)
BrHumInd; JEconLit.

Business and society review. v.1– , 1972– . Boston: Warren, Gorham & Lamont. Quarterly.
PersMgtAbst; SSI; WkRelAbst.

Business history review. v.1– , 1926– . Boston: Harvard Univ. Graduate School of Business Administration. Quarterly.

BusPerInd; Cc; MgtInd; PAIS; SSCI; WkRelAbst.

Business horizons. v.1– , 1958– . Bloomington: Indiana Univ. Graduate School of Business. Bimonthly.
BusPerInd; Cc; EM; PAIS; PersMgtAbst; SSCI; WkRelAbst.

Business quarterly: Canada's management journal. v.1– , 1933– . London, Ont.: Univ. of Western Ontario School of Business Adminstration. Quarterly.
Cc; CanInd; PAIS; SSCI.

California management review. v.1– , 1958– . Berkeley: Graduate School of Business Administration of the Univ. of California. Quarterly.
BusPerInd; Cc; EM; PAIS; PersMgtAbst; SSCI; WkRelAbst.

Cambridge journal of economics. v.1– , 1977– . London: Academic. Quarterly.
Cc; JEconLit.

Canadian journal of economics. v.1– , 1968– . Toronto: publ. by Univ. of Toronto Pr. for Canadian Economics Assn. Quarterly.
CanInd; Cc; PAIS; SSCI; SSI; WkRelAbst.

Challenge: the magazine of economic affairs. v.1– , 1952– . Armonk, N.Y.: M.E. Sharpe. Bimonthly.
WkRelAbst.

Chinese economic studies: a journal of translations. v.1– , 1967– . Armonk, N.Y.: M. E. Sharpe. Quarterly.
Cc; PAIS; SSCI.

Columbia journal of world business. v.1– , 1965– . New York: Trustees of Columbia Univ. Quarterly.
BusPerInd; Cc; PAIS; SSCI; WkRelAbst.

Decision sciences. v.1– . 1970– . Atlanta: American Inst. for Decision Sciences.
EM.

Econometrica. v.1– , 1933– . Chicago: Univ. of Chicago Pr. for Econometric Society. Bimonthly.
Cc; SSCI; SSI.

Economic inquiry. v.1– , 1962– . Long Beach: publ. by California State Univ. Dept. of Economics for Western Economic Assn. Quarterly.
Cc; JEconLit; PAIS; SSCI; SSI.

Economic journal. v.1– , 1891– . Cambridge: Royal Economic Society. Quarterly.
Cc; EM; PAIS; SSI; WkRelAbst.

Economica. v.1– , 1921– . London: London School of Economics and Political Science. Quarterly.
Cc; EM; JEconLit; PAIS; SSI.

Economy and society. v.1– , 1972– . London and Boston: Routledge & Paul. Quarterly.
SSCI.

European economic review. v.1– , 1969– . Amsterdam: North-Holland. Quarterly.
Cc; SSCI; SSI.

Explorations in economic history. v.1– , 1963– .
New York: Academic. Quarterly.
Cc; HistAbst; SSCI.

Financial management. v.1– , 1972– . Tampa:
Univ. of South Florida College of Business for
Financial Management Assn. Quarterly.
BusPerInd; Cc; SSCI.

George Washington journal of international law and
economics. v.1– , 1966– . Washington,
D.C.: George Washington Univ. National Law
Center. 3/yr.
Cc; SSCI.

Growth and change: a journal of regional development. v.1– , 1970– . Lexington: Univ. of
Kentucky College of Business and Economics.
Quarterly.
Cc; JEconLit; PAIS; SSCI; WkRelAbst.

Harvard business review. v.1– , 1922– . Boston:
Harvard Univ. Graduate School of Business
Administration. Bimonthly.
BusPerInd; Cc; IntBibZeit; PAIS; PersMgtAbst; PsychAbst; RG; SSCI; WkRelAbst.

History of political economy. (Duke Univ. Dept. of
Economics). v.1– , 1969– . Durham, N.C.:
Duke Univ. Pr. Quarterly.
Cc; HistAbst; JEconLit; SSCI; SSI.

Industrial and labor relations review. v.1– , 1947– .
Ithaca: New York State School of Industrial and
Labor Relations, Cornell Univ. Quarterly.
BusPerInd; Cc; JEconLit; PersMgtAbst;
PsychAbst; SSCI; SSI; WkRelAbst.

Industrial marketing management: an international
journal of industrial marketing and marketing
research. v.1– , 1971– . New York: Elsevier
North-Holland. Quarterly.
Cc; BusPerInd; SSCI.

Industrial relations: a journal of economy & society.
v.1– , 1961– . Berkeley: Univ. of California
Inst. of Industrial Relations. 3/yr.
BusPerInd; PersMgtAbst; WkRelAbst.

International economic review. v.1– , 1960– . Philadelphia and Osaka: publ. jointly by Univ. of
Pennsylvania Wharton School of Finance and
Commerce and Osaka Univ. Inst. of Social and
Economic Research Assn. 3/yr.
Cc; SSI.

International Monetary Fund. Staff papers. v.1– ,
1950– . Washington, D.C.: International
Monetary Fund. 3/yr.
BusPerInd; Cc; PAIS; SSCI.

Journal of accountancy. v.1– , 1905– . New York:
American Inst. of Certified Public Accountants.
Monthly.
BusPerInd; Cc; PAIS; SSCI.

Journal of accounting and economics. v.1– ,
1979– . Amsterdam: North-Holland. 3/yr.

Journal of accounting and public policy. v.1– .
1982– . New York: Elsevier. Quarterly.
PAIS.

Journal of accounting research. v.1– , 1963– . Chicago: Univ. of Chicago Graduate School of
Business for Inst. of Professional Accounting.
Semiannual.
BusPerInd; Cc; SSCI.

Journal of behavioral economics. v.1– , 1972– .
Macomb: Western Illinois Univ. Center for
Business and Economic Research. Semiannually.
JEconLit.

Journal of business. v.1– , 1928– . Chicago: Univ.
of Chicago Pr. Quarterly.
BusPerInd; Cc; JEconLit; PAIS; SSCI.

Journal of Common Market studies. v.1– , 1962– .
Oxford: Basil Blackwell. 4/yr.
Cc; PAIS; SSCI.

Journal of comparative economics. v.1– , 1977– .
(Assn. for Comparative Economic Studies)
New York: Academic. Quarterly.
JEconLit; SSI.

Journal of consumer affairs. v.1– , 1967– . Columbia: Univ. of Missouri Pr. for American
Council on Consumer Interests. Semiannual.
Cc; SSCI.

Journal of developing areas. v.1– , 1966– .
Macomb: Western Illinois Univ. Pr. Quarterly.
Cc; GeoAbst; HistAbst; SSCI.

Journal of development studies: a quarterly journal
devoted to economic, political and social development. v.1– , 1964– . London: Frank
Cass. Quarterly.
Cc; IntPolSciAbst; JEconLit; PAIS; SSCI; SSI;
WkRelAbst.

Journal of economic dynamics and control. v.1– ,
1979– . Amsterdam: North-Holland. Quarterly.
Cc.

Journal of econometrics. v. 1– , 1973– . Amsterdam: Elsevier. Monthly.
Cc; JEcon Lit.

Journal of economic education. v.1– , 1969– .
Washington: Heldref. Semianual.
Cc; CIJE; JEconLit; SSCI.

Journal of economic history. v.1– , 1941– . Wilmington, Del.: Economic History Assn.,
Eleutherian Mills Historical Library.
Quarterly.
Cc; SSCI; SSHI; SSI; WkRelAbst.

Journal of economic issues. v.1– , 1967– . Lincoln: Univ. of Nebraska Dept. of Economics for Assn. for Evolutionary Economics. Quarterly. Cc; JEconLit; PAIS; SSI.

Journal of economic literature. v.1– , 1963– . Nashville: American Economic Assn. Quarterly. Cc; SSCI.

Journal of economic theory. v.1– , 1969– . New York: Academic. Bimonthly. Cc; SSCI; SSI.

Journal of energy and development. v.1– , 1975– . Boulder: [Univ. of Colorado] Intl. Research Center for Energy & Economic Development. 2/yr. Cc; PAIS; SSCI.

Journal of European economic history. v.1– , 1972– . Rome: Banco di Roma. 3/yr. JEconLit; PAIS.

Journal of finance. v.1– , 1946– . New York: New York Univ. Graduate School of Business for American Finance Assn. 5/yr. BusPerInd; Cc; PAIS; SSCI.

Journal of financial and quantitative analysis. v.1– , 1966– . Seattle: Univ. of Washington Graduate School of Business Administration and Western Finance Assn. 5/yr. JEconLit; SSCI.

Journal of financial economics. v.1– , 1974– . Lausanne: Elsevier. Quarterly. Cc; JEconLit.

Journal of general management. v.1– , 1973– . Ruislip, Eng.: Business Pubs. Ltd. Quarterly. Cc; PAIS; SSCI; WkRelAbst.

Journal of health economics. v.1– , 1982– . Amsterdam: North-Holland. 3/yr. SSCI.

Journal of human resources. v. 1 – , 1966– . Madison: Univ. of Wisconsin Pr. for Industrial Relations Research Institute. Quarterly. BPIA; Cc; PersMgtAbst; SSCI; SSI; WkRelAbst.

Journal of industrial economics. v.– , 1952– . Oxford: Basil Blackwell. Quarterly. BPI; BPIA; Cc; PAIS; SSCI; WkRelAbst.

Journal of international economics. v.1– , 1971– Amsterdam: North-Holland. Quarterly. Cc; JEconLit; SSCI; SSI.

Journal of labor economics. v.– , 1983– . Chicago: Univ. of Chicago Pr. in association with the Economics Research Center/NORC (National Opinion Research Center). Quarterly. JEconLit; SSCI.

Journal of labor research. v.1– , 1980– . Fairfax, Va.: Dept. of Economics, George Mason Univ. Quarterly. BPIA; Cc; JEconLit; PAIS; SSCI.

Journal of law and economics. v.1– , 1958– . Chicago: Univ. of Chicago Law School. 2/yr. Cc; HistAbst; JEconLit; SSCI; SSI.

Journal of macroeconomics. v.1– , 1979– . Detroit: Wayne State Univ. Pr. Quarterly. Cc.

Journal of management information systems. v.1– , 1984– . Armonk, N.Y.: M. E. Sharpe. Quarterly. CompRev; DataProcDig.

Journal of marketing. v.1– , 1936– . Chicago: American Marketing Assn. Quarterly. BusPerInd; Cc; JEconLit; PsychAbst; SSCI.

Journal of marketing research. v.1– , 1964– . Chicago: American Marketing Assn. Quarterly. BusPerInd; Cc; PsychAbst; SSCI.

Journal of monetary economics. v.1– , 1975– . Amsterdam: North-Holland. 4/yr. BPIA; Cc; JEconLit; SSCI.

Journal of money, credit and banking. v.1– , 1969– . Columbus: Ohio State Univ. Pr. Quarterly. Cc; JEconLit: PAIS; SSI.

Journal of political economy. v.1– , 1892– . Chicago: Univ. of Chicago Pr. Bimonthly. Cc; JEconLit; SSCI; SSI.

Journal of post-Keynesian economics. v.1– , 1978– . Armonk, N.Y.: M.E. Sharpe. Quarterly. Cc.

Journal of public economics. v.1– , 1972– . Lausanne: Elsevier. Quarterly. Cc; EM; JEconLit; PAIS.

Kyklos: insternational review for social sciences. v.1– , 1947– . Basel: Kyklos-Verlag. Quarterly. BullAnal; Cc; EM; JEconLit; SSCI; SSI.

Land economics. v.1– , 1925– . Madison: Univ. of Wisconsin Pr. Quarterly. BullAnal; BusPerInd; Cc; EM; PAIS; SSCI.

Management science. v.1– , 1954– . Providence, R.I.: Inst. of Management Sciences. Monthly. BusPerInd; Cc; SSCI.

Management today. v.1– , 1966– . London: Management Publications. Monthly. EM; WkRelAbst.

Manchester School of Economic and Social Studies. v.1– , 1930– . Manchester, Eng.: Manchester School, Economics Dept., The Univ. 4/yr. BrHumInd; Cc; JEconLit; SSI; WkRelAbst.

National Institute economic review. v.1– , 1959– . London: National Inst. of Economic and Social Research. Quarterly. BusPerInd; PAIS.

Natural resources journal. v.1– , 1961– . Albuquerque: Univ. of New Mexico School of Law. Quarterly. Cc; IndLegPer; SSCI.

Omega: international journal of management science. v.1– , 1973– . Elmsford, N.Y.: Pergamon. Bimonthly. EM.

Organizational dynamics. v.1– , 1972– . New York: American Management Assn. Quarterly. PersMgtAbst; PsychAbst; SSCI; WkRelAbst.

Oxford bulletin of economics and statistics. v.1– , 1939– . Oxford: Basil Blackwell. 4/yr. Cc; SSCI.

Oxford economic papers. v.1– , 1938– . Oxford: Clarendon. 3/yr. BrHumInd; Cc; EM; JEconLit; PAIS; SSCI; SSI.

Problems of economics. v.1– , 1958– . Armonk, N.Y.: M.E. Sharpe. Monthly. Cc; PAIS; SSCI.

Public finance quarterly. v.1– , 1973– . Beverly Hills, Calif.: Sage. Quarterly. Cc: JEconLit: PAIS; SSCI.

Public relations journal: a journal of opinion in the field of public relations practice. v.1– , 1945– . New York: Public Relations Society of America. Monthly. BusPerInd.

Quarterly journal of economics. v.1– , 1886– . New York: Wiley for Harvard Univ. Quarterly. Cc; EM; JEconLit; SSCI; SSI; WkRelAbst.

Quarterly review of economics and business. v.1– , 1961– . Urbana: Bureau of Economic and Business Research, College of Commerce and Business Administration, Univ. of Illinois. Quarterly. Cc; JEconLit; PAIS; PersMgtAbst; WkRelAbst.

Rand journal of economics v.15– , 1984– . Washington, D.C.: Rand Corp. Quarterly. (Formerly: Bell journal of economics) BPIA; Cc; JEconLit; SSCI; SSI; WkRelAbst.

Review of black political economy. v.1– , 1970– . New Brunswick, N.J.: Transaction Periodicals Consortium. Quarterly. Cc; SSCI; WkRelAbst.

Review of economic studies. v.1– , 1933– . Clevedon, Eng.: Tieto. 3/yr. BrHumInd; JEconLit; SSCI; SSI.

Review of economics and statistics. v.1– , 1919– . Amsterdam: North-Holland for Harvard Univ. Quarterly. BusPerInd; Cc; EM; SSCI; SSI.

Review of income and wealth. series 1– , 1951– . New Haven, Conn.: Int. Assn. for Research in Income and Wealth. Quarterly. JEconLit.

Review of radical political economics. v.1– , 1969– . New York: Union for Radical Political Economics. Quarterly. WkRelAbst.

SAM advanced management journal. v.1– , 1936– . Cincinnati: Society for Advancement of Management. Quarterly. PersMgtAbst.

Sloan management review. v.1– , 1959– . Cambridge, Mass.: Alfred P. Sloan School of Management, MIT. 4/academic yr. BusPerInd; Cc; EngrInd; PAIS; PersMgtAbst; SSCI; WkRelAbst.

Southern economic journal. v.1– , 1933– . Chapel Hill: Univ. of North Carolina for Southern Economic Assn. Quarterly. Cc; PAIS; SSCI; WkRelAbst.

Soviet studies: a quarterly review of the social and economic institutions of the U.S.S.R. v.1– , 1949– . Harlow, Eng.: Univ. of Glasgow by Longman. Quarterly. Cc; HumInd; PAIS.

Third World quarterly. v.1– , 1979– . London: Third World Foundation for Social and Economic Studies. Quarterly. Cc.

Transportation journal. v.1– , 1961– . Louisville, Ky.: American Society of Traffic and Transportation. Quarterly.
Cc; SSCI.

Monograph Series

D810

Aldine treatises in modern economics. 1968– . Hawthorne, N.Y.: Aldine.

American economic history series. 1970– . New York: Wiley.

Annual accounting review. v.1– . New York: Harwood Academic Pubs., 1979– .

Brookings Institution. Studies in social economics. 1977– . Washington, D.C: The Institution.

——. Studies in the regulation of economic activity. 1981– . Washington, D.C.: The Institution.

——. Studies of government finance. no.1– , 1962– . Washington, D.C.: The Institution.

——. Transport research program. 1964– . Washington, D.C.: The Institution.

Cambridge Univ. Dept. of Applied Economics. Monographs. no.1– , 1948– . Cambridge: The University.

Canadian studies in economics. no.1– , 1954– . Toronto: Univ. of Toronto Pr.

Columbia essays on great economists. no.1– , 1971– . New York: Columbia Univ. Pr.

Columbia studies in economics. no.1– , 1968– . New York: Columbia Univ. Pr.

Committee for Economic Development. Research study. 1944– . New York: The Committee.

——. Supplementary paper. no.1– , 1959– . New York: The Committee.

Conference Board. Information bulletin. no.1– , 1975– . New York: The Board.

——. Report. no.501– , Oct. 1970– . New York. (Absorbed several publications issued by the board under its earlier name: National industrial conference board, q.v.)

Conference on Research in Income and Wealth. Studies in income and wealth. v.1– , 1937– . New York: National Bureau of Economic Research.

Contributions to economic analysis. v.1– , 1952– . Amsterdam: North-Holland.

Cowles Commission for Research in Economics/ Cowles Foundation for Research in Economics at Yale. Monographs. v.1– , 1934– . New York: Wiley; New Haven, Conn.: Yale Univ. Pr.

Economic handbook series. 1948– . New York: McGraw-Hill.

Harvard economic studies. v.1– , 1906– . Cambridge, Mass.: Harvard Univ. Pr.

Harvard studies in business history. v.1– , 1931– . Cambridge, Mass.: Harvard Univ. Pr.

Indiana University. International Development Research Center. Studies in development. no.1– , 1971– . Bloomington: Indiana Univ. Pr.

International economic papers. no.1– , 1951– . London and New York: Macmillan. (Translations prepared for the International Economic Assn.)

London School of Economics and Political Science. Studies in economics and commerce. v.1– , 1933– . London.

National Bureau of Economic Research. General series. v.1– , 1921– . New York.

——. Occasional papers. v.1– , 1940– . New York.

——. Special conference series. v.1– , 1949– . New York.

——. Studies in business cycles. v.1– , 1927– . New York.

——. Studies in international economic relations. no.1– , 1963– . New York.

National Industrial Conference Board. Studies in business economics. no.1– , 1945– . New York. (This organization's name is now Conference Board.) (Continued in: Conference Board. Reports.)

——. Studies in personnel policy. no.1– , 1937– . New York. (Continued in: Conference Board. Reports.)

National Institute of Economic and Social Research. Economic and social studies. no.1– , 1942– . Cambridge and New York: Cambridge Univ. Pr.

——. Occasional papers. no.1– ,1942– . Cambridge and New York: Cambridge Univ. Pr.

National Planning Assn. Case study. no.1– , 1953– . Washington, D.C.

——. [NPA] Report. no.1– , 1939– . Washington, D.C. (title varies)

——. Special report. no.1– , 1943– . Washington, D.C.

Political and Economic Planning. Broadsheet. v.1– , 1933– . London.

Studies in comparative economics. no.1– , 1962– . New Haven, Conn.: Yale Univ. Pr.

Twentieth Century Fund. Studies. various dates. New York: The Fund.

Yale studies in economic history. 1974– . New Haven, Conn.: Yale Univ. Pr.

Yale studies in economics. v.1– , 1950– . New Haven, Conn.: Yale Univ. Pr.

In addition, various university bureaus of business and economic research publish other important studies. See the annotation for Assn. for University Business and Economic Research, *Bibliography of publications of university bureaus of business and economic research* (D546). See also John Fletcher, ed., *Information sources in economics* (D511), especially chapters 6 (Unpublished material), 10 (International organizations' publications), and 12 (General economics).

Organizations

D811

American Agricultural Economics Assn. Lexington, Ky. Founded 1910.

American Assembly of Collegiate Schools of Business. St. Louis. Founded 1916.

American Economic Assn. Nashville. Founded 1885.

American Enterprise Institute for Public Policy Research. Washington, D.C. Founded 1943.

American Management Assn. New York. Founded 1923.

Assn. for University Business and Economic Research. Athens, Ga. Founded 1947.

British Institute of Management. London. Founded 1947.

Brookings Institution. Washington, D.C. Founded 1927.

Business and Professional Women's Foundation. Washington, D.C. Founded 1956.

Canadian Economic Council. Ottawa. Founded 1964.

Committee for Economic Development. New York. Founded 1942.

Conference Board. New York. Founded 1916 (as National Industrial Conference Board).

Council on Economic Priorities. Washington, D.C. Founded 1969.

Cowles Foundation for Research in Economics at Yale. New Haven, Conn. Founded 1955. (Continues work of Cowles Commission for Research in Economics, founded 1932.)

Econometric Society. New Haven, Conn. Founded 1930.

Economic History Assn. New York. Founded 1940.

Economic Research Council. London. Founded 1943.

European Institute of Business Administration (Institut Européen d'Administration des Affaires [*INSEAD*]). Paris. Founded 1958.

Gesellschaft für Wirtschafts- und Sozialwissenschaften (Verein für Sozialpolitik). Berlin. Founded 1872; refounded 1948.

Institute of Developing Economies (Ajia Keizai Kenkyusho). Tokyo. Founded 1958.

Institute of Management Sciences. Providence, R.I. Founded 1953.

Intl. Economic Assn. Paris. Founded 1949.

Joint Council on Economic Education. New York. Founded 1948.

National Assn. of Business Economists. Washington, D.C. Founded 1959.

National Bureau of Economic Research. New York. Founded 1920.

National Business Education Assn. Washington, D.C. Founded 1892.

National Institute of Economic and Social Research. London. Founded 1938.

National Planning Assn. Washington, D.C. Founded 1934.

Organization for Economic Cooperation and Development. Paris. Founded 1961.

Royal Economic Society. London. Founded 1890.

Society for Advancement of Management. Cincinnati. Founded 1912.

SRI International. Palo Alto, Calif. Founded 1946 (as Stanford Research Institute).

Twentieth Century Fund. New York. Founded 1919.

United Nations Economic and Social Commission for Africa. Addis Ababa. Founded 1958.

United Nations Economic and Social Council. New York. Founded 1945.

United Nations Economic Commission for Asia and the Pacific. Bangkok. Founded 1947.

United Nations Economic Commission for Europe. Geneva. Founded 1947.

United Nations Economic Commission for Latin America. Santiago, Chile. Founded 1948.

United Nations Economic Commission for Western Asia. Baghdad, Iraq. Founded 1973.

SOURCES OF CURRENT INFORMATION

D812 AACSB Newsline. 1– . 1971– . St. Louis: American Assembly of Collegiate Schools of Business. 6/yr.

D813 AEI economist. 1977– . Washington, D.C.: American Enterprise for Public Policy Research. Monthly.

D815 American journal of small business. v.1– , 1976– . Baltimore: Univ. of Baltimore. Quarterly.

D816 Bankers magazine. v.1– , 1846– . Boston: Warren, Gorham & Lamont. Quarterly.

D817 Barron's: national business and financial weekly. v.1– , 1921– . Chicopee, Mass.: Dow Jones. Weekly.

D818 Business America. v.1– , 1978– . Washington, D.C.: U.S. Dept. of Commerce. Biweekly.

D819 Business education forum. v.1– , 1947– . Reston, Va.: Natl. Business Education Assn. Monthly.

D820 Business marketing. v.68– , Apr. 1983– . Chicago: Business Marketing. Monthly. (Formerly: Industrial marketing)

D821 Business week. v.1– , 1929– . Highstown, N.J.: Business Week. Weekly.

D822 CEP newsletter. 1974– . New York: Council on Economic Priorities. Bimonthly.

D823 CEPAL review. 1976– . Santiago: United Nations Economic Commission for Latin America. Semiannual. Supersedes: Economic bulletin for Latin America.

D824 Canadian business: the magazine for management. v.1– , 1930– . Ottawa: Canadian Business. Monthly.

D825 Changing times. v.1– , 1947– . Washington, D.C.: Kiplinger Washington Editors. Monthly.

D826 Commercial and financial chronicle. v.1– , 1865– . Arlington, Mass.: National News Service. Semiweekly.

D827 Computer decisions. v.1– , 1969– . Rochelle Park, N.J.: Hayden. Monthly.

D828 Computerworld. v.1– , 1967– . Framingham, Mass.: C W Communications, Inc. Weekly.

D829 Consumer reports. v.1– , 1936– . Mount Vernon, N.Y.: Consumers Union of the United States. Monthly.

D830 Consumers' research magazine. v.56– , 1973– . Washington, D.C.: Consumers' Research. Monthly.

D831 DM: Data management. v.13– , 1975– . Park Ridge, Ill.: Data Processing Management Assn. Monthly.

D832 Data communications. v.1– , 1976– . New York: McGraw-Hill. Monthly.

D833 Development digest. (Prepared by National Planning Assn.) v.1– , 1962– . Washington, D.C.: Dept. of State, Agency for International Development. Quarterly.

D834 Dun's business month. v.1– , 1893– . New York: Dun & Bradstreet. Monthly. (Title varies)

D835 Economic bulletin for Africa. v.1– , 1961– . New York: UN Economic Commission for Africa. Semiannual.

D836 Economic bulletin for Asia and the Pacific. v.1– , 1950– . New York: UN Economic Commission for Asia and the Far East. Quarterly.

D837 Economic bulletin for Europe. v.1–32, 1949/50–80. New York: UN Economic Commission for Europe. 2/yr. (v.33– , 1981– , publ. by Pergamon for the United Nations.)

D838 Economic bulletin for Latin America. v.1– , 1956–74. New York: UN Economic Commission for Latin America. Semiannual. Superseded by: CEPAL review.

D839 Economic forum: first student edited journal in economics. v.10– , 1979– . Salt Lake City: Univ. of Utah Dept. of Economics. Quarterly.

D840 Economic outlook USA. v.1– , 1974– . Ann Arbor: Univ. of Michigan Survey Research Center. Quarterly.

D841 Economist. v.1– , 1843– . London. Weekly.

D842 Energy economics. v.1– , 1979– . Sussex: Butterworth Scientific. Quarterly.

D843 Enterprise. v.1– , 1977– . Washington, D.C.: National Assn. of Manufacturers. Monthly.

D844 Executive female. v.2– , 1979– . Huntington Station, N.Y.: National Assn. for Female Executives. Bimonthly.

D845 Federal Reserve bulletin. v.1– , 1915– . Washington, D.C.: Board of Governors of the Federal Reserve System. Monthly.

D846 Financial analysts journals. v.1– , 1945– . New York: Financial Analysts Federation. Bimonthly.

D847 Financial post: Canada's national weekly of business, investment, and public affairs. v.1– , 1907– . Toronto: Maclean-Hunter. Weekly.

D848 Financial world. v.1– , 1902– . New York: Macro Communications. Semimonthly.

D849 Forbes. v.1– , 1917– . New York: Forbes. Biweekly.

D850 Foreign economic trends and their implications for the United States. ET-68-1– , 1968– . Washington, D.C.: U.S. International Trade Administration. Irregularly.

D851 Fortune. v.1– , 1930– . Chicago: Time, Inc. Monthly.

D851 Inc. v.1– , 1979– . Boston: Inc. Quarterly
A

D852 Infosystems. v.1– , 1958– . Wheaton, Ill.: Hitchcock. Monthly.

D853 International labour review. v.1– , 1921– . Geneva: International Labour Organisation. Monthly.

D854 Journal of commerce and commercial. v.1– , 1827– . New York: Twin Coast Newspapers. Daily.

D855 Journal of small business management. v.1– , 1963– . (International Council for Small Business) Wichita, Kans.: Wichita State Univ., College of Business Administration. Quarterly.

D856 Journal of systems management. v.1– , 1950– . Cleveland: Assn. for Systems Management. Monthly.

D857 Labor law journal. v.1– , 1949– . Chicago: Commerce Clearing House. Monthly.

D858 Management accounting. v.1– , 1919– . New York: Natl. Assn. of Accountants. Monthly.

D859 Managerial planning. v.1– , 1952– . Oxford, Ohio: Planning Executives Institute. Bimonthly.

D860 Monthly labor review. v.1– , 1915– . Washington, D.C.: U.S. Bureau of Labor Statistics. Monthly.

D861 National business woman. v.1– , 1919– . Washington, D.C.: National Federation of Business and Professional Women's Clubs. 11/yr.

D862 Nation's business. v.1– , 1912– . Washington, D.C.: Chamber of Commerce of the United States. Monthly.

D863 OECD observer. v.1– , 1962– . Paris and Washington: Organisation for Economic Cooperation and Development. Bimonthly.

D864 Office administration and automation. v.44– , 1983– . New York: Geyer-McAllister. Monthly. (Formerly: Administrative management)

D865 Overseas business reports. OBR 62– . Washington, D.C.: U.S. Dept. of Commerce. Intl. Trade Administration. Irregularly.

D866 Population bulletin, no.1– , 1970– . Baghdad: UN Economic Commission for Western Asia, etc. Semiannual.

D867 Quarterly economic review. 1952– . London: Economist Intelligence Unit. Quarterly.

D868 Review of social economy. v.1– , 1944– . Chicago: DePaul Univ. (Association for Social Economics) 3/yr.

D869 Supervisory management. v.1– , 1955– . New York: American Management Assn. Monthly.

D870 Survey of current business. v.1– , 1921– . Washington, D.C.: U.S. Bureau of Economic Analysis. Monthly.

D871 Wall Street journal. Jan. 1, 1899– . New York: Dow Jones. Daily.

D872 Wall Street transcript: a professional publication for the business and financial community. v.1– , 1963– . New York: Wall Street Transcript Corp. Weekly.

D873 Women in business. v.1– , 1919– . (American Business Women's Assn.) Kansas City, Mo.: ABWA Co., Inc. 6/yr.

ONLINE DATABASES

D874

The growth of machine-readable databases in business and economics subjects—as in the other social science areas—continues apace. These databases may include information that is bibliographic, numeric (or statistical), textual, or graphic. The following are illustrative of the variety available:

ABI/INFORM (Louisville: Data Courier, 1971–) covers all phases of management (accounting, finance, marketing, production, etc.). Scans some 400 journals.

American Statistics Index (Washington, D.C.: Congressional Information Service, 1973–) offers citations to and abstracts from socioeconomic data produced by federal agencies. The publisher's Index to International Statistics (1983–) and Statistical Reference Index (1980–) are also online.

Chase Econometrics Associates (Bala Cynwyd, Pa.) offers economic analysis, forecasting, and consulting services for a variety of sectors of the U.S. economy and for selected foreign economies (financial, industrial production, iron and steel, agriculture, U.S. population, etc.).

Computer Contents (Belmont, Calif.: Information Access Co., 1983–) provides extensive coverage in the computer, telecommunications and electronics literature: journals, books, research reports, etc.

Data Resources, Inc. (Lexington, Mass.), relates developments on the national economic scene to detailed product, company, industry, and regional results. Economic, industrial, and financial statistics on the United States and more than 100 other countries.

Disclosure Incorporated (Bethesda, Md.) provides full-text copy of corporate reports, which the Securities Exchange Commission releases to the public: 10-K (annual business and financial report filed by U.S. public companies), 8-K (report of unscheduled material events of corporate changes of importance to shareholders or the SEC), proxy and registration statements, etc.

Dow Jones NEWS/RETRIEVAL (New York) provides news related to corporations listed on the New York and American stock exchanges and the National Association of Securities Dealers Automated Quotations Over-the-Counter Market.

Economic Information Systems (New York), through its EIS INDUSTRIAL PLANTS database, provides current information on industrial and mining firms and establishments of 20 or more people in the United States with annual sales of about $500,000 or more. Its EIS NONMANU-FACTURING ESTABLISHMENTS database (agriculture, construction, utilities, transportation, communications, trade, finance, services, etc.) provides comparable information for employers of 20 or more with annual sales of $250,000 or more. Each record contains: firm name, location, telephone number, principal product (4-digit SIC code), annual sales, estimated share of the market, employment level, and parent company information.

Management Contents (Belmont, Calif.: Information Access Co., 1974–) accesses books, research reports, periodicals and other serials.

Predicasts Terminal System (PTS) (Cleveland: Predicasts, Inc.) includes more than 3 million summaries of information taken from more than 2,500 newspapers, trade journals, government documents, bank letters, prospectuses, and reports from around the world.

Wiley J. Williams

5 Sociology

Survey of the Field

WHAT IS SOCIOLOGY?

In grandiose terms, sociology can be viewed as the study of human society. This, in fact, was what the early sociologists saw as their task—after debating whether a science of society was possible at all. Today we might think in terms of a more circumscribed definition: sociology is the attempt to understand patterns of human relationships. These patterns vary in scope from conversations to revolutions. What is common to all of them is the search for recurring modes of behavior to be explained by social factors.

For example, we are accustomed to thinking of the family in terms of an intimate, personal group whose behavior is likely to be idiosyncratic because it is based on emotional ties. But the sociologist will look at the family as an "institution," or set of interlocking roles. Mother-father, mother-son, sister-brother interactions show certain uniformities throughout a society because there are social expectations about the rights and responsibilities of these positions. The selection of a mate, the rearing of children, the choice of their schools—all of these seemingly personal matters are reinterpreted as socially determined patterns of behavior.

If such an analysis neglects some of the seeming individuality or variability of family lives, this is exactly sociology's intention. In his lively introduction to the field, Peter Berger calls this the "debunking" function of sociology. One might also refer to sociology's attempts to demystify the social world.

Sociology seizes upon familiar situations and asks, What is happening here? How did this come about? What are the consequences? For example, when a patient consults a doctor, what tensions will arise out of the fact that one is the expert while the other is but a layperson? What does the doctor do in the case of conflict between his or her status as physician and that of friend? How does the patient learn what kinds of questions he or she is entitled to ask? These are all questions the sociologist might raise. Indeed, the sociologist takes pride in the special way in which he or she poses problems for inquiry.

Many introductory texts discuss this "sociological perspective," in which human behavior is viewed as the product of external social forces. Because they see behavior in these terms, sociologists will ask a different set of questions from the psychologist or educator. For example, in examining barriers to higher education, they might wonder how the high school "manages" the process by its tracking procedures, its guidance policies, or even its athletic programs, so that certain groups are systematically routed to college while others are not. Questions about individual differences in motives, goals, or personality characteristics would come from the psychologist.

Sociologists employ a battery of special concepts that sensitize them to particular problems and guide their search for explanations. Thus, they will talk about role conflict or personal influence or unanticipated consequences. They also rely upon a kind of sociological instinct that is as difficult to nail down as it is to teach.

Sociology is still a developing field, struggling to be recognized as a science and to find a proper balance between academic and practical interests. *Footnotes,* the official newsletter of the American Sociological Association, airs many of these concerns. The journal *Society* represents the activist spirit within sociology. In the Kubat volume (E3), past presidents of the American Sociological Association talk about the needs of sociology as well as those of society. At present, there are more than 20 divisions in this professional organization, and sociology could be seen as the sum of these divisions—community, criminology, education, family, etc. But these categories are administrative devices for linking sociologies rather than intellectual compartments for separating areas. The processes of social control, social conflict, and social change overflow the divisional boundaries and run through all of sociology. Of course, sociology shares these concerns with other social sciences, but it has its own special perspective.

E1   Berger, Peter L. Invitation to sociology. Garden City, N.Y.: Doubleday, 1963. 191p.

E2   Gouldner, Alvin. The coming crisis of Western sociology. New York: Basic Books, 1970. 528p.

E3   Kubat, Daniel, ed. Paths of sociological imagination. New York: Gordon & Breach, 1971. 584p.

E4   Persell, Caroline Hodges. Understanding society: an introduction to sociology. New York: Harper, 1983. 704p.

ORIGINS OF SOCIOLOGY

It is generally agreed that sociology emerged from several disciplines: philosophy, law, economics, anthropology, and psychology. It is not clear, however, whether sociology simply splintered off from these fields or took over the empty spaces between them. Perhaps, in the last analysis, the question is not so important.

Sociology began as a very general inquiry into the nature of society and only later sought to differentiate itself from neighboring fields. The father of sociology is generally considered to be the nineteenth-century French philosopher, Auguste Comte. Together with the philosopher Claude-Henri Saint-Simon, Comte endeavored to develop a science of society that would account for both social order and social change.

Herbert Spencer wrote the first full-blown analysis of the sociological task, listing not only the institutions to be studied but also the interrelationships between the parts of society and the whole. His belief in the inevitability of social evolution has been discarded by modern social scientists, but his identification of the concepts of structure and function still belong in contemporary sociology.

Émile Durkheim defined sociology as the study of "social facts," characteristics of social life that cannot be reduced to individual properties. His general orientation, as well as his spectacular empirical contributions, assure him a firm place in sociology.

Max Weber, another giant in the history of sociology, is probably best known for his study linking the rise of capitalism to the spirit of Protestantism. His probing examinations of bureaucracy are equally important for the development of sociological theory.

Karl Marx's treatment of class stratification and of the processes of conflict and change have greatly influenced the content of sociology. Other towering figures from the nineteenth century are Vilfredo Pareto, Ferdinand Toennies, and Georg Simmel.

These early sociologists confronted the vast changes in their society and asked how social order could still be maintained in the face of the swift transformation to an industrial society. They maintained that society had an independent existence of its own, which could be studied as such. This was the proper role of sociology.

European sociology at the turn of the century thus offered a lofty, macroscopic interpretation of society's development. With the growth of the "Chicago School" in the 1920s, sociology took a more microscopic perspective. It fastened upon such topics as immigration, integration, and the tensions of urban life. Sometimes, it was hard to distinguish sociologists from the crusaders within social work or religion. Gradually, sociology's emphasis on the techniques and promise of empirical research gave it an identity of its own. It became an academic discipline, established first in the Midwest, where such important men as Robert Park, W. I. Thomas, Ellsworth Faris, George H. Mead, William F. Ogburn, and Lewis Wirth helped sociology to combine two themes: the empirical investigation of urban life and the theoretical speculation about the social development of the self. Then, as Shils describes, sociology spread from its first home eastward to Harvard and thence to Columbia. Shils calls this the "institutionalization of sociology" (E18). Lazarsfeld (E30) and his colleagues Lécuyer and Oberschall (E17) have taken a special interest in one form of institution—the social research bureau. They have linked this organization to the development of a whole new style of empirical research, where quantitative techniques and methodology became so important.

In the list of histories below, Coser's is especially recommended (E15). Many biographies of individuals may be found in v.18 of the *International encyclopedia of the social sciences: biographical supplement* (New York: Free Pr., 1979) **(E5)**.

Classics

E6   Auguste Comte and positivism: the essential writings. Ed. by Gertrud Lenzer. Chicago: Univ. of Chicago Pr., 1983.

E7   Durkheim, Émile. Suicide. Tr. by John Spaulding and George Simpson. New York: Free Pr., 1966. 405p.

E8   The Marx-Engels reader. Ed. by Robert C. Tucker. New York: Norton, 1972.

E9   Mead, George Herbert. Mind, self and society: from the standpoint of a social behaviorist. Ed. by Charles W. Morris. Chicago: Univ. of Chicago Pr., 1934. 401p.

E10   Park, Robert, and Ernest W. Burgess. Introduction to the science of sociology. Chicago: Univ. of Chicago Pr., 1921. 1,040p.

E11   Spencer, Herbert. The principles of sociology. 3d ed. New York: Appleton, 1910.

E12   Thomas, William I., and Florian Znaniecki. The Polish peasant in Europe and America. New York: Dover, 1958. 2v.

E13   Weber, Max. The Protestant ethic and the spirit of capitalism. Tr. by Talcott Parsons. London: Allen & Unwin, 1930. 292p.

Histories

E14   Aron, Raymond. Main currents in sociological thought. New York: Anchor, 1970. 2v.

E15   Coser, Lewis A. Masters of sociological thought. 2d ed. New York: HBJ, 1977. 611p.

E16   Faris, Robert E. L. Chicago sociology 1920–1932. Chicago: Univ. of Chicago Pr., 1967. 173p.

E17   Lécuyer, Bernard, and Anthony R. Oberschall. "The early history of social research." *In* International encyclopedia of the social sciences, ed. by David L. Sills, p.36–53. New York: Macmillan, 1968.

E18   Shils, Edward. "Tradition, ecology, and institution in the history of sociology." *Daedalus* 99:760–825 (Fall 1970).

SOCIAL THEORY

It must be said at the outset that there is no all-embracing deductive theoretical system in sociology. Instead, there is a series of pictures or orientations toward the social world. Turner sets up five of these major theoretical outlooks in his overview: functionalism, conflict theory, exchange theory, interactionism, and phenomenology (E33). Turner's book is especially helpful in contrasting the various approaches and in giving a state-of-the-art assessment of each one.

On the whole, contemporary sociology is still influenced by functionalism. The basic tenets of functionalism were adopted from anthropology by Harvard sociologist Talcott Parsons and biologist L. J. Henderson. A galaxy of sociologists emerged from the Harvard group, including Robert K. Merton, Wilbert Moore, and Kingsley Davis. It was Merton who proposed that sociology settle for "middle range theories," less abstract than a grand scheme but closer to empirical testing. Merton's own polished prose is the clearest exposition of his ideas.

Essentially, the functionalist asks how a particular belief or custom or institution has emerged and is sustained by other parts of the social system. The idea that a consequence can be a cause sounds almost paradoxical, but functionalists use the notions of reinforcement or feedback. Merton, for example, shows how the political machine assures a future for itself by serving various legal and illegal businesses in a way that other agencies would find impossible. Merton's distinctions between latent and manifest functions or between anticipated and unanticipated consequences have proved to be especially provocative. Thus, the political machine may grind in a corrupt manner, but it also serves to dole out food and favors to newly arriving immigrants who would be unable to manage without this help.

Conflict theorists like Dahrendorf have criticized functionalism for its undue emphasis on order and balance at the expense of conflict, discord, or oppression. According to conflict theory, social stability is the product of manipulation and subordination. The dominant class seeks to keep the lower class helpless and weak. It is the conflict between these opposing parties that will create radical social changes.

During the 1950s and 1960s, structural-functionalism, including offshoots such as exchange theory, reigned supreme in American sociology. But during the 1970s, a competing orientation, symbolic interactionism, was ascendant. This is an approach followed by a somewhat diverse group of sociologists who are interested in the ways individuals are guided to shape their worlds through social symbols. The question is not so much, What is real? as How do people create a sense of common reality? Erving Goffman is a well-known representative of this approach, as are the labeling theorists mentioned under the discussion of "social problems." (See below, E129–35.) Sociolinguists like Labov study language behavior and its connection to such social variables as class or interpersonal context. Labov has been particularly outspoken in his criticism of the notion of "cultural deprivation," maintaining that nonstandard English, though different, is not inferior to middle-class English. Harold Garfinkel, originator of ethnomethodology, wants to ascertain how sociologists can go about studying the social construction of reality. What are the best methods or techniques for identifying the taken-for-granted rules of everyday existence when even the sociologist lives according to these rules?

The symbolic interaction approach has its intellectual roots in the Chicago School of Herbert George Blumer, William I. Thomas, and George H. Mead, but it is no longer purely a midwestern phenomenon.

It is not really possible to claim that sociological theories have been tested through empirical research, in the style of the natural sciences. Theories have prompted questions for research as well as providing interpretations of empirical data. However, the relationship between theory and research is still somewhat untidy.

E19　Alexander, Jeffrey C. Theoretical logic in sociology; positivism, presuppositions, and current controversies. v.1. Berkeley: Univ. of Calif. Pr., 1982. 248p.

E20　Blau, Peter. Inequality and heterogeneity: a primitive theory of social structure. New York: Free Pr., 1977.

E21　Collins, Randall. Conflict sociology. New York: Academic, 1975. 592p.

E22　Dahrendorf, Ralf. Essays in the theory of society. Stanford, Calif.: Stanford Univ. Pr., 1967.

E23　Garfinkel, Harold. Studies in ethnomethodology. Englewood Cliffs, N.J.: Prentice-Hall, 1967. 288p.

E24　Goffman, Erving. Forms of talk. Philadelphia: Univ. of Pennsylvania Pr., 1981.

E25　Labov, William. Sociolinguistic patterns. Philadelphia: Univ. of Pennsylvania Pr., 1973.

E26　Merton, Robert K. Social theory and social structure. Enl. ed. New York: Free Pr., 1968. 702p.

E27　Parsons, Talcott. The system of modern societies. Englewood, N.J.: Prentice-Hall, 1971.

Commentaries

E28　Gouldner, Alvin. The two Marxisms: contradictions and anomalies in the development of theory. New York: Oxford Univ. Pr., 1982.

E29　Kinloch, Graham C. Sociological theory: its development and major paradigms. New York: McGraw Hill, 1976.

E30　Lazarsfeld, Paul F. "Sociology." *In* Main trends of research in the social and human sciences, p.61–165. Paris: UNESCO, 1970. Pt.1, social sciences.

E31　Mehan, Hugh, and Houston Wood. The reality of ethnomethodology. New York: Wiley, 1975.

E32　Mullins, Nicholas C. Theories and theory groups in contemporary American sociology. New York: Harper, 1973.

E33　Turner, Jonathan H. The structure of sociological theory. Rev. ed. Homewood, Ill.: Dorsey Pr., 1978. 446p.

METHODOLOGY AND EMPIRICAL RESEARCH

Empirical research is often divided into two spheres—the quantitative and the qualitative. It was Paul F. Lazarsfeld of Columbia University who sought to unite the two by clarifying the unique functions of each and their potential support for one another. This scrutiny of empirical studies in order to expose their tacit assumptions, their explanatory schemes, and their inner logic is called methodology. For the methodologist, structure and substance are interwoven.

In one sense, methodology grew out of the long-established tradition of the philosophy of science, but it also emerged from the newer development of survey research. During the late 1930s, sociologists began to use the sample survey to obtain information from a small group about the attitudes, behavior, and background characteristics of the larger population. So long as survey research limited itself to descriptive studies—social bookkeeping, as it were—no real methodological issues were raised. But when sample surveys were used as substitutes for controlled experiments in the analysis of causal relationships, they required closer examination. A whole new language of variates was created to describe the permutations of causal sequencing. Lazarsfeld and others present this language in their reader on methodology (E38). They explain how the sociologist captures social phenomena by developing concepts, forming indexes, and subjecting them to multivariate analysis. This is not a cookbook for research but rather an explication of what goes on underneath the statistics.

The Rosenberg book (E41) and that of Hirschi

and Selvin (E36) elaborate upon the Lazarsfeld approach. In a different vein, James S. Coleman, Raymond Boudon, Hubert Blalock, Jr., and Leo Goodman have introduced mathematics into sociological analysis. Through their efforts, sociology has been able to attack the study of processes. For a long time, quantitative research had been criticized for its atomistic approach to the social world. Where was the flow of reality when reduced to variates? Today, sociology is more equipped to counter these criticisms.

Qualitative research has prided itself on the study of processes—in the classroom, the family, the business firm, and the community. But qualitative research suffers from a lack of systematization. Field researchers were inclined to go their own ways, each equipped with his or her own interviewing guides and notebooks. Today, there are attempts at codification and at replication of earlier studies. One promising line of work, growing out of policy research, is the attempt to distinguish between social program designs and social program realities. This is called the study of the implementation process (see Williams and Elmore, E43). Patterns at one point in time must be compared with those at another in order to determine how the constellation has changed. For example, how did an ambitious federal program for career education go awry at the local school level? While some of these studies of social programs seek to combine quantitative and qualitative methods, other sociologists have developed new quantitative methods for analyzing event histories, such as marriage, childbirth, or work, within people's lives (E39).

As large-scale research grows increasingly expensive, sociologists have invented certain methodological economies. One way is to turn to secondary analysis, the reuse of existing data for new purposes (E37). Computerized data archives have facilitated this procedure. Another is to create larger studies out of a series of smaller ones, a kind of quasi-longitudinal research. The major problem lies in the conceptual integration of the separate pieces.

For those who would like a basic introduction to methodology, Cole (E34) is clear and concise.

E34   Cole, Stephen. The sociological method. 2d ed. Chicago: Rand McNally, 1976. 255p.

E35   Coleman, James S. Mathematics of collective action. Chicago: Beresford, 1973.

E36   Hirschi, Travis, and Hanan Selvin. Principles of survey analysis. New York: Free Pr., 1973.

E37   Hyman, Herbert. Secondary analysis of sample surveys: principles, procedures, and potentialities. New York: Wiley, 1972. 347p.

E38   Lazarsfeld, Paul F., and others, eds. Continuities in the language of social research. New York: Free Pr., 1972. 491p.

E39   Leinhardt, Samuel, ed. Sociological methodology 1982. San Francisco: Jossey-Bass, 1982.

E40   Merton, Robert K., and others, eds. Qualitative and quantitative social research: papers in honor of Paul F. Lazarsfeld. New York: Free Pr., 1979. 480p.

E41   Rosenberg, Morris. The logic of survey analysis. New York: Basic Books, 1968. 263p.

E42   Sudman, Seymour. Asking questions. San Francisco: Jossey-Bass, 1982. 397p.

E43   Williams, Walter, and Richard F. Elmore, eds. Social program implementation. New York: Academic, 1976. 299p.

SOCIOLOGY OF SCIENCE

What was once called a separate "sociology of sociology" has now been incorporated within the sociology of science, for the study of the interrelationships of scientific production and the social context has expanded to include social science knowledge. It was Robert Merton who began this line of work, focusing first on the institutional reward system that kept the scientific endeavor in motion. Although science itself was considered to be rational and empirical, scientists were working in a climate of conflicting values. For example, scientists were supposed to be humble about their own individual contributions, but prizes went to the individual scientists whose discoveries came first.

Science may be universal, but arrangements for research and development vary from one country to another, as the Merton and Gaston collection shows (E51).

Sociologists of science have produced an ingenious series of empirical studies on age and sex stratification in science, on the relationship between apprentices and masters, on the dynamics of winning the Nobel Prize, on the emergence of new specialties, on communications among scientists, and on the organization of scientific work. The most recent turn of topics is the study of the cognitive structure of the natural and social sciences. Cole, for example, uses authors' citations of one another to chart the career of Merton's theory of anomie (E47).

There is a certain reflexive quality to this work that can be confusing. All the time that the sociologist is analyzing, he or she too can be studied as a sociologist of science. Nevertheless, the entries listed below should convey exactly what the sociology of science is.

E44   Barnes, Barry, ed. Sociology of science: selected readings. Harmondsworth: Penguin, 1972.

E45   Ben-David, Joseph. The scientist's role in society: a comparative study with a new introduction. Chicago: Univ. of Chicago Pr., 1984. 236p.

E46   Cole, Jonathan R. Fair science: women in the scientific community. New York: Free Pr., 1979.

E47   Cole, Stephen. "The growth of scientific knowledge." *In* The idea of social structure, ed. by Lewis Coser. New York: HBJ, 1975.

E48   Crane, Diana. Invisible colleges. Chicago: Univ. of Chicago Pr., 1975. 214p.

E49   Kuhn, Thomas S. The structure of scientific revolutions. Rev. ed. Chicago: Univ. of Chicago Pr., 1972.

E50   Merton, Robert K. The sociology of science: theoretical and empirical investigations. Ed. by Norman Storer. Chicago: Univ. of Chicago Pr., 1973.

E51   ———, and Jerry Gaston, eds. The sociology of science in Europe. Carbondale: Southern Illinois Univ. Pr., 1977. 383p.

E52   Popper, Karl. The logic of scientific discovery. New York: Basic Books, 1959.

E53   Price, Derek J. de S. Little science, big science. New York: Columbia Univ. Pr., 1963.

E54   Zuckerman, Harriet. Scientific elite: Nobel laureates in the United States. New York: Free Pr., 1977. 335p.

MACROSOCIOLOGY

In recent years, sociology has returned to its origins: the search for broad-scale components of the social order. This renewed concern for the large, complex social units with which sociology began is called "macrosociology." Studies of modernization and development were the first products; these have now expanded into comparative analyses of the conditions under which various societal types emerge. One of the underlying goals is to help underdeveloped nations to come to maturity. Eisenstadt and Curelaru (E58) explain the field in a clear and leisurely fashion.

Macrosociology emerged out of uneasiness over the potential limitations of survey analysis, but macrosociologists have borrowed some of the tools of survey research for their studies. They have made great strides in constructing sociological variates such as "sense of community" out of observed differences between nations. They have used public opinion surveys to compare the distribution of values across nations. Thus, for example, they found that ambition is valued in Japan but not in Australia. Macrosociologists have also traced changes in values within a single country. The methodological problems of such studies are troubling. On what basis does the macrosociologist divide his terrain into manageable units? Can he develop standardized measurement techniques rather than improvised ones? How does he verify his insights? The Coleman collection provides a good introduction to the work.

Macrosociologists have not yet systematized the kind of interpretations they make so that their insights can be readily transferred from one site to the next. Most of their analyses are sketches rather than complete explanations of the phenomena they are studying.

E55   Almond, Gabriel, and Sidney Verba. The civic culture. Boston: Little, 1963. 379p.

E56   Coleman, James S., and others, eds. Macrosociology: research and theory. Boston: Allyn & Bacon, 1970. 189p.

E57   Eckstein, Harry. Division and cohesion in democracy: a study of Norway. Princeton, N.J.: Princeton Univ. Pr., 1966. 293p.

E58   Eisenstadt, S. N., and M. Curelaru. "Macrosociology." *Current sociology* 25: entire issue (1977, no. 2).

E59   Inkeles, Alex, and David H. Smith. Becoming modern: individual change in six developing countries. Cambridge, Mass.: Harvard Univ. Pr., 1974.

E60   Lenski, Gerhard E., and Jean Lenski. Human societies: an introduction to macrosociology. 3d ed. New York: McGraw-Hill, 1977.

E61   Sayigh, Rosemary. Palestinians: from peasants to revolutionaries. London: Zed, 1979. 206p.

E62   Scott, James C. The moral economy of the peasant: rebellion and subsistence in Southwest Asia. New Haven: Yale Univ. Pr., 1976. 246p.

E63   Skocpol, Theda. States and social revolutions: a comparative analysis of France, Russia and China. Cambridge: Cambridge Univ. Pr., 1979. 407p.

FUTURISM

No sooner do sociologists get a grip on the social world than they find it is changing. Whereas an understanding of the processes of social change would probably come from macrosociologists, predictions about the consequences of structural changes would emerge from the futurists.

Futurists make no claim to foresee events. They are preoccupied with the direction, speed, and possible effects of changes in institutions, in life patterns, or in technology. The field received considerable financial support from the American government and began with a somewhat disproportionate emphasis on weapons technology. However, the substance of the work has changed as more and more organizations have entered the field. Futuristic institutes such as the Rand Corporation, the Hudson Institute, and the Institute for the Future have expanded the content to include social-economic planning, environmental prediction, and demographic shifts.

Futurists have developed some special methods of their own for identifying future social problems and for extrapolating from existing social trends. One is the "Delphi technique," which assembles the forecasts of a group of experts, allows each to hear the others' predictions, and then progressively revises the forecasts. In the end, this method usually produces a high degree of consensus. Another method is the scenario where the futurist writes a script about the potential implications of alternative policies and maneuvers. Harrison (E67) discusses these methods as well as those borrowed from survey research or clinical prediction. His assessment of the limitations of each method is particularly instructive. His definition of forecasting is quite generous. Not all futurists would agree that the prediction of consumer purchases from consumer attitudes would fall under futurism, to be sure!

Surprisingly, there has been little concern for the accuracy of forecasting. Perhaps the staffs of the think tanks and corporate planning offices would prefer not to be challenged. Or perhaps it is difficult to design appropriate evaluations. What would be important is not a kind of pass-fail judgment but an assessment of why forecasting slips. Futurism is entwined with public policy. As policy changes, so should predictions. For example, a warning of food shortages should become outdated if an agricultural development program really works.

If futurists can reduce uncertainty about the coming years, one would surely wish to document their success through empirical evaluations.

E64   Bell, Daniel. The coming of post-industrial society: a venture in social forecasting. New York: Basic Books, 1973. 507p.

E65   ———, ed. Toward the year 2000: work in progress. Boston: Beacon, 1967.

E66   Bright, James, and Milton Schoeman, eds. A guide to practical technological forecasting. Englewood Cliffs, N.J.: Prentice-Hall, 1973.

E67   Harrison, Daniel P. Social forecasting methodology: suggestions for research. New York: Russell Sage, 1976. 94p. [Social science frontiers]

E68   Henshel, Richard. "Sociology and social forecasting." *In* Annual review of sociology, v.8. Palo Alto, Calif.: Annual Reviews, 1982.

E69   Oxenfeldt, Alfred. Futurism. New York: Columbia Univ. Bureau of Applied Social Research, July 1973. Mimeo.

STRATIFICATION

No subject has been dearer to the hearts of sociologists than the study of the consequences of social class stratification. In recent years, sex stratification has become an equally "hot" topic on the research agenda. Unfortunately, repeated demonstrations of the pervasive effects of social class, ethnic origins, or sex status on education and work run directly counter to the American Dream.

An important contribution to the literature is Featherman and Hauser's replication (E76) of an earlier study by Blau and Duncan. Both look at males' social origins to see how closely sons' schooling, occupation, and income match up with those of the parents. The latest study of "social mobility"—as this is called—suggests that there is a fair amount of mobility in the middle of the hierarchy but relatively little at the extremes. These researchers focus on starting points; others examine destinations for a better understanding of the processes of status attainment. Boudon's book (E72) is one such example. The literature in this field is highly technical and requires statistical knowledge. The two book reviews listed below are helpful reinterpretations (E77–78).

The social indicators movement is an outgrowth of the concern with stratification, though it goes far beyond the traditional indexes of social class. The idea is to collect periodic data on social states and conditions in such areas as crime, housing, family size, occupational prestige, religious behavior, and even quality of life. The *Social indicators newsletter,* a publication of the Social Science Research Council Center for Coordination of Research on Social Indicators, gives a concise summary of research, publications, and theoretical developments in the field. The essays in the Land and Spilerman book (E79) explain how social indicator models can help to investigate the specific processes that determine social conditions.

One of the most recent additions to the indicators armory is scientific activity. In 1973, the National Science Board published the first in a series of biennial indicators reports on trends in science, and, two years later, a group of social scientists, physical scientists, and philosophers met to examine the report and to speculate more generally about ways of estimating the condition of science as intellectual endeavor and as social institution. The conference was deemed to be a success, and the papers are published (E75).

E70   Blau, Peter M., and Otis Dudley Duncan. The American occupational structure. New York: Wiley, 1967.

E71   Blaxall, Martha, and Barbara Reagan, eds. Women and the workplace: the implications of occupational segregation. Chicago: Univ. of Chicago Pr., 1976. 312p.

E72   Boudon, Raymond. Education, opportunity, and social inequality: changing prospects in western society. New York: Wiley, 1974. 220p.

E73   Campbell, Angus, and others. The quality of American life: perceptions, evaluations, and satisfactions. New York: Russell Sage, 1976. 583p.

E74   Cott, Nancy F. The bonds of womanhood: "woman's sphere" in New England 1780–1835. New Haven, Conn.: Yale Univ. Pr., 1978.

E75   Elkana, Yehuda, and others, eds. Toward a metric of science: the advent of science indicators. New York: Wiley, 1978. 354p.

E76   Featherman, David L., and Robert M. Hauser. Opportunity and change. New York: Academic, 1978. 572p.

E77   Hauser, Robert M. "Review essay: on Boudon's model of social mobility." *American journal of sociology* 81:911–28 (Jan. 1976).

E78   Huber, Joan. "Ransacking mobility tables." *Contemporary sociology* 9:5–8 (Jan. 1980). [Review of Featherman and Hauser]

E79   Land, Kenneth, and Seymour Spilerman, eds. Social indicator models. New York: Russell Sage, 1975. 411p.

E80   Sheldon, Eleanor, and Wilbert Moore, eds. Indicators of social change. New York: Russell Sage, 1968. 822p.

SEX ROLES AND SOCIAL CHANGE

The sociology of sex roles is more than an adjunct to stratification analysis as described in the previous section. From the start of the women's movement in the early sixties, female sociologists have been both activists and scientific observers. They began to elucidate some of the problems that women had only dimly perceived, problems created by sweeping changes in the workplace and in the family. Not only were more women entering the labor market, but there was increased access to information on birth control, abortion, and divorce; more single-parent families; and increased longevity for both men and women (though widows would still outnumber widowers).

In the vein of "sex-roles research" (Astin and others, E81), sociologists documented widespread discrimination against women in educational, occupational, religious, and political spheres. For example, while the general educational level had risen, women still received less education than men of the corresponding age. Working women tended to be located in the poorly paid and dead-end jobs. Even when jobs were comparable, females earned less money than males. Such findings appeared to be especially surprising to male sociologists. Upon closer analysis, it became clear that sociology had become a science of male behavior—male mobility, male occupations, male crises. The authors in the Huber volume (E85) report how and why women are the victims of discrimination.

An official committee of the American Sociological Association has encouraged all members of the profession to guard against sexist bias in the choice of research problems, the selection of samples and techniques, and the interpretation of results. For example, the common questionnaire item asking for "head of household" makes no provision for the fact that there might be more than one.

The sociology of sex roles overlaps both with an older specialty—sociology of the family—and with one of the newest branches of sociology, the study of aging. The family provides a convenient site for exploring all of these topics. Thus, within the family setting, one can examine dual career patterns, division of labor in child-rearing and homemaking, the single-parent household, the decision to retire, the interactions between elderly parents and their adult children, the social response to widowhood, the social costs of aging, needed resources for the aged, etc.

Some skeptics ask whether there will even be a family 20 years from now. But Bane's review of empirical evidence gives her confidence that the institution of the family will survive (E82). Some alternatives, such as the Israeli Kibbutzim, the rural commune, or the Jesus-movement groups are described by Zablocki and Kanter (E92). The authors conclude that the specific life-style is less important than the processes by which people shift from one type of family life to another at different points in their lives. This "life-course perspective" has already infused much of the work on sex roles and is now being integrated with comparative historical analyses of women's place in bygone eras.

E81   Astin, Helen S., and others. Sex roles: a research bibliography. Washington, D.C.: National Institute of Mental Health, 1975.

E82   Bane, Mary Jo. American families in the twentieth century. New York: Basic Books, 1976. 195p.

E83   Epstein, Cynthia. Women's place: options and limits of professional careers. Berkeley: Univ. of California Pr., 1970. 221p.

E84   Haraven, Tamara K., and Kathleen J. Adams, eds. Aging and life course transitions: an interdisciplinary perspective. New York: Guilford, 1982. 281p.

E85   Huber, Joan, ed. "Changing women in a changing society." *American journal of sociology* 78: whole issue (Jan. 1973).

E86   Kanter, Rosabeth M. Men and women of the corporation. New York: Basic Books, 1977.

E87   Oakley, Ann, ed. The sociology of housework. New York: Pantheon, 1975. 264p.

E88   Rapaport, Rhona, and others. Fathers, mothers, and society: towards new alliances. New York: Basic Books, 1977. 421p.

E89   Riley, Matilda White, and others, ed. Aging from birth to death, v. 2: Sociotemporal perspectives. Boulder, Colo.: Westview, 1982. 228p.

E90   Sokoloff, Natalie J. Between money and love: the dialectics of women's home and market work. New York: Praeger, 1980. 320p.

E91   Tentler, Leslie Woodcock. Wage-earning women: industrial work and family life in the U.S., 1900–1930. New York: Oxford Univ. Pr., 1979.

E92   Zablocki, Benjamin D., and Rosabeth M. Kanter. "The differentiation of life-styles." *In* Annual review of sociology, v. 2. Palo Alto, Calif.: Annual Reviews, 1976.

SOCIOLOGY OF MEDICINE

Nowhere do the divisions between the subfields of sociology seem more arbitrary than in the case of medical sociology. Once restricted to the study of illness, medical practitioners, and hospitals, medical sociology now spills over into many of the broad social issues described elsewhere in this chapter: redefining professional control of standards, the unanticipated effects of new technologies, the ethics of research, the problems of an increasingly elderly population, the proper boundaries of social responsibility. Throughout, the emphasis is on the sociocultural forces and patterns that shape the need for and practice of medical care.

Like other sociologists, some medical sociologists teach in academic posts; others conduct applied research or serve as advisors to public agencies, hospitals, community organizations, or government agencies. In fact, most medical sociologists would find it difficult to keep up with the field without continuing experience in action settings. This means that in the future—as in many areas of applied sociology—a different sort of academic training may be necessary.

Medical sociology might be seen as starting with Talcott Parson's exploration of the social definition of illness. The person who is "certified" as ill receives a temporary exemption from his usual responsibilities, but at some point he is considered well enough to resume his usual role. Just how did physicians acquire the power to accredit illness? What are their distinctive outlooks and training? What are the conflicts between the roles of physicians and patients? Such questions have led to empirical studies of medical education and the process by which young men and women learn to take on the attitudes and problems of being physicians.

Illness was found to be socially distributed and socially generated. It is easy to imagine, for example, how heart disease or malnutrition might be linked to various income levels or occupational statuses; it is not quite so evident that even automobile accidents have their sociological components.

Since severely ill persons enter institutions, a logical subject for inquiry has been the social organization of the hospital. How does the hospital reconcile the conflicting demands of administrators, professionals, semiprofessionals, and patients so that the work of the hospital gets done? Glaser and Strauss, for example, have done some fascinating research on the ways in which the hospital "manages" the process of dying so as to keep it as unobtrusive as possible (E94).

Health is big business. Medical sociology must grapple with the economics of health care, the alternative modes of delivering health service, and the determination of health policy. Just how much of a society's limited resources should go to health care? How would one define the right to good health, in terms of actual services? Who is to make decisions about the allocation of scarce technology such as dialysis machines or life-sustaining equipment? Sociologists are clarifying some of these dilemmas; it remains to be seen whether they will be able to help resolve them.

Most of the major writers in the field are represented in the two readers listed. The Mechanic book (E96) is a good introductory text.

E93   Barber, Bernard. Informed consent in medical therapy and research. New Brunswick, N.J.: Rutgers Univ. Pr., 1980.

E94   Glaser, Barney G., and Anselm L. Strauss. Time for dying. Chicago: Aldine, 1968.

E95   Jaco, E. Gartly, ed. Patients, physicians, and illness: a sourcebook in behavioral science and health. 3d ed. New York: Free Pr., 1979. 479p.

E96   Mechanic, David. Medical sociology. 2d ed. New York: Free Pr., 1978.

E97   Schwartz, Howard D., and Cary S. Kart, eds. Dominant issues in medical sociology. Reading, Mass.: Addison-Wesley, 1978.

SOCIOLOGY OF EDUCATION

Sociology of education appears to have shifted its terrain. Once entrenched in the study of higher educational institutions and their effects, the field has shifted to a consideration of the entire educational system, its functions, its costs, and its social benefits. The field seethes with controversy, partly because the public has its own claims to educational expertise. Some debates are between scientists. Thus, remnants of the old "nature-nurture" controversy are surfacing in current writings on the origin and extent of racial differences in intellectual functioning. Other arguments—over busing or integration—involve scientists and the community.

Dissatisfaction with public education has prompted a series of efforts at change and a stream of studies to evaluate the efforts. Sociologists have studied the Head Start program, desegregation, decentralization, school voucher plans, open schools, alternative schools,

and, thus far, their research suggests that change is a painfully slow and incremental process. It may be years before the "real" effects of some of these innovations will appear in research. In the meantime, we probably need to know more about the sociology of learning, the mechanisms of peer-group influence, and the kinds of education that take place in family, church, or community rather than solely in the school.

Moreover, no matter what the reforms, it is not at all clear that they will result in greater economic or social equality. Jencks finds that family background is still the overwhelming determinant of economic success (E104). To achieve real equality would require more than tinkering with the classroom. Approaching from quite a different tack, theorists Bowles and Gintis (E99) come to similar conclusions, asserting that a capitalistic society uses education to perpetuate the advantage of the wealthy and to keep the poor submerged. Other sociologists might not take quite so strongly a Marxist position, but they do recognize that the schools, especially through their tracking procedures, channel children into educational and occupational careers on the basis of social class. Selections in the Sieber and Wilder book amplify this point of view.

Despite journals such as *Sociology of education,* the *Harvard educational review,* or the new *Educational evaluation and policy analysis,* sociology and education still have an uneasy partnership (E103).

E98   Boocock, Sarane Spence. Sociology of education: an introduction. 2d ed. Boston: Houghton, 1980. 360p.

E99   Bowles, Samuel, and Herbert Gintis. Schooling in capitalist America: educational reform and the contradictions of economic life. New York: Basic Books, 1976. 340p.

E100 Coleman, James S., and others. High school achievement: public, Catholic, and private schools compared. New York: Basic Books, 1982. 289p.

E101 Dore, Ronald. The diploma disease. Berkeley: Univ. of California Pr., 1976. 214p.

E102 Gordon, C. Wayne, ed. Uses of the sociology of education. Seventy-third yearbook of the National Society for the Study of Education, part II. Chicago: NSSE, 1974. 518p.

E103 Hansen, Donald A., and Joel Gerstl, eds. On education—sociological perspectives. New York: Wiley, 1967. 300p.

E104 Jencks, Christopher, and others. Who gets ahead? New York: Basic Books, 1979. 397p.

E105 Karabel, Jerome, and A. H. Halsey, eds. Power and ideology in education. New York: Oxford Univ. Pr., 1977.

E106 Leichter, Hope, ed. Families and communities as educators. New York: Teachers College Pr., 1979.

E107 Pavalko, Ronald M., ed. Sociology of education: a book of readings. 2d ed. Itasca, Ill.: Peacock Pub., 1976. 381p.

E108 Sieber, Sam D., and David Wilder, eds. The school in society: studies in the sociology of education. New York: Free Pr., 1973.

ORGANIZATIONAL ANALYSIS

There are hundreds of sociological studies of organizations, ranging from nunneries to nations. But despite the proliferation of studies, they can be divided into three types. The first asks about the effects of organizational structure upon its members. Thus, type of supervision has been linked to individual morale, work satisfaction, or research input. In a well-regarded book, Kanter describes all too vividly the ways by which large corporations restrict opportunities for women, and she proposes some reforms in hiring, in work hours, and in organizational positioning (E86). Indeed, ever since the famous Hawthorne researchers (E119) discovered that changes in social relations could directly affect industrial productivity, sociologists have studied organizations with the aim of changing them. This organizational counseling approach is exemplified by Argyris (E109), who has published extensively in the field.

The second type of sociological investigation probes the nature of organizational structure itself. The idea is to see along which dimensions organizations vary and which attributes seem to be determinants of others. For example, Blau has studied the links between organizational size and degree of specialization or expansion of the administrative machinery (E111). Despite common misgivings, increases in size can lead to economies of scale. Research such as this is helping to feed a theory of organizational behavior.

A third type of research goes beyond the single organization to look at its relationship with other sets of organizations, its interchanges with the broader environment. How do organizations cope with environmental uncertainty? What are institutional strategies for dealing with competition? What are the unique functions of the family vis à vis the school, and what functions should they share? Questions like these lead into the study of organizational processes—that is, organizational functioning over time and space. Such processes as innovation or implementation of social policy have recently attracted attention.

All three types of research are dependent upon the sociologist's ability to describe and measure differences among organizations and relations between them. Lazarsfeld and Menzel's early paper (E116) on conceptualizing organizational properties still applies today. It explains how information about individual members or global information about the organization can be used to construct indexes of organizations. Thus, a college could be characterized by "adding up" the attitudes of its students or by examining formal rules and regulations. But only recently have methodologists focused on processes rather than structure. This means that one can go beyond case studies to quantitative measures of institutional circles or communications networks. The Fischer volume illustrates the latter approach (E113).

Most of the titles listed below are empirical or theoretical analyses of organizations. The entries by Barton and by Etzioni and Lehman introduce the twin topics.

E109 Argyris, Chris. Intervention theory and method. Reading, Mass.: Addison-Wesley, 1970. 374p.

E110 Barton, Allen H. Organizational measurement and its bearing on the study of college environments. New York: College Entrance Examination Board, 1961. 82p.

E111 Blau, Peter M. The organization of academic work. New York: Wiley, 1973. 310p.

E112 Etzioni, Amitai, and Edward Lehman, eds. A comparative analysis of complex organizations. Rev. ed. New York: Free Pr., 1975.

E113 Fischer, Claude. To dwell among friends: personal networks in town and city. Chicago: Univ. of Chicago Pr., 1982. 451p.

E114 Hage, J., and K. Azumi, eds. Organizational systems: a text-reader in the sociology of organizations. London: Heath, 1972.

E115 Hage, J., and M. Aiken. Social change in complex organizations. New York: Random, 1970. 170p.

E116 Lazarsfeld, P., and H. Menzel. "On the relation between individual and collective properties." *In* Complex organizations, ed. by A. Etzioni. New York: Holt, 1961.

E117 March, J. G., ed. Handbook of organizations. Chicago: Rand McNally, 1964. 1,247p.

E118 Pressman, Jeffrey, and Aaron Wildavsky. Implementation. Berkeley: Univ. of California Pr., 1973. 182p.

E119 Roethlisberger, F. J., and William J. Dickson. Management and the worker: an account of a research program conducted by Western Electric Co. Boston: Harvard Business School, 1939.

E120 Rushing, William A., and Mayer N. Zald, eds. Organizations and beyond: selected essays of James D. Thompson. Lexington, Mass.: Lexington Books, 1976. 299p.

MASS COMMUNICATIONS

Early in the 1940s, in his classes at Columbia University, Paul Lazarsfeld designed a framework for communications research: the content of the media, the structure of the communications industry, and the relation between audience and effects. Today, that structure still stands. Wright gives a clear and concise overview of studies during the past decades (E128).

Content analysis of television programs, for example, tells a great deal about visible heroes and villains as well as those invisible citizens who never appear—the physicians who treat chicken pox, the fathers who do housework, or the women who manage large corporations. Gerbner, for one, asserts that the very distortions of television dramas teach the viewers what our society considers right and important (E125).

Studies of the mass media industry range from research on entire national systems to analyses of organizational arrangements of magazines. A useful introduction is the book by Davison and others (E122).

No area is more controversial than that of determining the effects of mass communications on specific audiences. Most of what is known at present is derived from studies of young people, not adults. Broadcasters have been forced to pay particular attention to the possible repercussions of violent content on children's behavior. Findings are still tentative, although short-run effects on some children seem to be substantiated. Research on "effects" is perplexing because of the methodological difficulties of disentangling the influence of prior experience or individual characteristics from the influence of the programs themselves. In addition, it is not easy to conduct the long-range research that is needed. Sociologists do not yet know under what conditions or for what groups of people television is really effective in raising the information level, transmitting propaganda, or changing attitudes. One

promising strategy is to focus upon how audiences "use" the mass media (E121). Early research pointed up the importance of interpersonal influences on behavior: many people use the media secondhand, as interpreted by friends and advisors (E126).

E121 Blumler, Jay G., and Elihu Katz, eds. The uses of mass communications. Beverly Hills, Calif.: Sage, 1975. 320p. [Annual views of communications research, v.3]

E122 Davison, W. Phillips, and others. Mass media systems and effects. New York: Praeger, 1976. 245p.

E123 Gans, Herbert J. Deciding what's news. New York: Pantheon, 1979. 393p.

E124 Gerbner, George, ed. Mass media policies in changing cultures. New York: Wiley, 1977. 291p.

E125 ———, and others, eds. The analysis of communication content: developments in scientific theories and computer techniques. New York: Wiley, 1969.

E126 Katz, Elihu, and Paul F. Lazarsfeld. Personal influence. New York: Free Pr., 1955.

E127 Milavsky, J. Ronald, and others. Television and aggression: a panel study. New York: Academic, 1982. 493p.

E128 Wright, Charles R. Mass communication. 2d ed. New York: Random, 1975. 179p.

SOCIAL PROBLEMS

When the Society for the Study of Social Problems was formed in the 1950s, it represented a distinct split with the sociological establishment. The new organization hoped to enable social scientists to apply their knowledge to the solution of social problems. Thirty years later, their mission sounds far less radical, but the real difficulty is that sociologists just do not quite know how to *apply* their insights.

Social problems readers began with an emphasis on deviant groups—the criminals, delinquents, addicts—who lived in the underworld of society. Now, problems have been redefined as public social issues: poverty, pornography, violence, etc. These problems do not surface automatically; they require identifiers, assessors, and carriers (E131). Spector and Kitsuse (E134) refer to this process as the construction of social problems.

Sociologists, however, have not lost interest in the study of deviance or social disorganization.

During the 1950s and '60s, Merton's theory of anomie stimulated myriad studies. His idea was that deviant behavior arose out of the discrepancy between the standard American goal of economic success and socially prescribed means of reaching that goal. Cloward and Ohlin made extensive use of Merton's theory in their own formulation of the opportunity theory of juvenile delinquency (E129). By the 1970s, the explanatory scaffolding had shifted somewhat, and labeling theory (as explained in Schur, E133) became the dominant mode of analysis. The central tenet is that deviance is created or reinforced by social definition and social rules. Thus, deviance is socially bestowed, but once labels are given, they are hard to shake off. The "ex-con" and the "released mental patient" carry their labels with them. Under labeling theory, the blind, the mentally ill, the crippled become the victims of the labeling process. Although labeling theory seems to concentrate on small-scale interactions, it also has turned to the analysis of collective rule-making organizations such as legislative bodies or federal commissions.

Sociologists have focused on several problem areas which were to be directly linked to social policy-making. One was the study of poverty. Whereas some sociologists stressed the attitudes, values, and life-styles that fostered the isolation of the poor, others hunted for the systematic ways by which our society engendered careers in poverty. When planning and action agencies were created to deal with these issues, sociologists took active roles. They tried to help sharpen goals, design modes of reaching low-income families, and evaluate the effectiveness of guaranteed income, manpower, or youth training programs. It soon became apparent that evaluation and experimentation in the social sciences were fraught with conceptual and methodological perils. A large literature ensued, and the Struening and Guttentag book provides a good sample (E130).

E129 Cloward, Richard A., and Lloyd E. Ohlin. Delinquency and opportunity: a theory of delinquent gangs. Glencoe, Ill.: Free Pr., 1960. 220p.

E130 Struening, E. L., and M. Guttentag, eds. Handbook of evaluation research. Beverly Hills, Calif.: Sage, 1975. 2v.

E131 Merton, Robert K., and Robert Nisbet, eds. Contemporary social problems. 4th ed. New York: HBJ, 1976. 782p.

E132 Rossi, Peter H., and others. Evaluation: a systematic approach. Beverly Hills, Calif.: Sage, 1979. 384p.

E133 Schur, Edwin M. Labeling deviant behavior. New York: Harper, 1971. 177p.

E134 Spector, Malcolm, and John I. Kitsuse. Constructing social problems. Menlo Park, Calif.: Cummings, 1977.

E135 Wiseman, J. P. "Toward a theory of policy intervention in social problems." *Social problems* 27:3–18 (1979).

USING SOCIOLOGY

For a long time, no one worried about what it meant to "use" sociology. While sociology was struggling to be recognized as an academic discipline, some were worried whether applied research was a worthy pursuit, but none questioned the possibility of applying research. The situation has changed radically within the past decade.

The debate over the basic-applied dimension seems to have subsided. There are still sociologists who prefer to start research with an eye to their own disciplines; there are others who select research that is geared toward policy decisions. In view of the shrinking opportunities for academic employment, the sociological practitioner has gained respectability and is using hard-won knowledge in practical ways. Such new journals as *Sociological practice* and *Knowledge: creation, diffusion, utilization* attest to this revised status. However, applied sociologists have found that there is a great deal to learn about utilizing sociology in the world of practical affairs.

Utilization is a lengthy process that involves many interconnected agencies—research funders, research mandators, research organizations, research clients, etc. Each has differing interests to express and protect. At every step in the utilization process, beginning with the policymaker's perception of a problem, each decision locks into the next, and each decision is a compound of knowledge and intuition. Lazarsfeld and others (E140) argue that detailed case studies of research utilization must be pressed toward a "theory of applications." Scott and Shore (E142) take a somewhat more extreme position, feeling that applied research is doomed to failure unless it is undertaken with policy concerns in mind. In other words, there is no haphazard application of research after the fact.

Most authors agree that there are both political and intellectual components to the utilization process. Exactly how does one translate a social problem into a research design? Is research alone expected to formulate new strategies or select from existing alternatives? What other considerations must be added? What does a researcher do to convert his study findings into recommendations for action?

It is not clear where applied research should be conducted. Independent research institutes, such as Abt Associates, Rand, or the Brookings Institution, have proven to be adept at obtaining federal contracts and grants for research. Lazarsfeld would prefer to locate applied research within the university because of the continuity in training from one generation to the next. Some universities have experimented with special degree programs in applied sociology, but no one yet knows exactly what mixture of academic and practical experience is the best preparation for applying knowledge and research.

As applied research increases, the ethical dilemmas multiply. The American Sociological Association is currently drafting a code of professional ethics that will not only ensure research objectivity and integrity but will protect the rights of human subjects to privacy, dignity, and informed consent.

E136 Coleman, James S. Policy research in the social sciences. Morristown, N.J.: General Learning Corp., 1972. 23p.

E137 Freeman, Howard E., and others, eds. Applied sociology: roles and activities of sociologists in diverse settings. San Francisco: Jossey-Bass, 1983. 490p.

E138 Holzner, Burkart, and John H. Marx. Knowledge application: the knowledge system in society. Boston: Allyn & Bacon, 1979. 388p.

E139 Komarovsky, Mirra, ed. Sociology and public policy: the case of presidential commissions. New York: Elsevier, 1975. 183p.

E140 Lazarsfeld, Paul F., and others. An introduction to applied sociology. New York: Elsevier, 1975. 196p.

E141 Lynn, Laurence E., Jr., ed. Knowledge and policy: the uncertain connection. Washington, D.C.: National Academy of Sciences, 1978. 183p.

E142 Scott, Robert, and Arnold Shore. Why sociology does not apply: a study of the use of sociology in public policy. New York: Elsevier, 1979. 265p.

E143 Weiss, Carol, ed. Using social research in public policy-making. Lexington, Mass.: Lexington Books, 1977. 256p.

E144 Williams, Walter. Social policy research and analysis: the experience in the federal social agencies. New York: American Elsevier, 1971. 204p.

Ann K. Pasanella

Survey of the Reference Works

GUIDES TO THE LITERATURE
General

E145 Bart, Pauline, and Linda Frankel. The student sociologist's handbook. 3d ed. Glenview, Ill.: Scott, Foresman, 1981. 249p.

Presents an overview of sociology in the first chapter, followed by chapters on the mechanics of writing a sociology paper and of library research, periodical literature in the field of sociology, and governmental and nongovernmental reference sources. The epilogue discusses career opportunities for sociologists. Appendixes outline the Dewey Decimal and Library of Congress classification systems for sociology. Index.

E146 Gruber, James, and others. Materials and methods for sociology research. New York: Libraryworks, 1980. 55, xii, 88p.

Designed to be used as a tool for teaching students of sociology about the basic reference books in the field (e.g., guides to the literature, dictionaries, encyclopedias, indexes, etc.) and how to use them, as well as specific research techniques and search strategies for obtaining information. The book is in two parts: (1) an instructor's manual and (2) a workbook (for students). The latter includes assignments.

E147 Cuvillier, Armand. Manuel de sociologie, avec notices bibliographiques. 5th ed. Paris: Presses Universitaires de France, 1963–67. 2v.

Two purposes are interwoven here. One is to interpret the subject matter of sociology (in 11 chapters) under 4 broad headings: history, object and methods, social morphology (or structure), and social physiology (or functional sociology); the other is to use this pattern of organization to order and discuss the literature. The result is an informative overview of sociological literature. A 20-page section in the beginning lists subject bibliographies, dictionaries, encyclopedias, periodicals, textbooks, general works, and handbooks. Each chapter concludes with a list of citations to support the discourse, paragraph by paragraph. Each volume has an extended list of publications, which complement these special bibliographies at the end of chapters. Indexes of principal concepts, methods, and theories; principal names; and location (with map) of peoples and tribes cited in the text. Emphasis is on European literature.

Specialized

Gale Research Company is publishing a number of separate "Information Guide" series pertaining to the social sciences, humanities, and current affairs. Many of the titles in the various series cover areas of sociology. A sampling of those published or soon to be published follows:

American Government and History Information Guide series:

E148   Buenker, John D., and Nicholas C. Burckel, eds. Immigration and ethnicity. 1977. 305p.

E149   Tingley, Elizabeth, and Donald F. Tingley. Women and feminism in American history. 1981. 289p.

American Studies Information Guide series:

E150   Mark, Charles, ed. Sociology of America. 1976. 454p.

Economics Information Guide series:

E151   Gagala, Kenneth L., ed. The economics of minorities. 1976. 212p.

Education Information Guide series:

E152   Cordasco, Francesco, and David N. Alloway, eds. Sociology of education. 1979. 266p.

E153   Wilkins, Kay S., ed. Women's education in the United States. 1979. 217p.

Ethnic Studies: An Information Guide series:

E154   Cordasco, Francesco. Italian Americans. 1978. 222p.

E155   Doezema, Linda Pegman. Dutch Americans. 1979. 314p.

E156   Douglass, William A., and Richard W. Etulain. Basque Americans. 1981. 169p.

E157   Keresztesi, Michael, and Gary R. Cocozzoli. German-American history and life. 1980. 372p.

E158   Sokolyszyn, Aleksander, and Vladimir Wertsman. Ukrainians in Canada and the United States. 1981. 236p.

E159   Trejo, Arnulfo D., ed. Bibliografia Chicana. 1975. 193p.

E160   Wertsman, Vladimir. The Romanians in America and Canada. 1980. 164p.

Health Affairs Information Guide series:

E161   Elling, Ray H., ed. Cross national study of health systems: countries, world religions, and special problems. 1980. 687p.

E162   Goldstein, Doris Mueller. Bioethics. 1982. 366p.

E163   Lee, Joel M., ed. Health care politics, policy and legislation.

E164   Maddox, George L., and others, eds. Social gerontology.

E165   Morris, Dwight A., and Lynne Darby Morris, eds. Health care administration. 1978. 264p.

E166   Weise, Frieda O., ed. Health statistics. 1980. 137p.

Man and the Environment Information Guide series:

E167   Meshenberg, Michael J., ed. Environmental planning. 1976. 492p.

E168   Owings, Loren C., ed. Environmental values, 1860–1972. 1976. 324p.

Psychology Information Guide series:

E169   Gottsegen, Gloria Behar, ed. Group behavior. 1979. 219p.

Social Issues and Social Problems Information Guide series:

E170   Garoogian, Andrew, and Rhoda Garoogian, eds. Child care issues for parents and society. 1977. 367p.

E171   Lester, David, and others, eds. Suicide. 1980. 294p.

E172   Sell, Kenneth D., and Betty H. Sell, eds. Divorce in the United States, Canada and Great Britain. 1978. 298p.

Urban Studies Information Guide series:

E173   Diner, Hasia R., ed. Women and urban society. 1979. 138p.

E174   Murphy, Thomas P., ed. Urban indicators. 1980. 234p.

E175 Palumbo, Dennis J., and George Taylor, eds. Urban policy. 1979. 198p.

Although the books in these series vary somewhat in format, they generally cover several aspects of the subject and include monographs, serials, and reference works. Most entries are annotated. All volumes have extensive indexes. Each book of the series lists other titles in the same series in press or in preparation.

E176 O'Block, Robert L. Criminal justice research sources. Cincinnati: Anderson, 1983. 121p.
Contains basic information about the card catalog, interlibrary loan, reference sources, microforms, databases, etc., of use to undergraduate and beginning graduate students in criminal justice.

The following bibliographies deal with minorities in the United States:

E177 Miller, Wayne Charles. A comprehensive bibliography for the study of American minorities. New York: New York Univ. Pr., 1976. 1,320p. 2v.
With more than 29,000 entries, many of them annotated, this undoubtedly is, as claimed in the preface, the most comprehensive bibliography on American minorities in existence. Lists bibliographies, guides to collections, encyclopedias, dictionaries, handbooks, periodicals, biographies, and autobiographies. The number of minority groups and breadth of subject matter covered is most impressive.

E178 Robinson, Barbara J., and J. Cordell Robinson. The Mexican American: a critical guide to research aids. Greenwich, Conn.: JAI Pr., 1980. 287p. [Foundations in library and information science, v.1]
Divided into two parts. Pt. 1, general reference works, includes general bibliographies, library guides, biographical, genealogical and statistical sources, directories, dictionaries, newspaper and periodical sources, and audiovisual sources. Pt. 2, subject bibliographies, covers education, folklore, history, labor, linguistics, literature, social and behavioral sciences, and women. Contains more than 650 entries with highly informative annotations. Author, title, and subject indexes.

E179 Abajian, James de T., ed. Blacks and their contributions to the American West: a bibliography and union list of library holdings through 1970. Boston: Hall, 1974. 487p.
The most comprehensive bibliography in its area, this work contains more than 4,000 entries covering a broad range of subjects. Includes bibliographies and finding aids, directories, census records, periodicals, and newspapers. Combined author and subject index.

E180 Miller, Elizabeth W. The Negro in America: a bibliography. 2d ed., rev. and enl. by Mary L. Fisher. Cambridge, Mass.: Harvard Univ. Pr., 1970. 351p.
A significant spin-off from studies of the black American initiated by the American Academy of Arts and Sciences. The 1970 edition has about 6,000 books, articles, official reports, etc., and emphasizes publications in the U.S. since 1954. "In content, it encompasses the clinical, empirical, prescriptive, and polemic, the scholarly and the journalistic. It seeks to make accessible to both layman and scholar significant writings and, at the same time, to identify problems and mark the urgency of their solutions" (preface). Mainly a classified bibliography with author index, it takes on the character of a guide in a concluding chapter that briefly introduces bibliographies, indexes, journals, and related tools available to support further research on the subject.

E181 Welsh, Erwin K. The Negro in the United States: a research guide. Bloomington: Indiana Univ. Pr., 1965. 142p.
Introduces books and, to a lesser extent, periodicals and bibliographies about blacks as of the mid-1960s. Alphabetical bibliography of about 450 works cited in the text, short directory of national and state organizations representing pro-integration and pro-segregation groups, and a short subject index.

REVIEWS OF THE LITERATURE AND RESEARCH

E182 American journal of sociology. v.1– , 1895– . Chicago: Univ. of Chicago Pr. Bimonthly.
One of the most cited journals in the field, each issue contains about 20 or more signed book reviews, generally from 2 to 4 pages in length. At the end of 1972, a "review symposium" appeared in which several scholars discussed a particular work. Soon thereafter, from 1 to 3 "review essays" became a regular feature. These are longer than book reviews and often list references.

E183 American sociological review. v.1– , 1936– . Washington, D.C.: American Sociological Assn. Bimonthly.
The other of the most cited journals in the field. Distinguished for its 36-year record of book reviewing, which was discontinued with v.36 (1971), when the association launched a separate journal for book reviews.

E184 L'Année sociologique. v.1–12, 1896–1912; new ser. v.1–2, no.2, 1923–24, 1924–25; 3d ser. v.1– , 1948– . Paris: Alcan, 1896–1925; Presses Universitaires de France, 1948– .

More than half of each volume of this respected publication (founded by Émile Durkheim) is devoted to a selective survey of the significant literature of sociology. Its 200–300 reviews a year vary in length from brief analyses to lengthy essays about significant contributions in a given subject area. Scope is international, but emphasis is on developments in French sociology. The signed reviews are grouped under major areas: general sociology; social structure; social systems and civilizations; sociology of knowledge, education, religion, etc. Has author and title indexes.

The gap between 1925 and 1948 was partially filled by *Annales sociologiques* (v.1–4, 1934–41), which was issued in 5 series: Sociologie générale, Sociologie réligieuse, Sociologie juridique et morale, Sociologie économique, and Morphologie sociale, langage, technologie, esthétique. Format the same as that of *L'Année*.

E185 Annual review of sociology. v.1– , 1975– . Palo Alto, Calif.: Annual Reviews, Inc.

"Annual reviews" now exist for many disciplines (the first was published in 1932) and have an excellent reputation. Sociology is one of the more recent ones to appear. Similar to others in the series, it is a compilation of essays by well-known specialists covering a wide range of subject categories, which vary from year to year, providing a broad overview and major source of information about progress in the discipline. An extensive list of literature cited accompanies each essay.

E186 British journal of sociology. v.1– , 1950– . London: London School of Economics and Political Science. Quarterly.

In addition to occasional review articles, this journal carries 15–25 critical reviews (450–1,800 words) in each issue. Book reviews are included in annual index.

E187 Contemporary sociology: a journal of reviews. v.1– , 1972– . Washington, D.C.: American Sociological Assn. Bimonthly.

With the inauguration of this journal, the effort to review all sociology books published in English was abandoned. *Contemporary sociology,* the editor writes, "is highly selective, reviewing only a portion of the sociological publications now issuing from the printing presses in unprecedented volume." The editors decided to concentrate on longer, more thoughtful reviews of those books judged most significant; to devote more space to review symposia and review essays; more grouping of titles for joint review; selected reviewing of foreign titles; occasional surveys of recent sociological literature in lesser-known languages; and continued reviewing of important books in related fields. A book review journal of high merit. Annual coverage has increased from about 400 to about 700 books.

E188 Current sociology. v.1- , 1952– . The Hague: Mouton. 3/yr.

Initially, alternate issues presented a world bibliography and trend reports on special subjects. In 1955, *International bibliography of sociology* (E236) became a separate publication. *Current sociology,* in turn, evolved into a continuous review, by staggered treatment of individual topics and research in the field as a whole. One result is a running inventory of progress and trends by subject: sociology in the USSR 1965–1975, sociology of popular culture, sociology in Spain, etc. These reviews, based on the accumulated literature, produce a succession of retrospective bibliographies that tend to be among the most definitive in the field.

E189 Sociology: reviews of new books. v.1– , 1973– . Washington, D.C.: Heldref. Bimonthly.

Short review articles which make up each number are listed in table of contents under subjects within the discipline. Author index in each issue, with annual cumulative author indexes.

Specialized Reviews of the Literature and Research

E190 Black books bulletin. v.1– , 1971– . Chicago: Institute of Positive Education. Quarterly.

Advertises on first page: "The Bulletin is the most comprehensive reviewing medium for books by and about Black people. Additionally, it presents the newest writings by some of our most gifted minds."

E191 Communication yearbook. v.1– , 1977– . New Brunswick, N.J.: Transaction Books. Annual.

Sponsored by the International Communication Association, "each volume in the series provides (1) disciplinary reviews and commentaries on topics of general interest to scholars and researchers . . . (2) overviews of general and specific developments in designated areas of communication theory and research [e.g., mass communication, organizational communication, intercultural communication], (3) current research in a variety of topics and (4) topic and author index." V.4 has more than 40 scholarly articles, each with a list of references.

E192 Family studies review yearbook. v.1– , 1983– . Beverly Hills, Calif.: Sage. Annual.

Volume one contains recent articles on such topics as family policy, family stress and coping, divorce, family violence, alcoholism and the family, work and family, family economics, marital enrichment, marital therapy, and family therapy.

E193 Journal of studies on alcohol. v.1– , 1940– . New Brunswick, N.J.: Rutgers Center of Alcohol Studies. Monthly.

Formerly *Quarterly journal of studies on alcohol.* "The contents of the Journal alternate monthly: Original articles appear in the odd-numbered months; current literature (informative abstracts, book reviews, bibliography and indexes) in the even-numbered months."

E194 Research in law and sociology. v.1– , 1978– . Greenwich, Conn.: JAI Pr. Annual.

Provides scholarly essays which "represent the current interests and perspectives of political scientists, psychologists, historians, lawyers and sociologists as they reflect upon significant problems concerning the relationships between law and social institutions, norms and values. . . . Some are primarily theoretical in orientation, a few have a methodological emphasis, and many focus on important social problems and have public policy orientation." Each volume contains about 10 essays, approximately 20 to 35 pages long, with appended lists of references. Two similar series by JAI Press were begun, in 1980 called *Research in the sociology of health care* (**E195**), and in 1981 called *Research in the sociology of work* (**E196**).

E197 Social forces. v.1– , 1922– . Chapel Hill: Univ. of North Carolina Pr. Quarterly.

Reviews about 30–40 books in each issue in the following categories: theory, methodology, studies in social structure, social psychology, social problems, social and cultural change, applications of sociology, and the discipline. No reviews of texts, readers, second editions, or books outside the field.

E198 Social service review. v.1– , 1927– . Chicago: Univ. of Chicago Pr. Quarterly.

This journal, devoted to the scientific and professional interests of social work, surveys the current books and public documents in long (400–2,000 words), critical, signed reviews. The approximately 10–30 reviews in each issue are generally restricted to English-language titles. Annual index of reviews. Also usually includes "Brief notices" about recent publications. "Doctoral dissertations in social work" was a regular feature from 1954 to 1974.

ABSTRACTS AND SUMMARIES
Comprehensive

E199 Bulletin signalétique. Section 521. Sociologie. Ethnologie.
Description at A149.

E200 Sociological abstracts. v.1– , 1952– . San Diego: Sociological Abstracts. 5/yr.

Primarily abstracts articles from journals, although also includes conference papers and (before 1973) some monographs. Concentrates on the core journals in sociology with selective coverage of journals in other disciplines when the articles were written by sociologists and/or pertain to sociology. *SA* began by covering seven journals in 1952; currently it covers more than 1,000 (about 140–200 per issue). Arranged according to broad professional interests or "files" (group interactions, social differentiation, sociology of religion, etc.). Includes subject, author, and source indexes. Each issue also provides a bibliography of book reviews from journals abstracted in that issue. A cumulative subject index is published within nine months of the following year. Cumulative indexes: v.1–10, 11–15.

Specialized

E201 Abstracts of popular culture: a quarterly publication of international popular phenomena. v.1– , 1976– . Bowling Green, Ohio: Bowling Green Univ. Popular Pr. Quarterly.

An attempt to gain bibliographic control over an elusive area, this abstracting service scans more than 600 domestic and foreign periodicals and plans to increase international coverage "constantly." A few of the topics covered are film, television, radio, popular literature, theater, amusements, urban and rural life, the counterculture, ethnic and women's studies, folklore, the family, leisure and work, and humor. Many of the periodicals scanned are not abstracted elsewhere.

E202 Criminology and penology abstracts. v.1– , 1961– . Deventer, Netherlands: publ. by Kugler for Criminologica Foundation. Bimonthly.

Formerly *Excerpta criminologica* and *Abstracts on criminology and penology*. A feature article in each issue is followed by classified, signed abstracts based on selected books and about 360 journals from 35 countries. Sociology and social work are included in the classification scheme. Author index cumulated annually.

E203 Criminal justice abstracts. v.1– , 1968– . Hackensack, N.J.: National Council on Crime and Delinquency. Quarterly.

Title and frequency vary. Formerly *Crime and delinquency literature*. Contains lengthy abstracts of selected current literature of international scope. Each issue has comprehensive review of a pertinent topic: victimless crime, marijuana, etc. About 375 abstracts an issue.

E204 "Current publications." *Studies in family planning*. no.1– , 1963– . New York: Population Council. Monthly.

Provides abstracts of books, pamphlets, reports, and journal articles related to family planning.

E205 Human resources abstracts. v.1– , 1966– . Beverly Hills, Calif.: Sage. Bimonthly. (More information at A161.)

E206 Language and language behavior abstracts. v.1– , 1967– . San Diego: Sociological Abstracts, Inc. Quarterly.

Includes a section on sociolinguistics. (More information at A163.)

E207 "The polls." *Public opinion quarterly*. v.4– , 1940– . New York: Columbia Univ. Pr. Quarterly.

Style of reporting and summarizing has varied. Thorough treatment of all available opinion polls from major U.S. polling organizations and occasional foreign polls from 1940 to 1950. After interruption, quarterly reporting was resumed in 1961, but the expansion of polling forced a change of style. Regular summaries of all major polls here and abroad had to give way to summaries based on topic ("Western partisanship in the Middle East") or period ("Polling in 1968").

Cumulative index to the Public opinion quarterly 1937–1967, volumes 1–31 (New York: American Assn. for Public Opinion Research, 1969; dist. by Columbia Univ. Pr. [110p.]) **(E208)**, indexes the preceding entry for the years indicated.

Other sources of current opinion are: *The Gallup opinion index: political, social and economic trends,* report no.1– , 1965– (Princeton, N.J.: Gallup Intl. [monthly]) **(E209)**, which regularly summarizes, for one of the major polling organizations, the results of recent polls on topics of current interest; *International Gallup polls,* v.1– , 1978– (Wilmington, Del.: Scholarly Resources [annual]) **(E210)**; and *Public opinion,* v.1– , 1978– (Washington, D.C.: American Enterprise Institute for Public Policy Research [bimonthly]) **(E211)**, which contains articles by eminent specialists about public opinion on currently significant topics. An "opinion roundup" in each issue uses charts and graphs to portray public opinion on a multitude of popular issues.

A number of retrospective polls are available: Hadley Cantril, *Public opinion, 1935–1946* (Princeton, N.J.: Princeton Univ. Pr., 1951 [1,191p.]) **(E212)**. This compilation reports more than 12,000 polls collected from 23 organizations in 16 countries, and limits itself to polls based on a national cross-section. Information for an entry includes (besides the name of the responsible organization) the place and date of the poll, the question, and a summary of the results.

George Horace Gallup, *The Gallup poll: public opinion, 1935–1971* (New York: Random, 1972 [2,388p.]) 3v. **(E213)** contains more than 7,000 Gallup poll reports from the founding of the Gallup poll in October 1935 through December 1971. An update appeared in 1978: *The Gallup poll: public opinion, 1972–1977* (Wilmington, Del.: Scholarly Resources, 1978 [1,334p.]) 2v. **(E214)**. Reports are in chronological order, with interviewing date provided for each poll. Subject indexes are included.

On the international scene, two European Gallup poll retrospective surveys have been published: George H. Gallup, *The Gallup international public opinion polls: France 1939, 1944–1975* (New York: Random, 1976 [1,257p.]) **(E215)**, and *The Gallup international public opinion polls: Great Britain 1937–1975* (New York: Random, 1976 [1,578p.]) **(E216)**.

Another useful source for public opinion research is *The Harris survey yearbook of public opinion: a compendium of American attitudes,* v.1– , 1970– (New York: Louis Harris and Associates) **(E217)**. So far, only 4 volumes of this "annual" have appeared.

E218 Resources in women's educational equity: abstracts/citations for the year 1976. Washington, D.C.: U.S. Dept. of Health, Education and Welfare; dist. by Supt. of Documents, 1977. 298p.

Includes citations about women relating to education, legal matters, career, sex differences, lifestyle, and health from several machine-readable databases: *Dissertation abstracts international* (DAI), *ERIC documents, ERIC journals, Sociological abstracts, Psychological abstracts,* etc. Subject and author indexes are provided.

E219 Sage family studies abstracts. v.1– , 1979– . Beverly Hills, Calif.: Sage. Quarterly.

Each issue provides approximately 250 abstracts referring to books, journal articles, government, and miscellaneous publications. Major categories covered are theory and methodology; life-styles; life cycles; marital and family processes; problems, therapy, and counseling; sex roles; and social issues. Author and subject indexes.

E220 Sage race relations abstracts. v.1– , 1975– . London and Beverly Hills, Calif.: Sage. Quarterly.

Published for the Institute of Race Relations in London, this quarterly abstracts articles from European and American periodicals, and some books and ephemera, dealing with immigration and race relations. Includes a bibliographic essay in each issue. Author and title indexes.

E221 Sage urban studies abstracts. v.1– , 1973– . Beverly Hills, Calif.: Sage. Quarterly.

Approximately 250 abstracts appear in each issue covering a broad range of topics on urban affairs, such as urban planning and land use; environment and energy; transportation and communication; housing and social services; social, economic, and political conditions. Books, articles, pamphlets, government publications, and miscellaneous fugitive materials are included. Annual cumulative subject and author indexes.

E222 Social research methodology abstracts. v.1– , 1979– . Rotterdam: SRM-Documentation Centre, Erasmus University. Annual.

An abstracting service focusing on the literature in the field of methods and techniques of empirical social research. Nearly 100 major English-language and foreign journals were abstracted in 1980. The abstracts are in two parts: "primary abstracts" which are original and "secondary abstracts" which refer to book reviews or abstracts "already provided by other sources," e.g., *Sociological abstracts*. Subject index and index of descriptors. See also *Social research methodology bibliography* (E244).

E223 Social work research and abstracts, v.1– , 1965– . Albany: National Assn. of Social Workers. Quarterly. Formerly Abstracts for social workers (v.1–13, no.1, Spring 1977).

Contains several original research papers as well as abstracts of articles previously published in social work and related fields selected from more than 250 journals. Abstracts are classified. Additional author and subject indexes, which cumulate annually.

E224 Straus, Murray A., and Bruce W. Brown. Family measurement techniques: abstracts of published instruments, 1935–1974. Rev. ed. Minneapolis: Univ. of Minnesota Pr., 1978. 668p.

Contains abstracts of 813 measurement techniques (319 in first edition) "that have been developed for quantitatively expressing the properties of the family or the behavior of people in family roles." There is no critical evaluation of the tests; they are included without regard to evidence of reliability and/or validity. Entries are topically arranged. Each one includes author(s) and test name, variables measured, test description, sample item, length, availability, and references. Author, test title, and subject indexes.

E225 Toronto Univ. School of Social Work. The research compendium: review and abstracts of graduate research, 1942–1962. Abstracts by Margaret Avison. Introductory essays by Margaret Avison and Albert Rose. Toronto: Univ. of Toronto Pr., 1964. 276p.

Presents results of 20 years of doctoral and master's research in Toronto's School of Social Work.

E226 U.S. Department of Housing and Urban Development. Socio-physical technology. Washington, D.C.: Govt. Print. Off., 1971. 11p.

Twenty bibliographies, selected by John Archea, ed. of *Man-environment systems,* as best covering the main issues of concern to those who are "attempting to understand, or modify, the complex set of relationships that link individual and collective human behavior with features of the natural and man-made physical environment."

E227 U.S. Urban Mass Transportation Administration, University Research and Training Program. Abstracts for university research projects. Washington, D.C.: Dept. of Transportation, UMTA; dist. by National Technical Information Service, Springfield, VA 22161, 1978. 263p.

Contains abstracts of published reports for research projects supported by UMTA's University Research and Training Grant Program. The abstracts are divided into 30 categories alphabetically arranged, including, for example, bibliographies, crime and crime prevention, elderly and handicapped, socioeconomic analysis, transportation analysis, and evaluation.

E228 Women studies abstracts. v.1– , 1972– . Rush, N.Y.: Women Studies Abstracts. Quarterly.

More than 300 periodicals are regularly abstracted and indexed in *WSA,* which includes book reviews, abstracts, and an extensive list of additional articles on a wide variety of topics pertaining to women such as education and socialization; employment; society and government; mental and physical health; family planning, childbirth and abortion; media; interpersonal relations; women's liberation movement. Annual name and subject indexes.

E229 World agricultural economics and rural sociology abstracts: abstracts of world literature. v.1– 6, April 1959–1964. Amsterdam: North-Holland, v.7– , 1965– . Slough, Eng.: Commonwealth Agricultural Bureaux; dist. by New York: Unipub. Monthly.

About 2,500 of the world's scholarly journals and government publications on agriculture and related sciences were scanned by the Commonwealth Bureau of Agricultural Economics in producing v.22, 1980, which contains nearly 9,000 abstracts. In the area of rural sociology, such subjects as demography and settlement, rural/urban relations and migration, sociology and social policy of rural areas, social stratification, sociology of the farm family, etc., are covered.

BIBLIOGRAPHIES OF BIBLIOGRAPHIES

Bibliographies in journals covered by *Sociological abstracts* (E200) are listed in the index under the heading "Bibliography(ies)." The section "Document analysis. Reference book" in each issue of *International bibliography of sociology* (E236) mainly lists bibliographies. Before 1972 this section was listed as "Reference books and bibliographies, collections." See also the listings of bibliographies in *Population index* (E241).

The strong interest in women's studies during the 1970s has produced various reference sources in this area, such as the following: Patricia K. Ballou, *Women: a bibliography of bibliographies* (Boston: Hall, 1980 [155p.]) (**E230**); Jane Williamson, *New feminist scholarship: a guide to bibliographies* (Old Westbury, N.Y.: Feminist Pr., 1980 [139p.]) (**E231**); and Maureen Ritchie, comp., *Women's studies: a checklist of bibliographies* (London: Mansell, 1980 [107p.]) (**E232**). All three have broad subject coverage; almost all entries in Ballou are annotated, about half in Williamson; Ballou includes publications with imprint dates from 1970 to 1979, while Williamson and Ritchie do not limit date of publication.

E233 Blazek, Ron, and others, comps. The black experience: a bibliography of bibliographies 1970–1975. Chicago: American Library Assn., 1978. 67p.

Relevant bibliographies of The Council of Planning Librarians publications are listed, as are separately published bibliographic works and bibliographic articles in journals (both annotated).

E234 Gubert, Betty Kaplan. Early black bibliographies, 1863–1918. New York: Garland, 1982. 380p. [Critical studies on black life and culture, v.25; Garland reference library of social science, v.103]

"The criteria for inclusion include rarity, originality, uniqueness, and scholarly significance. A special feature of the bibliographies is their inclusion of hard-to-find nineteenth-century periodical articles which report on contemporary issues, conferences, and events" (introduction).

E235 Davis, Bruce L., comp. Criminological bibliographies: uniform citations to bibliographies, indexes, and review articles of the literature of crime study in the United States. Westport, Conn.: Greenwood, 1978. 182p.

"A comprehensive source book of the secondary literature of crime study" (preface), intended primarily for social science researchers. Includes bibliographies of law review articles but not bibliographies of strictly legal materials such as statutes, judicial opinions, etc. No restrictions were placed on date of publication. The bibliography is divided into two parts with subcategories in each. Pt.1, Study of social problems, crime, delinquency, law, morality, ethics; pt.2, Criminal justice administration. Thoroughly indexed.

CURRENT BIBLIOGRAPHIES
Comprehensive

E236 International bibliography of sociology. v.1–9, 1951–59. Paris: UNESCO, 1952–61. v.10– , 1960– . London: Tavistock; Chicago: Aldine, 1962– . Annual.

Seeks to provide more or less complete coverage of scientific publications for the year without limitation as to country of origin, language, or form (books, articles, duplicated reports, etc.). A clear, logical classification scheme organizes the material. Time lag of about 2 years. No annotations. Author and subject indexes. V.1–4 (1951–54) appeared as issues of *Current sociology* (E188).

Specialized

E237 The criminal justice periodical index. v.1– , 1975– . Ann Arbor, Mich.: Univ. Microfilms Intl. 3/yr.

Nearly 100 periodicals are covered in this author and subject index. Many articles listed are available from Univ. Microfilms Intl.

E238 "Current publications in gerontology and geriatrics." *Journal of gerontology.* v.1– , 1964– . St. Louis: Gerontological Society. Quarterly.

Each quarterly issue carries extensive, serially numbered, classified list of books, articles, conference papers, and official publications of international scope. Thorough reviews of several books of special merit plus brief reviews of many other books.

E239 "Dissertations and theses in sociology." *American journal of sociology.* v.22–71, 1916/17–1965/66. Chicago: Univ. of Chicago Pr. Annual.

A current record (in 2 pts.) for 40 years. Pt. 1 lists Ph.D. and M.A. degrees conferred during the preceding year in U. S. and Canada, with the title of the research report in each case. Pt. 2 lists doctoral dissertations in progress. Beginning with v.69, these parts became "Doctor's degrees in sociology" and "Dissertations newly started."

E240 Index to periodical articles by and about blacks. (title varies) v.1– , 1950– . Boston: Hall. Annual.

Author-subject index to more than 20 black American periodicals compiled by the staff of the Hallie Q. Brown Memorial Library at Central State University, Wilberforce, Ohio. Decennial cumulations: 1950–59, 1960–70.

E241 Population index. v.1– , 1935– . Princeton, N.J.: Office of Population Research, Princeton Univ. and Population Assn. of America. Quarterly.

This scholarly index has a classified subject arrangement. Most entries are annotated and refer to books, periodicals, proceedings of professional meetings, publications of official U.S. and foreign governmental agencies, intergovernmental agencies, nongovernmental organizations, etc. Articles on topics of current interest, special charts, and statistical information are included. Geographical and author indexes. Annual cumulative index.

Population index bibliography cumulated 1935–1968 by authors and geographical areas (Boston: Hall, 1971) **(E242)** makes *Population index* more readily accessible: Author index, 4v.; Geographical index, 5v. It brings together some 150,000 entries, thus cumulating citations in 34v. of the ranking current bibliography of the subject.

E243 Research annual on intergroup relations. 1965– . Chicago: Quadrangle. Irregular.

Based on completed questionnaires sent to researchers throughout the world, briefly reports ongoing, completed, and proposed research in intergroup relations. Publisher varies. Anti-Defamation League of B'nai B'rith, Committee on Desegregation and Integration, Society for the Psychological Study of Social Issues, Committee on Intergroup Relations, and Society for the Study of Social Problems have cooperated in developing the series.

E244 Social research methodology bibliography. v.1– , 1979– . Rotterdam: SRM Documentation Centre, Erasmus University. Quarterly.

In coordination with the annual publication, *Social research methodology abstracts* (E222), this quarterly serves to provide "with a minimum of delay" information about recent literature in the field of methods and techniques of empirical social research.

E245 U.S. Department of Housing and Urban Development. *Housing and planning references.* n.s. v.1– , July/Aug. 1965– . Washington, D.C.: Govt. Print. Off. Bimonthly.

"This is a selection of publications and articles on housing and planning received by The Library of the Department of Housing and Urban Development." It updates the *Dictionary catalog* of the library (E285). Thoroughly indexed.

RETROSPECTIVE BIBLIOGRAPHIES
General

E246 Combined retrospective index to journals in sociology 1895–1974. Washington, D.C., and Inverness: Carrollton, 1978. 6v.

This massive bibliography indexes 128 English-language sociology journals, including some foreign ones, from the earliest volumes through 1974, "covering all periods and areas in the field of sociology." Included are "86 subject categories, each with its own chronological and keyword index." V.6 is an author index.

E247 Harvard Univ. Library. Sociology. Cambridge, Mass.: Harvard Univ. Library; dist. by Harvard Univ. Pr., 1973. [Widener Library shelflist, no. 45] 2v. (For more information see A257.)

E248 Lunday, G. Albert. Sociology dissertations in American universities, 1893–1966. Commerce: East Texas State Univ. Pr., 1969. 277p.

Lists by subject (with author index) close to 4,000 dissertations.

E249 Cordasco, Francesco, and Leonard Covello. Educational sociology: a subject index of doctoral dissertations completed at American universities, 1941–1963. New York: Scarecrow, 1965. 226p.

A classified list of 2,146 titles.

E250 Bibliographie zur deutschen Soziologie, 1945–1977 = Bibliography of German sociology [1945–1977]. Center for Intl. Comparative Studies (CICS), Univ. of Illinois Urbana u. Informationszentrum Sozialwiss. Bonn; hrsg. u. eingel. von Karl-Heinrich Bette, Matthias Herfurth, Günther Lüschen, unter Mitarb. von Gerhard Schonfeld . . . [and others]. Göttingen: Schwartz, 1980. 800p.

E251 Matthews, Mervyn, and T. Anthony Jones. Soviet sociology, 1964–75: a bibliography. New York: Praeger, 1978. 269p.

A 24-page introduction discusses the limitations of the discipline in the Soviet Union as well as the problem of availability of much work to outsiders. Despite these problems, this bibliography constitutes "something like the core of the discipline as published." Consists of 2,500 unannotated entries, mainly in the Russian language.

E252 Nanda, Yash, comp. The Durkheimian school: a systematic and comprehensive bibliography. Westport, Conn.: Greenwood, 1977. 457p.

Author's aim in producing this sizeable bibliography of more than 7,200 entries is "to bring to light an unknown Durkheim and his unnoticed work." Divided into three parts: (1) collective bibliographies of the periodical literature of the Durkheimian School, (2) systematic and comprehensive bibliography of the works by the members published outside *L'Année sociologique*, (3) bibliography of the works on the Durkheimian School and other works consulted.

E253 Remmling, Gunter W. The sociology of Karl Mannheim: with a bibliographical guide to the sociology of knowledge, ideological analysis, and social planning. New York: Humanities, 1975. 255p.

Includes a comprehensive bibliography of about 1,500 books and articles about Mannheim.

E254 Chubin, Daryl E. Sociology of sciences: an annotated bibliography on invisible colleges, 1972–1981. New York: Garland, 1983. 202p. [Garland bibliographies in sociology, v.2] [Garland reference library of social science, v.127]

Contains a bibliographic essay and more than 300 entries divided into sections on theories, methods, and comparative studies; citation research; physical science; biomedical science; social science; and lab-centered studies.

E255 Holland, Janet, and M. D. Steuer. Mathematical sociology: a selective annotated bibliography. London: Weidenfeld & Nicolson, 1969. 107p.

Seeks to facilitate the use of mathematical methods, first by reporting how these methods applied in 451 studies (340 articles, 111 books) over an 18-year period, and second by showing these methods to be too ubiquitous and fruitful for sociologists to remain innocent of their potential.

E256 Huber, B. J. "Studies of the future: a selected and annotated bibliography." *In* The sociology of the future: theory, cases and annotated bibliography, ed. by Wendell Bell and J. A. Mau. p.339–454. New York: Russell Sage, 1971.

Demography

E257 Bilsborrow, Richard E. Population in development planning: background and bibliography. Chapel Hill: Univ. of North Carolina, 1976. 216p. [TIS bibliography series; no.11]

Presents material on planning in economic models, migration, manpower, housing, agriculture, education, and health. Includes selected list of related bibliographies. Author index.

E258 Univ. of Texas Population Research Center. International population census bibliography. Austin: Univ. of Texas Bureau of Business Research, 1965–67. 6v.

Based on the holdings of leading research libraries, this series takes a long step toward a global chronological record of population census reports. Censuses on related subjects, such as agriculture and housing, are included. The volumes are devoted to Latin America and the Caribbean, Africa, Oceania, North America, Asia, and Europe. A 194-page supplement, embracing all nations, appeared in 1968.

Aging and the Aged

Numerous bibliographies have appeared in recent years covering basic sources on gerontology. Following are some of them: Willie M. Edwards and Frances Flynn, comp., *Gerontology: a core list of significant works* (Ann Arbor, Mich.: Institute of Gerontology, 1978 [160p.]) (**E259**), emphasizes items useful for a core collection, particularly in the area of social gerontology. Books, monographs, selected special issues of journals and U.S. government publications are listed. Another work by the same authors and also published by the Institute of Gerontology is *Gerontology: a cross-national core list of significant works* (1982 [365p.]) (**E260**), which is international in scope, with emphasis on American, Canadian, and British works.

B. McIlvaine and others, *Aging: a guide to reference sources, journals, and government publications* (Storrs: Univ. of Connecticut Library, 1978 [162p.] [Bibliography series no. 11]) (**E261**), lists mainly reference works published since 1970; international, national, and state government publications, 1975–77; and major journals. Most entries are annotated.

Linna Funk Place and others, *Aging and the aged: an annotated bibliography and library research guide* (Boulder, Colo.: Westview, 1981 [128p.]) (**E262**), has a chapter devoted to reference books, indexes, abstracts, journals, and organizations concerned with gerontology. Books, journal articles, and government publications published mainly between 1960 and 1970 are listed by subject under such broad categories as the physiological, psychological, environmental and social aspects of aging. Includes title and author indexes.

M. Leigh Rooke and C. Ray Wingrove, *Gerontology: an annotated bibliography* (Washington, D.C.: Univ. Pr. of America, 1978 [262p.]) (**E263**), lists books, monographs, substantial papers, and some government publications published for the most part between 1966 and early 1977. In two parts: general references and topical references. There are 33 subject categories under the latter. Author-editor index. More specialized are George F. Wharten, *Sexuality and aging: an annotated bibliography* (Metuchen, N.J.: Scarecrow, 1981 [251p.]) (**E264**), and Carroll Wetzel Wilkinson, *The rural aged in America 1975–1978: an annotated bibliography*. (Morgantown: West Virginia Univ. Pr., 1978 [66p.] [West Virginia Univ. Gerontology Center. Occasional papers on the rural aged, no.1]) (**E265**).

E266 Shock, Nathan W. A classified bibliography of gerontology and geriatrics. Stanford, Calif.: Stanford Univ. Pr., 1951. 599p.

E267 ——. ——. Supplement 1, 1949–1955. Stanford, Calif.: Stanford Univ. Pr., 1957. 525p.

E268 ——. ——. Supplement 2, 1956–1961. Stanford, Calif.: Stanford Univ. Pr., 1963. 624p.

The standard classical bibliography. Covers the subject from biochemistry and medicine to social science and social work as they concern the aged. 51,681 items (books, articles, reports, etc.), in many languages, are classified under 7 major headings with detailed subdivisions. Abstracts of articles are cited when available. Subject index refers to classification topics rather than individual references. Supplemented by lists in *Journal of gerontology*.

Migration

E269 Shaw, R. Paul. Migration theory and fact: a review and bibliography of current literature. Philadelphia: Regional Science Research Institute, 1975. 203p.

This review of the literature is divided into seven chapters which discuss establishing a theoretical perspective, selectivity and differentials in migration, spatial aspects, economic interpretations, subjective considerations in the decision to migrate, probabilistic and stochastic approaches, and directives for further research. Text refers to items in a separate bibliography section.

E270 Haskett, Richard C. "An introductory bibliography for the history of American immigration, 1607–1955." *In* George Washington Univ. A report on world population migrations as related to the United States of America, p.85–295. Washington, D.C.: The University, 1956. 449p.

A classified bibliography compiled as the first step in a research project on American immigration. More than 3,000 items deal with all aspects of immigration to the United States, internal migration movements, racial groups, and the immigrant's effect upon all aspects of American life. Covers 1607–1921, with final chapter on the period 1921–55. No index, but detailed table of contents. Some brief annotations.

E271 Lavell, Carr B., and Wilson E. Schmidt. "An annotated bibliography on the demographic, economic and sociological aspects of immigration." *In* George Washington Univ., A report on world population migrations as related to the United States of America, p.296–449. Washington, D.C.: The University, 1956. 449p.

750 monographs and periodical articles are arranged under 7 major headings with subdivisions: (1) General works, (2) International migration, (3) Immigration to the United States, (4) The immigrant in the United States, (5) Immigration and the nation, (6) Immigration control, and (7) Immigration policy. No index. Lengthy annotations.

E272 Price, Daniel O., and Melanie M. Sikes. Rural-urban migration research in the United States: annotated bibliography and synthesis. Bethesda, Md.: U.S. Dept. of Health, Education and Welfare, Center for Population Research; dist. by Supt. of Documents, 1975. 250p.

Deals with the massive redistribution of U.S. population from rural to urban areas. Pt. 1 is a synthesis of some of the findings in pt. 2, including a list of important areas where research is needed. Pt. 2 is an annotated bibliography of more than 1,200 entries, arranged alphabetically by author, of works published mainly from 1950 to 1972, with a few important works published before 1950. Pt. 3 is a topical index.

Social Ecology

E273 Zelinsky, Wilbur. A bibliographic guide to population geography. Chicago: Univ. of Chicago Dept. of Geography, 1962. 257p. [Dept. of Geography. Research paper no.80.]

This first comprehensive list to be devoted exclusively to population geography takes inventory of "all significant writings—a total of 2,588 items—that could be located by the compiler on all phases of population geography, as defined for purposes of this bibliography, published throughout the world since the beginning of specialized work in this discipline in the latter half of the Nineteenth Century through mid-1961" (introduction). Emphasis on the interaction between, and resultant characteristics of, places and people.

Rural Sociology

Rural sociology, v.1– , 1936– **(E274)**, a quarterly published by the Rural Sociological Society, is a source of first importance. *Twenty-year index*, v.1–20, 1936–55; *Cumulative index*, v.21–30, 1956–65; *Cumulative index*, v.31–40, 1966–75.

E275 Bertrand, Alvin L., ed. Seventy years of rural sociology in the United States: abstracts and articles and bulletin bibliography. New York: Essay Pr., 1972. 428p.

Pt. 1 consists of abstracts of nearly 2,000 articles on rural sociology from American scholarly journals. Pt. 2 is a bibliography of approximately 4,500 monographs, reports, and bulletins, many of which were issued by regional Agricultural Experiment Stations and originally listed in *Rural sociology* from 1936 to 1970.

E276 Anderson, Walfred A. Bibliography of researches in rural sociology. Ithaca: New York State College of Agriculture, 1957. 186p. [Rural sociology publication 52]

Excellent for older material in spite of some errors. Selects 2,500 books, articles, reports, and documents to consolidate and update (to 1956) the story of research in the United States, the birthplace of rural sociology. The annotated entries are arranged in 46 subject areas with an author index. The first of these, "Background Publications," has 15 subdivisions. The remaining 45 are arranged alphabetically and include class and caste, cooperatives, ecological studies, labor, migration and mobility, population, school, social trends, stratification, values, etc.

Urban Sociology

The Comparative Metropolitan Analysis Project sponsored by the Association of American Geographers produced three works of great value. One of them is described at E652. The other two are: John S. Adams, ed., *Contemporary metropolitan America* (Cambridge, Mass.: Ballinger, 1976) **(E277)**. In 4 parts: Pt. 1, Cities of the nation's historic metropolitan core (354p.); Pt. 2, Nineteenth century ports (314p.); Pt. 3, Nineteenth century inland centers and ports (507p.); Pt. 4, Twentieth century cities (350p.). Begins with a historic overview of the American city. In separate chapters describes 20 metropolitan regions—the physical environment, economy, population characteristics, special problems, etc., illustrated with hundreds of maps, charts, and photographs. Each chapter has an extensive bibliography. John S. Adams, *Urban policymaking and metropolitan dynamics: a comparative geographical analysis* (Cambridge, Mass.: Ballinger, 1976 [576p.]) **(E278)**, deals with urban problems and goals in metropolitan America, and progress made since 1960 toward solving and achieving them. Includes extensive bibliographies. Another work dealing with U.S. cities is Barbara Smith Shearer and Benjamin F. Shearer, comps., *Periodical literature on United States cities: a bibliography and subject guide* (Westport, Conn.: Greenwood, 1983 [574p.]) **(E279)**, which lists nearly 5,000 periodical articles published from 1970 through 1981 about U.S. cities with a population of 100,000 or more. For each city the possible categories of articles are: general, architecture and the arts, education and the media, environment, government and politics, housing and urban development, social and economic conditions, and transportation. Subject and author indexes.

E280 Bell, Gwen, and others. Urban environments and human behavior: an annotated bibliography. Stroudsburg, Pa.: Dowden, Hutchinson & Ross, 1973. 271p.

Cites more than 450 articles and books on the relation of the urban environment to human behavior. Includes a bibliography of bibliographies and list of related journals.

Making a general assessment of the position of urban studies under the aegis of the Social Science Research Council, Philip M. Hauser and Leo F. Schnore, eds., *The study of urbanization* (New York:

Wiley, 1965) **(E281)**, features a review of the literature. The 2,779 citations in Jon K. Meyers, *Bibliography of the urban crisis: the behavioral, psychological
and sociological aspects of the urban crisis* (Chevy
Chase, Md.: National Institute of Mental Health; dist.
by Supt. of Documents, 1969 [452p.], Public Health
Service Publication no. 1,948 **(E282)**, are listed under
10 broad headings that emphasize recent disorders,
their causes and effects, and responses to them. The
material falls mainly in the period 1954–68.

E283 Hoover, Dwight W. Cities. New York: Bowker,
      1976. 231p.
      Books, games, discs, films, and filmstrips are
featured in this annotated bibliography of more than
1,000 entries. Some of the topics covered are blacks,
ethnic groups, housing, education, transportation,
civil disorders, urban poverty, urban planning, urban
sociology and urban biographies. Includes a list of
journals on urban themes and a producer/distributor
directory.

E284 Paulus, Virginia, ed. Housing: a bibliography,
      1960–1972. New York: AMS Pr., 1974. 350p.
      Contains more than 3,500 entries on housing
with respect to urban planning, economics, sociology,
law, regional science, and public administration.
Books, journal articles, government documents, technical reports, and other materials are listed without
annotations. Author index and subject finding guide
are appended.

E285 U.S. Dept. of Housing and Urban Devel-
      opment, Library and Information Division.
      Dictionary catalog. Boston: Hall, 1973.
      14,956p. 19v. First supp., 1974. 2v. Second
      supp., 1975. 2v.
      "One of the richest and most diverse collections
of literature on urban affairs and community development ever assembled. [It] offers access to a sweeping
range of books, pamphlets, slides, films, microfilms,
local, state, Federal and foreign documents on the
urban environment." (foreword) Updated by E245.
      Pt. 1 of Martin H. Sable, *Latin American ur-
banization: a guide to the literature, organization
and personnel* (Metuchen, N.J.: Scarecrow, 1971
[1,077p.]) **(E286)**, is a multilingual list of about 7,000
books, articles, conference proceedings, and dissertations on urbanization, with primary attention given to
Latin American cities. Two additional parts consist of
directories of (1) research centers and organizations
at work on urban affairs and (2) specialists in these
fields. Stanley D. Brunn, *Urbanization in developing
countries: an international bibliography* (East Lansing:
Michigan State Univ., 1971 [693p.] [Latin American
Studies Center Research Report no.8]) **(E287)**, contains more than 7,000 unannotated entries "dealing
with all facets of urbanization" in Latin America, Africa, and Asia. Almost half the entries are in foreign
languages, mainly Spanish, Portuguese, and French.
The main body of the bibliography has a geographic
arrangement. Includes subject index.

Group and Intragroup Relations

E288 Stogdill, Ralph M. Leadership abstracts and
      bibliographies 1904–1974. Columbus: Ohio
      State Univ. College of Administrative Science,
      1977. 829p.
      Probably the best and scientifically most re-
sponsible bibliography on leadership anywhere. It lists
3,690 items, almost all of them annotated. "A considerable body of literature, mostly inspirational or
suggesting methods for being a good leader, was
ignored. As a result of this exclusion, the surviving
abstracts are concerned with attempts by professionally recognized scholars and researchers to arrive at a
scientifically valid understanding of leadership."

E289 Franklin, Jerome L. Organization develop-
      ment: an annotated bibliography. Ann Arbor:
      Univ. of Michigan Institute for Social Research,
      1973. 104p.
      Arranged alphabetically by author, the table of
contents is provided for each book discussed. All entries list topics covered. Many annotations are quite
lengthy. Includes topic and author indexes.
      Two bibliographies on community power quite
different in scope are: Willis D. Hawley and James H.
Svara, *The study of community power: a bibliographic
review* (Santa Barbara, Calif.: American Bibliographic Center/Clio Pr., 1972 [123p.]) **(E290)**, which is
confined to English-language publications and focuses
mainly on American community studies in the late
fifties and in the sixties, with most entries extensively
annotated, and Irving P. Leif, *Community power
and decision making: an international handbook*
(Metuchen, N.J.: Scarecrow, 1974 [170p.]) **(E291)**,
which includes works in English as well as other languages, is international in scope and is partially annotated.

E292 Raven, Bertram H. A bibliography of publica-
      tions relating to small groups. 3d ed. Los
      Angeles: Univ. of California Dept. of Psychol-
      ogy, 1965. 1v. (various paging)
      Extensive survey of the literature pertinent to
small-group research, based upon coded card file
established by the author. The 3,137 items (monographs, journal articles, dissertations, and published
and unpublished reports) are arranged alphabetically
by author, with subject index based upon the coding
system (which is outlined in supplement 1). A 653-item
supplement was published in May 1971. Restricted
almost wholly to English-language items. No annotations.

E293 Strodtbeck, Fred L., and A. Paul Hare. "Bib-
      liography of small group research (from 1900
      through 1953)." *Sociometry* 17:107–78 (May
      1954).
      The first comprehensive bibliography on small-
group research, this work lists research reports whose
emphasis is on the nature and consequences of face-to-
face interaction in small groups. The 1,407 items are
arranged by author, and monographs and articles con-

sidered to be important substantive and methodological contributions are starred. Updated by Hare, *Handbook of small group research* (E583).

Another slightly later work is Joseph E. McGrath and Irwin Altman, *Small group research: a synthesis and critique of the field* (New York: Holt, 1966 [601p.]) (**E294**).

A specialized branch of sociology that has in recent years been receiving increased attention is the field of social conflict. Jack Nusan Porter, *Conflict and conflict resolution: a historical bibliography* (New York: Garland, 1982 [115p.] [Garland bibliographies in sociology, v.1; Garland reference library of social science, v.107]) (**E295**) provides a historical overview of the field in this highly selective, partially annotated bibliography, which includes a chapter on reference books and several other chapters listing key sources throughout history from ancient to contemporary times. Author index.

Elise Boulding and others, comps., *Bibliography on world conflict and peace*, 2d ed. (Boulder, Colo.: Westview, 1979 [168p.]) (**E296**) deals mainly though not exclusively with international conflict. The main body of the bibliography is arranged alphabetically by author with subject descriptors for each entry. Three additional sections list collections, annuals, and series; periodicals; and bibliographies. No subject index.

E297 Intl. Sociological Assn. The nature of conflict: studies on the sociological aspects of international relations. Paris: UNESCO, 1957. 314p. [Tensions and technology series]

A comprehensive survey and evaluation of research by sociologists and social psychologists into the nature, conditions, and implications of human conflict, and particularly conflict between nations. Excludes (by definition) research in family conflict, culture conflict, crime, ideological conflict, etc. Consists of 4 essays that survey the then current knowledge, with references to a 1,160-item bibliography arranged under 4 major headings: (1) Sociology and psychosociology of intergroup conflicts, (2) International relations, (3) Racial conflicts, and (4) Industrial and agrarian conflicts. Includes books, articles, reports, etc., in many languages generally published between the mid-1940s and mid-1950s. Many items fully annotated. No index.

Albert J. Miller, *Confrontation, conflict and dissent: a bibliography of a decade of controversy, 1960–1970* (Metuchen, N.J.: Scarecrow, 1972 [562p.]) (**E298**), and Kurt Lang, *Military institutions and the sociology of war: a review of the literature with annotated bibliography*, especially p.157–280 (Beverly Hills, Calif.: Sage, 1972 [337p.]) (**E299**), cover related material.

E300 Russett, Bruce, and Alfred Stephan, eds. Military force and American society. New York: Harper, 1973. 371p.

Consists of several essays followed by "The new politics of national security: a selected and annotated research bibliography," which lists more than 2,500 items that cover many topics of interest to sociologists.

Stratification and Mobility

E301 Glenn, Norval D., and others. Social stratification: a research bibliography. Berkeley, Calif.: Glendessary. n.d. 466p.

The compilers concentrated on identifying, organizing, and describing major contributions limited to English-language works embodying or treating research but exclusive of dissertations, unpublished papers, etc., and mainly within the years 1940–68. Other bibliographies (in journals) deal with the subject tangentially, but one of the values of this volume is that it brings them together under "Bibliographies" (p.11–14). For more recent information, see "social classes" in *Bibliographic index* (A175). Also *Social forces* (E197).

Marriage and the Family

E302 Aldous, Joan, and Reuben Hill. International bibliography of research in marriage and the family, 1900–1964. Minneapolis: Minnesota Family Life Study Center and the Institute of Life Insurance; dist. by Univ. of Minnesota Pr., 1967. 508p.

The authors sought to include in this computer printout all contributions of research importance published since 1900 in books, journals, and pamphlets.

E303 Aldous, Joan, and Nancy Dahl. International bibliography of research in marriage and the family: v.II, 1965–1972. Minneapolis: Univ. of Minnesota Pr. in association with the Institute of Life Insurance for the Minnesota Family Study Center, 1974. 1,530p.

The 12,850 references listed in v.1, 1900–1964, are more than doubled in v.2, reflecting the growth in citations from about 200 per year in the 1940s to more than 1,200 per year in the early 1970s. Foreign-language publications increased from 12.1 percent in v.1 to 40 percent in v.2. The newer volume includes some additional titles for 1900–64 as well as more recent literature. The change in title, David H. L. Olsen and Nancy S. Dahl, *Inventory of marriage and family literature, 1973 and 1974*, for v.3 (St. Paul: Family Social Science, Univ. of Minnesota, 1975 [376p.]) (**E304**), indicates the new restriction to English-language publications in v.3, apparently due to the growth of literature in English and the expansion in subject matter—now no longer restricted to research and theory, as in the first two volumes. V.4 in this series was published by the Univ. of Minnesota, 1977. V.5–8, 1979–82, were published by Sage, Beverly Hills, Calif.

Complementing the preceding entries are: William J. Goode and others, *Social systems and family patterns: a propositional inventory* (Indianapolis: Bobbs-Merrill, 1971 [779p.]) (**E305**), which presents more than 8,000 propositions, e.g., "Stability of the final decision to divorce is not related to the number of children in the family." Each proposition is followed by a reference to a work supporting it. Gerald L. Soliday, ed., *History of the family and kinship: a select* *international bibliography* (Millwood, N.J.: Kraus, 1980 [410p.]) **(E306)**, aims "to provide its users with a selection of the best and most important scholarship on the history of kinship and the family" worldwide and including "all time periods from prehistory to the present." Arranged by country or region with the exception of one section on general works and one on classical antiquity. Contains 6,200 entries in English and foreign languages published through 1976, with a few items published in 1977 and 1978. James Wallace Milden, *The family in past time: a guide to the literature* (New York: Garland, 1977 [200p.] [Garland reference library of social science, v.32]) **(E307)** provides more than 1,300 annotated entries dealing with the family in European, American, and non-Western history.

E308 Mogey, John. "Sociology of marriage and family behavior, 1957–1968." *Current sociology*, v.17, no.1–3, 1969. The Hague: Mouton, 1971.

A trend report containing a bibliography of 2,090 items selected as among the most important contributions on the subject, from 39 countries.

Focusing on narrower issues are the following works: Ronald Freedman, *The sociology of human fertility: an annotated bibliography* (New York: Halsted Pr., 1975 [283p.]) **(E309)** and Katherine Ch'iu Lyle and Sheldon J. Segal, eds., *International family-planning programs, 1966–1975: a bibliography* (University, Ala.: Univ. of Alabama Pr., 1977 [207p.]) **(E310)**, which are international in scope and cover family planning literature. Freedman focuses on general population and fertility studies and is topically arranged. Lyle and Segal is arranged by country and is unannotated; Mary McKenney, *Divorce: a selected annotated bibliography* (Metuchen, N.J.: Scarecrow, 1975 [157p.]) **(E311)** contains more than 600 citations, most of which are annotated, covering such broad areas as legal, financial, psychological, sociological, religious, and moral aspects of divorce. Most items were published through 1972, with only a very few after this date. Subject and author indexes. Kenneth D. Sell, comp., *Divorce in the 70s: a subject bibliography* (Phoeniz: Oryx Pr., 1981 [191p.]) **(E312)** provides more than 4,700 unannotated entries published from 1970 through 1979, covering similar broad subject areas as McKenney. McKenney lists a few literary works and works about foreign countries, while Sell's bibliography excludes fiction and is limited to the United States. Author, geographic, and subject indexes. For an earlier work of Sell on divorce, see E172. Other works are Albert J. Miller, *Death: a bibliographical guide* (Metuchen, N.J.: Scarecrow, 1977 [420p.]) **(E313)**; Hannelore Wass and others, *Death education: an annotated resource guide* (Washington, D.C.: Hemisphere Pub. Corp., 1980 [303p.]) **(E314)**; and Benjamin Schlesinger, *The one-parent family: perspectives and annotated bibliography* (Toronto: Univ. of Toronto Pr., 1970 [138p.]) **(E315)**.

Ethnic Groups and Minorities
General

E316 Bentley, G. Carter. Ethnicity and nationality: a bibliographic guide. Seattle: Univ. of Washington Pr., 1982. 381p.

The author's goals in producing this bibliography of English-language materials published through 1979 were to offer "a representative selection of research from different academic disciplines concerned with ethnicity; to highlight important theoretical contributions to the understanding of ethnicity; and to provide a convenient guide to the literature that can be used as a starting point by a wide range of users."

E317 Cordasco, Francesco, and David N. Alloway. American ethnic groups: the European heritage: a bibliography of doctoral dissertations completed at American universities. Metuchen, N.J.: Scarecrow, 1981. 366p.

E318 Oaks, Priscilla. Minority studies: a selective annotated bibliography. Boston: Hall, 1975. 303p.

Much more modest in scope than Miller (E177), this work nonetheless should be useful to libraries starting to build a collection. Minority groups covered are limited to Native Americans, Spanish Americans, Afro-Americans, and Asian Americans. Some reference works and periodicals are listed. Another useful work is Jack F. Kinton, *American ethnic groups and the revival of cultural pluralism: evaluative sourcebook for the 70's*, 4th ed. (Aurora, Ill.: Social Science and Sociological Resources, 1974 [206p.]) **(E319)**, which lists books, journal articles, and reference works. The Canadian counterpart is Andrew Gregorovich, *Canadian ethnic groups bibliography: a selected bibliography of ethnocultural groups in Canada and the Province of Ontario* (Dept. of the Provincial Secretary and Citizenship of Ontario; dist. by Government of Ontario Bookstore, Toronto, Ont., Canada, 1972 [208p.]) **(E320)**.

Gail Ann Schlachter, *Minorities and women: a guide to the reference literature in the social sciences* (Los Angeles: Reference Service Pr., 1977 [349p.]) **(E321)**, lists fact books, biographical sources, documentary sources, directories, statistical sources, and citation sources on minorities in general, American Indians, Asian Americans, black Americans, Spanish Americans, and women.

Two very different works in the field of education are: Winnie Bengelsdorf and others, *Ethnic studies in higher education: state of the art and bibliography* (Washington, D.C.: American Assn. of State Colleges and Universities, 1972 [260p.]) **(E322)**, which contains some very extensive annotations; and Francesco Cordasco, *Immigrant children in American schools: a classified and annotated bibliography with selected source documents* (Fairfield, N.J.: Kelley, 1976 [381p.]) **(E323)**.

Specific

E324 New York Public Library. Schomburg Collection. Dictionary catalog of the Schomburg Collection of Negro literature and history. Boston: Hall, 1962. 9v.

Opens—by author, subject, and title—the contents of the best-supported separate collection of books, periodicals, newspapers, music, etc., in its field. Includes manuscripts and nonbook material, some of which is described.

Singular importance of the bibliography lies in bringing together literature by and about people of African descent, mainly outside Africa, since the beginning of the European phase of the slave trade. In documenting the career of the black since then, the project throws into relief significant aspects of Western society: race relations (about 2,500 references), slavery and the slave trade (approximately 6,500), civil rights, miscegenation, discrimination in education and employment, etc. First 5-year supplement (2v.), 1967; second supplement (4v.), 1972; third supplement (1974), 580p., 1976. Continued by New York Public Library. Schomburg Collection of Negro Literature and History, *Bibliographic guide to black studies*, 1975– (Boston: Hall, 1976– . Annual) **(E325)**.

Much of what has just been said about the Schomburg collection also applies to Howard Univ. Library, *Dictionary catalog of the Jesse E. Moorland Collection of Negro Life and History* (Boston: Hall, 1970 [9v.]) **(E326)**. The collection is somewhat smaller but older. It is strong in material on early European contacts with Africa, the slave trade, slavery, the antislavery movement, and post-emancipation history. Incorporated in the catalog is an African and American periodicals index.

These catalogs supplement one another and are supplemented by related bibliographies. Monroe N. Work, *A bibliography of the Negro in Africa and America* (New York: Wilson, 1928 [698p.]) **(E327)**, organizes 17,000 older documents, books, maps, articles, and pamphlets. Reprinted by Octagon in 1965 and 1970. Frank A. Ross and Louise V. Kennedy, *A bibliography of Negro migration* (New York: Columbia Univ. Pr., 1934 [251p.]) **(E328)**, a groundclearing survey for further research, supported by the Social Science Research Council, was reprinted by Burt Franklin in 1969.

Catalogs of other special collections on the black are Hampton Institute (Hampton, Va.), Collis P. Huntington Library, *A classified catalogue of the Negro collection*, compiled by the Writers' Program of the Work Projects Administration in the State of Virginia and sponsored by Hampton Institute (n.p.: 1940 [255p.]) **(E329)**, a list of 5,000 items; and Texas Southern Univ. Library, *Heartman Negro collection* (Houston: 1955– [325p.]) **(E330)**, a list of 15,000 items.

E331 Porter, Dorothy B., ed. The Negro in the United States: a selected bibliography. Washington, D.C.: Library of Congress; dist. by Supt. of Documents, 1970. 313p.

A select 1,781 titles, picked by one of the best bibliographers in the field "to meet the current needs of students, teachers, librarians, researchers, and the general public for introductory guidance to the study of the Negro in the United States." (preface) Guy T. Westmoreland, Jr., comp., *An annotated guide to basic reference books on the black American experience* (Wilmington, Del.: Scholarly Resources, 1974 [98p.]) **(E332)**, complements the Porter work.

Other lists in the same area are Richard Newman, *Black index: Afro-Americana in selected periodicals, 1907–1949* (New York: Garland, 1981 [266p.] [Critical studies on black life and culture, v.4; Garland reference library of social science, v. 65]) **(E333)**; San Fernando Valley State College Library, *The black experience in the United States: a bibliography based on the collections of the San Fernando Valley State College* (Northridge, Calif.: San Fernando Valley State College Foundation, 1970 [162p.]) **(E334)**; Erwin A. Salk, ed., *A layman's guide to Negro history* (Chicago: Quadrangle, 1966 [170p.]) **(E335)**; Augusta Baker, *The black experience in children's books* (New York: New York Public Library, 1971 [109p.]) **(E336)**; and Miles M. Jackson, Jr., and others, *A bibliography of Negro history and culture for young readers* (publ. by the Univ. of Pittsburgh Pr. for Atlanta Univ., 1968 [134p.]) **(E337)**. The last is an outgrowth of an Institute on Materials by and about Negro Americans sponsored by Atlanta University. *The black experience: a bibliography of books on black studies in the academic libraries of Brooklyn*, ed. by Tad Kumatz and Janyce Wolf (Brooklyn: Pratt Institute Library, 1971 [235p.]) **(E338)**, and *Blacks in America: bibliographical essays*, by James M. McPherson and others (New York: Doubleday, 1971 [336p.]) **(E339)**, are also useful.

E340 Negro in print: bibliographic survey. v.1–7, 1965–71. Washington, D.C.: Negro Bibliographic and Research Center. Bimonthly.

Annotated approximately 700 popular writings (fiction and nonfiction, books and articles) for schools and general readers. Some material on minorities other than the Negro. Ran features from time to time on selected topics, such as books for young readers, Negro history, black literary magazines, etc. A 5-year subject index (1965–70) by Dolores C. Leffal was published in 1971. Annual author and title indexes.

E341 West, Earle H. A bibliography of doctoral research on the Negro, 1933–66. Ann Arbor, Mich.: Univ. Microfilms, 1969. 134p.

Presents separately, in classified order, the dissertations in this field that are listed in *American doctoral dissertations* and *Dissertation abstracts*. More recent research is covered in Joan B. Peebles, *A bibliography of doctoral research on the Negro, 1967–77* (Ann Arbor, Mich.: Univ. Microfilms Intl. [1978?] [65p.]) **(E342)**.

A few more specialized bibliographies on the black are: Lenwood G. Davis and Janet Sims, *The black family in the United States: a selective bibliography of annotated books, articles, and dissertations on black families in America* (Westport, Conn.: Greenwood, 1978 [132p.]) **(E343)**, the introduction to which claims that it "is the most comprehensive and exhaustive bibliography ever compiled on the Black family." Other works by Davis are *The black aged in the United States: an annotated bibliography* (Westport, Conn.: Greenwood, 1980 [200p.]) **(E344)** and *The black woman in American society: a selected annotated bibliography* (Boston: Hall, 1975 [159p.]) **(E345)**. Also on the black woman is Janet L. Sims, comp., *The progress of Afro-American women: a selected bibliography and resource guide* (Westport, Conn.: Greenwood, 1980 [378p.]) **(E346)**. Equally useful but narrower in scope is Ora Williams, *American black women in the arts and social sciences: a bibliographic survey* (Metuchen, N.J. and London: Scarecrow, 1978 [197p.]) **(E347)**. Literature on the black child is comprehensively covered by Charlotte J. Dunmore, *Black children and their families: a bibliography* (San Francisco: R and E Research Associates, 1976 [103p.]) **(E348)**, and two works compiled by Hector F. Myers and others: *Black child development in America, 1927–1977: an annotated bibliography* (Westport, Conn.: Greenwood, 1979 [475p.]) **(E349)** and *Research in black child development: doctoral dissertation abstracts, 1927–1979* (Westport, Conn.: Greenwood, 1982 [737p.]) **(E350)**.

Ila Wales Brasch and Walter Milton Brasch, *A comprehensive annotated bibliography of American black English* (Baton Rouge: Louisiana State Univ. Pr., 1974 [289p.]) **(E351)** contains 10 classes of entries: research studies into American black English, general studies, pedagogy, general interest, reviews, folklore, slave narratives, literature, related materials, and the "disadvantaged" approach, each alphabetically arranged by author.

Indiana Univ. Pr. has published for the Newberry Library Center for the History of the American Indian a series of major reference works on the American Indian. Important for sociology are Russell Thornton and Mary K. Grasmick, *Sociology of American Indians: a critical bibliography* (Bloomington, 1980 [113p.]) **(E352)**, and Russell Thornton and others, *The urbanization of American Indians: a critical bibliography* (Bloomington, 1982 [87p.]) **(E353)**. More limited in scope is David H. Brumble III, *An annotated bibliography of American Indian and Eskimo autobiographies* (Lincoln: Univ. of Nebraska Pr., 1981 [177p.]) **(E354)**. Before the above were available, Jack W. Marken, *The Indians and Eskimos of North America: a bibliography of books in print through 1972* (Vermillion, S. D.: Dakota Pr., 1973 [200p.]) **(E355)**, helped fill a need in an area where not a great deal had been published. Lists more than 4,000

bibliographies, handbooks, autobiographies, myths and legends, and other books. Includes a selected subject index. Mary Jo Lass-Woodfin, ed., *Books on American Indians and Eskimos: a selection guide for children and young adults* (Chicago: American Library Assn., 1978 [237p.]) **(E356)**, is designed to aid librarians and teachers select the best; it comments on more than 800 books, estimates grade level, and rates whether worth buying (good, adequate, poor).

E357 Cordasco, Francesco, and Salvatore La Gumina. Italians in the United States: a bibliography of reports, texts, critical studies and related materials. New York: Oriole Editions, 1972. 137p.

Although Cordasco has contributed other bibliographies on Italian Americans, this is the most comprehensive for sociology. Lists more than 1,400 items, including bibliographies, serial publications, guides, and directories in the first section, followed by separate sections on such topics as Italian emigration to America, the sociology of Italian American life, the Italian American in the politico-economic context. While this books offers some references on religion, more thorough coverage of the subject is provided in Silvano M. Tomasi and Edward C. Stibili, *Italian Americans and religion: an annotated bibliography* (New York: Center for Migration Studies, 1978 [222p.]) **(E358)**.

E359 New York Public Library Reference Department. Dictionary catalog of the Jewish Collection. Boston: Hall, 1960. 14v.

One of the world's major research collections on the careers, problems, traditions, and achievements of the Jewish people.

E360 Schlesinger, Benjamin. The Jewish family: a survey and annotated bibliography. Toronto: Univ. of Toronto Pr., 1971. 175p.

Four articles, and references to literature on the subject in English. Of the 600 citations, about one fourth are works of fiction on Jewish life.

E361 Foster, David William, ed. Sourcebook of Hispanic culture in the United States. Chicago: American Library Assn., 1982. 352p.

Contains sections on selected topics, such as history, anthropology, sociology, sociolinguistics, education, literature, music, and art concerning Mexican Americans, continental Puerto Ricans, and Cuban Americans. Each topic has an introductory essay that is supposed to "establish the problems, controversies, and concerns of a specific discipline vis-à-vis a specific Hispanic American group" followed by an annotated bibliography. Author-title index.

E362 Robinson, Barbara J., and J. Cordell Robinson. The Mexican American: a critical guide to research aids. Greenwich, Conn.: JAI Pr., 1980. 287p.

Pt. 1 consists of general reference works, pt. 2 of subject bibliographies. Each annotation critically evaluates the entry according to arrangement, scope, content, coverage, and usage. Most materials are about the United States, with minor exceptions, and deal with the 19th and 20th centuries, except for a few historical and genealogical works on earlier times. Author, title, and subject indexes.

E363 Woods, Richard Donovan. Reference materials on Mexican Americans: an annotated bibliography. Metuchen, N.J.: Scarecrow, 1976. 190p.

Intended audience mainly scholars and users of academic libraries, though should be useful to public and school library clientele and others as well. Each of the 387 works listed is analyzed "from the point of view of purpose, scope, arrangement and evaluation." Geographical coverage is limited to the United States and only separately issued publications are included. Provides separate author, subject (including references and cross-references), and title indexes.

E364 Jordan, Lois B. Mexican Americans: resources for young people to build cultural understanding. Littleton, Colo.: Libraries Unlimited, 1973. 265p.

Aims to bring together books and audiovisual materials "on the historical backgrounds, cultural heritage and contemporary social, economic and political problems of Mexican Americans" suitable for young adults of junior and senior high school and college age. Includes more than 1,000 annotated entries.

E365 Stanford Univ. Center for Latin American Studies. The Mexican American: a selected and annotated bibliography. 2d ed. Ed. by Luis G. Nogales. Stanford, Calif.: The Center, 1971. 162p.

Lists 444 sources on the aspirations, problems, and achievements of Mexican Americans. Predominantly scholarly studies (books, articles, dissertations, etc.) but includes conference proceedings, official reports and hearings, a few bibliographies, and a list of about 60 Chicano periodicals published in 10 states. The alphabetical author list is supplemented by subject and (academic) field indexes. The latter approach by discipline shows a predominance of social science interests. Additional material is available in: Univ. of California Graduate School of Business, Div. of Research, *Mexican-American study project revised bibliography, with a bibliographical essay by Ralph Guzman* (Los Angeles: 1967 [99p.], Advance report 3) (**E366**); and U.S. Inter-Agency Committee on Mexican American Affairs, *A guide to materials relating to persons of Mexican heritage in the United States* (Washington, D.C.: 1969 [186p.]) (**E367**). More specialized are: Roberto Cabello-Argandoña and others, *The Chicana: a comprehensive bibliographic study* (Los Angeles: Bibliographic Research and Collection Development Unit, Chicano Studies Center, Univ. of California, 1975 [308p.]) (**E368**); and Mario A. Benitez and Lupita G. Villarreal, *The education of the Mexican American: a selected bibliography* (Rosslyn, Va.: National Clearinghouse for Bilingual Education, 1979 [270p.]) (**E369**).

E370 Vivo, Paquita, ed. The Puerto Ricans: an annotated bibliography. New York: Bowker, 1973. 299p.

This well-organized and comprehensive reference book is divided into four parts: 1, Books, pamphlets, and dissertations; 2, Government documents; 3, Periodical literature; 4, Audiovisual materials. Among the many subjects covered are folklore and traditions, language, migration and Puerto Ricans in the United States, population, and sociology. Includes separate subject, author, and title indexes.

Race Relations

E371 Phylon: the Atlanta University review of race and culture. v.1– , 1940– . Founded by W. E. B. duBois.

Although the emphasis is on blacks, this periodical features many articles on race relations, all races.

Several works on race relations in the United States appeared in the mid-1970s. *Bibliography on racism, 1972–1975*, v.2, Rockville, Md.: Dept. of Health, Education, and Welfare, Public Health Service, Alcohol, Drug Abuse, and Mental Health Administration, National Institute of Mental Health, Center for Minority Group Mental Health Programs (Washington, D.C.: dist. by Supt. of Documents, 1978 [various paging]) (**E372**) is an outgrowth of NIMH support of research into racism and mental health. This bibliography contains nearly 2,700 abstracts of books, periodical articles, government publications, and dissertations classified under the following major categories with numerous subcategories: white racism; American-Indians and Alaskan natives; Asian Americans and Pacific Islanders; blacks; and Hispanics. Author and subject indexes.

Constance E. Obudho, *Black-white racial attitudes: an annotated bibliography* (Westport, Conn.: Greenwood, 1976 [180p.]) (**E373**), cites nearly 500 books, articles, and dissertations dealing with racial attitude formation and change in children, racial attitudes in young people, racial attitude change in adults, concomitants of racial attitudes, and racial attitudes in adults. Author and subject indexes.

Francis Paul Prucha, *A bibliographical guide to the history of Indian-white relations in the United States* (Chicago and London: Univ. of Chicago Pr., 1977 [454p.]) (**E374**), totals more than 9,700 entries and is outstanding in depth and breadth of coverage. Even so, some restrictions were necessary owing to the vast amount of material available, e.g., most anthropological works are excluded. This bibliography is in two parts. The first part, Guides to sources, includes materials in the national archives, documents of the federal government, guides to manuscripts, and guides to other sources, e.g., newspapers, oral history, travel accounts, etc. Pt. 2 is a classified bibliography of published works covering many subjects, such as Indian affairs/Indian policy, the Indian Department, military relations, missions and missionaries, Indian education, Indians and Indian groups, to name only a few. Combined author and subject index. Updated by Francis Paul Prucha, *Indian-white relations in the United States: a bibliography of works published 1975–1980* (Lincoln: Univ. of Nebraska Pr., 1982 [179p.]) **(E375)**.

More information on race relations is available in "Race and schools and related topics: a bibliography," a regular feature in *Integrateducation*, v.1– , 1963– (Amherst: Integrated Education Associates, School of Education, Univ. of Massachusetts. Bimonthly) **(E376)**. A bibliography based largely on the bibliographies in earlier volumes of this journal is Meyer Weinberg, ed., *School integration: a comprehensive classified bibliography of 3,100 references* (Chicago: Integrated Education Associates, 1967 [137p.]) **(E377)**. More recent and still larger in scope is Leon Jones, *From Brown to Boston: desegregation in education, 1954–1974*, 2v. (Metuchen, N.J.: Scarecrow, 1979. v.1, Articles and books [1,065p.]; v.2, Legal cases and indexes [p.1,067–2,176]) **(E378)**. V.1 of this sizable bibliography contains annotations for more than 2,800 "articles" broadly defined to include, besides journal articles, such other materials as ERIC documents, pamphlets, and newspaper series, and for more than 400 books. V.2 contains more than 1,750 annotated references to legal materials. Entries in both volumes are arranged chronologically by year. Author-title, legal, and subject indexes.

Race relations in other areas of the world are dealt with in the following bibliographies: Dorothy Keyworth Davies, comp., *Race relations in Rhodesia: a survey for 1972–73* (London: R. Collings, 1975 [458p.]) **(E379)**; Robert M. Levine, *Race and ethnic relations in Latin America and the Caribbean: an historical dictionary and bibliography* (Metuchen, N.J.: Scarecrow, 1980 [252p.]) **(E380)**; Ambala-Vaner Silvanandan, *Coloured immigrants in Britain: a select bibliography*, 2d ed. (London: Institute of Race Relations, 1968 [82p.]) **(E381)**; and James Walvin, *The black presence; a documentary history of the Negro in England, 1555–1860* (New York: Schocken, 1972 [222p.]) **(E382)**.

Women

In an effort to gain bibliographic control over the enormous output of literature about women in the 1970s, numerous bibliographies have appeared. Barbara Haber, *Women in America: a guide to books, 1963–1975, with an appendix on books published 1976–1979* (Urbana: Univ. of Illinois Pr., 1981 [262p.]) **(E383)**, should be useful to educators, librarians trying to build a core collection, college students, and the general public. Covers a wide variety of topics, such as abortion, black women and native American women, crime and imprisonment, feminism, history, law and politics, life-styles, and sex roles. Each topic begins with a short essay. Annotations are often quite extensive and include evaluative remarks. Titles in the appendix are discussed in bibliographic essays. Excluded are fiction, poetry, drama, juvenile literature, highly technical studies, reference books, nonbook material, reprints and "books about women which do not relate to American life." Esther Stineman, *Women's studies: a recommended core bibliography* (Littleton, Colo.: Libraries Unlimited, 1979 [670p.]) **(E384)**, has descriptive and evaluative annotations and includes materials in the humanities as well as social sciences. Elizabeth H. Oakes and Kathleen E. Sheldon, *A guide to social science resources in women's studies* (Santa Barbara, Calif.: American Bibliographic Center–Clio Pr., 1978 [162p.]) **(E385)**, would serve as a good starting point for someone needing evaluations of the literature, especially academics choosing course material. This is a compilation of books, and a collection of articles in journals and books, with emphasis on those with an interdisciplinary and international focus. Arranged by discipline: anthropology, economics, history, psychology, sociology, with an added section on contemporary feminist thought. "The annotations describe the contents and thesis of the resource and critically evaluate it in terms of its use as an undergraduate text." Adequate indexing.

More comprehensive coverage of social science literature is provided in Marie Barovic Rosenberg and Len V. Bergstrom, comps. and eds., *Women and society: a critical review of the literature with selected annotated bibliography* (Beverly Hills, Calif.: Sage, 1975 [354p.]) **(E386)** and JoAnn Delores Een and Marie B. Rosenberg-Dishman, comps. and eds., *Women and society—citations 3601 to 6000: an annotated bibliography* (Beverly Hills, Calif.: Sage, 1978 [277p.]) **(E387)**. In these volumes the authors have tried to select works "that contribute to a general understanding of the economic, political, legal, military, social, moral, religious, educational, scientific, medical, philosophic, literary, and artistic aspects of women's roles in society." Their aim was also to give a cross-national and cross-cultural perspective. Divided into 10 subject categories, some subdivisions, and a special section of general reference works on women. Thorough indexing. Sue-Ellen Jacobs, *Women in perspective: a guide for cross-cultural studies* (Urbana: Univ. of Illinois Pr., 1974 [299p.]) **(E388)**, provides still another very good cross-cultural survey.

According to the author(s) Mei Liang Bickner, *Women at work: an annotated bibliography* (Los Angeles: Institute of Industrial Relations, Univ. of California, 1974) **(E389)**, v.1, and v.2 by the same author with others, *Women at work: an annotated bibliography 1973–1975* (Los Angeles: Institute of Industrial Relations, Univ. of California, 1977) **(E390)**, this bibliography "is intended primarily for persons who teach, conduct research, or are concerned students in the general area of working women"; only "serious studies, refereed journals, government publications, topical reports" and also, in the case of v.2, "court decisions," are included. Each volume contains approximately 600 entries organized by category and then by subcategory. V. 1 surveys post-1960 publications unless there are publications of "major significance" prior to that date, while v.2 contains material published 1973–75. Has separate author, title, category (including titles from other categories if relevant), and subject indexes.

Helen S. Astin and others, *Women: a bibliography on their education and careers* (Washington, D.C.: Human Service Pr., 1971 [243p.]) **(E391)**, abstracts and annotates 350 principal studies.

Albert Krichmar and others, *The women's movement in the seventies: an international English-language bibliography* (Metuchen, N.J.: Scarecrow, 1977 [875p.]) **(E392)**, provides excellent international coverage. "This partially annotated bibliography lists more than 8,600 English-language publications concerning the status of women in nearly 100 countries. . . . The emphasis is on change, attempted change, and continuing problems confronting women in the countries in which they live." Includes books, pamphlets, research reports, periodical articles, government documents, and doctoral dissertations published or reprinted between 1970 and 1976, including many 1976 publications. Time period covered extends from biblical to near present, although most of the material refers to the status of women in the 1970s. About 65 percent of the material deals with the status of women in the United States, the next highest being the United Kingdom with 6 percent. An earlier work by the same author is also worthwhile: *The women's rights movement in the United States 1848–1970: a bibliography and sourcebook* (Metuchen, N.J.: Scarecrow, 1972 [436p.]) **(E393)**.

The chief librarian of the U.S. Commission on Civil Rights, Marija Matich Hughes, has provided a rich lode of information about women in *The sexual barrier: legal, medical, economic and social aspects of sex discrimination* (Washington, D.C.: Hughes Pr., 1977 [843p.]) **(E394)**. Seventeen chapters cover just about every aspect of every topic where sex discrimination is an issue. 8,000 entries, some annotated, list sources from 1960 to 1975, including books, articles, pamphlets, and government documents from the United States, Great Britain, Australia, Canada, and other countries.

Irene Tinker and others, *Women and world development with an annotated bibliography* (New York: Praeger, 1976 [382p.]) **(E395)**, grew out of the American Association for the Advancement of Science seminar on Women in Development held in Mexico City in June 1975. The first half of the book is composed of "essays on selected issues" and proceedings of the seminar; the bibliography in the second half by Marya Buvinić with others focuses on "the effects of socio-economic development and cultural change on women and on women's reactions to these changes." Related works are Ayad Al-Qazzaz, *Women in the Middle East and North Africa: an annotated bibliography* (Austin: Center for Middle Eastern Studies, Univ. of Texas at Austin, 1977 [178p.]) **(E396)**; Kok-Sim Fan, *Women in Southeast Asia: a bibliography* (Boston: Hall, 1982 [415p.]) **(E397)**; Carol Sakala, *Women of South Asia: a guide to resources* (Millwood, N.Y.: Kraus, 1980 [517p.]) **(E398)**; Suzanne Smith Saulniers and Cathy A. Rakowski, *Women in the development process: a select bibliography on women in Sub-Saharan Africa and Latin America* (Austin: Institute of Latin American Studies, Univ. of Texas at Austin, 1977 [287p.]) **(E399)**; and United Nations. Dag Hammerskjold Library. *Status of women: a select bibliography 1965–1975* (White Plains, N.Y.: Unifo, 1976 [121p.]) **(E400)**.

Homosexuals

Vern L. Bullough and others, *An annotated bibliography of homosexuality* (New York: Garland, 1976 [v.1, 405p., v.2, 468p.]) (**E401**), contains more than 12,500 citations on homosexuality in the social sciences and humanities in English- and foreign-language publications. Despite the title, most citations are either unannotated or only very briefly annotated. Includes index of authors. William Parker, *Homosexuality: a selective bibliography of over 3,000 items* (Metuchen, N.J.: Scarecrow, 1971 [323p.]) (**E402**), and *Homosexuality bibliography: supplement, 1970–1975* (Metuchen, N.J.: Scarecrow, 1977 [337p.]) (**E403**) are arranged by type of publication, e.g., books, pamphlets and documents, newspaper articles, etc. Appendixes of *Supplement* list movies, television programs, audiovisual aids, and American laws applicable to consensual adult homosexuals (January 1, 1976). Separate subject and author indexes. Martin S. Weinberg and Alan B. Bell, *Homosexuality: an annotated bibliography* (New York: Harper, 1972 [550p.]) (**E404**), was prepared by the Institute for Sex Research. It contains more than 1,200 items on male and female homosexuality, including books, journal articles, dissertations, theses, and unpublished material in the English language (some translations from foreign journals). Divided into sections: physiological considerations; psychological considerations; sociological considerations; other bibliographies and dictionaries. Works that apply to more than one category are cross-referenced in the main body of the bibliography. Separate author and title indexes.

Communication and Opinion

E405 Blum, Eleanor. Basic books in the mass media: an annotated, selected booklist covering general communications, book publishing, broadcasting, editorial journalism, film, magazines, newspapers, and advertising. 2d ed. Chicago: Univ. of Illinois Pr., 1980. 427p.

Entries in the second, greatly revised edition increased from 665 to 1,179. Most of the new entries were published after April 1971, although a few significant older works were added. Includes many reference books, such as handbooks, directories, bibliographies, etc., and surveys, anthologies, texts, studies, histories. All titles deal with the subject in "broad general terms." Thus "no biographies either personal or institutional, and no books which treat too narrow an aspect of a subject" are included. Provides subject and author-title indexes.

Thomas F. Gordon and Mary Ellen Verna, *Mass communication effects and processes: a comprehensive bibliography, 1950–1975* (Beverly Hills, Calif.: Sage, 1978. [229p.]) (**E406**), presents more than 2,700 unannotated entries arranged alphabetically by author with a subject index.

Donald A. Hansen and J. H. Parsons, *Mass communication: a research bibliography* (Berkeley, Calif.: Glendessary, 1968 [144p.]) (**E407**), picks out 3,000 books, articles, and reports for some two decades from 1945 in an attempt to present as reliable a summary as possible of what was then known about the media and their programs and content, audiences, and social effects.

Reflecting the public interest in the effect of television on children is: Manfred Meyer and Ursula Nissen, comps., *Effects and functions of television: children and adolescents: a bibliography of selected research literature 1970–1978*, rev. ed. (New York: K. G. Saur, 1979 [172p.] [Communication research and broadcasting, no.2]) (**E408**). See also Charles K. Atkin and others, *Television and social behavior: an annotated bibliography on research, focusing on television's impact on children* (Rockville, Md.: National Institute of Mental Health, 1971 [150p.]) (**E409**), which has 550 research studies deemed significant from the standpoint of the Surgeon General's Scientific Advisory Committee on Television and Social Behavior, and annotates about 300 of the most important titles.

Leslie J. Friedman, *Sex role stereotyping in the mass media: an annotated bibliography* (New York and London: Garland, 1977 [324p.]) (**E410**), surveys broadcast media, film, print media, popular culture (e.g., music, comic strips, and books), and children's media for sex role stereotyping. Includes such subjects as advertising, media image of minority group women, media image of men, and impact of media stereotypes on occupational choices.

Ralph E. McCoy, *Freedom of the press: an annotated bibliography* (Carbondale: Southern Illinois Univ. Pr., 1968 [1v. unpaged]) (**E411**), lists some 8,000 books, articles, documents, films, and related materials on freedom of expression in speech, pictures, recordings, and other forms of communication. It is thoroughly indexed. McCoy's *Freedom of the press: a bibliocyclopedia ten-year supplement (1967–1977)* (Carbondale: Southern Illinois Univ. Pr., 1979 [557p.]) (**E412**), is a mammoth bibliography, limited to the English-speaking world, that lists books, pamphlets, journal articles, dissertations, films, and other materials on freedom of the press, broadly defined to include books, newspapers, motion pictures, recordings, radio and television broadcasting, and a few stage plays. The extensive, highly informative annotations make the new title given to the supplement appropriate.

Lynda Lee Kaid and others, *Political campaign communication: a bibliography and guide to the literature* (Metuchen, N.J.: Scarecrow, 1974 [206p.]) **(E413)** lists more than 1,500 books, periodical articles, pamphlets, government publications, and unpublished materials primarily on political campaign communication in the United States from 1950 through 1972, with a brief German and French supplement in order to present some "foreign perspectives on political communication."

A classic work in the area of propaganda is Harold D. Lasswell, *Propaganda and promotional activities: an annotated bibliography*. Ed. by Harold D. Lasswell and others, with a new introduction by Harold D. Lasswell. (Chicago: Univ. of Chicago Pr., 1969 [450p.]) **(E414)**. According to the editors, this work, originally published in 1935, gives "emphasis to the manipulative dimension and to researches having high empirical content."

Propaganda and promotional activities was followed by Bruce L. Smith and others, eds., *Propaganda, communication and public opinion: a comprehensive reference guide* (Princeton, N.J.: Princeton Univ. Pr., 1946 [435p.]) **(E415)**, which presents a classified list of almost 3,000 books and articles selected from the literature for the intervening years, 1934–43, plus a few major items published before 1934. Contains four introductory essays on the "science of mass communications" and, for general readers, 150 outstanding titles on propaganda, communication, and public opinion. The content focuses on propaganda goals and techniques, pressure groups, communication channels and specialists, research problems and methods, and control and censorship. A recent work more limited in scope is Robert Singerman, *Antisemitic propaganda: an annotated bibliography and research guide* (New York: Garland, 1982 [448p.] [Garland reference library of social science, v.112]) **(E416)**. The compiler states that he has tried "to identify, annotate, and locate all pertinent antisemitic books, pamphlets, and tracts published during the past century in the English language."

Robert M. Carter, *Communication in organizations: an annotated bibliography and sourcebook* (Detroit: Gale, 1972 [272p.]) **(E417)**, covers theories and systems of, and barriers to,

organizational communication, vertical and horizontal communication, communication media, informal communication channels, organizational change, and evaluation of the effectiveness of organizational communication. It also lists sourcebooks and articles, addresses of periodicals and publishers cited, and name, title, and subject indexes. Henry Voos, *Organizational communication: a bibliography* (New Brunswick, N.J.: Rutgers Univ. Pr., 1967 [251p.]) **(E418)**, surveys the literature on the transmission of meaning and understanding between and within groups, large and small, and emphasizes the importance of communication in all organized human activities.

An area in which there has been considerable interest among socio-linguists and social psychologists is nonverbal communication. Mary Ritchie Key, *Nonverbal communication: a research guide and bibliography* (Metuchen, N.J.: Scarecrow, 1977 [450p.]) **(E419)**, provides a thorough reference tool in this area.

SOCIAL CHANGE AND INNOVATION

A valuable source of information about social change in the United States is David W. Parish, *Changes in American society, 1960–1978: an annotated bibliography of official government publications* (Metuchen, N.J.: Scarecrow, 1980 [438p.]) **(E420)**, which contains informative annotations for more than 1,000 federal and state publications (mostly monographs) arranged under 34 broad subject categories, some with subcategories. Most entries indicate price or whether the item is free. Five appendixes list pertinent periodicals, out-of-print government publication book dealers, federal and state agency addresses, federal depositories, addresses of state libraries and document sales centers. Author, title, and subject indexes.

Michael Marien, *Societal directions and alternatives: a critical guide to the literature* (Lafayette, N.Y.: Information for Policy Design, 1976 [400p.]) **(E421)**, selected approximately 1,000 items, primarily books, for this guide because they addressed such questions as "Where are we? Where are we headed? What kind of society could we have? What are the possible strategies for achieving the desirable society?" Most entries are annotated, varying in length from very brief to a full page, and are rated for level of audience and quality. For the most part, only nonfiction, English-language books published in the 20th century, and works dealing with the developed nations are included. Updated by *Future survey annual 1979: a guide to the recent literature of trends, forecasts, and policy proposals*, ed. by Michael Marien and Lane Jennings (Washington, D.C.: World Future Society, 1980 [255p.]) **(E422)**. A related work is Mary Lee Bundy, ed., *Guide to the literature of social change*, v.1 (College Park, Md.: Urban Information Interpreters, 1977 [108p.]) **(E423)**; the literature of social change in this case means primarily materials for influencing social change.

A similar purpose is served by American Library Association Social Responsibilities Round Table, *Alternatives in print: an index and listing of some movement publications reflecting today's social change activities* (Columbus: Office of Educational Services, Ohio State Univ. Libraries, 1970–) **(E424)**. This "guide to publications available from non-profit, anti-profit, counter-culture, third-world and movement groups— the freepress" is intended to help "counteract the built-in censorship of the publishing establishment's distribution system." Originally designed to appear annually, latest was 3d ed., 1973. Contains a thesaurus of subject headings, subject index, list of social change publications, including price, and address list of social change publishers.

E425 Frey, Frederick W. and others. Survey research on comparative social change: a bibliography. Cambridge, Mass.: MIT Pr., 1969. Unpaged.

A mine of information produced as an aid to research on developing nations at MIT's Center for International Studies. The fully annotated, classified list of 2,174 entries, drawn from a search of about 250 journals, is liberally cross-referenced. Besides authors, the index includes countries in which surveys have been conducted (more than 100), major topics or groups covered (tribes, castes, etc.), special instruments used, their authors, and conclusions reached.

Garth N. Jones and others, *Planning, development and change: a bibliography on development administration* (Honolulu: East-West Center Pr., 1970 [180p.]) **(E426)** is an interdisciplinary work covering such topics as program budgeting, economic and social development, organizational theory and behavior, social change, etc. Includes a bibliography of bibliographies and supplementary references. Univ. of Minnesota Center for Political Analysis, *Bibliography on planned social change, with special reference to rural development and educational development* (Springfield, Va.: dist. by Natl. Technical Information Service, 1967. 3v. Prepared by the Center for the Agency for Intl. Development

and the Committee for Institutional Cooperation) **(E427)**, provides extensive coverage of the periodical literature (v.1, 636p.), books and book-length monographs (v.2, 204p.), and government reports, UN reports, and proceedings of special conferences (v.3, 184p.).

Eloise G. Requa and Jane Statham, *The developing nations: a guide to information sources concerning their economic, political, technical and social problems* (Detroit: Gale, 1965 [339p.]) **(E428)**, contains a wide range of materials on economic, political, and social development, and trade and development, in underdeveloped areas, together with materials on economic and technical assistance. Other related works are: Karl W. Deutsch and R. L. Merritt, *Nationalism and national development: an interdisciplinary bibliography* (Cambridge, Mass.: MIT Pr., 1970 [519p.]) **(E429)**; H. Kent Geiger, *National development, 1776–1966: a selective and annotated guide to the most important articles in English* (Metuchen, N.J.: Scarecrow, 1969 [247p.]) **(E430)**, and United Nations Economic Commission for Asia and the Far East, *Select annotated bibliography on social aspects of development planning* (1971 [61p.] [E/CN.11/989]) **(E431)**.

Recommended on city planning are: George C. Bestor and Holway R. Jones, *City planning bibliography: a basic bibliography of sources and trends.* 3d ed. (New York: American Society of Civil Engineers, 1972 [518p.]) **(E432)**, which contains more than 1,800 entries, about 75 percent of which are annotated, relating to the nature and form of cities, the history of cities and city planning, contemporary comprehensive planning, education for planning, general bibliographies, selected services, and periodicals in planning and related fields. Provides publishers' addresses. Author and subject indexes. Melville C. Branch, *Comprehensive urban planning: a selected bibliography with related materials* (Beverly Hills, Calif.: Sage, 1977 [477p.]) **(E433)**, focuses "almost entirely on experience, problems, and the future of cities in the United States."

The Council of Planning Librarians, *Exchange bibliography* (Monticello, Ill.: The Council, 1956–78) **(E434)**, includes a number of specialized bibliographies on planning.

Interest in the use of collective action to force change is reflected in Henry Bienen, *Violence and social change: a review of the literature* (Chicago: publ. by Univ. of Chicago Pr. for Adlai Stevenson Institute of Intl. Affairs, 1968 [119p.]) **(E435)**; Jarol B. Manheim and Melanie Wallace, *Political violence in the United States 1875–1974: a bibliography* (New York and London: Garland, 1975 [116p.] [Garland reference library of social science v.8]) (**E436**); and Ronald H. Chilcote, *Revolution and structural change in Latin America: a bibliography on ideology, development, and the radical left* (Stanford, Calif.: Hoover Institution Pr., 1971, 2v.) (**E437**). Relevant studies are also cited in "Collective violence," in American Academy of Political and Social Science, *Annals*, v.391 (Sept. 1970), 264p. (**E438**). *PAIS* lists additional bibliographies under "Violence" after 1964 and under "Force (violence)" before 1964.

Social Problems

Thorough coverage of the literature on drugs is provided in Joseph Menditto, *Drugs of addiction and nonaddiction, their use and abuse: a comprehensive bibliography, 1960–1969* (Troy, N.Y.: Whitston, 1970 [315p.]) (**E439**). Nine supplements have been published. The latest one is Elizabeth Goode, *Drug abuse bibliography for 1978 and 1979* (Troy, N.Y.: Whitston, 1983 [1817p.]) (**E440**); "It is a near complete bibliography of world literature surrounding drug abuse for the years 1978 and 1979" (preface), with a few citations prior to 1978. Theodora Andrews, *A bibliography of drug abuse, including alcohol and tobacco* (Littleton, Colo.: Libraries Unlimited, 1977 [306p.]) (**E441**) and *Supplement 1977–1980*, 1981 [312p.] (**E442**), have a similar focus. The annotations for more than 1,400 entries of the original work and supplement combined are highly informative. Most indicate price. The format of the two volumes is the same. Pt. 1 lists general reference sources. Pt. 2 covers a broad range of subjects. Introduction to the supplement states that the primary purpose of these volumes is "to provide guidance for reference service in all types of libraries, and to help researchers, practitioners, educators, and academic, public, and special librarians to select material from the large number of titles offered." Thorough indexing. A somewhat similar work with respect to U.S. minorities (blacks, Asian Americans, Mexican Americans, Puerto Ricans, and native Americans) is Patti Iiyama and others, *Drug use and abuse among U.S. minorities* (New York: Praeger, 1976 [247p.]) (**E443**).

Also see Eutychia G. Landos, *Compendium of current source materials for drugs* (Metuchen, N.J.: Scarecrow, 1982 [140p.]) (**E444**), which includes general reference materials, dictionaries, encyclopedias, directories, bibliographies and selected reading lists, lists of education, information and treatment centers, journals, newsletters, audiovisual catalogs and indexes, and computers/online data bases. The entries, annotated throughout, may represent "the most authoritative and accepted materials available" (p.i) at the time. Ernest L. Abel, comp., *A comprehensive guide to the cannabis literature* (Westport, Conn.: Greenwood, 1979 [699p.]) (**E445**), contains more than 8,000 entries arranged by author, with subject index. Many foreign journals are cited with titles of articles translated into English. No annotations. Coy W. Waller and others, *Marihuana: an annotated bibliography* (New York: Macmillan Information, a Division of Macmillan Publishing Co., 1976 [560p.]) (**E446**), is devoted to the international technical scientific literature on the subject, with more than 3,000 entries. Separate author and subject indexes. V.2 (New York: Macmillan Information, 1982 [620p.]) (**E447**) covers research from 1975 to 1979.

The international bibliography of studies of alcohol, ed. by Mark Keller, 3v. (New Brunswick, N.J.: Publications Div., Rutgers Center for Alcohol Studies, 1966–79) (**E448**), is intended to serve as a universal bibliographic resource for reports of whatever origin, found to be relevant to alcohol, its uses, and its effects. V.1, *References, 1901–1950*, compiled by Sarah S. Jordy (1966), contains 25,342 numbered entries arranged alphabetically by year of publication; v.2, compiled by Vera Efron and Sarah S. Jordy (1968), is a subject and author index to the basic volume. V.3, *References and indexes, 1951–1960*, was edited by Sarah S. Jordy and others (1979). Henrik Wallgren and Herbert Barry III, *Actions of alcohol* (New York: Elsevier, 1970 [2v.]) (**E449**), provides more selective coverage of the effects of alcohol on the organism, its complex relationship to behavior, and the implications for alcohol programs. More specialized are H. Paul Chalfant and Brent S. Roper, comps., with the assistance of Carmen Rivera-Worley, *Social and behavioral aspects of female alcoholism: an annotated bibliography* (Westport, Conn.: Greenwood, 1980 [145p.]) (**E450**); Grace M. Barnes, *Alcohol and youth: a comprehensive bibliography* (Westport, Conn.: Greenwood, 1982 [452p.]) (**E451**); Grace M. Barnes and others, *Alcohol and the elderly* (Westport, Conn.: Greenwood, 1980 [138p.]) (**E452**); and Patricia D. Mail and David R. McDonald, comps., *Tulapai to Tokay: a bibliography of alcohol use and abuse among native Americans of North America* (New Haven, Conn.: HRAF Pr., 1980 [356p.]) (**E453**).

Edwin D. Driver, *The sociology and anthropology of mental illness: a reference guide* (Amherst: Univ. of Massachusetts Pr., 1965 [146p.]) (**E454**), presents 1,585 contributions in a systematic attempt to "cover the literature on social and cultural aspects of mental illness and its treatment in Europe, Africa, Asia and Latin America as well as in the United States" (preface). Armando R. Favazza and Mary Oman, *Anthropological and cross-cultural themes in mental health: an annotated bibliography, 1925–1974* (Columbia: Univ. of Missouri Pr., 1977 [386p.] [Univ. of Missouri studies LXV]) (**E455**), complements the above. "Driver's book is more inclusive and covers the years 1956–1968, while our book is more exclusive, more anthropologically and cross-culturally oriented, and covers the years 1925–1974." (introduction)

Gale Research Company in one of its Social Issues and Social Problems Information Guide series provides a 1980 bibliography on suicide, see (E171). Anne E. Prentice, *Suicide: a selective bibliography of over 2,200 items* (Metuchen, N.J.: Scarecrow, 1974 [227p.]) (**E456**), lists books; theses and dissertations; articles in books; articles from the popular press and from religious, legal, medical and other scientific journals; literary works; films; tapes; and recordings. With a few exceptions, most of the material was published between 1960 and 1973. Separate author and subject indexes. The Suicide Prevention Center, Los Angeles, *Bibliography on suicide and suicide prevention* (Chevy Chase, Md.: National Institute of Mental Health; dist. by Supt. of Documents, 1969 [203p.], [Public Health Service Publication no.1,979]) (**E457**), has more than 3,000 selected items, which go back to 1897, the date of Émile Durkheim's monumental *Suicide: a study in sociology*, tr. by John A. Spaulding and George Simpson (E7), originally published with bibliographical footnotes in 1897.

Dorothy Pearl Wells, *Child abuse: an annotated bibliography* (Metuchen, N.J.: Scarecrow, 1980 [450p.]) (**E459**), and Beatrice J. Kalisch, *Child abuse and neglect: an annotated bibliography* (Westport, Conn.: Greenwood, 1978 [535p.] [Contemporary problems of childhood, no.2]) (**E460**), reflect the recent volume of literature on this subject. The citations from Wells (more than 2,400) and Kalisch (more than 2,000) are mainly from the 1960s and 1970s, though both contain a few earlier works (Kalisch dating back to the late 1800s). Both contain references to books, journal articles, dissertations, government publications, pamphlets, and miscellaneous publications. Wells includes some nonbook materials such as videocassettes, films, and a few foreign-language publications. All citations in Kalisch

are in English. Both include studies of causes, physical and psychological abuse, medical and legal aspects, and many other related topics. See also N. A. Polansky and others, *Child neglect: an annotated bibliography* (Washington, D.C.: U.S. Dept. of Health, Education, and Welfare, Social and Rehabilitation Service, Community Services Administration, 1976? [90p.]) (**E461**); *Child abuse and neglect audiovisual materials* (Washington, D.C.: Natl. Center on Child Abuse and Neglect; dist. by Supt. of Documents, 1980 [92p.]) (**E462**) and Benjamin Schlesinger, *Sexual abuse of children: a resource guide and annotated bibliography* (Toronto and Buffalo: Univ. of Toronto Pr., 1982 [200p.]) (**E463**). For more information on child abuse, see Psychology chapter.

Elizabeth Jane Kemmer, *Rape and rape-related issues: an annotated bibliography* (New York: Garland, 1977 [174p.] [Garland reference library of social science v.39]) (**E464**), contains about 350 references primarily from legal, medical, social science, and popular journals, and a few books and newspaper articles, published between 1965 and 1976. Subject index. Similar in scope is Dorothy L. Barnes, *Rape: a bibliography, 1965–1975* (Troy, N.Y.: Whitston, 1977 [154p.]) (**E465**), which lists books and periodical articles. Author index. Carolyn F. Wilson, *Violence against women: an annotated bibliography* (Boston: Hall, 1981 [111p.]) (**E466**), includes works about battered women, rape, sexual abuse of children, and pornography published mainly between 1975 and August 1980.

Maureen Muldoon, *Abortion: an annotated indexed bibliography* (New York: E. Mellen Pr., 1980 [151p.] [Studies in women and religion, 3]) (**E467**), contains about 3,400 entries, some of which are annotated, listed under such categories as bibliographies; ethical, theological, medical, social, and legal aspects of abortion; abortion studies in the states and in other countries; collected articles; and symposia proceedings. Additional material is contributed by Mary K. Floyd, *Abortion bibliography for 1970–* (Troy, N.Y.: Whitston, 1972– . Annual.) (**E468**), who cites books, government documents, and periodical articles dealing with abortion. Subject and author indexes. Charles Dollen, *Abortion in context: a select bibliography* (Metuchen, N.J.: Scarecrow, 1970 [150p.]) (**E469**), covers books and articles from 1967 to 1969 dealing with social as well as medical aspects of the problem.

Many sources are available on the topic of poverty. A recent work is Sharon M. Oster and others, *The definition and measurement of pov-*

erty, 2v. (Boulder, Colo.: Westview, 1978) **(E470)**. V. 1, which reviews the field, is divided into 12 chapters, each dealing with a separate topic, e.g., "historical definitions of poverty: an overview," "wealth/assets and consumption as measures of poverty," "determinants of the turnover rates of poor families," "social indicators," etc. V. 2, an annotated bibliography, indicates the chapter(s) of v.1 that refer to each entry. Dorothy Tompkins, *Poverty in the United States during the sixties: a bibliography* (Berkeley: Univ. of California Institute of Government, 1970 [542p.]) **(E471)**, treats poverty as the gap or disadvantage between people's daily life and their potential. U.S. Social Security Administration, *Poverty studies in the sixties: a selected annotated bibliography* (Washington, D.C.: Govt. Print. Off., 1970 [126p.]) **(E472)**, takes a broad view of poverty, relating it to other economic problems (housing, unemployment) and to education. *Culturally disadvantaged: a bibliography and Keyword-Out-of-Context (KWOC) index*, by Robert E. Booth and others (Detroit: Wayne State Univ. Pr., 1967 [803p.]) **(E473)**, indexes 1,400 books, research reports, microfiche, and other materials on the culturally and economically deprived, with strong emphasis on educational problems. The compilers provide "between 10 and 25 keywords or descriptors for each bibliographical item" to facilitate retrieval. It has indexes under subject headings and authors. Benjamin Schlesinger, *Poverty in Canada and the United States: overview and annotated bibliography* (Toronto: Univ. of Toronto Pr., 1966 [211p.]) **(E474)**, presents separate critical overviews of Canadian and American remedial programs, followed by selected policy, research, and popular contributions to the literature between 1960 and 1966. The Canadian Welfare Council, *Poverty: an annotated bibliography and references* (Ottawa: 1966 [136p.]) **(E475)**, and its four supplements (1967–69), cite and abstract about 2,000 books, articles, speeches, etc., featuring Canadian research reports and community action programs. J. Wayne Flynt and Dorothy S. Flynt, *Southern poor whites: a selected annotated bibliography of published sources* (New York: Garland, 1981 [320p.] [Garland reference library of social science, v.88]) **(E476)**, gives greatest weight to general reference sources and materials related to economics and folk culture; other topics covered include education, health, migration/urbanization, mountain poor whites, politics, race relations, religion, and women.

Howard M. Bahr, ed., *Disaffiliated man: essays and bibliography on skid row, vagrancy,*

and outsiders (Toronto: Univ. of Toronto Pr., 1970 [428p.]) **(E477)**, consists of an annotated list of items on the alienated and homeless, and contains 3 short interpretive essays.

Kenneth Keniston's very selective bibliography of approximately 300 items, *Radicals and militants: an annotated bibliography of empirical research on campus unrest* (Lexington, Mass.: D. C. Heath, Lexington Books, 1973 [415p.]) **(E478)** presents only studies done after 1945 that "report new findings on young American activists or radicals; or on the institutions where protests have occurred." Each entry includes "setting," "subjects" or "institutions," "methods," "results," and "comments" and is ranked by the author as to its importance. The annotated bibliography in U.S. President's Commission on Campus Unrest, *Campus unrest: the report*, p.467–518 (Washington, D.C.: Govt. Print. Off., 1970) **(E479)**, indicates the sources of the report and presents additional literature on campus unrest and related issues.

Helga Lende, *Books about the blind: a bibliographical guide to literature relating to the blind* (new rev. ed.; New York: American Foundation for the Blind, 1953 [357p.]) **(E480)**, contains more than 4,000 older citations on problems of the blind, programs of aid, literature and reading, biographies, and autobiographies. Mary Kinsey Bauman, comp., *Blindness, visual impairment, deaf-blindness: annotated listing of the literature, 1953–1975* (Philadelphia: Temple Univ. Pr., 1976 [537p.]) **(E481)**, updates the Lende work.

Richard L. Oram, *Transportation system management: bibliography of technical reports* (Washington, D.C.: Dept. of Transportation, Urban Mass Transportation Administration, Office of Policy and Program Development; for sale by National Technical Information Service, Springfield, VA 22161, 1976 [149p.]) **(E482)**, lists 150 "readily obtainable technical reports on operational transportation improvements." The U.S. Urban Mass Transportation Administration requested the preparation of Dawn E. Willis' *Urban mass transportation: a bibliography* (Washington, D.C.: Library Service Div., Office of Administrative Operations, Dept. of Transportation, 1971 [133p.] [Bibliographic list no. 6]) **(E483)**. It surveys research on transportation and related problems, new management procedures, and development of new systems and new applications for existing systems. The major older contributions are listed, but it is devoted mainly to the literature from 1960 to mid-1970. A complementary source is U.S. Urban Mass Transportation Administration, *An urban transporta-*

tion bibliography (Washington, D.C.: Govt. Print. Off., 1971 [109p.]) **(E484)**.

Deviant Behavior and Social Disorganization

Edward F. Mickolus, *The literature of terrorism: a selectively annotated bibliography* (Westport, Conn.: Greenwood, 1980 [553p.]) **(E485)**, provides a broad survey of the literature on terrorism with nearly 3,900 citations mainly to English-language sources. Entries are listed under geographic headings and topical headings such as tactics of terrorists, terrorist and guerrilla philosophies, state terrorism, media and terrorism, psychological and medical approaches to terrorism, fiction, bibliographies. Author and title indexes. More modest in scope is Augustus R. Norton and Martin H. Greenberg, *International terrorism: an annotated bibliography and research guide* (Boulder, Colo.: Westview, 1980 [218p.]) **(E486)**, which contains more than 1,000 entries and is also arranged in topical and geographic sections. An appendix lists a few core works for building a library on the subject of terrorism. Author index. The National Institute of Law Enforcement and Criminal Justice of the U.S. Department of Justice's LEAA has issued three annotated bibliographies on terrorism, all compiled by Guy D. Boston, two with associates: *Terrorism: a selected bibliography*, 1976 [45p.] **(E487)**; 2d ed., 1977 [62p.] **(E488)**; *Supplement to the second edition*, 1977 [63p.] **(E489)**; dist. by Govt. Print. Off.

Thomas F. Parker, ed., *Violence in the U.S.*, v.1, 1956–67; v.2, 1968–71 (New York: Facts On File, 1974) **(E490)**, consists of short articles chronicling major events of violence in the United States taken largely from earlier Facts On File publications. Marvin E. Wolfgang and Franco Ferracuti, *The subculture of violence: towards an integrated theory in criminology*, tr. from the Italian (London: Tavistock, 1967 [387p.]) **(E491)**, is a comprehensive analysis of the earlier literature by two internationally known criminologists. A related work of more recent date is Marvin E. Wolfgang and others, *The violent offender in the criminal justice system: a selected bibliography* (Washington, D.C.: U.S. Dept. of Justice, National Institute of Justice, 1982 [148p.]) **(E492)**.

Martin Wright, ed., *Use of criminology literature* (Hamden, Conn.: Archon Books, 1974 [242p.]) **(E493)**, provides a retrospective overview of the literature. Each chapter, beginning with "conducting a search for information in criminology," discusses the literature on a particular topic. Many categories are covered such as "sociological aspects of criminology," "alcoholism and crime—an introductory bibliography," "introduction to the literature of drug dependence," etc. Includes U.S. and British publications. Isabella Hopkins and others, comps., *Organized crime: a selected bibliography* (Austin: Criminal Justice Reference Library, Univ. of Texas School of Law, 1973 [99p.]) **(E494)**, covers general works, criminal organizations, organized crime involvement, organized crime control and prevention, and reference materials. Marvin E. Wolfgang and others, *Criminology index: research and theory in criminology in the United States, 1945–1972*, 2v. (New York: Elsevier, 1975) **(E495)**, is a major reference tool citing more than 3,000 articles and about 550 books or reports relating primarily to the "etiology of crime and delinquency published since 1945." Subjects not included are administration of justice, the police, courts, and corrections. Composed of three kinds of indexes: source document, paired-word subject, and criminology citation. The latter indicates where a work has been cited. For information on the administration of justice, see Sir Leon Radzinowicz and Roger Hood, *Criminology and the administration of justice: a bibliography* (Westport, Conn.: Greenwood, 1976 [400p.]) **(E496)**. "Our focus on criminology has been predominantly sociological rather than psychiatric and our interest in criminal justice and penology more concerned with issues of policy and the results of research than with day-to-day practical matters" (introduction). Most materials listed are English-language, a few are foreign, from the mid-1950s up to February 1976. A special work on the Soviet Union is provided by Peter H. Solomon, *Soviet criminology: a selected bibliography* (Cambridge: The Institute of Criminology, 1969 [55p.] [Bibliographical series, no.4]) **(E497)**.

Dorothy C. Tompkins, *The prison and the prisoner* (Berkeley: Univ. of California, 1972 [156p.] [Public policy bibliographies, no.1]) **(E498)**, contains nearly 1,100 references to journal and newspaper articles, government publications, etc., on the prison, state and federal prisons, administration of prisons, the prisoner, and proposals for prison reform. Index. Related works are Daniel Suvak, *Memoirs of American prisons: an annotated bibliography* (Metuchen, N.J.: Scarecrow, 1979 [227p.]) **(E499)**, and Keith Hawkins, *Parole: a select bibliography with spe-*

cial reference to American experience (Cambridge: The Institute of Criminology, 1969 [71p.] [Bibliographical series, no.3]) (**E500**).

Social Policy

An increasing number of scholars are concerned with the social implications of such bioethical issues as euthanasia, psychosurgery, human experimentation, genetic engineering, abortion, the definition of death, medical confidentiality, and the allocation of scarce medical resources. A huge compendium of English-language materials on such matters was compiled in the mid-1970s; LeRoy Walters, ed., *Bibliography of bioethics*, v.1, 225p.; v.2, 282p.; v.3, 348p.; v.4, 419p. (Detroit: Gale, 1975–78) (**E501**). Includes subject entry section, title and author indexes and bioethics thesaurus. *The bulletin of the atomic scientists*, v.1– , 1945– (Chicago: Educational Foundation for Nuclear Science [10/yr.]) (**E502**), has a long record of contributing to the debate on social policy issues relating to science and technology. Charles W. Triche III and Diane Samson Triche provide thorough coverage of a single issue in *The euthanasia controversy, 1812–1974: a bibliography with select annotations* (Troy, N.Y.: Whitston, 1975 [242p.]) (**E503**). It includes more than 1,350 references to books, essays, and periodicals, including newspaper articles and a few foreign publications. Author index.

U.S. Social Security Administration, *Basic readings in social security* (Washington, D.C.: Govt. Print. Off., 1970 [181p.]) (**E504**), is a partially annotated selection of books, articles, reports, and pamphlets on the history and features of U.S. social security and related programs. There are additional chapters on the social security programs of other nations, statistical publications, and bibliographies. Author index.

Ronald G. Havelock, *Bibliography on knowledge utilization and dissemination* (Ann Arbor: Univ. of Michigan Center for Research on Utilization of Scientific Knowledge, 1972 [239p.]) (**E505**), is one of the products of a program directed toward closing the gap between the advancement of knowledge and application of it.

Social Services

E506 Conrad, James H. Reference sources in social work: an annotated bibliography. Metuchen, N.J.: Scarecrow, 1982. 201p.

Covers works published between 1970 and early 1980 in such areas as history of social work, allied fields, fields of service, service methods, and the social work profession. Reference sources in social work as well as related disciplines, e.g., sociology, psychology, psychiatry, health care, public administration and criminology, are included. Appendixes provide lists of social work journals, social service organizations and social work libraries. Author, title, and subject indexes.

E507 Social service review: forty-year index, v.1–40, 1927–66. Chicago: Univ. of Chicago Pr., 1968. 172p. (Also Social service review 42:1–172 [1968])

This 3-part index covers much of the germinal thought of the 40-year period during which social work became well established. The parts consist of (1) an annotated list, by author, of articles and dissertation abstracts; (2) subject index of articles, notes and comments, and source materials; and (3) index, by author, of all books and official publications covered by the book review section. A coding system makes it easy to spot all contributions in a subdivision of the field.

E508 Patti, Rino J., comp., with the assistance of Phillip Osborne. Management practice in social welfare: an annotated bibliography. New York: Council on Social Work Education, 1976. 107p.

This thoroughly annotated "bibliography of current literature on social welfare administration . . . aims to provide an understanding of social welfare institutions and the forces that shape their direction and growth" (foreword). Culled from more than 2,000 potential sources are the most "highly pertinent" journal articles (384), books (235), monographs, and pamphlets published from 1965 to 1974. No index.

E509 Zimpfer, David G. Group work in the helping professions: a bibliography. Rochester, N.Y.: Univ. of Rochester Pr., 1976. 452p.

This publication, photo-offset from typescript, is a thorough unannotated bibliography on group work, including books, journal articles, dissertations, and unpublished documents. The president (1975–76) of the Association for Specialists in Group Work, a division of the American Personnel and Guidance Association, comments (opposite title page): "For the author, David Zimpfer, it represents a commitment over the last decade to assemble the most comprehensive printed bibliography available in the area of Group Work." Author index.

E510 Li, Hong-Chan. Social work education: a bibliography. Metuchen, N.J.: Scarecrow, 1978. 341p.

Tries to bring "together in one volume extensive sources of references in various forms on a wide range of issues in social work education," primarily in academic settings, and to classify "them as precisely as possible according to the subject matter." Includes about 3,000 unannotated references with some duplicate entries. Comprehensive coverage after 1960 and selected coverage prior to that date. Author index.

E511 Atkins, Jacqueline Marx, comp. Audiovisual resources for population education and family planning: an international guide for social work educators. New York: Intl. Assn. of Schools of Social Work, 1975. 148p.

Provides a brief introductory chapter on audiovisual equipment and its uses, and an annotated list of more than 200 audiovisual "aids," e.g., films, filmstrips, slides, transparencies, multimedia kits, etc., which should serve as a beginning guide for social work educators throughout the world in the classroom and on the job. Entries describe subject matter and indicate type of media, languages in which it is available, length of time and country or region of concern (when applicable), price (when known), and source. Includes a selected bibliography and 2 appendixes: addresses of sources for audiovisual materials and addresses of distributors of audiovisual equipment. Alphabetical title and topic indexes.

E512 Mental Health Materials Center, Inc., New York. A selective guide to materials for mental health and family life education. New York: The Center; dist. by Gale, 1976. 947p.

PERIODICALS

E513 Sussman, Marvin B., ed. Author's guide to journals in sociology and related fields. New York: Haworth Pr., 1978. 214p.

Designed to help sociologists and social scientists cope with the "publish or perish" dilemma by providing them with pertinent information about English-language journals selected mainly from *Sociological abstracts* and the 1976 edition of Ulrich's *International periodical directory*. Includes such information as "type of articles," "major content areas," "topics preferred," "inappropriate topics," "authorship restrictions," "style requirements," etc.

E514 Wepsiec, Jan. Sociology: an international bibliography of serial publications, 1880–1980. London: Mansell; dist. by Wilson, 1983. 183p.

Lists alphabetically by title about 2,300 serials published worldwide in sociology and related disciplines, with information as to where they are abstracted or indexed.

DIRECTORIES AND BIOGRAPHICAL INFORMATION

E515 American Sociological Assn. Directory of members, 1950– . Washington, D.C.: The Association. Annual.

Title varies. The 1980 directory listed about 14,000 members, more than 9,000 of whom were full members. Contains both an alphabetical list of members, with their preferred mailing addresses and section memberships in the association, and a geographical list.

E516 Guide to graduate departments of sociology. Washington, D.C.: American Sociological Assn. Annual.

The 1983 directory lists about 250 institutions, including a few foreign ones, with graduate departments of sociology. For each one, includes such information as name of person chairing the department, degree(s) offered, 1982–83 tuition, application deadlines, number of students admitted over 3-year period, graduate student enrollment, number of degrees granted, specialties, list of faculty members, and PhD's awarded in preceding year.

E517 Internationales Soziologen Lexikon, hrsg. von Wilhelm Bernsdorf. Stuttgart: F. Enke, 1959. 662p.

A companion volume to *Wörterbuch der Soziologie* (E558), this biographical dictionary lists more than 1,000 sociologists or those whose work is closely connected with sociological knowledge in a broad sense. International in scope. Includes the "founders" of sociology (Condorcet, Comte, Smith) as well as 20th-century sociologists. Each entry has (1) a brief biographical sketch, (2) analysis of the person's work and appraisal of the importance of its contribution to sociology, and (3) a listing of the titles and dates of principal works by and about each person. Each entry is signed by one of the 50 cooperating specialists. No index.

Demography

E518 Population: an international directory of organizations and information resources. Ed. by Thaddeus C. Trzyna and Joan Dickson Smith. Claremont, Calif.: Public Affairs Clearing House, 1976. 132p.

Lists intergovernmental organizations, international nongovernmental organizations, U.S. organizations, Canadian organizations, and organizations of other countries concerned with population and family planning, and provides information about their programs and activities, key personnel, and publications. Includes a bibliography, and organization and subject indexes.

Youth

E519 National children's directory: an organizational directory and reference guide for changing conditions for children and youth. Ed. by Mary Lee Bundy and Rebecca Glenn Whaley. College Park, Md.: Urban Information Interpreters, 1977. 303p.

E520 National directory of children and youth services: the reference handbook for professionals. Comp. by the eds. of Child Protection Report. Washington, D.C.: CPR Directory Services Co., 1979. 538p.

Aged and Aging

E521 A directory of resources for aging, gerontology, and retirement. Ed. by Charles Steube. Mankato: Minnesota Scholarly Pr., 1979. 211p.

E522 The emerging aging network: a directory of state and area agencies on aging. Comp. by the Select Committee on Aging, House of Representatives, Ninety-Fifth Congress, Second Session. Washington, D.C.: Govt. Print. Off., 1978. 132p. [Comm. Pub., No. 95–166.]

Urban Affairs

E523 National Assn. of Housing and Redevelopment Officials. NAHRO directory. Washington, D.C.: The Association, 1976– .

The 1976 directory lists more than 6,000 housing and redevelopment programs in the United States.

E524 Urban needs: a bibliography and directory for community resource centers, by Paula Kline. Metuchen, N.J.: Scarecrow, 1978. 257p.

"This bibliography is a resource for materials providing information on programs, services, organizations, agencies and individuals involved in the areas of education, employment, housing, community development, consumer protection, legal services, health care, recreation, social services and the information services provided by libraries, private organizations and government agencies" (introduction). Lists and describes hundreds of directories and handbooks relevant to sociology.

Ethnic Groups and Minorities

E525 Minority organizations: a national directory. 2d ed. Ed. by Katherine W. Cole. Garrett Park, Md.: Garrett Park Pr., 1982. 814p.

E526 Directory of special programs for minority group members: career information services, employment skills banks, financial aid sources: with an additional section on employment assistance services for women. 2d ed. Ed. by Willis L. Johnson. Garrett Park, Md.: Garrett Park Pr., 1975. 400p.

E527 Encyclopedic directory of ethnic organizations in the United States, by Lubomyr R. Wynar and others. Littleton, Colo.: Libraries Unlimited, 1975. 414p.

For each organization, includes address, principal officers, date founded, membership, scope (i.e., local, state, regional, national, international), publications, major conventions/meetings, comments about the purpose of the organization, and so forth.

Black Americans

E528 In black and white: a guide to magazine articles, newspaper articles, and books concerning more than 15,000 black individuals and groups. 3d ed.

Ed. by Mary Mace Spradling. Detroit: Gale, 1980. 2v.

Includes index of occupations and bibliography.

E529 Who's who among black Americans, 1976– . Northbrook, Ill.: Who's Who Among Black Americans, Inc.

The third edition, published in 1981, contains more than 16,000 biographical entries. Criteria for inclusion are based on "1) the position of responsibility held and 2) the level of significant achievement attained in a career of meritorious activity." Provides standard biographical data, e.g., profession, date and place of birth, members of family, education, accomplishments, address, etc. Geographic index and occupational index.

E530 Who's who in colored America: an illustrated biographical directory of notable living persons of African descent in the United States. 1927–50. Yonkers, N.Y.: Christian E. Burckel & Associates. Irregular.

Title and publisher vary. Contains biographical summaries for leaders (men and women) in all walks in which blacks gained prominence. With portraits. The 7 volumes in the series appeared in 1927, 1929, 1932, 1937, 1939, 1942, and 1950.

E531 Black list: the concise reference guide to publications and broadcasting media of black America, Africa and the Caribbean. New York: Panther, 1971. 289p. Looseleaf.

Gives addresses and principal officers of organizations concerned with publications and news. Afro-American section includes newspapers, periodicals, broadcasting stations, colleges and universities, publishers, book clubs, bookstores, advertising and public relations, literary agents. A similar grouping in the Africa and Caribbean section includes embassies and permanent missions to the United Nations.

E532 Race Relations Information Center. Directory of Afro-American resources. Ed. by Walter Schatz. New York: Bowker, 1970. 485p.

Directory of more than 2,000 U.S. institutions and organizations (public and private) and their approximately 5,350 collections of material that bear on the career of black Americans. Emphasis is on collections of primary sources. Includes bibliography, mostly of reference works (p.347–56); a main index of subjects, persons, places, and institutions; and a separate index of supervisory personnel.

Women

E533 Who's who and where in women's studies. Ed. by Tamar Burkowitz and others. Old Westbury, N.Y.: Feminist Pr., 1974. 308p.

From 1969 to 1974, women's studies programs grew from 2 to 112, and women's studies courses from 100 to more than 4,650. This directory lists women's studies courses in three ways: (1) colleges and universities; (2) faculty; (3) departments. Also lists schools offering women's studies programs.

E534 Women helping women: a state-by-state directory of services. New York: Women's Action Alliance; dist. by Neal Schuman, 1981. 179p.

Provides addresses and phone numbers for battered women and rape victim services, career counseling services, displaced homemaker programs, planned parenthood clinics, skilled trades training centers, women's centers, women's commissions, and women's health centers.

E535 Women's organizations and leaders directory, 1975–1976. Ed. by Myra E. Barrer. First intl. ed. Washington, D.C.: Today Publications and News Service, 1975. Irregular paging.

Contains five indexes: alphabetical, geographical, periodical (by title and by publisher), and subject. Each listing in the indexes refers to an entry number. The "text" provides descriptive information for more than 10,000 numbered entries representing more than 110 countries.

Social Problems

E536 American Correctional Assn. Directory of juvenile and adult correctional departments, institutions, agencies and paroling authorities, United States and Canada, 1955– . College Park, Md.: The Association.

Title varies. Most recent edition, 1975–76, describes the organization and administration of correctional and parole agencies, including those associated with federal and military facilities. Gives addresses of state law enforcement planning agencies.

E537 Directory of agencies serving the visually handicapped in the United States. 1926– . New York: American Foundation for the Blind. Biennial.

Title varies. Lists agencies and schools serving the visually handicapped.

Deviant Behavior

E538 Guerrilla and terrorist organisations: a world directory and bibliography. By Peter Janke. New York: Macmillan, 1983. 550p.

Describes nearly 550 terrorist organizations throughout the world, including their origins, ideology, makeup, activities, successes, or failures. Contains annotated bibliographies for each country.

Social Services

E539 Public welfare directory: 1979–80. Ed. by Michele Moore. Chicago: American Public Welfare Assn., 1979. 421p.

The 40th annual directory lists agencies and key personnel for all federal, state, territorial, county and major municipal public welfare agencies and related human service agencies, Canadian agencies, and international social services. Some descriptive material about agencies, programs, and services. Provides addresses and telephone numbers and where to write for specific requests.

E540 NASW professional social workers' directory. Washington, D.C.: Natl. Assn. of Social Workers, 1978. 1,733p.

Triple column listing of the names and addresses of the nearly 80,000 members of the NASW.

E541 NASW register of clinical social workers, 1976 edition; 1977 supplement. Washington, D.C.: National Assn. of Social Workers, 1976–77.

First ed. plus supplement. Provides such information as specialization, address, education, experience, and, if applicable to the state, certification.

E542 Schools of social work with accredited master's programs. New York: Council on Social Work Education, 1974. 19p. (Formerly Graduate professional schools of social work in Canada and the U.S.A.)

E543 Intl. Assn. of Schools of Social Work. IASSW directory: member schools and associations. New York: The Association, n.d.

Title and publisher vary.

E544 Social service organizations and agencies directory: a reference guide to national and regional social service organizations, including advocacy groups, voluntary associations, professional societies, federal and state agencies, clearinghouses and information centers. Comp. and ed. by Anthony T. Kruzas. Detroit: Gale, 1982. 525p.

E545 World guide to social work education. Comp. by Patricia J. Stickney and Rosa Perla Resnick. New York: International Assn. of Schools of Social Work, 1974. 297p.

E546 Directory of agencies: U.S. voluntary, international voluntary, intergovernmental. Washington, D.C: National Assn. of Social Workers, 1980. 104p.

E547 Family Service Assn. of America. Directory of member agencies. 1910?– . New York: The Association. Annual.

Lists accredited and provisional member agencies in U.S. and Canadian cities. For each entry provides agency name, address, executive director, and information on areas served by the agency.

E548 Helping others: a guide to selected social service agencies and occupations. Comp. and ed. by Norma Haimes. New York: Day, 1974. 208p.

The guide's "basic purpose is to describe the wide variety of agencies and occupations that exist whose goals are to ameliorate or eradicate the social problems that confront us today." Lists 74 private agencies, 27 federal agencies, and 44 state agencies and, for each, provides the following: statement about nature and purpose, occupation information (brief job description, experience and education required, salary range, etc.), where to write for futher information, and relevant bibliography titles. Includes bibliography, function index, and occupation index.

DICTIONARIES

E549 Hoult, Thomas Ford. Dictionary of modern sociology. Totowa, N.J.: Littlefield, 1969. 408p. Pbk. reprint, 1977.

Terms are arranged alphabetically, with definitions varying in length from a couple of lines to about half a page. Most definitions are accompanied by one or two illustrative quotations. Provides several lists of entries classified in terms of specialties; social organization, structure, and institutions; social problems, social disorganization; social psychology; other sociology and related; anthropology; and psychology. Lists works and authors cited.

E550 Theodorson, George A., and A. G. Theodorson. A modern dictionary of sociology. New York: Crowell, 1969. 469p.

Lacks the depth achieved by more restricted lists (e.g., E551) but has two advantages: it brings much of the nomenclature together in one place, and it provides brief definitions—too brief at times for precision, but beginners will find most of them helpful.

E551 Mitchell, Geoffrey D. A dictionary of sociology. Chicago: Aldine, 1968. 224p.

Includes about 300 terms too technical to be defined adequately by general dictionaries. Usually provides short description or definition, followed by historical reference to its uses, and (where possible) citation of works to put the term in context. Length ranges from a sentence or two to 2 or 3 pages. A number of biographical sketches of deceased sociologists are included. Longer entries are initialed, with contributors listed at front.

E552 La sociologie: les idées, les oeuvres, les hommes. Paris: Centre d'Etude et de Promotion de la Lecture, 1970. 544p.

Combines in a single volume features of a lexicon, biographical dictionary, bibliography, and handbook of learning. Ten articles of encyclopedic scope are arranged alphabetically together with definitions of 500 terms and short biographies of social thinkers since Comte. Footnotes and biographical sketches cite references to major contributions to the literature. Other reference features are tables ("Evolution of sociological thought," p.12–15), statistics ("Sociology of education," p.138–39), and numerous portraits.

E553 Abrams, Charles. The language of the cities: a glossary of terms. New York: Viking, 1971. 365p.

Definitions of urban terms range in length from a paragraph to more than a page, and are intended to aid expert and layperson alike. Emphasis is on American terminology, though an occasional foreign term is included.

E554 Interdisciplinary glossary on child abuse and neglect: legal, medical, social work terms. Washington, D.C.: Natl. Center on Child Abuse and Neglect; dist. by Supt. of Documents, 1978. 100p.

E555 Rush, George Eugene. Dictionary of criminal justice. Boston: Holbrook Pr., 1977. 374p.

"Combines the medical, legal, forensic, sociological, anthropological, psychological, and selected management terms *commonly* used in the broad interdisciplinary field of criminal justice" (preface).

E556 Elsevier's dictionary of criminal science in eight languages. Comp. and arranged on an English alphabetical base by Johann A. Adler. New York: Elsevier, 1960. 1,460p.

A multilingual glossary that covers criminal law, criminology, and criminalistics, as well as auxiliary sciences. Pt. 1 consists of 10,930 English/American terms, with indication of British or American usage and field of application (e.g., law, medicine, psychology, etc.) and translations into French, Italian, Spanish, Portuguese, Dutch, Swedish, and German. Pt. 2 is made up of alphabetical glossaries for each language above, with references to pt. 1.

ENCYCLOPEDIAS AND ENCYCLOPEDIC SETS

General

E557 Encyclopedia of sociology. Guilford, Conn.: Dushkin, 1974. 330p.

Contains 1,300 short articles alphabetically arranged and tied together by "see" and "see also" references. Historical as well as contemporary theories, institutions, leading figures, and events are included.

E558 Wörterbuch der Soziologie. 2. neubearb. u. erw. ausg. Bernsdorf, Wilhelm, and others. Stuttgart: Enke, 1969. 1,317p.

The 2d ed. is alphabetically arranged and treats major topics at length, with cross-references from smaller ones. Best described as a 1-volume encyclopedia, it is double the size of the 1955 edition, summarizes knowledge under bout 500 broad headings, and gives close attention to the literature and the evolution of sociological thought. Articles are signed by 165 contributors from 20 countries.

Ethnic Groups and Minorities

E559 Harvard encyclopedia of American ethnic groups. Ed. by Stephan Thernstrom and others. Cambridge, Mass.: Belknap, 1980. 1,076p.

This unique encyclopedia contains 106 entries (criteria for selection of ethnic groups are described in introduction), 29 thematic essays, 87 maps, and other supplementary material. Entries vary in length according to "estimated size of the group, the length and complexity of its history in the United States and the availability and nature of source material" (introduction). The 120 contributors, whom the editors describe as the most qualified individuals available, include historians, anthropologists, political scientists, geographers, economists, sociologists, and humanists.

E560 Encyclopedia of black America, Ed. by W.Augustus Low and Virgil A. Clift. New York: McGraw-Hill, 1981. 921p.

About 90 "scholars and authorities in many diversified fields and specialties" contributed to this work. Entries vary in length from a paragraph to more than 50 pages. Lengthier entries, such as for Afro-American history, education, and literature, often include a cluster of articles. Many entries are illustrated, and some provide statistical tables.

Social Problems and Deviant Behavior

E561 Encyclopedia of bioethics. 4v. Ed. by Warren T. Reich. New York: Free Pr., 1974. 1,933p.

Age-old issues as well as new ones created by modern technology are discussed in this encyclopedia, the first of its kind, which contains more than 300 essays written by highly qualified scholars. Each article includes a substantial bibliography of key sources. Appendix of codes and statements related to medical ethics.

E562 The concise encyclopedia of crime and criminals. Ed. by Harold R. Scott. London: Deutsch, 1961. 351p.

With the aid of other experts, a respected authority on police protection produced a comprehensive set of articles on crime and criminals in the Western world of the modern period. Includes biographies, 96 plates, and a select bibliography.

E563 Williams, Vergil L. Dictionary of American penology: an introductory guide. Westport, Conn.: Greenwood, 1979. 530p.

More than half of the entries in this encyclopedic work provide information about current ideological disputes, custodial and administrative devices for maintaining prison safety and security, recent historical events, and treatment and rehabilitation programs aimed at changing prisoner behavior. Most of the remaining ones deal with federal and state prison systems and famous individual prisons. Entries are 1–4 pages long and provide references. Appendixes give addresses of pertinent organizations and agencies as well as more than 200 pages of U.S. government statistics pertaining to correctional activities. Includes bibliography and index.

Social Services

E564 Encyclopedia of social work: successor to the Social work yearbook. Ed. by John Turner. New York: Natl. Assn. of Social Workers, 1965– . (17th issue 1977, 2v.)

1977 edition contains 192 articles on social work and social welfare activities in the United States, and 102 biographies of deceased Americans who made significant contributions to the development of social work. Each article includes a list of references. Also 54 statistical tables providing facts and figures about population, vital statistics, social and economic conditions and trends, and social welfare activities and programs in the United States.

E565 Social service organizations. 2v. Ed. by Peter Romanofsky. Westport, Conn.: Greenwood, 1978. 843p.

The histories in these 2 volumes of nearly 300 organizations representing the major social service fields vary in length from about 2 to 6 pages. Annotated references to secondary historical accounts, to the printed records of an organization, and to primary manuscript sources are useful additions.

Other Specialized Encyclopedias

E566 Encyclopedia of urban planning. Ed. by Arnold Whittick. New York: McGraw-Hill, 1974. 1,218p.

Articles in this huge, profusely illustrated encyclopedia, probably the first of its kind, were written by international experts. Alphabetically arranged, it includes planning terms and articles on planning in different countries, on planning in general, and on subjects closely related to it such as transportation, sociology, economics, and aesthetics. Short articles on well-known planners, architects, sociologists, reformers, writers, propagandists, etc. Extensive index.

E567 Fogarty, Robert S. Dictionary of American communal and utopian history. Westport, Conn.: Greenwood, 1980. 271p.

Provides biographical sketches of more than 140 individuals "who played a prominent role in developing, leading, or inspiring utopian settlements" and short articles about 59 of the most important or interesting colonies, mainly from the 18th, 19th, and early 20th centuries. Articles average about half a page to a page in length. Appendixes include an "Annotated list of communal and utopian societies, 1787–1919" by Otohiko Okugawa and "Communal history in America: a bibliographical essay." Contains selected bibliography and index.

E568 International encyclopedia of population. Ed. by John A. Ross. New York: Free Pr., 1982. 750p. 2v.

Funding for this project, in which more than 150 international scholars participated, was provided by the United Nations Fund for Population Activities and the Rockefeller, Mellon, and Hewlett foundations. Articles, which include bibliographies, are arranged alphabetically by topic. Numerous countries and regions serve as topics. Includes detailed subject index.

E569 World press encyclopedia. Ed. by George Thomas Kurian. New York: Facts On File, 1982. 1,202p. 2v.

According to the editor, the "World press encyclopedia is a definitive survey of the state of the press in 180 countries of the world. It brings together in an easily consultable form available information and statistics on the history and operation of the world's press as well as the political and economic climate in which it functions. In both scope and size, it is the most comprehensive survey of the world's press *ever* attempted" (p.xiii).

HANDBOOKS

A large number of handbooks relevant to various issues in sociology have been published in recent years. Handbooks range in scope from very broad to very specialized. A few of the more general ones are: Raj P. Mohan and Don Martindale, eds., *Handbook of contemporary developments in world sociology* (Westport, Conn.: Greenwood, 1979 [493p.]) **(E570)**; Robert E. L. Faris, *Handbook of modern sociology* (Chicago: Rand McNally, 1964 [1,088p.]) **(E571)**; George Gurvitch, ed., *Traité de sociologie*, 3d ed. (Paris: Presses Universitaires de France, 1967–) **(E572)**; William F. Ogburn and M. F. Nimkoff, *A handbook of sociology*, 5th ed., rev. (London: Routledge & Paul, 1965 [644p.]) **(E573)**; Heinz Maus, *A short history of sociology* (London: Routledge & Paul, 1962 [226p.]) **(E574)**.

Demography

E575 Goyer, Doreen S., and Eliane Domschke. The handbook of national population censuses: Latin America and the Caribbean, North America, and Oceania. Westport, Conn.: Greenwood, 1983. 711p.

Entries by country contain name of capital city, official statistical agency, national repository of census, and main U.S. repository for that country's census publications. Presents pertinent historical commentary and descriptions of individual censuses. Maps are provided for most countries.

E576 U.S. Bureau of the Census. The methods and materials of demography. By Henry S. Shyrock and others. Washington, D.C.: Govt. Print. Off., 1971. 2v.

A thorough, well-written handbook on how to gather and treat data to shed light on the composition and dynamics of population. Statistical data from international sources are used extensively.

Aged and Aging

Robert H. Binstock and Ethel Shanas, eds., *Handbook of aging and the social sciences* (New York: Van Nostrand Reinhold, 1976 [684p.]) **(E577)**, is a compilation of essays dealing with five areas of aging: social aspects of aging, aging and social structure, aging and social systems, aging and interpersonal behavior, aging and social intervention. Includes many articles in each of these areas. Extensive lists of references. Companion volumes in the Handbook of Aging series issued by the same publisher are: Caleb L. Finch and Leonard Hayflick, eds., *Handbook of the biology of aging*, 1977 [771p.]) **(E578)**, and James E. Birren and K. Warner Schaie, *Handbook of the psychology of aging*, 1977 [787p.]) **(E579)**.

Sourcebook on aging (Chicago: Marquis Academic Media, 1977 [662p.]) **(E580)** is an excellent reference book for recent information on the elderly. "Demographic breakdowns of those over 65 and facts on income, health status, education, and employment complement discussions of pension and insurance provisions, nutrition programs, the 'death and dignity' controversy, effects of age discrimination and continued recession on older workers, and the impact of an older population on education. Also examined are housing and transportation arrangements for the elderly, crime against senior citizens and demand for stringent legal action against the criminal, social and political activities by the elderly, as well as legislation affecting their economic and social rights" (preface). Includes many statistical tables and charts, texts of public laws and useful addresses. Information is fully documented. Subject and geographic indexes. Much information useful to the elderly is provided in Craig Norback and Peter Norback, *The older American's handbook: practical information and help on medical and nursing care, housing, recreation, legal services, employment, in-home services, food, associations and organizations, transportation, mental health and counseling for older and retired Americans* (New York: Van Nostrand Reinhold, 1977 [311p.]) **(E581)**. More detailed information on funding is given in Lilly Cohen and others, comps. and eds., *Funding in aging: public, private and voluntary*, 2d rev. and enl. ed. (Garden City, N.Y.: Adelphi Univ. Pr., 1979 [308p.]) **(E582)**.

Group Research

E583 A. Paul Hare, Handbook of small group research. 2d ed. New York: Free Pr., 1976. 781p.

This important reference book "summarizes the major trends and findings in theory and research on small groups from 1898 through 1974." It is organized in 3 parts: group process and structure, interaction variables, and performance characteristics. A bibliography section contains more than 6,000 references (first edition has less than 1,400). The 4 appendixes provide several small group experiments for use in classroom demonstrations, a review of the history of small group research, an outline of the most commonly used research methods, and an overview of the application of group dynamics in sensitivity training and related areas with a list of references to recent research. Author and subject indexes.

E584 Stogdill, Ralph Melvin. Stogdill's handbook of leadership: a survey of theory and research. Rev. and expanded ed. by Bernard M. Bass. New York: Free Pr., 1981. 856p.

This major reference source contains 8 sections with several chapters in each: introduction to leadership theory and research; the leader as a person; power and legitimacy; leader-follower interaction; management and styles of leadership: antecedents and consequences; situational aspects of leadership; special conditions; applications and implications. This revised and expanded edition of the handbook provides 5,000 references as opposed to 3,000 in the original (1974) edition. It gives more emphasis to such topics as leadership among women, blacks, and other cultures than in the earlier edition. For a bibliography on leadership by Stogdill, see E288.

The Black Experience

Library Journal and the American Library Association honored the first ed. (Harry A. Ploski and Roscoe C. Brown, comps., *The Negro almanac*, New York: Bellwether, 1967 [1,012p.]) (**E585**) of Harry A. Ploski and James Williams, comps., *The Negro almanac: a reference work on the Afro-American*, 4th ed. (New York: Wiley, 1983 [1,550p.]) (**E586**), as "one of the outstanding reference works of the decade." The fourth ed. contains a vast amount of information about black Americans, including historical, political, economic and social, as well as a great deal of biographical material about prominent blacks in many fields. Other subjects covered include education, the black press, black religious tradition, black organizations and the black woman. Also provides much statistical data in the form of tables, graphs, and charts. Two older handbooks, which also include a broad range of information about black Americans, are Mabel M. Smythe, *The black American reference book* (Englewood Cliffs, N.J.: Prentice-Hall, 1976 [1,026p.]) (**E587**), and editors of Ebony, *Ebony handbook* (Chicago: Johnson, 1974 [553p.]) (**E588**).

Women

E589 Alexander, Shana. State-by-state guide to women's legal rights. Los Angeles: Wollstonecraft; dist. by Price, Stern, Sloan, 1975. 224p.

In clear, concise, simple language, summarizes some of the more important laws in each state regarding marriage, children, abortion, divorce, rape, widowhood, employment, crime, and age of majority. A chapter is devoted to each of these topics, and each chapter contains a useful introduction.

E590 Women's rights almanac, 1974. Bethesda, Md.: Elizabeth Cady Stanton Pub., 1974. 620p.

Crammed full of facts and figures on politics, government, legal rights, employment, education, marriage and divorce, child care, birth and health, abortion, rape, consumer protection. Also includes women's organizations, historical landmarks, chronology of events, biographies of U. S. congresswomen, specific factual and statistical information for each state, etc.

E591 Harrison, Cynthia Ellen. Women's movement media: a source guide. New York: Bowker, 1975. 269p.

Until this guide was published, much of the information in it was widely scattered and difficult to retrieve. The word *media* is very broadly defined to include even "products by Feminists for Feminists." Contains more than 550 descriptive entries on publishers, distributors, news services, products, women's research centers and library research collections, U.S. and Canadian national and local women's organizations and centers, governmental and quasi-governmental organizations and agencies, and organizations with special interests, e.g., art and communication, education, employment, etc. Four indexes: geographic, media title, name of groups, and subject of groups.

E592 New York Radical Feminists. Rape: the first sourcebook for women. Ed. by Noreen Connell and Cassandra Wilson. New York: NAL, 1974. 283p.

Much useful information about how women can help themselves and others in dealing with the problem of rape. Includes articles on rape crisis centers, legal and medical issues, self-defense, political action, etc. Selected bibliography.

Social Services and Social Action

E593 Barkas, J. L. The help book. New York: Scribner, 1979. 667p.

Fifty-two chapters of practical information on subjects apt to interest the general public, such as aging, counseling, crime prevention, environment, housing, mental health, safety, transportation and travel, volunteerism, etc. Provides addresses and descriptions of hundreds of private and public organizations and agencies, but no telephone numbers. Annotated bibliographies for each chapter.

A useful looseleaf service is U.S. Executive Office of the President, Office of Management and Budget, *Catalog of federal domestic assistance, 1982* (Washington, D.C.: Govt. Print. Off., 1982) (**E594**). It contains full descriptions of nearly 1,000 financial and nonfinancial assistance programs, projects, services, and activities administered by federal agencies "which provide assistance or benefits to the American public." Includes five indexes: agency program, applicant eligibility, deadlines (for program applications), function, and subject.

E595 Encyclopedia of United States government benefits: a complete, practical, and convenient guide to United States government benefits available to the people of America. 2d ed. Ed. by Roy A. Grisham, Jr., and Paul D. McConaughy. Union City, N.J.: Wise, 1977. 1,013p.

E596 Human resources network: user's guide to funding resources. How to get money for: education, fellowships, scholarships, youth, the elderly, the handicapped, women, civil liberties, conservation, community development, arts and humanities, drug and alcohol abuse, health. Radnor, Pa.: Chilton, 1975. Irregular paging.
Purpose is to help all fund seekers from the most humble on up. Although the introduction claims, "what we do have is the most complete collection of funding information yet assembled," it also warns that it would be wise to use this book as a "road map" or starting point, since more detailed information is often found elsewhere.

E597 Taber, Merlin A., and others. Handbook for community professionals: an approach for planning and action. Springfield, Ill.: C. C. Thomas, 1972. 215p.
"Written as a practical guide on how to create community change," this handbook was based on a project "to develop and then implement a workable approach for directed change in community services for older people. The approach developed . . . was tried for one year in Champaign County." Chapters on the community professional and the bilateral planning and action approach, information necessary for action, translating information into action, etc. Includes glossary of terms and concepts, and 11-page bibliography.

E598 Klemer, Richard H., ed. Counseling in marital and sexual problems: a physician's handbook. Baltimore: Williams & Wilkins, 1965. 309p. Reprint, New York: Krieger, 1976.
Produced by a panel of experts under the direction of a psychologist.

E599 Andrews, Matthew. The parents' guide to drugs. New York: Doubleday, 1972. 192p.
Contains a directory (by state) of centers where emergency aid for drug problems may be obtained. Provides lists of educational films and organizations active in drug education. Details practical information about principal drugs (marijuana, heroin, LSD, amphetamines, barbiturates, etc.), including preparation, packaging methods, price, and use and symptoms, the environment of drug use, and available therapy.

E600 Onyx Group, Inc., comp. and ed. Environment U.S.A.: a guide to agencies, people and resources. New York: Bowker, 1974. 451p.
An enormous amount of information is packed into this volume. To name some: lists federal and state agencies, private organizations, officers of U.S. corporations, labor unions, education programs, and libraries concerned with environmental issues, and gives pertinent information about them. Discusses employment, fund raising, and legal matters. Includes 65-page bibliography, glossary of terms, and index.

The Population Institute, *The population activist's handbook* (New York: Collier Books, 1974 [176p.]) (**E601**), was written by individuals deeply concerned about the world problem of overpopulation for others who share their concern and want to do something about it. Gives specific suggestions about how to educate others about the problem and how to bring about changes in population policies. Provides information about what to read (important journals, books, pamphlets, audiovisual materials, government publications) and whom to contact. Mentions libraries with population collections, relevant organizations, college courses and counseling services, health service programs, and so forth.

E602 Burke, Joan Martin. Civil rights: a current guide to the people, organizations, and events. 2d ed. New York: Bowker, 1974. 266p.
Original edition compiled as a quick reference source for CBS News. Second edition is more recent and has an extra appendix. First half of book is devoted to summaries of activities of individuals and organizations involved with the civil rights movement. Five appendixes: (1) Congressional voting records on Civil Rights Acts from 1957 to 1970, (2) State and federal agencies with civil rights responsibilities, (3) Civil rights chronology from 1954 to 1974, (4) Leading black elected officials by state as of April 1973, and (5) Civil rights resources. The last describes special collections of various libraries in the U.S. Includes "suggested bibliography" and index.

Other Specialized Handbooks

Before the publication of Ithiel de Sola Pool and others, eds., *Handbook of communication* (Chicago: Rand McNally, 1973 [1,011p.]) (**E603**), no major review articles for subfields of the area of communication were available. This outstanding work fills that gap. Distinguished scholars present a wealth of information on research findings and developments in a broad range of subjects within the discipline. Tables, charts, and maps often illustrate trends and statistics. Extensive lists of references and additional readings accompany each article. See also E191.

Other, more specialized handbooks include David A. Goslin, ed., *Handbook of socialization theory and research* (Chicago: Rand McNally, 1969 [1,182p.]) **(E604)**; James G. March, ed., *Handbook of organizations* (see description at E117); Howard E. Freeman and others, eds., *Handbook of medical sociology*, 3d ed. (Englewood Cliffs, N.J.: Prentice-Hall, 1979 [516p.]) **(E606)**; and Louis Wekstein, *Handbook of suicidology: principles, problems and practice* (New York: Brunner/Mazel, 1979 [303p.]) **(E607)**.

YEARBOOKS

E608   American Jewish yearbook. v.1– , 1899– . Philadelphia: The Jewish Publication Society of America and the American Jewish Committee. Annual.

Short, well-documented articles, arranged by country, give a rounded account of world developments as seen from the point of view of the Jewish community. Also features a few lengthier "special articles." Like its predecessors, v.79 (1979) includes supplementary reference features: Jewish population statistics, directories of Jewish organizations and periodicals, a necrology, the Jewish calendar, annual report of the Jewish Publication Society of America, and an index to special articles in v.51–78, in addition to the annual index.

There is also an *American Jewish yearbook: index to volumes 1–50, 1899–1949* (New York: Ktav, 1967 [375p.]) **(E609)**.

E610   UNESCO yearbook on peace and conflict studies. v.1– , 1981– . Westport, Conn.: Greenwood; Paris: UNESCO. Annual.

E611   The women's annual: the year in review. v.1– , 1980– . Boston: Hall. Annual.

The intent of this publication, according to the editor, Barbara Haber, "is to record faithfully the progress and the setbacks that will inevitably occur during each given year" regarding the advancement of the position of women. Contains essays on such topics as domestic life, women and education, Third World women in America, politics and law, popular culture, violence against women, and women and work. Each essay includes a bibliography.

ORIGINAL SOURCES

The social indicator "movement" caught on in the late 1960s in the United States when social scientists from various disciplines began showing increasing interest in monitoring the qualitative

social conditions of society through the use of social indicators. Raymond Bauer, sometimes referred to as the "father" of the social indicator movement, edited an early work in this area, *Social indicators* (Cambridge, Mass.: MIT Pr., 1966 [357p.]) **(E612)**. Leslie D. Wilcox and others, *Social indicators and societal monitoring: an annotated bibliography* (San Francisco: Jossey-Bass, 1973 [464p.]) **(E613)**, is a basic book essentially superseding Bauer. Ralph M. Brooks in an introductory essay reviews the origin and development of social indicator research. Contains more than 1,000 references, about 600 of them annotated, which the authors "feel represent a cross section of relevant and related works on social indicators" (preface). Most references are American in origin, some from Europe and international organizations. Includes author, key word, subject, and address index. The latter provides names and addresses of institutes, agencies, and individuals involved in social indicator research.

Kevin J. Gilmartin and others, *Social indicators: an annotated bibliography of current literature* (New York: Garland, 1979 [123p.]) **(E614)**, supplements Wilcox and is the most complete bibliography for literature published between 1972 and 1978. Includes key historical works prior to 1972, state of the art overview of social indicators research, theoretical and methodological approaches to constructing social indicators, analyzing and reporting social indicators, examples of social indicators used or in use, and bibliographies of social indicators research. Author and subject indexes.

World handbook of political and social indicators, 3d ed., by Charles Lewis Taylor and David A. Jodice, 2v. (New Haven, Conn.: Yale Univ. Pr., 1983. v.1, Cross-national attributes and rates of change [305p.]; v.2, Political protest and government change [216p.]) **(E615)** presents comparative data for major countries of the world regarding many different political, social and economic variables. Provides more political events data than previous editions. The first *World handbook* was by Bruce M. Russett, and others (New Haven, Conn.: Yale Univ. Pr., 1964 [373p.]) **(E616)**. A 2d ed. by Charles Lewis Taylor and Michael C. Hudson appeared in 1972.

E617   Banks, Arthur S., and R. B. Textor. A crosspolity survey. Cambridge, Mass.: MIT Pr., 1963. 1,386p.

A comparison of 115 nations in terms of 57 variables that scholars generally consider indicative of the condition of a society, ranging from the state of literacy to the linguistic homogeneity of a population. The data consist of statistics and subjective judgments.

This pioneer work is amplified by Arthur S. Banks, *Cross-polity time series data* (Cambridge, Mass.: MIT Pr., 1971 [299p.]) (**E618**), which seeks to assemble and report objective data on some 102 topics as they apply to most independent nations of the world. Thirty-two serial publications, which contributed most of the information, are summarized and are cited in appendix 2.

E619 Mickiewicz, Ellen. Handbook of Soviet social science data. New York: Free Pr., 1973. 225p.

Mickiewicz, along with other noted scholars, has composed a unique reference book on the Soviet Union, providing and analyzing quantitative and social statistics in such areas as demography, agriculture, production, health, housing, education, communication, etc., obtained from Soviet sources. Karl W. Deutsch states in the introduction: "Dr. Mickiewicz's book represents a major step toward the possibility of true comparative political and social analysis—analysis in which the social system itself can be treated as a variable in comparing nations in addition to the customary variables of region, occupation, ethnicity, per capita income, rural-urban balance, and the like."

Some documentary sources on minorities include the following: Herbert Aptheker, ed., *A documentary history of the Negro people in the United States*. v.1, From colonial times to the founding of the N.A.A.C.P. in 1910; v.2, From the emergence of the N.A.A.C.P. to the beginning of the New Deal, 1910–1932 (New York: Citadel Pr., 1969); v.3, 1933–1945 (Secaucus, N.J.: Citadel Pr., 1974) (**E620**). "At long last we have this work which rescues from oblivion and loss, the very words and thoughts of scores of American Negroes who lived in slavery, serfdom and quasi-freedom in the United States of America from the seventeenth to the twentieth century. For fifteen years Dr. Aptheker has worked to find and select 450 documents to make an authentic record and picture of what it meant to be a slave in the Land of the Free, and what it meant to be free after the Emancipation Proclamation" (W. E. B. Dubois, preface to v.1).

E621 Fishel, Leslie H., Jr., and Benjamin Quarles, eds. The Negro American: a documentary history. New York: Morrow, 1970. 608p.

An anthology of 217 selections from contemporary sources that portrays the role of the black in American history and the importance of black history. An attractive volume, interesting to read and enlivened by numerous illustrations. Arranged by period, with subject subdivisions. Subject and title index.

Along with white women, black women gained increased attention in the reference literature of the 1970s as evidenced in *Black women in white America: a documentary history* (New York: Pantheon, 1972 [630p.]) (**E622**), ed. by Gerda Lerner. Contains quotes from ordinary anonymous women as well as recognized influential ones. Documents easily available elsewhere, such as on civil rights, prominent women in black culture, etc., are excluded while important unknown or little known documents are included.

Two outstanding, very different documentary histories of the American Indian appeared in the early 1970s. Virgil A. Vogel, *A documentary history of the American Indian* (New York: Harper, 1972 [473p.]) (**E623**), is intended for undergraduate students and ordinary citizens. Includes a wide variety of significant documents dating from pre-Columbian times to the late 1960s. Much valuable information is contained in the appendixes—roughly 40 percent of the book—such as on famous Americans of Indian descent, audiovisual aids, museums with significant collections relating to American Indians, government agencies concerned with Indians, Indian and Indian-interest organizations and publications. Provides a lengthy bibliography covering all periods of Indian history and an index. *The American Indian and the United States: a documentary history*, 4v. (New York: Random, 1973 [3,119p.]) (**E624**), by Wilcomb E. Washburn of the Smithsonian Institution, contains important governmental and legal documents; reports of the commissioners of Indian affairs; congressional debates on Indian affairs; acts, ordinances and proclamations; Indian treaties; and legal decisions. Includes map of Indian land cessions, 1776–1945, and an index. A less comprehensive but nonetheless important contribution is *Documents of United States Indian policy* (Lincoln: Univ. of Nebraska Pr., 1975 [278p.]) (**E625**), edited by Francis Paul Prucha, a well-known scholar in this field. Another rich source of primary data is provided in U.S. Bureau of Indian Affairs, *Letters received by the Office of Indian Affairs, 1824–80* (Washington, D.C.: National Archives, 1966, 962 reels, 35 mm. [National Archives microfilm publications, microcopy no.234]) (**E626**). Films available in whole or in part from National Archives. These letters received by the bureau from superintendents, agents, and other field officials offer information on such matters as population, emigration, education, health, medical care, land allotments, claims, complaints, etc. Edward E. Hill, *The Office of Indian Affairs, 1824–1880:*

historical sketches (New York: Clearwater, 1974 [246p.]) **(E627)**, is a guide to these microfilms.

A recent documentary work on homosexuals is Jonathan Ned Katz, *Gay/lesbian almanac: a new documentary* (New York: Harper, 1983 [764p.]) **(E628)**, which provides 364 historical "documents" from 1607 to 1950, with extensive introductory material and commentary, and a selected annotated bibliography.

STATISTICS

E629 American social attitudes data sourcebook 1947–1978. Philip E. Converse and others. Cambridge, Mass.: Harvard Univ. Pr., 1980. 441p.

Aided by a grant from the National Science Foundation, the editors used a database from the Institute for Social Research of the University of Michigan to compile this volume. Problems and limitations of the sourcebook are discussed in the introduction. Each chapter contains introductory remarks followed by statistical tables and graphs compiled from questionnaires submitted to various segments of the American population during several time periods. Covers the following topics: attitudes toward self and others; blacks and whites; women; family living; work and retirement; personal economic outlook; national economic outlook; government spending; and war and peace.

E630 Judge, Clark S. The book of American rankings. New York: Facts On File, 1979. 324p.

Presents overviews and recent statistical comparisons of states and major cities in the U.S. in 31 categories such as population, ethnicity, religion, education, crime, sports, government, etc., with more than 300 subcategories. Includes state summaries, glossary, bibliography, and index.

E631 U.S. Bureau of the Census. Bureau of the Census catalog. 1– , 1946– . Washington, D.C.: Govt. Print. Off. Quarterly, cumulative to an annual volume, with 12 monthly supp.

Lists and describes the bureau's publications, data files, and special tabulations. A few examples of publications of interest to sociology are: *The social and economic status of the black population in the United States: an historical view, 1790–1978* (1979), 266p.; *Characteristics of the population below the poverty level: 1977* (1979), 236p.; *World population: 1977—recent demographic estimates from the countries and regions of the world* (1978), 452p. The bureau's record is extended back to the first census by the U.S. Library of Congress, Census Library Project, *Catalog of United States census publications, 1790–1945* (Washington, D.C.: Govt. Print. Off., 1950 [320p.]) **(E632)**.

E633 ——. Negro population in the United States, 1790–1915. New York: Arno Pr. and the New York Times, 1968. 844p.

A reprint of a 1918 census report that "provides a wealth of information on every facet of Negro life susceptible of statistical study" (introduction).

E634 ——. Social indicators: selected data on social conditions and trends in the United States. Washington, D.C.: Dept. of Commerce, Office of Federal Statistical Policy and Standards, Bureau of the Census; dist. by Supt. of Documents, 1977– .

Contains hundreds of charts and tables in the following areas: population; the family; housing; social security and welfare; health and nutrition; public safety; education and training; work; income, wealth, and expenditures; culture, leisure, and the use of time; social mobility and participation. Includes subject index. The Canadian counterpart of this is *Statistics Canada, perspective Canada II: a compendium of social statistics, 1977* (Ottawa: Ministry of Supply and Services, 1977 [335p.]) **(E635)**.

E636 Bogue, Donald J. Population of the United States. Glencoe, Ill.: Free Pr., 1959. 873p. [Studies in population distribution, 14]

Describes and interprets U.S. population changes from 1950 to 1960 and summarizes principal trends. Statistics are drawn from hundreds of books, special government reports, and unpublished tabulations. 392 tables in 26 chapters, and an additional 69 tables in the appendix. Sources are cited for each table, often with critical comment. General index.

E637 Thompson, Warren S. Growth and changes in California's population. Los Angeles: Haynes Foundation, 1955. 377p.

A detailed analysis of permanent reference value, based on a 100-year record provided by the 11 state censuses. Summaries of extensive population data for the country as a whole for the period 1790–1930 are found in a reprint of a 1933 publication: Warren S. Thompson and P. K. Welpton, *Population trends in the United States* (New York: Gordon & Breach, 1969 [415p.]) **(E638)**.

E639 U.S. Department of Labor. Publications of the Bureau of Labor Statistics, 1886–1971. Bureau of Labor Statistics Bulletin no.1749. Washington, D.C.: Govt. Print. Off., 1972. 184p.

Lists the major publications of the Bureau of Labor Statistics, with a subject index of bulletins and reports. Updated by semiannual publications lists.

E640 U.S. Bureau of Labor Statistics. Directory of data sources on racial and ethnic minorities. Washington, D.C.: Govt. Print. Off., 1975. 83p.

E641 U.S. Federal Bureau of Investigation. Uniform crime reports for the United States and its possessions. v.1– , Aug. 1930– . Washington, D.C.: Govt. Print. Off.

Charts and tables provide all sorts of crime statistics for the United States, such as on different types of offenses, geographic breakdown of crime, crime trends, offenses cleared, persons arrested by age, sex, race, geographic breakdown of arrests, arrest trends, law enforcement personnel, etc.

E642 U.S. Department of Justice. Sourcebook of criminal justice statistics, 1978. Ed. by Nicolette Parisi and others. Washington, D.C.: Govt. Print. Off., 1974– . Annual.

1978 sourcebook offers hundreds of figures and tables on characteristics of the criminal justice system, public attitudes toward crime and criminal justice related topics, nature and distribution of known offenses, characteristics and distribution of persons arrested, judicial processing of defendants, and persons under correctional supervision.

E643 United Nations. Statistical Office. Demographic yearbook. 1948– . New York: 1949– . Annual.

A compilation of international demographic statistics, with accompanying technical notes and explanation, representing about 220 countries or areas. Many tables are published annually, including a world summary of basic demographic statistics, and "statistics on the size, distribution and trends in population, natality, foetal mortality, infant and maternal mortality, general mortality, nuptiality and divorce." Most feature a special topic, such as "International Migration Statistics" in the 1977 publication. A cumulative subject-matter index covers yearbooks from the beginning.

E644 Population Reference Bureau. World population growth and response: 1965–1975, a decade of global action. Washington, D.C.: The Bureau, 1976. 271p.

Offers overviews of the world population situation, of major regions of the world (Africa, Asia, Europe, Latin America, Caribbean Islands, Near East, North America, Oceania), and of individual countries. Discusses birth, mortality and growth rates, family planning policies and programs, external assistance for family planning, economic growth rates, special problems relating to poverty, health care, etc. Chapters on aid to developing countries and world demographic data. Includes numerous charts and graphs, and glossary.

E645 Keyfitz, Nathan, and Wilhelm Flieger. World population: an analysis of vital data. Chicago: Univ. of Chicago Pr., 1968. 672p.

Applying the mathematical methods available for demographic analysis, this book—as described by Conrad Taeuber (*American sociological review* 34:425 [1969])—is "a dramatic illustration of the new dimensions in the social sciences opened up by electronic computers guided by competence and imagination. The report undertakes to: (1) present official data on births, deaths, and population—all by age and sex—for as many periods of time and countries as possible; (2) calculate life tables that conform to these data; (3) facilitate comparisons of mortality and fertility among countries and moments in time; (4) establish a bench mark for work on future population; (5) analyze age distributions; (6) infer birth rates from age distributions as a means of checking the birth rates given in vital statistics; and (7) work out such measures of the combined action of mortality and fertility as (a) intrinsic rates of birth, death, and natural

increase, and (b) gross and net reproduction rates. This is accomplished in a set of 261 standard tables, given for 4 countries in Africa, 16 in North and Central America and the Caribbean, 6 in South America, 7 in East Asia, and 27 in Europe."

E646 Preston, Samuel H., and others. Causes of death: life tables for national populations. New York: Seminar Pr., 1972. 787p.

"The circumstances under which [people] die are closely related to the conditions under which they live. The extent of violence, poverty, passivity and ignorance in a population is reflected in the statistics of its causes and ages of death" (introduction). Presents cause of death statistics in tables for 48 countries, male and female, at various time intervals, which vary from country to country, a few dating back to the 19th century. Methods of calculation, accuracy and comparability of data, and sources of and adjustments to data are discussed.

E647 Walsh, Robert J. Reference data on socioeconomic issues of health. Chicago: American Medical Assn. Center for Health Services Research and Development, 1972. 148p.

E648 Boulding, Elise, and others. Handbook of international data on women. New York: Halsted Pr., 1976. 468p.

Financial support and encouragement for producing this handbook and much of the data came from the UN. It is essentially a series of tables ranking countries of the world for 107 indicators on women, covering economic activities; literacy and education; migration; marital status; life, death, and reproduction; and political and civic participation. Explanations of the indicators are given in an appendix.

E649 Vetter, Betty M., and others. Professional women and minorities: a manpower data resource service. 2d ed. Washington, D.C.: Scientific Manpower Commission, 1978. 272p.

Contains hundreds of statistical tables and charts presenting current and historical information relating to professional and academic degrees attained and occupational representation in the labor force of women and minorities. More than 200 published and unpublished sources were consulted in compiling this looseleaf notebook, which is supposed to be updated annually. Supplement no.1 was issued January 1980. 271p.

A worldwide survey of the mass media is presented in the United Nations Educational, Scientific and Cultural Organization, *World communication: a 200-country survey of press, audio, television and film*, 5th ed. (UNESCO; dist. by Unipub, 1975 [533p.]) **(E650)**.

E651 Sterling, Christopher H. and Timothy R. Haight. The mass media: Aspen Institute guide to communication industry trends. New York: Praeger, 1978. 457p.

Over 300 tables of statistical data on U.S. communication industry trends since 1900 are divided into seven sections dealing with growth, ownership and control, and economics of the media industries, employment and training in the media industries, content trends in the media, size and characteristics of media audiences, U. S. media industries abroad. Includes brief explanatory remarks about source reliability and validity for each table. Provides data from private correspondence, government, business, trade and academic sources.

ATLASES AND CHARTS

E652 Abler, Ronald, ed. A comparative atlas of America's great cities: twenty metropolitan regions. Washington, D.C.: Assn. of American Geographers, 1976. 503p.

A valuable book resulting from the Comparative Metropolitan Analysis Project sponsored by the Association of American Geographers. Combines maps and text to make comparisons of 20 metropolitan regions in numerous ways, such as land use, housing, socioeconomic characteristics, physical environments, open space for leisure time use, transportation and communication, etc. Includes discussion of sources used in compiling the atlas, appendixes, glossary, and index/gazetteer.

E653 North Carolina atlas: portrait of a changing southern state. Ed. by James W. Clay and others. Chapel Hill: Univ. of North Carolina Pr., 1975. 331p.

E654 Halvorson, Peter L., and William M. Newman. Atlas of religious change in America 1952–1971. Washington, D.C.: Glenmary Research Center, 1978. 95p.

SOURCES OF SCHOLARLY CONTRIBUTIONS

Journals

E655

Acta sociologica. (Scandinavian review of sociology.) v.1– , 1955– . Oslo: Universitetsforlaget. Quarterly. (Box 258, Irvington-on-Hudson, NY 10533)
Cc; PAIS; SSCI; SSI.

American journal of sociology. v.1– , 1895– . Chicago: Univ. of Chicago Pr. Bimonthly.
ABC; Cc; CIJE; EdAdmAbst; LLBA; SocAbst; SSCI; SSI.

American sociological review. v.1– , 1936– . Washington, D.C.: American Sociological Assn. Bimonthly.
Cc; PAIS; SSCI; SSI.

British journal of criminology, delinquency and deviant social behavior. v.1– , 1950– . London: Institute for the Study and Treatment of Delinquency. Quarterly.
BrEdInd; BrHumInd; Cc; PAIS; PsychAbst; SSCI; SSI.

British journal of sociology. v.1– , 1950– . London: Routledge & Paul. Quarterly.
BrEdInd; BrHumInd; Cc; PAIS; PsychAbst; SSCI; SSI.

Cahiers internationaux de sociologie. v.1– , 1946– . Paris: Presses Universitaires de France. Semi-annual.
SocAbst; SSCI.

Canadian review of sociology and anthropology. v.1– , 1964– . Canadian Sociology and Anthropology Assoc. Quarterly.
Cc; SSCI.

Criminology; an interdisciplinary journal. v.1– , 1963– . Beverly Hills, Calif.: Sage. Quarterly. (Formerly: Criminologica)
Cc; EM; PAIS; SSI.

International journal of comparative sociology. v.1– , 1960– . Leiden, The Netherlands: Dept. of Sociology, York Univ. (Canada). 4/yr.
Cc; SSCI; SSI.

International journal of social psychiatry. v.1– , 1955– . London: Avenue. Quarterly.
Cc; EM; PsychAbst; SocWkResAbst; SSCI; SSI.

Journal of criminal law and criminology. v.1– , 1910– . Chicago: Williams & Wilkins. Quarterly. (Formerly: Journal of criminal law, criminology and police science)
Cc; ChemAbst; EM; PAIS; PsychAbst; SSCI; SSI.

Journal of gerontology. v.1– , 1946– . Washington, D.C.: Gerontological Society. Bimonthly.
BiolAbst; Cc; ChemAbst; EM; NutrAbst; PAIS; PsychAbst; SSCI; SSI.

Journal of health and social behavior. v.1– , 1960– . Washington, D.C.: American Sociological Assn. Quarterly.
BiolAbst; Cc; EM; PsychAbst; SSCI; SSI.

Journal of marriage and the family. v.1– , 1938– . Minneapolis: National Council on Family Relations. Quarterly. (Formerly: Marriage and family living)
Cc; EM; PsychAbst; SocWkResAbst; SSI.

Journal of studies on alcohol. v.1– , 1940– . New Brunswick, N.J.: Rutgers Center of Alcohol Studies. Bimonthly. (Formerly: Quarterly journal of studies on alcohol)
BiolAbst; BullSig; ChemAbst; Cc; EM; HistAbst; NutrAbst; PsychAbst; SocWkResAbst; SSI.

Kölner Zeitschrift für Soziologie und Sozialpsychologie. v.1– , 1927– . Wiesbaden, W. Germany. 4/yr.
Cc; SocAbst; SSCI.

Perception. v.1– , 1977– . Ottawa: Canadian Council on Social Development. 5/yr. (Formerly: Canadian Welfare)
CanInd; PAIS; SocWkResAbst; SSCI.

Phylon: the Atlanta University review of race and culture. v.1– , 1940– . Atlanta: Atlanta Univ. Quarterly.
Cc; CIJE; PAIS; SSI; SSCI.

Polish sociological bulletin. v.1– , 1961– . Wroclaw, Poland: Ossolineum. Quarterly.
SSCI.

Population. v.1– , 1946– . Paris: Institut National d'Études Démographiques (INED). Bimonthly.
EM; SSCI.

Population bulletin. v.1– , 1945– . Washington, D.C.: Population Reference Bureau. 4/yr.
BiolAbst; Cc; PAIS; SSCI; SSI.

Population studies. v.1– , 1947– . London: London School of Economics. 3/yr.
BiolAbst; BrHumInd; Cc; EM; PAIS; SSCI.

Public opinion quarterly. v.1– , 1937– . New York: Elsevier. Quarterly.
Cc; HistAbst; IntBibSocSci; IntPolSciAbst; PAIS; PsychAbst; SSCI; SSI.

Revista internacional de sociologia. v.1– , 1941– . Madrid: Instituto de Sociologia Balmes. Quarterly.
HistAbst.

Revue française de sociologie. v.1– , 1960– . Paris: Editions du CNRS. Quarterly.
Cc; SSCI.

Rural sociology; devoted to scientific study of rural and small-town life. v.1– , 1936– . Knoxville, Tenn.: Rural Sociological Society. Quarterly.
HistAbst; PAIS; PsychAbst; SocAbst; SSI.

Social problems. v.1– , 1953– . Buffalo, N.Y.: Society for the Study of Social Problems, State Univ. College at Buffalo. 5/yr.
Cc; EM; PAIS; PsychAbst; SocAbst; SSCI; SSI.

Social psychology quarterly. v.1– , 1937– . Washington, D.C.: American Sociological Assn. Quarterly. (Formerly: Sociometry, social psychology)
Cc; PsychAbst; SSCI; SSI.

Social research; an international journal of political and social science. v.1– , 1934– . New York: New School for Social Research. Quarterly.
Cc; PAIS; SocAbst; SSI.

Sociologia internationalis. v.1– , 1963– . Berlin: Duncker und Humblot. Semiannual.

Sociological inquiry. v.1– , 1930– . Austin: Univ. of Texas Pr. (Alpha Kappa Delta—National Sociological Honor Society). Quarterly.
Cc; SocAbst; SSCI.

Sociological methods and research. v.1– , 1972– . Beverly Hills, Calif.: Sage. Quarterly.
Cc; PAIS; SocAbst; SSCI.

Sociological perspectives. v.1– , 1958– . Beverly Hills, Calif.: Sage. Quarterly. (Formerly: Pacific sociological review)
Cc; HistAbst; SocAbst; SocWkResAbst; SSCI.

Sociological quarterly. v.1– , 1960– . Carbondale, Ill.: Midwest Sociological Society, Dept. of Sociology, Southern Illinois Univ. Quarterly. (Formerly: Midwest sociologist)
AmH&L; Cc; HistAbst; PsychAbst; SocAbst; SocWkResAbst; SSCI.

Sociological review. v.1– , 1908– . Keele, Eng.: Univ. of Keele. Quarterly.
BrHumInd; Cc; PsychAbst; SSCI; SSI.

Sociology and social research; an international journal. v.1– , 1916– . Los Angeles: Univ. of Southern California. Quarterly.
Cc; HistAbst; PAIS; PsychAbst; SSCI; SSI.

Sociology of education. v.1– , 1927– . Washington, D.C.: American Sociological Assn. Quarterly.
Cc; EdInd; PAIS; PsychAbst; SSCI; SSI.

Teaching sociology. v.1– , 1973– . Beverly Hills, Calif.: Sage. Quarterly.
Cc; CIJE; SocAbst; SSCI.

Urban affairs quarterly. v.1– , 1965– . Beverly Hills, Calif.: Sage. Quarterly.
ABC; Cc; IntPolSciAbst; PAIS; SocAbst; SocWkResAbst; SSCI; SSI.

Monograph Series

E656

Arnold and Caroline Rose monograph series of the American Sociological Association. 1970?– . New York: Cambridge Univ. Pr.

California. University. University of California publications in sociology. v.1– , 1964– . Berkeley.

Centre d'Études Sociologiques. Travaux et documents. v.1– , 1969– . Paris.

France. Institut National d'Études Démographiques. Cahiers de travaux et documents. v.1– , 1946– . Paris: Institute.

Frankfurter Beiträge zur Soziologie. v.1–22, 1955–71. Frankfurt am Main: Institut für Sozialforschung.

Harvard Univ. Harvard sociological studies. no.1– , 1935– . Cambridge, Mass.

Yale Univ. Yale studies in attitude and communication. v.1– , 1957– . New Haven, Conn.

Organizations

E657

American Sociological Assn. Washington, D.C. Founded 1905.

British Sociological Assn. London. Founded 1951.

Centre d'Études Sociologiques. Paris. Founded 1946.

Columbia Univ. School of Social Work, Center for Research and Demonstration. New York. Founded 1956.

————. Industrial Social Welfare Center. New York. Founded 1969.

Cornell Univ. International Population Program. Ithaca, N.Y. Founded 1962.

Deutsche Gesellschaft für Soziologie. Munich. Founded 1910.

George Washington Univ. Social Research Group. Washington, D.C. Founded 1962.

Gerontological Society. Washington, D.C. Founded 1945.

Harvard Univ. Center for Population Studies. Boston. Founded 1964.

Intl. Assn. of Gerontology. Tokyo. Founded 1950.

Intl. Institute for Sociology. Cordoba, Argentina. Founded 1893.

Intl. Society of Criminology. Paris. Founded 1934.

Intl. Society for the Sociology of Knowledge. Founded 1972.

Intl. Sociological Assn. Montreal, Québec. Founded 1949.

Intl. Union for the Scientific Study of Population. Liège, Belgium. Founded 1928.

Kent State Univ. Consortium on Peace Research, Education and Development. Kent, Ohio. Founded 1970.

Massachusetts Institute of Technology. Center for Transportation Studies. Cambridge, Mass. Founded 1973.

National Conference on Social Welfare. Columbus, Ohio. Founded 1873.

Population Assn. of America. Washington, D.C. Founded 1932.

Princeton Univ. Office of Population Research. Princeton, N.J. Founded 1936.

Purdue Univ. Urban Development Institute. Hammond, Ind. Founded 1959.

Roper Public Opinion Research Center. Williamstown, Mass. Founded 1946.

Rutgers, The State Univ. Center of Alcohol Studies. New Brunswick, N.J. Founded 1939.

Sage (Russell) Foundation. New York. Founded 1907.

Scripps Foundation for Research in Population Problems. Miami Univ., Oxford, Ohio. Founded 1922.

Société Française de Sociologie. Paris. Founded 1962.

Univ. of California. Institute of Human Development. Berkeley. Founded 1927.

Univ. of California. Institute of Race and Community Relations. Berkeley. Founded 1975.

Univ. of Chicago. Community and Family Study Center. Chicago. Founded 1951.

Univ. of Chicago. National Opinion Research Center. Chicago. Founded 1941.

Univ. of Michigan. Center for Urban Studies. Dearborn. Founded 1964.

Univ. of Michigan. Research Center for Group Dynamics. Ann Arbor. Founded 1946.

Univ. of Minnesota. Minnesota Center for Social Research. Minneapolis. Founded 1965.

Univ. of North Carolina. Carolina Population Center. Chapel Hill. Founded 1966.

Univ. of Pennsylvania. Population Studies Center. Philadelphia. Founded 1961.

SOURCES OF CURRENT INFORMATION

E658 A.S.A. footnotes. v.1– , 1972– . Washington, D.C. American Sociological Assn. 9/yr. Tabloid.

E659 Canadian Sociology and Anthropology Association bulletin. v.1– , 1977– . Montreal: The Association. Concordia Univ. 2/yr.

E660 ISA [International Sociological Assn.] bulletin. no.1– , 1971– . Montreal. Triennial.
Reports activities of ISA research committees and the association, organization of congresses and meetings, news about national sociological associations and ISA members.

E661 NASW news. 1956– . Washington, D.C.: National Assn. of Social Workers. Monthly (except Aug. and Dec.).
Addressed to members of the association to keep them informed about organized professional activities, the development of welfare programs, and wider events that have a bearing on the future of social service.

E662 Social work education reporter. 1953– . New York: Council on Social Work Education. 3/yr.
Activities of the council, manpower requirements and programs, relevant publications, and other current developments.

E663 Sociolinguistics newsletter. 1966– . Missoula, Mont.: Scholars Pr., Univ. of Montana. Quarterly.

E664 Sociologists for women in society newsletter. v.1– , 1971– . Silver Spring, Md.: Penelope Maza (14163 Castle Blvd., No. 201). Quarterly.

E665 Washington report on medicine and health. 1947– . New York: McGraw-Hill. Weekly.
Title varies. Continuing report on legislation, court decisions, and other current developments in the field.

ONLINE DATABASES

E666

Numerous databases are available for searching by computer. For sociology, the most important is Sociological abstracts (Sociological Abstracts, Inc.). Others of interest are: America: history and life (ABC–Clio, Inc.), Child abuse and neglect (National Center on Child Abuse and Neglect), Commonwealth agricultural bureaux abstracts (Commonwealth Agricultural Bureaux), Comprehensive dissertation index (Xerox/University Microfilms), Current research information system (U.S. Dept. of Agriculture), Family resources (National Council on Family Relations), Foundation grants (The Foundation Center), Language and language behavior abstracts (Sociological Abstracts, Inc.), NCJRS (National Criminal Justice Reference Service), NICEM (National Information Center for Educational Media), NTIS (National Technical Information Service, U.S. Dept. of Commerce), PAIS international (Public Affairs Information Service, Inc.), Population bibliography (Univ. of North Carolina, Carolina Population Center), RILM (Repertoire International de la Littérature Musicale) Abstracts (City Univ. of New York, International RILM Center), Social scisearch (Institute for Scientific Information), SSIE current research (Smithsonian Science Information Exchange), U.S. political science documents (Univ. of Pittsburgh, Center for International Studies).

Marilyn L. Wertheimer

6 Anthropology

Survey of the Field

SYSTEMATIC SURVEYS

Anthropology's principal mission is the explanation of similarities and differences in the behavior of the membership of different sorts of human groups and societies. Cultural anthropology—or, if you like, sociocultural anthropology—has primary responsibilities for broad theoretical synthesis and for investigating modern and historic human groups and societies. The more sharply defined and more specialized sub-disciplines, including anthropological linguistics, anthropological archaeology, and biological anthropology, are listed here under separate headings but make their own characteristic and vital contributions to the field as a whole.

General syntheses of the field occur frequently in the form of textbooks or popular introductions. Because these present anthropology in a form most accessible to the nonspecialist, they are listed first.

F1   Anderson, Robert T. Anthropology: a perspective on man. Belmont, Calif: Wadsworth, 1972. 133p.

F2   Bates, Marston. Gluttons and libertines: human problems of being natural. New York: Random, 1967. 244p.

F3   Beals, Alan R. Culture in process. 3d ed. New York: Holt, 1979. 384p.

F4   Fox, Robin. Encounter with anthropology. New York: HBJ, 1973. 370p.

F5   Friedl, John. Cultural anthropology. New York: Harper's College Pr., 1976. 486p.

F6   Goldschmidt, Walter. Exploring the ways of mankind. 3d ed. New York: Holt, 1977, 566p.

F7   Olien, Michael D. The human myth: an introduction to anthropology. New York: Harper, 1978. 568p.

F8   Oswalt, Wendell H. Understanding our culture: an anthropological view. New York: Holt, 1970. 160p.

F9   Peacock, James L. The human direction: an evolutionary approach to social and cultural anthropology, 3d ed. Englewood Cliffs, N.J.: Princeton Univ. Pr., 1980. 333p.

F10   Pocock, David Francis. Social anthropology. 2d rev. ed. London: Sheed & Ward, 1971. 118p.

Although several journals and annual publications attempt systematic and technical review of the discipline as a whole, the complexity of the field appears to have had a generally discouraging effect upon the development of the more technical sorts of systematic surveys. A number of fairly general, but by no means exhaustive, surveys are listed here.

F11   Beals, Ralph L., and others. An introduction to anthropology. 5th ed. New York: Macmillan, 1977. 749p.

F12   Ember, Carol R., and Melvin Ember. Anthropology. Englewood Cliffs, N.J.: Prentice-Hall, 1977. 512p.

F13   Hockett, Charles F. Man's place in nature. New York: McGraw-Hill, 1973. 739p.

F14   Jarvie, Ian C. The story of social anthropology: the quest to understand human society. New York: McGraw-Hill, 1972. 131p.

F15   Keesing, Roger M. Cultural anthropology: a contemporary perspective. New York: Holt, 1976. 637p.

F16   Pfeiffer, John E. The emergence of society: a prehistory of the establishment. New York: McGraw-Hill, 1977. 512p.

More-recent works relevant to a general understanding of anthropology include the following:

F17   Alland, Alexander. To be human: an introduction to anthropology. New York: Wiley, 1980. 657p.

F18   Hoebel, E. Adamson, and others, eds. Crisis in anthropology: view from Spring Hill, 1980. New York: Garland, 1982. 546p.

F19   Kottak, Conrad. Anthropology: the exploration of human diversity. 3d. ed. New York: Random, 1982. 576p.

F20   Naroll, Raoul. The moral order: an introduction to the human situation. Beverly Hills, Calif.: Sage, 1983. 498p.

HISTORICAL DEVELOPMENT

A developing interest in the history of anthropology noted in the last edition of this volume has now born fruit in the publication of a large number of syntheses, biographies and commentaries written by anthropologists. Several professional historians of science have begun to specialize in anthropology. Existing histories, although they tend to agree upon the importance of such major categories as evolutionism, functionalism, or culture and personality, still fail to give us any strong picture of the development of anthropological ideas or of the very strong influences of anthropology upon adjoining fields. Unburdened by lavish and irrelevant detail about unimportant investigators, the briefer histories seem to provide a grander and more consistent picture.

F21   Brew, John Otis, ed. One hundred years of anthropology. Cambridge, Mass.: Harvard Univ. Pr., 1968. 276p.

F22   Darnell, Regna, ed. Readings in the history of anthropology. New York: Harper, 1974. 479p.

F23   deWall Malefijt, Annamarie. Images of man: a history of anthropological thought. New York: Knopf, 1974. 383p.

F24   Firth, Raymond William. Man and culture: an evaluation of the work of Bronislaw Malinowski. London: Routledge & Paul, 1968. 292p.

F25   Fortes, Meyer. Kinship and the social order: the legacy of Lewis Henry Morgan. Chicago: Aldine, 1970. 347p.

F26   Garbarino, Merwyn S. Sociocultural theory in anthropology: a short history. Ed. by Basic Anthropology Units and others. New York: Holt, 1977. 144p.

F27   Goldschmidt, Walter Rochs. The anthropology of Franz Boas: essays on the centennial of his birth. Washington, D.C.: American Anthropological Assn., 1959. 165p.

F28   Hays, Hoffman Reynolds. From ape to angel: an informal history of social anthropology. New York: Knopf, 1958. 440p.

F29   Henson, Hilary. British social anthropologists and language: a history of separate development. Oxford: Clarendon, 1974. 147p.

F30   Honigmann, John J. The development of anthropological ideas. Homewood, Ill.: Dorsey, 1976. 434p.

F31   Kaplan, David, and Robert A. Manners. Culture theory. Englewood Cliffs, N.J.: Prentice-Hall, 1972. 212p.

F32   Laguna, Frederica de, ed. Selected papers from the *American anthropologist*, 1888–1920.

Washington, D.C.: American Anthropological Assn., [c1960] 1977, 930p.

F33   Langness, L. L. The study of culture. San Francisco: Chandler, 1974. 181p.

F34   Lipset, David. Gregory Bateson: the legacy of a scientist. Englewood Cliffs, N.J.: Prentice-Hall, 1980. 360p.

F35   Lowie, Robert H. The history of ethnological theory. New York: Farrar & Rinehart, 1937. 296p.

F36   ———. Robert H. Lowie, ethnologist; a personal record. Berkeley and Los Angeles: Univ. of California Pr., 1959. 198p.

F37   Murphy, Robert F., ed. Selected papers from the *American anthropologist*, 1946–1970. Washington, D.C.: American Anthropological Assn., 1976. 424p.

F38   Stocking, George W., Jr. Race, culture and evolution: essays in the history of anthropology. New York: Free Pr., 1968. 380p.

F39   ———, ed. Selected papers from the *American anthropologist*, 1921–1945. Washington, D.C.: American Anthropological Assn., 1976. 485p.

F40   Voget, Fred W. A history of ethnology. New York: Holt, 1975. 879p.

Several biographical and autobiographical appraisals of the works of major figures in the development of anthropology have been published in recent years. Partly due to the biographical activities of Charles Wagley and his colleagues at Columbia University, biographies now exist for all but a few important figures in the history of the discipline. Some of these materials, along with a few collections of papers, are listed below. In addition see June Helm MacNeish, *Pioneers of American anthropology*, at F892.

F41   Herskovits, Melville Jean. Franz Boas: the science of man in the making. New York: Scribner, 1953. 131p.

F42   Kroeber, A. L., and others. Franz Boas: 1858–1942. Washington, D.C.: American Anthropological Assn., 1943. 119p. Reprint, New York: Kraus Intl. Pubs., 1969.

F43   Kroeber, Theodora. Alfred Kroeber: a personal configuration. Berkeley: Univ. of California Pr., 1970. 292p.

F44   Kuper, Adam. Anthropologists and anthropology: the British school, 1922–1972. New York: Pica Pr., 1973. 256p.

F45   Linton, Adelin Summer, and Charles Wagley. Ralph Linton. New York: Columbia Univ. Pr., 1971. 196p.

F47 Mead, Margaret. An anthropologist at work: writings of Ruth Benedict. Boston: Houghton, 1959. 583p.

F48 ———. Ruth Benedict. New York: Columbia Univ. Pr., 1973. 180p.

F49 Murphy, Robert Francis. Robert H. Lowie. New York: Columbia Univ. Pr., 1972. 179p.

F50 Resek, Carl. Lewis Henry Morgan: American scholar. Chicago: Univ. of Chicago Pr., 1960. 184p.

F51 Stern, Bernard Joseph. Lewis Henry Morgan: social evolutionist. New York: Russell & Russell, 1967. 221p.

F52 Steward, Julian Haynes. Alfred Kroeber. New York: Columbia Univ. Pr., 1973. 137p.

F53 Taylor, Walter W., and others. Culture and life: essays in memory of Clyde Kluckhohn. Carbondale: Southern Illinois Univ. Pr., 1973. 225p.

F54 Woodbury, Richard B. Alfred V. Kidder, New York: Columbia Univ. Pr., 1973. 220p.

As is true of many other disciplines, anthropology has been influenced by the interdisciplinary works of such people as Darwin and Wallace, Freud, Marx, Durkheim, Weber, Simmel, Mead, Spencer, and Ratzel. The beginnings of the organized discipline are usually set during the 1860s and '70s with the publication of the classic writings of Morgan, Tylor, and Maine. The second half of the nineteenth century and the early part of the twentieth saw the publication of a number of seminal works that were to have profound influence upon the development of the discipline. Some of these works, deemed most important for an understanding of the field, are:

F55 Bachofen, Johann Jakob. Das Mutterrecht. Mit unterstutsung von Harold Fuchs, Gustav Meyere und Karl Schefold. Hrsg. von Karl Meuli. Basel: B. Schwabe [c1861], 1948. 2v. 1,176p.

F56 ———. Myth, religion, and mother right: selected writings of J. J. Bachofen. Tr. by R. Manheim. Princeton, N.J.: Princeton Univ. Pr., 1967. 309p.

F57 Maine, Sir Henry S. Ancient law: its connection with the early history of society and its relation to modern ideas. London: J. Murray, 1861. 451p.

F58 ———. Lectures on the early history of institutions. Port Washington, N.Y.: Kennikat, 1966. 412p.

F59 ———. Village communities in the East and West. London: J. Murray, 1890. 413p.

F60 Morgan, Lewis Henry. Ancient society; or, Researchers in the lines of human progress from savagery, through barbarianism to civilization. New York: Holt, 1877. 560p.

F61 ———. Systems of consanguinity and affinity of the human family. Smithsonian, 1870. 590p.

F62 Pitt-Rivers, A. Lane-Fox. The evolution of culture and other essays. Ed. by J. L. Myres. Oxford: Clarendon, 1906. Reprint, New York: AMS Pr., 1979. 232p.

F63 Smith, William Robertson. Lectures on the religion of the Semites. New rev. ed. New York: Macmillan, 1927. 718p. (First series, The fundamental institutions.)

F64 ———. Lectures and essays of William Robertson Smith. Ed. by J. S. Black and G. Chrystal. London: A. & C. Black, 1912. 622p.

F65 Tylor, Edward Burnett. Anthropology: an introduction to the study of man and civilization. New York: Appleton, 1898. 448p.

F66 ———. Primitive culture. 5th ed. London: J. Murray, 1877, 1929. 2v.

F67 ———. Researches into the early history of mankind and the development of civilization. Ed. & abridged with an introd. by P. Bohannan. Chicago: Univ. of Chicago Pr. [c1865], 1964. 295p.

F68 Westermarck, Edward Alexander. The history of human marriage. 5th ed. New York: Macmillan, 1922. 3v.

F69 ———. The origin and development of the moral ideas. 2d ed. London: Macmillan, 1912–17. 2v.

From the time of Thomas Jefferson, such workers as Lewis and Clark, Schoolcraft, Morgan, Mooney, Putnam, and Mason had developed a lively applied and theoretical discipline in the United States, but it lacked a strong academic base. To remedy this deficiency, a distinguished German scholar who had already published important work on the diffusion of mythology on the northwestern coast and on Eskimo technology was brought in. By 1900, Franz Boas had established a department at Clark University and had published several articles establishing the paradigm for a scientific anthropology. In Boas' view, such an anthropology was to involve careful study of historical, environmental, and psychological factors leading to explanations of the development of cultural variation in each part of the world. All-encompassing schemes and worldwide generalizations were to be deferred until there was sufficient evidence to ensure that the data used in comparative research were genuinely comparable instead of merely similar in superficial appearance. As of the early part of the twentieth century, the major works in American anthropology were as follows:

F70 Lewis, Meriwether, and William Clark. The original journals of the Lewis and Clark Expedition, 1804–1806. Ed. with introd., notes, and index by R. G. Thwaites. New York: Antiquarian Pr. [c1904–5], 1959. 8v.

F71 Mason, Otis Tufton. Woman's share in primitive culture. New York: Appleton, 1894. 295p.

F72 ———. The origins of invention: a study of industry among primitive peoples. London: Scott, 1895. Reprint, Freeport, N.Y.: Books for Libraries Pr., 1972. 419p.

F73 Mooney, James. The Siouan tribes of the East. Washington, D.C.: Govt. Print. Off., 1894. Reprint, New York: Johnson Reprint Corp., 1970. 101p.

F74 ———. The ghost-dance religion and the Sioux outbreak of 1890. Chicago: Univ. of Chicago Pr., 1965. 359p.

F75 ———. The Swimmer manuscripts: Cherokee sacred formulas and medicinal prescriptions. Ed. by F. M. Obrechts. Washington, D.C.: Govt. Print. Off., 1932. 319p.

F76 Morgan, Lewis Henry. The Indian journals, 1859–62. Ed. with introd. by L. A. White. Ann Arbor: Univ. of Michigan Pr., 1959. 229p.

F77 ———. Houses and house life of the American aborigines. Chicago: Univ. of Chicago Pr., 1965. 319p.

F78 Powell, John Wesley. Indian linguistic families of America north of Mexico. 7th Annual Report of the Bureau of American Ethnology. Washington, D. C.: Govt. Print. Off., 1891. 142p.

F79 Putnam, Frederic Ward. The selected archaeological papers of Frederic Ward Putnam. New York: AMS Pr. for the Peabody Museum, 1973. 269p.

F80 Schoolcraft, Henry Row. Information respecting the history, condition, and prospect of the Indian tribes of the United States. New York: Paladin Pr. [c1951–57], 1969. 6v.

Although Boas' go-slow approach to the making of grand generalizations undoubtedly grated upon some of his students, most notably Margaret Mead and Ruth Benedict, a surprising number followed versions of the Boasian paradigm in their own research. Kroeber attempted to define the separate environments in which the cultures of North America developed and through the numerous publications of the Culture Element Distribution List sought to reconstruct the history of California Indian culture. Sapir, before he moved solidly into linguistics,

attempted to develop a set of rules for historical reconstruction. Redfield attempted to validate Park and Burgess' theories of urbanization by studying the development of culture in Yucatán. Taking a slightly different tack, Herskovits studied Afro-American culture from its possible roots in Dahomey (now Benin) to its various transformations in Guyana, Trinidad, Brazil, and the American South. Wissler, using the age-area, or diffusion, hypothesis, attempted to reconstruct the history of the Plains region. Boas himself organized the Jesup expedition in order to verify the hypothesis of prehistoric and historic interchanges across the Bering Straits. Some of the work of Boas and his students is listed below.

F81 Boas, Franz. Race, language and culture. New York: Macmillan, 1948. 647p.

F82 Benedict, Ruth. The chrysanthemum and the sword. Boston: Houghton, 1946. 324p.

F83 ———. Patterns of culture. 2d ed. Boston: Houghton, 1961. 290p.

F84 Goldenweiser, Alexander A. History, psychology and culture. New York: Knopf, 1933. 475p.

F85 ———. Anthropology: an introduction to primitive culture. New York: F. S. Crofts, 1946. 550p.

F86 Herskovits, Melville. Man and his works: the science of cultural anthropology. New York: Knopf, 1948. 678p.

F87 Kroeber, Alfred L. Anthropology. New York: Harcourt, 1923. 523p.

F88 ———. Configurations of culture growth. Berkeley: Univ. of California Pr., 1944. 882p.

F89 ———. Anthropology: race, language, culture, psychology, prehistory. New York: Harcourt, 1948. 856p.
See also *Anthropology today* (F951), edited by Kroeber.

F91 ———, and Clyde Kluckhohn. Culture: a critical review of concepts and definitions. Cambridge, Mass.: Peabody Museum, 1952. 223p.

F92 Lowie, Robert Harry. Culture and ethnology. New York: Basic Books, 1966. 189p.

F93 ———. Primitive religion. New York: Liveright, 1952. 382p.

F94 ———. The origin of the state. New York: Russell & Russell, 1954. 117p.

F95 ———. Social organization. New York: Holt, 1966. 465p.

F96 Mandelbaum, David G., ed. Selected writings in language, culture and personality. Berkeley: Univ. of California Pr., 1951. 617p.

F97 Mead, Margaret. Coming of age in Samoa. New York: Morrow, 1928. 297p.

F98 ———. Sex and temperament in three primitive societies. New York: Morrow, 1963. 335p.

F99 Radin, Paul. The method and theory of ethnology: an essay in criticism. New York: Basic Books, 1966. 278p.

F100 Redfield, Robert. The folk culture of Yucatan. Chicago: Univ. of Chicago Pr., 1941. 416p.

F101 Sapir, Edward. Language: an introduction to the study of speech. New York: Harcourt, 1921. 258p.

F102 Wissler, Clark. An introduction to social anthropology. New York: Holt, 1929. 392p.

F103 ———. Man and culture. New York: Crowell, 1923. 371p.

F104 ———. The American Indians: an introduction to the anthropology of the New World. New York: P. Smith [c1938], 1957. 435p.

The varieties of functionalism developed by Radcliffe-Brown and Malinowski quickly swept across England and took a firm root in the United States. Radcliffe-Brown contributed heavily to modern perceptions of the nature of cultural systems, while Malinowski was the first to formulate the basic principles of anthropological fieldwork. On the other hand, Radcliffe-Brown's reconstruction of Andaman Island culture was something of a disaster; so was Malinowski's attempt to develop a theory of culture around the concept of needs. Only a few major works by Radcliffe-Brown, Malinowski, and their students can be listed here.

F105 Barnes, John Arundel. Three styles in the study of kinship. Berkeley: Univ. of California Pr., 1973. 318p.

F106 Evans-Pritchard, Edward Evan. Social anthropology and other essays. New York: Free Pr., 1964. 354p.

F107 ———. Witchcraft, oracles and magic among the Azande. Oxford: Clarendon, 1950. 558p.

F108 Firth, Raymond William. We, the Tipokia: a sociological study of kinship in primitive Polynesia. 2d ed. Boston: Beacon, 1963. 488p.

F109 Forde, Cyril Daryll. Habitat, economy and society: a geographical introduction to ethnology. New York: Dutton, 1963. 500p.

F110 Fortes, Meyer. Marriage in tribal societies. Cambridge: Cambridge Univ. Pr., 1962. 157p.

F111 ———. The dynamics of clanship among the Tallensi: being the first part of an analysis of the social structure of a trans-Volta tribe. New York: Oxford Univ. Pr., 1945. 270p.

F112 ———. The web of kinship among the Tallensi: the second part of an analysis of the social structure of a trans-Volta tribe. New York: Oxford Univ. Pr., 1949. 358p.

F113 ———, and Edward Evan Evans-Pritchard, eds. African political systems. Oxford: Oxford Univ. Pr., 1940. 302p.

F114 Gluckman, Max. Custom and conflict in Africa. Oxford: Basil Blackwell, 1965. 173p.

F115 Hogbin, Herbert Ian. Social change. London: Watts, 1958. 257p.

F116 Kuper, Hilda. The uniform of colour: a study of white-black relationships in Swaziland. Johannesburg: Witwaterstrand Univ. Pr., 1947. 160p.

F117 ———. An African aristocracy: rank among the Swazi. London: Oxford Univ. Pr., 1961. 251p.

F118 Malinowski, Bronislaw. Coral gardens and their magic: soil tilling and agriculture in the Trobriand Islands, v. 1. Bloomington: Indiana Univ. Pr., 1965. 500p.

F119 ———. Argonauts of the Western Pacific: an account of native enterprise and adventure in the archipelagoes of Melanesian New Guinea. New York: Dutton, 1950. 527p.

F120 ———. Coral gardens and their magic: the language of gardening, v. 2. Bloomington: Indiana Univ. Pr., 1965. 350p.

F121 ———. Sex and repression in savage society. London: K. Paul, Trench, Trubner Co. Ltd., 1953. 285p.

F122 Middleton, John Francis, and David Tait, eds. Tribes without rulers: studies in African segmentary systems. London: Routledge & Paul, 1959. 234p.

F123 Nadel, Sigfried Frederick Stephen. The theory of social structure. Glencoe, Ill.: Free Pr., 1957. 159p.

F124 ———. The foundations of social anthropology. Glencoe, Ill.: Free Pr., 1951. 426p.

F125 Powdermaker, Hortense. Copper town: changing Africa, the human situation on the Rhodesian copperbelt. New York: Harper, 1962. 391p.

F126 ———. After freedom: a cultural study in the Deep South. New York: Viking Pr., 1968. 408p.

F127 Radcliffe-Brown, Alfred Reginald. A natural science of society. Glencoe, Ill.: Free Pr., 1957. 156p.

F128 ———. Structure and function in primitive society: essays and addresses. New York: Free Pr., 1965. 219p.

F129 ———, Alfred Reginald, and Cyril Daryll Forde, eds. African systems of kinship and marriage. Oxford: Oxford Univ. Pr., 1950. 399p.

F130 Richards, Audrey I. Land, labour and diet in Northern Rhodesia. London: Oxford Univ. Pr., 1939. 423p.

F131 ———. Hunger and work in a savage tribe. London: Routledge & Sons, 1932. 238p.

BIOLOGICAL ANTHROPOLOGY

Biological anthropology seeks understanding of the relationships between human culture and human biology. Early biological anthropology emphasized the measurement of human fossils and systematic comparison of existing human populations. Here, Boas was the first to question the existence of human races and the first to demonstrate the influence of culture and environment in the formation of supposedly racial traits such as head shape and stature. A few systematic surveys of biological anthropology are listed below, the older selections being mainly of historical interest.

F132 Birdsell, J. B. Human evolution: an introduction to the new physical anthropology. 3d ed. Palo Alto, Calif.: Houghton, 1981. 440p.

F133 Brace, C. Loring. The stages of human evolution: human and cultural origins. 2d ed. Englewood Cliffs, N.J.: Prentice-Hall, 1979. 116p.

F134 Buettner-Janusch, John. Physical anthropology: a perspective. New York: Wiley, 1973. 572p.

F135 Campbell, Bernard G., ed. Humankind emerging. 3d ed. Boston: Little, 1982. 514p.

F136 Harrison. G. A., and others. Human biology: an introduction to human evolution, variation, growth & ecology. 2d ed. New York: Oxford Univ. Pr., 1977. 499p.

F137 Hooton, Earnest A. Up from the ape. New York: Macmillan, 1931. 626p.

F138 Lerner, Isador Michael, and William J. Libby. Heredity, evolution, and society. San Francisco: Freeman, 1976. 431p.

F139 Poirier, Frank E. In search of ourselves: an introduction to physical anthropology. 2d ed. Minneapolis: Burgess, 1977. 478p.

F140 Weiss, Mark L., and Alan E. Mann. Human biology and behavior: an anthropological perspective. 2d ed. Boston: Little, 1978. 484p.

Traditional interests in variation among modern human beings are now largely expressed in terms of studies of genetic variation and human micro-evolution. Some recent and important works in this field include:

F141 Bodmer, W. F., and L. L. Cavalli-Sforza. Genetics, evolution and man. San Francisco: Freeman, 1976. 782p.

F142 Cavalli-Sforza, L. L. Elements of human genetics. 2d ed. Menlo Park, Calif.: Benjamin, 1977. 158p.

F143 Crawford, M. H., and P. L. Workman, eds. Methods and theories of anthropological genetics. Albuquerque: Univ. of New Mexico Pr., 1973. 509p.

F144 Dobzhansky, Theodosius Grigorievich. Genetic diversity and human equality. New York: Basic Books, 1973. 128p.

F145 Harrison, Geoffrey A., ed. Population structure and human variation. Cambridge: Cambridge Univ. Pr., 1977. 342p.

F146 ———, and Anthony J. Boyce, eds. The structure of human populations. Oxford: Clarendon, 1972. 447p.

F147 Lewontin, Richard C. The genetic basis of evolutionary change. New York: Columbia Univ. Pr., 1974. 346p.

F148 Roberts, D. F. Climate and human variability. 2d ed. Menlo Park, Calif.: Cummings, 1978. 123p.

F149 Salzano, Francisco M., ed. The role of natural selection in human evolution. Amsterdam: North-Holland, 1975. 439p.

F150 Speiss, E. B. Genetics in populations. New York: Wiley, 1977. 780p.

F151 Ward, Richard H., and Kenneth M. Weiss, eds. The demographic evolution of human populations. New York: Academic Pr., 1976. 158p.

The second major field within biological anthropology is the study of human and skeletal fossil remains. This most traditional field involves close collaboration with archaeologists and a profound understanding of evolutionary process. Recent and numerous finds, especially in Africa, have permitted increasingly sophisticated interpretations of the development of humanity.

F152 Brace, C. Loring, and others, eds. Atlas of human evolution. 2d ed. New York: Holt, 1979. 178p.

F153 Day, Michael H. Guide to fossil man: a handbook of human paleontology. 3d ed. London: Cassell, 1977. 346p.

F154 Isaac, Glynn, and Richard E. Leakey, eds. Human ancestors: readings from Scientific American. San Francisco: Freeman, 1979. 130p.

F155 Isaac, Glynn L., and Elizabeth R. McCown, eds. Human origins: Louis Leakey and the East

African evidence. Menlo Park, Calif.: Benjamin, 1976. 591p.

F156 Leakey, Richard, and Roger Lewin. People of the lake: mankind and its beginnings. Garden City, N.Y.: Anchor Books, 1978. 298p.

F157 Pfeiffer, John E. The emergence of man. 3d ed. New York: Harper, 1978. 477p.

F158 Poirier, Frank E. Fossil evidence: the human evolutionary journey. 2d ed. St. Louis: Mosby, 1977. 342p.

F159 Robinson, John Talbot. Early hominid posture and locomotion. Chicago: Univ. of Chicago Pr., 1972. 357p.

F160 Simons, Elwyn L. Primate evolution: an introduction to man's place in nature. New York: Macmillan, 1972. 321p.

F161 Washburn, Sherwood Larned, and Ruth Moore. Ape into humans: a study of human evolution. Boston: Little, 1980. 196p.

New methodologies and new fossil discoveries result in constant revision of anthropological interpretations of human evolution. A few recent and relevant works are listed below. See also Mark L. Weiss and Alan E. Mann, *Human biology and behavior: an anthropological perspective,* described at F130.

F162 Brain, C. K. The hunters or the hunted? An introduction to African cave taphonomy. Chicago: Univ. of Chicago Pr., 1981. 365p.

F163 Skinner, Mark F., and Geoffrey H. Sperber. Atlas of radiographs of early man. New York: Liss, 1982. 346p.

F165 Wolpoff, Milford H. Paleoanthropology. New York: Knopf, 1980. 412p.

Studies of microevolution and fossil hominids are now being illuminated by increased knowledge concerning the primate contemporaries of modern humanity. Field studies of primates as well as of other mammalian species have sharpened our understandings of the nature of humanity and of the probable course of human evolution.

F166 Bramblett, Claud A. Patterns of primate behavior. Palo Alto, Calif.: Mayfield, 1976. 320p.

F167 Dolhinow, Phyllis, ed. Primate patterns. New York: Holt, 1972. 425p.

F168 Hamburg, David A., and Elizabeth R. McCown, eds. The great apes. Menlo Park, Calif.: Benjamin-Cummings, 1979. 553p.

F169 Jolly, Alison. The evolution of primate behavior. New York: Macmillan, 1972. 397p.

F170 Kummer, Hans. Primate societies: group techniques of ecological adaptation. Chicago: Aldine, 1971. 160p.

F171 Lancaster, Jane Beckman. Primate behavior and the emergence of human culture. New York: Holt, 1975. 98p.

F172 Poirier, Frank E., ed. Primate socialization. New York: Random, 1972. 260p.

F173 Sussman, Robert W. Primate ecology: problem-oriented field studies. New York: Wiley, 1979. 596p.

F174 Tuttle, Russell H., ed. Socioecology and psychology of primates. The Hague: Mouton, 1975. 474p. (World anthropology series)

F175 van Lawick-Goodall, Jane. In the shadow of man. New York: Dell, 1971. 304p.

ARCHAEOLOGY: HISTORY AND PREHISTORY

The chief difference between archaeology and the more general field of cultural anthropology is that archaeologists obtain information about culture through the study of material remains. In archaeology, the questions and observations of the ethnographer are replaced by such real instruments as the shovel and the microscope. Many general surveys of archaeology and prehistory are available, some of the most recent being listed below:

F176 Chard, Chester S. Man in prehistory. 2d ed. New York: McGraw-Hill, 1975. 406p.

F177 Fagan, Brian M. In the beginning: an introduction to archaeology. 3d ed. Boston: Little, 1978. 562p.

F178 Knudson, S. J. Culture in retrospect: an introduction to archaeology. Chicago: Rand McNally, 1978. 555p.

F180 Thomas, David Hurst. Archaeology. New York: Holt, 1979. 510p.

F181 Willey, Gordon R., and Jeremy Sabloff. A history of American archaeology. San Francisco: Freeman, 1974. 252p.

See also, *The emergence of society* by John E. Pfeiffer described at F16.

During the 1940s, with the strong onset of functionalism and the corresponding decline in the importance of historical reconstruction and of the study of technology, social and cultural anthropology became increasingly separated from archaeology. There ceased to be grand theories of history uniting the two subdisciplines. During the past decade, the interests of workers in the two fields have begun to overlap at a number of points. The themes of space, ecology, population, and taxonomy have provided a solid basis for interaction. New theories about cultural change and development have led to further unification. In both fields, methodological innovation has provided more and better information for comparative purposes. The new archaeology—perhaps even the new, new archaeology—is best expressed in the following titles.

F182   Binford, Lewis R. An archaeological perspective. With a contribution by George I. Quimby. New York: Seminar Pr., 1972. 464p.

F183   Binford, Sally, and Lewis R. Binford, eds. New perspectives in archaeology. Chicago: Aldine, 1968. 373p.

F184   Butzer, Karl W. Environment and archeology: an ecological approach to prehistory. 2d ed. Chicago: Aldine, 1971. 703p.

F185   Chang, Kwang Chih. Settlement patterns in archaeology. Reading, Mass.: Addison-Wesley, 1972. 26p.

F186   Cohen, Mark Nathan. The food crisis in prehistory: overpopulation and the origins of agriculture. New Haven, Conn.: Yale Univ. Pr., 1977. 341p.

F187   Coles, John. Archaeology by experiment. New York: Scribner, 1974. 182p.

F188   Dora, Jay, and F. R. Hodson. Mathematics and computers in archaeology. Edinburgh: Edinburgh Univ. Pr., 1975. 381p.

F189   Hester, Thomas R., and others, eds. Field methods in archaeology. 6th ed. Palo Alto, Calif.: Mayfield, 1975. 408p.

F190   Hodder, Ian, ed. The spatial organization of culture. Pittsburgh: Univ. of Pittsburgh Pr., 1978. 310p.

F191   Ingersoll, Daniel, and others, eds. Experimental archaeology. New York: Columbia Univ. Pr., 1977. 423p.

F192   Lamberg-Karlovsky, C. C., ed. Hunters, farmers, and civilizations, old world archaeology: readings from *Scientific American*. San Francisco: Freeman, 1979. 306p.

F193   Redman, Charles L. Rise of civilization: early farmers to urban society in the ancient Near East. San Francisco: Freeman, 1978. 367p.

F194   ———, ed. Social archaeology: beyond subsistence and dating. New York: Academic, 1978. 471p.

F195   Renfrew, Colin, ed. The explanation of culture change: models in prehistory: proceedings of a meeting of the Research Seminar in Archaeology & Related Subjects held at the Univ. of Sheffield. London: Duckworth, 1973. 788p.

F196   Schiffer, Michael B. Behavioral archeology. New York: Academic, 1976. 222p.

F197   Sieveking, G. de G., and others, eds. Problems in economic and social archaeology. Boulder, Colo.: Westview, 1977. 626p.

F198   Smith, Philip E. L. Food production and its consequences. 2d ed. Menlo Park, Calif.: Cummings, 1976. 120p.

F199   Watson, Patty Jo, and others. Explanation in archaeology: an explicitly scientific approach. New York: Columbia Univ. Pr., 1971. 191p.

Traditionally, archaeology has been a strongly empirical discipline that conceived of itself as a handmaiden of history or as an impoverished recipient of theoretical leftovers from the rich banquet spread by those cultural anthropologists lucky enough to study the living or the only recently dead. During this decade, emboldened by new techniques and a wider vision of human conditions, the archaeologists have boldly, even recklessly, entered the arena of theory. Several of the works cited above and the following works attest to the strength of this efflorescence:

F200   Butzer, Karl W. Archaeology as human ecology: methods and theory for a contextual approach. New York: Cambridge Univ. Pr., 1982. 364p.

F201   Dickens, Roy S., Jr., ed. Archaeology of urban America: the search for pattern and process. New York: Academic, 1982. 468p.

F202   Gardes, Jean Claude. Archaeological constructs: an aspect of theoretical archaeology. New York: Cambridge Univ. Pr., 1980. 202p.

F203   Hassan, Fekri A. Demographic archaeology. New York: Academic, 1981. 312p.

F204   Joukowsky, Martha. A complete manual of field archaeology: tools and techniques of fieldwork for archaeologists. Englewood Cliffs, N.J.: Prentice-Hall, 1980. 630p.

F205   Paynter, Robert. Models of spatial inequality: settlement patterns in historical archaeology. New York: Academic, 1982. 308p.

F206   Renfrew, Colin, and Kenneth L. Cooke, eds. Transformations: mathematical approaches to culture change. New York: Academic, 1979. 515p.

ANTHROPOLOGICAL LINGUISTICS

Because the development of theories of language cannot take place within a discipline limited to information concerning Indo-European languages and their history, anthropological linguistics has always occupied a key position in the development of linguistic theory. The foundations of American linguistics were laid by Sapir and Bloomfield in the 1920s. For Sapir's work, *Language: an introduction to the study of speech,* see F101. An overview for beginners is Eastman, 1978. Also useful are Gleason, Austerlitz, and Greenberg, and the works on historical linguistics by Arlotto and Lehman.

Classical linguistics undertook the description and classification of the world's languages. To achieve this, simplifying assumptions were made concerning correct and incorrect usage. Thus, a grammar has been viewed as a device for processing vocabulary in order to produce correct sentences. More recently, linguists have begun to face the hard questions concerning the nature of language and the problem of producing sentences that are not just reasonably correct but are also meaningful and appropriate. Studies of animal communication, especially that of apes specifically trained to use various "languages," have acquired a considerable importance and have recently been reviewed with some enthusiasm by Linden.

The study of meaning is subsumed under the heading of sociolinguistics, a field not always easily distinguishable from parallel fields in ethnography and general anthropology. Works by Basso and Selby, Bauman and Scherzer, and Burling cover various aspects of sociolinguistics.

F207 Arlotto, Anthony. Introduction to historical linguistics. Houghton, 1972. 274p.

F208 Austerlitz, Robert, ed. The scope of American linguistics: The papers of the first Golden Anniversary symposium of the Linguistic Society of America. Lisse, Netherlands: Peter de Ridder Pr., 1975. 209p.

F209 Basso, Keith H., and Henry A. Selby, eds. Meaning in anthropology. Albuquerque: Univ. of New Mexico Pr., 1976. 255p.

F210 Bauman, Richard, and Joel Sherzer. Explorations in the ethnography of speaking. New York: Cambridge Univ. Pr., 1974. 501p.

F211 Bloomfield, Leonard. Language. New York: Holt, 1933. 564p.

F212 Burling, Robbins. Man's many voices: language in its cultural context. New York: Holt, 1970. 222p.

F213 Chomsky, Noam. Aspects of the theory of syntax. Cambridge, Mass.: MIT Pr., 1965. 251p.

F214 ———. Syntactic structures. The Hague: Mouton, 1957. 116p.

F215 Cook, Walter A. Introduction to tagmemic analysis. New York: Holt, 1969. 210p.

F216 Eastman, Carol M. Linguistic theory and language description. New York: Lippincott, 1978. 212p.

F217 ———. Aspects of language and culture. San Francisco: Chandler, 1975. 153p.

F218 Gleason, Henry Allen. An introduction to descriptive linguistics. Rev. ed. New York: Holt, 1961. 503p.

F219 Greenberg, Joseph H. A new invitation to linguistics. Garden City, N.Y.: Anchor Books, 1977. 147p.

F220 ———. Anthropological linguistics: an introduction. New York: Random, 1968. 212p.

F221 ———, ed. Universals of language: report. 2d ed. Cambridge: MIT Pr., 1966. 337p.

F222 Gumperz, John J., and Dell Hymes, eds. Directions in sociolinguistics: the ethnography of communication. New York: Holt, 1972. 598p.

F223 Hockett, Charles Francis. The view from language: selected essays, 1948–1974. Athens: Univ. of Georgia Pr., 1977. 338p.

F224 Hymes, Dell, ed. Language in culture and society: a reader in linguistics and anthropology. New York: Harper, 1964. 764p.

F225 Linden, Eugene. Apes, men, and language. Baltimore: Penguin, 1976. 304p.

F226 Lyons, John. Semantics. 2v. London: Cambridge Univ. Pr., 1977. v. 1: 371p.; v. 2: 897p.

F227 ———. Introduction to theoretical linguistics. London: Cambridge Univ. Pr., 1968. 519p.

F228 Nida, Eugene Albert. Componential analysis of meaning: an introduction to semantic structures. The Hague: Mouton, 1975. 272p.

F229 Pike, Kenneth L., and Evelyn G. Pike. Grammatical analysis. Dallas: Summer Institute of Linguistics, 1977. 505p.

F231 de Saussure, Ferdinand. Course in general linguistics. Ed. by C. Bally and A. Sechehaye. Tr. by W. Baskin. New York: McGraw-Hill, 1959. 240p.

F232 Voegelin, C. F., and F. M. Voegelin. Classification and index of the world's languages. Ed. by Charles F. Hockett. Amsterdam: Elsevier, 1977. 658p. [Foundations of linguistics]

F233 Whorf, Benjamin Lee. Language, thought and reality: selected writings. Ed. and introd. by John B. Carroll. Cambridge, Mass.: Technology Pr. of MIT, 1956. 278p.

Recent developments in linguistics are surveyed, sometimes all too briefly, by Hickerson. The other works cited below may give a further impression of the new thrusts of the discipline:

F234 Gumperz, John J. Discourse strategies. New York: Cambridge Univ. Pr., 1982. 228p.

F235 Hickerson, Nancy Parrott. Linguistic anthropology. New York: Holt, 1980. 168p.

F236 Lightfoot, David. The language lottery: toward a biology of grammars. Cambridge, Mass.: MIT Pr., 1982. 224p.

F237 Marcus, Mitchell P. A theory of syntactic recognition for natural language. Cambridge, Mass.: MIT Pr., 1980. 335p.

METHOD

Until the 1960s, knowledge of anthropological methodology diffused primarily by word of mouth from teacher to student. A sophisticated methodologist owned a copy of a statistics textbook, a manual of survey research, a few notes from Malinowski, and, perhaps, a book of instructions for the Thematic Apperception Test. During the 1960s, George and Louis Spindler added a series of works on method to their collection of case studies. At the same time, mathematical anthropology was beginning to emerge as a distinct subdiscipline, with the computer revolution leaving deep impressions upon everything from demography to folklore. Works edited by Golde, Jongmans and Gutkind, and Spindler provide individual accounts of the problems of fieldwork. Works by Thomas, Pelto, and Johnson provide rather different overviews of more technical methods. In addition see John J. Honigmann, *Handbook of social and cultural anthropology*, described at F946.

F238 Agar, Michael H. The professional stranger: an informal introduction to ethnography. New York: Academic, 1980. 227p. [Studies in anthropology]

F239 Ballonoff, Raul A. Mathematical foundations of social anthropology. The Hague: Mouton, 1976. 131p.

F240 Friedrichs, Jürgen, and Hartmut Lüdtke. Participant observation: theory and practice. Lexington, Mass.: Lexington Books, 1975. 257p.

F241 Golde, Peggy. Women in the field: anthropological experiences. Chicago: Aldine, 1970. 343p.

F242 Goodenough, Ward H. Description and comparison in cultural anthropology. Chicago: Aldine, 1970. 173p.

F243 Heider, Karl G. Ethnographic film. Austin: Univ. of Texas Pr., 1976. 166p.

F245 Johnson, Allen W. Quantification in cultural anthropology: an introduction to research design. Stanford, Calif.: Stanford Univ. Pr., 1978. 231p.

F246 Jongmans, D. G., and P. C. W. Gutkind, eds. Anthropologists in the field. Assen, Netherlands: Van Gorcum, 1967. 277p.

F247 Leinhardt, Samuel, ed. Social networks: a developing paradigm. New York: Academic, 1977. 465p.

F248 Levinson, David, ed. A guide to social theory: worldwide cross-cultural tests. 5v. New Haven, Conn.: Human Relations Area Files Pr., 1977.

F249 Lofland, John. Doing social life: the qualitative study of human interaction in natural settings. New York: Wiley, 1976. 328p.

F250 Pelto, Pertti J., and Gretel H. Pelto. Anthropological research: the structure of inquiry. 2d ed. Cambridge: Cambridge Univ. Pr., 1978. 333p.

F251 Spindler, George D., ed. Being an anthropologist: fieldwork in eleven cultures. New York: Holt, 1970. 304p.

F252 Thomas, David Hurst. Figuring anthropology: first principles of probability & statistics. New York: Holt, 1976. 532p.

ECOLOGY, DEMOGRAPHY, AND NUTRITION

Early anthropological approaches to the relationships between cultural systems and environments were rigidly deterministic and had to be rejected as soon as ethnographic research completed the demonstration that widely different cultural systems could exist in environments that were the same or similar. An ecological perspective in which the environment was seen as one of the powerful factors affecting the development of cultural systems was advocated by Franz Boas. Malinowski's concept of needs and of institutions dedicated to filling needs led easily into synoptic charts having a strong ecological tone.

The work of Daryll Forde, Aubrey Richards, and Evans-Pritchard in England and of Kroeber, Lloyd Warner, and Steward in the United States was profoundly influenced by the emerging field of biological ecology. These maiden attempts had relatively little influence upon the field as a whole, perhaps because popular culture of the time placed a heavy emphasis upon mastery of an environment viewed as essentially passive.

The emergence of ecology as a powerful influence upon anthropology as a whole can perhaps be placed at the beginning of the late 1950s following a survey of ecological studies published by Bates in *Anthropology today* and a survey of demography (Lorimer), both published in 1958. The many studies conducted during the 1960s ranged from those heavily emphasizing perceptions and cognitions about the environment to those emphasizing detailed descriptions of such activities as hunting and farming. Many studies were guided by a resurrected functionalism in which adaptation to the environment replaced maintenance of the social system as the principal explanation of every activity.

During the 1970s, as the field became increasingly institutionalized, good general surveys such as the works of Bennett, Hardesty, and Netting began to emerge. The excesses of the 1960s have led many ecologists into fields such as demography and nutrition, where research problems can be sharply defined and fairly elegant methodologies applied. Nutritional anthropology has not yet passed beyond the paper writing stage, but demographic anthropology has generated several important monographs and readers, notably those by Fix and Howell. See also a work by R. H. Ward and K. M. Weiss, *The demographic evolution of human populations,* described earlier at F151.

F253 Abernethy, Virginia. Population pressure and cultural adjustment. New York: Human Sci. Pr., 1979. 189p.

F254 Arnott, Margaret L., ed. Gastronomy: the anthropology of food and food habits. Chicago: Aldine, 1975. 354p.

F255 Acsadi, Gyorgy, and J. Nemeskeri. History of human life span and mortality. Budapest: Akademiai Kiado, 1970. 346p.

F256 Bennett, John W. The ecological transition: cultural anthropology and human adaptation. New York: Pergamon, 1976. 378p.

F257 Dyke, Bennett, and Warren T. Morrill, eds. Genealogical demography. New York: Academic, 1980. 255p.

F258 Fitzgerald, Thomas K., ed. Nutrition and anthropology in action. Assen, The Netherlands: Van Gorcum, 1977. 155p.

F259 Fix, Alan G. The demography of the Semai Senoi. Ann Arbor: Univ. of Michigan Museum of Anthropology, 1977. 123p. [Anthropological papers, no.62]

F260 Hardesty, Donald L. Ecological anthropology. New York: Wiley, 1977. 310p.

F261 Howell, Nancy. Demography of the Dobe Kung. New York: Academic, 1979. 389p.

F262 Lee, Richard Borshay. The Kung San: men, women and work in a foraging society. Cambridge: Cambridge Univ. Pr., 1979. 526p.

F263 Lorimer, Frank, ed. Culture and human fertility: a study of the relations of cultural conditions to fertility in non-industrial and traditional societies. Paris: UNESCO, 1954. 510p.

F264 MacCormack, Carol P., ed. Ethnography of fertility and birth. New York: Academic, 1982. 294p.

F265 Moran, Emilio F. Human adaptability. Boulder, Colo.: Westview, 1982. 404p.

F266 Netting, Robert McC. Cultural ecology. Menlo Park, Calif.: Cummings, 1977. 119p.

F267 Rappaport, Roy A. Pigs for the ancestors: ritual in the ecology of a New Guinea people. New Haven, Conn.: Yale Univ. Pr., 1967. 311p.

F268 Vayda, Andrew P., ed. Environment and cultural behavior: ecological studies in cultural anthropology. Garden City, N.Y.: Natural History Pr., 1969. 485p.

ECONOMIC ANTHROPOLOGY

Because the theoretical framework of economic science developed within Euro-American society, anthropologists have always encountered difficulty in relating this thoroughly Western science to the conditions of non-Western culture. Such figures as Polyani, Dalton, and Bohannan, labeled "substantivists," have argued that much of economics is simply inapplicable to anthropological materials. Others such as Firth and Schneider, labeled "formalists," have argued that the principles of economics ought to be universal and, if they are not, those principles are wrong.

With an increasing accumulation of information concerning non-Western economic systems, the debate between substantivists and formalists has receded into the background. Much of economic theory has undergone revision in the direction of greater sensitivity to cultural and psychological factors. Modern economists sometimes admit that classical and neoclassical economic theory does not always apply to Western societies either. Anthropologists, for their part, have found numerous instances where economic theory is useful in explaining behavior in other parts of the world. As a simple example, relationships between supply and demand exist in all societies, but they are rarely as straightforward as the traditional equation might suggest.

Although the general analysis of economic systems remains an important part of ethnographic research, much recent work in economic anthropology has involved the use of increasingly formal and sophisticated methods of analysis in sharply delimited problem areas. The development of decision-making approaches in economics has been balanced by a parallel development in anthropology. These and other formal approaches are exemplified in Plattner. Formal approaches to the study of regional systems, derived from George Skinner's work in China and based upon development in geography, are summarized in Smith. Much additional work has been completed but not yet published. Like many innovators, the proponents of these formal approaches have a somewhat limited view of the field. This is often expressed as direct contempt for those who fail to use regional analysis or alternative-decision making.

The appearance of Marxist economics in a number of university departments has corresponded with the appearance of increasing numbers of people who label themselves Marxist anthropologists. In some cases, this represents a political position embraced by people whose political education was completed before 1900, and it is chastening to see the errors of capitalist science magnified in their work. In other cases, the Marxist position triggers useful debate concerning inherent contradictions in various kinds of non-Western economic systems and concerning the relationships between small communities or tribes and the worldwide economic system. The works by Diamond, Godelier, and Leons and Stein provide an overview of Marxist approaches.

F270 Belshaw, Cyril S. Traditional exchange and modern markets. Englewood Cliffs, N.J.: Prentice-Hall, 1965. 149p.

F271 Boserup, Ester. The conditions of agricultural growth: the economics of agrarian change under population pressure. Chicago: Aldine, 1975. 124p.

F272 Dalton, George. Economic anthropology and development: essays on tribal and peasant economies. New York: Basic Books, 1971. 386p.

F273 Diamond, Stanley, ed. Toward a Marxist anthropology: problems and perspectives. Chicago: Aldine, 1979. 492p.

F274 Dumont, Louis. From Mandeville to Marx: the genesis and triumph of economic ideology. Chicago: Univ. of Chicago Pr., 1977. 236p.

F275 Firth, Raymond, ed. Themes in economic anthropology. London: Tavistock, 1967. 292p.

F276 ———, and B. S. Yamey. Capital, saving, and credit in peasant societies: studies from Asia, Oceania, the Caribbean, and Middle America. Chicago: Aldine, 1964. 399p.

F277 Godelier, Maurice. Perspectives in Marxist anthropology. Tr. by Robert Brain. Cambridge: Cambridge Univ. Pr., 1977. 243p.

F278 Herskovits, Melville Jean. Economic anthropology: a study in comparative economies. 2d rev. ed. New York: Knopf, 1952. 547p.

F279 Krader, Lawrence, ed. The ethnological notebooks of Karl Marx. Assen, Netherlands: Van Gorcum, 1972. 454p.

F280 LeClaire, Edward E., and Harold K. Schneider, eds. Economic anthropology: readings in theory and analysis. New York: Holt, 1968. 523p.

F281 Leons, Madeline Barbara, and Frances Roth Stein, eds. New directions in political economy: an approach from anthropology. Westport, Conn.: Greenwood, 1979. 350p.

F282 Moerman, Michael. Agricultural change and peasant choice in a Thai village. Berkeley: Univ. of California Pr., 1968. 227p.

F283 Nash, Manning. Primitive and peasant economic systems. San Francisco: Chandler, 1966. 166p.

F284 Neale, Walter C. Monies in societies. San Francisco: Chandler, 1976. 109p.

F285 Plattner, Stuart, ed. Formal methods in economic anthropology. Washington, D.C.: American Anthropological Assn., 1975. 215p.

F286 Sahlins, Marshall D. Stone age economies. Chicago: Aldine-Atherton, 1972. 348p.

F287 Schneider, Harold K. Economic man: the anthropology of economics. New York: Free Pr., 1974. 278p.

F288 Smith, Carol A., ed. Regional analysis. v. 1: Economic systems; v. 2: Social systems. New York: Academic, 1976. [Studies in anthropology]

F289 Terray, Emmanuel. Marxism and "primitive" societies: two studies. Tr. by Mary Klopper. New York: Monthly Review Pr., 1972. 186p.

KINSHIP AND SOCIAL STRUCTURE

Anthropologists developed an early interest in patterns of relatedness among the individuals in society. Starting with Lewis Henry Morgan in the 1870s, relationships among kinsmen have been given primary attention. This emphasis could be justified on the grounds that these were among the most important relationships for most known societies. The system of genealogical relationships embodied in the concepts of consanguinity and affinity has proved subject to simple algebraic analysis, and kin relations have proved to be a key to the understanding of a wide range of simple and complicated social systems.

Because kinship systems involve certain complexities akin to those possessed by bridge and chess puzzles, there are no explanations of kinship that can be characterized as easy for all people. The works of Fox, Pasternak, Graburn, and Buchler and Selby cited below are not ideal summaries, but they are a good place at which to begin a study of kinship. Also see *Three styles in the study of kinship* by John Barnes (F105); and M. Fortes, *Kinship and the social order,* cited at F25. At a higher level, the works of Barnes and Fortes are highly regarded, at least by some readers, and provide a sophisticated overview of the field. In addition to the historically interesting work of Morgan, the classics in the field consist of the works of Murdock and Lévi-Strauss. To an outside observer, it is not clear why these are classics since they both contain serious errors of planning and execution; nevertheless, it is these books more than any others that have stimulated discussion in the field. The works of Needham, Leach, and Gough and Schneider illustrate some of that discussion. See also a work cited earlier (F95), Robert Lowie's *Social organization.*

On the whole, especially as the study of kinship has become increasingly technical, anthropological interest in the study of kinship per se has receded. Most of the problems that needed to be solved in the analysis of kinship terminologies have been solved; other problems, such as the exact nature of this or that Australian kinship system, have proven intractable, although solutions are announced and rejected from time to time. In part, the declining interest in kinship has arisen primarily because it was too important to be left to the specialists. Psychological anthropology has drawn off much of the interest in how relatives behave toward each other, demographic and ecological anthropology have absorbed problems connected with relationships among kinship and population, and cognitive anthropology has swallowed the problem of kinship terminology along with its general interest in taxonomic problems. Kinship studies still exist and are still important, but they no longer dominate the field. Compared to the study of kinship systems, studies of other sorts of groupings have never been numerous, but there are excellent and recent works by Eisenstadt and Stewart. Other works on social organization can be found in the sections dealing with political anthropology, law, and urban anthropology.

F290   Barnes, John A. Three styles in the study of kinship. Berkeley: Univ. of California Pr., 1971. 318p.

F291   Barth, Frederick. Models of social organization. London: Royal Anthro. Inst. of Great Britain and Ireland, 1966. 32p. [Occasional papers no.23]

F292   Buchler, Ira R., and Henry Selby. Kinship and social organization: an introduction to theory and method. New York: Macmillan, 1968. 366p.

F293   Eisenstadt, Shmuel Noah. From generation to generation: age groups and social structure. New York: Free Pr., 1956. 357p.

F295   Fox, Robin. Kinship and marriage. Middlesex: Penguin, 1968. 271p.

F296   ———. The red lamp of incest. New York: Dutton, 1980. 271p.

F297   Goody, Jack, ed. The developmental cycle in domestic groups. Cambridge: Cambridge Univ. Pr., 1966. 145p.

F298   ———. The character of kinship. Cambridge: Cambridge Univ. Pr., 1973. 251p.

F299   Graburn, Nelson, ed. Readings in kinship and social structure. New York: Harper, 1971. 449p.

F300   Leach, Edmund R. Rethinking anthropology. London: Athlone Pr., 1971. 143p.

F301   Lévi-Strauss, Claude. The elementary structures of kinship. Rev. ed. Tr. and ed. by James Harle Bell and others. Boston: Beacon, 1969. 541p.

F302   Lowie, Robert. Social organization. New York: Rinehart [c1948], 1953. 465p.

F303   Murdock, George P. Social structure. New York: Macmillan, 1949. 387p.

F304   Needham, Rodney, ed. Rethinking kinship and marriage. London: Tavistock, 1971. 276p.

F305   Park, George K. The idea of social structure. Garden City, N.Y.: Anchor Books, 1974. 392p.

F306   Pasternak, Burton. Introduction to kinship and social organization. Englewood Cliffs, N.J.: Prentice-Hall, 1976. 167p.

F307   Schapera, Isaac, ed. Studies in kinship and marriage. London: Royal Anthro. Inst. of Great Britain and Ireland, 1963. 113p. [Occasional papers no.16]

F308   Schneider, David M., and Kathleen Gough, eds. Matrilineal kinship. Berkeley: Univ. of California Pr., 1961. 761p.

F309   Stewart, Frank Henderson. Fundamentals of age-group systems. New York: Academic, 1977. 381p.

THE ANTHROPOLOGY OF WOMEN

The importance of training women anthropologists competent to investigate and present woman's role in culture was recognized from the time of Boas in America and Tylor and Malinowski in England. Boas' students included, among others, Margaret Mead, Ruth Benedict, Gene Weltfish, Elsie Clews Parsons, and Ruth Bunzel. Those of Malinowski included Hortense Powermaker, Elizabeth Colson, Monica (Hunter) Wilson, Hilda Kuper, Audrey Richards, and Phyllis Kaberry. Perhaps because men were more accessible and foreign women anthropologists were often cast in a male role, the hope that training women anthropologists would lead to a feminist anthropology has proved futile. Of the distinguished women in anthropology in the past generation, only Kaberry and Mead concerned themselves in any detail with the role of women in society.

In recent years, a renewed interest in the condition of women has led to an increasing number of studies exclusively or largely concerned with woman's role and status. This concern has not always been supported by strong conceptions about what is to be meant by role and status. Indeed, the concept of woman as an underclass was advanced by Malinowski and repudiated by Kaberry quite a few years ago. Today, women anthropologists seem to interpret their role as one of providing people outside of anthropology with accurate information concerning the status of women in former and present times. Within anthropology, the availability of increasingly sophisticated information concerning the manner in which women perform their social roles may lead to a recasting of male-oriented concepts of power, authority, and family structure.

F310   Ardener, Shirley, ed. Perceiving women. New York: Wiley, 1975. 167p.

F311   Boserup, Ester. Woman's role in economic development. New York: St. Martin's, 1970. 283p.

F312   Caplan, Patricia, and Janet M. Bujra, eds. Women united, women divided: comparative studies of ten contemporary cultures. Bloomington: Indiana Univ. Pr., 1979. 288p.

F313   Friedl, Ernestine. Women and men: an anthropologist's view. New York: Holt, 1975. 148p.

F314   Giele, Janet Zollinger, and Audrey Chapman Smock, eds. Women: roles and status in eight countries. New York: Wiley, 1977. 443p.

F315   Hafkin, Nancy J., and Edna G. Bay, eds. Women in Africa: studies in social and economic change. Stanford, Calif.: Stanford Univ. Pr., 1976. 306p.

F316   Hammond, Dorothy, and Alta Jablow. Women in cultures of the world. Menlo Park, Calif.: Cummings, 1976. 158p.

F317   Martin, M. Kay, and Barbara Voorhies. Female of the species. New York: Columbia Univ. Pr., 1974. 432p.

F318   Reiter, Raymond, ed. Toward an anthropology of women. New York: Monthly Review Pr., 1975. 416p.

F319   Rohrlich-Leavitt, Ruby, ed. Women cross-culturally: change and challenge. Chicago: Aldine, 1975. 588p. [World anthropology series]

F320   Rosaldo, Michele Z., and Louise Lamphere, eds. Women, culture and society. Stanford, Calif.: Stanford Univ. Pr., 1974. 368p.

PSYCHOLOGICAL AND COGNITIVE ANTHROPOLOGY

Psychological anthropology has generally had to do with the cross-cultural application of the findings and theories of clinical psychology and psychoanalysis. In studies of child rearing and national character, the interest is often in the nature and development of the normal personality. Recent emphasis on the malleability of personality, and general criticism of the kinds of broad-brush labeling that often characterized the national character school, have caused extensive changes in the field. Still, it is safe to say that there is no way of applying personality terms to entire populations that will not draw heavy criticism. Cognitive anthropology arises partly out of a long tradition of studying "how people think" and partly out of a desire to find a more rigorous form of cross-cultural psychology. The field is not easily separated from ethnoscience or sociolinguistics.

An excellent and current review of the history and development of psychological anthropology is the volume edited by Spindler. Other useful surveys and viewpoints are those of Wallace, LeVine, Bourguignon, Hsu, and Barnouw. A sampling of widely divergent approaches to the field are provided by the recent works of Devereux, Munroe and Munroe, Rohner, and Wober. Works in psychological anthropology are listed below:

F321　Barnouw, Victor. Culture and personality. 3d ed. Homewood, Ill.: Dorsey Pr., 1979. 473p.

F322　Bourguignon, Erika. Psychological anthropology: an introduction to human nature and cultural differences. New York: Holt, 1979. 375p.

F323　Devereux, George. Ethnopsychoanalysis: psychoanalysis and anthropology as complementary frames of reference. Berkeley: Univ. of California Pr., 1978. 334p.

F324　Hsu, Francis L. K., ed. Psychological anthropology. New ed. Cambridge, Mass.: Schenkman, 1972. 623p.

F325　LeVine, Robert A. Culture, behavior, and personality: an introduction to the comparative study of psychological adaptation. 2d ed. Hawthorne, N.Y.: Aldine, 1982.

F326　Munroe, Robert L., and Ruth H. Munroe. Cross-cultural human development. Monterey, Calif.: Brooks/Cole, 1975. 181p.

F327　Rohner, Ronald P. They love me, they love me not: a world wide study of the effects of parental acceptance and rejection. New Haven, Conn.: HRAF Pr., 1975. 300p.

F328　Spindler, George D., ed. The making of psychological anthropology. Berkeley: Univ. of California Pr., 1978. 665p.

F329　Wallace, Anthony F. C. Culture and personality. 2d ed. New York: Random, 1970. 270p.

F330　Wober, Mallory. Psychology in Africa. London: Intl. African Inst., 1975. 247p.

Compared to the rather loose assortment of things that can be said to be "psychological anthropology," the field of cognitive anthropology seems to have a much stronger focus. The volume edited by Stephen Tyler gives a useful introduction to the field, although it has a heavy emphasis on kinship. Tyler's recent views on cognitive anthropology are to be found in his 1978 work. Much of the interest in cognitive matters has centered about taxonomic arrangements of various kinds as found in the listed works by Berlin and Kay, Berlin and others, and

Hunn. Other works by Agar and Spradley place emphasis on ways people do things, thus moving cognitive anthropology into close association with such fields as economic and political anthropology. Bouissac's work also involves some new method and theory.

Coming more from psychology than from anthropology, the work of Gay and Cole and the survey volume by Cole introduce a realistic search for means of identifying and interpreting differences between people in different cultures in the learning of mathematics and in the performance of various psychological tests. Sophisticated methodology also appears in the volume edited by Kay and the volumes edited by Romney and others. Without exactly pronouncing cognitive anthropology to be the wave of the future, we must nevertheless take note of the fact that it involves active methodological innovation and that it has successfully approached a variety of problems that were previously unsolved. Certainly, the conduct of anthropological fieldwork will never be the same.

F331　Agar, Michael. Ripping and running: a formal ethnography of urban heroin addicts. New York: Seminar Pr., 1973. 173p.

F332　Berlin, Brent, and Paul Kay. Basic color terms: their universality and evolution. Berkeley: Univ. of California Pr., 1969. 178p.

F333　Berlin, Brent, and others. Principles of Tzeltzal plant classification: an introduction to the botanical ethnography of a Mayan-speaking people of highland Chiapas. New York: Academic, 1974. 660p.

F334　Bouissac, Paul. Circus and culture: a semiotic approach. Thomas A. Sebeok, gen. ed. Bloomington: Indiana Univ. Pr., 1976. 206p. [Advance in semiotics]

F335　Cole, Michael. The cultural context of learning and thinking: an exploration in experimental anthropology. New York: Basic Books, 1971, 304p.

F336　———, and Barbara Means. Comparative studies of how people think: an introduction. Cambridge, Mass.: Harvard Univ. Pr., 1981. 222p.

F337　Gay, John, and Michael Cole. The new mathematics and an old culture: a study of learning among the Kepelle of Liberia. New York: Holt, 1967. 100p.

F338　Goody, John R. The domestication of the savage mind. Cambridge: Cambridge Univ. Pr., 1977. 179p.

F339　Hunn, Eugene S. Tzeltzal folk zoology: the classification of discontinuities in nature. New York: Academic, 1977. 368p.

F340 Kay, Paul, ed. Explorations in mathematical anthropology. Cambridge, Mass.: MIT Pr., 1971. 286p.

F341 Romney, Kimball A., and others, eds. Multidimensional scaling: theory and applications in the behavioral sciences. 2v. New York: Seminar Pr., 1972.

F342 Spradley, James P., ed. Culture and cognition: rules, maps and plans. San Francisco: Chandler, 1972. 400p.

F343 Tyler, Stephen A. The said and the unsaid: mind, meaning, and culture. New York: Academic, 1978. 487p.

F344 ———, ed. Cognitive anthropology; readings. New York: Holt, 1969. 521p.

ART, RELIGION, AND SYMBOLISM

The study of art and religion both have a long and independent history within anthropology. Durkheim attempted to establish a scientific foundation for the study of religion. Only a short time after that, Boas attempted to do the same for art. Both attempts ran afoul of the fact that both religion and art involve personal experience of great depth and complexity. Such personal experiences are crucial, but, like Heisenberg's electron, tend to disappear when measured. In his own approach to art, Kroeber emphasized style, and it is certainly the case that it is the pattern of change over time that is most easily measured and predicted.

With a few brilliant exceptions, ethnographic studies of art have had a tendency to degenerate into guided museum tours or courses in art appreciation. Studies of religion have been more fruitful and there has been a great deal of discussion of the various functions served by religious beliefs and practices. This utilitarian view may have reached its apogee with Rapaport's invention of the ritually regulated ecosystem, which turns out, however, to be not too different from Warner's ritually regulated social system. Rituals undoubtedly do possess a variety of economic and social functions and effects, but these often seem to pale beside the immense pleasure and excitement that rituals seem to generate. It is tempting to argue that holding these marvelous dramas is, in fact, the purpose of social life and that the function of everything else is the enhancement of religion, pleasure, and aesthetics.

The function of the organization vis-à-vis religion and the role of religion in the organization find their fruition in the newly evolving field of symbolism. The study of symbols dates back to the earliest psychoanalysts and is not clearly separate from parallel work in congnition, structuralism, and language. Although a few modern works such as that of Hatcher express a pursuit of real scientific goals that would have appealed to Malinowski or Boas, the bulk of work in the field of symbolism, like that in art and religion, expresses a humanistic frivolity that most linguists and cognitive anthropologists would be inclined to scorn. To be sure, symbolic anthropologists present abundant data.

F345 Baal, Jan van. Symbols for communication: an introduction to the anthropological study of religion. Assen, Netherlands: Van Gorcum, 1971. 295p.

F346 Babcock, Barbara A., ed. The reversible world: symbolic inversion in art and society. Ithaca, N.Y.: Cornell Univ. Pr., 1978. 302p.

F347 Banton, Michael, ed. Anthropological approaches to the study of religion. London: Tavistock, 1966. 176p.

F348 Biebuyck, Daniel, ed. Tradition and creativity in tribal art. Berkeley: Univ. of California Pr., 1969. 236p.

F349 Dolgin, Janet L., and others, eds. Symbolic anthropology: a reader in the study of symbols and meanings. New York: Columbia Univ. Pr., 1977. 523p.

F350 Douglas, Mary. Purity and danger: an analysis of concepts of pollution and taboo. New York: Praeger, 1966. 188p.

F351 ———. Natural symbols: explorations in cosmology. 2d ed. New York: Vintage, 1973. 219p.

F352 ———. Implicit meanings: essays in anthropology. Boston: Routledge & Paul, 1975. 325p.

F353 Firth, Raymond William, ed. Symbols: public and private. Ithaca, N.Y.: Cornell Univ. Pr., 1973. 469p.

F354 Graburn, Nelson H. H., ed. Ethnic and tourist arts: cultural expression from the fourth world. Berkeley: Univ. of California Pr., 1977. 412p.

F355 Grimes, Ronald L. Symbol and conquest: public ritual and drama in Santa Fe, New Mexico. Victor Turner, gen. ed. Ithaca, N.Y.: Cornell Univ. Pr., 1976. 281p. [Symbol, myth, and ritual]

F356 Hatcher, Evelyn Payne. Visual metaphors: a formal analysis of Navajo art. St. Paul: West, 1974.

F357 Needham, Rodney, ed. Right and left: essays on dual symbolic classification. Chicago: Univ. of Chicago Pr., 1973. 449p.

F358 Turner, Victor W. Dramas, fields and metaphors: symbolic action in human society. Ithaca, N.Y.: Cornell Univ. Pr., 1974. 309p.

F359 Wallace, Anthony F. C. Religion: anthropological view. New York: Random, 1967. 300p.

Although renewed interest in these fields arose more or less concurrently with the emergence of the new, new Marxist anthropology and the equally new racism of the sociobiologists, only the humanistic fields continue to yield extensive publication into the 1980s.

F360 Bloch, Maurice, and Jonathan Parry, eds. Death and the regeneration of life. New York: Cambridge Univ. Pr., 1982. 248p.

F361 Lincoln, Bruce. Priests, warriors, and cattle: a study in the ecology of religions. Berkeley: Univ. of California Pr., 1981. 256p.

F362 May, Elizabeth, ed. Musics of many cultures: an introduction. Berkeley: Univ. of California Pr., 1981. 451p.

F363 Todorov, Tzvetan. Symbolism and interpretation. Ithaca, N.Y.: Cornell Univ. Pr., 1982. 175p.

F364 Turner, Victor, ed. Celebration: studies in festivity and ritual. Washington, D.C.: Smithsonian, 1982. 318p.

POLITICAL AND LEGAL ANTHROPOLOGY

Political anthropology and the anthropology of law were originally conceived as distinct subfields. Political anthropology in the old tradition concerned itself with such things as the origin of the state and the development of other political institutions. Many of these traditional concerns remain in modified form. The works of Burling, Adams, Banton, Eisenstadt, and Cohen and Service represent continuing interest in administrative forms and in power and authority.

During the 1950s and 1960s, the attention of political anthropologists came to be directed increasingly toward the study of conflict and dispute. At first, there was a concern with the identification of factions and parties as aspects of social structure and with explication of the functional value of various kinds of conflict. If factions preserved the old society, that was good; but if they destroyed it, that was also good because it paved the way for a new society. The interest in cases, which Max Gluckman brought from law to political anthropology, was brilliantly developed by Victor Turner, who began to emphasize conflict processes through his concept of the social drama. The work of Beals and Siegel (published in 1966) and the work of Bailey (published in 1969) supplemented the concept of social drama with the concept of games in which parties or individuals adopted strategies and obtained spoils if they were successful.

This modern process-oriented view, emphasizing the game-like and dialog-like aspects of conflict, is consistent with the developing emphasis on decision making in cognitive and economic anthropology. On the other side, the movement of Victory Turner and the social drama into the field of ritual and symbolism, and the powerful emphasis on symbolism in the work of Cohen, foreshadows an increased emphasis on symbolism within political and legal anthropology.

With its movement into the field of disputes and dispute settlement, political anthropology has opened up a field largely neglected by legal anthropology. In the eyes of the law a dispute begins when the authorities are notified; in the eyes of the student of conflict, the dispute is deeply rooted in the internal strains characteristic of the society, and its movement into the public sphere is much closer to the end of the dispute process than it is to the beginning. From the political side, the most important recent theoretical approaches are to be found in Boissevain and Schmidt and others, while the work of Laura Nader and her students represents a strong attempt at reconciliation between the characteristic approaches of legal and political anthropology.

Orthodox legal anthropology remains a strong field based largely upon detailed analyses of particular legal systems. Pospisil's recent and clearly written summary of the ethnology of law is an excellent introduction to these materials. The work of Hamnett is also of interest here.

F365 Adams, Richard Newbold. Energy and structure: a theory of social power. Austin: Univ. of Texas Pr., 1975. 353p.

F366 Bailey, Frederick George. Stratagems and spoils: a social anthropology of politics. New York: Schocken, 1969. 240p.

F367 Balandier, Georges. Political anthropology. Tr. by A. M. Sheridan Smith. New York: Pantheon, 1970. 214p.

F368 Banton, Michael P., ed. Political systems and the distribution of power. New York: Praeger, 1965. 142p.

F369 Beals, Alan R., and Bernard J. Siegel. Divisiveness and social conflict: an anthropological approach. Stanford, Calif.: Stanford Univ. Pr., 1966. 185p.

F370 Boissevain, Jeremy. Friends of friends: networks, manipulators and coalitions. Oxford: Basil Blackwell, 1974. 285p.

F371 Britain, Gerald M., and Ronald Cohen, eds. Hierarchy and society: anthropological perspectives on bureaucracy. Beverly Hills, Calif.: Sage, 1982. 192p.

F372 Burling, Robbins. The passage of power: studies in political succession. New York: Academic, 1974. 322p.

F373 Cohen, Abner P. Two-dimensional man: an essay on the anthropology of power and symbolism in complex societies. Berkeley: Univ. of California Pr., 1974. 156p.

F374 Cohen, Ronald, and Elman R. Service, eds. Origins of the state: the anthropology of political evolution. Philadelphia: Inst. for the Study of Human Issues, 1978. 233p.

F375 Eisenstadt, Shmuel N. Political systems of empires. New York: Free Pr., 1963. 524p.

F376 Givens, R. Dale, and Martin A. Nettleship, eds. Discussions on war and human aggression. Chicago: Aldine, 1976. 231p. [World anthropology series]

F377 Gluckman, Max. Politics, law and ritual in tribal society. Chicago: Aldine, 1965. 339p.

F378 Hamnett, Ian. Social anthropology and the law. New York: Academic, 1977. 234p.

F379 Hoebel, Edward Adamson. The law of primitive man: a study in comparative legal dynamics. Cambridge, Mass: Harvard Univ. Pr., 1954. 357p.

F380 Leacock, Eleanor, and Richard Lee, eds. Politics and history in band societies. New York: Cambridge Univ. Pr., 1982. 500p.

F381 Malinowski, Bronislaw. Crime and custom in savage society. London: Routledge & Paul, 1926. 132p.

F382 Montague, Ashley. The nature of human aggression. London: Oxford Univ. Pr., 1976. 381p.

F383 Nader, Laura, ed. Law in culture and society. Chicago: Aldine, 1969. 454p.

F384 ———, and Harry F. Todd, Jr., eds. The disputing process: in ten societies. New York: Columbia Univ. Pr., 1978. 372p.

F385 Paine, Robert, ed. Politically speaking: cross-cultural studies of rhetoric. Philadelphia, Penn.: ISHI Pubs. 1982. 232p.

F386 Pospisil, Leopold J. The ethnology of law. 2d ed. Menlo Park, Calif.: Cummings, 1978. 136p.

F387 ———. The anthropology of law: a comparative theory. New York: Harper, 1971. 383p.

F388 Schmidt, Steffen W., and others, eds. Friends, followers, and factions: a reader in political clientelism. Berkeley: Univ. of California Pr., 1977. 512p.

F389 Swartz, Marc J., ed. Local level politics: social and cultural perspectives. Chicago: Aldine, 1968. 473p.

CHANGE AND DEVELOPMENT

Anthropologists, beginning with early theories of evolution, have always had strong interests in the mechanisms leading to cultural change. Although Kroeber and a very few other anthropologists had a general interest in the manner in which cultures changed, the overwhelming tendency has been to deal with the case at hand. This has been predominantly the case in which a small society or community is changing in response to the presence, often overwhelming, of a large society. Previous to World War II, anthropologists were frequently accused of wishing to maintain small societies as museum pieces; more recently, they have been accused of helping the forces of imperialism to alter such small societies. Plainly, there is no sort of partisan or even neutral approach to planned or directed change that can be acceptable to all parties. Some anthropologists have seen development, even conquest, as inevitable and been concerned to make it as painless as possible. Others, perhaps in other situations, have felt that applied anthropology was indefensible. Strictly speaking, however, there is no applied anthropology because there is no set of agreed upon principles that can be applied. Almost all anthropological work consists of supplying information about people studied. Such information can be used to promote stability or change, and such stability or change can be praised or found wanting. Perhaps the best moments of applied anthropology come when the anthropologist is in a position to explain options and to allow people to reach their own decisions about what is to be done.

Despite a recent emphasis on models in the two introductory surveys by Spindler and Galt, there is still a lack of any clear theory of cultural change. The slightly more technical works by Goodenough and Bee are still only ways of approaching or studying the field. Here it is a pity that no theoreticians have built upon the concepts of pattern or paradigm developed by Kroeber and Kuhn. As things stand, there are a great many cases reported in a great many collections such as those of Clifton, Pitt, Sanday, Spicer, and

Weaver, but the cases have no clear framework and do not seem to lead anywhere. The works of Belshaw, Foster, and Bastide provide a somewhat more organized presentation of applied anthropology, but again, the basis seems to be the individual case. For the present, then, it is sufficient that the cases are instructive.

F390 Bastide, Roger. Applied anthropology. Tr. by A. L. Morton. New York: Harper, 1973. 226p.

F391 Bee, Robert L. Patterns and processes: an introduction to anthropological strategies for the study of sociocultural change. New York: Free Pr., 1974. 260p.

F392 Belshaw, Cyril S. The sorcerer's apprentice: an anthropology of public policy. New York: Pergamon, 1976. 342p. [Frontiers of anthropology, 4]

F393 Bernard, Harvey R., and Pertti J. Pelto, eds. Technology and social change. New York: Macmillan, 1971. 354p.

F394 Clifton, James A., ed. Applied anthropology: readings in the uses of the science of man. Boston: Houghton, 1970. 286p.

F395 Dobyns, Henry F., and others, eds. Peasants, power and applied social change: Vicos as a model. Beverly Hills, Calif.: Sage, 1971. 237p.

F396 Eddy, Elizabeth M., and William L. Partridge, eds. Applied anthropology in America. New York: Columbia Univ. Pr., 1978. 484p.

F397 Foster, George M. Traditional societies and technological change. 2d ed. New York: Harper, 1973. 286p.

F398 Galt, Anthony H., and Larry Smith. Models and the study of social change. New York: Wiley, 1976. 180p.

F399 Goodenough, Ward H. Cooperation in change: an anthropological approach to community development. New York: Wiley, 1966. 543p.

F400 Pitt, David, ed. Development from below: anthropologists and development situations. The Hague: Mouton, 1976. 277p.

F401 Sanday, Peggy Reeves, ed. Anthropology and the public interest: fieldwork and theory. New York: Academic, 1976. 363p.

F402 Spicer, Edward H., ed. Human problems in technological change: a casebook. New York: Russell Sage, 1952. 301p.

F403 Spindler, Louise. Culture change and modernization: mini-models and case studies. New York: Holt, 1971. 177p.

F404 Weaver, Thomas, ed. To see ourselves: anthropology and modern social issues. Glenview, Ill.: Scott, Foresman, 1973. 485p.

Although development, especially community development, will probably remain the major emphasis of applied anthropology, major thrusts in the fields of medical and urban anthropology should not be neglected. Certainly, many of the most recent publications are in these fields.

F405 Bartlett, Peggy, ed. Agricultural decision making: anthropological contributions to rural development. New York: Academic, 1980. 378p.

F406 Brokensha, David, and others, eds. Indigenous knowledge systems and development. Washington, D.C.: Univ. Pr. of America, 1980. 466p.

F407 Hannerz, Ulf. Exploring the city: inquiries toward an urban anthropology. New York: Columbia Univ. Pr., 1980. 378p.

F408 Kleinman, Arthur. Patients and healing in the context of culture: an exploration of the borderland between anthropology, medicine, and psychiatry. Berkeley: Univ. of California Pr., 1980. 427p.

F409 Moore, Lorna G. The biocultural basis of health: expanding views of medical anthropology. St. Louis: Mosby, 1980. 278p.

F410 Young, James Clay. Medical choice in a Mexican village. New Brunswick, N.J.: Rutgers Univ. Pr., 1982. 233p.

F411 Zimmerman, Michael R. Foundations of medical anthropology: anatomy, physiology, biochemistry, pathology in cultural context. Philadelphia: Saunders. 1980. 214p.

SPECULATIVE ANTHROPOLOGY

Anthropology has long been afflicted by charlatans and gifted amateurs who have sought to bring the light of knowledge to those who foolishly tried to understand humanity by studying it. The voyages of Thor Heyerdahl have generated much heat and little light. For centuries, various romantics have insisted upon a separate origin for the American Indian. More recently, it has been claimed that they were established in their homeland by flying saucers and not by Atlanteans or Egyptians after all.

For several decades, anthropologists have been plagued by biologists and ethologists wishing to straighten out anthropological misconceptions about the nature of humanity. In this regard, the work of Konrad Lorenz and his followers and of Desmond Morris might be singled out for special opprobrium. More recently, under the leadership of Edmund Wilson, a number of biologists and even anthropologists have argued that a variety of human behaviors were genetic in nature. Some have embraced the view that a wide range of human behavior can be explained in terms of individual attempts to ensure the survival of the very same genes and alleles that they carry in their own bodies. Marshall Sahlins provides a useful critique of this pretentious nonsense.

The past few years have also seen the rise and fall of Carlos Castaneda. A close reading of Castaneda's work has caused some to question the reliability and even the existence of his informant. In the light of Castaneda, almost every elderly anthropological informant has acquired the radiance normally achieved only by the more sophisticated Hindu gurus. Done carefully and with real people, the presentation of anthropological informants as teachers and philosophers will be a valuable addition to the literature of anthropology.

More respectable, and perhaps more dangerous for that reason, is the work of Marvin Harris and his students. Here, instead of "inclusive fitness" as used by sociobiologists, the deus ex machina is technoenvironmental determinism. By this, Marvin Harris means to say that there is a direct relationship between such practices as cannibalism, war, food taboos, and witchcraft and problems posed by the interrelationship between environment and technology both narrowly conceived. Although it is evident that pressures from neighboring peoples or from the natural environment would exert pressures toward the rejection of wild and impractical behaviors, the prevailing opinion remains, as Boas noted in the 1890s, that the causation of social practices is multiple and is often different in different places. For example, there is no reason whatsoever to believe that food taboos are invariably designed to preserve scarce species or serve other obvious environmental functions. To date, Harris has not assembled convincing evidence to support his argument, and the two books cited here are characterized by a casual attitude toward the facts. This same casual attitude has been taken up by several of Harris' opponents and that would seem to be a good reason for relegating the entire topic of simple explanations for complex phenomena to a section on speculative anthropology.

F412 Barash, David P. Sociobiology and behavior. New York: Elsevier, 1977. 378p.

F413 Caplan, Arthur L., ed. The sociobiology debate: readings on ethical & scientific issues. New York: Harper, 1978. 514p.

F414 Harris, Marvin. Cows, pigs, wars and witches: the riddles of culture. New York: Random, 1974. 276p.

F415 ———. Cannibals and kings: the origins of cultures. New York: Random, 1977. 239p.

F416 Lumsden, Charles J., and Edward O. Wilson. Genes, mind, and culture: the coevolutionary process. Cambridge, Mass.: Harvard Univ. Pr., 1981. 428p.

F417 ———. Promethean fire: reflections on the origin of the mind. Cambridge, Mass.: Harvard Univ. Pr., 1983. 216p.

F418 Sahlins, Marshall. The use and abuse of biology: an anthropological critique of sociobiology. Ann Arbor: Univ. of Michigan Pr., 1976. 120p.

F419 Wilson, Edward O. Sociobiology: the new synthesis. Cambridge, Mass.: Belknap Pr. of Harvard Univ. Pr., 1975. 697p.

Alan R. Beals, with the assistance of James D. Armstrong,
James P. Barker, and Stanley C. Wilmoth

Survey of the Reference Works

GUIDES TO THE LITERATURE

A detailed discussion of the major works in this discipline can be found in the 1977 publication of Marilyn L. Haas, "Anthropology: a guide to basic sources," *Reference services review 5*, no.4:45–51 (73 references) **(F420)**, which provides the best available introduction to the basic specialized apparatus and a pragmatic discussion of the use, for anthropological purposes, of reference sources developed in other disciplines, including: *Social sciences citation index*, described at A231; *Resources in education*, described at H408; *Geo abstracts D (Social and historical geography)*, described at C481; *America: history and life*, described at B1491; *The combined retrospective index set to journals in history 1838–1974*, described at B1523; *Social sciences index*, described at A234; *The Humanities index*, described at A235; *Computer-readable databases: a directory and data sourcebook*, described at A373; *Monthly catalog of United States government publications*, described at I749; *Cumulative subject index to the Public Affairs Information Service bulletins 1915–74*, described at A227; *Psychological abstracts*, described at G458; *Historical abstracts*, described at B1492.

A less detailed article, Sol Tax, "Preface," *Anthropological bibliographies: a selected guide* **(F457)**, identifies the most indispensable reference books available to this discipline.

In 1976, Margaret Currier, who worked with several generations of anthropologists as librarian of the Tozzer Library in the Peabody Museum at Harvard University, reviewed the history and present status of "Problems in anthropological bibliography," *Annual review of anthropology* 5:15–34 (1976) **(F421)**. With lively charm, she explores the implications of the computer on bibliographic construction and identifies the ground-breaking products of this technology. Her discussion provides an excellent, basic guide in a series that is available in most academic libraries.

F422 O'Leary, Timothy J. "Ethnographic bibliography." *In* A handbook of method in cultural anthropology, ed. by Raoul Naroll and Ronald Cohen, p. 128–46. Garden City, N.Y.: publ. by Natural History Pr. for the American Museum of Natural History, 1970. 1,017p.

A classified list. Identifies the most useful bibliographies in each of 12 sections. This valuable source must be used with caution. The citations are irritatingly brief, and some volumes cited would be difficult to adequately identify with the information given. O'Leary's organization includes a section on bibliographies, followed by regional treatment of Asia, South Asia, East Asia, the Soviet Union, Europe, Africa, the Americas, the Pacific, and a review of general ethnographic subject bibliography. This reduces the need for us to develop retrospective depth, making it possible to concentrate on more recent publications.

F423 Nelson, B. R. "Anthropological research and printed library catalogs." *RQ* 19:159–70 (Winter 1979). Also in Nelson, Bonnie R., and Lee Ash. A guide to published library catalogs. Metuchen, N.J.: Scarecrow, 1982. 342p.

The "in-depth" cataloging of the great special and research libraries can often help the scholar identify sources. Some of the libraries that collect non-Western language materials provide the only cataloging available. Both subject libraries and libraries with great regional collections are comprehensively reviewed, and the special subject entries appropriate to the discovery of anthropological materials are discussed, especially when the subject headings in use are not those of the Library of Congress.

F424 Heizer, Robert F. Archaeology: a bibliographical guide to the basic literature. New York: Garland, 1980. 434p. [Garland reference library of social science, v.54]

First-start bibliographies with a heavy emphasis on American work. The bibliography of bibliographies is labeled "Primary source materials" in the table of contents. Does not provide an annotated guide to reference books or to continuing series with bibliographic sections. For example, there is no indication of the value of *Historical abstracts* (B1492), which covers nearly 60 journals with articles on African prehistory. Does not provide worldwide entry to the bibliographic record. An elaborate table of contents (118 subjects) introduces the classified arrangement of 9,318 entries with translations of foreign titles into English. There is an author index. Also useful are Frank G. Anderson, *Southwestern archaeology: a bibliography* (New York: Garland, 1982 [539p.], [Garland reference library of social science, v.69]) **(F425)**, and Linda Ellis, comp.

Laboratory techniques in archaeology: a guide to the literature: 1920–1980 (New York: Garland, 1982 [419p.], [Garland reference library of social science, v.110]) **(F426)**.

As to guides in special branches of anthropology, Jan Harold Brunvand's *Folklore: a study and research guide* (New York: St. Martin's, 1976 [144p.]) **(F427)** maintains a high standard of readability. In this student handbook, scholarly works in several languages are covered in the first chapter, which discusses leading theories and definitive works. A second chapter evaluates the standard reference works with an overwhelming emphasis on English-language sources. A third chapter discusses the production of research papers. An author index is included, and the table of contents provides a helpful subject outline. A more even conceptual control can be found in the much briefer Albert B. Friedman, *Myth, symbolic modes and ideology: a discursive bibliography* (Claremont, Calif.: Claremont Graduate School, 1976 [24p.]) **(F428)**. This is a valuable survey under 19 topical entries of definitive texts and bibliographies, with both historical depth and a clear command of more contemporary efforts to integrate the results of research in other disciplines into the investigation of myth, legend, fables, and folktales. The bibliography of references cited must be used with caution because few of the citations are complete.

In linguistics, two works merit special attention, although neither attempts serious international coverage: Aleksandra K. Wawrzyszko, *Bibliography of general linguistics: English & American* (Hamden, Conn.: Archon Books, 1971 [120p.]) **(F429)**, which serves linguists beyond the university level as a bibliographic guide to 344 items. Pt. 1 covers general sources and selected special topics. Pt. 2 covers linguistic periodicals and series. Also useful, Harold Byron Allen's *Linguistics and English linguistics*, 2d ed. (Arlington Heights, Ill.: AHM, 1977 [184p.] [Goldentree bibliographies in language and literature]) **(F430)**, selects 3,000 books and articles published in English up to 1975. Again, a table of contents guides the reader into the topical coverage. As a special feature, books of particular merit are marked by an asterisk, review citations are indicated by angle brackets, and specialized bibliographies appear at the beginning of relevant sections. It excludes documents available from ERIC, articles in collections, and unpublished dissertations. There is an author index.

Much of the world is still predominantly religious in value orientation. Since the great religions have elaborately developed scholarly traditions, work in complex societies often requires some guide that usefully integrates this facet of life into the scholarly traditions of the West. Charles J. Adams, ed., *A reader's guide to the great religions*, 2d ed. (New York: Free Pr., 1977 [521p.]) **(F431)**, includes 27 pages of thorough indexing. Each chapter, by a different specialist, includes an authoritative introduction and discussion of specialized topics, followed by evaluations of the works cited. Covers primitive religion, religions of China, religions of Japan, and religions of Mexico, Central and South America, the Sikhs, the Jainas, and the major religions— Hinduism, Buddhism, Judaism, Christianity, and Islam. Some chapters have appendixes that identify major reference books and periodicals. Aside from the subject index, there is an index of authors, compilers, translators, and editors. Also useful are the sections on the major religions in the American Historical Association's *Guide to historical literature*, described at B1435. *Research guide to religious studies*, by John F. Wilson and Thomas P. Slavens (Chicago: American Library Assn., 1982 [192p.] [Sources of information in the humanities, no.1]) **(F432)**, provides an evaluative survey of monographs in 110 pages. A second part lists and annotates major reference sources. For a classified arrangement of a select list that is annotated, consult *The religious life of man: guide to basic literature*, comp. by Leszek M. Karpinski (Metuchen, N.J.: Scarecrow, 1978 [399p.]) **(F433)**. Another more extensive list can be found in *Religions: a select, classified bibliography*, by Joseph F. Mitros (New York: Learned, 1973 [435p.]) **(F434)**.

REVIEWS OF THE LITERATURE

F435 Annual review of anthropology. Ed. by Bernard J. Siegel. v.1– , 1972– . Palo Alto, Calif.: Annual Reviews. Annual.

Continues the tradition established in *Biennial review of anthropology*, v.1–13, 1959–71 (Stanford, Calif.: Stanford Univ. Pr.; London: Oxford Univ. Pr.). Does provide timely evaluations of current research interests on carefully delimited problems. All subdisciplines of anthropology are touched on, but continuity of complete coverage of specific problems or geographic areas does not seem to be an editorial objective. The "Literature Cited," listed at the end of each review, forms a succession of retrospective bibliographies of serious work in anthropology. In terms of improved bibliographical control over research work, the cumulative benefits to anthropological scholarship are very considerable. An editorial flaw has been the erratic use of abbreviations in the bibliographies. A 5-year cumulative index covering v.3 to 7 is found in v.7. For bibliographic reviews from a more international point of view, but without the benefit of the considerable editorial talents of Bernard J. Siegel, consult "Anthropology" in *Bibliographische Berichte, im Auftrag des Deutschen Bibliographischen Kuratoriums,* bearb. von Erich Zimmerman. Jahrg 1, Hft. 1, 1959– (Frankfurt a. M.: Klostermann). Quarterly. Described at F463. Review articles can also be identified in the *Social sciences citation index* (A231), for which computer-readable databases are available, and the *Bibliographic index* (A175), which requires a substantial bibliography for inclusion.

F436 Reviews in anthropology. Westport, Conn.: Redgrave. v.1– , 1974– . Bimonthly.

Became bimonthly in 1976. Has sustained its objective of giving in-depth reviews of about 100 books a year in a format that leads to evaluative comparison of various contributions and to extensive bibliographies. The "Commentary" section gives authors an opportunity to reply. Coverage includes all subdisciplines in anthropology.

F437 Current anthropology: a world journal of the sciences of man. v.1– , 1960– . Chicago: Univ. of Chicago Pr. 5/yr.

An outgrowth of *Yearbook of anthropology* (F1007) and sponsored by the Wenner-Gren Foundation, *CA* embodies some of the features of an organ of general review. Program has emphasized 4 significant lines of effort: (1) a continuing review by teams of specialists of books and papers of general interest; (2) research reports; (3) current news, timely discussions, and reports of professional activities; and (4) cooperative production and publication of reference material. The review article, its hallmark, is used in two forms: (1) comprehensive presentation of a topic, subjected to extensive "CA comment" by critics, with a concluding rejoinder by the author or authors; and (2) "CA book review," based on the same treatment in depth. The result in either case approaches a definitive state-of-the-art review of a timely topic. Keyword index cumulates from volume to volume. Beginning with the August 1980 issue, *CA* plans twice-a-year publication of "Documentation in Anthropology," publishing the first issue in v.21, no.4:564–66. The regular identification of useful bibliographies and of newsletters for specialized groups is a useful feature.

F438 Yearbook of physical anthropology. v.23– , 1980– . New York: publ. by Alan R. Liss for the American Assn. of Physical Anthropology.

Beginning with v.24 (1981), this work will be issued as a supplement to *American journal of physical anthropology*, v.1– , 1918– (New York: publ. by Alan R. Liss for the American Assn. of Physical Anthropology), and included in the cost of that subscription. V.23 functions as an annual review not of the discipline as a whole, but certainly of selected topics in which developing research seems to justify a survey of the research to the date of publication. The new publication arrangement should make this valuable reference source less erratic in its publication schedule. For earlier volumes, see the section on Yearbooks.

Current Reviews of the Literature

F439 American anthropologist: journal of the American Anthropological Association. v.1– , 1888– . Washington, D.C. 6/yr.

Outstanding for coverage of the literature, this journal has increased the number of books and films reviewed each year to about 300, only to find the output climbing higher. Accordingly, the executive board of the association decided in 1970 to abandon the book review section in favor of a new program that was put into effect with v.73 (1971). The journal continues to have 6 issues per year consisting of separately edited series of "reviews issues" and "articles issues." This change provides better opportunity for planning and managing both programs. A "Current Book Review" issue normally leads off with a lengthy review article that attempts a synthesis of work in some strategic area. The main section consists of book reviews under broad headings, as general and theoretical, ethnology, political anthropology, development and change, religion, linguistics, archaeology, and physical anthropology. Other sections include film reviews, other new publications, and discussion and debate. The new policy fits in with a trend; the nineteenth-century organization of book reviewing is breaking down.

F440 Anthropologie. v.1– , 1890– . Paris: Masson. Bimonthly.

"Mouvement Scientifique" contains 100–150 critical, signed reviews (250–2,000 words) of contributions to prehistory, physical anthropology, and ethnography. "Bulletin bibliographique" briefly abstracts the contents of 60–70 journals and learned publications. Book reviews included in the index.

F441 Anthropos: revue international d'ethnologie et de linguistique. v.1– , 1906– . Fribourg, Switzerland: Anthropos-Institut. 3/yr.

The "Rezensionen" section contains 175–250 critical reviews per year (100–1,300 words). "Periodica" itemizes the contents of more than 100 journals of anthropological interest. Book reviews indexed by author, subject, and geographical area.

F442 Man: the journal of the Royal Anthropological Institute. v.1– , 1966– . London: The Institute. Quarterly.

Succeeds *Journal of the Royal Anthropological Institute* and *Man*, and inherits a tradition of high standards. Reviews 200–250 books and films per year. Annual index of authors and reviewers.

F443 Zeitschrift für Volkskunde: halbjahrs-schrift der Deutschen Gesellschaft für Volkskunde. v.1– , 1891– . Stuttgart: W. Kohlhammer. Semiannual.

Became a semiannual with v.54 (1958), and thereafter has devoted roughly half of each issue to reviewing world literature and reporting on scholarly activities in 2 sections: "Buchesprechungen" and "Bibliographische Hinweise." Annual index of books reviewed.

ABSTRACTS AND SUMMARIES

F444   Abstracts in anthropology. v.1– , 1970– . Westport, Conn.: Greenwood Periodicals. Quarterly.

While there has been a steady improvement in the coverage and quality of this serial publication, it has not reached maturity as a reference source. Entries are arranged under archaeology, subdivided by region; cultural anthropology, subdivided by topic; and sections on linguistics and physical anthropology. New issues are useful as a source for current awareness, but the indexes do not cumulate and are not professionally constructed.

F445   Abstracts in German anthropology. v.1– , 1980– . Gottingen, W. Germany: Greifswalder Weg 2, D2400.

Issued twice a year. Each issue of about 150 pages contains concise abstracts in English of all anthropological publications, including dissertations, appearing in German. To facilitate use, there is a subject and an author index. Includes all subdisciplines and all geographic areas including European ethnography.

F446   American Anthropological Assn. abstracts. 1960– . Washington, D.C. Annual.

Abstracts of papers and films for annual meetings beginning with the 59th in 1960. No index, but cross-references to the preliminary program.

F447   Bulletin signalétique. Secs.: 521 Sociologie-Ethnologie. 526 Art et archéologie. 524 Sciences du langage. 527 Sciences religieuses. 525 Préhistoire (especially 30[3][1977] 2,003 numbered items classed by cultures and geographic region). Description at A149.

Since 1972, available on the machine-readable database FRANCIS. For information write: Bulletin Signalétique, 54, Boulevard Raspail 75270 Paris, France.

F448   LLBA: language and language behavior abstracts. v.1– , 1967– . La Jolla, Calif.: Sociological Abstracts. Quarterly. Description at A163.

F449   Excerpta medica: the international medical abstracting service. v.1– , 1947– . Amsterdam: Excerpta Medica. Monthly.

A more general source. Section 1, "Anatomy, anthropology, embryology and histology," and several other subject sections have value to anthropological scholarship. See also *Cumulated index medicus*. v.1– , 1960– (Chicago: American Medical Assn.). Annual. (**F450**)

Retrospective Abstracts

Included in this section are discontinued abstracting services that have not been superseded and anthropological bibliographies with abstracts or annotations that are organized by date in order to reveal the historical development of themes or methods.

F451   Abstracts of folklore studies. v.1–13, 1963–75. Austin: Univ. of Texas Pr. Quarterly.

Arranged alphabetically by source. The annual index by author, title, and subject is difficult to use. A model indexing scheme that could turn this retrospective set into an important reference tool is available in *An analytical index to the* Journal of American folklore, comp. by Tristan P. Coffin, v.1–67, 68, 69, 70 (Philadelphia: American Folklore Society, 1958 [384p.] [American Folklore Society. Bibliographical and special series v.7]) (**F452**). This prototype index provides 8 approaches to material, including author, title, subject, and form (book reviews, tales, songs and rhymes). Separate indexes in the same volume for v.68 (1955), v.69 (1956), v.70 (1957).

F453   Favazza, Armando R. Anthropological and cross-cultural themes in mental health: an annotated bibliography, 1925–1974. Columbia: Univ. of Missouri Pr., 1977. 386p. [University of Missouri studies: 65]

3,600 English-language entries in chronological arrangement based on 68 journals, with brief descriptive abstracts. In the forward, Victor Barnouw reviews the anthropological publications and themes and includes tables of culture areas. There is a subject index in broad categories and an author index.

F454   Keesing, Felix M. Culture change: an analysis and bibliography of anthropological sources to 1952. Stanford, Calif.: Stanford Univ. Pr., 1953. 242p. [Stanford anthropological series, 1]

Pt. 1 is a chronological analysis of the progress of anthropological thought and a critique of research and the literature. Pt. 2 is a chronological list (4,212 items) of the works discussed. Most items are post-1865.

F455   Pas, H. T. Van der, comp. Economic anthropology, 1940–1972: an annotated bibliography. Oosterhout, Netherlands: Anthropological Pubns., 1973. 221p.

Long annotations. Organized by date and then by author with an author index.

F456   Van Willigen, John. Anthropology in use: a bibliographic chronology of the development of applied anthropology. Pleasantville, N.Y.: Redgrave, 1980. 149p.

Detailed introduction to each item. Organized by time period. Identifies and evaluates an illusive body of research. Author and geographical index.

BIBLIOGRAPHIES OF BIBLIOGRAPHIES

F457 Library-Anthropology Resource Group. Anthropological bibliographies: a selected guide. Ed. by Margo L. Smith and Yvonne M. Damien. South Salem, N.Y.: Redgrave, 1981. 307p.

Of the first importance. Covers bibliographies in books and journals as well as separately published items. Arranged first in six major geographic areas, each subdivided, followed by topical bibliographies on those with no specific geographical base. Some annotations. Excellent control over entry forms. Deserves careful study. Worldwide coverage of all aspects of anthropology.

Of the various sources that list bibliographies in anthropology, the Harvard University Peabody Museum Library *Catalogue* (F489–500) is outstanding. Consistently uses "Bibliography" as a special heading under major subjects such as anthropology, ethnography, ethnology, linguistics, technology, etc.

F458 Gibson, Gordon D. "A bibliography of anthropological bibliographies: the Americas." *Current anthropology* 1:61–75 (1960).

By concentrating on the most significant anthropological bibliographies originally published separately or in journals before 1955, this compilation forges a major link in the chain of control over earlier material. Use of the 290 bibliographies (which years of searching turned up) is facilitated by a geographical arrangement, supplemented by an index of subjects, authors, and, when necessary, names of periodicals. Compilations published in periodicals are included only when they are devoted chiefly or exclusively to anthropological literature concerning the Americas. The *International bibliography of social and cultural anthropology* (F468) seeks to cover material published since 1954.

F459 ———. "A bibliography of anthropological bibliographies: Africa." *Current anthropology* 10:527–66 (1969).

A research aid of exceptional importance. A thorough list of 872 bibliographies. For recent materials, consult the more general David Easterbrook, "Bibliography of African bibliographies, 1965–1975," *Africana journal* 7 (1976): 101–48 (**F460**). An alphabetical list of 664 items with a subject index. Followed by supplements. To date, *Africana journal* 8 (1977):232–42 (**F461**) and 9 (1978):293–306 (**F462**), bringing coverage to 1978.

F463 Bibliographische Berichte. Jahrg. 1– , 1959– . Frankfurt a. M.: Klostermann.

A general source with "Anthropology" as a section. Publisher varies, title varies, frequency varies. A classified listing of recent bibliographies in periodical articles and books as well as separate publications. Coverage is international, with a high percentage of German titles. Annual subject index. See also *Bibliographic index*, fully described at A175.

Regional bibliographies of bibliographies have great value. An example would be Bruno Basseches, *A bibliography of Brazilian bibliographies (Uma bibliografia das bibliografias brasileiras)* (Detroit: Blaine Ethridge, 1978 [185p.]) (**F464**), which lists 2,800 entries by subject or title with an author index. No subject index. More general bibliographic guides for countries can be useful. Titles available in *The world bibliographical series* can be identified both in *Publishers trade list annual* (A193) and American University, *Area handbooks* (F960).

Current Bibliographies
General

F465 Internationale Bibliographie der Zeitschriftenliteratur aus allen Gebieten des Wissens/International bibliography of periodical literature covering all fields of knowledge/Bibliographie internationale de la litterature periodique dans tous les domaines de la connaissance. v.1– , 1963/64– . Osnabrück, W. Germany: Felix Dietrich. Biannual.

10,000 periodicals published worldwide in all subjects are covered. Section A lists by key number the periodicals indexed. In section B, entries are listed under subject headings. References from English and French key words to German key words used for list headings are interfiled in the main alphabetical sequence. In section C, entries are arranged alphabetically by the author's name. Publication lag is less than a year. Provides subject entry to current periodical literature for all subdivisions of anthropology.

F466 Anthropological literature: an index to periodical articles and essays. Comp. by Tozzer Library, Peabody Museum of Archaeology and Ethnology, Harvard Univ. v.1– , Winter 1979– . Pleasantville, N.Y.: publ. for the Tozzer Library by Redgrave. Quarterly.

This publication brings the indexing of Tozzer Library to the research community in conventional form. In the geographic index, some subject headings have as many as 23 item numbers, and cumulations will be impossible unless these subject headings are expanded and subdivided. Available in subsections to individual scholars. Journals are selectively indexed, but a serious attempt is made to provide worldwide coverage for all of the subdisciplines of anthropology. Invaluable for physical anthropology and archaeology, and important because it maintains a bibliographic record. Improved organization is achieved by the ethnic, linguistic index; the archaeological site and culture index; and the joint author index.

F467 "Bibliographie." *In* Anthropologischer anzeiger. v.1– , 1924– . Stuttgart: E. Schweizerbart'sche Verlagsbuch-handlung. Quarterly.

More than 2,500 references per year in anthropology and related fields. Annual indexes by author and subject. Text in English and German, with occasional use of other European languages. Gap (from suspension) between v.19, no. 1/2 (1943–44), and v.20, no.1 (April 1956).

F468 International bibliography of social and cultural anthropology. v.1– , 1955– . London: Tavistock; Chicago: Aldine. Annual. [International bibliography of the social sciences]

Prepared by the International Committee for Social Sciences Documentation in cooperation with the International Congress of Anthropological and Ethnological Sciences. One of 4 current bibliographies that originated with an early UNESCO policy decision to help strengthen bibliographical control over social science literature. Area studies, linguistics, some human biology, anthropology and folklore are arranged according to a detailed classification scheme under 10 major categories, which are further divided by topic and geographical area. Book reviews are indicated by the abbreviation "CR." French and English titles are entered in the language of publication. For other entries, a translation of the title into English follows the language of publication. There is an author index and an alphabetical subject index in French and in English. Essentially an attempt to identify and organize work significant enough to be considered part of the global record of scholarship in the field. Experience has somewhat reduced the gap between the goal and the accomplishment. Selective list. See also *International bibliography of the social sciences* (A222).

F469 Anthropological index to current periodicals received in the Museum of Mankind Library. London: Royal Anthro. Inst. of Great Britain and Ireland. v.1– , 1963– . Quarterly.

Based on a strong collection of 450 journals. Title varies. Coverage includes European ethnography and ethnomusicology, human biology, archaeology, linguistics, and cultural anthropology. Absence of cumulative subject index reduces the ease with which this valuable reference tool can be used for retrospective searches. Completely accurate. Annual author index.

F470 Novaĭa inostrannaĭa literatura po obshchestvennym naukam: Istoriĭa, arkheologiĭa, ëtnografiĭa. Moskva: Akademiĭa nauk SSSR, In-t nauch. informafsii po obshchestvennym naukam. 1976– . Monthly. Preceding entry: Novaĭa inostrannaĭa literatura po istorii, arkheologii i ëtnografii (1947–75).

Lists new non-Russian-language literature on archeology and ethnography received by the Fundamental Library of Social Sciences.

F471 Novaĭa sovetskaĭa literatura po obshchestvennym naukam: Istoriĭa, arkheologiĭa, ëtnografiĭa. Moskva: Akademiĭa nauk SSSR, In-t nauch. informatsii po obshchestvennym naukam. 1976– . Monthly. Preceding title: Novaĭa sovetskaĭa literatura po istorii, arkheologii i ëtnografii (1947–75).

Called, 1949–69, *Fundamental'nakiia biblioteka obshchestvennykh nauk of the Akademiia nauk SSSR*. Provides subject entry into a range of Russian-language material that is worldwide in coverage. It maintains a monthly list of 1,000 titles of new Soviet literature, covers historical materialism, archaeology,

ethnology, bibliography, reviews of Soviet journals, and foreign books translated into Russian. The tables of contents of collections are given. There is no index. For Russian materials, reference can also be made to William S. Heiliger, *Bibliography of the Soviet social sciences, 1965–1975*, 2v. (Troy, N.Y.: Whitston, 1978 [996p.]) (**F473**).

Regional and Topical Bibliographies

F474 African affairs. v.1– , 1901– . London: Royal African Society. Quarterly.

Official journal of the society and longstanding forum for discussion of African problems. Features book reviews and a current international bibliography.

F475 Afrika-bibliographie. 1960/61– . Bonn: Deutsche Afrika-Gesellschaft. Irregularly.

German works only. Areas that receive primary emphasis are ethnology, linguistics, art, history, economics, and political and social science.

F476 "Bibliographie africainiste." *Journal de la Société des Africanistes*. v.1– , 1931– . Paris: Musée de l'Homme. Annual.

This important current bibliography of 1,000–2,500 items per year emphasizes archaeology, prehistory, anthropology, ethnography, linguistics, and sociology. Additional items on history and geography. Includes monographs, articles (since 1957), society publications, documents, etc., in all languages. No annotations.

F477 Bibliographie ethnographique de l'Afrique sud-saharienne. Tervuren, Belgium: Musée Royal de l'Afrique Centrale, 1925–30– . Annual.

Title, 1925–59: *Bibliographie ethnographique du Congo Belge et des régions avoisinantes*. Author list of books and articles, with subject index. Most items annotated. Cites reviews for more important items. International in coverage.

F478 Modern Language Assn. of America. MLA international bibliography of books and articles on the modern languages and literatures.

For description, see A224. Since 1970, has covered folklore studies. Reliable coverage of linguistics—William Bright is responsible for North American Indian languages. Each year 3 volumes are bound as one, and the first table of contents is to v.1 only. Table of contents to v.2 and v.3 can be located by a determined scholar.

F479 Internationale Volkskundliche Bibliographie/ International folklore bibliography/Bibliographie internationale des arts et traditions populaires. 1939/41– . Bonn: Rudolf Habelt Verlag. Every two years.

Comprehensive for Europe and the Western Hemisphere. Lists articles from 1,000 journals worldwide and includes books and essays in collections in a detailed classification system covering folk literature, music and dance, social traditions, symbols, folk medicine, etc. Subject classes are subdivided by linguistic group. Indispensable for European ethnography.

F480 Simmons, Merle Edwin. Folklore bibliography for 1973. Bloomington: publ. by the Indiana Univ. Research Center for Languages and Semiotic Studies for the Folklore Inst., 1975. 175p. [Indiana Univ. Folklore Institute monograph series, v.28]

F481 ———. Folklore bibliography for 1974. Bloomington: publ. by the Indiana Univ. Research Center for Language and Semiotic Studies for the Folklore Inst., 1977. 159p. [Indiana Univ. Folklore Institute monograph series, v.29]

F482 ———. Folklore bibliography for 1975. Philadelphia: Inst. for the Study of Human Issues, 1979. 186p. [Indiana Univ. Folklore Institute monograph series, v.31]

These reference sources are divided by subject area, with an author index. Irregular publication pattern. Provides continuity for the older "Folklore bibliography" in the quarterly *Southern folklore*, 1964–72 (Gainesville: Univ. of Florida Pr.) (**F483**), which was annual in its coverage of the New World, Spain, and Portugal.

F484 Demos: internationale ethnographische und folkloristische informationen. v.1– , 1960– . Berlin: Akademie Verlag. Quarterly.

A bulletin that classifies and fully annotates books, articles, and pamphlets in ethnography and folklore that originate in the cooperating countries. Prepared under the auspices of Institut für Deutsche Volkskunde an der Deutschen Akademie der Wissenschaft zu Berlin in cooperation with learned societies and ministries of culture in the Soviet Union, Czechoslovakia, Poland, Albania, Bulgaria, Romania, and Hungary. One section devoted to bibliography. Author index.

F485 Archäologische Bibliographie, 1913– , Beilage zum Jahrbuch des Deutschen Archäologischen Instituts. v.1– , 1914– . Berlin: de Gruyter. Annual.

International in scope, with broad coverage of books and articles.

F486 "Publications." *Journal de la Société des Américanistes.* v.54– , 1965– . Paris: Société des Américanistes. Semiannual.

Inventory of current publications of selected learned bodies and current contents of selected journals. Supersedes "Bibliographie" (new ser. v.10–53, 1919–64), a comprehensive list of books, articles, and society publications, with emphasis on anthropology, ethnography, linguistics, and archaeology.

F487 Bibliographie linguistique de l'année...et complément des années précédentes. v.1– , 1939– . Utrecht, The Netherlands: Spectrum. Annual, beginning with 1948.

Published by Permanent International Committee of Linguists. A comprehensive effort to list and organize the books and articles of significance for linguistic scholarship. More than 1,200 periodicals are represented. Uses a detailed classification system, supplemented by author index. Book reviews follow entries for book.

F488 Bibliographie linguistischer Literatur. Bd. 1– , 1976– . Frankfurt a. M.: Klostermann. Quarterly.

Continues *Bibliographie unselbstandiger Literatur. Linguistics* with v.4, 1978. A classified bibliography of periodical articles and essays in collection. Coverage is for Western languages only. Arranged by language with a subject breakdown. The 1971–75 volume included more than 13,000 items.

Retrospective Bibliographies

Five major tools for making a retrospective search of anthropological literature are the back files of (1) *Annual review of anthropology* (F435); (2) *International bibliography of social and cultural anthropology* (F468); (3) *International encyclopedia of the social sciences* (A415); (4) Harvard Univ., Peabody Museum of Archaeology and Ethnology, Library, *Catalogue* (F489); and (5) Library-Anthropology Resource Group, *Anthropological bibliographies: a selected guide* (F457). Supplementary retrospective aids include back files of abstracting services and current bibliographies. See also bibliographies of bibliographies and the retrospective sections of chapter 1.

Library Catalogs

F489 Harvard Univ. Peabody Museum of Archaeology and Ethnology. Library. Catalogue: subjects. Boston: Hall, 1963. 27v.

F490 ———. ———. Index to subject headings. Boston: Hall, 1963. 117p.

F491 ———. ———. First supplement. Boston: Hall, 1970. 6v.

Entries represent additions from 1963 through the first half of 1969.

F492 ———. ———. Second supplement. Boston: Hall, 1971. 3v.

Entries represent library acquisitions from the second half of 1969 through the first half of 1971, and several hundred volumes from the previously uncataloged libraries of G. G. MacCurdy, P. A. Means, and S. K. Lothrop. Provides list of serials indexed.

F493 ———. ———. Index to subject headings. Rev. ed. Boston: Hall, 1971. 237p.

Complete listing of headings and cross-references used in the subject sections of all catalogs hitherto published.

F494 ———. ———. Third supplement. Boston: Hall.

Entries through 1974. Includes supplement to the List of Serials.

F495 ———. ———. Fourth supplement. Boston: Hall.
V.4–7. Lists 274 serials added and indexed. Entries through August 1977.

F496 Harvard Univ. Peabody Museum of Archaeology and Ethnology. Library. Catalogue: authors. Boston: Hall, 1963. 26v.

F497 ———. ———. First supplement. Boston: Hall, 1970. 6v.
Contains entries from 1963 through the first half of 1969.

F498 ———. ———. Second supplement. Boston: Hall, 1971. 2v.
Covers entries from the second half of 1969 through the first half of 1971, and for volumes from the previously uncataloged libraries of G. G. MacCurdy, P. A. Means, and S. K. Lothrop.

F499 ———. ———. Third supplement. Boston: Hall.
Entries index through 1974.

F500 ———. ———. Fourth supplement. Boston: Hall.
Entries index through 1977. V.1–3.

F500 Index to anthropological subject headings. 2d
A rev. ed. Boston: Hall, 1981. 177p.

Explicitly states that the coverage for some periodicals is extensive while for others only one article may have been analyzed. There are some curious exclusions. The author index, for example, does not appear to list the contributions of O'Leary to the bibliographic control of cross-cultural studies (F510–12). Prehistoric and historic (but not Greek and Roman) archaeology, ethnology, biological anthropology, cultural anthropology, and linguistics (especially Western hemisphere) are covered. In the basic set, the historical archaeology of Europe, Asia, and Africa were not included. In the supplements, African linguistics, some Near Eastern archaeology, and some sociolinguistic studies of Europe are included. No discipline has a more comprehensive retrospective listing; but as the editors point out, even this effort "by no means represents international anthropology in all its dimensions." The catalogue appropriately reflects the broad research interests of Harvard University. It is weak in its coverage of the Middle East in comparison to its coverage of Middle America. It is strong in its coverage of Slavic language materials. The classification system, more appropriate to an earlier anthropology, remains adequate for area studies; this tool, however, should not be approached without an understanding of the classification system that is explained in the preface of the original set and in the introductions to the supplements. Also see F490, F493, and

F500A, *Index to anthropological subject headings*. Since this indexing no longer has the support of Harvard University, its continuation is imperiled.

Also of high rank, but more specialized and difficult to use, is the Deutsches Archäologisches Institut, Römische Abteilung, Bibliothek, *Katalog der Bibliothek des Kaiserlich Deutschen Archäologischen Instituts in Rom, von August Mau*...Neu bearb. von Eugen von Mercklin (Rome: Löscher; Berlin: de Gruyter, 1913–32 [2v. in 4]) (F501), with *1. Supplement; Ergänzungen zu Band I für die Jahre 1911–1925*, bearb. von Friedrich Matz (Berlin: de Gruyter, 1930 [516p.]) (F502), and *Kataloge der Bibliothek...; Autoren- und Periodica Kataloge; Systematischer Katalog; Zeitschriften-Autorenkatalog* (Boston: Hall, 1969 [13v.]) (F503). Opens wider access to one of the most eminent collections in the field. Particularly strong on the early history of humanity in European, African, and West Asian lands surrounding the Mediterranean.

For older contributions, consult *International catalogue of scientific literature: P, anthropology, 1900–14* (London: publ. by the Royal Society of London for the Intl. Committee, 1903–19 [14v. in 13]); reprint, New York: Johnson, 1968. 2v. (F504). Sec. P (one of 17) is valuable for inclusive coverage of its period and careful organization of the literature.

Other publications of library collections can be helpful for special purposes. For example, the American Museum of Natural History, New York, Library, *Research catalog of the Library of the American Museum of Natural History: classed catalog* (Boston: Hall, 1978 [12v.]) (F505), includes only holdings through the mid-1960s. Careful inspection of the guide to the classification scheme yields detailed entry to specific topics such as "circumcision" and "birth customs." Some collections are valuable for their predominantly contemporary focus. For example, Center for Applied Linguistics, Library, *Dictionary catalog of the Library of the Center for Applied Linguistics, Washington, D.C.* (Boston: Hall, 1974 [4v.]) (F506). See B. R. Nelson, "Anthropological research and printed library catalogs" (F423).

General Select Bibliographies

The American Universities Field Staff, *A select bibliography: Asia, Africa, Eastern Europe, Latin America* (New York: American Universities Field Staff, 1960 [534p.]) (F507), is a superior list that undertakes to skim the cream of books and journals (mainly in English) that interpret the culture of the peoples represented. A coding system helps identify important titles, and its annotations are of good quality. The original list of 7,000 titles is supplemented biennially (beginning with 1961) with about 500 titles, selected using the same high standards. Their 10-year cumulation has been published as American Universities Field Staff, *A select bibliography: Asia, Africa, Eastern Europe, Latin America: cumulative supplement 1961–1971* (New York: American Universities Field Staff, 1973 [357p.]) **(F508)**. 6,000 annotated items from this authoritative source. Updated by *Choice*.

One of the earliest select bibliographies of comparative studies is Selbald R. Steinmetz, *Essai d'une bibliographie systématique de l'ethnologie jusqu'à l'année 1911* (Brussels: Misch & Thron, 1911 [196p.]) [Instituts Solvay, Institut de Sociologie, monographies bibliographiques, 1] **(F509)**. It is a list of more than 2,100 books and articles that excludes studies of only one culture. A modern bibliography of cross-cultural studies can be found in Timothy J. O'Leary's "A preliminary bibliography of cross-cultural studies," *Behavior science notes* 4:1 [1969] 95–115 **(F510)**; "Bibliography of cross-cultural studies: supplement I," *Behavior science notes* 6:3 [1971] 191–206 **(F511)**; and "Bibliography of cross-cultural studies, supplement II," *Behavior science notes* 8:2 [1973] 123–34 **(F512)**. Selection for inclusion in these works reveals some theoretical bias. A better selective guide to material for cross-cultural studies can be found in Murdock's *Atlas of world cultures* (F926).

A number of monographs and bibliographic guides have become classics because of their comprehensive coverage of important material to the date of publication. Examples would include Wilfrid D. Hambly, *Source book of African anthropology* (Chicago: Field Museum of Natural History, 1937. 2v. in 1. [953p.] [Publication 394, 396; Anthropological series 26]) Reprint in 1v. by Kraus, 1968 **(F513)**. Hambly followed up the bibliographical section of his 1937 handbook with *Bibliography of African anthropology 1937–49; supplement to* Source book of African anthropology (Chicago: Field Museum of Natural History, 1952 [p. 155–292] [Fieldiana: Anthropology, v.37, no.2]) **(F514)**. Carleton Stevens Coon, *The origin of races* (New York: Knopf, 1962 [724p.]) **(F515)**, is valuable for summary of established fact, indexing, and documentation. See also William N. Stephens, *The family in cross-cultural perspective* (New York: Holt, 1963 [460p.]) **(F516)**. Dell Hymes, *Language in culture and society: a reader in linguistics and anthropology* (for description, see F224), is a classic for its bibliographic control over a large

number of topics. Steve Barnett, *Ideology and everyday life: anthropology, neomarxist thought, and the problem of ideology and the social whole* (Ann Arbor: Univ. of Michigan Pr., 1979 [179p.] [Anthropology series: Studies in cultural analysis]) **(F518)**, is noteworthy as well.

F519 Inventory of marriage and family literature. v.3– , 1973/74– . St. Paul: Univ. of Minnesota Family Social Science). Title varies. Formerly: *International bibliography of research in marriage and the family*.

A truly comprehensive coverage of English-language publications that brings the benefits of computer technology to its key-word index. Invaluable for first-start bibliographies on socialization, family, kinship, and marriage.

F520 Council of Planning Librarians. Exchange bibliography. v.1– , 1958– . Monticello, Ill.: Council of Planning Librarians.

The mimeo-like format has made it possible for anthropologists to publish a number of topical bibliographies, some with a very specialized focus of interest. Examples would include William W. Pilcher, *Urban anthropology*, Exchange bibliography, no.944–45 [1975] [106p.] **(F521)**; Darrell L. Whiteman, *On the evolution of human behavior: a preliminary bibliography*, Exchange bibliography, no.496 [1973] [19p.] **(F522)**; Theodore Reinhart and Linda A. Heck, *Economic anthropology: a working bibliography*, Exchange bibliography, no.373 [1973] [51p.] **(F523)**; William G. Lockwood, *Periodic markets: source materials on markets and fairs in peasant society*, Exchange bibliography, no.341 [1972] [22p.] **(F524)**; James Nwannukwu Kerri, *Voluntary associations in change and conflict—a bibliography*, Exchange bibliography, no.551 [1974] [13p.] **(F525)**; James C. Starbuck, *Geographic index to exchange bibliographies* (Monticello, Ill.: Council of Planning Librarians, 1974– [Exchange bibliography, Council of Planning Librarians; no.648–50, 683, 759, 883, 1002, 1127, 1238, 1346, 1483]) **(F526)**. Eleven volumes to date. In another series by the same publisher *Biosociocultural bibliography for interdisciplinary graduate research*, by Hope L. Isaacs and others (Monticello, Ill.: Vance Bibliographies, 1981 [304p.] [Public administration series, 638]) **(F527)**. Entry by detailed table of contents only.

F528 Field, Henry. Bibliography on Southwestern Asia. Coral Gables, Fla.: Univ. of Miami Pr., 1953–62.

1. 1953 [106p.], 2. 1955 [126p.], 3. 1956 [230p.], 4. 1957 [464p.], 5. 1958 [275p.], 6. 1959 [328p.], 7. 1962 [305p.]. Subject index to Bibliographies on Southwestern Asia: I–V, 1959–61 (19 parts) pt. 1. *Anthropogeography* by Edith W. Ware, 1961 [157p.]) **(F529)**.

This work is supplemented by *Bibliography on Southwestern Asia: supplement*, by Henry Field and Edith M. Laird (Coconut Grove, Fla.: Field Research Projects, 1968–72 [8v. in 7]) **(F530)**. V.1, 1968 [92p.]

IV *Anthropology, maps, botany and zoology*, 1969 [78p.]; VII *Anthropogeography, botany, and zoology*, 1972 [68p.]. Field and Laird's work is comprehensive on anthropogeography in all languages for the area, from Istanbul to the Hindu Kush on the north and from Aden to the Makran Coast on the south. Many works published by Field Research Projects, such as Rodman E. Snead, *Bibliography on the Makran regions of Iran and West Pakistan*, ed. by Henry Field (Coconut Grove, Fla.: Field Research Projects, 1970 [38p.]) **(F531)**, evade the normal channels of bibliographic review and distribution.

Folklore

F532 Peradotto, John. Classical mythology: an annotated bibliographical survey. Boulder, Colo: American Philological Assn., 1977. 76p. [American Philological Assn. bibliographical guides]

Goes beyond the sources familiar to students of classical mythology. Identifies reference books that can be useful in attempts to integrate the impact of theory developed in social science on modern scholarship in this area. Basically a classified arrangement under subject headings, e.g., "Myth and Psychology." For a wider range of coverage see Wilfrid Bonser, *A bibliography of folklore as contained in the first eighty years of the publications of the Folklore Society* (London: publ. by W. Glaisher for the Folk-Lore Society, 1961 [126p.] [Publications of the Folk-Lore Society, 121]) **(F533)**, and *A bibliography of folklore for 1958–1967: being a subject index to vols. 69–78 of the journal Folklore* (London: Folklore Society; distributed by W. Glaisher, 1969 [54p.] [Publications of the Folklore Society, 130]) **(F533A)**, limited only by the interests of the members of one of the principal learned societies in the field; and the Cleveland Public Library, John G. White Department, *Catalog of folklore, folklife, and folk songs*, 2d ed. (Boston: Hall, 1978 [3v.]) **(F534)**, based on a remarkable collection that includes folktales, medieval romances, fables and proverbs, music and chapbooks, as well as studies of beliefs and customs from various parts of the world.

The bulkiest segment of folk literature consists of folk narratives. Antti Aarne, *The types of the folktale; a classification and bibliography*, tr. and enl. by Stith Thompson, 2d rev. (Helsinki: Suomalainen Tiedeakatemia, 1981 [588p.] [Folklore Fellows Communications, no.184]) **(F535)**, is the foremost bibliographical source on the folktale. This work, originally published as Aarne's *Verzeichnis der Märchentypen* in 1910 (FFC, no.3), was first revised by Stith Thompson in 1928 (FFC, no.74). These two editions won a fundamental position in folklore scholarship for orderly study of the immense material they brought under better control.

F536 Flanagan, Cathleen. American folklore: a bibliography, 1950–1974. Metuchen, N.J.: Scarecrow, 1977. 406p.

3,600 entries arranged in 16 sections, with the first five arranged by form. A last section is devoted to a list of obituaries of prominent folklorists. Some brief annotations. Each item entered only once. Sections on bibliography dictionaries and archives are especially valuable.

Traditional Medicine

F537 Harrison, Ira E., and Sheila Grominsky. Traditional medicine: implications for ethnomedicine, ethnopharmacology, maternal and child health, mental health, and public health: an annotated bibliography of Africa, Latin America, and the Caribbean. New York: Garland, 1976–84. 2v. [Garland reference library of social science, v.19, 147]

A general section is followed by sections on Africa and the Latin America/Caribbean area. Each section is subdivided by topics such as health-care delivery, mental health, ethnomedicine, etc. An author index at the end of sections and a country index at the end of the volume. Some specialized regional bibliographies are available—for example: J. N. van Luijk, *Selected bibliography of sociological and anthropological literature relating to modern and traditional medicine in Africa south of the Sahara* (Leiden: Afrika-Studiecentrum, 1969 [62p.]) **(F538)**. "This. . . is the second part of a report on medical anthropological and medical sociological literature and research in a number of countries in Africa South of the Sahara." Excludes South Africa and the Portuguese and Spanish colonies. Items are coded for subject and area content. Covers period 1960–68. The first part discusses these items in Dutch. See also *Internationale Volkskundliche Bibliographie (International folklore bibliography)* (F479).

F539 Favazza, Armando R. Themes in cultural psychiatry: an annotated bibliography, 1975–1980. Columbia: Univ. of Missouri Pr., 1982. 194p.

Introduction includes a table of items relevant to geographic areas. Author and subject index.

Linguistics

F540 Gazdar, Gerald, comp. A bibliography of contemporary linguistic research. New York: Garland, 1978. 425p. [Garland reference library of the humanities, v.119]

5,000 entries. Monographs and book reviews dated earlier than 1970 are excluded. Main entry is by author. There are language and topical indexes, but they are difficult to use and are not professionally structured. See also *Bibliographie linguistischer literatur*, described at F488.

F541 Abrahamsen, Adele A. Child language: an interdisciplinary guide to theory and research. Baltimore: Univ. Park Pr., 1977. 381p.

1,500 items are annotated in a classified arrangement, with author and subject indexes.

F542 Mackey, William Francis. Bibliographie internationale sur le bilinguisme/International bibliography on bilingualism. Quebec: Presses de l'Université Laval, 1972. 203p.

11,006 items, including sociocultural studies, developmental studies, and studies of the relationship between language and culture, race and nation. Detailed analytical subject index in French and English. A substantial work, professionally executed.

F543   Université Laval. Centre international de recherches sur le bilinguisme/International Center for Research on Bilingualism. Linguistic composition of the nations of the world/Composition linguistique des nations du monde. Ed. by Heinz Kloss. Quebec: Presses de l'Université Laval, 1974–81. 4v. to date: v.1: Central and Western South Asia; v.2: North America; v.3: Central and South America; v.4 Oceania.

Assembles language statistics from all sources—official, professional, speculative. An attempt to establish the numerical limits of language communities. Additional volumes are promised.

Religions

William A. Lessa and Evon Z. Vogt, eds., *Reader in comparative religion: an anthropological approach*, 4th ed. (New York: Harper, 1979 [488p.]) **(F544)**, is a well-chosen list of studies with a general bibliography and an annotated list of "Selected monographs on non-Western religious systems." Religion in Africa is well supported by sound bibliographic work, including Robert Cameron Mitchell, comp., *A comprehensive bibliography of modern African religious movements* (Evanston, Ill.: Northwestern Univ. Pr., 1966 [132p.]) **(F545)**, with supplements by Harold W. Turner that appeared in 1968 and 1970 in the *Journal of religion in Africa* 1(3):173–211 and 3(3):161–208. Also, Harold W. Turner, *Bibliography of new religious movements in primal societies* (Boston: Hall, 1977– [Bibliographies and guides in African studies]) **(F546)**; v.1: *Black Africa*, 1977 (277p.), v.2: *North America*, 1978 (286p.). In this work, detailed tables of content give item numbers and pages and guide the reader to the bibliographic items. There is an author and a thematic index. Bibliographic control of scholarly contributions to the study of religion in Africa finds additional expansion in Patrick E. Ofori, *Black African traditional religion and philosophy: a select bibliographic survey of the sources from the earliest times to 1974* (Nendeln, Liechtenstein: Kraus-Thomson, 1975 [421p.]). Reprinted by Nendeln, Liechtenstein: KTO Pr., 1977 [1975] **(F547)**. Books, dissertations, and periodical articles in a classified arrangement. The regional sections are subdivided by country and then by tribe and again by subject. Traditional medicine is included. Author index. See also Irving I. Zaretsky and Cynthia Shambaugh, *Spirit possession and spirit mediumship in Africa and Afro-America: an annotated bibliography* (New York and London: Garland, 1978 [443p.] [Garland reference

library of social science, v.56]) **(F548)**. Annotated. Includes much material on psychology, social structure, and even art.

F549   Arab-Islamic bibliography: the Middle East Library Committee guide: based on Giuseppe Gabrieli's Manuale di bibliografia musulmana. Ed. by Diana Grimwood-Jones and others. Hassocks, Eng.: Harvester Pr.; Atlantic Highland, N.J.: Humanities, 1977. 292p.

Full and comprehensive coverage of the Islamic world. A truly remarkable work that covers reference sources and encyclopedias, provides in-depth studies of essential materials for studying Islam, and includes a directory of institutions and booksellers. It is not designed to reward a casual approach. For example, the user must infer from a table-of-contents entry "Bibliographies II Islam in general. New and Middle East (with or without North Africa: general and subjects)" that bibliographies of histories will include works of primary value to anthropologists. There is no subject index. Ibn Khaldun, for example, is listed and no fewer than four bibliographies of his life and work are included, but the absence of annotations means that the breadth of Ibn Khaldun's thought and its impact on the Arab mentality go unremarked. Similarly, particularly important editions or translations cannot be identified.

F550   Zoghby, Samir M., comp. Islam in sub-Saharan Africa: a partially annotated guide. Washington, D.C.: Library of Congress, 1978. 318p.

Superb scholarship organizes 2,682 annotated entries by historical period, then by region and then by subject. Covers material prior to December 1974 and provides a glossary, a list of periodicals, and an index.

F551   International bibliography of the history of religions/Bibliographie internationale de l'histoire des religions. v.1– , 1954– . Leiden, Liechtenstein: publ. by E. J. Brill for the Intl. Assn. for the History of Religions.

References to 2,500 books and articles from nearly 500 scholarly periodicals give worldwide coverage. The subject classification scheme includes the major religions, minor religions, Chinese religions, and Japanese religions. Book reviews follow the entry for the book. There is an author index.

F552   Lurker, Manfred. Bibliographie zur Symbolkunde. Baden-Baden: Verlag Heitz, 1964–68. 3v. [Bibliotheca bibliographica aureliana, v.12, 18, 24]

V.1 organizes 4,521 items under 14 subject headings, v.2 deals with types of symbols, and v.3 contains author and subject index. Can be updated by reference to *Bibliographie zur Symbolik, Ikonographie und Mythologie erghanzungsband*, v.1– , 1982– (Baden-Baden: Verlag V. Koerner) **(F553)**. Irregular. Previously *Bibliographie zur Symbolik: Ikonographie und Mythologie. International referateorgan*, Jahrg. 1– , 1968– (Baden-Baden: Verlag V. Koerner, D-757 Baden-Baden, Postfach 304, West Germany). Annual **(F553A)**. The volume for 1979 had 621 entries with an author and subject index. Identifies such anthropological material as Freerk C. Kamma, ed. *Religious text of the oral traditions of Western New Guinea* (v.12: item 282 [1979]).

Extensive bibliographies of some religious groups in the United States are available to the anthropologist. Examples would include Marta Weigle, *A penitente bibliography* (Albuquerque: Univ. of New Mexico Pr., 1976 [162p.]) **(F554)**, an annotated list arranged by form and by author thereunder with no index; Nelson P. Springer, comp., *Mennonite bibliography, 1631–1961* (Scottdale, Penn.: Herald Pr., 1977 [2v.]) **(F555)**, v.1: *International, Europe, Latin America, Asia, Africa*, v.2: *North America*. Indexes. 28,000 entries arranged geographically, then by broad subject and format with author, subject, and book review indexes; and Mary L. Richmond, comp., *Shaker literature: a bibliography* (Hancock, Mass.: Shaker Community, Inc., 1977 [2v.]) **(F556)**, v.1: *By the Shakers*, v.2: *About the Shakers*.

Expressive Culture

The *Annual review of anthropology* (F435) is the best single source for current bibliography on expressive culture. However, some regional bibliographies and reference books reflect the growing introduction of bibliographic order into this facet of investigation. Examples would include Charlotte Johnson Frisbie, *Music and dance research of Southwestern United States Indians: past trends, present activities, and suggestions for future research* (Detroit: Information Coordinators, 1977 [109p.] [Detroit studies in music bibliography, v.36]) **(F557)**. Well-documented bibliographic essays arranged by decade from 1880 to 1976, with an appendix for discographies, record companies, and archives. Also, Judith Lynne Hanna, "African dance research: past, present, and future," *Africana journal: a bibliographic library journal and review quarterly* 11[(1)(2)]:33–51 **(F558)**. An extensive review followed by a select bibliography of items discussed and a detailed guide to bibliographies and other research resources. Jaap Kunst, *Ethnomusicology: a study of its nature, its problems, methods and representative personalities to which is added a bibliography*, 3d ed. (The Hague: Nijhoff, 1974 [303, 46p.]) **(F559)**. *Primitive art* (Boston: Worldwide Books, 1969 [42p.] [Worldwide art books bibliography, v.4 (1)]) **(F560)** provides an annotated guide prepared by the staff of the Museum of Primitive Art in New York. Establishing a standard of excellence, Aubyn Kendall, *The art of archaeology of pre-Columbian middle America: an annotated bibliography of works in English* (Boston: Hall, 1977 [324p.]) **(F561)**.

Other Special Topics

The New York (City) Missionary Research Library, *Dictionary catalog of the Missionary research library, New York* (Boston: Hall, 1968 [17v.]) **(F562)**, has a wealth of documentation on the various cultures in which missionaries have lived and worked for many years. An example of the strength of this collection would be its holding of *Bibliografia missionaria* (Unione missionaria del clero in Italia) Isola del Liri, anno 1– , 1933– **(F563)**. A rarely held bibliographic entry into enormous amounts of ethnographic material produced by missionaries. See Godfrey Raymond Nunn, *Asia: reference works: a select annotated guide* (F694), for explicit entry to volumes devoted to Asia.

F564 Conklin, Harold C. Folk classification: a topically arranged bibliography of contemporary and background references through 1971. New Haven, Conn.: Yale Univ. Dept. of Anthropology, 1980. 521p.

Comprehensive. Includes analyses of systems of folk classification, comparisons of these analyses, and background literature on classification. Author index.

F565 Divale, William Tulio. Warfare in primitive societies: a bibliography. Rev. ed. Santa Barbara, Calif.: ABC–Clio, [1973]. 123p. [War/peace bibliography series 2]

1,655 entries in a classified arrangement. Part one is divided into 16 topics, and part two by geographical region. Author and tribe indexes.

F566 Bonser, Wilfrid. A prehistoric bibliography. Ext. and ed. by June Troy. Oxford: Basil Blackwell, 1976. 425p.

Arranged by the system of the Council of British Archaeologists to cover the British Isles. Index. In another area, prehistory is covered by James Douglas Pearson, *A bibliography of pre-Islamic Persia* (London: Mansell, 1975 [288p.] [Persian studies series, no.2]) **(F567)**. 7,300 items are classified under four major subject headings, with a detailed table of contents. Absolutely accurate.

F568 Jones, J. O. Index of human ecology. London: Europa, 1974. 169p.

The list of abstracting and indexing services by discipline is followed by a discussion of how to use these sources. The consolidated subject index is helpful.

F569 Lapointe, François. Claude Lévi-Strauss and his critics: an international bibliography of criticism (1950–1976): followed by a bibliography of the writings of Claude Lévi-Strauss. New York: Garland, 1977. 219p. [Garland reference library of the humanities, v.72]

Covers works about Lévi-Strauss followed by a chronological bibliography of his writings, including translations. Author and name index.

F570 Ritchie, Maureen, comp. Women's studies: a checklist of bibliographies. London: Mansell, 1980. 107p.

"Anthropology" as a section heading (p.15) and "Area studies" (p.17–26) are especially helpful. An unannotated list with an author and key-word index.

F571 Rosenstiel, Annette. Education and anthropology: an annotated bibliography. New York: Garland, 1977. 646p. [Garland reference library of social science, v.20]

English-language translations of foreign-language titles are given in this list of 3,435 books, articles, and dissertations in six languages. Topical, subject, and geographical indexes assist the user.

F572 Kemper, Robert V. The history of anthropology: a research bibliography. New York: Garland, 1977. 212p. [Garland reference library of social science, v.31]

This list of 2,400 entries in a classified arrangement has an author index. Provides students with a place to start.

DISSERTATIONS

F573 Reynolds, Michael M. A guide to theses and dissertations: an annotated international bibliography of bibliographies. Detroit: Gale, 1975. 599p.

Citations to lists of foreign and American theses and dissertations appearing in journals, books, and other published sources. These entries, retrospective through 1973, are arranged by geographic and subject area. It is hoped a promised supplement will contain a completely new index that brings together diverse elements of a subject. The present index does not reflect the scope of the lists. Authors and titles identified here should be searched for supplements in local card catalogs because some of the reference works itemized have been updated. Examples would include Jesse John Dossick, *Doctoral research on Russia and the Soviet Union, 1960–1975: a classified list of 3,150 American, Canadian, and British dissertations, with some critical and statistical analysis* (New York: Garland, 1976 [345p.] [Garland reference library in [i.e., of] social science, v.7]) (**F574**). Updated annually in the December issue of *Slavic review* since 1976 (**F575**). Another example, Standing Conference on Library Materials on Africa, *Theses on Africa, 1963–1975, accepted by universities in the United Kingdom and Ireland*, comp. by J. H. St. J. McIlwaine (London: Mansell, 1978 [123p.]) (**F576**).

Other recent publications of more general lists useful to anthropologists and published since the Reynolds work would include: Michael Sims, comp., *American & Canadian doctoral dissertations & master's theses on Africa, 1886–1974* (Waltham, Mass.: Brandeis Univ. African Studies Assn., 1976 [365p.]) (**F577**). 6,000 items arranged by geographic area and subdivided by subject. Carl W. Deal, *Latin America and the Caribbean: a dissertation bibliography* (Ann Arbor, Mich.: Univ. Microfilms Intl., 1978 [164p.]) (**F578**), lists 7,200 items in broad subject arrangement divided by country. Commonwealth Caribbean Resource Centre, comp., *Theses on the Commonwealth Caribbean, 1891–1973* (London, Ont.: Univ. of Western Ontario, Office of International Education, [1975] [139p.]) (**F579**), is an author list with geographic but no topical index. George Dimitri Selim, comp., *American doctoral dissertations on the Arab world, 1883–1974*, 2d ed. (Washington: Library of Congress, 1976 [173p.]) (**F580**). Superbly comprehensive. Oliver B. Pollak, *Theses and dissertations on Southern Africa: an international bibliography* (Boston: Hall, 1976 [236p.]) (**F581**). Broad subject arrangement divided by country. "Anthropology" 447 items. Author index. Entries includes author title, granting institution, and date. Pagination is usually included. *Doctoral dissertations on Asia*, v.1– , 1975– (Ann Arbor, Mich.: Assn. for Asian Studies [AAS Secretariat, 1 Lane Hall, Univ. of Michigan]) (**F582**). The latest edition seen (March 1980) contains 1,400 doctoral dissertations and includes names and addresses of many individuals. Items are entered only once and there is no subject index. The arrangement by region, then by country subdivided by time period, makes it difficult to use for a subject approach. William G. Coppell, *A bibliography of Pacific Island theses and dissertations* (Honolulu: Research School of Pacific Studies, Australian National Univ. in conjunction with the Institute for Polynesian Studies, Brigham Young Univ., Hawaii campus, 1983 [520p.]) (**F582A**) includes author, title, degree discipline from which degree was earned and pagination. Detailed index.

F583 Theses on Islam, the Middle East and Northwest Africa, 1880–1978: accepted by universities in the United Kingdom and Ireland. Comp. by Peter Sluglett. London: Mansell, 1983. 147p.

Classified arrangement with sections on Islamic and Christian studies followed by geographic arrangements subdivided by subject. Social studies and language are included.

F584 "Ph.D. dissertations in anthropology." *Current anthropology: a world journal of the sciences of man.* v.1– , 1960– . Chicago: Univ. of Chicago Pr. 5/yr.

The *Yearbook of anthropology, 1955* (F1007) lists more than 1,400 Ph.D. dissertations awarded at 61 institutions between 1870 and 1954. The first *CA* list (7:606–31 [1966]) attempts to bring it up to date. Various countries are represented. Arranged alphabetically by author and indexed by institutions submitting lists, but no subject breakdown. Supplemented by a comparable list, again with no duplication, in *Current anthropology* 9:590–606 (1968). And, again without duplication, *CA* 11:234 (1970), with an institutional index in *CA* 10:261–64.

F585 "Ph.D. dissertations in anthropology." In Guide to departments of anthropology. Described at F886.

A special feature. The current issue contains lists from preceding editions and includes some older titles from institutions new to the directory. The title of this feature changes frequently.

F586 McDonald, David R. Masters' theses in anthropology: a bibliography of theses from United States colleges and universities. New Haven, Conn.: HRAF Pr., 1977. 453p.

3,835 citations organize the work done in 109 institutions from 1898 to 1975. Subject, ethnic, national, cross-cultural, and institutional indexes greatly increase the value of this reference work. Subject index has multiple entries. A good piece of work.

F587 Dockstader, Frederick J., comp. The American Indian in graduate studies: a bibliography of theses and dissertations. New York: Museum of the American Indian, Heye Foundation, 1973–74. 2v. [Contributions from the Museum of the American Indian, Heye Foundation, v.25] v.1, 2d ed. of 1957 covers period 1890 to 1955; v.2, compiled by F. J. Dockstader and A. W. Dakstadea, covers period from 1955 to 1970. Edition by same title published as Contributions from the Museum of the American Indian, Heye Foundation, v.15.

The bibliography does not attempt to be critical, but about half the entries have brief, informative annotations. Arrangement is alphabetical by author, with the degree, date, institution, title, and pages for each entry and reference to the published version (if any). Indexed for topics, tribes, archaeological sites, geographical names, etc. 7,446 dissertations from 1890 to 1970. See also Gifford S. Nickerson, *Native North Americans in doctoral dissertations, 1971–1975: classified and indexed research bibliography* (Monticello, Ill.: Council of Planning Librarians, 1977 [77p.] [Council of Planning Librarians. Exchange bibliography, no. 1232]) (**F588**), which adds 500 dissertations. Planned as a supplement to Dockstader; however, limited to United States and Canada and includes only items listed in *Dissertations abstracts international* (A150).

F589 Montemayor, Felipe. 28 [i.e., Veintiocho] años de antropología: tesis de la Escuela Nacional de Antropología e Historia, 1944–1971. México: Instituto Nacional de Antropología e Historia, 1971. 615p.

"Catalogo...de las tesis de antropologia presentadas en la Escuela." Chronological listing with detailed abstracts and subject, place, and author indexes.

F590 White, Peter J. "Anthropological theses in Australia: a first listing (to 1974)." *Mankind* 10(2):Supp. (December 1975):1–20.

This 1975 publication includes all theses (including bachelors and diploma level) presented to anthropology and/or prehistory departments at Australian universities to date of cutoff. Additions are promised. An alphabetical list without indexes. Entries include author, title, date, degree, and granting institution.

F591 Westermark, George D., Robert L. Welsch. "A bibliography of North American anthropological doctoral theses on New Guinea." *Mankind* 11(1)(1977):26–32.

Sociocultural dissertations from the United States and Canada. Indicates availability in published form. Each listing includes author, date, and title of the thesis, followed by the university where the degree was granted. A code indicates province with which research was concerned but there is no index. For the Highlands, worldwide coverage is attempted by Terence E. Hays, *Anthropology in the New Guinea Highlands*. Fully described at F786.

F592 Dundes, Alan, comp. Folklore theses and dissertations in the United States. Austin: publ. for the American Folklore Society by the Univ. of Texas Pr., 1976. 610p. [Publications of the American Folklore Society, bibliographical and special series, v.27]

Arranged chronologically by years, then alphabetically by author within each year. Entries include author, title, degree, discipline, institution from which degree was earned, and pagination. Three indexes to subjects, authors, and institutions provide adequate entry to the list. A comprehensive bibliography on the subject within its defined limits.

F596 World catalogue of theses and dissertations relating to Papua New Guinea. Boroko, Papua New Guinea: Inst. of Applied Social and Economic Research, 1978. [124p.] [IASER bibliography: 2].

730 items by author, with a subject index.

PERIODICALS

F597 Library-Anthropology Resource Group. Serial publications in anthropology. 2d ed. Comp. by Library-Anthropology Resource Group; ed. by F. X. Grollig and Sol Tax. South Salem, N.Y.: Redgrave, 1982. 177p.

4,387 titles. Alphabetical by title, with a subject index. Some entries are sketchy. See also the anthropology sections of *Ulrich's international periodicals directory* (A381) and *Irregular serials and annuals: an international directory* (A382) and the list of periodicals indexed in the Harvard Univ. Peabody Museum of Archaeology and Ethnology *Catalogue* (F489–500). For regional lists, consult the guides listed in the section "Geographical bibliographies."

F598 Breedlove, James M., ed. The holdings of the Stanford University libraries on Latin American languages and linguistics. Stanford, Calif.: Resources Development Program, 1973. 63p.

A list of periodicals that are significant in the field.

F599 Linguistique: liste mondiale des périodiques spécialisés/Linguistics: world list of specialized periodicals. Paris: Mouton, 1971. 243p. [Maison des sciences de l'homme. Service d'échange d'informations scientifiques. Publications. Serie C: Catalogues et inventaires, 4.]

540 periodicals with information about publication and contents, arranged by country of origin and subdivided in a threefold hierarchy. English subject heading equivalents to the French are provided. Subject, title, and institutional indexes.

F600 Bloss, Ingeborg. Zeitschriftenverzeichnis Moderner Orient: Stand 1979/Union list of Middle East periodicals (up to 1979). Hamburg: Deutsches Orient-Institut, Dokumentations-Leitstelle Moderner Orient, 1980. 657p. [Dokumentationsdienst Moderner Orient; Reihe B. Bd. 1]

Geographic and subject index. Includes states of the Arab League, plus Turkey, Iran, Afghanistan, Israel, Pakistan, Malta, and Cyprus. Introduction in German and English.

F601 Auchterlonie, James Paul Crawford, ed. Union catalogue of Arabic serials and newspapers in British libraries. London: Mansell, 1977. 146p.

An alphabetical list of references to variant forms in indexes but not in the main body. Includes official publications; locations are given for each entry.

For union lists of Asian periodicals, consult Nunn's *Asia: reference works* (F694), and *The bibliography of South Asian periodicals: a union-list of periodicals*. South Asian Library Group, comp. by Graham W. Shaw and Salim Quraishi (Brighton, Sussex: Harvester Pr.; Totowa, N.J.: Barnes & Noble, 1982 [135p.]) (**F601A**). Includes periodicals published anywhere in South Asian languages and those in Arabic and Persian published in South Asia. Holdings in 6 major British libraries. Extensive cross reference to alternative spelling and titles.

GEOGRAPHICAL BIBLIOGRAPHIES

Sub-Saharan Africa

For basic entry into anthropological materials, consult: International African Institute, *Africa bibliography series: ethnography, sociology, linguistics and related subjects*, described at F622; the same institute's *Ethnographic survey of Africa*, described at F623; and the *International African bibliography*, described at F624. Use of the subject and regional entries in Library-Anthropology Resource Group, *Anthropological bibliographies* (F457), is essential to any complete search.

F602 Martin, Phyllis M., and Patrick O'Meara, eds. Africa. Bloomington: Indiana Univ. Pr., 1977. 482p.

24 articles from all disciplines, with anthropology well represented. The "Bibliography and sources for African studies" (p. 415–66), by Jean E.

Meeh Gosebrink, is well constructed as a guide to the literature. For most topics, references are given for (1) bibliographies, (2) continuing reference sources, (3) the major journals in the field, and (4) selected suggestions for additional reading. Emphasis is on works published after 1967. Includes Marxist contributions. Identifies titles on Africa in the *Case studies in cultural anthropology* (F1071). 27 maps and 16 pages of index. Does not supersede *The African experience*, ed. by J. N. Paden and E. W. Soja (Evanston, Ill.: Northwestern Univ. Pr., 1970 [3v. in 4]) (**F603**). An illuminating presentation by Hans E. Panofsky and others of reference sources for African studies and 31 essays by subject specialists. Its discussion of the African book trade can be enlightened by reference to *The African book world and press: a directory/Répertoire du livre et de la presse en Afrique*, comp. by the African Book Publishing Record and ed. by Hans M. Zell, 3d ed. (Oxford: Hans Zell; Detroit: Gale, 1983 [285p.]) (**F604**). Alphabetical order by country. Within countries, arrangement by 10 subjects, including libraries, booksellers and publishers, associations, and government printer for each of 51 countries. *African book publishing record*, v.1– , 1975– (Oxford: Hans Zell). Quarterly (**F605**). Supplements *African books in print*, v.1– , 1975– (London: Mansell) (**F606**). Publisher varies. *African book publishing record* lists books published or about to be published in Africa, arranged in three indexes: author, title and subject. Directory of publishers. V.6(3)(4) 1980 is a special issue devoted to "Publishing in Africa in the eighties," with a list of dealers in African books (p.191–93), several discussions of the African books trade including African imprint library services, and an extensive annotated bibliography of sources for book reviews on Africa (p.183–88). For retrospective depth in these reviews, see David Easterbrook, *Africana book reviews, 1885–1945* (F629). For comparative evaluation of recent work, see African Studies Assn., *A.S.A. review of books*, v.1–6, 1975–80 (Waltham, Mass.: African Studies Assn.). Annual (**F607**). Beginning with 1981, absorbed by *African studies review*, v.13– , April 1970– (Waltham, Mass.: African Studies Assn.) (**F607A**) Quarterly. Many review articles and groups of reviews, by theme, permit some critical comparison of scholarly production. Detailed table of contents guides the reader.

F608 Scheven, Yvette. Bibliographies for African studies, 1970–1975. Waltham, Mass.: Crossroads, 1977. 159p. [The archival and bibliographic series]

Essential for its coverage and currency. Superb organization of 993 bibliographies in a topical/geographical arrangement, with continuing bibliographies cited at the end of each section and an index of names, titles, and subjects. Most subject headings work for anthropological material. Thus, listed under "Nigeria" but not under "Anthropology" is Nduntuai G. Ita's *Bibliography of Nigeria: a survey of anthropological and linguistic writings from the earliest times to 1966* (London: Cass, 1971 [271p.]) (**F609**), which has 5,411 annotated items, *including*

Islamic studies, with the second section arranged by ethnic groups. Scheven identifies items in journals not covered by the major indexing services; the internal contents of books; and annotations and arrangements that lead to works whose titles barely reveal their ethnographic content, e.g., Angela Molnos, *Cultural source materials for population planning in East Africa* (Nairobi: East African Publishing House, 1973 [4v.]) **(F610)**, whose fourth volume consists of 181 pages of first-start bibliographies for 29 East African ethnic groups.

A second volume by Scheven, *Bibliographies for African studies, 1976–1979* (Waltham, Mass.: Crossroads, 1980 [142p.] [The archival and bibliographic series]) **(F611)**, and Yevette Scheven, *Bibliographies for African studies 1980–1983* (Oxford: Hans Zell; New York: Saur, 1984 [300p.]) **(F611A)**, follow the same selection standards as the earlier volume. Specific to the period and does not attempt to identify previously published base volumes. Identifies publications of African press, e.g., L. Neser, *Zulu ethnography: a classified bibliography* (Kwa-Dlangezwa: Kwazula Documentation Centre of the University of Zululand, 1976 [92p.] [Publications, Univ. of Zululand: Ser. 3 Specialized publications, no. 18]) **(F612)**, which has recently been supplemented by *Zulu ethnography: a supplementary bibliography* (Kwa-Dlangezwa: Univ. of Zululand, 1980 [71p.] [Publications, Univ. of Zululand: Ser. B, Specialized publications, no. 6]) **(F613)**.

For guidance into the basic bibliographic apparatus, consult Hans E. Panofsky, *A bibliography of Africana* (Westport, Conn.: Greenwood, 1975 [350p.] [Contributions in librarianship and information science, no.11]) **(F614)**. A discriminating knowledge of the literature of the whole of Africa makes this a basic guide. There is a subjct index but no author index. Freely assumes that the reader has exhausted Peter Duignan and Helen F. Conover's *Guide to research and reference works on Sub-Saharan Africa.* (Stanford, Calif.: Hoover Institution Pr., 1971(?) [1,102p.] [Stanford Univ. Hoover Institution on War, Revolution, and Peace, Bibliographical series, v.46]) **(F615)**, which selects, organizes, and annotates more than 3,127 treatises, abstracting services, bibliographies, directories, encyclopedias, atlases, and journals, and introduces organizations, libraries, and archives.

These guides provide entry into bibliographies of specific African cultures and culture complexes (such as the following), which exist in bountiful measure: Isaac Schapera, *Select bibliography of South African native life and problems* (London: Oxford Univ. Pr., 1941 [249p.]) **(F616)**. The first three supplements, published by the University of Cape Town School of Librarianship, Cape Town, 1958–64, are also available in reprint under the title, *Select bibliography of South African native life and problems: modern status and conditions: supplements I–III, 1939–1963* (New York: Kraus, 1969 [187p.]) **(F617)**. The fourth supplement, *South African native life and problems: modern status and condition: 1964–70*, by Stephanie

Alman (Cape Town: Univ. of Cape Town Libraries, 1974 [39p.] [Univ. of Cape Town School of Librarianship, Bibliographical series]) **(F618)**, omits periodical articles and government publications and is based on the collections of London libraries. See also Eckhard Strohmeyer and Walter Meritz, *Umfassende Bibliographie der Völker Namibiens (Südwestafrikas) und Südwestangolas/Comprehensive bibliography of the peoples of Namibia (South West Africa) and Southwestern Angola*. Bd 1 , 1975– (Starnberg, W. Germany: Max-Planck-Inst. zur Erforschung Lebensbedingungen Wissenschaftl.-Techn. Welt) **(F619)**. Title also in Portuguese, Afrikaans, and French. Chapter titles are in German, English, and French. V.1 is 349p. and is comprehensive to date of publication. General section, then arranged by ethnic groups. V.2 will cover the Bushman and provide an author index for both volumes. However, a classified Bushman bibliography of 290 items can be found in *The Bushmen: san hunters and herders of Southern Africa*, ed. by P. V. Tobias (Cape Town: Human & Rousseau, 1978 [206p.]) **(F620)**. *South African bibliography: a survey of bibliographies and bibliographical work*, 2d ed., by Reuben Musiker (Cape Town: D. Philip, 1980 [84p.]) **(F621)**, is an evaluative bibliography of bibliographies on South African topics, with coverage of neighboring territories Namibia, Botswana, Lesotho, and Swaziland. Annual supplements are planned.

F622 Intl. African Institute. Africa bibliography series: ethnography, sociology, linguistics and related subjects. Ed. by Ruth Jones. London: The Institute, 1958–61. 4v. to date.

Each volume is devoted to a different region: *West Africa* (1958), *Northeast Africa* (1959), *East Africa* (1960), *Southeast Central Africa and Madagascar* (1961). Series is based on the classified card index of the institute's library. Attempts to include all significant works. Each volume is subdivided territorially and then by subject. Some brief annotations. Indexes by author and ethnic and linguistic groups.

F623 Ethnographic survey of Africa/Monographies ethnologiques africaines. Ed. by Daryll Forde. London: Intl. African Inst., 1950– .

More than 50 volumes to date. First-start bibliographies and summary coverage under such titles as the *Southern Nilo-Hamites*; *The Gisu of Uganda*; *The central tribes of the Northeastern Bantu: the Kikuyu, including Embu, Maru, Mbere, Chuka, Mwimbi, Tharaka, and the Kamba of Kenya*; *The coastal tribes of the North-Eastern Bantu (Pokomo, Nyika, Teita)*; *The Swahili-speaking peoples of Zanzibar and the East African Coast: Arabs, Shirazi, and Swahili*; *Les Bira et les peuplades limitrophes*; *Mamvu-Mangutu et Baless-Mvuba*; *The Asande, and related peoples of the Anglo-Egyptian Sudan and Belgian Congo*; *The Nilotes of the Anglo-Egyptian Sudan and Uganda*; *Peoples of southwest Ethiopia and its borderland*; *Peoples of the Lake Nyama region*; *The central Nilo-Hamites*; *The Galla of Ethiopia: the Kingdoms of Kafa and Janjero*; *Peoples of the Horn of Africa: Somali, Afar, and Saho*. Purpose of the survey is a concise, accurate account of present knowledge of tribal groupings. Each monograph is prepared by an expert and devoted to a particular people or cluster of peoples. Indexed in U.S. Library of Congress, General Reference and Bibliographical Div., *Africa south of the Sahara: index to periodical literature, 1900–1970* (F632).

F624 International African bibliography. London: publ. by Mansell for the School of Oriental and African Studies, University of London, in association with the Intl. African Inst., v.1– , 1971– . Quarterly.

The first section covers Africa as a whole, with subdivisions for such subjects as ethnology, anthropology and sociology, religion and philosophy, language and literature. The remaining section covers regions of Africa, subdivided by countries. There is an annual author index. This series continues earlier coverage from *Africa: journal of the International African Institute*, v.1– , 1928– (London: Oxford Univ. Pr.) **(F625)**, in which there appeared a quarterly feature "Bibliography of current publications" through v.40, 1970. A journal still valuable for its book reviews and articles of international scope. A cumulation to the quarterly bibliographies published in *Africa* (1929–70) and in the *International African bibliography* for 1971 and 1972 can be found in International African Institute, Library, *Cumulative bibliography of African studies* (Boston: Hall, 1973 [6v.]) **(F626)**, with a divided subject and author catalogue; and *International African bibliography, 1973–1978: books, articles and papers in African studies*, ed. by J. D. Pearson (London: Mansell 1982 [343p.]) **(F627)**, with table of contents for classed arrangement.

F628 Asamani, J. O. Index Africanus. Stanford, Calif.: Hoover Institution Pr., 1975. 659p. [Stanford University. Hoover Institution on War, Revolution, and Peace. Bibliographical series, v.53.]

Covers 1885–1965. Significant articles from 200 journals, 20 memorial volumes, and 60 proceedings of conferences organized by geographical area and further subdivided by subject headings. 24,600 entries covering even the islands of Tristan da Cunha and Mauritius. Omits articles dealing with Islamic civilization. Author index. No subject index. The body of opinion that surrounded the books published in earlier scholarship can be found in David L. Easterbrook, *Africana book reviews, 1885–1945: an index to books reviewed in selected English-language publications* (Boston: Hall, 1979 [247p.] [Bibliographies and guides in African studies]) **(F629)**. A checklist of core books from 44 journals with a review index. Limited to English-language journals. Excludes Islamic studies.

Gibson's superb work "Bibliography of anthropological bibliographies: Africa," (F459) updated by Easterbrook's "Bibliography of African bibliographies, 1965–1975" and supplements (F460–62) makes it possible for us to concentrate on research aids of broader range. Passed over, except for a few examples, are bibliographies of African states that are often compiled in whole or in part from general sources such as the subject volumes of London Univ. School of Oriental and African Studies Library, *Library catalogue* (A264), and Boston Univ. Libraries, *Catalog of African government documents and African area index*, 2d rev. and enl. ed., comp. by Mary D. Herrick (Boston: Hall, 1964 [471p.]) **(F630)**. Arrangement follows LC schedules subnumbered for departments in governments. This source can be expanded by consulting Staatsbibliothek der Stiftung Preussischer Kulturbesitz, comp., *Catalogue of African official publications available in European libraries as of 1 May 1971* (Berlin: Intl. Federation of Library Assns., Committee for Official Publications, 1971 [251p.]) **(F631)**. Limited to independent countries. Includes government documents, state institutions, state libraries, and state universities. 1,186 items arranged by country, with author and title indexes.

F632 United States. Library of Congress. African Section. Africa south of the Sahara; index to periodical literature, 1900–1970. Boston: Hall, 1971. 4v.

First supplement, 1973 covers items added Jan. 1971 to June 1972. A second supplement provides coverage through 1976. This unit of LC now provides indexing to 3,000 journals. Arranged by area (region and country). Under subheadings of "anthropology and ethnology," and "language and linguistics," are broken down by tribe. Original indexing of journals received by the Library of Congress did not start until 1960. A working file with great variation in entries, but many journals covered here are not adequately indexed in other sources. Especially valuable for its inclusion of Russian- and French-language bibliographic services and, beginning in 1960, of *African abstracts*, v.1–25, 1950–75 (London: Intl. African Inst.) **(F633)**, which can be consulted directly as a retrospective source only with great labor since subject indexes were not designed to expand into cumulations. The second supplement contains finding aids: (1) an alphabetical list of personal authors and (2) an alphabetical list of all ethnic groups with variant names cross-referenced and with citations that identify the discussion of the tribes in George Peter Murdock, *Africa: its peoples and their culture history* (New York: McGraw-Hill, 1959 [456p.]) **(F634)**, which includes an index of almost 5,000 ethnic names and a large, folded map showing groups and culture areas. For former colonies of Great Britain, a more detailed subject entry can be found in Royal Commonwealth Society, *Subject catalogue* (A273).

F635 United States and Canadian publications and theses on Africa. v.1– , 1966– . Stanford, Calif.: Hoover Institution Pr., Annual.

Material arranged topically, e.g., "bibliographies." Subject, geographic, and author index. Beginning in the sixth issue, some doctoral dissertations are included. Comparable services are Standing Conference on Library Materials on Africa, *United Kingdom publications and theses on Africa* (1963–) (Cambridge: Heffer [annual]) **(F636)**, and *Afrika-bibliographie* (F475).

F637 Current bibliography on African affairs. 1962– . Farmingdale, N.Y.: Publ. by Baywood for the African Bibliographic Center. Monthly.

Preceded by series 1, v.1–6 (1962–68). An unevenly selected list of 250–350 items. Irregularly has additional features, occasional bibliographical essays being perhaps the most useful. For other current sources, consult the "General" section under the subheading "Continuing sources" in Yvette Scheven, *Bibliographies for African studies, 1970–1975* (F608) and *1976–1979* (F611).

F638 Witherell, Julian W., comp. The United States and Africa: guide to U.S. official documents and government-sponsored publications on Africa, 1785–1975. Washington, D.C.: Library of Congress, Govt. Print. Off., 1978. 949p.

A monumental work that sets a new standard of professional excellence. With superb control over the resources, this partially annotated bibliography of selected publications of the United States government relating to Africa (Egypt is excluded) provides ease of identification for many invaluable items. Includes indexing to annual reports of the Smithsonian Institution and national archive holdings. "Ethnology" is sometimes a subdivision under the names of countries, and direct entry can be made through the name of an ethnic group, e.g., Bakuba. Includes the translations of the Joint Publications Research Service. Identifies the mimeographed studies concerning American assistance programs prepared by or for federal government agencies. Arranged by geographic area and subdivided by topic. Indexing is by topic, issuing body, and main entry and is professionally structured. Maps are reached only under the index term "Geography and maps." Especially valuable for its identification of the Library of Congress bibliographies of the government documents of African nations.

F639 Blaudin de Thé, Bernard M. S., ed. Essai de bibliographie du Sahara français et des régions avoisinantes. 2d ed. Paris: Arts et Métiers Graphiques, 1960. 258p.

A classified bibliography of 9,301 books and articles related to French Africa. Author index. A source useful for updating this basic bibliography is the Library of Congress, African Section, *Africa south of the Sahara: index to periodical literature* (F632).

Recent examples of bibliographies covering a whole geographic unit or region include: Jacqueline Audrey Kalley, *The Transkei region of Southern Africa, 1877–1978: an annotated bibliography* (Boston: Hall, 1980 [218p.] [Bibliographies and guides in African studies]) (**F640**). Edition for 1976 published under title: *Transkeian bibliography: 1945 to independence, 1976*. A table of contents introduces a topical arrangement of 1,439 items supported by additional subject index and an author index. Annotated. Also S. A. Afre, *Ashanti region of Ghana: an annotated bibliography, from earliest times to 1973* (Boston: Hall, 1975 [494p.]) (**F641**). 2,781 annotated entries arranged in 34 main divisions, each with numerous subdivisions. Accurate and complete, with an author index.

F642 Armer, Michael. African social psychology: a review and annotated bibliography. New York: Africana, 1975. 321p. [African bibliography series, v.2]

863 annotated items in a broad classified arrangement, with author, country, and cross-classification indexes. Useful beyond the scope of its title in the identification of ethnographic sources.

F643 Anthropology of southern Africa in periodicals to 1950: an analysis and index. Comp. under direction of N. J. van Warmelo. Johannesburg: Witwatersrand Univ. Pr., 1977. 1,484p.

Indexed by linguistic group, place-name, and author. The linguistic group index is subdivided by subject, tribe or group, and person.

Middle East
North Africa and Southwest Asia (Excluding Pakistan)

The basic bibliographic apparatus for the study of Middle Eastern cultures includes (1) the indispensable *Index Islamicus*, a remarkable piece of work fully described at A292 that must be used with skill since each item is entered only once in a classified arrangement; (2) the *Encyclopedia of Islam*, described at F935; (3) the *Arab-Islamic bibliography*, fully described at F549, a detailed work in which the bibliography of bibliographies of the Arabian Peninsula, for example, lists 26 items; (4) Ruth Jones, *Northeast Africa* (F644); and (5) H. Field, *Bibliography on Southwestern Asia* (F528). To ensure complete bibliographic searching, use subject and area entries in Library-Anthropology Resource Group, *Anthropological bibliographies* (F457).

F644 International African Institute. North-east Africa. Comp. by Ruth Jones. London: Intl. African Inst., 1959. 51p. [Africa bibliography series: ethnography, sociology, linguistics and related subjects]

Provides best first entry into the literature, with 900 items selected for their anthropological importance. From this base, a continuous bibliographic record can be achieved by consulting "Bibliographie Maghrib-Sahara. Anthropologie, prehistoire, ethnographie," since 1961 in *Libyca: anthropologie, prehistoire, ethnographie*, v.1– , 1953– (Algeria: Service des antiques) (**F645**). Comprehensive for northeast Africa. The 1972 issue lists 10 bibliographies of ethnographic bibliographies.

F646 Simon, Reeva S. The modern Middle East: a guide to research tools in the social sciences. Boulder, Colo.: Westview, 1978. 283p. [Westview special studies on the Middle East, no.10]

Provides a most useful reference guide for the social scientist. The sections on "Specialized bibliography by countries" (p.53–89) and "bibliographies of dissertations" (p.90–94) have exceptional value. 724 annotated entries in Western and Middle Eastern languages cover all Arab countries, Afghanistan, Iran, Turkey, and Israel. Pagination is not given. Series information is sometimes missing. Extremely useful for its forthright format and range of coverage. Subject-author-title index. On the other hand, David W. Littlefield, *The Islamic Near East and North Africa: an annotated guide to books in English for nonspecialists* (Littleton, Colo.: Libraries Unlimited, 1977 [375p.]) **(F647)**, is a collection-building list of monographs. Remarkable for its selectivity, for its useful annotations, and for the completeness of its bibliographic citations. 1,166 titles in classified arrangement. Completely indexed. Seems to include everything in English that is fundamentally important. It cannot match *Middle East and Islam: a bibliographical introduction*, rev. and enl. ed., ed. by Diana Grimwood-Jones (Zug, Switzerland: Inter Documentation, 1979) [429p.] [Bibliotheca asiatica 15]) **(F648)**, for coverage of publications of scholarly value in all languages. Arranged by country and topics. Selected by a panel of scholars. Identifies out-of-print translations and includes a list of the most significant Islamic and Middle Eastern periodicals. Truly international in scope. Additional coverage of the countries of North Africa can be achieved by consulting the more general Hans E. Panofsky, *A bibliography of Africana* (F614).

F649 Anderson, Margaret. Arabic materials in English translation: a bibliography of works from the pre-Islamic period to 1977. Boston: Hall, 1980. 249p.

Arranged by subject classification and then alphabetically by author. The table of contents is useful. There is an author index in which "see-references" are given for variant forms.

F650 Atiyeh, George Nicholas, comp. The contemporary Middle East, 1948–1973: a selective and annotated bibliography. Boston: Hall, 1975. 664p.

Focuses on social conditions and related subjects but excludes Israel except for the Arab-Israeli conflict. Arranged by geographical area. Brief annotations ease the identification of relevant entries. Valuable for its range of coverage.

Among the available historical dictionaries, Carroll L. Riley, *Historical and cultural dictionary of Saudi Arabia* (Metuchen, N.J.: Scarecrow, 1972 [133p.] [Historical and cultural dictionaries of Asia, v.1]) **(F651)**, reflects the anthropological training of the author. This makes its bibliography especially helpful.

More-general bibliographic guides for countries can be useful. Titles available in the *World bibliographical series* can be identified in *Publishers trade list annual* (A193). An example of this series would be Shereen Khairallah's *Lebanon* (Santa Barbara, Calif.: Clio Pr., 1979 [154p.] [World bibliographical series]) **(F652)**. 650 entries give selective coverage to the customs, culture, religion, and social organization. Includes a section on social change and village life. Valuable indexing makes the contents easily accessible.

F653 The Middle East: abstracts and index. v.1– , 1978– . Pittsburgh: Northumberland Pr. Quarterly.

Abstracts about 2,000 items per issue. Divided into 19 sectons, with subarrangement by form so that dissertations or government documents, for example, can be searched by form. A topical and geographic index provides entry only to English-language publications. The term "Psychological and social studies" is a useful starting point for a search in anthropology.

F654 Middle East Institute. The Middle East: a selected bibliography of recent works, 1960–1970. Rev. ed. Washington, D. C.: Middle East Inst., 1972. 68p.

Arranged by topic and country to aid the undergraduate in the selection of English-language books. Substantial annual supplements to be cumulated every 10 years. Essential.

Other sources of current bibliographic information in continuing publications could include the following: *Bulletin signalétique, philosophie, sciences humaines* (Paris: Centre de Documentation, Sciences Humaines), fully described at A149, which can be used only if the diverse subdivisions are kept fully in mind. No geographic index is available. "Abstracta islamica" (Paris: Geuthner), described at A293, and the "Bibliographie africaniste," described at F476, which appears in the second issue each year of the *Journal* of the Société des Africainistes (Paris). "Bibliography of periodical literature," in *Middle East journal*, v.1– , 1947– (Washington, D.C. Middle East Inst.). Quarterly **(F655)**. Covers the major journals in all languages. Lists about 1,500 references per year. 300 journals of Middle Eastern, Islamic studies, and related fields. Covers North Africa and Muslim Spain, the Arab World, Israel, Turkey, the Transcaucasian states of the Soviet Union, Iran, Afghanistan, Pakistan, and Turkestan. Entries are classified under broad categories, including geography, social conditions, religion, language, and book reviews. The recently published *Articles on the Middle East 1947–1971: a cumulation of the bibliographies from the Middle East journal*, ed. by Peter M. Rossi and others (Ann Arbor, Mich.: Pierian, 1980 [4v.]) **(F656)**, provides a reprint of these quarterly records, with cumulative index. Provides entry to book reviews under an "Author/main entry/reviewer" index, giving a comprehensive approach to more than 42,000 references. A "Subject index: personal names" provides an approach to more than 9,200 references to the names of individuals treated as subjects in the cumulation. "Subject index: categories" identifies by page number the location of the subject areas classified in each quarterly bibliography. A list of periodicals indexed over the years is provided. Indispensable for access to an important body of periodical literature. Israel is excluded.

Any fieldworker going into the area will find *Middle East contemporary survey: volume one, 1976–77* (New York: Holmes & Meier) **(F659)**, a guide to the current situation in each country. Equally useful is the truly great *Middle East record*, v.1– , 1960– (Tel

Aviv: Israel Oriental Society; New York: Wiley) **(F660)**. Irregular. Its documentation in various languages has considerable scholarly value.

F661 Meghdessian, Samira Refidi. The status of the Arab woman: a select bibliography. London: Mansell, 1980. 176p.
Provides a separate section on each country. Subject index. Author index. In a more specialized focus, John Gulick has compiled *An annotated bibliography of sources concerned with women in the modern Middle East* (Princeton, N.J.: Princeton Univ. Program in Near Eastern Studies, 1974 [26p.] [Princeton Near East papers, no.17]) **(F662)**. See also Ingeborg Otto, *Frauenfragen im Modernen Orient: eine Auswahlbibliographie/Women in the Middle East and North Africa: a selected bibliography* (Hamburg: Deutsches Orient-Institut, Dokumentations-Leitstelle Moderner Orient, 1982. [247p.]) (Dokumentationsdienst Moderner Orient. Reihe A, Middle East documentation service. Ser. A; v.12) **(F663)**. 38 pages of index. Classified arrangement. Both Western languages and Arabic. 1,242 items.

F664 Université Saint-Joseph (Beirut). Centre d'Études pur le Monde arabe Moderne. Arab culture and society in change: a partially annotated bibliography of books and articles in English, French, German and Italian. Lebanon: Dar el-Mashreq [distributor: Near East Books Co., New York], 1973. 318p.
Integrates many periodicals not covered by the standard indexes.

F665 Rural politics and social change in the Middle East. Ed. by Richard Antoun and Iliya Harik. Bloomington: Indiana Univ. Pr., 1972. 498p. [Studies in development, no.5]
Includes specialized critique by H. Rosenfeld (p.45–74), which reviews the work of ethnographers and social anthropologists.

F666 The central Middle East: a handbook of anthropology and published research on the Nile Valley, the Arab Levant, southern Mesopotamia, the Arabian Peninsula, and Israel. Ed. by Louise E. Sweet. New Haven, Conn.: HRAF Pr., 1971. 323p.
Originally published in 1968 as a HRAFlex book. Now available in durable copy. Each of the five chapters provides a survey of a region, including religion and culture, with a lengthy, critical annotated bibliography. Dated but still a valuable first source. Also useful: the bibliographies in Richard V. Weekes, *Muslim peoples: a world ethnographic survey* (F930); and John Gulick, *The Middle East: an anthropological perspective* (Pacific Palisades, Calif.: Goodyear, 1976 [244p.]) (reprint, Univ. Pr. of America, 1983) **(F667)**. Organized around theoretical issues, with richly annotated bibliographies. Dense documentation.

F668 Antoun, Richard T. "Anthropology." *In* The study of the Middle East: research and scholarship in the humanities and the social sciences: a project of the Research and Training Committee of the Middle East Studies Association. Ed. by Leonard Binder. New York: Wiley, 1976. 648p.
Discusses the historical development and the problems of the anthropological work in the Middle East. Marked by informative footnotes and a selective bibliography. Includes tabulation of a survey of the work anthropologists are doing in the area. An appendix by David M. Hart reviews French contributions.

F669 Middle East Studies Assn. Bulletin. v.1– , 1967– . New York: New York Univ. Middle East Studies Assn. of North America.
State-of-the-art reviews for subject disciplines. Each issue lists doctoral dissertations completed. Bibliographic reviews of the anthropological literature. Includes Richard T. Antoun's 1971 "Three approaches to the cultural anthropology of the Middle East" (5:24–53) **(F670)**, which develops a syllabus and a 336-item bibliography, and John Gulick's 1969 "The anthropology of the Middle East" (3:1–14) **(F671)**, which provides a bibliographic review of early reports, child rearing, community studies, and social organization. Of more general value is its recent description of research libraries in the United States and Canada. Since the catalogues of so many Arabic collections have been published, the student who cannot travel has available the subject cataloging of many libraries. Consult the 1974 "Directory of library collections on the Middle East," v.17(1):22–48 **(F672)**.
Great centers of Arabic and Islamic studies can be identified in the subject index to *Commonwealth universities yearbook* (F891) and Florence Ljunggren and Charles L. Geddes, *An international directory of institutes and societies interested in the Middle East* (Amsterdam: Djambatan, 1962 [159p.]) **(F673)**, which contains some 350 societies, institutes and university departments interested in research and advanced instruction on the Middle East. Identifies serial publications of these institutions. Needs updating.

F674 Halliday, Fred. Arabia without sultans: a political survey of instability in the Arab world. New York: Vintage, 1975. 539p.
Addresses various "liberation" groups. A comprehensive analysis of the social structure by the editor of the *New left review*.

F675 Coult, Lyman H., and Karim Durzi. An annotated research bibliography of studies in Arabic, English and French, of the Fellah of the Egyptian Nile, 1798–1955. Coral Gables, Fla.: Univ. of Miami Pr., 1958. 144p.
Scholarly compilation of publications on the culture of the Fellahin. Author and subject indexes.

F676 Garsse, Yvan van. Ethnological and anthropological literature on the three southern Sudan provinces: Upper Nile, Bahr el Ghazal, Equatoria. Wien: Inst. f. Völkerkunde d. Unver. Univ. Wien, Engelbert Stiglmayr, 1972. 88p. [Acta ethnologica et linguistica, no.29. Series Africana, 7.]
1,072 entries arranged by author, with a subject index.

F677 Louis, Andre. Bibliographie ethno-socio-logique de la Tunisie. Tunis: Bascone for l'Institut des Belles Lettres Arabes, 1977. 393p. [Tunis. Institut des Belles Lettres Arabes. Publications. v.31.]

Title does not reveal scope of coverage. Includes some entry into materials on Tunisia, Algeria, Morocco. Includes also basic works, sources of review literature, bibliographies, a list of works most often cited, a list of journals, and festschrift. The thematic arrangement is detailed (47 subject headings). Ease of entry supported by an author and a subject index.

F678 Adam, André. Bibliographié critique de sociologie, d'ethnologie et de géographie humaine du Maroc: travaux de langues anglaise, arabe, espagnole et française. Algiers: Centre de recherches anthropolgiques, préhistoriques, et ethnographiques, Alger, 1972. 353p. [Mémoires du Centre de Recherches anthropologiques, préhistoriques et ethnographiques, Alger, 20]

A valuable bibliographic review, with a bibliography of bibliographies, a list of monographs most frequently cited, and an extensive list of journals. The bibliography proper is unnumbered and unannotated. Detailed classified arrangement is supported by an author index and an excellent topical index.

F679 Leupen, A. H. A. Bibliographie des populations touarègues: Sahara et Soudan centraux. Leyden, Netherlands: Afrika-Studie-centrum, 1978. 240p.

A substantial work. Annotates 1,415 items. Topical arrangement with some topic subdivisions. Author and subject index. The folding map of Tuareg lands illustrates their range over the Saharan map. Also useful is Richard I. Lawless, *Algerian bibliography: English language publications, 1830–1973* (London: Bowker for the Centre for Middle Eastern and Islamic studies of the Univ. of Durham, 1976 [114p.]) [Centre for Middle Eastern and Islamic Studies, publications no.4]) **(F680)**. 1,490 items arranged topically with cross-references. Excludes publications by United Nations agencies.

F681 Behn, Wolfgang. The Kurds in Iran: a selected and annotated bibliography. Munich: Verlag Dokumentation, 1977; dist. by Mansell, Salem, N.H. 76p.

First edition published in 1969 under the title: *The Kurds: a minority in Iran*. P.14–29 provides best available guide to Iranian study. Bibliography of bibliographies on p.28 under "General works." Substantial entry into specialized studies of Iran as a whole. Covers the years 1966–75 for books only and supplements the International Society Kurdistan's *ISK's Kurdish bibliography*, by S. Van Rooy (Amsterdam: The Society, 1968–) **(F682)**. Gives Library of Congress transliteration, where needed, and indexes in Persian, Latin, or Cyrillic alphabets. Descriptive annotations in English. See also *Bibliographical guide to Iran: the Middle East Library Committee guide*, ed. by L. P. Elwell-Sutton. (Sussex [East Sussex]: Har-

vester Pr.; Totowa, N.Y.: Barnes & Noble, 1983 [462p.]) **(F683)**. Classed arrangement, with author index.

F684 Beeley, Brian W. Rural Turkey: a bibliographic introduction. Ankara: Hacettepe Univ. Institute of Population Studies, 1969. 120p. (Hacettepe Univ. Publications no.10.)

The chapter "Background sources" provides a well-executed bibliographic review of both reference sources and studies of village and rural society. This is followed by an extensive bibliography arranged by author. There is no index.

F685 Suzuki, Peter T. Social change in Turkey since 1950: a bibliography of 866 publications. Heidelberg: High Speed Pr. Center (for the European Division of the Univ. of Maryland), 1969. 108p.

Numbered items entered alphabetically, with English translations of foreign-language titles indicated. Contributions based on fieldwork, including unpublished doctoral dissertations. No annotations. Adequate subject index.

F686 Franz, Erhard. Die ländliche Türkei im 20. Jahrhundert: eine bibliographische Einführung/Rural Turkey in the 20th century: a bibliographic introduction. Hamburg: Deutsches Orient-Institut, Dokumentations-Leitstelle Moderner Orient, 1974–75. 2v. (Dokumentationsdienst moderner Orient: Reihe A, 4, 6)

V.2 covers ethnology and includes indexing. An excellent source.

F687 Patai, Raphael. Jordan, Lebanon and Syria: an annotated bibliography. New Haven, Conn.: Human Relations Area Files, 1957. 289p. [Behavior science bibliographies]

A section on the area generally is followed by sections on each of the three countries. Out of date but still useful.

F688 Hanifi, M. Jamil. Annotated bibliography of Afghanistan. 4th ed. New Haven, Conn.: HRAF Pr., 1982. 545p. Revision of 3d ed. by Donald L. Wilbur (1968).

Classified arrangement. Comprehensive.

F689 Gazetteer of Arabia: a geographical and tribal history of the Arabian Peninsula. Ed. by Sheila A. Scoville. Graz, Austria: Akademische Druck, 1979. 4v.

First volume issued in 1979. Adds an interesting alphabetical entry with revision to include knowledge developed through 1970 to the earlier and still-valuable John Gordon Lorimer, *Gazetteer of the Persian Gulf, Oman, and Central Arabia* (official records of the Government of India), ed. by R. L. Birdwood (Calcutta: Supt. of Govt. Print., 1908–15 [2v.]) **(F690)**. V. I, historical (1915), v.II, geographical and statistical (1908). Reprint, Farnsborough, Mass.: Gregg, 1970. 2v. in 6.

Useful are the published catalogs of American collections and that of the Royal Commonwealth Society, London, Library, *Subject catalogue* (A273), which provides one entry into English contributions that are of the first importance in Middle Eastern studies and to its Arabic holdings. Among sources for American collections is the catalog *Arabic collection*, of the Univ. of Utah Middle East Library (Salt Lake City: Univ. of Utah Pr., 1968 [841p.] [Middle East Library. Catalogue series, v.1.]) **(F691)**. *Supplement 1–* , 1971– **(F692)** includes transliterated author and title indexes of considerable value to librarians who know little Arabic. For lists of libraries with relevant collections, see Simon's *Modern Middle East* (F646) using the index terms "libraries—directories" and "library catalogs."

Asia and the Pacific

F693 Siemers, Günter. Bibliographie asien- und ozeanienbezogener Bibliographien/Bibliography of bibliographies on Asia and Oceania. Hamburg: Institut für Asienkunde, Dokumentations-Leitstelle Asien, 1979. 172p. [Dokumentationsdienst Asien. Reihe A; 12.]
Oceania and Asia east of Pakistan. 902 titles from the holdings of 70 libraries. Extensively indexed. Fully describes even some of the extremely valuable pamphlets of N. L. H. Krauss that have been privately published and infrequently cataloged. A more general coverage can be found in London Univ. School of Oriental and African Studies. *Library catalogue* (A264), with three supplements. Integrates Asian and Pacific materials. Strong in anthropological materials.

Asia

F694 Nunn, Godfrey Raymond. Asia: reference works: a select annotated guide. London: Mansell, 1980. 365p. Earlier ed. published in 1971 by MIT Pr. as Asia: a selected and annotated guide to reference works.
Superb bibliographic control. Coverage organized by geographic units subdivided by form and then by subject. Encyclopedias and handbook, yearbooks, directories, atlases, theses, and dissertations are given accurate description. Though always accurate, the annotations are brief and cannot, for example, include the information that "Social anthropology" is a subject division in *Asian social science bibliography*, ed. by N. K. Goil, v.1– , 1966– (Delhi: Institute of Economic Research) **(F695)**. Nunn is especially valuable for the identification of the more general sources such as: Kokusai Bunka Shinkokai, *K. B. S. bibliography of standard reference books for Japanese studies with descriptive notes*, v.1– , 1959– (Tokyo: K. B. S.) **(F696)**, to be used with the series *An introductory bibliography for Japanese studies*, v.1– , 1974– (Tokyo: Univ. of Tokyo Pr.; Portland, Ore.: dist. by Intl. Scholarly Book Services) **(F697)** providing access to recent works in the social sciences written in Japanese with a focus on Japan. For China, Nunn identifies Ssu-yu Teng, comp., *An annotated bibliography of selected Chinese reference works*, 3d ed. (Cambridge, Mass.: Harvard Univ. Pr., 1971 [250p.] [Harvard-Yenching Institute studies, v.2]) **(F698)**, and

Noriko Kamachi, *Japanese studies of modern China since 1953: a bibliographical guide to historical and social science research on the nineteenth and twentieth centuries: supplementary volume for 1953–1969* (Cambridge, Mass.: East Asian Research Center, Harvard Univ.; dist. by Harvard Univ. Pr., 1975 [603p.] [Harvard East Asian monographs; v. 60]) **(F699)**, a supplement to John King Fairbank's invaluable *Japanese studies of modern China: a bibliographical guide to historical and social-science research on the 19th and 20th centuries* (Cambridge, Mass.: Harvard Univ. Pr., 1971 [331p.] [Harvard-Yenching Institute studies, v.26]) **(F700)**.

For recent material, refer to "Bibliography of Asian studies" (A243) and its two cumulations (A244), with the last (1966–70) showing a marked increase in the coverage of China and India. For American publishing efforts, a better subject entry can be found in the *Annual review of English books on Asia*, v.1– , 1974– (Provo, Utah: Brigham Young Univ. Pr.) **(F701)**. An accessions list with summaries of content for each title. Lists each item for form, by author, and by subject headings in multiple appearances. Also highly pertinent is *Annual bibliography of Indian archaeology*, v.1– , 1926– (Leyden, Netherlands: Instituut Ker, 1928–) **(F702)**, a comprehensive international bibliography of all scholarly writings relevant to the archaeology of India and contiguous territories to the east; also Indonesia, China, and Japan. Classified and serially numbered. Author index. Frequent references to reviews of cited books.

Southeast Asia

In the anthropological investigation of Southeast Asia, the essential first start is found in the works compiled by Frank M. LeBar, *Ethnic groups of mainland Southeast Asia* (New Haven, Conn.: Human Relations Area Files Pr., 1964 [288p.]) **(F703)**. Concise ethnographic descriptions in terms of major language stocks, with distinctions between lowland and upland groups. Provides selective first-start bibliographies for 151 groups, including those of southern China when they are culturally related. Ethnographic maps and ethnic indexes increase the reference value of this encyclopedia treatment. Frank M. LeBar, *Ethnic groups of insular Southeast Asia* (New Haven, Conn.: Human Relations Area Files Pr., 1972–75 [2v.])**(F704)**. V.1: *Indonesia, Andaman Island, and Madagascar*; v.2: *Philippines, Formosa, Sulu Sangihi, and Bolel Tobago*. Descriptive summaries are evaluative and supported by bibliographies. Ethnic and terminological indexes with ethnolinguistic maps. 19 recognized scholars contributed to this work. A fuller, unedited manuscript is available as Frank M. LeBar, comp., *Insular Southeast Asia: ethnographic studies* (New Haven, Conn.: Human Relations Area File Pr., 1976–77 [6v. in 4 sections]) **(F705)**. An older source, John Fee Embree, *Bibliography of the peoples and cultures of mainland Southeast Asia* (New York: Russell & Russell, 1972 [821p.]) **(F706)**, is an extensive bibliography of books and articles in English and European languages retrospective to the earliest studies. Entries are arranged first by general area, then by tribal groups, and finally by subject. Detailed table of contents but no indexes. Still valuable for its organization and scope.

F707 Southeast Asian research tools. Honolulu: Southeast Asian Studies, Asian Studies Program, Univ. of Hawaii, 1979– . 9v. [Southeast Asia paper; v. 16. Pts. 1–9.] Includes [1] Saito, S. Summary and needs, 64p.; [2] Char, L. H. Indonesia, 189p.; [3] Thwin, M. Burma, 67p.; [4] Roff, W. R. Malaysia, Singapore, Brunei, 61p.; [5] Baradi, E. R. The Philippines, 304p.; [6] Keyes, C. F. Thailand, 188p.; [7] Keyes, C. F. Laos, 69p.; [8] Keyes, C. F. Cambodia, 70p.; [9] Cotter, M. G. Vietnam, 49, 125p.

Sponsored by the Association for Asian Studies. A major contribution to bibliographic control. Evaluative guides to the reference sources for each area, including publications in the vernacular languages. The introductory and general bibliography sections cannot be ignored in anthropological searches. For example, the Koninklijk Instituut voor Taal-, Land- en Volkenkunde, *Bibliographical survey of Thailand: based on books in the library of the Royal Institute of Linguistics and Anthropology and on articles of the Journal of the Siam Society*, by G. A. Nagelkerke (Leyden, Netherlands: Library. Royal Institute of Linguistics and Anthropology, 1974 [63p.]) **(F708)**, is listed only in the "bibliography" section of the *Thailand* volume even though the author gives multiple listings to more useful works. Again, under "Bibliographies: General" in the volume *Malaysia, Singapore, Brunei*, nothing indicates the anthropological value of Karl Josef Pelzer, *West Malaysia and Singapore: a selected bibliography* (New Haven, Conn.: Human Relations Area Files Pr., 1971 [394p.] [Behavior science bibliographies]) **(F709)**, even though its section "Man and culture" (p.130–231) is specific to the interests of ethnologists and may be definitive for scholarly contributions. Again, listed in the volume *Burma*, under "Bibliographies" without explication of its limitations and with no indication of its anthropological importance, find Frank N. Trager, *Burma: a selected and annotated bibliography* (New Haven, Conn.: Human Relations Area Files Pr., 1973 [356p.] [Behavior science bibliographies]) **(F710)**, which excludes the invaluable articles in the *Journal* of the Burma Research society and many works of J. S. Furnival and C. H. Luce. Burma scholars should also consult J. D. Pearson's *South Asian bibliography*, fully described at **(F723)**. *Southeast Asian research tools* was undertaken as a survey and not as a reference guide. Subject indexing does not capture the more specific topical cover-

age of general works, and there is some unevenness of treatment. Thus, some volumes include the relevant work of LeBar listed above (F703–5) and some do not. Individual authors may have expected more general items to be published in a planned volume covering Southeast Asia as a whole. For this purpose, consult rather Donald Clay Johnson, *A guide to reference materials on Southeast Asia, based on the collections in the Yale and Cornell University libraries* (New Haven, Conn.: Yale Univ. Pr., 1970 [160p.] [Yale Southeast Asia studies, 6]) **(F711)**, which is still a major reference tool for anyone wishing to do research in the area. Organized by form rather than geographically.

F712 Johnson, Donald Clay. Index to Southeast Asian journals. 1960–1974: a guide to articles, book reviews, and composite works. Boston: Hall, 1977. 811p.

F713 ———. Index to Southeast Asian journals, 1975–1979: a guide to articles, book reviews, and composite works. Boston: Hall, 1982. 265p.

Limited to 41 scholarly journals. Classified arrangement of articles, with a second section for book reviews.

F714 United States. Library of Congress. Orientalia Division. Southeast Asia subject catalog. Boston: Hall, 1972– .

AACR2 form of entry: "Library of Congress. Orientalia Division." Six volumes in the basic set. Citations to books, journal articles, theses, and microforms in Western languages. Sections on each country are subdivided by subjects including "anthropology" and "archaeology." This control of Western-language materials is expanded by the Library of Congress, *Southeast Asia: Western-language periodicals in the Library of Congress*, comp. by A. Kohar Rony (Washington, D.C.: Library of Congress, 1979 [201p.]; for sale by the Supt. of Docs., Govt. Print. Off.) **(F715)**. For reference guides to serials in this area consult Godfrey Raymond Nunn, *Asia: reference works: a select annotated guide* (F694).

F716 Keyes, Charles F. "Ethnography and anthropological interpretation in the study of Thailand." *In* The study of Thailand: analyses of knowledge, approaches and prospects in anthropology, art history, economics, history, and political science, ed. by Eliezer B. Ayal. Athens: Ohio Univ. Center for International Studies, Southeast Asia Program, 1978. 257p. [Southeast Asia series; no.54], p. 1–59.

197 entries listed under references cited. 29 entries are annotated. Evaluative review of important work in the area.

F717 Saito, Shiro. Philippine ethnography: a critically annotated and selected bibliography. Honolulu: Univ. Pr. of Hawaii, 1972. 512p. [East-West bibliographic series]

Most comprehensive work to date. Includes books, journal articles, and official publications published in the major Western languages. Adequate subject and geographic entry.

F718 Koentjaraningrat, Raden Mas. Anthropology in Indonesia: a bibliographical review. The Hague: Nijhoff, 1975. 343p. [Instituut voor Taal-, Land- en Volkenkunde; 8]

A long, descriptive and evaluative essay followed by a list of references cited, listed alphabetically by author. An in-depth review of cultural anthropology for the area. Consult also G. A. Nagelkerke, *Bibliografisch overzicht uit periodieken over Indonesie 1930–1945/Bibliographical survey based on periodicals on Indonesia* (Leiden, Netherlands: Stationsplein 10: Bibliotheek Koninklijk Instituut voor Taal-, Land- en Volkenkunde, 1974 [232p.]) **(F719)**. Lists 3,159 articles, arranged geographically with a subject index. See also the older Raymond Kennedy, *Bibliography of Indonesian peoples and cultures*, 2d ed. (New Haven, Conn.: Southeast Asia Studies, Yale Univ., by arrangement with Human Relations Area Files, 1962 [207p.] [Behavior science bibliographies]) **(F720)**, which is still valuable for its arrangement by islands and then by peoples or tribes. No evaluation of items listed and no index.

F721 Cotter, Michael. Vietnam: a guide to reference sources. Boston: Hall, 1977. 272p.

Some 1,400 reference sources divided into sections for general reference followed by sections for the major disciplines. The introduction must be read for information on name forms used, for abbreviations, and for the coding practices that support the index and serve as annotations. Funded in part by the Vietnam Studies Group of the Assn. for Asian Studies.

South Asia

F722 Wasle, Iqbal, comp. Reference aids to South Asia. Toronto: Univ. of Toronto, 1977. 133p. [Reference series. Univ. of Toronto Library, no. 22]

Includes India, Bangladesh, Pakistan, Nepal, and Sri Lanka in a geographical arrangement with subdivisions by subject. Author/title index. Distributed at a reasonable cost. Adequate entry for most graduate students. J. D. Pearson's *South Asian bibliography: a handbook and guide*, comp. by the South Asia Library Group (Sussex, Eng.: Harvester Pr.; Atlantic Highlands, N.J.: Humanities, 1979 [381p.]) **(F723)**, supersedes all previous guides to that area. Twenty-six British scholars have compiled this extensive handbook of bibliographies, finding aids, and reference works. Subject bibliographies include "religion," "anthropology," "sociology," "art and archaeology," "music and dance," "language and literature," "history," "law," "economics," and "traditional sciences and technology." Section that covers regions and countries is subdivided into subjects. Afghanistan, Burma, the Maldives, the Himalayas, and Tibet are also included. Each of the 37 articles is professionally structured and maintains the model of excellence that makes this volume definitive for the area. More-general sources for areas must be consulted for topical subject coverage.

A general guide to one invaluable source of information can be found in Sashi Bhusan Chaudhuri, *History of the gazetteers of India* (New Delhi: Ministry of Education, Govt. of India, 1964 [231p.]) **(F724)**; see especially the appendixes (p.175–211). Useful for entry into *Imperial gazetteer of India*, rev. ed. (Oxford: Clarendon, 1907–31 [26v.]) **(F725)**, and the *Imperial gazetteer of India* (*provincial series*) (Calcutta: Supt. of Govt. Print., 1908–09 [25v.]) **(F726)**; reprint, New Delhi: Today and Tomorrow's Printers and Publishers, 1972–73.

F727 Pakistan and Bangladesh: bibliographic essays in social science. Ed. by W. Eric Gustafson. Islamabad: Univ. of Islamabad Pr., 1976. 364p.

This collection of bibliographical essays is a product of the National Seminar on Pakistan and Bangladesh, which has met at the Southern Asian Institute, Columbia University, since November 1970. Reasonably comprehensive bibliographic essays by recognized scholars on the subdisciplines of the social sciences, including anthropology. A supplementary bibliography divided into 16 categories and valuable for its selectivity and for its clear and concise annotations can be found in George L. Abernethy, comp., *Pakistan: a selected, annotated bibliography*, 4th ed. (Davidson, N.C.: Davidson College Publications Off., 1974 [50p.]) **(F728)**. Also valuable are Henry Field, *Bibliography on Southwestern Asia* (F528), with *Supplement* (F530) and *Subject index* (F529) and the "Bibliography of periodical literature" in the *Middle East journal*, described at F655.

Basic background information in the FASD *Area handbooks* (F960–78) provides a source of concise coverage for statistical and survey information, maps, and selective but general bibliographies. In addition, some historical dictionaries for the area reflect the anthropological training of their authors and provide useful survey bibliographies. For example, see Mohammed Jamil Hanifi, *Historical and cultural dictionary of Afghanistan* (Metuchen, N.J.: Scarecrow, 1976 [141p.] [Historical and cultural dictionaries of Asia, no. 5]) **(F729)**.

Also see Mohammed J. Hanifi's *Annotated bibliography of Afghanistan*, 4th ed. described at F688. This work is arranged by topic. Western, Slavic, and vernacular languages are covered.

F731 Sakala, Carol. Women of South Asia: a guide to resources. Millwood, N.Y.: Kraus, 1980. 517p.

The full and accurate annotations with selective entry into all aspects of South Indian culture make this reference book a preferred first entry into many aspects of the social sciences. A remarkable organization makes it easy to use. A substantial work that has value far beyond the scope of its title.

F732 Chaudhuri, Sibadas. Bibliography of Tibetan studies: being a record of printed publications mainly in European languages. Calcutta: The Asiatic Society, 1971; dist. by Columbia, Mo.: South Asia Books, 1973. 232p.

2,000 entries, including citations in Western languages and romanized Japanese. A classified subject index of 64 pages. Arranged in 13 categories, including bibliography, anthropology, ethnology, archaeology, dance, and linguistics.

F733   Goonetileke, H. A. I. A bibliography of Ceylon: a systematic guide to the literature on the land, people, history and culture published in Western languages from the sixteenth century to the present day. Zug, Switzerland: Inter Documentation Co., 1970–76. 3v. [Bibliotheca Asiatica 5, 14]

V.III supplements v.I and II, and contains additional materials up to June 1973. V.I and II were published in 1970; 2d ed. in 1973. This general bibliography of Ceylon has an organization that permits the identification of sections of interest to anthropologists such as section 9, physical anthropology and ethnology of racial and tribal groups; section 15, social organization; section 17, cultural and social change; section 18, religions; section 19, folk religion and popular religious cults; section 20, folklore; and section 30, games, sports, and amusements. Each section is arranged alphabetically by author. Predominantly Western language material, with only highly relevant articles in Asian languages, it includes books and journal articles and a few theses. Five-year supplements are planned.

F734   A bibliography of Nepal. Comp. by Basil C. Hedrick. Metuchen, N.J.: Scarecrow, 1973. 302p.

3,300 entries in subject categories, including "anthropology," "archaeology," and "sociology." There is an author index, and the preface promises annotations in the next edition. Includes unpublished manuscripts. Author index.

F735   Kanitkar, Helen A., comp. An anthropological bibliography of South Asia. The Hague: Mouton, 1976– .

Continuation of *An anthropological bibliography of South Asia*, by E. von Fürer-Haimendorf (F738). Lists 2,757 items. Drops physical anthropology and prehistoric archaeology. Adds coverage of South Asians overseas, tribal welfare, urbanization, political sociology, and sociolinguistics. One interesting appendix is devoted to the ethnology of India in literature, 1750 to the present. The publication lag makes it impossible for this source to identify recent contributions such as: Danesh A. Chekki, ed., *The social system and culture of modern India: a research bibliography* (New York: Garland, 1975 [843p.]) (F736), with 5,487 entries meticulously organized to include anthropology and social psychology, with a strong emphasis on modern India; and J. Troisi, *The Santals: a classified and annotated bibliography* (New Delhi: Manohar Book Service, 1976 [234p.]) (F737), in which 487 items are arranged in a classed arrangement, with adequate cross-references.

F738   Fürer-Haimendorf, Elizabeth von. An anthropological bibliography of South Asia, together with a directory of recent anthropological field work. Paris: Mouton, 1958–70. 3v. [Le Monde d'outre-mer passè et présent. 4. sér.: Bibliographies, 3–4, 8.]

The 3v. are *Basic works* (748p.), *1955–1962* (459p.), and *1960–1964* (562p.). A valuable tool, but restricted to India, Pakistan, Nepal, Sikkim, Bhutan, and Ceylon. V.3 has an appendix on ethnology of India as depicted in literature 500 A.D. to 1750 A.D. No annotations. Author index.

See also Calcutta, National Library, *Bibliography of Indology*, v.1 of *Indian anthropology* (Calcutta: National Library, 1960 [290p.]) (F739), which contains 2,067 entries arranged by 10 geographic regions. 1,004 entries are annotated. Author and subject indexes. "Physical anthropology," "linguistics," and "sociocultural anthropology" relating to the subcontinent of India. Journal articles are included only when coverage cannot be achieved from monographic sources. It cannot supersede David G. Mandelbaum's *Bibliography of the ethnology of India* (Berkeley: Univ. of California Dept. of Anthropology, 1949 [220p.]) (F740). A mimeographed publication, still valuable for its selectivity and organization.

F740   Roy, Ashim Kumar. Indus Valley civilization: a
A   bibliographic essay. Atlantic Highlands, N.J.: Humanities, 1982. 264p.

Bibliograhic essay of section is followed by a predominantly English language bibliography which includes articles, books, unpublished dissertations and newspaper articles. There is an addendum bibliography. The discussion of Harappan sites is exhaustive. No index.

East Asia

F741   Yang, Teresa Shu-yi Chin. East Asian resources in American libraries. New York: Paragon Book Gallery, 1977. 143p.

Includes T. S. Yang, "American library resources on East Asia"; T. C. Kuo, "East Asian collections in American libraries"; F. J. Shulma, "A bibliographical guide to East Asian resources in American libraries." Since East Asian materials are excluded from the national bibliographic control in the United States, the published catalogs of great local collections are indispensable to serious research. "Millions of volumes, serials, and newspapers can be identified only in these local sources" (p.36). The catalogs of many of the great collections have now been published. See B. R. Nelson's "Anthropological research and printed library catalogs" (F423).

A guide to the work of a new generation of scholars sensitive to the events in the Peoples Republic of China between 1949 and 1980 can be found in the "Annotated bibliography," in *Encyclopedia of China today*, ed. by Fredric M. Kaplan and others (Fair Lawn, N.J.: Eurasia Pr., 1980 [336p.]) (F742). The 1980 bibliography provides accurate and concise annotations in classified arrangement, with emphasis on English-language materials. Leads reader into older literature through John Lust's *Index sinicus: a catalogue of articles relating to China in periodicals and other collective publications, 1920–1955*. (Cambridge: W. Heffer, 1964 [663p.]) **(F743)**. Well organized by subjects, with subject and author-title index. The 1981 edition does not include or repeat the bibliographic guide of the first edition. It does, however, have several appendixes that identify and explain the use of several publication sources and a revised and updated but less useful bibliography. See *Encyclopedia of China today* (New York: Eurasia Pr., 1981 [446p.]) **(F744)**, bibliography, p.387–403. See also T'ung-li Yüan's *China in Western literature: a continuation of Cordier's bibliotheca sinica* (New Haven, Conn.: Far Eastern Pubs., Yale Univ., 1958 [802p.]) **(F745)** coverage of European language books appearing between 1921 and 1957. Lust and Yuan update the basic and still-useful work of Henri Cordier, *Bibliotheca sinica: dictionnaire bibliographique des ouvrages rélatifs à l'Empire Chinois*, 2d. ed., rév., corr. et considérablement augm. (Paris: Guilmoto, 1904–08 [4v.]) **(F746)**.

Some older guides are still valuable for the excellence of their annotations and for their superior organization. Examples: Peter Alexander Menquez Berton, *Contemporary China: a research guide*. (Stanford, Calif.: Hoover Institution Pr., 1967 [695p.] [Hoover Institution bibliographical series, 31]) **(F747)**. Mainland China from 1949, Taiwan and Hong Kong from 1945. Bibliographies and indexes, general references, selected documentary and serial publications, dissertations, and theses. Each topic is minutely subdivided. All entries are numbered serially and critically annotated. An author title index. Again, useful though dated. Secondly, Bernard S. Silberman, *Japan and Korea: a critical bibliography* (Tucson: Univ. of Arizona Pr., 1962 [120p.]) **(F748)**. For the identification of basic works in the English language.

F749 Wolff, Ernst. Chinese studies: a bibliographic manual. San Francisco: Chinese Materials Center, 1981. 152p. [Bibliographic series: Chinese Materials Center, v.1]

606 citations. 15 general bibliographies. 19 Western-language reference sources and 5 Russian sources. 53 bibliographic aids in Chinese. 514 works arranged by form—dictionaries, encyclopedias, newspapers, etc. See also Tsuen-hsuin Tsien, *China: an annotated bibliography of bibliographies* (Boston: Hall, 1978 [604p.]) (reprint, Greenwood, 1982) **(F750)**. Classified arrangement with author, title, and subject index.

F751 Skinner, George William. Modern Chinese society: an analytical bibliography. Stanford, Calif.: Stanford Univ. Pr., 1973. 3v.

Invaluable. Coverage is from 1644 to the present, integrated by a monumental application of computer technology and a complicated but useful scheme of annotation, classification, and indexing to provide a wide variety of approaches by subject, historical period, geographical area, and city versus rural society. 31,500 cited items. Its several indexes must be used for most searches.

F752 Dessaint, Alain Y. Minorities of Southwest China: an introduction to the Yi (Lolo) and related peoples and an annotated bibliography. New Haven, Conn.: HRAF Pr., 1980. 373p.

The annotations evaluate. An introduction to Yi studies. Excellent abstracts. Detailed and helpful indexes. Additional sources on the literature of ethnic groups in Southern China can be found in LeBar's *Ethnic groups of mainland Southeast Asia* (F703).

F753 Thompson, Laurence G. Studies of Chinese religion: a comprehensive and classified bibliography of publications in English, French, and German through 1970. Encino, Calif.: Dickenson, 1976. 190p.

Useful first-start bibliography for the major religions. For material beyond the scope of this work, consult P. Cohen's 1975 "A bibliography of the writings contributory to the study of Chinese folk religion," in American Academy of Religion, *Journal* 43(2):238–65 **(F754)**.

F755 Jokobson, Roman. Paleosiberian peoples and languages: a bibliographical guide. New Haven, Conn.: HRAF Pr., 1957. 222p. [Behavior science bibliographies] Reprint, Westport, Conn.: Greenwood, 1981.

An extensive bibliography dealing with the peoples of northeast Asiatic Russia (Gilyak, Chukehee, Yakaghir, and Yenisei). The 1,898 entries include a large number of Russian titles (translated) as well as material in other Western languages. Two general chapters are followed by one devoted to each of the 4 groups. Some brief explanatory annotations. No index. Also useful, Robert Arthur Rupen, *Mongols of the twentieth century* (Bloomington: Indiana Univ. Pr., 1964 [2v.]) [Indiana Univ. publications. Uralic and Altaic series, v.37.] **(F756)**, Also useful, American Council of Learned Societies, *Research and studies in Uralic and Altaic languages* (Project no. 66, v.2) **(F756A)**. Bibliography organizes by form 2,689 items with a detailed subject index.

F757 De Vos, George A. Socialization for achievement: essays on the cultural psychology of the Japanese. Berkeley: Univ. of California Pr., 1973. 597p.

The bibliography provides some entry into Western studies of Japan by social scientists. Systematic entry into the extensive Japanese contributions is provided through Richard King Beardsley, *Japanese sociology and social anthropology: a guide to Japanese reference and research materials* (Ann Arbor: Univ. of Michigan Pr., 1970 [276p.] [University of Michigan. Center for Japanese Studies. Bibliographical series, no.10]) **(F758)**. Bridges the gap between the way the Japanese organize their study and the way Westerners organize the same material. Out of date but useful.

For all things Japanese a good starting point even for more advanced students with some knowledge of Japan can be found in the English-language *Kodansha encyclopedia of Japan* (New York: Kodansha, 1983 [9v.]) **(F758A)**. Alphabetization is letter by letter disregarding all punctuation. 9,417 entries with an index volume that guides the reader into the internal content of 123 major articles; 1,429 medium length and 7,865 shorter entries. Most signed articles have suggestions for further reading. Japanese citations are not translated into English.

F759 Borton, Hugh, and others. A selected list of books and articles on Japan in English, French and German. Rev. and enl. ed. Cambridge, Mass.: publ. by Harvard Univ. Pr. for the Harvard-Yenching Inst., 1954. 272p.

A selective and critical bibliography of 1,781 works relating to the humanities and social sciences published to 1952. Analytical index of authors, titles, and subjects. This can be usefully updated by the less widely held Kokusai Bunka Kaikan, Tokyo, *Japan: International House of Japan Library acquisition list, 1955–1975* (Tokyo: Kokusai Bunka Kaikan, 1975 [242p.]) **(F760)**. An unannotated list of Western-language materials arranged by subject. Also, again by Kokusai Bunka Kaikan, Tokyo, *Modern Japanese literature in translation: a bibliography* (Tokyo: Kokusai Bunka Kaikan; New York: Kodansha, dist. by Harper, 1979 [311p.]) **(F761)**. Reference should also be made to Timothy O'Leary, "Ethnographic bibliography" (F422).

F763 *Studies on Korea: a scholar's guide*. Ed. by Han-Kyo Kim and Hong Kyoo Park. Honolulu: Univ. Pr. of Hawaii, 1980. 438p.

Largely English-language works of scholarly value. Classed arrangement with an author index. Professionally structured and executed.

The Pacific

The basic entry into this area is C. R. H. Taylor, *A Pacific bibliography* (F770), and John Greenway, *Bibliography of the Australian aborigines and native peoples of Torres Strait to 1959* (F765), with current coverage from the "Bibliographie de l'Océanie" (F764) and *Bibliography of periodical articles relating to the South Pacific* (F774A), and some coverage by the *Australian Public Affairs Information Service* (A242).

F764 "Bibliographie de l'Océanie." *Journal de las Société des Océanistes*. v.2– , 1946– . Paris: Musée de l'Homme. Annual.

This selective, classified bibliography covers Polynesia, Micronesia, Melanesia, and Australia (excludes the Philippines, Japan, and Indonesia). Emphasis is on anthropology, ethnology, acculturation, and linguistics, but also has material on history and geography, economics, art, and literature. The 1,000–1,500 items per year include books, articles, society publications, documents, theses, and newspaper articles that are significant. No index or annotations.

F765 Greenway, John. Bibliography of the Australian aborigines and the native peoples of Torres Strait to 1959. Sydney: Angus & Robertson, 1963. 420p.

A thorough international bibliography of monographic and serial publications. Arranged alphabetically by author. Detailed subject index. No annotations but some citations to reviews of major books. Supplemented and kept current by Australian Institute of Aboriginal Studies, *Partial accessions list*, no.1– , 1961/62– (Canberra: Australian Inst. of Aboriginal Studies, 1962– [semiannual]) **(F766)**. Title varies. Most recently: *Annual bibliography*, 1975– , issued in conjunction with its *Newsletter*. This list of books, articles, and parts of books on Australian aboriginal peoples does not purport to be exhaustive. Each issue is divided into 10 sections, ranging from social anthropology to prehistory and culture contact. Sections arranged alphabetically by author. No indexes. See also Norman James Brian Plomley, *An annotated bibliography of the Tasmanian aborigines* (London: Royal Anthro. Inst., 1969 [143p.] [Royal Anthropological Institute. Occasional paper no.28.]) **(F767)**, and Beryl F. Craig, comp., *North-west-central Queensland: an annotated bibliography* (Canberra: Australian Inst. of Aboriginal Studies, 1970 [137p.] [Australian aboriginal studies, v.41] [Bibliography series no.6]) **(F768)**. See also Norman Burnett Tindale, *Aboriginal tribes of Australia* (F990).

F769 Leeson, Ida. A bibliography of bibliographies of the South Pacific, publ. under the auspices of the South Pacific Commission. London and New York: Oxford Univ. Pr., 1954. 61p.

General and subject bibliographies appearing in books and periodicals. Index.

F770 Taylor, Clyde Romer Hughes. A Pacific bibliography: printed matter relating to the native peoples of Polynesia, Melanesia and Micronesia. 2d ed. Oxford: Clarendon, 1965. 692p.

Arranged by island group and subdivided by topics that are useful to anthropologists. Superb control of books and periodical articles. Definitive within its scope. Partially updated by Clyde Romer Hughes Taylor, *A bibliography of publications on the New Zealand Maori and the Moriori of the Chatham Islands* (Oxford: Clarendon, 1972 [161p.]) **(F771)**. 3,900 items. Author index provides abbreviated titles for authors with more than one item.

F772 Snow, Philip A. A bibliography of Fiji, Tonga and Rotuma. Coral Gables, Fla.: Univ. of Miami Pr., 1969. 418p.

Besides books and periodical articles, includes government documents and vernacular language items in a classed arangement of 10,000 for comprehensive coverage.

F773 New Guinea periodical index. v.1– , 1968– .
Papua New Guinea: Library, Univ. of Papua
New Guinea.
Alphabetical by author and subject. Attempts
worldwide coverage of articles published on any aspect
of New Guinea. Detailed indexing. For verification of
periodical titles, consult Brenda E. Moon, *Periodicals
for South-East Asian studies: a union catalogue of holdings in British and selected European libraries* (London: Mansell, 1979 [610p.]) **(F774)**. With cross-
reference to variant titles. Periodicals published in or
relating to Papua New Guinea, Melanesia, and
Polynesia are included. *Bibliography of periodical articles relating to the South Pacific*, 1976– (Suva, Fiji:
Univ. of South Pacific Library) **(F774A)**. Annual. Provides a classed index to a limited 200 journals. Scope is
all of Micronesia, Polynesia, and Melanesia.

F775 Marshall, Mac, and James D. Nason. Micronesia, 1944–1974: a bibliography of anthropological and related source materials. New
Haven, Conn.: HRAF Pr., 1975. 337p.
Excludes the Gilbert Islands. The computer
manipulates the codes in the main entry list, which is
alphabetically arranged and makes possible a guide to
topics and areas. Includes dissertations but excludes
government documents.

F776 O'Reilly, Patrick, and Édouard Reitman. Bibliographie de Tahiti et de la Polynésie française.
Paris: Musée de l'Homme, 1967. 1,048p. [Soci-
été des Océanistes. Publ. 14.]
A classified, annotated bibliography of 10,501
items.

F777 Klieneberger, Hans L. Bibliography of Oceanic
linguistics. London: Oxford Univ. Pr., 1957.
143p. [London Oriental bibliographies, v.1]
A useful bibliography of 2,100 references to
books and periodical articles covering the whole of
Oceania. Emphasizes linguistic works as such (dictionaries, grammars, individual and comparative studies), leaving aside the extensive literature published in
many South Seas languages. Entries are arranged by
region and subdivided by language. Some entries include references to reviews. Locates rare material. No
annotations. Index of personal and corporate authors.
All branches of the Summer Institute of Linguistics regularly publish local bibliographies. An example might be Elizabeth Murane, *Bibliography of the
Summer Institute of Linguistics, Papua New Guinea
Branch, 1956 to 1975* (Ukarumpa, Papua New Guinea:
The Institute, 1976. [64p.]) **(F778)**, and Thomas Edward Dutton, *A checklist of languages and present-day
villages of central and south-east mainland Papua*
(Canberra: Australian Natl. Univ., Research School
of Pacific Studies, Dept. of Linguistics, 1973 [80p.]
[Pacific linguistics, Ser. B monographs, v.24]) **(F779)**.

F780 Australian Natl. Univ. (Canberra) Dept. of Anthropology and Sociology. An ethnographic
bibliography of New Guinea. Canberra: Australian Univ. Pr., 1968. 3v.
Covers a century of Western-language books

and articles, from 1860 to 1964, on the present Territory of Papua, the trusteeship territory of New
Guinea, and Indonesian Irian Jaya. Extensive analytical indexing in v.2 and 3.

F781 Van Baal, J., K.W. Galis, and R M. Koentjaraningrat. West Irian: a bibliography. Dordrecht:
Foris, 1984. 305p. [Bibliographical series. Instituut voor Taal-, Land- en Volkenkunde, v.15].
Conceived as a guide. Assumes that the user will
trace the additional sources of information cited in the
works listed. Well organized by subject with regional
and tribal subdivisions as needed. Includes books and
journal articles and is especially valuable for its inclusion of unpublished materials in which much of the
information on West Irian has been recorded. Thus,
this work provides entry into the collection described
in 1968 by P. Nienhuis in his *Inventaris van het Kappor-
tenarchief Zaken*, 1968 which is reproduced as an
appendix. The collection numbers 921 documents
covering well over 25,000 pages and has been microfilmed.

F782 Cleverley, John, and Christabel Wescombe.
Papua New Guinea: guide to sources in education. Sydney: Sydney Univ. Pr., 1979. 150p.
A basic guide to the area includes directory
information to major institutes and centers of learning.
The bibliography of bibliographies is annotated with
great skill. A guide to research in the area regardless of
the discipline of interest. Includes: *New Guinea bibliography: a subject list of books published in the New
Guinea area and books dealing wholly or partially with
a New Guinea subject, published overseas*, v.1–14,
1967–80 (Port Moresby: Univ. of Papua New Guinea
Library) **(F783)**. Annual. Classed arrangement with
author/title and subject indexes to 1971. From 1972, a
dictionary catalogue form is adopted. Includes material that comes to University of Papua New Guinea
Library and discusses its relationship to the *Australian
national bibliography*, v.1– , 1961– (Canberra:
National Library of Australia) **(F784)**. Annual. Superseded by *Papua New Guinea national bibliography*,
1981– (Waigani: National Library Service of Papua
New Guinea) **(F784A)**. Annual.

F785 Potter, Michelle. Traditional law in Papua New
Guinea: an annotated and selected bibliogra-
phy. Canberra: Australian Natl. Univ. Dept. of
Law, Research School of Social Sciences, 1973.
132p.
A range of coverage beyond the scope of its title
makes this a valuable first-start source. Detailed index.
Cut off date is 1970.

F786 Hays, Terence E. Anthropology in the New
Guinea Highlands: an annotated bibliography.
New York: Garland, 1976. 238p. [Garland reference library in social science, v.17]
Broad subject headings include a general section of useful bibliographies and material by nonan-
thropologists. Includes doctoral dissertations, books,
and journal articles through 1974 in broad coverage of
all aspects of anthropology, with author and ethnolinguistic group indexes.

F787 Ord, Ian Geoffrey. Mental tests for pre-literates: resulting mainly from New Guinea Studies. London: Ginn, 1971. 270p.
Extensive bibliography.

F788 A bibliography of medicine and human biology of Papua New Guinea. Ed. by R. W. Hornabrook and G. H. F. Skeldon. Faringdon: Classey, 1977. 335p. [Monograph series: Papua New Guinea Institute of Medical Research; 5]
Covers ethnology and anthropometry as well as the more traditional interests of public health. Index.

The Americas

F789 Pan American Institute of Geography and History. Boletín bibliográfico do antropologiá Américana. v.1– , 1937– . Tacubaya, Mexico: Instituto Panamericano de Geografia e Historia. Irregular.
A general overview of anthropological developments in the Americas. Running account of research and organizational activity. Includes book reviews and reviews of contents of selected journals. Necrologies and ethnographic, regional, ethnohistorical, linguistic, and archaeological bibliographies are regular features. Includes Robert V. Kemper's 1971 "Bibliografía comentada sobre la anthropología urbana en américa latina" (v.33–34: 86–140) **(F790)**, which gives exhaustive coverage to his subject. Also includes H. N. Morales Chua's 1978 "Bibliografía anthropología de Guatemala 1975–1978," 40(49):79–86 **(F791)**, maintaining a continuing control of anthropologically important work in this region. Publication pattern highly irregular. Index volume covers the years 1937–67.

F792 Murdock, George Peter, and Timothy J. O'Leary. Ethnographic bibliography of North America. 4th ed. New Haven, Conn.: Human Relations Area Files Pr., 1975. 5v. v.1: General North America; v.2: Arctic and Subarctic; v.3: Far West and Pacific Coast; v.4: Eastern United States; v.5: Plains and Southwest.
40,000 entries for books and articles on native ethnic groups of North America. Coverage of the Southwest includes North Mexico to correspond to the *Handbook of North American Indians* (F989). Coverage has been extended to contemporary issues such as the relations of the governments of Canada and the United States to the Indians, pan-Indianism, urban Indians, and Canadian Indians as ethnic groups. Does not include ERIC documents or government documents, nonprint materials, or maps. The bulkiness of this publication makes it difficult to use. Scholarly output has expanded past the ability of this conceptual system to organize the materials. No author index.

F793 Guyot, Mireille. Bibliographie américaniste: archéologie et préhistoire, anthropologie et ethnohistoire. Paris: Musée de l'Homme, 1968– .
Conceptually little more than a reading list. Sponsorship validates this selection of scholarship representing the French approach. Contains a rich bibliography of bibliographies. Indexed by ethnic group, by region, and by author.

F794 Hasler, Juan A. Bibliographía americanística brevis. Medellín, Colombia: Universidad de Antioquia, 1973. 170p.
Extremely valuable for its identification of the focus of interest most useful to anthropologists in Latin American intellectual centers. Arranged topically both for regions and for subjects, this selective list is dominated by Spanish-language materials.

Latin America and the Caribbean

For a basic bibliographic apparatus, use J. H. Steward's *Handbook of South American Indians* (F983), Robert Wauchope's *Handbook of Middle American Indians* (F987), and for the West Indies, J. R. Swanton's *Indian tribes of North America* (F985). For bibliographic extension on a continuing basis, consult the comprehensive *Handbook of Latin American studies* (A245). Although the subject index of this magnificent series makes retrospective searches by region laborious, expansions on an annual basis have been regular. Entry to critical evaluation has been eased by *A guide to reviews of books from and about Hispanic America, 1972/Guía a las reseñas de libros de y sobre Hispanoamérica 1972*, v.1– , 1972– (Detroit: Blaine Ethridge) **(F795)**, which covers scholarly monographs for the years of issue and provides entry to book summaries and critical reviews in an author listing without subject index. Coverage is so comprehensive that the *Handbook of Latin American studies* (A245) can be used as a subject index. The Tulane Univ. Latin American Library, *Catalog of the Latin American Library of the Tulane University Library* (A277); the Florida Univ. Libraries, *Catalog of the Latin American collection* (A276); and the Univ. of Texas at Austin, *Catalog of the Latin American collection* (A275) are indispensable for serious in-depth scholarship. See also Library-Anthropology Resource Group, *Anthropological bibliographies* (F457).

F796 O'Leary, Timothy J. Ethnographic bibliography of South America. New Haven; Conn.: Human Relations Area Files Pr., 1963. 387p. [Behavior science bibliographies]
Provides an important tribal entry into bibliographic investigations in South American anthropology. 24,000 items, including articles from 650 journals, cover ethnography; pre-Columbian, colonial, and present-day Indians; social anthropology; archeology; linguistics; physical anthropology; and sociology. It is organized by cultural areas and within each area by tribal group. Tribal entry into the culture areas of Northern Mexico can be updated by reference to George Peter Murdock, *Ethnographic bibliography of North America* (F792). The bibliographic record for

the Suriname can be updated by G. A. Nagelkerke, *Bibliografisch overzicht van de Indianen in Suriname/ Bibliographical survey of the Indians of Surinam: 1700–1977* (Leiden, Netherlands: Caraïbische afdeling, Koninklijk Instituut voor Taal-, Land- en Volkenkunde, 1977 [55p.]) (**F797**). For studies of Latin American populations in the United States, Arnulfo D. Trejo's *Bibliografía Chicana: a guide to information sources* (Detroit: Gale, 1975 [193p.]) (**F798**), can be consulted with confidence. A well-balanced selective guide with informative annotations.

F799   Olien, Michael D. Latin Americans: contemporary peoples and their cultural traditions. New York: Holt, 1973. 408p.

Apendix B—"Reference materials on Latin America" (p.347–60)—serves as the best available select but unannotated bibliography of anthropological bibliographies of Latin America. Other sections of the 75-page bibliography in this text have considerable reference value. Appendix E is subdivided for Middle America, South America, the Caribbean, and Latin Americans in the United States and provides a list of monographs on Latin American societies and subcultures (in English) selected for anthropological emphasis. Less specifically useful for anthropological purposes is *Latin America: an acquisition guide for colleges and public libraries*, ed. by Earl J. Pariseau (Gainesville, Fla.: Consortium of Latin American Studies Programs, 1975 [754p.] [Publication-Consortium of Latin American Studies Programs; no.7]) (**F800**), in which more than 2,500 skillfully annotated items are placed in a classified arrangement with entry through a detailed table of contents. Each entry is complete and includes Library of Congress catalog number and price at the time of publication. Selected from a list of 7,500 items collected by the Spanish division of the Library of Congress and sponsored by the Latin American Studies Association, this publication was developed by 47 scholars with established reputations. Selection was based on appropriateness for teaching rather than for research, and devoted primarily to works in English. A general section is followed by 14 subject sections, and each section lists special bibliographies and guides before breaking down to geographic areas. The United States Books Exchange and a reprint project are discussed. This work, as a one-volume source, can be used to complement Stojan A. Bayitch's older but still useful *Latin America and the Caribbean: a bibliographic guide to works in English* (Coral Gables, Fla.: Univ. of Miami Pr., 1967 [943p.] [International legal studies no.10]) (**F801**). A single-volume bibliography arranged first by country, then by broad topic, and finally by author; A–Z without annotations.

F802   Coffin, Jean, and Crystal Graham. "Anthropology and folklore." *In* Indiana Univ. Libraries, Latin American studies research guide, p.94–107. Bloomington: Indiana Univ. Latin American Studies Program, 1978. 139p. [Latin American studies working papers, 8]

Fully annotated. Reflects the growing bibliographic control of work done in this region. Identifies

most of the basic monographic works devoted to specific geographic regions. Does not attempt to include items published in regional journals which update the basic works. Examples would include bibliographies of recent work that can be found as a regular feature in *Boletín Indigenista Venezolano*, v.1– , 1953– (Caracas: Ministerio de Justica. Comisíon Indigenista) (**F803**) (semiannual), and M. E. Bozzoli de Wille, "Bibliografía antropológica de Costa Rica: 1967–1972," *Estudios sociales centroamericanos* 3(7):164–83 (1974) (**F804**). Does not seem to include coverage of Bolivia for which useful guidance can be found in the work of Harold Key and Mary Key, *Bolivian Indian tribes: classification bibliography* (Norman, Okla.: Summer Institute of Linguistics 1967 [128p.]) [Summer Institute of Linguistics. University of Oklahoma. Publications in linguistics and related fields, no.15]) (**F805**), which provides both ethnographic and linguistic coverage with full annotations. Valuable for indexes by author and language group. This coverage can be expanded by reference to Dwight B. Heath's *Historical dictionary of Bolivia* (Metuchen, N.J.: Scarecrow, 1972 [324p.] [Latin American Historical Dictionaries, no.4]) (**F806**), which must be used with caution because of bibliographic errors. Nevertheless, nearly one-fifth of this work is devoted to a bibliographic essay that reflects the anthropological training of the author.

Brazilian studies have benefited from the publication of the catalog of the Canning House Library (A279), and William V. Jackson's *Library guide for Brazilian studies* (Pittsburgh: Univ. of Pittsburgh Book Centers, 1964 [197p.]) (**F807**). Jackson rewards examination by students of Brazil who would exploit American library resources. See also U.S. Library of Congress, *Catalog of Brazilian acquisitions of the Library of Congress, 1964–1974*, comp. by William V. Jackson (Boston: Hall, 1977 [751p.]) (**F808**), for recent publications. Excepting law organized by Library of Congress classification number, with adequate subject and author indexes. Also: *Brazil since 1930: an annotated bibliography for social historians* by Robert M. Levine (New York: Garland, 1980 [336p.] [Garland reference library of social science, v.59]) (**F808A**). 1,673 entries. Selected for interdisciplinary utility. Includes books, collections of essays, articles and dissertations. Index.

Some recently published catalogs of libraries have expanded the range of coverage discussed in B. R. Nelson's "Anthropological research and printed library catalogs" (F423). The Institute of Jamaica, West India Reference Library, *The catalogue of the West India Reference Library* (Millwood, N.Y.: Kraus, 1980– [2 parts in 6v.]) (**F809**), attempts to be comprehensive for Jamaica and the English-speaking Caribbean.

Control of resources in the major European languages has been eased by the publication of Ibero-Amerikanisches Institut (Berlin), *Schlagwortkatalog des Ibero-Amerikanischen Instituts: Preussischer Kulturbisitz in Berlin* (Boston: Hall, 1977–) (**F810**), which provides a classified arrangement by subject to monographs and articles from 2,000 periodicals, with

German subject headings. Spanish and English equivalency terms appear in the index and refer to the German term. Michel Lambert's *Bibliographie latino-américaniste: France 1959–1972* (Mexico: Institut Français d'Amèrique Latine, 1973 [159p.]) **(F811)**, provides a thematic index to 1,550 titles published in French between 1959 and 1972.

For subject searches, bibliographies with a specialized focus can offer substantial coverage of all facets of society and serve effectively as guides. For example, Meri Knaster's *Women in Spanish America: an annotated bibliography from pre-conquest to contemporary times* (Boston: Hall, 1977 [696p.]) **(F812)**. Annotates 2,435 items. Detailed subject arrangement with 45 pages of superb indexing. A companion guide can be found in the 1976 bibliographic review by Meri Knaster, "Women in Latin America: the state of the research," in *Latin American research review*, v.1– , 1965– (Chapel Hill: publ. by the Univ. of North Carolina Pr. for the Latin American Studies Assn. [v.11:3–74]) **(F813)**. An essential reference tool for anyone interested in family relationships in Latin America.

F814 Comitas, Lambros. The complete Caribbeana, 1900–1975: a bibliographic guide to the scholarly literature. Millwood, N.Y.: KTO Pr., 1977. 4v. 2,193p.

A bibliographic achievement that brings 17,000 unannotated references in all major European languages, including unpublished theses, into a classified arrangement in which 10 major topics are arranged into 67 chapters. Locations are cited. Agency produced documents are omitted unless "authored." When items cover two subjects, cross-references are used, but complete citation is given only once. There is an author index. The geographic index would benefit from subject expansion. Haiti, Cuba, Puerto Rico, and the Dominican Republic are excluded. Covers former colonies of Great Britain, France, the United States, and the Netherlands in the Caribbean region. Bibliographies of Central America that included British Honduras would be listed. Suriname, French Guiana, and Guyana on the South American coast are included. Some groups like the Maroons are given subject entry, but most subject headings label clusters of research. Since there is no subject index, this work cannot completely supersede other Caribbean bibliographies, such as Renè Mevis, *Inventory of Caribbean studies: an overview of social research on the Caribbean conducted by Antillean, Dutch and Surinamese scholars in the period 1945–1973: with an index of Caribbean specialists and a bibliography* (Leiden, Netherlands: Caribbean Dept., Royal Inst. of Linguistics and Anthropology, 1974 [181p.]) **(F815)**. Subject entry into Dutch-language materials. Includes a directory of Dutch and Surinamese scholars.

This has been continued by Theo M. P. Oltheten, *Inventory of Caribbean studies: an overview of social scientific publications on the Caribbean by Antillean, Dutch and Surinamese authors in the period 1945–1978/79* (The Hague: publ. by Smitts Drukkers-Uitgevers B.V. for the Dept. of Caribbean Studies,

Royal Inst. of Linguistics and Anthropology, Leiden, 1979 [278p.]) **(F816)**. Focused on French Guiana, Surinam, Guyana, and some coastal regions of South and Middle American countries, Belize, and the archipelago encircling the Caribbean Sea. Dutch, Surinamese, and authors of other nationalities if published in the Netherlands. Dutch titles are given English translations, and an index in English has been added. Books and periodicals are included. Again, since Comitas does not annotate, there is no device with which to alert the reader to the comprehensive bibliographic coverage of entries like Richard Price, *The Guiana Maroons: a historical and bibliographic introduction* (Baltimore: Johns Hopkins Univ. Pr., 1976 [184p.] [John Hopkins studies in Atlantic history and culture]) **(F817)**, which has a formal bibliography of 1,330 items with location symbols and an anthropological evaluation of his body of literature.

F817 Laguerre, Michel S. The complete Haitiana: A
A   bibliographic guide to the scholarly literature, 1900–1980. Millwood, N.Y.: Kraus, 1982. 2v.

Eleven major subject headings subdivided into 65 sections. Includes books, articles, dissertations, and theses, essays in books, encyclopedic works, government publications and reports. The introduction evaluates reference sources. All items have library location code. Covers history, population studies, ecological settings, culture, sociology, education, and health in a classed arrangement with author index.

For Cuba, which is excluded from Comitas, an important source of retrospective coverage is Univ. of Miami, Coral Gables, Library, *Catalog of the Cuban and Caribbean Library* (Boston: Hall, 1977 [6v.]) **(F818)**, and the 1950 work by J. F. Cordero, "Bibliografia sobre indigenismo en Cuba," *Revista de la Biblioteca Nacional*, 1:113–204 **(F819)**.

Few bibliographies of Latin American material adequately integrate the important class of agency publications. Consult Rosa Guintero's *Latin American serial documents* (Ann Arbor, Mich.: Univ. Microfilms Intl., 1968–) **(F820)**. Planned to provide entry into the documents of the 20 Latin American countries. For Brazil, consult also Mary Lombardi's *Brazilian serial documents: a selective and annotated guide* (Bloomington: Indiana Univ. Pr., 1974 [445p.]) **(F821)**, which brings the agency documents of one country into bibliographic control. An annotated list arranged by issuing agency. Serials of the federal universities, their faculties, and schools were omitted because they had been covered by a recent publication identified in the preface.

America North of Mexico

Research on the modern American Indian starts with the use of Frederick Webb Hodge, *Handbook of American Indians north of Mexico* (F982), which can be supplemented by reference to William Sturtevant's *Handbook of North American Indians* (F989); George P. Murdock's *Ethnographic bibliography of North America* (F792); the *Bibliographical series* (F826); and

Marilyn L. Haas' "Basic guide to reference sources for the study of the North American Indian," *RSR: reference services review* (Ann Arbor, Mich.: Pierian), v.7 [July–September]:15–35 **(F822)**. Haas is especially valuable for her discussion of computer readable databases, the basic tools of the discipline, and the value of more general reference sources. Identifies some hidden sources, i.e., the 1978 article by Michael L. Tate, "Studying the American Indian through government documents and the National Archives," in the bimonthly *Government publications review: an international journal*, v.1–6, 1974–79 (Elmsford, N.Y.: Pergamon) 5:285–94 **(F823)**, and a 1976 contribution by Harry Dees, "Basic bibliography for Native American law," *Law library journal*, v.1– , 1908– (Chicago: Assn. of Law Libraries), 69:78–89 **(F824)**. See also Timothy J. O'Leary, "General discussion," in *Ethnographic bibliography of North America*, p. xii–xxxvi, v.1, *Central North America* by George Peter Murdock and Timothy J. O'Leary (New Haven, Conn.: Human Relations Area Files Pr., 1975 [454p.] [Behavior sciences bibliographies]) **(F825)**. Less useful as a guide for the user is the Haas *Indians of North America: methods and sources for library research* (Hamden, Conn.: Library Professional Pub., 1983 [163p.]) **(F825A)**, which is valuable for its topical bibliographical section. The research tools most useful in expanding and updating bibliographies of the North American Indians are identified. Discusses the use of government documents, ERIC, theses and dissertations, manuscripts and archives, nonprint material, and maps. Guides the reader into research on Indian claims, but this section is not identified in the table of contents. See also Library-Anthropology Resource Group, *Anthropological bibliographies* (F457).

F825 Hirschfelder, Arlene B. Guide to research on
B   North American Indians. Chicago: American Library Assn., 1983. 330p.

The vast body of literature about the Native American Indian has become a serious obstacle to scholarly work. "From this mass of material, approximately 1,100 (English language) books, articles, government documents, and other written materials in twenty-seven fields of study have been selected and annotated for this guide" (p.ix). Encyclopedic monographs are boldly integrated with other standard reference sources. Coverage of Native Americans of the United States dominates selection with a serious effort to identify and select only the most important and comprehensive works on Canada, Mexico, Central and South America. The Table of Contents lends to bibliographic essays at the beginning of each section in which selected items are listed alphabetically by author with a segregated list of bibliographies at the end of each section. Given this skimpy organization much more comprehensive indexing would have been useful. A ten-page subject index is supported by an author-title index. Not designed for casual use, its annotations are so complete and its selectivity is so astute that any scholar will be richly rewarded for a thorough study of each section that touches on his interest. For guidance on the use of reference sources, as a technique, and the identification of continuing sources the works of Haas (F822) (F825A) make excellent companions.

F826 Bibliographical series. v.1– , 1976– . Bloomington: publ. for the Newberry Library by Indiana Univ. Pr., 1976– .

All volumes have a bibliographic essay, with items keyed by number to the bibliography provided at the rear of the volume. Directly preceding the bibliography is a list of five texts considered by the author to be basic. All volumes to date have been marked by excellence. Ideal first start. Usually less than 100 pages. Highly selective for scholarly value. Titles to date include: *The Plains Indian*, *The Apaches*, *The Indians of the Subarctic*, *Native American historical demography*, *The Ojibwas*, *The Navajos*, *The Cherokees*, *Indian missions*, *The Indians of the Northeast*, *The Delawares*, *Southeastern frontiers*, *The Indians of New England*, *The Yakimas*, *The Indians of the Great Basin*, *Canadian Indian policy*, *The urbanization of American Indians*. Rich annotations to many of these bibliographies can be found in *Guide to research on North American Indians* (F825B). Consult U.S. Library of Congress, *Monographic series*, v.1– , Jan./Mar. 1974– . (Washington, D.C.: Govt. Print. Off.) **(F827)**, under the series entry for full bibliographic information on individual titles and for additional titles as they appear.

Useful for consistent focus on the contemporary situation of the Indian is the irregular *Indian tribal series* (Phoenix: Indian Tribal Series Pubs., 2937 W. Indian School Rd.) **(F828)**. Edited in a contemporary tradition which relates the past to the present and predicts something of the future. Thin volumes, usually with a portrait of the present tribal chairman. Readable and inexpensive. All authors have carried out some fresh research on the reservations since the 1930s. Some of the tribes included are the Otoe-Missouria, Seneca, Kickapoos, the Havasupai, the Hopi, the Paiute, the Crow, the Osage, the Papago, the Yakima, the Mescalero Apache, the Creek, the Seminole, the Kalispel, the Cherokee, the Chickasaw, the "Three Affiliated Tribes," the Oneida, the Cocopah, the Comanche, the Southern Ute, the Kenaitze, the Chitimacha, the Quapaw, the Narrangansett, the Ponca, the Kaw, the Anishinabe of the Minnesota Chippewa, the Walapai, the Pawnee, the Coushatta, the Modoc, the Wichita, the Potawatomi, and the Eskimo.

F829   Hodge, William H. A bibliography of contemporary North American Indians, selected and partially annotated with study guides. New York: Interland, 1976. 296p.

2,600 items in a classified arrangement with an excellent index by tribes, states, areas, and regional groupings. Invaluable for its coverage of contemporary issues and subjects not available in other sources. Includes committee hearings and tribal government documents. Addresses such subjects as city living and migration patterns. There is an excellent section on music and dance (citations 1661–1715). This focus on concerns of the contemporary Indian is continued in Imre Sutton's *Indian land tenure: bibliographical essays and a guide to the literature* (New York: Clearwater, 1975 [290p.]) (**F830**), with 1,000 entries on aboriginals, covering such issues as occupancy, heirship, alienation, hunting territories, treaty rights, and colonial land policies.

F832   Prucha, Francis Paul. A bibliographical guide to the history of Indian-white relations in the United States. Chicago: Univ. of Chicago Pr., 1977. 454p.

9,705 books, journal articles, and dissertations with a cutoof 1974. Topically arranged under such headings as Indian policy, health, education, trade, and industrial tribes. A publication of the Center for the History of the American Indian of the Newberry Library.

F833   U.S. Dept. of the Interior. Library. Biographical and historical index to American Indians and persons involved in Indian affairs. Boston: Hall, 1966– . 8v.

Arranged by subject, this is a photo-reprint of a card file that dates back to the library of the Bureau of Indian Affairs, with coverage that extends to about 1965. Valuable primarily for its numerous analytical entries for articles, obscure pamphlets, and parts of books relating to Indians, Indian chiefs, and government officials. An extraordinarily rich repository of bibliographic and biographical data. Can be useful to the serious scholar.

F834   U.S. Dept. of the Interior. Library. Dictionary catalog of the Department Library. Boston: Hall, 1967. 37v. Four supplements to date.

Includes archival material, periodical articles, and many books on government relations with the Indian tribes, Indian constitutions, etc. Especially valuable as a biographical entry.

F835   "Bibliography, research and news." *American Indian quarterly*, v.1– , 1974– . Berkeley, Calif.: Native American Studies, Univ. of Calif. Quarterly.

Extensive coverage of recent research. Ethnomedicine is regularly included.

F836   U.S. Dept. of the Interior. Kappler's Indian affairs: laws and treaties. Washington, D.C.: U.S. Dept. of the Interior, 1979– . V.6 and 7 "revise and extend Kappler's compilation to include all treaties, laws, executive orders, relating to Indian affairs in force on Sept. 1, 1967." 1,708p.

Commonly known as the Kappler report. Originally published as *Indian affairs: laws and treaties*. Compiled between 1904 and 1941 and published as: 57th Congress, 1st session. Senate. Document 452; 62d Congress, 2d session. Senate. Document 719; 70th Congress, 1st session. Senate. Document 53; 76th Congress, 3d session. Senate. Document 194. Supplement published by U.S. Dept. of the Interior under title: *Kappler's Indian affairs*, 1975 (160p.).

F837   Johnson, Steven L. Guide to American Indian documents in the Congressional Serial Set: 1817–1899. New York: Clearwater, 1977. 503p. (The Library of American Indian affairs)

Indexing is based on examination of every document in the serials set. An enormous undertaking, professionally executed.

F838   Index to literature on the American Indian. 1970–73 4v. San Francisco: Indian Historian Pr., 1451 Masonic Ave., 94117.

Geographic and topical headings cover traditional anthropological concerns and extend into the interest of civil rights, hunting and fishing, and law. The 1971 volume has a list of Indian-related periodicals (p.191–230).

F839   Ortiz, Alfonso. Southwest. Washington, D.C.: Smithsonian; dist. by Supt. of Docs., Govt. Print. Off., 1979. 700p. [Handbook of North American Indians, 9]

Coverage of Pueblo people by 50 contributors. A detailed table of contents guides the reader, and the index has adequate subject-heading expansions. Professionally executed. Brilliantly edited. Pt. 2 has now been published: *Southwest* (Washington, D.C.: Smithsonian, 1983 [868p.]) [Handbook of North American Indians, v.10]. See F989. The necessary selectivity of the bibliographic coverage can be illustrated by referring to W. David Laird, *Hopi bibliography: comprehensive and annotated* (Tucson: Univ. of Arizona Pr., 1977 [735p.]) (**F840**). 2,935 items, accurately described with annotations arranged by author and with extensive cross-references and author and subject indexes. Excludes book reviews, letters to the editor, photographs without text, newspaper articles, etc. See also F989.

F841   Trigger, Bruce G. Northeast. Washington, D.C.: Smithsonian; dist. by Supt. of Docs., Govt. Print. Off., 1978. 924p. [Handbook of North American Indians, 15]

54 contributors. A truly great contribution to the ethnohistorical method. A concise and literate masterpiece. Detailed subject index. Following an introductory section, there is a division into 3 major regions, subdivided by tribes. Additional explication of the editorial viewpoint can be found in Bruce G. Trigger, *Time and traditions: essays in archaeological*

interpretation (New York: Columbia Univ. Pr., 1978 [273p.]) **(F842)**. See also F989.

F843 Heizer, Robert F. California. Washington, D.C.: Govt. Print. Off., 1978. 800p. [Handbook of North American Indians, v.8]

Tribal chapter followed by 25 chapters on subject topics. 44 articles by 33 leading specialists. The definitive and comprehensive review of California Indians, a monumental achievement. For a discussion of the series, see F989. The bibliography in this volume can be expanded to reference to Robert F. Heizer and Albert B. Elsasser, *A bibliography of California Indians: archaeology, ethnography, Indian history* (New York: Garland, 1977 [267p.] [Garland reference library of social science, v.48]) **(F844)**. 224 items are added to the previous and inexpensive Robert F. Heizer and others, *California Indian history: a classified and annotated guide to source materials* (Ramona, Calif.: Ballena Pr., 1975 [90p.] [Ballena Pr. publications in archaeology, ethnology and history, no.4]) **(F845)**. A carefully edited entry to 685 items. See also F989.

The monthly abstracting and indexing service of ERIC, *Research in education* [*RIE*], v.1– , 1966– (Washington, D.C.: Govt. Print. Off.) **(F846)**, can be invaluable in searches for North American Indian material. A random sample might include *American Indian education: a selected bibliography*, v.1– , 1969– (Las Cruces: ERIC Clearinghouse in Rural Education and Small Schools, New Mexico State Univ., 1969– [94p.]) **(F847)**. The publisher varies. Most recently by the National Educational Laboratory Publishers, Inc., 813 Airport Blvd., Austin, TX 78702. Supp. no.1, 1970 [124p.]; no.2, 1971 [286p.]; no.3, 1973 [437p.]; no.5, 1975 [396p.]; no.6, 1976 [242p.]; no.7, 1976 [278p.]. Long, detailed abstracts. The rules of inclusion seem to be anything an educator might find useful. For example, *Bibliographies of American Indian languages*, by Rudolph C. Troike, 1979 [180p.] (ED-016-200) **(F848)**. 12 bibliographies of 12 linguistic groups are given in-depth bibliographic coverage.

The concerns of medical anthropology are reflected in Mark V. Barrow, *Health and disease of American Indians north of Mexico: a bibliography, 1800–1969* (Gainesville: Univ. of Florida Pr., 1972 [147p.]) **(F849)**. Unannotated list of 483 books, journals, and government documents arranged by disease categories, with an author, subject, and tribal index. Does not include belief systems.

In 1981, Dianne R. Kelso and Carolyn L. Attneave's *Bibliography of North American Indian mental health* (Westport, Conn.: Greenwood [411p.]) **(F850)** organized 1,363 items, including unpublished research reports and government documents with elaborate indexes by tribe, subject, and author. See also *American Indian annotated bibliography of mental health*, ed. and indexed by Carolyn L. Attneave and Dianne R. Kelso (Seattle: Univ. of Washington Pr., 1977 [411p.]) **(F851)**. 500 entries, with detailed abstracts for about 250 entries. Covers nature healing practices, suicide, and witchcraft and includes belief systems as a focus of organization.

F852 Indians of the United States and Canada: a bibliography. Ed. by Dwight L. Smith. Santa Barbara, Calif.: ABC-Clio, 1974–83. 2v. [Clio bibliography series, 3, 9]

A compilation of descriptive annotations of literature of the years 1954–78. 9,905 Indian-related abstracts from *America: history and life* (B1491). Arranged by region and then by tribe. Author index. Detailed subject index. Also useful is Peter L. Storck, *A preliminary bibliography of early man in Eastern North America, 1839–1973* (Toronto: Royal Ontario Museum, 1975 [110p.] [Archaeology monograph, 4]) **(F853)**, with 1,242 journal articles, reviews, monographs, and books dealing in whole or in part with the subject of early man in eastern North America. For Canadian provinces east of Manitoba and, in the United States, east of the Mississippi. Geographic, subject, and site indexes.

F854 Haywood, Charles. A bibliography of North American folklore and folksong. New York: Dover, 1961. 2v.

An extensive bibliography of more than 40,000 books, articles, sets, recordings, etc. v.1, *American people north of Mexico*, subject headings are regional, ethnic group, and occupation. V.2, *American Indians north of Mexico including the Eskimos*, arranges most of its material by culture areas and is alphabetically subdivided by tribe. Music, in printed form and on records, is treated as equally important as other forms of folksong. Includes material of ethnographic importance for groups not included in George P. Murdock, *Ethnographic bibliography of North America* (F792).

F856 Garigue, Philippe. A bibliographical introduction to the study of French Canada. Westport, Conn.: Greenwood, 1977. 133p.

Reprint of the 1956 ed. Sensitive to the ethnographic studies of this modern, complex community. Dated but useful selection of early material.

F857 Abler, Thomas S., and others. Canadian Indian bibliography, 1960–1970. Toronto: Univ. of Toronto Pr., 1974. 732p.

3,038 entries. Part one is a topical arrangement of books, periodicals, theses, and unpublished reports. Part two is especially valuable for its inclusion of the "Case law digest," which attempts to bring together all case law related to Indian questions since July 1, 1867. A reference can also be made to Diamond Jenness, *The Indians of Canada*, described at F984.

F858 Burch, Ernst S., Jr. "The ethnography of northern North America: a guide to recent research." *Arctic anthropology* 16:62–146.

An introductory section provides an evaluative review in a classified arrangement, identifies major research institutes, and lists bibliographies and reference works. An exhaustive bibliography follows, arranged alphabetically by author. Can be complemented by Albert A. Dekin's less-useful *Arctic archaeology: a bibliography and history* (New York: Garland, 1978 [279p.] [Garland reference library of science and technology, v.1]) **(F859)**. The sections on "Explorers and ethnographers," "Chronologists and prehistorians," and "Archaeologists and anthropologists" reflect the impact of social science theory on archaeology. A brief list of important libraries and museums, with collections of Arctic material, is included. The best sources are identified in the 64-page bibliography of June Helm, *Subarctic* (Washington, D.C.: Govt. Print. Off., 1981 [836p.]) [Handbook of North American Indians, v.6] **(F859A)**. An encyclopedic summary of available knowledge on this region by a group of distinguished scholars.

F860 Arctic Institute of North America, Library. Catalogue of the Library of the Arctic Institute of North America, Montreal. Boston: Hall, 1971– .

Three supplements to date. In the second supplement, coverage of social science material reflects special efforts to strengthen holdings on northern peoples. The library provides analytics for journal articles (4,500 in the 1968 volume) from nonpolar journals, which are excluded from the annual Arctic Institute of North America, *Arctic bibliography*, v.1– , 1953– (Washington, D.C.: Govt. Print. Off.) **(F863)**.

Europe

For European anthropology, the most useful sources of bibliographic information are *Internationale Volkskundliche Bibliographie*, described at F479; *Geo abstracts D: social geography and cartography*, described at C481; the Royal Anthropological Institute of Great Britain and Ireland, Library, *Anthropological index to current periodicals received in the Museum of Mankind Library*, described at F469; and Bonser's *Bibliography of folklore as contained in the first eighty years of the publications of the Folk-lore Society* (F533). To identify continuing sources for individual countries, see "Documentation in anthropology" newsletter (F1061) and Library-Anthropology Resource Group, *Anthropological bibliographies* (F457).

F864 Kuter, Lois. The anthropology of Western Europe: a selected bibliography. Bloomington: West European Studies, Indiana Univ., 1978. 132p. [West European Studies, Indiana Occasional papers, no.1] 1,112 numbered items.

Strong in French and English sources. Section one provides a list of journals for the subject focus. Section two is divided geographically, with an alphabetical author listing under each area. There is an author index. As many as 150 numbers under a single subject in this index. Some unpublished dissertations are included. No annotations.

F865 Leeds. University. Brotherton Library. Catalogue of the Romany collection formed by D. U. McGrigor Phillips L.L.D. and presented to the University of Leeds. Edinburgh: publ. by Nelson for the Brotherton Collection, 1962. 227p.

A classified bibliography of more than 1,200 books and pamphlets, manuscripts, music items, letters, playbills, pictures, engravings, etc., relating to gypsies in many countries. Author and title index. Inclusion of manuscript items increases its importance. See also Dennis Binns, *A Gypsy bibliography: a bibliography of all recent books, pamphlets, articles, broadsheets, theses and dissertations pertaining to the Gypsies and other travellers that the author is aware of at the time of printing* (Chorltonville, Manchester: Dennis Binns Pubs., 1982 [110p.]) **(F865A)**.

F866 Pereira, Benjamin Enes. Bibliografía analítica de etnografia portuguesa. Lisboa: Centro de Estudos de Etnologia Peninsular, Instituto de Alta Cultura, 1965. 670p.

Annotated bibliography of books and periodical articles on the ethnology of Portugal. Subject arrangement of 3,834 items, with author index.

F867 González Ollè, Fernando. Manual bibliogràfico de estudios españoles. Pamplona: Ediciones Universidad de Navarra, 1976. 1,375p.

A substantial work with 22 main categories, each closely divided. A detailed table of contents and author and subject indexes guide the reader. Invaluable.

F868 Sanders, Irwin Taylor. East European peasantries: social relations: an annotated bibliography of periodical articles. Boston: Hall, 1976. 179p.

A bibliography of a 30-volume collection of periodical articles at the Mugar Library, Boston Univ. Geographical arrangement, with no index. Periodical articles only. Fully annotated. Covers the countries of Communist East Europe and Greece. Conceptually, a reading list.

F869 Halpern, Joel, ed. Bibliography of anthropological and sociological publications on Eastern Europe and the USSR (English language sources). Los Angeles: Univ. of California Russian and East European Studies Center, 1961. 142p. [Russian and East European Study Center series, v.1, no.2]

A preliminary but extensive bibliography of the most available books and articles in English. Entries are arranged geographically and cover the Slavs in general, Eastern Europe, the Balkans, Albania, Bulgaria, Czechoslavakia, Hungary, Poland, Romania, Yugoslavia, and the USSR. Entries for each area are classified by subject—for example, archaeology and history, ethnology, geography, linguistics, religion, demography, social change, etc. No index.

F870 Language and area studies: East Central and Southeastern Europe, a survey. Ed. by Charles Jelavich. Chicago: Univ. of Chicago Pr., 1969. 483p.

Consists of essays by several writers on the state of American scholarship in most of the social sciences and humanistic disciplines as they relate to the geographic areas. Sponsored by the Joint Committee of the American Council of Learned Societies and the Social Science Research Council in an effort to uncover the reasons for the relative neglect of these areas by American scholars.

F871 Gunar, Daniel. Contact des langues et bilinguisme en Europe orientale: bibliographie analytique/Language contact and bilingualism in Eastern Europe: analytical bibliography. Quebéc: Presses de l'Université Laval, 1979. 391p. (International Center for Research on Bilingualism)

1,656 items in an author list with magnificent indexing. A list of conceptual fields and a subject index expanded in great detail in both French and English.

F872 Horak, Stephan. Russia, the USSR, and Eastern Europe: a bibliographic guide to English language publications, 1964–1974. Littleton, Colo.: Libraries Unlimited, 1978. 488p.

F872 Horak, Stephan. Russia, the USSR, and East-
A   ern Europe, 1975–80. Littleton, Colo.: Libraries Unlimited, 1982. 279p.

These volumes update Paul Louis Horecky, *Southeastern Europe: a guide to basic publications* (Chicago: Univ. of Chicago Pr., 1969 [755p.]) (**F873**), an unusually lucid classified bibliography with evaluative annotations and an author-title-subject index that refers to serial numbers of the bibliography; Horecky's *East central Europe: a guide to basic publications* (Chicago: Univ. of Chicago Pr., 1969 [956p.]) (**F874**), which covers East Germany, Hungary, Czechoslovakia, and Poland in an annotated and classed bibliography in which the Slavic and Hungarian titles are translated into English; and his *Russia and the Soviet Union: a bibliographic guide to Western language publications* (Chicago: Univ. of Chicago Pr., 1965 [473p.]) (**F875**), which maintains high standards of selectivity and bibliographic construction. For current awareness and a more comprehensive coverage of recent scholarship, consult *American bibliography of Slavic and East European studies* (since 1973, comp. by the staff of the Slavic and Central European Division, U.S. Library of Congress), v.1– , 1967– (Palo Alto: History Dept., Stanford Univ.) (**F877**), which is arranged by subject and provides entry for "Anthropology," "Archaeology," "Folklore," and "Language and linguistics." For some Russian ethnic groups, the "Bibliography of periodical literature" in the *Middle East journal*, described at F655, is useful.

F881 Vlachos, Evan. Modern Greek society: continuity and change: an annotated classification of selected sources. Fort Collins: Colorado State Univ. Dept. of Sociology and Anthropology, 1969. 177p. [Colorado State Univ. Dept. of Sociology and Anthropology. Special monograph series, no.1.]

Covers such topics as the "Greek people," "Form and extent of groups in Greece," "Culture and personality," and "Nature and characteristics of Greek institutions." Long introductory sections with evaluative comments and bibliographic lists at the end of each section. Covers work since 1950, with a bias toward works in English and Greek. Author index.

For the identification of older but still very useful general bibliographies, Timothy J. O'Leary's "Ethnographic bibliographies" (F422) can be helpful. Examples might also include: Will Erich Peuckert, *Volkskunde: Quellen und Forschungen seit 1930* (Bern: Francke, 1951 [343p.] [Wisenschaftliche Forschungsberichte, geisteswissenschaftliche Reihe, Bd. 14]) (**F883**); Erling Grönland, *Norway in English: books on Norway and by Norwegians in English, 1936–1959: a bibliography; including a survey of Norwegian literature in English translation from 1742 to 1959* (Oslo: Norwegian Universities Pr., 1961 [152p.]) (**F884**), "Also published as vol. 19 of Norsk Bibliografisk Bibliotek"; Hilkka Aaltonen, *Books in English on Finland: a bibliographical list of publications concerning Finland until 1960, including Finnish literature in English translation; appendix: a selected list of books published from 1961 to 1963 inclusive* (Turku, Finland: Turku Univ. Library, 1964 [276p.] [Turku Univ. Library Publication, 8]) (**F885**). Topical entry is provided for anthropology. Organized by a classified arrangement with a persons index. Many of the more general sources could be valuable.

Unpublished dissertations are a valuable source for the vigorous activity in this area but can only be reached through more general reference. Sources listed under "Dissertations" (F573–96).

DIRECTORIES AND BIOGRAPHICAL INFORMATION

F886 Guide to departments of anthropology. 23rd ed. Washington, D.C.: American Anthropological Assn., 1982. 576p. Annual.

Name index gives most current address for 4,869 individuals holding positions in anthropology in the listed departments. Contains 3 divisions, each filled with useful information: (1) "Academic Departments." Detailed information, arranged alphabetically by university, about departments that offer graduate and/or undergraduate programs in anthropology: degrees offered; name, status, interest area(s) of all anthropologists in the department or elsewhere in the university; (2) "Museum Departments." Comparable information on staff, administration, programs (including institutional publications), and research facilities for museums with anthropological departments; (3) Recent Ph.D. dissertations in anthropology. Gives name, title, university, and area of specializaton.

F887 Fifth international directory of anthropologists. Chicago: Univ. of Chicago Pr., 1975. 496p. [Current anthropology resource series]

In contrast to the *Guide to departments of anthropology* (F886), this volume gathers essential information, including the published research of 4,765 anthropologists worldwide. Arranged in alphabetical order, with rich indexing by research interest and supplemented in *Current anthropology* (F437) by articles such as Christian Heilskov Rasmussen, "A biographical bibliography of Scandinavian anthropologists," *Current anthropology* 14:73–82 [1973]. See also *American men and women of science*, since anthropologists were retained when the social sciences were dropped in this series: *American men and women of science, 12th ed.: discipline index: the social and behavioral sciences* (New York: Jaques Cattell Pr./Bowker, 1974 [360p.]) **(F888)**; *The national faculty directory*, v.1– , 1970– (Detroit: Gale) **(F889)**; and *The archaeologists' yearbook 1973: an international directory of archaeology and anthropology* (Park Ridge, N.J.: Noyes Pr., 1973 [229p.]) **(F890)**. Coverage of societies and institutions in Great Britain seems to be exhaustive. Greece is not included. Uneven but valuable. See also *Commonwealth universities yearbook* (London: The Assn. of Commonwealth Universities, 1980 [4v.]) **(F891)**. Use v.4, section 2, "General indexes Subjects of study" (p.2,384–2,408), not only to identify faculty and study programs in anthropology and archaeology but also to identify programs relevant to anthropology, such as "Arabic."

F892 MacNeish, June Helm, ed. Pioneers of American anthropology: the uses of biography. Seattle: Univ. of Washington Pr., 1966. 247p. [American Ethnological Society monographs, 43]

Extensive attention to Boas; more limited attention to Erminie Smith, Alice Fletcher, Matilda Stevenson, Zelia Nuttall, Frances Densmore, and Elsie Clews Parsons.

F893 Directory of programs in linguistics in the United States and Canada. 4th ed. Washington, D.C.: Linguistic Society of America, 1984. 156p. [SLA bulletin 12, 1984]

Table of contents lists geographical guide to programs, institutional listing by regions, linguistic societies and organizations, an index of staff and to uncommonly taught languages.

F894 Nag, Moni. Population anthropology: an informational directory of contributors and their works. New York: Population Commission, Intl. Union of Anthropological and Ethnological Sciences, 1978. 96p.

Directories with a regional or subject focus are available. Examples would include Susan Tax Free-

man, *Europeanist social anthropologists in North America: a directory* (Washington, D.C.: American Anthropological Assn., 1975 [34p.] [A special publication of the American Anthropological Assn., no.5]) **(F895)**, and *Pacific anthropologists*, 1962– . Honolulu: Pacific Scientific Information Center, Bernice P. Bishop Museum, 1971 **(F896)**. Names arranged alphabetically, with addresses and fields of interest. Indexes by interest and residence. Also, *National directory of Latin Americanists: biographies of 2,695 specialists in the social sciences and humanities*, 2d ed. (Washington, D.C.: Govt. Print. Off., 1971 [684p.] [Hispanic Foundation bibliographical series, no.12]) **(F897)**. Reliable information on clearly professional personnel. A new edition covering 4,915 specialists has been promised for 1985.

F898 International directory of anthropological institutions. Ed. by William L. Thomas, Jr., and Anna M. Pikelis. New York: Wenner-Gren Foundation for Anthropological Research, 1953. 468p.

Geographical arrangement by countries or closely related groups of countries, with outline of the history and scope of anthropological research followed by information on individual institutions. Alphabetical indexes of institutions and of cities and towns. *Current anthropology* (F437) serves in its department of "Institutions" as an informal updating of the directory. See especially "Fourth international directory of anthropological institutions," *Current anthropology* 8:647–751 [1967]. A new edition is needed.

F899 Reference encyclopedia of the American Indian. Ed. by Barry T. Klein and Dan Icolari. 3d ed. Rye, N.Y.: Todd, 1978. 2v.

Primarily a directory of government agencies, associations, museums, reservations, etc. Biographical sketches of contemporary Indians can be found in v.2, "Who's Who." Contains a list of magazines and periodicals that capture some of the elusive writings by and about Indians. Other directories of value would include: U.S. Dept. of Commerce, *Federal and state Indian reservations and Indian trust areas*, rev. ed. (Washington: Govt. Print. Off., 1974 [604p.]) **(F900)**; Arnold Marquis, *A guide to America's Indians: ceremonials, reservations and museums* (Norman: Univ. of Oklahoma Pr., 1974 [267p.]) **(F901)**; and the *American Indian calendar, 1979* (Washington: Govt. Print. Off., 1979 [56p.]) **(F902)**.

DICTIONARIES

F903 International dictionary of regional European ethnology and folklore. Copenhagen: publ. by Rosenkilde & Bagger for the Intl. Commission on Folk Arts and Folklore, 1960–65.

Produced under a cooperative arrangement between the International Council for Philosophy and Humanistic Studies and UNESCO to provide definitions of general ethnological concepts. Languages include English, French, Spanish, German, and a Scandinavian language (usually Swedish). Citations to the literature. Volume one is the best available dictionary of ethnological concepts. Arranged by the English word. Definitions are thoroughly modern, with historical depth and adequate bibliographic references. Volume two is alphabetical for many languages and primarily focused on European folk traditions. Some terms excluded here can be found in Royal Anthropological Institute, *Notes and queries on anthropology,* 6th ed., rev. (London: Routledge & Paul, 1951 [403p.]) (**F904**). Valuable for its inclusion of physical anthropology and material culture. In encyclopedic arrangement, with subject index to terms.

F905 Winick, Charles. Dictionary of anthropology. New York: Philosophical Library, 1956. 578p. Reprint, Westport, Conn.: Greenwood, 1969, and Totowa, N.J.: Littlefield, 1970.

Errors of fact or interpretation detract from the usefulness of this work. Terms have been chosen from archaeology, cultural anthropology, linguistics, and physical anthropology.

Foreign-language dictionaries for anthropology abound, extending even to Malay and Tamil. For European languages: Roberto Bosi, *Dizionario di etnologia* (Milan: A. Mondadori, 1958 [364p.]) (**F906**). Short definitions, with good cross-referencing. Abelardo Martínez Cruz, *Léxico de antropología*, 3d ed. (Barcelona: Laia, 1975 [180p.] [Léxicos para el diálogo: 4]) (**F907**), and Garhard Heberer, *Anthropologie* (Frankfurt a.M.: Fischer, 1973 [318p.] [Das Fischer Lexikon: 15]) (**F908**).

F909 Champion, Sara. A dictionary of terms and techniques in archaeology. Oxford: Phaidon, 1980. 144p. Italian ed. by Garzanti (1983).

For sensitivity to recent developments, illustrations of superior quality, and reference to additional information, this dictionary is unexcelled.

F910 Heymer, Armin. Ethological dictionary: German-English-French. New York: Garland; Berlin: Paul Parey, 1977. 237p.

A 12-page bibliography of the biology of behavior comes at the end. 1,000 German terms arranged alphabetically with German definitions; the English term followed by treatment in French. Cross-references and a French and English index help the user.

F911 Hirschberg, Walter, ed. Wörterbuch der Völkerkunde. Stuttgart: Kroner, 1965. 508p. [Krhöners Taschenausabe, Bd. 205]

The style of treatment is encyclopedic. Extensive treatment of more important concepts, with short bibliographies. Some biographies. European emphasis.

F912 Coluccio, Felix. Diccionario del folklore americano (contribución). Buenos Aires: El Ateneo, 1954– .

Alphabetical dictionary of Latin American folklore. Main section is preceded by 3,394-item bibliography. References in each article refer to this bibliography.

F913 Leach, Maria, ed. Funk and Wagnalls standard dictionary of folklore, mythology and legend. New York: Funk & Wagnalls, 1972. 1,236p.

International in coverage. Includes 55 survey articles on subjects such as "Dance," "Folk and primitive," "Primitive and Folk Art." Maintains international directory of museums. Key to 2,035 culture areas, tribes, etc.

F914 Cotterell, Arthur. A dictionary of world mythology. New York: Putnam, 1980. 256p. Reprint, New York: Perigee, 1984.

Coverage is always accurate. Divided into seven geographic areas, with a comprehensive index.

F915 Brandon, S. G. F., ed. Dictionary of comparative religion. New York: Scribner, 1970. 704p.

Comprehensive coverage of religions other than Christian, with short, signed articles and bibliographic reference. Detailed subject index.

More-specialized dictionaries are often helpful in complex traditions. See Margaret Stutley and James Stutley, *Harper's dictionary of Hinduism: its mythology, folklore, philosophy, literature, and history* (New York: Harper, 1977 [372p.]) (**F916**). Definitions to 2,500 entries provide historical, philosophical, and religious analysis. More than 1,000 references are used to support the explanatory statements of the entries. Monier-William's Sanskrit-English dictionary is used as a standard for transliterations. Thomas Patrick Hughes, *A dictionary of Islam, being a cyclopaedia of the doctrines, rites, ceremonies, and customs, together with the technical and theological terms of the Muhammadan religion* (London: W. H. Allen, 1885; reprint, Delhi: Oriental Pubs., 1973; dist. by South Asia Books [Columbia, Mo.] [750p.]) (**F917**). A readable source for Muslim sects, place names, and technical terms. Heading terms are in English or romanized Arabic, with cross-references to the unused form. Each article has an index of terms in Arabic script. There are many cross-references between articles. It is less comprehensive and less obtuse than *Shorter encyclopedia of Islam,* ed. by Hamilton A. R. Gibb and J. H. Kramers on behalf of the Royal Netherlands Academy (Leiden, Netherlands: Brill; London: Luzac, 1953 [671p.]; reprint, Ithaca, N.Y.: Cornell Univ. Pr.) (**F918**). This volume reflects modern scholarship. Contains all articles on religion and law from the first edition and supplement of the *Encyclopedia of Islam* (F935).

F919 Moerman, Daniel E. American medical ethnobotany: a reference dictionary. New York: Garland, 1977. 527p. [Garland reference library of social science, v.34]

The same information is available in a better-organized form in Virgil J. Vogel's *American Indian medicine* (Norman: Univ. of Oklahoma Pr., 1970 [583p.] [Civilization of the American Indian series, v.95]) (**F920**).

F921 Ducrot, Oswald, and Tzvetan Todorov. Encyclopedic dictionary of the sciences of language. Baltimore: Johns Hopkins Univ. Pr., 1979. 380p.

Organized in a classified subject arrangement in which the single paragraphs are as autonomous as dictionary entries. The 11-page index is comprehensive. Critically compares the various methodological approaches; the transformational, the functional approach of French structuralism, and more traditional approaches are covered. The style is clear. The bibliography is reliable. The translation is solid. The anthropologist working with linguistic concepts will find this a valuable reference source. Also valuable is Jeanne Ambrose-Grillet's *Glossary of transformational grammar* (Rowley, Mass.: Newbury House, 1978 [166p.]) (F922), in which terms selected are taken from the standard theory of Noam Chomsky. Sources with a more conventional arrangement would include R. R. K. Hartmann and F. C. Stork, *Dictionary of language and linguistics* (New York: Wiley, 1972 [302p.]) (F923). Best general dictionary of linguistics. Covers terminology from all branches of linguistic scholarship. A companion volume that reflects the European tradition is Jean Dubois and others, *Dictionnaire de linguistique* (Paris: Larousse, 1973 [516p.]) (F924). Unusual organization helps place concepts in a related context. Indexed.

F925 Crystal, David. First dictionary of linguistics and phonetics. London: Andre Deutsch, 1980. 390p.

Each definition provides a reference to one of the 20 sources used by the author. Relevant to the contemporary usage.

ENCYCLOPEDIAS AND ENCYCLOPEDIC SETS

F926 Murdock, George Peter. Atlas of world cultures. Pittsburgh: Univ. of Pittsburgh Pr., 1981. 151p.

For the ethnologist, a preferred encyclopedic entry into the basic facts about the more completely described cultures of the world. A select sample of 563 cultures from the 1,264 cultures coded in installments of a feature called, "Ethnographic atlas," published in *Ethnology* (F1070). An added asterisk (H*) indicates that the society "was selected by HRAF for its so-called Probability Sample" (p.8). After the classification of each of these peoples, there is a bibliography of the definitive ethnographic record for that group. An interesting attempt to identify individual tribes for which the most encyclopedic record has been achieved has been made in "A standard ethnographic sample: preliminary edition," comp. by Raoul Naroll and others, *Current anthropology* 11(2)(1970):235–48. A list of published reports that record the work of investigators who stayed in the field for at least 12 months and learned the native language. Arranged first by region and then by the identify number given the tribe in Murdock's *Ethnographic atlas* (F1044).

F927 Encyclopedia of anthropology. Ed. by David E. Hunter and Phillip Whitten. New York: Harper, 1976. 411p.

An authoritative source of information for all aspects of anthropology. The editors solicit suggestions for improvement. Cross-references and a subject index are inadequate. Deals with concepts, theory, and leading figures in anthropology in 1,400 articles from 100 contributors. Can be supplemented by reference to Gould's *A dictionary of the social sciences* (A404) and the *International encyclopedia of the social sciences* (A415).

F928 Poirier, Jean. Ethnologie régionale. Paris: Gallimard, 1972–78. 2v. [Encyclopédie de la Pléiade, 33, 42]

Brilliantly edited, with signed articles and selective bibliographies (predominantly French-language). The indexing is a model of excellence and is sensitive to any conceivable scholarly interest. A good book.

English-language coverage for much of the world can be achieved by consulting compendiums or handbooks. For example, *Sixty cultures: a guide to the HRAF probability sample files*, ed. by Robert O. Lagace (New Haven, Conn.: Human Relations Area Files Pr., 1977 [507p.]) (F929), which is arranged alphabetically by tribe and provides a summary with sources of information cited and evaluated. A second volume of 60 more cultures is promised. There is an inadequate broad subject index. Many regional handbooks are encyclopedic. Richard V. Weekes, ed., *Muslim peoples: a world ethnographic survey*, 2d ed. (Westport, Conn.: Greenwood, 1984 [2v.]) (F930). Invited scholars contributed signed articles with bibliographies citing only works published after 1945. These articles usually include a description of the location of the group, ethnographic and demographic information, and social and political organization. Includes four maps of Muslim groups and three appendixes showing Muslim nationalities and Muslim ethnic groups. A valuable reference tool. See also *Peoples of Southern Africa* (Cape Town: Philip, 1978–) (F931). 14-volume series. The first volume, issued in 1978, covers the continent up to the period of modern colonization and is titled *The peopling of Southern Africa*, by R. Inskeep [160p.] (F932).

F933 Encyclopedia of Indians of the Americas. Ed. by Keith Irvine. St. Clair Shores, Mich.: Scholarly Pr., 1974– .

Disappointing popular treatment. Still far from complete. The first volume covers chronology from 2500 B.C. to 1974 A.D. and includes a conspectus. Should be compared with the more scholarly R. E. Taylor and Clement W. Meighan, *Chronologies in New World archaeology* (New York: Academic, 1978 [587p.] [Studies in archeology]) (F934), in which 18 leading New World archaeologists prepared essays of 30 to 40 pages that summarize the chronology of 13 archaeological regions in North and South America, with indexes to places, sites, and cultural terms.

F935 Encyclopedia of Islam. New ed. Leiden, Netherlands: Brill, 1960– .

F935 The encyclopaedia of Islam: a dictionary of the
A   geography, ethnography and biography of the
     Muhammadan peoples. 1st ed. Leiden, Nether-
     lands: Brill, 1913–36. 4v. and supplement
     (1938).
     Excellent bibliographies. Comprehensive cov-
erage of religion, history, and culture. Second edition
is into "K." Some new articles inferior to old. French,
German, and Turkish versions contain articles not in
English. Uses a German-based romanization system;
articles are arranged according to vernacular terms.
The basic reference for the serious student of Islam.

F936 Biasutti, Renato. Le razze e i popoli della terra.
     4th ed. Turin: Unione Tipografica-editrice Tor-
     inese, 1967. 4v.
     Comprehensive account of the physical and
cultural anthropology of the world, arranged on regional basis. Each chapter has a good bibliography.
Many illustrations, photographs, and maps. One of the
best general and not overly condensed surveys available. General index in v.4.

F937 Ebert, Max. Reallexikon der Vorgeschichte,
     unter Mitwirkung zahlreicher Fachgelehrter.
     Berlin: De Gruyter, 1924–32. 15v.
     Extensive and authoritative work on prehistory;
each article prepared by a specialist. Important articles
carry lengthy bibliographies, and shorter entries have
selected references. Each volume has about 130 plates
and maps, which the text refers to in detail. Includes
ancient history of various countries. V.15 is a general
index.

HANDBOOKS, MANUALS, AND SCHOLARLY COMPENDIUMS

F938 Varia folklorica. Ed. by Alan Dundes. The
     Hague: Mouton; Chicago: Aldine, 1978. 277p.
     Papers prepared for the 9th International Con-
gress of Anthropological and Ethnological Sciences,
Chicago, 1973, cover the more modern approach to
folklore without pretending to be encyclopedic. Excellent bibliographies. More-established methodologies
are found in Seán O Suilleabháin, *A handbook of Irish
folklore* (Dublin: publ. by the Educational Company
of Ireland, Ltd., for the Folklore of Ireland Society,
1942; reprint, Detroit: Singing Tree Pr., 1970 [699p.])
(F939). Folklore defined here as a comprehensive lore
of humanity and human activity. See also Kaarle
Krohn, *Folklore methodology formulated by Julius
Krohn and expanded by Nordic researchers* (Austin:
Univ. of Texas Pr., 1971 [192p.] [Publications of the
American Folklore Society. Bibliographical and special series, v.21.]) **(F940)**. The method is historical-
geographical and not concerned with psychological or
sociological issues.
     See also Stith Thompson, *Motif-index of folk-
literature: a classification of narrative elements in folk-*

*tales, ballads, myths, fables, medieval romances, exem-
pla, fabliaux, jestbooks and local legends,* rev. and enl.
ed. (Bloomington: Indiana Univ. Pr., 1955–58 [6 v.]) a
reprint (first issued 1932–36, as Indiana studies nos.
96–97, 100–101, 105–6, 108–12) **(F941)**. The standard
handbook in its field. A comprehensive, detailed classification scheme of 23 main divisions (e.g., mythological motifs, animals, taboos, deceptions, chance and
fate, society), each of which is minutely subdivided.
Many motifs have extensive bibliographical references. Ample cross-references of more than 40,000
listed and indexed motifs. V.6 is an alphabetical index
of motifs. Bacil F. Kirtley, *A motif-index of Polynesian, Melanesian, and Micronesian narratives* (New
York: Arno, 1980 [687p.]) **(F942)**, uses Thompson's
style of analysis and classification in treating myths,
tales, and legends, as does Katharine M. Briggs, *A
dictionary of British folk-tales in the English language,
incorporating the F. J. Norton Collection: part A, folk,
narratives; part B, folk legends* (Bloomington: Indiana
Univ. Pr., 1970–71 [4v.]) **(F943)** in part A (v. 1–2: *Folk
narratives*). Part B (v.1–2: *Folk legends*) cannot be
typed by this classification scheme. See also Ernest
Warren Baughman, *Type and motif-index of the folk-
tales of England and North America* (The Hague:
Mouton, 1966 [607p.] [Indiana Univ. Folklore ser.,
20]) **(F944)**. The alphabetical index in Stith Thompson,
Motif-index, serves for locating motif in this listing.
James T. Bratcher has provided the Aare-Thompson
classification system to a single journal in one section
of *Analytical index to publications of the Texas Folklore Society, volumes 1–36* (Dallas: Southern Methodist Univ. Pr., 1973 [322p.]) **(F945)**.

F946 Honigmann, John J. Handbook of social and
     cultural anthropology. Chicago: Rand Mc-
     Nally, 1973. 1,295p. [Rand McNally anthropol-
     ogy series]
     Review of research in various branches of
anthropology. Each chapter is by a specialist, with
extensive bibliographies. Subject index.

F947 Naroll, Raoul, and Ronald Cohen, eds. A hand-
     book of method in cultural anthropology. Gar-
     den City, N.Y.: publ. by Natural History Pr. for
     the American Museum of Natural History,
     1970. 1,017p.
     Its dual object is a reassessment of the position
of anthropology and a synthesis of critical insight into
scientific inquiry that will inform and guide the young
anthropologist. Linguistic analysis is ignored. Nonverbal communication was not covered but finds explication in Mary Ritchie Key's *Nonverbal communication:
a research guide & bibliography* (Metuchen, N.J.:
Scarecrow, 1977 [439p.]) **(F948)**. A 139-page review,
followed by an unannotated list of references arranged
by author. Bibliography, p.142–428.

F949 Murdock, George, and others. Outline of cul-
     tural materials. 4th ed. New Haven, Conn.:
     Human Relations Area Files Pr., 1982. 247p.
     Originally developed as a tool for the cross-
cultural survey instituted at Yale Univ. in 1937, this
classification scheme's ultimate purpose is the organization into "readily accessible form [of] the available

data on a statistically representative sample of all known cultures, primitive, historical and contemporary, for the purpose of testing cross-cultural generalizations, revealing deficiencies in the descriptive literature, and directory corrective research" (preface). It is the basic scheme of the HRAF, which divides all cultural and background information into 79 major and 619 minor divisions. Following the number and title of each category is a descriptive statement of the type of information included, with cross-references to other categories. Index. A sequel is Murdock's *Outline of world cultures*, 6th ed. rev. (New Haven, Conn.: HRAF, 1983 [259p.]) (**F950**), which classifies all known cultures in the world by geographical region, including extinct historical and prehistoric peoples.

F951   Anthropology today: an encyclopedic inventory. Prep. under the chairmanship of Alfred L. Kroeber. Chicago: Univ. of Chicago Pr., 1953. 966p.
See *Yearbook of anthropology* (F1007).

F952   Center for Applied Linguistics. A survey of materials for the study of the uncommonly taught languages. By Dora E. Johnson and others. Arlington, Va.: Center for Applied Linguistics, 1976. 8v.
Gives annotations for grammars, dictionaries, readers, and teaching aids. Assumes the teacher will also be a student of the language.

F953   Meillet, Antoine, and Marcel Cohen, eds. Les langues du monde. New ed. Paris: Centre Nationale de la Recherche Scientifique, 1952. 1,294p.
The main reference work in linguistics, covering more than 10,000 languages and dialects. Under each language group are sections on classification, features, syntax, and the various dialects as well as a comprehensive bibliography. Information for individual languages on phonology, grammar, phraseology, morphology, etc. Also, an annotated bibliography on classification and general linguistics. Appended is "Atlas des langues du monde," containing 21 maps and index of languages.

Works that illustrate the need for a new edition of this basic reference work with updated bibliographies include Čestmír Loukotka, *Classification of South American Indian languages* (Los Angeles: UCLA Latin American Center, 1968 [453p.] [California, University. University at Los Angeles, Latin American Center, Reference series, v.7.]) (**F954**). A classification of 117 South American languages. Includes 2,201 references in 12 European languages, including 346 unpublished manuscripts. Indexes of language families, languages and dialects, and of authors. Large linguistic map. Also, Charles Frederick Voegelin and M. F. Voegelin, *Classification and index of the world's languages* (F232). A good book. Arranged alphabetically by the names of groups of related languages. Biographic references are included in the discussion. Index of all names of groups, subgroups, languages, dialects, and tribes, with cross-reference to related names.

See also William S. Want, *CLIBOC: Chinese linguistics bibliography* (Cambridge: Cambridge Univ. Pr., 1970 [513p.] [Princeton-Cambridge studies in Chinese linguistics, v.1]) (**F956**). Articles arranged in three sections: (1) alphabetically by author, (2) subject index arranged by language and dialect, and (3) abstracts. Includes linguistic maps. Richard T. Parr, *A bibliography of the Athapaskan languages* (Ottawa: National Museums of Canada, 1974 [333p.] [Paper—ethnology division; no.14]) (**F957**). Arranged by ethnic group and subdivided by topic, this 5,000-item bibliography includes unpublished works. A new edition has been promised to bring coverage to 1980. Derek Fivaz, *African languages: a genetic and decimalised classification for bibliographic and general references* (Boston: Hall, 1977 [332p.] [Bibliographies and guides in African studies]) (**F958**). William Bright, *Bibliography of the languages of native California including closely related languages of adjacent areas* (Metuchen, N.J.: Scarecrow, 1982 [220p.] [Native American Bibliography series, no.3]) (**F959**). 1,077 entries. Includes all Yuman- and Numic-speaking peoples. Arranged alphabetically by author, with limited subject index.

Geographical Areas

F960   American Univ. Foreign Area Studies Division. Area handbooks. Washington, D.C.: American Univ. Pr., 1961–   .

The Foreign Area Studies Division of the Special Operations Research Office (SORO) serves as a research contractor for the Dept. of the Army. Most volumes in this unnumbered sequence appear as U.S. Dept. of the Army pamphlets in the 550– series. FASD has been prolific, producing important and influential social science research. Funded by the military, however, the work is affected by unresolved problems between the management of social science and the management of government. To identify all volumes in this "series," it is necessary to consult a wide range of basic bibliographic resources, of which the most important are the *National union catalog* (A261), the *Monthly catalog of United States Government publications* (I749), *PAIS bulletin* (A225), and *Selected Rand abstracts* (A164) (many area handbooks have been issued as Rand reports). Also consult American Univ., SORO, *Annotated bibliography of SORO publications* (Washington, D.C.: American Univ. Pr., 1965– [semiannual]) (**F961**).

Examples of FASD work are the area handbooks, all distributed in Washington by the Govt. Print. Off. and now cataloged by the Library of Congress under the name of the principal author. The handbooks can provide basic social science information, often for whole regions. For the Middle East, see Richard F. Nyrop's *Area handbook for the Yemens*, 1977 [266p.] (**F962**); his *Area handbook for the Republic of Turkey*, 2d ed., 1973 [415p.] (**F963**); his *Area handbook for Syria*, 1971 [357p.] (**F964**); his *Area handbook for Saudi Arabia*, 3d ed., 1977 [389p.] (**F965**); his *Area handbook for the Persian Gulf states*, 1977 [448p.] (**F966**); his *Area handbook for Morocco*, 1972 [403p.] (**F967**); his *Area handbook for Libya*, 2d ed., 1973 [317p.] (**F968**); his *Area handbook for the Hashermite Kingdom of Jordan*, 2d ed., 1974 [280p.] (**F969**); his *Area handbook for Egypt*, 3d ed., 1976 [454p.] (**F970**); his *Area handbook for Algeria*, 2d revision, 1972 [401p.] (**F971**); Howard C. Reese's *Area handbook for the Republic of Tunisia*, 1970 [415p.] (**F972**); Harvey Henry Smith's *Area handbook for Lebanon* [352p.] (**F973**); his *Area handbook for Israel* [456p.] (**F974**); his *Area handbook for Iran*, 1971 [653p.] (**F975**); his *Area handbook for Iraq*, 1971 [414p.] (**F976**); his *Area handbook for Afghanistan*, 1969 [435p.] (**F977**); and Stanford Research Institute's (SRI) *Area handbook for the peripheral states of the Arabian peninsula*, 1971 [201p.] (**F978**). Collectively these provide comprehensive coverage of the Middle East, but the coverage of the series is nearly worldwide in range. For recent editions covering Asia, reference can be made to G. Raymond Nunn, *Asia: reference works* (London: Mansell, 1980 [365p.]) (**F694**), first under geographic unit and then under the subject heading "Handbook."

Africa

F979   Bernatzik, Hugo A. Afrika: Handbuch der angewandten Volkerkunde. Innsbruck: Schlussel-Verlag, 1951. 2v. 1,429p.

This handbook of applied anthropology covers North Africa, Sudan, West Africa, East Africa, Congo, the Angola-Zambesi area, South Africa, and Madagascar. Information for each area on geography, history, and ethnography in relation to problems of applied anthropology. Each chapter has a select bibliography.

F980   Encyclopaedia of Southern Africa. Ed. by Eric Rosenthal. 7th ed. Cape Town: Juta, 1978. 577p.

"Southern Africa" here includes Rhodesia, Zambia, Malawi, South West Africa, Mozambique, Lesotho, Swaziland, and Botswania. This should be supplemented by referral to *The Bantu-speaking peoples of Southern Africa*, ed. by W. D. Hammond-Tooke (London: Routledge & Paul, 1974 [525p.]) (**F981**). A completely revised edition of I. Schapera's classic of the same title.

Western Hemisphere

F982   Hodge, Frederick W. Handbook of American Indians north of Mexico. Washington, D.C.: Govt. Print. Off., 1907–10. 2v. [U.S. Bureau of American Ethnology. Bulletin 30]. Reprint, St. Clair Shores, Mich.: Scholarly Pr., 1968.

An extensive compilation of authoritative information, arranged alphabetically, with a large number of cross-references. Aims to give a brief description of every linguistic stock, confederacy, tribe, subtribe or tribal division, and settlement, with information concerning ethnic relations, history, languages, manners and customs, arts, and industries. Each entry includes the origin and derivation of the name treated as well as a record of variant forms of the name, with references to the authorities. These "synonyms" are assembled, in alphabetical order, in

v.2 as cross-references. All cited sources are listed in an extensive bibliography in v.2. Many articles have illustrations.

F983   Steward, Julian H. Handbook of South American Indians. Washington, D.C.: Govt. Print. Off., 1946–59. 7v. [Bureau of American Ethnology. Bulletin 143]

Comprehensive synthesis of knowledge of the aboriginal population of South America that indicates deficiencies in this knowledge and the needs of future research. Centers attention on the culture of each tribe at the time of its first contact with Europeans: v.1, marginal tribes; v.2, Andean civilizations; v.3, tropical forest tribes; v.4, circum-Caribbean tribes; v.5, comparative ethnology; v.6, physical anthropology, linguistics, and cultural geography; v.7, general index. Each volume has a bibliography of all references cited in the text. Many useful maps and photographs.

F984   Jenness, Diamond. The Indians of Canada. Toronto: Univ. of Toronto Pr., 1977. 432p.

A standard source of information on Canadian Indians. Pt.1 treats the various aspects of Indian life under such headings as economic conditions, dwellings, social and political organization, religion, art and music, etc. Pt.2 treats the various tribes individually. The work is well documented and has a general index.

F985   Swanton, John R. Indian tribes of North America. Washington, D.C.: Govt. Print. Off., 1952. 726p. [Bureau of American Ethnology. Bulletin 145]

Especially useful for its coverage of the West Indies, which are not covered by Hodge's *Handbook of American Indians north of Mexico* (F982). Tribal entries are arranged alphabetically under each state. Information includes origin of tribal name and a brief list of important synonyms, tribal connections, the linguistic stock, location, history, population, and the "connection in which has become noted." 1650 is roughly the base date used in mapping tribal locations. References to the more important sources of information are included. Index of names and places. This work differs from Hodge in that it concentrates on tribal units and subunits, in contrast to the latter's more encyclopedic approach to all facets of American Indian cultures. Also useful is Swanton's *Indians of the southeastern United States* (Washington, D.C.: Govt. Print. Off., 1946 [943p.] [Bureau of American Ethnology. Bulletin 137]; reprint, Grosse Pointe, Mich.: Scholarly Pr., 1969) (**F986**).

F987   Wauchope, Robert, ed. Handbook of Middle American Indians. Austin: Univ. of Texas Pr., 1964–76. 16v. Supplement, v.1– , 1981– .

The bibliographies are incidental to the development of the text and are not intended to be comprehensive. As given at the end of chapters, citations are incomplete, and only the bibliography at the end of the volume provides full bibliographic descriptions. Covers the area south of Hodge's *Handbook of American Indians north of Mexico* (F982) and updates Steward's *Handbook of South American Indians* (F983).

F989 Handbook of North American Indians. Ed. by William C. Sturtevant. Washington: Smithsonian, 1978– ; for sale by the Supt. of Documents, Govt. Print. Off.

Published to date are: v.8, *California*, ed. by Robert F. Heizer and fully described at F843; v.15, *Northeast*, fully described at F841; v.9 and 10, *Southwest*, fully described at F839; and v.6, *Subarctic*, described at F859A. To be published in 20 volumes. Topics of the other volumes are: v.1, the introduction (gives general descriptions of anthropological and historical methods, and sources and summaries for the whole continent on social and political organization, religion, and the performing arts); v.2, Indians and Eskimos in contemporary society; v.3, environment, origins, and population (i.e., physical anthropology); v.4, the history of Indian-white relations; v.5, the Arctic; v.7, the Northwest Coast; v.11, the Great Basin; v.12, the Plateau; v.13, the Plains; v.14, the Southeast; v.16, technology and visual arts; v.17, languages; v.18 and 19, the biographical dictionary; and v.20, the index.

The unrelenting excellence of these volumes marks an editorial achievement of the first rank. They continue a tradition of anthropological scholarship in which reports are consolidated and published in a style that any educated person can understand. The bibliographies are extensive and the illustrations valuable and profuse. A scholarly achievement. This handbook will be the standard source for years to come.

The Pacific

F990 Tindale, Norman Burnett. Aboriginal tribes of Australia: their terrain, environmental controls, distribution, limits, and proper names. Berkeley: Univ. of California Pr., 1974. 404p.

An introductory statement includes detailed information on the tribal communities, their patterns of settlement, and the linguistics of tribal names. The catalog of tribes provides geographical location of individual tribes and their variant names. Arrangement is geographical by Australian states, and an appendix by Rhys Jones discusses Tasmanian tribes. The bibliography is extensive and the maps and illustrations valuable. An important contribution to the consolidation of anthropological knowledge.

F991 Anthropological studies in the eastern highlands of New Guinea. Ed. by Howard McKaughan. Seattle: Univ. of Washington Pr., 1972.

Nine volumes in all are planned. Published to date: v.1, *The languages of the eastern family of the east New Guinea highland stock*, ed. by Howard McKaughan, 1973 [817p.] (**F992**); v.2, *Physical anthropology of the eastern highlands of New Guinea*, by Robert Littlewood, 1972 [224p.] (**F993**); v.3, *Prehistory of the eastern highlands of New Guinea*, by Virginia Drew Watson and J. David Cole, 1977 [224p.] (**F994**); and v.4, *A New Guinea landscape: community, space, and time in the eastern highlands*, by K. J. Pataki-Schweizer, 1980 [165p.] (**F995**); v.5, *Tatrora culture*, by James B. Watson, 1983 [346p.] (**F995A**);

v.6, *Auyana: those who held onto home*, by Sterling Robbins, 1982 [254p.] (**F995B**). Planned are additional volumes on archaeology and ethnology.

Europe

F996 Bach, Adolf. Deutsche Volkskunde: Werke und Organisation, Probleme, System, Methoden, Ergebnisse und Aufgaben, Schrifttum. Mit 57 Skizzen und Karten. Heidelberg: Quelle & Heyer, 1960. 708p.

A detailed table of contents guides the reader. Extensive coverage of sociological and psychological facets of folk culture makes this source useful for European ethnography.

Asia

F997 Franke, Wolfgang. China handbuch. Düsseldorf: Bertelsmann, 1974. 1,768 columns.

Signed articles with bibliographic references. Primarily 19th and 20th century, with personal name and detailed subject indexes.

F998 Sanders, Alan J. K. The People's Republic of Mongolia: a general reference guide. London: Oxford Univ. Pr., 1968. 232p.

Very brief descriptions and pertinent short registries of institutions and social, economic, and political segments of a basically agricultural country. Chronology: 1921–67. Biographical notes, select bibliography, and subject index.

F999 Handbook of major Soviet nationalities. Ed. by Zev Katz. New York: Free Pr., 1975. 481p.

Divided into five parts: (1) Slavs, (2) Baltics, (3) Transcaucasians, (4) Central Asia, (5) other nationalities. All chapters are by recognized scholars, with selective bibliographies. A basic reference tool. Does not cover the religions of these groups. Each chapter deals with the territory, demography, language, and culture of 17 of the Soviet nations. References are cited, and there is an appendix of comparative tables for all groups.

F1000 Ramming, Martin. Japan-handbuch: nachschlagewerk der Japankunde. Im auftrage des Japaninstituts Berlin. Berlin: Steiniger, 1941. 740p.

An alphabetical dictionary of things Japanese. A remarkable book. Covers almost all aspects of Japanese culture in brief paragraphs. No references. Alphabetical arrangement.

Linguistic Anthropology, Psychological Anthropology

F1001 Current trends in linguistics. Ed. by Thomas A. Sebeok. The Hague: Mouton; dist. New York: Humanities. v.1– , 1963– .

Area survey articles with extensive bibliographies. Encyclopedic for the areas covered. Remarkable editorial control of regional linguistics and theoretical issues.

F1002 Handbook of Australian language. Ed. by R. M. W. Dixon and Barry J. Blake. Canberra: Australian Natl. Univ. Pr. v.1– , 1979– .

Makes available short grammatical sketches of Australian languages. The first volume includes one account of a living language and three accounts of dead or dying languages. Two additional volumes are planned.

F1003 Handbook of cross-cultural psychology. Ed. by Harry C. Triandis and others. Boston: Allyn & Bacon, 1980–81. 6v.

V.1, *Perspectives,* 1979 [392p.], has six major topics, each with 7 or 8 subheadings. Each article has a standard format that includes a content list, an abstract, an introduction, and the body of work with bibliography. Recognized authorities have contributed. V.2, *Methodologies,* 1979 [546p.], includes several articles of reference value, including Herbert Barry's "Description and uses of the Human Relations Area File" (p. 445–78) (**F1004**). Should be used in conjunction with *Encyclopedia of psychology*, ed. by Raymond Corsini (New York: Wiley, 1984 [4v.]) (**F1005**), which contains selective bibliographies of highly technical aspects of psychology.

F1006 Handbuch der Linguistik: allg. u. angewandte Sprachwiss. Aus Beitr. von Hans Arens... [et. al.] München: Nymphenburger Verlagshandlung, 1975. 584p.

Dictionary arrangement, with entries providing definitions and discussions of linguistic terms, sometimes several pages in length. Extensive bibliographies and a person and name index.

YEARBOOKS

F1007 International Symposium, Anthropology, New York, 1952. Yearbook of anthropology, 1955. New York: Wenner-Gren Foundation for Anthropological Research, 1955. 836p.

Launched as the first of an annual series that failed to materialize, it forms with *Anthropology today: an encyclopedic inventory,* prep. under the chairmanship of Alfred L. Kroeber, a major postwar professional assessment. (See F951 for description of the latter.) Divided into 6 parts, each consisting of essays by specialists, with bibliographies for each. In 1956, 19 of the essays were reprinted under the title *Current anthropology: a supplement to* Anthropology today, ed. by William L. Thomas, Jr. (Chicago: Univ. of Chicago Pr., 1956 [377p.]) (**F1009**).

Yearbook of physical anthropology, v.1–8, 1945–52, was superseded for 1953 by *Anthropology today* (F951) and for subsequent years by *Yearbook of physical anthropology* (v.10–15, 1962–67), which was published annually for the American Assn. of Physical Anthropologists by the Instituto de Investigaciones Históricas, Universidad Nacional Autónoma de Mexico, and the Instituto Nacional de Antropología e Historia, Córdoba (Mexico City: 1964–). This series picked up the numbering of the old series, with v.9,

Yearbook of physical anthropology, 1953–1961, covering 1953–61. The new series again picks up the numbering of the old series and becomes a forum for review articles. It is fully described at F438.

ORIGINAL SOURCES

F1011 Archives of archaeology. v.1– , 1960– . Madison: publ. jointly by the Society for American Archaeology and Univ. of Wisconsin Pr.

A new series on microcard of occasional publications of primary documentation of archaeological investigations and related materials. Hopes to make available the primary data from archaeological sites that are rarely published in any form.

F1012 Fay, George Emery. Charters, constitutions, and by-laws of the Indian tribes of North America. Greeley: Colorado State College Museum of Anthropology, 1967– . [Ethnology series]

Reproductions of the charters and other legal instruments governing present-day Indian tribal organizations, arranged by cultural and geographic areas. V.1 is *The Sioux tribes of South Dakota;* v.9 is *The Northwest and Alaska.* An important and imaginative contribution. Also consult Lester Hargrett, *A bibliography of the constitutions and laws of the American Indians* (Cambridge, Mass.: Harvard Univ. Pr., 1947 [124p.]) (**F1013**). It records all published Indian legal instruments prior to the reorganizaton of Indian tribal groups following the Act of 1934. Arranged by tribe. Locates copies in 50 libraries, public and private.

F1014 Washburn, Wilcomb E. The American Indian and the United States: a documentary history. New York: Random, 1973. 4v.

20 documents covering period 1763–1970. Presented chronologically under reports of the Commissioner of Indian Affairs, congressional debates, judicial decisions, treaties, and acts of Congress.

F1015 Hill, Edward E. The Office of Indian Affairs, 1824–1880: historical sketches. New York: Clearwater, 1974. 246p.

The National Archives and Records Service sells a 962-reel set of microfilm of the correspondence the BIA received between 1824 and 1880, which can be purchased in single reels, groups of reels, or as a complete set. This book opens up the entire collection to scholars. The introduction identifies the variety of entries under which data may be found. A jurisdictional index identifies agencies. The tribal index provides the official list of Indian tribes from the point of view of the U.S. government.

F1016 Ellis, Richard N. "Published source materials on Native Americans." *Western historical quarterly* 7:187–92 (April 1976).

An evaluation and comparison of 20 large and expensive sets.

F1017 Primary records in culture and personality. Ed. by Bert Kaplan. Madison, Wis.: Microcard Foundation, 1956– .

Purpose of this microcard series is to make hitherto unpublished source material and field data collected by anthropologists and psychologists available for interpretation and further research. The materials pertain primarily to individuals living outside the mainstream of Western culture. Each volume consists of a number of separate contributions and contains a set of data from a single culture. These data are of several types: Rorschachs, TATS (thematic apperception tests), dreams, and life histories. In addition, each contribution has an explanatory introduction by the contributor, describing the nature of the study being conducted at the time the material was collected, the locale and characteristics of the culture group, the methods used, and the conditions under which the samples were taken. Classified according to Murdock's *Outline of world cultures* (F950).

F1018 HRAF research guide. New Haven, Conn.: Human Relations Area Files Pr., n.d. 44p.

Social scientists are devising new research tools to aid in exploiting the data accumulating in data storage files. HRAF is an older, growing file of data on different societies that organizes the data according to a universal topical classification and is the hub of a research consortium. It has data on primitive and non-primitive societies, classified according to more than 700 categories of human behavior. Complete sets of files are located in more than 20 research centers. This brief introduction explains the setup, particularly the nature of the files and how to use them. Illustrated. See also Robert O. Legacé, *Nature and use of the HRAF files: a research and teaching guide* (New Haven, Conn.: Human Relations Area Files Pr., 1974 [49p.]) **(F1019)**.

F1022 Indiana University. Archives of Traditional Music. A catalog of phonorecordings of music and oral data held by the Archives of Traditional Music. Boston: Hall, 1975. 541p.

An important archival source of traditional music, verbal folklore, and oral data from North American Indian, African, and Latin American cultures. The indexing is comprehensive and professionally structured. One index provides entry by subject and cultural groups. A second index identifies the contributions of collectors, depositors, performers, and informants. A third index identifies the productions of particular recording companies. As a special feature, each item is given an HRAF number which relates that item to textual material. Also useful but more limited in scope is Ruth M. Stone and Frank J. Gillis' *African music and oral data: a catalog of field recordings, 1902–1975* (Bloomington: Indiana Univ. Pr., 1976 [412p.]) **(F1023)**. Indexed by subject and culture groups. Arranged by collector.

F1024 Field, Henry. Bibliography. Washington, D.C.: 1951– .

Includes a complete list of materials microfilmed in the American Documentation Institute.

F1025 Hill, Edward E. Guide to records in the National Archives of the United States relating to American Indians. Washington, D.C.: National Archives and Records Service, General Services Administration, 1981. 467p.

Chronological arrangement with detailed table of contents and 3,800 terms in the subject index.

ETHNOGRAPHIC FILM AND PHOTOGRAPHS

F1026 Asch, Timothy, and others. "Ethnographic film: structure and function." Annual review of anthropology 2:179–87 (1973).

A review article with a select bibliography organized to identify the reference value of film indexes, periodicals, and bibliographies and to provide a select list of books and articles for the beginning student.

F1027 Heider, Karl G. Films for anthropological teaching. 7th ed. Washington, D.C.: American Anthropological Assn., 1983. 312p. [A special publication of the American Anthropological Assn., no.1]

A select list of films and a list of major distributors. A more comprehensive list can be found in *Educational film locator of the Consortium of University Film Centers and R.R. Bowker Company*, 2d ed. (New York: Bowker, 1980 [2,611p.]) **(F1028)**, which standardizes entry into about 50 separate libraries. Lists 37,000 titles of educational value in all disciplines. The lending policy of each library is given. A subject, title, and audience-level index is followed by an alphabetical list of film descriptions, with holding information and producer/distributor identification. This is followed by a series listing, a foreign film title index, and producer/distributor lists. An excellent work.

Alfred M. Duggan-Cronin, *The Bantu tribes of South Africa: reproductions of photographic studies done by A. M. Duggan-Cronin* (Cambridge: Deighton, Bell, 1928–54 [4v. in 10]; reprint, Friends of the National Museum and Art Gallery, Gaborne, Botswana, 1984) **(F1029)**, is a beautifully executed anthropological record. The photographs focus on the landscape, scenes of daily life, costumes, adornments, and portraits of different tribes. They are accompanied by notes and an introductory essay by a specialist who describes the culture of the Bantus. H. Ian Hogbin, *Peoples of the Southwest Pacific: a book of photographs and introductory text* (New York: Day, 1946 [69p. of plates]) **(F1030)**, is an anthropologist's portrayal of how the Papuans of the Solomon Islands and New Guinea look and live.

Less accessible is Frederick McCarthy, *Australia's aborigines: their life and culture* (Melbourne: Colorgravure Pubs., 1957 [200p.]) **(F1031)**, which seeks to picture a way of life, as do John Collier, Jr., and Anibal Buitrón in *The awakening valley* (Chicago: Univ. of Chicago Pr., 1949 [199p.]) **(F1032)** for Indians of the Andes in Ecuador. Oliver LaFarge's *A pictorial history of the North American Indian* (New York: Crown, 1956 [272p.]) **(F1033)** is a vivid summary for the specialist and an introduction for the general reader. The coming of man to the New World is followed by chapters on cultural areas and a chapter on the Indian in the modern world. Its emphasis is on arts, crafts, and the Indian's way of life, examples of which are well chosen from early drawings, museum artifacts, and elsewhere. The text is clear and concise.

Three regional groups are portrayed by Leonard McCombe, *Navaho means people,* with photographs by Leonard McCombe and text by Evon Z. Vogt and Clyde Kluckhohn (Cambridge, Mass.: Harvard Univ. Pr., 1951 [159p.]) **(F1034)**; Emma L. Fundaburk, *Southeastern Indians: life portraits, a catalog of pictures, 1564–1860* (Metuchen, N.J.: Scarecrow, 1969 [reprint of 1958 ed., 136p.]) **(F1035)**; and Emma L. Fundaburk and Mary D. Foreman, *Sun circles and human hands: the Southeastern Indians— arts and industries* (Laverne, Ala.: Anchor, 1957 [232p.]) **(F1036)**. More recent is Cynthia Salvadori's *Maasai: photographs by Cynthia Salvadori* (London: Collins, 1973 [112p.]) **(F1037)**. A collection of black-and-white photographs, each accompanied by captions. Aldo Massola's *The aborigines of south-eastern Australia as they were* (Melbourne: Heinemann Australia, 1971 [167p.]) **(F1038)** is a mixture of old and new photographs. Philip John Crosskey Dark's *Kilenge life and art: a look at a New Guinea people* (London: Academy Editions, 1974 [33p.]) **(F1039)** features 246 black-and-white photographs. Text describes first field visit to the people by the author. Also, there is *The illustrated encyclopedia of mankind* (New York: Marshall Cavendish, 1978 [20v.]) **(F1040)**. Essays on 500 cultural groups and a wide range of topics by 100 specialists are enriched by color illustrations of ritual practices, housing, and the social activities of various peoples of the world, which Professor Fürer-Haimensdorf identifies as "an ethnographic record of considerable documentary value." (p.iv).

MAPS AND ATLASES

Leo Frobenius and Ritter von Wilm, *Atlas Africanus: belege zur morphologie der Afrikanischen kulturen* (hrsg. im auftrage des Forschungs-Institutes für Kulturmorphologie; Berlin: de Gruyter, 1921–31 [8pt.]) **(F1041)**, is a historic example of the use of mapping as an anthropological research tool. Interested in whether cultural similarities spring from human nature or from cultural contacts and migration, Frobenius and von Wilm used cartography for an empirical definition of the orbit, or range, of a culture (*Kulturkreise*). Later mapping of tribal and ethnic groups is illustrated by a well-known map in George P. Murdock's *Africa: its peoples and their culture history* (see F634), and by Alfred L. Kroeber's *Cultural and natural areas of native North America* (Berkeley: Univ. of California Pr., 1963 [240p.]) **(F1043)**, originally published in 1939 as v.38 of the University of California Publications in American Archaeology and Ethnology. The University of California, Berkeley, Library Photographic Service made copies available in 1984.

George P. Murdock's *Ethnographic atlas* (Pittsburgh: Univ. of Pittsburgh Pr., 1967 [128p.]) **(F1044)** undertakes to organize the uniform information gathered thus far on peoples of the world to aid comparative research. It considers about 50 economic, technological, social, and cultural factors; analyzes more than 400 societies for which such data are available; and systematically tabulates the results. The product is not an atlas in the usual sense but an intricate codification of data hitherto scattered, which was published in *Ethnology* in installments beginning in early 1962.

Robert F. Spencer and Elden Johnson, *Atlas for anthropology* (Dubuque, Iowa: W.C. Brown, 1968 [61p.]) **(F1045)**, compactly presents mappable subject matter for instruction purposes: five maps of cultural areas and tribal groups in North America, South America, Africa, Eurasia, and Oceania; five maps of language families in the same areas; four maps of Old and New World prehistory; and a map showing the racial distribution of humankind.

Harold E. Driver and others, *Indian tribes of North America* (Baltimore: Waverly, 1953 [30p.] [Indiana Univ. Publications in anthropology and linguistics, memoir 9]) (also as *Supplement* to *International journal of American linguistics,* v.19(3), July 1953) **(F1046)**, consists essentially of a map with explanatory notes, a bibliography of sources, and an index of tribal names. It is the third attempt to provide a continental map assigning definite tribal territories to 238 tribes. The earlier maps were included in Kroeber's *Cultural and natural areas of native North America* (F1043) and George P. Murdock's *Ethnographic bibliography of North America* (F792). See also Desmond J. Clark, *Atlas of African pre-history: maps by Eve Kemnitzer* (Chicago: Univ. of Chicago Pr., 1967 [12 maps, 38 overlays, 62p.]) **(F1047)**, a product of archaeological investigation that emphasizes the close relationship of culture to the environment. Graphic presentations of linguistic geography are well represented by Antoine Meillet and Marcel Cóhen, eds., *Les langues du monde,* new ed., with 26 maps (see description at F953); by Charles F. Voegelin and E. W. Voegelin, *Map of North American Indian languages* (New York: publ. by the American Ethnological Society in collaboration with Indiana Univ., 1944; dist. by J. J. Augustin, New York [97 × 90 cm.], Publication no.20, American Ethnological Society) **(F1049)**; and by Čestmír Loukotka, *Ethno-linguistic distribution of South American Indians* (Washington, D.C.: Assn. of American Geographers [1967], *Annals,* map supplement no.8) **(F1050)**, which is described more fully in the association's *Annals* 57:437–38 (1967).

"A world map of culture-areas for about 1500 A.D.," which concludes Gordon H. Hewes' *A conspectus of the world's cultures in 1500 A.D.*, p.1–22 (Boulder: Univ. of Colorado, 1954) [Univ. of Colorado Studies. Series in anthropology, no.4] **(F1051)**, is another summary of the results of research in cartographical form.

A recent addition to this type of investigation would be Jacquetta Hawkes and David Trump, *Atlas of early man* (New York: St. Martin's, 1976 [255p.]) **(F1052)**. Overview of eight "time-steps" between 5,000 B.C. and 500 A.D. Charts summarize economy, events, religion, technology, and inventions. A useful summary of the evidence for independent inventions with its implications for a universal mentality. David Whitehouse and Ruth Whitehouse, *Archaeological atlas of the world* (San Francisco: Freeman, 1975; Paris: Tallandier, 1978 [272p.]) **(F1053)**, offers 103 maps that provide an excellent synthesis of archaeological knowledge. 5,000 sites are identified.

F1054 Conklin, Harold C. Ethnographic atlas of Ifugao: a study of environment, culture, and society in Northern Luzon. New Haven, Conn.: Yale Univ. Pr., 1980. 116p.

Sets a new standard in showing how the relationships between humanity and the environment can be depicted. The author knows the people, their history, and what others have known about them. Destined to be a classic. 100 maps of which 28 are full-page. An excellent index and a two-page select bibliography.

F1055 Al-Faruqi, Isma'il Ragi, ed. Historical atlas of the religions of the world. New York: Macmillan, 1974. 346p.

65 maps in a cartographic treatment of the distribution of religions and sects, and special topics such as the use of stimulants in religious behavior. Informative text, with up-to-date bibliographies. An appendix of chronologies. An important reference book.

Bibliographies that provide detailed coverage for areas of anthropological importance continue to appear; i.e., C. E. Merrett, *A selected bibliography of Natal maps, 1800–1977* (Boston: Hall, 1979 [226p.]) **(F1057)**. *List of cartographic records of the Bureau of Indian Affairs*, comp. by Laura E. Kelsay (Washington, D.C.: General Services Administration, National Archives and Records Service, 1977 [187p.] [Special list, National Archives and Records Service no.13]) **(F1058)**, describes in detail the maps of the Bureau of Indian Affairs. Covers exploration routes, tribal lands, reservations, etc. Subject index.

Look under "Ethnography," "Ethnology," "Languages," and other headings in American Geographical Society, Map Department, *Index to maps in books and periodicals* (Boston: Hall, 1968 [10v.]) **(F1059)**, one can greatly extend this selected list of maps. Two supplements to date.

SOURCES OF CURRENT INFORMATION

One of the best current sources is *Current anthropology: a world journal of the sciences of man.* Description at F1070. A special feature, "Documentation in anthropology" **(F1061)**, published in this journal, lists newsletters of special interest to the discipline.

Most professional associations have newsletters that are circulated to all members and are available to others by subscription. These provide a compact source of current information on a broad band of professional interests and activities. Some have a discipline focus: *Anthropology newsletter*, v.1– , 1947– (Washington, D.C.: American Anthropological Assn.), 10/yr. **(F1062)**. *RAIN: Royal Anthropological Institute news*, v.1– , 1974– (London: The Institute), bimonthly **(F1063)**. Latin American Studies Assn., *Newsletter*, v.1– , 1969– (Urbana, Ill.: The Assn.) **(F1064)**. *African studies newsletter*, v.1– , 1968– (New York: African Studies Assn.), 6–9/yr. **(F1065)**.

The annual reports of foundations and professional societies are a source of information about their activities and publications; i.e., American Anthropological Assn., *Annual report and directory*, v.1– , 1969– (Washington, D.C.: American Anthropological Assn.) **(F1066)**; Wenner-Gren Foundation for Anthropological Research, *Report on the foundation's activities*, 1941– (New York: The Foundation), annual **(F1067)**; American Ethnological Society, *Newsletter*, 1959– (Seattle: The Society, c/o Univ. of Washington), annual **(F1068)**; *Folklore*, v.1– , 1878– (London: Folk-lore Society, c/o Univ. College), quarterly. Title varies. Carries annual reports and news and reports of meetings of the society. Cumulative index 1878–1958; supplement 1958–68. "Supplement," *Journal of American folklore*, 1888– (Austin: publ. by Univ. of Texas Pr. for American Folklore Society) **(F1069)**, annual. Not part of the *Journal* but issued supplemental to it. Contains annual report of the society, which includes—besides president's report—reports of other officers, editors, and committees; notices of future meetings and professional news; and full list of individual and institutional members.

SOURCES OF SCHOLARLY CONTRIBUTIONS

Journals

F1070

Africa: journal of the International African Institute. v.1– , 1928– . London: Oxford Univ. Pr. Quarterly.
AA; BrHumInd; BullSig; HistAbst; IntBibSocSci; IntBibZeit; LLBA; PAIS; SocAbst; SSCI.

American anthropologist. v.1– , 1888– . Washington, D.C.: American Anthropological Assn. 6/yr.
AA; AbstAnthro; AbstCrimPen; AbstFolk; BiolAbst; BullSig; Cc; EM; IntBibSocSci; IntBibZeit; LLBA; PsychAbst; SocAbst; SSCI; SSI.

American antiquity. v.1– , 1935– . Washington, D.C.: Society for American Archaeology. Quarterly.
Cc; ChemAbst; HistAbst; SSCI.

American journal of archaeology. v.1– , 1885– . Bryn Mawr, N.Y.: Archaeology Institute of America. Quarterly.
Cc; ChemAbst; SSCI.

American journal of physical anthropology. v.1– , 1918– . New York: American Assn. of Physical Anthropologists. Monthly.
Cc; EM; SSCI; SSI.

Anthropological linguistics. v.1– , 1959– . Bloomington; Indiana Univ. Dept. of Anthropology. 4/yr.
AbstrAnthro; Cc; SSCI.

Anthropological quarterly. v.1– , 1928– . Washington, D.C.: Catholic Univ. of America Pr. Quarterly.
Cc; SSCI; SSI.

Anthropologie. v.1– , 1890– . Paris: Masson. 4/yr.
BiolAbst; EM.

Anthropos: revue internationale d'ethnologie et de linguistique. v.1– , 1906– . Fribourg, Switzerland: St. Paul. 3/yr. Text in English, French, and German.
SSI.

Current anthropology: a world journal of the sciences of man. v.1– , 1960– . Chicago: Univ. of Chicago Pr. Bimonthly.
AbstAnthro; Cc; PsychAbst; SocAbst; SSCI; SSI.

Dialetical anthropology. v.1– , 1975– . Amsterdam: Elsevier. Quarterly.
Cc; LLBA.

Ethnology: an international journal of cultural and social anthropology. v.1– , 1964– . Pittsburgh: Univ. of Pittsburgh Dept. of Anthropology. Quarterly.
BiolAbst; Cc; SSCI; SSI.

Ethnos. v.1– , 1936– . Stockholm: Etnografiska Museet. 2/yr. Text in English and German.
SSCI.

Human biology: record of research. v.1– , 1929– . Detroit: Wayne State Univ. Pr. Quarterly.
AbstAnthro; BiolAbst; Cc; ChemAbst; EM; NutrAbst; PsychAbst.

Human organization. v.1– , 1941– . Washington, D.C.: Society for Applied Anthropology. Quarterly.
AbstAnthro; Cc; SSCI; SSI.

International journal of American linguistics. v.1– , 1917– . Chicago: Univ. of Chicago Pr. Quarterly.
AbstAnthro; Cc; LLBA; SSCI.

Journal of American folklore. v.1– , 1888– . Washington, D.C.: American Folklore Society. Quarterly.
AbstFolk; Cc; HistAbst; MusicInd; SSCI.

Journal of anthropological research. v.1– , 1945– . Albuquerque: Univ. of New Mexico Pr. Quarterly.
AbstAnthro; HistAbst; SSCI; SSI.

Journal of Asian studies. v.1– , 1941– . Coral Gables, Fla.: Univ. of Miami. 5/yr.
Cc; HistAbst; SSCI.

Man. v.1– , 1966– . London: Royal Anthropological Institute of Great Britain and Ireland. Quarterly.
BiolAbst; BrHumInd; Cc; EM; SSI.

Oceania: devoted to the study of the native peoples of Australia, New Guinea and the islands of the Pacific Ocean. v.1– , 1930– . New South Wales, Australia: Univ. of Sydney. Quarterly.
AustPAIS; Cc; SSCI; SSI.

Polynesian Society. Journal: a study of the native peoples of the Pacific area. v.1– , 1892– . Auckland, New Zealand: Polynesian Society. Quarterly.
Cc; SSCI.

Société des Amèricanistes. Journal. v.1– , 1895– . Paris: Société des Amèricanistes de Paris. Semi-annual.
SSCI.

Zeitschrift für ethnologie. v.1– , 1865– . Braunschweig, Germany: Deutsche Gesellschaft für Völkerkunde. 2/yr.
SSCI.

Monograph Series

F1071

American Anthropological Assn. Memoirs. v.1– , 1905– . Washington, D.C.

American Ethnological Society. Monographs. no.1– , 1940– . New York.

————. Publications. v.1– , 1907– . New York.

American Folklore Society. Memoirs. v.1– , 1894– . Philadelphia.

American Museum of Natural History. Anthropological papers. v.1– , 1907– . New York.

Bernice P. Bishop Museum. Memoirs. v.1–12, 1899–1949. Honolulu.

————. Bulletin. no.1– , 1922– . Honolulu.

Case studies in cultural anthropology. [Unnumbered.] New York: Holt, 1959– .

Chicago Natural History Museum. Fieldiana: Anthropology. v.1– , 1985– . Chicago.

Columbia Univ. Contributions to anthropology. v.1– , 1913– . New York.

Etnografiska Museet. Etnografiska studier. v.1– , 1935– . Göteborg, Sweden. (Text in English.)

Harvard Univ. Peabody Museum of Archaeology and Ethnology. Papers. v.1– , 1888– . Cambridge, Mass.

Kölner Ethnologische Mitteilungen. v.1– , 1960– . Cologne: Seminar für Völkerkunde, Universität Köln.

London Univ. London School of Economics and Political Science. Monographs in social anthropology. v.1– , 1940– . London.

Royal Anthropological Institute of Great Britain and Ireland. Occasional papers. v.1– , 1902– . London.

Smithsonian Institution. Miscellaneous collections. v.1– , 1862– . Washington, D.C.

Société d'Anthropologie de Paris. Bulletins et mémoires. v.1– , 1860– . Paris.

Society for Applied Anthropology. Monographs. no.1– , 1959– . Ithaca, N.Y.

U.S. Bureau of American Ethnology. Annual reports. v.1– , 1879–80– . Washington, D.C.

————. Bulletin. no.1– , 1886– . Washington, D.C.: Govt. Print. Off.

Universitè de Paris. Institut d'Ethnologie. Travaux et mémoires. v.1– , 1926– . Paris: Musée de l'Homme.

Universitet i Uppsala. Studia ethnographica Upsaliensia. v.1– , 1950– . Uppsala, Sweden. (Text in English, French, and German.)

Univ. of California. Anthropological records. no.1– , 1937– . Berkeley.

————. Folklore studies. v.1– , 1953– . Berkeley.

————. Publications in American archaeology and ethnology. v.1– , 1903– . Berkeley. Index. v.1–26, 1903–29.

Univ. of Oklahoma Pr. Civilization of the American Indian. v.1– , 1940– . Norman.

Wenner-Gren Foundation for Anthropological Research. Publications in anthropology. v.1– , 1943– . New York. (Formerly the Viking Fund, Inc.)

Yale Univ. Publications in anthropology. v.1– , 1936– . New Haven, Conn.

Organizations

F1072

American Anthropological Assn. Washington, D.C. Founded 1902.

American Ethnological Society. New York. Founded 1842.

American Folklore Society. Philadelphia. Founded 1888.

Bernice P. Bishop Museum. Honolulu. Founded 1889.

Bureau of American Ethnology. Washington, D.C. Founded 1879.

The Folk-lore Society. London. Founded 1878.

Harvard Univ. Peabody Museum of Archaeology and Ethnology. Cambridge, Mass. Founded 1866.

Heye Foundation. New York. Founded 1916.

Human Relations Area Files. New Haven, Conn. Founded 1949. (For a general description of this organization and its unique collection, see Gladys W. White, "The Human Relations Area Files," *College and research libraries* 19:111–17 [March 1958]).

Indiana Univ. Folklore Institute. Bloomington. Founded 1963.

Intl. African Institute. London. Founded 1926.

Intl. Union of Anthropological and Ethnological Sciences. Paris. Founded 1948.

Northwestern Univ. African Studies Center. Evanston, Ill. Founded 1948.

Polynesian Society, Inc. Wellington, New Zealand. Founded 1892.

Rhodes-Livingston Institute. Lusaka, Northern Rhodesia. Founded 1937.

Royal Anthropological Institute of Great Britain and Ireland. London. Founded 1843.

Société d'Anthropologie de Paris. Paris. Founded 1859.

Société des Africanistes. Paris, Musée de l'Homme. Founded 1931.

Société des Americanistes. Paris, Musée de l'Homme. Founded 1895.

Société des Océanistes. Paris. Founded 1937.

Society for American Archaeology. Ann Arbor, Mich. Founded 1934.

Society for Applied Anthropology. New York. Founded 1941.

Univ. of California. African Studies Center. Los Angeles. Founded 1959.

————. Center for the Study of Comparative Folklore and Mythology. Los Angeles. Founded 1960.

————. Robert H. Lowie Museum of Anthropology. Berkeley. Founded 1901.

Univ. of Michigan. African Studies Center. East Lansing. Founded 1960.

————. Museum of Anthropology. Ann Arbor. Founded 1926.

Univ. of North Carolina. Research Laboratories of Anthropology. Chapel Hill. Founded 1938.

Wenner-Gren Foundation for Anthropological Research, Inc. (Formerly the Viking Fund, Inc.) New York. Founded 1941.

Robert Westerman

7 Psychology

Survey of the Field
page 404

General psychology G1–14. *Systems, methodologies, and issues* G15–20. History of psychology G21–35. Systems of psychology G36–77. Statistics and psychometrics G78–101. *Experimental psychology* G102–14. Learning G115–37. Sensory and perceptual processes G138–54. Motivation and emotion G155–169. Thinking processes G170–84. *Physiological psychology* G185–206. *Developmental psychology* G207–31. *Personality* G232–67. *Social psychology* G268–307. *Clinical psychology* G308–50. *Educational psychology* G351–64. *Industrial and organizational psychology* G365–76.

Survey of the Reference Works
page 428

Guides to the literature. General G377–83. Specialized G384–403. *Reviews.* General G404–8. Specialized. Some major research fields in psychology G409–14. Developmental psychology G415–24. Clinical applications G425–29. Behavior modification G430–31. Mental retardation G432–35. Psychoanalysis G436–38. Test reviews and psychological assessment G439–57. *Abstracts and summaries.* General G458. Specialized G459–69. *Bibliographies of bibliographies* G470. *Current bibliographies* G471–75. *Retrospective bibliographies.* General G476–81. Specialized bibliographies G482–522. *Periodicals* G523–26. *Directories and biographical information.* Directories G527–39. Biography and history G542–49. *Dictionaries* G550–59. Foreign-language dictionaries G560–68. Specialized dictionaries G569–72. *Encyclopedias.* General G573–75. Specialized G576–79. *Handbooks.* Gen-

---

The late Robert I. Watson, Sr., completed his draft of this chapter shortly before he died. His mission, which he completed with distinction, was to provide an overview of the most significant literature in psychology as a social science up to about the middle of 1980. A number of important works have, of course, appeared between that cutoff date and the date of publication of this book, but it seemed inappropriate to try to update his selections without his personal consultation; changes, including selective deletion of some of the works he had included, would have destroyed the organized overview of the social science literature in psychology at the end of the 1970s that Watson's article provides. Therefore, while a small number of recent works for each of Watson's subdivisions have been added, they are appended at the end of each of Watson's subdivisions rather than integrated into the body of each section of the text. A few typographical and other inadvertent errors in Watson's text have also been corrected. —Michael Wertheimer, University of Colorado

Survey of the Field

Psychology, the scientific study of behavior and experience, in recent years has shown a considerable surge of growth both in numbers and in diversity of problems with which it concerns itself. Contact with its neighboring fields also occurs. On one hand, it has relations with the other social sciences, especially sociology, and, on the other, with the biological sciences, especially physiology. Since much psychological research is quantitative in nature, another direction of relationship is with mathematics, through the use of statistics and through quantitative theories, often stated in the form of computer programs. Still another characteristic of psychology arises from its being a profession as well as a science. This calls for relationships with physicians, psychoanalysts, teachers, and other individuals involved in matters of psychological importance. Consequently, works both by scientific and by professional colleagues are cited here if they have been accepted as integral to work in psychology. In keeping with this emphasis upon psychology as a social science, works concerned with the psychological study of other animal species are neglected.

A consistent classificatory scheme has been adopted so as to render the presentation more systematic and easier to follow from category to category. The first major category is that of books that survey the field in general. Thereafter, the categories are derived from those adopted by the American Psychological Association for classifying psychological literature (*Directory of the American Psychological Association*, Washington, D.C.: American Psychological Assn., 1978). From this classification, works concerned with systems of psychology, methodologies followed, and certain broad issues first receive consideration. Category sections devoted to experimental psychology, physiological psychology, developmental psychol-

ogy, personality, social psychology, clinical psychology, educational psychology, and industrial and organizational psychology follow.

The books selected for citation are perceived as meeting different needs. They are presented in the same sectional sequence throughout each category. First, historically important works are either cited directly or are represented by a classic secondary historical account. Standard textbooks follow. These books reflect the mainstream of thinking about a particular field. They are "accurate," "fair," and "judicious," and they "show relatively few biases," "are written so as to be comprehensible and comprehensive," and "devote their attention to the particular topic at hand." In other words, they are the textbooks in the best sense of the word that could be identified by this reviewer. Within the textbook section, whenever possible, a volume is identified that serves as a short introductory statement about the area under consideration. Two or more major textbooks that detail the subject at hand are cited. Appropriate handbooks or manuals may be identified. Books of readings—a sampling of articles and excerpts from research and theoretical literature—are often mentioned. Some books that are then cited are more specialized in the sense that they concentrate on one or another aspect of the topic in question.

In some instances, other books are included that "break new ground," "are provocative," "are illuminating," according to some competent judges; to other judges, however, these same books may be "inaccurate," "controversial," "unfair," "biased," "incomprehensible," and "not confined to a topic as it is generally understood." It is characteristic that these books do not always lend themselves readily to categorization. In the long run they may be seen to be of quite different merit. Sometimes they serve as the cutting edge of some area of psychological concern, but they may also prove to be ephemeral, reflecting a fad, stirring tremendous interest at one time only to fade into memory soon thereafter. Nevertheless, some such works demand inclusion.

GENERAL PSYCHOLOGY

General textbooks frequently serve as introductions to psychology at the level of the first course or first acquaintance. While reading a general text is by no means the only way to introduce oneself to psychology, it will serve unless one starts from a position of some already established specialized interest.

A book designed as a textbook that has become a classic is the *Principles of psychology* by William James, first published in 1890. In excellence of literary style, provocativeness of insight, and colorfulness of expression, no one has surpassed this book, published more than 90 years ago. A few years earlier, Wilhelm Wundt and Franz Brentano had published books that gave their versions of what the emerging science of psychology was to be. That each of the three later would serve at least as partial inspiration for a system of psychology does not detract from the fact that when they were written each was a personal vision of what the entire field of psychology was to be.

G1   Brentano, Franz. Psychology from an empirical standpoint. Tr. by A. C. Rancurello and others. New York: Humanities, 1973. 415p.

G2   James, William. The principles of psychology. New York: Holt, 1890. 2v.

G3   Wundt, Wilhelm. Principles of physiological psychology. 5th ed. Tr. by E. B. Titchener. New York: Macmillan, 1910. 347p.

The textbooks that follow show solid scholarship, breadth, and depth of coverage, and they present an eclectic, balanced approach. The books by Hilgard and by Zimbardo and their collaborators have been standard, widely adopted textbooks for years with proven staying power by periodic, thorough revision. The book by the Fernalds is perhaps more student-oriented in that they incorporate a variety of learning aids into the text itself. A newcomer is the volume edited by Meyer, with each chapter written by a specialist. A balanced book of readings drawn from the contemporary literature is provided by Bourne and Ekstrand.

G4   Bourne, Lyle E., and Bruce R. Ekstrand. Psychology: its principles and meanings. 3d ed. New York: Holt, 1979. 610p.

G5   Fernald, Lloyd Dodge, and Peter S. Fernald. Basic psychology. 4th ed. Boston: Houghton, 1979. 469p.

G6   Hilgard, Ernest R., and others. Introduction to psychology. 7th ed. New York: HBJ, 1979. 653p.

G7   Meyer, Merle E., ed. Foundations of contemporary psychology. New York: Oxford Univ. Pr., 1979. 726p.

G8   Zimbardo, Philip G., and Floyd L. Ruch. Psychology and life. 9th ed. Glenview, Ill.: Scott, Foresman, 1975. 788p.

Among recent significant works in general psychology are the following.

G9   Atkinson, Richard C., and others. Introduction to psychology. 8th ed. New York: HBJ, 1983. 701p.

G10   Bootzin, Richard, and others. Psychology today. 5th ed. New York: Random, 1983. 723p.

G11   Bourne, Lyle E., and Bruce R. Ekstrand. Psychology: its principles and meanings. 4th ed. New York: Holt, 1982. 581p.

G12   Gleitman, Henry. Psychology. New York: Norton, 1981. 745p.

G13   Kimble, Gregory A., and others. Principles of psychology. 6th ed. New York: Wiley, 1984. 661p.

G14   Krech, David, and others. Elements of psychology. 4th ed. New York: Knopf, 1982. 794p.

SYSTEMS, METHODOLOGIES, AND ISSUES

Books on the history of psychology and on systems of psychology are first cited. Statistics as a tool of research design is then considered. Psychometrics—i.e., test theory and construction—and survey methodology follows. Although called for by the classification of the American Psychological Association, discussion of methods of experimental observation and experimental design is deferred until the next major section on experimental psychology, since so often they draw their content from that field. Other more specific books on methodology are cited in other appropriate sections.

Among recent significant general works on systems, methodologies, and issues are the following.

G15   Cronbach, Lee J. Designing evaluations of educational and social programs. San Francisco: Jossey-Bass, 1982. 374p.

G16   ———. Essentials of psychological testing. 4th ed. New York: Harper, 1984. 656p.

G17   Gescheider, George A. Psychophysics: method, theory, and application. 2d ed. Hillsdale, N.J.: Erlbaum, 1984. 384p.

G18   Gottman, John M. Time-series analysis: a comprehensive introduction for social scientists. Cambridge: Cambridge Univ. Pr., 1981. 400p.

G19   Kazdin, Alan E. Single-case research designs: methods for clinical and applied settings. New York: Oxford Univ. Pr., 1982. 368p.

G20   Kidder, Louise H., ed. Selltiz, Wrightsman and Cook's Research methods in social relations. 4th ed. New York: Holt, 1981. 483p.

History of Psychology

Already mentioned as decisive in the history of psychology are the volumes by Brentano, James, and Wundt. The classic secondary account of the history of experimental psychology is that by Edwin G. Boring. It is a masterly discussion of the modern period, written more than 50 years ago and revised in 1950. It is still used as a textbook, although it needs supplementation for earlier periods and for the nonexperimental aspects of psychology.

G21   Boring, Edwin G. A history of experimental psychology. 2d ed. New York: Appleton, 1950. 777p.

In the current literature, well-written and factually correct introductory statements of the history of psychology have been prepared by Wertheimer and by Lowry. A more lengthy volume by Watson covers the history of psychology from the pre-Socratic Greeks to the beginnings of the contemporary period, and it is somewhat broader in coverage but less detailed in what it includes than the Boring. The book of readings prepared by Herrnstein and Boring presents articles and excerpts from longer works that range over some of the more salient topics in the history of psychology. Shorter, more elementary, and designed more to supplement textbooks is the book of readings edited by Watson, which contains selections and commentary on the basic works of 50 of the most important contributors to psychology.

Of the more specialized histories, two must be mentioned. The first, by Ellenberger, considers dynamic psychiatry, but in such fashion as to be directly relevant to the interests of the psychologist. The second is the volume edited by Postman, in which there is an examination in historical perspective of specialized problems in psychology, ranging from the mechanisms of hunger and thirst to the memory for form and to clinical versus statistical prediction in the field.

G22   Ellenberger, Henri F. The discovery of the unconscious: the history and evolution of dynamic psychiatry. New York: Basic Books, 1970. 932p.

G23   Herrnstein, Richard J., and Edwin G. Boring, eds. A source book in the history of psychology. Cambridge, Mass.: Harvard Univ. Pr., 1965. 636p.

G24   Lowry, Richard. The evolution of psychological theory: 1650 to the present. Chicago: Aldine-Atherton, 1971. 237p.

G25   Postman, Leo, ed. Psychology in the making: histories of selected research problems. New York: Knopf, 1962. 785p.

G26   Watson, Robert I. The great psychologists. 4th ed. New York: Harper, 1978. 645p.

G27   ———, ed. Basic writings in the history of psychology. New York: Oxford Univ. Pr., 1979. 420p.

G28   Wertheimer, Michael. A brief history of psychology. Rev. ed. New York: Holt, 1979. 168p.

Among major recent contributions to the history of psychology are the following.

G29   Kimble, Gregory A., and Kurt Schlesinger, eds. Topics in the history of psychology. 2v. Hillsdale, N.J.: Erlbaum, 1984.

G30   Leahey, Thomas H. A history of psychology: main currents in psychological thought. Englewood Cliffs, N.J.: Prentice-Hall, 1980. 431p.

G31   Lindzey, Gardner, ed. A history of psychology in autobiography, v.7. New York: Freeman, 1980. 498p. (See G545 for v.1–6.)

G32   Lowry, Richard. The evolution of psychological theory: a critical history of concepts and presuppositions. 2d ed. Hawthorne, N.Y.: Aldine, 1982. 246p.

G33   Robinson, Daniel N. An intellectual history of psychology. Rev. ed. New York: Macmillan, 1981. 484p.

G34   Schultz, Duane. A history of modern psychology. 3d ed. New York: Academic, 1981. 416p.

G35   Woodward, William R., and Mitchell G. Ash, eds. The problematic science: psychology in nineteenth-century thought. New York: Praeger, 1982. 384p.

Systems of Psychology

As exemplified by the books in general psychology already cited, and those on experimental psychology in a later section, there is some agreement among psychologists on the nature of their science. Nevertheless, there have been, and will continue to be, attempts to isolate areas within a larger framework. Systems of psychology, on the one hand, and theories such as those of personality and of learning, on the other, differ in emphasis. Systems are more extensive and may subsume narrower theories of personality and learning. For example, psychoanalysis and Gestalt psychology each include a distinctive personality theory. In contrast, theories of personality and learning make that particular contentual area central while treating other aspects of psychology as peripheral. Those books concerned with the broader systems will be examined at this juncture, leaving personality and learning theories for later discussion in the sections devoted to them.

The epoch-making books of Brentano, James, and Wundt each contributed to what later emerged as particular systems or schools of psychology—Brentano to phenomenology, James to functionalism, and Wundt to structuralism. Early in his career, Wundt's most influential American pupil, Edward Bradford Titchener, had every reason to believe that his version of his teacher's views was that of all psychology. Among the first to challenge this were the "functional psychologists," who insisted that Titchener's psychology should be called "structural" since he argued that prior study of the elements of the mind—mental anatomy as it were—was prior to and more important than the study of functional processes—their mental physiology. In the second decade of the century, structuralism disappeared as a viable point of view, while that of functionalism was absorbed into general psychology, so that the attitude it expresses is still very much present. Titchener's most representative book, originally published in 1909, and one from the functional camp by Angell, first appearing in 1904, are cited below.

G36 Angell, James R. Psychology: an introductory study of the structure and function of human consciousness. 4th ed. New York: Holt, 1908. 468p.

G37 Titchener, Edward B. A text-book of psychology. Enl. ed. New York: Macmillan, 1913. 565p.

Inclusive secondary accounts of the schools of psychology are available. Robert S. Woodworth and Mary R. Sheehan, in one of the two classic statements, have presented the various systems: behaviorism, Gestalt psychology, functionalism and various forms of psychoanalysis, and the like. In the second classic account, Edna Heidbreder, in a book published in 1933 and never revised (but still in print), presents a different view of essentially the same schools that Woodworth examined.

The book by Marx and Hillix contains consideration of the theoretical foundations for psychology—many of which deal with the systems —but includes chapters concerned with a host of other problems, which cut across theories and systems, such as field theory, varieties of S-R theory, operationism, and theoretical constructs. Chaplin and Krawiec organized their presentation around such topics as sensation, learning, and motivation as they are dealt with by the systems.

G38 Chaplin, James P., and T. S. Krawiec. Systems and theories of psychology. 4th ed. New York: Holt, 1979. 651p.

G39 Heidbreder, Edna. Seven psychologies. New York: Appleton, 1933. 450p.

G40 Marx, Melvin H., and William A. Hillix. Systems and theories in psychology. 3d ed. New York: McGraw-Hill, 1979. 513p.

G41 Woodworth, Robert S., and Mary R. Sheehan. Contemporary schools of psychology. 3d ed. New York: Ronald, 1964. 457p.

First expressed in talks and articles, the behaviorism of John B. Watson rapidly gained acceptance by many American psychologists at the expense of structuralism and functionalism during the second and third decades of this century. Watson advocated psychology conceived as a purely behavioral science, with the banishment of introspection and mentalistic thinking as relics of the past. One of his two most influential books, *Psychology from the standpoint of a behaviorist*, appeared in 1919. The views expressed in this volume changed over the years, until his authoritative, third revised edition. Nevertheless, it needs supplementation by a second statement, *Behaviorism*, written in more popular terms.

G42 Watson, John B. Psychology from the standpoint of a behaviorist. 3d rev. ed. Philadelphia: Lippincott, 1929. 458p.

G43 ———. Behaviorism. Rev. ed. Chicago: Univ. of Chicago Pr. 1930. 308p.

In 1910 Gestalt psychology came into being in Frankfurt as the result of an experiment conducted by Max Wertheimer, with Wolfgang Köhler and Kurt Koffka as subjects. These three psychologists were destined to maintain leadership in the development of this system. In the twenties and thirties they migrated to the United States, where their work became well known. The Gestalt movement was characterized by a vigorous attack on the view that would reduce mental life to elements such as sensory qualities. It espoused a phenomenological approach, recognizing that there are psychological properties of wholes that are not reducible to parts.

Wertheimer wrote no detailed, complete, and systematic statement of his views. However, Köhler and Koffka did.

G44   Koffka, Kurt. Principles of Gestalt psychology. New York: Harcourt, 1935. 720p.

G45   Köhler, Wolfgang. Gestalt psychology: an introduction to new concepts in modern psychology. Rev. ed. New York: Liveright, 1947. 369p.

Psychoanalysis is a more or less distinct field as a psychological system or theory, and many of its practitioners and theorists are allied with fields other than psychology, particularly psychiatry. Psychoanalysis grew out of Freud's work with neurotic adults, in the course of which he developed a method of diagnosis and treatment called free association; a conviction about the importance of unconscious functions, particularly sexual, as determinants of an individual's behavior; a theory of personality based upon so-called id, ego, and superego functioning; and a theory of the stages of psychosexual development.

Sigmund Freud was a productive writer for many years, living almost all of his life in Vienna. His *Collected works* have appeared in English and in German. Since a selection must be made, his *Interpretation of dreams,* first published in 1900, is a classic of the highest magnitude. If his *Introduction* and the supplement many years later, *The new introductory lectures,* are added, a reasonable preliminary coverage of his views is achieved.

G46   Freud, Sigmund. A general introduction to psycho-analysis: a course of 28 lectures delivered at the Univ. of Vienna. New York: Boni & Liveright, 1920. 406p.

G47   ———. New introductory lectures on psychoanalysis. Tr. by James Strachey. New York: Norton, 1965. 202p.

G48   ———. The interpretation of dreams. Tr. and ed. by James Strachey. New York: Basic Books, 1955. 692p.

Alfred Adler, who originally worked with Freud but broke with him on theoretical grounds, developed his own distinctive point of view; he called it individual psychology. He placed specific emphasis upon inferiority feelings, upon compensatory striving, and upon one's inherent social interest, along with general emphasis upon social factors. He published a great deal, but much of it was not systematically organized, being based on popular lectures delivered to audiences relatively unfamiliar with his work. The Ansbachers have reorganized selections from his writings and published them in two major volumes, along with annotations that are faithful to the original statements.

G49   Adler, Alfred. The individual psychology of Alfred Adler: a systematic presentation in selections from his writings. Ed. by Heinz L. Ansbacher and Rowena R. Ansbacher. New York: Basic Books, 1956. 503p.

G50   ———. Superiority and social interest: a collection of later writings. 2d rev. ed. Ed. by Heinz L. Ansbacher and Rowena R. Ansbacher. Evanston, Ill.: Northwestern Univ. Pr., 1970. 434p.

Carl Gustav Jung, another erstwhile Freudian collaborator, from Switzerland, was also prolific. His theory, referred to as analytical psychology, stressed unconscious factors, as did Freud's, but made the postulated energy of the libido nonsexual in nature. It includes a large collective component and depends heavily for evidence upon myths, legends, and cultural history, along with exploration of the mental life of disturbed individuals. Jung's complete works have now been published in a unified set of volumes. His style and topical organization, however, make it very difficult to suggest a representative selection. Probably his best systematic introduction is his *Modern man in search of a soul,* although it carries his work only to 1933. A judicious selection from his writings has been prepared by Jacobi and Hull.

G51   Jung, Carl G. Modern man in search of a soul. Tr. by W. S. Dell and C. F. Baynes. New York: Harcourt, 1933. 244p.

G52   ———. Psychological reflections: a new anthology of his writings, 1905–1961. Sel. and ed. by Jolande Jacobi and R. F. C. Hull. Princeton, N.J.: Princeton Univ. Pr., 1970. 391p. [Bollingen series, v.31]

Attention is now turned to modern modifications of these views. Neobehaviorism has often been expressed through the consideration of learning problems. Especially prominent are the publications by Guthrie, *The psychology of learning;* Hull, *A behavior system;* Skinner, *Science and human behavior* and *The behavior of organisms;* Spence, *Behavior theory and conditioning;* and Tolman, *Purposive behavior.* In varying degrees, each of these psychologists went beyond learning in carving out a system in which all problems, including learning, could be related to an overall point of view.

The thinking of Skinner attracts the most contemporary attention. The flourishing form of neobehaviorism for which he is the leader places emphasis upon operant conditioning and is represented by a division of the American Psychological Association on the "Experimental Analysis of Behavior." Almost needless to say, they are *not* the only psychologists who carry on this task. They merely give it their own particular meaning.

Thousands of individual research articles and many books have been published by others, but Skinner's books are outstanding. Skinner did not take a stand against all theory, as it is sometimes alleged. Rather, it was premature theory to which he objected. (One of his books—not cited here—had as a subtitle, "a theoretical analysis.") Nevertheless theory has only a minimal place in Skinner's approach; for example, when asked once to present his theories, he responded with an autobiographical statement of what he did in research. This is contained in his chapter in the second volume of the Koch series. Since learning was the focus of much of his earlier, more important research, two of his earlier books are to be cited in that section. An excursion into social planning through shaping behavior is given in his highly controversial *Beyond freedom and dignity.* Skinner's defense of behaviorism and his criticism of mentalism is the subject of a 1974 book, *About Behaviorism.* A collection of his papers, periodically updated, is supplied in his *Cumulative record.*

In the volume edited by Wann, Skinner and MacLeod considered behaviorism and phenomenology respectively as contrasting bases for psychology. Titles devoted to behavior modification as an applied aspect of the experimental analysis of behavior will be found in the section on clinical psychology. The volume by Kazdin cited there is particularly useful as a history of work in operant conditioning and in the experimental analysis of behavior.

G53   Skinner, B. F. Beyond freedom and dignity. New York: Knopf, 1971. 225p.

G54   ———, ed. Cumulative record: a selection of papers. 3d ed. New York: Appleton, 1972. 604p.

G55   ———. About behaviorism. New York: Knopf, 1974. 256p.

G56   Wann, T. W., ed. Behaviorism and phenomenology: contrasting bases for modern psychology. Chicago: Univ. of Chicago Pr., 1964. 190p.

Even during Freud's lifetime, changes within orthodox psychoanalysis were taking place. Emphasis on so-called ego functioning was a major development. Anna, Freud's daughter, published a major work in this area, as did Heinz Hartmann. In the same vein, David Rapaport, a psychologist, made a heroic effort to deal with psychoanalysis in a systematic way that would relate it to more general academic psychology. This is also the case in his chapter in v.3 of the series edited by Koch, *Psychology: a study of a science.* The examinations of the scientific status of psychoanalysis by Pumpian-Mindlin, by Fisher and Greenberg, and by others are valuable.

Views related to the psychoanalytic, but sufficiently distinct to warrant separate mention, have been expressed by the neo-Freudians. The neo-Freudians tend to assimilate a considerable amount of Freudian theory into a more distinctively social framework, which could have justified later mention in connection with social psychology. Three leading neo-Freudians whose books are cited are Fromm, Horney, and Sullivan. A text by Munroe considers not only the classic psychoanalytic tradition but these related neo-Freudian views. Other volumes by Fisher and Greenberg and edited by Pumpian-Mindlin are concerned with critiques of psychoanalysis.

G57   Fisher, Seymour, and Roger P. Greenberg. The scientific credibility of Freud's theories and therapy. New York: Basic Books, 1977. 502p.

G58   Freud, Anna. The ego and the mechanisms of defense. Rev. ed. New York: International Universities Pr., 1960. 191p. [Writings of Anna Freud, v.2]

G59   Fromm, Erich. Escape from freedom. New York: Holt, 1941. 305p.

G60   Hartmann, Heinz. Ego psychology and the problem of adaptation. Tr. by David Rapaport. New York: International Universities Pr., 1958. 121p.

G61   Horney, Karen. The neurotic personality of our time. New York: Norton, 1937. 299p.

G62   Munroe, Ruth L. Schools of psychoanalytic thought: an exposition, critique, and attempt at integration. New York: Holt, 1955. 670p.

G63   Pumpian-Mindlin, Eugene, ed. Psychoanalysis as science: the Hixon lectures on the scientific status of psychoanalysis. Stanford, Calif.: Stanford Univ. Pr., 1952. 174p.

G64   Rapaport, David. The structure of psychoanalytic theory: a systematizing attempt. New York: International Universities Pr., 1960. 158p. [Psychological issues, v.2, no.2. monograph no.6]

G65   Sullivan, Harry S. The interpersonal theory of psychiatry. New York: Norton, 1953. 393p.

An existential and phenomenological psychology, as amorphous as both its methodology and its boundaries may be, has been arousing considerable contemporary interest. Today it is less a school and more a point of view or method capable of being related to other systems—for example, psychoanalysis or Gestalt psychology. Its original impetus was to be found in the work of Franz Brentano, but it was his student Edmund Husserl who developed a philosophical approach called "pure phenomenology," cited here. Through the work of several European philosophers and psychiatrists, modern phenomenology and existential psychology and philosophy emerged from this beginning. A masterly account of this history in relation to both psychology and psychiatry is given by Spiegelberg. Giorgi placed a stress on psychology as a human rather than a natural science in his phenomenologically based account. The more exclusively scientific roots are stressed by MacLeod in the volume edited by Wann. Other interpretations are offered by the participants in the volume edited by Rollo May and others. Along with the phenomenological orientation, there is a strong humanistic emphasis in the books just mentioned. That is to say, the person is conceived as self-activated and self-actualized and as possessing an inherent dignity. Probably humanism's most important current representatives are Rollo May and Abraham Maslow. Although the latter was author of several books, his collection of papers perhaps reflects most adequately the systematic aspects of his particular humanistic orientation.

G66   Giorgi, Amedeo. Psychology as a human science: a phenomenologically based approach. New York: Harper, 1970. 240p.

G67   Husserl, Edmund. Ideas: general introduction to pure phenomenology. Tr. by W. R. Boyce Gibson. New York: Macmillan, 1931. 466p.

G68   Maslow, Abraham H. The farther reaches of human nature. New York: Viking, 1971. 423p.

G69   May, Rollo, and others, eds. Existence: a new dimension in psychiatry and psychology. New York: Basic Books, 1958. 445p.

G70   Spiegelberg, Herbert. Phenomenology in psychology and psychiatry: a historical introduction. Evanston, Ill.: Northwestern Univ. Pr., 1972. 411p.

Among significant recent works focused generally on systems of psychology or on particular systems are the following.

G71   Farrell, B. A. The standing of psychoanalysis. Oxford: Oxford Univ. Pr., 1981. 240p.

G72   Manaster, Guy J., and Raymond J. Corsini. Individual psychology. Itasca, Ill.: Peacock, 1982. 322p.

G73   Modgil, Suhan, and Celia Modgil, eds. Jean Piaget: consensus and controversy. New York: Praeger, 1982. 446p.

G74   Rapoport, Anatol. Mathematical models in the social and behavioral sciences. New York: Wiley, 1983. 507p.

G75   Robinson, Daniel N. Systems of modern psychology: a critical sketch. New York: Columbia Univ. Pr., 1979. 333p.

G76   Voyat, Gilbert E. Piaget systematized. Hillsdale, N.J.: Erlbaum, 1982. 214p.

G77   Wertheimer, Max. Productive thinking. Enl. ed. Chicago: University of Chicago Pr., 1982. 302p.

Statistics and Psychometrics

Statistics, a quantitative tool, is used in research design that is based on observational or experimental study. The larger problem of the experiment shades into the more specific issue of statistics used in experiments. This problem is a matter of concern in many of the books cited in the next category of experimental psychology.

In most instances, until about the beginning of the century, the use of statistics in psychology was confined to simple counting procedures. No authoritative or complete history is available. A book covering some aspects is that by Walker.

The handbook of multivariate methods edited by Raymond B. Cattell and the book by B. J. Winer are concerned with statistical manipulation and with research strategy and thus might have been mentioned in connection with experimental psychology. Set in an even broader context is the three-volume *Handbook of mathematical psychology,* edited by R. Duncan Luce and others. Not only are methodology and measurement considered, but chapters also are devoted to the application of mathematical psychology to the content areas of learning, language, audition, vision, concepts, and social interaction.

Books more specifically statistical in orientation, although in greater or lesser degree also concerned with research design, will now be considered. Although it requires some statistical background, a delightful book by Wallis and Roberts might be called statistics for the nonstatistically minded. Introductory texts in statistics are a popular publishing enterprise. Of this number, Klugh and Lindgren and others are cited. Both have a key word or phrase in the title that shows its particular strength—*essentials for research* for the first, *probability* for the second. A masterly general text, in which every word counts, was prepared by McNemar. Nevertheless, no book can cover all aspects. The more advanced texts suggest different emphases in their very titles: Cochran on *sampling,* Ferguson on *statistics* in psychology and *education,* Von Mises on *probability,* Hollander and Wolfe and Mosteller and Rourke on *nonparametric statistics,* and Torgerson on *scaling.*

G78   Cattell, Raymond B., ed. Handbook of multivariate experimental psychology. Chicago: Rand McNally, 1966. 959p.

G79   Cochran, William G. Sampling techniques. 3d ed. New York: Wiley, 1977. 428p.

G80   Ferguson, George A. Statistical analysis in psychology and education. 4th ed. New York: McGraw-Hill, 1976. 529p.

G81   Hollander, Myles, and Douglas A. Wolfe. Nonparametric statistical methods. New York: Wiley, 1973. 503p.

G82   Klugh, Henry E. Statistics: the essentials for research. 2d ed. New York: Wiley, 1974. 426p.

G83   Lindgren, B. W., and others. Introduction to probability and statistics. 4th ed. New York: Macmillan, 1978. 356p.

G84   Luce, R. Duncan, and others, eds. Handbook of mathematical psychology. New York: Wiley, 1963–65. 3v.

G85   McNemar, Quinn. Psychological statistics. 4th ed. New York: Wiley, 1969. 529p.

G86   Mosteller, Frederick, and Robert E. K. Rourke. Sturdy statistics: nonparametrics and order statistics. Reading, Mass.: Addison-Wesley, 1973. 395p.

G87   Torgerson, Warren S. Theory and methods of scaling. New York: Wiley, 1958. 460p.

G88   Von Mises, Richard. Probability, statistics and truth. 2d ed. New York: Macmillan, 1957. 244p.

G89   Walker, Helen M. Studies in the history of statistical method, with special reference to certain educational problems. Baltimore: Williams and Wilkins, 1929. 229p.

G90   Wallis, W. Allen, and Harry V. Roberts. The nature of statistics. New York: Free Pr., 1962. 218p.

G91   Winer, B. J. Statistical principles in experimental design. 2d ed. New York: McGraw-Hill, 1971. 907p.

Psychometric methods, which involve the development, validation, and application of psychological tests, are based on statistical methods but include problems of research design specific to themselves. Multivariate analysis as found in the volume edited by Cattell, above, is pertinent. Two stalwarts concerned with psychometric methods—one in its third and the other in its fourth edition—are the volumes expertly prepared by Anastasi and by Cronbach. A shorter, more introductory volume was prepared by Nunnally, while a book of readings was edited by Barnette.

G92   Anastasi, Anne. Psychological testing. 4th ed. New York: Macmillan, 1976. 750p.

G93   Barnette, Warren L., Jr., ed. Readings in psychological tests and measurements. 3d ed. New York: Oxford Univ. Pr., 1976. 415p.

G94   Cronbach, Lee. Essentials of psychological testing. 3d ed. New York: Harper, 1970. 752p.

G95   Nunnally, Jum C. Introduction to psychological measurement. 2d ed. New York: McGraw-Hill, 1970. 572p.

These books are concerned not only with the psychometric methods but also provide data about findings from tests applicable to educational, social, and clinical uses. They therefore are pertinent for several later categories. When emphasis is on use rather than method, psychometric books are also carried elsewhere, especially in the clinical section.

Among many important recent works on statistics or psychometrics are the following.

G96   Cochran, William G. Contributions to statistics. New York: Wiley, 1982. 1,835p.

G97   Downie, N. M., and Robert W. Heath. Basic statistical methods. 5th ed. New York: Harper, 1983. 371p.

G98   Ferguson, George A. Statistical analysis in psychology and education. 5th ed. New York: McGraw-Hill, 1981. 549p.

G99   Glass, Gene V, and Kenneth Hopkins. Statistical methods in education and psychology. 2d ed. Englewood Cliffs, N.J.: Prentice-Hall, 1984. 600p.

G100 Spence, Janet T., and others. Elementary statistics. 4th ed. Englewood Cliffs, N.J.: Prentice-Hall, 1983. 334p.

G101 Thorndike, Robert L. Applied psychometrics. New York: Houghton, 1982. 390p.

EXPERIMENTAL PSYCHOLOGY

The core of psychology is general experimental psychology, and the reference section of this chapter contains entries that will lead to its literature. Two will be mentioned here. The French handbook series edited by Paul Fraisse and Jean Piaget (G589) is a national counterpart to the six-volume series edited in the U.S. by Sigmund Koch, *Psychology: a study of a science* (G582), which is probably the most important single publication of recent years.

Only a year after Brentano's and Wundt's volumes (G1 and G3), psychology's first important experimental study was published by Hermann Ebbinghaus. It concerned memory and learning, with the results he found still cited as viable in the research literature.

G102 Ebbinghaus, Hermann. Memory: a contribution to experimental psychology. Tr. by H. L. Ruger. New York: Teachers College, Columbia Univ., 1913. 123p.

Textbooks in experimental psychology stress laboratory research design either with emphasis upon its content in sensation, perception, learning, psychophysics, motivation, emotion, and thinking or, more generally, upon the methods of research. Exemplification is to be found in two seminal books by Underwood. The first is less advanced, more leisurely, and more oriented toward particular content problems, while the second is advanced, terse, and oriented toward general research methodology and design. The volume by Andreas follows the more general approach first and then turns to the content areas. It is pitched at a somewhat lower level than Underwood's comparable volumes. A handbook of experimental methodology and instrumentation was prepared by Sidowski with the aid of very competent collaborators. An original and stimulating exploration of the power and complex possibilities of experimental and quasi-experimental designs for research is the theme of Campbell and Stanley. Relatively recently, an approach to experimental psychology through developing a model of information processing by identifying the cognitive stages intervening between stimuli and responses has attracted considerable attention. To relate the experimental method to this model is the task of Massaro. The influence that the experimenter's attitudes and expectancies can have upon the results obtained and how such bias is communicated and detected is the subject of the research reported by Rosenthal.

G103 Andreas, Burton G. Experimental psychology. 2d ed. New York: Wiley, 1972. 608p.

G104 Campbell, Donald T., and Julian C. Stanley. Experimental and quasi-experimental designs for research. Chicago: Rand McNally, 1966. 84p.

G105 Massaro, Dominic W. Experimental psychology and information processing. Chicago: Rand McNally, 1975. 651p.

G106 Rosenthal, Robert. Experimenter effects in behavioral research. Enl. ed. New York: Irvington, 1976. 500p.

G107 Sidowski, Joseph B., ed. Experimental methods and instrumentation in psychology. New York: McGraw-Hill, 1966. 803p.

G108 Underwood, Benton J. Experimental psychology. 2d ed. New York: Appleton, 1966. 678p.

G109 ———, and John J. Shaughnessy. Experimentation in psychology. New York: Wiley, 1975. 236p.

Among major recent general books on experimental psychology are the following.

G110 Jung, John. The experimenter's challenge: methods and issues in psychological research. New York: Macmillan, 1982. 429p.

G111 Kirk, Roger E. Experimental design: procedures for the behavioral sciences. 2d ed. Belmont, Calif.: Brooks/Cole, 1982. 911p.

G112 McGuigan, F. J. Experimental psychology. 4th ed. Englewood Cliffs, N.J.: Prentice-Hall, 1983. 381p.

G113 Plutchik, Robert. Foundations of experimental research. 3d ed. New York: Harper, 1983. 253p.

G114 Robinson, Paul W. Fundamentals of experimental psychology. 2d ed. Englewood Cliffs, N.J.: Prentice-Hall, 1981. 415p.

Learning

Learning is a major field of research in American psychology, although other fields are showing signs of assuming equal importance. On the basis of experimental evidence, many prominent psychologists have promoted a general, overall, theoretical point of view in which learning is made central, with the hope that eventually a broader system will emerge. With commendable caution, it is assumed that if one works thoroughly with the central issue of learning, the other problems in psychology—perhaps relatively neglected for the moment—will be seen in the perspective of the research findings of learning, making it possible to cope with them later. Those engaged in learning research do not deny that there are other problems in psychology; they merely insist that learning is a strategically appropriate place to begin to build the science of psychology.

Until recently, the field of learning has been dominated by somewhat older classic formulations. The major points of view are represented by Guthrie's contiguous conditioning, Hull's systematic behaviorism, Skinner's operant conditioning, Spence's modification of systematic behavior theory, and Tolman's sign-Gestalt, cognitive theory. Related to more inclusive systems, of the kind mentioned earlier, are Pavlovian conditioning and Köhler's Gestalt approach to learning. Many of these points of view are summarized by their proponents in v.2 of the handbook series edited by Koch, *Psychology: a study of a science*. Today, the Skinnerian operant conditioning approach clearly dominates the field, as attested to by the array of books mentioned in the section devoted to systematic views. A volume edited by Honig surveys operant conditioning research in 18 areas, thereby showing its considerable breadth.

G115 Guthrie, Edwin R. The psychology of learning. Rev. ed. New York: Harper, 1952. 310p.

G116 Honig, Werner K., ed. Operant behavior: areas of research and application. New York: Appleton, 1966. 865p.

G117 Hull, Clark L. A behavior system: an introduction to behavior theory concerning the individual organism. New Haven, Conn.: Yale Univ. Pr., 1952. 372p.

G118 Köhler, Wolfgang. The mentality of apes. Tr. from 2d rev. ed. by Ella Winter. New York: Harcourt, 1925. 342p.

G119 Pavlov, Ivan P. Conditioned reflexes: an investigation of the physiological activity of the cerebral cortex. Tr. and ed. by G. V. Anrep. London: Oxford Univ. Pr., 1927. 430p.

G120 Skinner, B. F. Science and human behavior. New York: Macmillan, 1953. 461p.

G121 ———. The behavior of organisms: an experimental analysis. New York: Appleton, 1938. 457p.

G122 Spence, Kenneth W. Behavior theory and conditioning. New Haven, Conn.: Yale Univ. Pr., 1956. 262p.

G123 Tolman, Edward C. Purposive behavior in animals and men. New York: Appleton, 1932. 463p.

A masterly secondary account that integrates the various approaches to learning has been prepared by Hilgard and Bower. Introductory statements have been published by Horton and Turnage and by Houston. Social learning theory, which draws heavily upon cognition, has incited much contemporary research. One of its leading protagonists, Bandura, has prepared a general introduction. Especially strong on research findings on memory are the volume written by Crowder and the volume edited by Tulving and Donaldson. Verbal learning is the topic of a book by Jung; motor learning of one edited by Bilodeau.

G124 Bandura, Albert. Social learning theory. Englewood Cliffs, N.J.: Prentice-Hall, 1977. 247p.

G125 Bilodeau, Edward A., ed. Acquisition of skill. New York: Academic, 1966. 539p.

G126 Crowder, Robert G. Principles of learning and memory. Hillsdale, N.J.: Erlbaum, 1976. 523p.

G127 Hilgard, Ernest R., and Gordon H. Bower. Theories of learning. 4th ed. Englewood Cliffs, N.J.: Prentice-Hall, 1975. 698p.

G128 Horton, David L., and Thomas W. Turnage. Human learning. Englewood Cliffs, N.J.: Prentice-Hall, 1976. 501p.

G129 Houston, John P. Fundamentals of learning. New York: Academic, 1976. 410p.

G130 Jung, John. Verbal learning. New York: Holt, 1968. 212p.

G131 Tulving, Endel, and Wayne Donaldson, eds. Organization of memory. New York: Academic, 1972. 423p.

Among significant recent books on learning and memory are the following.

G132 Bower, Gordon, and Ernest R. Hilgard. Theories of learning. 5th ed. Englewood Cliffs, N.J.: Prentice-Hall, 1981. 647p.

G133 Catania, A. Charles. Learning. 2d ed. Englewood Cliffs, N.J.: Prentice-Hall, 1984. 406p.

G134 Houston, John P. Fundamentals of learning and memory. 2d ed. New York: Academic, 1981. 639p.

G135 Schwartz, Barry. Psychology of learning and behavior. 2d ed. New York: Norton, 1983. 450p.

G136 Tarpy, Roger M. Principles of animal learning and motivation. Glenview, Ill.: Scott, Foresman, 1982. 403p.

G137 Underwood, Benton J. Studies in learning and memory: selected papers. New York: Praeger, 1982. 331p.

Sensory and Perceptual Processes

The psychological study of sensory and perceptual processes has been the work of many individuals. Its early history is best summarized by Boring in a 1942 book devoted precisely to this topic.

G138 Boring, Edwin G. Sensation and perception in the history of experimental psychology. New York: Appleton, 1942. 644p.

S. Howard Bartley's book on perception avowedly denies the classical distinction between sensation and perception, and tries to integrate them into a single, coherent pattern. If he does not fully succeed, he has still made a valuable contribution. Similarly, James Gibson presents a radical reformulation of the relationship between sensation and perception. Despite the valiant attempts of Bartley and of Gibson to reformulate sensation and perception in such fashion as to integrate them, some of the literature continues the distinction as well as relating their findings to physiology. Geldard's book *The human senses* first appeared in 1953 and was revised in 1972. Volume 1 of the series edited by Koch (G582) is directly relevant. The volume by Graham and others is more specialized in that it is devoted to vision. S. S. Stevens devoted much of his career to investigations of psychophysics in their "perceptual, neural and social relationships." It is summed up in a posthumous publication. Space perception, as arising through the primacy of a monocular factor, is a major theme of James Gibson. In more general terms, Eleanor Gibson related learning and developmental principles to perception.

A provocative, very important volume, which is hard to fit into the necessary straitjacket of categories, is *Cognitive psychology* by Neisser. The title might at first suggest thinking as the niche into which it should be placed, but in this volume Neisser is more concerned with perceptual acts. To Neisser, perception is an act of construction that leads to integration at a cognitive level, despite his inclusion of a culminating, final chapter on the thought processes. As can be recognized, it is also significant for the study of thinking.

Several volumes listed later under the category of physiological psychology and devoted to sen-sory processes are relevant. An authoritative, excellent introduction to the field of perception is supplied by Hochberg.

G139 Bartley, S. Howard. Principles of perception. 2d ed. New York: Harper, 1969. 518p.

G140 Geldard, Frank A. The human senses. 2d ed. New York: Wiley, 1972. 584p.

G141 Gibson, Eleanor J. Principles of perceptual learning and development. New York: Appleton, 1969. 537p.

G142 Gibson, James J. The perception of the visual world. Boston: Houghton, 1950. 235p.

G143 ———. The senses considered as perceptual systems. Boston: Houghton, 1966. 335p.

G144 Graham, Clarence H., ed. Vision and visual perception. New York: Wiley, 1965. 637p.

G145 Hochberg, Julian E. Perception. 2d ed. Englewood Cliffs, N.J.: Prentice-Hall, 1978. 280p.

G146 Neisser, Ulric. Cognitive psychology. Englewood Cliffs, N.J.: Prentice-Hall, 1967. 351p.

G147 Stevens, S. S. Psychophysics: introduction to its perceptual, neural and social prospects. New York: Wiley, 1975. 329p.

Among important recent works on sensory and perceptual processes are the following.

G148 Engen, Trygg. The perception of odors. New York: Academic, 1982. 202p.

G149 Hensel, Herbert. Thermal sensations and thermoreceptors in man. Springfield, Ill.: Thomas, 1982. 187p.

G150 Kubovy, Michael, and James R. Pomerantz, eds. Perceptual organization. Hillsdale, N.J.: Erlbaum, 1981. 506p.

G151 Mollon, J. D., and L. T. Sharpe, eds. Colour vision: physiology and psychophysics. New York: Academic, 1983. 613p.

G152 Rock, Irvin. The logic of perception. Cambridge, Mass.: MIT Pr., 1983. 365p.

G153 Uttal, William. A taxonomy of visual processes. Hillsdale, N.J.: Erlbaum, 1981. 1,097p.

G154 Wyszecki, Gunter, and W. S. Stiles. Color science: concepts and methods, quantitative data and formulae. 2d ed. New York: Wiley, 1982. 950p.

Motivation and Emotion

Motivation and emotion had an intertwined history in the nineteenth century through the work of Darwin on instinct and the expression of emotion. William James also contributed through attention to instinct and to will (G2). In the twentieth century, Cannon carried out research on emotion, in part stimulated by the work of James, and McDougall continued the emphasis on instincts.

G155 Cannon, Walter B. Bodily changes in pain, hunger, fear, and rage: an account of recent researches in the function of emotional excitement. 2d ed. Boston: Branford, 1953. 404p.

G156 Darwin, Charles R. The expression of the emotions in man and animals. Chicago: Univ. of Chicago Pr., 1965. 372p.

While not denying its biological-physiological base, contemporary interest in motivation and emotion has concentrated on deepening research and theory concerning their more psychological aspects. As expressed in the titles that follow these comments, some consider motivation, others emotion, but none of the writers fails to refer to the less dominant topic. Those who wish to show equal concern refer in their titles to both aspects. The major contribution of the book by Buck is systematically to draw motivation and emotion more closely together. Despite its appearance in 1964, still unexcelled in breadth of coverage is the volume on motivation prepared by Cofer and Appley. A wide range of major research figures in the study of emotion is sampled in the book of readings edited by Levine. The same function for motivation is provided by the book edited by Russell.

G157 Buck, Ross. Human motivation and emotion. New York: Wiley, 1976. 529p.

G158 Cofer, Charles N., and Mortimer H. Appley. Motivation: theory and research. New York: Wiley, 1964. 958p.

G159 Levine, Frederic M., ed. Theoretical readings in motivation: perspectives on human behavior. Chicago: Rand McNally, 1975. 480p.

G160 Russell, Wallace A., ed. Milestones in motivation: contributions to the psychology of drive and purpose. New York: Appleton, 1970. 572p.

Three books on motivation are more specialized in character. As the title implies, Jung provides an account of motivation that places it in the setting of a selective and experiencing person. Intrinsic motivation, which includes needs pertaining to competence and self-determination, has been presented in a pioneer volume by Deci. David McClelland and John W. Atkinson both have several books, separately and in collaboration, concerning the relation of motivation and achievement. While it has been difficult to select, the one chosen for inclusion,

edited by Atkinson and Raynor, has the advantage of implicitly and explicitly depending on earlier volumes and bringing out clearly how the study of achievement can lead to the study of other motives.

G161 Atkinson, John W., and J. O. Raynor, eds. Motivation and achievement. Washington, D.C.: Winston, 1974. 479p.

G162 Deci, Edward L. Intrinsic motivation. New York: Plenum, 1975. 324p.

G163 Jung, John. Understanding human motivation: a cognitive approach. New York: Macmillan, 1978. 518p.

Among recent significant works in motivation and emotion are the following.

G164 Fagen, Robert. Animal play behavior. New York: Oxford Univ. Pr., 1981. 684p.

G165 Field, Tiffany, and Alan Fogel, eds. Emotion and early interaction. Hillsdale, N.J.: Erlbaum, 1982. 299p.

G166 Lefcourt, Herbert M. Locus of control: current trends in theory and research. 2d ed. Hillsdale, N.J.: Erlbaum, 1982. 254p.

G167 McClelland, David C. Human motivation. Glenview, Ill.: Scott, Foresman, 1984. 608p.

G168 Rushton, J. Phillippe, and Richard M. Sorrentino, eds. Altruism and helping behavior: social, personality and developmental perspectives. Hillsdale, N.J.: Erlbaum, 1981. 456p.

G169 Wallach, Michael A., and Lise Wallach. Psychology's sanction for selfishness. San Francisco: Freeman, 1983. 307p.

Thinking Processes

The study of the thought processes has passed through three broad stages. The earlier or classic period is ably summarized in the historical account by Humphrey. Thereafter there was the modern study of thinking that has continuity with the earlier work and relates most directly with the rest of experimental psychology. It is still very much with us. Lastly, there is the "new look" in cognition which has overwhelmed some workers in the field. There is also a strong contemporary interest in the relation of computers to thinking.

G170 Humphrey, George. Thinking: an introduction to its experimental psychology. New York: Wiley, 1951. 331p.

D. E. Berlyne has given us an important account of a stimulus-response interpretation of thinking in the empirico-behavioristic tradition. A relatively broad description of the psychology of thinking is contained in the text by Vinacke. Jean Piaget has been developing his position concerning thinking through many books over many years. The one that proved to be most productive of validation studies of his ideas about thinking and reasoning was *The child's conception of physical causality*. It was followed by nearly 30 other books. In these later books he related thinking to problems of epistemology.

G171 Berlyne, D. E. Structure and direction in thinking. New York: Wiley, 1965. 378p.

G172 Piaget, Jean. The child's conception of physical causality. New York: Harcourt, 1930. 309p.

G173 Vinacke, William Edgar. The psychology of thinking. 2d ed. New York: McGraw-Hill, 1974. 616p.

Sharply differing views about the new look in cognition are extant. A 1958 publication, *Perception and communication,* by Broadbent helped to change the course of the cognitive revolution by presenting a model of human information processing. In the cited 1971 publication, he follows this with a blend of experiment and theory concerning cognition placed in a historical context. Another claimant for a different view, or views, is Neisser, already cited above (G146) in another work as well. Too complex for capsule summarization, these books make lively and impassioned reading and thus reflect the state of the inquiry into this aspect of the field itself.

Newell and Simon suggested nearly 20 years ago that a computer program could serve as a description of the thought processes, and recently they have given a sober, careful statement of how computer programming may be and is related to the experimental study of cognition. Although his scathing criticisms are not directed against Newell and Simon, a polemic against most of the research using computers for the study of thinking was prepared by Weizenbaum.

G174 Broadbent, Donald E. Decision and stress. New York: Academic, 1971. 522p.

G175 Neisser, Ulric. Cognition and reality: principles and implications of cognitive psychology. San Francisco: Freeman, 1976. 230p.

G176 Newell, Allen, and Herbert A. Simon. Human problem solving. Englewood Cliffs, N.J.: Prentice-Hall, 1972. 920p.

G177 Weizenbaum, Joseph. Computer power and human reason: from judgment to calculation. San Francisco: Freeman, 1976. 300p.

Among recent contributions to the psychology of thinking processes, or of cognition, are the following.

G178 Cohen, Gillian. The psychology of cognition. 2d ed. New York: Academic, 1983. 277p.

G179 Luria, Alexander R. Language and cognition. [Ed. by James V. Wertsch.] New York: Wiley, 1981. 271p.

G180 Neisser, Ulric, ed. Memory observed: remembering in natural contexts. San Francisco: Freeman, 1982. 433p.

G181 Shepard, Roger N., and Lynn A. Cooper. Mental images and their transformations. Cambridge, Mass.: MIT Pr., 1982. 364p.

G182 Simon, Herbert A. Models of thought. New Haven, Conn.: Yale Univ. Pr., 1979. 524p.

G183 Tulving, Endel. Elements of episodic memory. New York: Oxford Univ. Pr., 1983. 351p.

G184 Wexler, Kenneth, and Peter Culicover. Formal principles of language acquisition. Cambridge, Mass.: MIT Pr. 1980. 647p.

PHYSIOLOGICAL PSYCHOLOGY

Physiological psychology is a field in which there are several classic volumes prepared by nineteenth and early twentieth century physiologists and neurologists. Head's work on aphasia must be cited. So, too, must Helmholtz's classic research, on both audition and vision. Sherrington's early work on the integrative activity of the nervous system is also noteworthy. Somewhat later, the psychologist Lashley studied the relation of brain mechanisms to efficiency of psychological function. A modern classic, Geldard's volume on the senses (G140), contains much material relevant to physiological psychology.

G185 Head, Henry. Aphasia and kindred disorders of speech. New York: Hafner, 1963. 2v.

G186 Helmholtz, Hermann L. F. von. On the sensations of tone as a physiological basis for the theory of music. Tr. from 4th German ed. by A. J. Ellis. 3d ed. New York: Longmans, Green, 1895. 576p.

G187 ———. Treatise on physiological optics. Tr. from 3d German ed.; ed. by James P. Southall. Rochester, N.Y.: Optical Society of America, 1924–25. 3v.

G188 Lashley, Karl S. Brain mechanisms and intelligence: a quantitative study of injuries to the brain. Chicago: Univ. of Chicago Pr., 1929. 186p.

G189 Sherrington, Charles S. The integrative action of the nervous system. New Haven, Conn.: Yale Univ. Pr., 1906. 411p.

There is a wealth of good textbooks on physiological psychology. Length and the audience they address help to distinguish among them. The book by Isaacson, pertinently called a "primer," is the shortest and might be called an introduction to an introduction. Introductions at the next level were prepared by Leukel and by Schneider and Tarshis. Despite respectively using in their titles, "Essentials" and "Introduction," Grossman and Thompson both are pitched at still more advanced levels and give the most thorough coverage. They also happen to be very readable. Thompson also has edited an excellent book of readings of articles drawn from the pages of *Scientific American,* using, however, *psychobiology* as the operative term.

G190 Grossman, Sebastian P. Essentials of physiological psychology. New York: Wiley, 1973. 506p.

G191 Isaacson, Robert, and others. A primer of physiological psychology. New York: Harper, 1971. 295p.

G192 Leukel, Francis. Introduction to physiological psychology. 3d ed. St. Louis: Mosby, 1976. 514p.

G193 Schneider, Allen M., and Barry Tarshis. An introduction to physiological psychology. 2d ed. New York: Random, 1980. 528p.

G194 Thompson, Richard F. Introduction to physiological psychology. New York: Harper, 1975. 669p.

G195 ———, ed. Progress in psychobiology: readings from Scientific American. San Francisco: Freeman, 1976. 392p.

Reference in the title to Thompson's book of readings to "psychobiology" epitomizes an attempt to place physiological psychology in a perspective that includes evolution, genetics and communication. Many of these themes are explored in the volume edited by Gazzaniga and Blakemore.

There is a whole host of exciting, provocative books that may fall under this somewhat elusive and, as yet, not completely defined rubric. With the intent of broadening the scope of the field, Robinson considers its history and its underlying philosophical issues, while not neglecting its major research problems. Another unusual volume

at a more advanced level was written by Uttal. He organized the tremendously complex strands of the mind-body problem, has called attention to many of the relevant issues, and has related them to the evidence from physiology and psychology. Of course, neither he nor Robinson solved the mind-body problem. No one has. They do help by giving further approximations.

Jaynes boldly marshals many kinds of evidence to show that consciousness as we experience it emerged only when, in the course of evolution, the brain became less bicameral. Jerison, focusing on the problem of intelligence as related to brain and body weight, considers the brain's evolution in various species and emerges with a power law in the form of an encephalization quotient. Penfield, who had studied more than a thousand exposed, unanesthetized human brains and their verbal reports, arrived at the conclusion that the center for consciousness lies below the cerebral cortex where received opinion has placed it.

G196 Gazzaniga, Michael S., and Colin Blakemore, eds. Handbook of psychobiology. New York: Academic, 1975. 639p.

G197 Jaynes, Julian. The origin of consciousness in the breakdown of the bicameral mind. Boston: Houghton, 1977. 467p.

G198 Jerison, Harry J. Evolution of the brain and intelligence. New York: Academic, 1973. 482p.

G199 Penfield, Wilder, and others. The mystery of the mind: a critical study of consciousness and the human brain. Princeton, N.J.: Princeton Univ. Pr., 1975. 123p.

G200 Robinson, Daniel N. The enlightened machine: an analytical introduction to neuropsychology. Rev. ed. New York: Columbia Univ. Pr., 1980. 158p.

G201 Uttal, William R. The psychobiology of mind. Hillsdale, N.J.: Erlbaum, 1978. 785p.

Recent important works on physiological psychology include the following.

G202 Groves, Philip M., and Kurt Schlesinger. Introduction to biological psychology. 2d ed. Dubuque, Iowa: Brown, 1982. 737p.

G203 Hebb, D. O. Essay on mind. Hillsdale, N.J.: Erlbaum, 1980. 159p.

G204 Macphail, Euan M. Brain and intelligence in vertebrates. Oxford: Clarendon, 1982. 423p.

G205 Orbach, Jack, ed. Neuropsychology after Lashley. Hillsdale, N.J.: Erlbaum, 1982. 541p.

G206 Rosenzweig, Mark R., and Arnold L. Leiman.

Physiological psychology. Lexington, Mass.: Heath, 1982. 675p.

DEVELOPMENTAL PSYCHOLOGY

The term *developmental psychology* is used, rather than *child psychology,* because developmental psychology considers the entire life span, despite the preponderance of books devoted to younger ages. Developmental psychology, in its early history, originated in the area of child study. A collection of historical readings edited and with perspectives by Dennis provides an account of the earlier work and theory.

G207 Dennis, Wayne, ed. Historical readings in developmental psychology. New York: Appleton, 1972. 355p.

The four introductory texts cited here all have stood the test of repeated revision, since all are now in their fourth or fifth edition. Those by Hurlock, Jenkins and Shacter, and Watson and Lindgren are somewhat more elementary; those by Mussen and his collaborators are more advanced. The shorter version of the text by Mussen is sufficiently abbreviated to have made possible the addition of three chapters on adulthood.

A thorough reworking of Carmichael's classic *Handbook of child psychology* under the editorship of Mussen (G586) is the standard handbook source. A similar handbook on research methodology was also edited by Mussen.

More specialized books focus on segments of the life span. A carefully selected array of studies of infancy and early childhood is provided in the volume edited by Brackbill and Thompson. The first volume of a series edited by Hoffman and Hoffman contains several outstanding reviews of research in various areas of child development, e.g., the effects of infant care by Caldwell. The middle range of childhood is covered very adequately by the general texts mentioned earlier. A book of readings confined to the middle years, edited by Neugarten, is also available. Adolescence is the subject of the book by Garrison and Garrison. The psychology of aging (not just the psychology of the aged) is provided at the level of introductory texts in two excellent books. One is by Birren, the other by Botwinick.

G208 Birren, James E. The psychology of aging. Englewood Cliffs, N.J.: Prentice-Hall, 1964. 303p.

G209 Botwinick, Jack. Aging and behavior: a comprehensive integration of research findings. 2d ed. New York: Springer, 1978. 404p.

G210 Brackbill, Yvonne, and George G. Thompson, eds. Behavior in infancy and early childhood: a book of readings. New York: Free Pr., 1967. 692p.

G211 Garrison, Karl C., and Karl C. Garrison, Jr. Psychology of adolescence. 7th ed. Englewood Cliffs, N.J.: Prentice-Hall, 1975. 484p.

G212 Hoffman, Martin L., and Lois W. Hoffman, eds. Review of child development research. v.1. New York: Russell Sage, 1964. 547p. (6v. to date)

G213 Hurlock, Elizabeth B. Developmental psychology. 4th ed. New York: McGraw-Hill, 1975. 359p.

G214 Jenkins, Gladys G., and Helen S. Shacter. These are your children. 4th ed. Glenview, Ill.: Scott, Foresman, 1975. 366p.

G215 Mussen, Paul, and others. Child development and personality. 5th ed. New York: Harper, 1979. 579p.

G216 ———. Psychological development: a life-span approach. New York: Harper, 1979. 502p.

G217 Neugarten, Bernice L., ed. Middle age and aging: a reader in social psychology. Chicago: Univ. of Chicago Pr., 1968. 596p.

G218 Watson, Robert I., and Henry C. Lindgren. Psychology of the child and the adolescent. 4th ed. New York: Macmillan, 1979. 624p.

Some of the leading theoreticians and researchers on development have provided original accounts. The psychoanalytic neo-Freudian, the behavioral, the Gestalt, and the Piagetian points of view are represented in the titles now to be cited. The neo-Freudian tradition emphasizing social factors is dominated by the work of Erik H. Erikson, who presents a conceptualization of the stages of life from infancy to adulthood. The verbal learning theory as related to behavioral theory of Bandura represents another important theoretical position (G124). Heinz Werner was at least partially influenced by the Gestalt tradition in his theoretical approach to development. Lewin is also related to this tradition. His book, listed later, contains papers directed to his conceptualization of child development. There are also the freewheeling insights of Piaget, who casually tossed off provocative generalizations about childhood, supported by scraps of evidence from an unspecified but surely very small sample of children. Only two of his books are cited here—one has been mentioned earlier. It is not surprising that his work has brought forth several interpretive accounts. The one chosen for citation is the pioneer volume by Flavell. A book of readings, many by Piaget or Inhelder themselves, presents Genevan psychology and epistemology in a broad, well-selected sample of the topics that have occupied their efforts.

G219 Erikson, Erik H. Childhood and society. 2d ed. New York: Norton, 1963. 445p.

G220 Flavell, John H. The developmental psychology of Jean Piaget. Princeton, N.J.: Van Nostrand Reinhold, 1963. 472p.

G221 Inhelder, Bärbel, and Harold H. Chipman, eds. Piaget and his school: a reader in developmental psychology. New York: Springer-Verlag, 1976. 301p.

G222 Piaget, Jean. Judgment and reasoning in the child. Tr. by Marjorie Warden. New York: Humanities, 1962. 260p. (Reprint of 1928 ed.)

G223 ———. The language and thought of the child. Tr. by Marjorie Gabain. 3d enl. ed. New York: Humanities, 1959. 288p.

G224 Werner, Heinz. Comparative psychology of mental development. New York: Wiley, 1948. 564p.

There has been an explosion of publications in developmental psychology in recent years. Among major works are the following.

G225 Ambron, Sueann Robinson. Child development. 3d ed. New York: Holt, 1981. 558p.

G226 Baldwin, Alfred L. Theories of child development. 2d ed. New York: Wiley, 1980. 582p.

G227 Birren, James E., and others. Developmental psychology: a life-span approach. Boston: Houghton, 1981. 696p.

G228 Craig, Grace. Human development. 3d ed. Englewood Cliffs, N.J.: Prentice-Hall, 1983. 587p.

G229 Eichorn, Dorothy H., and others, eds. Present and past in middle life. New York: Academic, 1981. 500p.

G230 Gollin, Eugene, ed. Developmental plasticity: behavioral and biological aspects of variations in development. New York: Academic, 1981. 282p.

G231 Stone, L. Joseph, and Joseph Church. Childhood and adolescence. 5th ed. New York: Random, 1983. 640p.

PERSONALITY

When advancing a personality theory, a psychologist or psychiatrist most often attempts to account for the uniqueness of the individual, both in the relationship of one's broad patterns of behavior to one's experiences as well as one's commonality with and differences from other persons. Other psychological topics—for example, the aspects of general psychology—are minimized, if dealt with at all. This serves to distinguish a personality theory from a psychological system or school, which, by definition, must come to grips with these other aspects of psychology. The cruciality and prominence of personality concerns for the psychodynamic systems of Freud, Jung, Adler and their followers sometimes results in confusion on this point. That their views on personality must be taken into account is inescapable, as is the fact that they are the centers of differing schools of psychology.

While there were even earlier conceptualizations of personality by psychologists, a major pioneer account of personality by a psychologist was provided by Allport in a volume appearing in 1937. It was the first major modern attempt to bring integration to this elusive and amorphous field. Just a year later, the results of the cooperative research project supervised by Henry A. Murray, whose theoretical basis drew upon many sources, with earlier psychodynamic theories very prominent, was published. In 1950 Dollard and Miller related personality and psychotherapy, drawing primarily upon Pavlov's and Hull's approaches to learning and Freud's psychoanalytic theory. It presaged the emphasis that later psychologists were to place upon systematically relating general psychology to psychoanalysis.

G232 Allport, Gordon W. Personality: a psychological interpretation. New York: Holt, 1937. 588p.

G233 Dollard, John, and Neal E. Miller. Personality and psychotherapy: an analysis in terms of learning, thinking, and culture. New York: McGraw-Hill, 1950. 488p.

G234 Murray, Henry A., and others. Explorations in personality: a clinical and experimental study of fifty men of college age. New York: Wiley, 1938. 761p.

In a major secondary source, Hall and Lindzey bring together an account of the Freudian, neo-Freudian, Adlerian, and Jungian systems, as well as many of the theories to be considered later. A related book of primary theoretical and research source readings by the same editors has also been published. Volume 3 in the Koch-edited series, *Psychology: a study of a science* (G582) contains a somewhat disconnected array of worthwhile articles most directly related to personality, but peripherally related to social psychology. McClelland has written an eclectic book, using the device of relating each theoretical construct to the personality of one individual, whose experiences are the thread of coherence in his presentation. The stalwart of eclectic texts, now in its fourth edition, is that of Stagner. It is so organized that the various theories of personality are drawn upon for their contribution to the themes of development, description, dynamics, and determinants of personality. Recently, Sarason and Pervin have prepared textbooks with relatively more stress on related research findings than has been customary in the past. A textbook by Ryckman is shorter than most of the others, yet covers an adequate number of theories while still taking due account of relevant research findings. Maddi, as his subtitle implies, makes a comparative analysis of personality theories. While meant to be an introduction to personality theories, Mischel's text stresses social learning theory.

G235 Hall, Calvin S., and Gardner Lindzey. Theories of personality. 3d ed. New York: Wiley, 1978. 725p.

G236 Lindzey, Gardner, and Calvin S. Hall, eds. Theories of personality: primary sources and research. 2d ed. New York: Wiley, 1973. 486p.

G237 McClelland, David C. Personality. New York: Holt, 1951. 654p.

G238 Maddi, Salvatore R. Personality theories: a comparative analysis. 4th ed. Homewood, Ill.: Dorsey, 1980. 772p.

G239 Mischel, Walter. Introduction to personality. 2d ed. New York: Holt, 1976. 574p.

G240 Pervin, Lawrence A., and Hannah Levenson. Personality: theory, assessment, and research. 2d ed. New York: Wiley, 1975. 559p.

G241 Ryckman, Richard M. Theories of personality. New York: Van Nostrand Reinhold, 1978. 442p.

G242 Sarason, Irwin G. Personality: an objective approach. 2d ed. New York: Wiley, 1972. 601p.

G243 Stagner, Ross. Psychology of personality. 4th ed. New York: McGraw-Hill, 1974. 658p.

Certain theories of personality are sufficiently influential to be represented by primary sources by the theorists themselves. Going beyond his pioneer volume, Allport has worked out a theory of the development and organization of the personality that is of relatively wide scope. While doing so, he encompassed much eclectic material by making the concept of "trait" basic. The personal view of the world and the anticipations of what will happen on the basis of this view result in the "personal construct theory," developed by George Kelly. The recently revised classic study

of anxiety by May in a phenomenological setting pleads persuasively and eloquently for its all-pervasive character, although other facets of the personality are acknowledged. A collection of papers by Lewin give something of his view that any person is best studied in relation to the environmental field in which that person is to be found.

Raymond B. Cattell and Hans Eysenck, while critical of one another's work, are similar in that their goal is the construction of personality trait organization primarily through use of factor analytic procedures. They are also similar in that they are two of the most productive of contemporary psychologists. They are so intent in pursuing whatever facet of personality interests them at the moment that summaries of their work in a form desirable for inclusion in this account are difficult to come by. Fortunately, at least a partial contemporary summary of Cattell is available in the book by Cattell and Kline. We are not so fortunate in the case of Eysenck. Two of his books, both more than 20 years old, are more representative up to that point than would be his many more specific studies published since then.

G244 Allport, Gordon W. Pattern and growth in personality. New York: Holt, 1961. 593p.

G245 Cattell, Raymond B., and P. Kline. The scientific analysis of personality and motivation. New York: Academic, 1977. 385p.

G246 Eysenck, Hans J. The scientific study of personality. London: Routledge & Paul, 1952. 320p.

G247 ———. The structure of human personality. New York: Wiley, 1960. 448p.

G248 Kelly, George A. The psychology of personal constructs. New York: Norton, 1955. 2v.

G249 Lewin, Kurt. A dynamic theory of personality: selected papers. Tr. by D. K. Adams and K. E. Zener. New York: McGraw-Hill, 1935. 286p.

G250 May, Rollo. The meaning of anxiety. Rev. ed. New York: Norton, 1977. 425p.

Recently there has been a revival of interest in the subjective aspect of the personality, the self. An introductory volume is provided by Ziller. Wylie has thoroughly reviewed the methodology, theory, and research concerning the self-concept. The book of readings edited by Gordon and Gergen is an interdisciplinary blend that reflects their disciplinary identification as a sociologist and a psychologist.

G251 Gordon, Chad, and Kenneth J. Gergen, eds. The self in social interaction. (v.1. Classic and contemporary perspectives) New York: Wiley, 1968. 473p.

G252 Wylie, Ruth. The self-concept. Rev. ed. Lincoln: Univ. of Nebraska Pr., 1974–79. 2v.

G253 Ziller, Robert C. The social self. New York: Pergamon, 1973. 205p.

Intelligence is considered to be a specialized aspect of personality psychology. Three contrasting views of the nature of intelligence are described and defended respectively by Bindra, Guilford, and Hunt.

G254 Bindra, Dalbir. A theory of intelligent behavior. New York: Wiley-Interscience, 1976. 447p.

G255 Guilford, Joy P. The nature of human intelligence. New York: McGraw-Hill, 1967. 538p.

G256 Hunt, Joseph McVicker. Intelligence and experience. New York: Ronald, 1961. 416p.

A vehemently expressed, bitter, and well-publicized controversy rages about the validity of the intelligence quotient. The picture is thoroughly confused—much heat, very little light, many *ad hominem* arguments, all utterly impossible to summarize briefly. In order to simplify (really to oversimplify), a few among the many individuals conspicuous in this controversy will be lined up as for or against a heavy influence of heredity and the related validity of the I.Q.— Herrnstein (for), Jensen (for), Kamin (against), and Block and Dworkin in a book of readings (both for and against).

At the present time, the question of sex differences in intelligence, interests, and the entire gamut of personality characteristics is also very much a matter of intense and acrimonious debate. Maccoby and Jacklin carefully and systematically analyze the results of about 1,600 studies in terms of the presence or absence of sex differences. No volume in this field would be acceptable to all informed individuals. This is probably the most unbiased account available.

G257 Block, N. J., and Gerald Dworkin, eds. The IQ controversy: critical readings. New York: Pantheon, 1976. 557p.

G258 Herrnstein, Richard J. I.Q. in the meritocracy. Boston: Little, 1973. 235p.

G259 Jensen, Arthur R. Genetics and education. New York: Harper, 1972. 379p.

G260 Kamin, Leon J. The science and politics of IQ. Hillsdale, N.J.: Erlbaum, 1974. 183p.

G261 Maccoby, Eleanor E., and Carol N. Jacklin. The psychology of sex differences. Stanford, Calif.: Stanford Univ. Pr., 1974. 634p.

The books on testing by Cronbach (G94), Anastasi (G92), and Nunnally (G95) are also an aspect of the concern for personality. Books on mental retardation are also relevant here, but are cited in connection with clinical psychology. It has been customary to consider role theory an important point of articulation between psychology and sociology. Thus the earlier chapter on sociology should be consulted, particularly the works by Mead (*Mind, self and society*) and Merton (*Social structure and social theory*).

Among the many recent publications in the field of personality are the following.

G262 Anastasi, Anne. Psychological testing. 5th ed. New York: Macmillan, 1982. 784p.

G263 Byrne, Donn, and Kathryn Kelley. An introduction to personality. 3d ed. Englewood Cliffs, N.J.: Prentice-Hall, 1981. 591p.

G264 Liebert, Robert M., and Michael D. Spiegler. Personality: strategies and issues. 4th ed. Homewood, Ill.: Dorsey, 1982. 594p.

G265 Mischel, Walter. Introduction to personality. 3d ed. New York: Holt, 1981. 623p.

G266 Pervin, Lawrence A. Personality. 4th ed. New York: Wiley, 1984. 569p.

G267 White, Kathleen, and Joseph C. Spiesman. Research approaches to personality. Monterey, Calif.: Brooks/Cole, 1982. 261p.

SOCIAL PSYCHOLOGY

Social psychology is a branch not only of psychology but also of sociology: thus the appropriate section in that chapter also should be consulted.

A classic volume, which first appeared in 1908, is William McDougall's *An introduction to social psychology*. Although the instinct doctrine on which it is based has been superseded by other approaches to motivation, it had a pronounced influence upon American psychology, but to an even greater degree influenced British thinking on these matters. As if to emphasize the close relation between psychology and sociology, in the same year a second volume appeared written by a sociologist, Ross, who devoted his chapters to suggestibility, the crowd, imitation, conflict and compromise, and public opinion. His emphasis upon social influence proved to be rather more in keeping with current interest than did McDougall's emphasis upon drive.

G268 McDougall, William. An introduction to social psychology. Kennebunkport, Maine: Milford House, 1973. 524p.

G269 Ross, Edward A. Social psychology: an outline and source book. New York: Macmillan, 1908. 372p.

Textbooks in social psychology still reflect the diversity of approaches presaged by the McDougall and Ross volumes. Elementary textbooks can be expected to cover many topics in common and in not too unreasonable a manner, but also to stress one or more of these in the process. Consequently, they will be presented in terms of their emphases.

The older textbooks tend to be both longer and more eclectic. Two of them were prepared by Jones and Gerard, and by Krech. The former is strong in its skillful integration of the research literature; the latter in its adroit demonstration of the extension of principles of individual psychology into the social area. The Sherifs present another eclectic textbook, in which they carefully state their basic principles and then deal with social interaction, attitudes, and social change.

In their textbook, Harvey and Smith use an attributional approach; that is, they concentrate on how the individual attempts to understand and explain the relationships among events. In contrast, Carolyn Sherif's orientation tips in the direction of the sociological side of the McDougall-Ross dichotomy. She gives a heavy weight to reference groups. The orientation of Severy and his associates centers upon current social issues, racism, sexism, brainwashing, and politics, to mention some topics. A relatively well balanced reader is provided by Wrightsman and Brigham. A detailed and balanced analysis of research methodology in social psychology is very ably presented by McClintock.

The definitive *Handbook of social psychology* (G632) was edited by Gardner Lindzey and Elliot Aronson. Prepared by a large number of specialists, it covers the major aspects of social psychology under the headings of systematic positions, research methods, the individual in a social context, group psychology, the phenomena of interaction, and applied social psychology.

G270 Harvey, John H., and William P. Smith. Social psychology: an attributional approach. St. Louis: Mosby, 1977. 426p.

G271 Jones, Edward E., and Harold B. Gerard. Foundations of social psychology. New York: Wiley, 1967. 743p.

G272 Krech, David, and others. The individual in society: a textbook of social psychology. New York: McGraw-Hill, 1962. 564p.

G273 McClintock, Charles G., ed. Experimental social psychology. New York: Holt, 1972. 585p.

G274 Severy, Lawrence J., and others. A contemporary introduction to social psychology. New York: McGraw-Hill, 1976. 462p.

G275 Sherif, Carolyn W. Orientation in social psychology. New York: Harper, 1976. 441p.

G276 Sherif, Muzafer, and Carolyn W. Sherif. Social psychology. New York: Harper, 1969. 616p.

G277 Wrightsman, Lawrence S., and John C. Brigham, eds. Contemporary issues in social psychology. 3d ed. Monterey, Calif.: Brooks/Cole, 1977. 367p.

Discussed next are volumes that bring out some of the prominent theoretical strains in some of the specialized areas of research in social psychology. Devoted to the problem of group dynamics, the collection of readings edited by Cartwright and Zander is broad in scope and even suitable as a text. Another prominent research and theoretical problem is attitude study, which has been presented by Kiesler. Although somewhat dated, the volume edited by Daniel Katz on public opinion and propaganda is still very useful. At a relatively high level of difficulty, Tedeschi and Lindskold stress social influence theory.

G278 Cartwright, Dorwin, and Alvin Zander, eds. Group dynamics: research and theory. 3d ed. New York: Harper, 1968. 580p.

G279 Katz, Daniel, ed. Public opinion and propaganda: a book of readings. New York: Dryden, 1954. 779p.

G280 Kiesler, Charles, and others. Attitude change: a critical analysis of theoretical approaches. New York: Wiley, 1969. 386p.

G281 Tedeschi, James T., and Svenn Lindskold. Social psychology: interdependence, interaction, and influence. New York: Wiley, 1976. 705p.

The schools and systems have representative views of social psychology. Reinforcement theory, already examined in connection with learning, has very able representatives in social psychology. Miller and Dollard explain acquisition of social drives in terms of this theory. Bandura and Walters stress the influence of imitation on the study of the role of reinforcement learning. Skinner's *Verbal behavior* is an extrapolation of his general position to this social-psychological problem through his analyses of verbal behavior.

Gestalt psychology has been a major theoretical influence. Generally speaking, social perception is conceived as directed toward a state of order or simplicity. A representative volume in this tradition has been prepared by Asch in the setting of a general text. "Field theory" is closely related to, and a historical extension of, Gestalt psychology, and here Lewin, with his *Dynamic theory of personality* (G249) and his emphasis on motivation, is most prominent. The views of Festinger, expressed in the volume devoted to the influence of cognitive dissonance (which occurs when discrepant views are held simultaneously), are related to field theory, although they also reflect other influences.

Psychoanalytic theory also has been influential, and the volumes by Freud mentioned earlier are directly relevant. An additional volume concerned with social-psychological problems is his *Totem and taboo.* Erikson's major work, *Childhood and society* (G219), is in the neo-Freudian tradition in developmental psychology. *The authoritarian personality,* by Adorno and others, is a research study cast primarily in a psychoanalytic mold.

G282 Adorno, Theodor W., and others. The authoritarian personality. New York: Norton, 1969. 990p.

G283 Asch, Solomon E. Social psychology. New York: Prentice-Hall, 1952. 646p.

G284 Bandura, Albert, and Richard H. Walters. Social learning and personality development. New York: Holt, 1963. 329p.

G285 Festinger, Leon. A theory of cognitive dissonance. Stanford, Calif.: Stanford Univ. Pr., 1957. 291p.

G286 Freud, Sigmund. Totem and taboo: some points of agreement between the mental lives of savages and neurotics. Tr. by James Strachey. New York: Norton, 1950. 172p.

G287 Miller, Neal E., and John Dollard. Social learning and imitation. New Haven, Conn.: Yale Univ. Pr., 1962. 341p.

G288 Skinner, B. F. Verbal behavior. New York: Appleton, 1957. 478p.

The psychology of art is sometimes considered an aspect of social psychology. A comprehensive integrated survey of the field that helps materially to establish it systematically was prepared by the Kreitlers.

G289 Kreitler, Hans, and Shulamith Kreitler. Psychology of the arts. Durham, N.C.: Duke Univ. Pr., 1972. 514p.

Psychologists and others from related fields have been concerned with communication and language. Blumenthal recently published an excellent account of the history of psycholinguistics that may serve as an introduction to the field. A standard book on communication is supplied by Miller. Communication in its mathematical aspects is the concern of Shannon and Weaver. Whorf, as edited by Carroll, presents a stimulating and controversial account of the relation of thought to the structure of language.

G290 Blumenthal, Arthur L. Language and psychology: historical aspects of psycholinguistics. New York: Wiley, 1970. 248p.

G291 Miller, George A. The psychology of communication; seven essays. New York: Basic Books, 1967. 197p.

G292 Shannon, Claude E., and Warren Weaver. The mathematical theory of communication. Urbana: Univ. of Illinois Pr., 1949. 117p.

G293 Whorf, Benjamin L. Language, thought, and reality: selected writings. Ed. by John B. Carroll. Cambridge, Mass.: Technology Pr. of MIT, 1956. 278p.

The new psycholinguistics of the last 15 years or so is certainly an exciting, controversial, and rapidly expanding field. The books by Fodor and by Glucksberg and Danks are introductory. Psycholinguistics in terms of original studies or contemporary overviews is reported in the other books that follow by Anderson, Brown, Chomsky, Miller and Johnson-Laird, and Wales and Walker. All that can be said succinctly is that one can rely upon the fact that their titles do not belie their content.

G294 Anderson, John R. Language, memory, and thought. Hillsdale, N.J.: Erlbaum, 1976. 546p.

G295 Brown, Roger. A first language: the early stages. Cambridge, Mass.: Harvard Univ. Pr., 1973. 437p.

G296 Chomsky, Noam. Aspects of the theory of syntax. Cambridge, Mass.: MIT Pr., 1965. 251p.

G297 ———. Language and mind. New York: HBJ, 1972. 194p.

G298 Fodor, Jerry A., and others. The psychology of language: an introduction to psycholinguistics and generative grammar. New York: McGraw-Hill, 1974. 537p.

G299 Glucksberg, Sam, and Joseph H. Danks. Experimental psycholinguistics: an introduction. Hillsdale, N.J.: Erlbaum, 1975. 233p.

G300 Miller, George A., and Philip N. Johnson-Laird. Language and perception. Cambridge, Mass.: Harvard Univ. Pr., 1976. 760p.

G301 Wales, Roger J., and Edward Walker, eds. New

approaches to language mechanisms: a collection of psycholinguistic studies. New York: North-Holland, 1976. 296p.

Recent major texts in social psychology include the following.

G302 Freedman, Jonathan, and others. Social psychology. 4th ed. Englewood Cliffs, N.J.: Prentice-Hall, 1981. 686p.

G303 Hollander, Edwin P. Principles and methods of social psychology. 4th ed. New York: Oxford Univ. Pr., 1981. 558p.

G304 Shaw, Marvin E. Group dynamics: the psychology of small group behavior. 3d ed. New York: McGraw-Hill, 1981. 531p.

G305 ———, and Phillip Costanzo. Theories of social psychology. 2d ed. New York: McGraw-Hill, 1982. 482p.

G306 Worchel, Stephen, and Joel Cooper. Understanding social psychology. 3d ed. Homewood, Ill.: Dorsey, 1983. 684p.

G307 Wrightsman, Lawrence S., and Kay Deaux. Social psychology in the eighties. 3d ed. Monterey, Calif.: Brooks/Cole, 1981. 760p.

CLINICAL PSYCHOLOGY

Clinical psychology is a major branch of professional psychology, with its practitioners offering clinical services to the public. The major tasks of the clinical psychologist are diagnostic assessment and treatment. Other than to the parent science of psychology, its greatest intellectual debt is to psychiatry.

In the nineteenth century, Wilhelm Wundt's psychiatrist student Emil Kraepelin did much to establish a description of and nomenclature for the mental ills of humankind. In the second decade of this century, Hermann Rorschach, a psychiatrist, developed the Rorschach inkblot test, an early "projective" technique, in which the respondent is free to interpret ambiguous stimuli according to his or her own personal inclinations. Clinical psychology was also influenced by the contact that its practitioners had with patients seeking help. The book by Frederic Wells, published in 1927, shows how an adequately trained academic psychologist, when placed in relation with patients, can develop the sensitivity and skills to help with their problems.

All three pioneers were concerned primarily with the assessment phase of the clinical method, although in a broader sense their intent was therapeutic. It was only after World War II that heavy involvement of psychologists in psychotherapy took place. In 1942 Carl Rogers, a psychologist, published a book that for the first time allowed his fellow psychologists to conceive that there was an approach to psychotherapy that was their very own.

G308 Kraepelin, Emil. Clinical psychiatry: a textbook for students and physicians. 7th ed. Tr. and abstr. by A. R. Diefendorf. New York: Macmillan, 1907. 562p. Reprint, Delmar, N.Y.: Scholars' Facsimiles & Reprints, 1981.

G309 Rogers, Carl R. Counseling and psychotherapy: newer concepts in practice. Boston: Houghton, 1942. 450p.

G310 Rorschach, Hermann. Psychodiagnostics: a diagnostic test based on perception. Tr. by Paul Lemkau and Bernard Kronenberg. 5th ed. New York: Grune & Stratton, 1951. 263p.

G311 Wells, Frederic L. Mental tests in clinical practice. Yonkers, N.Y.: World Book, 1927. 315p.

Garfield has prepared a lucid, well-written introductory text, devoting attention to diagnostic appraisal and psychotherapeutic and behavior change. An even shorter introduction was prepared by Rotter. There are also two more advanced texts: one written by Korchin, the other edited by Weiner. The handbook edited by Wolman gives wide coverage, including research methods, theories, diagnostic methods, psychopathology, methods of treatment, and psychology as a profession.

G312 Garfield, Sol L. Clinical psychology: the study of personality and behavior. Chicago: Aldine, 1974. 461p.

G313 Korchin, Sheldon J. Modern clinical psychology: principles of intervention in the clinic and community. New York: Basic Books, 1976. 672p.

G314 Rotter, Julian B. Clinical psychology. 2d ed. Englewood Cliffs, N.J.: Prentice-Hall, 1971. 117p.

G315 Weiner, Irving B., ed. Clinical methods in psychology. New York: Wiley, 1976. 678p.

G316 Wolman, Benjamin B., and others, eds. Handbook of clinical psychology. New York: McGraw-Hill, 1965. 1,596p.

The diagnostic phase of the clinical task was covered in the general texts mentioned earlier. There are also special volumes devoted to specific instruments. Characteristic of high-caliber books that examine the literature on a particular widely used intelligence test is the volume prepared by Matarazzo on Wechsler's measures of adult intelligence. After more than 10 years' experience with the instrument, Hathaway and Meehl published a survey of their findings with the Minnesota Multiphasic Personality Inventory. As distinguished from a projective device such as the Rorschach test, this is the most widely used structured personality test in clinical psychology.

G317 Hathaway, Starke R., and Paul Meehl. An atlas for the clinical use of the MMPI. Minneapolis: Univ. of Minnesota Pr., 1951. 799p.

G318 Matarazzo, Joseph D., and David Wechsler. Wechsler's measurement and appraisal of adult intelligence. 5th ed. Baltimore: Williams & Wilkins, 1972. 572p.

Books devoted to psychotherapy and behavior modification concern another important aspect of clinical psychology. The book by Rogers, already mentioned (G309), is supplemented by two others. The reference to "A Complete Guide to Therapy" in the title of Kovel's book is made with tongue in cheek. It is actually a delightful and clear introduction for the layperson or undergraduate to a broad spectrum of psychotherapeutic efforts. The work edited by Garfield and Bergin is, as its title indicates, devoted to psychotherapy and behavioral change. Addressed to counseling psychologists, Patterson's book contains admirable summaries of many approaches to psychotherapy and counseling. Probably the most important single book directly initiating research on behavior modification as an approach to treatment was written by Wolpe, who was more influenced in his thinking by Pavlov and Hull than by the Skinnerians. While bearing the title *History of behavior modification,* and serving that function, Kazdin's volume also is an excellent statement about the contemporary status of experimental research in the field. The British tradition in behavior modification is represented by the volume edited by the indefatigable Eysenck. A leading researcher of the therapeutic relationship is Strupp. His collected papers bring out the scope and depth of his inquiries. Case studies along with orienting commentary for psychodynamic, humanistic, and behavior therapies are provided by Morse and Watson. Among the therapists included are Freud, Rogers, Perls, Ellis, Wolpe, and Strupp.

G319 Eysenck, Hans, ed. Experiments in behaviour therapy: readings in modern methods of treatment of mental disorders derived from learning theory. New York: Macmillan, 1964. 558p.

G320 Handbook of psychotherapy and behavior change: an empirical analysis. 2d ed. Ed. by Sol L. Garfield and Allen E. Bergin. New York: Wiley, 1978. 1,024p.

G321 Kazdin, Alan E. History of behavior modification: experimental foundations of contemporary research. Baltimore: Univ. Park Pr., 1978. 468p.

G322 Kovel, Joel A. A complete guide to therapy: from psychoanalysis to behavior modification. New York: Pantheon, 1976. 284p.

G323 Morse, Stephen J., and Robert I. Watson, Jr. Psychotherapies: a comparative casebook. New York: Holt, 1977. 421p.

G324 Patterson, Cecil H. Theories of counseling and psychotherapy. 3d. ed. New York: Harper, 1980. 685p.

G325 Rogers, Carl R. Client-centered therapy, its current practice, implications, and theory. Boston: Houghton, 1951. 560p.

G326 ———. On becoming a person: a therapist's view of psychotherapy. Boston: Houghton, 1961. 420p.

G327 Strupp, Hans. Psychotherapy: clinical, research, and theoretical issues. New York: Aronson, 1973. 816p.

G328 Wolpe, Joseph. Psychotherapy by reciprocal inhibition. Stanford, Calif.: Stanford Univ. Pr., 1958. 239p.

While psychopathology is considered to be an aspect of clinical psychology in the American Psychological Association classification, most textbook writers and publishers still prefer the term "abnormal psychology." Among the textbooks appearing recently there is a significant tendency to move away from the illness model learned from psychiatry, in the direction of other models shortly to be specified.

In the more conventional manner of heavy reliance upon the disease entity illness model, Coleman and Page each supply a standard text at a high level of competence. The three-volume handbook of psychiatry edited by Arieti is clearly the most important single source for the medical model. While still relying in some measure upon that model, other texts consider others. An excellent introduction is provided by Price. He explains why and how different perspectives— psychoanalytic, illness, learning, moral, humanistic, and social—give different views of abnormal behavior. In their book, the Sarasons use the unifying theme of maladaptive behaviors. Davison and Neale give consideration to the statistical, medical, and learning models. White and Watt offer a book in the extended psychoanalytic tradition. Maher escapes reliance upon the illness model by stressing the experimental research potential of problems in psychopathology. A group of British investigators under the editorship of Eysenck have published a handbook in the experimental tradition. Books of readings have been prepared by Sarason and Sarason, and by Zax and Stricker.

The controversial psychiatrist Thomas Szasz has devoted many years to a series of merciless criticisms of psychiatry and, by a not unreasonable extension, to large segments of abnormal psychology. The title of one of his earlier works, *The myth of mental illness,* epitomizes his aim. For first reading, however, his book on schizophrenia is recommended.

G329 Arieti, Silvano, ed. American handbook of psychiatry. 2d ed. New York: Basic Books, 1974. 3v.

G330 Coleman, James C., and others. Abnormal psychology and modern life. 6th ed. Glenview, Ill.: Scott, Foresman, 1980. 702p.

G331 Davison, Gerald C., and John M. Neale. Abnormal psychology: an experimental clinical approach. 2d ed. New York: Wiley, 1978. 686p.

G332 Eysenck, Hans J., ed. Handbook of abnormal psychology. 2d ed. San Diego: Knapp, 1973. 906p.

G333 Maher, Brendan A. Principles of psychopathology: an experimental approach. New York: McGraw-Hill, 1966. 525p.

G334 Page, James D. Psychopathology: the science of understanding deviance. 2d ed. Chicago: Aldine, 1975.

G335 Price, Richard H. Abnormal behavior: perspectives in conflict. 2d ed. New York: Holt, 1978. 278p.

G336 Sarason, Irwin G., and Barbara A. Sarason. Abnormal psychology: the problem of maladaptive behavior. 3d ed. Englewood Cliffs, N.J.: Prentice-Hall, 1980. 573p.

G337 ———, comps. Readings in abnormal psychology: the problem of maladaptive behavior. New York: Appleton, 1972. 367p.

G338 Szasz, Thomas. Schizophrenia: the sacred symbol of psychiatry. New York: Basic Books, 1976. 237p.

G339 White, Robert W., and Norman F. Watt. The abnormal personality. 4th ed. New York: Ronald, 1973. 628p.

G340 Zax, Melvin, and George Stricker, eds. The study of abnormal behavior: selected readings. 3d ed. New York: Macmillan, 1974. 582p.

Mental retardation is of concern to the clinical psychologist. The standard introductory textbook on mental retardation was prepared by Sarason, in the most recent editions with a collaborator. It manages to strike a middle-of-the-road stance in an admirable fashion. The volume edited by the Clarkes is useful as both a text and reference book. It is thorough and fair, with individual chapters prepared by experts. What can be done for and with the mentally retarded is the theme of Baroff's book. Since these books consider the care and treatment of the mentally retarded, they are more appropriately mentioned here, rather than in the subdivision on intelligence in the section on personality, but they are obviously relevant there as well.

G341 Baroff, George S. Mental retardation: nature, cause, and management. New York: Hemisphere, 1974. 504p.

G342 Clarke, Ann M., and A. D. B. Clarke, eds. Mental deficiency: the changing outlook. 3d ed. New York: Free Pr., 1975. 886p.

G343 Sarason, Seymour B., and John Doris. Psychological problems in mental deficiency. 4th ed. New York: Harper, 1969. 483p.

Among the many significant publications in abnormal and clinical psychology during the last few years are the following.

G344 Coleman, James, and others. Abnormal psychology and modern life. 7th ed. Glenview, Ill.: Scott, Foresman, 1984. 701p.

G345 Davison, Gerald C., and John M. Neale. Abnormal psychology: an experimental clinical approach. 3d ed. New York: Wiley, 1982. 823p.

G346 Garfield, Sol L. Clinical psychology: the study of personality and behavior. 2d ed. Hawthorne, N.Y.: Aldine, 1983. 471p.

G347 Smith, Mary Lee, and others. The benefits of psychotherapy. Baltimore: Johns Hopkins Univ. Pr., 1980. 269p.

G348 Sundberg, Norman D., and others. An introduction to clinical psychology. Englewood Cliffs, N.J.: Prentice-Hall, 1983. 496p.

G349 Weiner, Irving, ed. Clinical methods in psychology. 2d ed. New York: Wiley, 1983. 726p.

G350 White, Robert W., and Norman F. Watt. The abnormal personality. 5th ed. New York: Wiley, 1981. 793p.

EDUCATIONAL PSYCHOLOGY

Educational psychology has long outgrown its early stage, when it was essentially the application of general psychology to educational matters. Two rather different approaches have been attempted. There was the playfully presented but deeply serious association with education that stirred in William James when, in 1899, he considered consciousness, association, habit, will, and other less conventional rubrics of psychology; and there was the thorough, solid approach of Edward L. Thorndike in 1903 when he translated facts about the original nature of human beings and the psychology of learning and individual differences into an educational setting.

G351 James, William. Talks to teachers on psychology, and to students on some of life's ideals. New York: Norton, 1958. 191p.

G352 Thorndike, Edward L. Educational psychology. New York: Teachers College, Columbia Univ., 1913–14. 3v.

A leading text in educational psychology is that of Cronbach. It covers thoroughly the traditional topics of development, motivation, learning, and individual differences, as did Thorndike, but now on the basis of research by educational psychologists. From among the many others that merit attention, the books by Mathis and others, and Gage and Berliner, are here suggested. At a more introductory level, Lindgren's book is representative. A book of readings was edited by the Sprinthalls. A specific aspect of educational psychology that has received considerable attention recently is the psychology of teaching. The volume by Biehler is recommended in this field. Books cited in the chapter on education should also be consulted.

G353 Biehler, Robert F. Psychology applied to teaching. 3d ed. Boston: Houghton, 1978. 873p.

G354 Cronbach, Lee J. Educational psychology. 3d ed. New York: HBJ, 1977. 875p.

G355 Gage, Nathaniel L., and David C. Berliner. Educational psychology. 2d ed. Chicago: Rand McNally, 1979. 800p.

G356 Lindgren, Henry C. Educational psychology in the classroom. 5th ed. New York: Wiley, 1976. 521p.

G357 Mathis, B. Claude, and others. Psychological foundations of education: learning and teaching. New York: Academic, 1970. 778p.

G358 Sprinthall, Richard C., and Norman A. Sprinthall, comps. Educational psychology: selected readings. New York: Van Nostrand Reinhold, 1969. 361p.

Among the many important works on educational psychology of the last few years are the following.

G359 Biehler, Robert F., and Jack Snowman. Psychology applied to teaching. 4th ed. New York: Houghton, 1982. 733p.

G360 Gage, N. L., and David C. Berliner. Educational psychology. 3d ed. New York: Houghton, 1984. 809p.

G361 Hopkins, Kenneth D., and Julian C. Stanley. Educational and psychological measurement and evaluation. 6th ed. Englewood Cliffs, N.J.: Prentice-Hall, 1981. 517p.

G362 Lindgren, Henry Clay. Educational psychology in the classroom. 6th ed. New York: Oxford Univ. Pr., 1980. 796p.

G363 Sprinthall, Richard C., and Norman A. Sprinthall. Educational psychology: a developmental approach. 3d ed. Reading, Mass.: Addison-Wesley, 1981. 605p.

G364 Worell, Judith, ed. Psychological development in the elementary years. New York: Academic, 1982. 479p.

INDUSTRIAL AND ORGANIZATIONAL PSYCHOLOGY

Although there were some studies before the turn of the century, industrial psychology did not emerge fully as a field of psychological interest and effort until the twentieth century. A book that directly relates to that trend appeared in 1913, written by Hugo Münsterberg, concerned with applied experimental psychology and the psychology of work.

G365 Münsterberg, Hugo. Psychology and industrial efficiency. New York: Houghton, 1913. 320p.

Traditionally, industrial psychology concerned selection, placement, and training of industrial workers; organizational psychology added the newer areas of work motivation, and organization theory and development. Contemporary books generally stress both. A consistent leading textbook that successfully made the transition from industrial to an inclusion of organization psychology, and now in its third edition, was written by Gilmer, one of the pioneers in organization psychology. Bass and Barrett have prepared a text encompassing both areas. Leavitt is more specifically concerned with organizational psychology. A book of readings was edited by Deci and others.

G366 Bass, Bernard M., and Gerald V. Barrett. Man, work, and organizations: an introduction to industrial and organizational psychology. Boston: Allyn & Bacon, 1972. 673p.

G367 Deci, Edward L., and others. Readings in industrial and organizational psychology. 3d ed. New York: McGraw-Hill, 1972. 527p.

G368 Gilmer, B. von Haller, and others. Industrial and organizational psychology. 4th ed. New York: McGraw-Hill, 1977. 496p.

G369 Leavitt, Harold J. Managerial psychology: an introduction to individuals, pairs, and groups in organizations. 4th ed. Chicago: Univ. of Chicago Pr., 1978. 385p.

Among significant recent works on industrial and organizational psychology are the following.

G370 Kantowitz, Barry H., and Robert D. Sorkin. Human factors: understanding people-system relationships. New York: Wiley, 1983. 699p.

G371 McCormick, Ernest J., and Mark Sanders. Human factors in engineering and design. 5th ed. New York: McGraw-Hill, 1982. 615p.

G372 McCormick, Ernest J., and Daniel R. Ilgen. Industrial psychology. 7th ed. Englewood Cliffs, N.J.: Prentice-Hall, 1980. 464p.

G373 Maier, Norman R. F., and Gertrude Casselman Verser. Psychology in industrial organizations. 5th ed. New York: Houghton, 1982. 652p.

G374 Naylor, James C., and others. A theory of behavior in organizations. New York: Academic, 1980. 299p.

G375 Robbins, Stephen P. Organizational behavior: concepts, controversies and applications. 2d ed. Englewood Cliffs, N.J.: Prentice-Hall, 1983. 564p.

G376 Schultz, Duane P. Psychology and industry today: an introduction to industrial and organizational psychology. 3d ed. New York: Macmillan, 1982. 509p.

Robert I. Watson, Sr., with Michael Wertheimer

Survey of the Reference Works

GUIDES TO THE LITERATURE

General

G377 Elliott, Charles K. A guide to the documentation of psychology. London: Bingley, 1971. 134p.
Three chapters orient the student to psychology, to the organization of the library as a bibliographical tool, and to reasons why documentary skills are essential for research. Discusses other basic research tools, searching technique, and utilization of the results. Ten appendixes include select lists of organizations, journals, newsletters, handbooks, dictionaries, bibliographical guides, KWIC indexes of abstracting and indexing services, and sources for reviews.

G378 Louttit, Chauncey M. Handbook of psychological literature. Bloomington, Ind.: Principia Pr., 1932. 273p.
A pioneer systematization of and introduction to the scattered literature.

The following four items are written with the needs of undergraduates in mind:

G379 Bell, James E. A guide to library research in psychology. Dubuque, Iowa: Brown, 1971. 211p.

Four chapters acquaint the student with the college library, useful reference tools, and steps to take in preparing a paper that involves library research. Chapter 5 and two appendixes supplement this presentation with a detailed bibliography of reference and monographic works in psychology and lists of further aids, from additional introductions to the library to an outline of the Library of Congress (LC) classification.

G380 Noland, Robert L. Research and report writing in the behavioral sciences: psychiatry, psychology, sociology, educational psychology, cultural anthropology, managerial psychology. Springfield, Ill.: Thomas, 1970. 98p.
Intended primarily for students of psychology, this work provides a practical, step-by-step introduction to preparation of library research reports. About half of the guide is devoted to literature searching and to the literature on research methods.

G381 Reed, Jeffrey G., and Pam M. Baxter. Library use: a handbook for psychology. Washington, D.C.: American Psychological Assn., 1983. 138p.
Among the subjects discussed in this guide, intended primarily for undergraduate and beginning graduate students, are selection and defining of research topics in psychology; relevant sources of information for psychology, such as *Psychological abstracts,* government publications, and computer data-

bases and searches; tests and measurements; and inter-library loan.

G382 Sarbin, Theodore R., and William C. Coe. The student psychologist's handbook: a guide to sources. Cambridge, Mass.: Schenkman, 1969. 104p.

Teaches the beginner how to prepare a research paper. Introduces the scope of psychology, purposes and procedures of research, and pays special attention to the literature in a chapter on journals and handbooks.

A guide designed for the more advanced researcher is Raymond G. McInnis, *Research guide for psychology* (Westport, Conn.: Greenwood Pr., 1982 [604p.] [Reference sources for the social sciences and humanities, no.1]) (**G383**), which aims to help library users to "discover, quickly and systematically, appropriate bibliographic and substantive sources" on their topics of investigation. Covers general reference sources and information sources, including research guides, literature reviews, and bibliographic sources, for 16 subdivisions of psychology. The model for the classification scheme is *Psychological abstracts*. Approximately 1,200 titles, most of which were published prior to 1980, are discussed in bibliographic essays. Index of authors, titles, and selected subjects.

Specialized

Psychology Information Guide series is one of many series of bibliographies published by Gale Research Company. The first volume in the psychology series is Wayne Viney and others, eds., *History of psychology: a guide to information sources* (Detroit: Gale, 1979 [502p.]) (**G384**), which lists about 3,000 English-language books and journal articles, more than 1,200 of which are annotated. The entries are divided into five major categories: general reference works; references in the history of psychology; systems and schools of psychology; histories and major works in selected content areas of psychology; histories of related fields. Each of these categories includes many subcategories. Name, title, and subject indexes.

Each volume in the Gale series is subtitled "A Guide to Information Sources," and provides access to the literature of the particular area of psychology specified by the title. Others published so far are Gloria B. Gottsegen, ed., *Group behavior* (1979 [219p.]) (**G385**); A. George Gitter and Robert Grunin, eds., *Communication* (1980 [157p.]) (**G386**); Charles N. Cofer, ed., *Human motivation* (1980 [178p.]) (**G387**); Henry Leland and Marilyn Deutsch, eds., *Abnormal behavior* (1980 [261p.]) (**G388**); Gloria B. Gottsegen and Abby J. Gottsegen, eds., *Humanistic psychology* (1980 [185p.]) (**G389**). In preparation

are Dorothy H. Eichorn, ed., *Child and adolescent development* (**G390**); John F. Feldhusen, ed., *Educational and school psychology* (**G391**); Carol Filipczak, ed., *B. F. Skinner and behaviorism* (**G392**); Reuben Fine, ed., *Freud and psychoanalysis* (**G393**); Durand F. Jacobs and Jack G. Wiggins, Jr., eds., *Psychology in health and rehabilitation* (**G394**); Helen R. Kearney, ed., *Psychology of women* (**G395**); Milton V. Kline, ed., *Altered states of consciousness* (**G396**); David L. Margules, ed., *Psychopharmacology* (**G397**); David L. Margules, ed., *Physiological psychology* (**G398**); Robert B. Meager, Jr., ed., *Personality* (**G399**); Elizabeth Ann Robertson-Tchabo, ed., *Adult development and aging* (**G400**); Sydney Schultz and Duane Schultz, eds., *Psychology and industry* (**G401**); Ethel Tobach, ed., *Animal behavior* (**G402**).

In Gale's Philosophy and Religion Information Guide series, of interest to psychology is Donald Capps and others, eds., *Psychology of religion: a guide to information sources* (1976 [352p.]) (**G403**). Contains mainly English-language materials (some are annotated) published from 1950 to 1974, with a few influential works prior to 1950. Includes general works and mythological, ritual, experimental, dispositional, social, and directional dimensions of religion. Each of these categories has several subdivisions. Bibliographies are found under "general works." Author, title, and subject indexes.

REVIEWS
General

G404 Advances in the study of behavior. v.1– , 1965– . New York: Academic. Irregular.

Reports recent developments in research on all aspects of behavior using both animal and human subjects. Aims to include "intensive factual reviews of recent work, reformulations of persistent problems, and historical and theoretical essays, all oriented toward the facilitation of current and future progress."

G405 Annual review of psychology. v.1– , 1950– . Stanford, Calif.: Annual Reviews. Annual.

An authoritative, widely used reference source of approximately 20 articles every year, each written by an expert who critically reviews a special topic in psychology. Each article contains a lengthy bibliography ranging from about 100 to 400 citations. The major areas of the field are covered periodically but not in as systematic a fashion as originally envisioned. A new "continuous" feature initiated in 1979 is a prefatory chapter written by a distinguished psychologist.

G406 Psychological bulletin. v.1– , 1904– . Washington; D.C.: American Psychological Assn. Bimonthly.

An official periodical of the American Psychological Association, this prestigious journal publishes evaluative reviews of particular research areas in all fields of psychology. High rejection rate assures top-level quality. Policy is to report "original research only when it illustrates some methodological problem or issue."

G407 L'Année psychologique. v.1– , 1894– . Paris: Presses Universitaires de France. Semi-annual.

Three main sections in each fascicle: (1) original research reports, each with brief summaries in English and French and a bibliography; (2) critical reviews of progress in selected areas of research, each with short summaries in English and French and a bibliography; (3) classified reviews of about 50 books. International in scope. Index of authors of books reviewed. List of books received.

G408 Contemporary psychology: a journal of reviews. v.1– , 1956– . Washington, D.C.: American Psychological Assn. Monthly.

This is the American Psychological Association's official book review journal, the most complete such journal in the world. Most of each issue is devoted to one- to three-page book reviews with biographical information about the author(s). Also includes brief reviews, notices about conference proceedings and reports of major research projects, "previews" of psychology textbooks, "On the Other Hand" (presenting readers' comments on reviews and books reviewed), and a list of books received. Publishes consolidated reviews of introductory psychology textbooks every few years.

Specialized

There are now so many specialized review series that it is inappropriate to present an exhaustive list of them here. This section includes representative selections of these works.

Some Major Research Fields in Psychology

G409 The psychology of learning and motivation: advances in research and theory. Ed. by Gordon H. Bower, v.1– , 1967– . New York: Academic. Irregular.

G410 Advances in the psychology of human intelligence. v.1– , 1982– . Hillsdale, N.J.: Erlbaum. Semiannual.

G411 Behavioral primatology: advances in research and theory. v.1– , 1977– . Hillsdale, N.J.: Erlbaum. Irregular.

Reviews scientific studies of the behavior of nonhuman primates.

G412 Progress in psychobiology and physiological psychology. v.1– , 1966– . New York: Academic. (Formerly: Progress in physiological psychology, 1966–75)

G413 Advances in experimental social psychology. Ed. by Leonard Berkowitz, v.1– , 1964– . New York: Academic. Irregular.

Prominent scholars provide overviews and theoretical integrations of specialized areas of research in the field.

G414 Progress in experimental personality research. v.1– , 1964– . New York: Academic. Irregular.

Papers "reflect the main themes of contemporary work in the field of personality," including both normal and abnormal behavior.

Developmental Psychology

G415 Review of child development research. New York: Russell Sage, v.1–2; Chicago: Univ. of Chicago Pr. v.3– , 1964– . Irregular.

Prepared under the auspices of the Society for Research in Child Development, "the aim in these volumes is to provide the practitioner or researcher with a critical review and analysis of the research literature on selected topics, to present a summary of the current status of our knowledge and questions yet to be answered on these issues, and, when possible, to relate findings drawn from research to practical problems." Extensive bibliographies. Author and subject indexes.

G416 Advances in child development and behavior. v.1– , 1963– . New York: Academic. Irregular.

Offers scholarly, well-documented articles that critically review, summarize, and integrate recent advances in the field. Emphasis is on research dealing with "problems of current and significant interest."

G417 Advances in infancy research. v.1– , 1981– . Norwood, N.J.: Ablex.

G418 Advances in developmental psychology. v.1– , 1981– . Hillsdale, N.J.: Erlbaum.

G419 Advances in applied developmental psychology. v.1– , 1983– . New York: Academic. Annual.

G420 Life-span development and behavior. v.1– , 1978– . New York: Academic. Annual.

G421 Annual review of gerontology and geriatrics. v.1– , 1980– . New York: Springer. Annual.

Purpose is "to present a comprehensive description and analysis of the recent literature and of the salient issues in the fields of aging, from the biological and behavioral sciences to social and health sciences." Plan is continually to provide "critical syntheses of advances and evolving issues in relevant areas."

G422 Advances in behavioral pharmacology. v.1– , 1977– . New York: Academic. Irregular.

G423 Current developments in psychopharmacology. v.1– , 1975– . Jamaica, N.Y.: S P Books. Irregular.

G424 Stress and anxiety. v.1– . 1975– . Washington. D.C.: Hemisphere. Irregular; about 1v./yr.

Clinical Applications

G425 Year book of psychiatry and applied mental health. 1970– . Chicago: Year Book Medical Publishers. Annual.

Emphasizing psychiatric journals, this series aims to survey the literature on mental health. Subjects of chapters vary from year to year, as research developments require, but each volume seeks to "make available in detailed abstract form the working essence of the cream of recent international medico-scientific literature."

G426 Annual progress in child psychiatry and child development. 1968– . New York: Brunner/Mazel. Annual.

Primarily directed toward workers in the field as an aid to keeping abreast of significant new work ranging from the sociocultural, perceptual-cognitive, behavioral, and clinical to the biochemical and neurophysiological. Articles present original research as well as reviews of the status of knowledge in a particular area.

G427 Advances in clinical child psychology. v.1– , 1977– . New York: Plenum. Annual.

G428 Progress in community mental health. v.1– , 1969– . New York: Brunner/Mazel. Irregular.

G429 Annual review of the schizophrenic syndrome. v.1– , 1971– . New York: Brunner/Mazel. Biennial.

Behavior Modification

G430 Annual review of behavior therapy theory and practice. v.1– , 1973– . New York: Brunner/Mazel. Annual.

G431 Progress in behavior modification. v.1– , 1975– . New York: Academic. Irregular.

The editors believe that due to "the publication explosion in behavior modification, there is a real need for a review publication that undertakes to present yearly in-depth evaluations that include a scholarly examination of theoretical underpinnings, a careful survey of research findings, and a comparative analysis of existing techniques and methodologies. In this serial publication we propose to meet this need. . . . The range of topics will include, but will not be limited to, studies of fear behavior, measurement and modification of addictive behaviors, modification of classroom behaviors, remedial methods for the retarded and physically handicapped, descriptions of animal analogs, the effects of social influences on behavior, the use of drugs in behavioral approaches, and the contribution of behavior therapy to the treatment of physical illness" (preface). Extensive list of references accompanies each article. V.9 was published in 1980.

Mental Retardation

G432 Advances in mental handicap research. v.1– , 1980– . New York: Wiley. Irregular.

V.1 concentrates on language, social interaction, basic learning processes, and comprehensive intervention. Based on research findings, it attempts to be relevant to education and other services for the mentally handicapped.

G433 International review of research in mental retardation. v.1– , 1966– . New York: Academic. Annual.

Designed to inform the professional of recent progress, this review aims to present the findings of high-quality research dealing with both applied and basic issues.

G434 Mental retardation and developmental disabilities: an annual review. v.1– , 1970– . New York: Grune & Stratton. Annual. (Formerly: Mental retardation: an annual review)

Scholarly review of recent developments in the field. Usually features one or more articles by a foreign professional. Lengthy bibliography with each article. Subject index.

G435 Progress in learning disabilities. v.1– , 1968– . New York: Grune & Stratton. Irregular.

Psychoanalysis

G436 Annual survey of psychoanalysis. 1952– . New York: International Universities Pr. Annual.

G437 The psychoanalytic study of the child. v.1– , 1945– . New York: International Universities Pr. v.1–4; New Haven, Conn.: Yale Univ. Pr. v.5– . Annual.

Articles fall into broad categories such as contributions to psychoanalytic theory, problems of development, clinical contributions, applications of psychoanalysis, etc. Bibliography with each article. Subject index.

G438 Jahrbuch der Psychoanalyse. v.1– , 1964– . Berne: Hans Huber. Irregular.

Text in German, summaries in English. V.1–2 published by West Deutscher Verlag, Cologne.

Test Reviews and Psychological Assessment

Probably the most thorough job of trying to provide comprehensive and responsible reference information about psychological tests was done by the late Oscar Krisen Buros.

G439 Mental measurements yearbook. Ed. by Oscar Krisen Buros. 1938– . Highland Park, N.J.: Gryphon Pr. Irregular.

The eight yearbooks published to date are the most important sources of information available on tests published as separates in English-speaking countries. Test entries are arranged according to broad subject categories, with subcategories, and provide basic facts such as title, description of groups for which test is intended, cost, scoring and reporting services, author, publisher, etc. Contains test reviews written especially for the yearbooks by qualified individuals, excerpts of test reviews from professional journals, and references on the construction, use, and validity of the tests, as well as much other relevant information. Although the yearbooks include several indexes, only very general subject indexing is provided. A detailed subject index would be useful. The eighth *MMY* published in 1978 supplements but does not supersede *Tests-in-print II* (G444). More recent reviews can be located through such indexes as *Social sciences citation index* (Permutation Subject Index), *Psychological abstracts*, etc. Buros died shortly before publication of the eighth *MMY*; the University of Nebraska at Lincoln plans to continue the series.

Several more specialized monographs have been published. *Personality tests and reviews II* (Highland Park, N.J.: Gryphon Pr., 1975 [841p.]) **(G440)** and *Reading tests and reviews*, 2v. (Highland Park, N.J.: Gryphon Pr., 1968–75.) **(G441)** are reprints of the relevant sections of the seventh *MMY* and *TIP II*; *Intelligence tests and reviews* (Highland Park, N.J.: Gryphon Pr., 1975 [1,129p.]) **(G442)** is a reprint of relevant sections of the first seven *MMY*s and *TIP II*.

Tests-in-print; a comprehensive bibliography of tests for use in education, psychology and industry, ed. by Oscar Krisen Buros (Highland Park, N.J.: Gryphon Pr., 1961 [479p.]) **(G443)** is a cumulative index to the first five *Mental measurements yearbooks*. It is now mainly of historic interest. *Tests-in-print II: an index to tests, test reviews and the literature of specific tests* (Highland Park, N.J.: Gryphon Pr., 1974 [1,107p.]) **(G444)** is a master index to the first seven *Mental measurements yearbooks* and to the first edition of *Personality tests and reviews*. It is a classified bibliography of tests in print as of early 1974 and of tests that have gone out of print since *TIP I*. Includes "Standards for Educational and Psychological Tests" of the American Psychological Association, American Educational Research Association, and National Council on Measurement in Education. Contains a publishers directory, indexes of titles and names, and a scanning index. *Tests-in-print III: an index to tests, test reviews, and the literature on specific tests*, ed. by James V. Mitchell, Jr. (Lincoln: Buros Institute of Mental Measurements, Univ. of Nebraska-Lincoln; dist. by the Univ. of Nebraska Pr., 1983 [714p.]) **(G445)**, describes nearly 2,700 tests in print that are commercially available for purchase, including tests still in print and reviewed in the previous eight *Mental measurements yearbooks*. Provides more than 12,000 references on specific tests; a directory of test publishers with index to their tests; a title index of in-print tests and tests out of print since previous listings; a name index for test authors, reviewers, and authors of references; and a classified subject index of tests.

G446 Lake, Dale G., and others, eds. Measuring human behavior: tools for the assessment of social functioning. New York: Teachers College Pr., 1973. 422p.

Index to about 100 measuring instruments designed to assess "social functioning," defined as "the

properties of the individual (cognitive/perceptual, motivational, and overt behavioral) as he or she takes part in social interaction, and . . . the properties of the immediate social system involved (dyads, small groups, organizations)." Provides information on each instrument's development, reliability, and validity as well as other details.

G447 Advances in psychological assessment. Palo Alto, Calif.: Science & Behavior, v.1–2; San Francisco: Jossey-Bass, v.3– , 1968– .

Purpose is threefold: to "describe and evaluate new tests, techniques and innovative directions"; to "review the literature and bring the reader up to date on standard, widely used assessment techniques"; to "provide helpful background material to assessment psychologists . . . on philosophical and methodological bases, on historical background and on relevant topics from related fields." (preface)

Although test experts might caution against the dissemination of information about tests whose reliability and validity have not been rigorously established, such a list is available in the following:

G448 Ki-Taek, Chun, and others. Measures for psychological assessment: a guide to 3,000 original sources and their application. Ann Arbor: Survey Research Center of the Institute for Social Research, Univ. of Michigan, 1975. 664p.

The authors point out that while reviews of published tests are readily available in Buros' publications, no comparable systematic coverage exists of the "much greater number of less formal and often ad hoc assessment devices" that have been "developed and described in journal articles." This book is designed to help remedy the situation by providing "a comprehensive bibliography relating to all measures of mental health and related concepts. Since inclusiveness is a most desirable feature here, an attempt has been made to cite all measures, whether they are popular or infamous, visible or obscure, and recent or old. The entries in this volume are based on our search of 26 measurement-related journals in psychology and sociology from the period 1960–1970. . . ." A "primary reference" section lists about 3,000 references to journal articles or other publications in which measures were first described, and an "applications" section cites references to approximately 6,600 instances where these measures have been used. Includes author and descriptor indexes.

Specialized reference books are available for some specific tests, such as the following on the Rorschach test or the Minnesota Multiphasic Personality Inventory.

G449 Lang, Alfred. Rorschach-bibliography, 1921–1964. Berne–Stuttgart: Hans Huber, 1966. 191p.

3,855 classified titles, with author index.

G450 Butcher, James N., and Paolo Pancheri. A handbook of cross-national MMPI research. Minneapolis: Univ. of Minnesota Pr., 1976. 470p.

G451 Dahlstrom, W. Grant, and others. An MMPI handbook, v.I: Clinical interpretation. Rev. ed.

Minneapolis: Univ. of Minnesota Pr., 1972. 507p. v.II: Research applications. Rev. ed. Minneapolis: Univ. of Minnesota Pr., 1975. 586p.

G452 Good, Patricia King-Ellison, and John P. Brantner. A practical guide to the MMPI: an introduction for psychologists, physicians, social workers and other professionals. Rev. and exp. ed. Minneapolis: Univ. of Minnesota Pr., 1974. 102p.

G453 Swenson, Wendell M., and others. An MMPI source book: basic item, scale, and pattern data on 50,000 medical patients. Minneapolis: Univ. of Minnesota Pr., 1973. 150p.

G454 Taulbee, Earl S., and others. The Minnesota Multiphasic Personality Inventory (MMPI): a comprehensive, annotated bibliography (1940–1965). Troy, N.Y.: Whitston, 1977. 603p.

There are also specialized reference books that focus on tests for particular subgroups of the population, such as the following two on children and on the aged:

G455 Johnson, Orval G. Tests and measurements in child development: handbook II. San Francisco: Jossey-Bass, 1976. 2v.

The purpose of this handbook and of its predecessor—Orval G. Johnson and James W. Bommarito, *Tests and measurements in child development: a handbook* (San Francisco: Jossey-Bass, 1971 [518p.]) **(G456)**—is to provide a source of information on "unpublished measures suitable for children" referred to in professional journals and other sources. Handbook I lists measures suitable for ages 0–12, Handbook II for ages 0–18. The measures described in Handbook I were obtained from a search of the literature published from 1956 to 1965, those in Handbook II of the literature from 1966 through 1974.

Entries are arranged alphabetically by name under each of 11 categories and subcategories. The following information is presented for each measure: name of measure (provided by author or person writing description), author, age for which measure is appropriate, variable, type of measure, source from which measure may be obtained, description, reliability and validity, and a bibliography.

G457 Mangen, David J., and Warren A. Peterson, eds. Research instruments in social gerontology, v.1: Clinical and social psychology. Minneapolis: Univ. of Minnesota Pr., 1982. 652p.

The editors of this projected three-volume series intend to develop a reference source on more than 400 measurements to assess individual and social behaviors, attitudes, and traits among the aging. The present volume details the theoretical conceptualization, validity, reliability, and relevance of tests in 11 categories, including intellectual functioning, personality, adaptation, and self-concept and self-esteem. Subject and name (but no test) indexes.

ABSTRACTS AND SUMMARIES
General

G458 Psychological abstracts. v.1– , 1927– . Washington, D.C.: American Psychological Assn. Monthly.

The most important abstracting service for psychology and related disciplines. Abstracts are nonevaluative and cover serials and monographs. More than 950 journals, many of which are foreign, are regularly searched and selectively abstracted. Some entries, such as for secondary sources and materials considered peripheral to psychology, are unannotated or briefly annotated.

The abstracts are arranged under 16 major categories, some of which have subcategories. Each monthly issue has author and subject indexes with cumulative indexes every six months. Three-year cumulations are available. Subject headings are reviewed annually and revised as interests shift and grow.

The predecessor to *Psychological abstracts* is *Psychological index*. See G478.

Several new derivatives, published quarterly by the American Psychological Association, were initiated early in the 1980s. They supply for various fields of psychology abstracts from subcategories of the PsycINFO Database from which *Psychological abstracts* is produced. These are *PsycSCAN: applied psychology; PsycSCAN: clinical psychology; PsycSCAN: developmental psychology;* and *PsycSCAN: LD/MR* (learning disorders and mental retardation), dist. by American Psychological Association, 1400 N. Uhle St., Arlington, VA 22201.

Bulletin signalétique. Sec. 390, Psychologie, psychopathologie, psychiatrie. Description at A149.

Specialized

G459 Abstracts and reviews in behavioral biology. v.1–14, 1968–74. Baltimore: Natl. Education Consultants. Monthly.

Formerly (through 1971) *Communications in behavior biology*, pt.B, *Abstracts and index*.

G460 Child development abstracts and bibliography, v.1– , 1927– . Chicago: Society for Research in Child Development. 3/yr.

Contains about 1,200 abstracts per year from approximately 190 professional periodicals. Heavy emphasis on general experimental, social, and clinical psychology. Other subject areas included are biology, public health, medicine, and education. Reviews about 75 books annually, related to the growth and development of children; lists books received. Author and subject indexes.

G461 Developmental disabilities abstracts. v.1–13, 1964–78. Washington, D.C.: Dept. of Health, Education, and Welfare, Office of Human Development, Developmental Disabilities Office. Quarterly. (Formerly: Mental retardation abstracts: mental retardation and developmental disabilities)

Classified abstracts of periodical literature and books, with author and subject indexes.

G462 French-language psychology. v.1– , 1980– . New York: North-Holland. V.1 in 4 issues.

Designed to inform English-speaking psychologists about the literature of psychology in French-speaking countries, primarily Belgium, Canada, France, and Switzerland. Lists abstracts or reviews books and articles published in French since January 1979, with full-page summaries for the most outstanding items. Also publishes general articles on the progress and current state of psychology in these countries.

G463 The German journal of psychology; a quarterly of abstracts and review articles. v.1– , 1977– . Toronto: C. J. Hogrefe. Quarterly.

Published under the auspices of the International Union of Psychological Science, the *GJP* provides nonevaluative abstracts in English of German-language works on psychology published in Austria, the Federal Republic of Germany, the German Democratic Republic, and Switzerland. Abstracts are of journal articles, books, and psychological tests and are arranged alphabetically by author within broad subject categories. English translation of title precedes German title. It also "publishes review articles on selected topics of current research and university training in psychology, and on the status of applied psychology in the German-speaking countries."

G464 Psychopharmacology abstracts. v.1– , 1961– . Chevy Chase, Md.: National Inst. of Mental Health; dist. by Supt. of Documents. Quarterly.

Aim of this information service is to provide rapid access to the world's literature regarding new developments and research results in the field of psychopharmacology. Classified arrangement with author and subject indexes, which cumulate with each volume.

G465 Research relating to children: bulletin no.1–42, Dec. 1948–Feb. 1979. Urbana, Ill.: ERIC Clearinghouse on Early Childhood Education; dist. by Supt. of Documents.

For more than 30 years, the bulletin reported on research completed or in progress relating to such matters as growth and development of children; special groups of children; the child in the family; socioeconomic, cultural, and educational factors affecting children; and social, health, and educational services for children. Information supplied for each research project included name(s) of investigator(s), purpose, subjects, methods, findings (if available), duration, cooperating group(s), and publication(s), if any. A special section was devoted to long-term research.

Carrie Lee Rothgeb produced *Abstracts of the standard edition of the complete psychological works of Sigmund Freud* (New York: Aronson, 1973 [315p.]) (**G466**) and coproduced with Siegfried M. Clemens *Abstracts of the collected works of C. G. Jung* (Rockville, Md.: National Inst. of Mental Health; dist. by Supt. of Documents, 1978 [1v., various paging]) (**G467**).

G468 Schizophrenia bulletin. Rockville, Md.: National Inst. of Mental Health; dist. by Supt. of Documents. v.1– , 1969– . Quarterly.

"Purpose is to facilitate the dissemination and exchange of information about schizophrenia and to provide abstracts of the recent literature on the subject." International in scope.

G469 USSR and Eastern Europe scientific abstracts. Biomedical and behavioral sciences. Arlington, Va.: U.S. Joint Publications Research Service; Springfield, Va.: dist. by National Technical Information Service. No.1– , March 13, 1973– . (Formerly: USSR and Eastern Europe scientific abstracts. Biomedical sciences.)

BIBLIOGRAPHIES OF BIBLIOGRAPHIES

G470 Louttit, Chauncey M. Bibliography of bibliographies in psychology, 1900–1927. Washington, D.C.: National Research Council, 1928. Reprint, New York: Burt Franklin, 1970. 108p. [National Research Council. Bulletin 65.]

Lists 2,134 bibliographies in books or articles that (1) contain no less than 50 specific references, (2) rate high for complete coverage of the subject, and (3) provide good historical orientation. Four main parts: a list of periodicals and general works searched; "Further bibliographical sources"—indexes, abstracts, review journals; main list of bibliographies, arranged by author; and subject index with numerous cross-references. Some titles published as early as 1850 are included because of their historical importance.

With *Psychological abstracts* (G458), this bibliography of bibliographies succeeds in providing continuous coverage of psychological bibliographies through the twentieth century. *Psychological abstracts* has, from its beginning in 1927, served as a current bibliography of bibliographies by its inclusion of "Bibliographies" ("Bibliography" before 1947) in the index. Starting with only 4 bibliographies for 1927, the number has risen at times to more than 100 per year as bibliographical studies have increased.

CURRENT BIBLIOGRAPHIES

G471 "Checklist for ordering recent materials in psychology." *In* Perceptual and motor skills. v.8– , 1958– . Perceptual and Motor Skills, P.O. Box 9229, Missoula, MT 59807. Bimonthly. 2v./yr.

Since the mid-fifties, *Perceptual and motor skills* has featured this checklist, which is an unannotated list alphabetically arranged by author of books and a few other works in all areas of psychology. Usually includes price.

G472 Personnel literature. v.1– , 1941– . Washington, D.C.: U.S. Office of Personnel Management Library; dist. by Supt. of Documents. Monthly. (Formerly issued by U.S. Civil Service Commission Library)

Lists alphabetically by subject materials in the field of personnel administration received in the library. Includes monographs and articles from periodicals. Annual name and subject index. Several subject bibliographies are published annually in the Personnel Bibliography series.

G473 "Psychopharmacology—a recurring bibliography." *In* Psychopharmacology bulletin. Rockville, Md.: Dept. of Health, Education, and Welfare, Public Health Service, Alcohol, Drug Abuse, and Mental Health Administration, National Inst. of Mental Health, Washington, D.C.; dist. by Supt. of Documents. v.11, no.2, April 1975– .

In 1975 "Psychopharmacology—a recurring bibliography" became a continuing feature of the bulletin. It is a subject and author bibliography of recent papers on psychopharmacology from the world literature, computer-generated by the Medical Literature Analysis and Retrieval System (MEDLARS) of the National Library of Medicine, National Institute of Health.

G474 Zeitschrift für experimentelle und angewandte Psychologie. v.1– , 1953– . Göttingen: Verlag für Psychologie. 4/yr.

Zeitschrift für Psychologie und Physiologie der Sinnesorgane (v.1–156, 1890–1944) provided world coverage of psychological literature from 1890–1916, when it was interrupted. Indexed only German literature for 1925–44. For the years 1926–29, psychological literature published outside Germany was indexed in *Archiv für die gesamte Psychologie* (v.62–79, 1928–31). Beginning in 1911, *Zeitschrift* adopted the pattern of *Psychological index*: some 1,000 items (books, articles, dissertations) listed under 3 main areas with 33 subdivisions, supplemented with author index. Summaries in French and English. Current coverage revived by *Zeitschrift für experimentelle und angewandte Psychologie* in 1965. The gap has been largely filled by:

G475 Wellek, Albert. Gesamtverzeichnis der deutschsprachigen psychologischen Literatur der Jahre 1942 bis 1960. Göttingen: Verlag für Psychologie, 1965. 876p.

Extends the annual record of German psychological literature from 1944, the year *Zeitschrift für Psychologie* suspended publication of its index service, to 1960. Lists more than 15,000 monographs and articles in German.

RETROSPECTIVE BIBLIOGRAPHIES

General

G476 Columbia University. Libraries. Psychology Library. Author index to Psychological index, 1894–1935, and Psychological abstracts, 1927–1958. Boston: Hall, 1960. 5v.

The result of publishing a card index prepared at Columbia by clipping each new issue of *PI* and *PA*, this project provides comprehensive control over the professional literature for most of the scientific period. The 5 volumes bring all 320,000 entries of the two series together in a single alphabet. First supplement, 1959–63. Compiled by Psychology Library. Columbia Univ. (Boston: Hall, 1965). Second supplement, 1964–68. 2v. Compiled by the staff of G. K. Hall (Boston: Hall, 1970). Indexes: 1969–71; 1972–74; 1975–77 (Washington, D.C.: American Psychological Assn., 1972–78).

G477 Psychological abstracts. Cumulated subject index to Psychological abstracts, 1927–1960. Boston: Hall, 1966. 2v. First supplement, 1961–65. Second supplement, 1966–68. 2v. (Boston: Hall, 1968–71). Indexes, 1969–71, 2v.; 1972–74, 2v.; 1975–77, 2v.; 1978–80, 2v. (Washington, D.C.: American Psychological Assn., 1968–81).

In volumes for 1975–77, specialized bibliographies can be located under heading "Bibliography"; for biographical material see such headings as "Autobiography," "Biography," "Obituary." Headings vary in earlier volumes. For a general description of *Psychological abstracts*, see G458.

G478 Psychological index, 1894–1935: an annual bibliography of the literature of psychology and cognate subjects. Princeton, N.J.: Psychological Review Corp., 1894–1936. 42v.

Begun as a supplement to *Psychological review*, this annual bibliography informally continued Rand's *Bibliography of philosophy, psychology and cognate subjects* (G480) and provided extensive coverage of all the literature of psychology and allied fields (150,844 items). Listed original publications in all languages—books, articles, and translations—and new editions in English, German, French, and Italian. Indexed about 3,000 titles a year in 350 periodicals. Classified arrangement with alphabetical author index. Its task of listing psychological literature was absorbed by *Psychological abstracts*.

G479 Psychological register. Ed. by Carl Murchison. Worcester, Mass.: Clark Univ. Pr., 1929–32. v.2–3.

Has brief biographies with full bibliographies of prominent psychologists throughout the world, arranged by country. V.1, designed to include psychologists from ancient times to 1929, was never published. V.2 (1929), with 1,250 psychologists from 29 countries, was entirely superseded by v.3 (1932), with 2,400 psychologists from 40 countries. Each entry gives name, address, place and date of birth, education and degrees, positions held, professional memberships, and bibliography of published contributions. No cumulative name index.

G480 Rand, Benjamin. Bibliography of philosophy, psychology and cognate subjects. New York: Macmillan, 1905. 2v.

Forms v.3 of *Dictionary of philosophy and psychology* (G550). Pt. 1 of this volume, "History of philosophy," includes works by and about the great philosophical thinkers from Thales to Spencer. Pt.2, arranged systematically, devotes sec. G (p.913–1,192) to psychology as a separate subject. More than 14,000 items are arranged by author under 43 major subject headings. No index. Sec. G, which brings the literature to 1902, is continued by *Psychological index* (G478).

G481 Dambauer, J., ed. Bibliographie der deutsch-sprachigen psychologischen Literatur. Frankfurt: Klostermann. 8v. 1972–79.

A compendium that provides access to the German-language literature in psychology.

Specialized Bibliographies

The specialized bibliographies in the field of psychology cover an enormous range of detailed subareas, from the hyperkinetic child through factor analysis, from the perception of time to psychological research in a particular country during particular years. This section includes a selection from this heterogeneous group, published by a wide variety of sources. For example, a decade of research on memory (1960–69) is traced in a series of bibliographies published in *Perceptual and motor skills* 25:573–82, 825–39, 921–48 (1967); 28:903–26 (1969); 32:99–124 (1971) (G471); the United States government sometimes publishes bibliographies relevant to psychology which can be located through the *U.S. monthly catalog*. Interspersed among the following items are instances of such government-sponsored bibliographies, dealing especially with issues in mental health and/or mental retardation.

G482 Abrams, Susan, and Sandra Ciufo. Cooperative studies in mental health and behavioral sciences: an annotated bibliography summarizing two decades of cooperative research in mental health and behavioral sciences, 1956–1975. Washington, D.C.: U.S. Veterans Administration, Dept. of Medicine and Surgery, 1975. 71p.

G483 Feldman, Saul, and others, eds. Mental health administration: an annotated bibliography. Rockville, Md.: Dept. of Health, Education and Welfare, Public Health Service, Alcohol, Drug Abuse, and Mental Health Administration, National Inst. of Mental Health, Staff College, 1978. 449p.

More than a thousand fully annotated entries from literature of the period 1965–75, including journal articles, books, government publications, etc., cover such topics as roles and training of the mental health administrator, planning and decision making, program description, management information, staffing, and personnel management, mental health administration abroad, and so forth.

G484 Flax, James W., and others. Mental health and rural America: an overview and annotated bibliography. Rockville, Md.: Dept. of Health, Education, and Welfare, Public Health Service, Alcohol, Drug Abuse, and Mental Health Administration, National Inst. of Mental Health, Division of Mental Health Service Programs; dist. by Supt. of Documents, 1979. 216p.

Contains more than 350 entries listed under four main categories: profiles of rural America, mental health programs and problems, clinical issues, and manpower issues. Thorough summary of each work.

G485 Fox, Rita. Mental health planning: an annotated bibliography. [Hyattsville, Md.]: Dept. of Health, Education, and Welfare, Public Health Service, Health Resources Administration, Bureau of Health Planning, National Health Planning Information Center; dist. by Supt. of Documents, 1978. 159p. [Health planning bibliography series; 11]

Alcoholism, community health, drug abuse, mental retardation and developmental disabilities, psychiatric services, and state and regional planning are some of the areas of mental health planning treated in this bibliography. Lengthy annotations.

G486 Kelso, Dianne R., and Carolyn L. Attneave, comps. Bibliography of North American Indian mental health. Prepared under the auspices of the White Cloud Center. Westport, Conn.: Greenwood, 1981. 411p.

Provides more than 1,350 citations pertaining to North American native peoples (including Indians, Aleuts, Eskimos, and Metis) and mental health issues, intended to be of use primarily to scholars and those engaged in mental health service delivery. All entries are in the English language, the majority of them being articles in referenced journals published in the 1970s, though many of them are of earlier dates.

G487 Newton, Frank, and others. Hispanic mental health research: a reference guide. Berkeley: Univ. of California Pr., 1982. 685p.

Contains about 2,000 annotated entries about Hispanics ("all people of Spanish speaking/surname origin residing in the United States or Puerto Rico") and mental health issues, including works related to anthropology, education, psychology, psychiatry, sociology, and social work published through 1977, with a few titles for 1978 and 1979. Annotations are not evaluative.

G488 Summerlin, Florence A. Religion and mental health: a bibliography. Rockville, Md.: Dept. of Health and Human Services, Public Health Service, Alcohol, Drug Abuse, and Mental Health Administration, National Inst. of Mental Health; dist. by Supt. of Documents, 1980. 401p.

Contains more than 1,800 abstracts of journal articles, reports, and books on topics pertaining to religion and mental health, of interest primarily to psychologists, psychiatrists, clergy, social workers, and other professionals.

G489 U.S. National Institute of Mental Health. NIMH research on the mental health of the aging. Washington, D.C.: Govt. Print. Off., 1972. 74p.

G490 Coelho, George V., and Richard I. Irving, eds. Coping and adaptation: an annotated bibliography and study guide. Rockville, Md.: National Inst. of Mental Health; dist. by Supt. of Documents, 1981. 480p.

"Provides mental health researchers and practitioners with recent, relevant mental health information on theoretical, developmental, clinical, behavioral, and social issues concerning coping and adaptation. The key substantive areas include major psychosocial and developmental transitions in the life cycle, stressful situations of rapid change, life-threatening crises of severe injury or illness, and seriously detrimental and handicapping conditions of individual or social origin" (introduction).

G491 Heber, Rick, and others [for] U.S. President's Panel on Mental Retardation. Bibliography of world literature on mental retardation, Jan. 1940–March 1963. Washington, D.C.: U.S. Dept. of Health, Education, and Welfare; dist. by Supt. of Documents, 1963. 564p.

G492 ———. ———. Supplement, March 1963–Dec. 31, 1964. Washington, D.C.: U.S. Dept. of Health, Education, and Welfare; dist. by Supt. of Documents, 1965. 99p.

These older works emphasize scientific and professional literature that directly discusses mental retardation, and literature on conditions and diseases known to be associated with retardation.

Various bibliographies emphasize child research, or problems with particular subgroups of children. The old works are listed in Louis N. Wilson, *Bibliography of child study: 1898–1912* (Worcester, Mass.: Clark Univ. Pr., and Washington, D.C.: U.S. Govt. Print. Off., 1899–1912; reprint, New York: Arno, 1975 [135p.]) **(G493)**.

Two major retrospective bibliographies published by the American Psychological Association were derived from *Psychological abstracts* and the PsycINFO Database, the first consisting of 4,000 abstracts on learning and psychoneurological disorders; communication, hearing, language, speech, and behavior disorders; and dyslexia and hyperkinesis, and the second consisting of 3,600 abstracts on autism and mild to severe mental retardation. Both include orig-

inal research, case histories, practical applications, and reviews of the literature. *PsycINFO retrospective: learning and communication disorders, 1971–1980* (1982 [508p.]) **(G494)**, and *PsycINFO retrospective: mental retardation, 1971–1980* (1982 [468p.]) **(G495)**.

G496 Winchell, Carol Ann. The hyperkinetic child: a bibliography of medical, educational, and behavioral studies. Westport, Conn.: Greenwood, 1975. 182p.

Contains close to 1,900 entries representing primarily the 1950s through mid-1974, with a few "classic" studies from the early twentieth century. Includes journal articles, books, chapters in books, conference reports, proceedings of symposia, government documents, pamphlets, and theses and dissertations. Classified arrangement with author index and selective key-word subject index. Supplemented by the author's *The hyperkinetic child: an annotated bibliography, 1974–1979* (Westport, Conn.: Greenwood, 1981 [451p.] [Contemporary problems of childhood, no.4]) **(G497)**.

G498 U.S. National Institute of Mental Health. Bibliography on the hyperkinetic behavior syndrome. Rockville, Md.: Dept. of Health, Education, and Welfare, Public Health Service, Alcohol, Drug Abuse, and Mental Health Administration, National Inst. of Mental Health, 1978. 40p.

Unannotated references to recent literature about the hyperkinetic behavior syndrome, drug treatment, and other treatments or hypotheses about the hyperkinetic behavior syndrome. "The National Institute of Mental Health proposes that this publication be used to increase awareness and understanding of the sociopsychological, physiological, and pharmacological dimensions of the hyperkinetic behavior syndrome" (foreword).

G499 Benson, Hazel B. Behavior modification and the child: an annotated bibliography. Westport, Conn.: Greenwood, 1979. 398p. [Contemporary problems of childhood, no.3]

Contains approximately 2,150 annotated entries, which refer to English-language publications, including popular and professional journal articles, books, chapters in books, conference reports, government documents, pamphlets, and doctoral dissertations published mainly from 1956 to 1977, with a few items from earlier years. An unannotated addendum lists about 150 works from late 1977 and 1978. Covers such areas as general introductory material, behavioral techniques for specific behaviors and for the handicapped child, educational applications, use by professions, training, and research in behavior modification. Appendixes include basic bibliographic tools, audiovisual materials, and a glossary. Author index and selective key-word subject index.

Bibliographies on behavior modification are not limited to its use with children, as indicated by William R. Morrow and others, *Behavior therapy bibliography, 1950–1969; annotated and indexed* (Columbia: Univ. of Missouri Pr., 1971 [165p.]) **(G500)**.

The older literature on psychotherapy in general is surveyed in the following title.

G501 Strupp, Hans H., and Allen E. Bergin. Research in individual psychotherapy: a bibliography. Chevy Chase, Md.: National Inst. of Mental Health, 1969. 167p. [Public Health Service publication 1944]

A contribution to understanding the process, effect, and spread of psychotherapy. Its 2,741 citations deal with clinical, educational, and scientific problems, with emphasis upon studies showing rigorous research design and quantitative results. Index to the content areas within which the research falls.

The following items sample the tremendously variegated kinds of retrospective bibliographies available in other areas relevant to psychology.

G502 Alvarez, Walter C. Minds that came back. Philadelphia: Lippincott, 1961. 384p.

The narratives of 75 persons who had once been neurotic or psychotic are followed by an annotated bibliography of works (p.339–73) by people who, having been ill over many years, have written about their experiences.

G503 Crabtree, J. Michael, and Kenneth E. Moyer. Bibliography of aggressive behavior: a reader's guide to the research literature. New York: Alan R. Liss, 1977. 416p.

A substantial bibliography with classified arrangement of more than 3,800 references mainly to English-language books and journal articles dealing with human and animal aggression, broadly defined, published during the 50 years preceding the mid–1970s. Availability of items to most users was a consideration in selection. Should be useful to the novice as well as to the advanced researcher. Kenneth E. Moyer and Michael Crabtree, *Bibliography of aggressive behavior: a reader's guide to the literature, volume II* (New York: Alan R. Liss, 1981 [459p.]) (**G504**) provides more than 3,600 additional entries of works published in the 1970s. This volume gives broader coverage of the field of aggressive behavior and cites more foreign publications than the original volume.

G505 DeMause, Lloyd, ed. A bibliography of psychohistory. New York: Garland, 1975. 81p. [Garland reference library in social science, v.6]

Lists journal articles, books, unpublished papers, and doctoral dissertations, including some foreign works, on psychohistory—"broadly defined as the use of modern psychology in interpreting history." Divided into six sections: methodology and general, history of childhood, ancient, medieval, and Renaissance, modern, Asia. *Appendix: a guide to the interdisciplinary literature of the history of childhood,* by Manuel D. Lopez, is an annotated bibliography of miscellaneous works.

G506 Hinman, Suki, and Brian Boltan. Factor analytic studies, 1971–1975. Troy, N.Y.: Whitston, 1979. 386p.

G507 Lystad, Mary H. Social aspects of alienation: an annotated bibliography. Chevy Chase, Md.: National Inst. of Mental Health; dist. by Supt. of Documents, 1969. 92p. [Public Health Service publication 1978]

Annotated list of 225 studies directed toward the meaning of alienation and who is alienated. Project was undertaken "as a first step toward critical evaluation of the problems of alienation in modern society." Emphasis is on empirical studies in the years 1959–68.

G508 Nelson, David. Bibliography of British psychological research 1960–1966. London: Her Majesty's Stationery Office. Social Science Research Council; dist. by Redwood City, Calif.: Pendragon, 1971. 210p.

The main source for entries and pattern for classification scheme is *Psychological abstracts.* Each section begins with an assessment of British work by an expert in that field.

G509 Watson, Robert Irving. The history of psychology and the behavioral sciences: a bibliographic guide. New York: Springer, 1978. 241p.

This broad guide to the history of psychology and allied fields is designed primarily for the graduate student and specialist. It lists nearly 800 English- and foreign-language titles, almost all of them annotated, which are divided into five major sections—general resources, historical accounts, methods of historical research, historiographic fields, and historiographic theories—each of which has numerous subsections. No index.

G510 Wright, Logan. Bibliography on human intelligence. National Clearinghouse for Mental Health Information: an extensive bibliography. Washington, D.C.: Govt. Print. Off., 1969. 222p. [Public Health Service publication 1839]

Approximately 6,700 references provide inclusive coverage of the literature on intelligence and cognition. Main list of citations is arranged by author; classified and topical indexes.

G511 Young, Mary E. Child abuse and neglect (a bibliography with abstracts). Report for 1971–March 1979. Springfield, Va.: National Technical Information Service, 1979. 83p.

For more information on child abuse see Sociology chapter.

G512 Zelkind, Irving, and Joseph Sprug. Time research: 1172 studies. Metuchen, N.J.: Scarecrow, 1974. 253p.

Lists more than a thousand books, journal articles, and dissertations dealing with time, published between 1886 and 1973, arranged alphabetically by author, with independent, dependent, or other relevant variables identified for each work. Six indexes: frequency of citation, monographs (including books and chapters in books), dissertations, journals (studies grouped under journals in which they appeared), chronological (main entries arranged by date of publication), and variables (subject index).

G513 Zukerman, Elyse. Changing directions in the treatment of women: a mental health bibliography. Rockville, Md.: Dept. of Health, Education, and Welfare, Public Health Service, Alcohol, Drug Abuse, and Mental Health Administration, National Inst. of Mental Health, 1979. 494p.

The 400 items included in this bibliography are from 1960 through early 1977, except for some older psychoanalytic material. "The literature selected for inclusion goes beyond psychotherapy to include all efforts that help women grow and develop, cope with the crises that women experience, and deal with the pain and problems created by their social situation in our culture." Abstracts, which are often as long as a page to a page and a half, summarize contents of each work; there are no evaluations of research. Many articles from psychology journals are included.

Bibliographies are available for each of the major early psychoanalytic schools. The one on classical Freudian psychoanalysis is Alexander Grinstein, *Sigmund Freud's writings: a comprehensive bibliography* (New York: International Universities Pr., 1977 [181p.]) (**G514**); Jung's analytical psychology is covered in Joseph F. Vincie and Margreta Rathbauer-Vincie, *C.G. Jung and analytical psychology: a comprehensive bibliography* (New York: Garland, 1977 [325p.] [Reference library of social science, v.38]) (**G515**); Harold H. Mosak and Birdie Mosak, *A bibliography for Adlerian psychology* (Washington, D.C.: Hemisphere Pub. Co.; dist. by Halsted Pr., 1975 [320p.]) (**G516**), surveys Adler's individual psychology. A broad general reference tool for psychoanalysis is:

G517 Grinstein, Alexander. The index of psychoanalytic writings. New York: International Universities Pr., 1956–66. 9v.; 1971–75. 5v.

The first 5 volumes link up with J. Rickman's basic *Index psychoanalyticus, 1893–1926* (London: Woolf, 1968) (**G518**), to bring the record of books, monographs, articles, reviews, and abstracts published in every language through 1952. The 37,121 numbered entries are arranged alphabetically by author. V.5 is a subject index. For foreign works that did not appear in English, translation of title is provided. All known reviews and abstracts are noted for each title. V.6–9 continue the record through 1959, v.10–14 through 1969. V.9 and 14 are subject indexes.

Current literature is surveyed in *Annual survey of psychoanalysis* (G436).

Catalogs have been published for several specialized libraries, such as the following two:

G519 Geneva. Bibliothèque publique et universitaire. Catalog of the Jean Piaget archives, University of Geneva/Catalogue des archives Jean Piaget, Université de Genève. Boston: Hall, 1975. 384p.

Divided into three parts: Pt.1 includes all publications by Piaget from 1907 to June 1974; Pt. 2, papers of Piaget's collaborators at Geneva University; and Pt. 3, secondary literature related to Piagetian theory and research.

G520 Indiana Univ. Institute for Sex Research. Library. Catalog of the social and behavioral sciences monograph section. Boston: Hall, 1975. 4v.

G521 ———. Catalog of the periodical literature in the social and behavioral sciences section; including supplement to monographs, 1973–75. Boston: Hall, 1976. 4v.

A grant from the National Institute of Mental Health enabled the institute to produce catalogs of most of its library's holdings, comprising at the time more than 30,000 monographs, journals, and reprints relevant to sexual behavior, which may well be one of the world's largest collections in this area. The catalog contains journal articles and monographs catalogued up to November 1975. Erotic art and literature are not included; however, "bibliographies and censorship studies of such materials are included." The monographic collection consists mainly of 19th- and 20th-century works in Western languages, though many different languages and periods are represented. More recent literature collected by the institute may be found in *Sex studies index, 1980*, by the Alfred C. Kinsey Institute for Sex Research, Indiana Univ. (Boston: Hall, 1982 [219p.]) (**G522**), which lists works mainly published in 1979–80 (with a few for 1978) in two indexes: author and subject. A special vocabulary developed by the institute for classifying its collection, specified in its *Sexual nomenclature: a thesaurus* (see G570), is used in the subject index.

PERIODICALS

There are two fairly recent and relatively comprehensive guides to psychological periodicals:

G523 Markle, Allan, and Roger C. Rinn, eds. Author's guide to journals in psychology, psychiatry and social work. New York: Haworth Pr., 1977. 256p.

Designed to help scholars locate those journals most likely to accept their work for publication. More than 950 English-language journals are listed alphabetically by title, with such information supplied for each as manuscript submission address; major content areas; types of articles usually accepted, e.g., research, theoretical, review; topics preferred; inappropriate manuscripts; where indexed/abstracted; subscription address and cost; acceptance rate; style requirements; circulation.

G524 Tompkins, Margaret, and Norma Shirley. Serials in psychology and allied fields. 2d ed. Troy, N.Y.: Whitson, 1976. 472p.

Second edition, which more than doubles number of entries in 1969 edition, lists in alphabetical order more than 900 currently published nongovernmental, mostly English-language serials. Each entry usually provides such data as frequency of publication, subscription rate, name of editor, address, date of first issue, circulation, copyright, where indexed, objectives. Subject listing of publications as well as combined title and subject index. An older international list is:

G525 Psychologie: liste mondiale des périodiques spécialisés. Psychology; world list of specialized periodicals. Paris: Mouton, 1967. 165p.

Alphabetical list by country (with separate list for international organizations) of periodicals that publish original studies in psychology. Descriptive information for each title includes location, editor, sponsor, some title changes, size of issue, and scope of interest.

Narrower in scope is:

G526 Arnold, Darlene Baden, and Kenneth O. Doyle, Jr. Educational psychology journals: a scholar's guide. Metuchen, N.J.: Scarecrow, 1975. 143p.

Lists 122 journals "that intersect psychology and education" and for each one provides such information as editor and editorial address, publisher and copyright holder, subscription data (cost, frequency, etc.), typical content areas of articles, intended audience, special features, acceptance/rejection criteria and procedures, style requirements, payment, and whether or not reprints are available. Subject index.

DIRECTORIES AND BIOGRAPHICAL INFORMATION

Directories

G527 American Psychological Assn. Directory. 1916– . Washington, D.C.: The Assn.

Title varies. The main section of the 1983 directory is a biographical roster that provides name, address, APA divisional membership status, and other itemized information for more than 56,000 fellows, members, and associates. This is followed by a geographical index, divisional membership roster, and diplomate rosters of the American Board of Professional Psychology and the American Board of Psychological Hypnosis. In addition, includes lists of APA officers, concise information about the association, bylaws, ethical standards of psychologists, standards for providers of psychological services, psychology laws in the United States and Canada, and other information.

G528 American Psychological Assn. Membership register. Washington, D.C.: 1967– .

Issued annually in years when the fuller directory is not published. Provides mailing addresses, telephone numbers, and membership status of current APA members. Also contains divisional membership rosters and lists of diplomates of the American Board of Professional Psychology and the American Board of Psychological Hypnosis.

G529 Canadian Psychological Assn. Directory. Ottawa: The Assn. Irregular.

Contains list of members, bylaws, code of ethics. Text is in English and French.

G530 Psychonomic Society. Membership directory. Austin: Publications Office, Psychonomic Society, 1979. 48p.

Lists and provides institutional affiliation for more than 2,000 members of the society. To become a member, an individual must be actively engaged in empirical research in psychology.

G531 International directory of psychologists. 3d ed. Ed. by E.H. Jacobson and others. New York: North-Holland, 1980. 606p.

Provides, for psychologists outside of the United States and Canada, information similar to that listed in the *American psychological association directory.*

G532 Wolman, Benjamin B. International directory of psychology: a guide to people, places, and policies. New York: Plenum, 1979. 279p.

Presents information about psychology in 66 countries, obtained from questionnaires sent to executive offices of national psychological organizations, governmental bodies, or other authorized persons. Although not always uniform, usually includes information for each country about the national psychological organization (official name, address, internal structure, membership, major activities), education and training of psychologists, legal status, research and publications, occupational distribution, and opportunities for foreign psychologists.

G533 National register of health service providers in psychology. Washington, D.C.: Council for the National Register of Health Service Providers in Psychology, 1980. 390p.

Lists approximately 12,300 psychologists (or about two-thirds of all those eligible according to the register's criteria). Application for listing is voluntary. In order to be listed, a psychologist must have a doctorate degree in psychology from an accredited institution and two years of supervised experience in health service, and must be currently licensed or certified by a state board of examiners of psychology to engage in independent practice of psychology. Alphabetical listing and geographical index.

G534 Reference encyclopedia of American psychology and psychiatry. Ed. by Barry T. Klein. Rye, N.Y.: Todd, 1975. 459p.

This "encyclopedia" contains the following lists (with supplementary information for most items in each list): associations, societies, and organizations; research centers; periodicals; special libraries; foundation grants and awards; audiovisual aids; psychiatric hospitals; mental health centers; psychology graduate schools; psychiatric training programs. A subject-category index ties items in the various lists together by subject.

G535 The national directory of mental health: A Guide to Adult Out-patient Mental Health Facilities and Services throughout the United States. Comp. and prep. by Neal-Schuman Publishers, Inc. New York: John Wiley, 1980. 543p.

Pt. 1 suggests criteria to consider when seeking help with a mental health problem; it also lists state mental health associations and national "hot line" numbers. Pt. 2 lists approximately 3,600 outpatient facilities by state. Entries include address, telephone number, services provided, staff, types of therapy, referral fee, and waiting time. Pt. 3 contains an index to facilities and an index to services and therapies.

G536 U.S. National Institute of Mental Health. Mental health directory, 1977. Rockville, Md.: Dept. of Health, Education, and Welfare, Public Health Service, Alcohol, Drug Abuse, and Mental Health Administration; dist. by Supt. of Documents, 1977. 620p.

Provides names, addresses, and, usually, telephone numbers for regional alcohol, drug abuse, and mental health administration offices of DHEW, and for state mental health authorities, facilities, and services. Some entries indicate geographic areas served, auspices or "type of agency operating and establishing policy for the facility," and services provided. Appendix lists voluntary mental health associations, self-help organizations for mental health, and other information sources connected with mental health.

G537 Directory, federally funded community mental health centers. Rockville, Md.: Dept. of Health, Education, and Welfare, Public Health Service, Alcohol, Drug Abuse, and Mental Health Administration, National Inst. of Mental Health; dist. by Supt. of Documents, 1979. 85p.

Lists federally funded community mental health centers by state and for each provides address, telephone number, director, board chairperson, and type of grant received, e.g., construction grant, initial operations grant, consultation and education grant, etc.

G538 Directory of national information sources on handicapping conditions and related services. Washington, D.C.: Dept. of Health, Education, and Welfare, Office of Human Development, Office for Handicapped Individuals, Clearinghouse on the Handicapped; dist. by Supt. of Documents, 1976. 405p.

Lists national organizations providing direct services to the physically and mentally handicapped, and for each organization supplies such information as address, phone number, handicapping conditions served, scope of activities, and services offered. Provides similar information for "federal information sources." Index.

G539 International directory of mental retardation resources. 2d ed. Ed. by Rosemary F. Dybwad and Florence Heller. Rev. 1977–78. Washington, D.C.: Dept. of Health, Education, and Welfare, Office of Human Development Services, President's Committee on Mental Retardation, 1978. 360p.

Pt.1 provides information about services offered for the mentally retarded by the United Nations and its specialized agencies as well as by other international organizations, governmental and non-governmental. Pt.2 supplies reports on 87 individual countries, with varying amounts of information regarding government agencies with mental retardation responsibility, voluntary organizations, research, publications, brief descriptive notes on program areas, and other information.

Biography and History

Useful sources of biographical and bibliographical information about the major figures in the history of psychology are Robert I. Watson, *The great psychologists,* described at G26; and Edwin G. Boring, *A history of experimental psychology,* described at G21. Other sources of psychological biography are listed below.

G542 Benjamin, Ludy T., Jr., and Kathryn L. Heider. "History of psychology in biography: a bibliography." Journal supplement abstract service, Catalog of selected documents in psychology 6 (1976). Ms No.1276. 21p.

G543 Benjamin, Ludy T., Jr. "Prominent psychologists; a selected bibliography of biographical sources." Journal supplement abstract service, Catalog of selected documents in psychology 4 (1974). Ms No.535. 32p.

G544 Hilgard, Ernest R., ed. American psychology in historical perspective: addresses of the presidents of the American Psychological Association, 1892–1977. Washington, D.C.: American Psychological Assn., 1978. 558p.

Provides one-page biographies of each of the presidents of the association, and either the full text or a brief abstract of each presidential address.

G545 A history of psychology in autobiography. 6v. 1930–74. Publisher varies.

This series grew out of Boring's recognition that it is impossible to get the important facts on the scientific development of many psychologists except from the individuals themselves. Clark Univ. Pr. published 3 volumes before the original selection committee, led by Carl Murchison, disbanded. With a new publisher, Boring and others edited v.4 and 5. V.6, edited by Gardner Lindzey, was published in 1974; v.7 in 1980 (see G31).

A related work is T. S. Krawiec, ed., *The psychologists*, 2v. (New York: Oxford Univ. Pr., 1972,

1974); v.3, *The psychologists: autobiographies of distinguished living psychologists* (Brandon, Vt.: Clinical Psychology, 1978) **(G546)**.

So far, three volumes of this series have appeared. In each, about a dozen prominent psychologists in various areas of the discipline reminisce (in approximately 25 to 50 pages by each psychologist) about their lives. Includes a portrait and list of references for each autobiographee. A biographical index identifies persons referred to in the autobiographies.

G547 Watson, Robert I., Sr., ed. Eminent contributors to psychology: v.1, A bibliography of primary references. 469p.; v.2, A bibliography of secondary references. 1,158p. New York: Springer, 1974–76.

V.1 lists 538 individuals who lived between 1600 and 1967 and who were "selected because of their contributions to psychology"; for each one, cites primary sources ranging from 1 to 80, totaling about 12,000 references. Provides birth and death dates, country or countries where "principal work was done," "major field of endeavor," and "eminence rating score," determined by an international panel of experts. V.2 lists about 55,000 secondary references for these same individuals.

A useful companion to Watson is Leonard Zusne, *Names in the history of psychology: a biographical sourcebook* (Washington, D.C.: Hemisphere; dist. by Halsted, 1975 [489p.]) **(G548)**. The author's 526 biographees are selected largely from the same roster of names compiled by Edwin G. Boring and Robert I. Watson, used by the latter as the basis for the above. Like Watson, Zusne is interested in the individual's contribution to psychology, and his short biographies are based on this criterion. Information for each biographee includes "rating of eminence" using same rating as Watson, birth and death dates, highest degree, relevant positions held, and biographic references. Vernon Nordby and Calvin S. Hall, *A guide to psychologists and their concepts* (San Francisco: Freeman; dist. by Scribner, 1975 [187p.]) **(G549)**, is intended for those with little knowledge of psychology. It provides brief biographical sketches of 42 psychologists (19 of whom are European, the rest American) selected primarily because their ideas are still viable and influential in today's world. More than 400 "first, second and third-order concepts" are mentioned and defined in the various biographies. They are listed in the subject index. Also includes name index.

DICTIONARIES

G550 Baldwin, James M. Dictionary of philosophy and psychology, including many of the principal conceptions of ethics, logic, aesthetics, philosophy of religion, mental pathology, anthropology, biology, neurology, physiology, economics, political and social philosophy, philology, physical science and education, and giving a terminology in English, French, German and Italian. New York: Macmillan, 1901–5. 3v. in 4. Reprint, Gloucester, Mass.: Peter Smith, 1960.

Strives to understand the principal terms and concepts in philosophy, psychology, and cognate fields and define them lucidly. Attempts to set terms and concepts, particularly those of larger significance, into the context of the intellectual movements that gave them standing. In consequence, there are entries of 4 kinds: (1) concise definitions, (2) definitions plus explanatory information, (3) longer articles of 1,000–5,000 words, and (4) some biography. Many citations of supporting literature. Authoritative for the period.

G551 Chaplin, J. P. Dictionary of psychology. New rev. ed. New York: Dell, 1975. 576p.

Intent is to present "accurate, concise, and meaningful definitions" of technical terms used in the literature of psychology, including some terms from the related disciplines of psychoanalysis, psychiatry, and biology. A number of semipopular terms and terms from the literature of pseudo-psychology and spiritualism are also included. Some entries are in the form of "extended articles," such as on the central concepts and schools of psychology, and special names. Includes six appendixes providing additional information.

G552 Drever, James. A dictionary of psychology. Rev. ed. by Harvey Wallerstein. Harmondsworth, Eng.: Penguin, 1971. 320p.

Competent dictionary of some 4,000 concisely defined terms. Adequate cross-references. Includes foreign terms.

G553 English, Horace B., and Alva C. English. A comprehensive dictionary of psychological and psychoanalytical terms: a guide to usage. New York: McKay, 1958. 594p.

A bit old, but still useful; defines and explains moot or obscure points for more than 13,000 terms. Includes not only the basic nomenclature for psychology but also relevant terms from mathematics, medicine, and other related fields. Specialized terms or usages of a branch of science, school, or individual are so labeled. Extensive cross-references.

G554 Harriman, Philip L. Handbook of psychological terms. Totowa, N.J.: Littlefield, 1965. 222p.

Satisfactory for most commonly encountered terms and concepts where terse definitions, without variations of usage, are sufficient. Well-chosen illustrations and diagrams enhance its value.

G555 Heidenreich, Charles A. A dictionary of general psychology: basic terminology and key concepts. Dubuque, Iowa: Kendall/Hunt, 1970. 307p.

A dictionary intended for the undergraduate student and the interested layperson. Eclectic in orientation, it provides brief definitions of basic terms used by psychologists (and sociologists) regarding personality, social adjustment, and personality development, and of key concepts in general psychology.

G556 Longman dictionary of psychology and psychiatry. Ed. by Robert M. Goldenson and Walter D. Glanze. New York: Longman, 1984. 816p.

Claims to be the "first dictionary of its kind," both in size (over 21,000 entries, over three-quarter million words) and in scope—encompassing the vocabulary of all the psychosciences as well as terms from hundreds of fields with which the psychosciences interact" (methodological notes).

G557 Warren, Howard C. Dictionary of psychology. Boston: Houghton, 1934. 372p.

A distinguished group, assembled by Warren, compiled this work after his death. It attempted to supersede Baldwin's work (G550) by providing still more precise definitions. Many cross-references, German and French equivalents, glossaries.

G558 Wilkening, Howard E., and others. The psychology almanac: a handbook for students. Monterey, Calif.: Brooks/Cole, 1973. 241p.

The bulk of this volume, "designed primarily for the psychology major, both undergraduate and graduate," is a dictionary of approximately 5,000 terms. More than 800 books and about 500 periodicals were examined in the search for terms to include. Provides 70 pages of statistical tables as well as ethical standards of psychologists and other special features.

G559 Wolman, Benjamin B., comp. and ed. Dictionary of behavioral science. New York: Van Nostrand Reinhold, 1973. 478p.

Ninety scholars contributed to this work, which purports to cover "all areas of psychology such as experimental and developmental psychology, personality, learning, perception, motivation, and intelligence. It also includes all aspects of applied psychology, such as diagnosis and treatment of mental disorders, and social, industrial and educational psychology. The Dictionary covers the disciplines of psychiatry, biochemistry, psychopharmacology and clinical practice." Two appendixes: classification of mental disorders by American Psychiatric Association, and ethical standards of psychologists by American Psychological Association.

Foreign-Language Dictionaries

G560 Asanger, Roland, and Gerd Wenninger, eds. Handwörterbuch der Psychologie. Weinheim: Beltz Verlag, 1979. 608p.

G561 Dorsch, Friedrich, and others. Psychologisches Wörterbuch 9, vollständig neubearb. Aufl. Berne: Hans Huber, 1976. 774p.

Continuation and expansion of an early dictionary by Fritz Giese, first published in 1920. Uses encyclopedic style similar to Baldwin (G550) in treating psychological terms. Gives Latin and Greek antecedents and cross-references, and refers to original authors.

G562 Duijker, Hubert C. J. Trilingual lexicon of psychology. 2d ed. Berne: Hans Huber, 1975. 3v.

V.1: English/French/German; v.2: Français/Allemand/Anglais; v.3: Deutsch/Englisch/Französisch.

G563 Haas, Roland. Dictionary of psychology and psychiatry. English-German. Published under the auspices of the Centre for Psychological Information and Documentation at the University of Trier, West Germany. Toronto: C. J. Hogrefe, 1980. 453p.

Presents translations for more than 30,000 terms used in psychology and psychiatry, as well as in related fields, such as neuroanatomy, neurophysiology, cybernetics, statistics, psycholinguistics, sexology, biology, sociology, and educational science. A companion German-English volume is in preparation.

Another English-German dictionary is Alfred H. Berger, *Dictionary of psychology: English-German* (New York: Ungar, 1977 [133p.]) **(G564)**; its counterpart is Hugo G. Beigel, *Dictionary of psychology and related fields: German-English* (New York: Ungar, 1971 [256p.]) **(G565)**.

G566 Hehlmann, Wilhelm. Wörterbuch der Psychologie. Mit 33 Abbildungen. 5, erg. Aufl. Stuttgart: A. Kröner, 1968. 703p.

A standard German dictionary with more than 3,500 entries. References to the literature accompany all main entries. Information on individual psychologists, including their principal publications. Extensive entries on the schools and branches of psychology. Chronology of significant names and events. Appendix on psychological literature.

G567 Piéron, Henri. Vocabulaire de la psychologie. 5e éd. rem. et augm. ss la dir. de François Bresson et Gustave Durup. Paris: Presses Universitaires de France, 1973. 562p.

This French dictionary defines about 4,000 terms and relates them to thinkers and movements that helped shape their meanings. Definitions are signed. Some English terms as well as German and English equivalents, synonyms, and antonyms. Adequate cross-references. Alphabetical index of names cited. Includes common abbreviations, symbols (there is a list of symbols for scoring such tests as the Rorschach), and tables, including one on pharmacology.

G568 Sury, Kurt F. von. Wörterbuch der Psychologie und ihrer Grenzgebiete. 3, vollständig neubearb. und stark erw. Aufl. Basel: Schwabe, 1967. 324p.

Contains more than 3,700 entries, with numerous cross-references. A section by Willy Canziani (p.289–324) brings biographical and bibliographical data together for 150 deceased psychologists, three-fourths of them German or French.

Specialized Dictionaries

G569 Battro, Antonio M. Piaget: dictionary of terms. Tr. and ed. by Elizabeth Rütschi-Herrmann and Sarah F. Campbell. New York: Pergamon, 1973. 186p.

Terms used by Piaget and his collaborators are arranged alphabetically and illustrated by quotations from his works, which explain the terms. References for the quotations are to works listed in a bibliography that makes up part of this book.

G570 Brooks, JoAnn, and Helen C. Hofer, comps. Sexual nomenclature: a thesaurus. Indiana Univ. Institute for Sex Research. Boston: Hall, 1976. 403p.

Contains special vocabulary developed by the institute in order to provide subject access to its collection. Consists of about 2,000 single- and multiple-word descriptors with broader, narrower, and related terms, and scope notes; includes also references from terms not used to those used.

G571 Fann, William E., and Charles E. Goshen. The language of mental health. St. Louis: Mosby, 1973. 132p.

Designed for students and laypersons who are beginning to become acquainted with the mental health field. The terminology is divided by category: abnormal psychology, human behavior, treatment, administrative and legal terms, and words from related sciences. When more than one discipline uses the same term, the authors have tended to select the definition in current use in the profession considered responsible for the term. They have also tried to make the definitions simple rather than academic and to avoid using one technical term to define another. Appendixes provide: (1) abbreviations, slang, and colloquial English terms and (2) brief biographies of persons influential in the field of mental health.

G572 Thesaurus of psychological index terms. 3d ed. Washington, D.C.: American Psychological Assn., 1982. 258p.

Developed from terms appearing in *Psychological abstracts* as index terms or used in titles and abstracts, and "from key words in context (KWIC) lists produced from 10,000 titles of journal articles, books, separates, and dissertations." Broader, narrower, and related terms are given as well as "use" references, directing the reader from terms not used as index terms in *Psychological abstracts* to ones that are. Both current terms and those discontinued since the first edition (1974) are searchable by computer. [Current terms can be searched online from the time they were included in the thesaurus; discontinued terms can be searched for the period they were used.]

ENCYCLOPEDIAS
General

G573 Encyclopedia of psychology. Ed. by H. J. Eysenck and others. New York: Herder, 1972. 3v.

Does not match in depth the treatment of psychology in the *International encyclopedia of the social sciences* (A415) or the *International encyclopedia of psychiatry, psychology, psychoanalysis, and neurology* (G574) but provides an authoritative general treatment for anybody—specialist or layperson—interested in the subject. Entries of two kinds: ordinary definitions of a line or two, and specially written articles covering important terms and concepts ranging up to 4,000 words and containing carefully selected bibliographies for further study.

G574 International encyclopedia of psychiatry, psychology, psychoanalysis, and neurology. Ed. by Benjamin B. Wolman. 12v. Produced for Aesculapius Pubs. by Van Nostrand Reinhold, 1977. [5,627p.]

This huge scholarly encyclopedia contains articles on topics in the fields of psychiatry, psychology, psychoanalysis, neurology, and related disciplines, written by 1,500 specialists mainly from the United States, some from other countries. Each article is signed and most include a selected bibliography. Volume 12 has a complete list of articles, and name and subject indexes.

G575 Psychology encyclopedia 73/74. Ed. by Stanley Schindler. Guilford, Conn.: Dushkin, 1973. 311p.

A well-organized, copiously illustrated encyclopedia for the nonspecialist, with more than 1,000 short articles tied together by cross-references and 12 subject "maps." Longer articles are signed. Includes an extensive bibliography.

Specialized

G576 Encyclopedia of human behavior, psychiatry and mental health. Ed. by Robert M. Goldenson. New York: Doubleday, 1970. 1,472p. 2v.

This substantial set of 1,000 essays of varying length, illustrated and well indexed, is intended primarily for the lay reader.

G577 Encyclopaedic handbook of medical psychology. Ed. by Stephen Krauss. Boston: Butterworth, 1976. 585p.

Contains one- to five-page articles written mainly by practicing psychiatrists on a wide range of topics, many of which are pertinent to psychopathology or to general psychology as well as to psychiatry. Most articles have a list of references.

G578 Wright, Logan, and others. Encyclopedia of pediatric psychology. Baltimore: Univ. Park Pr., 1979. 933p.

"Our goal has been to provide broad coverage of the entire field of pediatric medicine, but particularly those areas in which behavioral and psychological problems constitute an important component of the problem." (preface)

G579 The new encyclopedia of child care and guidance. Ed. by S. M. Gruenberg. Garden City, N.Y.: Doubleday, 1968. 1,016p.

This somewhat dated resource defines terms, lists relevant organizations, contains extensive annotated bibliography, and features 30 chapters by specialists on various aspects of child care and guidance.

HANDBOOKS

Psychology has an unusually large number of scholarly handbooks, many of which will not be easy for the nonpsychologist to understand. The following list is intended to be representative rather than exhaustive:

General

G580 Die Psychologie des 20. Jahrhunderts. v.1– , 1976– . Zürich: Helmut Kindler Verlag.
V.1, *Die Europäische Tradition*; v.2, *Freud und die Folgen (1)*; v.3, *Freud und die Folgen (2)*; v.4, *Pawlow und die Folgen*; v.5, *Binet und die Folgen*; v.6, *Lorenz und die Folgen*; v.7, *Piaget und die Folgen*; v.8, *Lewin und die Folgen*; v.9, *Ergebnisse für die Medizin (1)*; v.10, *Ergebnisse für die Medizin (2)*; v.11, *Konsequenzen für die Pädagogik (1)*; v.12, *Konsequenzen für die Pädagogik (2)*; v.13, *Anwendungen im Berufsleben*; v.14, *Auswirkungen auf die Kriminologie*; v.15, *Transzendenz, Imagination und Kreativität.*
This mammoth undertaking, coordinated by Gerhard Strube, seeks to provide a complete overview of psychology in the twentieth century. Each of the 15v., most of which are more than a thousand pages in length, is edited by an expert in its field. After examining the general European background of psychology, the work describes the contributions of major figures and their followers—Freud, Pavlov, Binet, Lorenz, Piaget, and Lewin—and then devotes a number of volumes to applications of psychology to medicine, education, the world of work, and criminology. The last volume concentrates on religion, parapsychology, literature, and art.

G581 Katz, David, and Rosa Katz, eds. Handbuch der Psychologie. 2, Aufl. Basel: Schwabe, 1960. 666p.

G582 Koch, Sigmund, ed. Psychology: a study of a science. New York: McGraw-Hill, 1959–63. 6v.
This massive work was intended to provide an overview of all of psychology; it was sponsored by the American Psychological Association and funded by APA and the National Science Foundation. A stellar group of psychologists took part in writing the essays in these volumes. The first three volumes, entitled v.1, *Sensory, perceptual, and physiological formulations;* v.2, *General systematic formulations, learning, and special processes*; and v.3, *Formulations of the person and the social context*, were written either by the originators of the theories analyzed or by authors "creatively associated" with them. V. 4–6, entitled v.4, *Biologically oriented fields: their place in psychology and in biological science*; v.5, *The process areas, the person, and some applied fields: their place in psychology and in science*; and v.6, *Investigations of man as socius: their place in psychology and the social sciences*, were written by individuals whose "primary affiliation" was with one of the fields considered. A planned seventh "integrative volume" never appeared.

G583 Thomae, Hans, and others, eds. Handbuch der Psychologie. Toronto: C. J. Hogrefe, 1959–1980. 12v.
V.1, *Allgemeine Psychologie I: Der Aufbau des Erkennens*, in 2 parts: (1) Wahrnehmung und Bewusstsein, and (2) Lernen und Denken; v.2, *Allgemeine Psychologie II: Motivation*; v.3, *Entwicklungspsychol-*

ogie; v.4, *Persönlichkeitsforschung und Persönlichkeitstheorie*; v.5, *Ausdruckspsychologie*; v.6, *Psychologische Diagnostik*; v.7, *Sozialpsychologie* in 2 parts: (1) Theorien und Methoden and (2) Forschungsbereiche; v.8, *Klinische Psychologie*, in 2 parts; v.9, *Betriebspsychologie*; v.10, *Pädagogische Psychologie*; v.11, *Forensische Psychologie*; v.12, *Marktpsychologie.*
The volumes and half-volumes of this massive series range in number of pages from about 600 to more than 2,000 pages each. Many volumes have been reprinted or have come out in revised editions. V.12 was still in preparation in 1980.

G584 Wolman, Benjamin B., ed. Handbook of general psychology. Englewood Cliffs, N.J.: Prentice-Hall, 1973. 1,006p.

G584 A Yaremko, R. M., and others. Reference handbook of research and statistical methods in psychology: for students and professionals. New York: Harper, 1982. 335p.

Developmental

G585 Adelson, Joseph, ed. Handbook of adolescent psychology. New York: Wiley-Interscience, 1980. 632p.

G586 Mussen, Paul, ed. Handbook of child psychology. 4th ed. v.1, History, theories, and methods; v.2, Infancy and biological bases of development; v.3, Cognitive development; v.4, Socialization, personality and social development. New York: Wiley, 1983.

G587 Osofsky, Joy D. Handbook of infant development. New York: Wiley, 1980. 954p.

G588 Wolman, Benjamin B., ed. Handbook of developmental psychology. Englewood Cliffs, N.J.: Prentice-Hall, 1982. 960p.

Experimental

G589 Fraisse, Paul, and Jean Piaget, eds. Traité de psychologie expérimentale. Paris: Presses Universitaires de France, 1963–67. 9v.

G590 Gazzaniga, Michael S., ed. Handbook of cognitive neuroscience. New York: Plenum, 1983. 425p.

G591 Kling, Julius William, and others. Woodworth and Schlosberg's experimental psychology. 3d ed. New York: Holt, 1971. 1,279p.

G592 Puff, Richard C., ed. Handbook of research methods in human memory and cognition. New York: Academic, 1982. 474p.

Clinical

G593 American Psychiatric Assn. Task Force on Nomenclature and Statistics. Diagnostic and statistical manual of mental disorders. 3d ed. Washington, D.C.: American Psychiatric Assn., 1980. 494p.

This volume, generally known as the *DSM III*, is the current standard diagnostic manual for classification of mental disorders, developed over a period of many years by the American Psychiatric Association. Since *DSM III* is substantially different from its predecessor, the following guide is recommended by the American Psychiatric Association for use in conjunction with it: *DSM-III training guide for use with the American Psychiatric Association's diagnostic and statistical manual of mental disorders*, 3d ed., ed. by Linda J. Webb and others (New York: Brunner/Mazel, 1981[158p.]) **(G594)**.

See also *Handbook of abnormal psychology*, ed. by H. J. Eysenck at G332, and Silvano Arieti, *American handbook of psychiatry*, described at G329.

G595 Anchin, Jack C., and Donald J. Kiesler, eds. Handbook of interpersonal psychotherapy. New York: Pergamon, 1982. 346p.

G597 Bellack, Alan S., and others, eds. International handbook of behavior modification and therapy. New York: Plenum, 1982. 1,021p.

G598 Corsini, Raymond J., ed. Handbook of innovative psychotherapies. New York: Wiley, 1981. 969p.

G600 Filskov, Susan B., and Thomas J. Boll, eds. Handbook of clinical neuropsychology. New York: Wiley-Interscience, 1981. 806p.

G601 Garfield, Sol L., and Allen E. Bergin. Handbook of psychotherapy and behavior change: an empirical analysis. 2d ed. New York: Wiley, 1978. 1,024p.

G602 Golann, Stuart E., and Carl Eisdorfer, eds. Handbook of community mental health. New York: Appleton, 1973. 982p.

G603 Goldberger, Leo, and Shlomo Breznitz. Handbook of stress: theoretical and clinical aspects. New York: Free Pr., 1982. 804p.

G604 Goldstein, Alan, and Edna B. Foa, eds. Handbook of behavioral interventions: a clinical guide. New York: Wiley, 1980. 760p.

G605 Grossman, Herbert J., ed. Manual on terminology and classification in mental retardation. Washington, D.C.: American Assn. on Mental Deficiency, 1973. 180p. [Special publication no.2]

G606 Gurman, Alan S., and David P. Kniskern, eds. Handbook of family therapy. New York: Brunner/Mazel, 1981. 796p.

G607 Hersen, Michel, and others, eds. The clinical psychology handbook. Elmsford, N.Y.: Pergamon, 1983. 864p.

G608 Jeger, Abraham M., and Robert S. Slotnick, eds. Community mental health and behavioral-ecology: a handbook of theory, research and practice. New York: Plenum, 1982. 510p.

G609 Kellerman, Henry, and Anthony Burry. Handbook of psychodiagnostic testing: personality analysis and report writing. New York: Grune & Stratton, 1981. 222p.

G610 Kendall, Philip C., and James N. Butcher, eds. Handbook of research methods in clinical psychology. New York: Wiley, 1982. 728p.

G611 Langsley, Donald G., and others. Handbook of community mental health: a practical guide to the operation of community mental health centers and the services they provide. Garden City, N.Y.: Medical Examination Pub. Co., 1981. 274p.

G612 Matson, Johnny L., and James A. Mulick, eds. Handbook of mental retardation. Elmsford, N.Y.: Pergamon, 1983. 616p.

G613 Millon, Theodore, and others. Handbook of clinical health psychology. New York: Plenum, 1982. 608p.

G614 Rie, Herbert E., and Ellen D. Rie, eds. Handbook of minimal brain dysfunctions. New York: Wiley-Interscience, 1980. 744p.

G615 Tuma, June M., ed. Handbook for the practice of pediatric psychology. New York: Wiley, 1982. 356p.

G616 Turner, Samuel M., and others, eds. Handbook of clinical behavior therapy. New York: Wiley, 1981. 765p.

G617 Walker, C. Eugene, and Michael C. Roberts, eds. Handbook of clinical child psychology. New York: Wiley, 1983. 1,436p.

G618 Wiener, Daniel N. A consumer's guide to psychotherapy. Rev. ed. New York: Hawthorn, 1975. 314p.

G619 Wolman, Benjamin B., and George Stricker, eds. Handbook of family and marital therapy. New York: Plenum, 1983. 575p.

Other Specialized

Following are two outstanding reference works in the field of aging: James E. Birren and R. Bruce Sloan, eds., *Handbook of mental health and aging* (Englewood Cliffs, N.J.: Prentice-Hall, 1980 [1,064p.]) **(G620)**, contains original contributions by specialists covering such areas as current social issues, genetics, learning, memory, personality, adjustment, environment, depression, sexuality, relaxation, and exercise. Leonard W. Poon, ed., *Aging in the 1980s: psychological issues* (Washington, D.C.: American Psychological Assn., 1980 [656p.]) **(G621)**, covers nine major areas of aging: clinical, neuropsychological, psychophysiological, psychopharmacological, cognitive, environmental and methodological issues, stress and coping, and interpersonal relations.

There are useful handbooks for students of particular areas of psychology such as G622 and G623 for biopsychology. See also the *Handbook of mathematical psychology*, 3v., ed. by R. Duncan Luce and others at G84.

G622 Ford, Donald H., and J. P. Schade. Atlas of the human brain. 2d rev. ed. New York: Elsevier, 1971. 234p.

G623 Iversen, Leslie L., and others, eds. Handbook of psychopharmacology. New York: Plenum, 1975– .

G624 Carterette, Edward C., and Morton P. Friedman, eds. Handbook of perception. v.1–10, 1974–78. New York: Academic.

Aims "to bring together essential aspects of the very large, diverse, and widely scattered literature on human perception and to give a précis of the state of knowledge in every area of perception." The following volumes have been published: v.1, *Historical and physiological roots of perception* (1974); v.2, *Psychophysical judgment and measurement* (1974); v.3, *Biology of perceptual systems* (1973); v.5, *Seeing* (1975); v.6a, *Tasting and smelling* (1978); v.6b, *Feeling and hurting* (1978); v.8, *Perceptual coding* (1978); v.9, *Perceptual processing* (1978); v.10, *Perceptual ecology* (1978).

G625 Dunnette, Marvin D., ed. Handbook of industrial and organizational psychology. Chicago: Rand McNally, 1976. 1,740p.

G626 Gambrill, Eileen D. Behavior modification: handbook of assessment, intervention, and evaluation. San Francisco: Jossey-Bass, 1977. 1,231p.

G627 Johnson, Margo, and Michael Wertheimer, eds. Psychology teacher's resource book: first course. 3d ed. Washington, D.C.: American Psychological Assn. 1979. 209p.

Although intended primarily for the high school teacher, this work is also useful at the college level. Provides reviews of introductory textbooks, books of readings, and laboratory manuals. Other features include lists of supplementary readings, basic sources of information, and audiovisual materials, as well as information about instruments used in teaching and research, and ethical guidelines for psychology teachers. Outlines of a wide variety of courses in psychology are provided in Paul J. Woods, ed., *Source book on the teaching of psychology*, 2v. (Roanoke, Va.: Scholars' Pr., 1980) **(G628)**.

G629 Kiesler, Charles A., and others, eds. Psychology and national health insurance: a sourcebook. Washington, D.C.: American Psychological Assn., 1979. 647p.

G630 Knutson, Jeanne N., ed. Handbook of political psychology. San Francisco: Jossey-Bass, 1973. 543p.

Not surprisingly, the contributors to this handbook represent several disciplines—psychology, political science, and sociology. Although "political psychology" has been around for several decades, "the conceptual and methodological inadequacies of much past work" became apparent to the authors, who have tried to remedy the situation with this handbook. The first chapter integrates "the intellectual traditions which have flowed into political psychology." Fourteen further chapters are divided into four areas: basic psychological constructs; forming and maintaining stable orientations; nexus of individual and polity; methods of inquiry. Concluding chapter provides an overview of the field. Includes extensive bibliography, and author and subject indexes.

G631 Landsberg, Gerald, and others, eds. Evaluation in practice: a sourcebook of program evaluation studies from mental health care systems in the United States. Rockville, Md.: Dept. of Health, Education, and Welfare, Public Health Service, Alcohol, Drug Abuse, and Mental Health Administration, National Inst. of Mental Health; dist. by Supt. of Documents, 1979. 288p.

Concern with accountability led to greatly increased sophistication during the 1970s in research to evaluate the effectiveness of intervention programs, including in the area of mental health. This sourcebook provides models of formative and summative evaluation procedures, with sections on such areas as needs assessment, patterns of use, client outcome, cost effectiveness, and quality assurance.

G632 Lindzey, Gardner, and E. Aronson, eds. The handbook of social psychology. 2d ed. Reading, Mass.: Addison-Wesley, 1968–69. 5v.

A slightly out of date, but still very useful, massive overview of the field.

G634 Rosenberg, Sheldon, ed. Handbook of applied psycholinguistics; major thrusts of research and theory. Hillsdale, N.J.: Erlbaum, 1982. 615p.

G635 Sternberg, Robert J., ed. Handbook of human intelligence. New York: Cambridge Univ. Pr., 1982. 1,031p.

G636 Stone, George C., and others. Health psychology—a handbook: theories, applications, and challenges of a psychological approach to the health care system. San Francisco: Jossey-Bass, 1979. 729p.

G637 Triandis, Harry C., ed. Handbook of cross-cultural psychology. 6v. Rockleigh, N.J.: Allyn & Bacon, 1980.

According to the editor, "This is the first handbook of cross-cultural psychology. It is an attempt to assemble in one place the key findings of cross-cultural psychologists" (preface). More than 60 experts have contributed to the 6 volumes of this comprehensive handbook: v.1, *Perspectives*; v.2, *Methodology*; v.3, *Basic processes*; v.4, *Developmental psychology*; v.5, *Social psychology*; v.6, *Psychopathology*.

G638 White, Willo P., ed. Resources in environment and behavior. Washington, D.C.: American Psychological Assn., 1979. 376p.

This handbook for the new field of environmental psychology provides an annotated bibliography, historical background, a directory of psychologists identified with the field, and information about career opportunities, graduate programs, funding sources, and teaching innovations.

G639 Wolman, Benjamin B., ed. Handbook of human sexuality. Englewood Cliffs, N.J.: Prentice-Hall, 1980. 384p.

G640 ———. Psychological aspects of obesity. New York: Van Nostrand Reinhold, 1982. 318p.

Psychology as a Career

The American Psychological Association (Washington, D.C.) has published a number of works designed to help students interested in psychology to plan their education and to inform students and professionals about career opportunities in psychology. Following are some of them: Paul J. Woods, ed., *The psychology major: training and employment strategies* (1979 [331p.]) (**G641**). Divided into five parts: preparation and strategies for employment; job prospects: potential and real; training for careers in community service, mental health, and public affairs; the undergraduate major: surveys, models, and problems. Pt.5 includes 4 appendixes, one of which is an annotated bibliography of curriculum and careers in psychology. Bruce R. Fretz and David J. Stang, *Preparing for graduate study in psychology: NOT for seniors only* (1980 [87p.]) (**G642**), discusses such topics as deciding whether to go to graduate school, choosing a specialty and type of degree, learning about and choosing graduate schools, and financial aid. *Graduate study in psychology and associated fields, 1983* (1983 [895p.]) (**G643**). This annual publication is an indispensable resource for anyone contemplating a career in psychology. The current edition presents information obtained from questionnaires concerning more than 500 graduate programs in psychology. It lists facilities by state. Most entries provide name of institution, address, and department; programs and degrees offered; application, admission, and degree requirements; student statistics (proportion of applicants accepted, minimum acceptable undergraduate grade average, minimum acceptable performance on the Graduate Record Examination, etc.); teaching opportunities; information about tuition and housing, financial assistance, internships, special programs for minorities, and additional comments about the program. Also lists programs by degree offered. *Careers in psychology* (1978 [30p.]) (**G644**) presents concise information about major types of careers in psychology. Paul J. Woods, ed., *Career opportunities for psychologists: expanding and emerging areas* (1976 [307p.]) (**G645**), "attempts to broaden the horizons for prospective psychologists and to contribute to changes in professional preparation. The book also provides options not ordinarily considered by psychologists wishing to change careers or those who currently may be unemployed or underutilized" (foreword). As for the specific field of careers in mental health, the following work describes particular career options: Paul Schmolling and others, *Helping people: a guide to careers in mental health* (Englewood Cliffs, N.J.: Prentice-Hall, 1981 [168p.]) (**G646**). Of interest to researchers seeking funding is Robert P. Lowman and others, *APA guide to research support* (1981 [376p.]) (**G647**). An indispensable resource for every person who hopes to publish anything in the technical literature is:

G648 Publication manual of the American Psychological Association. 3d ed. Washington, D.C.: American Psychological Assn., 1983. 208p.

Changes in reference format and other style changes were incorporated into the third edition, and some new material was added, such as "guidelines for non-sexist language in APA journals" and "suggestions for avoiding ethnic bias." Like earlier editions of the manual, this one is "intended to aid authors in the preparation of manuscripts." Contains information on the content and organization of a manuscript, writing style, APA editorial style as well as details about typing, mailing, and proofreading. Includes a list of APA journals with policy statements about their coverage, and a bibliography.

Standards for Psychologists

The American Psychological Association has published the official standards of the association relating to such matters as ethics, testing, and providers of psychological services. Following are some of the more recent ones: *Ethical principles in the conduct of research with human participants* (1982 [64p.]) (**G649**). *Ethical principles of psychologists* (1981 [11p.]) (**G650**). *Standards for educational and psychological tests*. Prepared by a joint committee of the American Psychological Association, American Educational Research Association [and] National Council on Measurement in Education (1974 [76p.]) (**G651**). *Standards for providers of psychological services* (1977 [16p.]) (**G652**).

AUDIOVISUAL MATERIALS

The most general survey of audiovisual material relevant to psychology is by James B. Maas and Carol M. Howe, chapter 6, in *Psychology teacher's resource book*, ed. by Margo Johnson and Michael Wertheimer (Washington, D.C.: American Psychological Assn., 1979 [209p.]). (See G627.) It lists film catalogs, film series and special collections, television courses, slides and overhead transparencies, audio catalogs and programs, and a topical listing of films and filmstrips. Includes addresses of distributors.

G653 American Psychological Assn. The master lecture series on psychology. 1974– . Washington, D.C.: The Assn. Annual.

Five to eight "Master Lectures on Psychology" have been presented each year, beginning in 1974, at the annual convention of the American Psychological Association, as part of the association's continuing education program. "Each year a different area of psychology is selected and experts in the field are invited to review the relevant issues, methodologies, and advances in research." Topics covered so far are physiological psychology (1974), developmental psychology (1975), behavior control (1976), brain-behavior relationships (1977), psychology of aging (1978), sex and gender (1979), cognitive psychology (1980), psychotherapy research and behavior change (1981), psychology and the law (1982), and psychology and health (1983). All of these lectures are available on tape, and some are available on fiche, or in manuscript form, from the APA (1200 17th St., N.W., Washington, DC 20036).

Some specialized resources are also available, such as:

G654 Child abuse and neglect audiovisual materials. National Center on Child Abuse and Neglect; dist. by Supt. of Documents (issued Feb. 1978; revised June 1980). 92p.

Lists and describes more than 350 films, filmstrips-tapes, slides-tapes, video materials, audio materials, and multimedia packages. For each entry, includes such information as purchase price, rental price, length of film, videocassette, address where item may be obtained, etc. Producer, subject, and title indexes.

SOURCES OF SCHOLARLY CONTRIBUTIONS

Journals

G655

Psychological abstracts lists more than 1,100 journals that publish original scholarly contributions in psychology. Following are some that may be of general interest.

American journal of psychology. v.1– , 1887– . Urbana: Univ. of Illinois Pr. Quarterly. BiolAbst; Cc; ChemAbst; PsychAbst; SSCI; SSI.

American psychologist. v.1– , 1946– . Washington, D.C.: American Psychological Assn. Monthly. BiolAbst; Cc; ChemAbst; PsychAbst; SSCI; SSI.

Animal learning and behavior. v.1– , 1973– . Austin: Psychonomic Society. Quarterly. BiolAbst; EM; PsychAbst.

Behavior research methods and instrumentation. v.1– , 1968– . Austin: Psychonomic Society. Bimonthly. BiolAbst; Cc; PsychAbst.

Behavioral neuroscience. v.1– , 1983– . Washington, D.C.: American Psychological Assn. Bimonthly. (Supersedes in part (1947–82) Journal of comparative and physiological psychology) BiolAbst; ChemAbst; EM; PsychAbst.

Behavioral science. v. 1– , 1956– . Louisville, Ky.: Society for General Systems Research. Bimonthly. BiolAbst; PsychAbst; SocAbst; SSCI.

British journal of psychology. v. 1– , 1904– . London: British Psychological Society. 4/yr. BioAbst; BrEdInd; BrHumInd; Cc; LLBA; PsychAbst; SSCI; SSI.

British journal of social psychology. v. 1– , 1981– . London: British Psychological Society. Quarterly. (Supersedes in part British journal of social and clinical psychology) BiolAbst; Cc; LLBA; PsychAbst; SocEdAbst; SSCI.

Canadian journal of psychology. v. 1– , 1947– . Ottawa: Canadian Psychological Assn. Quarterly. BiolAbst; Cc; PsychAbst; SSCI; SSI.

Child development. v. 1– , 1930– . Chicago: Univ. of Chicago Pr. Quarterly. BiolAbst; Cc; EdInd; LLBA; SSCI; SSI.

Cognitive psychology. v.1– , 1970– . New York: Academic. Quarterly. Cc; PsychAbst; SSCI.

Contemporary psychology. v. 1– , 1956– . Washington, D.C.: American Psychological Assn. Monthly. BiolAbst; Cc; SSCI.

Developmental psychology. v. 1– , 1969– . Washington, D.C.: American Psychological Assn. Bimonthly. BiolAbst; Cc; PsychAbst; SSCI.

Educational and psychological measurement. v.1– , 1941– . Durham, N.C.: College Station. Quarterly. ChemAbst; EdInd; PsychAbst; SSCI.

The Italian journal of psychology. v.1– , 1974– .
Bologna, Italy: Società editrice il Mulino. 3/yr.
PsychAbst.

Journal de psychologie normale et pathologique.
v.1– , 1904– . Paris: Presses Universitaires
de France. 4/yr.
EM; PsychAbst.

Journal of abnormal psychology. v.1– , 1906– .
Washington, D.C.: American Psychological
Assn. Quarterly.
BiolAbst; Cc; EM; PsychAbst; SSCI; SSI.

Journal of applied psychology. v.1– , 1917– .
Washington, D.C.: American Psychological
Assn. Quarterly.
BiolAbst; Cc; EdInd; EM; PsychAbst; SSCI;
SSI.

Journal of clinical psychology. v.1– , 1945– . Bran-
don, Vt.: Clinical Psychology Publ. Co.
Quarterly.
BiolAbst; Cc; ChemAbst; EM; PsychAbst;
SSCI.

Journal of comparative psychology. v.1– , 1983– .
Washington, D.C.: American Psychological
Assn. Quarterly. (Supersedes in part Journal of
comparative and physiological psychology)

Journal of consulting and clinical psychology. v.1– ,
1968– . Washington, D.C.: American Psychological Assn. Bimonthly.
BiolAbst; Cc; EM; PsychAbst; SSCI; SSI.

Journal of counseling psychology. v.1– , 1954– .
Washington, D.C.: American Psychological
Assn. Quarterly.
Cc; EdInd; PsychAbst; SSCI; SSI.

Journal of educational psychology. v.1– , 1910– .
Washington, D.C.: American Psychological
Assn. Bimonthly.
BiolAbst; EdInd; PsychAbst; SSCI.

Journal of experimental psychology: animal behavior
processes. v.1– , 1975– . Washington, D.C.:
American Psychological Assn. Quarterly.
BiolAbst; PsychAbst.

Journal of experimental psychology: general. v.1– ,
1975– . Washington, D.C.: American Psychological Assn. Quarterly.
BiolAbst; Cc; PsychAbst.

Journal of experimental psychology: human percep-
tion and performance. v.1– , 1975– .
Washington, D.C.: American Psychological
Assn. Bimonthly.
Cc; PsychAbst.

Journal of experimental psychology: learning, memory, and cognition. v.1– , 1975– . Washington, D.C.: American Psychological Assn.
Quarterly. (Formerly: Journal of experimental
psychology: human learning and memory)
Cc; BiolAbst; PsychAbst.

Journal of experimental social psychology. v.1– ,
1965– . New York: Academic. Bimonthly.
BiolAbst; Cc; PsychAbst; SSCI; SSI.

Journal of general psychology: experimental, phys-
iological and comparative psychology. v.1– ,
1927– . Provincetown, Mass.: Journal Pr.
Quarterly. 2v./yr.
BiolAbst; CIJE; Cc; ChDevAbst; DSHAbst;
EM; PsychAbst; SSCI.

Journal of genetic psychology: developmental and
clinical psychology. v.1– , 1891– . Provincetown, Mass.: Journal Pr. Quarterly. 2v./yr.
BiolAbst; Cc; ChDevAbst; DSHAbst; EM;
LLBA; PsychAbst; SocEdAbst; SSCI.

Journal of personality. v.1– , 1932– . Durham,
N.C.: Duke Univ. Pr. Quarterly.
BiolAbst; Cc; EdInd; PsychAbst; SSCI.

Journal of personality and social psychology. v.1– ,
1965– . Washington, D.C.: American Psychological Assn. Monthly.
BiolAbst; Cc; PsychAbst; SSCI; SSI.

Journal of personality assessment. v.34– , 1970– .
Portland, Ore.: Society for Personality Assessment. Bimonthly. (Formerly: Journal of projective techniques and personality assessment)
Cc; EM; PsychAbst.

Journal of psychology: the general field of psychology.
v.1– , 1936– . Provincetown, Mass: Journal
Pr. Bimonthly. 3v./yr.
BiolAbst; CIJE; ChemAbst; ChDevAbst;
DSHAbst; EM; LLBA; PsychAbst; SSCI.

Journal of social issues. v.1– , 1944– . New York:
Society for the Psychological Study of Social
Issues. Quarterly.
Cc; PsychAbst; SSCI; SSI.

Journal of social psychology. v.1– , 1929– . Provincetown, Mass.: Journal Pr. Bimonthly.
3v./yr.
BiolAbst; Cc; ChDevAbst; DSHAbst; EM;
LLBA; PsychAbst; SSCI; SocEdAbst; SSI.

Journal of the history of the behavioral sciences.
v.1– , 1965– . Brandon, Vt.: Clinical
Psychology Pub. Co. Quarterly.
Cc; PsychAbst; SocAbst; SSCI.

Journal of verbal learning and verbal behavior. v.1– ,
1962– . New York: Academic. Bimonthly.
Cc; PsychAbst; SSCI; SSI.

Memory and cognition. v.1– , 1973– . Austin:
Psychonomic Society. Bimonthly.
BiolAbst; Cc; EM; PsychAbst; SSCI.

Perception and psychophysics. v.1– , 1966– . Austin: Psychonomic Society. Monthly.
BiolAbst; Cc; EM; PsychAbst; SSCI.

Perceptual and motor skills. v.1– , 1949– . Box
9229, Missoula, MT 59807. Bimonthly 2v./yr.
BiolAbst; Cc; DSHAbst; EM; PsychAbst.

Physiological psychology. v.1– , 1973– . Austin: Psychonomic Society. Quarterly.
BiolAbst; Cc; PsychAbst.

Professional psychology: research and practice. v.1– , 1969– . Washington, D.C.: American Psychological Assn. Bimonthly.
Cc; PsychAbst; SSCI.

Psychological bulletin. v.1– , 1904– . Washington, D.C.: American Psychological Assn. Bimonthly.
BiolAbst; Cc; PsychAbst; SSCI.

Psychological documents. v.1– , 1971– . Washington, D.C.: American Psychological Assn. Semiannually. (Formerly: JSAS catalog of selected documents in psychology)
PsychAbst.

Psychological issues. v.1– , 1959– . New York: International Universities Pr. 4/yr.
PsychAbst; SSCI.

Psychological reports. v.1– , 1955– . Box 9229, Missoula, MT 59807. Bimonthly. 2v./yr.
BiolAbst; Cc; EM; LLBA; PsychAbst; SSCI; SSI.

Psychological research; an international journal of perception, learning and communication. v.1– , 1921– . New York: Springer-Verlag. 4/yr.
Cc; PsychAbst; SSCI.

Psychological review. v.1– , 1894– . Washington, D.C.: American Psychological Assn. Quarterly.
BiolAbst; Cc; PsychAbst; SSCI; SSI.

Psychologie française. v.1– , 1956– . Paris: Société Française de Psychologie. Quarterly.
BiolAbst; PsychAbst; SSCI.

Psychologische Beiträge; Vierteljahresschrift für alle Gebiete der Psychologie. v.1– , 1953– . Koenigstein, W. Germany: Deutsche Gesellschaft für Psychologie. 4/yr.
Cc; PsychAbst; SSCI.

Psychologische Rundschau; Überlick über die Fortschritte der Psychologie in Deutschland, Osterreich und der Schweiz. v.1– , 1949– . Göttingen, W. Germany: Verlag für Psychologie. Quarterly.
PsychAbst.

Psychology of women quarterly. v.1– , 1976– . New York: Human Sciences Pr. Quarterly.
Cc; ChDevAbst; CIJE; PsychAbst; SocAbst; SSCI; WomStudAbst.

Psychonomic society. Bulletin. v.1– , 1973– . Austin: Psychonomic Society. Bimonthly.
Cc; PsychAbst; SSCI.

Quarterly journal of experimental psychology: section A: human experimental psychology; section B: comparative and physiological psychology. v.1– , 1948– . London and New York: Experimental Psychology Society. 4/yr.
BiolAbst; BrEdInd; Cc; PsychAbst; SSCI.

Teaching of psychology. v.1– , 1974– . Washington, D.C.: American Psychological Assn. Quarterly.
Cc; PsychAbst.

Zeitschrift für Psychologie: mit Zeitschrift für angewandte Psychologie. v.1– , 1890– . Leipzig, E. Germany: Johann Ambrosius Barth Verlag. 4/yr.
BiolAbst; PsychAbst; SSCI.

Monograph Series

During the earlier decades of this century, many universities such as the University of California at Berkeley, Stanford, and Columbia issued monograph series with a specialized focus, and various journals (e.g., the journals of the American Psychological Association, the *British journal of psychology,* and *Psychological reports*), published longer research reports as supplements from time to time. This practice greatly diminished in the 1960s and 1970s. A massive series, published for four decades, was *Archives of psychology,* nos. 1–300, 1906–45. New York: Columbia Univ. Pr. The American Psychological Association also published 233 *Psychological monographs, general and applied,* from 1895 to 1966, for a total of 80 volumes. Among the few remaining monograph series are the following:

G656

Genetic psychology monographs: child behavior, animal behavior and comparative psychology. v.1– , 1926– . Provincetown, Mass.: Journal Pr. Quarterly.

Nebraska symposium on motivation. v.1– , 1953– . Lincoln: Univ. of Nebraska Pr. Annual. Cumulative index: 1953–58.

Psychological issues. v.1– , 1959– . New York: International Universities Pr. 4/yr.

Society for Research in Child Development. Monographs. v.1– , 1936– . Chicago.

Selected Organizations

The chief psychological organization in the United States is the American Psychological Association (1200 17th St., N.W., Washington, D.C., 20036; founded 1892) with a membership of more than 56,000 (**G656A**). Its membership is subdivided by primary interest into about 40 divisions, each of which is a separate organization in itself. The names of the divisions indicate how the national organization subdivides its own discipline: General Psychology, Teaching of Psychology, Experimental Psychology, Evaluation and Measurement, Physiological and Comparative Psychology, Developmental Psychology, Personality and Social Psychology, Society for the Psychological Study of Social Issues, Psychology and the Arts, Clinical Psychology, Consulting Psychology, Industrial and Organizational Psychology, Educational Psychology, School Psychology, Counseling Psychology, Psychologists in Public Service, Military Psychology, Adult Development and Aging, Society of Engineering Psychologists, Rehabilitation Psychology, Consumer Psychology, Philosophical and Theoretical Psychology, Experimental Analysis of Behavior, History of Psychology, Community Psychology, Psychopharmacology, Psychotherapy, Psychological Hypnosis, State Psychological Association Affairs, Humanistic Psychology, Mental Retardation, Population and Environmental Psychology, Psychology of Women, Psychologists Interested in Religious Issues, Child and Youth Services, Health Psychology, Psychoanalysis, Clinical Neuropsychology. Regional associations are: Eastern Psychological Association, Midwestern Psychological Association, New England Psychological Association, Rocky Mountain Psychological Association, Southeastern Psychological Association, Southern Society for Philosophy and Psychology, Southwestern Psychological Association, and Western Psychological Association. Every state has a psychological association, and some municipal and other small units also exist.

Additional organizations that are relevant to psychological concerns include:

G657

American Assn. for the Advancement of Science. Washington, D.C. Founded 1848.

American Assn. of State Psychology Boards. Montgomery, Alabama. Founded 1962.

American Board of Professional Psychology. Washington, D.C. Founded 1947.

American Educational Research Assn. Washington, D.C. Founded 1915.

American Personnel and Guidance Assn. Falls Church, Va. Founded 1952.

American Society of Clinical Hypnosis. Des Plaines, Ill. Founded 1957.

Animal Behavior Society. Washington, D.C. Founded 1964.

Assn. for the Advancement of Psychology. Washington, D.C. Founded 1974.

Assn. for Women in Psychology. Columbus, Ohio. Founded 1969.

Assn. of Black Psychologists. Washington, D.C. Founded 1968.

Brain Research Foundation. An affiliate of the Univ. of Chicago. Chicago. Founded 1953.

British Psychological Society. London. Founded 1902.

Canadian Psychological Assn. (Société Canadienne de Psychologie). Ottawa. Founded 1939.

Center for Advanced Study in the Behavioral Sciences. Stanford, Calif. Founded 1953.

Cheiron: Intl. Society for the History of the Behavioral and Social Sciences. Address varies. Founded 1968.

Deutsche Gesellschaft für Psychologie. Mainz. Founded 1903.

Educational Testing Service. Princeton, N.J. Founded 1947.

ERIC Clearinghouse for Social Studies/Social Science Education. Boulder, Colo. Founded 1970.

ERIC Clearinghouse on Science, Mathematics, and Environmental Education. Ohio State University, Columbus. Founded 1966.

Human Resources Research Organization. Alexandria, Va. Founded 1951.

Institute for Personality and Ability Testing. Champaign, Ill. Founded 1949.

Intl. Association of Applied Psychology. Paris. Founded 1920.

Intl. Council of Psychologists. New York. Founded 1942.

Intl. Union of Psychological Science. Dept. of Psychology, Michigan State Univ. East Lansing. Founded 1953.

Intl. Union of Scientific Psychology. Paris. Founded 1951.

National Academy of Sciences. Washington, D.C. Founded 1863.

National Council for the Social Studies. Washington, D.C. Founded 1921.

National Institute of Education. Washington, D.C. Founded 1972.

National Institute of Mental Health. Rockville, Md. Founded 1949.

National Science Foundation. Washington, D.C. Founded 1950.

Psychonomic Society. Psychology Dept., Univ. of Wisconsin. Madison. Founded 1959.

Social Science Education Consortium. Boulder, Colo. Founded 1963.

Society for Multivariate Experimental Psychology. College of Human Development, Pennsylvania State Univ. University Park. Founded 1960.

Society for Research in Child Development. Lafayette, Ind. Founded 1933.

SOURCES OF CURRENT INFORMATION

The best way to obtain up-to-date information is personal inquiries directed to major associations or to scholars currently engaged in the field of interest, attending lectures and symposia at national and regional psychology conventions, or attending colloquiums presented by major scholars at institutions of higher education. The following are further resources for obtaining relatively recent material:

G658 APA Monitor. v.1– , 1970– . Washington, D.C.: American Psychological Assn. Monthly.
This newsletter contains articles on recent and pending legislation of interest to psychologists, on activities of the association's boards and committees, on the research and practice of prominent psychologists, etc., as well as classified advertisements and announcements of position openings for psychologists.

G659 American psychologist: the official journal of the American Psychological Assn. v.1– , 1946– . Washington, D.C. Monthly.
Carries official papers and reports of the association and its committees and substantive papers likely to be of profession-wide interest.

G660 British Psychological Society. Bulletin. v.1– , 1948– . Leicester, Eng.: The Society. Monthly.
An official organ of the society, the bulletin offers a continuous review of developments of interest to members, formal papers selected to help keep members abreast of the profession as a whole, abstracts of papers read before the society, reports of organized activities, correspondence, and other news or discussion of general interest to the profession.

G661 Canadian psychological review: Psychologie canadienne. v.1– , 1951– . Ottawa: Canadian Psychological Assn. Quarterly. (Formerly: Canadian Psychologist)
Publishes official papers and proceedings of the association, names of officers, announcements and reports of professional activities, comments on psychological affairs, evaluative reviews likely to be of general interest, and original papers (mainly on psychological theory).

G662 High school psychology teacher. v.1– , 1969– . Washington, D.C.: Clearinghouse on Precollege Psychology, American Psychological Assn. 4/yr. (Formerly: Periodically)
Includes news of interest to high school psychology teachers—such as information about summer institutes, funding opportunities, and recent relevant publications; publishes suggestions for classroom demonstrations and for how to teach various subtopics in psychology, and provides reviews of text materials intended for the high school audience.

G663 International journal of psychology: journal international de psychologie. v.1– , 1966– . Paris: Dunod. Quarterly.
House organ of International Union of Psychological Science. "Devoted to cross-cultural comparative and cooperative research in general, genetic and social psychology throughout the world. . .and gives information on activities of the IUPS and national psychological member societies" (statement of purpose, v.1).

G664 Psychologia: an international journal of psychology in the Orient. v.1– , 1957/58– . Kyoto: Psychologia Society. Quarterly.
In English. Conceived as a channel of communication between East and West and as a forum for international discussion. Contributors of different nationalities. Publishes reviews, world news, brief reports, and discussions, especially from Japan, India, and other Asian countries.

G665 Psi Chi newsletter. v.1– , 1934– . Washington, D.C.: Psi Chi National Office. Quarterly.
This official publication of the national honor society in psychology contains news of general interest to the membership, activities of selected chapters, occasional general articles of interest to undergraduate psychology students, lists of officers and new members of its component chapters, and other information pertaining to Psi Chi.

G666 Psychologie française. v.1– , 1956– . Paris: Société Française de Psychologie. Quarterly.
Each issue has a section, "Nouvelles de la psychologie."

G667 Psychology today. v.1– , 1967– . Washington, D.C.: American Psychological Assn. Monthly.
This monthly for the general public carries primarily articles intended to have broad popular appeal, such as on personality, sex, or social interaction. Typically articles are solicited on more or less recent developments that are apt to be of wide interest. Ac-

quired by the APA early in 1983, it will probably provide broader coverage of the entire discipline of psychology in future years—but with the intended audience remaining the general public.

COMPUTERIZED DATABASES

G668

Numerous databases are available for searching by computer. For psychology, the most important is PsycINFO (American Psychological Assn.), which contains all of the material from *Psychological abstracts*. PsycALERT (American Psychological Assn.) provides full bibliographic information and brief indexing of very recent material; records are deleted from PsycALERT when they are fully indexed and become available on PsycINFO, so there is no duplication in the two files. Others include Child Abuse and Neglect (National Center on Child Abuse and Neglect); Comprehensive Dissertation Index (Xerox Univ. Microfilms); Conference Papers Index (Data Courier, Inc.); ERIC (Educational Resources Information Center); Foundation Grants (The Foundation Center); MLA Bibliography (Modern Language Association); Mental Health Abstracts (National Clearinghouse for Mental Health Information, National Institute of Mental Health; IFI/Plenum Data Company); NICEM (National Information Center for Educational Media); NTIS (National Technical Information Service, U.S. Dept. of Commerce); Population Bibliography (Univ. of North Carolina, Carolina Population Center); RILM (Répertoire International de la Littérature Musicale) Abstracts (City Univ. of New York, International RILM Center); Scisearch 1974–1977 (Institute for Scientific Information); Scisearch 1978–present (Institute for Scientific Information); SSIE Current Research (Smithsonian Science Information Exchange); Social Scisearch (Institute for Scientific Information).

Marilyn L. Wertheimer

8 Education

Survey of the Field

Survey of the Reference Works

Survey of the Field

INTRODUCTION

The term *education* has several meanings. Etymologically, it is derived from *educatus* and *educare* (Latin, to rear or raise). The basic meaning was defined by John Dewey in 1911 in Paul Monroe's *Cyclopedia of education* (H569): "Speaking generally, education signifies the sum total of processes by means of which a community or social group, whether small or large, transmits its acquired power and aims with a view to securing its own continuous existence and growth." With relation to the immature individual, Dewey defined education "as a process of the continuous reconstruction of experience with the purpose of widening and deepening its social content, while, at the same time, the individual gains control of the methods involved." There are other and somewhat contrasting definitions, both in the present and all through history, but all usually consider education from the standpoint of the community and the individual.

Education is also a body of knowledge and technique that is designed to prepare professional teachers through the study of psychology and sociology and their applications to school problems, the history and philosophy of schools and the learning process, the teaching and administrative procedures, and the like. It is also applied to a scholarly discipline that seeks to discover new and authenticated knowledge through the various processes of objective scientific research, such as the historical and experimental methods. Education draws upon other disciplines for its basic content, but it deals with this material in a way that the other fields do not, that is, with reference to school learning processes, administration, and problems, as well as the broader issues involving influences on knowledge, attitudes, and behavior of individuals and groups.

The following analysis of educational literature is mainly limited to books, although there are numerous articles and pamphlets of considerable reference value. It is too much to expect even the specialist in the literature to be familiar with all the important "smaller" writings in the many branches of education. Familiarity with the bibliographies and indexes will be sufficient, in most instances, to locate contributions that are published in the better journals.

CLASSICS

Pedagogical literature is as old as recorded history. The masterworks of thought of all peoples have either been devoted to education or have contained thoughts on raising children and related questions. Thus the book of Proverbs in the Bible, Confucius' writings, Plato's *Republic* (**H1**), Cicero's essays and orations, and many other great books, from the remote past to the present, have had something significant to say about the various aspects of education. So far as special pedagogical works are concerned, there is a long list of writings, such as Plutarch's essay on the education of children in his *Moralia* (**H2**); Quintilian's *Institutes of oratory* (**H3**); Erasmus' *Education of a Christian prince* (**H4**); John Locke's *Some thoughts concerning education* (**H5**); Jean-Jacques Rousseau's *Emile* (**H6**); the numerous writings by Johann Heinrich Pestalozzi, Johann Friedrich Herbart, and Friedrich Froebel; the annual reports of Horace Mann; the books by Sir Richard Livingstone, John Dewey, Georg Kerschensteiner, Maria Montessori, Anton S. Makarenko, Rabindranath Tagore, and other educators of many nations. The major works of this nature can be located with little delay in the standard biographies of the writers, books on educational history and theory, the educational encyclopedias, and specialized bibliographies. The bibliographer in education will often find it useful to compile lists of the educators, more or less influential, of the various countries, together with some biographical facts and the titles of the chief works.

In addition to the seminal studies of educational theory that date from ancient times, there is a vast corpus of volumes on different aspects of education intended for the prospective and the practicing teacher, the scholar in education, and the educational research worker. Such books began to appear with increasing frequency from the early nineteenth century onward, although monographs on educational history go back at least three centuries earlier. Obviously, it is impossible for the most advanced scholar to be familiar, let alone intimate, with this abundance of writings in the field of education. Even the educational historian would find it very difficult to know all the important works of the past and present in his area in the major languages.

Professor Will Seymour Monroe pointedly observed in his *Bibliography of education* (New York: Appleton, 1897, p. xi) (see H460 for description), that "the literature on education is now admittedly large and is growing daily." That was in 1897, and the literature nine decades later has attained a tremendous size. Accordingly, it is clear that the subject bibliographer in education must be selective and critical in order to achieve mastery of the literature of the field. Also necessary is constant reading and scanning to broaden the acquaintance with the significant books and other sources in at least the more common languages.

INTRODUCTORY WORKS

From about the early nineteenth century onward there was an increasing number of systematic treatises on pedagogy that offered an introduction to and overview of the entire field, or major portions of it. Among the classic works are Johann Friedrich Herbart's *Allgemeine Pädagogik* (1806) (**H8**), Tuiskon Ziller's *Vorlesungen über allgemeine Pädagogik* (1876) (**H9**), and Alexander Bain's *Education as a science* (1879) (**H10**). These books influenced generations of educators and teachers, in their native countries and abroad.

There are still some older works that have much to offer the reader, even if they are outdated with respect to some particular detail and statistics. Chapman and Counts treat the interrelationship of education with society, psychology, and the nature of the school. Klapper's approach is to consider education as physical, social, economic, and mental adjustment.

The introductory treatises are designed mainly for the prospective teacher, but might also be consulted with profit by teachers in service, administrators, and others who wish to obtain a general and fundamental notion of education and the American school system. All consider similar subject matter to a greater or lesser extent—principles, administration and organization, methods and materials of learning and teaching, the relation to society, and the like.

Chris A. DeYoung's *An introduction to American education,* which was co-authored for several editions by Richard Wynn, is now under the sole authorship of the latter (H32). It retains the stress on administration and organization, and includes chapters on international education and issues of recent and current concern.

Thayer and Levit are concerned with such issues as racial segregation, academic freedom, church and state in relation to schools, federal aid, and criticism of public schools. Pounds and Bryner analyze the historical and current relationships of the schools to the community, the socioeconomic problems of education, contrasting conceptions of the school, and education on an international scale.

Callahan combines textual matter and source readings in his approach to the past, present, and probable future of education. Of special value is Kneller's compilation of essays on the historical, sociological, philosophical, administrative, and international foundations of education.

The subject bibliographer should be acquainted with at least a sampling of the foreign general works on education.

The introductory works of the 1970s and 1980s reflect the newer developments and concerns, particularly in American education. Ikenberry deals with the social, historical, international, and philosophical foundations, adding school organization and administration and the nature and problems of the teaching profession. Covering similar ground, Van Scotter *et al.* also include political and economic factors, case studies of racism and sexism, and "alternative, global, and future perspectives." Problems, issues, and such concerns as social mobility and the urban future are featured in Crary and Petrone. To Hunt, the significant educational questions are interrelated with crime, religion, racial-ethnic relations, sexism, and ecology. The Bredemeier volume, which places education and the school within the social setting, offers orientation on the learning process, the school experience, the teacher's functions, and strategies for change in curriculum, instruction, and organization. A leading educational critic of American life, Joel Spring, presents an introduction to the American educational system emphasizing the social, political, and economic contradictions between education and society.

Hubert offers a standard, comprehensive introduction. Schneider deals mainly with the theoretical structure and problems of historical, philosophical, and scientific foundations of education, together with current problems in Italy and elsewhere. García Hoz treats these topics, and also a variety of other themes, including comparative education. Planchard presents the relation of education to psychology and sociology, and analyzes administration, school reform, and education in developing countries. In Nicolin's book are reprinted essays (1806–1966) concerned with the nature of education and on education as a discipline. Finally, account should be taken of the introductory books published in the USSR. Ilina's work is an introduction to education from the communist viewpoint, with special reference to the USSR. The volumes by Boldyrev and Ogorodnikov, better-known writers, are more advanced.

H11   Boldyrev, N. I., N. K. Goncharov, and others. Pedagogika. Moscow: Prosveschenie, 1968. 525p.

H12   Bredemeier, Mary E. and Harry C. Bredemeier. Social forces in education. Sherman Oaks, Calif.: Alfred Pubs., 1978. 390p.

H13   Callahan, Raymond E. An introduction to education in American society. 2d ed. New York: Knopf, 1960. 467p.

H14   Chapman, J. Crosby and George S. Counts. Principles of education. Boston: Houghton, 1924. 645p.

H15   Crary, Ryland W. and Louis A. Petrone. Foundations of education. New York: Knopf, 1971. 473p.

H16   García Hoz, Victor. Principios de pedagogía sistemática. 4th ed. Madrid: Ediciones Rialto, 1968. 558p.

H17   Hubert, René and Gaston Mialaret. Traité de pédagogie générale. 7th ed. Paris: Presses Universitaires de France, 1970. xii, 689p.

H18   Hunt, Maurice P. Foundations of education: social and cultural perspectives. New York: Holt, 1975. 563p.

H19   Ikenberry, Oliver S. American education foundations: an introduction. Columbus, Ohio: Merrill, 1974. 488p.

H20   Ilina, T. A. Pedagogika. Moscow: Prosveshchenie, 1969. 576p.

H21   Klapper, Paul. Contemporary education: its principles and practice. New York: Appleton, 1929. 660p.

H22   Kneller, George F., ed. Foundations of education. 3d ed. New York: Wiley, 1971. 674p.

H23   Morando, Dante. Pedagogia. 3d ed. Brescia, Italy: Morcelliana, 1951. 431p.

H24   Nicolin, Friedhelm, ed. Pädagogik als Wissenschaft. Darmstadt, W. Germany: Wissenschaftliche Buchgesellschaft, 1969. 467p.

H25   Ogorodnikov, I. T. Pedagogika. Moscow: Prosveshchenie, 1968. 373p.

H26   Planchard, Emile. Introduction à la pédagogie. 3d ed. Louvain, Belgium: Nauwelaerts, 1969. 237p.

H27   Pounds, Ralph L. and James R. Bryner. The school in American society. 3d ed. New York: Macmillan, 1973. 618p.

H28   Schneider, Friedrich. Einführung in die Erziehungswissenschaft. 2d ed. Graz, Austria: Styria, 1953. 427p.

H29   Spring, Joel. American education: an introduction to social and political aspects. 2d ed. New York: Longman, 1982. 276p.

H30   Thayer, V. T. and Martin Levit. The role of the school in American society. 2d ed. New York: Dodd, 1966. 589p.

H31   Van Scotter, Richard D., Richard J. Kraft, and John D. Haas. Foundations of education: social perspectives. Englewood Cliffs, N.J.: Prentice-Hall, 1979. 416p.

H32   Wynn, Richard, Chris A. DeYoung, and Joanne Lindsay Wynn. American education. 8th ed. New York: McGraw-Hill, 1977. 441p.

EDUCATIONAL HISTORY

The student of the history of education can find short sketches of the subject in ancient, medieval, and Renaissance writings. Occasionally there are longer treatments, as in the histories prepared by Chinese scholars from the Han Dynasty onward and in the works of Leonardo Bruni and Flavio Blondo in Italy in the middle of the fifteenth century. A historical treatise published in 1517 by Robert Goulet on the genesis of the University of Paris is one of the earliest books devoted exclusively to educational history—in the Western world at least. During the succeeding three centuries there were several books of broad scope, such as Heinrich Conring's *De antiquitatibus academicis dissertationes septem,* in three editions—1651, 1674, 1739 (**H33**)—on the history of higher education, and Claude Fleury's *Traité des choix et de la méthods des études* (1685) (**H34**) on the general history of education. But there were many more specialized histories of individual universities or schools and biographies of educators. For example, Cotton Mather included a history of Harvard College in the fourth book of his classic *Magnalia Christi Americana* (1702) (**H35**).

It was toward the end of the eighteenth century that the modern movement in the writing of the history of education may be said to have begun. During the nineteenth century the most comprehensive and influential general works were by Germans: Karl von Raumer (1847), Karl Schmidt (1860–62), and K. A. Schmid (1884–1902). The work by von Raumer appeared in English in Henry Barnard's *American journal of education* (**H36**) and provided the content for some of the leading American books on the history of education. In the United States there were various writings on educational history, mainly concerned with colleges, before the publication of the first general treatment, Henry I. Smith's *History of education, ancient and modern* in 1842.

As can very well be imagined, there is a plenitude of published material on the history of education, both general and specialized, in a variety of forms and in every literate language. The specialist is at a loss even to be acquainted with a small segment of it. The best that can be done is to select a sampling of books, including those that have enjoyed wide circulation. Let the reader bear in mind that all branches and sub-branches in the field of education have a history. Some of these historical writings are of greater value than others. In several instances it is still necessary to write the history of a specific area or problem in education. It is noteworthy that, as international interdependence increases in the various areas of activity and thought, the scholar and the student—and the librarian, too—in the history of education will have to derive his knowledge from publications and sources in various languages to a greater extent than heretofore.

In educational historiography, the general works, as a rule, treat educational ideas, content, methods, institutions, and personalities from antiquity to the twentieth century, many stressing the Western world. Typical of this group are the volumes by Cubberley (H53), by Eby and Arrowood, by Butts, by Larroyo, by Boyd, and by Good and Teller. Günther and his East German colleagues cover this ground from the Marxist viewpoint. Giraldi gives special attention to Italy. Bowen's comprehensive survey, in three volumes, ends with the sixteenth century. A work that seeks to balance the educational history of the Occident and the Orient is Myers' adaptation to education of Arnold J. Toynbee's historical compendium and interpretation. Brickman surveys the international interrelationships in higher learning throughout history.

Another category of historical literature in education considers a specific country or area, period, institution, idea, subject of instruction, or teaching procedure. In addition, there is a type of historiography that traces the origin and growth of educational problems or issues. Among the many examples, only a few can be cited. Although there are various treatments in English and other languages of twentieth-century education, Connell's work is unusual not only in its recency, but also in its addition of Asia and Africa to Europe and the United States. Battle and Lyons deal with aspects of modern African educational developments. Lowndes analyzes the changes in English and Welsh education from 1895 to 1965. Prost presents over a century and a half of French education, and includes documents. Over two-thirds of Konstantinov is concerned with modern Russian and Soviet education.

Medieval Arab education, an infrequent subject in English, is described in an informative but uneven work by Nakosteen. The scholarly volumes by Ballauff give intensive coverage to German education from the sixteenth to the twentieth century. Among the thorough studies of ancient education, special notice should be given to Woody's on Asia and classical Greece and Rome and to Marrou's on Greco-Roman education. Riché's scholarly study, now available in English, covers the early medieval period in central and western Europe.

The history of educational thought in the West is delineated by Ulich and by Curtis and Boultwood. Nash's volume has scholarly essays on educational thought from Plato to B. F. Skinner. There are other works in several languages that explore a similar range, but with emphasis on other thinkers. Brubacher's contribution is a historical analysis of specific educational problems and issues, as well as educational theory, from ancient times to the present. The recent interest in the history of children is represented by scholarly essays from ancient times to the nineteenth century in Mause's volume.

Owing to the richness of all types of specialized writings in educational history, it will be possible to mention only a small number—without necessarily implying that they are better than those omitted. In the literature on American education, Monroe offers a comprehensive, but largely undocumented, analysis from the colonial era until 1865. Cremin's work is a thoroughly documented study, beginning with the European origins of American colonial education, and continuing to 1876, with a comprehensive bibliographical essay (H51–52). Butts and Church interpret the sweep of American educational history. A careful historical presentation of Catholic education in the United States is that of Buetow. The history of Negro education in the Southern United States is given good treatment by Bullock. Curti discusses and fully documents the views of the most influential American educator of the nineteenth and twentieth centuries. Newer historical approaches on black education are provided in Franklin and Adamson. A comprehensive historical treatment of the education of racial and ethnic minorities in the United States is given by Weinberg.

Collections of source materials and documents are important to anyone studying the history of education in any depth. Ulich combines Western and Eastern classics of educational thought (H79). Cubberley includes pertinent documents from ancient times to the twentieth century (H54). Knight and Hall, and Calhoun cover American educational sources from colonial times to the twentieth century, with the latter adding an informative introduction and bibliographical essay. (See also Sol Cohen, *Education in the United States: a documentary history* at H604.) The documents in Sylvester and Maclure illuminate over a millennium of education in England. Smirnov's book is a documentary history of Russian and Soviet education.

There are still many varieties of monographs in educational history to which attention might be invited. Some will be included in the branches of education to be discussed later in this chapter.

H37   Ballauff, Theodor. Pädagogik: Eine Geschichte der Bildung und Erziehung. Freiburg i. Br., W. Germany: Alber, 1969–73. 3v. (v.2–3 with Klaus Schaller)

H38   Battle, Vincent M. and Charles H. Lyons, eds. Essays in the history of African education. New York: Teachers College Pr., 1970. 123p.

H39   Bowen, James. A history of Western education. 3v. New York: St. Martin's, 1972–81.

H40   Boyd, William. The history of Western education. 10th ed., rev. by Edmund J. King. London: Black, 1972. 515p.

H41   Brickman, William W. Two millennia of international relations in higher education. Norwood, Pa.: Norwood Edns., 1976. 263p.

H42   Brubacher, John S. A history of the problems of education. 2d ed. New York: McGraw-Hill, 1966. 659p.

H43   Buetow, Harold A. Of singular benefit: the story of Catholic education in the United States. New York: Macmillan, 1970. 526p.

H44   Bullock, Henry A. A history of Negro educa-

tion in the South: from 1619 to the present. Cambridge, Mass.: Harvard Univ. Pr., 1967. 339p.

H45   Butts, R. Freeman. Public education in the United States: from revolution to reform. New York: Holt, 1978. 436p.

H46   ———. The education of the West: a formative chapter in the history of civilization. New York: McGraw-Hill, 1973. 631p.

H47   Calhoun, Daniel, ed. The education of Americans: a documentary history. Boston: Houghton, 1969. 644p.

H48   Church, Robert L. Education in the United States: an interpretive history. New York: Free Pr., 1976. 489p.

H50   Connell, W. F. History of education in the twentieth century world. New York: Teachers College Pr., 1980. 478p.

H51   Cremin, Lawrence A. American education: the colonial experience, 1607–1783. New York: Harper, 1970. 688p.

H52   ———. American education: the national experience, 1783–1976. New York: Harper, 1980. 607p.

H53   Cubberley, Ellwood P. The history of education: educational practice and progress considered as a phase of the development and spread of Western civilization. Boston: Houghton, 1920. 849p.

H54   ———. Readings in the history of education. Boston: Houghton, 1920. 648p.

H55   Curti, Merle. The social ideas of American educators. New York: Scribner, 1935. 613p.

H56   Curtis, S. J. and M. E. A. Boultwood. A short history of educational ideas. 5th ed. London: Universal Tutorial Pr., 1977. 685p.

H57   Eby, Frederick and Charles F. Arrowood. The development of modern education. 2d ed. Englewood Cliffs, N.J.: Prentice-Hall, 1964. 719p.

H58   ———. The history and philosophy of education: ancient and medieval. New York: Prentice-Hall, 1940. 966p.

H59   Franklin, Vincent P. and James D. Anderson, eds. New perspectives on black educational history. Boston: Hall, 1978. 213p.

H60   Giraldi, Giovanni. Storia italiana della pedagogia. Rome: Armando, 1966. 522p.

H61   Good, Harry G. and James D. Teller. A history of Western education. 3d ed. New York: Macmillan, 1969. 630p.

H62   Günther, Karl-Heinz and others, eds. Geschichte der Erziehung. 12th ed. Berlin: Volk & Wissen, 1976. 730p.

H63   Knight, Edgar W. and Clifton L. Hall. Readings in American educational history. New York:

Appleton, 1951. 781p.; New York: Greenwood, 1970. 799p.

H64 Konstantinov, N. A. and others. Istoriya pedagogiki. 4th ed. Moscow: Prosveshchenie, 1974. 446p.

H65 Larroyo, Francisco. Historia general de la pedogogía. 14th ed. Mexico City: Poorua, 1977. 800p.

H66 Lowndes, G. A. N. The silent social revolution: an account of the expansion of public education in England and Wales, 1895–1965. 2d ed. London: Oxford Univ. Pr., 1969. 387p.

H67 Maclure, J. Stuart, ed. Educational documents: England and Wales, 1816 to the present day. 4th ed. New York: Methuen, 1973. 416p.

H68 Marrou, H. I. A history of education in antiquity. New York: Sheed & Ward, 1956; Madison: Univ. of Wisconsin Pr., 1982. 466p.

H69 DeMause, Lloyd, ed. The history of childhood. New York: Psychohistory Pr., 1974. 450p.

H70 Monroe, Paul. Founding of the American public school system. New York: Macmillan, 1940; New York: Hafner, 1971. 520p.

H71 Myers, Edward D. Education in the perspective of history. New York: Harper, 1960. 388p.

H72 Nakosteen, Mehdi. History of Islamic origins of Western education, A.D. 860–1350. Boulder: Univ. of Colorado Pr., 1964. 765p.

H73 Nash, Paul and others, eds. The educated man. New York: Wiley, 1965. Reprint, Huntington, N.Y.: Krieger, 1980. 421p.

H74 Prost, Antoine. Histoire de l'enseignement en France, 1800–1967. Paris: Colin, 1968. 524p.

H75 Riché, Pierre. Education and culture in the barbarian West: sixth through eighth centuries. Columbia: Univ. of South Carolina Pr., 1976. 557p.

H76 Smirnov, V. Z. Khrestomatiya po istorii pedagogiki. Moscow: Uchpedgiz, 1957. 534p.

H77 Sylvester, D. W. Educational documents, 800–1816. London: Methuen, 1970. 290p.

H78 Ulich, Robert. History of educational thought. Rev. ed. New York: American Book, [1968]. 452p.

H79 ———, ed. Three thousand years of educational wisdom; selections from great documents. 2d ed. Cambridge, Mass.: Harvard Univ. Pr., 1954. 668p.

H80 Weinberg, Meyer. A chance to learn: the history of race and education in the United States. Cambridge: Cambridge Univ. Pr., 1977. 471p.

H81 Woody, Thomas. Life and education in early societies. New York: Macmillan, 1949. Reprint, New York: Hafner, 1970. 825p.

EDUCATIONAL PHILOSOPHY

This type of educational literature comprises general works, such as Brubacher's, Wingo's, and Butler's, which analyze fundamental principles and the viewpoints of the various schools of thought; an exposition of a single theory, such as Breed's volume; and collections of statements by different thinkers. A basic work is Dewey's *Democracy and education,* which represents pragmatism or experimentalism but must be supplemented by his later and critical book, *Experience and education.* Another influential work exemplifying the pragmatic standpoint is the book by Kilpatrick. Brameld treats contrasting schools of educational thought as well as the author's own position of reconstructionism. Idealism is expressed by Horne; the Catholic educational philosophy is presented by Redden and Ryan; and the principles of realism are stressed by Broudy. Woelfel analyzes in detail the theories of seventeen American educators of different shades of thought. A distinctive position is held by Berkson, who links educational theory with practice. The historical context in educational theory is represented by Price. Morris and Pai present philosophic schools of thought as a basis for decision-making on current educational issues. A critique of liberal theories underlying American education is provided by Feinberg.

Symposia offer viewpoints by proponents of various schools of thought. Scheffler's collection draws upon the writings of the general philosophers. Park collects essays on various trends, including existentialism and philosophical analysis, aiming to enable the student to think philosophically. Archambault brings together writings by British representatives of the school. Morris and Strain present recent writings on various positions in educational theory.

H82 Archambault, Reginald D., ed. Philosophical analysis and education. London: Routledge & Paul, 1965. New York: Humanities, 1972. 212p.

H83 Berkson, I. B. Ethics, politics, and education. Eugene: Univ. of Oregon Pr., 1968. 348p.

H84 Brameld, Theodore. Patterns of educational philosophy: divergence and convergence in culturological perspective. New York: Holt, 1971. 615p.

H85 Breed, Frederick S. Education and the new realism. New York: Macmillan, 1939. 237p.

H86 Broudy, Harry S. Building a philosophy of education. 2d ed. Englewood Cliffs, N.J.: Prentice-Hall, 1961; Huntington, N.Y.: Krieger, 1977. 410p.

H87   Brubacher, John S. Modern philosophies of education. 4th ed. New York: McGraw-Hill, 1969. 393p.

H88   Butler, J. Donald. Four philosophies and their practice in education and religion. 3d ed. New York: Harper, 1968. 528p.

H89   Dewey, John. Democracy and education. New York: Macmillan, 1916. 434p.

H90   ———. Experience and education. New York: Macmillan, 1938. 116p.

H91   Feinberg, Walter. Reason and rhetoric: the intellectual foundations of twentieth century liberal educational policy. New York: Wiley, 1975. 287p.

H92   Horne, Herman H. The philosophy of education. New York: Macmillan, 1904. 295p.

H93   Kilpatrick, William H. Philosophy of education. New York: Macmillan, 1951. 465p.

H94   Morris, Van Cleve, ed. Modern movements in educational philosophy. Boston: Houghton, 1969. 381p.

H95   ——— and Young Pai. Philosophy and the American school. Boston: Houghton, 1976. 476p.

H96   Park, Joe, ed. Selected readings in the philosophy of education. 4th ed. New York: Macmillan, 1974. 367p.

H97   Price, Kingsley. Education and philosophical thought. 2d ed. Boston: Allyn & Bacon, 1967. 605p.

H98   Redden, John D. and Francis A. Ryan. A Catholic philosophy of education. Rev. ed. Milwaukee: Bruce, 1956. 601p.

H99   Scheffler, Israel, ed. Philosophy and education. 2d ed. Boston: Allyn & Bacon, 1966. 387p.

H100   Strain, John P., ed. Modern philosophies of education. New York: Random, 1971. 555p.

H101   Wingo, G. Max, ed. Philosophies of education: an introduction. Lexington, Mass.: Heath, 1974. 367p.

H102   Woelfel, Norman. Molders of the American mind. New York: Columbia Univ. Pr., 1933; New York: Octagon, 1974. 304p.

EDUCATIONAL SOCIOLOGY

The field of educational sociology was inaugurated around the turn of the twentieth century by sociologists who applied the principles of their discipline to the problems of education. After a period, during which it was developed by educators such as E. George Payne and Harold Rugg, who injected a social emphasis into the study of education, it has attracted greater attention by professional sociologists. One indication of change has been the transformation of the *Journal of educational sociology* into *Sociology of education.*

Levine and Havighurst introduce the reader to the impact of social structure and forces upon teachers and students, including minorities. Brookover and Gottlieb treat education within the social order, as well as the influence of the school on personal and interpersonal development. The many school-community relations are clarified in Graham. Brembeck deals in detail with the interaction of students and teachers with the school and community. The growing interest in the sociology of education in Germany is exemplified by the introductory work of Kippert, the more extensive study by Stieglitz, and the comprehensive treatment in Bornemann and Mann-Tiechler of the interrelationship of family, social agencies, and school in an age of crisis.

The general works are supported by books of essays, readings, and studies. Among the increasing number of such volumes are those edited by Swift and by Stanley and others. Halsey placed education, sociology, and economics in international perspective. The essays in Miles and Charters stress the social psychology of education. The anthropological approach to intercultural education is featured in Landes. The Berelson and Steiner volume is a summary and synthesis of sociological research basic to education. Carl Weinberg treats a variety of educational problems in social perspective. The newer concern with the problems of, and solutions for, the education of the economically, racially, and other disadvantaged, especially in an urban setting, is exemplified by Bernstein and by Passow. On a more specialized basis, the essays in Meyer Weinberg's collection treat the issue of the education of the blacks, while Cordasco and Bucchioni, and Carter stress the problems of educating the Spanish-speaking pupils in the United States. Folger and Nam interpret in social terms the significance of the 1960 census for American education. The increasing interest in the interrelationship of economics, sociology, and education is illustrated in the compilations by Anderson and Bowman and by Bowman.

Only a few examples of the recent extensive and specialized literature on the sociology of education can be cited. The increasing recognition of the importance of minorities in American society is treated in Henderson's volume on the backgrounds, characteristics, and sociocultural status of the various constituent racial and ethnic groups, with a focus on educational guidance. Hyman and Wright indicate the relationship between the school and the individual's ethical development. The impact of a rapidly changing society on Catholic education since the mid-1960s is examined by Greeley and others. The collection of papers edited by Calhoun and Ianni treats education in formal schools and outside institutional framework, as well as the relation between language and education. The growing emphasis on teacher preparation in various minority, racial, and cultural groups is illustrated by Banks's study of the theory and practice of multiethnic education.

H103 Anderson, C. Arnold and Mary J. Bowman, eds. Education and economic development. Chicago: Aldine, 1965. 436p.

H104 Banks, James A. Multiethnic education: theory and practice. Boston: Allyn & Bacon, 1981. 326p.

H105 Berelson, Bernard and Gary A. Steiner. Human behavior; an inventory of scientific findings. New York: Harcourt, 1964. 712p.

H106 Bernstein, Abraham. The education of urban populations. New York: Random, 1967. 398p.

H107 Bornemann, Ernst and Gustav V. Mann-Tiechler, eds. Handbuch der Sozialerziehung. Freiburg i. Br., W. Germany: Herder, 1963–64. 3v.

H108 Bowman, Mary J. and others. Readings in the economics of education. Paris: UNESCO, 1968. 945p.

H109 Brembeck, Cole. Social foundations of education. 2d ed. New York: Wiley, 1971. 661p.

H110 Brookover, Wilbur B. and David Gottlieb. A sociology of education. 2d ed. New York: American Book, 1964. 488p.

H111 Calhoun, Craig J. and Francis A. J. Ianni, eds. The anthropological study of education. The Hague: Mouton, 1976. 360p.

H112 Carter, Thomas P. Mexican Americans in school: a history of educational neglect. New York: College Entrance Examination Board, 1970. 235p.

H113 Cave, William M. and Mark A. Chesler, eds. Sociology of education: an anthology of issues and problems. New York: Macmillan, 1974. 552p.

H114 Cordasco, Francesco and Eugene Bucchioni, eds. Puerto Rican children in mainland schools. Metuchen, N.J.: Scarecrow, 1968. 465p.

H115 Folger, John K. and Charles B. Nam. Education of the American population. Washington, D.C.: U.S. Dept. of Commerce, 1967; New York: Arno, 1976. 290p.

H116 Graham, Grace. The public school in the new society. New York: Harper, 1969. 404p.

H117 Greeley, Andrew M., William C. McCready, and Kathleen McCourt. Catholic schools in a declining church. Kansas City, Mo.: Sheed & Ward, 1976. 483p.

H118 Halsey, A. H. and others, eds. Education, economy, and society. New York: Free Pr., 1965. 625p.

H119 Levine, Daniel and Robert J. Havighurst. Society and education. 6th ed. Boston: Allyn & Bacon, 1984.

H120 Henderson, George, ed. Understanding and counseling ethnic minorities. Springfield, Ill.: Thomas, 1979. 535p.

H121 Hyman, Herbert H. and Charles R. Wright. Education's lasting influence on values. Chicago: Univ. of Chicago Pr., 1979. 161p.

H122 Kippert, Klaus, ed. Einführung in die Soziologie der Erziehung. Freiburg i. Br., W. Germany: Herder, 1970. 355p.

H123 Landes, Ruth. Culture in American education: anthropological approaches to minority and dominant groups in the schools. New York: Wiley, 1965. 330p.

H124 Miles, Matthew B. and W. W. Charters, Jr. Learning in social settings; new readings in the social psychology of education. Boston: Allyn & Bacon, 1970. 751p.

H125 Passow, A. Harry, ed. Developing programs for the educationally disadvantaged. New York: Teachers College Pr., 1968. 364p.

H126 Stanley, William O. and others, eds. Social foundations of education. New York: Dryden, 1956. 638p.

H127 Stieglitz, Heinrich. Soziologie und Erzichungswissenschaft. Stuttgart: Enke, 1970. 608p.

H128 Swift, D. F., ed. Basic readings in the sociology of education. London: Routledge & Paul, 1970. 301p.

H129 Weinberg, Carl. Education and social problems. New York: Free Pr., 1970. 350p.

H130 Weinberg, Meyer, ed. Integrated education. Beverly Hills, Calif.: Glencoe Pr., 1968. 376p.

COMPARATIVE AND INTERNATIONAL EDUCATION

This study of the national system of education or an educational problem in perspective of the development of one or more other nations has achieved some popularity in recent decades, especially during the 1950s. As a field of research and writing, however, it is well over a century and a half old. The literature includes reference books, compilations, theoretical works, documentary collections, textbooks, yearbooks, periodicals, analyses of observations, and so forth. Among such writings are the yearbooks of Teachers College of Columbia University and the University of London Institute of Education (H598), and the International Bureau of Education (H588), the volumes of the World Survey of Education, issued by UNESCO (H570), the *Comparative education review* (H630), and the monographic reports on education published by the U.S. Office of Education (H612), the Organization for Economic Cooperation and Development (H608), the Council of Europe, and other organizations.

In recent years the field of international education has been brought closer to comparative education. One example of this trend is the title change from Comparative Education Society to Comparative and International Education Society. The fundamental theoretical work by Schneider throws light on the nature of comparative education and on educational questions in international perspective. The classic study *Comparative education,* by Kandel, considers eight issues (national character, state and school, teacher education, etc.) in five countries of Europe and in the United States. To some extent his later volume is an abbreviated and updated treatment of these and other problems. Hans, also a pioneer in the field, deals with language, race, religion, and other factors underlying national educational systems, as well as a comparison of the school systems of England, France, the USSR, and the United States. Cramer and Browne emphasize school administration, organization, and other problems in several countries in Asia, Europe, Australia, and North America. King, utilizing the approach of national systems, devotes attention to four European countries, the United States, Japan, and India.

In recent years the number of general works has multiplied considerably. Bereday offers the principles of research methodology with illustrative examples and a comprehensive bibliography. The combination of history, theory, and research in comparative education is presented by Schneider (1961). Hilker, Tusquets, Vexliard, Noah and Eckstein, and Thut and Adams analyze the role of historical and cultural forces in the formation of educational systems, while Ulich treats the development of national systems in broad, humanistic, historical, and international perspective.

Another recent trend is the proliferation of composite publications. Among these are Gezi and Kazamias and Epstein. Fischer contains essays showing the approaches to comparative education through anthropology, sociology, political science, and economics. Eckstein and Noah stress the quantitative approach to research, while Thomas is concerned with curriculum change in various societies.

The specialized studies include monographs on the school systems of several or single countries, sometimes in comparison with other countries. Many are concerned with one or more educational problems in the context of one or more foreign cultures. An example of the latter is the compilation edited by Schultze, which covers various phases and problems of education in the West European countries. De Witt's study is a careful examination of the educational system of the Soviet Union, with special reference to the training of scientists and engineers and with consideration of the comparable situation in the United States. Merriam discusses citizenship education in several European countries and the United States. Adams and Bjork indicate the educational problems of the emergent nations of Asia and Africa. Shimoniak stresses the USSR, but includes the communist countries of Eastern Europe, Asia, and Cuba. Springer's study in comparative curriculum is exemplary. Clayton compares church-state-school relations in three West European countries with the United States. Ashby offers a comparative-historical study of British higher educational policy, while Qubain presents a careful study of higher and professional education in seven Arab countries. Husén and colleagues contribute an original statistical study in which mathematics achievement is compared in twelve countries.

Students of the literature can profit from the use of recent reference works that are discussed at length in this book. In comparative education, the *International guide to educational documentation* is a valuable, annotated compilation of documentary material and other works concerning education all over the world. Bristow and Holmes is an excellently selected and indexed bibliography of works and studies in English. Sasnett and Sepmeyer contains detailed outlines of the educational systems of African nations. Sketchy, but suggestive, is Beck's outline of the educational systems of fifty countries.

The literature on the various types of educational contact among the nations has also been increasing, particularly since 1945. A satisfactory introduction to the field of international education is furnished by the essays in Scanlon and Shields. The Fraser and Brickman volume collects documentary materials illustrating such relations in the nineteenth century, while Johnson and Colligan concentrate on the historical development of the Fulbright exchanges. The recent history of efforts at establishing an international university is traced by Zweig. Coombs depicts the facts and the strategies involved in international educational problems. Sanders and Ward analyze the recent international programs of American colleges and universities.

Recent writings are characterized by many works on education in developing countries, on the systems of the USSR and the People's Republic of China, and on various specialized topics. Parkinson's book is a comparative study of three African countries, two Asian, and one South American with reference to the impact of foreign aid. The comparative testing in six subjects of pupils in several countries, carried on by the International Association for the Evaluation of Educational achievement, is analyzed in Purves and Levine. Grandpré surveys coeducation, with special reference to Catholic education, in fifteen countries. The movements for educational reform in a dozen countries in Europe, the Far East, and the United States are reviewed in Röhrs. Szyliowicz analyzes educational change in the Arab countries, Iran, and Turkey. The USSR makes available detailed statistical data on education at periodic intervals. A valuable work is the survey and appraisal by Spaulding and Flack of research literature on the experience of foreign students in the United States.

H131 Adams, Don and Robert M. Bjork. Education in developing areas. New York: McKay, 1969. 161p.

H132 Ashby, Eric. Universities: British, Indian, African. Cambridge, Mass.: Harvard Univ. Pr., 1966. 558p.

H133 Beck, Carlton E., ed. Perspectives on world education. Dubuque, Ia.: W. C. Brown, 1970. 434p.

H134 Bereday, George Z. F. Comparative method in education. New York: Holt, 1964. 302p.

H135 Bristow, Thelma and Brian Holmes. Comparative education through the literature. Hamden, Conn.: Archon Books, 1968. 181p.

H136 Clayton, A. Stafford. Religion and schooling: a comparative study. Waltham, Mass.: Blaisdell, 1969. 254p.

H137 Coombs, Philip H. The world educational crisis: a systems analysis. New York: Oxford Univ. Pr., 1968. 241p.

H138 Cramer, John F. and George S. Browne. Contemporary education. New York: Harcourt, 1965. 598p.

H139 De Witt, Nicholas. Education and professional employment in the USSR. Washington, D.C.: Govt. Print. Off., 1962. 856p.

H140 Eckstein, Max A. and Harold J. Noah, eds. Scientific investigations in comparative education. New York: Macmillan, 1969. 428p.

H141 Fischer, Joseph, ed. The social sciences and the comparative study of educational problems. Scranton, Pa.: International Textbook, 1970. 533p.

H142 Fraser, Stewart E. and William W. Brickman, eds. A history of international and comparative education: nineteenth century documents. Glenview, Ill.: Scott, Foresman, 1968. 495p.

H143 Gezi, Kalil I., ed. Education in comparative and international perspectives. New York: Holt, 1971. 562p.

H144 Grandpré, Marcel de. La coéducation dans les écoles de 45 pays. Sherbrooke, Quebec: Editions Paulines, 1973. 334p.

H145 Hans, Nicholas. Comparative education: a study of educational factors and traditions. 3d ed., rev. London: Routledge & Paul, 1967. 334p.

H146 Hilker, Franz. Vergleichende Padagogik: eine Einführung in ihre Geschichte, Theorie und Praxis. Munich: Hueber, 1962. 185p.

H147 Husén, Torsten and others, ed. International study of achievement in mathematics. New York: Wiley, 1967. 2v.

H148 International guide to educational documentation: 1955–1960. Paris: UNESCO, 1963. 700p.

H149 International guide to educational documentation: 1960–65. Paris: UNESCO, 1971. 575p.

H150 Johnson, Walter and Francis J. Colligan. The Fulbright program: a history. Chicago: Univ. of Chicago Pr., 1965. 380p.

H151 Kandel, I. L. Comparative education. Boston: Houghton, 1933. Reprint, Westport, Conn.: Greenwood, 1970. 922p.

H152 ———. The new era in education: a comparative study. Boston: Houghton, 1955. 388p.

H153 Kazamias, Andreas M. and Erwin H. Epstein, eds. Schools in transition: essays in comparative education. Boston: Allyn & Bacon, 1968. 421p.

H154 King, Edmund J. Other schools and ours. 4th rev. ed. New York: Holt, 1973. 520p.

H155 Merriam, Charles E. The making of citizens. New York: Teachers College Pr., 1966. 460p.

H156 Noah, Harold J. and Max A. Eckstein. Toward a science of comparative education. New York: Macmillan, 1969. 222p.

H157 Parkinson, Nancy and others. Educational aid and national development: an international comparison of the past and recommendations for the future. London: Macmillan, 1976. 411p.

H158 Purves, Alan C. and Daniel U. Levine, eds. Educational policy and international assessment: implications of the IEA surveys of achievement. Berkeley, Calif.: McCutchan, 1975. 184p.

H159 Qubain, Fahim I. Education and science in the Arab world. Baltimore: Johns Hopkins Univ. Pr., 1966. Reprint, New York: Arno, 1979. 538p.

H160 Röhrs, Hermann, ed. Die Schulreform in den Industriestaaten. Frankfurt am Main: Akademische Verlagsgesellschaft, 1971. 313p.

H161 Sanders, Irwin T. and Jennifer C. Ward. Bridges to understanding; international programs of American colleges and universities. New York: McGraw-Hill, 1970. 285p.

H162 Sasnett, Martena and Inez Sepmeyer. Educational systems of Africa; interpretations for use in the evaluation of academic credentials. Berkeley: Univ. of California Pr., 1966. 1,550p.

H163 Scanlon, David G. and James J. Shields, eds. Problems and prospects in international education. New York: Teachers College Pr., 1968. 399p.

H164 Schneider, Friedrich. Triebkräfte der Pädagogik der Völker; eine Einführung in die Vergleichende Erziehungswissenschaft. Salzburg: Otto Müller, 1947. 503p.

H165 ———. Vergleichende Erziehungswissenschaft; Geschichte, Forschung, Lehre. Heidelberg: Quelle & Meyer, 1961. 218p.

H166 Schultze, Walter, ed. Schools in Europe. Weinheim, Berlin: Beltz, 1968–70. 3v. in 6pt.

H167 Shimoniak, Wasyl. Communist education; its history, philosophy, and politics. Chicago: Rand McNally, 1969. 506p.

H168 Spaulding, Seth and Michael J. Flack, eds. The world's students in the United States: a review and evaluation of research on foreign students. New York: Praeger, 1976. 520p.

H169 Springer, Ursula K. Recent curriculum developments in France, West Germany, and Italy; a study of trends at the middle level of education. New York: Teachers College Pr., 1969. 169p.

H170 Szyliowicz, Joseph S. Education and modernization in the Middle East. Ithaca, N.Y.: Cornell Univ. Pr., 1973. 477p.

H171 Thomas, R. Murray and others, eds. Strategies for curriculum change: cases from thirteen nations. Scranton, Pa.: International Textbook, 1968. 386p.

H172 Thut, I. N. and Don Adams. Educational patterns in contemporary societies. New York: McGraw-Hill, 1964. 494p.

H173 Tusquets, Juan. Teoría y práctica de la pedagogía comparada. Madrid: Editorial Magisterio Español, 1969. 366p.

H174 Ulich, Robert. The education of nations; a comparison in historical perspective. 2d ed. Cambridge, Mass.: Harvard Univ. Pr., 1967. 365p.

H175 U.S.S.R. Tsentralnoe Statisticheskoe Upravlenie. Otdel statistiki kultury. Narodnoe obrazovanie, nauka i kultura v SSSR: statisticheskii sbornik. Moscow: Izdatelstvo "Statistika," 1971. 403p.

H176 Vexliard, Alexandre. La pédagogie comparée: méthodes et problèmes. Paris: Presses Universitaires de France, 1967. 215p.

H177 Zweig, Michael. The idea of a world university. Carbondale: Southern Illinois Univ. Pr., 1967. 204p.

EDUCATIONAL PSYCHOLOGY, MEASUREMENT, AND GUIDANCE

As in the other branches of education, there are various classes of books in educational psychology, measurement, and guidance. Some are broad in scope, embracing such topics as intelligence, learning, growth, behavior, and the like. Examples of these are the works of Mathis and DeCecco and Crawford. Others concentrate on the different aspects of the learning process, with particular reference to learning in school. Among these are Klausmeier and Ripple, and Lindgren. In addition, there are specialized, scholarly analyses, such as the volumes by Gagné and by Hilgard and Bower on the learning process. Some works contain chapters by specialists on learning and other subjects; among these are Bloom, Shulman and Keislar, and Clarizio.

The books on measurement by Thorndike, by Ebel, by Gronlund, by Thorndike and Hagen, and by Glass and Hopkins are comprehensive in scope and treatment.

Among the recent works in this field are a comparative analysis of the application of psychoanalytical and other modern psychological theories to education. Good and Brophy aim at the integration of the principles and practices of psychology in relation to classroom practice. Airasian and others present the background, goals problems, and issues of the competency testing movement of the early 1970s.

The growing field of guidance is well represented by the detailed work of Hutson. Weinberg, and Zaccaria and Bopp illustrate the tendency to relate society and education to guidance.

H178 Airasian, Peter W., George F. Madaus, and Joseph J. Pedulla. Minimal competency testing. Englewood Cliffs, N.J.: Educational Technology Pubns., 1979. 225p.

H179 Bloom, Benjamin S. and others. Handbook on formative and summative evaluation of student learning. New York: McGraw-Hill, 1971. 923p.

H180 Clarizio, Harvey F. and others, eds. Contemporary issues in educational psychology. 2d ed. Boston: Allyn & Bacon, 1974. 727p.

H181 DeCecco, John P. and William R. Crawford. The psychology of learning and instruction: educational psychology. 2d ed. Englewood Cliffs, N.J.: Prentice-Hall, 1974. 604p.

H182 Ebel, Robert L. Essentials of educational measurement. 3d ed. Englewood Cliffs, N.J.: Prentice-Hall, 1979. 388p.

H183 Gagné, Robert. The conditions of learning. 3d ed. New York: Holt, 1977. 339p.

H184 Glass, Gene V. and Kenneth D. Hopkins. Statistical methods in education and psychology. 2d ed. Englewood Cliffs, N.J.: Prentice-Hall, 1984.

H185 Good, Thomas L. and Jere E. Brophy. Educational psychology: a realistic approach. 2d ed. New York: Holt, 1980. 658p.

H186 Gronlund, Norman E. Measurement and evaluation in teaching. 5th ed. New York: Collier Bks., 1985.

H187 Hilgard, Ernest R. and Gordon H. Bower. Theories of learning. 5th ed. Englewood Cliffs, N.J.: Prentice-Hall, 1981. 647p.

H188 Hutson, Percival W. The guidance function in education. 2d ed. New York: Appleton, 1968. 786p.

H189 Lindgren, Henry C. Educational psychology in the classroom. 6th ed. New York: Oxford Univ. Pr., 1980. 796p.

H190 Mathis, B. Claude and others. Psychological foundations of education: learning and teaching. New York: Academic Pr., 1970. 778p.

H191 Klausmeier, Herbert J. and Richard E. Ripple, eds. Learning and human abilities: educational psychology. 3d ed. New York: Harper, 1971. 810p.

H192 Roberts, Thomas M., ed. Four psychologies applied to education: Freudian, behavioral, humanistic, and transpersonal. New York: Schenkman, Wiley, 1975. 588p.

H193 Shulman, Lee S. and Evan R. Keislar, eds. Learning by discovery. Chicago: Rand McNally, 1966. 224p.

H194 Thorndike, Robert L., ed. Educational measurement. 2d ed. Washington, D.C.: American Council on Education, 1971. 768p.

H195 ——— and Elizabeth P. Hagen. Measurement and evaluation in psychology and education. 4th ed. New York: Wiley, 1977. 693p.

H196 Weinberg, Carl. Social foundations of educational guidance. New York: Free Pr., 1969. 398p.

H197 Zaccaria, Joseph S. and Stephen G. Bopp. Approaches to guidance in contemporary education. 2d ed. Cranston, R.I.: Carroll Pr., 1981. 311p.

CURRICULUM AND INSTRUCTION

The expression "curriculum and instruction" has been commonly used in educational circles in recent years, and displaced the traditional terms "general methods" and "special methods" of teaching. A comprehensive treatment of the past and present, and of the future possibilities of curriculum from the kindergarten through grade 12, is provided by Gwynn and Chase. Covering the elementary and secondary school curricula, but from a more theoretical standpoint, is the work by Crary. A unique contribution is Dolch's fully documented survey of 2,500 years of the curriculum in the Western world.

Among the specialized books, Barlow presents the history of industrial education, while Thompson emphasizes a multifaceted approach to vocational education. The history of physical education is treated by Van Dalen and Bennett.

Rubin presents readings which cover the subject-matter fields, current movements and methods of instruction. The theory and practice of curriculum development and evaluation on a global level, especially in developing countries, are analyzed in Lewy. Curriculum design and decision-making are stressed in Goodlad's introductory work.

In methodology, a basic handbook is the compilation of research studies edited by Gage.

The historical background of the reading problem is given by Mathews, while Chall emphasizes the history of the controversy on reading methods in the United States, while Robinson analyzes reading instruction in various subjects. A standard work on the methods and materials of audiovisual instruction is the comprehensive text by Dale.

The improvement of teaching skills with stress on individualized and open learning is the theme of Good and Brophy. The particular problems of teaching in urban and multicultural environments are explored in the books by Lemlech, Cross, Baker, Stiles, and Banks. Becker's compilation, dealing with the principles, content, and methods of world-centered education in elementary and secondary schools, aims at the reduction of ethnocentrism. Purpel and Ryan offer readings on teaching practices in values clarification and other aspects of moral education, a subject of increasing concern.

During the 1960s there has been a proliferation of newer techniques of teaching, such as the computer and the teaching machine, as well as other innovations. Lumsdaine and Glaser is an important source book of studies from the 1920s throughout the 1950s of teaching machines and programmed procedures. Saettler's historical study of instructional technology furnishes a framework, while Tickton's collection is an encyclopedic appraisal of the field.

H198 Banks, James A. Teaching strategies for ethnic studies. 3d ed. Boston: Allyn & Bacon, 1984. 479p.

H199 Barlow, Melvin A. History of industrial education in the United States. Peoria, Ill.: Bennett, 1967. 512p.

H200 Becker, James M., ed. Schooling for a global age. New York: McGraw-Hill, 1979. 345p.

H201 Chall, Jeanne S. Learning to read: the great debate. Updated ed. New York: McGraw-Hill, 1983. 372p.

H202 Crary, Ryland W. Humanizing the school; curriculum development and theory. New York: Knopf, 1969. 481p.

H203 Cross, Dolores E., Gwendolyn C. Baker, and Lindley J. Stiles, eds. Teaching in a multicultural society: perspectives and professional strategies. New York: Free Pr., 1977. 221p.

H204 Dale, Edgar. Audio-visual methods in teaching. 3d ed. New York: Dryden Pr., 1969. 719p.

H205 Dolch, Josef. Lehrplan des Abendlandes: Zweieinhalb Jahrtausende Seiner Geschichte. 3d ed. Darmstadt, W. Germany: Wissenschaftliche Buchgessellschaft, 1982. 483p.

H206 Gage, N. L., ed. Handbook of research on teaching. Chicago: Rand McNally, 1963. 1,218p.

H207 Good, Thomas L. and Jere E. Brophy. Looking in classrooms. 3d ed. New York: Harper, 1984.

H208 Goodlad, John I. and others. Curriculum inquiry: the study of curriculum practice. New York: McGraw-Hill, 1979. 371p.

H209 Gwynn, J. Minor and John B. Chase, Jr. Curriculum principles and social trends. 4th ed. New York: Macmillan, 1969. 661p.

H210 Lemlech, Johanna K. Handbook for successful urban teaching. New York: Harper, 1977. Reprint, Lanham, Md.: Univ. Pr. of America, 1984. 316p.

H211 Lewy, Arieh, ed. Handbook of curriculum evaluation. Paris: UNESCO, 1977. 306p.

H212 Lumsdaine, A. A. and Robert Glaser, eds. Teaching machines and programmed learning. Washington, D.C.: National Education Assn., 1960. 724p.

H213 Mathews, Mitford M. Teaching to read; historically considered. Chicago: Univ. of Chicago Pr., 1966. 218p.

H214 Nelson, Lois N., ed. The nature of teaching. Waltham, Mass.: Blaisdell, 1969. 323p.

H215 Purpel, David and Kevin Ryan, eds. Moral education . . . it comes with the territory. Berkeley, Calif.: McCutchan, 1976. 424p.

H216 Robinson, H. Alan. Teaching reading, writing, and study strategies: the content areas. 3d ed. Boston: Allyn & Bacon, 1983. 329p.

H217 Rubin, Louis, ed. Curriculum handbook. Boston: Allyn & Bacon, 1977. 2v.

H218 Saettler, L. Paul. A history of instructional technology. New York: McGraw-Hill, 1968. 399p.

H219 Taylor, Marvin J., ed. An introduction to Christian education. Nashville: Abingdon, 1966. 412p.

H220 Thompson, John F. Foundations of vocational education: social and philosophical. Englewood Cliffs, N.J.: Prentice-Hall, 1973. 260p.

H221 Tickton, Sidney G., ed. To improve learning: an evaluation of instructional technology. New York: Bowker, 1970–71. 2v.

H222 Van Dalen, Deobold B. and Bruce L. Bennett. A world history of physical education: cultural, philosophical, comparative. 2d ed. Englewood Cliffs, N.J.: Prentice-Hall, 1971. 694p.

PRESCHOOL AND ELEMENTARY EDUCATION

Books in this category generally treat principles, curriculum, practice, and related topics. Some works have been mentioned under "Curriculum and instruction," while others will appear in other sections.

Ragan and Shepherd covers the whole range—history, sociology, organization, curriculum, and evaluation. The ideas of more than 1,000 elementary school textbooks in the nineteenth century in the United States are analyzed by Elson.

The volume on elementary education by Glickman and Esposito is concerned with the goals, principles, methods, appraisal, curriculum modification, and alternative school models.

The increasing interest in preschool education, especially in its innovative aspects, is illustrated by the essays in Zigler and Valentine: the development and evaluation of the Head Start Program (1964–74) for "economically disadvantaged children." In a more general way, Foster and Headley treat in detail the principles and practices of kindergarten education.

H223 Elson, Ruth M. Guardians of tradition. Lincoln: Univ. of Nebraska Pr., 1964. 424p.

H224 Foster, Josephine and Neith Headley. Education in the kindergarten. New York: Van Nostrand, 1966. 564p.

H225 Glickman, Carl D. and James P. Esposito. Leadership guide for elementary school improvement: procedures for assessment and change. Boston: Allyn & Bacon, 1979. 334p.

H226 Ragan, William B. and Gene D. Shepherd. Modern elementary curriculum. 6th ed. New York: Holt, 1982. 510p.

H227 Zigler, Edward and Jeanette Valentine, eds. Project Head Start: a legacy of the war on poverty. New York: Free Pr., 1979. 610p.

SECONDARY EDUCATION

The history of secondary education in Western Europe and the United States by Kandel has not been superseded after four decades. Krug's monograph is a detailed study of American secondary education from 1880 to 1941. Bent, Hoover, and Blount and Klausmeier are introductions to the principles and practices of secondary education. French adds an emphasis on historical development to the general content.

There is a growing literature on specialized aspects and new approaches to secondary education; many of these are summarized in Unruh and Alexander. Typical of the many writings on the trend toward independent study is Alexander's informative book. The critique of high-school textbooks of American history by Fitzgerald may inspire a reexamination of the content of this course.

On an international scale, King offers a comparative analysis of upper secondary education in five West European countries, with special reference to structure, curriculum, sociological aspects, and possible future changes.

H228 Alexander, William M. and others. Independent study in secondary schools. New York: Holt, 1968. 200p.

H229 Bent, Rudyard K. and others. Principles of secondary education. 6th ed. New York: McGraw-Hill, 1970. 460p.

H230 Blount, Nathan S. and Herbert J. Klausmeier. Teaching in the secondary school. 3d ed. New York: Harper, 1968. 582p.

H231 FitzGerald, Frances. America revised: history textbooks in the twentieth century. Boston: Little, 1979, 240p.

H232 French, William M. American secondary education. 2d ed. New York: Odyssey, 1967. 587p.

H233 Hoover, Kenneth H. Learning and teaching in the secondary school. 3d ed. Boston: Allyn & Bacon, 1972. 633p.

H234 Justman, Joseph. Theories of secondary education in the United States. New York: Bureau of Publications, Teachers College, Columbia Univ., 1940. Reprint, New York: AMS Pr., 1972. 481p.

H235 Kandel, I. L. History of secondary education. Boston: Houghton, 1930. 577p.

H236 King, Edmund J., Christine H. Moor, and Jennifer A. Mundy. Postcompulsory education. London; Beverly Hills, Calif.: Sage, 1974–75. 2v.

H237 Krug, Edward A. The shaping of the American high school. New York: Harper, 1964, 1972. 2v.

H238 Monroe, Paul, ed. Principles of secondary education. New York: Macmillan, 1914. 790p.

H239 Unruh, Glenys G. and William M. Alexander. Innovations in secondary education. 2d ed. New York: Holt, 1970. 280p.

HIGHER EDUCATION

A unique reference work on the various aspects of higher education all over the world, past and recent, is Asa S. Knowles, *The international encyclopedia of higher education*, described at H568, which stresses administration, governance, finance, planning, professional education, and international cooperation. Also of international reference value are UNESCO's worldwide outline of higher education and Eurich's comparative analysis of twelve higher educational systems on four continents. An example of a history of a national system of higher and professional education is the volume by Harris. The twentieth-century university in various countries is treated, in greater or lesser detail, in Schairer and Hoffmann, in Bereday and Lauwerys, in Cueto Fernandini, in Steger, and in Waardenburg.

The historical development of higher education in the United States from the colonial period to the present era is clearly and comprehensively, if not exhaustively, covered by Brubacher and Rudy. More specialized historical accounts are contributed by Hofstadter and Metzger, by Veysey, by Curti and Nash, and by Rudolph. An indispensable collection of significant documents on the history of American higher education is presented in Hofstadter and Smith. Flexner's study, contrasting American universities with those of England and Germany, is controversial and provocative but is nonetheless an important classic in the literature, and has been reprinted twice with different introductions. Among the more recent comparative works are *Reform and expansion of higher education in Europe* and Burn's study of higher education in four West European nations, the USSR, Canada, Australia, Japan, and India.

Newer approaches to administration and to methods and materials of instruction are discussed in MacKenzie and others, Miller, and in Jencks and Riesman. Heiss offers enlightenment on changes in the doctoral and other graduate programs. Sanford's basic compilation of studies on the social and psychological problems and context of the college in the United States remains a valuable contribution to the literature. In addition, see Asa S. Knowles, *Handbook of college and university administration,* described in detail at H576.

Few subjects have attracted and held as much worldwide concern as the accelerated student revolution in the 1960s. An enormous literature has resulted from the widespread demonstrations and the consequent changes in administration, policy, and program of institutions of higher education. Feuer presents the historical development of the student revolt in Germany, Russia, and the United States (especially at the University of California, Berkeley); Lipset and Altbach, and Brickman and Lehrer are among those who provide international perspectives. Wallerstein and Starr is a valuable compilation of source materials.

H240 Bereday, George Z. F. and Joseph A. Lauwerys, eds. Higher education: 1959. Yonkers, N.Y.: World Book, 1959. Reprint, Freeport, N.Y.: Books For Libraries Pr., 1972. 520p.

H241 Brickman, William W. and Stanley Lehrer, eds. Conflict and change on the campus. New York: School & Society Books, 1970. 528p.

H242 Brubacher, John S. and Willis Rudy. Higher education in transition: a history of American colleges and universities, 1636–1976. 3d ed. New York: Harper, 1976. 536p.

H243 Burn, Barbara B. and others. Higher education in nine countries. New York: McGraw-Hill, 1971. 387p.

H244 Clarke, Martin L. Higher education in the ancient world. London: Routledge & Paul; Albuquerque: Univ. of New Mexico Pr., 1971. 188p.

H245 Cueto Fernandini, Carlos, ed. La universidad en el siglo XX. Lima: Universidad Nacional Mayor de San Marcos, 1951. 408p.

H246 Curti, Merle and Roderick Nash. Philanthropy in the shaping of American higher education. New Brunswick, N.J.: Rutgers Univ. Pr., 1965. 340p.

H247 Eurich, Nell P. Systems of higher education in twelve countries: a comparative view. New York: Praeger, 1981. 153p.

H248 Feldman, Kenneth and Theodore M. Newcomb. The impact of college on students. San Francisco: Jossey-Bass, 1973. 2v.

H249 Feuer, Lewis S. The conflict of generations. New York: Basic Books, 1969. 543p.

H250 Flexner, Abraham. Universities: American, English, German. London; New York: Oxford Univ. Pr., 1968. 381p.

H251 Harris, Robin S. A history of higher education in Canada, 1663–1960. Toronto: Univ. of Toronto Pr., 1976. 715p.

H252 Heiss, Ann H. Challenges to graduate schools. San Francisco: Jossey-Bass, 1970. 328p.

H253 Hofstadter, Richard and Walter P. Metzger. The development of academic freedom in the United States. New York: Columbia Univ. Pr., 1955. 527p.

H254 Hofstadter, Richard and Wilson Smith, eds. American higher education: a documentary history. Chicago: Univ. of Chicago Pr., 1961. 2v.

H255 Hook, Sidney, Paul Kurtz, and Miro Todorovich, eds. The university and the state: what role for government in higher education? Buffalo: Prometheus Books, 1978. 296p.

H256 Jencks, Christopher and David Riesman. The academic revolution. Chicago: Univ. of Chicago Pr., 1977. 580p.

H259 Levin, Arthur. Handbook on undergraduate curriculum. San Francisco: Jossey-Bass, 1978. 662p.

H260 Lipset, Seymour M. and Philip G. Altbach, eds. Students in revolt. Boston: Beacon, 1970. 561p.

H261 MacKenzie, Norman and others. Teaching and learning: an introduction to new methods and resources in higher education. 2d ed. Paris: UNESCO, 1976. 224p.

H262 Miller, Richard I. The assessment of college performance. San Francisco: Jossey-Bass, 1979. 374p.

H263 Reform and expansion of higher education in Europe: national reports, 1962–1967. Strasbourg: Council for Cultural Co-operation, 1967. 264p.

H264 Rudolph, Frederick. Curriculum: a history of the American undergraduate course of study since 1636. San Francisco: Jossey-Bass, 1977. 362p.

H265 Sanford, Nevitt, ed. The American college: a psychological and social interpretation of the higher learning. New York: Wiley, 1962. 1,084p.

H266 Schairer, Reinhold and Conrad Hoffmann, eds. Die Universitätsideale der Kulturvölker. Leipzig: Quelle & Meyer, 1925. 125p.

H267 Steger, Hanns-Albert, ed. Grundzüge des lateinamerikanischen Hochschulwesens. Baden-Baden: Nomos, 1965. 306p.

H268 Touraine, Alain. The academic system in American society. New York: McGraw-Hill, 1974. 319p.

H269 UNESCO. World guide to higher education: a comparative survey of systems, degrees, and qualifications. 2d ed. New York: Unipub, 1982. 369p.

H270 Veysey, Laurence R. The emergence of the American university. Chicago: Univ. of Chicago Pr., 1965. 505p.

H271 Waardenburg, Jean-Jacques. Les Universités dans le monde arabe actuel: documentation et essai d'interprétation. Paris: Mouton, 1966. 2v.

H272 Wallerstein, Immanuel and Paul Starr, eds. The university crisis reader. New York: Vintage, 1971. 2v.

H273 Wilson, Logan. The academic man. New York: Oxford Univ. Pr., 1942. Reprint, New York: Octagon, 1976. 248p.

TEACHER EDUCATION

A historical account of the teacher from ancient times to the twentieth century is narrated by Castle. The training, activities, and status of the teacher in America from the colonial period to the twentieth century is presented by Elsbree. Borrowman describes the programs for the education of the American teacher from the early nineteenth century onward, with special reference to the relation of general to professional studies, and supplements this study with a volume of documents. Monroe traces the full history of teaching-learning theory in connection with the evolution of the aims and practices in teacher education. The struggle between the National Education Association and the American Federation of Teachers is depicted by Stinnett (H296). Peterson's book contains biographical essays of influential teachers and professors, American and foreign, by their pupils (H292).

The development of the higher educational profession in England is delineated by Perkin, while Gönner recounts the advancement of teacher education in Austria from the late eighteenth to the mid-twentieth century.

The various facets of the status of the teacher as a member of a profession are analyzed in the standard work by Stinnett (H295). The Hortons present readings on recent problems and developments in teacher education. The professional status of teachers, their compensation, organization, and collective bargaining are discussed in Gerwin. Teachers' ideas, ideals, self-images, and perceptions by others are studied by Lortie. Borich analyzes teacher competency, performance, and accountability. Peterson and Walberg offer readings on the significance of the results of research for teacher education (H293). Older but still useful for reference is the encyclopedic compilation of research studies concerning the teaching process and problems, edited by Robert M. W. Travers, and published in 1973. For a full description, see the annotation on *Second handbook of research on teaching*, at H579. Harris's volume is a functional treatment of methods of advancing the qualifications of the teacher in service. An evaluation of the international background and interests of teachers in the United States is made by Harold Taylor on the basis of a national survey. Stone describes various experimental programs for the preparation of teachers.

On the international scene, the International Association of University Professors and Lecturers furnishes a report on the selection and training of higher educational personnel in sixteen countries (H294). Majault's book is a survey of programs of elementary and secondary school teachers' preparation in West European countries. The use of radio and television in teacher education is the theme of a report, edited by Mertens, of a conference under the auspices of the UNESCO Institute for Education in Hamburg.

The problems of teacher education in England are elucidated by Taylor. Of similar scope, but with more reference to the world scene, is the compilation edited by Krug. The impact by the National Union of Teachers on educational policy in England and Wales since World War II is analyzed by Manzer. The Morrison and McIntyre book examines research studies on teacher behavior in schools, teachers' roles, the background and training of teachers, and other pertinent subjects, with special reference to Britain. Bokelmann and Scheuerl's work contains essays by specialists on the issues involved in curriculum planning in relation to the West German teaching profession, including some attention to the situation in East Germany.

H274 Bokelmann, Hans and Hans Scheuerl, eds. Der Aufbau erziehungswissenschaftlicher Studien und der Lehrberuf. Heidelberg: Quelle & Meyer, 1970. 370p.

H275 Borich, Gary D. An appraisal of teaching: concepts and process. Reading, Mass.: Addison-Wesley, 1977. 396p.

H276 Borrowman, Merle L. The liberal and technical in teacher education. New York: Bureau of Publications, Teachers College, Columbia Univ., 1956. Reprint, Westport, Conn.: Greenwood, 1977. 247p.

H277 ———, ed. Teacher education in America: a documentary history. New York: Teachers College Pr., 1965. 252p.

H278 Castle, Edgar B. The teacher. London: Oxford Univ. Pr., 1970. 246p.

H279 Elsbree, Willard S. The American teacher: evolution of a profession in a democracy. New York: American Book, 1939. Reprint, Westport, Conn.: Greenwood, 1970. 566p.

H280 Gerwin, Donald, ed. The employment of teachers: some analytical views. Berkeley, Calif.: McCutchan, 1974. 440p.

H281 Gönner, Rudolf. Die österreichische Lehrerbildung von der Normalschule bis zur Pädagogischen Akademie. Vienna: Oesterreichischer Bundesverlag für Unterricht, Wissenschaft und Kunst, 1967. 376p.

H282 Harris, Ben M. and others. In-service education: a guide to better practice. Englewood Cliffs, N.J.: Prentice-Hall, 1969. 432p.

H283 Horton, Lowell and Phyllis Horton, eds. Teacher education: trends, issues, innovations. Danville, Ill.: Interstate, 1974. 366p.

H284 King, Edmund J., ed. The teacher and the needs of society in education. Oxford: Pergamon, 1970. 319p.

H285 Lortie, Dan C. Schoolteacher: a sociological study. Chicago: Univ. of Chicago Pr., 1975. 284p.

H286 Majault, Joseph. Teacher training. Strasbourg: Council for Cultural Co-operation, Council of Europe, 1965. 211p.

H287 Manzer, Ronald A. Teachers and politics in England and Wales; the role of the National Union of Teachers in the making of national educational policy since 1944. Toronto: Univ. of Toronto Pr., 1970. 164p.

H288 Mertens, J., ed. L'emploi de la radio et de la télévision dans la formation des maîtres. Hamburg: UNESCO Institute for Education, 1969. 129p.

H289 Monroe, Walter S. Teacher-learning theory and teacher education: 1890 to 1950. Urbana: Univ. of Illinois Pr., 1952. Reprint, New York: Greenwood, 1969. 426p.

H290 Morrison, A. and D. McIntyre. Teachers and teaching. 2d ed. Harmondsworth, Eng.: Penguin, 1969. 206p.

H291 Perkin, Harold. Key profession: the history of the Association of University Teachers. New York: Kelley, 1969. 268p.

H292 Peterson, Houston, ed. Great teachers: portrayed by those who studied under them. New Brunswick, N.J.: Rutgers Univ. Pr., 1946. 351p.

H293 Peterson, Penelope L. and Herbert J. Walberg, eds. Research on teaching. Berkeley, Calif.: McCutchan, 1979. 298p.

H294 The recruitment and training of university teachers. Ghent: International Assn. of University Professors and Lecturers, 1967. 223p.

H295 Stinnett, T. M. Professional problems of teachers. 3d ed. New York: Macmillan, 1968. 541p.

H296 ———. Turmoil in teaching: a history of the original struggle for America's teachers. New York: Macmillan, 1968. 406p.

H297 Stone, James C. Breakthrough in teacher education. San Francisco: Jossey-Bass, 1968. 206p.

H298 Taylor, Harold. The world and the American teacher; the preparation of teachers in the field of world affairs. Washington, D.C.: American Assn. of Colleges for Teacher Education, 1968. 311p.

H299 Taylor, William. Society and the education of teachers. London: Faber, 1969. 304p.

ADULT EDUCATION

The development of adult education in the context of various societies, from primitive man to the twentieth century in America, is provided by Grattan, with the developments during the past century and a half more fully described than those of previous centuries. Grattan also presents a useful collection of documents illustrating the evolution of the theory of adult education in America. A substantial historical account of American adult education is provided by Knowles. Predeek supplies a meticulously documented historical account of libraries in Britain and the United States. Shera offers a scholarly monograph on more than two centuries of the New England public library; Bode traces the development of the lyceum as an institution of American adult education; and Gould recounts the growth and decline of the Chautauqua form of adult education in America. A volume edited by Knowles provides encyclopedic information on all phases of adult education in the United States. Recent and contemporary developments and issues are covered by Liveright and by Knowles with the latter stressing the contribution by universities. For a well-annotated bibliography of the study of liberal arts subjects in adult education, especially in the universities, the librarian can turn to the comprehensive compilation of Mezirow and Berry. The status, issues, and approaches toward solutions in American adult education are identified in the report to the Ford Foundation by Hunter and Harman.

A century of the services of English universities to the development of adult education is traced by Jepson. The historical problems of English adult education are analyzed critically by Newman.

A comparative study of adult education in Western Europe and the United States in a historical context is provided by Ulich. MacKenzie presents case studies of open adult education in countries on three continents. Jeffries describes the work of UNESCO and the United Nations in alleviating illiteracy around the world. A more substantial study is that by Zischka, an analysis on a global basis of the efforts toward solutions of illiteracy. By way of contrast, Goody's volume contains case studies of countries, mainly in Asia and Africa, that have promoted literacy. The role of adult education in the development of the newer nations is studied by Lowe.

H301 Bode, Carl. The American lyceum; town meeting of the mind. New York: Oxford Univ. Pr.,
1956. Reprint, Carbondale: Univ. of Illinois Pr., 1968. 265p.

H302 Goody, Jack, ed. Literacy in traditional societies. Cambridge: Cambridge Univ. Pr., 1968. 347p.

H303 Gould, Joseph E. The Chautauqua movement; an episode in the continuing American Revolution. Albany: State Univ. of New York Pr., 1961. 108p.

H304 Grattan, C. Hartley. In quest of knowledge: a historical perspective on adult education. New York: Association Pr., 1955. Reprint, New York: Arno, 1971. 337p.

H305 ———, ed. American ideas about adult education, 1710–1951. New York: Columbia Univ. Teachers College, Bureau of Publications, 1959. 140p.

H306 Hunter, Carmen St. John and David Harman. Adult illiteracy in the United States: a report to the Ford Foundation. New York: McGraw-Hill, 1979. 206p.

H307 Jeffries, Sir Charles. Illiteracy: a world problem. New York: Praeger, 1967. 204p.

H308 Jepson, N. A. The beginnings of English university adult education—policy and problems; a critical study of the early Cambridge and Oxford University extension lecture movements between 1873 and 1907, with special reference to Yorkshire. London: Joseph, 1973. 372p.

H309 Knowles, Malcolm S. Higher adult education in the United States. Washington, D.C.: American Council on Education, 1969. 105p.

H310 ———. The adult education movement in the United States. New York: Holt, 1962. 335p.

H311 ———, ed. Handbook of adult education in the United States. Chicago: Adult Education Assn. of the U.S.A., 1960. 624p.

H312 Liveright, A. A. A study of adult education in the United States. Syracuse, N.Y.: Syracuse Univ. Pr., 1968. 138p.

H313 Lowe, John, ed. Adult education and nation-building; a symposium on adult education in developing countries. Edinburgh: Univ. Pr., 1970. 258p.

H314 MacKenzie, Norman, Richmond Postgate, and John Scuphan. Open learning: systems and problems in post-secondary education. Paris: UNESCO, 1975. 498p.

H315 Mezirow, J. D. and Dorothea Berry, comps. The literature of liberal adult education: 1945–1957. New York: Scarecrow, 1960. 308p.

H316 Newman, Michael. The poor cousin: a study of adult education. London, Boston: Allen & Unwin, 1979. 249p.

H317 Predeek, Albert. A history of libraries in Great Britain and North America. Tr. by Lawrence S.

Thompson. Chicago: American Library Assn., 1947. 177p.

H318 Shera, Jesse H. Foundations of the public library: the origins of the public library movement in New England, 1629–1855. Chicago: Univ. of Chicago Pr., 1949. Reprint, Hamden, Conn.: Shoe String, 1974. 308p.

H319 Ulich, Mary E. Patterns of adult education: a comparative study. New York: Pageant, 1965. 205p.

H320 Zischka, Anton. Welt ohne Analphabeten. Gütersloh, W. Germany: Bertelsmann, 1964. 351p.

SPECIAL EDUCATION

Special education comprises the study of the educational problems and programs of all types of children who deviate from the "normal"—the physically, mentally, and emotionally handicapped, as well as those who are gifted or talented in academic, artistic, or other creative ways. Telford and Sawrey offer study of the identification of the intellectually superior and the intellectually and physically retarded, including the problems of the aged. Perry's book is a highly detailed analysis of the characteristics, curriculum, and methods involved in teaching the trainable mentally retarded. Kirk and Lord present articles by specialists on the history and recent research on the retarded. Dunn's compilation emphasizes children with learning disabilities, but also a chapter on superior children.

Essays on the various aspects of special education are furnished by Cruickshank and Johnson and by Jones. A detailed, comprehensive treatment of the administration of programs of special education is the contribution of Meisgeier and King. Hildreth treats the identification, psychology, teaching, curriculum, guidance, and other aspects of the education of gifted children. Gold concentrates on the nature and curriculum of the academically talented, and adds a section on teacher training. A recent composite survey and appraisal of the education of gifted children is edited by Passow. Stanley and his co-editors compile studies of the mathematically, musically, and artistically gifted, adding to the original work by Lewis M. Terman. Even more specialized is the collection of papers under Keating's editorship on the identification of and programs for mathematically talented children and youth. Tannenbaum stresses intellectual and creative abilities.

H321 Cruickshank, William M. and G. Orville Johnson, eds. Education of exceptional children and youth. 3d ed. Englewood Cliffs, N.J.: Prentice-Hall, 1975. 708p.

H322 Dunn, Lloyd M., ed. Exceptional children in the schools: special education in transition. 2d ed. New York: Holt, 1973. 610p.

H323 Gold, Milton J. Education of the intellectually gifted. Columbus: Merrill, 1965. 472p.

H324 Hildreth, Gertrude H. Introduction to the gifted. New York: McGraw-Hill, 1966. 572p.

H325 Jones, Reginald L., ed. Problems and issues in the education of exceptional children. Boston: Houghton, 1971. 424p.

H326 Keating, Daniel P., ed. Intellectual talent: research and development: proceedings of the sixth annual Hyman Blumberg Symposium on Early Childhood Education. Baltimore: Johns Hopkins Univ. Pr., 1976. 346p.

H327 Kirk, Samuel A. and Francis E. Lord, eds. Exceptional children: educational resources and perspectives. Boston: Houghton, 1974. 503p.

H328 Meisgeier, Charles H. and John D. King, comps. The process of special education administration. Scranton, Pa.: International Textbook, 1970. 730p.

H329 Passow, A. Harry, ed. The gifted and the talented: their education and development. Chicago: Univ. of Chicago Pr., 1979. 473p.

H330 Perry, Natalie. Teaching the mentally retarded child. 2d ed. New York: Columbia Univ. Pr., 1974. 751p.

H331 Stanley, Julian C., William C. George, and Cecilia H. Solano, eds. The gifted and the creative: a fifty-year perspective: revised and expanded proceedings of the seventh annual Hyman Blumberg Symposium on Research in Early Childhood Education. Baltimore: Johns Hopkins Univ. Pr., 1977. 284p.

H332 Tannenbaum, Abraham J. Gifted children: psychological and educational perspectives. New York: Macmillan, 1983. 527p.

H333 Telford, Charles W. and James M. Sawrey. The exceptional individual. 4th ed. Englewood Cliffs, N.J.: Prentice-Hall, 1981. 532p.

EDUCATIONAL RESEARCH

The field of educational research has grown greatly. Some indications of this are the expansion of the American Educational Research Association, the increase in the number of journals and reference works, the development of the Educational Resources Information Centers (ERIC), and the dissertation explosion. A great deal of emphasis is evident on empirical, experimental, and statistical studies in the behavioral areas of education. Historical, theoretical, sociological, and comparative studies in education have also increased, but they seem to be numerically overwhelmed by the other types of research.

Of the introductory works, Van Dalen's covers a broad spectrum: concepts, step-by-step procedures, and tools with respect to experimental, historical, and descriptive research. Mouly stresses the interpretation of research findings. Tuckman's treatise discusses theory but lays stress on quantitative methods and the applicability in scholastic settings. Also dealing with the application of quantitative procedures, mainly derived from the behavioral sciences, and related research to educational problems is the volume by Asher. Good is an older work which describes various research methods and furnishes abundant references. Considerably briefer are the introductions in German by Röhrs and in Italian by Visalberghi. Cronbach and Suppes, both of them recognized research scholars, bring together papers by specialists on the future possibilities of educational research in the light of past and recent experience. A unique contribution is the collection of papers, edited by Broudy and others, relating educational theory to the concepts and issues of research.

The status of educational research in West Germany, the United States, Britain, Sweden, and the Soviet Union is treated comparatively in the volume edited by Lemberg.

H334 Asher, J. William. Educational research and evaluation methods. Boston: Little, 1976. 358p.

H335 Broudy, Harry S., Robert H. Ennis, and Leonard I. Krimerman, eds. Philosophy of educational research. New York: Wiley, 1973. 942p.

H336 Cronbach, Lee J. and Patrick Suppes, eds. Research for tomorrow's schools: disciplined inquiry for education. New York: Macmillan, 1969. 281p.

H337 Good, Carter V. Essentials of educational research: methodology and design. 2d ed. New York: Appleton, 1972. 429p.

H338 Lemberg, Eugen, ed. Das Bildungswesen als Gegenstand der Forschung. Heidelberg: Quelle & Meyer, 1963. 312p.

H339 Mouly, George. Educational research: the art and science of investigation. Boston: Allyn & Bacon, 1978. 390p.

H340 Röhrs, Hermann. Forschungsmethoden in der Erziehungswissenschaft. Stuttgart: Kohlhammer, 1971. 176p.

H341 Thouless, Robert H. Map of educational research. Slough, Eng.: National Foundation for Educational Research in England and Wales, 1969. 331p.

H342 Tuckman, Bruce W. Conducting educational research. 2d ed. New York: Harcourt, 1978. 479p.

H343 Van Dalen, Deobold B. Understanding educational research: an introduction. 4th ed. New York: McGraw-Hill, 1979. 547p.

H344 Visalberghi, Aldo. Problemi della ricérca pedagogica. Florence: La Nuova Italia, 1965. 162p.

EDUCATIONAL ADMINISTRATION AND SUPERVISION

From the 1950s onward the trend in this field has been toward an emphasis on administrative theory, policy making, and decision making. More recently, considerable attention has been given to the contribution of the behavioral sciences toward the better administration and organization of school systems. With the rise of the roles of teachers, students, and parents in administrative policies and processes, it can be said that the area of educational administration is in a state of flux. A convenient guide to the literature of a more placid era in educational administration, before 1947, is the book by Sears. Morphet deals with concepts, practices, and issues, as does Campbell. Walton employs a theoretical approach to administrative problems. The essays in Rosenthal derive from political science and sociology in pointing up the impact of political power and pressure on the formation of public educational policy. The compilation edited by Griffiths studies the historical and theoretical frameworks of the implications of behavioral science for the profession.

Of rising significance is the subject of teacher negotiations with boards of education. The issues associated with negotiations are studied in detail in Lieberman and Moskow.

The field of supervision is represented by Marks' exhaustive volume, which lays stress on the practical aspects. Neagley covers much of the same territory, in less space. Focus on the improvement of teaching and curriculum is the characteristic of Harrison's treatment of the supervisor as an educational leader.

The economics of education, including school finance as a foundation of educational administration, has been attracting increasing attention in recent decades. Johns and Morphet is a basic work, while the volume by Garius and colleagues studies the economic and political forces affecting the formation of public educational policy and issues. The Robinson and Vaizey compilation adds an international dimension to educational finance.

The techniques of developing and interpreting educational policy to pupils, parents, teachers, and the public are analyzed in Kindred, Bagin, and Gallagher. Wynne presents reports by undergraduate students of the functioning of 167 public and private schools during 1972–79 in and near Chicago. Lipham and Hoeh concentrate on the theories underlying the work of the principal, as well as specific activities. A study of special interest is Gosden's thoroughly documented account of the organization of British educational activities and welfare services for children, and the beginnings of educational reconstruction during 1939–45.

School law has long been a significant component in the preparation of school administrators. Peterson's volume is a comprehensive presentation of the subject, as is the one by Yudof. The Edwards and Garber treatise is an updated edition of a classic work.

H345 Benson, Charles S. The economics of public education. 3d ed. Boston: Houghton, 1978. 413p.

H346 Campbell, Roald F. and others. The organization and control of American schools. 3d ed. Columbus: Merrill, 1975. 468p.

H347 Edwards, Newton and Lee O. Garber. The courts and the public schools. 3d ed. Chicago: Univ. of Chicago Pr., 1971. 710p.

H348 Elsbree, Willard S. and others. Elementary school administration and supervision. 3d ed. New York: American Book, 1967. 520p.

H349 Garms, Walter L., James W. Guthrie, and Lawrence C. Pierce. School finance: the economics and politics of public education. Englewood Cliffs, N.J.: Prentice-Hall, 1978. 466p.

H350 Gauerke, Warren E. and Jack R. Childress, eds. The theory and practice of school finance. Chicago: Rand McNally, 1967. 437p.

H351 Gosden, P. H. J. H. Education in the Second World War: a study in policy and administration. London: Methuen, 1976. 527p.

H352 Griffiths, Daniel E., ed. Behavioral science and educational administration. Chicago: Univ. of Chicago Pr., 1964. 360p.

H353 Harrison, Raymond H. Supervisory leadership in education. New York: American Book, 1968. 414p.

H354 Johns, Roe L., Edgar L. Morphet, and Kern Alexander. The economics and financing of education: a systems approach. 4th ed. Englewood Cliffs, N.J.: Prentice-Hall, 1983. 371p.

H355 Kindred, Leslie W., Don Bagin, and Donald R. Gallagher. The school and community relations. 3d ed. Englewood Cliffs, N.J.: Prentice-Hall, 1984. 339p.

H356 Lieberman, Myron and Michael H. Moskow. Collective negotiations for teachers. Chicago: Rand McNally, 1966. 745p.

H357 Lipham, James M. and James A. Hoeh, Jr. The principalship: foundations and functions. New York: Harper, 1974. 372p.

H358 Marks, James R. and others. Handbook of educational supervision. 2d ed. Boston: Allyn & Bacon, 1978. 699p.

H359 Morphet, Edgar L., Roe L. Johns, and Theodore C. Reller. Educational organization and administration: concepts, practices, and issues. 4th ed. Englewood Cliffs, N.J.: Prentice-Hall, 1982. 422p.

H360 Neagley, Ross L. and N. Dean Evans. Handbook for effective supervision in instruction. 3d ed. Englewood Cliffs, N.J.: Prentice-Hall, 1980. 374p.

H361 Peterson, Le Roy J., Richard A. Rossmiller, and Martin M. Volk. The law and public school operation. New York: Harper, 1978. 528p.

H362 Robinson, E. A. G. and J. E. Vaizey, eds. The economics of education; proceedings of a conference held by the International Economic Association. London: Macmillan; New York: St. Martin's, 1966. 781p.

H363 Rosenthal, Alan, ed. Governing education. Garden City, N.Y.: Doubleday, 1969. 500p.

H364 Sears, Jesse B. Public school administration. New York: Ronald, 1947. 433p.

H365 Walton, John. Administration and policymaking in education. Rev. ed. Baltimore: Johns Hopkins Univ. Pr., 1969. 228p.

H366 Wynne, Edward A. Looking at schools; good, bad, and indifferent. Lexington, Mass.: Lexington Books, 1980. 235p.

H367 Yudof, Mark G. and others. Kirp and Yudof's educational policy and the law: cases and materials. 2d ed. Berkeley, Calif.: McCutchan, 1982. 863p.

EDUCATIONAL CRITICISM AND CONTROVERSY

Ever since the 1950s the tempo of dissatisfaction with education in the United States and other countries has accelerated greatly. Many books and other writings have appeared in response to the interest of the public and the profession. Some of this literature attacks educational abuses, and indeed the school itself, another segment defends and explains education in a better light, and some publications seek to steer a middle course.

Controversies in the United States have centered on such questions as progressive education, church-state-school relations, racial integration, academic freedom, athleticism, and ethnic-racial-religious-sex discrimination. (Some of these issues also are included in works cited in other categories in this chapter.) The critics of yesteryear have faded into the historical hinterland, but their places have been taken by neocritics. The cycle of criticism has turned from anti-progressive to anti-establishment.

Criticism of education has been flourishing on all continents and in the newer nations of Asia and Africa. In the USSR, where criticism may be rewarded with a rest period in a mental hospital, voices have been heard against the excessive homework assignments given pupils.

In various countries in Western Europe, criticism of secondary education has resulted in movements to transform the traditional secondary school into a comprehensive institution with enlarged opportunities for higher and professional education. A leader in the "comprehensivization" of secondary education has been Sweden, which passed a law to that effect early in the 1950s. A full account of the European reforms since World War II remains to be written.

The historical context of several educational controversies in the United States is furnished by Rudy. A critique of the American educational system as the perpetuator of a static school and a class-dominated social order is found in the papers by educational historians identified as radicals, under the editorship of Karier and others. The thesis of Bowles and Gintis is the bankruptcy of liberal educational reform. Their solution emphasizes "a socialist strategy" comprising "a system of participatory power" exercised by students, teachers, parents, and the public, and "a program of revolutionary reforms." Oliver's "radical critique" involves educational reform to improve the community and the quality of life.

An objective treatment of a broad range of issues is given in Ehlers, a standard work. Elam summarized public opinion on many aspects and problems of education. Among the recent controversies are the basic rights of parents in education, argued by Coons and Sugarman; the validity of the Intelligence Quotient in relation to society and education, presented by Block and Dworkin; the issue of creationism versus evolutionism in textbooks, analyzed by Nelkin; and

the impact of racial segregation and desegregation in schools on achievement, social contact, language development, and other outcomes, studied by Kluger and Gerard and Miller, and in the essays compiled by Rist.

Some newer criticism of American education is frequently reminiscent of the strictures raised in the 1920s and 1930s by the progressives, who championed the cause of the child against the traditional school curriculum and practices. The collection of essays by Gross and Gross features the leading radical, anti-establishment critics.

Silberman's elaborate work is a many-sided critique of schools in the United States, to a large extent because they are joyless and debilitating. The most radical critic is the cosmopolitan Illich, whose thesis is the withering away of the school as he says it is presently constituted in the United States and elsewhere.

American critics have been prone to point with approbation to the pedagogical system of another country in an effort to elevate our own educational establishment. First it was Germany, then the Soviet Union, in the early 1970s England, and in the early 1980s Japan. That all, however, is not serene across the Atlantic is clear from a reading of the book by Froome, a primary school headmaster who defends the traditional approach against the inroads of the "open classroom" and other innovations. Calò pointed up weaknesses in Italian education of the late 1950s, and recent and current events indicate that his critique is still pertinent. Picht's critical examination of West German education continues to arouse comment. The detailed, documented critique of West German education, compiled by Becker and others of the Deutsches Pädagogisches Zentralinstitut of East Berlin, is not comparable in objectivity to Picht's work.

A review of the literature is mercifully spared the responsibility of predicting the future. The Hegelian triad may bring to the fore, some time in the future, a wave of countercriticism of the current crop of critics, but no higher synthesis, however much desired, is yet discernible in the literature.

H368 Becker, Horst and others, comps. Die westdeutsche Bildungskrise. Berlin: Volk & Wissen, 1967. 255p.

H369 Block, N. J. and Gerald Dworkin, eds. The IQ controversy: critical readings. New York: Pantheon, 1976. 559p.

H370 Bowles, Samuel and Herbert Gintis. Schooling in capitalist America: educational reform and the contradictions of economic life. New York: Basic Books, 1976. 340p.

H371 Calò, Giovanni. Problemi attuali della pedagogia e della scuola. Bologna: Malipiero, 1958. 294p.

H372 Coons, John E. and Stephen E. Sugarman. Education by choice: the case for family control. Berkeley: Univ. of California Pr., 1978. 249p.

H373 Ehlers, Henry and others, eds. Crucial issues in education. 7th ed. New York: Holt, 1981. 306p.

H374 Elam, Stanley M., ed. A decade of Gallup polls of attitudes toward education, 1969–1978. Bloomington, Ind.: Phi Delta Kappa, 1978. 377p.

H375 Froome, Stuart. Why Tommy isn't learning. London: Stacey, 1970. 159p.

H376 Gerard, Harold B. and Norman Miller. School desegregation: a long-term study. New York: Plenum, 1975. 315p.

H377 Gross, Ronald, and Beatrice Gross, eds. Radical school reform. New York: Simon & Schuster, 1971. 350p.

H378 Illich, Ivan. Deschooling society. New York: Harper, 1971. 117p.

H379 Karier, Clarence, Paul C. Violas, and Joel Spring, eds. Roots of crisis: American education in the twentieth century. Chicago: Rand McNally, 1973. 243p.

H380 Kluger, Richard. Simple justice: a history of Brown v. Board of Education and black Americans' struggle for equality. New York: Knopf, 1976. 823p.

H381 Nelkin, Dorothy. Science textbook controversies and the politics of equal time. Cambridge, Mass.: MIT Pr., 1977. 174p.

H382 Oliver, Donald W. Education and community: a radical critique of innovative schooling. Berkeley, Calif.: McCutchan, 1976. 415p.

H383 Picht, Georg. Die deutsche Bildungskatastrophe. Olten, W. Germany: Walter-Verlag, 1964. 247p.

H384 Rist, Ray C., ed. Desegregated schools: appraisals of an American experiment. New York: Academic Pr., 1979. 242p.

H385 Rudy, [Solomon] Willis. Schools in an age of mass culture. Englewood Cliffs, N.J.: Prentice-Hall, 1965. 374p.

H386 Silberman, Charles E. Crises in the classroom. New York: Random, 1970. 552p.

H387 Weinberg, Meyer. Minority students: a research appraisal. Washington, D.C.: U.S. Govt. Print. Off., 1977. 398p.

William Brickman

Survey of the Reference Works

GUIDES TO THE LITERATURE

H388 Berry, Dorothea M. A bibliographic guide to educational research. 2d ed. Metuchen, N.J.: Scarecrow, 1980. 215p.

Designed to serve as a guide to the literature for students in education courses, this work also has many sections of particular value to the practicing classroom teacher. Substantially updated, this edition contains annotated references to over 750 sources, covering books, periodicals, research studies, government publications, children's literature, classroom textbooks, tests, audiovisual materials, programmed and computer-assisted instruction, reference works, methodology, and style manuals. Includes author, title, and subject indexes.

H389 Burke, Arvid J. and Mary A. Burke. Documentation in education. New York: Teachers College Pr., 1967. 413p.

A classic guide to the literature, this source is still valuable for its basic and comprehensive approach to the education literature. Pt. 1, on the storage and retrieval of information, is the most dated; the material in Pt. 2 (dealing with education reference works) and Pt. 3 (on the techniques of in-depth bibliographic research) holds up well, but needs to be supplemented with more recent sources.

H390 Humby, Michael. A guide to the literature of education. 3d ed. London: Univ. of London Institute of Education Library, 1975. 142p. (Education libraries bulletin. Supp. 1.)

A selected bibliography of over 500 sources, this

work is especially valuable for its European coverage. It covers the standard categories of education reference works, including classification schemes for education and libraries and information systems in the field. Very useful annotations and an author/title index.

H391 Willingham, Warren W. The source book for higher education: a critical guide to literature and information on access to higher education. New York: College Entrance Examination Board, 1973. 481p.

The final product of the College Board's Access Research Office, this guide covers all factors influencing access to higher education: aspirations, social and financial barriers, and determinants of the worth of a college education. It is divided into sections on access processes (such as decision, finance, admissions), the system, students, access agents, and sources of information. This work is characterized by really informative and evaluative annotations. Includes author and subject indexes.

H392 Woodbury, Marda. A guide to sources of educational information. 2d ed. Arlington, Va.: Information Resources Pr., 1982. 430p.

Coverage is almost entirely American and the most current available in a work of this kind. While most of the material involves printed sources or computer access, other types of information are surveyed: information centers and clearinghouses, organizations and government agencies, and special search or bibliographic services. Has sections dealing with effective research, printed research tools, and works on specialized subjects, such as funding, legislation, special education, guides to instructional materials, and tests and assessment instruments. The last section of the book deals with nonstandard and nonprint sources of information, including computerized retrieval systems, state library services, and institutional sources of information. Has a combined author, title, and subject index.

REVIEWS OF THE LITERATURE

General

H393 Review of educational research. v.1– , 1931– . Washington, D.C.: American Educational Research Assn. Quarterly.

Publishes critical and integrative reviews of the research literature of education, often drawing on the social and behavioral sciences. Since 1969, the *Review* has published unsolicited research reviews on topics of the contributors' choosing. Before that time, review articles were solicited with each of 15 general topics being covered every 3 years.

H394 Review of research in education. v.1– , 1973– . Washington, D.C.: American Educational Research Assn. Annual.

Intends to survey educational research through critical and synthesizing essays. While the topics in each volume vary over time, broad coverage is achieved in all areas relating to education. Articles are accompanied by substantive bibliographies and each volume includes a subject index.

Specialized

H395 Progress in learning disabilities. v.1– , 1968– . New York: Grune & Stratton.

Appearing at intervals of 3 to 4 years, these volumes are designed to present students of this field with a current review of research findings related to the psychoneurological study of childhood.

H396 Review of child development research. v.1–5, 1964–75. Chicago: Univ. of Chicago Pr.

Published under the auspices of the Society for Research in Child Development, the purpose of this series was to disseminate advances in child study to practitioners by selecting topics "ripe for review" and of general interest for which no other current review exists and for which a significant body of information exists. Many of the topics relate directly to education. Author and subject indexes.

H397 Review of special education. v.1–2, 1973–74. Philadelphia: JSE. v.3–4, 1976–80. New York: Grune & Stratton.

Reviews areas critical to the education of exceptional children. Includes an author/subject index.

Other sources which review the literature, but are listed elsewhere in this chapter, are the *Encyclopedia of educational research* (H575), the *Handbook of research on teaching* (H580), the *Second handbook of research on teaching*, (H579), and some of the works listed in the Yearbooks section (H584–602). Because of the interrelatedness of the social sciences, much material relevant to education can also be found in other review series in the behavioral sciences, such as *Advances in child development and behavior*, *Annual progress in child psychiatry and child development*, and the *Annual review of psychology* (G405).

Books

H398 Educational studies: a journal in the foundations of education. v.1– , 1970– . Gainesville, Fla.: Norman Hall, Univ. of Florida for the American Education Studies Assn. Quarterly.

Originally devoted entirely to book reviews, this journal has now widened its scope to include research and review articles; nonetheless, about half of each issue is still devoted to book reviews. The reviews are split into broad subject categories. "Books received" are also noted.

H399 Review of education. v.1– , 1975– . South Salem, N.Y.: Redgrave. Quarterly.

Entirely devoted to book reviews, this series provides readable and critical analyses of the current literature written by qualified experts. Most books appear to be reviewed within a year of publication.

Many educational journals publish reviews of books within their scope. Reviews of specific books may be located through *Education index* or standard book review sources.

Tests

H400 Mental measurements yearbook. Ed. by Oscar Buros. 1938–78. Highland Park, N.J.: Gryphon. Irregularly.

This series of yearbooks (and related works) forms the authoritative work in this field. Published on an irregular schedule (1938, 1940, 1949, 1953, 1959, 1965, 1972, and 1978), the series is designed to assist test users in education, industry, psychiatry, and psychology in locating, selecting, evaluating, and using standardized tests of all types. The *MMY*s were preceded by three substantial bibliographies of educational, psychological, and personality tests issued by Buros in 1933, 1935, and 1937. In their present format, the *MMY*s present bibliographies of standardized tests published in English-speaking countries, along with reviews both written for the yearbook and excerpted from reviews published elsewhere, and bibliographies of references to specific tests from the literature.

In general, the yearbooks are arranged with the tests in a broad subject sequence, followed by sections on books in the field of testing (and their reviews), a directory of test publishers, indexes by title and personal name, and a classified list of tests.

The eighth *MMY* (1978) carries coverage through 1977 for tests and through 1975 for references. The title index in the eighth *MMY* lists all the tests listed in that edition along with all the titles listed in *Tests in print II* (a companion volume listing all tests in print as of late 1974). The title index in *Tests in print II* is a master index to the previous *MMY*s and so guides one to information on tests out of print but listed in earlier *MMY*s. The index leads to the most recent entry in a *MMY* volume, but each entry, in turn, leads to entries in earlier volumes. It is therefore possible to trace a history of reviews and references for long-used tests and their various editions. The many editions of the yearbooks do not supersede each other but rather build on the information contained in the previous volumes.

Other related products have been published by Buros in specific subject areas, such as *Vocational tests and reviews, Personality tests and reviews, Intelligence tests and reviews*, and others. For the most part, these volumes are subsections of the full yearbooks.

CSE Test evaluation series:

H401 CSE Criterion-referenced test handbook. 1979.

H402 CSE elementary school test evaluations. 1976.

H403 CSE-ECRC preschool/kindergarten test evaluations. 1971.

H404 CSE-RBS test evaluations: tests of higher-order cognitive, affective, and interpersonal skills. 1972.

H405 CSE secondary school test evaluations. 1974.

Los Angeles: Center for the Study of Evaluation, Graduate School of Education, Univ. of California.

Aside from the *MMY*s, the only major evaluative listing of tests in this area. Ratings are made in the areas of measurement validity, examinee appropriateness, administrative usability, normed technical excellence, and overall worth.

ABSTRACTS AND SUMMARIES
General

H406 Education abstracts. v.1–16, 1949–64. Paris: UNESCO. Monthly.

Now primarily useful for historical bibliography, this series supplied descriptive bibliography of technical materials relevant to fundamental education throughout the world. Published under the title *Fundamental education abstracts and bibliography* from 1949 to 1951. Listings are by country and specialized topic and are in English, French, and Spanish. Annual index in the Dec. issue.

H407 Education digest. v.1– , 1935– . Ann Arbor, Mich.: Prakken. 9/yr.

Published monthly from Sept. to May, this series digests new books and articles in education selected from over 400 publications. News notes, book reviews and a classified list of additional educational materials are included at the end of each issue. Yearly author index.

H408 Resources in education (RIE). v.1– , 1966– . Washington, D.C.: Govt. Print. Off. Monthly.

Funded by the National Institute of Education and produced by ERIC (Educational Resources Information Center), a nationwide information network of 16 specialized clearinghouses for acquiring, abstracting, indexing, and disseminating education-related reports. Currently adding over 13,000 documents a year of many types: research reports, meeting papers, curriculum guides, dissertations, tests and questionnaires, numerical data, and others. Most documents cited are available from the ERIC Document Reproduction Service (EDRS), but even those not available from EDRS must list a source. The monthly issues include the abstracts (called resumes), and indexes by subject, personal author, institution, and publication type. Cumulated semiannual indexes; Oryx Press has published annual indexes to *RIE* since 1979. Access is by the subject descriptors listed in the *Thesaurus of ERIC descriptors*. Formerly called *Research in education*. The entire file may be accessed by means of computerized searching.

Specialized

H409 College student personnel abstracts. v.1– , 1965– . Claremont, Calif.: Claremont Institute for Administrative Studies. Quarterly.

Covers journal articles, conference proceedings, and research reports dealing with college student characteristics, attitudes, and behavior, with faculty, and with student services. Entries are arranged by broad topics, with author and subject indexes; the last issue of each volume contains the annual author/subject index. Entries are drawn from over 120 journals on a regular basis.

H410 Educational administration abstracts. v.1– , 1965– . Beverly Hills, Calif.: Sage in cooperation with the University Council for Educational Administration. Quarterly.

Lists approximately 250 abstracts an issue, drawn from about 140 journals in education and related areas including personnel management and public administration. Abstracts are listed in a broad topical arrangement, covering administrative tasks and processes, organizational variables, societal factors influencing education, educational administration programs, theory and research, and planning and futurology. There are ample cross-references and an author index. Includes a listing of dissertations in the area of educational administration from UCEA member schools.

H411 Exceptional child education resources. v.1– , 1969– . Reston, Va.: Council for Exceptional Children. Quarterly.

Designed as a resource for administrators, researchers, teachers, psychologists, and others concerned with the topic, this series gives comprehensive coverage of important publications in special education. More than 200 journals are regularly scanned for input, along with research reports, curriculum guides, and other educational documents. Many of the documents are input into the ERIC system and are available through the same channels as the documents listed in *RIE*. Each issue includes an author, title, and subject index, with a volume index in the winter issue. Indexing is by use of the *Thesaurus of ERIC descriptors*. Formerly called *Exceptional child education abstracts*. The entire file is available for computerized searching.

H412 Language teaching. v.1– , 1968– . Comp. by the English-Teaching Information Centre and the Centre for Information on Language Teaching and Research. London: Cambridge Univ. Pr. Quarterly.

Formerly called *Language teaching and linguis-*

tics abstracts and, before that, *Language teaching abstracts*. Covers articles in almost 400 journals dealing with the study and teaching of foreign languages, including English as a second language. Also lists research in progress in Europe. Entries are arranged in a broad classed arrangement, with author and subject indexes; a cumulated author and subject index appears in the last issue of the year. A survey article is sometimes included and books with brief reviews are listed in a separate section.

H413 Research into higher education abstracts. v.1– , 1967– . Abingdon, Eng.: Carfax for the Society for Research into Higher Education. 3/yr.

Aims to provide complete coverage of the United Kingdom and selected coverage overseas. Primarily concerned with research articles, but reference works, reviews, and some general interest articles are included. Entries are arranged in a general classed arrangement with an author index. Thesis and dissertation titles are also listed.

H414 Resources in vocational education. v.1– , 1967– . Columbus, Ohio: National Center for Research in Vocational Education, Ohio State Univ. Bimonthly.

Formerly called *Abstracts of research and instructional materials in vocational and technical education (AIM-ARM)*, from 1967–77. Abstracts of educational documents (which are also listed in *RIE* and available through EDRS), and projects in progress. Includes subject, author, and institutional indexes. Indexing is by the *Thesaurus of ERIC descriptors*. Starting with v.14 (1981–82), the publication has been reorganized so that each issue is devoted to a specific segment of the file: Selected abstracts from ERIC, Curriculum resources, Directory of vocational educational personnel, or State program improvement projects.

H415 Sociology of education abstracts. v.1– , 1965– . Abingdon, Eng.: Carfax. Quarterly.

A listing of some 600 books and journal articles each year covering the sociology of education. With v.19 has given up its faceted indexes (covering theory, method, empirical situations, and data); annual author and subject index appears in the final issue of each volume.

The interdisciplinary nature of the social sciences means that much material of significance to educational researchers can be found in other social science abstracting services: *Child development abstracts and bibliography* (G460), *Dissertations abstracts international* (A150), *Language and language behavior abstracts* (A163), *Human resources abstracts* (A161), *Psychological abstracts* (G458), *Sociological abstracts* (E200), *Sage family studies abstracts* (E219), *Women studies abstracts* (E228), *Re-*

search relating to children (G465). Many of these sources can be searched by computer.

Another important abstracting service is *Bulletin signaletique: Section 520: Sciences de l'education*, especially for its international scope. More information at A149.

BIBLIOGRAPHIES OF BIBLIOGRAPHIES

H416 Besterman, Theodore. Education: bibliography of bibliographies. Totowa, N.J.: Rowman & Littlefield, 1971. 306p.

A reprinting of the education section of his *World bibliography of bibliographies*. More information at A172.

H417 Monroe, Walter S. and Louis Shores. Bibliographies and summaries in education to July 1, 1935. New York: Wilson, 1936. 470p.

Important annotated catalog of more than 4,000 bibliographies published from 1910 to 1935. Annotations for each entry indicate the time period covered, the number of references in the bibliography, the degree of completeness, the types of materials, and the general character of the summaries.

H418 Reynolds, Michael M. A guide to theses and dissertations: an annotated international bibliography of bibliographies. Detroit: Gale, 1975. 599p.

A retrospective, international list of bibliographies of dissertations and theses completed through 1973, which includes a section on education. Includes series appearing in journals. Indexed by institution, name, title, and subject.

CURRENT BIBLIOGRAPHIES

H419 Australian education index. v.1– , 1957– Hawthorn, Australia: Australian Council for Educational Research. Quarterly (March, June, Sept., with a cumulated annual volume in Dec.).

Covers books, journal articles, research reports, conference papers, tests, legislation, and curriculum materials on education and educational psychology published in Australia. Includes works by Australian educators or about Australian education published elsewhere. Entries are arranged by broad subject grouping with an author/institution index. The subject index now uses a version of the *Thesaurus of ERIC descriptors*, modified to be consistent with Australian usage. Since 1979, the machine-readable records are available through AUSINET as the Australian education database.

H420 British education index. v.1– , 1954– . London: British Library, Bibliographic Services Div. 3/yr. and an annual cumulated volume.

Indexes over 300 English-language periodicals published or distributed in the British Isles. Originally compiled by librarians at several institutes of education and cumulated biennially, the production of the index was taken over by the British Library in 1970. Each issue consists of a subject list of articles and an author list.

H421 Business education index. v.1– , 1940– St. Paul, Minn.: Delta Pi Epsilon Graduate Business Education Society National Office, Gustavus Adolphus College. Annual.

Author-subject index of articles compiled from a selected list of periodicals and yearbooks. The comprehensive *Bibliography of research studies in business education, 1920–1940* preceded this series. Volume usually appears in the summer following the year covered.

H422 Canadian education index/Répertoire canadien sur l'education. Toronto: Canadian Education Assn. 3/yr. (3d issue is an annual cumulation)

An author/subject index to books, pamphlets, reports and a selected list of more than 200 Canadian education journals. Includes an author list of monographs and a list of French to English cross-references. Entries are indexed using the *Canadian education subject headings (CanESH)*, ed. by Deborah C. Sawyer (Toronto: Canadian Education Assn., 1979).

H423 Current index to journals in education (CIJE). v.1– , 1969– . Phoenix, Ariz.: Oryx. Monthly with semiannual cumulations.

Comprehensive index to the educational periodical literature, covering more than 17,000 articles a year from over 750 journals in education and education-related disciplines. Indexing is done by the 16 ERIC clearinghouses. Cited items are indexed to considerable depth using the *Thesaurus of ERIC descriptors*. Each issue consists of a main entry section (entries include short annotations), subject index, author index, and a journal contents index. *CIJE* is a companion work to *Resources in education (RIE)*, the ERIC index to the report literature. Part of the ERIC database.

H424 Education index. 1929– . New York: Wilson. Monthly (except July and Aug.) with annual cumulations.

An author-subject index to the professional literature. From 1929 to 1961, the *Index* covered nearly all current references from significant American sources and some British publications. Coverage included books, many education periodicals, association yearbooks, bulletins, reports, special publications, and most publications of the National Education Association and the U.S. Office of Education. Reviews were listed alphabetically by author under the heading "Book reviews." Three-year cumulations were issued from 1929 to 1953 and two-year cumulations from 1954 to 1963.

Coverage was curtailed in 1961, when many author entries were deleted and the *Index* discontinued indexing books, book reviews, many government documents, research reports, and other monographic publications. Book reviews were reinstated in 1970, author entries are once more included, and the *Index* now provides author-subject coverage of over 300 journals. While not as comprehensive in its coverage as *CIJE*, its advantages include a shorter time lag in indexing and coverage of book reviews. Author and subject entries are arranged in one alphabet, with most subject entries subdivided. A key to the abbreviations and a list of indexed periodicals are included.

H425 Educational documentation and information. v.1– , 1926– . Paris: UNESCO. Quarterly.

Formerly the *Bulletin of the International Bureau of Education*, this journal now has a theme approach. Each issue contains an article and a bibliography on the same subject. Before 1970, the *Bulletin* published the major accessions to the library of the International Bureau of Education in Geneva, which were then cumulated yearly into the *Annual educational bibliography of the International Bureau of Education* (Geneva: International Bureau of Education, 1955–69). This series ceased when the *Bulletin* changed to its present format.

H426 El-hi textbooks in print. 1927– . New York: Bowker. Annual.

This series has a varied history: first published as part of *Publishers weekly* and then as *American education catalog*, the title changed in 1956 to *Textbooks in print*, and in 1970 to its present name. The 1983 edition lists over 27,000 current items; while the emphasis is on class texts, also included are reference books for elementary and high schools, maps, tests, programmed learning materials, and teaching aids. Supplementary reading materials and audiovisual materials not connected with a text are excluded. There are 4 indexes: subject, author, title, and series. Includes a list of publishers and their addresses.

H427 Master's theses in education. 1951/52– . Cedar Falls, Ia.: Research Pubns. Annual.

Annual listing of master's theses in education written in the United States and Canada. Classified arrangement with an institutional index.

H428 Research studies in education: a subject and author index of doctoral dissertations, reports and field studies; and a research methods bibliography. Comp. by Mary Louise Lyda and others. 1953–70. Bloomington, Ind.: Phi Delta Kappa. Annual.

Listed dissertations complete and under way and a research methods bibliography, arranged alphabetically by topic. This index continued earlier compilations in the same vein: *Research studies in education, a subject index of doctoral dissertations, reports, and field studies, 1941–1951* (a subject list with looseleaf supplements), compiled by Mary Louise Lyda and Stanley B. Brown (Boulder, Colo.: Phi Delta Kappa, 1953 [121p.]); U.S. Office of Education, Library, *Bibliography of research studies in education, 1926/27–1940/41* (Washington, D.C.: Govt. Print. Off., 1929–42 [published in the U.S.O.E. Bulletin, 1928–41]); and Monroe's *Ten years of education research, 1918–1927* (Urbana, Ill.: Univ. of Illinois Pr., 1928 [377p.]).

H429 State education journal index. v.1– , 1964– . Westminster, Colo.: State Education Journal Index. Semiannual.

An annotated subject index to journals published by state education associations. Published in Feb. and July.

RETROSPECTIVE BIBLIOGRAPHIES

With the development of databases corresponding to most of the major indexing and abstracting sources and the advent of bibliographies tailored to individual interests produced from these computerized information sources, the need for the published retrospective bibliography is not as great. Increasingly, researchers will have computerized literature searches run to match their specific needs rather than refer to a published bibliography which does not correspond exactly to their interests (and which itself may have been produced by means of a computer search). However, bibliographies covering the period before the late 1960s and those covering the book literature, which is still not as comprehensively covered in these databases as the journal and report literature, will continue to be of great use to anyone using the education literature.

H430 Altbach, Philip G. Higher education in developing nations: a selected bibliography, 1969–1973. New York: Praeger, 1975. 229p.

Published in cooperation with the International Council for Educational Development, this source lists about 2,400 entries from 85 countries. While most of the entries are in English, Spanish, French and German also appear. Entries are arranged by continent, subarranged by country. This continues an earlier bibliography by Altbach, *Higher education in developing countries* (Cambridge, Mass.: Harvard Univ. Center for International Affairs, 1970) which covered the period before 1969.

H431 ———, Gail P. Kelly, and David H. Kelly. International bibliography of comparative education. New York: Praeger, 1981. 300p.

A bibliographic source for the discipline of comparative education, this work incudes an extensive essay on the field, a bibliography covering both the definition and development of the discipline as well as topics of major interest within comparative education, and ends with a bibliography of education in various countries and regions of the world (both developed and undeveloped areas, but excluding the United States). Most of the material listed is in English, but key works in French, German and Spanish are included. The regional and national bibliography is additionally indexed by the same subject categories used in the first section.

H432 Beach, Mark. A bibliographic guide to American colleges and universities: from colonial times to the present. Westport, Conn.: Greenwood, 1975. 314p.

Over 2,800 entries covering the history of individual universities and colleges. Arranged by state, and then alphabetically by institution. Name and subject index.

H433 Bibliography of publications of the United States Office of Education 1867–1959. With an introduction by Francesco Cordasco. Totowa: N.J.: Rowan & Littlefield, 1971. 3v. in 1.

A very handy reprint of the lists of U.S. Office of Education publications for this time period, which originally appeared in the Office's *Bulletin* in 1910, 1937, and 1960.

H434 Bibliography of research in instructional media. Comp. by Taher A. Razik and Delgea M. Ramroth. Englewood Cliffs, N.J.: Educational Technology Pubns., 1974. 441p.

Valuable because it gathers materials from the large number of fields and organizations working in this area. Covering the period from 1915 to 1973, this source lists almost 3,500 references in a subject arrangement. Related is *Media and adult learning, a bibliography with abstracts, annotations, and quotations*, by John Ohleger and David Gueulett (New York: Garland, 1975 [486p.]) (**H435**).

H436 Blaug, Mark. Economics of education: a selected annotated bibliography. 3d ed. Oxford, New York: Pergamon, 1978. 421p.

Covering the material to Sept. 1975, this is a large (over 1,900 items), annotated bibliography of English, French and German items, including material on both developed and undeveloped countries. Includes an author and country index.

H437 Boydston, Jo Ann and Kathleen Paulos. Checklist of writings about John Dewey. 2d ed. Carbondale, Ill.: Southern Illinois Univ. Pr., 1978. 476p.

Spanning the period from 1887 to 1977, this source lists over 2,500 items grouped into the following categories: published works about Dewey, unpublished works about Dewey, reviews of Dewey's work, and reviews of works about Dewey. Another useful compilation is M. H. Thomas' *John Dewey: a centennial bibliography* (Chicago: Univ. of Chicago Pr., 1962).

H438 Cordasco, Francesco. A bibliography of vocational education: an annotated guide. New York: AMS Pr., 1977. 245p.

A selective guide to the literature of vocational, industrial, manual, trade, and career education, covering material from the early 20th century to the end of 1975. Author and subject indexes.

H439 ——— and David N. Alloway. Sociology of education: a guide to information sources. Detroit: Gale, 1979. 266p.

A listing of over 1,500 sources on the sociology of education, this work aims to be a representative guide to the literature. Arranged by subject with author, title, and subject indexes. This volume is one of the *Education information guide series* published by Gale; others in the series include:

H440 The psychological foundations of education by Olga K. Baatz and Charles Albert Baatz. 1981.

H441 Women's education in the United States by Kay S. Wilkins. 1979.

H442 Bilingual education in American schools by Francesco Cordasco with George Bernstein. 1979.

H443 U.S. higher education by Franklin Parker and Betty June Parker. 1980.

H444 The history of American education by Francesco Cordasco, David N. Alloway, and Marjorie Seilken Friedman. 1979.

H445 The philosophy of education by Charles Albert Baatz. 1980.

H446 Durnin, Richard G. American education: a guide to information sources. Detroit: Gale, 1982. 247p.

This bibliography covers books on the history, philosophy, sociology and biography of American schooling on the elementary, secondary, and higher education levels. Listings, briefly annotated, are grouped by subject. Includes a name index. Similar volumes are: *American educational history: a guide to information sources*, by Michael W. Sedlak and Timothy Walch (Detroit: Gale, 1981) (**H447**), which is limited in scope to the historical background of American education, and *A bibliography of American educational history*, by Francesco Cordasco and William W. Brickman (New York: AMS Pr., 1975) (**H448**).

H449 Exceptional children research review. Ed. by G. Orville Johnson and Harriett D. Blank. Washington, D.C.: Council for Exceptional Children, 1968. 336p.

A follow-up to the original work by Samuel A. Kirk and B. S. Weiner, *Behavioral research on exceptional children* (Washington, D.C.: Council for Exceptional Children, 1963 [360p.]) (**H450**). This source lists studies on the gifted, mental retardation, visual and aural handicaps, cerebral dysfunction, orthopedic disabilities, speech, language, and communication disorders, and behavioral disorders. Topical arrangement with an author index. A related work is *The gifted student: an annotated bibliography*, compiled by Jean Laubenfels (Westport, Conn.: Greenwood, 1977) (**H451**).

H452 Hall, Granville Stanley. Hints toward a select and descriptive bibliography of education. Boston: Heath, 1886. Reprint, Detroit: Gale, 1973. 135p.

Basically a guide to Hall's pedagogical course at Johns Hopkins in 1880, this list is also a reflection of American education at the time. A classed list, with author index.

H453 Hamilton, Malcolm, ed. Education literature, 1907–1932. New York: Garland, 1979. 26v. in 12.

This extensive work is a reprint of the *Bibliography of education from 1907–1911/12* and *Record of current educational publications 1 January 1912–January/March 1932*, published by the U.S. Office of Education, primarily in its *Bulletin* and the only index coverage for materials on education during this time period. However, this work is more than a simple reprint since it includes cumulative name and subject indexes—including those years never indexed originally. Subject headings are those used at the time.

H454 Higher education: a bibliographic handbook. Ed. by D. Kent Halstead. Washington, D.C.: U.S. Dept. of Education, Office of Education Research and Improvement, National Institute of Education. v.2. 1981.

Planned to be 2 volumes and to cover 38 topics (including, among others, management, philosophy, economics, campus planning, faculty, curriculum), this work has extensive annotations for each entry. Individual chapters were compiled by specialists knowledgeable in the field and the emphasis is on current theory and practice. A preliminary version of this source was *Higher education planning: a bibliographic handbook*, ed. by D. Kent Halstead (Washington, D.C.: Govt. Print. Off., 1979).

H455 International education: the American experience, a bibliography. Compiled by Agnes N. Tysse. Metuchen, N.J.: Scarecrow, 1974. 2v. in 3.

Covers educational, cultural, scientific and technical exchange, focusing on foreign students in the United States, Americans overseas, and nonreturning students. V.1 covers dissertations and theses, arranged by author with a subject index. V.2 covers articles from some 700 periodicals, some dating as far back as the late 19th century. Arranged topically, with name and subject indexes.

H456 Jones, Leon. From Brown to Boston: desegregation in education, 1954–1974. Metuchen, N.J.: Scarecrow, 1979. 2v.

Spanning the period between two major legal decisions—*Brown* vs. *Board of Education* in 1954 to *Milliken* vs. *Bradley* in 1974, this bibliography lists over 5,000 references, all with substantial and informative annotations. The work is split into 3 sections by type of material: articles, books, and legal materials. Within each grouping, material is arranged by year. There are indexes by author-title, cases and legal issues, and subject.

H457 Lauerhass, Ludwig, Jr. and Vera Lucia Oliveira de Araujo Haugse. Education in Latin America: a bibliography. Los Angeles: UCLA Latin American Center; Boston: Hall, 1980. 431p.

Intended as a reference volume for research on education in all of Latin America, reaching from pre-Columbian times until the mid-1970s. Over 9,800 entries are listed, grouped by country and subdivided by topic. Covers Mexico, Central America, the Caribbean, Spanish South America and Brazil. Includes an index to corporate and proper names. Lists books, monographs, and pamphlets; serials exclusively dedicated to the subject are listed but individual journal articles are not.

H458 McCarthy, Joseph M. International list of articles on the history of education published in non-educational serials, 1965–1974. New York: Garland, 1977. 228p.

Designed to deal with the large number of articles on the history of education which appear in journals not covered by the usual educational abstracting and indexing sources. Entries are broken down by country, with an author index.

H459 Marks, Barbara S., comp. The New York University list of books in education. New York: Citation, 1968. 527p.

A comprehensive and well-annotated listing of works with which faculty at the NYU School of Education felt a graduate student should be familiar. Over 2,800 works are listed in a subject arrangement, with numerous cross-references.

H460 Monroe, Walter S. Bilbiography of education. New York: Appleton, 1897. Reprint, Detroit: Gale, 1968. 202p.

More than 3,000 books and pamphlets, mostly in English. Especially important for the national, state, and city reports listed.

H461 Parker, Franklin and Betty June Parker. Women's education, a world view. Westport, Conn.: Greenwood, 1979–81. 2v.

This work covers training and education for women. Peripheral areas such as feminism, the suffrage movement, and women's studies are included if the work treats women's education in a significant way. Likewise, biographies of women are included if they are of educators or treat the biographee's education. The first volume covers doctoral dissertations and the second books and reports. Coverage is limited to English-language materials. Entries are arranged alphabetically by author; both volumes have subject indexes.

H462 Quay, Richard H., comp. Index to anthologies on postsecondary education, 1960–1978. Westport, Conn.: Greenwood, 1980. 342p.

Over 220 anthologies are indexed in this work, giving access to a type of material (individually authored chapters) not often covered in standard secondary sources. Most of the material here was originally published in these anthologies and not indexed elsewhere; for works originally published elsewhere, the primary source is listed. Entries are arranged by broad topic, with added name and subject indexes.

H463 Rosenstiel, Annette. Education and anthropology: an annotated bibliography. New York: Garland, 1977. 646p.

Designed to reflect the historical influences, current trends, theory and practical methodology at the juncture of these two disciplines. Over 3,400 references are drawn from the social sciences from 1689 to 1976. Arranged in author order with a subject index and a people and place index.

H464 Sources for the history of education. Ed. by C. W. J. Higson. London: Library Assn., 1967. 196p.

A listing of books on education, school textbooks, children's books from the 15th century to 1870, and government publications relating to education until 1918 which are owned by 17 British libraries (mostly of Institutes of Education) as of 1964. Continued by the *Supplement to sources for the history of education*, ed. by C.W.J. Higson (London: Library Assn., 1976 [221p.]) **(H465)**, which covers materials added to these same and a few additional libraries in the period from 1965 to 1974.

H466 Tests: a comprehensive reference for assessments in psychology, education and business. Ed. by Richard C. Sweetland and Daniel J. Keyser. Kansas City: Test Corp. of America, 1983.

Over half of this book is devoted to educational tests. A listing of over 3,000 tests arranged by 3 broad groups and subdivided by topic. In the education section, these topics range over academic subject, achievement and aptitude tests, intelligence tests, special education, reading, sensory-motor skills, speech, hearing and vision, and student and teacher evaluations. Entries list level, purpose, description, timing, range, scoring, cost and publisher of the test; no validity and reliability data is supplied. Includes a publisher index, title index, author index, scoring service index, and an index of tests for the visually impaired.

H467 United States. Office of Education. Educational Resources Information Center. Office of Education research reports: resumes and indexes, 1956–1965. Washington, D.C.: Govt. Print. Off., 1967. 2v.

This reference work provides access to a variety of research projects sponsored by the U.S. Office of Education for the period before the publication of *Research in education* and, later, *Resources in education* (H408), where this kind of report is now covered. The first volume contains the abstracts describing the projects and the second volume offers access by author, institution, subject, and report number indexes.

H468 Weinberg, Meyer. The education of poor and minority children: a world bibliography. Westport, Conn.: Greenwood, 1981. 2v.

A large (over 40,000 entries) and wide-ranging bibliography, this work draws from education, law, history, and other social sciences. Almost a quarter of the material relates to non–United States areas. Arrangement is by broad subject categories, with an author index.

Library Catalogs

H469 Columbia University. Teachers College Library. Dictionary catalog of the Teachers College Library. Boston: Hall, 1970. 36v.
———. 1st supp. 1971. 5v.
———. 2nd supp. 1973. 2v.
———. 3rd supp. 1977. 10v.

Provides bibliographical information by author, title, and subject on the holdings of the ranking separate collection of educational literature in the United States. Supplemented since 1978 by the *Bibliographic guide to education* (Boston: Hall, annual), which lists nonserial publications cataloged by the Teachers College Library and selected works in education cataloged by the Research Libraries of the New York Public Library.

H470 Harvard University Library. Education and education periodicals. Cambridge, Mass.: The Library, 1968; dist. by Harvard Univ. Pr. 2v. (Widener shelflist, v.16–17)

Lists more than 30,000 works held by Harvard. More information at A257.

H471 United States. Department of Health, Education, and Welfare Library. Author/title catalog of the department library. Boston: Hall, 1965. 29v.
———. First supp., 1974. 7v.
———. Subject catalog of the department catalog. 1965. 20v.

This library is rich in education-related materials. More information at A281.

H472 University of London. Institute of Education. Library. Catalogue of the Comparative Education Library. Boston: Hall, 1971. 6v.
———. First supp. 1975. 3v.

One of the preeminent collections in this area. Includes the holdings listed in the Institute Library's *Catalogue of the collection of education in tropical areas*, published by Hall in 1964.

Dissertations

H473 American dissertations on foreign education: a bibliography with abstracts. Ed. by Franklin Parker and Betty June Parker. Troy, N.Y.: Whitson, 1971– .

Heavily annotated, volumes so far in the series have covered Canada, India, Japan, Africa, Scandinavia, China, Korea, Mexico, South America, Central America, Pakistan and Bangladesh, Iran and Iraq, Israel, and the Middle East. Author and subject indexes.

An older, valuable bibliography in this field is Walter C. Eells' *American dissertations on foreign education, 1884–1958* (Washington, D.C.: National Education Assn., Committee on International Relations, 1959 [300p.]) **(H474)**. This work lists some 1,600 doctoral dissertations and 4,000 master's theses completed at American universities and colleges. Studies are arranged by continent and country. Author and subject indexes.

H475 Blackwell, Annie M., ed. A list of researches in education and educational psychology, presented for higher degrees in the universities of the United Kingdom, Northern Ireland, and the Irish Republic. London: Newnes, 1950. 2v.

First published covering the period 1918 to 1948 and then updated by a second list and 3 supplements, extending coverage to 1957. Continued by *Current researches in education and educational psychology* (1959/60–1968/69) (London: National Foundation for Educational Research in England and Wales) (**H476**).

H477 Cordasco, Francesco and Leonard Covello, comps. Educational sociology: a subject index of doctoral dissertations completed at American universities, 1941–1963. New York: Scarecrow, 1965. 226p.

More than 2,000 entries in a classed arrangement, with an author index.

DIRECTORIES AND BIOGRAPHICAL INFORMATION

A primary source of information on educational directories is:

H478 Guide to American educational directories. Ed. by Barry T. Klein. 5th ed. Rye, N.Y.: Todd, 1980. 202p.

Extensive list of several thousand educational directories. Entries are arranged in a broad subject arrangement; each entry includes title, publisher, price, revision, and a resume. Covers association, government and research agencies, foundations, educational and research personnel, colleges and universities, publishers, exchange students, financial aid, and libraries, among other categories. Title index.

Educators

H479 Biographical dictionary of American educators. Ed. by John F. Ohles. Westport, Conn.: Greenwood, 1978. 3v.

Listing of 1,655 eminent American educators, who had reached the age of 60, retired, or died by January 1, 1975. Included are state and national leaders, as well as subject matter specialists, over the last 200 years. Each entry includes the vital statistics, education, employment, contribution to education and participation in professional activities, as well as further sources of information. Each sketch attempts to give some indication of the significance of the person. Appendixes list entries by state of birth, state of major service, field of work, a chronology of birth years, and important dates in American education.

H480 College and university administrators directory: a guide to officers, deans, managers, and other administrative personnel in American colleges and universities. Detroit: Gale, 1980. 937p.

A directory to more than 355,000 administrative personnel included in the HEGIS XIII institution profile computer tapes of the National Center for Education Statistics. Three parts include: an alphabetical name and address listing, administrators classed by function as defined by DHEW manpower codes, and a state-by-state guide to the over 3,000 institutions covered and their administrative personnel.

H481 Graduate programs and faculty in reading. Ed. by Paula Blomenberg. 4th ed. Newark, Del.: International Reading Assn., 1981. 375p.

Includes information on over 300 graduate programs in reading in the United States and Canada. For each entry, lists the director, overview of the program, degrees offered and number awarded, application procedures, tuition, financial aid, and names of faculty.

H482 International who's who in education. Ernest Kay, ed. director. 2d ed. Cambridge: International Who's Who in Education, 1981. 490p.

Successor to *Who's who in education* (1974), this edition has been expanded to include leading eminent teachers, academics, and administrators on an international scale, especially to include the United States and Canada. Includes the usual biographical and professional information.

H483 Leaders in education. Ed. by Jacques Cattell Pr. 5th ed. New York: Bowker, 1974. 1,309p.

Nearly 17,000 biographical sketches are included in this latest edition of the directory, which was first published in 1932. Criteria for inclusion are achievement in education, research activity of a high level, or a position of substantial responsibility. A diverse group is covered, including officers and deans in higher education, professors of education, directors and staff of education research institutions, state and provincial commissioners of education, leading figures in public education, staff of the Office of Education, and educational authors. Geographic and specialty indexes are included.

H484 National Center for Education Statistics. Education directory: state education agency officials. 1969/70–1971/73, 1976– . Comp. by Joanell Porter. Washington, D.C.: Govt. Print. Off. Annual.

A listing of administrative personnel in state education agencies responsible for elementary, secondary, and vocational education. Information includes the 50 states, the District of Columbia, and outlying areas. Entries are arranged by state and a name index is included. Formerly titled *Education directory: state governments*.

H485 National education directory. Ed. by John T. Grupenhoff. Rockville, Md.: Aspen Systems, 1982. 483p.

Designed to enable individuals to locate personnel in Congress, federal agencies, state departments of education, or state, national, or regional education associations. Lists key congressional education subcommittees, federal agencies, and education association personnel; gives information on congressional delegations, including location of local offices. Indexed by name.

H486 National faculty directory. 14th ed. Detroit: Gale, 1983. 3v.

Over 597,000 entries, listing name, departmental affiliation, and institutional address, from over 3,400 American colleges and universities and 145 Canadian institutions. Revised annually using questionnaires and course catalogs.

H487 Who's who biographical record: child development professionals. Chicago: Marquis Who's Who, 1976. 515p.

Using the same format as *Who's Who in America*, this directory lists over 9,000 persons in the United States in the area of child guidance and child development, including child psychologists and guidance counselors, special education teachers, day care and preschool professionals, and professors of education and educational psychology. A similar directory of elementary and secondary school administrators is *Who's who biographical record: school district officials* (Chicago: Marquis Who's Who, 1976 [666p.] (**H487A**).

H488 Who's who in American education: a biographical directory of eminent living university and college professors, superintendents and principals of schools, state and national school officials, librarians and miscellaneous educators. 1928–1968. Hattiesburg, Miss.: Who's Who in American Education. Biennial.

Now mainly of historical value, a good source of biographical information about educators, many not covered by other sources, during the mid-20th century. Many portraits were included in the earlier volumes.

H489 World who's who of women in education. Ernest Kay, ed. director. Cambridge; New York: International Biographical Centre, 1978. 559p.

An international women's faculty directory, this is a listing of standard directory information on women teaching in all disciplines.

In addition to these directories, more general sources are valuable for information about educators. Another type of source is the membership directory as, for example, those issued by educational associations, such as the American Educational Research Association, Teachers of English to Speakers of Other Languages, and the National Association of Elementary School Principals.

Organizations

H490 Encyclopedia of associations. 18th ed. Detroit: Gale, 1983. 5v.

Valuable general source of identification of nonprofit organizations. Sizable section on educational and education-related associations. Description at A348.

H491 Directory of educational research institutions. Prepared by the International Bureau of Education and the Division of Structures, Content, Methods and Techniques of Education, UNESCO. Paris: UNESCO, 1980. 208p.

Put together by questionnaire response, this directory lists over 550 institutions covering 117 countries. For each organization is listed: official name, director, staff size, type of research and objectives, publications, and work in progress. Keyword index in English, French and Spanish.

H492 Directory of research organizations in education: research, development, dissemination, evaluation and policy studies. Ed. by Rolf Leming. San Francisco: Far West Laboratory for Educational Research and Development, 1982. 411p.

Lists over 2,400 organizations in the United States that perform research activities in education. Includes school districts, state education agencies, postsecondary education units, and private organizations; excludes federal agencies. Arrangement is state by state, subdivided by zip code. Two indexes are provided: by broad subject and by educational level.

H493 National Education Association of the United States. NEA Handbook. v.1– , 1945/46– . Washington, D.C.: The Association. Annual.

The principal source of information on the objectives, structure and activities of the NEA and its affiliated organizations. Provides information on all divisions, departments, commissions, and committees, including historical background, current officers, summaries of activities, and publications. State and local affiliates are arranged geographically by state. Includes name and subject indexes.

H494 UNESCO. International Bureau of Education. Directory: documentation and information services. Paris: UNESCO, 1977. 70p.

This lists international, national, and regional services. Entries appear in either French or English and include name, address, year of creation, parent body, staff, services, user group, collection, publications, and scheme used. Other useful directories of education information centers include the *Subject directory of special libraries and information centers— Volume 2: Education and information science libraries*, ed. by Brigitte T. Darnay, 8th ed. (Detroit: Gale, 1983) (**H495**) and the *Encyclopedia of information systems and services* ed. by John Schmittroth, 5th ed. Detroit: Gale, 1982) (**H496**).

H497 U.S. Office of Education. Directory of education associations. 1912– . Washington, D.C.: Govt. Print. Off. Annual.

Formerly one part of the U.S.O.E. *Education directory*, this is a comprehensive listing of all types of educational associations: national, regional, international, state, foundations, religious associations, professional, honor societies, and national recognition societies. Entries include address, phone, and key officers. Indexed by name and by keyword.

H498 World Confederation of Organizations of the Teaching Profession. Directory of member organizations. 2d ed. Morges, Switzerland: The Confederation, 1976. 225p.

First published in 1967, this directory provides the address, history, purpose, membership, governance, international relations, officers, activities, and publications. Most entries are in English, with some in Spanish, French or Portuguese. Arrangement is alphabetical by country.

Higher Education and Research Institutes

H499 Accredited institutions of postsecondary education: programs, candidates. 1964– . Washington, D.C.: American Council on Education. Annual.

Published for the Council on Postsecondary Accreditation by the American Council on Education, this is a directory of accredited institutions, professionally accredited programs, and candidates for accreditation. Listings are arranged alphabetically by state, with information including date of first accreditation, calendar, specialized accreditations, and chief officers. Candidates for accreditation are listed in a separate section. Valuable for its appendix on the accrediting process and listing of accrediting agencies.

H500 American universities and colleges. Comp. and ed. by the American Council on Education. 12th ed. New York; Berlin: de Gruyter, 1983. 2,156p.

More than 1,700 institutions are listed in this detailed directory of American higher education. Sizable profiles are arranged by state and include information on programs offered, history, characteristics of freshmen, admission requirements, specialized programs, degrees conferred, enrollment, faculty size, fees and financial aid, buildings and grounds, and administration. Also valuable for its supplementary information: essays on higher education in the United States, a section on professional education, academic costume and ceremony, and summary data on institutions listed. Includes both institution and general indexes.

H501 An assessment of research-doctorate programs in the United States/Committee on an Assessment of Quality-Related Characteristics of Research-Doctorate Programs in the United States. Ed. by Lyle V. Jones, Gardner Lindzey, and Porter E. Coggeshall. Washington, D.C., National Academy Pr., 1982. 5v.

The 5 volumes cover the social and behavioral sciences, the biological sciences, engineering, the humanities, and the mathematical and physical sciences. This study was done under the aegis of the Conference Board of Associated Research Councils; 228 universities participated and almost 5,000 faculty responded to the reputational survey, covering 32 disciplines in all. Measures used in assessment covered factors related to program size, characteristics of graduates, reputational survey results, university library size, research support, and publication records. Earlier, reputable works in the same vein include *A rating of graduate programs*, by Kenneth D. Roose and Charles J. Andersen (Washington, D.C.: American Council on Education, 1970) (**H502**) and *An assessment of quality in graduate education*, by A.M. Cartter (Washington, D.C.: American Council of Education, 1966) (**H503**).

H504 Cass, James and Max Birnbaum. Comparative guide to American colleges for students, parents, and counselors. 10th ed. New York: Harper, 1981. 778p.

Geared toward those making a choice of college, this source sees itself as a consumer's guide to higher education. In addition to the usual directory information, includes graduate career data, giving the actual career paths of graduates of each school. Usefulness is enhanced by indexes listing schools by state, by selectivity in their admissions, by religious affiliation, and by selected fields of study. Descriptions vary in length, depending on the reputation of the school, its desire to seek a national student body, willingness to reveal information, and applicability to this book. Other sources which share this slant toward college choice include *Barron's profiles of American colleges*, 14th ed. (Woodbury, N.Y.: Barron, 1984) (**H505**), whose 2 volumes cover descriptions of the colleges and an index to major areas of study, respectively; *Peterson's annual guide to undergraduate study*, 17th ed. (Princeton, N.J.: Peterson's Guides, 1983) (**H506**), which covers admissions test scores, majors offered and descriptions of the institutions; and *Lovejoy's college guide*, 1953/54– (New York: Simon & Schuster, biennial) (**H507**), which includes, in addition to the descriptions, listing of career curricula and special programs such as cooperative, correspondence, and external curricula, special calendars, and programs for the handicapped. New in the 16th edition is a sports index.

H508 The college blue book. 1923– . New York: Macmillan. Irregular.

Now in its 19th edition, this source has a 3-volume format, covering over 3,200 institutions of higher education in the United States and Canada. *Volume 1: Narrative descriptions* offers a concise profile of each school, including facts about the campus, community, entrance requirements, costs, collegiate and community environment, and acceptance rate. *Volume 2: Tabular data* lists each institution with very abbreviated information about costs, accreditation, enrollment, faculty, chief administrators, admission plans and policy, library holdings, and so on. *Volume 3: Degrees offered by college and subject* is in 2 parts: one lists colleges by state and the degrees they offer and the other lists subjects and the schools which offer degrees in those fields. Includes an index of institutions with cross-references for mergers, name changes, and closures.

H509 The college handbook. 1941– . New York: College Entrance Examination Board. Biennial.

The 1982–83 edition lists over 3,000 institutions of higher education, including community and junior colleges, with full descriptions for 2,545. Designed for the students choosing a college, entries include enrollment, calendar, location, curriculum, admissions, expenses, and financial aid. Index by institutions is included.

H510 Commonwealth universities yearbook. 1914– . London: Assn. of Commonwealth Universities. Publication suspended 1941–46; annual since 1947.

The primary publication of the Association, this source lists factual information about Commonwealth universities in good standing. Serves as both a directory to the universities and as the handbook of the Association. Information is arranged by country, with the entries for the larger countries preceded by an article on the university systems. Information is provided by the registrar or secretary of each university, including history, activities, course and entry requirements, statistics, teaching staff, computers, labs, and publications. Appendixes cover special topics, such as university admissions requirements, students from abroad, the Commonwealth Scholar and Fellowship plan, the Association, and a select bibliography. Indexes are included for abbreviations, institutions and subjects of study, and names.

H511 Education directory: colleges and universities. Washington, D.C.: National Center for Education Statistics. Annual.

Successor to one part of the *Education directory*, which has been published in one form or another by the U.S. Office of Education since 1895 (first as one chapter in the annual report of the U.S. Commissioner of Education 1895–1911, then as part of the bulletin series from 1912 to 1941, and then separately as the *Education directory*). This source lists institutions in the United States and outlying areas which are legally authorized to offer and do offer at least a one-year program of college-level studies leading to a degree. Appendixes list changes, statewide agencies of higher education, higher education associations, consortia, and abbreviations.

H512 Community, junior, and technical college directory. 1927– . Washington, D.C.: American Assn. of Community and Junior Colleges. Annual.

Formerly called the *Junior college directory,* this lists more than 1,200 institutions, excluding proprietary schools. Includes brief information in tabular form, such as location, chief executive officer, control, accreditation, calendar, enrollment, faculty size, administration size, tuition and fees. Lists community and junior college organizations and state administrators. Another good source of information on community and junior colleges is *Barron's guide to the two-year colleges*, 7th ed. (Woodbury, N.Y.: Barron's, 1981 [2v.]) (**H513**). This 2-volume work gives descrip-

tions of over 1,100 2-year colleges and 390 2-year programs at 4-year colleges; the first volume lists the descriptions and the second lists schools by occupational program.

H514 International handbook of universities and other institutions of higher education. 8th ed. New York; Berlin: de Gruyter for the International Assn. of Universities, 1981. 1,205p.

First published in 1959, this is a companion volume to the *Commonwealth universities yearbook* (H510) and *American universities and colleges* (H500). Covers 112 countries and territories outside the United States and the Commonwealth. Arranged in national chapters, entries include listings of colleges and their deans, brief history, language of instruction, and the usual directory information. Appendix includes information on the International Association of Universities, its officers, and member institutions. Institutional index with names listed in the language of the country and in English translation.

H515 Doughty, Harold R. and Herbert B. Livesey. Guide to American graduate schools. 4th ed. New York: Penguin, 1982. 559p.

Basic information for prospective graduate students. Describes over 600 American institutions offering graduate or professional study. Indexed by state and field of study. Another major source of graduate school information is *Peterson's annual guides to graduate study*, 1966– . (Princeton, N.J.: Peterson's Guides) (**H516**). Split into 5 volumes: (1) graduate institutions: an overview, (2) humanities and social sciences, (3) biological, agricultural, and health sciences, (4) physical sciences, and (5) engineering and applied sciences. The set covers over 200 selected degree fields in 1,100 graduate institutions in the United States and Canada.

H517 Occupational education. New York: Macmillan, 1983. 1,006p.

First published in 1972, this work is now one segment of the *College blue book* (H508). This reference work lists just over 9,000 schools offering occupational programs. Entries are arranged by state, with an index by curricula and programs of instruction. Another valuable source of this type of information is the *Directory of postsecondary schools with occupational programs, 1978*, compiled by Evelyn R. Kay (Washington, D.C.: National Center for Education Statistics, 1978 [376p.]) (**H518**), which lists public and private non-collegiate schools which offer one or more occupational programs in preparation for a specific career in addition to 2- and 4-year colleges which offer occupational programs leading to a certificate or degree at less than the baccalaureate level. It is supplemented by *Programs and schools* (Washington, D.C.: National Center for Education Statistics, 1978 [330p.]) (**H519**), which supplied names and addresses of noncollegiate postsecondary schools, by program.

H520 Ohles, John F. and Shirley M. Ohles. Private colleges and universities. Westport, Conn.: Greenwood, 1982. 2v.

Consists of institutional sketches of 1,291 American private colleges and universities. Compiled from college catalogs, published histories, descriptions written specifically for the project, and material such as alumni magazines and standard reference works. References are given for most profiles; material is current up to 1980.

H521 Research centers directory. 9th ed. Detroit: Gale, 1984. 1,100p.

Extensive directory of research centers, foundations, laboratories, and similar nonprofit institutions and programs, which is heavily used in educational research and information work. More information at A353.

H522 Songe, Alice H. American universities and colleges: a dictionary of name changes. Metuchen, N.J.: Scarecrow, 1978. 264p.

Includes entries for the new names, the old names, and for closures from 1964 to 1977. Full information is listed under the new name, including location, type, present administration, original name, founding name and date, history of changes and mergers, and changes in location or administrative control.

H523 World guide to universities/Internationales Universitats Handbuch. 2d ed. New York: Bowker; Munich: Verlag Dokumentation, 1976. 4v.

Pt. 1 covers Europe in 2 volumes, and Pt. 2 covers Africa, Asia, Oceania, and the Americas in another 2 volumes. Arranged by country, each entry includes name, address, founding, enrollment, administration, library, faculties, affiliated schools or institutes, and academic staff. There is a keyword index to subject and a name index listing over 95,000 names.

H524 World list of universities/Liste mondiale des universites. Paris: International Assn. of Universities. Triennial.

Directory of more than 6,000 institutions of higher education in 151 countries and a guide to the principal national and international organizations concerned with higher education. Each national chapter has a list of the higher education institutions followed by information about national academic, governmental, administrative, and student organizations. Learned societies are not listed. Entries are in alphabetical order by English titles, with indexes to both English and French titles.

H525 Who offers part-time degree programs? Patricia Consolloy, ed. coordinator. Princeton, N.J.: Peterson's Guides, 1981. 349p.

Over 2,000 schools are listed alphabetically, by state; usual directory information is given. There are specialized listings of programs by type: part-time evening, part-time weekend, part-time summer, and external degree.

H526 World of learning. 1947– . London: Europa. Annual.

Most comprehensive listing of universities, colleges, libraries, museums and archives, art galleries, learned societies, and research institutes throughout the world. Provides basic information about institutions, arranged by country. Has an institutional index.

Scholarships, Fellowships, and Grants

H527 The complete grants sourcebook for higher education. Prepared by the Public Management Institute. Washington, D.C.: American Council on Education, 1980. 605p.

Pt. 1 outlines a systematic approach to grant-seeking, from original preparation through the follow-up period. Pt. 2 is a listing of over 500 funding sources, with information on areas of interest, financial data, eligibility applications and policy. Funding sources are indexed by type, areas of interest, and by state or region.

H528 The grants register. Ed. by Craig Alan Lerner and Roland Turner. 1969/70– . London: Macmillan. Biennial.

Now in its 8th edition, this source lists over 2,000 scholarships, fellowships, research grants, exchange opportunites, travel grants, grants-in-aid, competitions, and professional and vocational awards intended for nationals of the United States, Canada, United Kingdom, Ireland, Australia, New Zealand, South Africa, and developing countries. Intended for students at or above the graduate level and for further professional or advanced vocational training. Indexed by awards and awarding bodies, and by subject.

H529 Feingold, S. Norman and Marie Feingold. Scholarships, fellowships and loans. v.7. Arlington, Mass.: Bellman, 1982. 796p.

Descriptions of over 1,350 funds, covering 262 different vocational areas. A special section, "Vocational goals index," is a tabular listing by fields and fund, displaying required level of study, sex, type of award, legal requirements, affiliation (ethnic, religious, veteran, etc.), citizenship, and number of awards available.

H530 Financial aids for higher education catalog. 10th ed. Comp. by Oreon Keeslar. Dubuque, Iowa: W. C. Brown, 1982. 1,016p.

Designed for high school seniors, this source describes programs of aid and how to qualify for them.

H531 Scholarships, fellowships, grants, and loans. New York: Macmillan, 1983. 763p.

The 1,849 entries in this source are divided into 10 broad subject categories, each broken down into finer subdivisions. Each entry lists title, field, level, amount of award, eligibility, deadlines, and application information. Indexes cover titles, sponsoring agencies, level of awards, and subjects. Part of the *College blue book* series.

H532 Study abroad: international scholarships, international courses. v.1– , 1948– . Paris: UNESCO. Biennial.

Over 100 countries contributed information to the latest edition of *Study abroad*, which calls attention to those offers of financial aid and programs which are open to a wide range of international applicants. There are 2 sections: scholarships and courses. Entries can be in English, French, or Spanish and list name and duration of programs, fields of study, description of assistance, and application instructions. Organization, national institution, and subject indexes.

Study and Employment Abroad

H533 Institute of International Education. Handbook on international study for U.S. nationals. 6th ed. New York: The Institute, 1976. 2v.

Arranged by country, these guides provide information on awards, study and exchange programs, volunteer and trainee opportunities, organizations and agencies providing services, government regulations, and fields of study. Material is indexed by institution, fields of study, and organization. Two volumes are available: v.1—*Study in Europe*, and v.2—*Study in the American Republics*.

The Institute of International Education publishes other guides of interest in this area. *The learning traveler. Volume 2: Vacation study abroad* (**H534**) (formerly *Summer study abroad*) covers programs sponsored by U.S. and foreign institutions, with information on courses, costs, scholarships, and accommodations. *Teaching abroad* lists over 150 sponsors and organizations conducting teaching programs abroad for U.S. teachers. *The learning traveler. Volume 1: U.S. College-sponsored programs abroad: academic year* (**H535**) is an annual guide to graduate and undergraduate programs. Related is their *Handbook on U.S. study for foreign nationals* (**H536**).

Other useful, but more specialized, volumes in this vein are *Higher education in the United Kingdom, 1982–84: a handbook for students and their advisors* (New York: Longman, 1982) (**H537**), which is geared towards students coming to the U.K. for study, and *Higher education in the European Community; a handbook for students*, ed. by Manfred Stassen, 2d ed. (Brussels: Commission for the European Communities, 1979) (**H538**).

H539 Mathies, Lorraine and William G. Thomas. Overseas opportunities for American educators: perspectives and possibilities. New York: Macmillan, 1973. 369p.

Has sections dealing with the variety of overseas possibilities, elementary and secondary schools designed for American youth, schools and organizations which sponsor overseas educational programs and provide employment opportunities, and considerations in obtaining an overseas position. A more recent directory, which lists only addresses, of English-language oriented schools and colleges in over 160 countries is the *Teachers' guide to overseas teaching*, compiled by Louis A. Bajkai (La Jolla, Calif.: Teach Overseas, 1977 [140p.]) (**H540**).

H541 Garraty, John A. and others. The new guide to study abroad. 1981–82 ed. New York: Harper, 1981. 464p.

Geared toward the student or scholar planning to go abroad, this guide is full of practical information. Includes a list of programs sponsored by both American and foreign colleges, universities, and organizations. Also has information on programs for high school students and on teaching abroad.

Secondary, Elementary, and Preschool Education

H542 CIC's school directory, 1978/79. Denver: Curriculum Information Center, 1978.

Formerly called the *School Universe Data Book*, this source is available in 2 formats: the State Edition in 51 individual softcover volumes and the Regional Edition in 7 volumes. Produced from CIC's databank, this is a comprehensive directory of public schools, Catholic schools, and other independent schools in the 50 states and the District of Columbia. Lists names of state and diocesan level administrators and principals, addresses and phone numbers of districts, enrollment, grade spans and types of district and schools, and an indication of special programs. Gives statistical summaries by county and district.

H543 Directory for exceptional children: a listing of educational and training facilities. 9th ed. Boston: Sargent, 1981. 1,384p.

First published in 1954, this reference work lists more than 3,000 public and private facilities. Intended to be used by both parent and professional, the directory is arranged by type of special need: learning disabled, emotionally disturbed, autistic children, psychiatric and guidance clinics, residential and day facilities for orthopedic and neurologic handicaps, facilities for the mentally retarded, visual handicaps, aural handicaps, and speech handicaps. In addition to standard information, entries include the therapy in use, rates, structure, and type of handicaps accepted. Also includes a listing of national organizations, societies, foundations, and federal and state agencies concerned with exceptional children.

H544 National Center for Education Statistics. Education directory: local education agencies. 1968/69– . Washington, D.C.: Govt. Print. Off. Annual.

Within state groupings, entries are arranged alphabetically by the name of the district. Each entry lists location, county, grade spans, enrollment, and number of schools. Formerly called *Education directory: public school systems*.

H545 Patterson's American education. v.1– , 1904– . Mount Prospect, Ill.: Educational Directories. Annual.

A comprehensive directory, first published as *Patterson's American educational directory*. Pt.1 is a state-by-state listing of schools. Each state section begins with a listing of state officials, followed by a city-by-city listing of public school districts, secondary schools, private or parochial high schools, colleges, universities, and community colleges. After the state sections is a listing of Roman Catholic, Seventh Day

Adventist, and Lutheran school superintendents. Pt.1 concludes with a directory of educational associations. Pt.2 is a classified directory of 7,000 schools by type of program: business schools, home study schools, junior colleges, and universities and colleges listed by programs of study. The volume ends with an index to the classified directory.

H546 Private independent schools. 35th ed. Wallingford, Conn.: Bunting & Lyon, 1982.

First published in 1943 and considered the "blue book" of private schools. Contains full-length descriptive articles and brief listings of approximately 1,300 schools in the United States, Canada, and 52 other countries. Arranged by state, entries include the history, philosophy, campus facilities, student body, academic program, student activities, admission, and costs. There is an institutional index and a geographic and classified index.

Another standard reference for private schools, the annual *Handbook of private schools*, v.1– , 1915– (Boston: Sargent) **(H547)** includes a listing of the "Leading private schools" with descriptions, a section called "Private schools illustrated" with paid announcements, a listing of summer academic programs and camps, and listing of other schools not included in the first section due to insufficient information or since they have local enrollments or special programs.

DICTIONARIES

H548 Good, Carter V. and Winifred R. Merkel, eds. Dictionary of education. 3d ed. New York: McGraw-Hill, 1973. 681p.

A scholarly and comprehensive dictionary whose first edition appeared in 1945, this work now has more than 33,000 entries. Due to the growth of the terminology, this edition is limited to English language terms, primarily from the United States. Prepared under the auspices of Phi Delta Kappa, this dictionary is still one of the best in the field. Includes many cross-references and has a special section for Canada, England, and Wales.

H549 Hills, P. J., ed. A dictionary of education. London; Boston: Routledge & Paul, 1982. 284p.

This dictionary is in 2 parts: the initial section contains very brief essays on the 15 basic subdivisions covered (such as administration, curriculum development, comparative education, economics, psychology and sociology of education, and other topics) and the second part lists the terms and definitions. Largely restricted to British usage.

H550 Page, G. Terry and J. B. Thomas, eds. International dictionary of education. Cambridge, Mass.: MIT Pr., 1980. 384p.

A practical guide to the international language of education from preschool to postdoctoral levels, with over 10,000 entries. Includes wide coverage of international and major national institutions and asso-

ciations. Has extensive cross-references and some biographical entries. Usually gives the country of origin for terms peculiar to one country. Appendixes list abbreviations for associations and U.S. honor societies, fraternities, and sororities along with their addresses.

H551 National Center for Education Statistics. Combined glossary: terms and definitions from the handbooks of the state educational records and report series. Washington, D.C.: National Center for Education Statistics, 1974. 293p.

The terms listed here are taken from the 11 handbooks of the *State Educational records and reports series* and, in a sense, this serves as an index to these handbooks by indicating the source of each term. An extremely useful tool for educational administrators. The appendix lists Chapter 6 of Handbook 6: "Standard terminology for curriculum and instruction in local and state school systems," which contains definitions of terms about subject matter areas and cocurricular activities.

H552 Palmer, James C. and Anita Y. Colby, comps. Dictionary of educational acronyms, abbreviations, and initialisms. Phoenix, Ariz.: Oryx, 1982. 88p.

In the continually growing and changing acronymic maze, this source is a valuable listing in the area of education. A good general source is *Acronyms, initialisms, and abbreviations dictionary*, 9th ed. (ed. by Ellen T. Crowley, Detroit: Gale, 1984) **(H552A)**.

H553 Rowntree, Derek. A dictionary of education. Totowa, N.J.: Barnes & Noble, 1982. 354p.

This dictionary lists both United Kingdom and U.S. terms, including those likely to puzzle the reader from the other country as well as those which have different meanings in the two countries. Some proper names are included, primarily those which are often cited without explanation.

Specialized

H554 Davis, William E. Educator's resource guide to special education: terms–laws–tests–organizations. Boston: Allyn & Bacon, 1980. 259p.

The bulk of this work is the dictionary of terms used in special education. Examples are often given within the definition, as well as considerable cross-references. Other sections include acronyms and abbreviations, a listing of tests used in the field, key legislation, and a listing of associations and organizations in special education. A related work is *A dictionary of special education terms*, by Byron C. Moore, Willard Abraham, and Clarence R. Laing (Springfield, Ill.: Thomas, 1980 [117p.]) **(H555)**.

H556 Educational technology: a glossary of terms. Washington, D.C.: Assn. for Educational Communications and Technology, 1979. 371p.

Produced by the AECT Task Force on Definition and Terminology, the glossary is split into sections dealing with theory, research, design, materials, production, evaluation, selection, devices, techniques, logistics, utilization, organization management, personnel mangement, people and settings. This sectional division is made easy to use by a combined index. This source is good for very technical terminology, which is not dealt with in such depth in the standard dictionaries.

H557 Gatti, Richard and David J. Gatti. Encyclopedic dictionary of school law. West Nyack, N.Y.: Parker, 1975. 316p.

Covers areas such as constitutional rights of teachers, administrators, and students, liability of teachers, contract rights and responsibilities, collective bargaining, parochial school aid, tenure laws, discrimination, and school board powers and duties. Tries not only to explain the law but to give guidelines for action. Cites statutes, education codes, and cases. There are extensive cross-references and a classified index.

H558 Harris, Theodore L. and Richard E. Hodges, coeditors. A dictionary of reading and related terms. Newark, Del.: International Reading Assn., 1981. 382p.

Designed to meet the needs of a wide range of users, this volume lists over 5,000 terms. Terms are drawn primarily from the field of reading, but many other disciplines contributed terms: language, physiology, psychology, and pedagogy among others.

H559 National Center for Higher Education Management Systems. Glossary of standard terminology for postsecondary education. Comp. by Sherrill Cloud. Boulder, Colo.: The Center, 1979.

Intended to promote standardization in terminology used in postsecondary education at the institutional, state, and national levels, this source lists definitions for the most common terms and categories used in reporting information. Reflecting standards set by national groups such as the National Association of College and University Business Officers and the American Association of Collegiate Registrars and Admissions Officers, the glossary lists over 350 entries, with an appendix listing the terms grouped into reporting categories.

Thesauri

H560 International standard classification of education (ISCED). Paris: UNESCO, 1976.

Presents codes and definitions for 518 programs of education, 21 fields of study, and 8 levels of education for use in classifying statistics on regular, special, and adult education. This volume is designed as an instrument for assembling, compiling, and presenting statistics in a uniform manner both within individual countries and internationally.

H561 Educational Resources Information Center. Thesaurus of ERIC descriptors. 10th ed. Phoenix, Ariz.: Oryx, 1984. 640p.

The starting point for any search of the educational literature through *Resources in education* (H408) or *Current index to journals in education* (H423), in either printed or computerized form. Also used in many smaller, more specialized bibliographies. The main part of the thesaurus consists of the alphabetic list of descriptors, each of which is listed with broader, narrower, and related terms. Synonymous forms are controlled by "use" and "used for" references. Scope notes and parenthetic qualifiers are used to clarify usage when necessary. Other parts of the thesaurus include a rotated descriptor display, showing each element of the descriptor in alphabetical order, and a two-way hierarchical display. Also included is the list of broad groups of descriptors, along with the terms in each group. A particularly useful feature is the addition of the number of postings for each term in *RIE* or *CIJE*, as of October 1981, and the date of entry of the term into the system. A cumulated list of descriptors added since the publication of this edition appears in current issues of *RIE* and *CIJE*. This edition includes an introductory essay on indexing guidelines for the ERIC system, which will be useful to searchers.

H562 Terminology: UNESCO: IBE education thesaurus. Paris: UNESCO, 1978. 348p.

This thesaurus was first constructed by the International Bureau of Education in 1973 for the international indexing and retrieval of documents and data in the field of education. Used by those working in UNESCO programs and in the development of databases by IBE, a decentralized system utilizing a number of centers and institutions. Terms appear in English, French and Spanish (this ed. is the printed English version); it is intended to be published in 3-year cycles with one language published each year. The thesaurus consists of a list of general headings, an alphabetic array of descriptors and identifiers (including scope notes, cross-references, and broader, narrower, and related terms), a faceted arrangement of descriptors by broad subject, and a rotated list of descriptors. Specialized glossaries published by UNESCO include: *Terminology of adult education* (Paris: UNESCO, 1980) (**H563**), *Terminology of special education* (Paris: UNESCO, 1978) (**H564**), and *Terminology of technical and vocational education* (Paris: UNESCO, 1979) (**H565**).

ENCYCLOPEDIAS AND ENCYCLOPEDIC SETS

H566 Dejnozka, Edward L. and David E. Kapel. American educators' encyclopedia. Westport, Conn.: Greenwood, 1982. 634p.

A one-volume ready reference with almost 2,000 short articles covering the terminology and names frequently encountered in the professional literature. Entries include a short list of references. A useful selection of appendixes include such items as the Code of Ethics for the education profession, past presidents of various educational associations, past U.S. Commissioners of Education, and a chronology of important legislation affecting education.

H567 Encyclopedia of education. Ed. by Lee C. Deighton. New York: Macmillan, 1971. 10v.

The first comprehensive encyclopedia of education since Monroe's *Cyclopedia of education*, published in 1911 (H569). Has more than 1,000 signed articles, most with short bibliographies. Arranged alphabetically by topic, the articles cover all aspects and levels of education, including academic programs, learning and instruction, educational and vocational guidance, and social issues. While primarily geared to American education, it also describes the educational systems of some 100 countries in detail. Intended for educational practitioners and decision makers (principals, school board members, and legislators). Index volume includes a guide to articles by title and author's name, with extensive cross-references from subject headings to article titles and vice versa.

H568 International encyclopedia of higher education. Ed. by Asa S. Knowles. San Francisco: Jossey-Bass, 1977. 10v.

A comprehensive work on all aspects of higher education throughout the world. Has articles which deal with the higher education systems in 198 countries and territories, topical essays discussing the political, economic, social, historical, scientific, and contemporary issues in the field, articles on fields of study intending to provide information both on the nature of the field and on programs of study, articles on 14 educational associations, a listing of 91 centers and institutes of higher education research, reports on the future of postsecondary education, a directory of documentation and information centers throughout the world, and a glossary of terms in use throughout the world. The *Encyclopedia* covers studies of national, international, and comparative scope. Has approximately 1,300 entries in 10 volumes. Most articles include bibliographies.

H569 Monroe, Paul, ed. Cyclopedia of education. New York: Macmillan, 1911–13. 5v.

A classic view of education in America at the beginning of this century. Articles were written by more than 1,000 specialists, many of great eminence. For example, there are entries on anthropology by Franz Boaz, on philosophy of education by John Dewey, on education of the blind by Helen Keller, and on psychology by Robert M. Yerkes. Education throughout the world and throughout history is presented in over 7,000 entries. Much biographical material and bibliographies are included with the more substantial entries.

H570 World survey of education. Paris: UNESCO, 1955–71. 5v.

While not a general education encyclopedia, attempted to provide comparable data on over 200 countries and territories. Each volume covers a different aspect of education: v.1: *Handbook of education organizations and statistics* (1955) includes reports from 194 national and official agencies dealing with all aspects of education from kindergarten to university. V.2: *Primary education* (1958) provides a detailed picture of primary schooling in 100 countries and territor-

ies. V.3: *Secondary education* (1961) includes 200 national studies and deals with world trends. V.4: *Higher education* (1966) contains reports and plans in 200 countries. V.5: *Educational policy, legislation, and administration* (1971) considers the aims, administration, policy, and legal basis of the educational system in each of the countries. Until 1969, this set was updated by the *International yearbook of education* (H588) and more recently by the *International guide to educational systems* (H589). Much comparative statistical data can be found in the current UNESCO *Statistical yearbook* (A497).

A more recent source containing comparative data on higher education systems throughout the world is the *World guide to higher education: a comparative survey of systems, degrees, and qualifications*, 2d ed. (Paris: UNESCO, 1982 [369p.]) (**H571**), which describes the state of postsecondary education in over 150 countries.

HANDBOOKS, MANUALS, AND COMPENDIA

H572 Council of Chief State School Officers. Education in the states. Washington, D.C.: National Education Assn., 1969. 2v.

V.1: *Historical development and outlook* reports a nationwide study of state departments of education and traces the historical development, since 1900, of each state and U.S. territory department of education. V.2: *Nationwide development since 1900* contains in-depth reviews of major concerns at this level, including topics such as state financing of elementary and secondary education, curriculum, adult education, pupil personnel services, and public relations. Intended for school board members, legislators, educational administrators, teachers, and citizens.

H573 Encyclopedia of education. Ed. by Edward Blishen. New York: Philosophical Library, 1970. 882p.

Compact handbook of useful information on the British educational system and its history. Includes some biographical entries and short reading lists after many entries. Appendix lists universities, colleges of education, examining bodies, and educational journals.

H574 Encyclopedia of education evaluation: concepts and techniques for evaluating education and training programs. Ed. by Scarvia B. Anderson and others. San Francisco: Jossey-Bass, 1975. 515p.

Extremely readable and understandable definitions for this field; short bibliographies accompany most terms. Includes a name index, a subject index, and an extensive bibliography.

H575 Encyclopedia of educational research. Ed. by Harold E. Mitzel. 5th ed. Sponsored by the

American Educational Research Assn. New York: Free Pr., 1982. 4v.

First published in 1941, and at approximately 10-year intervals since, the *Encyclopedia* is a reference work of central, continuing importance. Considerably expanded since the last edition, it authoritatively covers various areas of specialization at all levels of education, making it a convenient source of information about major developments in the field. Not limited to the time period since the last edition, its articles deal with persistent educational problems and continuing education concerns. Contributors are recognized authorities who present concise summaries in their specialties, along with well-selected bibliographies. Arranged alphabetically by broad topic, with a substantial subject index.

H576 Handbook of college and university administration. Ed. by Asa S. Knowles. New York: McGraw-Hill, 1970. 2v.

More than 200 chapters covering administration in American higher education. V.1: *General* covers general administrative areas. V.2: *Academic* covers academic programs, standards, policies, academic personnel, and student personnel administration. Contributors include over 160 authors selected for their expertise. Arranged by broad topic, with a substantial index.

H577 Handbook of contemporary education. Comp. and ed. by Steven E. Goodman. New York: Bowker, 1976. 622p.

This compilation of essays includes information on specific programs so researchers can locate human resources in addition to the literature. Over 100 articles are grouped into 8 areas: educational changes and planning, administration, teacher/faculty issues, education and training of teachers and administrators, students and parents, special interest groups, teaching and learning strategies, and alternatives and options in education. Includes bibliographies, author index, and a broad term subject index which uses ERIC descriptors.

H578 Handbook of special education. Ed. by James M. Kauffman and Daniel P. Hallahan. Englewood Cliffs, N.J.: Prentice-Hall, 1981. 807p.

Aimed at students, professionals and practitioners involved in the education of exceptional chidren. A compendium of articles ranging from the theoretical to the practical, the manual is divided into 5 sections: the introduction (covering history, trends and European practice), conceptual foundations (dealing with the various types of disabilities and special characteristics), delivery systems, curriculum and methods, and environmental management.

H579 Second handbook of research on teaching. Ed. by Robert M. W. Travers. Chicago: Rand McNally, 1973. 1,400p.

A worthy successor to the earlier *Handbook of research on teaching,* ed. by Nathaniel L. Gage (see H206), and sponsored by the American Educational Research Association, this scholarly work summarizes and analyzes research in the field. Chapters are grouped under 4 main headings: an introductory section on research and teaching, methods and techniques of teaching, research on special problems of teaching, and research on the teaching of school subjects. Arranged in 42 chapters, with extensive bibliographies and a name and subject index.

H581 Woellner, Elizabeth H. Requirements for certification. Ed.1– , 1935– . Chicago: Univ. of Chicago Pr. Annual.

Standard reference work on certification requirements for teachers, administrators, counselors, and librarians as established by the states. In addition to the state-by-state listing of requirements, includes the recommendations of regional and national accrediting associations, and sources of information regarding teacher applications in U.S. positions and territories. Other sources for related information include: *A manual on standards affecting school personnel in the United States,* ed. by T. M. Stinnett, (Washington, D.C.: National Educational Assn., 1974 [184p.]) **(H582)** and *Handbook of certification/licensure requirements for school psychologists,* rev. ed., compiled by Douglas T. Brown, Timothy J. Sewall, and John P. Lindstrom (Washington, D.C.: National Assn. of School Psychologists, 1977) **(H583)**.

YEARBOOKS

H584 Association for Supervision and Curriculum Development. Yearbook. 1944– . Alexandria, Va.: The Association.

Formerly published as the *Yearbook of the National Education Association Department of Supervision and Curriculum Development.* The series is a basic work in curriculum studies. Each volume has a distinct title.

H585 Claremont College Reading Conference. Yearbook. 1936– . Claremont, Calif.: The Conference.

Each volume in this series has a distinct theme. Another yearly series devoted to reading is the *National Reading Conference Yearbook,* 1952– (Clemson, S.C.: National Reading Conference) **(H586)**.

H587 Educational media yearbook. 1973– . Littleton, Colo.: Libraries Unlimited.

Meant as a ready reference for media specialists in schools at all levels, media designers, producers, and publishers, and for students and teachers of educational technology. The latest edition is in 6 parts: educational technology abroad, review of the past year, a guide to media-related organizations, data on graduate programs, sources of funding, and a mediagraphy. Includes a directory of producers, publishers, and distributors, and a substantial index.

H588 International yearbook of education. v.1– , 1933– . (Publication suspended 1940–45, 1970–79) Paris: UNESCO.

In the new series (1980–), this work provides different information in alternate years: profiles of national education systems alternating with a comparative study of educational trends. The most recent volumes give profiles for 91 countries and the study of trends is based on material provided by governments when surveyed by the International Bureau of Education in Geneva for the period 1974–78. Before resumption of publication in 1980, an interim volume detailing education systems throughout the world was published by IBE: *International guide to education systems*, prepared by Brian Holmes (Paris: UNESCO, 1979) **(H589)**.

H590 International yearbook of educational and instructional technology, 1982/83. London: Kogan Page, 1982. 537p.

Produced under the auspices of the Association of Educational and Training Technology (formerly APLET) to provide a survey of the field for both practitioners and newcomers. Covers trends and developments in the field, resources in educational technology, a directory of centers and organizations concerned with educational technology, a list of producers and distributors of programs and software, and a guide to AV hardware.

H591 Journal of Negro education. Yearbook issue. v.1– , 1932– . Washington, D.C.: Howard Univ. Bureau of Educational Research.

The summer issue each year is devoted to a state-of-the-art review of a major aspect of black education. Articles in this issue are by invitation only.

H592 National Business Education Association. Yearbook. 1963– . Reston, Va.: The Association.

Each volume has a separate theme.

H593 National Council for the Social Studies. Yearbook. v.1–47, 1931–77. Arlington, Va.: The Council.

Each of the 47 volumes in this series addressed a different theme, usually the same as the national conference for that year.

H594 National Council of Teachers of Mathematics. Yearbook. 1926– . Washington, D.C.: The Council.

Each year the yearbook is developed around a topic of current interest.

H595 National Society for the Study of Education. Yearbook. v.1– , 1902– . Chicago: Univ. of Chicago Pr.

Issued in 2 volumes each year, each devoted to different topics, this series remains one of the most scholarly and readable collections of material in educational thought and practice. Each volume is compiled under the direction of an editor selected by the society's board of directors. The papers in each volume are indexed in the *Education index*.

H596 Sourcebook of equal educational opportunity. 3d ed. Chicago: Marquis Academic Media, 1979. 601p.

Originally called the *Yearbook of equal educational opportunity*, this series uses statistical, narrative, and resource data to trace the struggles of minorities for equal access and quality in education. After a general introduction, the books deal with various aspects of the access problem for blacks, native Americans, Asian-Americans, disadvantaged/white ethnic groups, Hispanics, and women. Includes subject and geographic indexes.

H597 Standard education almanac. 1968– . Chicago: Marquis. Annual.

Designed to give a comprehensive current overview of educational enterprise in the United States and Canada. A combination of statistical, narrative, and directory information, the latest edition covers the areas of education in general, elementary and secondary education, higher education, vocational and continuing issues, research and policy. There is also a directory listing of information sources.

H598 World yearbook of education. 1932–40, 1948–74. London: Evans; New York: Harcourt. 1979– . New York: Nichols.

Early volumes in this series were called the *Yearbook of education* and were produced by the University of London Institute of Education; these covered statistical information from many countries and covered general themes. After this, the series began to devote each edition to a major theme of international interest. Since 1953, it was sponsored by the University of London Institute of Education and Teachers College, Columbia University. Title changed to *World yearbook of education* in 1965. These yearbooks are valuable as a source of comparative studies.

H599 Yearbook of adult and continuing education, 1980–81. 6th ed. Chicago: Marquis, 1980.

While format has changed over the years, the current edition features a collection of articles reflecting the field of continuing education ranging over adult education, international aspects, basic education, continuing professional education, career education, community education, and a section on current issues and non-traditional approaches. Earlier editions have contained statistical summaries.

H600 Yearbook of higher education. 1969– . Chicago: Marquis.

Now in its 16th edition, this series attempts a statistical and narrative description of higher education in the United States and Canada. Pt.1 is a directory of the institutions of higher education with information such as the type of control, calendar, enrollment, and administrative personnel. Pt.2 lists resources in higher education, including associations, consortia, and ERIC clearinghouses. Pt.3 includes standard statistical summaries of higher education, with sources of data cited.

H601 Yearbook of school law. 1933– . Ed. by Philip K. Piele. Topeka, Kan.: National Organization on Legal Problems of Education.

Begun by M. M. Chambers in 1933 and designed for those interested in the application of law to educational problems. Published by NOLPE since 1972, the series gives concise reference to the latest court decisions affecting education. Covers all of the previous year's state appellate court and federal court decisions that affect schools, as well as any other significant school law decisions. All education-related cases reported in *West's regional, federal, and Supreme Court reports* are included. For a time, the *Yearbook of higher education law*, ed. by D. Parker Young (Topeka, Kan.: NOLPE, 1977–81) provided similar information for court cases involving higher education. Beginning in 1982, the *Yearbook of school law* once again includes material on higher education.

H602 Yearbook of special education, 1980–81. 6th ed. Chicago: Marquis.

Aimed at both professional personnel and the handicapped and their families, this yearbook contains current information on the education of those with special needs. Includes descriptions of research, activities, statistics, legislation—mostly reprinted from other sources. The 6th edition reflects current issues in the field with separate chapters addressing minimum competency testing, PL 94–142, cultural diversity, sensory handicaps, learning and behavior handicaps, the gifted, and professionals in the field.

SOURCEBOOKS

H603 Bremner, Robert H., ed. Children and youth in America; a documentary history. Cambridge, Mass.: Harvard Univ. Pr., 1970–74. 3v. in 5.

A sourcebook of documents relating to American children. The 3 volumes cover the periods 1600 to 1865, 1866 to 1932, and 1933 to 1973, with an index in the last volume.

H604 Cohen, Sol. Education in the United States: a documentary history. New York: Random, 1974. 5v.

Brings together and places in context the most significant documents on American education from the 16th and 17th century English and European background through colonial beginnings to the present time.

H605 Kersey, Shirley Nelson, comp. Classics in the education of girls and women. Metuchen, N.J.: Scarecrow, 1981. 323p.

Originally compiled to compensate for the lack of an available text for a course on the "History of the education of girls and women in the Western world," this is a compilation of original works ranging from ancient Greece through early Christian times, the Renaissance, Reformation and the Enlightenment to the 19th century.

See also J. Maclure, *Educational documents: England and Wales, 1816 to the present day* (H67) for a sourcebook of official documents tracing the development of the public system of education in England and Wales.

STATISTICAL SOURCES

H607 Educational statistics of OECD member countries. Paris: Organisation for Economic Co-operation and Development 1981. 231p.

Compiled by the OECD Secretariat under the guidance of the Education Committee on Educational Statistics and Indicators, this sourcebook is valuable for data on OECD members. Its purpose is to provide a data set tracing the development of educational systems in OECD member countries. New to this edition is material on public expenditures on education and new entrants to higher education. The work lists its sources of data by country. The older edition, *Education statistics yearbook* (Paris: OECD, 1974–75 [2v.]) (**H608**), covered some different areas of data and is still valuable for that reason.

H609 1981–82 Fact book for academic administrators. Comp. by Charles J. Andersen. Washington, D.C., American Council on Education, 1981.

The purpose of this annual series is to condense data from documented governmental and private sources into graphs and tables which emphasize trends and relationships in higher education. Covers demographics and economics, enrollment, institutions, faculty and staff, students, and earned degrees. It is a successor to the Council's *Fact book on higher education.*

H610 Hamilton, Malcolm. Directory of educational statistics: a guide to sources. Ann Arbor, Mich.: Pierian, 1974. 71p.

Lists sources of educational statistics, both current and historical (some data go as far back as 1870). While the majority of sources listed are from the United States, there are some British and international sources. Especially valuable for its listing of sources outside the standard U.S.O.E. and NEA sources and for its year-by-year listing of information about the publication history of many of the series cited. Contains a subject and title index.

H611 Higher education: international trends, 1960–1970. Paris: UNESCO, 1975.

A quantitative analysis of major international trends in the development of higher education during the previous decade. A statistical analysis is presented for each continent or world region, using a common format. Includes an informative chapter on general trends in higher education.

H612 National Center for Education Statistics. Digest of education statistics. 1962– . Washington, D.C.: Govt. Print. Off. Annual.

Originally published by the U.S. Office of Education, this series continues the *Biennial survey of education*, and is an abstract of statistical information on American education from kindergarten through graduate school. Information is gathered from statistical surveys and estimates made by various governmental and nongovernmental agencies. Data on a wide range of topics are included: enrollment, numbers of schools and colleges, teachers, finances, educational attainment, graduates, libraries, federal funds, research and development activities; to be included, data must be nationwide in scope and of current interest and value. Therefore, the material covered changes over the years as more and different data are collected. Many series of data, some dating as far back as 1870, are shown to provide historical perspective. A substantial subject index is included and all sources of data are listed.

This volume is especially useful as a starting place in a search for data; it leads into many other valuable series produced by NCES: *Earned degrees conferred* (**H613**), *Financial statistics of institutions of higher education* (**H614**), *Statistics of public elementary and secondary school systems* (**H615**), and others. Two companion volumes of special note are the Center's *Condition of education* (**H616**) and *Projections of educational statistics* (**H617**). The *Condition of education* is an annual report describing conditions in education as well as those in society at large which affect education within a social indicators framework. It is especially good at the social context of education (education and work, education and community, school environment, educational outcomes, as examples). *Projections of education statistics* presents trends for approximately 9 years ahead on enrollments, instructional staff, graduates and finances in elementary, secondary, and postsecondary education in the United States.

H618   National Center for Higher Education Management Systems. A reference guide to postsecondary education data sources. Boulder, Colo.: The Center, 1975.

Intended for institutional, local, and national planners, decision makers and researchers, this is a directory to data sources which correspond to items in the Center's *Statewide measure inventory* (**H619**). Includes a very detailed annotated bibliography of data sources that are national in scope and related to at least one measure in the *Statewide measure inventory*. While linked to the *Inventory*, this directory is useful in its own right, as an index to over 200 sources of statistical data.

H620   National Education Association. Rankings of the states. 1948–   . Washington, D.C.: The Association. Annual.

States are ranked in educational categories such as enrollment, attendance, teachers, educational attainment, general financial resources, school revenues, and expenditures. Another useful series of reports, published from 1958 to 1973, is the Association's Research Division's *Research reports* (**H621**) providing surveys and interpreting studies on educational problems such as salaries, tenure conditions, economic status of teachers, and school size.

H622   Sessions, Vivian T., ed. Directory of data bases in the social and behavioral sciences. New York: Science Associates, 1974. 300p.

This listing of almost 700 data banks and archives provides, for each entry, the name of the organization, address, subject fields, file title, chronological and geographical scope of the file, data sources and collection, storage media, hardware/software, output

media, data products, documentation, publications, and access. Includes subject, institutional, personnel, and geographic indexes.

A similar source is the National Center for Education Statistics' *Directory of federal agency education data tapes*, 2d ed. (Washington, D.C.: NCES, 1979 [229p.]) (**H623**), with descriptions of databases covering areas such as elementary and secondary education, postsecondary education, demographics, manpower supply and demand, libraries, and federal outlays for education.

H624   Statistics of students abroad, 1969–73. Paris: UNESCO, 1976. 345p.

This volume is an updating of the first in the series on student exchanges, covering 1962–68. Information on foreign students in institutions of higher education has been utilized to provide profiles of nationals by their country of origin. Pt.1 includes the methodology of the study and an analysis of world trends. Pt.2 contains the country tables, in which students abroad are presented by host country and field of study.

H625   UNESCO statistical yearbook. 1963–   . Paris: UNESCO. Annual.

Data presented here cover education, science and technology, libraries, museums, theatre, book production, newspapers and other periodicals, cultural expenditure, film and cinema, radio, and television. Data are drawn from UNESCO questionnaires and official publications for over 200 countries and territories. Presents data for the last year available and in a comparative format. Introductory material to chapters is given in English, French, and Spanish. Supersedes UNESCO's *Basic facts and figures*.

H626   U. S. Department of Education. Office for Civil Rights. Directory of public elementary and secondary schools, and schools in selected school districts: school year 1978–1979. Washington, D.C.: U.S. Dept. of Education. Office for Civil Rights, 1981. 2v.

Best source for enrollment figures broken down by race/ethnicity and sex. Categories used are American Indian or Alaskan native, Asian or Pacific Islander, Black, White, or Hispanic. The survey has been expanded to collect data related to special education and Title IX-related matters. Data was drawn from a sample of over 6,000 school districts and over 54,000 individual schools. Enrollment figures are subdivided by race/ethnicity and sex for categories such as various disabilities, courses of study (such as science, business, industrial arts) and disciplinary actions. Also given are data by sex for interscholastic athletic teams and enrollment in home economics and industrial arts classes. Includes national and state by state summaries.

A similar survey is Racial, ethnic and sex enrollment data from institutions of higher education: Fall, 1976 (Washington, D.C.: Govt. Print. Off., 1978) (**H627**). This source lists institutions receiving federal financial assistance and lists enrollment by institution, by state, by type of institutions, by major field of study, and by class level.

H628 U.S. Office of Education. Biennial survey of education in the United States. 1916–58. Washington, D.C.: Govt. Print. Off. Irregularly.

A valuable statistical profile of education in the United States for these years. Information on public and nonpublic education including enrollment, expenditure, salaries, and per capita costs. Some years included data on libraries, special schools and rural schools. Continued by the *Digest of educational statistics* **(H629)**.

SOURCES OF SCHOLARLY CONTRIBUTIONS

Journals

H630

American educational research journal. v.1– , 1964– . Washington, D.C.: American Educational Research Assn. Quarterly.
Cc; EdInd; LLBA; PsychAbst; SSCI.

American journal of education. v.1– , 1893– . Chicago: Univ. of Chicago Pr. Quarterly. (Formerly: School review)
Cc; CIJE; EdAdmAbst; EdInd; PsychAbst; SocAbst; SSCI.

British journal of educational psychology. v.1– , 1931– . Edinburgh: Scottish Academic Pr. 3/yr.
BioAbst; BrEdInd; Cc; ChDevAbst; EdInd; PsychAbst; SSCI.

British journal of educational studies. v.1– , 1952– . Oxford: Basil Blackwell. 3/yr.
BrEdInd; Cc; CIJE; EdInd; SSCI.

Child development. v.1– , 1930– . Chicago: Univ. of Chicago Pr. (for the Society for Research in Child Development) Quarterly.
BioAbst; Cc; ChDevAbst; DSHAbst; LLBA; PsychAbst; SSCI; SSI.

Comparative education review. v.1– , 1956– . Chicago: Univ. of Chicago Pr. 3/yr.
Cc; EdInd; SSCI.

Curriculum inquiry. (formerly Curriculum theory network) v.1– , 1968– . New York: Wiley. Quarterly.
Cc; CIJE; EdInd; ResHighEd; SocEdAbst; SSCI.

Educational administration quarterly. v.1– , 1964– . Beverly Hills, Calif.: Sage. Quarterly.
Cc; EdAdmAbst; EdInd; SSCI.

Educational and psychological measurement. v.1– , 1941– . Durham, N.C.: Educational and Psychological Measurement. Quarterly.
ChemAbst; EdInd; PsychAbst; SSCI.

Educational review. v.1– , 1948– . Abingdon, Eng.: Carfax. 3/yr.
BrEdInd; Cc; CIJE; EdInd; SSCI.

Elementary school journal. v.1– , 1900– . Chicago: Univ. of Chicago Pr. 5/yr.
Cc; CIJE; DSHAbst; EdAdminAbst; EdInd; LLBA; PsychAbst; SSCI.

Exceptional children. v.1– , 1934– . Reston, Va.: Council for Exceptional Children. 6/yr.
ChDevAbst; EdInd; PsychAbst; SSCI.

Harvard educational review. v.1– , 1931– . Cambridge, Mass.: Harvard Univ. Graduate School of Education. Quarterly.
Cc; CIJE; EdInd; PAIS; PsychAbst; SocAbst; SocEdAbst; SSCI.

Higher education. v.1– , 1971– . Amsterdam: Elsevier. Bimonthly.
BrEdInd; Cc; CIJE; CollStudPersAbst; EdInd; SocAbst; SocEdAbst; SSCI.

Instructional science. v.1– , 1971– . Amsterdam: Elsevier. Quarterly.
BrEdInd; Cc; CIJE; EdInd; PsychAbst; SocAbst; SocEdAbst; SSCI.

Journal of curriculum studies. v.1– , 1968– . Basingstoke, Eng.: Taylor & Francis. Quarterly.
Cc; CIJE; EdAdmAbst; SocEdAbst; SSCI.

Journal of educational measurement. v.1– , 1964– . Washington, D.C.: National Council on Measurement in Education. Quarterly.
Cc; EdInd; PsychAbst; SSCI.

Journal of educational psychology. v.1– , 1910– . Washington, D.C.: American Psychological Assn. Bimonthly.
Cc; ChDevAbst; CIJE; CollStudPersAbst; DSHAbst; EdAdmAbst; EdInd; LangTeach; LLBA; PsychAbst; ResHighEd; SocAbst; SSCI; WomStudAbst.

Journal of educational research. v.1– , 1920– . Washington, D.C.: Heldref. Bimonthly.
Cc; CIJE; EdAdmAbst; EdInd; LLBA; PsychAbst; SocAbst; SSCI.

Journal of higher education. v.1– , 1930– . Columbus: Ohio State Univ. Pr. Bimonthly.
CollStudPersAbst; EdAdmAbst; EdInd; PsychAbst; SSCI.

Journal of learning disabilities. v.1– , 1968– . Chicago: Professional Pr. Monthly.
BioAbst; Cc; CIJE; EdInd; LLBA; PsychAbst; SSCI.

Journal of reading behavior. v.1– , 1969– . Rochester, N.Y.: National Reading Conference. Quarterly.
Cc; EdInd; PsychAbst; SSCI.

Journal of school psychology. v.1– , 1963– . New York: Human Sciences Pr. Quarterly.
Cc; CIJE; EdInd; PsychAbst; SSCI.

Journal of special education. v.1– , 1966– . New York: Grune & Stratton. Quarterly.
Cc; EdInd; PsychAbst.

Language learning. v.1– , 1948– . Ann Arbor:

University Hospital, Univ. of Michigan. Semiannual.
Cc; EdInd; SSCI.

New Zealand journal of educational studies. v.1– , 1966– . Wellington: New Zealand Council for Educational Research. Semiannual.
Cc; PsychAbst; SocEdAbst.

Phi Delta Kappan. v.1– , 1915– . Bloomington, Ind.: Phi Delta Kappa. Monthly (Sept.–June).
Cc; CIJE; EdInd; SSCI.

Programmed learning & educational technology. v.1– , 1964– . London: Kogan Page. Quarterly. (Formerly: Programmed learning)
Cc; SSCI.

Psychology in the schools. v.1– , 1964– . Brandon, Vt.: Clinical Psychology Pub. Quarterly.
ChDevAbst; EdInd; PsychAbst; SSCI.

Reading research quarterly. v.1– , 1965– . Newark, Del.: International Reading Assn. Quarterly.
Cc; ChDevAbst; EdInd; PsychAbst; SSCI.

Reading teacher. v.1– , 1947– . Newark, Del.: International Reading Assn. 9/yr.
Cc; EdInd; PsychAbst.

Review of educational research. v.1– , 1931– . Washington, D.C.: American Educational Research Assn. Quarterly.
EdInd; PsychAbst; SSCI.

Studies in higher education. v.1– , 1976– . Abingdon, Eng.: Carfax. Semiannual.
Cc; CIJE; PsychAbst; SSCI.

TESOL quarterly. v.1– , 1967– . Washington, D.C.: Teachers of English to Speakers of Other Languages. Quarterly.
Cc; EdInd.

Teachers College record. v.1– , 1900– . New York: Columbia Univ. Teachers College Record. Quarterly.
Cc; CIJE; EdAdmAbst; EdInd; PsychAbst; SocAbst; SSCI.

Monograph Series

H631 Advances in lifelong education. v.1– , 1976– . Oxford: Pergamon and the UNESCO Institute for Education, Hamburg.

H632 CSE monograph series in evaluation. v.1– , 1973– . Los Angeles: Center for the Study of Evaluation, Univ. of California.
Continues, in purpose, the AERA monograph series on curriculum evaluation (v.1–7, 1967–74. Chicago: Rand McNally).

H633 University of Chicago. Department of Education. Supplementary education monographs. 1917–1968. Chicago: Univ. of Chicago Pr.

H634 John Dewey Society. Lectureship series. 1958– . Carbondale, Ill.: The Society.

H635 The library of education. 1962–1967. New York: Center for Applied Research in Education.
Authoritative 100v. series, with a cumulative index, covering curriculum and teaching, administration and finance, psychology, history, philosophy, social foundations, and professional skills.

H636 National Society for the Study of Education. Yearbook. 1902– . Chicago: Univ. of Chicago Pr.

H637 Ontario Institute for Studies in Education. Monograph series. 1965– . Toronto: The Institute.

H638 Phi Delta Kappa symposia on educational research. 1959–1976. Bloomington, Ind.: Phi Delta Kappa.

H639 Society for Research in Child Development. Monographs. 1936– . Chicago: Univ. of Chicago Pr.

Organizations

H640

American Assn. for Higher Education. Washington, D.C. Founded 1870.

American Assn. of Colleges for Teacher Education (formerly the American Assn. of Teacher's Colleges). Washington, D.C. Founded 1918.

American Assn. of Community and Junior Colleges. Washington, D.C. Founded 1920.

American Assn. of School Administrators. Arlington, Va. Founded 1865.

American Assn. of University Professors. Washington, D.C. Founded 1915.

American Council on Education. Washington, D.C. Founded 1918.

American Educational Research Assn. Washington, D.C. Founded 1915.

Assn. for Childhood Education Intl. Wheaton, Md. Founded 1892.

Assn. for Supervision and Curriculum Development. Alexandria, Va. Founded 1921.

Assn. of American Colleges. Washington, D.C. Founded 1915.

Assn. of American Universities. Washington, D.C. Founded 1900.

Carnegie Foundation for the Advancement of Teaching. Princeton, N.J. Founded 1905.

College Entrance Examination Board. New York. Founded 1900.

Council for Exceptional Children. Reston, Va. Founded 1922.

Education Commission of the States. Denver. Founded 1966.

Education Resources Information Center (ERIC). Washington, D.C. Founded 1966.

Educational Testing Service. Princeton, N.J. Founded 1947.

Institute of International Education. New York. Founded 1919.

Intl. Assn. of Universities. Paris. Founded 1950.

Intl. Bureau of Education. Geneva. Founded 1925.

Intl. Reading Assn. Newark, Del. Founded 1956.

John Dewey Society. Columbia, S.C. Founded 1935.

National Assn. for the Education of Young Children. Washington, D.C. Founded 1926.

National Assn. of Elementary School Principals. Reston, Va. Founded 1921.

National Assn. of Secondary School Principals. Reston, Va. Founded 1916.

National Business Education Assn. Reston, Va. Founded 1892.

National Council for the Social Studies. Washington, D.C. Founded 1921.

National Council of Teachers of English. Urbana, Ill. Founded 1911.

National Council of Teachers of Mathematics. Reston, Va. Founded 1920.

National Education Assn. Washington, D.C. Founded 1857.

National PTA (formerly the National Congress of Parents and Teachers). Chicago. Founded 1897.

National Science Teachers Assn. Washington, D.C. Founded 1895.

Society for Research in Child Development. Chicago. Founded 1933.

Society for Research into Higher Education. Guildford, U.K. Founded 1964.

UNESCO Institute for Education. Hamburg. Founded 1951.

SOURCES OF CURRENT INFORMATION

H641

Good general sources include the *New York times* and the *Times* (London). More specialized publications that report on educational developments are listed below:

AAHE bulletin. v.1– , 1948– . Washington, D.C.: American Assn. for Higher Education. 10/yr.

AGB reports. v.1– , 1959– . Washington, D.C.: Assn. of Governing Boards of Universities and Colleges. Bimonthly.

Academe: bulletin of the AAUP. v.1– , 1915– . Washington, D.C.: American Assn. of University Professors. 6/yr.

American education. v.1– , 1965– . Washington, D.C.: U.S. Office of Education. 10/yr.

Change. v.1– , 1969– . Washington, D.C.: Heldref Pubs. for the Council on Learning. 8/yr.

Chronicle of higher education. v.1– , 1966– . Washington, D.C.: The Chronicle. Weekly.

COMPACT. v.1– , 1966– . Denver: Education Comm. of the States. Quarterly.

Community and junior college journal. v.1– , 1930– . Washington, D.C.: American Assn. of Community and Junior Colleges. 8/yr.

EDUCOM bulletin. v.1– , 1966– . Princeton, N.J.: Interuniversity Communications Council. Quarterly.

ERIC Newsletters. 1966– .
Each of the subject-oriented clearinghouses in the ERIC network produces a newsletter to provide current information to the community it serves.

Education U.S.A. 1958– . Arlington, Va.: National School Public Relations Assn. Weekly.

Educational record. v.1– , 1920– . Washington, D.C.: American Council on Education. Quarterly.

Educational researcher. v.1– , 1964– . Washington, D.C.: American Educational Research Assn. Monthly.

Higher education and national affairs. v.1– , 1952– . Washington, D.C.: American Council of Education. 40/yr.

Nation's school report. v.1– , 1928– . Washington, D.C.: Capitol Pubs. monthly.

NEA reporter. 1962– . Washington, D.C.: National Education Assn. Monthly.

Principal (formerly National elementary principal). v.1– , 1921– . Arlington, Va.: National Assn. of Elementary School Principals. 5/yr.

Times (London). Educational Supplement. 1910– London: Times Newspapers Ltd. Weekly.

Times (London). Higher education supplement. 1971– . London: Times Newspapers Ltd. Weekly.

Camille Wanat

9 Political Science

Survey of the Field

Survey of the Reference Works

94. Special topics I1995–1025. *Encyclopedias and enclyopedic sets* I1026–34. *Handbooks, manuals, and compendia* I1035–51. U.S. politics and government I1052–68. Comparative politics and government I1068A–83. *Yearbooks* I1084–1105. *Original sources* I1106–44. Treaties I1145–55. *Statistical sources* I1156–67A. U.S. elections I1168–80. *Atlases, maps, and pictorial works* I1181–85. *Sources of scholarly contributions.* Journals I1186. Monograph series I1187. Organizations I1188. *Sources of current information* I1189–99.

Survey of the Field

INTRODUCTION

Political science is as broad as its subject matter, politics. Michael J. Oakeshott defines the latter as an attending to the arrangements of society; David Easton defines it as the authoritative allocation of values influenced by the distribution and use of power. Benjamin Lippincott characterizes the study of politics as an analysis of the relations that do, may, or ought to arise in the act of governance; Harold Lasswell and Abraham Kaplan see political science as the study of the shaping and sharing of power. These definitions, found in the citations below, epitomize the range of contemporary political science.

I1   Easton, David. The political system: an inquiry into the state of political science. 2d ed. New York: Knopf, 1971. 377p.

I2   Lasswell, Harold, and Abraham Kaplan. Power and society. New Haven, Conn.: Yale Univ. Pr., 1950. 295p.

I3   Oakeshott, Michael J. Rationalism in politics, and other essays. London: Methuen, 1962. 333p.

I4   UNESCO. Contemporary political science: a survey of methods, research and teaching. Liege, Belgium: G. Thone, 1950. 713p.

This broad focus on politics camouflages even greater diversity in disciplinary approaches to political studies. Politics involves both ends and means. The study of ends largely has been a decidedly normative one, while the study of means tended to be either descriptive or explanatory and variously has emphasized the role of institutions, processes, systemic and structural determinants, rational choice, technology, and much more. Then too, the human materials from which elites and masses are drawn have come to be an important aspect of the study of politics. Such studies draw freely from cognate disciplines, including biophysiology, biopsychology, sociobiology, psychology, social psychology, economics, sociology, and anthropology. And in a more reflective mode, political science also has turned considerable attention to the logic of inquiry and discovery, methods of design and analysis, and the philosophy of knowledge itself.

The separate academic discipline and professional group knowing itself as "political science" is less than a century old. This type of self-consciousness and style of designation emerged first in the United States with the founding of the School of Political Science at Columbia University and the founding of the American Political Science Association in 1903. The latter event also marked the formal separation of political science from economics and history. The spirit of American political science only slowly has disseminated to other countries, perhaps because long-standing intellectual traditions on the continent and elsewhere define politics as an epiphenomenon of economics and history. About three-fourths of the world's political scientists practice their craft in the United States. A history of American political science can be found in:

I5   Somit, Albert, and Joseph Tanenhaus. The development of American political science: from Burgess to behavioralism. Boston: Allyn & Bacon, 1967, 220p.

Topical inventories of contemporary political science can be found in:

I6   Finifter, Ada W., ed. Political science: the state of the discipline. Washington, D.C.: American Political Science Assn., 1983. 614p.

I7   Graham, George J., Jr., and George W. Carey, eds. The post-behavioral era: perspectives on political science. New York: McKay, 1972. 305p.

I8   Greenstein, Fred I., and Nelson Polsby, eds. Political science: scope and theory. Reading, Mass.: Addison-Wesley, 1975. 414p.

Most political scientists would agree that political science should provide a theoretical basis for the organization and analysis of things political. Many also would agree that politics is more than a reflection of fundamental economic and historical forces and that it thus deserves study in its own right. Although this consensus helps distinguish political science from other disciplines, it neither defines "the things political" nor provides a unifying theory of politics. The discipline lacks what Thomas Kuhn calls a "paradigm." This dissension periodically erupts into serious controversy over "scope and methods."

I9   Bluhm, William T., ed. The paradigm problem in political science. Durham, N.C.: Carolina Academic Pr., 1982. 227p.

I10   DeGrazia, Alfred. The Velikovsky affair: the warfare of science and scientism. New Hyde Park, N.Y.: Universe, 1966. 260p.

I11   Kuhn, Thomas S. The structure of scientific revolutions. 2d ed., enl. Chicago: Univ. of Chicago Pr., 1970. 210p.

I11A Ricci, David M. The tragedy of political science: politics, scholarship, and democracy. New Haven, Conn.: Yale Univ. Pr., 1984. 335p.

The enormous scope of political inquiry is witnessed by the extraordinary body of knowledge to which political science is heir. Reaching back to biblical times and classical Greece and growing through the centuries, the discipline has inherited a plethora of normative and empirical questions, concepts, theories, and analytical tools. All of these contribute to the cacophony of modern political science and its themes of discord, ranging from cognitive versus non-cognitive and empirical versus normative to deductive versus inductive and nomothetic versus idiographic.

I12   Sabine, George S. History of political theory. 3d ed. New York: Holt, 1962. 948p.

Controversies over scope are not readily separable from those over method. Competing epistemologies range from logical positivism to hermeneutic phenomenology. Debates over justification pose essentialists against intuitionists, and both against value relativists. And debates on the logic of empirical inquiry find statistical researchers fending off mathematical modelers, and both of these attacking the work of political scientists who see science as the piecemeal accumulation and interpretation of idiographic data. The latter sometimes hail their work as insightful and artful, while the political statisticians and mathematicians focus on the need for intersubjectively verifiable knowledge.

I13   Brecht, Arnold. Political theory: the foundations of twentieth century political thought. Princeton, N.J.: Princeton Univ. Pr., 1959. 603p.

I14   Feigl, Herbert, and May Brodbeck, eds. Readings in the philosophy of science. New York: Appleton, 1953. 811p.

I15   Kaplan, Abraham. The conduct of inquiry: methodology for behavioral science. San Francisco: Chandler, 1964. 428p.

I16   Laslett, Peter, and W. G. Runciman, eds. Philosophy, politics and society. 2d ser. New York: Barnes & Noble, 1962. 229p.

I17   Oppenheim, Felix. Moral principles in political philosophy. New York: Random, 1968. 202p.

I18   Pocock, J. G. A. Politics, language, and time: essays on political thought and history. New York: Atheneum, 1971. 291p.

I19   Popper, Karl. The logic of scientific discovery. 3d ed., rev. London: Hutchinson, 1968. 480p.

I20   ———. The poverty of historicism. New York: Harper, 1957. 166p.

I21   Weldon, Thomas Dewar. The vocabulary of politics. London: Penguin, 1953. 199p.

THE HERITAGE

As indicated, political science is heir to a tradition rooted particularly in classical Greece. In three works that come to us as *The republic, The statesman*, and *The laws*, Plato sets forth a systematic discussion about the nature of man, society, and state, both as they are and as they ought to be. Aristotle's *Politics* and *Ethics* both questioned and elaborated upon Plato's teachings. Aristotle also introduced the comparative method of political inquiry, which established him as the father of modern political science. From Plato, Aristotle, and their Greek predecessors, we inherit Western notions of citizenship—that citizens are equal before the law, that neither magistrate nor citizen is above the law, and that government might serve a useful purpose in the individual's pursuit of the good life.

This great dialogue continued in ancient Rome. Roman jurists such as Cicero developed the foundations of modern constitutionalism. They argued, for example, that laws of nature or "justice" were common to or observed by peoples of all customs and that "man-made" (positive) law, magisterial decrees, and even the will of the "sovereign" were subject to this universal law or spark of divine reason. From this reasoning derive notions and practice of social contracts (e.g., *Mayflower Compact*) and self-evident universal truths that check the powers of human government (e.g., *Declaration of Independence* and *Bill of Rights*).

Christianity forcefully brought further dimensions to the great dialogue of political philosophy. St. Paul resurrected the ancient Stoic doctrine of human equality, defining the worth and dignity of individuals not in terms of skills or capacity but in terms of their relation to God. From St. Augustine through St. Thomas Aquinas, spokespersons for the medieval church emphasized the differences between moral ideals and existing practices, thereby establishing and maintaining a critical dualism between higher standards (the church) and accepted practices (the state). The resulting tension between what is and what ought to be provides one foundation for later notions of progress and the progressive state.

The decline of medievalism brought into political discourse a host of new views on the nature of humanity, society, and state. Machiavelli and Hobbes ushered a darker view of human nature back into political philosophy, and perhaps both saw the secular state as the ultimate source of sovereignty. John Locke dramatically reintroduced natural laws and rights that transcend and limit the secular state. Locke's atomistic individualism then was modified through the works of Rousseau and the Scottish Moralists (e.g., Hume, Smith), who extolled the virtues of conscience and community.

Strands of this great dialogue are synthesized in what some consider to be America's greatest contribution to political thought, *The federalist papers*. Here the designers of the American Constitution elaborated upon the greatest feat of political engineering known to humankind. The individual, alternately moved by passion and reason, was thought to find himself or herself in a society of diverse and divisive social and economic interests. The Constitution, inter alia, promised to protect citizens against themselves, establish a union that could make laws and rules for a diverse society, and still preserve those fundamental elements of human rights that transcend the opinions of minorities and majorities.

Just as political science is heir to a philosophic tradition it also is heir to the political practice informing and informed by that tradition. Political dialogue is intricately bound with two millenia of Western history. The Greek city-state (or polis, from which derives "political" and its cognates) alternately served as the thesis for Plato's antithesis and then embodied the principles of government analyzed by Aristotle. The Greek and Roman empires fostered the search for universal laws transcending custom. The fact that there was a Roman Republic, then Roman Empire, and finally a Holy Roman Empire encapsulates much of the early political dialogue. And certainly the rise of nation-states in the sixteenth and seventeenth centuries raised numerous practical questions about the relation between the individual and the state. Forms of rule, whether monarchy, oligarchy, democracy, or tyranny, have been factually related to the quality of life, and conceptions of the good life can be found in such varied credos as liberty, equality, fraternity, nationalism, and imperialism.

The theory and practice of politics reflect the efforts of the many or the few who seek to take into their hands the course of human history. Just as politics is central to the enterprise of collective life, so is political science, whether in the rudimentary form of the great dialogues or the more contemporary analyses of relations that do, may, or ought to arise in the act of governance. The political role of political science is hard to miss. Socrates died for his vision of the collective good, as did thousands of lesser mortals in the battles between church and state. The works of Machiavelli and Hobbes gave a justification for totalitarianism, while Locke and Jefferson helped justify revolution. Even in more mundane ways like citizenship training and public policy analysis, political science remains in the thick of politics. In this, political science differs from the other social sciences, and from this difference derives part of its disciplinary identity and internal dissension.

The following works provide an overview of the great political dialogues and their relation to political practice. (Note: This discussion focuses on political science in the United States, and thus most of the citations are of domestic publications. The fact that components of American political science were born in Europe and brought mature to the United States makes it necessary to cite those foreign publications that have played an integral role in the American elaboration and evolution. An impressive interaction over the past 50 years between American scholars and the British in particular make certain British citations especially appropriate.)

I22   Anderson, William. Man's quest for political knowledge: the study and teaching of politics in ancient times. Minneapolis: Univ. of Minnesota Pr., 1964. 381p.

I23   Barker, Ernest. Greek political theory: Plato and his predecessors. 4th ed. London: Methuen, 1951. 403p.

I24   ———. Principles of social and political theory. Oxford: Clarendon, 1951. 284p.

I25   Becker, Carl. The heavenly city of the eighteenth-century philosophers. New Haven, Conn.: Yale Univ. Pr., 1946. 168p.

I26   Bury, John Bagnell. The idea of progress: an inquiry into its origins and growth. New York: Dover, 1955. 357p.

I27   Carritt, Edgar F. Morals and politics: theories of their relation from Hobbes and Spinoza to Marx and Bosanquet. Oxford: Clarendon, 1935. 216p.

I28   Dunning, William A. A history of political theories. New York: Macmillan, 1902, 1905, 1920. 3v.

I29   Gettell, Raymond G. History of political thought. New York: Century, 1924. 511p.

I30   Hacker, Andrew. The study of politics: the Western tradition and American origins. New York: McGraw-Hill, 1963. 105p.

I31   Murray, Alexander R. M. An introduction to political philosophy. London: Cohen & West, 1953. 240p.

I32   Murray, Robert H. The history of political science from Plato to the present. 2d ed. New York: Appleton, 1930. 439p.

I33   Pollack, Frederick. An introduction to the history of the science of politics. Boston: Beacon, 1960. 128p.

I34   Shaw, L. Earl, ed. Modern competing ideologies. Lexington, Mass.: Heath, 1973. 428p.

I35   Sibley, Mulford Q. Political ideas and ideologies: a history of political thought. New York: Harper, 1970. 611p.

I36   Skinner, Quentin. The foundations of modern political thought. Cambridge: Cambridge Univ. Pr., 1978. 2v.

I37   Strauss, Leo. Natural right and history. Chicago: Univ. of Chicago Pr., 1953. 327p.

I38   ———, and Joseph Cropsey, eds. History of political philosophy. Chicago: Rand McNally, 1963. 790p.

I39   Troeltsch, Ernest. The social teaching of the Christian churches. Tr. by Olive Wyon. New York: Macmillan, 1931. 2v.

I40   Weldon, Thomas Dewar. States and morals: a study in political conflicts. London: John Murray, 1946. 302p.

I41   Willoughby, W. W. An examination of the nature of the state: a study in political philosophy. New York: Macmillan, 1896. 448p.

I42   Wolin, Sheldon S. Politics and vision. Boston: Little, 1960. 529p.

I43   Woolsey, Theodore D. Political science; or, the state theoretically and practically considered. New York: Scribner, Armstrong, 1878. 2v.

RISE OF POLITICAL SCIENCE IN THE UNITED STATES

The traditions inherited by political science were taught in American colleges and universities throughout the eighteenth and nineteenth centuries under such rubrics as "moral philosophy," "classics of politics," and "political economy." Interest in the social sciences grew rapidly after the Civil War, and hundreds of American students enrolled for advanced study in European and particularly German universities. Upon their return these newly trained scholars, among them John W. Burgess, sought to establish centers of advanced social science training in the United States, and many favored an instructional program based on the German model. Burgess finally succeeded in 1880 when the trustees of Columbia College authorized advanced training in political science. Its success catapulted Columbia to the forefront of advanced training in political science, and with Johns Hopkins, the Columbia School began staffing other fledging programs, particularly in the Midwest.

As noted earlier, political science largely had become a self-conscious discipline shortly after the turn of the century. The American Political Science Association appeared in 1903, and an increasing number of colleges and departments joined the ranks of Ph.D.–granting institutions in political science. Their curricula and research largely were formalistic and legalistic, and, apart from a common focus on the state, the province of political science was difficult to distinguish from that of history, philosophy, and the other social sciences. However, the ferment of ideas begun here would provide the catalyst for a more distinctive political science that emerged in the following generations.

American political science differs from its progenitors, but only because it has added to rather than replaced its original constituent parts. The study of ancient and modern political philosophy remains an integral part of most political science programs. The study of foreign governments—comparative government, or, more lately, comparative politics—inaugurated by Aristotle has from the beginning been a "field" of specialization. The study of international relations, less of classical and more of modern European origins, likewise has long been a field of specialization. However, much of what political science has concerned itself with has been peculiarly and often intensely American; this probably was inevitable and, some would argue, desirable as well. American government has at all times been a prominent field of specialization. Indeed, it has often been divided into fields of subspecialization—national government, state government, local government, federalism, and intergovernmental relations—or divided along other lines, such as constitutional law, political parties, and public opinion. The increased emphasis on human behavior in political situations in the post–World War II period has added further depth to an increasingly diverse field of study.

Its drive toward science most clearly distinguished American political science from its European cognates. To be sure, Aristotle customarily is credited as being the first "political scientist" in the stricter or physical science sense of scientific inquiry. Aristotle's concerns went beyond the gathering and ordering of data, for he systematically raised and attempted to answer questions of cause and effect. Other participants in the great dialogue did likewise, including Machiavelli, Hobbes, the authors of the *Federalist*, Bentham, and Marx. But it has been a distinctly American effort to develop a program of research and teaching that consciously emphasized stricter standards of science. The very choice of the name *political science* rather than *politics* or *government* officially signified a commitment with considerable programmatic implications.

Such was the basis of John W. Burgess' training program at Columbia. He felt that students should first learn habits of critical reading and thinking so that they might separate fact from fiction. Next he expected students to search for causal patterns in the facts or data of politics and finally to establish the larger meaning of these causal patterns. Other major spokesmen for a strict scientific method in the study of politics included James Bryce, Arthur Bentley, and Charles Beard. In the post–World War I period the focus of political science qua science shifted to Charles Merriam and the Department of Political Science at the University of Chicago. That school became extremely influential in efforts to apply scientific knowledge to social problems and produced a number of scholars influential in the further elaboration of American political science. Among these students were Harold Lasswell, perhaps the most distinguished political scientist of the twentieth century, and Herbert Simon, a recent Nobel laureate.

The rise of a science of politics in the United States is ironic, particularly when considered in light of European fears over the leveling effect of American democracy and vulgar populism. To be sure, American colleges and universities often were targets of anti-intellectualism, and only slowly and partially did they insulate themselves from the nuances of public opinion. Fortuitously, however, the growth of advanced training in political science parallels the rise of middle-class progressivism and its search for a scientific politics that might remove corruption and establish good government at all levels of the American polity. In this context it is important to note that Charles Merriam, like fellow political scientist President Woodrow Wilson, was a scholar-politician of progressivism. Wilson sought to bring science to politics through the Democratic party, while Merriam attempted much the same through the Republican party.

Political science thus has been intermingled with "reformism" of various kinds, and it has at all times been engaged—sometimes centrally, sometimes marginally—with the enterprises of citizenship education and training for public service. Even those not captured by the progressive spirit have believed that the discipline owed much to the democratic polity that gave it a home. In the latter connection, it may be noted that a specialization known as "public administration" developed in the twenties and thirties and another known as "public policy analysis" developed in the seventies.

Apart from those previously mentioned, the following citations further aid a study of the rise and early development of American political science.

I44   Crick, Bernard. The American science of politics: its origins and conditions. Berkeley: Univ. of California Pr., 1959. 252p.

I45   Gettell, Raymond G. Introduction to political science. Rev. ed. Boston: Ginn, 1922. 421p.

I46   Haddow, Anna. Political science in American colleges and universities, 1636–1900. New York: Appleton, 1939. 308p.

I47   Hyneman, Charles S. The study of politics: the present state of American political science. Urbana: Univ. of Illinois Pr., 1959. 232p.

I48   Karl, Barry D. Charles E. Merriam and the study of politics. Chicago: Univ. of Chicago Pr., 1974. 337p.

I49   Mackenzie, W. J. M. The study of political science today. London: Macmillan, 1970. 96p.

I50   Mathews, John Mabry, and James Hart, eds. Essays in political science in honor of Westel Woodbury Willoughby. Baltimore: Johns Hopkins Univ. Pr., 1937. 364p.

I51   Merriam, Charles E. New aspects of politics. Chicago: Univ. of Chicago Pr., 1925. 253p.

I52   Somit, Albert, and Joseph Tanenhaus. American political science: a profile of a discipline. New York: Atherton, 1964. 173p.

I53   Waldo, Dwight. Political science in the United States of America: a trend report. Paris: UNESCO, 1956. 84p.

BEHAVIORALISM AND BEYOND

In the generation following World War II, political science became the battlefield for another drive toward science commonly known as the behavioral revolution or persuasion, depending upon one's point of view. The new science was more reflective than its predecessors, favoring the contemplative over the activist role. The movement thus repudiated the progressive activism of Merriam and others, for it sought to withhold political advice until the bases of its knowledge were more secure and scientific. Bitter battles in the 1950s led to the temporary ascendancy of behavioralism in the 1960s. Events of that decade, however, soon demanded a "relevance" from political scientists before which the stricter forms of behavioralism were remarkably defenseless. The post-behavioral era that emerged by the 1970s reintroduced an uneasy alliance between political science and political action.

To say that behavioralism dominated the post–World War II era does not mean that other cleavages within the discipline disappeared; rather, behavioralism crystallized diverse antagonisms against a common enemy that, in turn, gave the discipline a false sense of its own coherency. The behavioral persuasion modeled a science of politics on the methodology of the natural sciences. It also hailed itself as the first step toward an integrated or unified science of politics with human *behavior* as its ultimate focus—not what laws say or what institutions should do, or even what goals society should seek. Finally, behavioralism made survey research a primary source of data.

The broad-gauged offensive of behavioralism united its diverse opponents into a temporary alliance that collapsed quickly once political science moved into its latest self-conscious phase of relevance to political action. The behavior persuasion emphasized the need for description, explanation, and verification and, concomitantly, deemphasized the role of prescription, ethical inquiry, and action. The later deemphasis mobilized normative theorists against behavioralism. Its emphasis on the cumulation of reliable empirical knowledge pitted behavioralism against the idiographic work of case-study specialists. And its assertion that the accumulation of reliable empirical knowledge necessarily precedes its deployment in the solution of practical problems offended committed activists within the discipline. Its devotion to general theory and the strictest standards of science alienated those political scientists who preferred ad hoc theory or low-level generalizations and a less stringent test of scientific adequacy. Finally, its emphasis on survey research and other forms of quantifiable data brought a concomitant emphasis on quantitative methodology that gave an aura of sophistication to those with these tools and generated insecurity and hostility among those without them.

Perhaps these tenets were the central ones, although no one emerged as the authoritative sine qua non of behavioralism. Indeed, behavioralists argued much among themselves, particularly after the heady wine of self-proclaimed victory brought them to overestimate the permanency of their revolution. With behavioralism as the center of the disciplinary controversy during the 1950s and 1960s, the focus of the discipline also changed, at least until post-behavioralism. Research on political institutions declined as the focusing on political behavior increased. Normative and empirical theorizing became more careful and penetrating, and the disciplinary dissension produced high-quality examinations of epistemology, the logic of scientific inquiry, verification, and justification. The emphasis on survey research dramatically expanded the study of voting behavior and public opinion, elite-mass linkages, and political socialization. The discipline also became less intensely American in its focus. In part this shift represents the decreased parochialism of political scientists in the wake of World War II. In part this shift also captures the changing disciplinary alliances from law, jurisprudence, philosophy, and history toward psychology, economics, sociology, and to a lesser extent anthropology and biology.

The behavioralist dynasty had begun crumbling by the late 1960s as social conditions, students, and the so-called "Caucus for a New Political Science" demanded more disciplinary relevance and action in the solution of pressing social problems, rather than a continued accumulation of basic political knowledge. Postbehavioralism also denied the desirability or possibility of a value-free science, and thus called upon political scientists to assume their share of the burden in protecting the humane values of civilization. From its origin, the post-behavioral movement was more a repudiation of certain behavioral tenets than it was a blueprint for a new political science. This repudiation brought together conservative and radical critics of behavioralism, but their differences were too fundamental to permit a permanent alliance. Old cleavages arose from the cacophony that ensued, although the following decade witnessed a rekindled interest in public policy studies reminiscent of the pre-behavioral era.

Political science of the 1980s lacks the protagonist or set of antagonists necessary for its self-conscious identity. Knowing what one believes in or alternately what one opposes provides a basis for disciplinary organization and continuity. Behavioralism brought an increased range of interests and inquiries to political science, but its demise as the dominant mood has allowed these and older interests and inquiries to blur if not bankrupt disciplinary identity. The rise of technical concentrations with their own jargon and tools, the proliferation of specialized journals, the declining membership in the central organization (the American Political Science Association), pressures toward secession bottled only by increasingly tight university budgets, and its self-proclaimed interdisciplinary status are some signs of the times. A comparison of the program of the annual convention of the American Political Science Association in recent years with one of a generation ago is instructive. Earlier presentations were made under the rubrics of 6 or 7 recognized and fairly stable "fields." Recent programs, however, list presentations under some 15 or 20 headings, of wide variety and changing status.

Works that pertain especially to the behavioral movement include the following. Some are apologias, some present commentary and interpretation, some (e.g., Storing and Voegelin) are critical.

I54   Charlesworth, James C., ed. Contemporary political analysis. New York: Free Pr., 1967. 380p.

I55   ———. A design for political science: scope, objectives, and methods. Philadelphia: American Academy of Political and Social Science, 1966. 254p. [Monograph series no.6]

I56   ———. The limits of behavioralism in political science. Philadelphia: American Academy of Political and Social Science, 1962. 123p.

I57   Connolly, William. Political science and ideology. New York: Atherton, 1967. 179p.

I58   Dahl, Robert A. Modern political analysis. 3d ed. Englewood Cliffs, N.J.: Prentice-Hall, 1976. 166p.

I59   Easton, David, ed. Varieties of political theory. Englewood Cliffs, N.J.: Prentice-Hall, 1966. 154p.

I60   Eulau, Heinz. The behavioral persuasion in politics. New York: Random, 1963. 141p.

I61   ———, Samuel J. Eldersveld, and Morris Janowitz, eds. Political behavior: a reader in theory and research. Glencoe, Ill.: Free Pr., 1956. 421p.

I62   Eulau, Heinz, and James G. March, eds. Political report of the behavioral and social science survey committee. Englewood Cliffs, N.J.: Prentice-Hall, 1969. 160p.

I63   Isaak, Alan C. Scope and methods of political science: an introduction to the methodology of political inquiry. Homewood, Ill.: Dorsey Pr., 1969. 257p.

I64   Pool, Ithiel de Sola, ed. Contemporary political science—toward empirical theory. New York: McGraw-Hill, 1967. 276p.

I65   Ranney, Austin, ed. Essays on the behavioral study of politics. Urbana: Univ. of Illinois Pr., 1962. 251p.

I66   Storing, Herbert J., ed. Essays on the scientific study of politics. New York: Holt, 1962. 333p.

I67   Van Dyke, Vernon. Political science: a philosophical analysis. Stanford, Calif.: Stanford Univ. Pr., 1960. 253p.

I68   Voegelin, Eric. The new science of politics: an introduction. Chicago: Univ. of Chicago Pr., 1952. 193p.

I69   Young, Roland, ed. Approaches to the study of politics. Evanston, Ill.: Northwestern Univ. Pr., 1958. 283p.

Works that sample the currents of postbehavioralism include:

I70   Green, Philip, and Sanford Levinson, eds. Power and community: dissenting essays in political science. New York: Pantheon, 1970. 396p.

I71   Greenstein, Fred, and Nelson Polsby, eds. Handbook of political science. Reading, Mass.: Addison-Wesley, 1975. 9v.

I72   Kariel, Henry S. The promise of politics. Englewood Cliffs, N.J.: Prentice-Hall, 1966. 120p.

I73   Landau, Martin. Political theory and political science: studies in the methodology of political inquiry. New York: Macmillan, 1972. 244p.

I74   Lindblom, Charles E., and David K. Cohen. Usable knowledge: social science and social problem solving. New Haven, Conn.: Yale Univ. Pr., 1979. 129p.

I75   McCoy, Charles, and John Playford, eds. Apolitical politics: a critique of behavioralism. New York: Crowell, 1967. 246p.

I76   MacRae, Duncan, Jr. The social function of social science. New Haven, Conn.: Yale Univ. Pr., 1976. 352p.

I77   Marini, Frank, ed. Toward a new public administration: the Minnowbrook perspective. Scranton, Pa.: Chandler, 1971. 372p.

I78   Meehan, Eugene. Value judgment and social science: structures and processes. Homewood, Ill.: Dorsey Pr., 1969. 159p.

I79   Ostrom, Elinor, ed. Strategies of political inquiry. Beverly Hills, Calif.: Sage, 1982. 224p.

I80   Surkin, Marvin, and Alan Wolfe, eds. An end to political science. New York: Basic Books, 1970. 324p.

SEARCH FOR A FOCUS

Political science often has been as unsure of what it is not as it has been unsure of what it is. This amorphous self-consciousness is traced largely to the discipline's failure to agree upon the fundamental building blocks of political inquiry and consequently the skills fundamental to political inquiry. Is the nation-state the cornerstone of politics? What of power? Or the political system? Institutions? Groups? Behavior? Policies? Each of these, and others, has been offered as the basic building block or fundamental unit of analysis appropriate to political inquiry. However, there has been no single concept that has captured the imagination of most political scientists. The lack of a common foundation consequently prevented theory construction that might unite the disparate elements of political science into a general framework for political inquiry. And absent that conceptual and theoretical foundation, disparate tools or methodologies further separate researchers within the discipline. In short, political scientists utilize so many different analytic concepts, organizing

theories, and methods of inquiry that they find themselves in need of translators when members of the same discipline attempt to speak among themselves.

The State Concept

Perhaps the oldest conceptual category is the state and, for modern political science particularly, the nation-state as it developed from the sixteenth and seventeenth centuries to the present day. That this concept became the focus of the Columbia program in the 1880s is not surprising, particularly given the European, and especially German, emphasis on Staatswissenschaft (science of the state). From this focus derive a number of questions. Who is the sovereign? That is, who holds final or supreme power in the nation-state? What are the necessary and sufficient grounds for political obligation? That is, who must we obey, when, and why? Similarly, what of nationalism? Authority? And what of constitutionalism?

The following illustrate usage of the state concept and some derivative questions.

I81   Bluntschli, J. K. The theory of the state. Oxford: Clarendon, 1895. 550p.

I82   Flathman, Richard. Political obligation. New York: Atheneum, 1972. 334p.

I83   Hobhouse, L. T. Liberalism. New York: Oxford Univ. Pr., 1964. 130p.

I84   Kohn, Hans. The idea of nationalism. New York: Collier Macmillan, 1944. 735p.

I85   Lindsay, A. D. The modern democratic state. New York: Oxford Univ. Pr., 1962. 286p.

I86   McIlwain, Charles H. Constitutionalism: ancient and modern. Rev. ed. Ithaca, N.Y.: Cornell Univ. Pr., 1947. 180p.

I87   MacIver, R. M. The modern state. London: Oxford Univ. Pr., 1955. 504p.

I88   Minogue, Kenneth R. Nationalism. New York: Basic Books, 1967. 168p.

I89   Skocpol, Theda. States and social revolutions. Cambridge: Cambridge Univ. Pr., 1979. 407p.

I90   Smith, Anthony D. Theories of nationalism. London: Dockworth, 1971. 344p.

I91   Willoughby, William F. An introduction to the study of government of modern states. New York: Century, 1919. 455p.

I92   Wilson, Woodrow. The state: elements of historical and practical politics. Boston: Heath, 1889. 686p.

The Power Concept

Research using the state concept tended to be philosophical, legalistic, institutional, or simply descriptive. Such results fell short of a science of politics, and although the concept never lost a place in the discipline and indeed has witnessed a resurgence in the past decade, its earlier preeminence was eclipsed by the concept of political power. In a renewed drive toward a science of politics, power became the analogue of wealth in economics. The concept was thought to be the source from which political functions like decision making derived their substance. Political scientists focused on potential and in-use resources for power, the accumulation and dispersion of power and resources, the exercise of power, and its impact. But power was too elusive in its definition, operationalization, and measure to unify and organize the discipline.

The following argue the case for the power concept, illustrate its use, or offer critical commentary thereon. In addition, see Harold D. Lasswell and Abraham Kaplan, *Power and society,* described at I2.

I93   Catlin, George E. G. The science and method of politics. New York: Knopf, 1927. 360p.

I94   Dahl, Robert A. Who governs? New Haven, Conn.: Yale Univ. Pr., 1961. 335p.

I95   Horowitz, Irving, ed. Power, politics, and people: the collected essays of C. W. Mills. New York: Ballantine, 1963. 657p.

I96   Hunter, Floyd. Community power structure: a study of decision-makers. Chapel Hill: Univ. of North Carolina Pr., 1953. 297p.

I97   Jouvenel, Bertrand de. On power: its nature and the history of its growth. Tr. by J. F. Huntington. New York: Viking, 1949. 421p.

I98   Katznelson, Ira. The politics of power: a critical introduction to American government. 2d ed. New York: HBJ, 1979. 435p.

I99   Lasswell, Harold D., ed. A study of power. Glencoe, Ill.: Free Pr., 1950.
Contains three studies of power: Lasswell, "World politics and personal insecurity" (307p.); Charles E. Merriam, "Political power" (331p.); T. V. Smith, "Power and conscience: beyond conscience" (373p.).

I101   Löwenstein, Karl. Power and the governmental process. 2d ed. Chicago: Univ. of Chicago Pr., 1965. 464p.

I102   Merriam, Charles E. Political power. New York: Collier, 1964. 317p.

I103   Mills, C. Wright. The power elite. New York: Oxford Univ. Pr., 1956. 423p.

I104   Moore, Barrington. Political power and social theory: seven studies. New York: Harper, 1965. 243p.

I105   Morgenthau, Hans J. Scientific man versus power politics. Chicago: Univ. of Chicago Pr., 1946. 224p.

I106   Russell, Bertrand. Power: a new social analysis. New York: Norton, 1938. 315p.

I107   Wrong, Dennis H. Power: its forms, bases, and uses. New York: Harper, 1979. 236p.

Systems Theory

A third claimant to the throne of a unified political science is the concept of *political systems* or *systems theory* more generally. This approach waxed strongly during the 1960s but quickly waned in the 1970s, although it still has some proponents. The rise of systems theory in political science followed the emergence of a systems paradigm in sociology and anthropology. General systems theory emphasized the interactions and mutual dependencies of elements in a universe of inquiry, such as human society. Because these interactions and dependencies were thought to converge toward equilibrium, its proponents thought it possible to develop a unified science of society that specified the necessary functions and, in the case of structural functionalism, the attendant structures implied by a convergence toward equilibrium. The political system, in turn, was seen as one of the subsystems for systems maintenance.

The potentially conservative emphasis on systems maintenance became the focus of bitter complaint by action-oriented political scientists during the late 1960s and early 1970s, and efforts to include a change of system (as opposed to systems transformation) within the general theory weakened its intellectual coherency. A theory of convergence toward equilibrium plus a theory permitting system succession raised obvious questions about dividing lines between the two phenomena and severely taxed available systems schema in the search for answers. The declining appeal of general systems theory coincided, perhaps spuriously, with a renewed interest in collective violence, mass unrest, and revolution.

In addition to some works previously cited (e.g., Easton), those that follow further exemplify the systems approach, criticize it, or look at collective violence and revolution as agents of system change.

I108   Almond, Gabriel A., and G. Bingham Powell, Jr. Comparative politics: a developmental approach. Boston: Little, 1966. 348p.

I109 Arendt, Hannah. On violence. New York: Harcourt, 1970. 106p.

I110 Bluhm, William T. Theories of the political system. Englewood Cliffs, N.J.: Prentice-Hall, 1965. 502p.

I111 Gurr, Ted Robert. Why men rebel. Princeton, N.J.: Princeton Univ. Pr., 1970. 421p.

I112 Hibbs, Douglas. Mass political violence: a cross-national causal analysis. New York, Wiley, 1973. 253p.

I113 Kariel, Henry. Open systems. Itasca, Ill.: Peacock, 1969. 148p.

I114 Mitchell, William C. Sociological analysis and politics: the theories of Talcott Parsons. Englewood Cliffs, N.J.: Prentice-Hall, 1967. 222p.

I115 Sears, David, and John McConahay. The politics of violence: the new urban blacks and the Watts riot. Boston: Houghton, 1973. 244p.

I116 Tilly, Charles. From mobilization to revolution. Reading, Mass.: Addison-Wesley, 1978. 349p.

Process Perspectives

Three related concepts fall under what might loosely be termed "process perspectives" in political science. They are *group theory* and *pluralism, cybernetics*, and *decision making*. The first holds that groups crystallize and pursue social interests in the political arena. The push and pull of organized interests supposedly leads to a political balance among competing interests. This view was set forth early in the century in a remarkable book by Arthur F. Bentley, and particularly after its exposition and application by David Truman in 1951 became widely popular. With its substitution of groups for individuals, group theory has been described as a laissez-faire theory of politics. This approach, much like systems theory, came under considerable attack in the late 1960s and early 1970s. Theodore Lowi, the political scientist judged by colleagues as the most influential during the 1970s, argued that pluralism had become the dogma of government as well as scholarship, and that consequently liberal governments could not plan because they had become captives of interest groups.

Cybernetics refers to control through communication. It, like pluralism, focused ultimately on decision making. While pluralism emphasized the role of organized groups, cybernetics focused on the substance and process of communication as it affected decision making. Neither theory fully captured the range of phenomena covered by decision making, and a number of alternate approaches to decision making can be found, including psychological, social psychological, and rational choice. So broad is the decision-making umbrella that even *power* justly falls under its aegis. Such breadth is, of course, its weakness, for the concept of decision making covers a host of nonintegrated theories about human choice and action.

Works in which one or more of these focuses are expounded upon or exemplified include the following.

I117 Allison, Graham. Essence of decision: explaining the Cuban missile crisis. Boston: Little, 1971. 338p.

I118 Arrow, Kenneth. Social choice and individual values. 2d ed. New Haven, Conn.: Yale Univ. Pr., 1963. 124p.

I119 Bentley, Arthur F. The process of government. Ed. by Peter H. Odegard. Cambridge, Mass.: Belknap, 1967. 501p.

I120 Berelson, Bernard, and others. Voting. Chicago: Univ. of Chicago Pr., 1954. 395p.

I121 Black, Duncan. The theory of committees and elections. Cambridge: Cambridge Univ. Pr., 1958. 241p.

I122 Braybrooke, David, and Charles Lindblom. A strategy of decision: policy evaluation as a social process. New York: Free Pr. 1963. 268p.

I123 Buchanan, James, and Gordon Tullock. The calculus of consent: logical foundations of constitutional democracy. Ann Arbor: Univ. of Michigan Pr., 1962. 361p.

I124 Campbell, Angus, and others. The American voter. New York: Wiley, 1960. 573p.

I125 Connolly, William. The bias of pluralism. New York: Atherton, 1969. 261p.

I126 Dahl, Robert. A preface to democratic theory. Chicago: Univ. of Chicago Pr., 1956. 155p.

I127 ———, and Charles Lindblom. Politics, economics, and welfare. New York: Harper, 1963. 557p.

I128 Deutsch, Karl W. The nerves of government. New Haven, Conn.: Yale Univ. Pr., 1963. 316p.

I129 Downs, Anthony. An economic theory of democracy. New York: Harper, 1957. 310p.

I130 Farquharson, Robin. Theory of voting. New Haven, Conn.: Yale Univ. Pr., 1969. 183p.

I131 Fishburn, Peter. The theory of social choice. Princeton, N.J.: Princeton Univ. Pr., 1973. 264p.

I132 George, Alexander L. Presidential decision-making in foreign policy: the effective use of information and advice. Boulder, Colo.: Westview, 1980. 267p.

I133 Harsanyi, John C. Rational behavior and bargaining equilibrium in games and social situations. New York: Cambridge Univ. Pr., 1977. 314p.

I134 Lane, Robert. Political ideology. New York: Free Pr., 1962. 509p.

I135 Lasswell, Harold. Psychology and politics. Chicago: Univ. of Chicago Pr., 1930. 285p.

I136 ———. Decision-making: seven categories of functional analysis. College Park: Bureau of Governmental Research, College of Business and Public Administration, Univ. of Maryland, 1956. 23p.

I137 ———, and others. Language of politics: studies in quantitative semantics. New York: G. W. Stewart, 1949. 398p.

I138 Lazarsfeld, Paul, and others. The people's choice. 2d ed. New York: Columbia Univ. Pr., 1948. 178p.

I139 Leites, Nathan. A study of bolshevism. Glencoe, Ill.: Free Pr., 1953. 639p.

I140 Lindblom, Charles. The intelligence of democracy. New York: Free Pr., 1965. 352p.

I141 Lowi, Theodore. The end of liberalism. 2d ed. New York: Norton, 1979. 331p.

I142 Olson, Mancur. The logic of collective action: public goods and the theory of groups. Rev. ed. Cambridge, Mass.: Harvard Univ. Pr., 1971. 186p.

I142A Peleg, Bezalel. Game theoretic analysis of voting in committees. New York: Cambridge Univ. Pr., 1984. 169p.

I143 Riker, William. The theory of political coalitions. New Haven, Conn.: Yale Univ. Pr., 1962. 300p.

I144 ———. Liberalism against populism: a confrontation between the theory of democracy and the theory of social choice. San Francisco: Freeman, 1982. 311p.

I145 ———, and Peter Ordeshook. An introduction to positive political theory. Englewood Cliffs, N.J.: Prentice-Hall, 1973. 387p.

I146 Schelling, Thomas C. The strategy of conflict. Cambridge, Mass.: Harvard Univ. Pr., 1960. 309p.

I147 Simon, Herbert. Administrative behavior: a study of decision-making processes in administrative organization. 3d ed. New York: Free Pr., 1976. 364p.

I148 Snyder, Richard C., and others. Decision making as an approach to the study of international politics. Princeton, N.J.: Foreign Policy Analysis Project, 1954. 120p.

I149 ———. Foreign policy decision making: an approach to the study of international politics. New York: Free Pr., 1962. 274p.

I150 Truman, David B. The governmental process. New York: Knopf, 1951. 544p.

CONTEMPORARY STRUCTURE

Perhaps early political science could be divided into a finite number of subcurricula such as American government and politics, comparative government, international relations, and theory and methodology. However, these categories shed only dim light on the diversity of contemporary political science. If classifications serve to distinguish the similar from the dissimilar and thus provide the foundations for comparison, systematic accumulation of knowledge, or synthesis, then existing classifications are as dysfunctional as they are functional. Although most political scientists recognize the shortcomings of traditional categories, there are almost as many alternative classification schemes as there are political science programs. Part of this flux follows from the different constellation of faculty interests across universities, part from the ebb and flow of topical interests in the discipline, and much from the diverse nature of a discipline without a central organizing paradigm.

Given the lack of any functional and widely accepted classification scheme, that used here will reflect the schema used to classify book reviews in the *American political science review:* (1) American government and politics, (2) comparative politics and other area studies, (3) international relations, (4) normative theory, (5) empirical theory, and (6) methodology. In addition to these distinctions, others might include units of analysis such as individuals, groups, institutions, processes, society and culture, nation-states, or transnational organizations. Alternately, if decision making were the organizing concept, the classification might distinguish between and among problem discovery and/or definition, political agenda setting, policy formation, policy implementation, and policy evaluation.

Few extended works address the classification of political science subcurricula, although the topic often is addressed in works designed to introduce students to the discipline or in historical overviews of the discipline. Some of these are:

I151 Catlin, George E. G. Systematic politics: elementa politica et sociologica. Toronto: Univ. of Toronto Pr., 1962. 434p.

I152 Eulau, Heinz. "Political science." *In* A reader's guide to the social sciences. Rev. ed. Ed. by Bert F. Hoselitz. p.129–237. New York: Free Pr., 1970.

I153 Haas, Michael, and Henry S. Kariel, eds. Approaches to the study of political science. Scranton, Pa.: Chandler, 1970. 541p.

I154 Irish, Marian D., ed. Political science: advance of the discipline. Englewood Cliffs, N.J.: Prentice-Hall, 1963. 248p.

I155 MacKenzie, William J. M. Politics and social science. Baltimore: Penguin, 1967. 424p.

I156 Murphy, Robert E. The style and study of political science. Glenview, Ill.: Scott, Foresman, 1970. 135p.

I157 Rodee, Carlton Clymer, and others. Introduction to political science. 3d ed. New York: McGraw-Hill, 1976. 466p.

I158 Sorauf, Francis. Political science: an informal overview. Columbus, Ohio: Merrill, 1966. 115p.

I159 Wasby, Stephen L., and others. Political science: the discipline and its dimensions: an introduction. New York: Scribner, 1970. 586p.

I160 Weinstein, Michael A., ed. The political experience: readings in political science. New York: St. Martin's, 1972. 388p.

I161 Welsh, William A. Studying politics. New York: Praeger, 1973. 260p. [Basic concepts in political science]

I162 Young, Oran R. Systems of political science. Englewood Cliffs, N.J.: Prentice-Hall, 1968. 113p.

AMERICAN GOVERNMENT AND POLITICS

American government long has been a central concern of political science. Data on the American polity are perhaps the most available in the world, and the multitude of governments at the national, state, and local levels permit numerous points of scholarly access. In addition, American government is the mainstay of virtually all political science programs, particularly those in public institutions of higher education, where state laws or accreditation requirements demand systematic training in American governmental processes, institutions, and politics. Then, too, student interest continues strong in these areas. Finally, the effort to be relevant and the personal sense of civic duty further contribute to American political scientists' study of their government and politics.

Masses and Elites

Although not the oldest component of American government and politics, the study of masses and elites has become an extremely important segment of political science. Research on individual choice or decision making has drawn to

political science a number of researchers from sociology, psychology, economics, geography, and anthropology. The scope of these studies has become so broad and so interdisciplinary in focus that only a small portion of the relevant literature can be cited here, although two early works deserve particular attention. Stuart Rice's now-classic *Farmers and workers in American politics* focused attention on the voting patterns of certain portions of the American electorate. Although later works would substitute survey research for Rice's reliance on aggregate data, his approach still influences the quantitative study of political history where survey research data is nonexistent. Harold Lasswell's path-breaking *Psychopathology and politics* first used clinical psychology techniques in the study of political elites. That work, in turn, has spawned considerable research in personality development as it affects politics.

The early work on voting and later efforts at mass political history relied on aggregate- as opposed to individual-level data. Thus country- or state-level data has become the basis for inferences about individual motives and behavior. Statistically, of course, such inferences are unreliable, but the advent of survey research and scientific sampling procedures provided a methodological device for examining the motives and behavior of individuals without relying solely upon aggregate data-based inferences. The early pioneer work in this area was Lazarsfeld and others, *The people's choice,* a study of the vote decision among Erie County, Ohio, voters in the presidential campaign of 1940. Another study on Elmira, New York, follows for the 1948 elections (see Berelson and others, *Voting,* I120); and in *The American voter* (I124), a study of the 1956 presidential election, Campbell and others firmly established the importance of national surveys in electoral behavior research. (Other national surveys had been conducted and were reported upon for the 1944, 1948, and 1952 national elections.) Lazarsfeld and the Columbia School dominated voting research during the 1940s and into the 1950s, but Campbell and the Michigan School had become the dominant center for voting research by the 1960s. About this time the extraordinarily influential V. O. Key, Jr., turned to Gallup polls to begin questioning the findings of the Michigan researchers. Although he died before publication of his *The responsible electorate,* the volley fired there became the basis for what might be loosely called a Chicago-Harvard alternative to the dim view of mass electoral behavior presented in the Michigan work. This alternative, perhaps best exemplified in Nie and others, *The changing American voter* (I180), also began drawing upon surveys conducted by the National Opinion Research Center at the University of Chicago. The relatively friendly rivalry between these two schools of thought has focused attention on such areas as the extent of issue voting, the extent of ideological conceptualization among ordinary men and women, and a host of related matters. Other themes and debates within political science include the nature, durability, and function of partisanship in the vote choice; the role of candidates and issues; contextual influences on voting; and the role of self-interest, personality, group identification, and personal values on voting choice and the structure of opinion.

The following list includes a sampling of major works in this area that have not been cited previously in this essay.

I163   Abramson, Paul R. Political attitudes in America. San Francisco: Freeman, 1983. 353p.

I164   Asher, Herbert B. Presidential elections and American politics. Rev. ed. Homewood, Ill.: Dorsey Pr., 1980. 336p.

I165   Burdick, Eugene, and Arthur Brodbeck, eds. American voting behavior. Glencoe, Ill.: Free Pr., 1959. 475p.

I166   Burnham, Walter Dean. Critical elections and the mainspring of American politics. New York: Norton, 1970. 210p.

I167   Campbell, Angus, and others. The voter decides. Evanston, Ill.: Row, Peterson, 1954. 242p.

I168   ———, and others. Election and the political order. New York: Wiley, 1966. 385p.

I169   Fiorina, Morris. Retrospective voting in American national politics. New Haven, Conn.: Yale Univ. Pr., 1981. 249p.

I170   Ginsberg, Benjamin. The consequences of consent: elections, citizen control and popular acquiescence. Reading, Mass.: Addison-Wesley, 1982. 271p.

I171   Hinckley, Barbara. Congressional elections. Washington, D.C.: Congressional Quarterly Pr., 1981. 173p.

I172   Jacobson, Gary C. The politics of congressional elections. Boston: Little, 1983. 216p.

I173   ———, and Samuel Kernell. Strategy and choice in congressional elections. New Haven, Conn.: Yale Univ. Pr., 1981. 111p.

I174   Kessel, John H. Presidential campaign politics: coalition strategies and citizen response. Homewood, Ill.: Dorsey Pr., 1980. 298p.

I175   Key, V. O., Jr. Public opinion and American democracy. New York: Knopf, 1961. 566p.

I176   ———. The responsible electorate. Cambridge, Mass.: Belknap, 1966. 158p.

I177   Lane, Robert E. Political life: why people get involved in politics. Glencoe, Ill.: Free Pr., 1959. 374p.

I179   Milbrath, Lester. Political participation. Chicago: Rand McNally, 1965. 195p.

I180   Nie, Norman, and others. The changing American voter. Enl. ed. Cambridge, Mass.: Harvard Univ. Pr., 1979. 430p.

I181   Page, Benjamin I. Choices and echoes in presidential elections. Chicago: Univ. of Chicago Pr., 1978. 336p.

I182   Patterson, Thomas E. The mass media election: how Americans choose their president. New York: Praeger, 1980. 203p.

I183   Pomper, Gerald. Voter's choice: varieties of American electoral behavior. New York: Dodd, 1975. 259p.

I184   Rice, Stuart A. Farmers and workers in American politics. New York: Columbia Univ. Pr., 1924. 231p.

I185   Rogin, Michael Paul. The intellectuals and McCarthy: the radical specter. Cambridge, Mass.: MIT Pr., 1967. 366p.

I186   Verba, Sidney, and Norman H. Nie. Participation in America: political democracy and social equality. New York: Harper, 1972. 428p.

Political psychology and the intensive study of American political elites has grown considerably since Lasswell. Once again these endeavors tend to be interdisciplinary, whether scholars from psychology or social psychology turn their attention to political matters or whether political scientists seek and use these cognate theories and conceptualizations for their own disciplinary purposes. Among the more important are:

I187   Barber, James David. The presidential character: predicting performance in the White House. Englewood Cliffs, N.J.: Prentice-Hall, 1972. 479p.

I188   George, Alexander L., and Juliett L. George. Woodrow Wilson and Colonel House: a personality study. New York: Day, 1956. 362p.

I189   Kearns, Doris. Lyndon Johnson and the American dream. New York: Harper, 1976. 432p.

While intensive studies focus upon a few individuals, thereby sacrificing generality in favor of depth, extensive studies choose to sacrifice depth in the interests of generality. Again researchers in American politics have produced numerous books in the areas of political socialization, political personality, elite recruitment, and so forth. Some of the important works in this area include:

I190　Adorno, T. W., and others. The authoritarian personality. New York: Harper, 1950. 990p.

I191　Barber, James D. The lawmakers: recruitment and adaptation to legislative life. New Haven, Conn.: Yale Univ. Pr., 1965. 314p.

I192　Easton, David, and Jack Dennis. Children in the political system: origins of political legitimacy. New York: McGraw-Hill, 1969. 440p.

I193　Greenstein, Fred I. Children and politics. New Haven, Conn.: Yale Univ. Pr., 1965. 199p.

I194　Hess, Robert D., and Judith Torney. The development of political attitudes in children. Chicago: Aldine, 1967. 288p.

I195　Jennings, M. Kent, and Richard G. Niemi. Generations and politics: a panel study of young adults and their parents. Princeton, N. J.: Princeton Univ. Pr., 1981. 427p.

I196　Rokeach, Milton. The open and closed mind: investigations into the nature of belief systems and personality systems. New York: Basic Books, 1960. 447p.

I197　Seligman, Lester G., and others. Patterns of recruitment: a state chooses its lawmakers. Chicago: Rand McNally, 1974. 269p.

I198　Verba, Sidney, and Gary R. Orren. Economic and political equality: the attitudes of American leaders. Cambridge, Mass.: JFK School of Govt., 1983. 60p.

Game theory, rational man modeling, and public choice is another area of research on individuals in American government and politics. Most of this literature, however, appears in article form in the major journals, and thus extended book treatments are indeed few. (Explicit theoretical treatments of this matter can be found in the empirical theory section below.) In addition to titles listed under decision making (above), some of the relevant titles include:

I199　Axelrod, Robert. Conflict of interest. Chicago: Markham, 1970. 216p.

I200　Claunch, John M., ed. Mathematical applications in political science. Dallas: Arnold Foundation, Southern Methodist Univ., 1965. 85p.

I201　Enelow, James N., and Melvin J. Hinich. The spatial theory of voting: an introduction. New York: Cambridge Univ. Pr., 1984. 238p.

I202　Herndon, James F., and Joseph L. Bernd, eds. Mathematical applications in political science. Charlottesville: Univ. of Virginia Pr., 1971. 92p.

I203　Mitchell, William C. Public choice in America: an introduction to American government. Chicago: Markham, 1971. 396p.

I204　Niemi, Richard G., and Herbert F. Weisberg, eds. Probability models of collective decision making. Columbus, Ohio: Merrill, 1972. 414p.

I205　Rapoport, Anatol, ed. Mathematical models in the social and behavioral sciences. New York: Wiley, 1983. 507p.

Groups and Processes

The extraordinary importance of pluralism in American political science has made the study of groups in the American political process one of the more enduring. Past research has shown the role of interest groups in defining political problems and getting them onto the political agenda, as well as their role in the policy formulation and implementation process. Their ubiquity was, in fact, one basis for Lowi's complaint, noted earlier, against the theory and practice of American government. Important representative works on interest groups include:

I206　Bauer, Raymond, and others. American business and public policy: the politics of foreign trade. New York: Atherton, 1963. 499p.

I207　Boneparth, Ellen, ed. Women, power and policy. Elmsford, N.Y.: Pergamon, 1982. 319p.

I208　Herring, E. Pendleton. Group representation before Congress. Baltimore: Johns Hopkins Univ. Pr., 1929. 309p.

I209　Latham, Earl. The group basis of politics: a study in basing-point legislation. Ithaca, N.Y.: Cornell Univ. Pr., 1952. 244p.

I210　McConnell, Grant. Private power and American democracy. New York: Knopf. 1967. 397p.

I211　Ornstein, Norman J., and Shirley Elder. Interest groups, lobbying, and policymaking. Washington, D.C.: Congressional Quarterly, 1978. 245p.

I212　Karnig, Albert K., and Susan Welch. Black representation and urban policy. Chicago: Univ. of Chicago Pr., 1980. 179p.

I213　Zeigler, Harmon. Interest groups in American society. Englewood Cliffs, N.J.: Prentice-Hall, 1964. 343p.

INSTITUTIONS AND PROCESSES

Given the discipline's European origins, the oldest orientation toward American government and politics focuses upon institutions. Because the founding fathers deliberately sought to fragment the institutions exercising power, American government provides a vast panorama for political research. By design, institutional power is fragmented horizontally and vertically. The horizontal fragmentation can be seen in the separation of powers among the executive, legislative, and judicial branches of government, and the vertical fragmentation can be seen in the federal arrangements with power and function distributed among national, state, and local governments. These formal divisions are further supplemented by political parties and a plethora of bureaucracies.

Congress

For each institution, substantial political research has not been wanting. The volume of material written on Congress, for example, is simply astonishing. So too is the diversity of tools and conceptual approaches. Congressional researchers have used mathematical models, statistical analyses of roll calls, budgets, elite opinion, biographical and historical description, and even case studies of single committees. The conceptual frameworks include systems theory, group theory, game theory, and even communications theory, to name but a few. The list that follows reflects a small portion of this enormous body of research.

I214   Bailey, Stephen K. Congress makes a law. New York: Columbia Univ. Pr., 1950. 282p.

I215   Burnham, James. Congress and the American tradition. Chicago: Regnery, 1959. 363p.

I216   Clausen, Aage R. How congressmen decide: a policy focus. New York: St. Martin's, 1973. 243p.

I217   Dodd, Lawrence C., and Bruce I. Oppenheimer, eds. Congress reconsidered. 2d ed. Washington, D.C.: Congressional Quarterly, 1981. 442p.

I218   Fenno, Richard F. The power of the purse: appropriations politics in Congress. Boston: Little, 1966. 704p.

I219   Fiorina, Morris P. Representatives, roll calls and constituencies. Lexington, Mass.: Lexington Books, 1974. 143p.

I220   Froman, Lewis A., Jr. The congressional process: strategies, rules, and procedures. Boston: Little, 1967. 217p.

I221   Hayes, Michael T. Lobbyists and legislators. New Brunswick, N.J.: Rutgers Univ. Pr., 1981. 200p.

I222   Jackson, John E. Constituencies and leaders in Congress. Cambridge, Mass.: Harvard Univ. Pr., 1974. 217p.

I223   Jones, Charles O. The United States Congress: people, place, and policy. Homewood, Ill.: Dorsey Pr., 1982. 477p.

I224   Kingdon, John W. Congressmen's voting decisions. 2d ed. New York: Harper, 1981. 313p.

I225   Matthews, Donald. U.S. senators and their world. Chapel Hill: Univ. of North Carolina Pr., 1960. 303p.

I226   Mayhew, David R. Congress: the electoral connection. New Haven, Conn.: Yale Univ. Pr., 1974. 194p.

I227   Morrow, William L. Congressional committees. New York: Scribner, 1969. 261p.

I228   Orfield, Gary. Congressional power: Congress and social change. New York: HBJ, 1975. 339p.

I229   Peabody, Robert L. Leadership in Congress: stability, succession, and change. Boston: Little, 1976. 522p.

I230   Saloma, John S., III. Congress and the new politics. Boston: Little, 1969. 293p.

I231   Sundquist, James L. The decline and resurgence of Congress. Washington, D.C.: Brookings, 1981. 500p.

I232   Truman, David B. The congressional party: a case study. New York: Wiley, 1959. 336p.

I233   Turner, Julius. Party and constituency: pressures on Congress. Baltimore: Johns Hopkins Univ. Pr., 1952. 190p.

I234   Wahlke, John C., and others. The legislative system: explorations in legislative behavior. New York: Wiley, 1962. 517p.

I235   Wildavsky, Aaron. The politics of the budgetary process. 3d ed. Boston: Little, 1979. 311p.

I236   Wilson, Woodrow. Congressional government. Cleveland: World Publishing, 1885. 344p.

The Presidency

In theory, Congress has charge of policy formation and the president implements that policy. We have witnessed trends over the past century in which the president has assumed a greater role in policy formation, exemplified in the presidential budget, the State of the Union address, and so on. At the same time, as we shall see below, the bureaucracy has become the focus of policy implementation, often without either direct control or supervision by the president. The role of the president, his staff, relations with Congress, and many other matters are examined in the following sampling of research on the American presidency.

I237 Binkley, Wilfred. President and Congress. New York: Knopf, 1947. 312p.

I238 Chamberlain, Lawrence H. The president, Congress, and legislation. New York: Columbia Univ. Pr., 1947. 478p.

I239 Corwin, Edward S. The president: office and powers. 4th ed. New York: New York Univ. Pr., 1964. 519p.

I240 Cronin, Thomas E. The state of the presidency. Boston: Little, 1975. 355p.

I241 Davis, Vincent Post, ed. The post-imperial presidency. New Brunswick, N.J.: Transaction Bks., 1980. 190p.

I242 Edwards, George C., III. Presidential influence in Congress. San Francisco: Freeman, 1980. 216p.

I243 Fenno, Richard F. The president's cabinet. Cambridge, Mass.: Harvard Univ. Pr., 1959. 326p.

I244 Finer, Herman. The presidency: crisis and re-generation. Chicago: Univ. of Chicago Pr., 1960. 374p.

I245 Hargrove, Erwin C. The power of the modern presidency. New York: Knopf, 1974. 353p.

I246 Heclo, Hugh. A government of strangers: ex-ecutive politics in Washington. Washington, D.C.: Brookings, 1977. 272p.

I247 Koenig, Louis W. The chief executive. 3d ed. New York: HBJ, 1975. 452p.

I248 Laski, Harold J. The modern presidency. New York: Harper, 1940. 278p.

I248A Lowi, Theodore. The personal president: pow-er invested, promise unfulfilled. Ithaca, N.Y.: Cornell Univ. Pr., 1985. 221p.

I249 Neustadt, Richard E. Presidential power: the politics of leadership from FDR to Carter. New York: Wiley, 1980. 286p.

I249A Page, Benjamin I., and Mark P. Petracca. The American presidency. New York: McGraw-Hill, 1983. 418p.

I250 Reedy, George E. The twilight of the presi-dency. New York: NAL, 1971. 191p.

I251 Rossiter, Clinton. The American presidency. 2d ed. New York: Harcourt, 1960. 281p.

I252 Schlesinger, Arthur M., Jr. The imperial pres-idency. Boston: Houghton, 1973. 505p.

I253 Sundquist, James L. Politics and policy: the Eisenhower, Kennedy, and Johnson years. Washington, D.C.: Brookings, 1968. 560p.

The Judiciary

Studies of the judicial system in America, par-ticularly of the Supreme Court and constitutional law, are among the oldest produced by American political scientists. In the last generation these studies have expanded to include a host of mate-rials on judicial behavior or, more generally, patterns underlying and reasons for judicial deci-sion making. During the past 15 years or so, the empirical study of criminal justice institutions has dramatically accelerated, so much so that this area has become an established part of many political science curricula, paralleling similar de-velopments in sociology and psychology. Once again the scope and amount of research in this area forbids more than a sampling of literature in the study of American judicial institutions.

I254 Abraham, Henry J. Freedom and the court. 2d ed. New York: Oxford Univ. Pr., 1972. 397p.

I255 Becker, Theodore L. Comparative judicial poli-tics: the political functioning of courts. Chicago: Rand McNally, 1970. 407p.

I256 Berger, Raoul. Government by judiciary: the transformation of the Fourteenth Amendment. Cambridge, Mass.: Harvard Univ. Pr., 1977. 483p.

I257 Bickel, Alexander M. The Supreme Court and the idea of process. New York: Harper, 1970. 210p.

I258 Cole, George F., ed. Criminal justice: law and politics. 3d ed. North Scituate, Mass.: Duxbury, 1980. 479p.

I259 Cox, Archibald. The Warren Court: constitu-tional decisions as an instrument of reform. Cambridge, Mass.: Harvard Univ. Pr., 1968. 144p.

I260 Eisenstein, James, and Herbert Jacob. Felony justice: an organizational analysis of criminal courts. Boston: Little, 1977. 322p.

I261 Feeley, Malcolm M. The process is punishment: handling cases in a lower criminal court. New York: Russell Sage, 1979. 330p.

I262 Goldman, Sheldon. Constitutional law and Supreme Court decision-making: cases and essays. New York: Harper, 1982. 800p.

I263 Konvitz, Milton R. A century of civil rights. New York: Columbia Univ. Pr., 1961. 272p.

I264 Kurland, Philip B. Politics, the Constitution, and the Warren Court. Chicago: Univ. of Chi-cago Pr., 1970. 222p.

I265 McCloskey, Robert G. The American Supreme Court. Chicago: Univ. of Chicago Pr., 1960. 260p.

I266 Mason, Alpheus T., and William M. Beaney. American constitutional law. 6th ed. Engle-wood Cliffs, N.J.: Prentice-Hall, 1978. 787p.

I267 Mendelson, Wallace, ed. The Constitution and

the Supreme Court. New York: Dodd, 1959. 520p.

I268 Miller, Arthur Selwyn. The Supreme Court: myth and reality. Westport, Conn.: Greenwood Pr., 1978. 260p.

I269 Murphy, Walter F., and C. Herman Pritchett, eds. Courts, judges, and politics. 3d ed. New York: Random, 1979. 769p.

I270 Pritchett, C. Herman. The American Constitution. 3d ed. New York: McGraw-Hill, 1977. 719p.

I270A ———. Constitutional law of the federal system. Englewood Cliffs, N.J.: Prentice-Hall, 1984. 382p.

I270B ———. Constitutional civil liberties. Englewood Cliffs, N.J.: Prentice-Hall, 1984. 406p.

I271 Rohde, David W., and Harold J. Spaeth. Supreme Court decision making. San Francisco: Freeman, 1976. 229p.

I272 Schubert, Glendon A. Judicial policy-making: the political role of the courts. Chicago: Scott, Foresman, 1965. 212p.

I273 ———. The judicial mind: attitudes and ideologies of Supreme Court justices. Evanston, Ill.: Northwestern Univ. Pr, 1965. 295p.

I274 ———. The judicial mind revisited: psychometric analysis of Supreme Court ideology. New York: Oxford Univ. Pr., 1974. 183p.

I275 Shapiro, Martin. Courts: a comparative and political analysis. Chicago: University of Chicago Pr., 1981. 245p.

I276 ———, and Douglas S. Hobbs. American constitutional law: cases and analyses. Cambridge, Mass.: Winthrop, 1978. 766p.

I277 Swisher, Carl B. American constitutional development. 2d ed. Boston: Houghton, 1954. 1,145p.

I278 Ulmer, S. Sidney, ed. Courts, law, and judicial processes. New York: Macmillan, 1981. 564p.

I279 Weinreb, Lloyd L. Denial of justice: criminal process in the United States. New York: Free Pr., 1977. 177p.

The Bureaucracy

Although not in the master blueprint of the founding fathers, the contemporary bureaucracy further fragments power at the federal and state level. Contrary to the once-popular image that bureaucracies are under the control of the executive, whether the president or the governor, the bureaucracies have proven remarkably intransigent. Some are independent agencies, but even those under the nominal control of the executive branch know how to use their legislative contracts to counterbalance executive influence. Bureaucratic politics have become another focal point for extensive political science research. Representative works include:

I280 Fried, Robert C. Performance in American bureaucracy. Boston: Little, 1976. 470p.

I281 Krislov, Samuel. Representative bureaucracy. Englewood Cliffs, N.J.: Prentice-Hall, 1974. 149p.

I282 Meltsner, Arnold J. Policy analysis in the bureaucracy. Berkeley: Univ. of California Pr., 1976. 310p.

I283 Niskanen, William A. Bureaucracy and representative government. Chicago: Aldine, 1971. 241p.

I284 Pressman, Jeffrey L., and Aaron Wildavsky. Implementation. Berkeley: Univ. of California Pr., 1973. 182p.

I285 Rourke, Francis E. Bureaucracy, politics, and public policy. 2d ed. Boston: Little, 1976. 208p.

I286 Seitz, Steven Thomas. Bureaucracy, policy, and the public. St. Louis: Mosby, 1978. 216p.

I287 Weiss, Carol H., and Allen H. Barton, eds. Making bureaucracies work. Beverly Hills, Calif.: Sage, 1980. 309p.

I288 Wilson, James Q., ed. The politics of regulation. New York: Basic Books, 1980. 468p.

I289 Woll, Peter. American bureaucracy. 2d ed. New York: Norton, 1977. 260p.

Federalism

While the separation of powers horizontally fragments the exercise of power in the American polity, the principles and practices of federalism do so vertically. No debate has been more pointed or bitter than that over the proper role of the states and localities vis-à-vis the national government. In fact, this is the only issue over which Americans fought a civil war. The importance of this issue has long been recognized in political science, and contemporary political scientists continue perspicacious analyses of federalist problems, promises, and performances. Some important works include:

I290 Barfield, Claude E. Rethinking federalism: block grants and federal, state, and local responsibilities. Washington, D.C.: American Enterprise Institute for Public Policy Research, 1981. 99p.

I291 Derthick, Martha. Between state and nation: regional organization of the United States. Washington, D.C.: Brookings, 1974. 242p.

I292 Elazar, Daniel J. American federalism: a view from the states. New York: Crowell, 1966. 228p.

I293 Friedrich, Carl J. Trends of federalism in theory and practice. New York: Praeger, 1968. 193p.

I294 Goldwin, Robert A., ed. A nation of states: essays on the American federal system. Chicago: Rand McNally, 1963. 148p.

I295 Hanus, Jerome, ed. The nationalization of state government. Lexington, Mass.: Lexington Books, 1981. 169p.

I296 Hawkins, Robert B., ed. American federalism: a new partnership for the republic. San Francisco: Institute for Contemporary Studies, 1982. 281p.

I297 Reagan, Michael D., and John Sanzone. The new federalism. 2d ed. New York: Oxford Univ. Pr., 1981. 196p.

I298 Wildavsky, Aaron, ed. American federalism in perspective. Boston: Little, 1967. 277p.

State and Local Governments

Related to the general issue of federalism is an emphasis on the study of state and local governments as alternative seats of the American democracy. Although early works in these areas were largely ideographic, a substantial body of comparative literature has developed in the field of state politics, once again following the lead of V. O. Key, Jr. Some of the more important, including Key's two classics, are listed below:

I299 Adrian, Charles R. Governing our fifty states and their communities. 4th ed. New York: McGraw-Hill, 1978. 138p.

I300 Anderson, William, and others. Government in the fifty states. New York: Holt, 1960. 509p.

I301 Dye, Thomas R. Politics in states and communities. 3d ed. Englewood Cliffs, N.J.: Prentice-Hall, 1977. 494p.

I302 Fenton, John H. Midwest politics. New York: Holt, 1966. 244p.

I303 Francis, Wayne L. Legislative issues in the fifty states. Chicago: Rand McNally, 1967. 129p.

I304 Jacob, Herbert, and Kenneth Vines, eds. Politics in the American states: a comparative analysis. 3d ed. Boston: Little, 1976. 509p.

I305 Jewell, Malcolm E. The state legislature: politics and practice. New York: Random, 1962. 146p.

I306 Key, V. O., Jr. American state politics: an introduction: New York: Knopf, 1966. 289p.

I307 ———. Southern politics in state and nation. New York: Knopf, 1949. 675p.

I308 Lockard, Duane. New England state politics. Princeton, N.J.: Princeton Univ. Pr., 1959. 347p.

I309 Sharkansky, Ira. The maligned states: accomplishments, problems, and opportunities. 2d ed. New York: McGraw Hill, 1978. 162p.

Early studies of county and local government often were excessively formal or reft by moral indictment. But as America became an urban society, and that surprisingly only during the past generation, political science began focusing its inquiry on metropolitan problems and governance. The literature has expanded enormously over the past two decades, and some of the key contributions include:

I310 Aggar, Robert E., and others. The rulers and the ruled: political power and impotence in American communities. New York: Wiley, 1964. 789p.

I311 Banfield, Edward C. Political influence. Glencoe, Ill.: Free Pr., 1961. 345p.

I312 ———. The unheavenly city: the nature and future of our urban crisis. Boston: Little, 1968. 308p.

I313 ———. The unheavenly city revisited. Boston: Little, 1974. 358p.

I314 ———, and James Q. Wilson. City politics. Cambridge, Mass.: MIT Pr. and Harvard Univ. Pr., 1963. 362p.

I315 Dommel, Paul R., and others. Decentralizing urban policy: case studies in community development. Washington, D.C.: Brookings, 1982. 271p.

I316 Greenstone, J. David, and Paul E. Peterson. Race and authority in urban politics. Chicago: Univ. of Chicago Pr., 1973. 364p.

I317 Greer, Scott. Governing the metropolis. New York: Wiley, 1962. 150p.

I318 Gulick, Luther H. The metropolitan problem and American ideas. New York: Knopf, 1962. 166p.

I319 Katznelson, Ira. City trenches. New York: Pantheon, 1981. 267p.

I320 Lineberry, Robert, and Ira Sharkansky. Urban politics and public policy. 3d ed. New York: Harper, 1978. 421p.

I321 Peterson, Paul. City limits. Chicago: Univ. of Chicago Pr., 1981. 268p.

I322 Presthus, Robert. Men at the top: a study in community power. New York: Oxford Univ. Pr., 1964. 485p.

I323 Sayre, Wallace, and Herbert Kaufman. Governing New York City. New York: Russell Sage, 1960. 815p.

I324 Shank, Allan. Political power and the urban crisis. Boston: Holbrook, 1970. 532p.

I325 Wilson, James Q., ed. City politics and public policy. New York: Wiley, 1968. 300p.

I326 ———. Varieties of police behavior: the management of law and order in eight communities. Cambridge, Mass.: Harvard Univ. Pr., 1968. 309p.

Political Parties

Two extra-constitutional institutions also require our attention: political parties and the press. Political scientists ignored these institutions long after their practical importance had been established, almost as if the constitutional blueprints created blindspots when viewing the real political world. The increased emphasis on an empirical political science helped remedy these deficiencies, and the literature on parties has become an integral part of virtually all political science curricula. Some of the more important works include:

I327 Binkley, Wilfred. American political parties: their natural history. New York: Knopf, 1943. 420p.

I328 Burns, James M. The deadlock of democracy. Englewood Cliffs, N.J.: Prentice-Hall, 1963. 388p.

I329 Chambers, William Nisbet. Political parties in a new nation: the American experience, 1776–1809. New York: Oxford Univ. Pr., 1963. 231p.

I330 Crotty, William J., and Gary C. Jacobson. American parties in decline. Boston: Little, 1980. 267p.

I331 Eldersveld, Samuel J. Political parties: a behavioral analysis. Chicago: Rand McNally, 1964. 613p.

I332 Greenstone, J. David. Labor in American politics. (Phoenix ed.) Chicago: Univ. of Chicago Pr., 1977. 458p.

I333 Hofstadter, Richard. The idea of a party system: the rise of legitimate opposition in the United States 1780–1840. Berkeley: Univ. of California Pr., 1969. 280p.

I334 Key, V. O., Jr. Politics, parties and pressure groups. 5th ed. New York: Crowell, 1964. 738p.

I335 Ladd, Everett C., Jr., and Charles D. Hadley. Transformations of the American party system. 2d ed. New York: Norton, 1978. 406p.

I336 Leiserson, Avery. Parties and politics: an institutional and behavioral approach. New York: Knopf, 1958. 379p.

I337 Lipset, Seymour Martin, ed. Party coalitions in the 1980s. San Francisco: Institute for Contemporary Studies, 1981. 480p.

I338 Macridis, Roy C., ed. Political parties: contemporary trends and ideas. New York: Harper, 1967. 268p.

I339 Mazmanian, Daniel A. Third parties in presidential elections. Washington, D.C.: Brookings, 1974. 163p.

I340 Petrocik, John R. Party coalitions: realignments and the decline of the New Deal party system. Chicago: Univ. of Chicago Pr., 1981. 215p.

I341 Pomper, Gerald M., ed. Party renewal in America. New York: Praeger, 1980. 204p.

I342 Ranney, Austin, and Willmoore Kendall. Democracy and the American party system. New York: Harcourt, 1956. 550p.

I343 Schattschneider, Elmer E. Party government. New York: Rinehart, 1942. 219p.

I344 Sorauf, Frank J. Political parties in the American system. Boston: Little, 1964. 194p.

The Media

Studies of the media and their relation to American government and politics is one of the latest additions to legitimate political inquiry. The role of media manipulation in campaigning and efforts to influence public opinion has become the object of considerable scrutiny. Some contributions to this literature include:

I345 Agranoff, Robert. The new style election campaign. 2d ed. Boston: Holbrook Pr., 1976. 392p.

I346 MacKuen, Michael Bruce, and Steven Lane Coombs, eds. More than news: media power in public affairs. Beverly Hills, Calif.: Sage, 1981. 231p.

I347 Patterson, Thomas E., and Robert D. McClure. The unseeing eye: the myth of television power in national politics. New York: Putnam, 1976. 218p.

I348 Rosenbloom, Henry. Politics and the media. Rev. ed. Fitzroy, Australia: Scribe Pubs., 1978. 160p.

I349 Rubin, Bernard. Media, politics, and democracy. New York: Oxford Univ. Pr., 1977. 192p.

THE STUDY OF SOCIETY AND CULTURE

The study of American society and culture has taken on reinvigorated meaning in light of the comparative research that follows in the next section. Studies of other countries have uncovered national traditions, habits, and "national character" that help explain politics within these nations. From here it was a short step for American political scientists to realize that their understanding of government and politics might be parochial and lacking generalization without some knowledge of the broader social and cultural context within which American politics occurs and from which American politics might be compared with that of other nations. These studies often come from cognate disciplines and take on a variety of conceptual and methodological forms. Some of the more important include:

I350 Boorstin, Daniel. The genius of Amerian politics. Chicago: Univ. of Chicago Pr., 1953. 201p.

I351 Glazer, Nathan, and Daniel Patrick Moynihan. Beyond the melting pot. Cambridge, Mass.: MIT Pr. and Harvard Univ. Pr., 1963. 360p.

I352 Hartz, Louis. The liberal tradition in America. New York: Harcourt, 1955. 329p.

I353 Hofstadter, Richard. The American political tradition. New York: Knopf, 1965. 378p.

I354 Lippmann, Walter. Essays in the public philosophy. New York: NAL, 1956. 144p.

I355 Potter, David M. People of plenty. Chicago: Univ. of Chicago Pr., 1954. 219p.

COMPARATIVE GOVERNMENT AND POLITICS

The study of countries other than the United States always has been a part of American political science, but like the study of American government, these area studies largely were legalistic and formalistic. The emphasis focused on the constitutional democracies of Europe until World War II, when it became increasingly clear that the continents of Asia, Africa, and South America no longer could be ignored by students of comparative government. Political scientists, many of whom had served the United States government in military and nonmilitary roles, also began focusing on dictatorships as permanent alternatives to constitutional democracy. The proliferation of new nation-states following World War II provided further incentive for the expansion of area studies curricula within political science.

The confluence of personal experience and the dramatic expansion in the number of nation-states led to a veritable explosion in comparative research focusing on the politics as well as the governments of other nations. This expanded scope of comparative political inquiry was further intensified by the behavioral movement within political science. Although behavioralism's impact on area studies was at first modest, its long-range impact proved enormous, eventually resulting in a split between area specialists and cross-national researchers. The former relied on description and modest analytic techniques inherited from historiography, while the latter emphasized bolder tools of concept formation and operationalization, classification and comparison, theory and explanation. The area specialists concentrated on intensive ideographic analyses while the cross-national researchers focused upon extensive and nomothetic analyses.

Masses and Elites

Systematic study of foreign voting behavior has been limited, so much so that the cumulative research on all foreign countries combined pales in comparison to the volume of material written on American voting behavior. Limited funds, scarce survey research facilities, and limited interest among foreign colleagues have contributed to this imbalance. The slow diffusion of American political science as a *science* further hinders foreign research in this area. Lacking the resources and institutional bases for extensive survey research overseas, many American political scientists turned to elite interviewing and other methods for bringing behavioral tools to the study of comparative politics without the attendant costs of mass-based survey research. One consequence of the greater comparativist emphasis on elites has been a tendency to present a less balanced picture regarding the role of elites versus masses in politics than that found in the research on American political process.

Comparative mass-based research includes:

I356 Allardt, Erik, and Stein Rokkan, eds. Mass politics: studies in political sociology. New York: Free Pr., 1969. 400p.

I357 Almond, Gabriel, and Sidney Verba. The civic culture: political attitudes and democracy in five nations. Princeton, N.J.: Princeton Univ. Pr., 1963. 562p.

I358 ———, eds. The civic culture revisited: an analytic study. Boston: Little, 1980. 421p.

I359 Barnes, Samuel H., and others. Political action: mass participation in five Western democracies. Beverly Hills, Calif.: Sage, 1979. 607p.

I360 Butler, David, and others, eds. Democracy at the polls: a comparative study of competitive national elections. Washington, D.C.: American Enterprise Institute, 1981. 367p.

I361 Butler, David, and Donald Stokes. Political change in Great Britain: the evolution of electoral choice. 2d ed. New York: Macmillan, 1974. 500p.

I362 Czudnowski, Moshe M. Comparing political behavior. Beverly Hills, Calif.: Sage, 1976. 178p.

I362A Dalton, Russel, J., and others, eds. Electoral change in advanced industrial democracies: realignment or dealignment? Princeton, N.J.: Princeton Univ. Pr., 1984. 504p.

I363 Di Palma, Giuseppe. Mass politics in industrial societies: a reader in comparative politics. Chicago: Markham, 1972. 411p.

I364 Dogan, Mattei, and Richard Rose, eds. European politics: a reader. Boston: Little, 1971. 590p.

I365 Inglehart, Ronald. The silent revolution: changing values and political styles among Western publics. Princeton, N.J.: Princeton Univ. Pr., 1977. 482p.

I365A Noelle-Neumann, Elisabeth. The spiral of silence: public opinion—our social skin. Chicago: Univ. of Chicago Pr., 1984. 184p.

I366 Rose, Richard, ed. Electoral behavior: a comparative handbook. New York: Free Pr., 1974. 753p.

I367 Szabo, Stephen F. The successor generation: international perspectives of postwar Europeans. London: Butterworth, 1983. 183p.

I368 Verba, Sidney, and others. Participation and political equality: a seven-nation comparison. New York: Cambridge Univ. Pr., 1978. 394p.

The study of political elites is, as mentioned, much more common. Some contributions in this area include:

I369 Aberbach, Joel D., and others. Bureaucrats and politicians in Western democracies. Cambridge, Mass.: Harvard Univ. Pr., 1981. 308p.

I370 Bendix, Reinhard. Kings or people: power and the mandate to rule. Berkeley: Univ. of California Pr., 1979. 692p.

I371 Cohen, Abner. The politics of elite culture: explorations in the dramaturgy of power in a modern African society. Berkeley: Univ. of California Pr., 1981. 257p.

I372 Kautsky, John. The politics of aristocratic empires. Chapel Hill: Univ. of North Carolina Pr., 1982. 416p.

I373 Janowitz, Morris. The military in the political development of new nations: an essay in comparative analysis. Chicago: Univ. of Chicago Pr., 1964. 134p.

I374 Putnam, Robert D. The comparative study of political elites. Englewood Cliffs, N.J.: Prentice-Hall, 1976. 246p.

I375 Pye, Lucian W., ed. Communications and political development. Princeton, N.J.: Princeton Univ. Pr., 1963. 381p. [Studies in political development I]

Groups and Processes

The American study of pressure groups, interest groups, and more generally organized interests has provided an orientation that has influenced if not motivated similar studies in other countries. Comparative research has documented the role of such groups at all stages of decision making, from the definition of political problems and aggregation of social interests, through agenda setting and policy formation, to the process of implementing and evaluating public policy. Although interest groups may not have the same power in other countries that they wield in the United States, it is clear that they do perform important functions in totalitarian as well as democratic societies. Some examples of this research include:

I376 Eckstein, Harry. Pressure group politics. Stanford, Calif.: Stanford Univ. Pr., 1960. 168p.

I377 Ehrmann, Henry, ed. Interest groups on four continents. Pittsburgh: Univ. of Pittsburgh Pr., 1958. 316p.

I378 Finer, Samuel E. The anonymous empire. Rev. ed. London: Pall Mall, 1966. 173p.

I379 La Palombara, Joseph. Interest groups in Italian politics. Princeton, N.J.: Princeton Univ. Pr., 1964. 452p.

I380 Millen, Bruce H. The political role of labor in developing countries. Washington, D.C.: Brookings, 1963. 148p.

I381 Palamountain, Joseph. The politics of distribution. London: Faber, 1961. 395p.

I382 Skilling, H. Gordon, and Franklyn Griffiths. Interest groups in Soviet politics. Princeton, N.J.: Princeton Univ. Pr., 1971. 433p.

INSTITUTIONS AND PROCESSES

The study of governmental institutions is the oldest component of comparative government and politics. The tradition dates back to Aristotle's *Politics*, and similar examples can be found in the later classics such as Montesquieu's *The spirit of the laws*. The last generation of comparative government studies reflects a curious mix of *Staatswissenschaft* from early American political science and more recent behavioral approaches. Some examples of the more formalistic research include:

I383   Andrews, William G., ed. European political institutions: a comparative government reader. 2d ed. Princeton, N.J.: Van Nostrand Reinhold, 1966. 587p.

I384   Bagehot, Walter. The English constitution. Ithaca, N.Y.: Cornell Univ. Pr., 1966. 310p.

I385   Blaustein, Albert P., and Eric B. Blaustein, eds. Constitutions of dependencies and special sovereignties. Dobbs Ferry, N.Y.: Oceana, 1975. 2v.

I386   Blondel, Jean. An introduction to comparative government. New York: Praeger, 1969. 557p.

I387   Bryce, James. Modern democracies. New York: Macmillan, 1921. 2v.

I388   Fainsod, Merle. How Russia is ruled. Cambridge, Mass.: Harvard Univ. Pr., 1963. 684p.

I389   Finer, Herman. Theory and practice of modern government. Rev. ed. New York: Holt, 1949. 954p.

I390   Finer, Samuel E. Comparative government. New York: Basic Books, 1971. 615p.

I391   Friedrich, Carl J. Constitutional government and democracy. 4th ed. Waltham, Mass.: Blaisdell, 1968. 728p.

I392   ———, and Zbigniew Brzezinski. Totalitarian dictatorship and autocracy. 2d ed. New York: Praeger, 1966. 439p.

I393   Spiro, Herbert J. Government by constitution. New York: Random, 1959. 496p.

I394   Wheare, Kenneth C. Modern constitutions. New York: Oxford Univ. Pr., 1951. 216p.

I395   Young, Roland. The British parliament. London: Faber, 1962. 259p.

I396   Zurcher, Arnold J., ed. Constitutions and constitutional trends since World War II. 2d ed. New York: New York Univ. Pr., 1955. 351p.

More recent institutional studies include:

I397   Bertsch, Gary K., and others. Comparing political systems: power and policy in three worlds. New York: Wiley, 1978. 515p.

I398   Bill, James A., and Robert L. Hardgrave, Jr. Comparative politics: the quest for theory. Columbus, Ohio: Merrill, 1973. 261p.

I399   Blondel, Jean. Comparative legislatures. Englewood Cliffs, N.J.: Prentice-Hall, 1973. 173p.

I400   Dahl, Robert A. Polyarchy: participation and opposition. New Haven, Conn.: Yale Univ. Pr., 1971. 257p.

I400A Dodd, Lawrence C. Coalitions in parliamentary government. Princeton, N.J.: Princeton Univ. Pr., 1976. 282p.

I401   Fogelman, Edwin, and John V. Gillespie. Comparative politics: conditions for effective democracy. Boston: Little, 1972. 190p.

I402   Jackman, Robert W. Politics and social equality: a comparative analysis. New York: Wiley, 1975. 225p.

I403   Katz, Richard. A theory of parties and electoral systems. Baltimore: Johns Hopkins Univ. Pr., 1980. 151p.

I404   Kornberg, Allan, ed. Legislatures in comparative perspective. New York: McKay, 1973. 457p.

I405   La Palombara, Joseph. Politics within nations. Englewood Cliffs, N.J.: Prentice-Hall, 1974. 625p.

I405A Lijphart, Arend. Democracies: patterns of majoritarian and consensus government in twenty-one countries. New Haven, Conn.: Yale Univ. Pr., 1984. 229p.

I406   Lipset, Seymour Martin. Political man: the social bases of politics. Expanded ed. Baltimore: Johns Hopkins Univ. Pr., 1981. 586p.

I407   MacRae, Duncan, Jr. Parliament, parties and society in France, 1946–1958. New York: St. Martin's, 1967. 375p.

I408   Macridis, Roy C., and Bernard E. Brow. Comparative politics: notes and readings. 4th ed. Homewood, Ill.: Dorsey Pr., 1972. 534p.

I409   Nordlinger, Eric A. On the autonomy of the democratic state. Cambridge, Mass.: Harvard Univ. Pr, 1981. 239p.

I410   Powell, G. Bingham. Contemporary democracies: participation, stability, and violence. Cambridge, Mass.: Harvard Univ. Pr., 1982. 279p.

I411   Rae, Douglas. The political consequences of electoral laws. New Haven, Conn.: Yale Univ. Pr., 1967. 173p.

Political Parties

From political oppositions in Western democracies to the totalitarian parties of the East, the political party has been the object of sustained comparative research. In contrast to its less formal role in American politics, the political party abroad often serves a formal electoral and governing function. The European parliamentary system organizes its executive through party victory in the legislative elections, and party discipline is generally much stronger than in the United States. The totalitarian party in the Eastern bloc, similarly, formally engages in problem definition, agenda setting, policy formation, implementation, and even evaluation. Such functions imply long-range planning by foreign political parties, and in this respect they differ most from those in the U.S. Some representative works on parties include:

I412 Alford, Robert R. Party and society: the Anglo-American democracies. Chicago: Rand McNally, 1963. 396p.

I413 Allardt, Erik, and Yrjö Littunen, eds. Cleavages, ideologies and party systems: contributions to comparative political sociology. Helsinki: Transactions of the Westermarck Society, 1964. 463p.

I414 Blondel, Jean. Voters, parties and leaders: the social fabric of British politics. Rev. ed. Baltimore: Penguin, 1974. 272p.

I415 Budge, Ian, and Dennis Farlie. Voting and party competition: a theoretical critique and synthesis applied to surveys from ten democracies. New York: Wiley, 1977. 555p.

I416 Dahl, Robert A., ed. Political oppositions in Western democracies. New Haven, Conn.: Yale Univ. Pr., 1966. 458p.

I417 Duverger, Maurice. Political parties. 2d ed., rev. New York: Wiley, 1962. 439p.

I418 Epstein, Leon D. Political parties in Western democracies. New York: Praeger, 1967. 374p.

I419 Hodgkin, Thomas. African political parties: an introductory guide. Baltimore: Penguin, 1961. 217p.

I420 La Palombara, Joseph, and Myron Weiner, eds. Political parties and political development. Princeton, N.J.: Princeton Univ. Pr., 1966. 487p.

I421 Lijphart, Arend. The politics of accommodation: pluralism and democracy in the Netherlands. 2d ed., rev. Berkeley: Univ. of California Pr., 1975. 231p.

I422 Lipset, Seymour M., and Stein Rokkan. Party systems and voter alignments: cross-national perspectives. New York: Free Pr., 1967. 554p.

I423 McDonald, Neil A. The study of political parties. New York: Random, 1963. 97p.

I424 Neumann, Sigmund, ed. Modern political parties. 4th ed. New York: Knopf, 1962. 460p.

I425 Ostrogorski, M. I. Democracy and the organization of political parties. New York: Haskell House, 1970. 2v.

Politics and Development

The relation of government and politics to society and culture has become a matter of considerable interest since World War II. Reasons for this interest include the rapid spread of communist ideology, the social and cultural origins for totalitarianism and democracy, the social and cultural bases for economic and political development, and the problems of political order under conditions of rapid social change. The following represent works on one or more of these topics, including political modernization and political development.

I427 Almond, Gabriel. The appeals of communism. Princeton, N.J.: Princeton Univ. Pr., 1954. 415p.

I428 ———, and James Smoot Coleman. The politics of the developing areas. Princeton, N.J.: Princeton Univ. Pr., 1960. 591p.

I429 Apter, David E. The politics of modernization. Chicago: Univ. of Chicago Pr., 1965. 481p.

I430 Arendt, Hannah. The origins of totalitarianism. Rev. ed. New York: HBJ, 1973. 527p.

I431 Banfield, Edward C. The moral basis of a backward society. Glencoe, Ill.: Free Pr., 1958. 204p.

I432 Bell, Daniel. The coming of post-industrial society: a venture in social forecasting. New York: Basic Books, 1973. 507p.

I433 Edinger, Lewis J., ed. Political leadership in industrial societies: studies in comparative analysis. New York: Wiley, 1967. 76p.

I434 Friedrich, Carl J., ed. Totalitarianism. Cambridge, Mass.: Harvard Univ. Pr., 1954. 346p.

I435 Holt, Robert T., and John E. Turner. The political basis of economic development. Princeton, N.J.: Van Nostrand Reinhold, 1966. 410p.

I436 Huntington, Samuel. Political order in changing societies. New Haven, Conn.: Yale Univ. Pr, 1968. 488p.

I437 Inkeles, Alex. Exploring individual modernity. New York: Columbia Univ. Pr., 1983. 376p.

I438 Kautsky, John H. Political change in underdeveloped countries: nationalism and communism. New York: Wiley, 1962. 347p.

I439 La Palombara, Joseph, ed. Bureaucracy and political development. Princeton, N.J.: Princeton Univ. Pr., 1963. 487p.

I440 Lasswell, Harold D., and others. The comparative study of symbols. Stanford, Calif.: Stanford Univ. Pr., 1952. 87p.

I441 Lasswell, Harold D., and Daniel Lerner, eds. World revolutionary elites. Cambridge, Mass.: MIT Pr., 1965. 478p.

I442 Lerner, Daniel. The passing of traditional society: modernizing the Middle East. Glencoe, Ill.: Free Pr., 1958. 466p.

I443 Levy, Marion J. Modernization and the structure of society: a setting for international affairs. Princeton, N.J.: Princeton Univ. Pr., 1966. 855p.

I444 Moore, Barrington, Jr. The origins of dictatorship and democracy: lord and peasant in the making of the modern world. Boston: Beacon, 1966. 559p.

I445 Neumann, Franz L. The democratic and authoritarian state. New York: Free Pr., 1957.
303p.

I446 Organski, A. F. K. The stages of political development. New York: Knopf, 1965. 229p.

I447 Pye, Lucian. Politics, personality, and nation-
building: Burma's search for identity. New
Haven, Conn.: Yale Univ. Pr., 1962. 307p.

I448 ——, and Sidney Verba, eds. Political culture
and political development. Princeton, N.J.:
Princeton Univ. Pr., 1965. 574p.

I449 Riggs, Fred W. Administration in developing
countries: the theory of prismatic society. Boston: Houghton, 1964. 477p.

I450 Rustow, Dankwart A. A world of nations:
problems of political modernization. Washington, D.C.: Brookings, 1967. 306p.

I451 Talmon, Jacob L. The origins of totalitarian
democracy. London: Secker & Warburg, 1952.
366p.

I452 Triska, Jan F. Political development and political change in Eastern Europe: a comparative
study. Denver: Univ. of Denver Pr., 1975. 74p.

I453 Ulam, Adam B. The new face of Soviet totalitarianism. Cambridge, Mass.: Harvard Univ.
Pr., 1963. 233p.

Cross-National Research

Perhaps the most impressive and controversial
development in comparative research during the
past generation has been the enormous proliferation of cross-national studies and data archives.
Here the nation-state becomes the unit of analysis, and data for different countries on a host of
variables provide a foundation for systematic
comparison and analysis. This approach again
illustrates the impact of behavioralism on comparative analysis; only here, unlike the survey
research cited earlier, the focus is on the state
itself, and the methodological tools are more
econometric than psychometric. Apart from
some already mentioned, additional contributions to this literature include:

I454 Banks, Arthur S., and Robert B. Textor. A
cross-polity survey. Cambridge, Mass.: MIT
Pr., 1963. 1476p.

I455 Dogan, Mattei, and Stein Rokkan, eds. Social
ecology. Cambridge, Mass.: MIT Pr., 1974.
607p.

I455A Dogan, Mattei, and Dominque Pelassy. How to
compare nations: strategies in comparative politics. Chatham, N.J.: Chatham, 1984. 185p.

I456 Merritt, Richard L., and Stein Rokkan. Comparing nations: the use of quantitative data in
cross-national research. New Haven, Conn.:
Yale Univ. Pr., 1966. 585p.

I457 Przeworski, Adam, and Henry Teune. The
logic of comparative social inquiry. New York:
Wiley-Interscience, 1970. 153p.

I458 Russett, Bruce M., and others. World handbook of political and social indicators. New
Haven, Conn.: Yale Univ. Pr, 1964. 373p.

I459 Taylor, Charles, and Michael C. Hudson.
World handbook of political and social indicators. 2d ed. New Haven, Conn.: Yale Univ. Pr.,
1972. 443p.

INTERNATIONAL POLITICS, LAW, AND ORGANIZATION

The developmental evolution of international
relations within political science closely parallels
that found in American government. The early
phase heavily emphasized historiography, case
study, description, and/or legal and administrative formalisms. The second phase witnessed a
growing interest in nomothetic reasoning—that
is, a focus on patterns across events as opposed to
the idiosyncrasies of specific events, coupled
with some effort to explain these patterns. The
third, or scientific, phase emerged after World
War II under the guise of the behavioral movement. This phase emphasized the need for testa-
bility in explanations and the expectation that
empirical testing would be made. The fourth
phase, generally associated with applied mathematical reasoning, emerged within the last 15 or
20 years. This persuasion, like its analogue in
American government and politics (i.e., the
study of rational choice and public choice at the
micro level, and forecasting at the macro level)
focused upon the need to ground empirically
testable hypotheses within a larger framework of
explicit assumptions and propositions. That is,
the need to specify the relation among hypotheses became more important than the need for
empirical testing.

Like American goverment and politics, the
study of international relations simultaneously
houses representatives from all these traditions.
The study of comparative government and politics differs from American and IR (international
relations) in that the fourth phase has few practitioners, and, indeed, its third phase is generally
less developed than its analogues in American
and IR. This diversity is a continued source of
tension and it further contributes to the fragmentation of an already diverse discipline.

Researchers from all four "traditions" share certain substantive concerns such as the causes and prevention of war. These concerns cover all phases of the decision process, from problem discovery and definition to the evaluation of government actions. One major debate, found in a variety of forms, centers upon a distinction between idealists and realists, with the former emphasizing moral, legal, and generally more formal solutions to the problem of war, while the latter focus on power and self-interest. Idealists have sometimes been accused of naiveté while "realists" were in turn accused of being Machiavellian or amoral, focusing as they did on political (e.g., power) solutions to the problem of war.

Still, methodological differences are perhaps the most decisive, and these differences also tend to be reflected in the units of analysis most likely emphasized in each tradition's analyses. There is, for example, far greater focus on individuals in the quasi-historical and descriptive research. Conversely, the later approaches focus more on social, cultural, and nation-state variables, although some excellent micro-level mathematical treatments of international relations also have emerged in recent years.

The Traditional Study of Individuals

The study of diplomat and statesperson, as noted above, concentrates among phase one researchers, although some excellent examples also appear in phase two research. Because historical studies and biographies of statespersons are too numerous to list here, and given their often marginal contribution to political science as science, only a few important citations will be made here.

I460   Lasswell, Harold D. World politics and personal insecurity. London: Whittlesey; New York: McGraw-Hill, 1935. 307p.

I461   Rogow, Arnold. James Forrestal: a study of personality politics and policy. New York: Macmillan, 1963. 397p.

I462   Wolfenstein, E. Victor. The revolutionary personality: Lenin, Trotsky and Ghandi. Princeton, N.J.: Princeton Univ. Pr., 1967. 330p.

The Study of Nation-States

Without question the most common unit of analysis found in the international relations literature is the nation-state. Among the contributions in this area are:

I463   Aron, Raymond. Peace and war: a theory of international relations. Tr. by Richard Howard and Annette B. Fox. New York: Doubleday, 1966. 820p.

I464   Brodie, Bernard. Strategy in the missile age. Princeton, N.J.: Princeton Univ. Pr., 1959. 423p.

I465   Claude, Inis L., Jr. Power and international relations. New York: Random, 1962. 310p.

I466   Falk, Richard. Human rights and state sovereignty. New York: Holmes & Meier, 1980. 251p.

I467   Frankel, Joseph. International relations in a changing world. New York: Oxford Univ. Pr., 1979. 211p.

I468   Halpern, Morton H. Limited war in the nuclear age. New York: Wiley, 1963. 191p.

I469   Herz, John H. Political realism and political idealism: a study in theories and realities. Chicago: Univ. of Chicago Pr., 1951. 275p.

I470   ———. International politics in the atomic age. New York: Columbia Univ. Pr., 1959. 360p.

I471   Hoffman, Stanley. Duties beyond borders: on the limits and possibilities of ethical international politics. Syracuse, N.Y.: Syracuse Univ. Pr., 1981. 252p.

I472   Kahn, Herman. On thermonuclear war: three lectures and several suggestions. 2d ed. New York: Free Pr., 1969. 668p.

I473   Kissinger, Henry A. The necessity for choice: prospects of American foreign policy. New York: Harper, 1961. 387p.

I474   Knorr, Klaus E. The war potential of nations. Princeton, N.J.: Princeton Univ. Pr., 1956. 310p.

I475   ———, and Thornton Read, eds. Limited strategic war. Princeton, N.J.: Princeton Univ. Pr., 1960. 258p.

I476   Morgenthau, Hans J. Politics among nations: the struggle for power and peace. 5th ed. New York: Knopf, 1972. 617p.

I477   ———. In defense of the national interest: a critical examination of American foreign policy. New York: Knopf, 1951. 283p.

I478   Organski, A. F. K. World politics. 2d ed. New York: Knopf, 1968. 509p.

I479   Osgood, Robert E. Ideals on self-interest in America's foreign relations: the great transformation of the twentieth century. Chicago: Univ. of Chicago Pr., 1953. 491p.

I480   Snyder, Glenn H. Deterrence and defense: toward a theory of national security. Princeton, N.J.: Princeton Univ. Pr., 1961. 294p.

I481   Sprout, Harold H., and Margaret Sprout. Foundations of international politics. Princeton, N.J.: Van Nostrand Reinhold, 1962. 734p.

Contemporary research in international relations may utilize middle-range theories, quantitative data and analyses, and in some cases sophisticated mathematical models in the study of war and peace. Examples of works in these areas include the following. See also, Thomas C. Schelling, *The strategy of conflict*, described at I146.

I482 Ashley, Richard K. The political economy of war and peace. London: Frances Pinter, 1980. 384p.

I483 Azar, Edward. Probe for peace: small state hostilities. Minneapolis: Burgess, 1973. 89p.

I484 Bueno de Mesquita, Bruce. The war trap. New Haven, Conn.: Yale Univ. Pr., 1981. 223p.

I485 Choucri, N., and Robert C. North. Nations in conflict: national growth and international violence. San Francisco: Freeman, 1975. 356p.

I486 Deutsch, Karl W. The analysis of international relations. 2d ed. Englewood Cliffs, N.J.: Prentice-Hall, 1978. 312p.

I487 Fox, William T. R., ed. Theoretical aspects of international relations. Notre Dame, Ind.: Notre Dame Univ. Pr., 1959. 118p.

I488 Gilpin, Robert. War and change in world politics. New York: Cambridge Univ. Pr, 1981. 272p.

I489 Hoffman, Stanley. Contemporary theory in international relations. Englewood Cliffs, N.J.: Prentice-Hall,1960. 203p.

I490 Hollist, W. Ladd, ed. Exploring competitive arms processes: applications of mathematical modeling and computer simulation in arms policy analysis. New York: Dekker, 1978. 279p.

I491 Holsti, Ole R. Crisis, escalation, war. Montreal: McGill-Queen's Univ. Pr., 1972. 290p.

I492 Jervis, Robert. Perception and misperception in international politics. Princeton, N.J.: Princeton Univ. Pr., 1976. 445p.

I493 Kaplan, Morton A. System and process in international politics. New York: Wiley, 1957. 280p.

I494 ———, ed. New approaches to international relations. New York: St. Martin's, 1968. 518p.

I495 Katzenstein, Peter J. Between power and plenty: foreign economic policies of advanced industrial states. Madison: Univ. of Wisconsin Pr., 1978. 344p.

I496 Kelman, Herbert C., ed. International behavior: a social psychological analysis. New York: Holt, 1965. 626p.

I496A Keohane, Robert O. After hegemony: cooperation and discord in the world political economy. Princeton, N.J.: Princeton Univ. Pr., 1984. 290p.

I497 Knorr, Klaus E., and James Rosenau, eds. Contending approaches to international relations. Princeton, N.J.: Princeton Univ. Pr., 1969. 297p.

I498 Knorr, Klaus, and others, eds. The international system: theoretical essays. Princeton, N.J.: Princeton Univ. Pr., 1961. 237p.

I499 Liska, George. International equilibrium: theoretical essays on the politics and organization of security. Cambridge, Mass.: Harvard Univ. Pr., 1957. 223p.

I500 McClelland, Charles A. Theory and the international system. New York: Macmillan, 1966. 138p.

I501 Mueller, John E., ed. Approaches to measurement in international relations. New York: Appleton, 1969. 311p.

I502 Organski, A. F. K., and Jacek Kugler. The war ledger. Chicago: Univ. of Chicago Pr., 1980. 292p.

I503 Richardson, L. Arms and insecurity: a mathematical study of the causes and origins of war. Pittsburgh: Principia, 1960. 307p.

I504 Rosecrance, Richard N. Action and reaction in world politics. Boston: Little, 1963. 314p.

I505 Rosenau, James. The scientific study of foreign policy. Rev. ed. New York: Nichols, 1980. 577p.

I506 Rummel, Rudolph. Understanding conflict and war. Beverly Hills, Calif.: Sage, 1981. 5v.

I507 Russett, Bruce M. International regions and the international system: a study in political ecology. Chicago: Rand McNally, 1967. 252p.

I508 ———, ed. Economic theories of international politics. Chicago: Markham, 1968. 542p.

I509 ———, and Harvey Starr. World politics: the menu for choice. San Francisco: Freeman, 1981. 596p.

I510 Saaty, Thomas L. Mathematical models of arms control and disarmament. New York: Wiley, 1968. 190p.

I511 Schelling, Thomas C. Arms and influence. New Haven, Conn.: Yale Univ. Pr., 1966. 293p.

I513 Singer, Joel D., ed. Quantitative international politics: insights and evidence. New York: Free Pr., 1968. 394p.

I514 ———, and Melvin Small. The wages of war: 1816–1965. New York: Wiley, 1972. 419p.

I515 Waltz, Kenneth N. Theory of international politics. Reading, Mass.: Addison-Wesley, 1979. 251p.

I516 Zinnes, Dina. Contemporary research in international relations: a perspective and a critical appraisal. New York: Free Pr., 1976. 477p.

I517 ———, and John V. Gillespie, eds. Mathematical models in international relations. New York: Praeger, 1976. 397p.

International Law and Organizations

The study of international law and organizations has been an integral part of international relations since the early years of American political science. Political scientist and President Woodrow Wilson demonstrated his interest if not his political savvy through championing the League of Nations, the forerunner of the United Nations. Much of the early literature was and remains excessively formal and legalistic, focusing on law and legislation, treaties, organizational structures, and charters. Examples include:

I518 Brierly, James L. The law of nations: an introduction to the international law of peace. 6th ed. Ed. by H. Waldock. New York: Oxford Univ. Pr., 1963. 442p.

I519 Friedmann, Wolfgang, G. The changing structure of international law. New York: Columbia Univ. Pr., 1964. 410p.

I520 Kensen, Hans. The law of the United Nations: a critical analysis of its fundamental problems. New York: Praeger, 1950. 903p.

I521 ———. Principles of international law. 2d ed. New York: Holt, 1966. 602p.

I522 Lauterpacht, Hersch. The function of law in the international community. Oxford: Clarendon, 1933. 469p.

Although quantitative and mathematical studies in this area are rare, there has been a growing body of literature in the analytical and conceptual mode. Examples here include:

I523 Barkun, Michael. Law without sanctions: order in primitive societies and the world community. New Haven, Conn.: Yale Univ. Pr., 1968. 178p.

I524 Coplin, William. The functions of international law. Chicago: Rand McNally, 1966. 294p.

I525 Deutsch, Karl, and Stanley Hoffman. The relevance of international law. Cambridge, Mass.: Schenkman, 1968. 280p.

I526 Falk, Richard. The status of law in international society. Princeton, N.J.: Princeton Univ. Pr., 1970. 678p.

I527 Hovet, Thomas. Bloc politics in the United Nations. Cambridge, Mass.: Harvard Univ. Pr., 1960. 197p.

I528 Kaplan, Morton, and Nicholas DeB. Katzenbach. The political foundations of international law. New York: Wiley, 1961. 372p.

I529 Levi, Werner. Law and politics in the international society. Beverly Hills, Calif.: Sage, 1976. 191p.

The emergence of new nation-states, the continued pressures of nationalism within nations, the dependency of some nations upon others, and the political and economic needs for transnational regional cooperation have been the focus of considerable attention, particularly since World War II. Some of these contributions include:

I530 Claude, Inis L., Jr. Swords into plowshares: the problems and progress of international organization. 4th ed. New York: Random, 1971. 514p.

I531 Deutsch, Karl W. Nationalism and social communication: an inquiry into the foundation of nationality. 2d ed. Cambridge, Mass.: MIT Pr., 1966. 345p.

I532 ———, and others. Political community and the North Atlantic area. Princeton, N.J.: Princeton Univ. Pr., 1957. 228p.

I533 Etzioni, Amitai. Political unification. New York: Holt, 1965. 346p.

I534 Falk, Richard. A study of future worlds. New York: Free Pr., 1975. 506p.

I535 Haas, Ernst. Beyond the nation-state: functionalism and international organization. Stanford, Calif.: Stanford Univ. Pr., 1964. 595p.

I536 ———. The unification of Europe. Stanford, Calif.: Stanford Univ. Pr., 1958. 552p.

I537 ———. The obsolescence of regional integration theory. Berkeley: Inst. of International Studies, Univ. of California Pr., 1975. 123p.

I538 Keohane, Robert O., and Joseph Nye, eds. Power and interdependence: world politics in transition. Boston: Little, 1977. 273p.

I539 Nye, Joseph S. Peace in parts: integration and conflict in regional organization. Boston: Little, 1971. 210p.

NORMATIVE POLITICAL THEORY

The search for ideals; the distinction between good and bad, right and wrong; the process of justification; and the effort to delineate what one ought or ought not do have long been parts of traditional political science. For a time, the drive toward a science of politics isolated this segment of the discipline, but the demand for relevance over the past 15 years again found a home for this form of discourse within political science. Normative theorists point out that what we do and do not study reflects our values, that empirical findings are subject to abuse, and that in any event intellectuals have a fundamental obligation to help refashion and rethink the values of civilization.

These and other problems define a considerable role for normative political theory. Its mission includes an epistemological vigil, keeping the discipline apprised of the assumptions and implications of various forms of empirical inquiry. Also, it serves as its own critic through discourse on competing principles of justification. And singularly important, normative theory protects and nourishes the grand search for the good life, the good state, etc., both as ends in themselves and as means to illumine and inform empirical inquiry. In a sense, therefore, normative theory might be considered the "queen mother" of the discipline.

The classical study of political theory focuses upon the works of major political theorists from Plato and Aristotle to the present. Surveys of political theorists usually include Greek and Roman political theory, medieval (especially Catholic) theory, Renaissance theory, and more recent literature such as utilitarianism and Marxism. These broad sweeps have taken two general forms. The first—history of political thought—approaches its subject matter as an intellectual historian, focusing as much on context and why the ideas rose as upon the ideas themselves. The second approach is topical or analytical, focusing more upon the ideas, comparisons among ideas, and extrapolation of their relevance to modern problems. (Like many distinctions found throughout this essay, the dividing lines are not clear-cut or universally accepted.) References to the works of specific classical theorists are too numerous to list here. Surveys of the history of political thought will include ample reference to these primary texts. Examples of such surveys, in addition to those mentioned at the outset of this essay, include:

I540 Catlin, George E. G. The story of the political philosophers. New York: Whittlesey, 1939. 802p.

I541 Coker, Francis W. Recent political thought. New York: Appleton, 1934. 574p.

I542 McIlwain, Charles H. The growth of political thought in the West. New York: Macmillan, 1932. 417p.

I543 Merriam, Charles E. History of American political theories. New York: Russell & Russell, 1968. 364p.

I544 Strauss, Leo. Liberalism, ancient and modern. New York: Basic Books, 1968. 276p.

Some examples of topical or analytical approaches to normative political theory include:

I545 Arendt, Hannah. The human condition. New York: Doubleday, 1958. 332p.

I546 ———. On revolution. New York: Viking, 1963. 343p.

I547 Barry, Brian M. Sociologists, economists, and democracy. London: Collier-Macmillan, 1970. 202p.

I548 ———. The liberal theory of justice: a critical examination of the principal doctrines. Oxford: Clarendon, 1973. 168p.

I549 Bay, Christian. The structure of freedom. Stanford, Calif.: Stanford Univ. Pr., 1958. 419p.

I550 Berlin, Isaiah. Four essays on liberty. New York: Oxford Univ. Pr., 1969. 213p.

I551 Eisenach, Eldon J. Two worlds of liberalism: religion and politics in Hobbes, Locke, and Mill. Chicago: Univ. of Chicago Pr., 1981. 262p.

I551A Fishkin, James S. Beyond subjective morality: ethical reasoning and political philosophy. New Haven, Conn.: Yale Univ. Pr., 1984. 201p.

I552 Flathman, Richard E. Concepts in social and political philosophy. New York: Macmillan, 1973. 532p.

I553 ———. The public interest: an essay concerning the normative discourse of politics. New York: Wiley, 1966. 197p.

I554 ———. The practice of rights. Cambridge: Cambridge Univ. Pr., 1977. 250p.

I555 Fuller, Lon. Anatomy of law. New York: Praeger, 1968. 122p.

I556 Habermas, Jürgen. Knowledge and human interests. Boston: Beacon, 1971. 356p.

I557 Hallowell, John H. The moral foundation of democracy. Chicago: Univ. of Chicago Pr., 1954. 134p.

I558 Hart, H. L. A. The concept of law. London: Oxford Univ. Pr., 1961. 262p.

I559 Hayek, Friedrich A. The road to serfdom. Chicago: Univ. of Chicago Pr., 1956. 248p.

I560 Marcuse, Herbert. Reason and revolution. New York: Oxford Univ. Pr., 1941. 431p.

I561 Nozick, Robert. Anarchy, state, and utopia. New York: Basic Books, 1974. 367p.

I562 Pitkin, Hanna Fenichel. The concept of representation. Berkeley: Univ. of California Pr., 1967. 323p.

I563 Rawls, John. A theory of justice. Cambridge, Mass.: Belknap, 1971. 607p.

I564 Shklar, Judith. After utopia. Princeton, N.J.: Princeton Univ. Pr., 1957. 309p.

I565 Thorson, Thomas L. The logic of democracy. New York: Holt, 1962. 162p.

I566 Tussman, Joseph. Obligation and the body politic. New York: Oxford Univ. Pr., 1960. 144p.

Normative political theorists also have reminded colleagues about their historical role in the process of civilization and that, in particular, the intellectuals must bear a heavy burden in carrying forth the values of civilization as well as reinvigorating or redefining those value foundations. Although this view of the role of intellectuals is perhaps foreign to the American democratic spirit, its appeals have not fallen upon deaf ears within the discipline. Two works written abroad but widely read in the United States are:

I567 Benda, Julien. The treason of the intellectuals. New York: Norton, 1969. 244p.

I568 Cobban, Alfred. In search of humanity: the role of the enlightenment in modern history. London: Cape, 1960. 254p.

Normative theory's epistemological vigil has produced a considerable body of commentary on the drive toward science, its epistemological problems, and its shortcomings. Many of these have been referenced earlier in the discussion of behavioralism. Under the aegis of normative political theory have emerged several competing theories of "doing" proper reseach in the social sciences. One attempts to adapt the principles of natural science to the less uniform and more obtrusive subject matter of the social sciences. Another emphasizes the inherent limits of all knowledge, and that science, like other forms of knowing, is bound to its historical context. Here knowledge is cumulative within a paradigm but less so across paradigms. A third theory emphasizes the mental and/or social construction of reality as the proper explanation for action. This phenomenological approach (in part derived from the influential work of Alfred Schütz) contrasts with the more mechanical "black-box" perspective of behavioral psychologists like B. F. Skinner.

Note that *behaviorism* is a stimulus-response method for studying behavior without substantive reference to the intervening organism. *Behavioralism* refers to the drive for science in political science. Although the terms sometimes are confused, their distinction is essential for a basic understanding of contemporary political science.

A fourth competing theory, known as the common language tradition and deriving its impetus from Ludwig Wittgenstein, argues that the search for causes of human action ought to be replaced with the search for *reasons* for human action. Some examples of political theory's epistemological vigil include:

I569 Apel, Karl Otto. Analytic philosophy of language and the Geisteswissenschaften. Dordrecht, Holland: D. Reidel, 1967. 67p.

I570 Berger, Peter L., and Thomas Luckmann. Social construction of reality: a treatise in the sociology of knowledge. Garden City, N.Y.: Doubleday, 1966. 203p.

I571 Cohen, Morris R. Reason and nature: an essay on the meaning of scientific method. 2d ed. Glencoe, Ill.: Free Pr., 1964. 470p.

I572 Cowling, Maurice. Nature and limits of political science. Cambridge, Mass.: Cambridge Univ. Pr., 1963. 213p.

I573 Dallmayr, Fred R. Beyond dogma and despair: toward a critical phenomenology of politics. Notre Dame, Ind.: Univ. of Notre Dame Pr., 1981. 358p.

I574 Frohock, Fred M. The nature of political inquiry. Homewood, Ill.: Dorsey Pr., 1967. 218p.

I575 ———. Normative political theory. Englewood Cliffs, N.J.: Prentice-Hall, 1974. 118p.

I576 Germino, Dante. Beyond ideology: the revival of political theory. New York: Harper, 1967. 254p.

I577 Gunnell, John G. Political theory: tradition and interpretation. Cambridge, Mass.: Winthrop, 1979. 170p.

I578 Hampshire, Stuart. Thought and action. London: Chatto & Windus, 1959. 276p.

I578A Kaplan, Morton A. Science, language and the human condition. New York: Paragon, 1984. 394p.

I579 Kateb, George. Political theory: its nature and uses. New York: St. Martin's, 1968. 102p.

I580 Mannheim, Karl. Ideology and utopia. New York: Harcourt, 1936. 318p.

I581 Meehan, Eugene J. Contemporary political thought: a critical study. Homewood, Ill.: Dorsey Pr., 1967. 437p.

I582 ———. The theory and method of political analysis. Homewood, Ill.: Dorsey Pr., 1965. 227p.

I583 Nozick, Robert. Philosophical explanations. Cambridge, Mass.: Harvard Univ. Pr., 1981. 764p.

I584 Oakeshott, Michael. Experience and its modes. Cambridge: Cambridge Univ. Pr., 1933. 359p.

I585 Schütz, Alfred. The phenomenology of the social world. Evanston, Ill.: Northwestern Univ. Pr., 1967. 255p.

I586 Strauss, Leo. What is political philosophy? and other studies. Glencoe, Ill.: Free Pr., 1959. 345p.

I587 Winch, Peter. The idea of a social science and its relation to philosophy. London: Routledge & Paul; New York: Humanities, 1958. 143p.

EMPIRICAL POLITICAL THEORY

One major consequence of behavioralism was an increased interest and conscientious effort at empirical theory construction and testing. These efforts, paralleling the distinction between phase three and four researchers discussed above, tend to occur along two not entirely consistent dimensions. The first uses statistical inference to identify empirical patterns and then seeks to explain these patterns through what might be called "post-facto theorizing." The second uses mathematical deduction to identify expected empirical patterns as these derive from a priori postulates and assumptions. To be sure, theories based on empirical patterns, as well as the empirical patterns themselves, inform the development of more deductive theories. While the latter can bring more rigor to the former, the sad fact remains that statistically inferred theories tend to be ad hoc and lacking universality, while more deductive theory often provides an ill fit with empirical reality. Still, the effort is being made to develop scientific theories of politics, and major developments can be expected in this area in the decades that follow.

Inductive efforts to forge empirical theory rest not only upon quantitative studies of politics but also upon experimental and quasi-experimental research. These efforts focus on a variety of units of analysis, from the individual and group through nation-states as primary actors. Some examples of these efforts, including some very early ones, include:

I588 Bennett, W. Lance. The political mind and the political environment. Lexington, Mass.: Lexington Books, 1975. 207p.

I589 Cantril, Hadley. Human nature and political systems. New Brunswick, N.J.: Rutgers Univ. Pr., 1961. 112p.

I590 Cnudde, Charles F., and Dean E. Neubauer, eds. Empirical democratic theory. Chicago: Markham, 1969. 534p.

I591 Davies, James C. Human nature in politics: the dynamics of political behavior. New York: Wiley, 1963. 403p.

I592 Dawson, Richard, and Kenneth Prewitt. Political socialization: an analytical study. Boston: Little, 1969. 226p.

I593 Edelman, Jacob Murray. The symbolic uses of politics. Urbana: Univ. of Illinois Pr., 1964. 201p.

I594 ———. Politics as symbolic action: mass arousal and quiescence. Chicago: Markham, 1971. 188p.

I595 Greenstein, Fred I. Political socialization: a study in the psychology of political behavior. Glencoe, Ill.: Free Pr., 1959. 175p.

I596 Langton, Kenneth P. Political socialization. New York: Oxford Univ. Pr., 1967. 215p.

I597 Lasswell, Harold D. Power and personality. New York: Viking, 1962. 250p.

I598 Mohr, Lawrence B. Explaining organizational behavior: the limits and possibilities of theory and research. San Francisco: Jossey-Bass, 1982. 260p.

I599 Tufte, Edward. Political control of the economy. Princeton, N.J.: Princeton Univ. Pr., 1978. 168p.

I600 Wallas, Graham. Human nature in politics. 3d ed. New York: Knopf, 1921. 313p.

Mathematical approaches to politics date back to the Greeks, but before the last decade and a half most contributions in this area came from researchers in economics. That pattern abruptly changed, and now a growing segment of mathematically oriented and/or deductively analytical political scientists has produced sophisticated research and theory. Some important contributions in this area, in addition to those already cited, include:

I601 Alker, Hayward R., Jr. Mathematics and politics. London: Macmillan, 1965. 152p.

I602 ———, and others, eds. Mathematical approaches to politics. Amsterdam, N.Y.: Elsevier, 1973. 479p.

I602A Axelrod, Robert. The evolution of cooperation. New York: Basic Books, 1984. 241p.

I603 Baumol, William J. Welfare economics and the theory of the state. 2d ed. Cambridge, Mass.: Harvard Univ. Pr., 1965. 212p.

I604 Brams, Steven J. Game theory and politics. New York: Free Pr., 1975. 212p.

I605 Buchanan, James M. The limits of liberty: between anarchy and leviathan. Chicago: Univ. of Chicago Pr., 1975. 210p.

I606 Curry, Robert L., Jr., and Larry L. Wade. A theory of political exchange: economic reasoning in political analysis. Englewood Cliffs, N.J.: Prentice-Hall, 1968. 110p.

I607 Frohlich, Norman, and others. Political leadership and collective goods. Princeton, N.J.: Princeton Univ. Pr., 1971. 161p.

I607A Shubik, Martin. A game-theoretic approach to political economy. Cambridge, Mass.: MIT Pr., 1984. 744p.

I608 Simon, Herbert A. Models of man; social and rational. New York: Wiley, 1957. 287p.

I609 Tullock, Gordon. Toward a mathematics of politics. Ann Arbor: Univ. of Michigan Pr., 1967. 176p.

I610 ———, ed. Toward a science of politics. Blacksburg, Va.: Public Choice Center, Virginia Polytechnic Institute and State Univ., 1981. 130p.

I611 Von Neumann, John, and Oskar Morgenstern. The theory of games and economic behavior. 3d ed. New York: Wiley, 1964. 641p.

POLITICAL METHODOLOGY

The growing sense of science within political science has brought with it a keen interest in empirical methodology. This literature includes such topics as polimetrics (the measure of political phenomena) and research design (how to go about getting the data necessary to answer empirical questions). For decades political science borrowed these resources from other disciplines, but this has become less frequent in the past decade or so. This has been a welcomed development, because the approaches of other disciplines never fully matched the needs of political science, but absent its own core of sophisticated methodologists, the discipline could not readily address its own needs. The behavioral persuasion, however, changed that, and the discipline's cadre of methodologists increased rapidly during the 1960s and 1970s, providing the needed internal source for methodological instruction and development. A journal (*Political methodology*) is devoted to problems of design and analysis in political research. The references below indicate some of the available methodology textbooks.

I612 Asher, Herbert B. Causal modelling. 2d ed. Beverly Hills, Calif.: Sage, 1983. 96p.

I613 Garson, G. David. Political science methods. Boston: Holbrook Pr., 1976. 540p.

I614 Gurr, Ted Robert. Polimetrics: an introduction

to quantitative macropolitics. Englewood Cliffs, N.J.: Prentice-Hall, 1972. 214p.

I615 Key, V. O., Jr. A primer of statistics for political scientists. New York: Crowell, 1966. 209p.

I616 Manheim, Jarol B., and Richard C. Rich. Empirical political analysis: research methods in political science. Englewood Cliffs, N.J.: Prentice-Hall, 1981. 359p.

I617 Nachmias, David, and Chava Nachmias. Research methods in the social sciences. 2d ed. New York: St. Martin's, 1981. 585p.

I618 Nie, Norman H., and others. Statistical package for the social sciences. 2d ed. New York: McGraw-Hill, 1975. 675p.

I619 Palumbo, Dennis. Statistics in political and behavioral science. Rev. ed. New York: Columbia Univ. Pr., 1977. 469p.

I620 Rai, Kul B., and John C. Blydenburgh. Political science statistics. Boston: Holbrook Pr., 1973. 255p.

I621 Shively, W. Phillips. The craft of political research: a primer. Englewood Cliffs, N.J.: Prentice-Hall, 1974. 174p.

I622 Stokey, Edith, and Richard Zeckhauser. A primer for policy analysis. New York: Norton, 1978. 356p.

I623 Tufte, Edward. Data analysis for politics and policy. Englewood Cliffs, N.J.: Prentice-Hall, 1974. 179p.

INSTRUCTION

The past decade has witnessed growing interest in the art of teaching political science. A journal (*Teaching political science*) now is available, and the American Political Science Association regularly publishes a newsletter on teaching political science. Book-length treatments on the subject are still few, although there has been a rapid growth of computer-based instructional texts called *Supplementary empirical teaching units in political science,* or *SETUPS,* covering American, cross-national, and world politics. Although the discipline has become more conscientious about its teaching mission, research on pedagogical matters has not assumed the same priority as research on politics. The following materials illustrate political scientists' pedagogical research.

I624 American Political Science Association, Committee for the Advancement of Teaching. Goals for political science. New York: Sloane, 1951. 319p.

I625 Connery, Robert H. Teaching political science:

a challenge to higher education. Durham, N.C.: Duke Univ. Pr., 1965. 284p.

1626 Guetzkow, Harold S., and others. Simulation in international relations: developments for research and teaching. Englewood Cliffs, N.J.: Prentice-Hall, 1963. 248p.

1627 Molitor, André. The university teaching of social sciences: public administration. Paris: UNESCO, 1959. 192p.

1628 Reed, Thomas H., and Doris D. Reed. Preparing college men and women for politics. New York: Citizenship Clearing House, 1952. 180p.

1629 Riker, William H. The study of local politics: a manual. New York: Random, 1959. 126p.

1630 Robson, William A. The university teaching of social sciences: political science. Paris: UNESCO, 1954. 249p.

1631 Sweeney, Stephen B., and others, eds. Education for administrative careers in government service. Philadelphia: Univ. of Pennsylvania Pr., 1958. 366p.

FUSION AND FISSION: WHITHER POLITICAL SCIENCE?

Because of the diversity of their fields, political scientists maintain considerable interdisciplinary contacts. Traditional area studies rsearchers maintain contact with history and other colleagues in area studies programs. Those who study constitutional law, criminal procedure, and related topics often maintain contacts with law schools. Behavioral researchers have contacts with economists, psychologists, and sociologists. And those interested in special topics like women's studies, black studies, or Hispanic studies find colleagues in other social science disciplines as well. Finally, those using mathematical models are developing closer ties with mathematicians, engineers, and other applied mathematical fields.

What are the implications of this interdisciplinary mingling? To be sure, part of the problem arises from the simple fact that the disciplinary classifications do not always correspond with the actual divisions of intellectual labor. But who wins in a struggle between organized disciplines and cross-disciplinary rsearch? A decade ago, some political scientists feared that cognate disciplines would come to dominate those areas of cross-disciplinary research in which political scientists took part. Even though lip service was given to interdisciplinary work, it often went unrewarded or under-rewarded, save in those in-

stances where the cross-disciplinary work was housed in a separate adminstrative unit. Although the competition for scarce resources remains a source of considerable anguish, political science borrowed what it needed from cognate disciplines and then came to dominate many of those collaborative ventures. In part this might reflect the lack of a unifying paradigm in political science, allowing a freedom of intellectual development less available in disciplines with defined paradigms. Further, distinctly political topics such as political psychology, political economy, or political sociology draw more from the intellectual baggage of political science than from their co-disciplines.

The situation is less promising with area specialists. Their tools are more similar to historiography than to political science, and except for their emphasis on current events and problems, these area researchers are intellectually closer to historians than to contemporary political scientists. Because many historians feel, however, that events unfolding now cannot be analyzed with the necessary objectivity, their departments are seldom quick to accommodate area researchers from political science. In some universities, depending upon available funds, this potential conflict was resolved through establishment of area studies programs and institutes where historians and area studies specialists can meet as colleagues without threatening disciplinary norms and integrity. For a more favorable assessment, see:

1632 Pye, Lucian W., ed. Political science and area studies: rivals or partners? Bloomington: Indiana Univ. Pr., 1975. 245p.

The largely peaceful co-existence between law schools and political science dates back to the founding of the discipline. Political scientists bring to the study of law several elements not dominant in law schools. (Many law schools have included some of these elements in their curricula, however.) First, political scientists seldom see law as a universal lever of causation. That is, they recognize that law must operate within the boundaries of legitimacy and that other behavioral factors often outweigh the simple dictates of law. Second, political scientists are considerably more interested in the politics of law than in its substance as an end in itself. Third, political scientists are more likely to look at law in theoretical and philosophical terms. Also, political scientists have access to an undergraduate clientele that law schools generally choose to avoid. For these and a host of other reasons, it is quite likely that peaceful co-existence between law-oriented political scientists and law schools will continue.

Two recent developments also deserve mention. First, science and technology programs have grown rapidly in the 1980s, and these programs have drawn political scientists into interdisciplinary arenas with physicists, engineers, biologists, and other natural scientists as well as philosophers, classicists, and more. At this point it is unclear what consequences are likely to follow from the evolving programs in science and technology. Second, fledgling peace science and peace studies programs have begun to appear on various campuses across the nation. Peace science programs typically emphasize sophisticated mathematical methodology and bring together political scientists, mathematicians, engineers, and the like. Peace studies programs typically are more action-oriented and tend toward more humanistic disciplines. The divisions within political science are in a sense reflected in the divisions between the peace studies and peace science programs as well.

Economics

Over the past 15 years, economics has become the premier cognate discipline for political science. That status relates in part to a growing interest in policy analysis, which, in turn, demands increased familiarity with evaluation tools common in business and economics. Additionally, however, the rigor of economics has provided an important model as behavioralism matured into a more mathematical phase within the discipline. That rigor and parsimony of deductive economic theory provided an attractive template for political research. Finally, the demand for relevance in the discipline once again helped inspire interest in political economy, and political scientists thus found economic concepts and theories directly relevant to their substantive research agenda. The role of economics in political science is sufficiently important that a recent president of the American Political Science Association was an economist by training but wrote prolifically in the area of political economy. Some examples of the political economy literature widely used in political science include:

I633 Boulding, Kenneth. Conflict and defense: a general theory. New York: Harper, 1962. 349p.

I634 Haveman, Robert H., and Julius Margolis, eds. Public expenditure and policy analysis. 2d ed. Chicago: Rand McNally, 1977. 591p.

I635 Heilbroner, Robert L. The economic transformation of America. New York: HBJ, 1977. 276p.

I636 Heller, Walter W. New dimensions of political economy. New York: Norton, 1967. 203p.

I637 Hirschman, Albert O. Essays in trespassing: economics to politics and beyond. New York: Cambridge Univ. Pr., 1981. 310p.

I638 ———. Exit, voice, and loyalty: responses to decline in firms, organizations, and states. Cambridge, Mass.: Harvard Univ. Pr., 1970. 162p.

I639 Ilchman, Warren F., and Norman T. Upholff. The political economy of change. Berkeley: Univ. of California Pr., 1969. 316p.

I640 Lindblom, Charles. Politics and markets. New York: Basic Books, 1977. 403p.

I641 Nagel, Stuart S., ed. Improving policy analysis. Beverly Hills, Calif.: Sage, 1980. 264p.

I642 Quade, E. S. Analysis for public decisions. 2d ed. New York: Elsevier, 1982. 322p.

I643 Scott, Andrew M. Competition in American politics: an economic model. New York: Holt, 1970. 134p.

I644 Sharkansky, Ira. Policy analysis in political science. Chicago: Markham, 1969. 476p.

I645 Wildavsky, Aaron. How to limit government spending. Berkeley: Univ. of California Pr., 1980. 197p.

Psychology and Social Psychology

Human nature has long been a central interest to political theorists, from the ancient Greeks to the present day. Most classical theorists offered their views and modern political scientists continue efforts to understand human nature as it affects politics. Although considerable effort is now made within the discipline, some influential contributions not previously mentioned include:

I646 Allport, Gordon W. Pattern and growth in personality. New York: Holt, 1961. 593p.

I647 Centers, Richard. The psychology of social classes. Princeton, N.J.: Princeton Univ. Pr., 1949. 244p.

I648 Holland, Paul W., and Samuel Leinhardt, eds. Perspectives on social network research. New York: Academic, 1979. 532p.

I649 McClelland, David C. The achieving society. New York: Free Pr., 1961. 512p.

Sociology

In its drive toward science following World War II, political science often turned to sociology for theory and methodology. Thus, sociology had an enormous influence on the early behavior movement. By the end of the 1960s, however, the poverty of social theory as a means of illuminating political matters had become more apparent, particularly given the often nonautonomous status assigned political processes. Still, the sociologists' concern with concept formation, theory construction, and theory testing provided needed guidance as the discipline sought to establish its own scientific credentials. Much the same holds for methodology. In the early years after World War II, political science borrowed as much statistical know-how from sociology as it borrowed from psychology. As the discipline matured, however, economics provided more assistance. Now, as mentioned before, the discipline is moving into a more self-sufficient state of methodological expertise. Some major sociological sources include:

I650 Bell, Daniel. The end of ideology: on the exhaustion of political ideas in the fifties. Rev. ed. Glencoe, Ill.: Free Pr., 1967. 474p.

I651 Blalock, Hubert. Social statistics. Rev. 2d ed. New York: McGraw-Hill, 1979. 625p.

I651A ————, ed. Causal models in panel and experimental designs. New York: Aldine, 1985. 287p.

I652 ————, and Ann Blalock, eds. Methodology in social research. New York: McGraw-Hill, 1968. 493p.

I653 Blau, Peter M. Exchange and power in social life. New York: Wiley, 1964. 352p.

I654 Dahrendorf, Ralf. Class and class conflict in industrial society. Stanford, Calif.: Stanford Univ. Pr., 1959. 336p.

I655 Etzioni, Amitai. The active society: a theory of societal and political processes. New York: Free Pr., 1968. 698p.

I656 Kornhauser, William. The politics of mass society. New York: Free Pr., 1959. 256p.

I657 MacIver, Robert M. The web of government. New York: Macmillan, 1947. 498p.

I658 Merton, Robert. Social theory and social structure. New York: Free Pr., 1957. 645p.

I659 Michels, Robert. Political parties: a sociological study of the oligarchical tendencies of modern democracy. New York: Free Pr., 1962. 379p.

I660 Parsons, Talcott. The social system. Glencoe, Ill.: Free Pr., 1951. 575p.

I661 ————. The structure of social action. New York: Free Pr., 1966. 817p.

I662 Tönnies, Ferdinand. Community and society. Tr. and ed. by Charles O. Loomis. East Lansing: Michigan State Univ. Pr., 1957. 298p.

I663 Weber, Max. The theory of social and economic organization. Tr. by A.M. Henderson and Talcott Parsons. New York: Free Pr., 1947. 436p.

Fission: International Studies

Although political science has done well in its cross-disciplinary endeavors, there have been pressures from within that threaten to divide the discipline on a permanent basis. We already have seen the problem with area studies researchers who, partly because of their closer affinity with history than with modern political science, are drawn when budgets permit into area studies programs and institutes. For almost the opposite reason, international studies has moved further from the political science fold. Membership of these researchers in the American Political Science Association is down, they participate less at the annual meetings, and they have instead substituted the International Studies Association, replete with journals and annual meetings. The movement toward the ISA has attracted a disproportionately large segment of the more rigorously scientific scholars. The fact that international studies has moved ahead of many other segments of the discipline in its drive for science, coupled with the discipline's heavy American emphasis, might help explain this secession. Although centers and institutes for international studies have expanded over the past two decades, the fact remains that restrictive budget conditions have helped check this centrifugal tendency.

Fission: Vocational Programs

On the whole, political science prides itself upon being an academic discipline. It has, however, given birth to two vocational strains: one following the drive for applied scientific knowledge after World War I (Merriam and others), and the second following the drive for relevance at the close of the 1960s. The first fostered an interest in a science of government now commonly known as "public administration" and the second fostered an interest in policy analysis and prescription often represented by the term "public policy studies." Both orientations have deep-seated practical goals and, consequently, might be termed "vocational spin-offs" from political science.

The subdiscipline of public administration emerged in the 1920s under the tutelage of Leonard D. White and W. F. Willoughby. Building upon the long struggle for civil service reform that dated back to the Garfield administration, these scholars sought to combine political science with the tools of scientific management in a training program for government servants. These practical and vocational objectives distinguished public administration from other segments of political science, and its applied status tended to isolate its practitioners from other scholars. These tensions eventually led to the formation of the American Society for Public Administration (ASPA) in 1940. Scholarly members of ASPA also tend to maintain membership in the American Political Science Association, but ASPA's membership also includes large numbers of practicing administrators.

Policy studies is a relative newcomer, but it appears to be following an evolutionary path similar to public administration. Some colleges and universities have established separate policy studies programs, most remain as a subcurriculum within political science, and a few others have been combined with public administration. Although both are, generally speaking, vocationally oriented, policy studies is more methodological than public administration. Like public administration, policy studies has its own national organization (Policy Studies Organization) and publishes its own journal. Its members generally have maintained their affiliation with the American Political Science Association, and it is not unusual for scholars to be members of all three organizations. Some early signs indicate that organizational loyalties might well be moving away from the American Political Science Association.

Because both programs have a captive clientele outside academia, and because both directly or indirectly train for a ready job market outside the university, both have sources of funding and political support that are unavailable to more traditional segments of the discipline. This situation, in turn, helps to explain the continued and largely successful drive to separate public administration from its political science host as well as the proliferation of public policy institutes across the nation. (The National Association of Public Administrators' peer review process now expects that public administration programs should have a separate and identifiable budget, administration, and teaching staff.)

The area studies specialists also have their own journals, but they lack the external resources necessary to establish their independence within colleges and universities, save in instances where the area studies programs were established in days before lean budgets. The long-standing and now easily identifiable external clientele of public administration has made its secession easier, although in small colleges and some universities the ties with political science still remain strong. Policy studies programs have had less time to build a similar track record, but indications do point toward a trend away from political science as the host department, as resources (both external and internal) permit. At this time, however, most policy studies programs remain affiliated with political science departments.

Some examples of the public administration literature include:

I664   Charlesworth, James C., ed. Theory and practice of public administration: scope, objectives, and methods. Philadelphia: American Academy of Political and Social Science, 1968. 336p. [Monograph 8]

I665   Dimock, Marshall E., and G. O. Dimock. Public administration. 4th ed. New York: Holt, 1969. 634p.

I666   Golembiewski, Robert T., and others, eds. Public administration: readings in institutions, processes, behavior, policy. 3d ed. Chicago: Rand McNally, 1976. 726p.

I667   Nigro, Felix A. Modern public administration. 2d ed. New York: Harper, 1970. 490p.

I668   Waldo, Dwight. The administrative state: a study of the political theory of American public administration. New York: Ronald, 1948. 227p.

I669   ———. The study of public administration. New York: Random, 1955. 72p.

I670   Williams, J. D. Public administration: the people's business. Boston: Little, 1980. 585p.

The volume of policy-relevant literature is simply enormous, and some of it is technically sophisticated. Much less, however, contributes to cumulative disciplinary knowledge. Some examples of important perspectives in policy studies include:

I671   Brewer, Gary D., and Peter deLeon. The foundations of policy analysis. Homewood, Ill.: Dorsey Pr., 1983. 476p.

I672   Dror, Yehezkel. Approaches to policy sciences. Santa Monica, Calif.: Rand Corp., 1969. 8p.

I673 Nagel, Stuart, ed. Policy studies and the social sciences. Lexington, Mass.: Heath, 1979. 315p.

I674 Rein, Martin. Social science and public policy. New York: Penguin, 1976. 272p.

I675 Rivlin, Alice M. New approaches to public decision-making. Ottawa: Information Canada, 1972. 37p.

I676 Wildavsky, Aaron. Speaking truth to power: the art and craft of policy analysis. Boston: Little, 1979. 431p.

Steven Seitz

Survey of the Reference Works

GUIDES TO THE LITERATURE

General

I677 Brock, Clifton. The literature of political science; a guide for students, librarians, and teachers. New York: Bowker, 1969. 232p.

A fine guide, now much in need of a revision. The first section is a survey of types of information sources (e.g., catalogs, indexes and abstracts, government publications), describing their use and giving valuable tips on research. Section 2 is a straightforward listing of the most important sources in political science, American government and politics, political behavior and public opinion, public administration, international relations, comparative politics and area studies, and world communism.

Bibliographies are listed first in each chapter, followed by a selection of handbooks, yearbooks, dictionaries, chronologies, and other reference works. Strong organization and excellent, often detailed annotations.

I678 Harmon, Robert B. Political science: a bibliographical guide to the literature. New York: Scarecrow, 1965. 388p.

Explicit attempt to update Laverne Burchfield, *Student's guide to materials in political science* (New York: Holt, 1935 [426p.]) (**I679**), the prototype for sources included in this section.

A listing of monographs and reference works on general political science, comparative government, political parties and theory, law and jurisprudence, public administration, and international relations. Goal of comprehensiveness is admirable, but the guide is disappointing both in its arrangement—with many titles awkwardly placed—and in its scarcity of annotations, particularly for monographs (somewhat compensated for by brief, informative introductory and linking notes).

Three supplements, published by Scarecrow 1968–74, rectify some of the flaws in organization, but infrequency of annotation and absence of subject index keep it from being first rate.

Harmon's *Developing the library collection in political science* (Metuchen, N.J.: Scarecrow, 1976 [198p.]) (**I680**) is a generally useful listing of basic monographs (by subject), reference materials (by type), and major periodicals.

I681 Holler, Frederick L. Information sources of political science. 3d ed. Santa Barbara, Calif.: ABC-Clio, 1981. 278p.

Excellent examination of reference works and bibliographies of value for political science research. Following an illuminating introductory essay, "The retrieval of political information," individual chapters are concerned with general reference sources; social sciences reference sources; American government, politics, and public law; international relations and organizations; comparative and area studies; political theory; and public administration.

Among other features, fullness of annotations, useful integration of computer databases with traditional information sources, and citation of relevant sources from other disciplines where gaps in coverage exist (e.g., political theory) are especially noteworthy. Subject, author, and title indexes. In terms of continuity and currency, an indispensable guide to political science literature.

I681A Information sources in politics and political science: a survey worldwide. Ed. by Dermot Englefield and Gavin Drewry. London: Butterworths, 1984. 509p.

Bibliographic essays on the literature of international politics, from a British perspective. In 4 parts: (1) resources (library and bibliographical aids), (2) approaches to the study of politics and government, (3) politics and government: United Kingdom, and (4) politics and government: overseas. The 24 contributed essays are full and well-written. A major limitation is the 7-page subject index. No index to works cited.

I682   Mason, John B. Research resources; annotated guide to the social sciences. Santa Barbara, Calif.: ABC-Clio, 1968–71. 2v.

Each volume is oriented toward political science research. v.1, *International relations and recent history: indexes, abstracts and periodicals*, lists relevant sources in chapters by form. In addition to the categories mentioned in the title, coverage includes books (primarily reference works and bibliographies), national and trade bibliographies, U.S. government publications, and the American and foreign press. Although more than half the 1,300 items listed are standard general or social science sources, the specialized tools are well covered. Generous, frequently critical annotations. Name and title indexes. No subject index but numerous cross-references. v.2, *Official publications: U.S. government, United Nations, international organizations, and statistical sources*, highlights major federal documents and series and has a subject index.

I683   Vose, Clement E. A guide to library sources in political science: American government. Washington, D.C.: American Political Science Assn., 1975. 135p. [Instructional resource monograph, 1]

Intended to introduce students and teachers to library resources on American government. Pt. 1 discusses major tools for researching government publications, the Constitution, and the three branches. Pt. 2 describes four types of reference books (almanacs, biographies, political dictionaries, and encyclopedias). Library basics and files, archives, and manuscripts are covered in pt. 3. Lively prose and very helpful photographs, which depict groups of sources in shelf displays. A major flaw: subject bibliographies (other than indexes and abstracts, discussed briefly) are barely mentioned, let alone cited, despite their great importance to students and teachers.

Similar in approach: Richard L. Merritt and Gloria J. Pyszka, *The student political scientist's handbook* (Cambridge, Mass.: Schenkman, 1969 [171p.]) (**I684**), which discusses basic research tools, the study of politics, use of the library, composition of term papers, and careers in political science; and Carl Kalvelage and others, *Bridges to knowledge in political science: a handbook for research* (Pacific Palisades, Calif.: Palisades, 1984 [153p.]) (**I685**), a succinct guide to research and term paper presentation.

Specialized

I686   Bemis, Samuel F., and Grace Griffin. Guide to the diplomatic history of the United States, 1775–1921. Washington, D.C.: Govt. Print. Off., 1935. 979p. Reprint, Gloucester, Mass.: Peter Smith, 1959.

An important guide, listing nearly 6,000 printed and manuscript sources. Pt.1 contains the bibliographic chapters, topically and chronologically arranged. Includes documents, histories, letters, maps, and manuscript materials. Pt.2 analyzes printed state papers and locates manuscripts. Author index and index to collections of personal papers.

For additional locations of archives and manuscripts, consult the *National union catalog of manuscript collections* (B1626) and the directory issued by the National Historical Publications and Records Commission (B1477).

Succeeded, but not replaced, by *Guide to American foreign relations since 1700* (I688).

I687   Goehlert, Robert U. Congress and law-making: researching the legislative process. Santa Barbara, Calif.: Clio, 1979. 168p.

"Designed to help users trace congressional legislation and to familiarize them with the major sources of information about Congress" (preface). Goehlert goes well beyond outlining techniques for researching the legislative history of a bill by providing information on a variety of official and commercially published sources for researching legislators and the legislative process. Appendixes show how to cite government publications and list U.S. depository libraries. Exemplary annotations and clear illustrations of sources add to the value of this fine guide.

Similar in design and quality: Robert U. Goehlert and Fenton S. Martin, *The presidency: a research guide* (Santa Barbara, Calif.: ABC-Clio [1984]) (**I687A**). The appendixes, which tabulate sources and approaches for presidential research, are especially useful.

I688   Guide to American foreign relations since 1700. Ed. by Richard D. Burns. Santa Barbara, Calif.: ABC-Clio, 1983. 1,311p.

Massive, superbly organized introduction to research in U.S. foreign relations. Chapter 1 surveys reference aids. The remaining 39 chapters are arranged chronologically and have subdivisions for reference sources, overviews of the period, major personalities, and themes. In addition to the full annotations for each cited work, brief notes are given for some 3,000 citations repeated in related chapters. Indexes for authors, topics, and individuals. Compilation supported by the Society for Historians of American Foreign Relations.

The *Guide* expands and updates Bemis and Griffin's *Guide to the diplomatic history of the United States, 1775–1921* (I686), which remains valuable for its references to earlier writings and unpublished manuscript sources.

I689   Harmon, Robert B. The art and practice of diplomacy: a selected and annotated guide. Metuchen, N.J.: Scarecrow, 1971. 355p.

Compiled for "the student who would like to know a little more about contemporary diplomacy as an important factor in international affairs" (preface). Well-organized guide describing 900 monographs, articles, and reference works. In 7 sections: nature and objectives of diplomacy; historical evolution of diplomacy; modern diplomatic methods; foreign affairs administration; language of diplomacy; selected reference and auxiliary sources; diplomatic documents and organization. Includes list of studies and manuals for 34 nations, a short glossary of diplomatic terms, and illustrative examples of diplomatic documents. Very brief annotations, but full, informative introductions to each section. Index of works cited.

I690 Robinson, Jacob. International law and organization: general sources of information. Leyden, The Netherlands: A.W. Sijthoff, 1967. 560p.

A detailed guide to encyclopedias, dictionaries, bibliographies, biobibliographies, serials, periodicals, and yearbooks for research in public international law and organization. Outstanding features: (1) numerous references to abstracts and book reviews, (2) citations to biobibliographical material for 1,248 prominent figures.

I691 Simpson, Antony E. Guide to library research in public administration. New York: Center for Productive Public Management. John Jay College of Criminal Justice, 1976. 210p.

Well-conceived and -executed introduction to the dispersed literature of public administration. Much of the strength is derived from the preliminary sections, including a preface by Marc Holzer on historical/conceptual approaches to public administration and the author's discussion of the nature of library search strategies in the discipline. Lengthy, informative annotations characterize the chapters on reference sources (listed by form), except for subject bibliographies, which are cited but not described. Concluding chapters are concerned with computer literature searching, archives and unpublished sources, and writing the research paper. In many respects, a model guide.

Documents

I692 Aufricht, Hans. Guide to League of Nations publications: a bibliographical survey of the work of the League, 1920–1947. New York: Columbia Univ. Pr., 1951. 682p. Reprint, New York: AMS Pr., 1966.

The most comprehensive bibliographic guide to the documents of the League and its autonomous affiliates. Selectively lists the most significant publications, including some confidential and "not on public sale" items. Arranged by organizational unit or broad topic. Introductory and chapter notes sketch history and structure of the League. Appendixes of basic League documents and analytical subject index.

Standard lists of League documents: Marie J. Carroll, *Key to League of Nations documents placed on public sale, 1920–1929*, and 4 supplements, *1930–36* (Boston: World Peace foundation, 1930–36) **(I693)**; and League of Nations, *Catalogue of publications, 1920–1935*, and 5 supplements, *1936–1945* (Geneva: 1935–45) **(I694)**. A systematic reworking of these lists is also available: Mary E. Birchfield, *Consolidated catalog of League of Nations publications offered for sale* (Dobbs Ferry, N.Y.: Oceana, 1976 [477p.]) **(I695)**. For a thorough enumeration of the many series issued by the League, see Victory Y. Ghébali and

Catherine Ghébali, *A repertoire of League of Nations serial documents, 1919–1947/Répertoire des séries de documents de la Société des Nations, 1919–1947* (Dobbs Ferry, N.Y.: Oceana, 1973 [2v.]) **(I696)**, produced under the auspices of the Carnegie Endowment for International Peace.

I697 Bishop, Olga B. Canadian official publications. Oxford and New York: Pergamon, 1981. 297p. [Guides to official publications, 9] Well-illustrated survey of Canadian documents.

I698 Fetzer, Mary K. United Nations documents and publications: a research guide. New Brunswick, N.J.: Rutgers Univ. Graduate School of Library Service, 1978. 61p.

For years, the best general guide to U.N. documents was Brenda Brimmer and others, *A guide to the use of United Nations documents, including reference to the specialized agencies and special UN bodies* (Dobbs Ferry, N.Y.: Oceana, 1962 [272p.]) **(I699)**. With the multitude of changes in and increasing complexity of UN documentation, the need for a new guide to replace Brimmer has been evident. Several publications, none of which is entirely adequate, have appeared in recent years. Of these, Fetzer's guide is the most useful for a clear introduction to UN publications. Covering basic resources (depository libraries, indexes), types of publications, research problems (e.g., republished documents), and special United Nations processes, this modest guide suggests approaches to locating the wealth of UN materials rather than describing them in depth. Does not cover publications of related intergovernmental organizations, such as UNESCO.

The UN documentation system is treated rather fully in Peter I. Hajnal, *Guide to United Nations organization, documentation and publishing, for students, researchers, librarians* (Dobbs Ferry, N.Y.: Oceana, 1978 [450p.])**(I700)**, but the organization of this work, a combination of handbook and bibliographic guide, tends to confuse rather than illuminate. Luciana Marulli, *Documentation of the United Nations system; co-ordination in its bibliographic control* (Metuchen, N.J.: Scarecrow, 1979 [225p.]) **(I701)**, originally a library school thesis, contains useful information on lists produced by the UN and related agencies; however, it is a critical overview of coordination activities, not a guide. For concise profiles of UN-related organizations and their basic lists, reference sources, and periodicals, Harry N. Winton, *Publications of the United Nations system: a reference guide* (New York: Bowker, 1972 [202p.]) **(I702)**, has some value.

I703 Jeffries, John. A guide to the official publications of the European communities. 2d ed. London: Mansell, 1981. 318p.

Helpful guide to the intricate system of Common Market documentation. Includes selective bibliography of nonofficial sources, list of documentation centers and depository libraries, and index.

I704 Morehead, Joe. Introduction to United States public documents. 3d ed. Littleton, Colo.: Libraries Unlimited, 1983. 309p. [Library science text series]

Covers the vast range of federal government publications and policy issues relating to them in a clear, informative manner. Preliminary chapters deal with the publishing/distribution apparatus: the Government Printing Office, the Superintendent of Documents, the depository library system, and technical report literature (NTIS, ERIC, etc.) and other classes of documents excluded from the depository program. In this section, the author provides a stimulating perspective on a number of controversial topics, such as governmental versus commercial publication, increased distribution in microform, impact of information technology on public access, and adequacy of bibliographic control. The remaining chapters describe reference guides to federal and legal publications and key documents of the three branches and their auxiliaries. Numerous illustrations and tables enhance the utility of this classic guide.

Also see: Edward Herman, *Locating United States government information: a guide to sources* (Buffalo: Hein, 1983 [250p.]) (**I705**), a straightforward, selective treatment featuring a wide variety of specimens for documents and indexes; James A. Downey, *U.S. federal official publications: the international dimension* (Oxford and New York: Pergamon, 1978 [352p.] [Guides to official publications, 2]) (**I706**), which offers a British outlook on the importance of U.S. documents and problems of foreign access to them; and Frederic J. O'Hara, *A guide to publications of the executive branch* (Ann Arbor, Mich.: Pierian, 1979 [287p.]) (**I707**), a richly detailed examination of the output of the executive agencies, with agency, title, and subject indexes.

An earlier work that set the standard for the guides noted above: Laurence F. Schmeckebier and Roy B. Eastin, *Government publications and their use*, 2d rev. ed. (Washington, D.C.: Brookings, 1969 [502p.]) (**I708**), contains a wealth of valuable material and remains the best source for historical data on important publications.

I709   Official publications of the Soviet Union and Eastern Europe, 1945–1980: a select annotated bibliography, ed. by Gregory Walker. London: Mansell; New York: dist. in the U.S. and Canada by Wilson, 1982. 620p.

Because of its breadth and authority, serves as an excellent guide to government documents of the USSR and its satellites. For each country, discusses the governmental publication system and describes the major national and general bibliographies, constitutional documents, codes and other legislative documents, party organs, statistical sources, works of party leaders, and sources of information on international, military, economic, social, and cultural affairs. Index. Most of the contributors are librarians working with Slavonic and East European collections in Great Britain.

The same standards of excellence are observed in *Official publications of Western Europe*, ed. by Eve Johansson (London: Mansell; New York: dist. in the

U.S. and Canada by Wilson, 1984– , v.1–) (**I709A**). V.1 treats documents of Denmark, Finland, France, Ireland, Italy, Luxembourg, Netherlands, Spain, and Turkey. A projected second volume will cover the rest of Western Europe.

I710   Palic, Vladimir M. Government publications: a guide to bibliographic tools. 4th ed. Washington, D.C.: Library of Congress, 1975. 441p.

Prepared by the Library of Congress' specialist in government documents bibliography, the guide "outlines bibliographic aids in the field of official publications issued by the United States, foreign countries, and international governmental organizations" (preface). Includes official and commercially published lists of documents. Author, title, and country indexes.

Palic builds on the works of James B. Childs, editor of the first three editions, and largely supersedes an excellent earlier guide, Everett S. Brown, *Manual of government publications: United States and foreign* (New York: Appleton, 1950 [121p.]) (**I711**). For a supplementary list by Palic, see *Government organization manuals: a bibliography* (I797).

I712   Rodgers, Frank. A guide to British government publications. New York: Wilson, 1980. 750p.

Massive explication of the nature and extent of British documents. Part 1 discusses the British constitution and government, official printing and publishing, and general catalogs and indexes. Part 2 outlines the documentation of parliamentary activity. In part 3, the publications of the executive agencies, including those of Scotland, Wales, and Northern Ireland, are described and discussed. Selected secondary references for official bodies are listed and a brief glossary provided.

Whereas Rodgers is exhaustive, James G. Ollé, *An introduction to British government publications*, 2d ed. fully rev. and enl. (London: Assn. of Assistant Librarians, 1973 [175p.]) (**I713**), attempts to provide a manageable survey of the broad range of British documents. Another excellent guide, John E. Pemberton, *British official publications*, 2d rev. ed. (Oxford and New York: Pergamon, 1973 [328p.]) (**I714**), is notable for its inclusion of specimen pages.

For a helpful introduction to the parliamentary papers and their locators, see Percy Ford and Grace Ford, *A guide to parliamentary papers: what they are, how to find them, how to use them*, 3d ed. (Shannon, Ireland: Irish Univ. Pr., 1972 [87p.]) (**I715**).

REVIEWS OF THE LITERATURE

I716   American political science review. v.1– , 1906– . Washington, D.C.: American Political Science Assn. Quarterly.

Significant American review source. Extensive, classified arrangement of about 600 reviews per year. Occasional bibliographic essays.

Through 1966, also included bibliographies of selected articles and documents. In 1968 an annual listing of doctoral dissertations in political science was transferred to the association's newsletter, *P.S.* (I1196).

I717 Foreign affairs, v.1– , 1922– . New York: Council on Foreign Relations. 5/yr.

A useful bibliographic section appears in each issue. In 2 pt.: "Recent books on international relations" (400–500 per year), classified by subject and annotated with brief evaluative comments, and "Source material," a selective, unannotated list of official documents and pamphlets. The book notes form the basis for *Foreign affairs bibliography* (I804).

I718 International affairs, v.1– , 1922– . London: Royal Institute of Intl. Affairs. Quarterly.

British counterpart to *Foreign affairs*. The book review section is an important source for the more notable contributions to Western politico-economic literature. Includes more than 600 books a year, grouped by subject and area. Substantial, evaluative reviews.

I719 Neue Politische Literatur: Berichte über das internationale Schrifttum. v.1– , 1956– . Frankfurt: Europäische Verlagsanstalt. Quarterly.

German-language reviews of international political science literature. Signed review articles and individual reviews for 300–500 significant titles a year. Annual author and subject indexes.

I720 Perspectives: monthly reviews of new books on government/politics/international affairs. v.1– , 1972– . Washington, D.C.: Heldref Publications. 10/yr.

Evaluations of about 300 English-language (predominantly American) books per year. Each issue is arranged by general topics: United States—politics and public policy; United States—foreign policy and national security; international relations, law, and organization; comparative politics, theory, and methodology; Asia; Western Hemisphere; Africa/Middle East; Europe/USSR. Annual index by authors reviewed. Most reviews appear within 2 to 6 months of publication date.

I721 The political science reviewer. v.1– , 1971– . Bryn Mawr, Pa.: Intercollegiate Studies Institute. Annual.

Each volume covers some 15 titles in 9–10 reviews and critical bibliographic essays, with related readings footnoted. Contributions have depth and authority, and attempt is made to accomodate a broad range of political persuasion. Reviews of textbooks, reprints, and classics, as well as more recent literature.

I722 Revue française de science politique. v.1– , 1951– . Paris: Fondation Nationale des Sciences Politiques. Bimonthly.

Each issue has a survey of current literature. "Notes bibliographiques" has signed reviews of 30–50 significant works a year. "Informations bibliographiques" contains short book notes or abstracts for more than 1,000 titles, arranged by subject. Some review articles. International in scope, treating all aspects of political science and many cognate areas.

ABSTRACTS AND SUMMARIES

I723 International law reports. v.1– , 1919/22– London: Longmans, 1919–38; London: Butterworth, 1938–76; Cambridge: Grotius, 1978– Irregular.

Volumes for 1919/22–49 issued as *Annual digest and reports of public international law cases* (with slight variations in title). Important source for accurate digests of cases under 11 general headings (e.g., states as international persons, jurisdiction, the individual in international law, treaties, war, and neutrality). Summary of facts and decision for each case, followed by extensive quotation from the court's opinion. Index and tables of cases reported and cited.

I724 International political science abstracts. v.1– , 1951– . Oxford: Blackwell, 1951–72; Paris: Intl. Political Science Assn., 1973– Bimonthly.

Abstracts articles from a selected world list of periodicals in political science and related areas. More than 5,000 entries per year, arranged under 6 major headings: political science, political thinkers and ideas, governmental and administrative institutions, political process, international relations, and national and area studies. Short abstracts in English of English-language articles and in French of those in other languages. Subject and author indexes and list of periodicals are cumulated annually.

I725 Peace research abstracts journal. v.1– , 1964– . Dundas, Ont.: Peace Research Inst. Monthly.

Intricately classified and coded arrangement of abstracts. Major classifications: the military situation; limitation of arms; tension and conflict; ideology and issues; international institutions and regional alliances; nations and national policies; pairs of countries and crisis areas; international law, economics, and diplomacy; decision making and communications; methods and miscellaneous.

1–3 main classes covered each issue. Annual subject index ordered by classification code number, necessitating reference to accompanying coding manual. A large percentage of the 6,000–7,000 abstracts per year are supplied by the author or reprinted from other abstracting services. Monthly and annual author indexes. Despite complexity, a valuable control for a proliferating body of literature.

The excellent *Arms control and disarmament: a quarterly bibliography with abstracts and annotations* (Washington, D.C.: Govt. Print. Off., v.1–9, 1964–74) **(I726)**, now discontinued, is a useful record for the period covered.

I727   Sage public administration abstracts: an international information service. v.1– , 1974– . Beverly Hills, Calif.: Sage. Quarterly.

Broad-based service, offering subject access to English-language books, articles, pamphlets, government publications, and fugitive material on public administration. Approximately 1,000 entries per year, arranged under such headings as administrative structure, administration and politics, bureaucracy, and social services administration. Author and topical subject indexes for each issue cumulated annually.

I728   United States political science documents. v.1– , 1975– . Pittsburgh: Univ. Center for Intl. Studies, Univ. of Pittsburgh. Annual.

Published in conjunction with the American Political Science Association, USPSD is an ambitious, promising research tool. From a core of about 120 American journals in political science and related disciplines, more than 3,600 articles are fully described and abstracted, with a variety of indexing approaches provided. Document descriptions (v.2) include standard bibliographic details, the abstract, key subjects and geographical areas treated, and, if applicable, persons cited in the article and special features (e.g., tables, maps). Indexes (v.1) are broken down by authors/contributors, subjects, geographical areas, proper names, and journals covered. Subject descriptors are derived from the *Political science thesaurus* (1970), but many nonthesaurus terms are also included in the "proper names index," which consists primarily of organizational names. This practice leads to some awkwardness in searching, as with the terms "Watergate" and "Polish-Americans," which are not approved descriptors and will be found only in the proper names index. Future plans include indexing of book reviews from the journals surveyed and indexing and abstracting of books.

I729   U.S. Library of Congress. Congressional Research Service. Digest of public general bills and resolutions. 74th Cong.– , 1936– . Washington, D.C.: Govt. Print. Off., 1936– .

Brief digest of bills and resolutions introduced in Congress, with somewhat fuller information for reported measures. As bills become law or receive action, status and summary are given in preliminary sections. Sponsor, subject, and bill name indexes. Each session's cumulations and supplements result in a permanent volume.

I730   Whiteman, Marjorie M. Digest of international law. Washington, D.C.: Govt. Print. Off., 1963–73. 15v.

Digests published and unpublished sources on international law. Unofficial publications included, but sources are primarily documents of international bodies and national agencies. Index to set in v.15. Dept. of State publication, reflecting U.S. viewpoint.

Whiteman succeeds, but does not replace, 2 earlier works: John B. Moore, *Digest of international law* (Washington, D.C.: Govt. Print. Off., 1906 [8v.]) **(I731)**, and Green H. Hackworth, *Digest of international law* (Washington, D.C.: Govt. Print. Off., 1940–44 [8v.]) **(I732)**.

CURRENT BIBLIOGRAPHIES

I733   ABC pol sci: a bibliography of contents: political science and government. v.1– , March 1969– . Santa Barbara, Calif.: ABC-Clio. 6/yr.

Current contents source for political science. Lists tables of contents (excluding letters to the editor, book reviews, etc.) for current issues of about 300 domestic and foreign journals in political science, law, and other social science disciplines. Each issue's indexes of subjects and authors cumulate annually, thereby allowing for retrospective as well as current searches. Most issues covered are 2–6 months old. Two five-year cumulative indexes, covering 1969–78, have been published.

I734   "Doctoral dissertations in political science in universities of the United States." *P.S.* v.1– , 1968– . Washington, D.C.: American Political Science Assn.

Annual listing (in 2 sections): (1) dissertations in preparation, announcing additions, changes, and deletions since the previous listing, and (2) dissertations completed since the previous listing. Classified under 8 subject areas. Continues the annual (1911–67) list in *American political science review* (I716).

I735   International bibliography of political science. v.1–8, 1952–59. Paris: UNESCO, 1954–61; v.9– , 1960– . London: Tavistock, 1962– . Annual.

A component of the UNESCO-sponsored series *International bibliography of the social sciences* (A222) prepared by the International Committee for Social Science Information and Documentation. Extensive (4,000–5,000 items a year) but selective, classified bibliography of books, periodical articles, pamphlets, and documents exhibiting "scientific" character. Political science is broadly interpreted, with material in related fields included. References to articles analyzed in *International political science abstracts* (I724), and occasional book reviews. Author and subject indexes. Despite lag of 2–3 years, the essential current bibliography in political science.

Documents

I736   Bibliographic guide to government publications—U.S. Boston: Hall, 1976– . Annual.

Designed as a supplement to New York (City) Public Library, Research Libraries, *Catalog of government publications* (I849). Lists documents cataloged by the New York Public Library during the previous year, with additional entries from Library of Congress MARC tapes. Provides, in one alphabet, access by author, agency, title, series, and subject. Foreign documents are similarly indexed in the annual companion series, *Bibliographic guide to government publications—foreign* (Boston: Hall, 1976–   ) **(I737)**.

I738   Congressional Information Service. CIS index to publications of the United States Congress. v.1–   , Jan. 1970–   . Washington, D.C.: CIS. Monthly.

A valuable service. Attempts comprehensive abstracting and indexing of current congressional documents (except the bills themselves, publications relating to private bills, and documents that serve a ceremonial or housekeeping function). Basic arrangement by committee, subdivided by type of publication (documents, hearings, prints, reports, etc.). Gives complete bibliographic data for each item, information on availability, and brief summary of content. Indexes by subjects and names; titles; bill, report, and document numbers; committee and subcommittee chairmen. Major features: (1) full analysis of hearings, with testimony of each witness detailed, (2) extensive indexing, especially useful because of inclusion of hearing witnesses' names.

Annual cumulation of document abstracts incorporates additional material and appends a section on legislative histories. Indexes cumulate quarterly and annually; five-year cumulative indexes also available. The publishers offer a microfiche set of listed publications.

Another commercial service, Commerce Clearing House, *Congressional index* (75th Cong.–   , 1937/38–   ) (Chicago) **(I739)**, gives up-to-date information on congressional matters and also serves as a key to legislative publications. Loose-leaf format, with new material issued twice a week.

While both of the above titles are expensive, they offer solid help for users of current congressional publications.

I740   Great Britain. Stationery Office. Government publications. London: HMSO, 1923–   . Monthly.

Also known as *Catalogue of government publications*. Includes all priced items, parliamentary and nonparliamentary, sold or published by HMSO. In 3 sections: (1) parliamentary publications, (2) classified list by department or agency, (3) periodicals. Annual cumulations paged consecutively for 5 years to coordinate with the quinquennial consolidated index. A convenient merging of the indexes has been produced: Great Britain. Stationery Office. *Cumulative index to the annual catalogues of Her Majesty's Stationery Office publications, 1922–1972* (Washington, D.C.: Carrollton, 1976 [2v.]) **(I741)**. Preceded by *Quarterly list* from 1897 to 1921.

I742   Index to current urban documents. Westport, Conn.: Greenwood, July 1972–   . Quarterly.

A systematic effort to reveal the richness of local U.S. municipal and county publications. Documents are listed geographically by state and city/county, then by government agency. Information provided includes short annotations for many publications for which titles do not convey full content. Subject index includes as many as 12 or more entries for documents examined, fewer for those derived from accessions lists. Most publications listed are available by subscription or individually through the publisher's *Urban documents microfiche collection*. Quarterly issues cumulated into permanent annual volumes.

I743   United Nations. UNDOC: current index. v.1–   , Jan. 1979–   . New York: United Nations, 1979–   . Monthly.

Major list of UN publications. Issued each month, except July and August, UNDOC includes (1) a comprehensive checklist, arranged by agency; and (2) subject, author, and title indexes, both parts replaced by annual cumulations. Frequent references to "limited" documents, which are not sent to depository libraries, and omission of "restricted" (confidential) publications cause some frustration in use.

Bibliographic coverage of UN documents has varied in completeness and structure over the years. Prior to 1950, the principal lists were the UN Library's *Check list of United Nations documents* (1949–53) **(I744)**, which covered the period 1946–49, and *Documents of international organizations*, v.1–3, Nov. 1947–Sept. 1950 (Boston: World Peace Foundation) **(I745)**, a selective, quarterly bibliography. The UN's *United Nations documents index*, v.1–24 (Lake Success, N.Y.: UN, 1950–73) **(I746)**, originally listed all documents, including those of specialized agencies but excepting restricted and internal materials. With v.14, 1963, publications of most affiliates were omitted and a pattern of annual cumulative checklists and indexes was assumed. A cumulation of the indexes to v.1–13, 1950–62, was published in 4v. by Kraus-Thomson, New York, in 1974, with a separate cumulation for v.14–24 planned. The 1974–78 period is covered by the UN's *UNDEX* **(I747)**, issued in three parts: (1) Series A: subject index; (2) Series B: country index; (3) Series C: list of documents issued.

I748   U.S. Library of Congress. Processing Services. Monthly checklist of state publications. v.1–   , 1910–   . Washington, D.C.: Govt. Print. Off. Monthly.

Records, with full bibliographic information, state documents received by LC (currently more than 19,000 annually). Alphabetical arrangement by state, territory, or possession. Special monthly sections: publications of associations of state officials and regional organizations; state library surveys, studies, manuals, and statistical reports. Content notes for composite reports. Cumulation of periodicals in December issue. Annual index.

I749   U.S. Superintendent of Documents. Monthly catalog of United States government publications. v.1–   , Jan. 1895–   . Washington, D.C.: Govt. Print. Off., 1895–   . Monthly.

Essential listing of publications, including congressional and departmental documents, issued by all branches of the government. Entries (some 27,000 per year) are grouped alphabetically by agency, with monthly indexes cumulated semiannually and annually. Two major changes were instituted in July 1976: (1) full bibliographic description of items, including Library of Congress subject headings; and (2) detailed indexing by author, title, subject, and series/report numbers. Limitations of description and indexing access for the earlier volumes, as well as data on history and structure of the *Catalog*, are given in John G. Burke and Carol D. Wilson, *The monthly catalog of United States government publications: an introduction to its use* (Hamden, Conn.: Linnet, 1973 [113p.]) **(I750)**.

The *Monthly catalog*, the major documents bibliography since 1941, has attempted (since 1947) to provide comprehensive coverage, with moderate success. For best coverage through 1940, see *Catalog of the public documents of the Congress . . .* (I857). Information on ordering and depository libraries. Annual serials supplement lists periodicals and related publications.

Decennial/quinquennial indexes from 1941. A useful merger of subject entries from these and the earlier annual indexes: *Cumulative subject index to the Monthly catalog of United States government publications, 1900–1971*, comp. by William W. Buchanan and Edna M. Kanely (Washington: Carrollton, 1973–75 [15v.] **(I751)**. *Cumulative title index to United States public documents, 1789-1976* (Arlington, Va.: U.S. Historical Documents Institute, 1979–   ) **(I752)**, projected for 16v., is a title index to the shelflist (by Superintendent of Documents number) of the Government Printing Office Library; although not directly keyed to the *Monthly catalog* and its predecessors, the inclusion of date for each entry allows for systematic searches of the documents bibliographies.

Also of interest: *Publications reference file* **(I753)**, begun in 1977, a microfiche listing of items for sale from the Government Printing Office. Complete cumulations every other month, with new listings in alternate months. By GPO stock number, Superintendent of Documents classification, and alphabetically by title, series, key words and phrases, subjects, and personal authors.

RETROSPECTIVE BIBLIOGRAPHIES

The increasing number of quality subject bibliographies published during the last decade is a boon for the researcher. To the bibliographer faced with space limitations, it is also a source of some frustration. The list that follows is far from comprehensive, with several bibliographies of merit and most topical bibliographies published before 1965 excluded.

General

I754 A bibliography for students of politics. London: Oxford Univ. Pr., 1971. 113p.

"Primarily intended as a guide to reading for the politics papers in the Oxford Honour Schools of Philosophy, Politics and Economics" (preface). A well-selected, classified list of books and some important articles. No annotations or index.

I755 Bracher, Karl D., and others. Bibliographie zur Politik in Theorie und Praxis. Aktualis. Neuaufl. Düsseldorf: Droste, 1976. 574p. [Bonner Schriften zur Politik und Zeitgeschichte, 13]

Extensive reading list of books and articles on all aspects of political science. Almost 8,000 entries, unannotated, for English and German (and a small number of other Western-language) writings. Detailed classification, with table of contents. Author index.

I756 California Univ. (Berkeley) Institute of Governmental Studies. Subject catalog. Boston: Hall, 1970. 26v. First supplement: Hall, 1978. 5v.

Topical analysis of the institute's collection of pamphlets, documents, and periodicals. Covers a broad range of subjects relating to governmental affairs. Selective indexing of periodicals.

I757 C.R.I.S., the combined retrospective index set to journals in political science, 1886–1974, with an introduction and user's guide by Evan I. Farber. Executive ed.: Annadel N. Wile. Washington, D.C.: Carrollton, 1977–78. 8v.

Despite problems inherent in a project of its scope, this is a highly valuable contribution to the control of periodical literature relevant to political science.

The basic design of the C.R.I.S. project is as follows: From a core of 531 English-language journals in history, sociology, and political science, some 400,000 articles have been identified and classified into 570 hierarchical subject categories. Within each category, individual key words or terms in titles are extracted and arrayed alphabetically. Author indexes have been similarly created and a numerical coding system and the use of abbreviations employed to save space. Counterpart sets for history (11v.) and sociology (6v.) are also published by Carrollton.

The political science set lists about 115,000 articles under 95 subject categories in v.1–6 and by author in v.7–8. Categories are broad, even in the subclasses. (Example: Public Administration—Financial Administration—Taxes and Other Income.) Articles may be listed in more than one category. Major limitations: (1) dependence on key words in titles to indicate intellectual content of an article, as titles frequently do not convey either the specificity or breadth found in the best indexing; (2) use of category labels which often do not lead the searcher to the appropriate section, compounded by a scarcity of cross-references and the lack of an alphabetical topical key to indicate where a commonly expressed term (e.g., the American presidency) can be found. Minor problems with computer sorting also exist. Major strengths include the magnitude of the project, with many of the journals and backfiles indexed for the first time, and the inclusion of political science materials published in the core history and sociology periodicals.

For many topics, the researcher might be better served by one of the specialized retrospective bibliographies noted in this and other guides. However, *C.R.I.S./political science* is a major tool that will provide expanded approaches for the persistent searcher.

I758   Harvard Univ. Library. Government: classification schedule, classified listing by call number, author and title listing, chronological listing. Cambridge, Mass.: dist. by Harvard Univ. Pr., 1969. 263p. [Widener Library shelflist, 22]

Computer-produced display of the Widener Library's holdings in general government and civil law. Main list arranged by library's classification scheme, with author, title, and chronological approaches also provided. Approximately 7,000 titles of a general, historical, comparative, or theoretical nature. Works relating to specific countries or areas are covered in history volumes of the series. See also *Widener Library shelflist* (A257).

I759   Stanford Univ. Hoover Institution on War, Revolution and Peace. The library catalogs . . . ; catalog of the Western language collections. Boston: Hall, 1969. 63v. First supplement: Hall, 1972. 5v. Second supplement: Hall, 1977. 6v.

The major collections of the internationally renowned research library are represented in this reproduction of its card catalog. Contains more than 1 million cards in more than 30 languages. v.1–56 list books alphabetically, with author, title, and subject entries interfiled. Remaining volumes cover various special collections, including government documents and society publications. Focus of the collections is on political, social, and economic change in the 20th century. Major coverage for Eastern and Western Europe, the Middle East, Africa south of the Sahara, Latin America, and the Far East. Collections on Germany, France, Russia, and Africa are comprehensive. Material on the U.S. and Great Britain is primarily limited to their participation in the 2 world wars and influence in international affairs. Monumental.

Hall also published the following Hoover catalogs in 1969: *Catalogs of the Western language serials and newspaper collections* (3v.) (**I760**), *Catalog of the Japanese collection* (7v.) (**I761**) *Catalog of the Chinese collection* (13v.) (**I762**), *Catalog of the Arabic collection* (902p.) (**I763**), and *Catalog of the Turkish and Persian collections* (670p.) (**I764**). The catalogs of the Chinese and Japanese collections were each supplemented in 1972 and 1977.

U.S. Politics and Government

I765   Goehlert, Robert U., and John R. Sayre. The United States Congress: a bibliography. New York: Free Pr.; London: Collier Macmillan, 1982. 376p.

Timesaving gathering of references to 5,620 books, journal articles, dissertations, essays in compilations, and selected federal documents on the history, development, and legislative process of Congress. Arranged under 14 broad categories (e.g., committee structure and work, leadership in Congress, pressures on Congress), subdivided by specific aspects.

Although unannotated, the careful grouping of entries and a detailed 44-page subject index provide ready access to items cited.

I766   Greenstein, Fred I., and others. Evolution of the modern presidency: a bibliographical survey. Washington, D.C.: American Enterprise Inst. for Public Policy Research, 1977. 369p. [Studies in political and social processes]

Thoroughgoing effort to document the expanding role of the president, from the first Roosevelt administration (1932) through the Ford incumbency. The core of the bibliography lists for each president: general historical accounts and biographies; papers, memoirs; compendia and bibliographies; selected material on pre-presidential background; writings on advisers and advisory relations; references on specific events, activities and policies; and writings dealing with additional aspects and themes. Other chapters cover basic reference sources, selected government documents, and various topical matters (presidential constituencies, the vice presidency, etc.). 2,500 entries, selectively annotated. Author index.

The American presidency: a historical bibliography (Santa Barbara, Calif.: ABC-Clio, 1984 [376p.] [Clio bibliography series, 15]) (**I766A**) pulls together some 3,500 citations from the publisher's abstracting service, *America, history and life*. Covers writings of the 1973–82 period, exhaustively indexed. For a quick overview of source and secondary materials on each president, plus readings on selected topics (e.g., first ladies, problems of the presidency), see Kenneth E. Davison, *The American presidency: a guide to information sources* (Detroit: Gale, 1983 [467p.] [American studies information guide series, 11]) (**I766B**).

I767   McCarrick, Earlean M. U.S. Constitution: a guide to information sources. Detroit: Gale, 1980. 390p. [American government and history information guide series, 4]

Fully annotated bibliography of primary and secondary sources on the Constitution. Preliminary chapters list reference sources, general interpretive works, and studies of the background, framing, ratification, and basic principles of the document. The remaining sections deal with the individual articles, the Bill of Rights, and the amendments. Author and title indexes and detailed subject index. Two related, unannotated bibliographies: Stephen M. Millett, *A selected bibliography of American constitutional history* (Santa Barbara, Calif.: Clio Pr., 1975 [116p.]) (**I768**), which is similar in structure to McCarrick; and Alpheus T. Mason and D. Grier Stephenson, *American constitutional development* (Arlington Heights, Ill.: AHM, 1977 [166p.] [Goldentree bibliographies in American history]) (**I769**), arranged by topic.

Of special value to scholars is the systematic approach offered by Kenneth L. Hall, *A comprehensive bibliography of American constitutional and legal history, 1896–1979* (Millwood, N.Y.: Kraus, 1984 [5v.]) (**I769A**). Includes 68,000 entries for more than 18,000 unique citations, carefully classified and with separate author and subject indexes (v.5). Covers 1896–1979 "published writings of an analytically historical nature that are generally accessible to American scholars" (introd.). No annotations.

I770 Manheim, Jarol B., and Melanie Wallace. Political violence in the United States, 1875–1974: a bibliography. New York: Garland, 1975. 116p.

Unannotated listing of materials on such topics as race, riots, anarchism and terrorism, assassination, vigilantism, and gun control.

I771 Maurer, David J. U.S. politics and elections: a guide to information sources. Detroit: Gale, 1978. 213p. [American government and history information guide series, 2]

A survey of generally available literature of interest to the student of American political history. Sources are grouped in chronological order, with a final chapter devoted to general works. Selection limited to 20th-century books (periodical articles are not included). Critical, but very brief, annotations. Author, title, and subject indexes.

I772 Mills, William. The image makers: a bibliography of American presidential campaign biographies. Metuchen, N.J.: Scarecrow, 1979. 254p.

Specialized listing of works that "attempt, through a recounting of the lives of candidates or would-be candidates, to assist in the process of persuading the electorate to nominate and elect contenders for the presidency" (introd.). Arranged chronologically by campaign, then by aspirant. Entries receive full bibliographic description, except for size. Useful as a preliminary survey of a unique form of American political artifact.

I773 Smith, Dwight L., and Lloyd W. Garrison. The American political process: selected abstracts of periodical literature (1954–1971). Santa Barbara, Calif.: ABC-Clio, 1972. 630p.

2,274 brief abstracts, drawn from the publisher's reference journals, *Historical abstracts,* and *America: history and life.* Major classifications: political parties; American elections; political behavior; political institutions. Useful section on political behavior describes references on the influence of ethnic groups, women, and polls in American politics. Extensive combined index.

Also culled from ABC-Clio's abstracting services: *The American electorate: a historical bibliography* (Santa Barbara, Calif.: ABC-Clio, 1984 [388p.] [ABC-Clio research guides, 8]) **(I773A).**

Special aspects of the political process are treated in the following: Lubomyr R. Wynar, *American political parties: a selective guide to parties and movements of the 20th century.* (Littleton, Colo.: Libraries Unlimited, 1969 [427p.]) **(I774),** which lists more than 3,000 books, articles, documents, dissertations, and convention proceedings; Lynda L. Kaid and others, *Political campaign communication: a bibliography and guide to the literature* (Metuchen, N.J.: Scarecrow, 1974 [26p.] **(I775),** which features a supplement of French and German writings on American political communication (unannotated, as is the principal bibliography); Kalman S. Szekely, *Electoral college: a selective annotated bibliography* (Littleton, Colo.: Libraries Unlimited, 1970 [125p.]) **(I776),** a listing of some 800 pro and con items on a persistently controversial topic in American government; and Charles O. Jones and Randall B. Ripley, *The role of political parties in Congress: a bibliography and research guide* (Tucson: publ. by Univ. of Arizona Pr. for the Institute of Govt. Research, 1966 [41p.]) **(I777).**

I778 Stanwick, Kathy, and Christine Li. The political participation of women in the United States: a selected bibliography, 1950–1976. Center for the American Woman and Politics, Eagleton Institute of Politics, Rutgers Univ. Metuchen, N.J.: Scarecrow, 1977. 160p.

Contains more than 1,500 entries, grouped by form of publication (books, articles, dissertations, research in progress, etc.). Author and biographical index. Lack of classified arrangement and/or subject index lessens usefulness, as writings on particular topics (e.g., black women) can only be found by scanning each page.

Updating Stanwick and Li, Barbara J. Nelson's *American women and politics: a selected bibliography and resource guide* (New York: Garland, 1984 [255p.]) **(I778A)** has about the same number of citations, grouped under 15 topics, and a fair subject index. Unannotated, as is the earlier work.

I779 Stephenson, D. Grier. The Supreme Court and the American republic; an annotated bibliography. New York: Garland, 1981. 281p.

Most useful feature is highlighting of major court decisions and analytical materials relating to the institutional development of the Court and constitutional interpretation. Also includes sections on reference aids, general works, and biographical/autobiographical materials on individual justices. Author and case indexes.

I780 Walton, Hanes. The study and analysis of black politics: a bibliography. Metuchen, N.J.: Scarecrow, 1973. 161p.

Good attempt to identify writings on the political activity of Afro-Americans published through the early 1970s. Topics include black political socialization, political parties, candidates, and political thought. Author index. No subject index, but topical arrangement and chapter introductions facilitate use.

I781 Wilson, David E. National planning in the United States: an annotated bibliography. Boulder, Colo.: Westview, 1979. 279p.

Drawing on the literature of public administration, political science, economics, and sociology, Wilson provides a sturdy bibliographic supplement to his book, *The national planning idea in U.S. public policy: five alternative approaches,* also published by Westview in 1979. Sequence is historical, tracing the development of national planning efforts and focusing on activities in the 1970s. Good annotations. No indexes.

State and Local Government

I782 Bollens, John C. American county government, with an annotated bibliography. Beverly Hills, Calif.: Sage, 1969. 433p.

Major portion of this study is devoted to an extensive bibliographical commentary on post-1945 writings on county government. Classified arrangement, covering aspects of finance, intergovernmental relations, organization, politics, reform, and services. Most sections include works on individual states, as well as general studies. Exceptionally full, analytical annotations. Preliminary chapters discuss literature and research needs and the political vitality of the county as a unit. Author and title indexes.

I783 Government Affairs Foundation (New York). Metropolitan communities: a bibliography, with special emphasis upon government and politics. Chicago: Public Administration Service, 1957. 392p. Supplements 1955–70. Public Administration Service, 1960–72. 4v.

Comprehensive listing of monographs, plus selected articles, on urban development. Two main parts, subdivided by area and topic. Pt.1 includes writings on the functions, problems, services, organization, and politics of metropolitan governments; pt.2 lists studies on the social, economic, and demographic characteristics of cities and environs. Supplements 2–4 sponsored by the Institute of Governmental Studies, Univ. of California, Berkeley.

For foreign materials, see International Union of Local Authorities, *Metropolis: a select bibliography of administrative and other problems in metropolitan areas throughout the world*, comp. by D. Halász (The Hague: Nijhoff, 1967 [265p.]) (**I784**), which covers Europe, Australia, India, Latin America, and other areas. Geographical arrangement by country, subdivided by topic (administration and organization, housing, transport and traffic, etc.). Excludes writings on the U.S. and Canada.

I785 Municipal government reference sources: publications and collections. Ed. for the American Library Assn. Government Documents Round Table by Peter Hernon and others. New York: Bowker, 1978. 341p.

The value of this source for identifying key city documents and series (e.g., publications checklists, directories, codes) is immeasurably enhanced by inclusion of data on library and archival sources for gaining access to the publications. Arranged by state and city, with brief discussions of the nature, extent, and availability of the municipality's documents. Includes information on local newspaper indexing. Generally limited to 1970s publications, but includes many annuals and other series. A pioneering inventory and, as such, incomplete (for example, data on Charleston, West Virginia, and Erie, Pennsylvania, are reported as unavailable). Invaluable, nonetheless.

Also see *Index to current urban documents* (I742).

I786 Murphy, Thomas P. Urban politics: a guide to information sources. Detroit: Gale, 1978. 248p. [Urban studies information guide series, 1]

Books and articles are listed under the following headings: urban governmental structure; political leadership and political parties; participatory decision making; socioethnic politics; urban public policy issues; metropolitan organization and suburbanization; and federalism and urban governments. Full annotations and author, title, and subject indexes contribute to the usefulness of the bibliography for research in U.S. municipal politics.

Special aspects are treated in: John D. Hutcheson and Jann Shevin, *Citizen groups in local politics: a bibliographic review* (Santa Barbara, Calif.: Clio Pr., 1976 [275p.]) (**I787**), which is skillfully organized and annotated; Willis D. Hawley and James H. Svara, *The study of community power: a bibliographic review* (Santa Barbara, Calif.: ABC-Clio, 1972 [123p.]) (**I788**), with in-depth annotations for published studies and accompanying listings of dissertations; and Irving P. Leif, *Community power and decision-making: an international handbook* (Metuchen, N.J.: Scarecrow, 1974 [170p.]) (**I789**).

I790 Parish, David W. State government reference publications: an annotated bibliography. 2d ed. Littleton, Colo.: Libraries Unlimited, 1981. 355p.

Classified, annotated list of major serials and representative monographs issued by state agencies. By publication type (e.g., legislative manuals, statistical abstracts, bibliographies), with sublisting by state. Especially useful for data on state blue books and publications checklists. Agency addresses given in appendix. Indexes.

I791 Selected bibliography on state government, 1959–1972. Comp. by Regis Koslofsky and others. Lexington, Ky.: Council of State Governments, 1972. 237p.

Consists of a master list of more than 1,000 books and scholarly articles, an author index, and a key-word-in-context subject index. No annotations. Also see the Council of State Governments, *State government: an annotated bibliography, containing periodically revised sources of comparative data* (Chicago: The Council, 1959 [46p.]) (**I792**), and Susan A. MacManus, *Selected bibliography on state government, 1973–1978.* (Lexington, Ky.: Council of State Governments, 1979 [148p.]) (**I793**).

Public Administration and Policy

I794 Ashford, Douglas E., and others. Comparative public policy: a cross-national bibliography. Beverly Hills, Calif.: Sage, 1978. 272p.

Attempts to identify studies pertaining to key issues of public policy for five individual advanced states (United States, Great Britain, France, West Germany, and Japan), as a means for enhancing research of a comparative nature. Policy areas covered are administrative reform, economic management, local and regional reorganization, labor relations, race and migration, social security, higher education, and science and technology. For each country, a brief overview precedes the bibliography, which is partially annotated. Two appendixes list readings in comparative public policy and official sources of current policy information for each country. An outgrowth of the Comparative Public Policy Project at Cornell University's Center for International Studies.

I795   Great Britain. Ministry of Overseas Development. Library. Public administration: a select bibliography. 3d rev. ed. London: Overseas Development Administration Library, 1973.

Classified, unannotated list of predominantly British sources. Periodicals and related bibliographies are noted. 1976 and 1978 supplements.

I796   Murin, William J., and others. Public policy: a guide to information sources. Detroit: Gale, 1981. 283p. [American government and history information guide series, 13]

"Almost exclusively devoted to public policy within the American political system" (introd.). Individual chapters treat theories and concepts, decision making, state and local policy processes, urban policy, intergovernmental aspects, implementation and evaluation, and policy issues (business, education, science and technology, etc.). Expert annotations for the 1,300 books and articles cited.

I797   Palic, Vladimir M. Government organization manuals: a bibliography. Washington, D.C.: Library of Congress, 1975. 105p.

Unannotated list of sources for administrative structure of national governments. Includes official and unofficial publications. Index. Also see Richard I. Korman, *Checklist of government directories, lists, and rosters* (Westport, Conn.: Meckler Pub.: Cambridge: Chadwyck-Healey, 1982 [51p.]) (I798), which notes some additional publications but inexplicably omits a number of countries (e.g., Argentina, Italy, all of Scandinavia) from the survey.

I799   Palumbo, Dennis J., and George A. Taylor. Urban policy: a guide to information sources. Detroit: Gale, 1979. 198p. [Urban studies information guide series, 6]

Focuses on the study of public policy and its impact on urban areas. Includes books, essays, and selected articles on such topics as models and theories of analysis, determinants of policy, policy goals, formation and implementation, and evaluation of policy. Brief, descriptive annotations. Indexes.

I800   Rouse, John E. Public administration in American society: a guide to information sources. Detroit: Gale, 1980. 553p. [American government and history information guide series, 11]

Classified, fully annotated examination of the role of public administration in American life, as reflected in the literature. Areas covered include federalism and administrative structure, governmental divisions, discipline and practice of public administration, governmental discrimination and equal employment, productivity, centralization and decentralization, and comparative and developmental administration. Appendixes include information on the American Society of Public Administration and on the National Association of Schools of Public Affairs and Administration and their membership. Author, title, and subject indexes. Rouse's claim that this is probably the first comprehensive annotated bibliography on the topic is justified. A significant, well-executed effort.

William G. Hills and others, *Administration and management: a selected and annotated bibliography* (Norman: Univ. of Oklahoma Pr., 1975 [182p.]) (I801), stresses the pragmatic in its treatment of some 250 important books. Excellent annotations.

International Relations

I802   Blackstock, Paul W., and Frank L. Schaf. Intelligence, espionage, counterespionage, and covert operations: a guide to information sources. Detroit: Gale, 1978. 255p. [International relations information guide series, 2]

Critical assessments of selected English-language materials on a vital, controversial area of international relations activity. Chapter introductions give valuable overviews of the literature. Includes separate list of 50 essential books. Author and title indexes.

I803   Burns, Richard D. Arms control and disarmament: a bibliography. Santa Barbara, Calif.: ABC-Clio, 1977. 430p. [War/peace bibliography series, 6]

Extensive, unannotated listing of nearly 9,000 books, articles, and documents. Classified under 13 broad topics (League of Nations/UN; inspection, verification, and supervision; limitation of weapons and personnel; etc.), with detailed subgroupings. Author and subject indexes. Considering the great volume of literature available in this area, a useful starting point for the researcher.

I804   Foreign affairs bibliography: a selected and annotated list of books on international relations [1919–32, 1932–42, 1942–52, 1952–62, 1962–72]. New York: publ. by Harper (1933–35) and Bowker (1964–76) for the Council on Foreign Relations. 5v.

Comprehensive but selective listing of monographs, primarily in English and major West European languages. Based on bibliographic notes in the quarterly *Foreign affairs* (I717), with additional titles. Three major headings—general international relations, the world since 1914, and the world by regions—subdivided by subject and/or area. Covers history, politics, diplomacy, economics, international law, world organization, social problems, racial problems, etc. Few government documents included. Very brief annotations. Author index.

A related source, *The foreign affairs 50-year bibliography,* ed. by Byron Dexter (New York: Bowker, 1972 [832p.]) (I805), offers new evaluations of

2,130 of the most important books published in international relations, 1920–70.

I806   Foreign Relations Library. Catalog. Boston: Hall, 1969. 9v. 1st suppl. Hall, 1980. 3v.
Reproduction of the Council on Foreign Relations' holdings on all phases of international relations since 1918.

I807   Groom, A. J. R., and C. R. Mitchell. International relations theory: a bibliography. London: Frances Pinter Ltd.; New York: Nichols, 1978. 222p.
Theoretical and conceptual aspects of international relations are treated in 14 bibliographic essays. Emphasis of the contributions is on recent English-language books, although some articles are also noted. Chapters discuss writings on methodology and research methods, foreign policy analysis, psychological aspects of international relations, etc. No indexes.
Robert I. Pfaltzgraff, *The study of international relations: a guide to information sources* (Detroit: Gale, 1977 [155p.] [International relations information guide series, 5]) (**I808**), covers much the same ground. 360 annotated entries (all books), a list of major international relations journals, and author, title, and subject indexes. Moorhead Wright and others, *Essay collections in international relations: a classified bibliography* (New York: Garland, 1977 [172p.]) (**I809**), analyzes more than 200 anthologies published between 1945 and 1975, and provides a topical subject index.

I810   Norton, Augustus R., and Martin H. Greenberg. International terrorism: an annotated bibliography and research guide. Boulder, Colo.: Westview, 1980. 218p.
Research interest in the phenomenon of terrorism is reflected in the simultaneous publication of two related sources, Norton and Greenberg's *International terrorism* and Edward F. Mickolus, *The literature of terrorism: a selectively annotated bibliography* (Westport, Conn.: Greenwood, 1980 [553p.]) (**I811**). Although there is some overlap in coverage between the two, each is independently valuable.
The Norton-Greenberg compilation consists of about 1,000 entries, of which a third are annotated, covering general works, philosophical concerns, legal perspectives, terrorist tactics, individual world areas, efforts to combat terrorism, etc. Mickolus's work, which is somewhat more broadly based and includes nearly 3,900 items, follows a similar scheme; the section on responses to terrorist activities is extensive, and the sections on the media and psychological/medical approaches are especially useful. Both sources list selected fiction dealing with terrorism.
Indexing is weak in each. Norton and Greenberg includes only an author index. Mickolus also indexes by title, but these 76 pages would have been better used for a subject or title keyword index.

I812   Plischke, Elmer. U.S. foreign relations: a guide to information sources. Detroit: Gale, 1980. 715p. [American government and history information guide, 6]

"Designed to assist the serious student of American diplomacy" (preface), this extensive listing of reference sources, books, articles, and documents fulfills its aim. Following a section on diplomacy and diplomats in general, the core of the bibliography cites secondary sources on the conduct of U.S. foreign relations and its many aspects (executive and legislative concerns, the military, crisis diplomacy, etc.). Final sections discuss official sources and resources and enumerate memoirs and biographical literature. Author-agency index, but no subject index. Generally limited to English-language materials.
Bibliographies covering U.S. relations with special areas include: Thomas A. Bryson, *United States/Middle East diplomatic relations, 1784–1978: an annotated bibliography* (Metuchen, N.J.: Scarecrow, 1979 [205p.]) (**I813**); David F. Trask and others, *A bibliography of United States–Latin American relations since 1810: a selected list of eleven thousand published references* (Lincoln: Univ. of Nebraska Pr., 1968 [441p.]) (**I814**); and Michael C. Meyer, *Supplement to a bibliography of United States-Latin American relations since 1810* (Lincoln: Univ. of Nebraska Pr., 1979 [193p.]) (**I815**).
For a carefully classified and indexed list of more than 3,800 items relating to security aspects of U.S. foreign relations, see Arthur D. Larson, *National security affairs: a guide to information sources* (Detroit: Gale, 1973 [411p.] [Management information guide, 27]) (**I816**).

I817   Remington, Robin A. The international relations of Eastern Europe: a guide to information sources. Detroit: Gale, 1978. 273p. [International relations information guide series, 8]
General and country-specific sources are succinctly described. List of basic books appended. Author, title, subject indexes.
Other regional volumes of this series include: Ann Schulz, *International and regional politics in the Middle East and North Africa: a guide to information sources* (Detroit: Gale, 1977 [244p.]) (**I818**); W. A. E. Skurnik, *Sub-Saharan Africa: a guide to information sources* (Detroit: Gale, 1977 [130p.]) (**I819**); Richard J. Kozicki, *International relations of South Asia, 1947–80: a guide to information sources* (Detroit: Gale, 1981 [166p.]) (**I820**); and John J. Finan and John Child, *Latin America: international relations: a guide to information sources* (Detroit: Gale, 1981 [236p.]) (**I821**).

I822   Swarthmore College. Peace Collection. Catalog of the Peace Collection. Boston: Hall, 1982. 3v.
Catalog of the Friends Historical Library at Swarthmore. Books and serials entered under authors, titles, and subjects, with separate sections for periodicals and audiovisual materials in v.3.
Related research aids: Robert S. Woito, *To end war: a new approach to international conflict* (New York: Pilgrim Pr., 1982 [755p.]) (**I823**), which includes, in addition to bibliographic references, discussions of ideas, contexts, and actions relating to the promotion of peace and lists of world affairs organizations and periodicals; and Berenice A. Carroll and others, *Peace and war: a guide to bibliographies* (Santa

Barbara, Calif.: ABC-Clio, 1983 [580p.]) **(I824)**, which analyzes nearly 1,400 bibliographies, literature reviews, and reading list sections of books, and has a detailed subject index.

I825 United Nations. Library, Geneva. League of Nations & United Nations monthly list of selected articles: cumulative, 1920–1970: political questions. Ed. by Norman S. Field. Dobbs Ferry, N.Y.: Oceana, 1971–73. 6v.

Contents: v.1, 1920–28; v.2, 1929–45; v.3, 1946–60; v.4, 1961–70; v.5, Special problems, 1920–70; v.6, Security and international peace, 1920–70.

Important index to articles on international relations and law, drawn from about 3,000 periodicals. v.1–4 are arranged by country and date of article. v.5–6 list articles by topics, including geographical areas, with a chronological subarrangement. Special and security problems covered include colonies, minorities, pan-Americanism, the two world wars, disarmament, and war prevention.

International Organizations and Law

I826 Atherton, Alexine L. International organizations: a guide to information sources. Detroit: Gale, 1976. 350p. [International relations information guide series, 1]

Primarily concerned with the structure and activities of the United Nations, with lesser coverage for the League of Nations and other bodies. Well-organized guide, useful both for pinpointing bibliographies and other reference sources of value and for identifying important English-language books. Short, critical annotations. Author, title, and subject indexes.

Whereas Atherton is highly selective and narrowly focused, Michael Haas, *International organization: an interdisciplinary bibliography* (Stanford, Calif.: Hoover Institution Pr., 1971 [944p.] [Hoover Institution bibliographical series, 41]) **(I827)**, casts a broad net (7,935 books and scholarly articles in English) and deals with a variety of major organizations. In 7 parts: international organizations in general, early international organizations, League of Nations system, United Nations system, regional international organizations, nongovernmental organizations, proposals for world government. Occasional brief comments to clarify content; otherwise, no annotations. Author index. Minimal subject index.

I828 Dimitrov, Théodore D. World bibliography of international documentation. Pleasantville, N.Y.: UNIFO, 1981. 2v.

V.1, International organizations; v.2, Politics and world affairs. Revision and expansion of Dimitrov's *Documents of international organisations: a bibliographic handbook covering the United Nations and other intergovernmental organisations* (London: Intl. Univ. Pubs.; Chicago: American Library Assn., 1973 [301p.]) **(I829)**. Despite its impressive title and scope (more than 9,500 items in most major languages),

almost unusable. For one thing, general and specialized books, serials, and documents are listed alphabetically within a section, without annotation and in undifferentiated fashion. While this works reasonably well in sections with a limited number of entries (as in those relating to smaller specialized agencies), it presents real problems in a section as large as that on the UN, with more than 1,000 works cited. Selection criteria also seem uncertain, especially in the sections under "Bibliographic Control of International Documents," where a vast quantity of library literature with little or no direct relationship to international documents is listed. Most of v.2 is taken up by three long lists under topics (world politics, nuclear weapons control, peace) that have been well covered in classified, annotated bibliographies. Finally, the 4-page subject index is inadequate, particularly in view of the organizational problems noted.

I830 Hüfner, Klaus, and Jens Naumann. The United Nations system: international bibliography/Das System der Vereinten Nationen; internationale Bibliographie. München: Verlag Dokumentation, 1976–79. 3v. in 5.

Contents: v.1, Learned journals and monographs, 1945–65 (originally published in 1968 as *Zwanzig Jahre Vereinte Nationen: internationale Bibliographie*); v.2A, Learned journals, 1965–70; v.2B, Learned journals, 1971–75; v.3A, Monographs and articles in collective volumes, 1965–70; v.3B, Monographs and articles in collective volumes, 1971–75. (Note: v.3B publ. by K. G. Saur, München.)

Unannotated bibliography of English, French, and German writings on the UN during its first 30 years. Literature grouped as follows: general bibliographic materials, the UN system (general considerations), institutional and organizational arrangements (including material on specialized agencies), actual and potential areas of activity (e.g., disarmament and security, decolonization, natural resources, conventions). Author indexes in each volume. A major contribution.

I831 Kujath, Karl. Bibliographie zur europäischen Integration, mit Ammerkungen/Bibliographie sur l'intégration européenne, annotée/Bibliography on European integration, with annotations. Bonn: Europa Union Verlag, 1977. 777p.

Produced under the auspices of the Institute of European Politics, this massive effort "is directed at anyone concerned at all with the problems of Europe and its unification" (intro.). Emphasis is on the European Communities and its members states; also covers the Council of Europe, the Benelux Economic Union, the Organization for Economic Co-operation and Development, the Atlantic Community, and others. Annotations in English, French, or German, depending on the language of the original. Includes principal documents as well as secondary literature. Author index.

Also see the lightly annotated list of books and dissertations in English, J. Bryan Collester, *The European Communities: a guide to information sources* (Detroit: Gale, 1979 [265p.] [International relations information guide series, 9]) **(I832)**.

I833 Merrills, J. G. A current bibliography of international law. London: Butterworths, 1978. 277p.

Attempt is made to identify recent (1970s) articles and selected monographs on a wide range of international law topics, including sources, statehood, the law of the sea, air and space law, human rights, international claims, and the law of war. All entries receive informative annotations. Most of the source journals are English-language law reviews. Author index.

Ingrid Doimi di Delupis, *Bibliography of international law* (London and New York: Bowker, 1975 [670p.]) **(I834)**, includes materials in all Western languages and is expertly classified; unfortunately, it lacks annotations, a subject index, and a key to the numerous periodical abbreviations. Wesley I. Gould and Michael Barkun, *Social science literature: a bibliography for international law* (Princeton, N.J.: publ. by Princeton Univ. Pr. for the American Society of International Law, 1972 [641p.]) **(I835)**, surveys the scholarly literature of the social sciences in general to locate materials relevant to international law. Because of this interdisciplinary focus, it serves as a useful complement to Merrills, Delupis, and other lists. Excellent annotations. A supplement or new edition would be welcomed.

Documents

I836 Birchfield, Mary E. The complete reference guide to United Nations sales publications, 1946–1978. Pleasantville, N.Y.: UNIFO, 1982. 2v.

Contents: v.1, Catalogue; v.2, Sales number, title, and key-word-in-context indexes.

Although sales publications (those considered useful for public information needs) comprise only one segment of the UN's extensive program of documentation, they are widely known and frequently cited. Citations commonly refer to the document's sales publication number rather than to the "document symbol" classification system used by most UN documents collections.

Besides providing a convenient one-stop list of these publications over a 23-year period, the guide has two other major values: (1) basic arrangement by UN document symbol, either official or fabricated (where no official symbol was originally assigned); (2) variety of access points provided by the indexes in v.2. The 228-page key-word-in-context index to title words, compiled by Jacqueline Coolman, is especially and uniquely valuable for researching UN documents.

I837 Browne, Cynthia E. State constitutional conventions, from independence to the completion of the present Union, 1776–1959: a bibliography. Westport, Conn.: Greenwood, 1973. 250p.

Supplemented by Susan R. Yarger, *State constitutional conventions, 1959–1975: a bibliography* (Westport, Conn.: Greenwood, 1976 [50p.]) **(I838)**, and Bonnie Canning, *State constitutional conventions, revisions, and amendments, 1959–1976: a bibliography* (Westport, Conn.: Greenwood, 1977 [47p.]) **(I839)**.

Includes "all publications of state constitutional conventions, commissions, and legislative or executive committees, and all publications for or relating to these conventions and commissions issued by other agencies of state governments" (preface). A microfiche set of the original documents is also available.

I840 Great Britain. Parliament. House of Commons. General alphabetical index to the bills, reports, estimates, accounts and papers printed by order of the House of Commons and to the papers presented by command. 1801– . London: HMSO, 1853– .

The basic index to the parliamentary papers. Annual sessional indexes are consolidated into decennial indexes, and these in turn into 50-year cumulative indexes. Three of the latter have been issued to date: 1801–52, 1852–99, and 1900–1949. Excludes papers of the House of Lords (unless they are duplicated in the Commons papers) and the publications of bureaus and departments. Arranged alphabetically by large subject. Gives locational information.

I841 ——. ——. ——. Hansard's catalogue and breviate of parliamentary papers, 1696–1834. Repr. in facsimile with an intro. by Percy Ford and Grace Ford. Oxford: Basil Blackwell, 1953. 220p.

Classified listing of the most significant parliamentary papers under 26 major subject headings (e.g., education, agriculture, trade and manufactures, public works). Each entry indicates location of and topics covered by the paper. Limited to papers on "public" subjects, with material on foreign and diplomatic affairs largely excluded. General index. The reprint contains a select list of House of Lords' papers not included in the original of 1834.

Hansard's catalogue is continued by Percy Ford and Grace Ford, *A select list of British parliamentary papers, 1833–1899* (Oxford: Basil Blackwell, 1953 [165p.]) **(I842)**, which cites and classifies 4,500 papers. Similar in scope to the earlier work but less detailed in description.

For the 20th century, the same authors have compiled *A breviate of parliamentary papers, 1900–1916* (Oxford: Basil Blackwell, 1957 [470p.]) **(I843)**; *A breviate of parliamentary papers, 1917–1939* (Oxford: Basil Blackwell, 1951 [571p.]) **(I844)**; *A breviate of parliamentary papers, 1940–1954* (Oxford: Basil Blackwell, 1961 [515p.]) **(I845)**; and *Select list of British parliamentary papers, 1955–1964* (Shannon: Irish Univ. Pr., 1970 [117p.]) **(I846)**. Each of the breviates includes a subject list of papers (under 16 major headings, with topical subdivisions); a synopsis of each paper, stating terms of reference, argument, conclusions, and recommendations made; a keyword subject index; and an index of chairpersons and authors. These lists provide an indispensable key to the major committee and departmental reports in the parliamentary papers for 1696 to 1964.

I847 Hasse, Adelaide R. Index to United States documents relating to foreign affairs, 1828–1861. Washington, D.C.: Carnegie, 1914–21. 2v. Reprint, New York: Kraus, 1965.

Indexes published records, documents, papers, correspondence, legislation, and judicial decisions on international and diplomatic questions. Alphabetical subject arrangement, with many entries for individuals. Fills the indexing gap between class 1 of the *American state papers* (I1130) and *Foreign relations of the United States* (I1139).

For a detailed examination of relevant legislative documents, 1789–1969, see Igor I. Kavass and Michael J. Blake, *United States legislation on foreign relations and international commerce: a chronological and subject index of public laws and joint resolutions of the Congress of the United States* (Buffalo: W. S. Hein, 1977–78 [4v.]) **(I848)**.

I849 New York (City) Public Library. Research Libraries. Catalog of government publications. . . . Boston: Hall, 1972. 40v.

Reproduction of the NYPL catalog, representing more than one million U.S. and foreign documents. Arranged alphabetically by country, state, or city; subdivided by agency. Major holdings for the U.S., Great Britain and the Commonwealth nations, and Western Europe. Supplement for 1974 published in 1976. Continued on an annual basis by two series of the *Bibliographic guide to government publications* (I736, I737).

I850 Rohn, Peter H. World treaty index. 2d ed. Santa Barbara, Calif.: ABC-Clio, 1983–84. 5v.

Contents: v.1, Reference volume; v.2, Main entry section, pt.1, 1900–59; v.3, Main entry section, pt.2, 1960–80; v.4, Party index; v.5, Keyword index.

Much improved, expanded, and simplified over the first edition (ABC-Clio, 1974), which covered 1920–70. The complex set, produced from the computer database of the Treaty Research Center, University of Washington, provides basic data on 44,000 treaties and cites the sources of texts, including the complete series of the League of Nations and the United Nations, as well as 120 national sources. Main list (v.2–3) is arranged chronologically by signature date and gives source citation, name/title, registration and force dates, language(s), topic (assigned from a thesaurus in v.1), parties, and annexes showing post-signature activity. Party index (v.4) is arranged alphabetically by country or international organization, with subarrangement by treaty partner/date for bilateral treaties and by date for multilateral treaties; main topic and brief citation are also supplied for each entry. Keyword index (v.5) lists treaties by title words and indicates dates and signatories. Following instructions for use and the thesaurus, the bulk of v.1 is devoted to the extensive (622p.) "Treaty Profiles" section, a revised treatment of Rohn's 1976 publication with the same title. The profiles consist of statistical tabulations designed to show global, regional, and national patterns and topical concerns during the 1946–75 period. The *Index* is a well-organized, valuable key to 20th-century treaty documentation.

Access to multiparty treaties, especially those of the earlier period or those that have appeared in miscellaneous sets and anthologies, is provided by Harvard Univ. Law School Library, *Index to multilateral treaties: a chronological list of multi-party international agreements from the sixteenth century through 1963,* with citations to their text (Cambridge, Mass.: The Library, 1965 [301p.]) **(I851)**. Subject and regional index to 3,859 cited texts. Treaty sources published since 1780 are described in United Nations, Office of Legal Affairs, *List of treaty collections* (New York: United Nations, 1956 [174p.]) **(I852)**. Three major sections: general collections, collections by subject matter, collections by states. Also see the earlier, complementary list: Denys P. Myers, *Manual of collections of treaties and of collections relating to treaties* (Cambridge, Mass.: Harvard Univ. Pr., 1922 [685p.]) **(I853)**.

I854 U.S. Congress. Senate. Library. Index of congressional committee hearings (not confidential in character) prior to January 3, 1935 in the United States Senate Library. Washington, D.C.: Govt. Print. Off., 1935. 1,056p.

The library's holdings of hearings for both chambers, arranged by subject, committee, and bill number. Gives date, Congress, and session of the hearing and indicates published form (House report, Senate report, etc.). Supplements cover 1935–78.

Other hearings lists: U.S. Congress, House Library, *Index of congressional committee hearings in the library of the United States House of Representatives prior to January 1, 1951* (Washington, D.C.: Govt. Print. Off., 1954 [485p.]) **(I855)**, and Harold O. Thomen, *Checklist of hearings before congressional committees through the Sixty-seventh Congress* (Washington, D.C.: Library of Congress, Legislative Reference Service, 1941–58 [9v.]) **(I856)**. Thomen lists and locates more than 5,000 printed hearings, as recorded in various sources.

From 1970, best indexing for hearings (and other congressional documents) is provided by Congressional Information Service, *CIS index to publications of the United States Congress* (I738).

I857 U.S. Superintendent of Documents. Catalog of the public documents of the Congress and of all departments of the Government of the United States. . . . v.1–25, March 4, 1893–Dec. 31, 1940. Washington, D.C.: Govt. Print. Off., 1896–1945.

Complete and permanent register of U.S. documents published 1893–1940. Dictionary arrangement of author (corporate and personal), subject, and (when necessary) title entries. Full bibliographic information, including congressional serial set numbers. Commonly referred to as the *Document catalog*.

Coverage for the earlier years is less satisfactory, but the following can be consulted: Adolphus W. Greely, *Public documents of the first fourteen Congresses, 1789–1817: papers relating to early congressional documents* (Washington, D.C.: Govt. Print. Off., 1900 [903p.]) **(I858)**; Benjamin P. Poore, *A descriptive catalogue of the government publications of the United States, September 5, 1774–March 4, 1881* (Washington, D.C.: Govt. Print. Off., 1885 [1,392p.]) **(I859)**; and John G. Ames, *Comprehensive index to the publications of the United States Government, 1881–1893* (Washington, D.C.: Govt. Print. Off., 1905 [2v.]) **(I860)**. A rich source of bibliographic detail is the Supt.

of Documents library shelflist, *Checklist of United States public documents, 1789–1909*, 3d ed. rev. and enl. (Washington, D.C.: Govt. Print. Off., 1911 [1,707p.]) **(I861)**. Arranged by department, the *Checklist* is especially useful for descriptions of the serial set volumes and for historical data on agencies and their publications. A projected index volume was never published.

Best coverage after 1940 is provided by the Supt. of Documents, *Monthly catalog of United States government publications* (I749). Information on useful retrospective indexes to the principal documents bibliographies is included in the *Monthly catalog* entry.

Miscellaneous

I862 Beck, Carl, and J. Thomas McKechnie. Political elites: a select computerized bibliography. Cambridge, Mass.: MIT Pr., 1968. 661p.

Extensive list of conceptual and theoretical studies of elite behavior. The major section is arranged by title keywords, augmented by locale designations if not clearly expressed in title. A full citation listing of the books and articles also includes codes for 7 analytical topics (e.g., general elite theory, definition of elites, methodology of elites). Index of main and secondary authors.

I863 Deutsch, Karl W., and Richard L. Merritt. Nationalism and national development: an interdisciplinary bibliography. Cambridge, Mass.: MIT Pr., 1970. 519p.

Classified arrangement of more than 5,000 books and articles in the major Western languages, with sections on "building blocks" of nationalism, growth of nations, the rise of settler nations, and nationalism outside the Western world. Computer-produced, with author index and KWIC subject index. The latter, unfortunately in two alphabets, depends on whether the keyword is capitalized in the bibliography. Few annotations.

An elaborate scheme of selection criteria was employed to arrive at the 350 items included in H. Kent Geiger, *National development, 1776–1966: a selective and annotated guide to the most important articles in English* (Metuchen, N.J.: Scarecrow, 1969 [247p.]) **(I864)**. Chronological, with author-title-subject index. Detailed, evaluative annotations. More than half of the "articles" cited are books. Allan A. Spitz, *Developmental change: an annotated bibliography* (Lexington: Univ. Pr. of Kentucky, 1969 [316p.]) **(I865)**, lists 2,493 items, mainly post-1960 journal articles. Six major sections: social factors and problems, economic factors and problems, political factors and problems, public administration, units and areas, and international assistance. Annotations are objective, resembling short abstracts. Journal and author indexes and unannotated bibliography of about 1,000 books.

For additional references on national development, see the retrospective bibliographies listed under "Social change and innovation" in chapter 5.

I866 Heggie, Grace F. Canadian political parties, 1867–1968: a historical bibliography. Toronto: Macmillan of Canada, 1977. 603p.

Thorough, well-crafted source for materials published up to 1970. Pt.1 lists studies on the history of political parties, collectively and individually. Pt.2 is concerned with government and political institutions (e.g., dominion-provincial relations, government organization, the executive, Parliament). Appendixes of sources consulted and periodicals examined. Author and subject indexes. Most entries accompanied by a brief note on content.

I867 Muller, Robert H., and others. From radical left to extreme right: a bibliography of current periodicals of protest, controversy, advocacy, or dissent. 2d ed., rev. and enl. Ann Arbor, Mich.: Campus Publishers, 1970 (v.1); Metuchen, N.J.: Scarecrow, 1972–76 (v.2–3). 3v.

V.3 edited by Theodore J. Spahn and Janet P. Spahn, Muller's collaborators on v.1–2.

Invaluable guide, largely devoted to the American alternative political press. Scope is best illustrated by the chapter headings, which include "Radical left," "Marxist-socialist left," "Underground," "Anarchist," "Libertarian," "Racial and ethnic pride," "Conservative," "Anti-Communist," and "Race supremacist," and, in the more recent volumes, "Radical professional," "Conservation and ecology," "Feminist," and "Gay liberation." In addition to basic data (address, frequency, format, etc.) for each title, gives full, objective review of policy and content and indicates publisher's reaction to the review. Geographical and editor-publisher-opinion indexes. Title index (cumulative in v.3). Excellent source of information on 1,300-plus elusive publications, many of which have ceased.

For a historical approach to America's leftist press, see Walter Goldwater, *Radical periodicals in America, 1890–1950: a bibliography with brief notes. With a genealogical chart and a concise lexicon of the parties and groups which issued them*, rev. ed. (New Haven, Conn.: Yale Univ. Library, 1966 [51p.]) **(I868)**.

I869 Whetten, Lawrence L. Current research in comparative communism: an analysis and bibliographic guide to the Soviet system. New York: Praeger, 1976. 159p.

Lists 1965–75 writings in English on aspects of change in the Soviet system. Classified under broad topics (e.g., economic development and political change, post-industrial society, man and society, Communist elites, collective leadership, ideological and political culture, culture and socialist morality). No annotations, but audience level and general nature of the citation are given. Preliminary sections discuss the research design, the state of comparative communism studies, etc.

Related works of value: Thomas T. Hammond, *Soviet foreign relations and world communism: a selected, annotated bibliography of 7,000 books in 30 languages* (Princeton, N.J.: Princeton Univ. Pr., 1965 [1,240p.] **(I870)**, a massive, scholarly effort; Witold S. Sworakowski, *The Communist International and its front organizations: a research guide and checklist of holdings in American and European libraries* (Stanford, Calif.: Hoover Institution Pr., 1965 [493p.] [Hoover Institution bibliographical series, 21]) **(I871)**, a specialized tool for identifying and locating publications by and on the Comintern network; and the general, annotated list, Peter H. Vigor, *Books on communism and the Communist countries: a selected bibliography*, 3d ed. (London: Ampersand, 1971 [444p.]) **(I872)**.

Best survey of the literature on American communism: Joel I. Seidman, *Communism in the United States: a bibliography* (Ithaca, N.Y.: Cornell Univ. Pr., 1969 [526p.]) **(I873)**, which describes nearly 7,000 items and attempts to provide a balanced selection of pro- and anti-Communist writings.

DIRECTORIES AND BIOGRAPHICAL INFORMATION

Biography

International

I874 Bartke, Wolfgang. Who's who in the People's Republic of China. English translation by Franciscus Verellen. Armonk, N.Y.: M. E. Sharpe, 1981. 729p.

A publication of the Institute of Asian Affairs, Hamburg. Intended as "a reference guide to the current active leadership of China" (preface), gives for those profiled: (1) posts held as of March 1980, (2) narrative sketches of varying length and detail, (3) chronologies of political activity (appointments, elections, important speeches, purges, etc.), (4) photographs, if available. Separate section for biographies of 25 important deceased and purged cadres. Data culled from the official Chinese press. An extensive appendix on the organization of the PRC adds to the value of this impressive, unique source. See also B1647 and B1649, *Biographical dictionary of republican China* and *Biographic dictionary of Chinese Communism, 1921–1965*.

I875 Dictionnaire des parlementaires français: notices biographiques sur les ministres, sénateurs et députés français de 1889 à 1940. Ed. by Jean Jolly. Paris: Presses Universitaires de France, 1960–77. 8v.

Long biographical entries emphasizing the political activity of each biographee. Preliminary lists in v.1 include ministries of France 1871–1940, presidents of the Senate 1876–1940, and senators 1876–1945.

Adolphe Robert and others, *Dictionnaire des parlementaires français* (Paris: Bourloton, 1891 [5v.]) **(I876)**, covers the period 1789–1889.

I877 Dod's parliamentary companion. 1832– . London: Dod's Parliamentary Companion, Ltd. Annual.

Publisher varies. Brief biographies of members of Parliament. Also lists the constituencies and votes cast at the most recent elections and major government offices and officials. Biographical sketches of House of Commons members and an analysis of the 1983 election are contained in Times, London, *The Times guide to the House of Commons, June 1983* (London: Times Books, 1983 [368p.]) **(I878)**. Earlier editions published irregularly (after elections) since 1945.

A useful gathering of sketches from *Dod's* with supplementary material: *Who's who of British members of Parliament: a biographical dictionary of the House of Commons, based on annual volumes of "Dod's parliamentary companion" and other sources*, ed. by Michael Stenton and Stephen Lees (Hassocks, Sussex: Harvester Pr.; Atlantic Highlands, N.J.: Humanities, 1976–81 [4v.]) **(I879)**. Covers all members, 1832–1979, by chronological period. Also see: *Biographical dictionary of modern British radicals*, ed. by Joseph O. Baylen and Norbert J. Gossman (Hassocks, Sussex: Harvester Pr.; Atlantic Highlands, N.J.: Humanities, 1979– . v.1– .) **(I880)**, to be completed in 3v. for 1770–1970. Intended to supplement the *Dictionary of national biography* (B1660) and the *Dictionary of labour biography*, ed. by Joyce M. Ballamy (London: Macmillan, 1972– **[I880A]**), by augmenting material contained in those sources and providing sketches for individuals not included therein.

I881 European Consortium for Political Research. Directory of European political scientists. 3d fully rev. ed. Comp. and ed. by Jean Blondel and Carol Walker. Oxford: H. Zell, 1979. 461p.

Reflecting the growing recognition in Europe of political science as a discipline and designed to increase communication and professionalism, gives data on 2,153 individuals. Information includes date of birth, address, degrees awarded, title of doctoral thesis, previous and current appointments, publications, and fields of interest. Index by subjects and regions based on field of interest data.

I882 Lazić, Brako M. Biographical dictionary of the Comintern. Stanford, Calif.: Hoover Institution Pr., 1973. 458p. [Hoover Institution publications, 121]

Attempts to assemble reliable data on major figures of the Communist International, using published and unpublished sources considered accurate and avoiding those sources (e.g., Soviet documents of the Stalinist era) likely to contain factual errors or omissions. Includes more than 700 sketches, with 300 devoted to the Comintern's overall directorate.

I883 Saur, Karl O. Who's who in German politics: a biographical guide to 4,500 politicians in the Federal Republic of Germany. New York: Bowker, 1971. 342p.

Short sketches on leading political figures. In German.

For historical biography, see Wilhelm Kosch, *Biographisches Staatshandbuch: Lexikon der Politik, Presse und Publizistik* (Bern: Francke, 1963 [2v.]) **(I884)**, which provides sketches for political personalities of the German-speaking countries from the 19th century forward and is especially useful for minor figures and bibliographic references; and Max Schwarz, *MdR: biographisches Handbuch der Reichstage* (Hannover: Verlag für Literatur und Zeitgeschehen, 1965 [832p.]) **(I885)**, which lists the cabinets and parliaments of the First, Second, and Third reichs and gives brief data on the political career of each member.

I886   Who's who in the United Nations and related agencies. New York: Arno, 1975. 785p.

Valuable source for personal data on 3,500 key members of the UN and its affiliates. Full entries indicate title, nationality, languages, career positions, education, awards, etc. Organizational roster and other reference material (e.g., UN installations). Index by nationality.

Also see the biographical section of the *International yearbook and statesmen's who's who* (A436), and the "Biography and News" issues of *Current world leaders* (I907).

United States

I887   American Political Science Assn. Biographical directory. 1st ed., 1945– . Washington, D.C.: The Assn. Irregular.

Basic information on members of the association. Each listing includes vital statistics, educational background, fellowships and honors, professional employment, professional and public service, publications, fields of specialization, and address. Appendixes list members geographically and by general and specialized fields of interest.

As new editions appear infrequently (6th ed., 1973, is the latest), reference should also be made to the association's *Membership directory* (see I956) for new members and current addresses.

I888   Biographical dictionary of American mayors, 1820–1980: big city mayors. Ed. by Melvin G. Holli and Peter d'A. Jones. Westport, Conn.: Greenwood, 1981. 451p.

Serves a useful function by providing fairly lengthy, signed sketches of 679 mayors of 15 major cities. The cities selected for treatment (Baltimore, Boston, Buffalo, Chicago, Cincinnati, Cleveland, Detroit, Los Angeles, Milwaukee, New Orleans, New York, Philadelphia, Pittsburgh, San Francisco, and St. Louis) are those deemed to have a consistent pattern of leadership and historical importance. Appendixes give statistical and tabular data, including lists of mayors by city, political party affiliation, ethnic background, religious affiliation, and place of birth. Additional volumes projected.

I889   Biographical dictionary of the federal judiciary. Comp. by Harold Chase and others. Detroit: Gale, 1976. 381p.

Consists primarily of sketches extracted from the Marquis publications, *Who's who in America* and *Who was who in America,* giving basic information on federal judges, 1789–1974. Incorporates some new material from state historical societies and other sources. Appendix lists judges by appointing president.

I890   Biographical directory of the governors of the United States, 1780–1978. Ed. by Robert Sobel and John Raimo. Westport, Conn.: Meckler, 1978. 4v.

Collection of short, somewhat critical profiles, written by historical society researchers, librarians, historians, etc. Grouped first by state, then chronologically. Location of papers and/or bibliographic references given in most entries. Complete name index to set in each volume. Considering the difficulties in finding information on many of the individuals who have served as governors, a useful compilation.

John Raimo, *Biographical directory of American colonial and revolutionary governors, 1607–1789* (Westport, Conn.: Meckler, 1980 [521p.]) **(I891)**, covers the earlier period and adds a chronology and bibliography at the beginning of each state section. Straightforward personal and career sketches will be found in v.2–3 of Joseph E. Kallenbach and Jessamine S. Kallenbach, *American state governors, 1776–1976* (Dobbs Ferry, N.Y.: Oceana, 1977–82 [3v.]) **(I892)**. For discussion of electoral data in v.1, see I1172.

I893   Kane, Joseph N. Facts about the president: a compilation of biographical and historical information. 4th ed. New York: Wilson, 1981. 456p.

Classic source for ready reference information on the presidents. Pt.1 provides for each incumbent, through Ronald Reagan, basic career data, details on parents and family, election information, names of cabinet members and Supreme Court appointees, important dates, data on the vice-president, and additional (anecdotal) information. Pt.2 contains comparative data on a wide variety of topics, from the most basic (e.g., states represented, dates and places of birth) to those of a more trivial nature (zodiacal signs, occupations of wives' fathers, physical appearance, mountains named for presidents, among many others). Most information is presented in tabular form or in short paragraphs. Includes portraits and a topical index. Those seeking fast access to reliable information on presidents will do well to try Kane first.

For brief, scholarly essays on each president, see *The presidents: a reference history*, ed. by Henry F. Graff (New York: Scribner, 1984 [700p.]) **(I893A)**. Sketches accompanied by helpful evaluative bibliographies of important books. Also see William A. DeGregorio, *The complete book of U.S. presidents* (New York: Dembner, 1984 [691p.]) **(I893B)**, whose format is a cross between the fact book approach of Kane and the narrative style of *The presidents*.

Key executive staff are treated in two sources: Robert I. Vexler, *The vice-presidents and cabinet members: biographies arranged chronologically by administration* (Dobbs Ferry, N.Y.: Oceana, 1975 [2v.]) **(I894)**, and *Biographical directory of the United States executive branch, 1774–1977*, Robert Sobel, ed. (Westport, Conn.: Greenwood, 1977 [503p.]) **(I895)**, expanded from a work first published in 1971. Entries and bibliographies in Vexler are lengthier than in Sobel. Arrangement in Sobel is alphabetical by name, with special indexes and comparative tabulations. Information contained in both is similar; allowing for stylistic differences, many of the entries are nearly identical.

I896 Political profiles. Ed. by Eleanora W. Schoenebaum. New York: Facts On File, 1976–
       v.1– .
       v.1, The Truman years; v.2, The Eisenhower years; v.3, The Kennedy years; v.4, The Johnson years; v.5, The Nixon-Ford years.
       Exceptional in quality and significance, this set not only provides well-written, interesting sketches of prominent personalities associated with each presidentia. administration, but it also captures the unique political and cultural essence of the period itself.
       Among the many virtues: (1) selection of individuals profiled, which is primarily devoted, but not limited, to government officials and includes a number of influential people from other spheres (e.g., Arthur Miller, George Meany, Jane Fonda, Walter Cronkite); (2) volume introductions, which concisely summarize the key events of the administration; (3) appendixes containing useful chronologies, rosters, and bibliographies; and (4) indexes by career of individual and names/topics. Some individuals, such as Hubert Humphrey, appear in several volumes, with each sketch focusing on activities during that administration. Cross-references from volume to volume, as well as within each volume. A sixth volume, *The Carter years,* is projected. *Political profiles* sets the standard for reference works on post–World War II U.S. political biography.
       Investigative journalism characterizes the lively profiles found in Ronald Brownstein and Norma Easton, *Reagan's ruling class: portraits of the president's top one hundred officials* (New York: Pantheon, 1983 [759p.]) **(I896A)**. Introduction by Ralph Nader.

I897 Rutgers Univ. Center for the American Woman and Politics. Women in public office: a biographical directory and statistical analysis. Comp. by the Center for the American Woman and Politics, Eagleton Institute of Politics, Rutgers—The State University of New Jersey. Project staff: Kathy Stanwick and others. 2d ed. Metuchen, N.J.: Scarecrow, 1978. 68p., 510p.
       Identifies more than 17,000 women serving as local, state, and federal officials in 1977 and, where available, gives basic biographical data (except for members of state boards and commissions). Illuminating 68-page "Profile of Women Holding Office" precedes directory listings by state. Name index.

Esther Stineman, *American political women: contemporary and historical profiles* (Littleton, Colo.: Libraries Unlimited, 1980 [228p.]) **(I898)**, contains portraits of 60 of the most notable or representative women officeholders in all levels of government (e.g., Frances Berkins, Margaret Chase Smith, Ella Grasso, Patricia Harris, Shirley Temple Black). Short bibliographies for each entry and a good general bibliography. For sketches of all women senators and representatives through 1972, see Rudolf Engelbarts, *Women in the United States Congress, 1917–1972: their accomplishments: with bibliographies* (Littleton, Colo.: Libraries Unlimited, 1974 [184p.]) **(I899)**.

I900 U.S. Congress. Biographical directory of the American Congress, 1774–1971. . . . Washington, D.C.: Govt. Print. Off., 1971. 1,972p.
       More than 10,800 biographies of congressmen and the members of the Continental Congress. Also contains a chronological list of executive officers, a list of delegates to the Continental Congress, and a listing of congresses through the 86th, with dates, officers, and members.
       The barest of essentials are included in Congressional Quarterly, Inc., *Members of Congress since 1789,* 2d ed. (Washington, D.C.: Congressional Quarterly, 1981 [180p.]) **(I901)**. Party affiliation, state represented, birth and death dates, dates of incumbency. Family relationships to other members noted, where applicable.

I902 United States. Dept. of State. Biographic register. 1869– . Washington, D.C.: Govt. Print. Off. Annual.
       Concise biographic information on personnel of the Dept. of State and other federal government agencies in foreign affairs. In 1974, the *Register* was restricted to limited official use; current editions are no longer available to the general public.

I903 Who's who in American politics: a biographical directory of United States political leaders. 1st ed.– , 1967–68–   New York: Bowker, 1967– . Biennial.
       Vital source of information on persons active in American political life. Entries give full name, address, political party affiliation, birthplace and date, education, family data, present and previous political and business positions, and achievements. Includes nationally prominent figures but is especially useful for inclusion of state and local officials, convention delegates, officers of political organizations, and other lesser-known persons. Earlier editions alphabetical by individual, with geographical index. With 7th ed. (1979–80), the 23,000 entries are arranged by state, with a name index provided.
       An unrelated source, useful for basic data on historical figures: Dan Morris and Inez Morris, *Who was who in American politics: a biographical dictionary of over 4,000 men and women who contributed to the United States political scene from colonial days up to and including the immediate past* (New York: Hawthorn, 1974 [637p.]) **(I904)**. Based on material in standard reference sources.

I905 Who's who in government. 1st ed.– , 1972/
73– . Chicago: Marquis. Irregularly.

Complements *Who's who in American politics*
(above) in that it gives information on many officeholders who are not active in the political arena. Profiles
nearly 18,000 officials and administrative staff on all
levels of government. Basic Marquis *Who's who* format. Indexed by geographical area and/or function.

Directories of Governments and Officials

International

I906 Bottin administratif et documentaire. Paris:
Didot-Bottin, 1942– . Annual.

Exhaustive directory of the national and regional governments of France, arranged by functions.
Indexes by major administrative headings and by
names of officials. Maps, organization charts, historical tables, etc. Information previously contained in
Bottin.

I907 Current world leaders. v.1– , 1958– . Santa
Barbara, Calif.: Intl. Academy at Santa Barbara. Monthly.

Minor variations in title, format, and place of
publication. "Almanac issue" (published in April,
August, and December) gives up-to-date listings of
major governmental officials of world states, as well as
officers of major international organizations and
alliances. Information obtained from official sources,
unless otherwise indicated.

Changes in government are reported in other
issues of each volume. "Speeches and Reports" (3/yr.)
and "Biography and News" (6/yr.). The latter is an
excellent source for current political biography.

Similar in intent: U.S. Central Intelligence
Agency, *Chiefs of state and cabinet members of foreign
governments* (Washington, D.C.: CIA, 1979?–)
(I908), part of the CIA's National Foreign Assessment
Center's Reference aid series, is completely revised
each month and includes a personal name index.

Communications are emphasized in the annual
*Lambert's worldwide government directory, with inter-
governmental organizations* (Washington, D.C.: Lambert, 1981–) **(I909)**. Gives addresses, telephone
numbers, and telex and cable information on heads of
state, cabinet members (including many deputy ministers and undersecretaries), court officers, banking
officials, and national trade and resources directors.
These unique features help to justify the expense
($250/yr.) of *Lambert's*.

I910 Great Britain. Civil Service Dept. The civil service year book. 1974– . London: HMSO.
Annual.

Volumes for 1809–1973 published as the *British
imperial calendar and civil service list*. Major list of
British government offices and officials, grouped as
follows: (1) the royal households and offices;
(2) parliamentary offices; (3) ministers and departments; (4) libraries, museums, galleries, research

councils, and other organizations; (5) departments
and other organizations of Northern Ireland, Scotland, and Wales. Separate table of salaries, and name
index.

D. A. Pickrill, *Ministers of the Crown* (London
and Boston: Routledge & Paul, 1981 [135p.]) **(I911)**,
consists of chronological lists of British officeholders,
by ministry, from earliest times to the present.

The organization of the Diplomatic Service and
brief biographies of staff are found in: Great Britain,
Foreign and Commonwealth Office, *The diplomatic
service list*, 1966– (Annual) **(I912)**.

I913 Henige, David P. Colonial governors from the
fifteenth century to the present: a comprehensive list. Madison: Univ. of Wisconsin Pr., 1970.
461p.

Well-documented lists of administrators of
European colonial possessions, as well as those of
Japan and the United States. The colonies of each
nation are grouped together, and the listing for each
colony is accompanied by historical notes and sources.
Compiler attempts (with considerable success) to provide full name and dates of incumbency for each
governor. Bibliographies of primary and secondary
sources. General and name indexes.

I914 Institut zur Erforschung der UdSSR. Party and
government officials of the Soviet Union, 1917–
1967. Comp. by the Institute for the Study of the
USSR (Munich). Ed. by Edward L. Crowley
and others. Metuchen, N.J.: Scarecrow, 1969.
214p.

In 2 pts.: Communist party officials by congress,
and government officials by agency. Notes, statistical
tables, organization charts, and general and name indexes. The institute also has compiled *The Soviet
diplomatic corps, 1917–1967*, ed. by Edward L.
Crowley (Metuchen, N.J.: Scarecrow, 1970 [240p.])
(I915), which lists key diplomatic personnel by function and area of service and has alphabetical section
and biographical sketches stressing diplomatic activity. Chronology of noteworthy diplomatic acts and
events. General and name indexes.

I916 Repertorium der diplomatischen Vertreter aller
Länder seit dem Westfälischen Frieden (1648).
(Repertory of the diplomatic representatives of
all countries since the Peace of Westphalia
[1648]). Oldenburg: G. Stalling; Zürich: Fretz
& Wasmuth; Graz: Böhlaus Naehf., 1936–65.
3v.

V.1 covers 1648–1715; v.2, 1716–63; and v.3,
1764–1815. Under each major country, representatives are listed by the country to which they were sent.
For each envoy, gives name, capacity, dates of mission, and source of information. Personal name and
country indexes in each volume.

I917 Ross, Martha, and Bertold Spuler. Rulers and
governments of the world. London and New
York: Bowker, 1977–78. 3v.

Contents: v.1, Earliest times to 1491; v.2, 1490–
1929; v.3, 1930–1975. v.1 by Ross; v.2–3 translated

from Spuler's *Regenten und Regierungen der Welt,* with revisions.

Enormously valuable compilation, consisting of chronological lists of rulers, heads of state, etc., for territories, dynasties, sees, hordes, and countries, as well as lists of cabinets for major modern nations. Personal name indexes in each volume. v.1 includes table, showing forms of names in various languages, and a bibliography. Difficulties in determining dates and names, which abound in an enterprise such as this, are discussed in the prefaces.

Less comprehensive but convenient: Alan R. Langville, *Modern world leaders: a chronology* (Metuchen, N.J.: Scarecrow, 1979 [360p.]) **(I918)**, gives names of heads of government for all nations independent for at least 20 years since 1800, with earlier rulers also listed for the major countries. U.S. state governors and Canadian provincial leaders included. Historical headnotes. Name index.

Expanding coverage of major cabinet officials in the 20th century are volumes by Robin L. Bidwell in the series Bidwell's guide to government ministers. So far published: *The major powers and Western Europe, 1900–1971* (London: F. Cass, 1973 [297p.] [v.1.]) **(I919)**; *The Arab world, 1900–1972* (London: F. Cass, 1973 [124p.] [v.2]) **(I920)**; *The British Empire and successor states, 1900–1972* (London: F. Cass, 1974 [156p.] [v.3]) **(I921)**; and an unnumbered volume for all of Africa, 1950–76, *Guide to African ministers* (London: Collings, 1978 [79p.]) **(I922)**. In addition to heads of state and heads of government, includes ministers of foreign affairs, war/defense, the interior, and finance for all countries. Ministers of justice, the navy, and trade/commerce are given for the major powers, and ministers of oil for the major Arab nations. No indexes. Listings by function in chronological order; sublistings by country groups seem arbitrary and are somewhat confusing.

I923   U.S. Dept. of State. Diplomatic list. 1893– . Washington, D.C.: Govt. Print. Off. Quarterly.
Lists members of the diplomatic corps and staff members of foreign embassies and legations in Washington, by country and rank. A related State Dept. publication, *Foreign consular offices in the United States* (1932–   ) **(I924)**, provides an annual listing of each office's jurisdictions and personnel.

I925   U.S. Central Intelligence Agency. Directory of Soviet officials. Washington, D.C.: CIA, 1982–83. [3v.]
V.1, National organizations; v.2, Republic organizations; v.3, Science and education.
Issued as part of the Reference aid series of the CIA's National Foreign Assessment Center. New editions published irregularly from the 1960s (previously by the State Department's Bureau of Intelligence and Research). In addition to party and government officials (by function), lists key personnel in cultural and professional organizations, propaganda organizations, academies and institutions, religious denominations, the media, and international organizations. Indicates date when position was assumed and birth date, when known. Name index.

Similar information is provided for other socialist governments in several volumes of the Reference aid series, among them: *Directory of officials of the Socialist Republic of Romania* **(I926)**; *Directory of officials of the People's Republic of China* **(I927)**; *Directory of officials of the Socialist Federal Republic of Yugoslavia* **(I928)**; *Directory of officials of the Democratic People's Republic of Korea* **(I929)**; *Directory of officials of the Republic of Cuba* **(I930)**; *Directory of officials of the German Democratic Republic* **(I931)**; *Directory of officials of the Bulgarian People's Republic* **(I932)**; *Directory of officials of the People's Socialist Republic of Albania* **(I933)**; *Directory of officials of the Hungarian People's Republic* **(I934)**; *Directory of officials of the Polish People's Republic* **(I935)**; *Directory of officials of the Czechoslovak Socialist Republic* **(I936)**; and *Directory of officials of the Socialist Republic of Vietnam* **(I937)**. New editions of most of these directories have appeared since 1979.

I938   Wood, Alan. The Times guide to the European Parliament, 1984. London: Times Books, 1984. 287p.
Handbook on the second election for the European Parliament gives background and statistical data but is primarily of interest for brief biographical sketches, accompanied by photographs, of the members. A 1979 guide also published. See the looseleaf *Official handbook of the European Parliament* (Herstmonceux, Hailsham, East Sussex: Dod's Parliamentary Companion, 1980–   ) **(I939)** for revised and new entries on members.

United States

I940   National directory of women elected officials, 1981. Washington, D.C.: National Women's Political Caucus, 1981. 150p.
Names and addresses of women legislators (federal and state), mayors, and members of the Republican and Democratic national committees. Concise statistical summaries of women officeholders for each state.

I941   National roster of black elected officials. 1970– . Washington, D.C.: Joint Center for Political Studies. Annual.
For each state, gives names and addresses of federal, state, county, and municipal incumbents, as well as judicial officials, police chiefs, local school board members, and school superintendents. Includes statistical tables and name index.

I942   Solomon, Samuel R. The governors of the American states, commonwealths, and territories, 1900–1980. Lexington, Ky.: Council of State Governments, 1980. 79p.
Arranged first by jurisdiction, then chronologically. Includes term of office, name of governor, party, residence, notes, birthdate, birthplace, and date of death. Also see I890, I892.

I943   State elective officials and the legislatures. Lexington, Ky.: Council of State Governments, 1963– . Biennial.
Issued as a supplement to the council's *Book of*

the states (see I1055). Gives names of major state officials and Supreme Court justices, and provides names and addresses of legislators. Two other biennial supplements to the *Book of the states* are *State legislative leadership, committees and staff* (Lexington, Ky.: Council of State Governments, 1979–) **(I944)**, which gives a state-by-state breakdown of legislative organization and lists, by function, selected officials, committee chairmen, and staff; and *State administrative officials classified by function* (Lexington, Ky.: Council of State Governments, 1967–) **(I945)**, which provides names, addresses, and phone numbers of key state officers listed under 100 areas of responsibility (consumer protection, liquor control, transportation, etc.).

Functional groupings of administrative officials are also featured in *The national directory of state agencies* (Arlington, Va.: Information Resources Pr., 1974/75–) **(I946)**, published biennially. Category headings and data supplied are almost identical to the council's list, noted above. Also lists agencies by state.

Susan Lukowski and Cary T. Grayson, *State information book* (Washington, D.C.: Potomac, 1980 [305p.]) **(I947)**, is a handy listing of major administrative officers and services, legislative officials, Supreme Court justices, and state offices of federal agencies. New editions or supplements published at 2- to 3-year intervals since 1973.

I948 Taylor's encyclopedia of government officials, federal and state. 1967/68– . Dallas: Political Research. Biennial.

Most of the information in this directory can be found in standard sources, but the following features are noteworthy: (1) complete lists of state legislators by district, (2) maps of congressional and state districts for each state, showing party control, and (3) extensive pictorial material, including photographs of major federal and state officials. Also gives names and addresses of national convention delegates. Colorful, attractive presentation. Subscription price ($225) includes cumulated quarterly updates, other supplementary matter, and a toll-free telephone look-up service.

I949 United States. Congress. Official congressional directory. 1809?– . Washington, D.C.: Govt. Print. Off. Annual.

Published irregularly by private firms until 1864. Currently issued for each session of Congress. Includes biographical sketches of members, arranged by state; state delegations; alphabetical list of members, with addresses, phone numbers, etc.; terms of service; committee and subcommittee assignments; administrative assistants and secretaries; sessions of Congress; governors of states; votes cast for congressmen; biographical sketches of cabinet members and lists of officials in each department; biographies of members of the Supreme Court and a list of courts; officials of independent agencies; international organization delegations; foreign and U.S. diplomatic officers; press galleries; and maps of congressional districts. Detailed table of contents and an index of individuals. Very useful.

Data from the earliest directories, plus related broadsides and pamphlets, are conveniently gathered in United States, Congress, *The United States congressional directories, 1789–1840*, ed. by Perry M. Goldman and James S. Young (New York: Columbia Univ. Pr., 1973 [417p.]) **(I950)**.

An annual companion publication, *Congressional staff directory* (Washington, D.C.: Congressional Staff Directory, 1959–) **(I951)**, lists the staffs of senators, representatives, and committees and subcommittees. Also sketches of key staff personnel, lists of major officials and their liaison staffs, and the congressional districts and representatives of 9,900 cities and towns. Personal name index. A prepublication supplement, *Advance locator*, gives most recent information on changes and a current directory of offices, phone numbers, etc.

I952 United States. Dept. of State. Key officers of foreign service posts: guide for business representatives. Feb. 1964– . Washington, D.C.: Govt. Print. Off. Quarterly.

Gives address and telephone number of foreign embassies, missions, and consulates of the U.S. In addition to the ambassador, names other major personnel, such as economic officer, consular officer, political officer, and scientific attache.

The State Dept.'s quarterly *Foreign Service list* (1929–75) **(I953)**, now discontinued, included staff members of the Foreign Service, Agency for International Development, Peace Corps, U.S. Information Agency, Dept. of Agriculture, and the army, navy, and air force.

I954 Washington information directory. 1975/76– . Washington, D.C.: Congressional Quarterly. Annual.

Extensive, well-organized guide to executive, congressional, and private agencies in the Washington area. Listings arranged in 16 chapters (e.g., communications and the media, economics and business, equal rights, national security) with topical subdivisions. Each entry includes address, telephone number, principal officer, and statement of purpose or responsibility. Appendix section contains rosters for congressional committees, executive departments, White House staff, foreign embassies, national labor unions, state and local governments, etc. Subject and agency/organization indexes.

Addresses and telephone numbers of key agencies and individuals are given in the inexpensive annual *Duke's Washington pocket directory: a citizen's guide to major government offices and information services* (Washington, D.C.: WANT, 1982?–) **(I955)**. *Duke's* highlights consumer contacts and Washington tourist attractions.

See also *United States government manual* (I1066) and *Encyclopedia of governmental advisory organizations* (I1067), both included under "Handbooks, Manuals, and Compendia" in this chapter.

Miscellaneous

1956   American Political Science Assn. Membership directory. 1974– . Washington, D.C. Annual.

Supplements the association's *Biographical directory* (I887). Alphabetical listing of members gives basic addresses, affiliations, and areas of specialization. Indexes by field of interest and geographical location.

Special lists issued by the APSA include: *Roster of women in political science*, 4th ed. (Washington, D.C.: Committee on the Status of Women in the Profession, 1976 [152p.]) **(I957)**; *Directory of black Americans in political science*, 1st ed. (Washington, D.C.: Committee on the Status of Blacks in the Profession, 1977 [106p.]) **(I958)**; and *Roster of Chicanos in political science*, 2d ed. (Washington: Committee on the Status of Chicanos in the Profession, 1976 [31p.]) **(I959)**. Recent editions of the *Membership directory* include lists of women and minority members.

1960   Directory of organizations and individuals professionally engaged in governmental research and related activities. 1935– . Ocean Gate, N.J.: Governmental Research Assn. Biennial.

In six sections: (1) local and state agencies, including independently organized research agencies, taxpayers' associations, citizens' and voters' leagues, college and university governmental research divisions, legislative reference agencies, and tax-supported agencies, by state and city; (2) national agencies concerned directly or indirectly with governmental research; (3) individual members of the assn. not listed in pts.1 and 2; (4) index of legislative organizations concerned with program evaluation; (5) index of organizations; and (6) index of individuals. Basic information (founding date, address, executive officer, etc.) for each organization.

1961   Guide to graduate study in political science. 1st ed.– , 1972– . Washington, D.C.: American Political Science Assn. Annual.

Alphabetical list of institutions, displaying for each: (1) degrees offered; (2) tuition; (3) application deadline; (4) requirements for admission; (5) financial aid; (6) requirements for degree; (7) program description; (8) faculty, with degrees and areas of specialization noted. Numerical charts indicate total number of students admitted, women students, black students, foreign students, size of faculty. Faculty and geographical indexes.

Similar information for schools offering degrees in public administration is provided in *Programs in public affairs and public administration directory* (Washington, D.C.: National Assn. of Schools of Public Affairs and Administration) **(I962)**, published biennially since 1974, with variations in title.

1963   North American human rights directory. 3d ed. Comp. by Laurie S. Wiseberg and Hazel Sirett. Washington, D.C.: Human Rights Internet, 1984. 264p.

Describes goals and programs of international, governmental, and nongovernmental groups and lists addresses, telephone numbers, principal officers, and publications of each. Organizations are indexed by type of concern and geographical area of concern. Covers U.S. and Canadian groups. Related directories, published by the Human Rights Internet, an international communications network and clearinghouse, include: *Human rights directory: Latin America, Africa, Asia* (Washington, D.C.: 1981 [243p.]) **(I964)**; and *Human rights directory: Western Europe* (Washington, D.C.: 1982 [335p.]) **(I965)**.

1966   Roeder, Edward. PACs Americana: a directory of Political Action Committees (PACs) and their interests. Washington, D.C.: Sunshine Services, 1982. 859p., plus appendixes.

Scope is indicated by additional title-page information: "An encyclopedic directory of all non-party political action committees formed in time to legally contribute more than $1,000 to a 1982 election campaign; lists more than 3,100 PACs, their sponsors and affiliates, their political/economic interests, and 7,000 PAC officials; contains detailed breakdown of PAC contribution records, by type of candidate."

Provides a massive amount of data on federal financing sources and their spheres of interest and persuasion. The two largest sections are especially useful: "PACs and Their Spending Records," which gives sponsor, treasurer, contact, address, telephone number, and 1979–80 expenditures for federal office (broken down by seat, party affiliation, incumbent/challenger status, and election outcome for each office supported); and "Political and Economic Interest Categories," which arranges sponsors and their PACs by a classification scheme of areas of interest. Other sections cover research methodology; PAC sponsors and unsponsored PACs, arranged alphabetically; alternative names, acronyms, and former names; affiliate organizations; and major contributors by candidate type.

Containing some of the same kinds of data but differing significantly in focus is the complementary source, Marvin I. Weinberger and David U. Greevy, *The PAC directory: a complete guide to political action committees* (Cambridge, Mass.: Ballinger, 1982 [various paginations, approx. 1,500p.]) **(I967)**. Whereas Roeder gives no names of individual candidates and profiles PAC contributions only for 1979–80 races, *PAC directory* provides detailed breakdowns of funding for each candidate in 1977–78, as well as 1979–80, in the 2 principal sections: "The Committees—Party and Non-party PAC Contributions" and "Index of Selected Candidate Support." On the other hand, Roeder's directory information is better organized and more complete, the interest category treatment is more original and useful than the *PAC directory's* Standard Industrial Classification index (limited to corporate PACs), and the sponsor/PAC affiliate links are examined systematically. New edition of *The PAC directory*, covering the 1982 election cycle, published by Ballinger in 1984.

Despite the surge of interest in political action committees, it seems questionable that two plump, expensive ($185–$200) directories are needed. Potential buyers should examine these or future editions with an eye to the differences noted above.

I968 Szabo, Stephen F. Research support for political scientists: a guide to sources of funds for research fellowships, grants, and contracts. 2d ed. Washington, D.C.: Departmental Services Program, American Political Science Assn., 1981. 126p.

Describes governmental and private sources. Bibliography of basic information sources appended.

I969 Washington representatives. 1st ed.– , 1977– . Washington, D.C.: Columbia Books. Annual.

Described in recent editions as "a compilation of Washington representatives of the major national associations, labor unions and U.S. companies, registered foreign agents, lobbyists, lawyers, law firms and special interest groups, together with their clients and areas of legislative and regulatory concern." Main alphabetical list by individual or law firm. Entries include address, telephone number, notes on background, and organizations/clients represented. Three indexes: (1) Organizations represented, (2) Selected subjects, (3) Foreign interests (by country). First three editions published as *Directory of Washington representatives of American associations and industry*.

See also *Encyclopedia of governmental advisory organizations* (I1067) (included under "Handbooks, Manuals and Compendia" in this chapter).

Note: For a good directory of English-language scholarly journals that describes important political science periodicals, see *Political and social science journals: a handbook for writers and reviewers* (Santa Barbara, Calif.: ABC-Clio, 1983 [236p.] [**I969A**]).

DICTIONARIES

I970 Beck, Carl, and others. Political science thesaurus II. Rev. and exp. 2d ed. Pittsburgh: Univ. Center for Intl. Studies, Univ. of Pittsburgh, 1979. 675p.

Published in conjunction with the American Political Science Assn. Aims to regulate terminology in political science and cognate fields, thereby promoting accuracy in retrieval from computerized information systems and assisting writers to achieve precision in usage.

Basic list arrays approved descriptors (i.e., subject headings) alphabetically, with sublistings under each entry for related, broader, and narrower descriptors listed elsewhere in the thesaurus. Entries also indicate alternative headings that are not used but refer to the heading being consulted. Scope notes, indicating content covered by a descriptor, sometimes provided.

Other lists include: (1) approved geographical descriptors (not entered in the main list); (2) a rotated descriptor display, ordered by key words in the descriptors; and (3) hierarchical displays, with headings

grouped under 38 broad subject and 10 geographical divisions. Methodology and sources consulted (primarily social science journals) discussed in the introductory sections and appendixes. The thesaurus is used in the preparation of indexes for *United States political science documents* (I728) and is a basic tool for users of the printed and computerized versions.

PSTII succeeds in its goal of providing improved terminological control and precision. Although not a dictionary in the conventional sense, the thesaurus promotes improved understanding and systematic examination of the political science vocabulary.

I971 Cranston, Maurice W., and Sanford A. Lakoff. A glossary of political ideas. New York: Basic Books, 1969. 180p.

Short articles on 51 basic concepts (e.g., authority, justice, sovereignty) discuss historical context and usage for each term. Cross-references and suggestions for further reading.

I972 Davis, Robert R. Lexicon of historical and political terms. Palo Alto, Calif.: R & E Research Associates, 1982. 133p.

Competently written explanations for about 250 terms. Designed to supplement texts for survey courses in political science and history.

I973 Dunner, Joseph, ed. Dictionary of political science. New York: Philosophical Library, 1964. 585p.

A collection of short articles on ideas, personalities, events, political areas, and organizations important for the study of world politics. Signed entries, contributed by some 200 prominent scholars, are generally informative and well written.

I974 Elliott, Florence. A dictionary of politics. 7th ed. Harmondsworth, Eng.: Penguin, 1973. 522p.

Small encyclopedia of world affairs. Concise articles on nations and sketches of contemporary political figures.

I975 Görlitz, Axel, ed. Handlexikon zur Politikwissenschaft. 2. erw. Aufl. München: Ehrenwirth, 1972. 518p.

Signed articles, of considerable length, on major concepts and processes, accompanied by bibliographies.

A standard source, Walter Theimer, *Lexikon der Politik: politische Grundbegriffe und Grundgedanken*, 8. neubearb. Aufl. (München: Francke, 1975 [315p.]) (**I976**), is also useful for terms and includes numerous entries for countries and personalities.

I977 Heimanson, Rudolph. Dictionary of political science and law. Dobbs Ferry, N.Y.: Oceana, 1967. 188p.

Glossary of politico-legal terms and phrases. Most definitions are amplified by discussions of legal origins or contexts and have citations to statutes and decisions. Variations and differences in meaning noted.

I978 Laqueur, Walter A., ed. A dictionary of politics. Rev. ed. New York: Free Pr., 1974. 565p.

Competent source for identification of people, places, events, and terms important in world politics. Emphasis on the modern period. Fully cross-referenced.

I979 Montgomery, Hugh, and Philip G. Cambray. A dictionary of political phrases and allusions, with a short bibliography. London: S. Sonnenschein, 1906. 406p. Repr., Detroit: Gale, 1968.

Still occasionally useful for terms of historical importance in British politics.

I980 Parodi, Jean Luc, ed. La politique. Paris: Hachette, 1971. 511p.

Mixture of 10 long, signed articles on broad concepts (e.g., political institutions, role of the mass media, the Third World) and 500 shorter entries for terms, organizations, individuals, etc. Text in French, with English equivalents supplied for entry words and an English-French index included. Contains charts and tables. Numerous margin notes and cross-references.

I981 Polec: dictionary of politics and economics. (Dictionnaire de politique et d'economie. Lexikon für Politik und Wirtschaft.) By Harry Back and others. 2. verb. und erw. Aufl. Berlin: de Gruyter, 1967. 1,037p.

Ingenious arrangement places 17,000 English, French, and German expressions in a single alphabet, with definition in the language of the entry term and cross-references to counterpart entries for the other languages. Example: entry for "collegial system" gives definition in English and refers user to the French *système collégial* and the German *Kollegialsystem.* Good selection and numerous references to related terms.

A related source, Hans E. Zahn, *Wörterbuch zur Politik und Wirtschaftspolitik/Dictionary of politics and economic policy/Dictionnaire politique et de politique économique; mit englischen und französischen Erläuterungen zum Regierungssystem der Bundesrepublik Deutschland,* v.1– (Frankfurt a.M.: F. Knapp, 1975–) **(I982),** lists English and French equivalents under the German form. Appendix provides extended discussions, in English and French, of 92 terms relating to the political and parliamentary system of the Federal Republic of Germany.

I983 Political science dictionary. By Jack C. Plano and others. Hinsdale, Ill.: Dryden Pr., 1973. 418p.

Excellent general-purpose dictionary. Defines about 2,000 terms, ranging from significant events, institutions, and processes to political philosophies, theories, and methodologies. Reasonably full definitions. Numerous cross-references.

Definitions of some 200 terms, with brief discussions of their significance, are included in Jack C. Plano and others, *Dictionary of political analysis,* 2d ed. (Santa Barbara, Calif.: ABC-Clio, 1982 [197p.] [Clio dictionaries in political science, 3]) **(I984).**

I985 Roberts, Geoffrey K. A dictionary of political analysis. London: Longmans, 1971. 229p.

A plea for and an attempt at precision in defining some 400 key concepts, processes, institutions, and ideologies. Complex and ambiguous terms are supplied with examples and suggestions for further reading. Numerous cross-references.

I986 Scruton, Roger. A dictionary of political thought. London: Macmillan, 1982. 499p.

Stressing the conceptual, Scruton has selected for brief explication "the principal ideas through which modern political beliefs find expression" (preface). Skillful use of cross-references. Provocative and valuable.

U.S. Politics and Government

I987 Findling, John E. Dictionary of American diplomatic history. Westport, Conn.: Greenwood, 1980. 622p.

Contains 1,000 entries, evenly divided between (1) sketches of ambassadors and other diplomatic personnel and selected influential nondiplomats and (2) discussions of important topics, treaties, and events. Cites suggested readings in each entry. Appendixes include a chronology and a list of key diplomatic personnel by presidential administration. Detailed index.

I988 McCarthy, Eugene J. Dictionary of American politics. New York: Macmillan, 1968. 182p.

Good, popular dictionary featuring brief, clear entries and attractive illustrations (mostly political cartoons).

I989 Mitchell, Edwin V. An encyclopedia of American politics. New York: Doubleday, 1946. 338p. Reprint, New York: Greenwood, 1968.

Still-useful glossary, with entries ranging from a sentence to several pages. Text of summary of major documents.

I990 Plano, Jack C., and Milton Greenberg. The American political dictionary. 7th ed. New York: Holt, 1985. 606p.

Effectively organized source. In 14 topical chapters (e.g., political ideas, civil liberties, the legislative process, foreign policy and national defense), with alphabetical listings of terms followed by important agencies, cases, and statutes. Good definitions and statements of significance for each term. Index of main and secondary entries.

Similar in arrangement: James B. Whisker, *A dictionary of concepts on American politics* (New York: Wiley, 1980 [285p.]) **(I991),** designed as an auxiliary to American government textbooks; gives definitions in topical clusters and cites significant cases. Jeffrey M. Elliot and Sheikh R. Ali, *The presidential-congressional political dictionary* (Santa Barbara, Calif.: ABC-Clio, 1984 [365p.] [Clio dictionaries in political science, 9]) **(I991A)** follows the Plano-Greenberg scheme of subject-matter groupings of terms, defining and discussing those that have special relevance to the executive office and the legislature. Appendixes and general index.

I992 Safire, William L. Safire's political dictionary: an enlarged up-to-date edition of The new language of politics. 3d ed. New York: Random, 1978. 845p.

Lively treatment. Omits many standard terms found in other political science dictionaries but includes such contemporary or offbeat expressions as "rubber-chicken circuit," "at that point in time," and "brain drain." Origins are outlined somewhat discursively and with a liberal sprinkling of quotations. Index of sources and persons quoted. Entertaining and witty, as well as useful.

I993   Smith, Edward C., and Arnold J. Zurcher. Dictionary of American politics. 2d ed. New York: Barnes & Noble, 1968. 434p.

Useful, compact list of more than 3,800 terms, phrases, nicknames, slogans, and abbreviations. Short, clear definitions. A standard work.

I994   Sperber, Hans, and Travis Trittschuh. American political terms: an historical dictionary. Detroit: Wayne State Univ. Pr., 1962. 516p.

Patterned after *Oxford English dictionary, APT* is a successful attempt to provide similar treatment for the American political vocabulary. Has fewer entries than other works in this section, but each term is defined and traced historically, with quotations supplied to illustrate variations or changes in usage. Bibliography of sources consulted.

Special Topics

I995   Abraham, Louis A. Abraham and Hawtrey's parliamentary dictionary. 3d ed. Ed. by Stephen C. Hawtrey and H. M. Barclay. London: Butterworth, 1970. 248p.

Helpful guide to expressions in common use in the houses of Parliament, with definitions and explanations of procedures. Cross-references and brief index.

A similar work, Norman W. Wilding and Philip Laundy, *An encyclopaedia of Parliament*, rev. 4th ed. (London: Cassell, 1972 [931p.]) **(I996)**, incorporates material for other Commonwealth nations and outlines historical origins of terms and procedures. Appendixes include lists of officials and a bibliography.

These 2 dictionaries are designed as practical guides. For the definitive source from which both draw, see Thomas E. May, *Erskine May's treatise on the law, privileges, proceedings and usage of Parliament*, 20th ed., ed. by Sir Charles Gordon (London: Butterworth, 1983 [1,200p.]) **(I997)**.

I998   Black, Henry C. Black's law dictionary: definitions of terms and phrases of American and English jurisprudence, ancient and modern. 5th ed. St. Paul: West Pub., 1979. 1,511p.

The standard source for explication of legal terms, abbreviations, and maxims, as well as the legal meaning of standard English words. Includes Anglo-American terms of all periods. Concise definitions, with references to legal decisions and authoritative comments. 5th ed. extensively revised, with 10,000 new or changed entries.

Hand dictionaries for use by lawyers and law students include: Max Radin, *Law dictionary*, 2d ed.

rev., ed. by Lawrence G. Greene (Dobbs Ferry, N.Y.: Oceana, 1970 [122p., 402p., 36p.]) **(I999)**; Steven H. Gifis, *Law dictionary* (Woodbury, N.Y.: Barron's, 1975 [227p.]) **(I1000)**; and Charles R. Hemphill and Phyllis D. Hemphill, *The dictionary of practical law* (Englewood Cliffs, N.J.: Prentice-Hall, 1979 [231p.]) **(I1001)**. The nonspecialist is well served by (among others) *The plain-language law dictionary*, ed. by Robert E. Rothenberg (Harmondsworth, Eng. New York: Penguin, 1981 [430p.]) **(I1002)**.

I1003   Chandler, Ralph C., and Jack C. Plano. The public administration dictionary. New York: Wiley, 1982. 406p.

Much-needed glossary of important terms and concepts. Classified under six broad headings (e.g., public policy, personnel administration), entries offer full definitions and illuminating discussions of significance. Cross-references and index. In addition to standard vocabulary, a good source for such fashionable expressions as *entropy*, *satisficing*, and *zero-base budgeting*.

For quick look-ups of key concepts and theories, D. A. Cutchin, *Guide to public administration* (Itasca, Ill.: Peacock, 1981 [159p.]) **(I1004)**, is handy. Also includes brief annotated bibliographies of reference sources, journals, indexes and abstracting services.

I1005   Coston, Henry. Dictionnaire de la politique française. Paris: Publications Henry Coston (Diffusion: La Librairie Française), v.1– , 1967–   .

V.2 (1972) and 3 (1979) serve as updates to v.1, each having its own A–Z sequence. Collectively, an illustrated guide to the modern French political scene. Some term definitions, but the bulk of entries are for politicians, political movements and parties, organizations, and influential media.

I1006   Parkinson, Roger. Encyclopedia of modern war. London: Routledge & Paul, 1977. 226p.

Short historical articles on battles, weapons, and individuals of note for the period 1793–1975. Useful section of maps. Topical index.

Emphasis is on weapons in Edward Lutwak, *A dictionary of modern war* (New York: Harper, 1971 [224p.]) **(I1007)**, which includes 96 vivid photographs. For succinct definitions of 800 terms relating to military systems and strategy, see Wolfram F. Hanrieder and Larry V. Buel, *Words and arms: a dictionary of security and defense terms, with supplementary data* (Boulder, Colo.: Westview, 1979 [265p.]) **(I1008)**. Statistical tables and charts included.

I1009   Plano, Jack C., and Roy Olton. The international relations dictionary. 3d ed. Santa Barbara, Calif.: ABC-Clio, 1982. 488p. [Clio dictionaries in political science, 2]

Intended "to serve as a guide to the rich, technical language of international relations" (preface). Terms are grouped in 12 chapters by subject (e.g., ideology and communication, American foreign policy, international organization), with definitions and statements of significance provided. Cross-references and alphabetical index increase its usefulness.

Supplementary sources include: Jack E. Vincent, *A handbook of international relations: a guide to terms, theory and practice* (Woodbury, N.Y.: Barron's, 1969 [456p.]) **(I1010)**, which has lengthy entries for international organizations and terms relating to international law and diplomacy; United States, Dept. of State, Library, *International relations dictionary*, 2d ed. (Washington, D.C.: The Library, 1980 [80p.]) **(I1011)**, an excellent, well-documented glossary of current foreign affairs jargon, with many entries for influential organizations (e.g., Trilateral Commission, Third World Forum); and Melquiades J. Gamboa, *A dictionary of international law and diplomacy* (Quezon City, Philippines: Phoenix Pr.; Dobbs Ferry, N.Y.: dist. by Oceana, 1973 [351p.]) **(I1012)**, notable for numerous references to and excerpts from relevant documents.

For multilingual approaches to terminology in international relations and international law, see Günther Haensch, *Wörterbuch der internationalen Beziehungen und der Politik, systematisch und alphabetisch: Deutsch, Englisch, Französisch, Spanisch/Dictionary of international relations and politics, systematic and alphabetical: German, English, French, Spanish*, 2 völlig neubearb, u. erw. Aufl (München: Max Hueber, 1975 [781p.]) **(I1013)**, a classified display of equivalent expressions, with indexes in each of the 4 languages; *Dictionnaire de la terminologie du droit international*, publié sous le patronage de l'Union académique internationale (Paris: Sirrey, 1960 [755p.]) **(I1014)**, which gives authoritative, fully documented definitions in French and indexes counterpart terms in English, Spanish, Italian, and German; and Yvette Renoux, *Glossary of international treaties: in French, English, Spanish, Italian, Dutch, German, and Russian* (Amsterdam: Elsevier, 1970 [212p.]) **(I1015)**.

I1016 Rossi, Ernest E., and Jack C. Plano. The Latin American political dictionary. Santa Barbara, Calif.: ABC-Clio, 1980. 261p.

Definitions and discussions of significance of terms are grouped in topical chapters (corresponding to areas covered in textbooks on Latin America), as follows: (1) geography, population, and social structure; (2) historical perspective; (3) political culture and ideology; (4) revolutionary and counter-revolutionary forces; (5) political parties, pressure groups, and elections; (6) the military; (7) governmental institutions and processes; (8) economic modernization and political development; (9) international law and organization; (10) United States–Latin American relations. Index of main and secondary terms. A valuable aid for an increasingly important area of study.

Related dictionaries published by ABC-Clio: Lawrence Ziring, *The Middle East political dictionary* (1984 [452p.]) **(I1017)**; Claude S. Phillips, *The African political dictionary* (1984 [245p.]) **(I1018)**; and Barbara P. McCrea and others, *The Soviet and East European political dictionary* (1984 [367p.]) **(I1019)**.

I1020 Wilczynski, Jozef. An encyclopedic dictionary of Marxism, socialism and communism: economic, philosophical, political and sociological theories, concepts, institutions and practices—classical and modern, East-West relations included. Berlin and New York: de Gruyter, 1981. 660p.

Designed to provide "a quick reference, explaining doctrines, terms and phrases for the student of the social sciences and the educated or curious public" (preface). Distinguished by clear, highly informative entries. In addition to terms, also discusses organizations, individuals, and significant writings (e.g., *Ten days that shook the world*). Extensively cross-referenced.

A dictionary of Marxist thought, ed. by Tom Bottomore (Oxford: Basil Blackwell, 1983 [587p.]) **(I1021)**, is very similar to Wilczynski in coverage and quality. Lengthy articles accompanied by reading lists, a general bibliography, and an excellent index.

Edward Hyams, *A dictionary of modern revolution* (London: Allen Lane, 1973 [322p.]) **(I1022)**, contains far fewer entries than the above but is expansive for those topics discussed. As in Wilczynski, cross-references abound. Explication of key Marxist concepts may be found in James Russell, *Marx-Engels dictionary* (Westport, Conn.: Greenwood, 1980 [140p.]) **(I1023)**.

Two older sources remain valuable: Robert N. C. Hunt, *A guide to Communist jargon* (New York: Macmillan, 1957 [169p.]) **(I1024)**; and Lester DeKoster, *Vocabulary of communism: definitions of key terms, summaries of central ideas, short biographies of leading figures, descriptions of significant things and events* (Grand Rapids, Mich.: Eerdmans, 1964 [224p.]) **(I1025)**.

ENCYCLOPEDIAS AND ENCYCLOPEDIC SETS

I1026 Academie Diplomatique Internationale. Dictionnaire diplomatique, publié sous la direction de A.-F. Frangulis . . . v.1– , 1933– . Paris: L'Academie.

The components of this complex set comprise a useful encyclopedia of diplomacy. The basic work, published in 2v. in 1933, has been augmented over the years, with supplements (called v.3–7) appearing in 1937, 1948, 1954, 1957, and 1968. Of special note is v.5, a biographical dictionary of diplomats from the Middle Ages to the mid-1950s. In the other volumes, articles on nations, organizations, and diplomatic topics are often accompanied by bibliographies and the texts of treaties and related documents.

For a Soviet approach to diplomatic concepts, events, and persons in the modern world, see *Diplomaticheskii slovar'*, ed. by A. A. Gromyko (Moskva: Politizdat, 1971–73 [3v.]) **(I1027)**.

I1028 Cyclopedia of American government. Ed. by Andrew C. McLaughlin and Albert B. Hart.

New York: Appleton, 1914. 3v. Reprint, Gloucester, Mass.: Peter Smith, 1963.

Age has diminished the value of this source. Contains signed articles on all aspects of American government, entry bibliographies, cross-references, and an index. Of historical interest, but still occasionally useful for biography, as well as lesser-known events and catchwords.

I1029 Encyclopedia of American foreign policy: studies of the principal movements and ideas. Ed. by Alexander DeConde. New York: Scribner, 1978. 3v.

Superior reference source, achieving an admirable balance of scholarship and readability. Consists of 95 essays (arranged alphabetically), a section of biographical articles, and an analytical index. Essays (typically 6–12 pages in length) are written by specialists and deal with such broad issues as anti-imperialism, détente, the military-industrial complex, national security, and public opinion. Each concludes with a bibliography and references to related essays in the encyclopedia. Will be the standard work in the field for years to come.

I1029 Encyclopedia of American political history:
A studies of the principal movements and ideas. Ed. by Jack P. Greene. New York: Scribner, 1984. 3v.

Joins its counterpart for American foreign policy (above) in the select group of superb subject encyclopedias available to students of political science. Following an introductory essay on historiography of American politics, discusses 90 major concepts ranging (alphabetically) from agricultural policy to women's rights. Bibliographies, cross-references, and index. Contributed essays written by American scholars.

I1030 Handwörterbuch der Staatswissenschaften. hrsg. von Ludwig Elster, Adolf Weber, Friedrich Wieser. 4. gänz. umgearb. Aufl. Jena: F. Fischer, 1923–29. 8v. and supplements.

The only comprehensive encyclopedia of political science, unfortunately now very much out of date. Lengthy articles prepared by specialists, with full bibliographies. Subject index in v.8. Succeeded by the broader-based *Handwörterbuch der Sozialwissenschaften* (A416).

I1031 Marxism, Communism and Western society: a comparative encyclopedia. Ed. by Claus D. Kernig. New York: Herder, 1972–73. 8v.

Impressive collection of essays on Soviet and democratic societies, focusing on their differences in approach and outlook on a wide variety of topics and problems. Long, signed articles by an international panel of contributors, with extensive bibliographies following each entry. Topics include not only those of a politico-economic nature, such as capitalism and land reform, but also those relating to cultural aspects (e.g., the arts, origin of Christianity, literature). Also published in German as *Sowjetsystem und demokratische Gesellschaft: eine vergleichende Enzyklopädie* (Freiburg: Herder, 1966–72 [3v.]) **(I1032)**.

I1033 Staatslexikon: Recht, Wirtschaft, Gesellschaft. hrsg. von der Görres-Gesellschaft. 6. völlig neubearb. und crw. Aufl. Freiburg: Herder, 1957–63. 8v.

Standard German work containing some 4,000 signed articles written from the Roman Catholic point of view. Covers basic problems and special aspects of government, law, economics, and sociology. Bibliographies.

I1034 Strupp, Karl. Wörterbuch des Völkerrechts. In völlig neu bearb. 2. Aufl., hrsg. von Hans-Jürgen Schlochauer. . . . Berlin: de Gruyter, 1960–62. 4v.

Comprehensive encyclopedia of international law. Especially good for post-1945 period, although historical matters are included, where required, for full understanding of the development of international law and diplomacy. Extensive cross-references and bibliographies. v.4 is an index.

HANDBOOKS, MANUALS, AND COMPENDIA

I1035 Annuaire des communautés européenes et des autres organisations européenes/European Communities yearbook and other European organizations. 1st ed.– . Bruxelles: Editions Delta, 1977– . Annual.

Fact-filled source of information on the structure, personnel, and activities of the European Community and related bodies. Also includes brief data on such groups as the European Free Trade Association, the Benelux Economic Union, and the European Space Agency. Practical information (embassies, holidays, etc.), schools and institutes for European studies, professional associations, diplomatic corps, and press corps. Indexes. Text in French and English.

Political and Economic Planning, *A handbook of European organizations*, by Michael Palmer and others (New York: Praeger, 1968 [519p.]) **(I1036)**, although somewhat dated, is expertly prepared and offers a historical perspective on the major organizations.

I1037 Cook, Chris, and John Paxton. European political facts, 1789–1848. New York: Facts On File, 1981. 195p.

I1038 ———. European political facts, 1848–1918. New York: Facts On File, 1978. 342p.

I1039 ———. European political facts, 1918–1973. New York: Facts On File, 1978. 363p.

Although content and organization vary somewhat among the volumes, this set is generally useful as a potpourri of ready reference data on European political history. Included are chronologies, glossaries of people and terms, rosters of heads of state and ministers, lists of treaties, descriptions of parliamentary systems and political parties, and numerous statistical tables for population, education, economic output, elections, etc. Arrangement of material requires some study, as indexing is minimal. Distributed in Great Britain by the original publisher, Macmillan of London.

Comparable in handiness: David Butler and Anne Sloman, *British political facts, 1900–1979*, 5th ed. (New York: St. Martin's, 1980 [492p.]) (**I1040**); Chris Cook and John Paxton, *Commonwealth political facts* (New York: Facts On File, 1979 [293p.]) (**I1041**); Chris Cook and David Killingray, *African political facts since 1945* (New York: Facts On File, 1981 [263p.]) (**I1042**); and Colin Campbell, *Canadian political facts 1945–1976* (Toronto and New York: Methuen, 1977 [151p.]) (**I1043**).

I1044 Everyone's United Nations. 9th ed. New York: United Nations, 1979. 477p.

Official handbook that clearly explains the structure, functions, and work of the UN and related intergovernmental agencies. The 9th ed. is in reality a supplementary update of the 8th ed., published under the former title, *Everyman's United Nations*, in 1968. The two volumes form a synopsis of and guide to United Nations activities, 1945–78.

Another approach to historical data on the UN is provided by *A chronology and fact book of the United Nations, 1941–1979*, 6th ed., by Thomas Hovet and Erica Hovet (Dobbs Ferry, N.Y.: Oceana, 1979 [304p.]) (**I1045**). In 3 parts: (1) chronology of events, with index; (2) major documents (e.g., UN charter, General Assembly rules of procedure); and (3) tables, primarily for memberships of councils and other bodies.

Also see Peter I. Hajnal, *Guide to United Nations organization, documentation and publishing* (I700).

I1046 Mickolus, Edward F. Transnational terrorism: a chronology of events, 1968–1979. Westport, Conn.: Greenwood, 1980. 967p.

Attempts to provide hard data on incidents of nondomestic terrorism, to support objective analysis of terrorist patterns and tactics. Chronology describes events (including some historical and domestic acts, for illustrative purposes), giving basic information on location, means used, perpetrator (if known), and outcome. Especially important or controversial incidents are discussed in greater detail. Introduction includes various tables, derived from computer sorting of the data, showing numbers of incidents and casualties, patterns of national involvement, chronological frequencies, etc. Indexed by location, type of attack, and responsible group. Lays a solid foundation for further research.

I1046 Schiavone, Giuseppe. International organiza-
A   tions; a dictionary and directory. London: Macmillan, 1983. 321p.

Although a directory of major organizations, by type, is included, the principal value of this work is the "dictionary," an alphabetical sequence of sketches on the organizations, giving history and purpose of each.

I1047 Thanassecos, Luc. Chronologie des relations internationales, 1914–1971: exposés thématiques. Paris and La Haye: Mouton, 1972. 690p.

Important events in 20th-century world politics, closely classified by topic, then by date. Includes maps. Geographical and personal name indexes.

I1048 Treaties and alliances of the world. 3d ed. Comp. and written by Henry W. Degenhardt. Harlow, Essex: Longmans, 1981. 409p.

A Keesing's reference publication, this accomplished survey of world treaty activity benefits both the specialist and lay researcher. Narrative discussions, accompanied by full texts of (or generous excerpts from) treaties, grouped in 19 topical chapters. Coverage includes early international agreements and their later expansion, World War II, the United Nations, nuclear and conventional disarmament, international cooperation, NATO, the Communist world, and world regions. Maps, tables, diagrams, index.

I1049 World armies. Ed. by John Keegan. London: Macmillan, 1979. 843p.

Extraordinarily valuable sourcebook on the domestic and external military affairs of 151 countries. Alphabetical by nation, each profile includes historical background; military strength and budget; command and constitutional status; role, commitment, deployment, and recent operations; organization; recruitment, training, and reserves; equipment and arms industry; rank, dress, and distinctions; and current developments. Written by 16 authorities, about half of whom are on the faculty of the Royal Military Academy, Sandhurst. The political and social role of the armed forces is emphasized.

Less ambitious in scope, but useful for data on personnel and weaponry: Trevor N. Dupuy and others, *The almanac of world military power*, 4th ed. (San Rafael, Calif.: Presidio, 1980 [418p.]) (**I1050**); and *Armed forces of the world: a reference handbook*, 4th ed., ed. by Robert C. Sellers (New York: Praeger, 1977 [278p.]) (**I1051**).

U.S. Politics and Government

I1052 The almanac of American politics 1972– . Boston: Gambit, 1972–73; New York: Dutton, 1975–79; Washington, D.C.: Barone, 1981– . Biennial.

Current subtitle: "The president, the senators, the representatives, the governors—their records and election results, their states and districts."

Concise, topical information, presented in a well-organized, readable fashion. For each state and district, gives a colorfully written summary of the political scene, census data, voter makeup, and recent election results. State overviews also indicate federal tax burden, outlays by federal agency, and economic base. In addition to personal/professional data and a photograph, the material on individual congressmen includes committee and subcommittee assignments, ratings by political interest groups (e.g., Americans for Democratic Action, National Association of Businessmen), and votes on recent key or controversial bills. Congressional committee rosters, district maps, and name index. Given the problems of attaining objectivity in an undertaking of this nature, the authors seem reasonably unbiased, although the interpretive descriptions of geographical areas might invite rebuttal. A basic source.

Politics in America: members of Congress in Washington and at home, ed. by Alan Ehrenhalt (Washington, D.C.: Congressional Quarterly, 1981 [1,382p.] **(I1053)**, invites comparison as a competitor to the *Almanac*. Although much of the information contained (state and district profiles, voter data, committee assignments, key votes, interest group ratings, etc.) is presented in a similar fashion, there is one major difference: *Politics in America*'s profiles of the congressmen are longer and more detailed, having been based substantially on assessments of colleagues offered in interviews with the members of both houses. A polished, attractive effort. Updated editions published in 1983 and 1985.

For a thorough presentation of legislators' voting records, see CQ's annual *Congressional roll call: a chronology and analysis of votes in the House and Senate*, 91st Congress– (Washington, D.C.: Congressional Quarterly, 1970–) **(I1054)**.

I1055 Book of the states. v.1– , 1935– . Lexington, Ky.: Council of State Governments. Biennial.

Provides information on the structure, working methods, financing, and functional activities of the state governments. Articles on the 3 branches, intergovernmental relations, and major state services, surveying current developments and tabulating pertinent statistical data. "State pages" give basic facts and list major officials. For supplements issued by the Council of State Governments, see *State elective officials and the legislatures* (1943), *State legislative leadership, committees and staff* (1944), and *State administrative officials classified by function* (1945).

I1056 Congressional Quarterly, Inc. Congress and the nation. v.1– , 1965– . Washington, D.C.: Congressional Quarterly. Quadrennial.

Excellent synthesis of governmental and political developments of the post–World War II period. v.1 covered 1945–64; subsequent volumes deal with events of each 4-year presidential term. Currently arranged by 15 areas of activity: politics and national issues; foreign policy; national security; economic policy; commerce and transportation; agricultural policy; labor and manpower; housing and urban affairs; energy policy; environmental policy; health, education, and welfare; law and justice; general government; inside Congress; the presidency. Generous provision of statistical tables, charts, chronologies, key votes, and lists of officials throughout text and appendixes. Detailed table of contents and index. Based on material from the publisher's *CQ weekly report* and *Congressional Quarterly almanac* (I1189). Highly valued.

I1057 Congressional Quarterly's guide to Congress. 3d ed. Washington, D.C.: Congressional Quarterly, 1982. 1,185p.

Full, well-organized gathering of information on the legislative branch. Major sections: origins and development of Congress; powers; procedures; hous-

ing and support; Congress and the electorate; pressures on Congress; qualifications and conduct of members. Treatment is basically narrative, with tables, fact boxes, and bibliographies interspersed. Appendix, containing documents, statistics, biographical notes, congressional rules, etc., and an index add reference value.

Essentially the same format has been used in the CQ companion volume, *Congressional Quarterly's guide to the U.S. Supreme Court* (Washington, D.C.: Congressional Quarterly, 1979 [1,022p.]) **(I1058)**. Special features: excellent profiles of the 101 justices, 1789–1979; chronological list and discussion of major decisions; and a separate case index. The topical chapters are expertly done.

I1059 Government agencies. Ed. by Donald R. Whitnah. Westport, Conn.: Greenwood, 1983. 683p. [Greenwood encyclopedia of American institutions, 7]

Fills a long-standing need for a ready-reference source of historical/critical data on important government bodies. The 100-plus agency profiles fall somewhere between the brevity of *United States government manual* sketches and the expansiveness of volumes in the Praeger library of U.S. government departments and agencies series. Written by a panel of scholarly contributors, each essay traces the agency's origin and development, discusses its functional mission, and comments on successes and failures in achieving its goals. Sources for additional information noted. General index. While not comprehensive—notable omissions include the Library of Congress and the National Institutes of Health—coverage is good for executive and independent bodies. Some defunct agencies (e.g., Works Progress Administration) are included.

I1060 The municipal year book. 1934– . Washington, D.C.: Intl. City Management Assn. Annual.

Combined statistical almanac and review of current activity for urban areas. Includes topical articles on trends in municipal government, salaries, and management and services, but emphasis is on statistical and directory information. Among the useful tabulations: basic profiles of individual cities of more than 10,000 in population; salaries of municipal officials and workers in key service areas; and a directory of municipal officials in cities of 2,500 or more. Contains subject lists of information sources and a five-year cumulative index to the series.

I1061 National party conventions 1831–1980. Washington, D.C.: Congressional Quarterly, 1983. 245p.

Summarizes highlights of the conventions, through discussion of the balloting and excerpts from the platforms. In addition to chronological profiles, briefly describes preconvention politics and the nominating process, shows voting on key ballots, and provides sketches of political parties and presidential/vice-presidential candidates. Includes bibliographies and an index. Useful compendium.

Interesting essays on the major platform issues of each convention are found in Edward W. Chester, *A guide to political platforms* (Hamden, Conn.: Archon, 1977 [373p.]) **(I1062)**. Introduction discusses contextual and comparative aspects. Annotated bibliography and name-topic index.

Also historical in approach, Richard C. Bain and Judith H. Parris, *Convention decisions and voting records*, 2d ed. (Washington, D.C.: Brookings, 1973 [350, 120p.]) **(I1063)**, summarizes convention activity 1832–1972 and gives detailed voting records.

I1064 Reagan's first year. Washington, D.C.: Congressional Quarterly, 1982. 171p.

Part of CQ's annual review series on the American presidency. Surveys the year's activities in general, as well as discusses major issues, programs advanced, and problems. About half of the volume is devoted to appendixes, which list presidential nominations and sources of support, provide a chronology, and reproduce selected messages, addresses, and news conferences. Index.

Earlier volumes follow a similar scheme. Titles for given years vary: 1969–73 called *Nixon: the first [second, etc.] year of his presidency*; 1974–77 called *Presidency 1974 [1975, etc.]*; 1978–80 called *President Carter, 1978 [1979, etc.]*.

I1065 Schapsmeier, Edward L., and Frederick H. Schapsmeier. Political parties and civic action groups. Westport, Conn.: Greenwood, 1981. 554p. [Greenwood encyclopedia of American institutions, 4]

Pulls together a body of information previously found in scattered sources and arranges it alphabetically in illuminating essays. Of special value are the many entries for pressure groups, lobbying organizations, and other bodies established to influence the political process. Historical in approach, articles contain references to further reading and notes on the organizations' publications. Chronological lists of presidential candidates and votes for the major parties. Appendixes: organizations by primary function (agricultural, civic improvement, peace, etc.); chronology, by foundation date; glossary. Cross-references and index.

I1066 United States government manual. 1935– . Washington, D.C.: Govt. Print. Off. Annual.

Published by the National Archives' Office of the Federal Register. Earlier vols. called *United States government organization manual*.

Serves as both handbook and directory of the federal government, with official information on the organization, functions, and major personnel of principal agencies in the 3 branches. Also describes independent establishments and government corporations (e.g., Federal Communications Commission); selected boards, committees, and commissions; quasi-official agencies; major multilateral and bilateral international organizations; and abolished and transferred agencies. Sources for further information noted. Appendixes include abbreviations and acronyms, organization charts, and listings of regional agencies. Name, subject, and agency indexes.

Complementing the *USGM* is *Encyclopedia of governmental advisory organizations*, 4th ed., ed. by Denise A. Adzigian (Detroit: Gale, 1983 [964p.]) **(I1067)**, which bears the subtitle "A reference guide to permanent, continuing, and ad hoc U.S. presidential advisory committees, pubic advisory committees, interagency committees, and other government-related boards, panels, task forces, commissions, conferences, and other similar bodies serving in a consultative, coordinating, advisory, research, or investigative capacity." Grouped under 10 categories (e.g., agriculture, education, and social welfare), each entry contains, as available, name, address, telephone number, executive secretary, history and authority, program, recommendations, membership, staff, subsidiary units, publications and reports, meetings, and remarks. Alphabetical and keyword index also lists administrative agencies that are sometimes mistaken for advisory bodies and refers to their inclusion in the *Government manual* or *Official congressional directory*. Update service, *New governmental advisory organizations*, available. Important and valuable.

Federal regulatory directory (1979/80– ; Washington, D.C.: Congressional Quarterly; annual) **(I1068)** provides a wealth of information on the background, powers, commissioners, organization, and offices of the government's regulatory agencies. Introductory sketches on regulatory history, practice, and influence. Index.

Comparative Politics and Government

I1068 Degenhardt, Henry. Political dissent: an
A   international guide to dissident, extra-parliamentary, guerrilla and illegal political movements. General editor: Alan J. Day. Harlow, Essex: Longman; Detroit: distr. by Gale, 1983. 592p.

Companion volume to Day and Degenhardt's *Political parties of the world* (I1079). Describes parties and groups which exhibit "political opposition outside the legal structure of the state concerned, i.e., forces which constitute an actual or potential threat to the stability of the state" (introd.). By continent, then country, with national overviews and, for each group, a concise discussion of its history, purpose, activity, and leadership. Bibliography and indexes. Another in the useful Keesing's reference publication series.

Similar in coverage and arrangement: Peter Janke and Richard Sim, *Guerrilla and terrorist organisations: a world directory and bibliography* (Brighton, Sussex: Harvester, 1983 [531p.]) **(I1068B)**. Separate bibliographies for each country and a list of widely used acronyms are special features.

I1069 European electoral systems handbook. Ed. by Geoffrey Hand and others. London and Woburn, Mass.: Butterworth, 1979. 252p.

Articles on systems employed in the member states of the European Communities. Each country's electoral process is outlined according to a uniform plan of topics, which include method of voting, elections, parties, individual candidates, and dissemination of election results. Ballot facsimiles, tables, bibliographies. Useful comparative approach.

I1070 Herman, Valentine, and Françoise Mendel. Parliaments of the world: a reference compendium. Berlin and New York: de Gruyter, 1976. 985p.

Results of a massive survey conducted by the Inter-Parliamentary Union, detailing the workings of 56 national legislative bodies. Data are displayed in 70 tables classified under 6 broad areas: (1) composition of parliament, (2) organization and operation, (3) legislative function, (4) powers over finance, (5) control of the executive, (6) other functions. Emphasis is on comparative aspects with each table accompanied by an analytical summary of findings. Bibliography and topical index.

For brief statements on lawmaking and election processes, by country, see John Paxton, *World legislatures* (New York: St. Martin's, 1974 [169p.]) **(I1071)**. Data on individual states, provinces, territories, etc., for Australia, Canada, France, West Germany, the USSR, and the United States.

I1072 International handbook of political science. Ed. by William G. Andrews. Westport, Conn.: Greenwood, 1982. 464p.

Ground-breaking survey of professional/educational activity in 26 countries since 1945. Designed to both reflect and describe recent trends in the discipline, contributions on each country vary in coverage but most include: introductory statement; state of political science in 1945; intellectual structure of the discipline; teaching, research, and association activities; relationship to practical politics; and present state and future prospects. Four preliminary essays discuss political science from an international perspective. Appendixes include a useful list of national professional associations by country, with addresses, major personnel, and publications. Despite the omission of several countries (e.g., Mexico, South Africa) for which no contribution was forthcoming, a revealing look at the discipline as perceived and advanced by a variety of cultures.

I1073 Marxist governments: a world survey. Ed. by Bogdan Szajkowski. New York: St. Martin's, 1981. 3v.

Collection of scholarly articles on the Communist nations. The 25 expert contributors generally follow the same plan of arrangement: origin and history of Marxist activity, prominent parties, governmental structure, internal and external affairs, basic facts, bibliography. Includes maps, tables, and indexes.

Witold S. Sworakowski, *World communism: a handbook* (Stanford, Calif.: Hoover Institution Pr., 1973 [576p.]) **(I1074)**, also authoritative and excellent, focuses on the historical development of the communist movement. Alphabetical arrangement of essays on 106 countries in which there has been Communist party activity, as well as entries for the major world Marxist organizations. Signed articles by scholars. De-

signed as a retrospective companion to the annual *Yearbook on international Communist affairs* (I1100).

I1075 Political handbook of the world: governments, regional issues, and intergovernmental organizations. 1927– . New York: publ. by McGraw-Hill for the Council on Foreign Relations. Annual.

Convenient source for quick reference on the current political status of world regions and nations. Reports for each country include general data; names of chief officials; brief descriptions of political background, constitution and government, foreign relations, and current issues; leaders and programs of the political parties; composition of the parliamentary body; names of cabinet members; major components of the news media and their political affiliations; and intergovernmental representation. Useful profiles of intergovernmental organizations. Indexes to countries, organizations, and personal names. Publisher and frequency variations; present arrangement established with 1975 vol.

The annual *Countries of the world and their leaders yearbook* (1st ed.– ; Detroit: Gale, 1974–) **(I1076)** is also handy; however, its contents consist of reproductions of the Department of State's *Background notes* for nations, plus other State Dept. and CIA publications, which may normally be found in government documents collections.

For other annual factbooks covering world politics, see *Annual register of world events* (A432), *The Europa yearbook* (A435), *International yearbook and statesmen's who's who* (A436), *Statesman's yearbook* (A437), and *Yearbook of international organizations* (A438).

I1077 The Times survey of foreign ministries of the world. Selected and ed. by Zara Steiner. London: Times Books, 1982. 624p.

Specialized examination of principal foreign affairs offices of 24 countries. Written by experts, each section contains a full discussion of the history and importance of the ministry; organization charts; and a bibliography. Index. Emphasis is on the major industrialized nations.

I1078 World encyclopedia of political systems & parties. Ed. by George E. Delury. New York: Facts On File, 1983. 2v.

Scholarly profiles of the contemporary political/governmental apparatus of 169 nations and 8 dependent territories. Discusses the basic system of government; the electoral system; the history, policy, membership, financing, and leadership of major parties; minor parties and opposing factions; and national prospects. Suggestions for further reading for each country. General index. Only currently active parties are covered. Extremely valuable.

Focus on the current scene also characterizes Alan J. Day and Henry W. Degenhardt, *Political parties of the world*, 2d ed. (Harlow, Essex: Longman; Detroit: distr. by Gale, 1984 [602p.]) **(I1079)**, a Keesing's reference publication. General data for each country, followed by ready-reference sketches of major and minor parties. Also serves as directory by providing addresses, titles of publications, and international affiliations of most parties. Excludes illegal/unofficial parties, which are described in the authors' *Political dissent* (I1068A).

Historical data on a wide range of parties, active and defunct, will be found in volumes of the *Greenwood historical encyclopedia of the world's political parties.* Published to date: *Political parties of the Americas: Canada, Latin America, and the West Indies*, ed. by Robert J. Alexander (Westport, Conn.: Greenwood, 1982 [2v.]) **(I1080)**; and *Political parties of Europe*, ed. by Vincent E. McHale (Westport, Conn.: Greenwood, 1983 [2v.]) **(I1081)**. In addition to data on the parties, both sets include historical profiles of each country's political life, tables, chronologies, party genealogies, ideological and interest group lists, and extensive indexes. Also see *Lexikon zur Geschichte der Parteien in Europa*, ed. by Frank Wende (Stuttgart: Kröner, 1981 [890p.]) **(I1082)**, for solid information on European parties. These works, together with Schapsmeier and Schapsmeier, *Political parties and civic action groups*, for the U.S. (I1065), and a projected Greenwood volume for Australasia and Africa, form a vital component for historical background on world party activity.

Kenneth Janda, *Political parties: a cross-national survey* (New York: Free Pr.; London: Collier Macmillan, 1980 [1,019p.]) **(I1083)**, analyzes basic data on 158 parties of 53 countries during the period 1950–62. An outcome of the International Comparative Political Parties Project and "intended to impose intellectual order upon the mass of facts about political parties . . . and harness them in the service of comparative analysis" (preface), the survey uses an extensive set of variables (grouped under broad terms, such as governmental status, issue orientation, and centralization of power) to arrive at findings for each party examined. Complex, important study.

YEARBOOKS

I1084 L'Année politique. 1st ser., 1874–1905; 2d ser., 1944–45– . Paris: Presses Universitaires de France, 1876–1906, 1945–75; Editions du Grande Siècle, 1976– . Annual.

Title varies; recent vols. called *L'Année politique, économique et sociale en France.* Chronological reviews of the year's major political, economic, and social events in France. Abundant organizational and statistical material. Index. Invaluable guide for French politics and foreign affairs.

I1085 Annuaire européen/European yearbook. v.1– , 1948– . Publ. under the auspices of the Council of Europe. The Hague: Nijhoff, 1955– . Annual.

Valuable source for basic documents and information about European organizations and for articles on their functions and activities. Introductory articles are in English or French, with summaries in the other language. The extensive documentary section contains a chronology or summary of events for each of the principal organizations and gives the texts of agreements they have concluded or their basic constitutional documents (in French and English on facing pages). Rosters of officers. A bibliographical section lists books, pamphlets, and articles on European cooperation. Name and general indexes. Classified cumulative list of articles in v.1–22 published in v.22. Publication lag of two years.

I1086 Annual of power and conflict: a survey of political violence and international influence. 1971– . London: Inst. for the Study of Conflict. Annual.

Survey of revolutionary, subversive, and terrorist movements in more than 100 countries. Emphasis on internal security challenges. Grouped by world regions, each nation's entry includes basic statistics, discussion of challenges (stressing revolutionary parties and organizations), and a chronology of events.

I1087 British year book of international law. v.1– , 1920/21– . London: Oxford Univ. Pr. Annual.

In addition to articles on current legal questions and international relations, contains books reviews, a documentary survey of British court decisions and other United Kingdom materials on international law, and a table showing multilateral agreements signed during the year. Topic and case indexes.

Other annual surveys of current topics and writings include: *Annuaire français de droit international* (v.1– , 1955– ; Paris: Centre National de la Recherche Scientifique, 1956–) **(I1088)**; *German yearbook of international law* (v.1– , 1948– ; Berlin: Duncker & Humblot) **(I1089)**, called *Jahrbuch für internationales Recht* through 1975; and *Canadian yearbook of international law* (v.1– , 1963– ; Vancouver: Univ. of British Columbia Pr.) **(I1090)**.

I1091 Canadian annual review of politics and public affairs. 1973– . Toronto: Univ. of Toronto Pr. Annual.

Breezy but solid account of the year's politico-economic developments in Canada. Articles grouped in 4 sections: (1) parliament and politics, (2) the provinces, (3) external affairs and defense, and (4) the national economy. Includes calendar of events, obituary notes, and index. Contributors are Canadian scholars. Supersedes *Canadian annual review*, 1960–70.

I1092 Die international Politik. 1955– . München: Oldenbourg, 1958– . Annual.

Yearbook of the Forschungsinstitut der Deutschen Gesellschaft für Auswärtige Politik. Scholarly survey of international relations. Supplementary vols. contain documents and chronologies.

I1092 Unesco yearbook on peace and conflict studies. A 1980– . Paris: Unesco; Westport, Conn.: Greenwood, 1981– . Annual.

Signed essays, treating aspects of peace research documentation and data collection. Aims to promote improved information exchange among international scholars.

I1093 United Nations. Yearbook. 1946/47– . New

York: UN Dept. of Public Information. Annual.

Records the year's activities of the UN and its specialized agencies. The various subjects (political, security, economic, social, trusteeship, legal, administrative, and budgetary questions) are treated in detailed essays, to which are appended documentary references and in many cases the text of (and vote on) relevant resolutions. General information on the specialized agencies. Rosters of officials. Subjects, names, and resolutions indexes. 2–3-year publication lag.

Somewhat more timely is the compact *Annual review of United Nations affairs* (1949– ; Dobbs Ferry, N.Y.: Oceana) **(I1094)**, which is similarly arranged and includes summaries of statements made at the General Assembly's general debate.

I1095 World armaments and disarmament: SIPRI yearbook. 1968/69– . Stockholm: Almqvist & Wiksell, 1969–77; London: Taylor & Francis, 1978– . Annual.

Collaboratively published in the U.S. by Humanities, MIT Pr., Crane Russak, etc.

Issued by the Stockholm International Peace Research Institute, a continuing "analysis of the world's arms races, and the attempts to stop them . . ." (preface, 1981 ed.). Covers developments in armaments and arms control for the previous year, and trends of the last several years. Thorough articles on major issues accompanied by a broad range of graphs, maps, chronologies, and statistical tables. Includes material on world military expenditures, arms trade with industrialized and Third World countries, nuclear explosions, arms limitations agreements, etc. Reflective, well documented, indispensable.

The International Institute for Strategic Studies' annual *Strategic survey* (London: The Institute, 1966–) **(I1096)** is a useful analysis of general and national developments in international security and strategic policy. Also issued by the institute is the statistical annual *The military balance*, discussed in the "Statistical Sources" section of this chapter (I1166).

I1097 Year book of world affairs. v.1– , 1947– .
Publ. under the auspices of the London Inst. of World Affairs. London: Stevens. Annual.

Currently includes about 20 articles on topics of contemporary interest and notes articles from earlier volumes that relate to issues of recent or continuing importance. v.25 (1971) includes cumulative index to articles in the first 25 vols. Useful bibliographic essays discontinued with v.26 (1972).

I1098 Yearbook on human rights. New York: United Nations, 1946– . Annual.

Review of the year's major national developments in human rights. Information for each country is arranged by the pertinent articles of the Universal Declaration of Human Rights and includes references to and summaries of laws, constitutions, and judicial decisions. Also surveys international developments and tabulates data on the status of major international human rights agreements. Subject index. 5-year time lag in publication.

For up-to-date country summaries concerning treatment of political prisoners, see the annual *Amnesty International report* (London: Amnesty Intl. Pubs., 1961/62–) **(I1099)**. Also contains data on Amnesty International activities and publications.

I1100 Yearbook on international Communist affairs. 1966– . Stanford, Calif.: Hoover Institution Pr., 1967– . Annual.

Scholarly presentation of data on the structures, activities, and publications of world Communist organizations. Main section consists of signed profiles on individual parties, arranged alphabetically by region and country. Also sketches of international Communist-front organizations and their meetings, selected bibliography, party/front membership totals, and name index. Authoritative, fact-filled source.

The following important yearbooks ceased publication during the 1970s:

I1101 Survey of international affairs. 1920/23–63. London: Oxford Univ. Pr., 1925–77. Annual.

I1102 Documents on international affairs. 1928–63. London: Oxford Univ. Pr., 1929–73. Annual.

Published under the auspices of the Royal Institute of International Affairs, these prominent companion series reviewed events of international significance through overviews of world areas and compilations of official statements, communications, resolutions, etc. A consolidated index to both series through 1938 was published in 1967.

I1103 The United States in world affairs. 1931–70. New York: Harper, 1932–67; Simon & Schuster, 1968–72. Annual.

I1104 Documents on American foreign relations. 1938/39–70. New York: Harper, 1939–67; Simon & Schuster, 1968–73. Annual.

I1105 American foreign relations: a documentary record. 1971–78. New York: New York Univ. Pr., 1976–79. Annual.

The Council on Foreign Relations inaugurated *The United States in world affairs* to provide background information and critical commentary on U.S. participation in international affairs. *Documents*, originally published under the sponsorship of the World Peace Foundation, was taken over by the council in 1952 as a complementary source for major addresses and other public statements. *American foreign relations* continued these two series, combining the survey and documentary features of each.

ORIGINAL SOURCES

I1106 Blaustein, Albert P., and Gisbert H. Flanz. Constitutions of the countries of the world: a series of updated texts, constitutional chronologies and annotated bibliographies. Permanent ed. Dobbs Ferry, N.Y.: Oceana, 1971– .

Multivolume looseleaf service, providing up-to-date constitutions in English, with historical summaries of constitutional developments. Subscription includes cumulative supplements for changes between country revisions, and binders for older constitutions. Because of the currency afforded by the format, the best available source for world constitutions. This role was previously assumed by the excellent set, Amos Peaslee, *Constitutions of nations*, 4th rev. ed., by Dorothy Peaslee Xydis (The Hague: Nijhoff, 1974–) **(I1107)**, which appears in new editions at 5- to 10-year intervals.

Complementary for international coverage: *Constitutions of dependencies and special sovereignties,* ed. by Albert P. Blaustein and Eric B. Blaustein, which appears in 2 volumes (I385), and also published in looseleaf format; and Amos Peaslee, *International governmental organizations: constitutional documents*, rev. 3d ed. in 5 parts, prep. by Dorothy Peaslee Xydis (The Hague: Nijhoff, 1974–79 [5v.]) **(I1109)**, which arranges organizations according to type of activity (agriculture, education, science, etc.). Also see the special compilation for Communist countries, *The constitutions of the Communist world*, ed. by William B. Simons (Alphen aan den Rijn; Germantown, Md.: Sijthoff & Noordhoff, 1980 [644p.]) **(I1110)**.

Standard source for the U.S.: Columbia Univ., Legislative Drafting Research Fund, *Constitutions of the United States, national and state*, 2d ed. (Dobbs Ferry, N.Y., 1974–) **(I1111)**, a looseleaf service that reproduces current constitutions for U.S. possessions and territories, as well as for states.

I1112 A comprehensive handbook of the United Nations: a documentary presentation in two volumes. Ed. by Min-Chuan Ku. New York: Monarch, 1978–79. 2v.

"Consists of basic laws, rules and regulations dealing with both substantive and procedural matters of all important organs of the United Nations and its affiliated agencies" (preface). As intended, a full (more than 1,500 pages) display of documents for the student of the UN and its specialized agencies. Especially useful section of documents on the background of the UN's formation. Includes some charts, tables, and lists; a bibliography; and a sketchy index.

I1113 Great Britain. Foreign and Commonwealth Office. British and foreign state papers. v.1–170, 1812–1968. London: HMSO, 1841–1977.

An invaluable source of information on British and international affairs, with treaties (including some to which Britain was not a party), English-language texts of national constitutions, official correspondence, and other documents of historical interest and importance. Vols. contained both documents of the year in question and earlier papers not previously made public. Chronological list of documents and subject-country index in each volume, with 6 cumulative general indexes. Series has ceased but continues to be useful for sources on 19th- and 20th-century international relations.

I1114 Great Britain. Parliament. Parliamentary debates. v.1–41 (1803–20); n.s., v.1–25 (1820–30); 3d ser., v.1–356 (1830–90/91); 4th ser., v.1–199 (1892–1908); 5th ser.: Commons, v.1–1,000 (1909–80), Lords, v.1– (1909–); 6th ser.: Commons, v.1– (1980–). London: 1804– .

Often referred to as Hansard's debates, after the publisher of the first 3 series, T. C. Hansard. Series 1–4 are neither complete nor verbatim, and not all division lists are given in full. Since 1909, when it became official, substantially a verbatim record. Issued daily during sessions; cumulated in sessional volumes with general, detailed index.

The period before 1803 is covered by William Cobbett, *Parliamentary history of England from the earliest period to the year 1803* (London: Hansard, 1806–20 [36v.]) **(I1115)**, a retrospective compilation based on various records and sources.

I1116 Historic documents. 1972– . Washington: Congressional Quarterly, 1973– . Annual.

Although the scope of topics treated in documents selected for this excellent series is broad, most of the texts relate to domestic or international governmental affairs. The 70–80 documents included each year consist of complete texts of or excerpts from speeches, treaties, court opinions, congressional documents, presidential commission reports, etc., and are arranged by date. Each is introduced by a statement giving background, context, and importance of the document. 5-year cumulative topical index in each volume. For convenience of use and high editorial quality, *Historic documents* cannot be overvalued.

I1117 Independence documents of the world. Ed. by Albert P. Blaustein and others. Dobbs Ferry, N.Y.: Oceana, 1977.

Gathers the "declarations of independence" for those nations of the world that have such establishing or founding documents. The various manifestos, proclamations, treaties, resolutions, etc., are arranged by country, with each prefaced by a brief historical statement. English-language translations provided for foreign-language documents. Numerous facsimiles of original texts.

I1118 International organization and integration: annotated basic documents and descriptive directory of international organizations and arrangements. Ed. by P. J. G. Kapteyn and others. 2d completely rev. ed. The Hague and Boston: Nijhoff; Hingham, Mass.: dist. in the U.S. and Canada by Kluwer Boston, 1981– , v.1– .

Extensive, multivolume revision of an excellent sourcebook first published in 1968. Two volumes have appeared so far: IA, The United Nations Organization; and IIA, European Communities. Both contain full texts of major documents, with annotations, and a subject index. Future volumes devoted to organizations related to the UN, organizations and arrangements of the Northern Hemisphere and outside the Northern Hemisphere, and functional organizations and arrangements.

I1119 Johnson, Donald B. National party platforms. Rev. ed. Urbana: Univ. of Illinois Pr., 1978. 2v. v.1, 1840–1956; v.2, 1960–76. Platforms of parties whose size, performance, and historical significance made them important in American politics. Also includes platforms of influential splinter groups (e.g., the States' Rights Party in 1948). Subject and name indexes. Supplement for 1980 published in 1982.

Similar for Canada: D. Owen Carrigan, *Canadian party platforms, 1867–1968* (Urbana: Univ. of Illinois Pr., 1968 [363p.]) **(I1120)**. *British general election manifestos, 1900–1974*, rev. ed., ed. by Fred W. S. Craig (London: Macmillan, 1975 [484p.]) **(I1121)**, presents party-prepared summaries of policy for the Conservative, Labour, and Liberal parties.

I1122 Schlesinger, Arthur M., ed. History of American presidential elections, 1789–1968. New York: Chelsea, 1971. 4v.

Each election is discussed in a scholarly essay, followed by a selection of documents (letters, editorials, speeches, etc.) evoking the contemporary political climate. Interesting, useful sourcebook.

Of comparable value is the companion set edited by Schlesinger, *History of U.S. political parties* (New York: Chelsea, 1973 [4v.]) **(I1123)**.

I1124 The Third World without superpowers: the collected documents of the non-aligned countries. Ed. by Odetter Jankowitsch and Karl P. Sauvant. Dobbs Ferry, N.Y.: Oceana, 1978– , v.1– .

The rationale and principal value of this set is to bring together the previously scattered texts of meetings and conferences relating to the origins and development of the nonaligned movement. Arrangement of v.1–4 is broadly chronological, from the Belgrade Summit of 1961 through 1977, with documents reproduced in unaltered form. Chronology (v.1) lists all relevant meetings, including those for which no documents were issued. Bibliography, list of abbreviations, and excellent index in v.4; v.5–6 document the Havana Summit (1979).

While the above compilation traces the rise of political influence among the developing countries, a companion set, Group of 77, *The Third World without superpowers, 2nd series: the collected documents of the Group of 77*, ed. by Karl P. Sauvant (New York: Oceana, 1981–82 [6v.]) **(I1125)**, chronicles activities on economic matters, in the UN and elsewhere. Texts relating to the Group of 77, an economic caucus for more than 120 developing nations, are presented without alteration.

I1126 United States. Federal register. March 14, 1936– . Washington, D.C.: Govt. Print. Off. Daily except Sat. and Sun.

Primary purpose is to make available to the public regulations and legal notices, including proposed changes and new rules, used by federal administrative agencies. Also contains presidential proclamations and executive orders (except those that have no general applicability or legal effect), agency organization procedures, and documents or classes of documents determined to have general applicability and effect. Monthly indexes (cumulating throughout the year) and annual index.

The *Code of federal regulations* (Washington, D.C.: Govt. Print. Off., 1938–) **(I1127)**, based on material from the *Federal register*, incorporates provisions currently in force. In 50 topical titles, similar to those in the *United States code*. Currently, each title is revised annually, if needed. General index.

I1128 United States. United States statutes at large. 1789– . Boston: Little, 1845–73; Washington, D.C.: Govt. Print. Off., 1873– .

Sessional compilation of laws passed, arranged chronologically by date of passage. Contains public laws, private laws, concurrent resolutions, reorganization plans, executive proclamations, etc. Preliminary numerical lists, subject and individual indexes, and marginal notes in each volume. Legislative histories included, beginning in 1975. Official place of publication for treaties through 1949 (from 1950, in *United States treaties and other international agreements* (I1151)).

General and permanent laws in force on Jan. 14, 1983, are codified in United States, *United States code*, 1982 ed. (Washington, D.C.: Govt. Print. Off., 1983 [25v.]) **(I1129)**. Classified under 50 titles (education, highways, public lands, etc.), with chapter and section subdivisions. Popular name and general index. Tables, showing inclusion of statues in the *Code*. First published in 1926; currently revised every 6 years, with cumulative supplements issued annually.

I1130 United States. Congress. American state papers. . . . Washington, D.C.: Gales & Seaton, 1832–61. 38v.

Venerable, classic source of early legislative and executive documents, which for years has provided the only readily accessible texts of documents of the first 14 Congresses. Chronological, within 10 classes: (1) foreign relations, (2) Indian affairs, (3) finance, (4) commerce and navigation, (5) military affairs, (6) naval affairs, (7) post office, (8) public lands, (9) claims, and (10) miscellaneous. Final volume in each class has an index.

Not to be confused with *ASP* is the commercially published *New American state papers* **(I1131)**, a miscellany of reprinted documents for the period 1789–1860. Issued in 11 subject sets (176 volumes) by Scholarly Resources of Wilmington, Delaware, in 1972–73, this project purports to replace and expand the original *ASP* but has been challenged in terms of its editorial soundness, selection of texts, organization, and expense (see *American archivist*, v.36, Oct. 1973, p.523–36).

Another commercial venture, which offers a careful recompilation and expansion of material in the *ASP*, is *National state papers of the United States, 1789–1817* (Wilmington, Del.: Michael Glazier, 1977–) **(I1132)**. Two components published to date: *The Congressional journals of the United States, 1789–1817* in 65v. (1977); *Texts of documents: administration of John Adams, 1797–1801* in 24v. (1980). *Texts of documents: administration of George Washington, 1789–1797*, is in progress. Documents arranged in strict chronological order, with no division into topical classes.

I1133 United States. Congress. Congressional record: proceedings and debates of the . . . Congress. 43rd Congress, March 1873– . Washington, D.C.: Govt. Print. Off., 1873– .

Basic account of legislative activity. Issued daily

while Congress is in session, with revised permanent edition for each session. In 4 parts for each day: proceedings of the Senate; proceedings of the House; extensions of remarks, for material not read on the floor but inserted later; and the daily digest, a summary of activity. Biweekly and permanent indexes in two sections: alphabetical index of names and subjects, and history of bills and resolutions, by number. Athough the *Record* includes congressional speeches and debates, it does not contain the text of bills. Further, it is not truly a verbatim account, as members reserve the right to revise or exclude remarks. See Schmeckebier, *Government publications and their use* (I708), and Morehead, *Introduction to United States public documents* (I704), for details on these and other limitations.

For proceedings before 1873, see *Annals of Congress, 1789–1824* (42v., 1834–56) **(I1134)**, *Register of debates, 1824–37* (14v. in 29, 1825–37) **(I1135)**, and *Congressional globe, 1833–73* (46v. in 108, 1834–73) **(I1136)**. Accounts of the bills, resolutions, and amendments introduced each day, as well as complete lists of bills and resolutions, can be found in the journals of each chamber: U.S. Congress, House of Representatives, *Journal* (v.1– , 1789– ; Washington, D.C.: Govt. Print. Off.) **(I1137)**; and U.S. Congress, Senate, *Journal* (v.1– , 1789– ; Washington, D.C.: Govt. Print. Off.) **(I1138)**. Issued annually, the journals do not include the texts of debates or bills. Indexes.

I1139 United States. Dept. of State. Foreign relations of the United States. 1861– . Washington, D.C.: Govt. Print. Off., 1862– . Irregular.

Important series, constituting "the official record of the foreign policy of the United States." Contains the texts of diplomatic communications, exchanges of notes, reports, presidents' annual messages to Congress, some treaties, and other official papers relating to the foreign relations and diplomacy of the United States. Currently published in several parts for each year or group of years, with individual volumes covering geographical areas. Each volume is indexed and 2 general indexes cover the time period 1861–1918. Conflict between attempt to adhere to "principles of historical objectivity" and concern for confidentiality and security results in two major shortcomings: (1) the series is not a complete record, as pertinent material may be omitted, and (2) the time lag in publication (currently about 30 years) is crucially long.

Diplomatic documents for the period 1789–1828 can be found in class 1, "Foreign relations," of *American state papers* (I1130). For a key to material published between 1828 and 1861, see Hasse, *Index to United States documents relating to foreign affairs, 1828–1861* (I847).

I1140 United States. President. Weekly compilation of presidential documents. v.1– , 1965– . Washington, D.C.: Govt. Print. Off. Weekly.
Source of current releases by the White House. Includes transcripts of news conferences, messages to Congress, public speeches, proclamations, executive

orders, etc. Indexes cumulate in each issue and annually.

Weekly compilation serves as the basis for current volumes of an important series: U.S. President, *Public papers of the presidents of the United States* (Washington, D.C.: Govt. Print. Off., 1958–) **(I1141)**. Annual volumes for recent administrations and, retrospectively, with coverage thus far extended back to 1929 (except for the papers of Franklin D. Roosevelt, published commercially). Volumes from the Truman administration onward do not contain most proclamations and executive orders, but references are made to their inclusion in the *Federal register.* Cumulated indexes, by administration, published by KTO Pr.

When completed, the Public papers series will supersede an earlier set: U.S. President, *A compilation of the messages and papers of the presidents, 1789–1902,* ed. by James D. Richardson (New York: Bureau of National Literature and Art, 1903–04 [10v.]) **(I1142)**.

Two useful collections of major presidential addresses are U.S. President, *The State of the Union messages of the presidents, 1790–1966,* ed. by Fred L. Israel (New York: Chelsea, 1966 [3v.]) **(I1143)**, and U.S. President, *The presidents speak: the inaugural addresses of the American presidents, from Washington to Nixon,* 3d ed., annotated by David Lott (New York: Holt, 1969 [308p.]) **(I1144)**, which sets the stage for each address by providing background commentaries and marginal notes.

Treaties

I1145 Israel, Fred. L., comp. Major peace treaties of modern history, 1648–1967. New York: Chelsea, 1967. 4v.
Contains about 100 treaties grouped by period, area, or topic, with chapter commentaries sketching historical background and effects of the treaties. All texts in English, 17 of them published for the first time. Includes 28 maps and a detailed index.

A convenient one-volume source for important treaties:

I1146 John A. S. Grenville. The major international treaties 1914–1973: a history and guide with texts. New York: Stein & Day, 1974. 575p.

I1147 Parry, Clive, comp. The consolidated treaty series. v.1– . Dobbs Ferry, N.Y.: Oceana, 1969– .
Ambitious attempt to bring together texts of treaties signed between 1648 and 1918, thereby providing retrospective link to the UN and League of Nations treaties series (see below). The treaties, in the original language(s), are reproduced from existing treaty collections, and some previously unpublished agreements are included. Where available, translations in English or French accompany the original. Basic set of 226v. completed in 1981. Appendix of Dutch colonial agreements (v.227–) and a separately numbered index-guide in progress.

I1148 Timberlake, Charles E. Detente: a documentary record. New York: Praeger, 1978. 231p.

Drawn mostly from Dept. of State publications, a chronological presentation of treaties (bilateral and selected multilateral), press releases, etc., tracing the progress of detente from 1972 through 1977. In eight chapters, with introductory notes. Subject index.

I1149 United Nations. Treaty series. v.1– . 1946– . New York: UN.

Texts of treaties and international agreements registered or filed and recorded with the Secretariat of the UN since Dec. 14, 1946. Reproduced in the original language(s), with English and French translations. Each volume contains an annex, recording ratifications, accessions, etc., to treaties published earlier. General index for every 50 or 100 vols. With its predecessor, League of Nations, *Treaty series* (Geneva: 1920–46 [205v.]) (**I1150**), provides substantial world coverage of treaties from 1918. For earlier treaties, see I1147.

I1151 United States. Treaties, etc. United States treaties and other international agreements. v.1– , 1950– . Washington, D.C.: Govt. Print. Off., 1952– . Annual.

Published by the Dept. of State. From 1950, the official place of publication and legal evidence for treaties involving the United States. Treaties are printed in the language(s) appearing in the original. Includes country/subject indexes. Arranged in numerical order as originally published in pamphlet form in the department's *Treaties and other international acts series*, the primary source for recent texts.

Prior to 1950, treaties were officially published in *United States statutes at large* (I1128). They have also appeared as source material in *Foreign relations of the United States: diplomatic papers* (I1139) since 1861.

A retrospective compilation brings together the pre-1950 treaties: U.S. Treaties, etc., *Treaties and other international agreements of the United States, 1776–1949*, comp. by Charles I. Bevans (Washington, D.C.: Govt. Print. Off., 1968–76 [13v.]) (**I1152**). Includes multilateral treaties by date (v.1–4) and bilateral treaties by country (v.5–12). Cumulated analytical index in v.13. English texts or official English translations only. The above set replaces, for most purposes, two earlier compilations: U.S. Treaties, etc., *Treaties, conventions, international acts, protocols, and agreements between the United States of America and other powers, 1776–1937* (Washington, D.C.: Govt. Print. Off., 1919–38 [4v.]) (**I1153**), which is often referred to as *Malloy's treaties* after the compiler of v.1–2, William M. Malloy; and U.S. Treaties, etc., *Treaties and other international acts of the United States of America*, ed. by Hunter Miller (Washington, D.C.: Govt. Print. Off., 1931–48 [8v.]) (**I1154**), commonly cited by the editor's name.

The annual State Dept. publication, *Treaties in force: a list of treaties and other international agreements of the United States in force* (Washington, D.C.: 1929–) (**I1155**) lists bilateral treaties (by country and

subject) and multilateral treaties (by subject) active as of Jan. 1 each year. Citations to original sources of the texts.

STATISTICAL SOURCES

I1156 Craig, Fred W. S. British electoral facts, 1832–1980. 4th ed. Chichester, England: Parliamentary Research Services, 1981. 203p.

Convenient collection of statistical summaries for elections in England, Wales, Scotland, and Northern Ireland. In addition to tables for general elections and by-elections, includes data on such peripheral matters as candidates' expenses, electorate and turnout, gains and losses, public opinion polls, and women candidates.

Companion volumes edited by Craig, giving breakdown by constituency, are: *British parliamentary election results, 1832–1885* (London: Macmillan, 1977 [692p.]) (**I1157**); *British parliamentary election results, 1885–1918* (London: Macmillan, 1974 [698p.]) (**I1158**); *British parliamentary election results, 1918–1949*, rev. ed. (London: Macmillan, 1977 [785p.]) (**I1159**); *British parliamentary election results, 1950–1973*, 2d ed. (Chichester, Eng.: Parliamentary Research Services, 1983 [780p.]) (**I1160**); *Britain votes 2: British parliamentary election results, 1974–1979* (Chichester, Eng.: Parliamentary Research Services, 1980 [292p.]) (**I1161**); and *Britain votes 3: British parliamentary election results 1983* (Chichester, Eng.: Parliamentary Research Services, 1984 [141p.]) (**I1161A**).

I1162 ———, and Thomas T. Mackie. Europe votes 1: European parliamentary election results 1979. Chichester, Eng.: Parliamentary Research Services, 1980. 152p.

For each member country of the European Community, gives brief data on electoral systems, followed by rosters of candidates, votes cast, and seats won in the first election to the European Parliament. Volume projected for the 1984 election results.

I1163 Mackie, Thomas T., and Richard Rose. The international almanac of electoral history. 2d ed. London: Macmillan, 1982. 422p.

Purpose is "to provide a complete and accurate compilation of election results in Western nations since the beginning of competitive national elections" (preface). Within the stated limitation (only Western European states, Australia, Canada, and the U.S. are covered), a handy sourcebook. Country tables—by date from the earliest competitive election—show total votes, percentage of votes, seats won, and percentage of seats won for each party involved. Short historical sketches and sources for electoral data accompany the country tabulations. Appendix for the 1979 European Parliament election results.

I1164 United States. Arms Control and Disarmament Agency. World military expenditures and arms transfers, 1972–1982. Washington, D.C.: Govt. Print. Off., 1984. 121p.

Fifteenth of a series begun in 1965. Traces the development of munitions acquisition and costs for 145 countries over the course of a decade in 2 principal tables: (1) military expenditures, armed forces, gross national product, central government expenditures, and population; (2) value of arms transfers and total imports and exports by region, organization, and country. Preliminary essays and analyses of highlights center on U.S. and USSR roles in armament. Sources noted.

Ruth L. Sivard's annual *World military and social expenditures* (Leesburg, Va.: World Priorities, 1974–) **(I1165)** describes itself as an "accounting of the use of world resources for social and for military purposes" in order to provide "an objective basis for assessing relative priorities." Drawing on statistical sources of U.S. agencies, intergovernmental organizations, and independent research bodies, compares and ranks political/geographical regions and individual nations on such factors as number of military personnel versus teachers and physicians, public expenditure per soldier versus expenditure per capita, life expectancy, nutrition, drinking water, etc. Graphs, maps, and tables. Anti-war editorial perspective.

For a valuable annual survey of military personnel, expenditure, and major weaponry of countries, with comparative analyses of the world military powers, see *The military balance* (London: Intl. Institute for Strategic Studies, 1963–) **(I1166)**.

I1167 United States. Bureau of the Census. Census of governments, 1982. Washington, D.C.: Govt. Print. Off., 1983–

Results of special census taken every 5 years since 1957, provides an extensive statistical analysis of state, local, and municipal government in the U.S. In 8 sections: (1) governmental organization, (2) taxable property values and assessment, (3) public employment, (4) government finances, (5) local government in metropolitan areas, (6) topical studies, (7) guide to the 1982 census of governments, (8) procedural history.

I1167 Vital statistics on Congress. 1980– . Washing-
A   ton, D.C.: American Enterprise Inst. for Public Policy Research. Biennial.

Employing a variety of tables and charts, traces trends in the collective activity and behavior of Congress in recent years. Arranged in 8 topical chapters, with interpretive introductions: members of Congress; elections; campaign finance; committees; congressional staff and operating expenses; workload; budgeting; and voting alignments. Contains data on topics of general interest (e.g., blacks and women in Congress, PAC contributions) but is most useful in providing such flavorful statistical summaries as "ratio of bills passed to bills introduced, 80th–97th congresses" and "relatively uncontrollable federal outlays under present law, fiscal years 1967–1984." Appendix gives selected data on individual members. Although most of the figures are derived from standard sources, such as *Congressional directory* and Congressional Quarterly publications, the assemblage and presentation of such a wide range of information in one handy

volume make this compendium especially valuable and vital.

U.S. Elections

I1168 America votes: a handbook of contemporary American election statistics. v.1– , 1956– . Washington: publ. by Congressional Quarterly for the Elections Research Center. Biennial.

V. 1–2 published by Macmillan; v.3–5 published by Univ. of Pittsburgh Pr. This very useful series continues the work for earlier years done by Burnham, Robinson, etc. (see I1176 and I1177), and goes further by including the votes for governors, senators, and congressmen. Presidential summaries (elections from 1948 and tallies for recent primaries) precede the state profiles. Data for each state: (1) incumbent governor, senators, and representatives; (2) postwar vote for governors and senators; (3) map of the state, showing counties and congressional districts; (4) tabulation by county/congressional district (and by ward for major cities) for president, senators, and representatives in the most recent election; and (5) notes on the tables, including votes for candidates of parties other than Democratic or Republican.

Very similar in content and arrangement: Warren J. Mitofsky, comp. and ed., *Campaign '78: a comprehensive political handbook* (New York: Arno, 1980 [539p.]) **(I1169)**. A CBS News publication, also includes national overview, selected state ballot issues, and analyses of state voting patterns and political demography. Earlier volume for the 1976 campaign published in 1977.

Retrospective chronological series of state voting for presidential, gubernatorial, senate, and house candidates highlight the statistical handbook, *Congressional Quarterly's guide to U.S. elections* (Washington, D.C.: Congressional Quarterly, 1975 [1,103p.]) **(I1170)**. As in other CQ guides, a variety of charts, lists, and chronologies, plus name indexes, are included. Supplement for 1976 elections published 1977. Second edition scheduled for publication in 1985.

I1171 Glashan, Roy R. American governors and gubernatorial elections, 1775–1978. Westport, Conn.: Meckler, 1979. 370p.

Provides election results for each state, with breakdowns by major party votes, other significant votes, and scattered votes for each election. Also gives selected personal data (e.g., birthplace, birth date, occupation) and includes quotations from speeches and writing of governors (a superfluous feature). No index.

Most of the same statistical data are included in v.1 of Joseph E. Kallenbach and Jessamine S. Kallenbach, *American state governors, 1776–1976* (published in 3 volumes) (see I892). Kallenbach is better organized and more legible and offers historical procedural summaries for each state. V.2–3 contain biographical sketches.

I1173 Miller, Warren E., and others. American national election studies data sourcebook, 1952–1978. Cambridge, Mass.: Harvard Univ. Pr., 1980. 388p.

Companion volume to *American social attitudes data sourcebook, 1947–1978* (E629); gives time series tabulations of voter attitudes and behavior derived from surveys conducted in 14 postwar election years. Divided into 6 broad groupings: (1) social characteristics of the electorate (age, sex, religion, etc.), (2) partisanship (i.e., party or persuasion identification), (3) positions on public policy issues, (4) support of the political system (e.g., trust in government, citizen duty factors), (5) involvement and turnout, and (6) the vote. Methodological introductions and notes. This compendium, based on data produced by the Center for Political Studies, will be a gold mine for anyone attempting to analyze the American electorate's collective sensibilities.

I1174 Presidential elections since 1789. 3d ed. Washington, D.C.: Congressional Quarterly, 1983. 211p.

Quick-reference source for state data on presidential candidates and elections through 1980. Tables include primary returns, by state, from 1912; popular returns for party candidates, by state, from 1824; and electoral college votes from 1789. Also contains selected handbook-style data, such as balloting at nominating conventions, biographical sketches of candidates, and texts of major election laws. Index.

The above draws upon the pioneering work, Svend Petersen, *A statistical history of American presidential elections, with supplementary tables covering 1968–1980* (Westport, Conn.: Greenwood, 1981 [250p. plus supplement]) (**I1175**), an updated reprint of the 1968 edition. Petersen also includes specialized analyses of interest (e.g., states as barometers, high/low percentages of winners and losers of states, unsuccessful parties). Only state figures tabulated.

Breakdowns by counties, with details on county organization and party control, are provided by the scholarly compilation, W. Dean Burnham, *Presidential ballots, 1836–1892* (Baltimore: Johns Hopkins Univ. Pr., 1955 [956p.]) (**I1176**). Burnham is a backward extension of two earlier works by Edgar E. Robinson: *The presidential vote, 1896–1932* (Stanford, Calif.: Stanford Univ. Pr., 1934 [403p.]) (**I1177**) and *They voted for Roosevelt: the presidential vote, 1932–1944* (Stanford, Calif.: Stanford Univ. Pr., 1947 [207p.]) (**I1178**). In both studies, the major table, "Party vote for electors by state and county," gives totals for the Democratic party, the Republican party, and other parties, with the composition of the "other vote" spelled out in the appendixes. County-by-county data for 12 20th-century elections can be found in Governmental Affairs Institute, Washington, D.C., Elections Research Center, *America at the polls: a handbook of American presidential election statistics, 1920–1964*, compiled and ed. by Richard M. Scammon (Pittsburgh: Univ. of Pittsburgh Pr., 1965 [521p.]) (**I1179**). Chief source for presidential election statistics

by county (and major cities) from 1954 is *America votes* (I1168).

For a richly detailed presentation of data on 6 modern presidential elections and their contexts, see John H. Runyon and others, *Source book of American presidential campaign and election statistics, 1948–1968* (New York: Ungar, 1971 [380p.]) (**I1180**). In addition to election results, this excellent study contains tabulations and other data on the primaries, conventions, campaign staffs, campaign itineraries, campaign costs, media exposure, and public opinion polls.

ATLASES, MAPS, AND PICTORIAL WORKS

I1181 Kidron, Michael, and Ronald Segal. The new state of the world atlas; a Pluto Press project. New York: Simon & Schuster, 1984. 57maps, 52 unnumbered pages of text.

Vivid color maps depicting comparative national/regional aspects of public issues (e.g., trade power, harmworkers and healthworkers, urban blight). Informative notes provided for each map.

Cited as one example of several available atlases of world or regional politics. Most of these lose their currency value shortly after publication but continue to have some interest as time-capsules of the period depicted.

I1182 Kinnear, Michael. The British voter: an atlas and survey since 1885. London: Batsford Academic and Educational, 1981. 172p.

Depicts outcomes of the general elections and shows areas of party and other types of influence for selected elections (e.g., Liberal Unionists 1886–1910, the mining vote in 1921).

I1183 Martis, Kenneth C., ed. The historical atlas of United States congressional districts, 1789–1983. Ruth A. Rowles, cartographer and assistant ed. New York: Free Pr., 1982. 302p.

Beautifully produced volume, tracing the evolution of the districts during the first 97 congresses. For each congress chronologically, gives: (1) map of the U.S., showing the location of each district, with special insets for Hawaii, Alaska, and major cities; (2) alphabetical roster of representatives, with their states and districts indicated. Introduction discusses history, purpose, and methodology of the project, which is based on work originally undertaken by the Works Progress Administration's Historical Records Survey in the 1930s and 1940s. "Legal district descriptions" gives details on geographical composition (e.g., counties included) of each district over the years. Personal name index. Clarity and readability of the maps is exceptional. Two projected atlases will map political party representation and critical congressional votes.

Stanley B. Parsons and others, *United States congressional districts, 1788–1841* (Westport, Conn.: Greenwood, 1978 [416p.]) (**I1184**) also depicts geographical boundaries of the districts for the first 27 congresses, but in rather different fashion. Maps for individual states show district locations in reference to counties, and membership lists include party affiliation and city and county of residence. Selected demographic and geographic data (overall and slave populations, square-mile size, and population density) for counties. Maps are commonplace but adequate.

I1185 Sallnow, John, and Anna John. An electoral atlas of Europe, 1968–1981: a political geographic compendium including 76 maps. Cartography by Sarah K. Webber. London and Boston: Butterworth, 1982. 149p.

Graphic display of political party influence in nations and national regions of Europe. Following overview, groups countries by location or characteristic into 4 groups: Central Europe, maritime Europe, Mediterranean Europe, and Nordic Europe. Maps for each country accompanied by narrative analysis and election tables.

SOURCES OF SCHOLARLY CONTRIBUTIONS

Journals

I1186

Academy of Political Science. Proceedings. v.1– , 1910– . New York. Irregularly.
ABC; AmH&L; Cc; HistAbst; IntBibPolSci; IntlPolSciAbst; PAIS; SSCI; SSI; USPSD.

Administrative science quarterly. v.1– , 1956– . Ithaca, N.Y.: Cornell Univ. Graduate School of Business and Public Administration. Quarterly.
ABC; AmH&L; Cc; HistAbst; IntPolSciAbst; PAIS; PsychAbst; SagePubAdminAbst; SocAbst; SSCI; SSI; USPSD.

American journal of international law. v.1– , 1907– . Washington, D.C.: American Society of Intl. Law. Quarterly.
ABC; AmH&L; Cc; HistAbst; IndLegPer; IntBibPolSci; IntPolSciAbst; PAIS; SSCI; SSI; USPSD.

American journal of political science. v.1– , 1957– . Austin: Univ. of Texas Pr. for the Midwest Political Science Assn. Quarterly.
ABC; AmH&L; Cc; CommunAbst; HistAbst; HumResAbst; IntBibPolSci; IntPolSciAbst; SagePubAdminAbst; SocAbst; SSCI; SSI; USPSD.

American political science review. v.1– , 1906– . Washington, D.C.: American Political Science Assn. Quarterly.
ABC; AmH&L; Cc; CommunAbst; HistAbst; HumResAbst; IntBibPolSci; IntPolSciAbst; SagePubAdminAbst; SocAbst; USPSD.

American politics quarterly. v.1– , 1973– . Beverly Hills, Calif.: Sage. Quarterly.
ABC; AmH&L; Cc; CommunAbst; HistAbst;

HumResAbst; IntBibPolSci; IntPolSciAbst; PAIS; SagePubAdminAbst; SSCI; SSI; USPSD.

British journal of political science. v.1– , 1971– . Cambridge: Cambridge Univ. Pr. Quarterly.
ABC; AmH&L; Cc; HistAbst; IntPolSciAbst; PAIS; SSCI; SSI.

Canadian journal of political science. v.1– , 1968– . Waterloo, Ont.: Wilfrid Laurier Univ. Pr. for the Canadian Political Science Assn. Quarterly.
ABC; AmH&L; Cc; CommunAbst; IntBibPolSci; IntPolSciAbst; PAIS; SocAbst; SSCI; SSI.

Comparative political studies. v.1– , 1968– . Beverly Hills, Calif.: Sage. Quarterly.
ABC; AmH&L; Cc; CommunAbst; HistAbst; HumResAbst; IntBibPolSci; IntPolSciAbst; PAIS; SagePubAdminAbst; SSCI; SSI; USPSD.

Comparative politics. v.1– , 1968– . New York: City Univ. of New York. Quarterly.
ABC; AmH&L; Cc; CommunAbst; HistAbst; IntBibPolSci; IntPolSciAbst; PAIS; SagePubAdminAbst; SSCI; SSI; USPSD.

Comparative strategy: an international journal. v.1– , 1978– . New York: Crane Russak. Quarterly.
Cc; IntBibPolSci; IntPolSciAbst; SSCI; USPSD.

Congress and the presidency: a journal of capitol studies. v.1– , 1972– . Washington, D.C.: American Univ. Center for Congressional and Presidential Studies. 2/yr.
ABC; AmH&L; Cc; HistAbst; IntPolSciAbst; PAIS; SSCI.

Cooperation and conflict: Nordic journal of international politics. v.1– , 1965– . Olso: Universitetsforlaget for Nordic Cooperation Committee for Intl. Politics. Quarterly.
ABC: AmH&L; HistAbst; IntBibPolSci; IntPolSciAbst; PAIS.

European journal of political research: official journal of the European Consortium for Political Research. v.1– , 1973– . Amsterdam: Elsevier. Quarterly.
ABC; AmH&L; Cc; CommunAbst; IntBibPolSci; IntPolSciAbst; SocAbst; SSCI.

Foreign affairs. v.1– , 1922– . New York: Council on Foreign Relations. 5/yr.
ABC; AmH&L; Cc; HistAbst; IntBibPolSci; IntPolSciAbst; PAIS; RG; SSCI; SSI; USPSD.

Foreign policy. no.1– , 1970– . Washington, D.C.: Carnegie Endowment for Intl. Peace. Quarterly.
ABC; Cc; AmH&L; HistAbst; IntBibPolSci; IntPolSciAbst; PAIS; RG; SSCI; SSI; USPSD.

Government and opposition: a journal of comparative politics. v.1– , 1965– . London: London

School of Economics and Political Science. Quarterly.
ABC; AmH&L; Cc; HistAbst; IntBibPolSci; IntPolSciAbst; PAIS; SocAbst; SSCI; SSI.

History of political thought. v.1– , 1980– . Exeter, Eng.: Imprint Academic. Quarterly.
AmH&L; HistAbst; IntPolSciAbst; PhilInd.

International affairs. v.1– , 1922– . Guildford, Eng.: Butterworth for Royal Institute of Intl. Affairs. Quarterly.
ABC; AmH&L; BrHumInd; Cc; IntBibPolSci; IntPolSciAbst; PAIS; SSCI; SSI.

International organization. v.1– , 1947– . Cambridge, Mass.: MIT Pr. for World Peace Foundation. Quarterly.
ABC; AmH&L; Cc; CommunAbst; IntBibPolSci; IntPolSciAbst; PAIS; SSCI; SSI; USPSD.

International political science review. v.1– , 1980– . Beverly Hills, Calif.: Sage for Intl. Political Science Assn. Quarterly.
ABC; IntPolSciAbst; USPD.

International security. v.1– , 1976– . Cambridge, Mass.: MIT Pr. for Harvard Univ. Center for Science and Intl. Affairs. Quarterly.
ABC; AmH&L; Cc; HistAbst; IntBibPolSci; IntPolSciAbst; PAIS; SSCI; USPSD.

International studies quarterly: journal of the Intl. Studies Assn. v.1– , 1957– . Guildford, Eng.: Butterworth. Quarterly.
ABC; AmH&L; Cc; HistAbst; IntBibPolSci; IntPolSciAbst; SSCI; SSI; USPSD.

Journal of commonwealth and comparative politics. v.1– , 1961– . London: Frank Cass. 3/yr.
ABC; AmH&L; Cc; HistAbst; IntBibPolSci; IntPolSciAbst; SSCI.

Journal of conflict resolution: research on war and peace between and within nations. v.1– , 1957– . Beverly Hills, Calif.: Sage. Quarterly.
ABC; AmH&L; Cc; HistAbst; IntBibPolSci; IntPolSciAbst; PAIS; PsychAbst; SocAbst; SSCI; SSI.

Journal of international affairs. v.1– , 1947– . New York: Columbia Univ. School of Intl. Affairs. Semiannual.
ABC; AmH&L; HistAbst; HumResAbst; IntBibPolSci; IntPolSciAbst; PAIS; SagePubAdminAbst; SSCI; SSI; USPSD.

Journal of peace research. v.1– , 1964– . Oslo: Universitetsforlaget for Intl. Peace Research Institute. Quarterly.
ABC; Cc; HistAbst; IntBibPolSci; IntPolSciAbst; PAIS; SocAbst; SSCI; SSI.

Journal of policy analysis and management. v.1– , 1981– . New York: Wiley for Assn. for Public Policy Analysis and Management. Quarterly. (Formerly: Public policy).

ABC; Cc; CommunAbst; HistAbst; HumResAbst; IntBibPolSci; IntPolSciAbst; PAIS; SagePubAdminAbst; SocAbst; SSCI.

Journal of politics. v.1– , 1939– . Gainesville, Fla.: Southern Political Science Assn. Quarterly.
ABC; AmH&L; Cc; CommunAbst; HistAbst; IntBibPolSci; IntPolSciAbst; PAIS; SocAbst; SSCI; SSI; USPSD

Journal of public policy. v.1– , 1981– . Cambridge: Cambridge Univ. Pr. Quarterly.
ABC; HumResAbst; IntPolSciAbst; PAIS; SocAbst.

Journal of strategic studies. v.1– , 1978– . London: Frank Cass. Quarterly.
AmH&L; Cc.; HistAbst; IntBibPolSci; IntPolSciAbst.

Legislative studies quarterly. v.1– , 1976– . Iowa City: Univ. of Iowa Comparative Legislative Research Center. Quarterly.
ABC; Cc; IntBibPolSci; IntPolSciAbst; SagePubAdminAbst; USPSD.

Micropolitics. v.1– , 1981– . New York: Crane Russak. Quarterly.
ABC; IntPolSciAbst; SocAbst.

Millennium: journal of international studies. v.1– , 1971– . Oxford: Martin Robertson. 3/yr.
ABC; AmH&L; BritHumInd; HistAbst; IntBibPolSci; IntPolSciAbst; PAIS.

Orbis: a journal of world affairs. v.1– , 1957– . Philadelphia: Foreign Policy Research Inst. Quarterly.
ABC; AmH&L; Cc; HistAbst; IntBibPolSci; IntPolSciAbst; PAIS; SSCI; SSI; USPSD.

Parliamentary affairs. v.1– , 1947– . London: Oxford Univ. Pr. Quarterly.
ABC; AmH&L; BrHumInd; Cc; HistAbst; IntBibPolSci; IntPolSciAbst; PAIS; SagePubAdminAbst; SocAbst; SSCI; SSI.

Policy and politics. v.1 , 1972– . Bristol, Eng.: School for Advanced Urban Studies. Quarterly.
ABC; Cc; IntBibPOlSci; SSCI.

Policy studies review. v.1– , 1981– . Urbana: Univ. of Illinois Policy Studies Organization. Quarterly.
ABC; AmH&L; HistAbst; HumResAbst; IntPolSciAbst; PAIS; SagePubAdminAbst; SocAbst.

Political behavior. v.1– , 1979– . New York: Agathon Pr. Quarterly.
IntPolSciAbst; PsychAbst; SocAbst; USPSD.

Political communication and persuasion. v.1– , 1980– . New York: Crane Russak. Quarterly.
ABC; CommunAbst; IntPolSciAbst; PAIS; SocAbst; USPSD.

Political methodology. v.1– , 1974– . Los Altos, Calif.: Geron-X. Quarterly.
ABC; IntPolSciAbst; USPSD.

Political quarterly. v.1– , 1930– . London: Political Quarterly. Quarterly.
ABC; BrHumInd; Cc; CommunAbst; IntBibPolSci; IntPolSciAbst; PAIS; SSCI; SSI.

Political science quarterly. v.1– , 1886– . New York: Academy of Political Science. Quarterly.
ABC; AmH&L; Cc; HistAbst; IntBibPolSci; IntPolSciAbst; PAIS; SagePubAdminAbst; SSCI; SSI; USPSD.

Political studies. v.1– , 1953– . Guildford, Eng.: Butterworth for Political Studies Assn. of the United Kingdom. Quarterly.
ABC; AmH&L; BrHumInd; Cc; HistAbst; IntBibPolSci; IntPolSciAbst; PAIS; SagePubAdminAbst; SocAbst; SSCI; SSI.

Political theory: an international journal of political philosophy. v.1– , 1973– . Beverly Hills, Calif.: Sage. Quarterly.
ABC; Cc; AmH&L; HistAbst; IntBibPolSci; IntPolSciAbst; SSCI; USPSD.

Politics and society. v.1– , 1970– . Los Altos, Calif.: Geron-X. Quarterly.
ABC; Cc; AmH&L; HistAbst; IntBibPolSci; IntPolSciAbst; SSCI; SSI; USPSD.

Politique étrangère de la France. v.1– , 1935– . Paris: Documentation Française. Quarterly.
ABC; IntBibPolSci; IntPolSciAbst.

Politische Vierteljahresschrift: Zeitschrift der Deutschen Vereinigung für Politische Wissenschaft. v.1– , 1960– . Opladen: Westdeutscher Verlag. Quarterly.
AmH&L; HistAbst; IntBibPolSci; IntBibZeit; IntPolSciAbst; SSCI.

Polity. v.1– , 1968– . Amherst, Mass.: Northeastern Political Science Assn. Quarterly.
ABC; Cc; HistAbst; HumResAbst; IntBibPolSci; IntPolSciAbst; SagePubAdminAbst; SSCI; USPSD.

Presidential studies quarterly. v.1– , 1972– . New York: Center for the Study of the Presidency. Quarterly.
ABC; AmH&L; HistAbst; HumResAbst; IntBibPolSci; IntPolSciAbst; SagePubAdminAbst; USPSD.

Public administration. v.1– , 1923– . London: Royal Inst. of Public Administration. Quarterly.
ABC; AmH&L; BrHumInd; Cc; HistAbst; IntBibPolSci; IntPolSciAbst; PAIS; SSCI.

Public administration review. v.1– , 1940– . Washington, D.C.: American Society for Public Administration. Bimonthly.
Cc; IntPolSciAbst; PAIS; SagePubAdminAbst; SSCI; SSI; USPSD.

Public choice. v.1– , 1966– . The Hague: Nijhoff. Bimonthly.
ABC; Cc; HumResAbst; IntBibPolSci; Int-

PolSciAbst; SagePubAdminAbst; SocAbst; SSCI; USPSD.

Public interest. no.1– , 1965– . New York: Natl. Affairs. Quarterly.
ABC; AmH&L; Cc; HistAbst; HumResAbst; IntBibPolSci; IntPolSciAbst; PAIS; SocAbst; SSCI; SSI; USPSD.

Publius; the journal of federalism. v.1– , 1971– . Philadelphia: Temple Univ. Center for the Study of Federalism. Quarterly.
ABC; AmH&L; Cc; HistAbst; IntPolSciAbst; SagePubAdminAbst; SocAbst; SSCI; USPSD.

Review of international studies. v.1– , 1975– . Guildford, Eng.: Butterworth. Quarterly.
AmH&L; HistAbst; IntBibPolSci; IntPolSciAbst.

Review of politics. v.1– , 1939– . Notre Dame, Ind.: Univ. of Notre Dame. Quarterly.
ABC; AmH&L; Cc; HistAbst; IntBibPolSci; IntPolSciAbst; SSCI; SSI; USPSD.

Revue du droit public et de la science politique en France et à l'étranger. v.1– , 1894– . Paris: Libraire Générale de Droit et de Jurisprudence. Bimonthly.
IntBibPolSci; IntPolSciAbst.

Revue française de science politique. v.1– , 1951– . Paris: Fondation Nationale des Sciences Politiques. Bimonthly.
AmH&L; HistAbst; IntBibPolSci; IntPolSciAbst; SSCI.

SAIS review. v.1– , 1981– . Washington, D.C.: Johns Hopkins Univ. School of Advanced Intl. Studies. Semiannual.
ABC: AmH&L: HistAbst; PAIS.

Scandinavian political studies. New series, v.1– , 1978– . Publ. by Universitetsforlaget for Nordic Political Science Assn. Quarterly.
ABC; AmH&L; HistAbst; IntBibPolSci; IntPolSciAbst.

State government. v.1– , 1930– . Lexington, Ky.: Council of State Governments. Quarterly.
ABC; AmH&L; Cc; HistAbst; HumResAbst; PAIS; SagePubAdminAbst; SSCI; SSI.

Washington quarterly. v.1– , 1978– . New Brunswick, N.J.: Rutgers Univ. for Georgetown Univ. Center for Strategic and Intl. Studies. Quarterly.
ABC; AmH&L; Cc; HistAbst; IntBibPolSci; USPSD.

West European politics. v.1– , 1978– . London: Frank Cass. 3/yr.
ABC; AmH&L; HistAbst; IntBibPolSci; IntPolSciAbst; PAIS; SagePubAdminAbst; SocAbst.

Western political quarterly. v.1– 1948– . Salt Lake City: Univ. of Utah for Western Political Science Assn., Pacific Northwest Political Science

Assn., and Southern California Political Science Assn. Quarterly.
ABC; AmH&L; Cc; HistAbst; IntBibPolSci; IntPolSciAbst; SagePubAdminAbst; SSCI; SSI; USPSD.

Women and politics. v.1– , 1980. New York: Haworth Pr. Quarterly.
IntPolSciAbst; PAIS; SocAbst; WomStudAbst.

World affairs: a quarterly review of international problems. v.1– , 1837– . Washington, D.C.: American Peace Society. Quarterly.
ABC; AmH&L; Cc; HistAbst; IntBibPolSci; IntPolSciAbst; SSCI; SSI; USPSD.

World politics: a quarterly journal of international relations. v.1– , 1948– . Princeton, N.J.: Princeton Univ. Pr. for Center of Intl. Studies. Quarterly.
ABC; AmH&L; Cc; HistAbst; IntBibPolSci; IntPolSciAbst; PAIS; SSCI; SagePubAdminAbst; SSI; USPSD.

Zeitschrift für die gesamte Staatswissenschaft. Bd. 1– , 1844– . Tübingen, W. Germany: J. C. B. Mohr. Quarterly.
IntBibPolSci; IntBibZeit; IntPolSciAbst; PAIS.

Zeitschrift für Politik. N.S. v.1– , 1954– . Cologne: Heymanns. Quarterly.
ABC; AmH&L; HistAbst; IntBibPolSci; IntBibZeit; IntPolSciAbst.

Monograph Series

I1187

Bibliothèque de droit international. v.1– , 1957– . Paris: Librairie Générale de Droit et de Jurisprudence.

Fondation Nationale des Sciences Politiques. Cahiers. v.1– , 1947– . Paris.

Harvard political studies. 1930– . Cambridge, Mass.: Harvard Univ. Pr.

Nomos: yearbook of the American Society for Political and Legal Philosophy. v.1– , 1958– . New York: New York Univ. Pr.

Princeton Univ. Center of Intl. Studies. Research monograph. no.1– , 1959– . Princeton, N.J.: Princeton Univ. Pr.

Sage international yearbook of foreign policy studies. v.1– , 1973– . Beverly Hills, Calif.: Sage.

Sage yearbooks in politics and public policy. v.1– , 1975– . Beverly Hills, Calif.: Sage.

Stanford Univ. Hoover Institution on War, Revolution and Peace. Publications. v.1– , 1932– . Stanford, Calif.: Hoover Institution Pr.

Tulane studies in political science. v.1– , 1952– . New Orleans: Tulane Univ. Pr.

Yale studies in political science. v.1– , 1954– . New Haven, Conn.: Yale Univ. Pr.

Organizations

I1188

Académie Internationale de Science Politique et d'Histoire Constitutionelle. Paris. Founded 1936.

Academy of Political Science. New York. Founded 1880.

American Enterprise Institute for Public Policy Research. Washington, D.C. Founded 1943.

American Political Science Assn. Washington, D.C. Founded 1903.

American Society for Public Administration. Washington, D.C. Founded 1939.

Carnegie Endowment for International Peace. Washington, D.C. Founded 1910.

Council of State Governments. Lexington, Ky. Founded 1925.

Council on Foreign Relations. New York. Founded 1921.

Deutsche Vereinigung für Politische Wissenschaft. Hamburg. Founded 1951.

European Consortium for Political Research. Colchester, England. Founded 1970.

Fondation Nationale des Sciences Politiques. Paris. Founded 1945.

Foreign Policy Assn. New York. Founded 1918.

Inter-University Consortium for Political and Social Research. Ann Arbor, Mich. Founded 1962.

Intl. City Management Assn. Washington, D.C. Founded 1914.

Intl. Institute of Administrative Sciences. Brussels. Founded 1930.

Intl. Political Science Assn. Paris. Founded 1949.

Intl. Studies Assn. Columbia, S.C. Founded 1959.

Istituto per gli Studi di Politica Internazionale. Milan. Founded 1934.

Public Administration Service. McLean, Va. Founded 1933.

Royal Institute of Intl. Affairs. London. Founded 1920.

Stockholm Intl. Peace Research Institute. Stockholm. Founded 1966.

SOURCES OF CURRENT INFORMATION

I1189 CQ weekly report. v.1– , 1943– . Washington, D.C.: Congressional Quarterly. Weekly.

Good source for current facts, figures, and unbiased commentary on all aspects of congressional activity. Covers major issues, committee activities, floor action (including roll-call votes), and the status of major legislation. Valuable, timely profiles of emerging issues and personalities. The annual *Congressional Quarterly almanac* serves as a digest of material contained in the weekly reports.

Congressional Quarterly's monitoring of government processes and activities is of inestimable benefit to both political scientists and the general public. In addition to publications noted elsewhere in this chapter, CQ issues a variety of inexpensive paperbacks on important topics. Recent titles include *Financing politics, Media power in politics, The Washington lobby, Elections '84*, and *Candidates '84*.

I1190 Campaigns and elections: the journal of political action. v.1– , 1980– . McLean, Va.: Stanley F. Reed. Quarterly.

Focuses on nuts-and-bolts political strategy. Brief articles on election laws, fund-raising techniques, the media, use of the computer, etc. Main value for political scientists is its highlighting of current trends and issues in practical politics.

I1191 Congressional digest. v.1– , 1921– . Washington, D.C.: Congressional Digest. Monthly.

Each issue is devoted to a major controversial topic of national importance. The factual background is given, followed by a pro and con section consisting of selections from congressional testimony, speeches, articles, etc. Also includes summary of the month's activities in Congress.

I1192 Current American government. Fall 1961– . Washington, D.C.: Congressional Quarterly. Semiannual.

CQ's survey of recent significant developments in national government and politics. Contains sections on Congress, the president and executive branch, the Supreme Court, lobbies, and politics.

I1193 Department of State bulletin. v.1– , 1939– . Washington, D.C.: Govt Print. Off. Monthly.

Provides information on developments in U.S. foreign relations. Includes press releases on foreign policy, statements and addresses of the president and officers of the department, special articles, and information pertaining to treaties and international agreements.

I1194 Europa Archiv: Zeitschrift für internationale Politik. v.1– , 1946– . Bonn: publ. by Verlag für International Politik für Deutsche Gesellschaft für Auswärtige Politik e. V. Semimonthly.

A journal of political documentation, whose articles are usually followed by notes on sources and texts of pertinent documents. Also notes recent publications on international political questions and includes a chronology.

I1195 National journal. v.1– , 1969– . Washington, D.C.: National Journal. Weekly.

Provides "intelligence" reports on federal policymaking and a weekly summary of federal activity. Also features checklists of major issues, items on Washington personalities, and statistical tables. Semiannual indexes of topics, personal names, and governmental and private organizations. Lively and informative.

I1196 P. S. v.1– , 1968– . Washington, D.C.: American Political Science Assn. Quarterly.

The association's news organ. Contains news notes on professional activities, research and training support, APSA committees, conferences, individual contributions and awards, etc. For information about its annual list of doctoral dissertations, see I734.

I1197 Revue politique et parlementaire: economie, finance, urbanisme. no.1– , 1894– . Paris. Bimonthly.

Short articles on political activity in France and elsewhere.

I1198 U.S. news and world report. v.1– , 1933– . Washington, D.C. Weekly.

News magazine, offering comment on and interpretation of developments in contemporary political and economic affairs.

I1199 World today. v.1– , 1945– . Oxford: Oxford Univ. Pr. Monthly.

Issued under the auspices of the Royal Institute of International Affairs. Each issue carries 4–6 objective reports on all aspects of the international scene. Good for interpretive articles on current conditions in individual countries or areas.

See also lists of current digests and selected daily newspapers in "Social Science Literature" chapter.

Phillip A. Smith

Index

Index prepared by Answers Unlimited, Inc.

Index numbers refer to serial entry numbers, not to pages.

The form of alphabetization used in this index is basically word-by-word. Punctuation and nonalphabetic signs and symbols, except as noted below, are ignored.

Numerals, arabic and roman, are alphabetized as if they were spelled out. Modified letters and diacritics are treated like their plain equivalents in the English alphabet. The ampersand is filed as its spelled-out language equivalent. Abbreviations and acronyms are arranged as written except titles such as Mr. (Mister) and St. (Saint). Names beginning with the letters Mc are alphabetized as if they began with the letters Mac.

Some names (such as those beginning de, der, den, di, du, la) and some words with variant spellings (such as source book and sourcebook, hand book and handbook) are filed as one word for the convenience of the index user.

In access points beginning with a surname, all terms of honor and address are disregarded for filing purposes.

Where title entries are identical, the entries are arranged by the author's last name which appears in parentheses, e.g., (Miller), or by a descriptor such as (database) or (periodical). Where a title entry and a subject entry are identical, the title entry appears before the subject entry.

Barrett, Gerald V.
Man, work, and organizations, G366
Barro, Robert J.
Macroeconomics, D120A
Money, employment, and inflation, D90
Barron's guide to the two-year colleges, H513
Barron's: national business and financial weekly, D817
Barron's profiles of American colleges, H505
Barrow, Mark V.
Health and disease of American Indians north of Mexico, F849
Barry, Brian M.
The liberal theory of justice, I548
Sociologists, economists, and democracy, I547
Barry, Herbert
"Description and uses of the Human Relations Area File," F1004
Barry, Herbert, III
Actions of alcohol, E449
Barry, Rozanne M.
African newspapers in selected American libraries, a union list, A313
Bart, Pauline
The student sociologist's handbook, E145
Barth, Frederick
Models of social organization, F291
Barth, Hans Karl
Egypt, C594
Bartke, Wolfgang
Who's who in the People's Republic of China, I874
Bartlett, Peggy
Agricultural decision making, F405
Bartley, Numan V.
The rise of massive resistance, B1282
Bartley, S. Howard
Principles of perception, G139
Barton, Allen H.
Making bureaucracies work, I287
Organizational measurement and its bearing on the study of college environments, E110
The bases of economic geography, C196
"Basic bibliography for Native American law," F824
Basic books in the mass media, E405
"Basic business handbooks and dictionaries," D689
Basic color terms, F332
"Basic guide to reference sources for the study of the North American Indian," F822
Basic history of American business, D327
Basic library of management, D598

Basic maps of the U.S. economy, 1967-1990, D794
Basic psychology, G5
Basic readings in social security, E504
Basic readings in the sociology of education, H128
Basic statistical methods, G97
Basic statistics of the community, A488
Basic writings in the history of psychology, G27
Basque Americans, E156
Bass, Bernard M.
Man, work, and organizations, G366
Basseches, Bruno
A bibliography of Brazilian bibliographies, F464
Bassett, Keith
"Numerical methods for map analysis," C471
Basso, Keith H.
Meaning in anthropology, F209
Bassols Batalla, Angel. See Batalla, Angel Bassols
Bastide, Roger
Applied anthropology, F390
Batalla, Angel Bassols
Bibliografía de México, C575
Bater, James H.
"Soviet town planning," C472
Bates, Marston
Gluttons and libertines, F2
BATESON, GREGORY, F34
Bath, B. H. Slicher van. See Slicher van Bath, B. H.
Bath University of Technology
Design of information systems in the social sciences, A15
Investigation into information requirements of the social sciences, A14
Batson, Harold E.
A select bibliography of modern economic theory, 1870-1929, D597
Battis, Emery
Saints and sectaries, B584
Battle, Vincent M.
Essays in the history of African education, H38
Battles won and lost, B1222
Battro, Antonio M.
Piaget, G569
Bauer, Jeffrey C.
Issues in health economics, D389
Bauer, K. Jack
The Mexican-American War, 1846-1848, B877
Bauer, P. T.
Equality, the Third World, and economic delusion, D490
Bauer, Raymond
American business and public policy, I206
Social indicators, E612
Baughman, Ernest Warren
Type and motif-index of the folktales of England and North America, F944
Bauman, Mary Kinsey
Blindness, visual impairment, deaf-blindness, E481

Bauman, Richard
Explorations in the ethnography of speaking, F210
Baumann, Duane D.
Water resources for our cities, C390
Baumol, William J.
Contestable markets and the theory of industry structure, D363A
Economic dynamics, D91
Welfare economics and the theory of the state, D416, I603
Bautier, Robert H.
The economic development of medieval Europe, B98
Bawerk, Eugen Böhm von. See Böhm von Bawerk, Eugen
Baxter, Maurice G.
Daniel Webster and the Supreme Court, B740
Baxter, Mike
"Estimation and inference in spatial interaction models," C472
Baxter, Pam M.
Library use, G381
Baxter, William
People or penguins, D377
Bay, Christian
The structure of freedom, I549
Bay, Edna G.
Women in Africa, F315
The Bay of Pigs: the leaders' story of Brigade 2506, B1403
Bay of Pigs: the untold story, B1404
Bayitch, Stojan A.
Latin America and the Caribbean, F801
Baylen, Joseph O.
Biographical dictionary of modern British radicals, I880
Bayley, Edwin R.
Joe McCarthy and the press, B1306
Beach, Mark
A bibliographic guide to American colleges and universities, H432
Beale, Howard K.
The critical year, B932
Theodore Roosevelt and the rise of America to world power, B1079
Beales, Derek
The risorgimento and the unification of Italy, B364
Beals, Alan R.
Culture in process, F3
Divisiveness and social conflict, F369
Beals, Ralph L.
An introduction to anthropology, F11
Beaney, William M.
American constitutional law, I266
Beard, Charles A.
An economic interpretation of the Constitution of the United States, B686

Bellack, Alan S.
International handbook of behavior modification and therapy, G597
Bellush, Bernard
The failure of the NRA, B1160
Belshaw, Cyril S.
The sorcerer's apprentice, F392
Traditional exchange and modern markets, F270
Belz, Herman
A new birth of freedom, B937
Bemis, Samuel F.
The diplomacy of the American Revolution, B674
Guide to the diplomatic history of the United States, 1775-1921, I686
Jay's treaty, B745
John Quincy Adams and the foundations of American foreign policy, B764
John Quincy Adams and the union, B773
The Latin American policy of the United States, B769
Pinckney's treaty, B746
Ben-David, Joseph
The scientist's role in society, E45
Benda, Julien
The treason of the intellectuals, I567
Bendix, Reinhard
Kings or people, I370
Benedict, Michael Les
A compromise of principle, B939
The impeachment and trial of Andrew Johnson, B940
Benedict, Ruth
The chrysanthemum and the sword, F82
Patterns of culture, F83
BENEDICT, RUTH, F47-F48
Benefit-cost analysis of government programs, D423
The benefits of psychotherapy, G347
Bengelsdorf, Winnie
Ethnic studies in higher education, E322
Benitez, Mario A.
The education of the Mexican American, E369
Benjamin Franklin (Clark), B615
Benjamin Franklin (Van Doren), B613
Benjamin Franklin and a rising people, B614
Benjamin Franklin and American foreign policy, B677
Benjamin, Ludy T., Jr.
"History of psychology in biography," G542
"Prominent psychologists," G543
Bennett, Bruce L.
A world history of physical education, H222
Bennett, Carl A.
Evaluation and experiment, A104
Bennett, Edward M.
Recognition of Russia, B1185

Bennett, John W.
The ecological transition, F256
Bennett, John W. Wheeler. *See* Wheeler-Bennett, John W.
Bennett, Robert J.
European progress in spatial analysis, C42
Geography of public finance, C189
Quantitative geography, C41
Bennett, W. Lance
The political mind and the political environment, I588
Benoist, Jean-Marie
The structural revolution, A112
Benson, Charles S.
The economics of public education, H345
Benson, Hazel B.
Behavior modification and the child, G499
Benson, Lee
The concept of Jacksonian democracy, B792
Bent, Rudyard K.
Principles of secondary education, H229
Bentham, Jeremy
Economic writings, D24
Bentley, Arthur F.
The process of government, I119
Bentley, G. Carter
Ethnicity and nationality, E316
Bercovitch, Sacvan
The Puritan origins of the American self, B579
Bereday, George Z. F.
Comparative method in education, H134
Higher education, H240
Berelson, Bernard
The behavioral sciences today, A22
Human behavior, H105
Voting, I120
Berger, Alfred H.
Dictionary of psychology, G564
Berger, Peter L.
Invitation to sociology, E1
The social construction of reality, A70
Social construction of reality, I570
Berger, Raoul
Government by judiciary, I256
Berghe, Pierre L. van den
Man in society, A110
Bergin, Allen E.
Handbook of psychotherapy and behavior change, G320, G601
Research in individual psychotherapy, G501
Bergman, Edward F.
Modern political geography, C173
Bergson, Abram
The economics of Soviet planning, D223
The Soviet economy, D224
Bergstrom, Len V.
Women and society, E386
Berichte zur deutschen Landeskunde, C581

Berki, Sylvester E.
Hospital economics, D385
Berkowitz, Leonard
Advances in experimental social psychology, G413
Berkson, I. B.
Ethics, politics, and education, H83
Berle, Adolf
The modern corporation and private property, D364
Berleant Schiller, Riva
Directory of business and financial services, D799
Berlin, Brent
Basic color terms, F332
Principles of Tzeltzal plant classification, F333
Berlin, Isaiah
Four essays on liberty, I550
Historical inevitability, B3
Berliner, David C.
Educational psychology, G355, G360
Berlyne, D. E.
Structure and direction in thinking, G171
Berman, Ronald
America in the sixties, B1340
Berman, William C.
Politics of civil rights in the Truman administration, B1272
Bernard, Harvey R.
Technology and social change, F393
Bernard, Jessie
Origins of American sociology, A37
Bernard, Luther L.
Origins of American sociology, A37
Bernatzik, Hugo A.
Afrika, F979
Bernd, Joseph L.
Mathematical applications in political science, I202
Bernsdorf, Wilhelm
Internationales Soziologen Lexikon, E517
Wörterbuch der Soziologie, E558
Bernstein, Abraham
The education of urban populations, H106
Bernstein, Carl
All the president's men, B1351
The final days, B1352
Bernstein, George
Bilingual education in American schools, H442
Bernstein, Irving
The lean years, B1135
Turbulent years, B1173
Berry, Brian J. L.
A bibliographic guide to the economic regions of the United States, C534
Central place studies, C552
Comparative urbanization, C266
Contemporary urban ecology, C257
Geographic perspectives on urban systems with integrated readings, C255

603

Blum, Eleanor
Basic books in the mass media, E405
Blum, Jerome
Lord and peasant in Russia from the ninth century to the nineteenth century, B378
Blum, John Morton
The national experience, B495
The Republican Roosevelt, B1065
V was for victory, B1248
Woodrow Wilson and the politics of morality, B1074
BLUM, LEON, B426
Blum, Walter J.
The uneasy case for progressive taxation, D404
Blume, Helmut
The Caribbean islands, C404
Blumenthal, Arthur L.
Language and psychology, G290
Blumer, Herbert
Symbolic interactionism, A57
Blumler, Jay G.
The uses of mass communications, E121
Blunden, John R.
Geographical aspects of health, C375C
Bluntschli, J. K.
The theory of the state, I81
Blydenburgh, John C.
Political science statistics, I620
BNA policy and practice series, D800
Board, Christopher
"Map design and evaluations," C472
"Maps and mapping," C472
"Maps in the mind's eye," C472
Boas, Franz
Race, language and culture, F81
BOAS, FRANZ, F27, F41-F42
Boateng, E. A.
A political geography of Africa, C190
Boatner, Mark M.
Civil War dictionary, B1683
Encyclopedia of the American Revolution, B1682
Bode, Carl
The American lyceum, H301
Bodily changes in pain, hunger, fear, and rage, G155
Bodmer, W. F.
Genetics, evolution and man, F141
Boehm, Eric H.
Blueprint for bibliography, A140
Historical periodicals, B1685
Historical periodicals directory, B1684
Boehnke, Barbara
The spatial analysis of crime, C515
Boer, S. P. de. See de Boer, S. P.
Boesch, Hans
Japan, C448
Bogardus, Emory S.
The development of social thought, A38

Bogue, Donald J.
Population of the United States, E636
Bohannan, P.
Researches into the early history of mankind and the development of civilization, F67
Bohlen, Charles E.
Witness to history, 1929-1969, B1383
Böhm von Bawerk, Eugen
Capital and interest, D79
Boissevain, Jeremy
Friends of friends, F370
Bok, Derek C.
Labor and the American community, D280
Bokelmann, Hans
Der Aufbau erziehungswissenschaftlicher Studien und der Lehrberuf, H274
Boldyrev, N. I.
Pedagogika, H11
Boletín bibliográfico do antropologiá Américana, F789
Boletín Indigenista Venezolano, F803
Bolgar, R. R.
The classical heritage and its beneficiaries, B158
BOLIVIA, F805-F806
Bolivian Indian tribes, F805
Boll, Thomas J.
Handbook of clinical neuropsychology, G600
Bollens, John C.
American county government, I782
The Bolsheviks, B390
Boltan, Brian
Factor analytic studies, 1971-1975, G506
BONAPARTE, JOSEPH, B303
Bonbright, James C.
Principles of public utility rates, D370
Bond guide, D804
Bond survey, D802
Bonds of womanhood, E74
Boneparth, Ellen
Women, power and policy, I207
Bonnardel, Regine van Chi-. See van Chi-Bonnardel, Regine
Bonner, Thomas N.
The contemporary world, A39
Bonser, Wilfrid
An Anglo-Saxon and Celtic bibliography (450-1087), B1585
A bibliography of folklore as contained in the first eighty years of the publications of the Folk-Lore Society, F533
A bibliography of folklore for 1958-1967, F533A
A prehistoric bibliography, F566
A Romano-British bibliography (55 B.C.-A.D. 449), B1586
The bonus march, B1151
Boocock, Sarane Spence
Sociology of education, E98
The book of American rankings, E630

Book of the states, I1055
Book of the states: state administrative officials classified by function, 1945; state elective officials and the legislatures, I1943; state legislative leadership, committees and staff, I1944
Book review digest, A132
Book review index, A215
Book review index to social science periodicals, A216
Booker T. Washington, B969
Books about the blind, E480
Books for college libraries, A256
Books in American history, B1628
Books in English on Finland, F885
Books in print, A192
Books in series in the United States, A502
Books on American Indians and Eskimos, E356
Books on communism and the Communist countries, I872
The bookseller, A206
Boorman, Howard L.
Biographical dictionary of republican China, B1647
Boorstin, Daniel J.
The Americans: the colonial experience, B527; the democratic experience, B986; the national experience, B827
The genius of American politics, I350
The lost world of Thomas Jefferson, B717
Booth, Robert E.
Culturally disadvantaged, E473
Boots, Barry N.
"Population density, crowding and human behaviour," C472
"Probability model approach to map pattern analysis," C472
Bootzin, Richard
Psychology today, G10
Bopp, Stephen G.
Approaches to guidance in contemporary education, H197
Borden, Morton
Parties and politics in the early Republic, 1789-1815, B709
"The borderlands of geography as a social science," C7
Borg, Dorothy
The United States and the Far Eastern crisis of 1933-1938, B1190
Borgstrom, Georg
Too many, C381
Borich, Gary D.
An appraisal of teaching, H275
Boring, Edwin G.
A history of experimental psychology, G21
A history of psychology in autobiography, G545
Sensation and perception in the history of experimental psychology, G138

Index

Dictionary of banking and finance
(Davids), D666

Dictionary of banking and finance
(Rosenberg), D667

Dictionary of behavioral science,
G559

A dictionary of British folk-tales
in the English language,
incorporating the F.J. Norton
Collection, F943

Dictionary of business and
economics, D663

Dictionary of Canadian biography,
B1657

Dictionary of comparative
religion, F915

A dictionary of concepts on
American politics, I991

Dictionary of criminal justice,
E555

Dictionary of economic and
statistical terms, D686

Dictionary of economics, D685

A dictionary of economics
quotations, D677A

Dictionary of education (Good),
H548

A dictionary of education (Hills),
H549

A dictionary of education
(Rountree), H553

Dictionary of educational
acronyms, abbreviations, and
initialisms, H552

A dictionary of general
psychology, G555

The dictionary of human
geography, C618

A dictionary of international law
and diplomacy, I1012

Dictionary of international
relations and politics,
systematic and alphabetical,
I1013

A dictionary of Islam, F917

Dictionary of labour biography,
I880A

Dictionary of language and
linguistics, F923

A dictionary of Marxist thought,
I1021

Dictionary of Mexican American
history, B1704

The dictionary of modern
economics, D683

A dictionary of modern
revolution, I1022

Dictionary of modern sociology,
E549

A dictionary of modern war,
I1007

Dictionary of national biography,
from the earliest times to
1900, B1660

Dictionary of occupational titles,
D699

Dictionary of personnel
management and labor
relations, D684

Dictionary of philosophy and
psychology, G550

Dictionary of political analysis
(Plano), I984

A dictionary of political analysis
(Roberts), I985

Dictionary of political economy,
D682

A dictionary of political phrases
and allusions, with a short
bibliography, I979

Dictionary of political science,
I973

Dictionary of political science and
law, I977

A dictionary of political thought,
I986

A dictionary of politics (Elliott),
I974

A dictionary of politics (Laqueur),
I978

Dictionary of politics and
economic policy, I982

The dictionary of practical law,
I1001

Dictionary of psychology
(Chaplin), G551

Dictionary of psychology (Drever),
G552

Dictionary of psychology
(Warren), G557

Dictionary of psychology and
psychiatry, G563

Dictionary of psychology and
related fields, G565

Dictionary of psychology:
English-German, G564

A dictionary of reading and
related terms, H558

Dictionary of social science, A412

A dictionary of sociology, E551

A dictionary of special education
terms, H554

A dictionary of statistical terms,
A405, D676

A dictionary of terms and
techniques in archaeology,
F909

A dictionary of the social sciences
(Gould), A404

A dictionary of the social sciences
(Reading), A410

Dictionary of world history,
B1700

A dictionary of world mythology,
F914

Dictionnaire de la géographie,
C621

Dictionnaire de la politique
française, I1005

Dictionnaire de la terminologie du
droit international, I1014

Dictionnaire de linguistique, F924

Dictionnaire des parlementaires
français (Jolly), I875

Dictionnaire des parlementaires
français (Robert), I876

Dictionnaire diplomatique, I1026

Dictionnaire politique et de
politique éconimique, I982

di Delupis, Ingrid Doimi. *See*
Doimi di Delupis, Ingrid

Diderot, B249

DIDEROT, DENIS, B249

Dienes, Leslie
The Soviet energy system, C421
"The differentiation of life-styles,"
E92

DIFFUSION (GEOGRAPHY),
C114-C118A, C471. *See also*
SPATIAL SYSTEMS (GEOGRAPHY)

"Diffusion research in geography,"
C471

Digest of education statistics,
H612

Digest of educational statistics,
H629

Digest of international law
(Hackworth), I732

Digest of international law
(Moore), I731

Digest of international law
(Whiteman), I730

Digest of public general bills and
resolutions, I729

Diggins, John P.
The American left in the
twentieth century, B1335

Dilke, Margaret S.
"Perception of the Roman
world," C471

Dilke, O. A. W.
"Perception of the Roman
world," C471

Dilthey, Wilhelm
Selected writings, A68

Dimitrov, Thèodore D.
Documents of international
organisations, I829
World bibliography of
international
documentation, I828

Dimock, G. O.
Public administration, I665

Dimock, Marshall E.
Public administration, I665

Diner, Hasia R.
Women and urban society,
E173

Dinerstein, Herbert S.
The making of a missile crisis,
October 1962, B1407

Diogenes, A501

Dion, Louise
Introduction aux ouvrages de
référence en géographie,
C463

Di Palma, Guiseppe
Mass politics in industrial
societies, I363

The diploma disease, E101

Diplomacy during the Civil War,
B928

Diplomacy for victory, B1231

The diplomacy of annexation,
B871

The diplomacy of the American
Revolution, B674

Diplomatic history, B1755

A diplomatic history of the
American people, B496

Diplomatic list [of the U.S.
Department of State], I923

Diplomatic prelude, B447

The diplomatic service list, I912

Diplomaticheskii slovar', I1027

Directions in economic
development, D136

Directions in geography, C52

Directions in sociolinguistics,
F222

DIRECTORIES, A297-A302. *See also*
subdivision DIRECTORIES under
specific subjects and
geographic names

The Directory, B291

Dorn, Walter L.
  Competition for empire,
    1740-1763, B235
Dornbusch, Rudiger
  Macroeconomics, D88
  Open economy
    macroeconomics, D467
Dorsch, Friedrich
  Psychologisches Wörterbuch 9,
    vollständig neubearb, G561
Dossick, Jesse John
  Doctoral research on Russia and
    the Soviet Union,
    1960-1975, F574
Dotson, Lillian O.
  Bibliography of the peoples and
    cultures of mainland
    Southeast Asia, B1558
Doughty, Harold R.
  Guide to American graduate
    schools, H515
Doughty, Robin W.
  "Environmental theology,"
    C472
Douglas, David C.
  English historical documents,
    B1725
  The Norman achievement,
    1050-1100, B115
  The Norman fate, B116
Douglas, Mary
  Implicit meanings, F352
  Natural symbols, F351
  Purity and danger, F350
Douglas, Paul H.
  The theory of wages, D265
DOUGLAS, STEPHEN A., B894-B895
Douglass, William A.
  Basque Americans, E156
Dovring, Folke
  Land and labor in Europe in
    the 20th century, D238
Dow Jones-Irwin business and
    investment almanac, D700
Dow Jones NEWS/RETRIEVAL,
    D874
Downey, Glanville
  Constantinople in the age of
    Justinian, B87
Downey, James A.
  U.S. federal official
    publications, I706
The downfall of the Liberal Party,
    1914-1935, B422
Downie, N. M.
  Basic statistical methods, G97
Downing, Paul B.
  Air pollution and the social
    sciences, A283
Downs, Anthony
  An economic theory of
    democracy, D419, I129
Downs, Robert Bingham
  American library resources,
    A365
  Bibliography, A144
Downs, Roger M.
  "Geographic space perception,"
    C471
  "Geography of the mind," C127
  Maps in minds, C133
Doyle, Kenneth O.
  Educational psychology journals,
    G526

Dramas, fields and metaphors,
    F358
Drawers of water, C384
Dream and thought in the
    business community,
    1860-1900, B980
The Dred Scott case, B882
Drever, James
  Dictionary of psychology, G552
Drewry, Gavin
  Information sources in politics
    and political science, I681A
Driessen, E. J.
  Biographical dictionary of
    dissidents in the Soviet
    Union, B1664
Driver, Edwin D.
  The sociology and anthropology
    of mental illness, E454
Driver, Harold E.
  Indian tribes of North America,
    F1046
Dror, Yehezkel
  Approaches to policy sciences,
    I672
  Design for policy sciences, A102
Drucker, Peter F.
  An introductory view of
    management, D310
  Technology, management &
    society, D309
DRUG ABUSE, E439-E453, E599.
    See also ALCOHOL ABUSE
Drug abuse bibliography for 1978
    and 1979, E440
Drug use and abuse among U.S.
    minorities, E443
Drugs of addiction and
    nonaddiction, their use and
    abuse, E439
Drury, Peter
  "Some spatial aspects of health
    service developments,"
    C472
DSM-III training guide for use
    with the American Psychiatric
    Association's diagnostic and
    statistical manual of mental
    disorders, G594
Dubin, Robert
  Human relations in
    administration, D311
Dubofsky, Melvyn
  Industrialism and the American
    worker, 1865-1920, B978
Dubois, A.
  Collection des économistes et
    des réformateurs sociaux de
    la France, D40
Dubois, Jean
  Dictionnaire de linguistique,
    F924
DuBois, W. E. B.
  Black Reconstruction in
    America, 1860-1880, B936
  The suppression of the African
    slave-trade to the United
    States of America,
    1638-1870, B807
DUBOIS, W. E. B., B971-B972
Duby, George
  The early growth of the
    European economy, B94

Ducharry, Monique
  Géographie du transport aérien,
    C243
Ducrot, Oswald
  Encyclopedic dictionary of the
    sciences of language, F921
Dudon, Paul
  St. Ignatius of Loyola, B182
Duesenberry, James
  Income, savings, and the theory
    of consumer behavior,
    D188
Duffield, B. S.
  Recreation in the countryside,
    C251
Duggan-Cronin, Alfred M.
  The Bantu tribes of South
    Africa, F1029
Duignan, Peter
  Guide to research and reference
    works on Sub-Saharan
    Africa, F615
  The United States and the
    African slave trade,
    1619-1862, B809
Duijker, Hubert C. J.
  Trilingual lexicon of psychology,
    G562
du Jonchay, Ivan
  Atlas international Larousse,
    politique et économique,
    C671
Duke's Washington pocket
    directory, I955
Dulles, Foster R.
  America's rise to world power,
    1898-1954, B1040
  Labor in America, B520
DULLES, JOHN FOSTER,
    B1399-B1401
Dulles over Suez, B1399
Dumont, Louis
  From Mandeville to Marx, F274
Dumont, Maurice E.
  Aardrijkskundige bibliografie
    van België, C580
Dun & Bradstreet, Inc.
  Industry norms and key
    business ratios, D755
  Middle market directory, D643
  Million dollar directory, D644
  Principal international
    businesses, D645
  Reference book of corporate
    managements, D623
Duncan, James S.
  "The transfer of ideas into
    Anglo-American human
    geography," C472
Duncan, Otis Dudley
  The American occupational
    structure, E70
Dundes, Alan
  Folklore theses and dissertations
    in the United States, F592
  Varia folklorica, F938
Dunlop, John T.
  Industrial relations systems,
    D281
  Labor and the American
    community, D280
  Labor in the twentieth century,
    D282

Federal Bureau of Investigation. *See* United States. Federal Bureau of Investigation
The federal investment in knowledge of social problems, A6
Federal register, I1126
Federal regulatory directory, I1068
Federal Reserve bulletin, D759, D845
Federal tax citator, D803
Federal tax course (Commerce Clearing House), D801
Federal tax course (Prentice-Hall), D803
Federal tax handbook, D803
Federal tax policy, D412
Federal tax service, cumulative, D803
FEDERALISM (U.S.), I290-I298
The Federalist era, 1789-1801, B691
The Federalists, B693
Feeley, Malcolm M.
The process is punishment, I261
Fehrenbacher, Don E.
The Dred Scott case, B882
Feigl, Herbert
Readings in the philosophy of science, I14
Feinberg, Walter
Reason and rhetoric, H91
Feingold, Marie
Scholarships, fellowships and loans, H529
Feingold, S. Norman
Scholarships, fellowships and loans, H529
Feis, Herbert
The atomic bomb and the end of World War II, B1375
Between war and peace, B1235
The China tangle, B1253
Churchill-Roosevelt-Stalin, B1245
Contest over Japan, B1389
From trust to terror, B1368
The road to Pearl Harbor, B108
Feldhusen, John F.
Educational and school psychology, G391
Feldman, Arnold S.
Labor commitment and social change in developing areas, D299
Feldman, Kenneth
The impact of college on students, H248
Feldman, Saul
Mental health administration, G483
Feldstein, Martin
Hospital costs and health insurance, D385A
Feldstein, Paul J.
Health care economics, D386
Fellmann, Jerome D.
International list of geographical serials, C693
Fellner, William
Trends and cycles in economic activity, D112
Fellows of the Social Science Research Council, 1925-1951, A344

FELLOWSHIPS, H527-H532. *See also* GRANTS AND AWARDS
Felony justice, I260
Fels, Rendigs
Recent advances in economics, D520
Female of the species, F317
The feminine mystique, B1342
Fennell, John L.
The emergence of Moscow, 1304-1359, B228
Ivan the Great of Moscow, B229
Fenno, Richard F.
The power of the purse, I218
The president's cabinet, I243
Fenton, John H.
Midwest politics, I302
Ferguson, George A.
Statistical analysis in psychology and education, G80, G98
Ferguson, Jack
Specialized social science information services in the United States, A145
Ferguson, John A.
Bibliography of Australia, B1548
Ferguson, Wallace K.
Europe in transition, 1300-1520, B138
The Renaissance in historical thought, B156
The ferment of reform, 1830-1860, B826
Fernald, Lloyd Dodge
Basic psychology, G5
Fernald, Peter S.
Basic psychology, G5
Fernandini, Carlos Cueto. *See* Cueto Fernandini, Carlos
Ferracuti, Franco
The subculture of violence, E491
Ferrell, Robert H.
American diplomacy, B501
American diplomacy in the Great Depression, B1181
Harry S. Truman and the modern American presidency, B1290
Peace in their time, B1180
Festinger, Leon
A theory of cognitive dissonance, G285
FESTSCHRIFTEN. *See* subdivision FESTSCHRIFTEN under subjects
Fetridge, Clark
Office administration handbook, D721
Fetzer, Mary K.
United Nations documents and publications, I698
The feudal monarchy in France and England, B117
Feudal society, B103
Feudalism, B104
FEUDALISM, B103-B104, B112-B120
Feuer, Lewis S.
The conflict of generations, H249
Fichtenau, Heinrich
The Carolingian Empire, B100

Field, Henry
Bibliography, F1024
Bibliography on Southwestern Asia, F528, F530
Bibliography on the Makran regions of Iran and West Pakistan, F531
FIELD METHODS. *See* headings beginning METHODOLOGY
Field methods in archaeology, F189
Field study in American geography, C17
Field, Tiffany
Emotion and early interaction, G165
Field training in geography, C15
Fieldhouse, David K.
Economics and empire, 1830-1914, B316
Fieldiana: Anthropology, F1071
Fielding, Gordon J.
Geography as social science, C136
The fifteen weeks (February 21-June 5, 1947), B1381
The fifteenth century, B149
Fifth international directory of anthropologists, F887
Le figaro, A521
Figuring anthropology, F252
FIJI, F772
Filby, P. William
American and British genealogy and heraldry, B1631
Filipczak, Carol
B. F. Skinner and behaviorism, G392
Filler, Louis
The crusade against slavery, 1830-1860, B828
Crusaders for American liberalism, B1062
FILMS. *See* AUDIOVISUAL MATERIALS
Films for anthropological teaching, F1027
Filskov, Susan B.
Handbook of clinical neuropsychology, G600
The final days, B1352
Finan, John J.
Latin America, I821
FINANCE, D346, D348-D357, D359-D361. *See also* PERSONAL FINANCE
BIOGRAPHICAL DIRECTORIES, D630
CURRENT SOURCES, D817, D826, D845-D848
DICTIONARIES, D666-D667
DIRECTORIES, D653-D654, D662
ENCYCLOPEDIAS, D671, D681
HANDBOOKS, D706, D709A
ONLINE DATABASES, D874
PERIODICALS, D807
RESEARCH, D521
STATISTICS, D759, D762, D778
FINANCE, PUBLIC. *See* PUBLIC FINANCE
Financial aids for higher education catalog, H530
Financial analysts journals, D846
Financial handbook, D706
Financial management, D807

659

A guide to theses and dissertations, F573, H418

A guide to trade and securities statistics, D747

Guide to United Nations organization, documentation and publishing, for students, researchers, librarians, I700

Guide to U.S. elections, I1170

Guide to U.S. government directories, A3B

Guide to U.S. government publications, A314

A guide to western manuscripts and documents in the British Isles relating to South and Southeast Asia, B1451

Guidebook to labor relations, D709, D801

Guides to manuscript materials for the history of the United States, B1447

Guilford, Joy P.
The nature of human intelligence, G255

Guintero, Rosa
Latin American serial documents, F820

Gulick, John
An annotated bibliography of sources concerned with women in the modern Middle East, F662
"The anthropology of the Middle East," F671
The Middle East, F667

Gulick, Luther H.
The metropolitan problem and American ideas, I318

Gumina, Silvatore La. *See* La Gumina, Silvatore

Gumperz, John J.
Directions in sociolinguistics, F222
Discourse strategies, F234

Gunar, Daniel
Contact des langues et bilinguisme en Europe orientale, F871

Gunnell, John G.
Political theory, I577

The guns of August, B394

Guns, sails and empires, B185

Günther, Karl-Heinz
Geschichte der Erziehung, H62

Gurley, John G.
Money in a theory of finance, D351

Gurman, Alan S.
Handbook of family therapy, G606

Gurr, Ted Robert
Polimetrics, I614
Why men rebel, I111

Gurtov, Melvin
The first Vietnam crisis, B1419

Gurvitch, George
Traité de sociologie, E572

Gustafson, W. Eric
Pakistan and Bangladesh, F727

Gustavus Adolphus and the rise of Sweden, B226

Guth, Delloyd J.
Late medieval England, 1377-1485, B1575

Guthrie, Edwin R.
The psychology of learning, G115

Guthrie, James W.
School finance, H349

Gutkind, P. C. W.
Anthropologists in the field, F246

Gutman, Herbert G.
The black family in slavery and freedom, 1750-1925, B822

Guttentag, M.
Handbook of evaluation research, E130

Guyot, Mireille
Bibliographie américaniste, F793

Guzman, Frank
Mexican-American study project revised bibliography, with a bibliographical essay, E366

Gwynn, J. Minor
Curriculum principles and social trends, H209

GYPSIES, F865-F865A
A gypsy bibliography, F865A

Haas, Ernst
Beyond the nation-state, I535
The obsolescence of regional integration theory, I537
The unification of Europe, I536

Haas, John D.
Foundations of education, H31

Haas, Marilyn L.
"Anthropology," F420
"Basic guide to reference sources for the study of the North American Indian," F822
Indians of North America, F825A

Haas, Michael
Approaches to the study of political science, I153
International organization, I827

Haas, Roland
Dictionary of psychology and psychiatry, G563

Haavelmo, Trygve
A study in the theory of investment, D156

Habakkuk, H.J.
American and British technology in the 19th century, D208A

Haber, Barbara
Women in America, E383

Haber, Samuel
Efficiency and uplift, B1048

Haberler, Gottfried von
Prosperity and depression, D114
The theory of international trade, with its applications to commercial policy, D456

Habermas, Jürgen
Toward a rational society, A79
Knowledge and human interests, A78, I556

Habitat, economy and society, F109

Hacker, Andrew
The study of politics, I30

Hackworth, Green H.
Digest of international law, I732

Haddow, Anna
Political science in American colleges and universities, 1636-1900, I46

Hadley, Charles D.
Transformations of the American party system, I335

Hadrill, John M. Wallace. *See* Wallace-Hadrill, John M.

Haensch, Günther
Wörterbuch der internationalen Beziehungen und der Politik, systematisch und alphabetisch, I1013

Hafen, LeRoy R.
Western America, B505

Hafkin, Nancy J.
Women in Africa, F315

Hafner, James A.
Perspectives on poverty, C512

Hagan, Kenneth J.
American foreign policy, B498

Hage, J.
Organizational systems, E114
Social change in complex organizations, E115

Hagen, Elizabeth P.
Measurement and evaluation in psychology and education, H195

Hagen, Everett
On the theory of social change, D131

Hägerstrand, Torsten
Innovation diffusion as a spatial process, C114

Haggett, Peter
Geography, C2
Locational analysis in human geography, C106
Models in geography, C43
Network analysis in geography, C44
"The spatial economy," C105

Hahn, Frank H.
General competitive analysis, D150

Haight, Timothy R.
The mass media, E651

Haile, Harry G.
Luther, B170

Haimendorf, Elizabeth von Fürer. *See* Fürer-Haimendorf, Elizabeth von

Haimes, Norma
Helping others, E548

Haines, Charles G.
The role of the Supreme Court in American government and politics, 1789-1835, B742

Haining, R. P.
"Analysing univariate maps," C472

Hajnal, Peter I.
Guide to United Nations organization, documentation and publishing, for students, researchers, librarians, I700

Halász, D.
Metropolis, I784

Hansen, Alvin H.
  Business-cycle theory, its
    development and present
    status, D115
  Economic policy and full
    employment, D93
Hansen, Chadwick
  Witchcraft at Salem, B587
Hansen, Donald A.
  Mass communication, E407
  On education–sociological
    perspectives, E103
Hansen, Marcus L.
  The immigrant in American
    history, B988
Hanson, Agnes O.
  Executive and management
    development for business
    and government, D809
Hanson, Norwood Russell
  Patterns of discovery, A42
Hanson, Perry O., III
  The spatial analysis of crime,
    C515
Hanus, Jerome
  The nationalization of state
    government, I295
The Hapsburg Empire, 1790-1918,
  B321
The Hapsburg monarchy,
  1867-1914, B369
Haraven, Tamara K.
  Aging and life course
    transitions, E84
Harbaugh, William H.
  The life and times of Theodore
    Roosevelt, B1068
Harberger, Arnold C.
  Taxation and welfare, D407
Harbison, Winfred A.
  The American Constitution,
    B516
Harcourt, G. C.
  Some Cambridge controversies
    in the theory of capital,
    D83
Hard times, B1147
Harden, Donald B.
  The Phoenicians, B42
Hardesty, Donald L.
  Ecological anthropology, F260
Hardgrave, Robert L., Jr.
  Comparative politics, I398
The Harding era, B1139
HARDING, WARREN G.,
  B1137-B1139, B1179
Hare, A. Paul
  "Bibliography of small group
    research (from 1900
    through 1953)," E293
  Handbook of small group
    research, E583
Hare, F. Kenneth
  Man and environment, C388
Harfax directory of industry data
  sources, D563
Hargrett, Lester
  A bibliography of the
    constitutions and laws of
    the American Indians,
    F1013
Hargrove, Erwin C.
  The power of the modern
    presidency, I245

Harik, Iliya
  Rural politics and social change
    in the Middle East, F665
Haring, Clarence H.
  The Spanish Empire in
    America, B539
Harlan, Louis R.
  Booker T. Washington, B969
Harlem, B1121
Harlem renaissance, B1122
Harman, David
  Adult illiteracy in the United
    States, H306
Harmon, Robert B.
  The art and practice of
    diplomacy, I689
  Developing the library collection
    in political science, I680
  Political science, I678
Harper, Alan
  The politics of loyalty, B1299
Harper encyclopedia of the
  modern world, B1706
Harper, Robert A.
  Modern metropolitan systems,
    C297
Harper's dictionary of Hinduism,
  F916
Harries, Keith D.
  Crime, C145
  The geography of laws and
    justice, C147
Harriman, Philip L.
  Handbook of psychological
    terms, G554
Harrington, Michael
  The other America, B1325
Harris, Ben M.
  In-service education, H282
Harris, Chauncy D.
  Annotated world list of selected
    current geographical serials,
    C694
  Bibliography of geography,
    C455
  Cities of the Soviet Union,
    C317
  Guide to geographical
    bibliographies and reference
    works in Russian or on the
    Soviet Union, C585
  International list of geographical
    serials, C693
  United States of America,
    bibliography of geography,
    C570A
  "Urban geography in Japan,"
    C551
Harris, Marvin
  Cannibals and kings, F415
  Cows, pigs, wars and witches,
    F414
  The rise of anthropological
    theory, B29
Harris, Richard
  "Residential segregation and
    class formation in the
    capitalist city," C472
Harris, Richard Colebrook
  Canada before Confederation,
    C87
  The seigneurial system in early
    Canada, C88

Harris, Robin S.
  A history of higher education in
    Canada, 1663-1960, H251
The Harris survey yearbook of
  public opinion, E217
Harris, Theodore L.
  A dictionary of reading and
    related terms, H558
Harrison Church, Ronald J.
  Africa and the islands, C428
Harrison, Cynthia Ellen
  Women's movement media,
    E591
Harrison, Daniel P.
  Social forecasting methodology,
    E67
Harrison, Geoffrey A.
  Human biology, F136
  Population structure and human
    variation, F145
  The structure of human
    populations, F146
Harrison, Ira E.
  Traditional medicine, F537
Harrison, James D.
  The perception and cognition of
    environment, C516
Harrison, Raymond H.
  Supervisory leadership in
    education, H353
Harriss, Barbara
  "Development studies," C472
Harriss, John
  "Development studies," C472
Harrod, Roy F.
  International economics, D457
  Towards a dynamic economics,
    D132
Harry S. Truman and the modern
  American presidency, B1290
Harsanyi, John C.
  Rational behavior and
    bargaining equilibrium in
    games and social situations,
    I133
The harsh lands, C212
Harsin, Paul
  Oeuvres completes [of John
    Law], D28
Hart, Albert B.
  Cyclopedia of American
    government, I1028
Hart, Albert G.
  Anticipations, uncertainty, and
    dynamic planning, D167
Hart, Basil Liddell. *See* Liddell
  Hart, Basil
Hart, H. L. A.
  The concept of law, I558
Hart, James
  Essays in political science in
    honor of Westel Woodbury
    Willoughby, I50
Hart, John F.
  The look of the land, C167
Hartman, Mary S.
  Clio's consciousness raised,
    B350
Hartmann, Heinz
  Ego psychology and the problem
    of adaptation, G60
Hartmann, R. R. K.
  Dictionary of language and
    linguistics, F923

663

Human Relations Area Files,
F1072
Survey of world cultures, A503
Human relations in
administration, D311
HUMAN RESOURCE DEVELOPMENT.
See PERSONNEL MANAGEMENT
Human resources abstracts, A161,
D531, E205
Human resources network, E596
Human Resources Research Office
(George Washington
University), A504
Human Resources Research
Organization, G657
HUMAN RIGHTS, I1098-I1099,
1963-1965. *See also* CIVIL
RIGHTS
Human rights and state
sovereignty, I466
Human rights directory: Latin
America, Africa, Asia, 1964;
Western Europe, 1965
The human senses, G140
Human settlement in the
perspective of geography,
C540
The human side of enterprise,
D316
Human societies, E60
Human spatial behavior, C121
Human understanding, A50
HUMANISM (PSYCHOLOGY),
G68-G69, G389
HUMANISM (RENAISSANCE),
B156-B161
Humanistic geography, C124
Humanistic psychology, G389
Humanities index, A235
Humanizing the school, H202
Humankind emerging, F135
Humby, Michael
A guide to the literature of
education, H390
Hume, David
Writings on economics, D18
Humlum, Johannes
Kulturgeografisk atlas, C675
Hummel, Arthur W.
Eminent Chinese of the Ching
period, B1648
Humphrey, George
Thinking, G170
The Hundred Years War, B143
HUNGARY, C584, I934
Hunger and work in a savage
tribe, F131
Hunn, Eugene S.
Tzeltzal folk zoology, F339
Hunt, Elgin F.
Social science, A27
Hunt, Joseph McVicker
Intelligence and experience,
G256
Hunt, Maurice P.
Foundations of education: social
and cultural perspectives,
H18
Hunt, Robert N. C.
A guide to communist jargon,
I1024
Hunter, Carmen St. John
Adult illiteracy in the United
States, H306

Hunter, David E.
Encyclopedia of anthropology,
F927
Hunter, Floyd
Community power structure,
I96
Hunter, John Melton
The geography of health and
disease, C375
Hunters, farmers, and
civilizations, old world
archaeology, F192
The hunters or the hunted? F162
Huntington, Samuel
Political order in changing
societies, I436
Hurlock, Elizabeth B.
Developmental psychology,
G213
Hurst, Michael E. Eliot. *See* Eliot
Hurst, Michael E.
Hurwicz, Leonid
Studies in resource allocation
processes, D151
Husén, Torsten
International study of
achievement in
mathematics, H147
Husserl, Edmund
The crisis of European sciences
and transcendental
phenomenology, A69
Ideas, G67
Hutcheson, John D.
Citizen groups in local politics,
I787
HUTCHINSON, ANNE, B583
Hutchinson, Harry D.
Money, banking, and the U. S.
economy, D354
HUTCHINSON, THOMAS, B672
Hutchinson, William Kenneth
American economic history,
D509
Hutchison, T. W.
Knowledge and ignorance in
economics, D48
Hutson, Percival W.
The guidance function in
education, H188
Huxley, Aldous
Grey eminence, B213
Hyams, Edward
A dictionary of modern
revolution, I1022
Hyde, John K.
Padua in the age of Dante,
B152
Hydro-abstracts, A162
Hyman, Harold M.
Stanton, B909
Hyman, Herbert H.
Education's lasting influence on
values, H121
Secondary analysis of sample
surveys, E37
Hymes, Dell
Directions in sociolinguistics,
F222
Language in culture and society,
F224
Hyneman, Charles S.
The study of politics, I47

Hynes, Mary C.
List of theses and dissertations
on Canadian geography,
C633
The hyperkinetic child: a
bibliography of medical,
educational and behavioral
studies, G496
The hyperkinetic child: an
annotated bibliography,
1974-1979, G497

Ianni, Francis A. J.
The anthropological study of
education, H111
IASSW directory, E543
Ibero-Americana, A503
Ibero-Amerikanisches Institut
(Berlin)
Schlagwortkatalog des
Ibero-Amerikanischen
Instituts Preussischer
Kulturbisitz in Berlin, F810
Icolari, Dan
Reference encyclopedia of the
American Indian, F899
The icon and the ax, B377
The idea of a party system, B710,
I333
The idea of a social science and
its relation to philosophy,
I587
The idea of a Southern nation,
B847
The idea of a world university,
H177
The idea of history, B8
The idea of nationalism, I84
The idea of pre-history, B32
The idea of progress, I26
The idea of social structure, F305
Ideals on self-interest in America's
foreign relations, I479
Ideas, G67
The ideas of the woman suffrage
movement, 1820-1920, B1055
Identities and interactions, A60
The ideological origins of the
American Revolution, B642
Ideology and everyday life, F518
Ideology and utopia, I580
Ideology, science, and human
geography, C51
IGNATIUS OF LOYOLA, SAINT, B182
IIS. *See* Index to international
statistics
Iiyama, Patti
Drug use and abuse among U.S.
minorities, E443
Ikenberry, Oliver S.
American education
foundations, H19
Ilbery, Brian W.
"Agricultural decision-making,"
C472
Ilchman, Warren F.
The political economy of
change, I639
Ilgen, Daniel R.
Industrial psychology, G372
Ilina, T. A.
Pedagogika, H20
Illich, Ivan
Deschooling society, H378

Mabbutt, J. A.
Desertification world bibliography update, 1976-1980, C568A
Mabogunje, Akin L.
Regional mobility and resource development in West Africa, C354
Urbanization in Nigeria, C321
MacArthur, Douglas
Reminiscences, B1397
MACARTHUR, DOUGLAS, B1396-B1397
Macartney, Carlile A.
The Hapsburg Empire, 1790-1918, B321
Independent Eastern Europe, B429
McBride, Theresa M.
The domestic revolution, B276
McCall, George
Indentities and interactions, A60
McCardell, John
The idea of a Southern nation, B847
McCarrick, Earlean M.
U.S. Constitution, I767
McCarthy, Eugene J.
Dictionary of American politics, I988
MacCarthy, Frederick
Australia's aborigines, F1031
McCarthy, Joseph M.
International list of articles on the history of education published in non-educational serials, 1965-1974, H458
MCCARTHY, JOSEPH R., B1297-B1307
McClelland, Charles A.
Theory and the international system, I500
McClelland, David C.
The achieving society, D331, I649
Human motivation, G167
Personality, G237
McClintock, Charles G.
Experimental social psychology, G273
McCloskey, Robert G.
American conservatism in the age of enterprise, 1865-1910, B984
The American Supreme Court, I265
McClure, Robert D.
The unseeing eye, I347
Maccoby, Eleanor E.
The psychology of sex differences, G261
MacCombe, Leonard
Navaho means people, F1034
McConahay, John
The politics of violence, I115
McConaughy, Paul D.
Encyclopedia of United States government benefits, E595
McConnell, Grant
Private power and American democracy, I210

MacCormack, Carol P.
Ethnography of fertility and birth, F264
McCormick, Ernest J.
Human factors in engineering and design, G371
Industrial psychology, G372
McCormick, Richard P.
The second American party system, B799
McCourt, Kathleen
Catholic schools in a declining church, H117
McCown, Elizabeth R.
The great apes, F168
Human origins, F155
McCoy, Charles
Apolitical politics, I75
McCoy, Donald R.
Calvin Coolidge, B1141
McCoy, Ralph E.
Doctoral dissertations in labor and industrial relations, D613
Freedom of the press: a bibliocyclopedia ten-year supplement, E412
Freedom of the press: an annotated bibliography, E411
McCrea, Barbara P.
The Soviet and East European political dictionary, I1019
McCready, William C.
Catholic schools in a declining church, H117
McCullagh, Patrick
Quantitative techniques in geography, C35
McCulloch, John R.
Early English tracts on commerce, D43
The literature of political economy, D607
A select collection of scarce and valuable tracts on money, D42
McCullough, David
The path between the seas, B1090
McDiarmid, Orville J.
Unskilled labor for development, D269
McDonald, David R.
Masters' theses in anthropology, F586
Tulapai to Tokay, E453
McDonald, Forrest
Alexander Hamilton, B713
The presidency of George Washington, B695
We the people, B688
McDonald, Neil A.
The study of political parties, I423
McDougall, William
An introduction to social psychology, G268
McFadden, Daniel
Production economics, D155
McFeely, William S.
Grant, B912
Yankee stepfather, B945
Macfie, Samuel
Central America, C576

Manufacturing and mining activities in Latin America, C574
McGaugh, Maurice E.
Geographies, atlases, and special references on the states and provinces of Anglo-America, C646
McGee, Terence G.
"The persistence of the protoproletariat," C471
The urbanization process in the Third World, C318
"Western geography and the Third World," C397
McGlashan, Neil D.
Geographical aspects of health, C375C
McGrath, Joseph E.
Small group research, E294
McGraw-Hill dictionary of modern economics, D679
McGraw Hill real estate handbook, D718A
McGregor, Douglas
The human side of enterprise, D316
McGuigan, F. J.
Experimental psychology, G112
McHale, Vincent E.
Political parties of Europe, I1081
Machlup, Fritz
International payments, D474
The methodology of economics and other social sciences, D52
McIlvaine, B.
Aging, E261
McIlwain, Charles H.
Constitutionalism, I86
The growth of political thought in the West, I542
Macinko, George
Beyond the urban fringe, C328
McInnis, Raymond G.
Research guide for psychology, G383
Social science research handbook, A128
McIntosh, Donald
The foundations of human society, A30
McIntyre, D.
Teachers and teaching, H290
MacIver, Robert M.
The modern state, I87
The web of government, I657
McKaughan, Howard
Anthropological studies in the eastern highlands of New Guinea, F991
The languages of the eastern family of the east New Guinea highland stock, F992
McKean, Roland N.
The economics of defense in the nuclear age, D424
McKechnie, J. Thomas
Political elites, I862
McKelvey, Blake
The emergence of metropolitan America, 1915-1966, B314

MANUFACTURERS
DIRECTORIES, D637, D649, D652, D658-D659
STATISTICS, D741, D754
Manufacturing: a study of industrial location, C221
Manufacturing and mining activities in Latin America, C574
MANUFACTURING GEOGRAPHY, C216-C230, C471-C472, C523-C526
Manuscript sources in the Library of Congress for research on the American Revolution, B1471
MANUSCRIPTS AND ARCHIVES, B1444-B1454, B1456-B1457, B1461-B1462, B1471-B1478, B1626, B1635
Manzer, Ronald
Teachers and politics in England and Wales, H287
Map collections in the United States and Canada, C655
"Map design and evaluations," C472
Map of educational research, H341
Map of North American Indian languages, F1049
Map use, C32
Mapping the land, C26
MAPS, C634-C651, C652-C655. *See also* ATLASES; GAZETTEERS; and subdivisions ATLASES and GAZETTEERS under geographical headings
Maps and diagrams, C28
"Maps and mapping," C472
Maps, distortion, and meaning, C31
Maps in minds, C133
"Maps in the mind's eye," C472
Marathon, B1358
Marble, Duane F.
Spatial analysis, C38
March, James G.
A behavioral theory of the firm, D308
Handbook of organizations, E117
Organizations, D315
Political report of the behavioral and social science survey committee, I62
Marcus, Mitchell P.
A theory of syntactic recognition for natural language, F237
Marcus, Robert D.
Grand Old Party, B955
Marcus, Steven
Engels, Manchester and the working class, B274
Marcuse, Herbert
One dimensional man, A81
Reason and revolution, I560
Margolis, Julius
Public expenditure and policy analysis, D408, I634
Margules, David L.
Physiological psychology, G398
Psychopharmacology, G397

Marien, Michael
Future survey annual 1979, E422
Societal directions and alternatives, E421
Marihuana, E446-E447
MARIHUANA, E445-E447. *See also* DRUG ABUSE
"Marine resources and environment," C472
Marini, Frank
Toward a new public administration, I77
Mark, Charles
Sociology of America, E149
Marken, Jack W.
The Indians and Eskimos of North America, E355
The market for labor, D252
Market guide, D758
Market structure and innovation, D337
Market structure, organization, and performance, D366
MARKETING
ABSTRACTS, D528
ATLASES AND MAPS, D797-D798
CURRENT SOURCES, D820
DIRECTORIES, D656-D657
DISSERTATIONS, D611-D612
HANDBOOKS, D711
LITERATURE GUIDES, D516
PERIODICALS, D807
STATISTICS, D742, D753, D758, D766, D769, D772-D774
See also ADVERTISING
Marketing and distribution abstracts, D528
Marketing doctoral dissertation abstracts, 1974/75, D611
MARKETING GEOGRAPHY, C231-C234, C472, C528
Marketing geography with special reference to retailing, C231
Marketing information, D516
MARKETING RESEARCH, D634
Markets and hierarchies, D369
Markham, Felix
Napoleon and the awakening of Europe, B295
Markle, Allan
Author's guide to journals in psychology, psychiatry and social work, G523
Markowitz, Harry
Portfolio selection, D356
Marks, Barbara S.
The New York University list of books in education, H459
Marks, Frederick W.
Velvet on iron, B1080
Marks, James R.
Handbook of educational supervision, H358
Marks, Sally
The illusion of peace, B417
Markus, Robert A.
Christianity in the Roman world, B80
Marouzeau, Jules
Dix années de bibliographie classique...1914-1924, B1505

Marquis, Arnold
A guide to America's Indians, F901
MARRIAGE. *See* FAMILIES
Marriage in tribal societies, F110
Marrou, H. I.
A history of education in antiquity, H68
Marsden, B. S.
Bibliography of Australian geography theses, C633A
Marsden, George M.
Fundamentalism and American culture, B1132
Marshall, Alfred
Principles of economics, D3
MARSHALL, GEORGE C., B1226
Marshall, Joan K.
Serials for librarians, A318
MARSHALL, JOHN, B739, B741-B742
Marshall, Mac
Micronesia, 1944-1974, F775
The martial spirit, B1037
Martin, A.
Bibliographie des travaux publiés de 1866 à 1897 sur l'histoire de la France de 1500 à 1789, B1573
Martin, Fenton S.
The presidency, I687A
Martin, Geoffrey J.
All possible worlds, C54
The Association of American Geographers, C66
Martin, J. E.
"Location theory and spatial analysis," C472
Martin, James K.
A respectable army, B663
Martin, Kingsley
French liberal thought in the eighteenth century, B244
Martin, M. Kay
Female of the species, F317
Martin, Michael R.
Encyclopedia of Latin-American history, B1703
Martin, Phyllis M.
Africa, F602
Martindale, Don
Handbook of contemporary developments in world sociology, E570
Martines, Lauro
Power and imagination: city-states in Renaissance Italy, B155
Martínez Cruz, Abelardo
Léxico de antropología, F907
Martinson, Tom L.
Introduction to library research in geography, C459
Martis, Kenneth C.
The historical atlas of United States congressional districts, 1789-1983, I1183
Marulli, Luciana
Documentation of the United Nations system, I701
Marx-Engels dictionary, I1023
The Marx-Engels reader, E8
Marx, John H.
Knowledge application, E138
Marx, Karl
Capital, B21

METHODOLOGY OF ANTHROPOLOGY,
F180-F189, F191, F199,
F204, F238-F252
HANDBOOKS, F947-F950
LITERATURE GUIDES, F426
The methodology of economics,
D44
METHODOLOGY OF ECONOMICS,
D44-D54
The methodology of economics
and other social sciences, D52
METHODOLOGY OF EDUCATION,
H178-H273, H334-H344. *See
also* CURRICULUM AND
INSTRUCTION
METHODOLOGY OF GEOGRAPHY,
C14-C52, C71A, C472. *See
also* QUANTITATIVE
METHODOLOGY (GEOGRAPHY)
METHODOLOGY OF POLITICAL
SCIENCE, I13-I21, I612-I623,
I651-I652
METHODOLOGY OF PSYCHOLOGY,
G15-G20, G92-G95, G584A,
G592, G610. *See also*
PSYCHOMETRICS; STATISTICS
(PSYCHOLOGY)
METHODOLOGY OF SOCIAL SCIENCES,
A114-A115, A422
METHODOLOGY OF SOCIOLOGY,
E34-E43
ABSTRACTS, E222, E224
CURRENT BIBLIOGRAPHIES, E244
PERIODICALS, E655
RETROSPECTIVE BIBLIOGRAPHIES,
E255
The methods and materials of
demography, E576
Methods and theories of
anthropological genetics, F143
Methods in futures studies, A98
Methods of regional analysis,
D170
Metropolis, I784
Metropolitan communities, I783
METROPOLITAN GOVERNMENT. *See*
LOCAL GOVERNMENT
The metropolitan problem and
American ideas, I318
"Metropolitan regional analysis,"
C471
Metternich and the times, B305
Metzger, Walter P.
The development of academic
freedom in the United
States, H253
Meuli, Karl
Das mutterrecht, F55
Mevis, Renè
Inventory of Caribbean studies,
F815
The Mexican American, E178
The Mexican American: a critical
guide to research aids, E362
The Mexican American: a selected
and annotated bibliography,
E365
Mexican-American study project
revised bibliography, with a
bibliographical essay by Frank
Guzman, E366
MEXICAN-AMERICAN WAR,
B871-B877
The Mexican-American War,
1846-1848, B877

Mexican Americans, E364
MEXICAN AMERICANS , E178
BIOGRAPHY, B1704
EDUCATION, H112
HISTORY, B1704
LITERATURE GUIDES, E178
RETROSPECTIVE BIBLIOGRAPHIES,
E361-E369
Mexican Americans in school,
H112
The Mexican Revolution,
1914-1915, B1092
The Mexican War, B875
MEXICO
ANTHROPOLOGY, F410, F589
GEOGRAPHY, C367, C575
HISTORY, B1091-B1093, B1507,
B1596, B1704
Mexico. Dirección de Geografía y
Meteorología
Bibliografía de México, C575
Mexico views manifest destiny,
1821-1846, B873
Meyer, J. R.
The economics of competition
in the transportation
industries, D175
The urban transportation
problem, D174
Meyer, James T.
"Geography of the mind," C127
Meyer, Karl E.
The Cuban invasion, B1402
Meyer, Klaus
Bibliographie zur
osteuropäischen Geschichte,
B1563
Meyer, Manfred
Effects and functions of
television, E408
Meyer, Merle E.
Foundations of contemporary
psychology, G7
Meyer, Michael C.
Supplement to a bibliography of
United States-Latin
American relations since
1810, I815
Meyere, Gustav
Das Mutterrecht, F55
Meyers, Jon K.
Bibliography of the urban crisis,
E282
Meyers, Marvin
The Jacksonian persuasion,
B793
Meyers, Patricia Gober. *See*
Gober-Meyers, Patricia
Meynen, Emil
Gazetteers and glossaries of the
geographical names of the
member countries of the
United Nations and the
agencies in relationship
with the United Nations,
C622A
Orbis geographicus 1980/1984,
C611, C700
Mezirow, J. D.
The literature of liberal adult
education, H315
Mialaret, Gaston
Traité de pédagogie générale,
H17

Miami, University of. *See*
University of Miami
Michels, Robert
Political parties, I659
Michigan, University of. *See*
University of Michigan
Mickiewicz, Ellen
Handbook of Soviet social
science data, E619
Mickolus, Edward F.
The literature of terrorism,
E485, I811
Transnational terrorism, I1046
Microeconomic analysis, D70
MICRONESIA, F770, F775, F942
Micronesia, 1944-1974, F775
Micropolitics, I1186
Middagh, Mark
Human settlement in the
perspective of geography,
C540
Middle age and aging, G217
MIDDLE AGES, B83, B92-B135
BIBLIOGRAPHIES OF
BIBLIOGRAPHIES, B1501
CHRONOLOGIES, B1720
CURRENT BIBLIOGRAPHIES,
B1513-B1514
DICTIONARIES, B1691-B1692
ENCYCLOPEDIAS, B1672-B1674
LITERATURE GUIDES,
B1439-B1440
LITERATURE REVIEWS, B1490
RETROSPECTIVE BIBLIOGRAPHIES,
B1440, B1522,
B1540-B1542
SOURCE MATERIAL, B1728
Middle America, C403
MIDDLE AMERICA. *See* CENTRAL
AMERICA
Middle-class democracy and the
revolution in Massachusetts,
1691-1780, B640
"Middle East," C472
MIDDLE EAST
ANTHROPOLOGY, F644-F692
ARCHAEOLOGY, F567
DISSERTATIONS, F583
ECONOMICS, D811
EDUCATION, H170
FOREIGN RELATIONS, I813, I818
GAZETTEERS, F689-F690
GEOGRAPHY, C367, C436, C472,
C697
HANDBOOKS, F962-F978
HISTORY, B36-B47,
B1441-B1442, B1453
PERIODICALS, F600
POLITICS AND GOVERNMENT,
I1017
WOMEN, E396
YEARBOOKS, A448, A452-A453
The Middle East: a geographical
study, C436
The Middle East: a physical,
social, and regional
geography, C435
The Middle East: a selected
bibliography of recent works,
1960-1970, F654
The Middle East: abstracts and
index, F653
The Middle East: an
anthropological perspective,
F667

706

The People's Republic of
Mongolia, F998
Peoples of Southern Africa, F931
Peoples of southwest Ethiopia and
its borderland, F623
Peoples of the Horn of Africa,
F623
Peoples of the Lake Nyama
region, F623
Peoples of the Southwest Pacific,
F1030
The peopling of Southern Africa,
F932
PEP. *See* Political and Economic
Planning
Peradotto, John
Classical mythology, F532
Perceiving women, F310
Perception (Hochberg), G145
Perception (periodical), E655
The perception and cognition of
environment, C516
Perception and misperception in
international politics, I492
Perception and psychophysics,
G655
The perception of odors, G148
"Perception of the Roman world,"
C471
The perception of the visual
world, G142
Perceptual and motor skills, G655
PERCEPTUAL GEOGRAPHY,
C127-C133A, C471-C472,
C516-C517
Perceptual organization, G150
PERCEPTUAL PROCESSES. *See*
SENSORY AND PERCEPTUAL
PROCESSES
Pereira, Benjamin Enes
Bibliografía analítica de
etnografía portuguesa, F866
Performance in American
bureaucracy, I280
Pergamon world atlas, C663
PERICLES, B57-B58
Pericles and Athens, B57
The perils of prosperity, 1914-32,
B1094
Period and place, C71A
"Periodic market-places and
periodic marketing," C472
Periodic markets, F524
Periodic markets, daily markets
and fairs, C528
Periodical literature on United
States cities, E279
PERIODICALS
ANTHROPOLOGY, F597-F601A,
F1070
DIRECTORIES, A381-A388
ECONOMICS, D807-D809
EDUCATION, H420-H421,
H423-H424, H429, H630,
H641
GEOGRAPHY, C693-C698
HISTORY, B1062, B1684-B1686,
B1755
POLITICAL SCIENCE, I1867-I1868,
I1186
PSYCHOLOGY, G523-G526,
G655, G658-G667
RETROSPECTIVE BIBLIOGRAPHIES,
A314-A321

SOCIAL SCIENCES, A381-A388,
A501, A505-A520
SOCIOLOGY, E513-E514,
E655-E665
Periodicals for South-East Asian
studies, F774
Perjury, B1298
Perkin, Harold
Key profession, H291
Perkins, Bradford
Castlereagh and Adams, B765
The first rapprochement, B748
The great rapprochement,
B1041
Prologue to war, B758
Perkins, Dexter
A history of the Monroe
Doctrine, B766
The new age of Franklin
Roosevelt, 1932-1945,
B1146
Perlman, Mark
Health, economics, and health
economics, D391A
Perlman, Selig
A theory of the labor
movement, D286
Perloff, Harvey S.
Regions, resources and
economic growth, D182
Perroy, Edouard
The Hundred Years War, B143
Perry, Natalie
Teaching the mentally retarded
child, H330
Perry, P. J.
"Beyond Domesday," C472
Persell, Caroline Hodges
Understanding society, E4
The Persian Empire, B54
PERSIAN EMPIRE, B54, F567
"The persistence of the
protoproletariat," C471
"Personal construct theory, the
repertory grid method and
human geography," C472
PERSONAL FINANCE, D732
Personal income taxation, D415
Personal influence, E126
Personal knowledge, A46
The personal president, I248A
Personality (McClelland), G237
Personality (Pervin), G266
PERSONALITY, G232-G267
LITERATURE GUIDES, G399
LITERATURE REVIEWS, G414,
G440, G449-G454
PERIODICALS, G655
Personality: a guide to the
information sources, G399
Personality: a psychological
interpretation, G232
Personality: an objective
approach, G242
Personality and psychotherapy,
G233
Personality: strategies and issues,
G264
Personality tests and reviews II,
G440
Personality theories, G238
Personality: theory, assessment,
and research, G240
Personnel administration
handbook, D722

Personnel and training abstracts,
D528
Personnel communications, D803
Personnel literature, G4712
PERSONNEL MANAGEMENT
ABSTRACTS, D528, D536
BUSINESS SERVICES, D800; D803
DICTIONARIES, D684
HANDBOOKS, D691, D712, D722,
D733
MONOGRAPH SERIES, D810
RETROSPECTIVE BIBLIOGRAPHIES,
D603
Personnel management abstracts,
D536
Personnel policies and practices,
D803
Perspective on the nature of
geography, C56
Perspectives, I720
Perspectives in Marxist
anthropology, F277
Perspectives on environment,
C377
Perspectives on poverty, C512
Perspectives on social network
research, I648
Perspectives on world education,
H133
Pertz, Georg H.
Monumenta Germaniae
Historica, B1728
Pervin, Lawrence A.
Personality, G266
Personality: theory, assessment
and research, G240
Pescow, James K.
Encyclopedia of accounting
systems, D702
Pessen, Edward M.
Jacksonian America, B798
Petchenik, Barbara Bartz
The nature of maps, C33
PETER I, B230-B231
Peter the Great and the
emergence of Russia, B230
Petermanns geographische
Mitteilungen, C697
Peters, Thomas J.
In search of excellence, D318
Petersen, Svend
A statistical history of American
presidential elections, with
supplementary tables
covering 1968-1980, I1175
Peterson, H. C.
Opponents of war, 1917-1918,
B1102
Peterson, Houston
Great teachers, H292
Peterson, Le Roy J.
The law and public school
operation, H361
Peterson, Merrill D.
The Jeffersonian image in the
American mind, B718
Thomas Jefferson and the new
nation, B719
Peterson, Paul E.
City limits, I321
Race and authority in urban
politics, I316
Peterson, Penelope L.
Research on teaching, H293

Sheehan, Mary R.
  Contemporary schools of
    psychology, G41
Sheehy, Eugene P.
  "Atlases," C648
  "Gazetteers," C622
  Guide to reference books, A121
Sheffrin, Steven M.
  Rational expectations, D125
Sheldon, Eleanor
  Indicators of social change, E80
Sheldon, Kathleen E.
  A guide to social science
    resources in women's
    studies, E385
Sheldon's retail, D655
Shepard, Roger N.
  Mental images and their
    transformations, G181
Shepherd, Gene D.
  Modern elementary curriculum,
    H226
Shepherd, William G.
  Public policies toward business,
    D368A
Shepherd, William R.
  Historical atlas, B1750
Shepherd's historical atlas, B1750
Sheppard, Helen E.
  Acronyms, initialisms &
    abbreviations dictionary,
    A402
Sheppard, Julia
  British archives, B1450
Shera, Jesse H.
  Foundations of the public
    library, H318
Sherif, Carolyn W.
  Orientation in social psychology,
    G275
  Social psychology, G276
Sherif, Muzafer
  Social psychology, G276
Sherman, H.
  Comparing economic systems,
    D236
Sherrington, Charles S.
  The integrative action of the
    nervous system, G189
Sherwin, Martin J.
  A world destroyed, B1256
Sherzer, Joel
  Explorations in the ethnography
    of speaking, F210
Shevin, Jann
  Citizen groups in local politics,
    I787
Shields, James J.
  Problems and prospects in
    international education,
    H163
Shils, Edward
  "Tradition, ecology, and
    institution in the history of
    sociology," E18
Shimoniak, Wasyl
  Communist education, H167
SHIPPING INDUSTRY, C241
Shirer, William L.
  The rise and fall of the Third
    Reich, B465
Shirley, Norma
  Serials in psychology and allied
    fields, G524

Shively, W. Phillips
  The craft of political research,
    I621
Shklar, Judith
  After utopia, I564
Shock, Nathan W.
  A classified bibliography of
    gerontology and geriatrics,
    E266-E268
Shonfield, Andrew
  Modern capitalism, D442
Shore, Arnold
  Why sociology does not apply,
    E142
Shores, Louis
  Bibliographies and summaries
    in education to July 1,
    1935, H417
Short, J. R.
  "Political geography," C472
Short, John R.
  "Residential mobility," C472
A short history of educational
  ideas, H56
A short history of socialism, B270
A short history of sociology, E574
The shorter Cambridge medieval
  history, B1673
Shorter encyclopedia of Islam,
  F918
Shotskii, Vladimir P.
  Eastern Siberia, C209
Shoup, Paul S.
  The East European and Soviet
    data handbook, A482
Shub, David
  Lenin, B412
Shubik, Martin
  A game-theoretic approach to
    political economy, I607A
Shulman, Lee S.
  Learning by discovery, H193
Shy, John
  A people numerous and armed,
    B667
Shyrock, Henry S.
  The methods and materials of
    demography, E576
Sibley, Mulford Q.
  Political ideas and ideologies,
    I35
SICILY, B114. *See also* ITALY
Siddall, William R.
  Transportation geography, C531
Sidowski, Joseph B.
  Experimental methods and
    instrumentation in
    psychology, G107
Sieber, Sam D.
  The school in society, E108
Siebert, W. Stanley
  The market for labor, D252
Sieg heil! B1744
Siegel, Bernard J.
  Annual review of anthropology,
    F435
  Divisiveness and social conflict,
    F369
Siegfried, John J.
  Recent advances in economics,
    D520
Siemers, Günter
  Bibliographie asien- und
    ozeanienbezogener
    Bibliographien, F693

Sieveking, G. de G.
  Problems in economic and
    social archaeology, F197
Sigmann, Jean
  1848, B318
Sigmund Freud's writings, G514
The significance of territory, C188
Sikes, Melanie M.
  Rural-urban migration research
    in the United States, E272
Silberman, Bernard S.
  Japan and Korea, B1557, F748
Silberman, Charles E.
  Crises in the classroom, H386
The silent revolution, I365
The silent social revolution, H66
Sills, David L.
  "Geography," C8
  International encyclopedia of
    the social sciences, A415,
    D8
Silvanandan, Ambala-Vaner
  Coloured immigrants in Britain,
    E381
Sim, Richard
  Guerilla and terrorist
    organisations, I1068B
Simkins, Francis B.
  Pitchfork Ben Tillman, B965
Simmons, Ian Gordon
  The ecology of natural
    resources, C379
  "Natural resources and their
    management," C472
  "Resource management and
    conservation," C472
Simmons, J. L.
  Identities and interactions, A60
Simmons, James W.
  Systems of cities, C275
  "Urban and regional systems...,"
    C472
Simmons, Merle Edwin
  Folklore bibliography for 1973,
    F480; ...for 1974, F481; ...
    for 1975, F482
Simon, David
  "Third world colonial cities in
    context," C472
Simon, Herbert A.
  Administrative behavior, D320,
    I147
  Human problem solving, G176
  Models of man, I608
  Models of thought, G182
  Organizations, D315
Simon, Reeva S.
  The modern Middle East, F646
Simonett, David S.
  Remote sensing of environment,
    C21
Simons, Elwyn L.
  Primate evolution, F160
Simons, Henry C.
  Personal income taxation, D415
Simons, William B.
  Constitutions of the Communist
    world, I1110
Simple justice, B1276, H380
Simpson, Antony E.
  Guide to library research in
    public administration, I691
Simpson, Donald H.
  Biography catalogue, A274

Smith *(Continued)*

Area handbook for Israel, F974
Area handbook for Lebanon, F973
Smith, Henry Nash
Virgin land, B1001
Smith, James M.
Freedom's fetters, B725
Smith, James Ward
Religion in American life, B1603
Smith, Joan Dickson
Population, E518
SMITH, JOHN, B556
Smith, Justin H.
War with Mexico, B874
Smith, Larry
Models and the study of social change, F398
Smith, Margo L.
Anthropological bibliographies, F457
Smith, Mary Lee
The benefits of psychotherapy, G347
Smith, Neil
"Geography, science and post-positivist modes of explanation," C472
Smith, P. J.
The Prairie provinces, C401
Smith, Page
John Adams, B723
Smith, Philip E. L.
Food production and its consequences, F198
Smith, Robert E. F.
A Russian-English dictionary of social science terms, A411
Smith, Robert H. T.
"Periodic market-places and periodic marketing," C472
Smith, Robert S.
Modern labor economics, D256
Smith, Stephen L. J.
Recreation geography, C251A
Smith, Susan J.
Exploring social geography, C153A
Smith, V. Kerry
Scarcity and growth reconsidered, D383
Smith, William P.
Social psychology, G270
Smith, William Robertson
Lectures and essays, F64
Lectures on the religion of the Semites, F63
Smith, Wilson
American higher education, H254
Smithsonian Institution
Miscellaneous collections, F1071
Smithsonian Science Information Exchange
SSIE current research, E666, G668
Smock, Audrey Chapman
Women, F314
Smolensk under Soviet rule, B449
Smythe, Mabel M.
The black American reference book, E587

Snead, Rodman E.
Bibliography on the Makran regions of Iran and West Pakistan, F531
Snell, John L.
Illusion and necessity, B467
The meaning of Yalta, B1233
Snider, Delbert A.
International monetary relations, D477
Snow, Philip A.
A bibliography of Fiji, Tonga and Rotuma, F772
Snowman, Jack
Psychology applied to teaching, G359
Snyder, Glenn H.
Deterrence and defense, I480
Snyder, Louis L.
The blood and iron chancellor, B361
Snyder, Richard C.
Decision making as an approach to the study of international politics, I148
Foreign policy decision making, I149
Sobel, Robert
Biographical directory of the governors of the United States, 1780-1978, I890
Biographical directory of the United States executive branch, 1774-1977, I895
The great bull market, B1134
Soboul, Albert
The French Revolution, 1787-1799, B286
The Parisian sansculottes and the French Revolution, 1793-94, B289
SOCIAL ACTION, E597, E600-E602
Social action & the law, A514
Social and behavioral aspects of female alcoholism, E450
Social and behavioral science programs in the National Science Foundation, A5
The social and economic history of the hellenistic world, B63
Social anthropology, F10
Social anthropology and other essays, F106
Social anthropology and the law, F378
Social archaeology, F194
Social areas in cities, C139
Social aspects of alienation, G507
Social aspects of interaction and transportation, C271
Social behavior, A65
The social burdens of environmental pollution, C288
Social change, F115
SOCIAL CHANGE, E420-E438, E435, F115, F390-F404
SOCIAL CHANGE AND SEX ROLES. *See* SEX ROLES
Social change in complex organizations, E115
Social change in Turkey since 1950, F685
Social choice and individual values, D195, I118

SOCIAL CONFLICT, E21, H241, I506
PERIODICALS, A501
RETROSPECTIVE BIBLIOGRAPHIES, E295-E300, F565
See also CONFLICT THEORY
The social construction of reality, A70, I570
Social Darwinism in American thought, B981
SOCIAL DISORGANIZATION, E485-E500
Social ecology, I455
SOCIAL ECOLOGY. *See* POPULATION (GEOGRAPHY)
Social experimentation, A107
Social forces, A501, E197
Social forces in education, H12
Social forecasting methodology, E67
Social foundations of education (Brembeck), H109
Social foundations of education (Stanley), H126
Social foundations of educational guidance, H196
The social foundations of German unification, 1858-1871, B359
The social function of social science, A29, I76
"Social geography" (Eyles), C134
"Social geography..." (Jackson), C472
"Social geography" (Robson), C472
SOCIAL GEOGRAPHY, C134-C157, C471-C472, C481, C509-C515
The social geography of medicine and health, C375D
A social geography of the city, C267
Social geography of the United States, C140
Social gerontology, E164
The social ideas of American educators, H55
Social indicator models, E79
Social indicators, E612
SOCIAL INDICATORS, E75-E80, E612, E634
Social indicators: an annotated bibliography of current literature, E614
Social indicators and societal monitoring, E613
Social indicators: selected data on social conditions and trends in the United States, A462
Social indicators III, D789
The social interpretation of the French Revolution, B287
Social justice and the city, C156
Social learning and imitation, G287
Social learning and personality development, G284
Social learning theory, G124
Social networks, F247
"Social networks as metaphors, models and methods," C472
Social organization, F95
SOCIAL POLICY, E501-E505
Social policy research and analysis, E144
Social problems, A501, E655

765

Contributors

Alan R. Beals, Department of Anthropology, University of California, Riverside

William W. Brickman, Graduate School of Education, University of Pennsylvania

Stanley Chodorow, Dean of Arts and Humanities, University of California, San Diego

Chauncy D. Harris, Department of Geography, University of Chicago

Bert F. Hoselitz, Department of Economics, University of Chicago

Howard Jones, Department of History, University of Alabama

Roger T. Kaufman, Department of Economics, Smith College, Northampton, Massachusetts

Ann K. Pasanella, Center for the Social Sciences, Columbia University

Steven Seitz, Department of Political Science, University of Illinois, Urbana

Ted P. Sheldon, Universities Libraries, University of Missouri, Kansas City

Phillip A. Smith, Library, University of California, San Diego

Stephen K. Stoan, Social Sciences Librarian, Wichita State University, Wichita, Kansas

Camille Wanat, Physics Library, University of California, Berkeley

Robert I. Watson, late Professor of Psychology, University of New Hampshire

William H. Webb, formerly of the Library, University of California, San Diego

Marilyn L. Wertheimer, University Libraries, University of Colorado, Boulder

Michael Wertheimer, Department of Psychology, University of Colorado, Boulder

Robert Westerman, Library, University of California, San Diego

Wiley J. Williams, School of Library Science, Kent State University, Kent, Ohio

Andrew S. Zimbalist, Department of Economics, Smith College, Northampton, Massachusetts